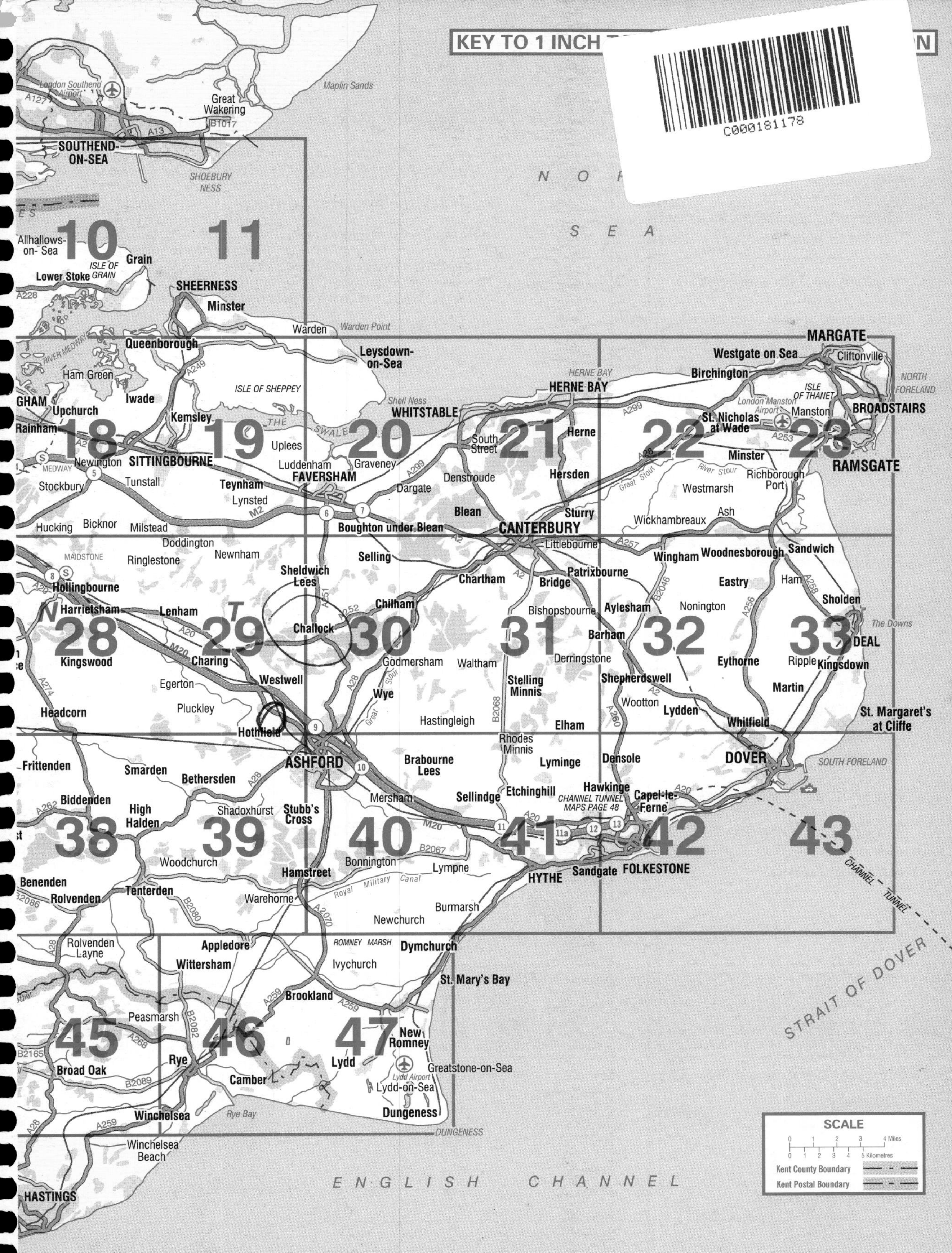
KEY TO 1 INCH … N
Maplin Sands
London Southend Airport
A127
Great Wakering
B1017
A13
SOUTHEND-ON-SEA
SHOEBURY NESS
NORTH SEA
10
11
Allhallows-on- Sea
ISLE OF GRAIN
Grain
Lower Stoke
A228
SHEERNESS
Minster
Warden
Warden Point
RIVER MEDWAY
Queenborough
Leysdown-on-Sea
Ham Green
A249
ISLE OF SHEPPEY
Iwade
GHAM
Upchurch
Kemsley
Shell Ness
WHITSTABLE
HERNE BAY
Westgate on Sea
MARGATE
Cliftonville
Birchington
NORTH FORELAND
ISLE OF THANET
London Manston Airport
Manston
BROADSTAIRS
St. Nicholas at Wade
Rainham
18
19
THE SWALE
20
21
22
23
A299
Herne
South Street
A28
A253
Newington
SITTINGBOURNE
Uplees
Luddenham
Graveney
Minster
RAMSGATE
MEDWAY
River Stour
Richborough Port
Stockbury
Tunstall
Teynham
FAVERSHAM
Dargate
Denstroude
Hersden
Great Stour
Westmarsh
Lynsted
M2
Blean
Sturry
Ash
Wickhambreaux
Hucking
Bicknor
Milstead
Boughton under Blean
CANTERBURY
Littlebourne
A257
Wingham
Woodnesborough
Sandwich
MAIDSTONE
Doddington
Ringlestone
Newnham
Selling
Sheldwich Lees
Chartham
Bridge
Patrixbourne
Eastry
Ham
A258
Hollingbourne
A251
A252
Chilham
B2046
Sholden
Harrietsham
Lenham
Challock
Bishopsbourne
Aylesham
Nonington
A256
The Downs
28
29
30
31
32
33
DEAL
A20
Barham
M20
Kingswood
Charing
Godmersham
Waltham
Derringstone
Eythorne
Ripple
Kingsdown
A274
Egerton
Westwell
Stelling Minnis
Shepherdswell
Martin
A28
Wye
B2068
A2
Wootton
Lydden
Headcorn
Pluckley
A260
St. Margaret's at Cliffe
Hastingleigh
Elham
Whitfield
Hothfield
Rhodes Minnis
Frittenden
ASHFORD
Brabourne Lees
Lyminge
Densole
DOVER
SOUTH FORELAND
Smarden
Bethersden
Biddenden
Sellindge
Etchinghill
Hawkinge
Capel-le-Ferne
CHANNEL TUNNEL MAPS PAGE 48
High Halden
Shadoxhurst
Stubb's Cross
Mersham
A262
38
39
40
41
42
43
Woodchurch
Bonnington
B2067
Lympne
HYTHE
Sandgate
FOLKESTONE
Benenden
Hamstreet
Royal Military Canal
CHANNEL TUNNEL
Rolvenden
Tenterden
Warehorne
B2086
B2080
A2070
Burmarsh
Newchurch
Rolvenden Layne
Appledore
ROMNEY MARSH
Dymchurch
Wittersham
Ivychurch
STRAIT OF DOVER
St. Mary's Bay
Brookland
A259
Peasmarsh
B2082
45
46
47
A268
New Romney
B2165
Rye
Lydd
Broad Oak
Camber
Greatstone-on-Sea
Lydd Airport
Lydd-on-Sea
B2089
Winchelsea
Rye Bay
Dungeness
DUNGENESS
A28
Winchelsea Beach
ENGLISH CHANNEL
HASTINGS
SCALE
0 1 2 3 4 Miles
0 1 2 3 4 5 Kilometres
Kent County Boundary
Kent Postal Boundary

REFERENCE TO 1 INCH TO 1 MILE STREET MAP SECTION

Motorway	M2
Motorway Junction Numbers	
Unlimited Interchange	4 Limited Interchange 3
Motorway Service Area	(S) MEDWAY
Mileages - between Motorway Junctions	4
Primary Route	A2
North & South Circular Roads	
Primary Route Destination	DOVER
A Road	A274
B Road	B2162
Other Selected Roads	
Dual Carriageway	
Transport for London Road Network (Red Route) Primary Route	
North & South Circular Roads	
A Road	
One-Way Road (Motorway, Primary Route & A Road only - Traffic flow indicated by a heavy line on the driver's left)	
Tunnel	
Major Road Under Construction	
Major Road Proposed	
Junction Name	KESTON MARK
Toll	TOLL
Ferry	

Railway and Croydon Tramlink	
Level Crossing and Tunnel	
Railway Station	SEVENOAKS
London Underground Station	ROTHERHITHE
D.L.R. Station and Tramlink Stop	SOUTH QUAY
Local Authority Boundary	
Posttown & London Postal District Boundaries	
Postcode Boundary within Posttown	
Map Continuation for 1 Inch to 1 Mile Street Mapping (Blue Pages)	5
to 3 Inches to 1 Mile Street Mapping (Red Pages)	89 or 223
Airport	LONDON BIGGIN HILL AIRPORT
Airport Runway	
Built-up Area	
National Grid Reference	580
Place of Interest	• Chartwell
River or Canal	

Sporting Venues

		Stadium	
Cricket		Horse Racing	
Football		Motor Racing	
Golf Course		Rugby	
18 Hole 9 Hole		Tennis	

Tourist Information Centre

Open all year	i	Open Summer only	i

Viewpoint	180° 360°
Wood, Park, Cemetery, Etc.	

SCALE   1 Inch (2.54 cm) to 1 Mile
1.58 cm to 1 Kilometre

0   ½   1   2 Miles
0   1   2   3 Kilometres

1:63,360

The following features are shown only in those areas of Kent not covered by 3 Inches to 1 Mile Street Mapping (Red Pages)

Building	☐	**Fire Station**	■
Car Park - selected	P	**Hospital**	H
		Post Office	★
Church or Chapel	†	**Toilet**	▽

AZ KENT

CONTENTS

Geographers' A-Z Map Company Ltd.

Head Office : Fairfield Road, Borough Green, Sevenoaks, Kent TN15 8PP
Telephone : 01732 781000 (Enquiries & Trade Sales) 01732 783422 (Retail Sales)
www.a-zmaps.co.uk

Edition 2* 2004 Copyright © Geographers' A-Z Map Company Ltd. 2004

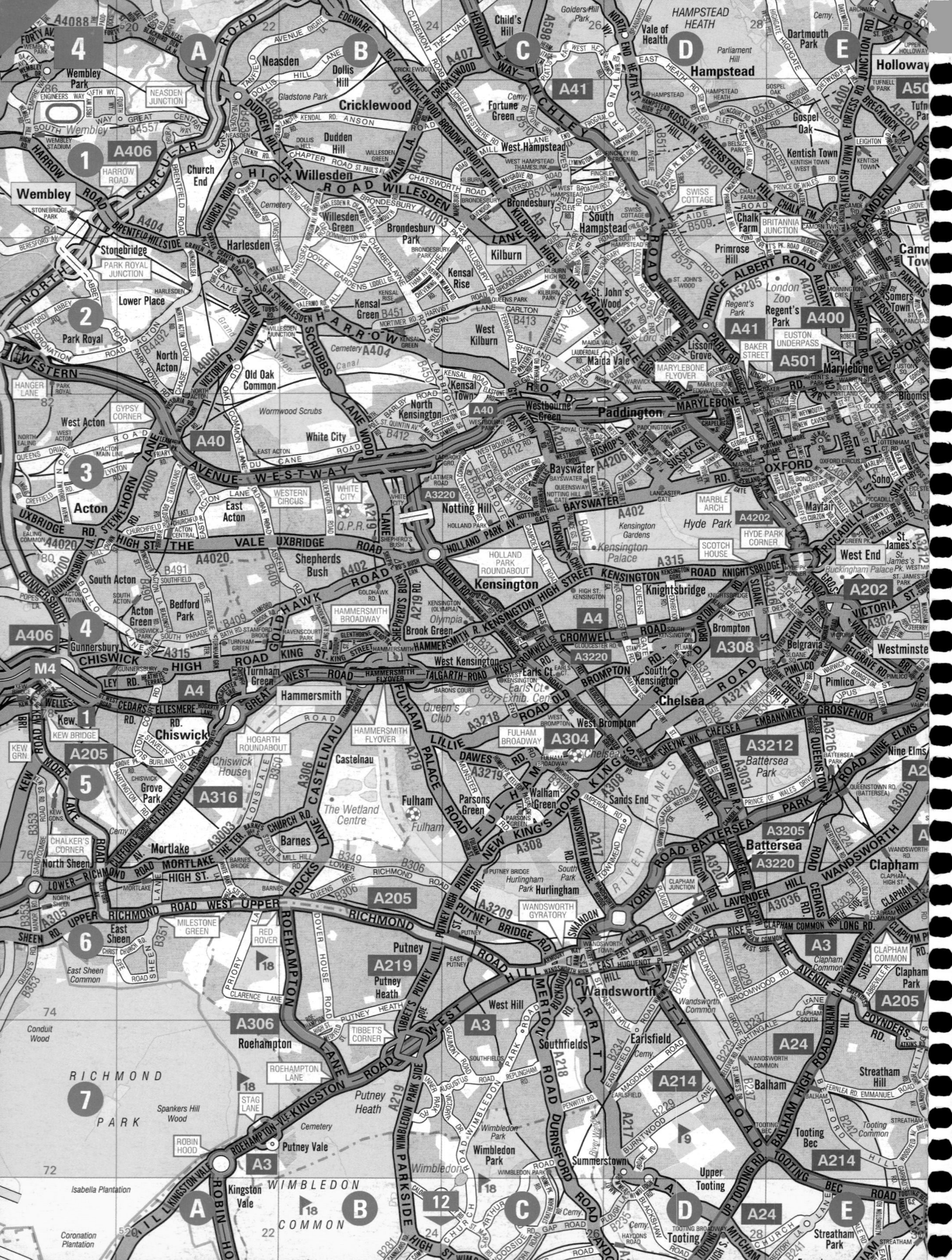
4
A
B
C
D
E
1
2
3
4
5
6
7
12
Wembley Park
Wembley
Neasden
Dollis Hill
Cricklewood
Dudden Hill
Child's Hill
Fortune Green
West Hampstead
Vale of Health
HAMPSTEAD HEATH
Hampstead
Parliament Hill
Dartmouth Park
Holloway
Gospel Oak
Kentish Town
Church End
Willesden
Willesden Green
Brondesbury
Brondesbury Park
Kilburn
South Hampstead
Swiss Cottage
Chalk Farm
Primrose Hill
Camden Town
Stonebridge
Harlesden
Kensal Rise
Kensal Green
St. John's Wood
London Zoo
Regent's Park
Somers Town
Lower Place
Park Royal
North Acton
Old Oak Common
West Kilburn
Maida Vale
Lisson Grove
Marylebone
Kensal Town
North Kensington
Wormwood Scrubs
White City
Westbourne Green
Paddington
West Acton
Acton
East Acton
Notting Hill
Bayswater
Oxford Circus
Soho
Mayfair
Hyde Park
Kensington Gardens
Kensington Palace
West End
St. James's
Buckingham Palace
Shepherds Bush
South Acton
Acton Green
Bedford Park
Kensington
Knightsbridge
Brompton
Brook Green
Olympia
West Kensington
Belgravia
Westminster
Gunnersbury
Turnham Green
Hammersmith
Earls Ct.
South Kensington
Chelsea
Pimlico
Victoria
Kew
Chiswick
Queen's Club
West Brompton
Nine Elms
Grove Park
Chiswick House
Castelnau
Fulham
Battersea Park
Walham Green
Parsons Green
Sands End
The Wetland Centre
Mortlake
Barnes
North Sheen
Battersea
Clapham
Hurlingham
South Park
East Sheen
Putney
Wandsworth
Clapham Common
Clapham Park
East Sheen Common
Putney Heath
West Hill
Wandsworth Common
Conduit Wood
Roehampton
Southfields
Earlsfield
RICHMOND PARK
Spankers Hill Wood
Streatham Hill
Balham
Wimbledon Park
Summerstown
Tooting Bec
Putney Vale
Tooting Common
Isabella Plantation
Kingston Vale
WIMBLEDON COMMON
Upper Tooting
Tooting
Coronation Plantation
Streatham Park
A406
A404
A4088
A41
A5
A407
A502
A5200
A40
A4000
A219
A404
A3220
A402
A4020
A315
A4202
A202
A4
A308
A3212
A304
A3216
A205
A316
A306
A3003
A3205
A3220
A3036
A3
A219
A3209
A217
A214
A24
A218
M4
B4557
B510
B520
B451
B413
B450
B412
B405
B491
B409
B317
B350
B349
B306
B305
B351
B353
B229
B237
B234
B235
B242
B241
NORTH CIRCULAR ROAD
HARROW ROAD
WESTERN AVENUE
WESTWAY
UXBRIDGE ROAD
GOLDHAWK ROAD
CHISWICK HIGH ROAD
GREAT WEST ROAD
KENSINGTON HIGH STREET
CROMWELL ROAD
KING'S ROAD
FULHAM ROAD
PICCADILLY
OXFORD ST.
MARYLEBONE RD.
EDGWARE ROAD
KILBURN HIGH RD.
MAIDA VALE
FINCHLEY ROAD
PRINCE ALBERT ROAD
BAYSWATER RD.
HOLLAND PARK AV.
KINGSTON ROAD
UPPER RICHMOND ROAD
BATTERSEA PARK ROAD
WANDSWORTH ROAD
TRINITY ROAD
GARRATT LANE
PUTNEY HIGH ST.
HAMMERSMITH FLYOVER
HOLLAND PARK ROUNDABOUT
HAMMERSMITH BROADWAY
HOGARTH ROUNDABOUT
KEW BRIDGE
WANDSWORTH GYRATORY
TIBBET'S CORNER
SCOTCH HOUSE
HYDE PARK CORNER
MARBLE ARCH
MARYLEBONE FLYOVER
BAKER STREET
EUSTON UNDERPASS
BRITANNIA JUNCTION
SWISS COTTAGE
NEASDEN JUNCTION
PARK ROYAL JUNCTION
HANGER LANE
GYPSY CORNER
WESTERN CIRCUS
CHALKER'S CORNER
MILESTONE GREEN
RED ROVER
ROEHAMPTON LANE
STAG LANE
ROBIN HOOD
CLAPHAM JUNCTION
CLAPHAM COMMON
FULHAM BROADWAY

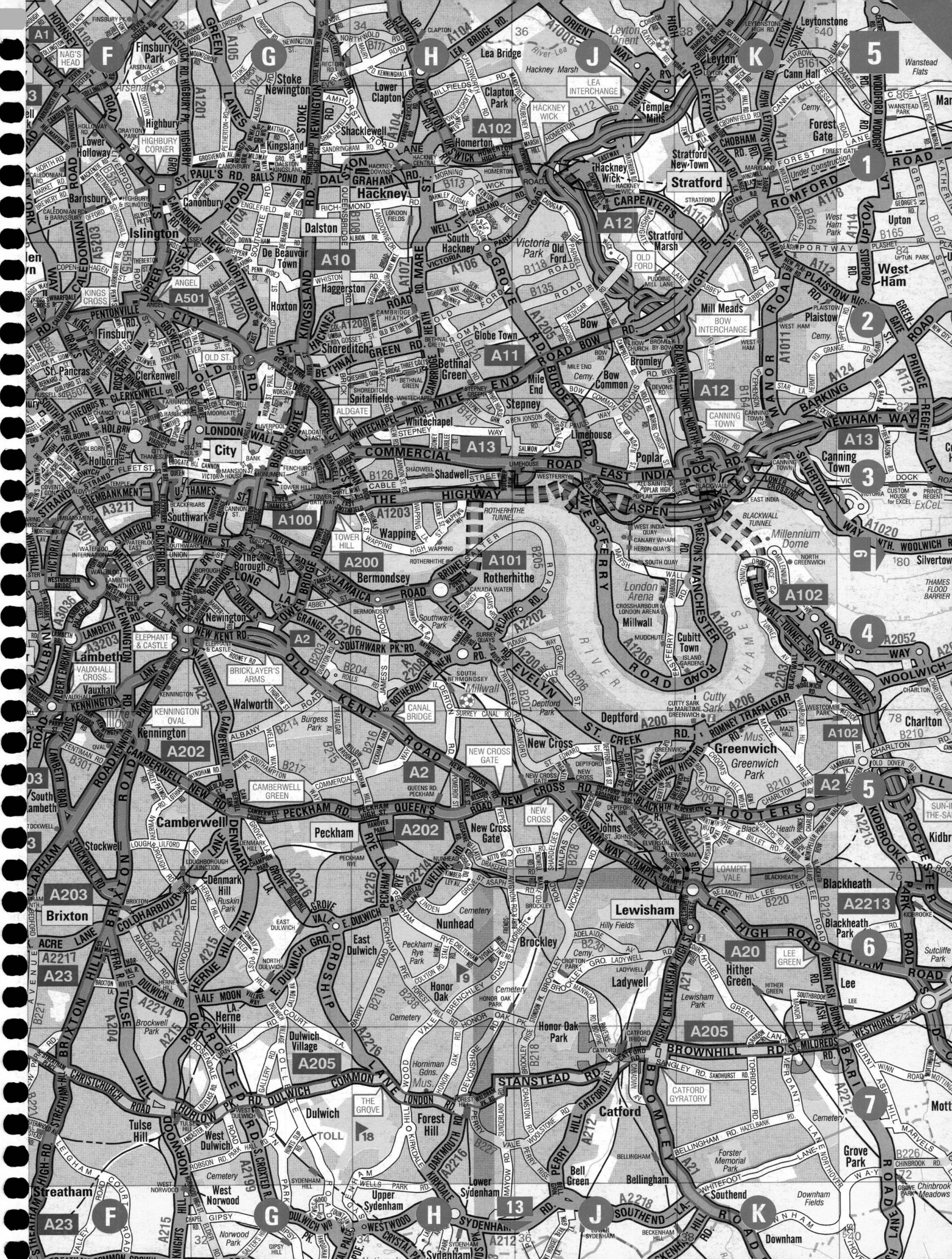

F
G
H
J
K
5
Finsbury Park
Stoke Newington
Lower Clapton
Clapton Park
Lea Bridge
Hackney Marsh
Leyton Orient
Leyton
Leytonstone
Cann Hall
Forest Gate
Wanstead Flats
Highbury
Lower Holloway
Highbury Corner
Kingsland
Shacklewell
Homerton
Hackney Wick
Temple Mills
Stratford New Town
Stratford
Lea Interchange
Barnsbury
Canonbury
Islington
Hackney
Dalston
De Beauvoir Town
South Hackney
Victoria Park
Old Ford
Stratford Marsh
West Ham Park
Upton
West Ham
Angel
Kings Cross
Haggerston
Hoxton
Finsbury
Pentonville
St. Pancras
Clerkenwell
Shoreditch
Globe Town
Bethnal Green
Bow
Bromley
Mill Meads
Plaistow
Bow Interchange
Mile End
Stepney
Bow Common
Spitalfields
Whitechapel
Aldgate
Holborn
City
Limehouse
Poplar
Canning Town
Shadwell
Wapping
Rotherhithe Tunnel
Tower Hill
Southwark
Borough
Bermondsey
Rotherhithe
Canada Water
Blackwall Tunnel
Millennium Dome
North Greenwich
Silvertown
Custom House for ExCeL
Thames Flood Barrier
London Arena
Millwall
Cubitt Town
Island Gardens
Canary Wharf
Heron Quays
South Quay
Mudchute
Crossharbour & London Arena
Newington
Elephant & Castle
Lambeth
Vauxhall
Vauxhall Cross
Walworth
Kennington
Kennington Oval
Southwark Park
Surrey Quays
Deptford
Deptford Park
Cutty Sark
Greenwich
Greenwich Park
Charlton
Burgess Park
Camberwell Green
Camberwell
New Cross
New Cross Gate
Peckham
St. Johns
Blackheath
Kidbrooke
Stockwell
Denmark Hill
Ruskin Park
Brixton
Nunhead
East Dulwich
Peckham Rye Park
Brockley
Lewisham
Hilly Fields
Ladywell
Hither Green
Lee
Blackheath Park
Lee Green
Sutcliffe Park
Herne Hill
Brockwell Park
Dulwich Village
Honor Oak
Honor Oak Park
Lewisham Park
Horniman Gdns.
Catford
Catford Gyratory
Forest Hill
Dulwich
Tulse Hill
West Dulwich
Bell Green
Bellingham
Forster Memorial Park
Grove Park
Southend
Downham Fields
Streatham
West Norwood
Norwood Park
Upper Sydenham
Lower Sydenham
Sydenham
Downham
Chinbrook Meadows
A1
A10
A102
A12
A11
A13
A501
A100
A200
A101
A2
A202
A203
A205
A20
A2213
A23
A2217
A1020

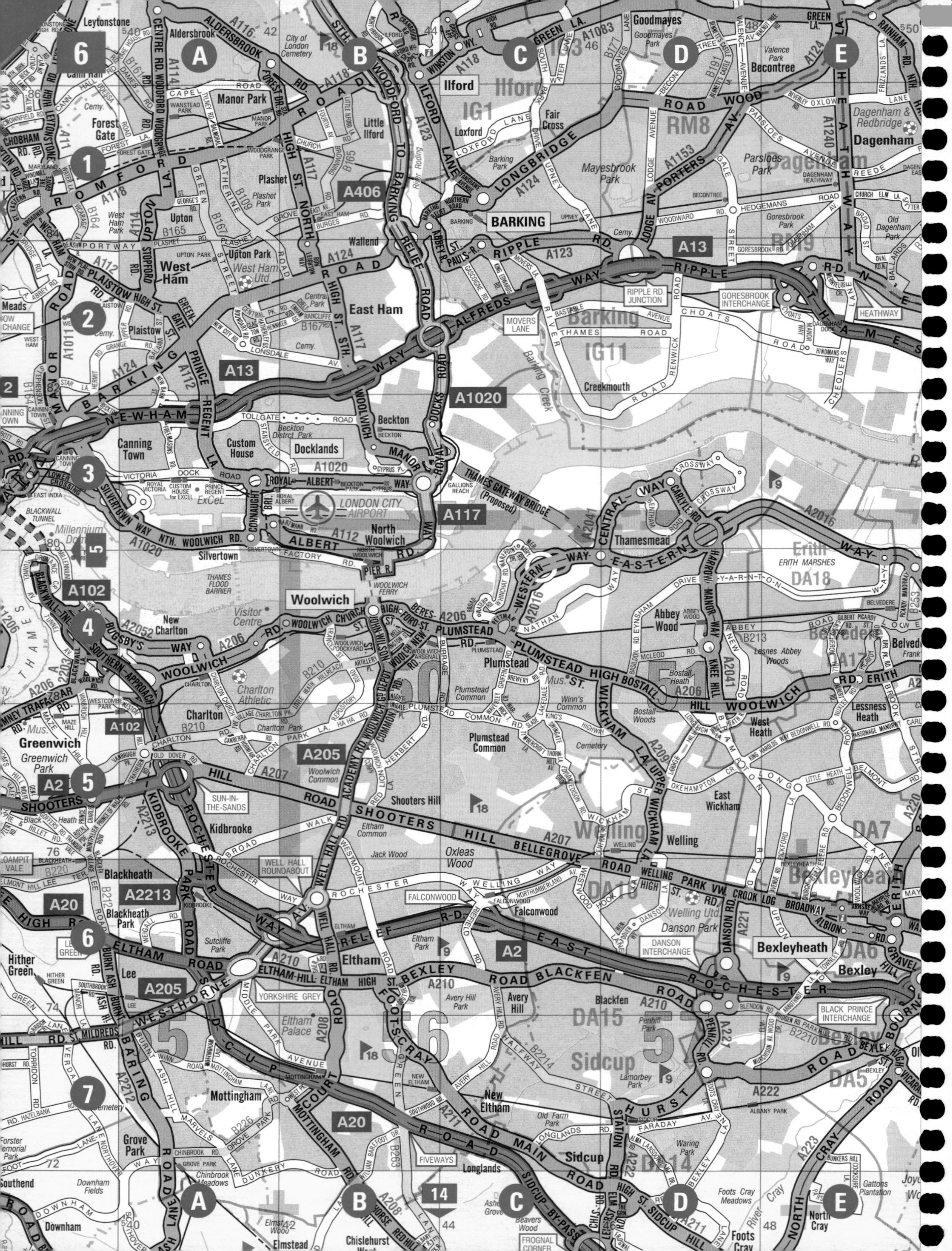

6
A
B
C
D
E
1
2
3
4
5
6
7
Leytonstone
Aldersbrook
City of London Cemetery
Goodmayes
Goodmayes Park
Valence Park
Becontree
Manor Park
Ilford
IG1
Forest Gate
Little Ilford
Loxford
Fair Cross
RM8
Dagenham & Redbridge
Dagenham
Barking Park
Mayesbrook Park
Parsloes Park
Plashet
Plashet Park
A406
BARKING
Upton
West Ham Park
Upton Park
West Ham
West Ham Utd.
Wallend
Goresbrook Park
Old Dagenham Park
A13
East Ham
Central Park
Plaistow
RIPPLE RD JUNCTION
GORESBROOK INTERCHANGE
HEATHWAY
MOVERS LANE
Barking
IG11
Creekmouth
A1020
Beckton
Beckton District Park
Canning Town
Custom House
Docklands
LONDON CITY AIRPORT
ExCeL
THAMES GATEWAY BRIDGE (Proposed)
A117
North Woolwich
Silvertown
Thamesmead
Erith
ERITH MARSHES
DA18
THAMES FLOOD BARRIER
Woolwich
WOOLWICH FERRY
A102
New Charlton
Visitor Centre
Abbey Wood
Lesnes Abbey Woods
Plumstead
Plumstead Common
Charlton Athletic
Charlton
Greenwich
Greenwich Park
Bostall Heath
Bostall Woods
Winn's Common
Lessness Heath
West Heath
A205
Shooters Hill
A2
SUN-IN-THE-SANDS
Kidbrooke
Eltham Common
Jack Wood
Oxleas Wood
Welling
East Wickham
DA7
Blackheath
WELL HALL ROUNDABOUT
A2213
A20
Blackheath Park
FALCONWOOD
Falconwood
Welling Utd.
Danson Park
DANSON INTERCHANGE
Bexleyheath
Bexley
DA6
Eltham Park
Sutcliffe Park
Eltham
Hither Green
Lee
YORKSHIRE GREY
Avery Hill Park
Avery Hill
Blackfen
DA15
BLACK PRINCE INTERCHANGE
Eltham Palace
Penhill Park
Sidcup
Lamorbey Park
DA5
Mottingham
New Eltham
Old Farm Park
Waring Park
Grove Park
Chinbrook Meadows
FIVEWAYS
Longlands
Foots Cray Meadows
Gattons Plantation
North Cray
Southend
Downham Fields
Downham
14
Elmstead
Chislehurst
Foots Cray
Beavers Wood
FROGNAL CORNER

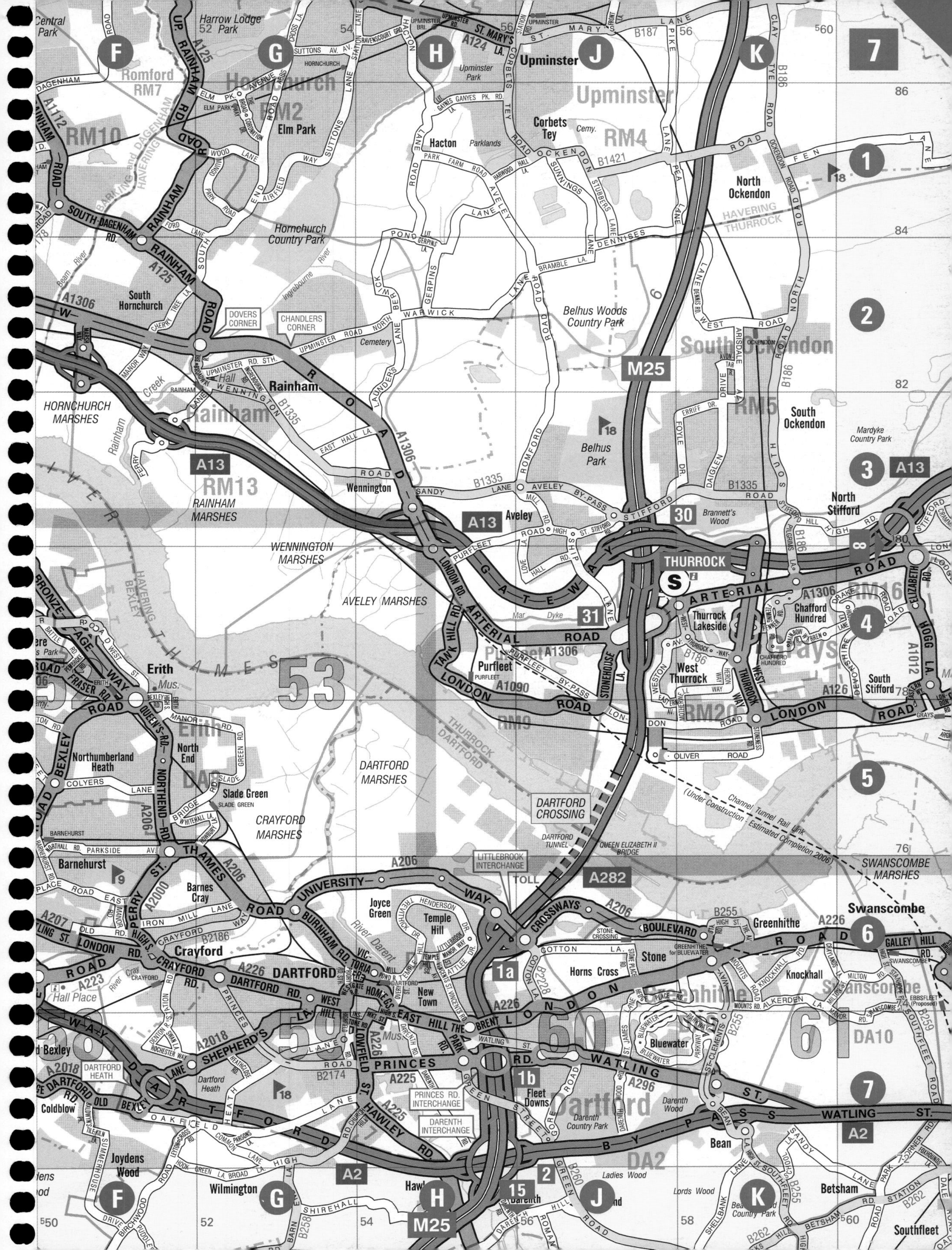
7
Upminster
Hornchurch
Romford RM7
RM2
RM10
Elm Park
Hacton
Corbets Tey
RM4
North Ockendon
Hornchurch Country Park
South Hornchurch
Belhus Woods Country Park
South Ockendon
Rainham
RM13
Rainham Marshes
Wennington
Aveley
Belhus Park
Wennington Marshes
Aveley Marshes
Thurrock
Thurrock Lakeside
Chafford Hundred
West Thurrock
Purfleet
North Stifford
South Stifford
Grays
RM16
RM20
Erith
North End
Northumberland Heath
Slade Green
Dartford Marshes
Crayford Marshes
Dartford Crossing
Barnehurst
Barnes Cray
Crayford
Dartford
Joyce Green
Temple Hill
New Town
Stone
Horns Cross
Greenhithe
Swanscombe
Knockhall
Bluewater
Swanscombe Marshes
Fleet Downs
Darenth Wood
Darenth Country Park
Dartford Heath
Coldblow
Joydens Wood
Wilmington
Bean
Betsham
Southfleet
DA2
DA10
53
59
60
61
M25
A13
A2
A282
THE QUEEN ELIZABETH II BRIDGE
Channel Tunnel Rail Link (Under Construction - Estimated Completion 2006)

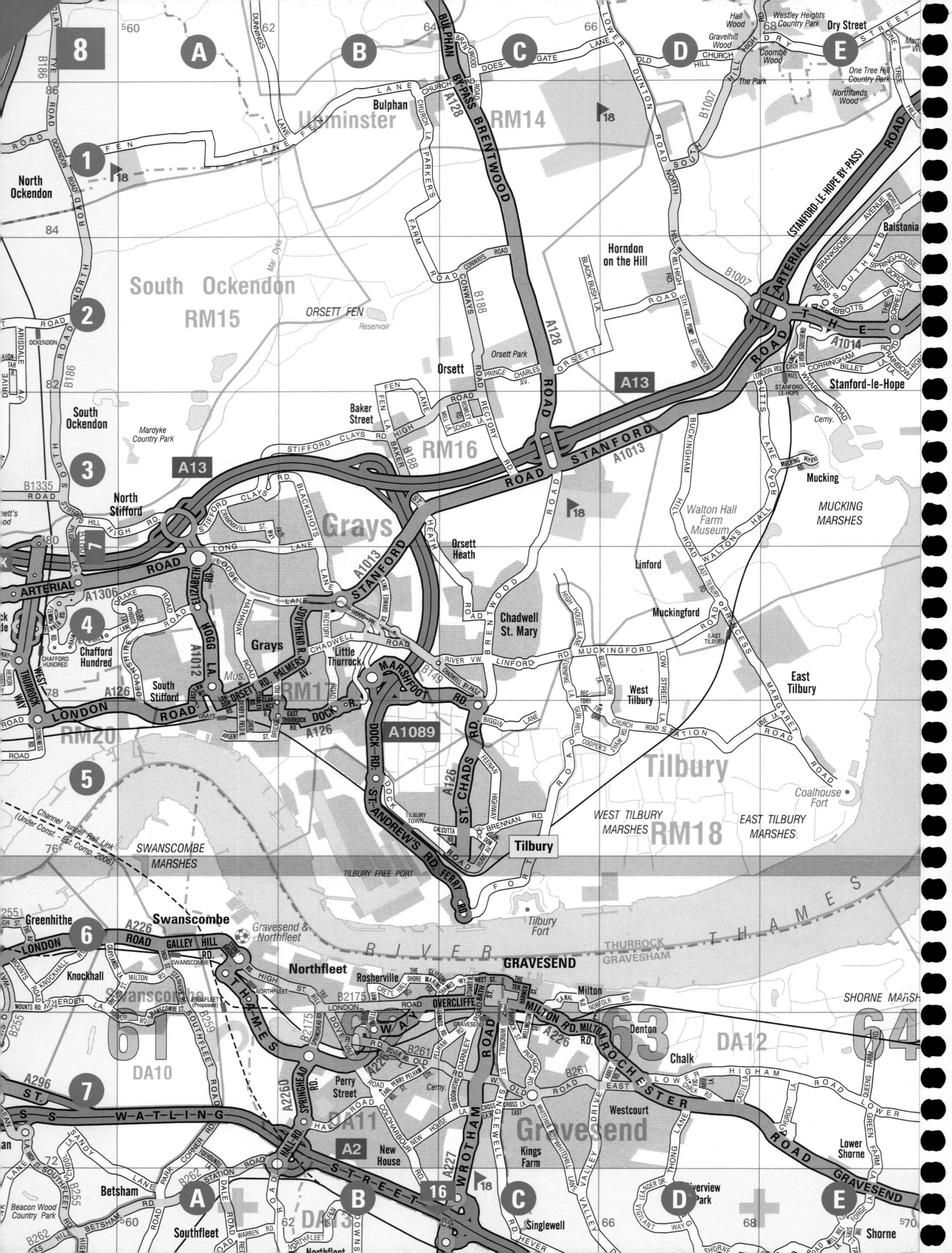
A
B
C
D
E
1
2
3
4
5
6
7
Upminster
RM14
Bulphan
North Ockendon
South Ockendon
RM15
ORSETT FEN
Reservoir
Orsett
Orsett Park
Horndon on the Hill
Baker Street
RM16
Mardyke Country Park
North Stifford
Grays
Orsett Heath
Chadwell St. Mary
Linford
Mucking
MUCKING MARSHES
Walton Hall Farm Museum
Muckingford
Chafford Hundred
Little Thurrock
South Stifford
RM17
RM20
West Tilbury
East Tilbury
Tilbury
RM18
Coalhouse Fort
WEST TILBURY MARSHES
EAST TILBURY MARSHES
Stanford-le-Hope
Balstonia
Westley Heights Country Park
Dry Street
One Tree Hill Country Park
Northlands Wood
Hall Wood
Gravelhill Wood
Coombe Wood
The Park
SWANSCOMBE MARSHES
Channel Tunnel Rail Link (Under Const. Est. Comp. 2006)
TILBURY FREE PORT
Tilbury Fort
RIVER THAMES
THURROCK
GRAVESHAM
Greenhithe
Swanscombe
Gravesend & Northfleet
Knockhall
Northfleet
Rosherville
GRAVESEND
Milton
Denton
Chalk
SHORNE MARSH
DA10
DA11
DA12
DA13
61
62
63
64
Perry Street
Westcourt
Gravesend
New House
Kings Farm
Lower Shorne
Riverview Park
Betsham
Beacon Wood Country Park
Southfleet
Singlewell
Shorne
A13
A128
A1013
A1014
A1089
A126
A1306
A1012
A226
A2
A227
A2260
A296
B186
B188
B1007
B1335
B149
B2175
B261
B262
B255
B259
16
18
7
ARTERIAL ROAD
STANFORD ROAD
BRENTWOOD ROAD
LONDON ROAD
WATLING STREET
ROCHESTER ROAD
GRAVESEND ROAD
DOCK RD.
ST. ANDREW'S RD.
FERRY RD.
ST. CHADS RD.
MARSHFOOT RD.
HOGG LA.
ELIZABETH RD.
HIGH ST.
OVERCLIFFE
MILTON RD.
WROTHAM ROAD
SPRINGHEAD RD.
GALLEY HILL RD.
Tilbury

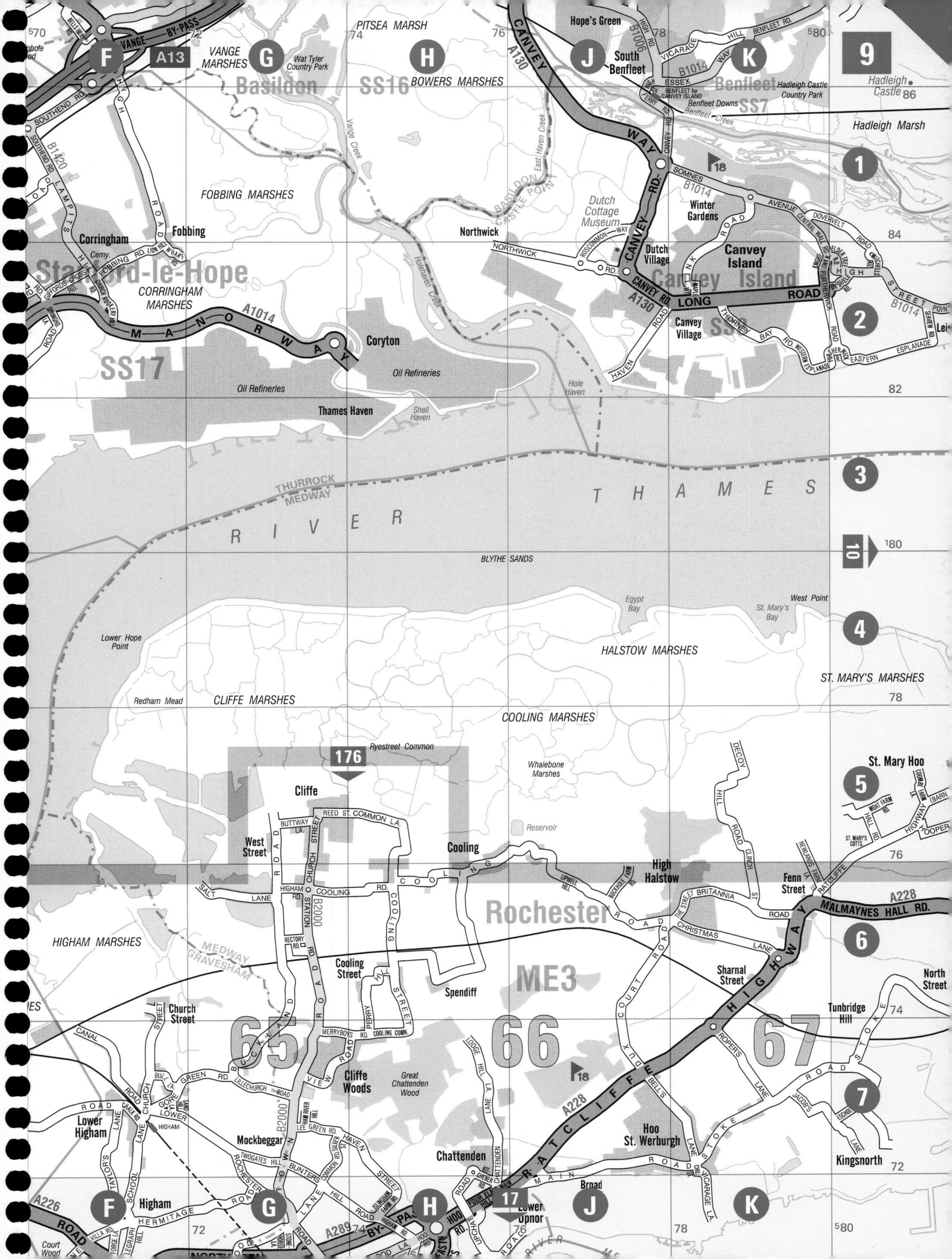
Hope's Green
PITSEA MARSH
VANGE MARSHES
Wat Tyler Country Park
Basildon
SS16
BOWERS MARSHES
South Benfleet
Benfleet
SS7
Hadleigh Castle Country Park
Hadleigh Castle
Benfleet Downs
Benfleet Creek
Hadleigh Marsh
A13
VANGE BY-PASS
SOUTHEND RD.
CANVEY WAY
A130
FOBBING MARSHES
Fobbing
Corringham
Stanford-le-Hope
CORRINGHAM MARSHES
MANOR WAY
A1014
Coryton
SS17
Oil Refineries
Thames Haven
Shell Haven
Hole Haven
Northwick
Dutch Cottage Museum
Dutch Village
Winter Gardens
Canvey Island
Canvey Village
LONG ROAD
THORNEY BAY RD.
EASTERN ESPLANADE
RIVER THAMES
THURROCK
MEDWAY
BLYTHE SANDS
Egypt Bay
St. Mary's Bay
West Point
Lower Hope Point
HALSTOW MARSHES
ST. MARY'S MARSHES
Redham Mead
CLIFFE MARSHES
COOLING MARSHES
Ryestreet Common
Whalebone Marshes
St. Mary Hoo
Cliffe
West Street
Reservoir
Cooling
High Halstow
Fenn Street
A228
MALMAYNES HALL RD.
Rochester
HIGHAM MARSHES
MEDWAY
GRAVESHAM
Cooling Street
Spendiff
ME3
Sharnal Street
North Street
Tunbridge Hill
Church Street
65
66
67
Cliffe Woods
Great Chattenden Wood
Lower Higham
Mockbeggar
Chattenden
Hoo St. Werburgh
Kingsnorth
Higham
A226
A289
Broad
Lower Upnor
Court Wood

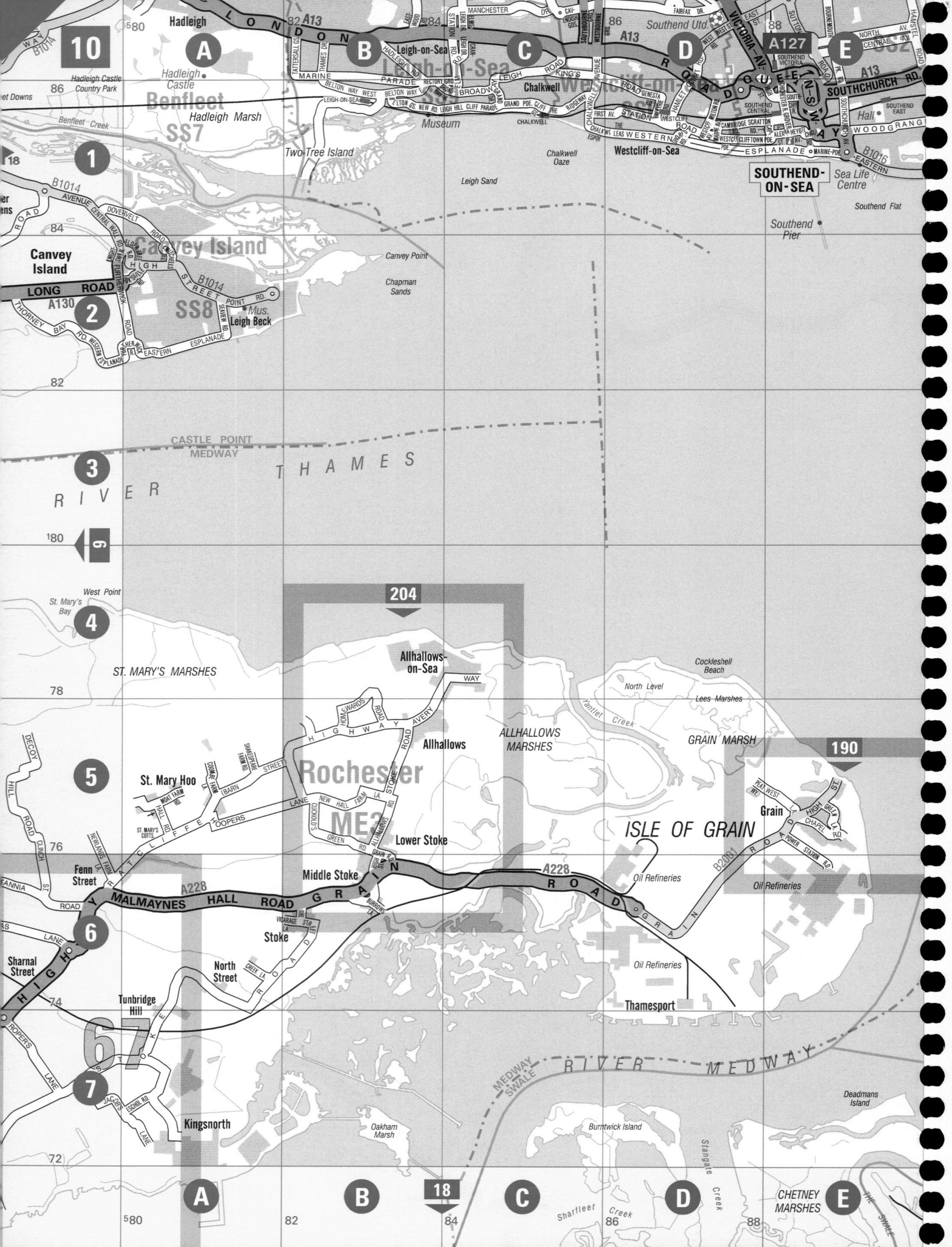

Hadleigh
Leigh-on-Sea
Westcliff-on-Sea
Southend Utd.
SOUTHEND-ON-SEA
Sea Life Centre
Southend Pier
Southend Flat
Hadleigh Castle
Hadleigh Castle Country Park
Benfleet
Hadleigh Marsh
SS7
Benfleet Creek
Two Tree Island
Museum
Chalkwell
Chalkwell Oaze
Leigh Sand
Canvey Island
Canvey Point
Chapman Sands
LONG ROAD
A130
SS8
Leigh Beck
CASTLE POINT
MEDWAY
RIVER THAMES
West Point
St. Mary's Bay
ST. MARY'S MARSHES
Allhallows-on-Sea
Allhallows
ALLHALLOWS MARSHES
Rochester
ME3
St. Mary Hoo
Lower Stoke
Middle Stoke
Stoke
North Street
Fenn Street
Sharnal Street
Tunbridge Hill
Kingsnorth
MALMAYNES HALL ROAD
A228
GRAIN ROAD
ISLE OF GRAIN
Grain
Oil Refineries
Thamesport
Yantlet Creek
North Level
Lees Marshes
Cockleshell Beach
GRAIN MARSH
B2001
RIVER MEDWAY
MEDWAY SWALE
Oakham Marsh
Burntwick Island
Stangate Creek
Sharfleet Creek
Deadmans Island
CHETNEY MARSHES
204
190
67
18
9

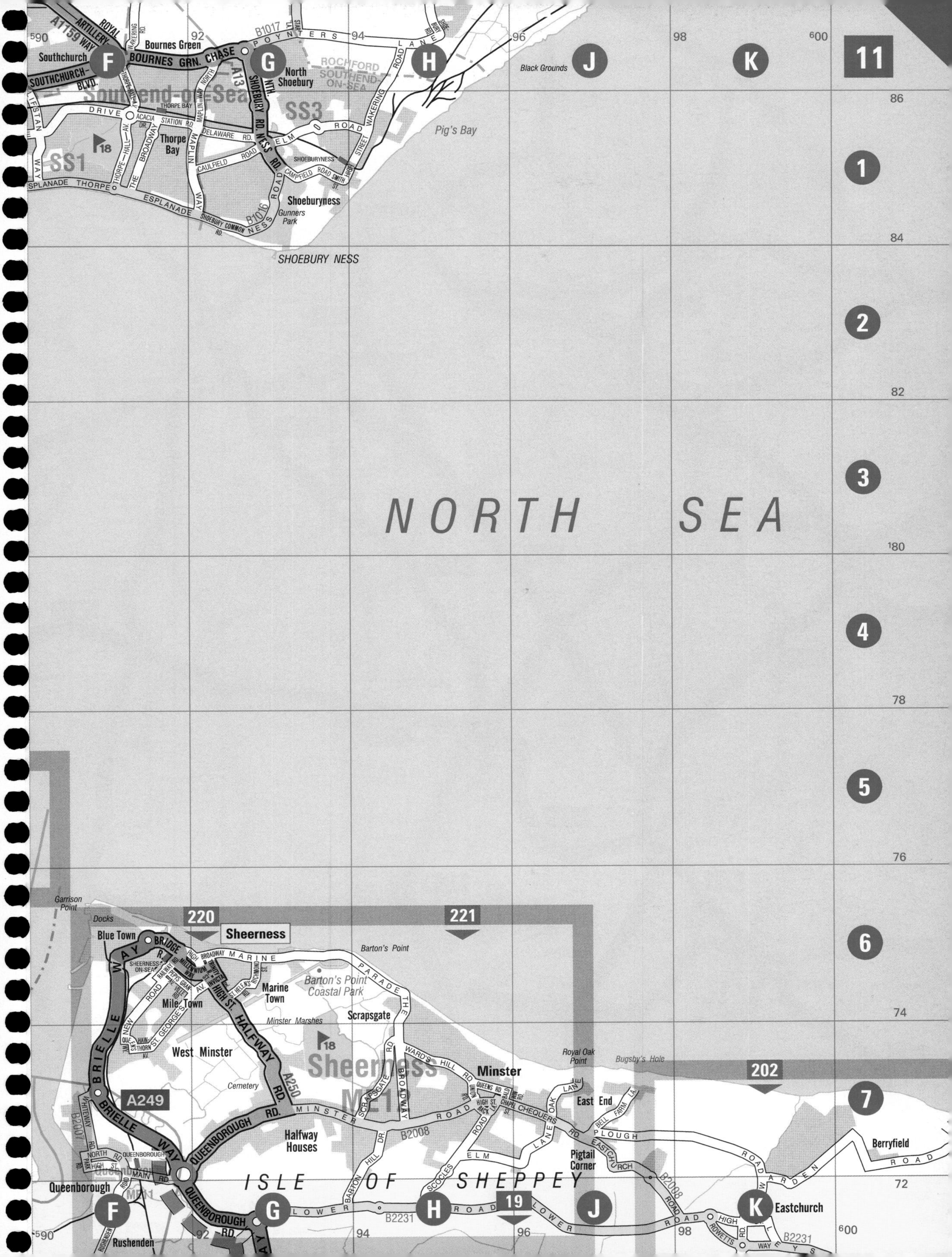
NORTH SEA
Southchurch
Bournes Green
BOURNES GRN. CHASE
North Shoebury
ROCHFORD
SOUTHEND-ON-SEA
Southend-on-Sea
SS3
SS1
Thorpe Bay
Pig's Bay
Black Grounds
Shoeburyness
Gunners Park
SHOEBURY NESS
Garrison Point
Docks
Blue Town
Sheerness
Barton's Point
Barton's Point Coastal Park
Marine Town
Mile Town
Scrapsgate
Minster Marshes
West Minster
Cemetery
Sheerness ME12
Minster
Royal Oak Point
Bugsby's Hole
East End
Halfway Houses
Pigtail Corner
Berryfield
Eastchurch
Queenborough
Rushenden
ISLE OF SHEPPEY
220
221
202
19
A249
A250
B2008
B2231
B2007
A13
B1016
B1017
A1159

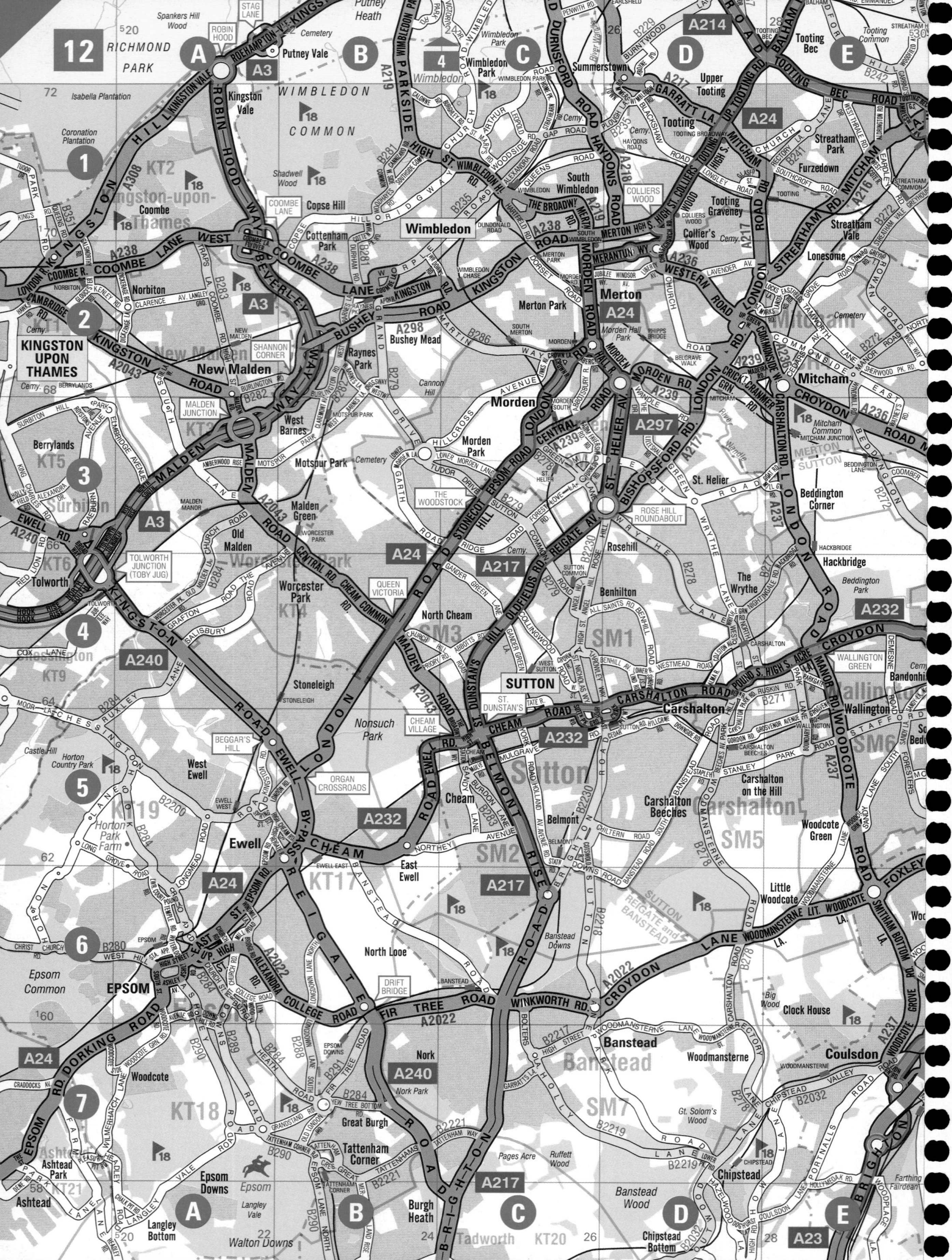
12
RICHMOND PARK
Putney Vale
Putney Heath
Wimbledon Park
Summerstown
Upper Tooting
Tooting Bec
Tooting Common
Isabella Plantation
Coronation Plantation
Kingston Vale
WIMBLEDON COMMON
Tooting
Streatham Park
Furzedown
Kingston-upon-Thames
Coombe
Shadwell Wood
Copse Hill
Cottenham Park
Wimbledon
South Wimbledon
Tooting Graveney
Collier's Wood
Streatham Vale
Lonesome
Norbiton
KINGSTON UPON THAMES
New Malden
Raynes Park
Bushey Mead
Merton Park
Merton
Morden Hall Park
Mitcham
Mitcham Common
Berrylands
Surbiton
West Barnes
Motspur Park
Morden
Morden Park
St. Helier
Beddington Corner
Tolworth
Old Malden
Malden Green
Worcester Park
Rosehill
Hackbridge
The Wrythe
Benhilton
North Cheam
Beddington Park
Stoneleigh
SUTTON
Carshalton
Wallington
Bandonhill
Nonsuch Park
Castle Hill
Horton Country Park
West Ewell
Cheam
Carshalton Beeches
Carshalton on the Hill
Belmont
Woodcote Green
Horton Park Farm
Ewell
East Ewell
Little Woodcote
Banstead Downs
North Looe
Epsom Common
EPSOM
Big Wood
Clock House
Banstead
Woodmansterne
Coulsdon
Nork
Woodcote
Nork Park
Great Burgh
Tattenham Corner
Gt. Solom's Wood
Ashtead Park
Epsom Downs
Pages Acre
Ruffett Wood
Chipstead
Ashtead
Langley Vale
Burgh Heath
Banstead Wood
Langley Bottom
Walton Downs
Tadworth
Chipstead Bottom
Farthing Fairdean

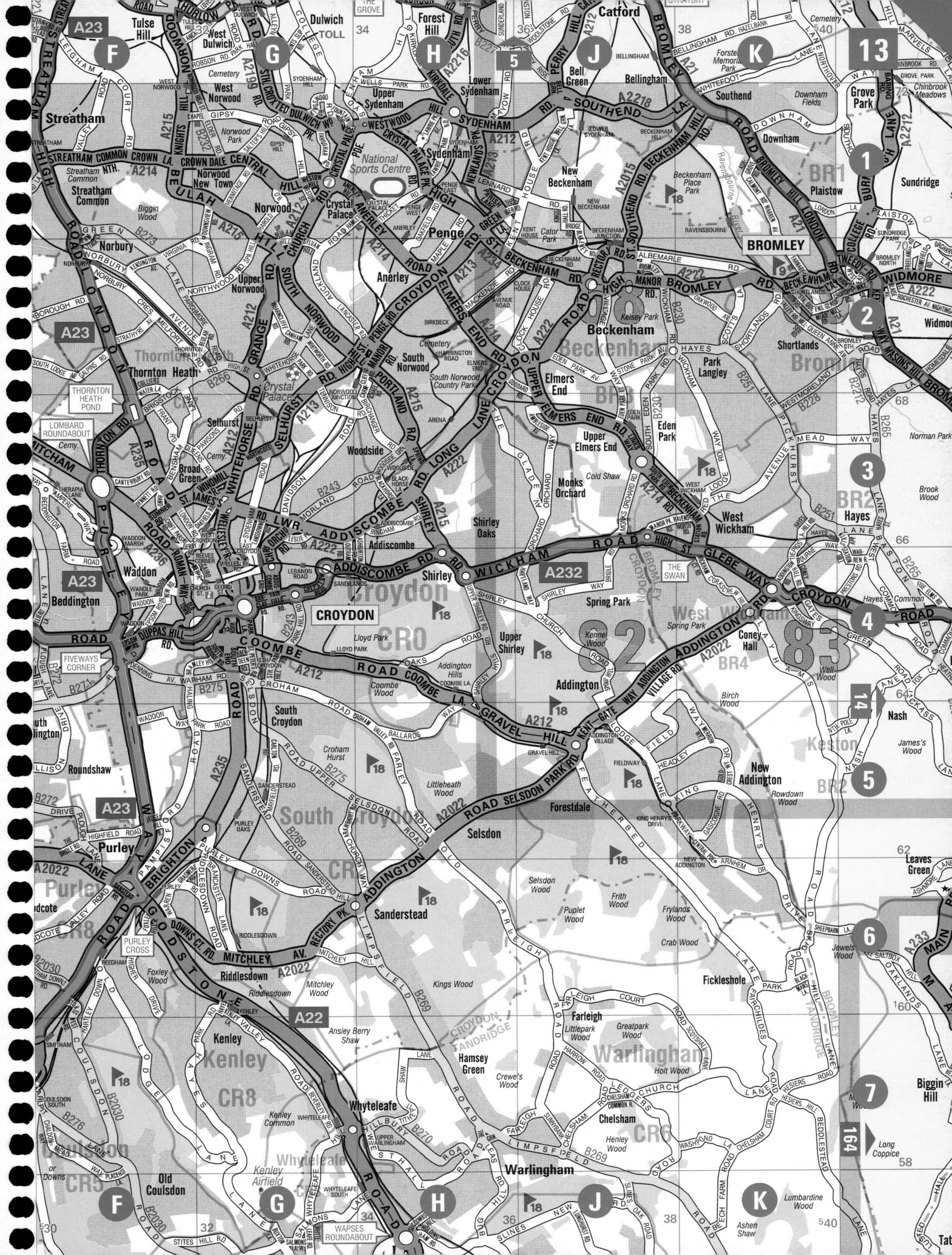
Tulse Hill
West Dulwich
Dulwich
Forest Hill
Catford
Streatham
West Norwood
Upper Sydenham
Lower Sydenham
Sydenham
Bell Green
Bellingham
Southend
Downham
Grove Park
Sundridge
Plaistow
Streatham Common
Norwood New Town
Norwood
National Sports Centre
Crystal Palace
Penge
New Beckenham
Beckenham Place Park
BROMLEY
Norbury
Upper Norwood
Anerley
Beckenham
Shortlands
Bromley
Thornton Heath
THORNTON HEATH POND
LOMBARD ROUNDABOUT
South Norwood
South Norwood Country Park
Elmers End
Park Langley
Selhurst
Woodside
Upper Elmers End
Eden Park
Broad Green
Monks Orchard
West Wickham
Hayes
Norman Park
Brook Wood
Shirley Oaks
Addiscombe
Waddon
Beddington
Shirley
CROYDON
Croydon
Spring Park
West Wickham
THE SWAN
FIVEWAYS CORNER
Lloyd Park
Upper Shirley
Addington Hills
Addington
Coney Hall
Well Wood
Coombe Wood
South Croydon
Birch Wood
Nash
Keston
James's Wood
Croham Hurst
Littleheath Wood
New Addington
Rowdown Wood
Roundshaw
Forestdale
South Croydon
Selsdon
Purley
Leaves Green
Selsdon Wood
Frith Wood
Puplet Wood
Frylands Wood
Sanderstead
Crab Wood
PURLEY CROSS
Jewels Wood
Foxley Wood
Riddlesdown
Mitchley Wood
Kings Wood
Fickleshole
Farleigh
Littlepark Wood
Greatpark Wood
Ansley Berry Shaw
Kenley
Warlingham
Hamsey Green
Crewe's Wood
Holt Wood
Biggin Hill
Kenley Common
Whyteleafe
Chelsham
Henley Wood
Long Coppice
Coulsdon
Old Coulsdon
Kenley Airfield
Warlingham
WAPSES ROUNDABOUT
Lumbardine Wood
Ashen Shaw
A23
A22
A232
CR0
CR8
CR6
CR5
BR1
BR2
BR3
BR4
82
83
F
G
H
J
K
1
2
3
4
5
6
7
14
164

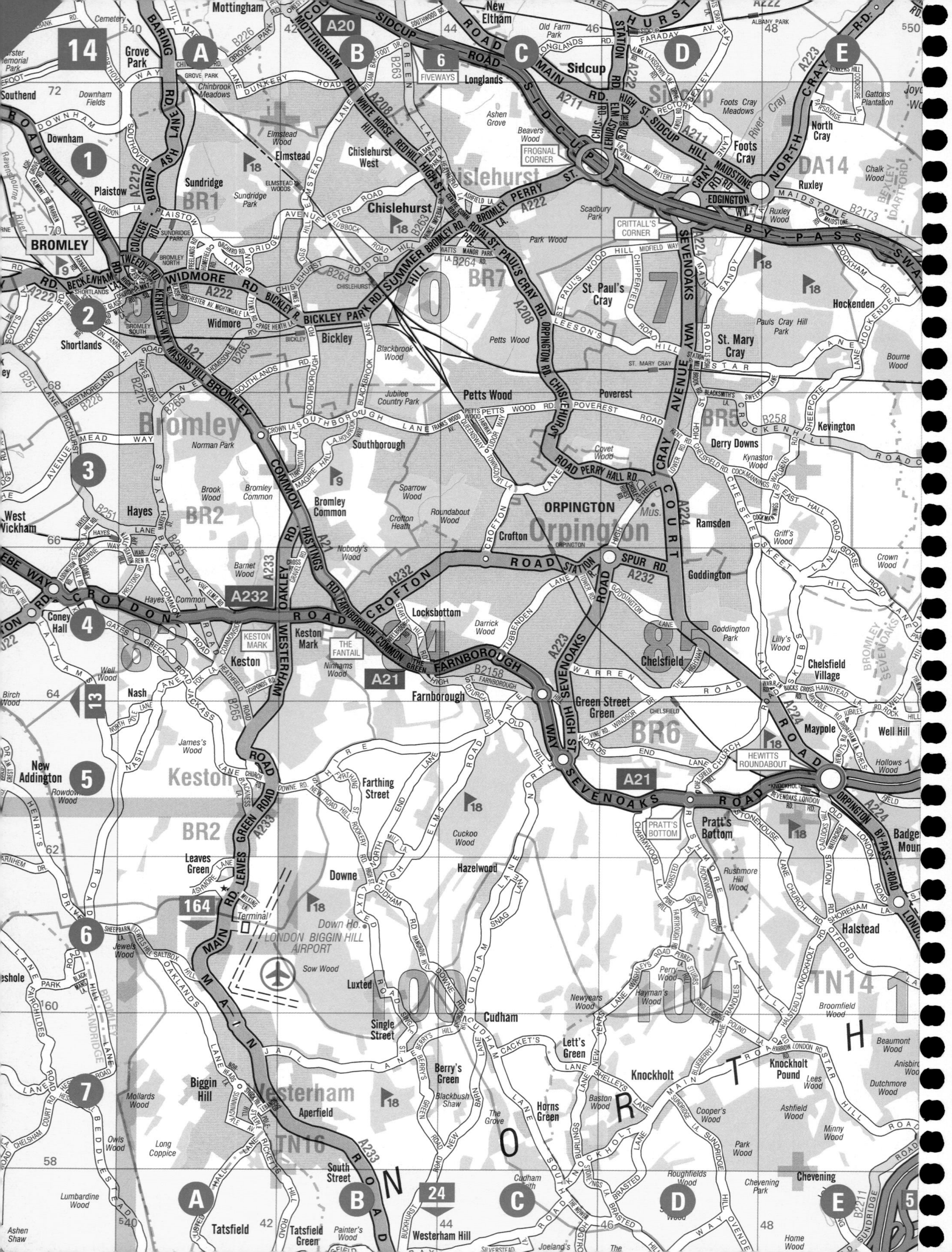

14
A
B
C
D
E
1
2
3
4
5
6
7
Mottingham
New Eltham
Old Farm Park
Grove Park
Southend
Downham Fields
Downham
Plaistow
Sundridge
Sundridge Park
BR1
BROMLEY
Chinbrook Meadows
Elmstead Wood
Elmstead
Chislehurst West
Chislehurst
Ashen Grove
Beavers Wood
FROGNAL CORNER
Longlands
Sidcup
FIVEWAYS
A20
6
Foots Cray Meadows
Foots Cray
North Cray
Gattons Plantation
DA14
Chalk Wood
Ruxley
Ruxley Wood
EDGINGTON
Scadbury Park
CRITTALL'S CORNER
Park Wood
BR7
St. Paul's Cray
St. Mary Cray
Pauls Cray Hill Park
Hockenden
Bourne Wood
Widmore
Shortlands
Bickley
Blackbrook Wood
Petts Wood
Jubilee Country Park
Poverest
BR5
Kevington
Derry Downs
Kynaston Wood
Bromley
Norman Park
Southborough
Covet Wood
Sparrow Wood
Roundabout Wood
Crofton Heath
Crofton
ORPINGTON
Orpington
Mus.
Ramsden
Griff's Wood
Crown Wood
Brook Wood
Bromley Common
Hayes
BR2
West Wickham
Barnet Wood
Hayes Common
A232
Nobody's Wood
Goddington
Coney Hall
KESTON MARK
Keston Mark
THE FANTAIL
Locksbottom
Darrick Wood
Goddington Park
Lilly's Wood
Chelsfield Village
Well Wood
Keston
Ninhams Wood
A21
Farnborough
Chelsfield
Green Street Green
BR6
Well Hill
Nash
Birch Wood
13
James's Wood
New Addington
Rowdown Wood
HEWITTS ROUNDABOUT
Maypole
Hollows Wood
Keston
Farthing Street
Cuckoo Wood
PRATT'S BOTTOM
Pratt's Bottom
Badgers Mount
BR2
Leaves Green
Downe
Hazelwood
Rushmore Hill Wood
164
Terminal
Down Ho.
LONDON BIGGIN HILL AIRPORT
Jewels Wood
Sow Wood
Halstead
Luxted
Perry Wood
Newyears Wood
Hayman's Wood
TN14
Broomfield Wood
Single Street
Cudham
Lett's Green
Knockholt
Knockholt Pound
Beaumont Wood
Lees Wood
Dutchmore Wood
Berry's Green
Blackbush Shaw
Biggin Hill
Westerham
Aperfield
Mollards Wood
Baston Wood
Horns Green
The Grove
Cooper's Wood
Ashfield Wood
Minny Wood
Owls Wood
Long Coppice
TN16
Park Wood
South Street
Cudham Frith
Roughfields Wood
Chevening Park
Chevening
Lumbardine Wood
24
Ashen Shaw
Tatsfield
Tatsfield Green
Painter's Wood
Westerham Hill
Home Wood
Joeland's
N O R T H
40
42
44
46
48
50
72
70
68
66
64
62
60
58

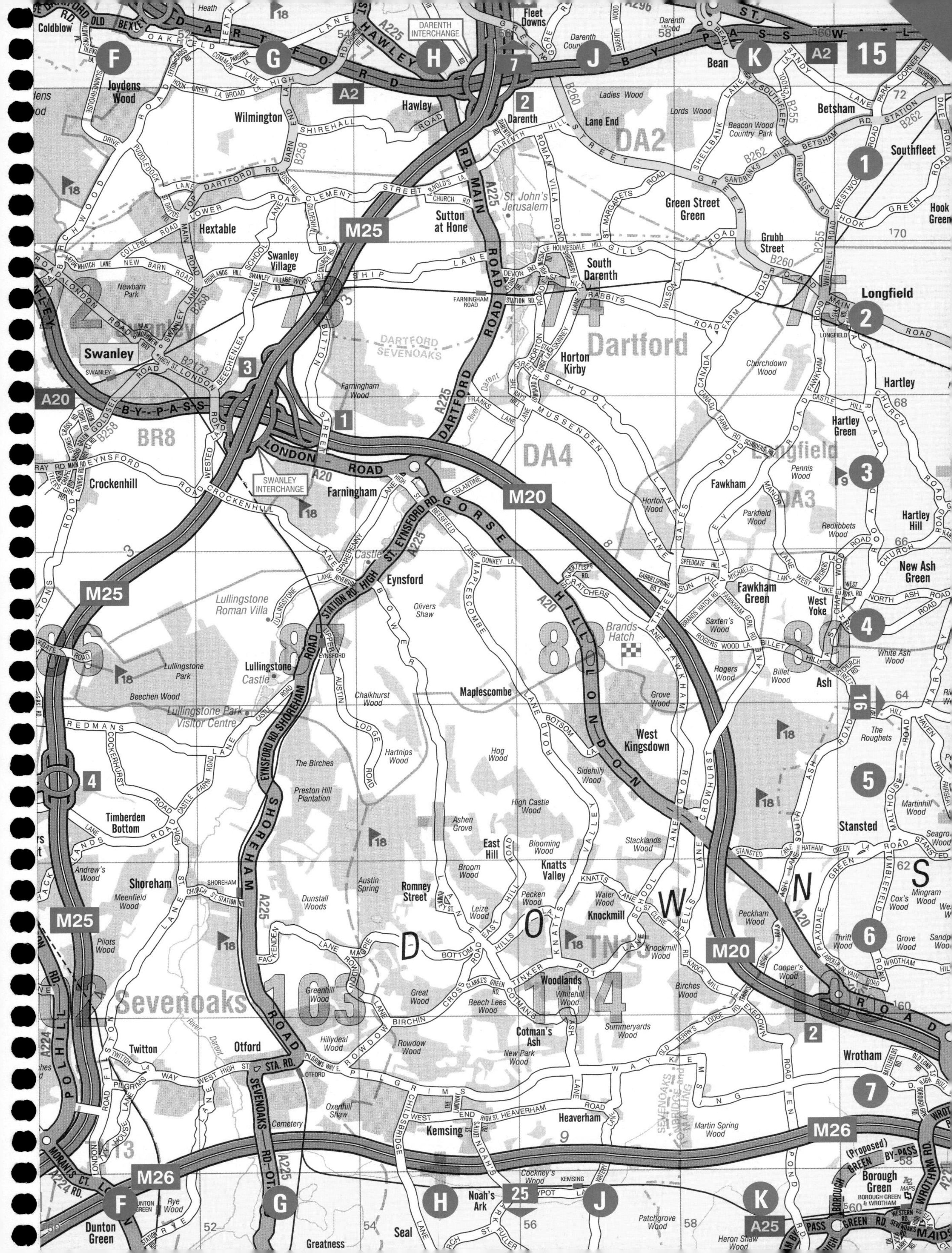

15
Coldblow
Heath
Fleet Downs
Darenth County
Bean
DARENTH INTERCHANGE
DARTFORD BY-PASS
A2
A225
A296
Joydens Wood
Wilmington
Hawley
Darenth
Ladies Wood
Lane End
Lords Wood
Betsham
Beacon Wood Country Park
DA2
Southfleet
Hextable
Sutton at Hone
St. John's Jerusalem
Green Street Green
Grubb Street
Hook Green
Swanley Village
South Darenth
Longfield
Newbarn Park
Swanley
Horton Kirby
Dartford
DARTFORD SEVENOAKS
Churchdown Wood
Hartley
Farningham Wood
BR8
DA4
Hartley Green
Longfield
Pennis Wood
DA3
SWANLEY INTERCHANGE
Crockenhill
Farningham
Fawkham
Horton Wood
Parkfield Wood
Redlibbets Wood
Hartley Hill
New Ash Green
Castle
Eynsford
Olivers Shaw
Lullingstone Roman Villa
Fawkham Green
West Yoke
Saxten's Wood
Brands Hatch
White Ash Wood
Lullingstone Park
Lullingstone Castle
Rogers Wood
Billet Wood
Ash
Beechen Wood
Chalkhurst Wood
Maplescombe
Grove Wood
Lullingstone Park Visitor Centre
The Roughets
West Kingsdown
Hog Wood
Hartnips Wood
The Birches
Sidehilly Wood
Preston Hill Plantation
High Castle Wood
Martinhill Wood
Timberden Bottom
Ashen Grove
Stansted
Stacklands Wood
Blooming Wood
East Hill
Andrew's Wood
Broom Wood
Knatts Valley
Shoreham
Austin Spring
Romney Street
Dunstall Woods
Meenfield Wood
Pecken Wood
Water Wood
Knockmill
Leize Wood
Peckham Wood
Cox's Wood
Mingram Wood
Pilots Wood
Knockmill Wood
Thrift Wood
Grove Wood
TN15
Cooper's Wood
Sevenoaks
Greenhill Wood
Great Wood
Woodlands
Whitehill Wood
Birches Wood
Beech Lees Wood
Summeryards Wood
Hillydeal Wood
Rowdow Wood
Cotman's Ash
Twitton
Otford
New Park Wood
Wrotham
Oxenhill Shaw
Cemetery
Kemsing
Heaverham
SEVENOAKS TONBRIDGE and MALLING
Martin Spring Wood
TN13
Cockney's Wood
Borough Green
Noah's Ark
Rye Wood
Dunton Green
Patchgrove Wood
Seal
Greatness
Heron Shaw Wood
D O W N S
M25
M20
M26
A20
A25
A224
A225

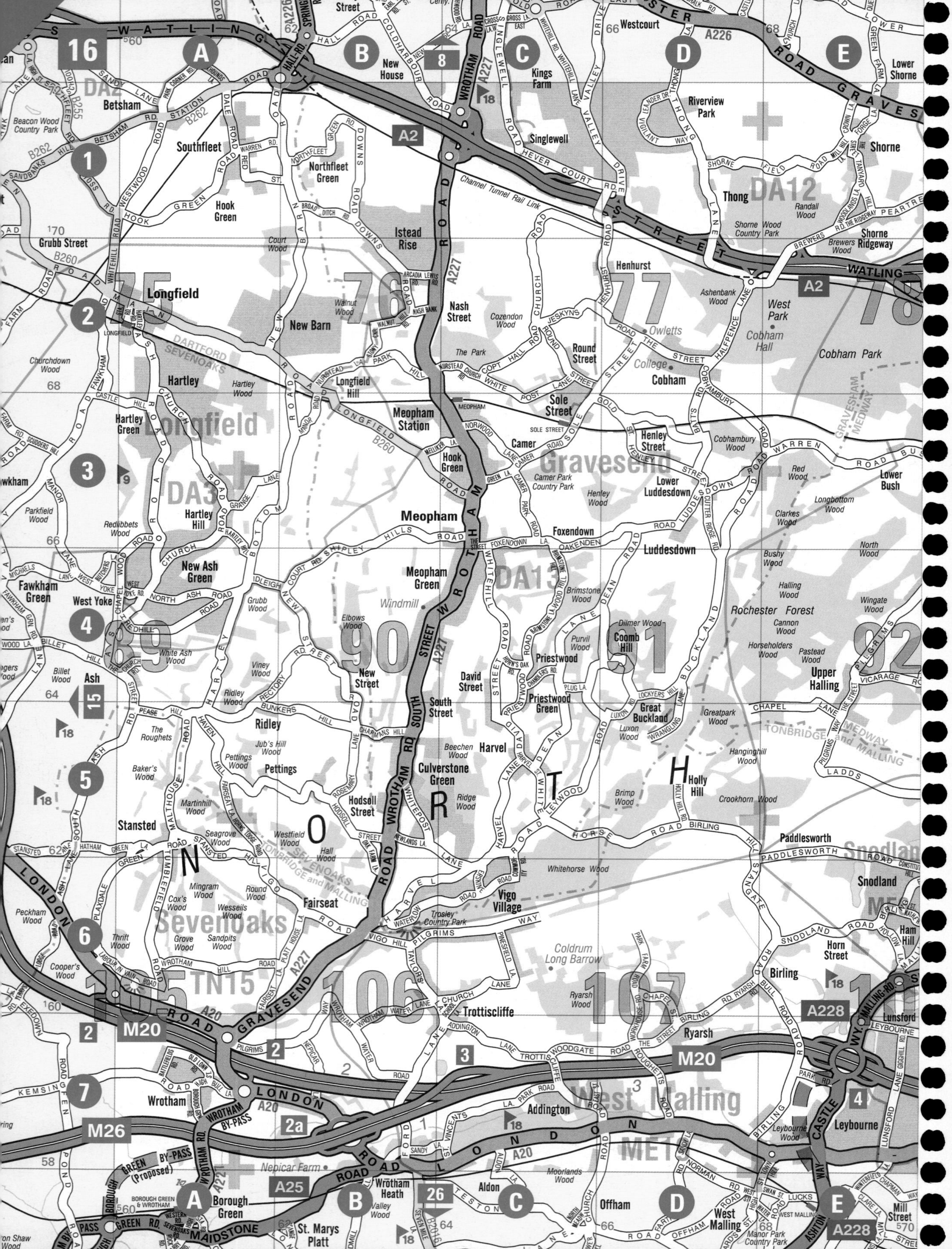

16
Betsham
Southfleet
Northfleet Green
Hook Green
Grubb Street
Longfield
New Barn
Istead Rise
Nash Street
Henhurst
Cobham
Hartley
Longfield Hill
Meopham Station
Sole Street
Camer
Hartley Green
Hook Green
Henley Street
Lower Luddesdown
Gravesend
Hartley Hill
Meopham
Foxendown
Luddesdown
New Ash Green
Fawkham Green
West Yoke
Meopham Green
Ash
Ridley
New Street
South Street
David Street
Priestwood
Priestwood Green
Great Buckland
Upper Halling
Harvel
Culverstone Green
Pettings
Stansted
Hodsoll Street
Paddlesworth
Snodland
Vigo Village
Fairseat
Sevenoaks
Trottiscliffe
Birling
Horn Street
Ryarsh
Wrotham
Addington
West Malling
Leybourne
Borough Green
Wrotham Heath
Aldon
Offham
St. Marys Platt
Mill Street
Westcourt
New House
Kings Farm
Singlewell
Riverview Park
Thong
Shorne
Lower Shorne
Shorne Ridgeway
West Park
Cobham Park
Rochester Forest
Holly Hill
Lunsford
Ham Hill
WATLING STREET
GRAVESEND ROAD
WROTHAM ROAD
LONDON ROAD
M20
M26
A2
A20
A25
A226
A227
A228
DA2
DA3
DA12
DA13
TN15
NORTH
75
76
77
78
89
90
91
92
105
106
107

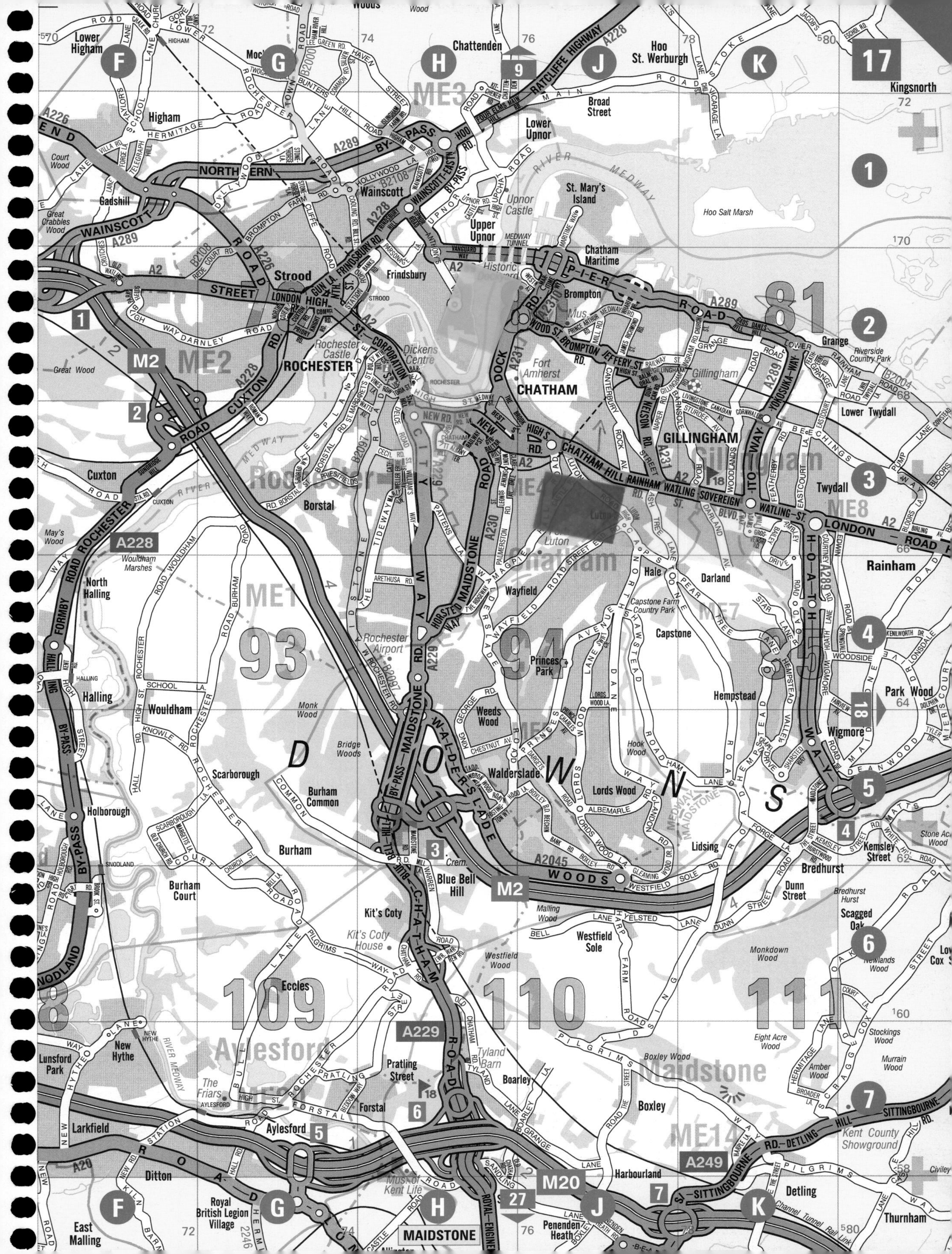

17
Lower Higham
Higham
Chattenden
Hoo St. Werburgh
Kingsnorth
Broad Street
Lower Upnor
Upper Upnor
Upnor Castle
St. Mary's Island
Hoo Salt Marsh
RIVER MEDWAY
Chatham Maritime
Wainscott
Gadshill
Court Wood
Great Crabbles Wood
Strood
Frindsbury
Brompton
Rochester Castle
Dickens Centre
ROCHESTER
Fort Amherst
CHATHAM
Gillingham
GILLINGHAM
Grange
Riverside Country Park
Lower Twydall
Twydall
Rainham
Great Wood
Cuxton
May's Wood
Wouldham Marshes
North Halling
Halling
Borstal
Luton
Hale
Darland
Wayfield
Capstone Farm Country Park
Capstone
Rochester Airport
Princes Park
Hempstead
Park Wood
Wigmore
Wouldham
Monk Wood
Weeds Wood
Bridge Woods
Scarborough
Burham Common
Walderslade
Lords Wood
Hook Wood
Holborough
Burham
Blue Bell Hill
Lidsing
Bredhurst
Kemsley Street
Stone Acre Wood
Burham Court
Kit's Coty
Kit's Coty House
Malling Wood
Westfield Sole
Dunn Street
Bredhurst Hurst
Scagged Oak
Westfield Wood
Monkdown Wood
Newlands Wood
Eccles
Eight Acre Wood
Stockings Wood
Aylesford
Tyland Barn
Boxley Wood
Maidstone
Murrain Wood
Amber Wood
Lunsford Park
New Hythe
The Friars
Pratling Street
Boarley
Boxley
Forstal
Larkfield
Kent County Showground
Ditton
Harbourland
Detling
Civiley
Mus. of Kent Life
Royal British Legion Village
East Malling
Penenden Heath
Thurnham
MAIDSTONE
Channel Tunnel Rail Link
ME1
ME2
ME3
ME4
ME5
ME7
ME8
ME14
ME20
M2
M20
A2
A20
A226
A228
A229
A230
A231
A249
A289
A2045
B2000
B2097
B2108
B2004
93
94
95
109
110
111
81
D O W N S

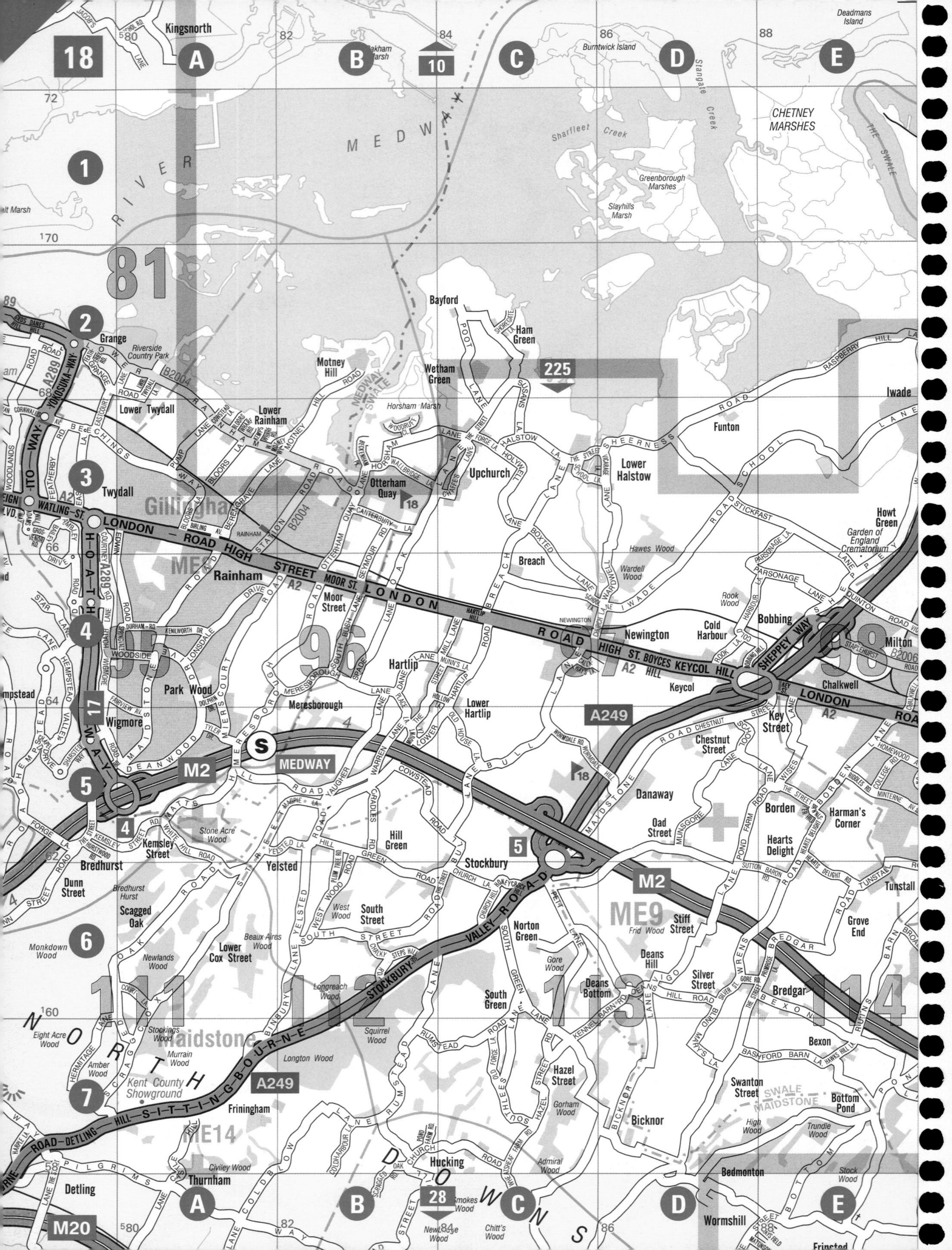

18
Kingsnorth
10
Deadmans Island
Burntwick Island
RIVER MEDWAY
Stangate Creek
CHETNEY MARSHES
Sharfleet Creek
THE SWALE
Greenborough Marshes
Slayhills Marsh
81
Grange
Riverside Country Park
Lower Twydall
Motney Hill
Lower Rainham
Bayford
Ham Green
Wetham Green
225
Horsham Marsh
Funton
Iwade
Twydall
Gillingham
Otterham Quay
Upchurch
Lower Halstow
Howt Green
Garden of England Crematorium
Hawes Wood
Wardell Wood
Breach
Rainham
Moor Street
Newington
Cold Harbour
Bobbing
Milton
Rook Wood
A2
A249
A289
B2004
M2
95
96
97
98
Park Wood
Hartlip
Keycol
Chalkwell
Meresborough
Lower Hartlip
Key Street
Chestnut Street
Wigmore
MEDWAY
Danaway
Borden
Harman's Corner
Oad Street
Hearts Delight
Kemsley Street
Stone Acre Wood
Hill Green
Stockbury
Bredhurst
Yelsted
Dunn Street
Bredhurst Hurst
Scagged Oak
West Wood
South Street
Norton Green
ME9
Frid Wood
Stiff Street
Tunstall
Grove End
Monkdown Wood
Beaux Aires Wood
Lower Cox Street
Newlands Wood
Longreach Wood
Gore Wood
Deans Hill
Deans Bottom
Silver Street
Bredgar
South Green
111
112
113
114
NORTH DOWNS
Eight Acre Wood
Stockings Wood
Maidstone
Squirrel Wood
Murrain Wood
Longton Wood
Bexon
Amber Wood
Kent County Showground
Hazel Street
Swanton Street
Bottom Pond
Fríningham
Gorham Wood
Bicknor
SWALE
MAIDSTONE
High Wood
Trundle Wood
ME14
Hucking
Civiley Wood
Admiral Wood
Bedmonton
Stock Wood
Detling
Thurnham
28
Smokes Wood
Chitt's Wood
New House Wood
Wormshill
Frinsted
M20
A
B
C
D
E
1
2
3
4
5
6
7

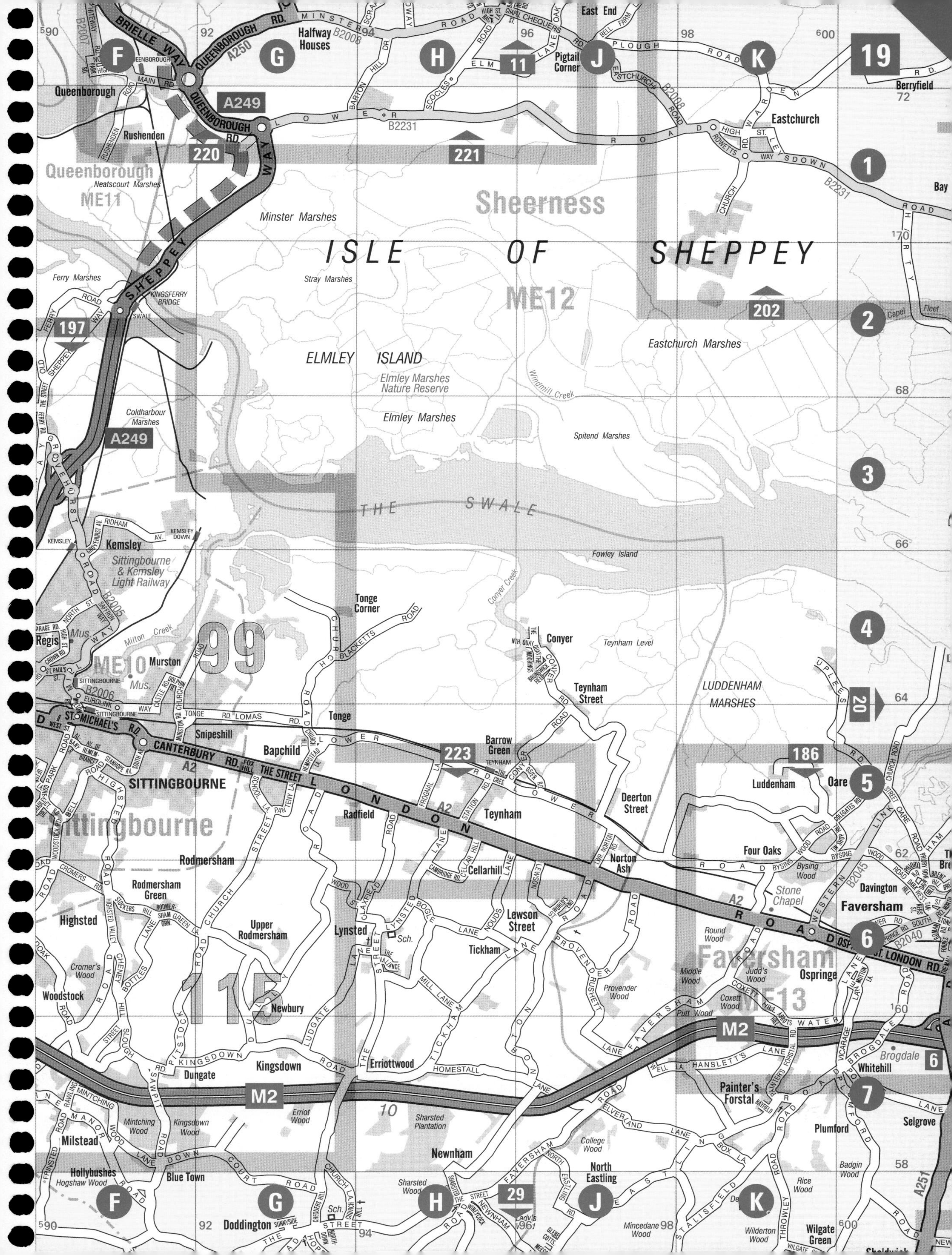
19
Queenborough
Rushenden
Halfway Houses
East End
Pigtail Corner
Berryfield
Eastchurch
Bay
Queenborough
Neatscourt Marshes
ME11
Sheerness
Minster Marshes
ISLE OF SHEPPEY
Ferry Marshes
Stray Marshes
ME12
Kingsferry Bridge
ELMLEY ISLAND
Elmley Marshes Nature Reserve
Elmley Marshes
Eastchurch Marshes
Windmill Creek
Coldharbour Marshes
Spitend Marshes
THE SWALE
Fowley Island
Kemsley
Sittingbourne & Kemsley Light Railway
Conyer Creek
Tonge Corner
Milton Creek
Conyer
Teynham Level
ME10
Murston
Teynham Street
LUDDENHAM MARSHES
Tonge
Snipeshill
Barrow Green
Bapchild
Luddenham
Oare
SITTINGBOURNE
Sittingbourne
Radfield
Teynham
Deerton Street
Four Oaks
Rodmersham
Cellarhill
Norton Ash
Bysing Wood
Davington
Stone Chapel
Faversham
Rodmersham Green
Highsted
Lynsted
Upper Rodmersham
Lewson Street
Tickham
Round Wood
Faversham
Cromer's Wood
Middle Wood
Judd's Wood
Ospringe
Provender Wood
Coxett Wood
ME13
Woodstock
Newbury
Putt Wood
Brogdale
Whitehill
Dungate
Kingsdown
Erriottwood
Painter's Forstal
Mintching Wood
Kingsdown Wood
Erriot Wood
Sharsted Plantation
College Wood
Plumford
Selgrove
Milstead
Newnham
North Eastling
Badgin Wood
Rice Wood
Hollybushes
Hogshaw Wood
Blue Town
Sharsted Wood
Doddington
Mincedane Wood
Wilderton Wood
Wilgate Green
A249
A250
A2
M2
B2231
B2008
B2006
B2005
B2045
B2040
A251
220
221
202
197
223
186
11
20
29
99
115

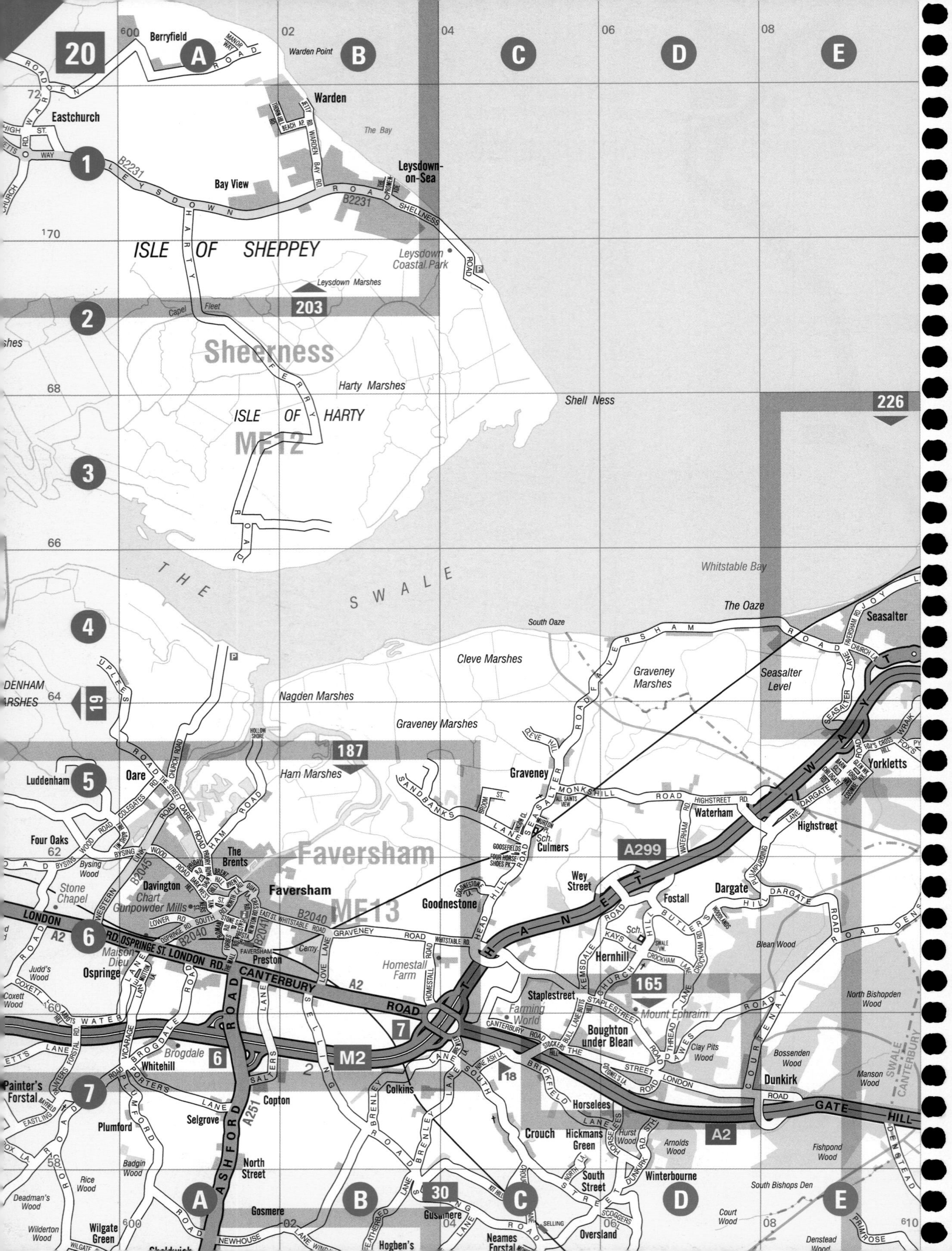

Berryfield
Warden Point
Warden
The Bay
Eastchurch
Leysdown-on-Sea
Bay View
ISLE OF SHEPPEY
Leysdown Coastal Park
Leysdown Marshes
203
Sheerness
Harty Marshes
ISLE OF HARTY
ME12
Shell Ness
226
THE SWALE
Whitstable Bay
The Oaze
South Oaze
Seasalter
Cleve Marshes
Graveney Marshes
Seasalter Level
Nagden Marshes
19
187
Ham Marshes
Graveney
Yorkletts
Luddenham
Oare
Waterham
Highstreet
Four Oaks
The Brents
Culmers
Faversham
Bysing Wood
Stone Chapel
Davington
Chart Gunpowder Mills
ME13
Goodnestone
Wey Street
Fostall
Dargate
Hernhill
Blean Wood
Maison Dieu
Ospringe
Preston
Judd's Wood
Homestall Farm
165
Staplestreet
Mount Ephraim
North Bishopden Wood
Coxett Wood
Farming World
Boughton under Blean
Clay Pits Wood
Bossenden Wood
Whitehill
Brogdale
M2
Dunkirk
Manson Wood
Painter's Forstal
Colkins
Copton
Horselees
Selgrove
Plumford
Crouch
Hickmans Green
Hurst Wood
Arnolds Wood
Fishpond Wood
Badgin Wood
North Street
Rice Wood
South Street
Winterbourne
South Bishops Den
Deadman's Wood
30
Gosmere
Court Wood
Wilderton Wood
Wilgate Green
Hogben's
Neames Forstal
Oversland
Denstead Wood
A2
A299
A251
B2231
B2040
B2045

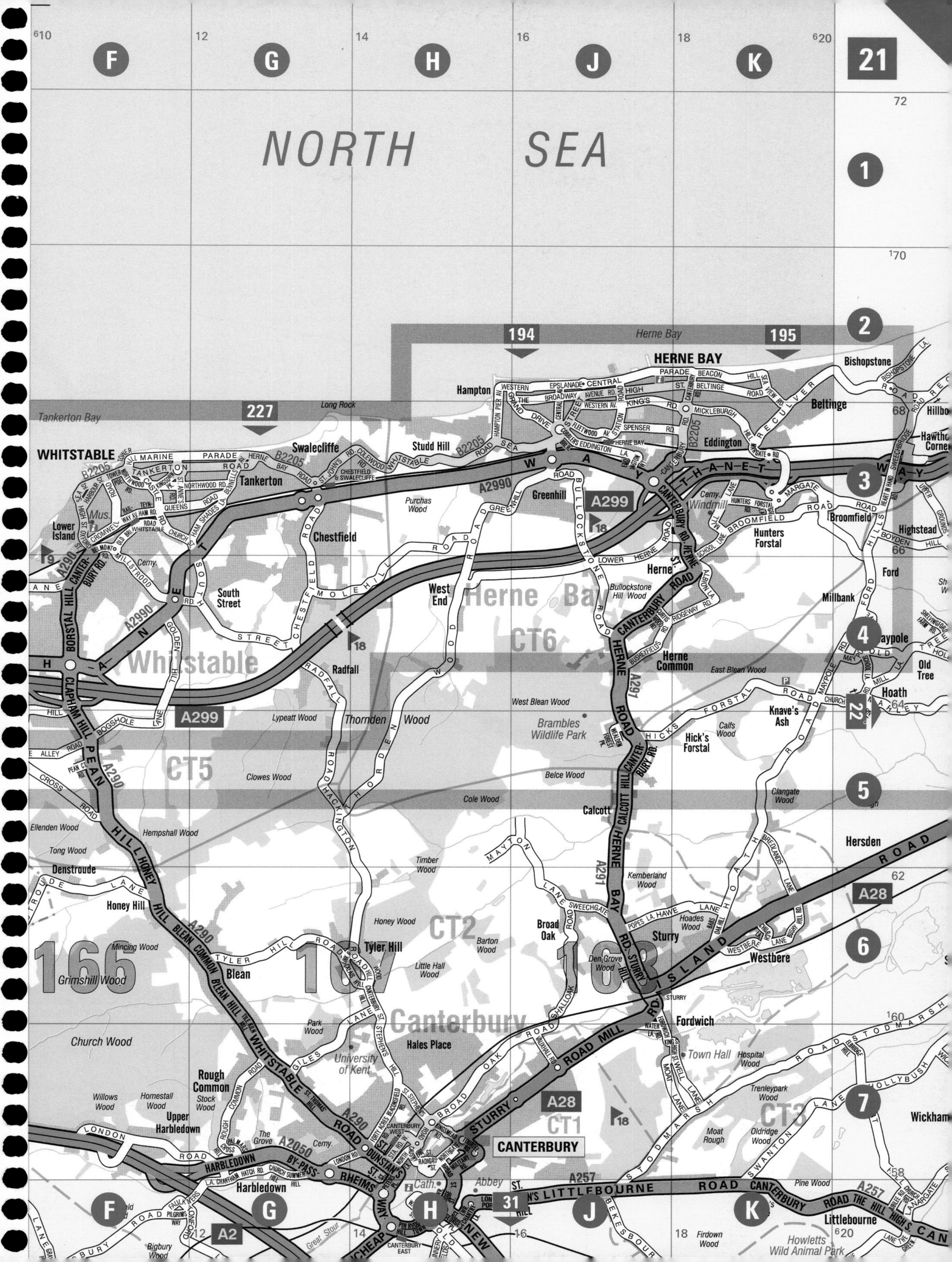

NORTH SEA
F
G
H
J
K
1
2
3
4
5
6
7
Herne Bay
HERNE BAY
194
195
227
Tankerton Bay
Long Rock
WHITSTABLE
Tankerton
Swalecliffe
Studd Hill
Hampton
Bishopstone
Beltinge
Eddington
Greenhill
Chestfield
Purchas Wood
A299
A2990
A290
A291
A28
A2050
A257
A2
B2205
Lower Island
South Street
West End
Herne Bay
Herne
Bullockstone Hill Wood
Hunters Forstal
Broomfield
Highstead
Ford
Millbank
Maypole
Old Tree
Hoath
Herne Common
East Blean Wood
CT6
Whitstable
Radfall
Thornden Wood
Lypeatt Wood
West Blean Wood
Brambles Wildlife Park
Knave's Ash
Hick's Forstal
Calfs Wood
CT5
Clowes Wood
Belce Wood
Cole Wood
Calcott
Clangate Wood
Ellenden Wood
Hempshall Wood
Tong Wood
Denstroude
Hersden
Timber Wood
Kemberland Wood
Honey Hill
Honey Wood
CT2
Broad Oak
Hoades Wood
Sturry
Barton Wood
Westbere
166
167
168
Mincing Wood
Grimshill Wood
Blean
Tyler Hill
Little Hall Wood
Den Grove Wood
Canterbury
Fordwich
Park Wood
Church Wood
University of Kent
Hales Place
Town Hall
Hospital Wood
Rough Common
Willows Wood
Homestall Wood
Stock Wood
Upper Harbledown
Trenleypark Wood
Wickham
The Grove
Cemy.
CT1
CANTERBURY
CT3
Moat Rough
Oldridge Wood
Harbledown
Cath.
Abbey
31
Pine Wood
Littlebourne
Bigbury Wood
Great Stour
Firdown Wood
Howletts Wild Animal Park

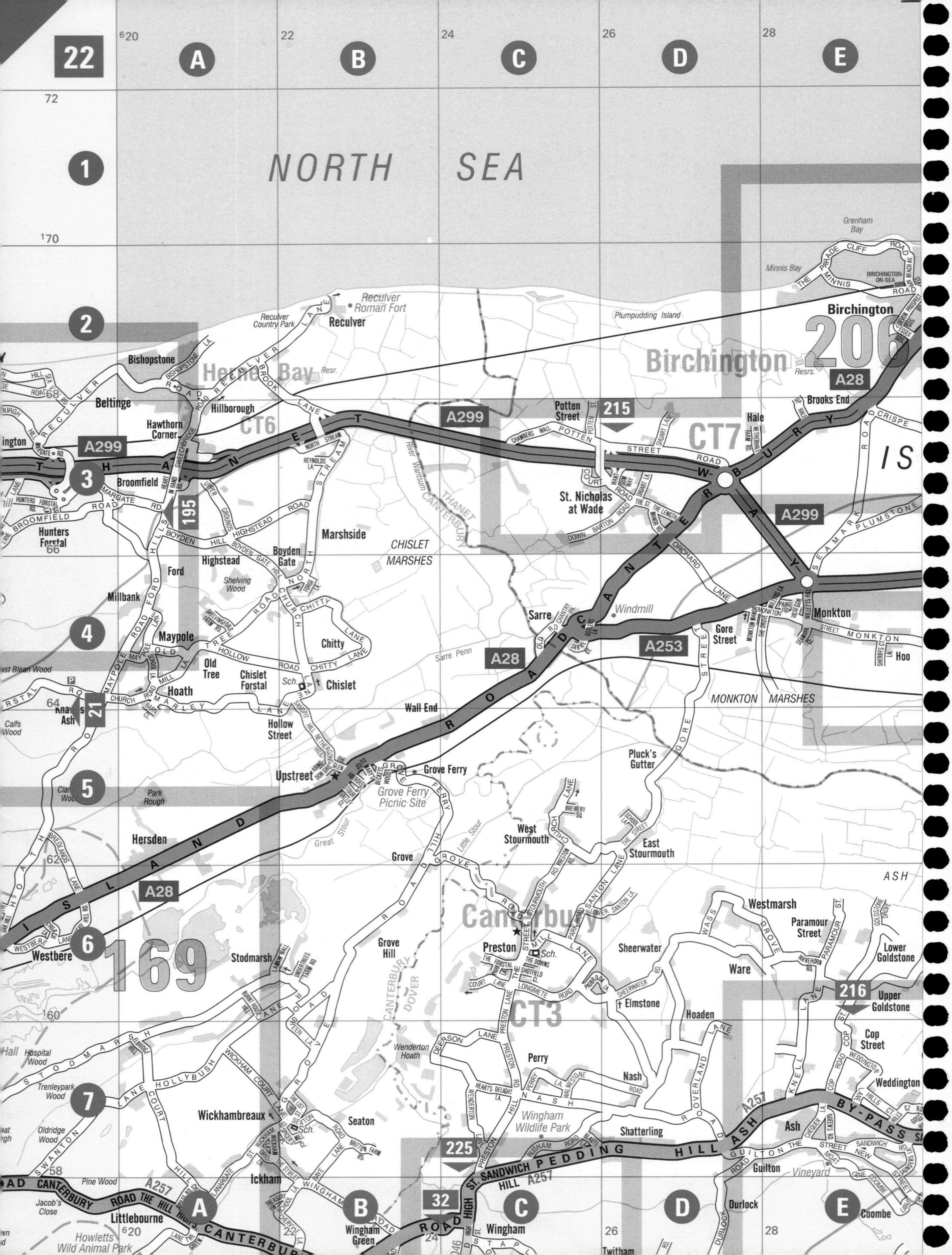

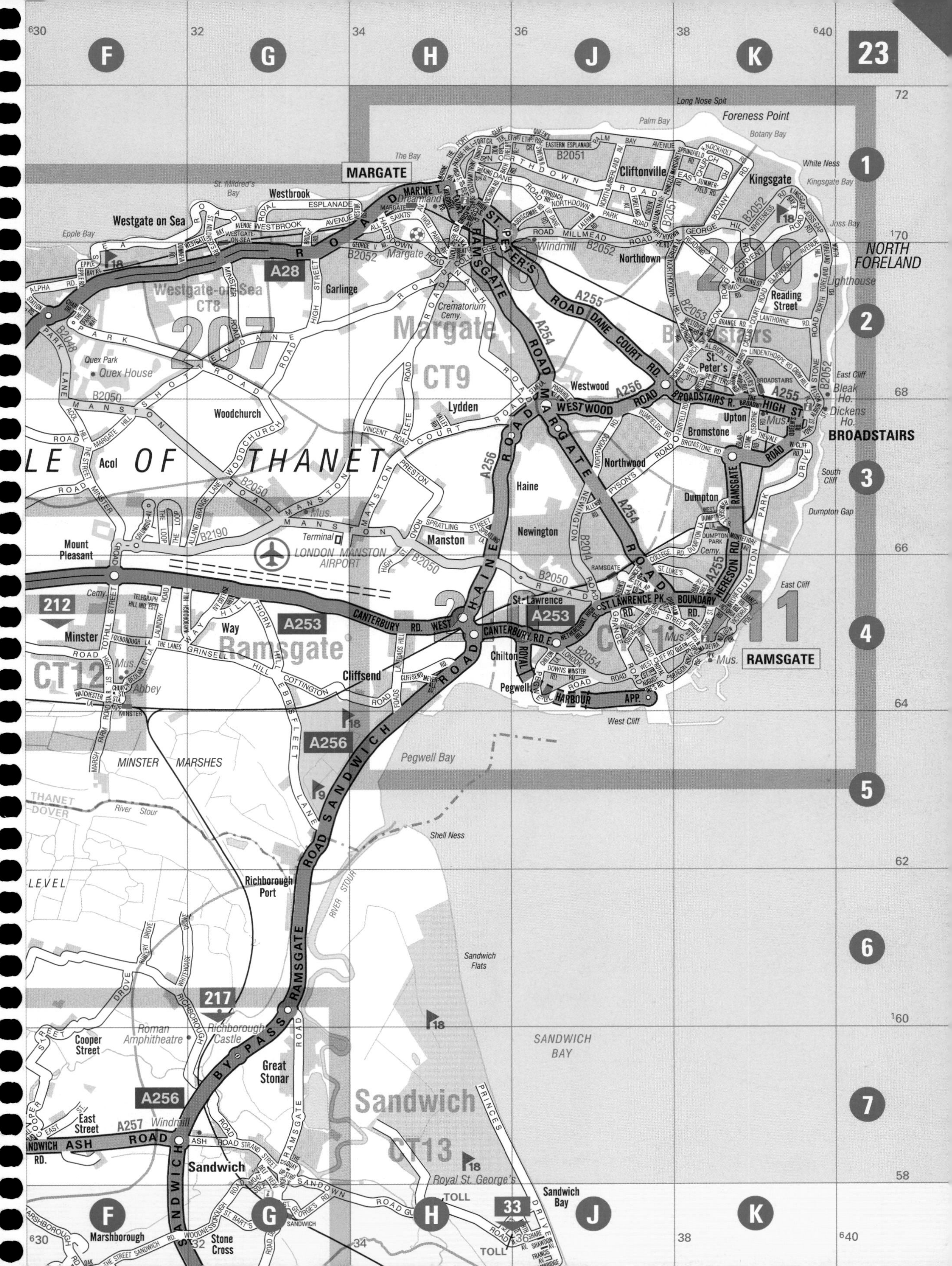
MARGATE
Westgate on Sea
Westbrook
Garlinge
Margate
CT9
Westgate-on-Sea
CT8
Cliftonville
Kingsgate
Northdown
NORTH FORELAND
Lighthouse
Reading Street
Broadstairs
St. Peter's
Westwood
Lydden
Woodchurch
Quex Park
Quex House
Acol
ISLE OF THANET
Haine
Northwood
Upton
Bromstone
BROADSTAIRS
Bleak Ho.
Dickens Ho.
Dumpton
Dumpton Gap
Newington
Manston
Mount Pleasant
LONDON MANSTON AIRPORT
Terminal
Minster
CT12
Way
Ramsgate
Cliffsend
Chilton
Pegwell
St. Lawrence
RAMSGATE
CT11
Pegwell Bay
MINSTER MARSHES
Shell Ness
Richborough Port
Sandwich Flats
SANDWICH BAY
Roman Amphitheatre
Richborough Castle
Cooper Street
Great Stonar
East Street
Sandwich
CT13
Royal St. George's
Sandwich Bay
Marshborough
Stone Cross
A28
A253
A254
A255
A256
A257
B2050
B2052
Foreness Point
Long Nose Spit
Palm Bay
Botany Bay
White Ness
Kingsgate Bay
Joss Bay
East Cliff
South Cliff
West Cliff
The Bay
St. Mildred's Bay
Epple Bay
207
208
209
210
211
212
217
33

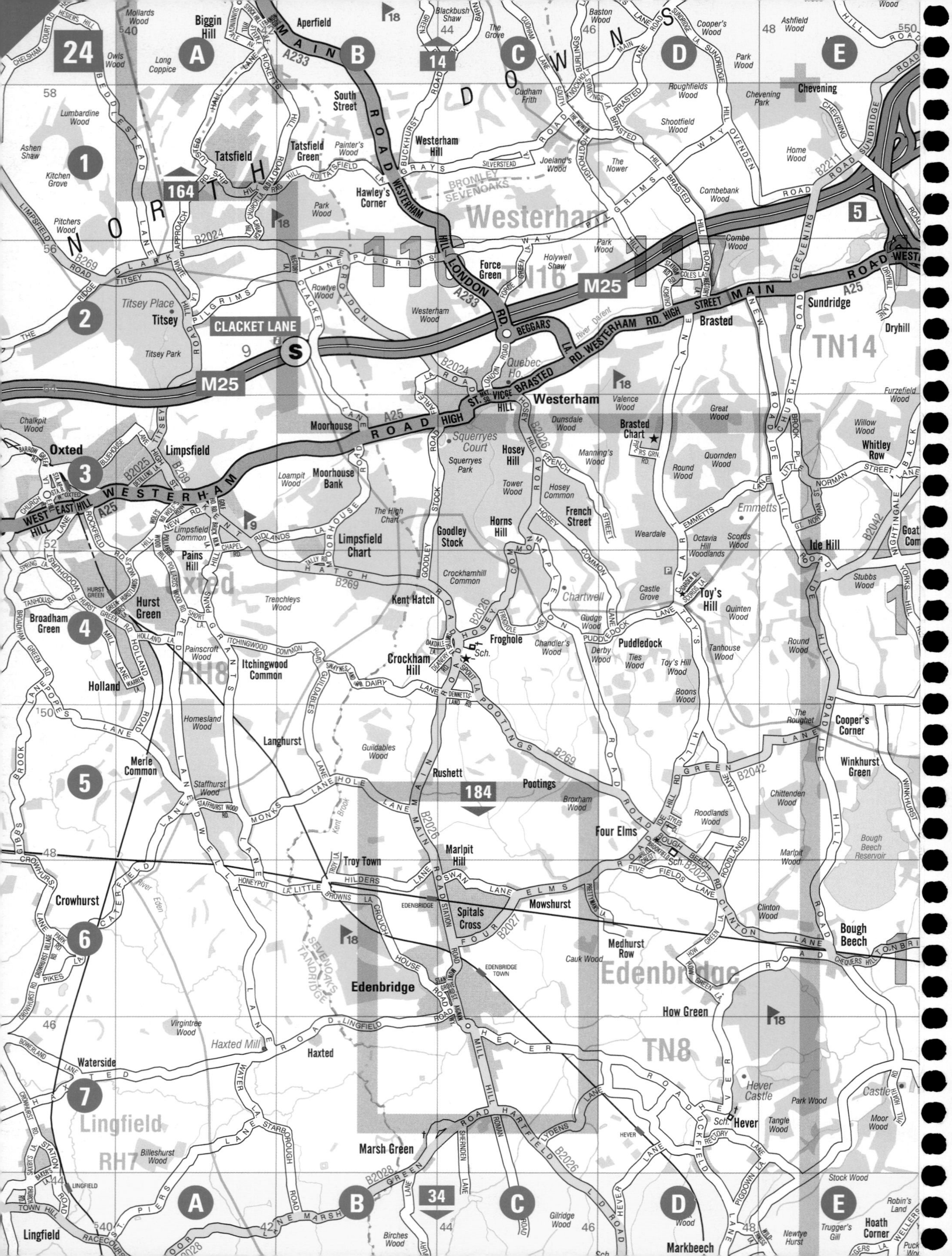

24
A
B
C
D
E
1
2
3
4
5
6
7
164
14
184
34
NORTH DOWNS
Biggin Hill
Aperfield
South Street
Tatsfield
Tatsfield Green
Westerham Hill
Hawley's Corner
Cudham Frith
Chevening
Chevening Park
Westerham
Force Green
TN16
M25
Clacket Lane
Titsey
Titsey Place
Titsey Park
Sundridge
Brasted
Dryhill
TN14
Oxted
Limpsfield
Moorhouse
Moorhouse Bank
Squerryes Court
Squerryes Park
Hosey Hill
Brasted Chart
Whitley Row
Emmetts
Ide Hill
Limpsfield Common
Pains Hill
Limpsfield Chart
Goodley Stock
Horns Hill
French Street
Weardale
Hurst Green
Kent Hatch
Crockhamhill Common
Chartwell
Toy's Hill
Broadham Green
Holland
Itchingwood Common
Crockham Hill
Froghole
Puddledock
RH8
Merle Common
Langhurst
Rushett
Pootings
Cooper's Corner
Winkhurst Green
Four Elms
Marlpit Hill
Troy Town
Crowhurst
Spitals Cross
Mowshurst
Medhurst Row
Bough Beech
Bough Beech Reservoir
Edenbridge
How Green
TN8
Waterside
Haxted
Haxted Mill
Lingfield
RH7
Hever
Hever Castle
Marsh Green
Markbeech
Hoath Corner

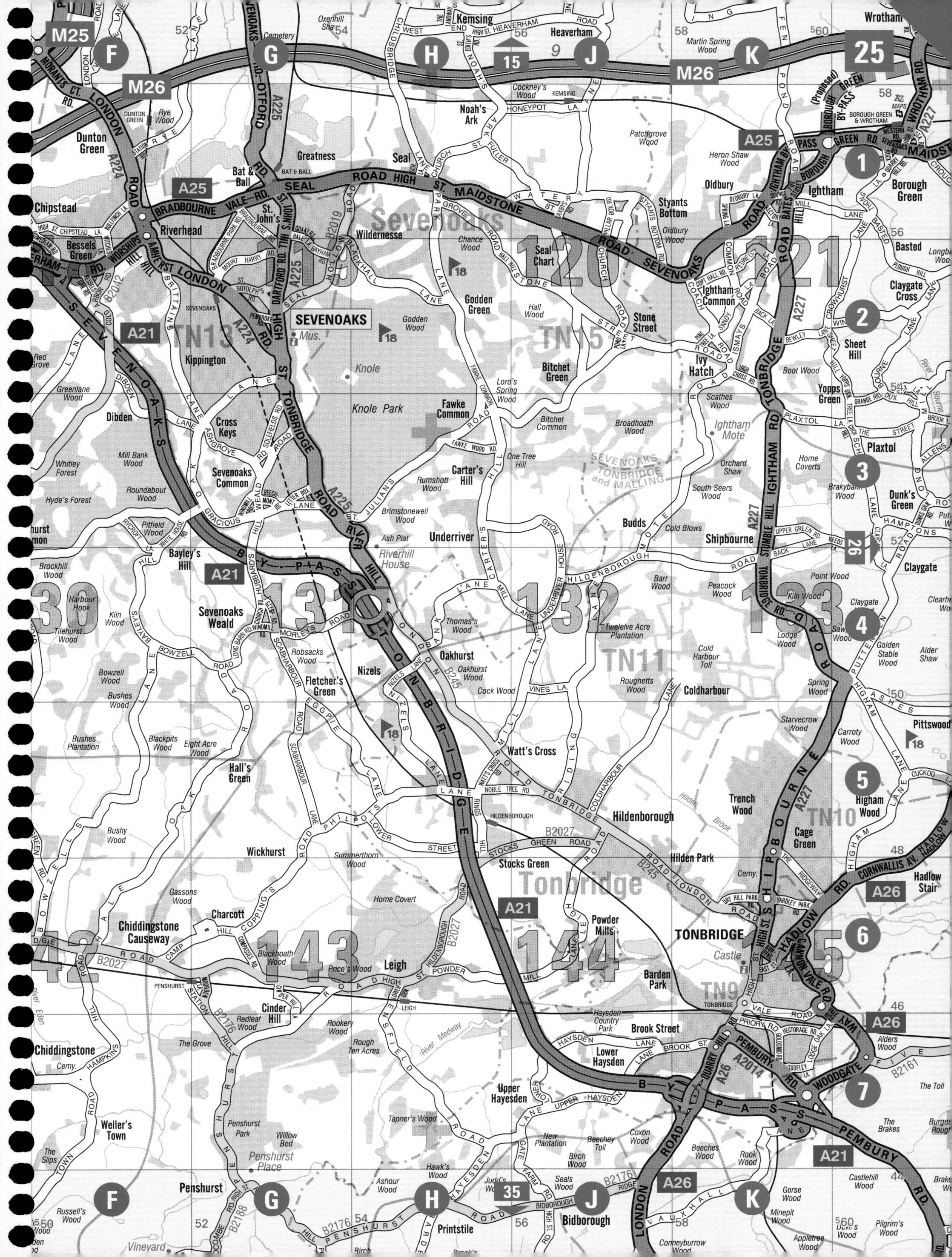

M25
M26
A25
A21
A26
A225
A224
A227
A2014
B245
B2027
B2176
B2188
B2019
B2042
B2161
25
15
26
35
F
G
H
J
K
1
2
3
4
5
6
7
119
120
121
130
131
132
133
142
143
144
145
TN13
TN15
TN11
TN10
TN9
Kemsing
Heaverham
Wrotham
Oxenhill Shaw
Cemetery
Martin Spring Wood
Noah's Ark
Cockney's Wood
Patchgrove Wood
Dunton Green
Rye Wood
Greatness
Seal
Bat & Ball
Heron Shaw Wood
Oldbury
Styants Bottom
Ightham
Borough Green
Chipstead
Bessels Green
Riverhead
St. John's
Sevenoaks
Wilderness
Chance Wood
Seal Chart
Oldbury Wood
Basted
Longbury Wood
SEVENOAKS
Mus.
Godden Wood
Godden Green
Hall Wood
Stone Street
Ightham Common
Claygate Cross
Red Grove
Kippington
Knole
Bitchet Green
Ivy Hatch
Sheet Hill
Greenlane Wood
Dibden
Cross Keys
Knole Park
Fawke Common
Lord's Spring Wood
Bitchet Common
Broadhoath Wood
Scathes Wood
Ightham Mote
Boot Wood
Yopps Green
Plaxtol
Whitley Forest
Mill Bank Wood
Sevenoaks Common
One Tree Hill
Carter's Hill
Rumshott Wood
SEVENOAKS TONBRIDGE and MALLING
Orchard Shaw
Home Coverts
Roundabout Wood
Hyde's Forest
Brimstonewell Wood
South Seers Wood
Brakybank Wood
Dunk's Green
Pitfield Wood
Ash Plat
Underriver
Riverhill House
Budds
Cold Blows
Shipbourne
Claygate
Brockhill Wood
Bayley's Hill
Harbour Hook
Kiln Wood
Tilehurst Wood
Sevenoaks Weald
Thomas's Wood
Barr Wood
Peacock Wood
Point Wood
Kiln Wood
Claygate Wood
Clearheart Wood
Twelve Acre Plantation
Lodge Wood
Golden Stable Wood
Alder Shaw
Robsacks Wood
Oakhurst
Oakhurst Wood
Cold Harbour Toll
Bowzell Wood
Bushes Wood
Fletcher's Green
Nizels
Cock Wood
Roughetts Wood
Coldharbour
Spring Wood
Starvecrow Wood
Carroty Wood
Pittswood
Bushes Plantation
Blackpits Wood
Eight Acre Wood
Watt's Cross
Hall's Green
Trench Wood
Higham Wood
Hildenborough
Cage Green
Bushy Wood
Wickhurst
Summerthorn Wood
Stocks Green
Hilden Park
Tonbridge
Cemy.
Hadlow Stair
Gassons Wood
Charcott
Home Covert
Chiddingstone Causeway
Blackhoath Wood
Price's Wood
Leigh
Powder Mills
TONBRIDGE
Castle
Barden Park
Penshurst
Cinder Hill
Redleaf Wood
Rookery Wood
Hayesden Country Park
Brook Street
Lower Haysden
Alders Wood
The Grove
Rough Ten Acres
River Medway
River Eden
Chiddingstone
Upper Hayesden
The Toll
The Brakes
Burges Rough
Weller's Town
Penshurst Park
Willow Bed
Tapner's Wood
New Plantation
Beechey Toll
Coxon Wood
Beeches Wood
Birch Wood
The Slips
Penshurst Place
Hawk's Wood
Judd's Wood
Seals Wood
Rook Wood
Ashour Wood
Penshurst
Bidborough
Gorse Wood
Castlehill Wood
Russell's Wood
Printstile
Minepit Wood
Pilgrim's Wood
Devil's Wood
Appletree Wood
Conneyburrow Wood
Vineyard

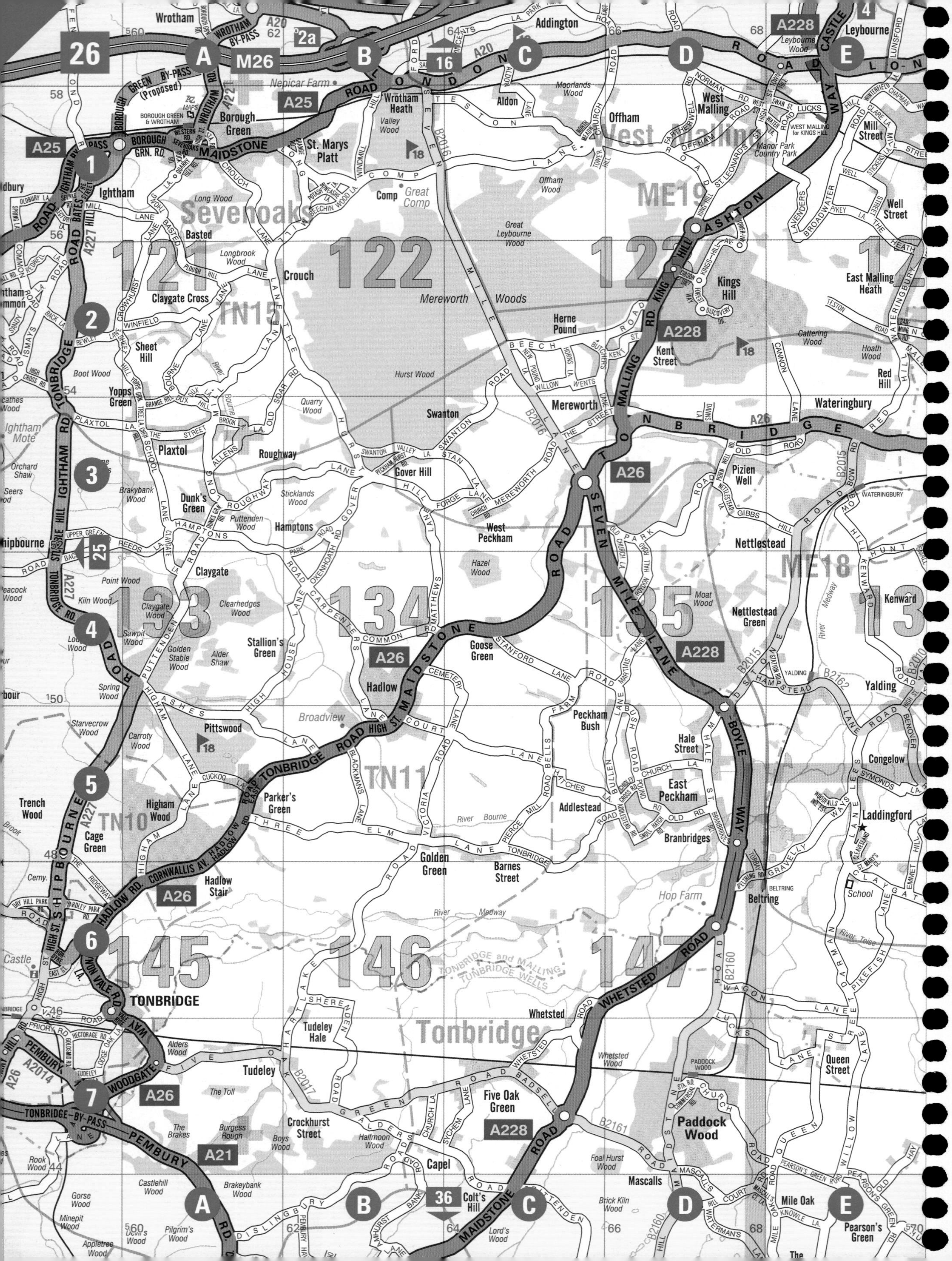
A
B
C
D
E
1
2
3
4
5
6
7
M26
A20
A25
A26
A227
A228
A21
A2014
B2016
B2015
B2017
B2160
B2161
B2162
ME19
ME18
TN15
TN11
TN10
121
122
123
133
134
135
145
146
147
16
25
36
4
2a
Wrotham
Addington
Leybourne
Nepicar Farm
Wrotham Heath
Valley Wood
Borough Green
St. Marys Platt
Aldon
Offham
West Malling
Moorlands Wood
Manor Park Country Park
Mill Street
Ightham
Sevenoaks
Long Wood
Basted
Comp
Great Comp
Offham Wood
Great Leybourne Wood
Well Street
Longbrook Wood
Crouch
Claygate Cross
Mereworth Woods
Kings Hill
East Malling Heath
Sheet Hill
Herne Pound
Kent Street
Cattering Wood
Hoath Wood
Red Hill
Boot Wood
Hurst Wood
Yopps Green
Quarry Wood
Swanton
Mereworth
Wateringbury
Ightham Mote
Plaxtol
Roughway
Gover Hill
Pizien Well
Orchard Shaw
Seers Wood
Brakybank Wood
Dunk's Green
Sticklands Wood
Puttenden Wood
Hamptons
West Peckham
Nettlestead
Shipbourne
Claygate
Point Wood
Hazel Wood
Kiln Wood
Peacock Wood
Claygate Wood
Clearhedges Wood
Moat Wood
Nettlestead Green
Kenward
Sawpit Wood
Golden Stable Wood
Alder Shaw
Stallion's Green
Goose Green
Hadlow
Yalding
Spring Wood
Starvecrow Wood
Broadview
Peckham Bush
Carroty Wood
Pittswood
Hale Street
Congelow
Trench Wood
Higham Wood
Parker's Green
Addlestead
East Peckham
Laddingford
Cage Green
River Bourne
Branbridges
Golden Green
Barnes Street
Hadlow Stair
Hop Farm
Beltring
School
River Medway
River Teise
Castle
TONBRIDGE
TONBRIDGE and MALLING
TUNBRIDGE WELLS
Whetsted
Tudeley Hale
Tonbridge
Alders Wood
Tudeley
Whetsted Wood
Queen Street
Paddock Wood
The Toll
Five Oak Green
The Brakes
Burgess Rough
Crockhurst Street
Boys Wood
Halfmoon Wood
Capel
Foal Hurst Wood
Mascalls
Rook Wood
Castlehill Wood
Brakeybank Wood
Gorse Wood
Minepit Wood
Colt's Hill
Brick Kiln Wood
Mile Oak
Pearson's Green
Pilgrim's Wood
Devil's Wood
Appletree Wood
Lord's Wood
TONBRIDGE-BY-PASS
PEMBURY ROAD
MAIDSTONE ROAD
SEVEN MILE LANE
BOYLE WAY
WHETSTED ROAD
TONBRIDGE ROAD
LONDON ROAD
ASHTON WAY
CASTLE WAY
KING HILL
MALLING RD.
SHIPBOURNE RD.
HIGH ST.
WOODGATE WAY
VALE RD.
FIVE OAK GREEN ROAD
HADLOW RD.
CORNWALLIS AV.

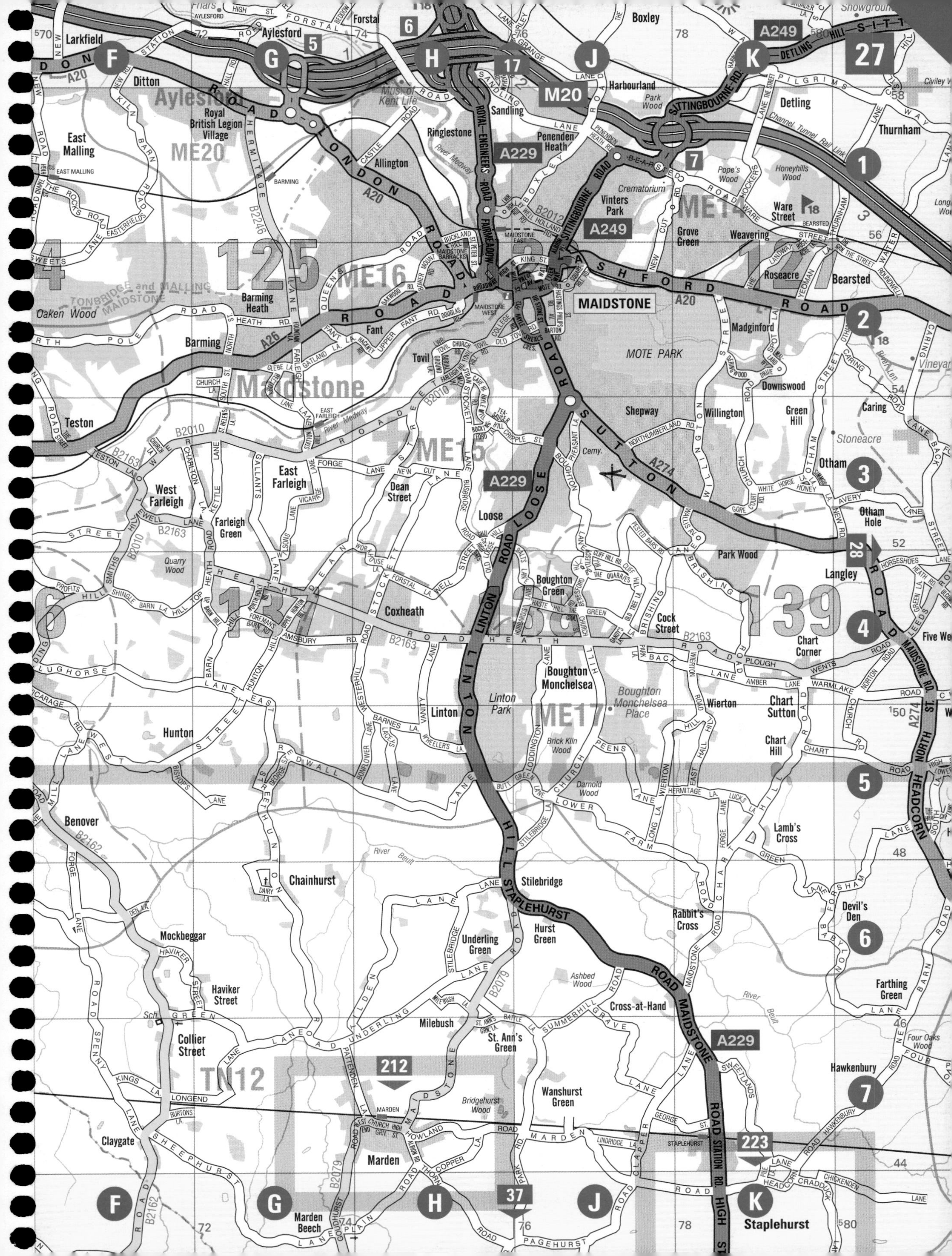

27
Aylesford
Larkfield
Ditton
Boxley
Detling
Thurnham
Harbourland
Sandling
Ringlestone
Penenden Heath
Allington
Royal British Legion Village
East Malling
Barming Heath
Barming
Maidstone
MAIDSTONE
Bearsted
Weavering
Grove Green
Vinters Park
Roseacre
Madginford
Downswood
Mote Park
Shepway
Willington
Green Hill
Caring
Otham
Otham Hole
Langley
Park Wood
Teston
West Farleigh
East Farleigh
Farleigh Green
Dean Street
Loose
Tovil
Fant
Coxheath
Boughton Green
Cock Street
Chart Corner
Boughton Monchelsea
Linton
Linton Park
Wierton
Chart Sutton
Chart Hill
Hunton
Benover
Chainhurst
Stilebridge
Lamb's Cross
Rabbit's Cross
Devil's Den
Mockbeggar
Underling Green
Hurst Green
Haviker Street
Farthing Green
Collier Street
Milebush
St. Ann's Green
Cross-at-Hand
Hawkenbury
Wanshurst Green
Claygate
Marden
Marden Beech
Staplehurst
M20
A20
A26
A229
A249
A274
B2010
B2163
B2162
B2079
ME14
ME15
ME16
ME17
ME20
TN12
125
127
137
138
139
212
223
37

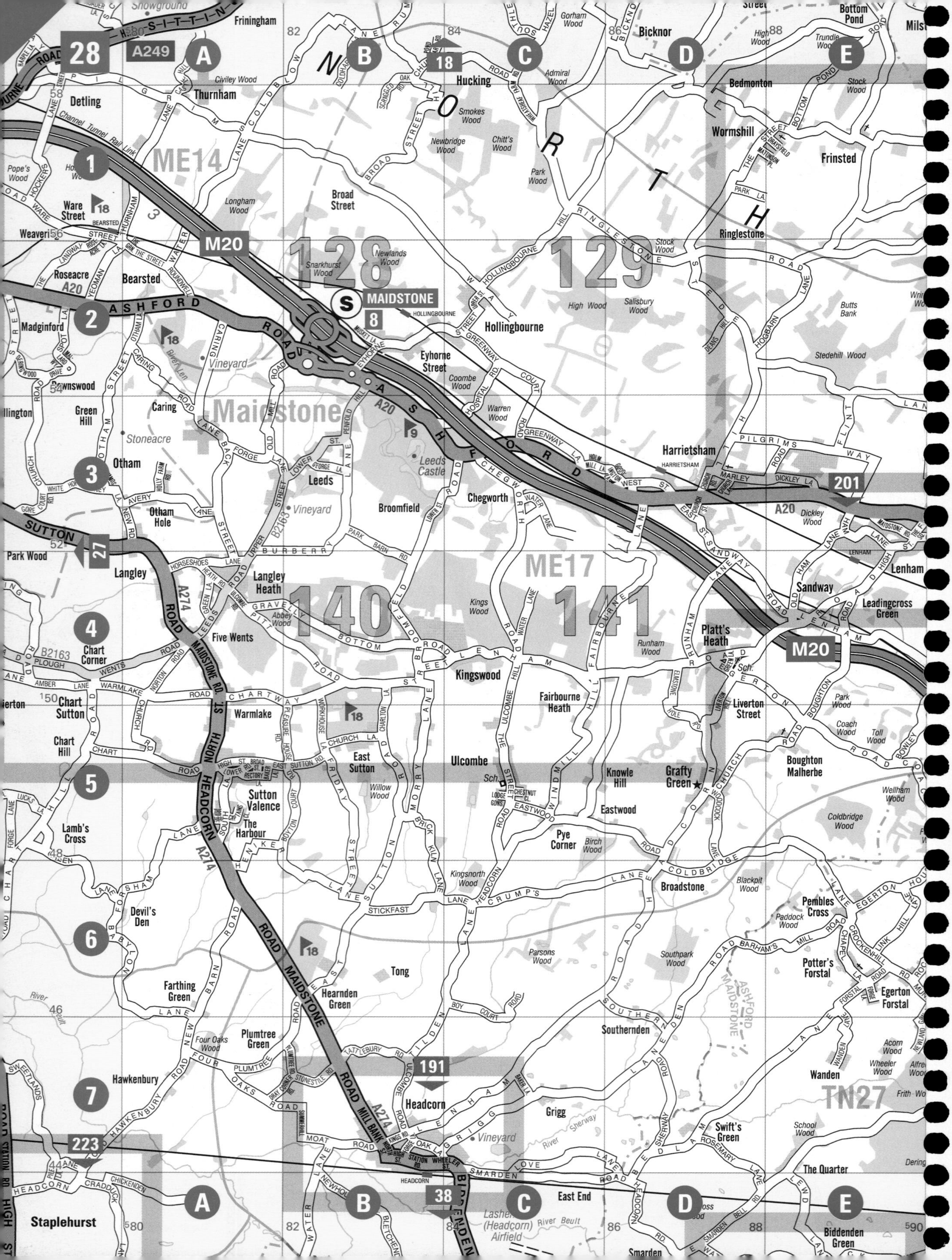

28
128
129
140
141
Maidstone
ME14
ME17
TN27
M20
A20
A274
A249
B2163
MAIDSTONE
Detling
Thurnham
Bearsted
Roseacre
Madginford
Otham
Langley
Chart Sutton
Sutton Valence
Headcorn
Hollingbourne
Harrietsham
Lenham
Ulcombe
Kingswood
Broomfield
Leeds
Leeds Castle
Staplehurst
Wormshill
Frinsted
Hucking
Bicknor
Grafty Green
Boughton Malherbe
Smarden
Biddenden Green
East Sutton
Langley Heath
Chegworth
Eyhorne Street
Platt's Heath
Sandway
Egerton Forstal
Hawkenbury
Tong
Grigg
Southernden
Broadstone
Lashenden (Headcorn) Airfield
River Beult
18
201
191
223
38
27
8

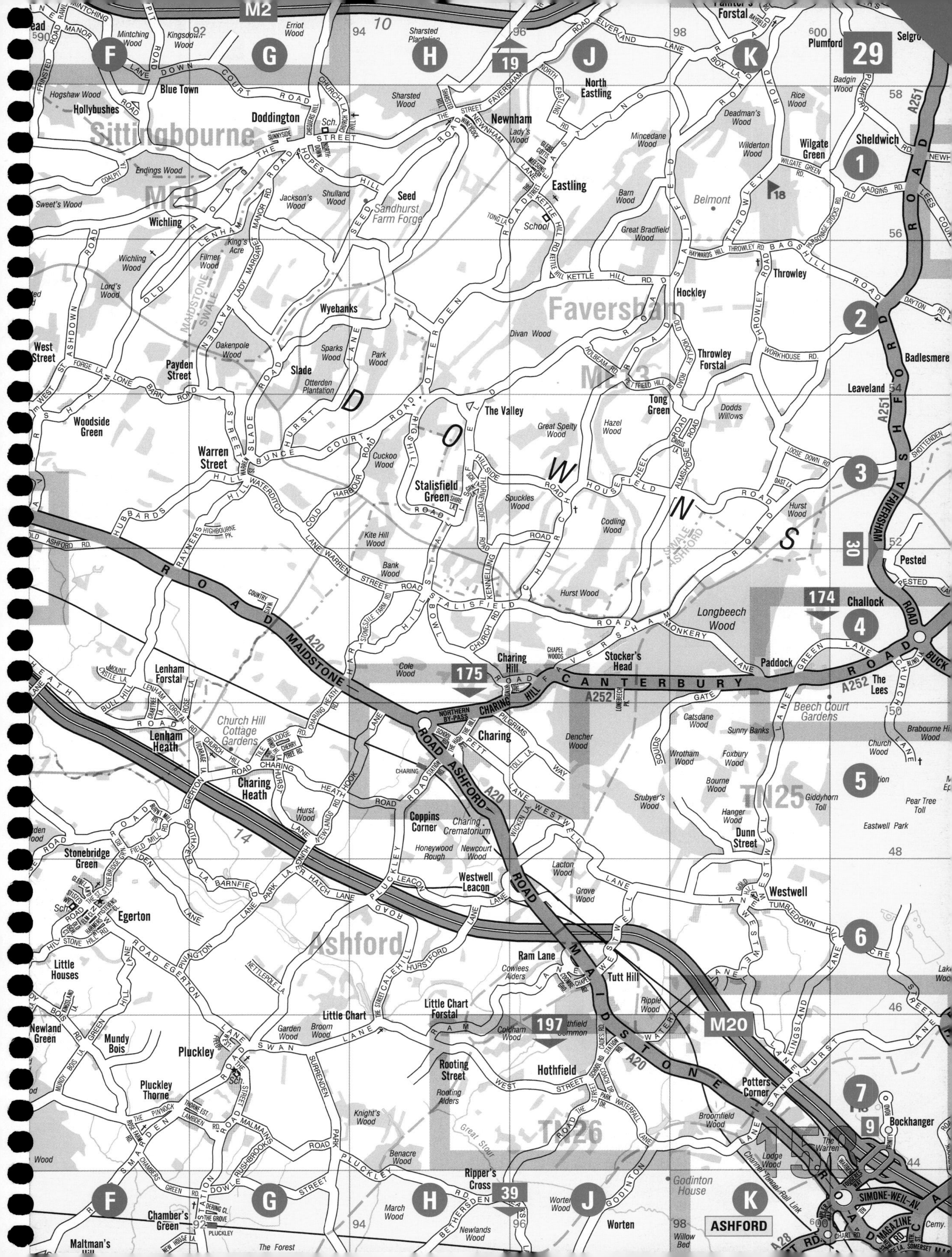
29
M2
M20
A20
A251
A252
Sittingbourne
Faversham
Ashford
ME9
ME13
TN25
TN26
DOWNS
Doddington
Newnham
Eastling
North Eastling
Sheldwich
Wilgate Green
Throwley
Hockley
Throwley Forstal
Badlesmere
Leaveland
Tong Green
Challock
Paddock
The Lees
Stalisfield Green
Charing
Charing Hill
Charing Heath
Lenham Heath
Lenham Forstal
Warren Street
Payden Street
Wichling
Seed
Wyebanks
Slade
Woodside Green
West Street
Hollybushes
Blue Town
Egerton
Stonebridge Green
Little Houses
Newland Green
Mundy Bois
Pluckley
Pluckley Thorne
Little Chart
Little Chart Forstal
Coppins Corner
Westwell Leacon
Westwell
Dunn Street
Tutt Hill
Ram Lane
Hothfield
Rooting Street
Ripper's Cross
Potters Corner
Bockhanger
Worten
Chamber's Green
Maltman's
Godinton House
ASHFORD
Plumford
Painter's Forstal
Pested
Stocker's Head
Belmont
Church Hill Cottage Gardens
Beech Court Gardens
Sandhurst Farm Forge
Charing Crematorium
Eastwell Park
Channel Tunnel Rail Link
Great Stour

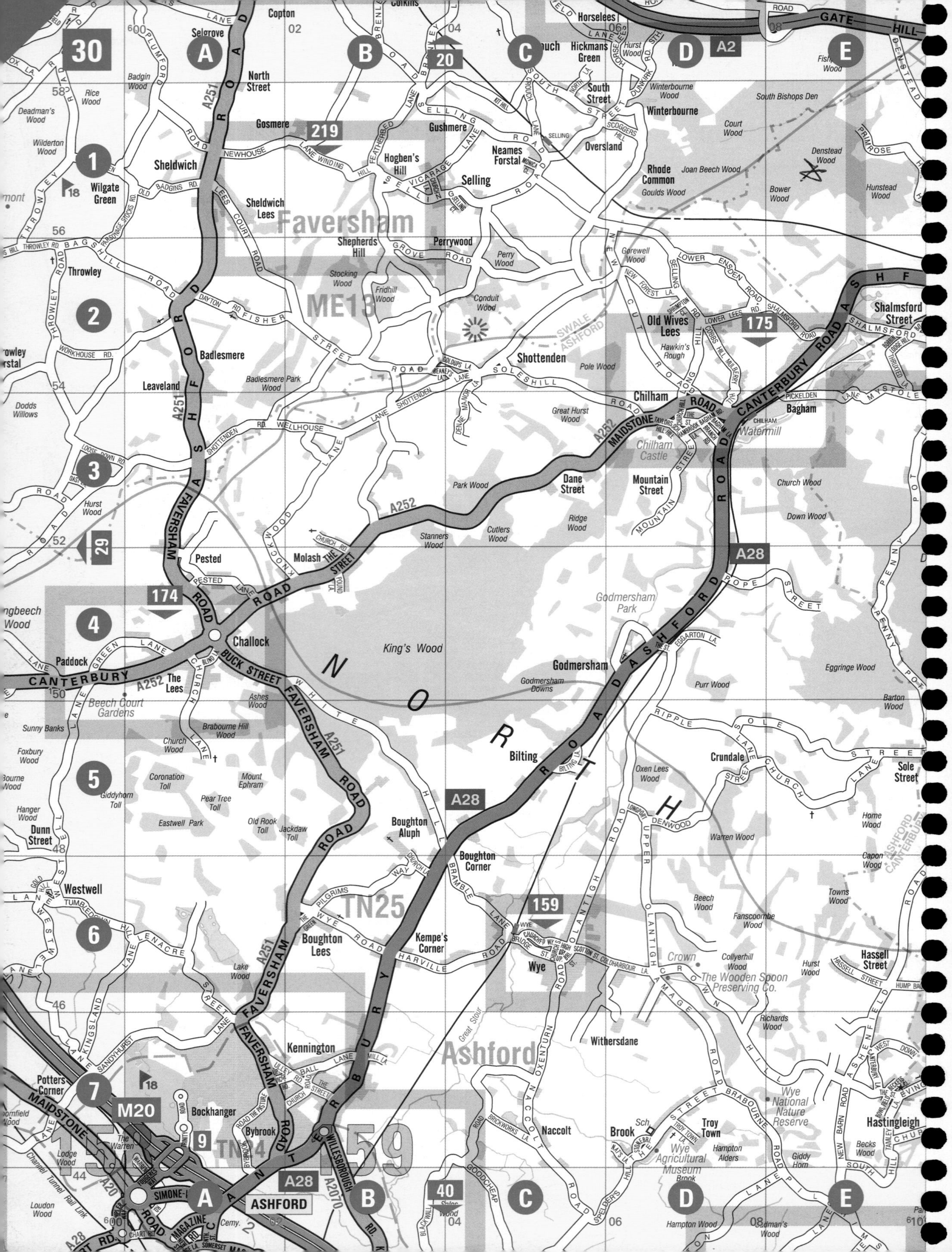

30
A
B
C
D
E
1
2
3
4
5
6
7
Faversham
ME13
TN25
Ashford
ASHFORD
NORTH
Selgrove
Copton
North Street
Sheldwich
Wilgate Green
Sheldwich Lees
Gosmere
Gushmere
Hogben's Hill
Selling
Neames Forstal
Shepherds Hill
Perrywood
South Street
Hickmans Green
Horselees
Winterbourne
Oversland
Rhode Common
Throwley
Badlesmere
Leaveland
Shottenden
Old Wives Lees
Chilham
Bagham
Shalmsford Street
Dane Street
Mountain Street
Chilham Castle
Chilham Watermill
Molash
Pested
Challock
Paddock
The Lees
King's Wood
Godmersham
Godmersham Park
Bilting
Crundale
Sole Street
Boughton Aluph
Boughton Corner
Westwell
Dunn Street
Boughton Lees
Kempe's Corner
Wye
Crown
The Wooden Spoon Preserving Co.
Withersdane
Kennington
Potters Corner
Bockhanger
Bybrook
Naccolt
Brook
Troy Town
Wye National Nature Reserve
Wye Agricultural Museum
Hastingleigh
Hassell Street
A251
A252
A28
A2
A20
A2070
M20
219
175
174
159
20
29
40
9

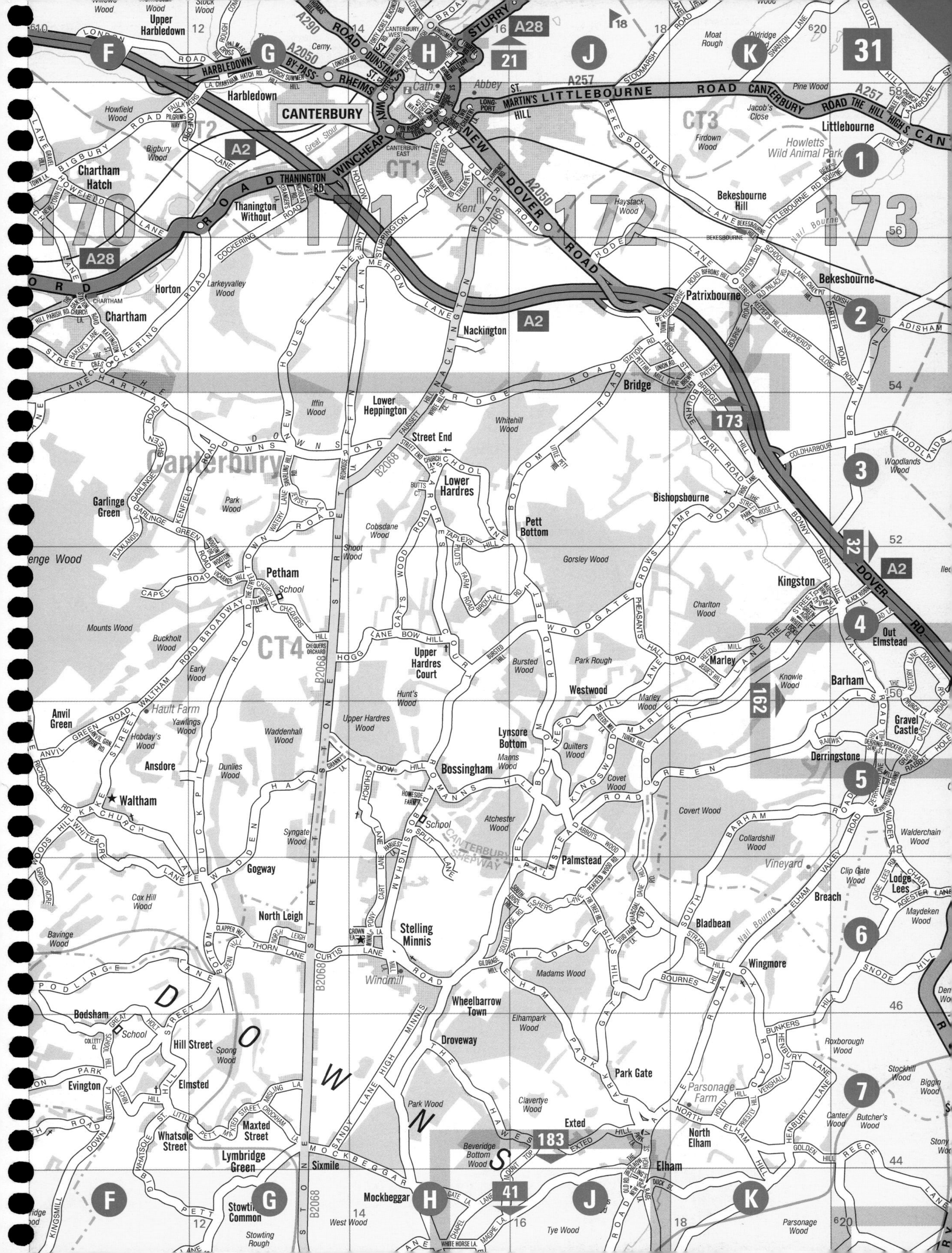

31
F
G
H
J
K
A28
21
A2050
A290
A257
A2
A2050
B2068
CANTERBURY
CT1
CT2
CT3
CT4
170
171
172
173
Upper Harbledown
Harbledown
Howfield Wood
Bigbury Wood
Chartham Hatch
Thanington Without
Horton
Larkeyvalley Wood
Chartham
Cath.
Abbey
Kent
Haystack Wood
Firdown Wood
Jacob's Close
Pine Wood
Moat Rough
Littlebourne
Howletts Wild Animal Park
Bekesbourne Hill
Bekesbourne
Patrixbourne
Nackington
Bridge
Lower Heppington
Iffin Wood
Whitehill Wood
Street End
Lower Hardres
Pett Bottom
Bishopsbourne
Woodlands Wood
Canterbury
Garlinge Green
Park Wood
Cobsdane Wood
Shoot Wood
Gorsley Wood
Kingston
Petham
School
Charlton Wood
Out Elmstead
Mounts Wood
Buckholt Wood
Early Wood
Upper Hardres Court
Bursted Wood
Park Rough
Marley
Barham
Knowle Wood
Westwood
Marley Wood
Hunt's Wood
Hault Farm
Anvil Green
Yawlings Wood
Hobday's Wood
Upper Hardres Wood
Waddenhall Wood
Lynsore Bottom
Quilters Wood
Gravel Castle
Derringstone
Ansdore
Dunlies Wood
Bossingham
Manns Wood
Covet Wood
Waltham
Atchester Wood
Covert Wood
Walderchain Wood
Syngate Wood
Collardshill Wood
Palmstead
Vineyard
Clip Gate Wood
Lodge Lees
Gogway
Breach
Maydeken Wood
Cox Hill Wood
North Leigh
Stelling Minnis
Bladbean
Bavinge Wood
Wingmore
Windmill
Madams Wood
Wheelbarrow Town
Bodsham
School
Elhampark Wood
Hill Street
Spong Wood
Droveway
Roxborough Wood
Evington
Elmsted
Park Gate
Stockhill Wood
Biggin Wood
Park Wood
Clavertye Wood
Parsonage Farm
Maxted Street
Whatsole Street
Exted
North Elham
Canter Wood
Butcher's Wood
Beveridge Bottom Wood
183
Lymbridge Green
Sixmile
Elham
Mockbeggar
41
Stowting Common
West Wood
Tye Wood
Parsonage Wood
Stowting Rough
DOWNS
DOVER RD.
32
162

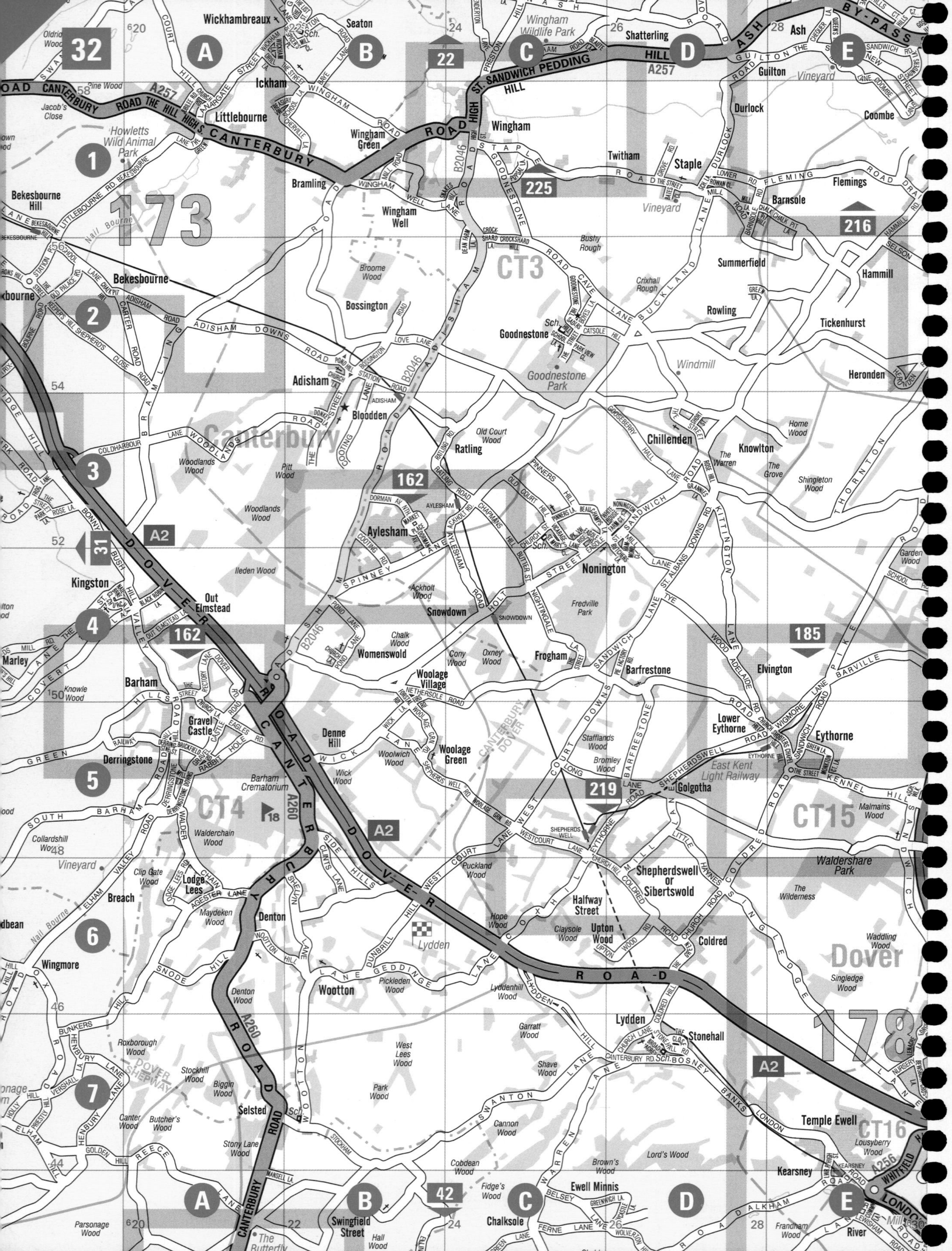
A
B
C
D
E
22
216
225
173
CT3
Canterbury
162
31
185
219
CT4
CT15
Dover
178
CT16
A2
A257
A260
A256
B2046
42
Wickhambreaux
Seaton
Wingham Wildlife Park
Shatterling
Ash
Ickham
Littlebourne
Wingham Green
Wingham
Guilton
Durlock
Coombe
Howletts Wild Animal Park
Jacob's Close
Bekesbourne Hill
Bekesbourne
Bramling
Wingham Well
Twitham
Staple
Flemings
Barnsole
Broome Wood
Bushy Rough
Summerfield
Hammill
Bossington
Crixhall Rough
Rowling
Tickenhurst
Goodnestone
Goodnestone Park
Windmill
Heronden
Adisham
Bloodden
Old Court Wood
Ratling
Chillenden
Knowlton
Home Wood
The Warren
The Grove
Shingleton Wood
Woodlands Wood
Pitt Wood
Aylesham
Nonington
Garden Wood
Kingston
Out Elmstead
Ileden Wood
Ackholt Wood
Snowdown
Fredville Park
Marley
Chalk Wood
Womenswold
Cony Wood
Oxney Wood
Frogham
Barfrestone
Elvington
Barham
Knowle Wood
Woolage Village
Gravel Castle
Denne Hill
Woolage Green
Stafflands Wood
Bromley Wood
Lower Eythorne
Eythorne
East Kent Light Railway
Golgotha
Derringstone
Barham Crematorium
Woolwich Wood
Wick Wood
Shepherds Well
Malmains Wood
Collardshill Wood
Walderchain Wood
Vineyard
Clip Gate Wood
Lodge Lees
Puckland Wood
Shepherdswell or Sibertswold
Waldershare Park
Breach
Maydeken Wood
Denton
Halfway Street
The Wilderness
Hope Wood
Claysole Wood
Upton Wood
Coldred
Lydden
Waddling Wood
Wingmore
Denton Wood
Wootton
Pickleden Wood
Lyddenhill Wood
Singledge Wood
Roxborough Wood
Garratt Wood
Stonehall
West Lees Wood
Stockhill Wood
Biggin Wood
Shave Wood
Park Wood
Selsted
Canter Wood
Butcher's Wood
Cannon Wood
Temple Ewell
Lousyberry Wood
Stony Lane Wood
Lord's Wood
Brown's Wood
Kearsney
Cobdean Wood
Fidge's Wood
Ewell Minnis
Parsonage Wood
Swingfield Street
Hall Wood
Chalksole
Frandham Wood
River
The Butterfly
Canterbury Road
Dover Road
Sandwich Road

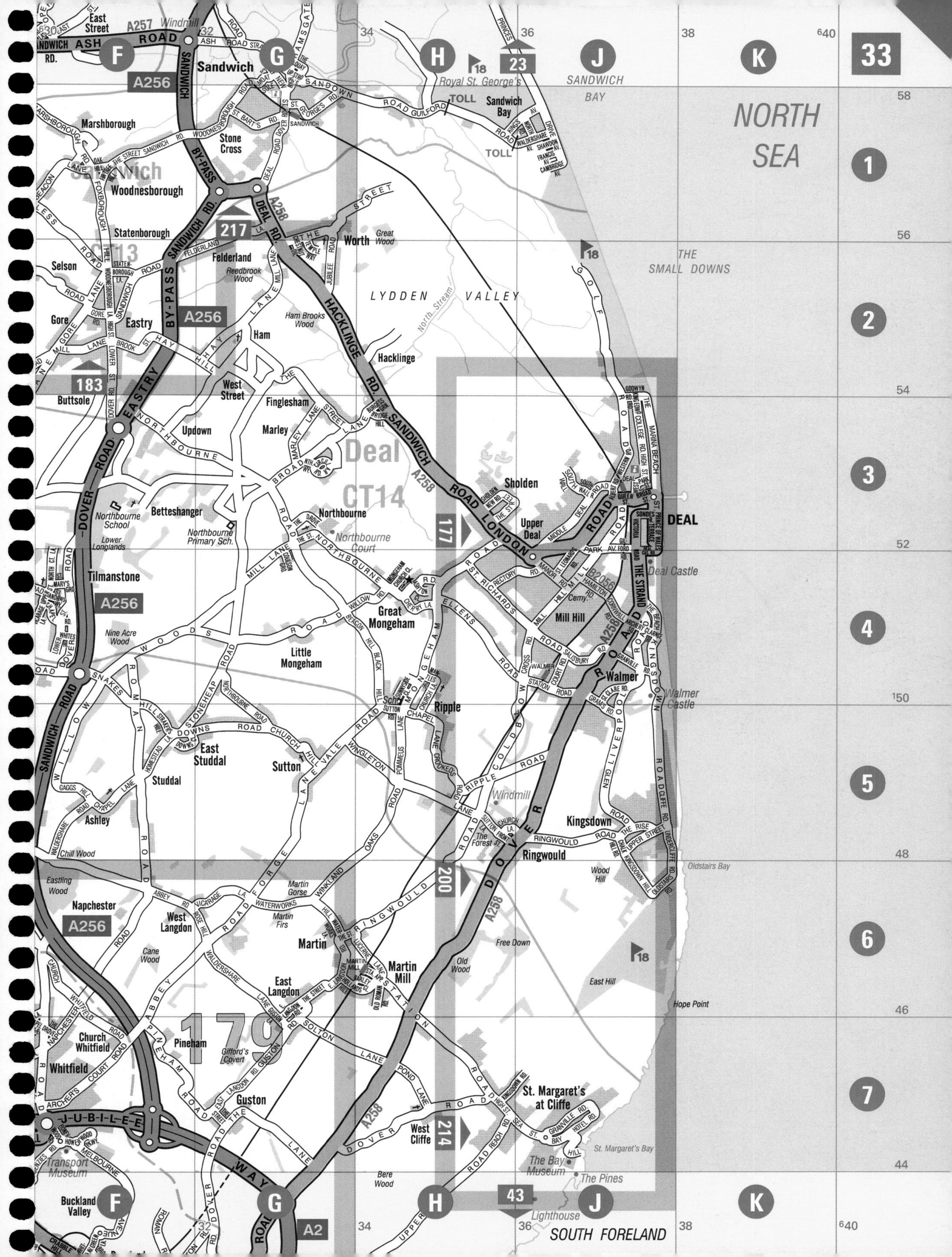
NORTH SEA
SANDWICH BAY
THE SMALL DOWNS
Sandwich
Sandwich Bay
Royal St. George's
Marshborough
Stone Cross
Woodnesborough
Statenborough
Worth
Great Wood
Selson
Felderland
Reedbrook Wood
LYDDEN VALLEY
North Stream
Gore
Eastry
Ham Brooks Wood
Ham
Hacklinge
Buttsole
West Street
Finglesham
Updown
Marley
Deal
CT13
CT14
Sholden
Upper Deal
DEAL
Betteshanger
Northbourne School
Lower Longlands
Northbourne Primary Sch.
Northbourne
Northbourne Court
Deal Castle
Tilmanstone
Great Mongeham
Mill Hill
Nine Acre Wood
Little Mongeham
Walmer
Walmer Castle
Ripple
East Studdal
Studdal
Sutton
Windmill
Kingsdown
Ashley
The Forest
Ringwould
Chill Wood
Wood Hill
Oldstairs Bay
Eastling Wood
Napchester
Martin Gorse
West Langdon
Martin Firs
Cane Wood
Martin
Free Down
Martin Mill
Old Wood
East Langdon
East Hill
Hope Point
Church Whitfield
Whitfield
Pineham
Gifford's Covert
Guston
St. Margaret's at Cliffe
West Cliffe
St. Margaret's Bay
Transport Museum
The Bay Museum
The Pines
Bere Wood
Buckland Valley
Lighthouse
SOUTH FORELAND
A256
A257
A258
A2
B2056
SANDWICH BY-PASS
DEAL RD.
HACKLINGE RD.
SANDWICH ROAD
LONDON ROAD
DOVER ROAD
SANDWICH ROAD
JUBILEE WAY
THE STRAND
217
183
177
200
214
23
43
179
F
G
H
J
K
1
2
3
4
5
6
7
30
32
34
36
38
640
58
56
54
52
150
48
46
44

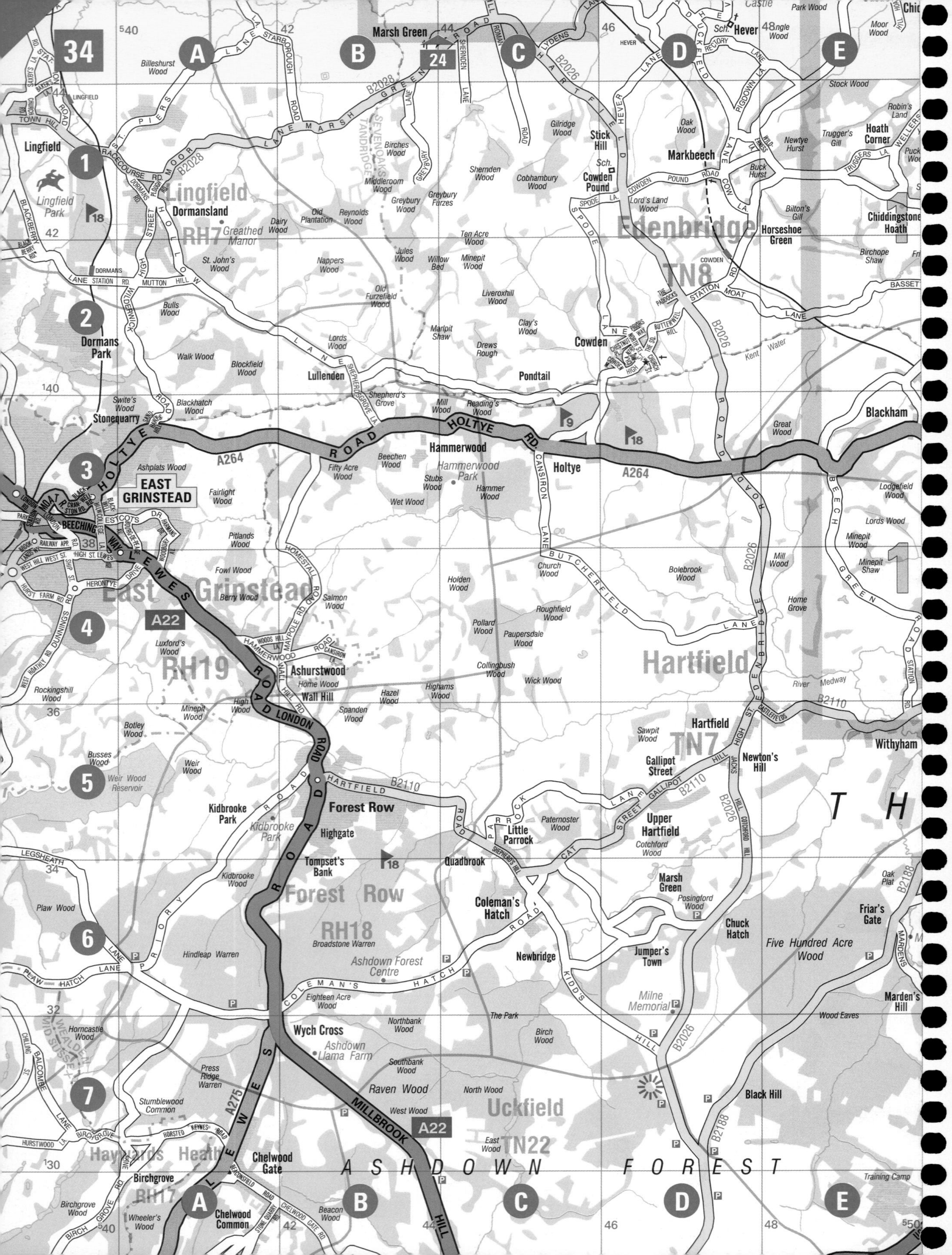

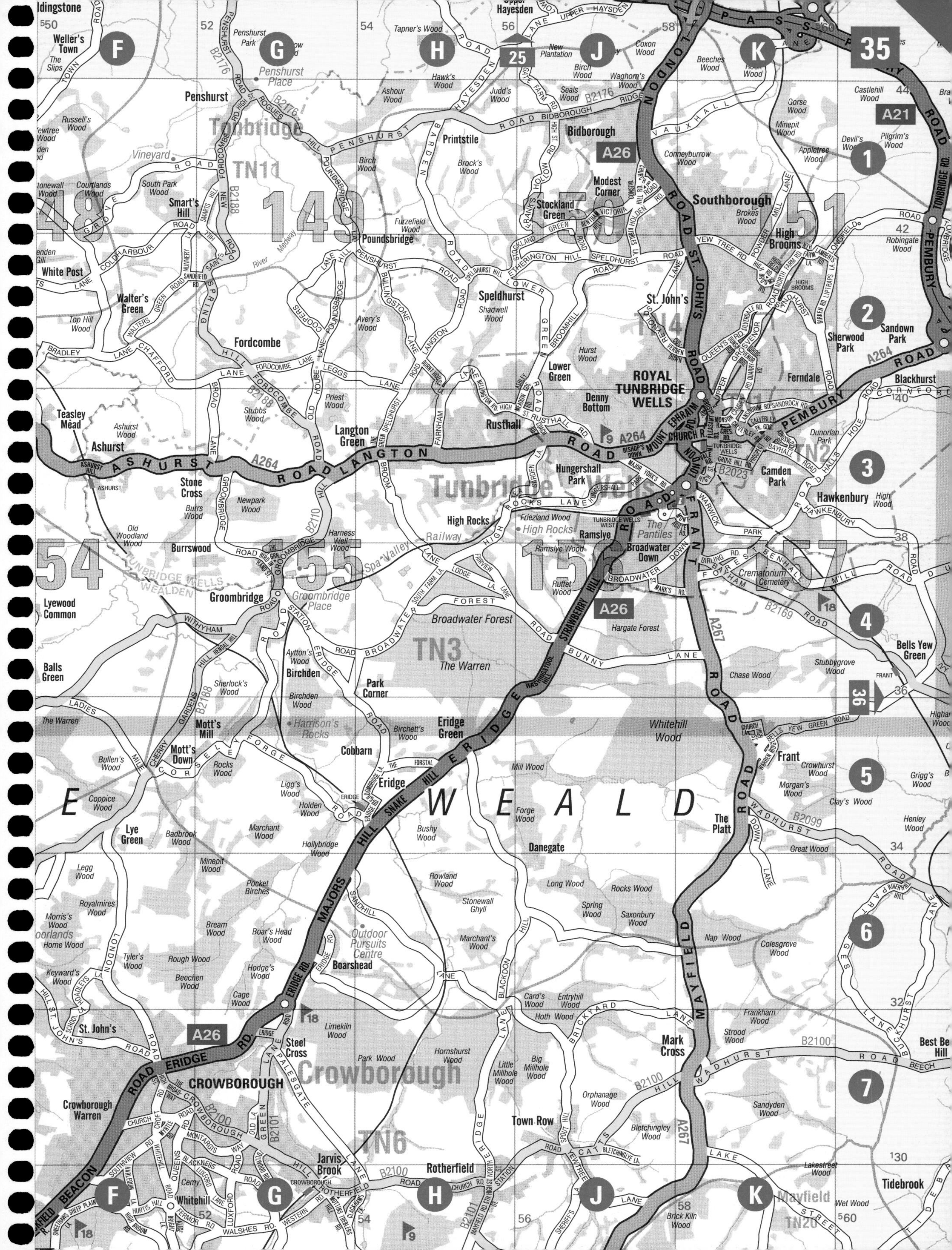
35
Penshurst
Penshurst Place
Tonbridge
TN11
Poundsbridge
Printstile
Bidborough
Southborough
Modest Corner
Stockland Green
High Brooms
Speldhurst
St. John's
TN4
ROYAL TUNBRIDGE WELLS
Rusthall
Denny Bottom
Lower Green
Langton Green
Fordcombe
Walter's Green
White Post
Smart's Hill
Ashurst
Teasley Mead
Stone Cross
Burrswood
Groombridge
Groombridge Place
Tunbridge Wells
High Rocks
Ramslye
Broadwater Down
Hungershall Park
Camden Park
Hawkenbury
Sherwood Park
Sandown Park
Ferndale
Blackhurst
TN2
TN3
The Warren
Broadwater Forest
Birchden
Park Corner
Eridge Green
Eridge
Cobbarn
Frant
The Platt
Bells Yew Green
Mott's Mill
Mott's Down
Balls Green
Lyewood Common
Lye Green
WEALD
Danegate
Boarshead
Outdoor Pursuits Centre
Steel Cross
Crowborough
CROWBOROUGH
Crowborough Warren
St. John's
Whitehill
Jarvis Brook
TN6
Rotherfield
Town Row
Mark Cross
Mayfield
TN20
Tidebrook
Best Beech Hill
A26
A264
A267
A21
B2176
B2188
B2110
B2169
B2099
B2100
B2101
B2023
149
150
151
154
155
156
157
148
F
G
H
J
K
1
2
3
4
5
6
7
25
36

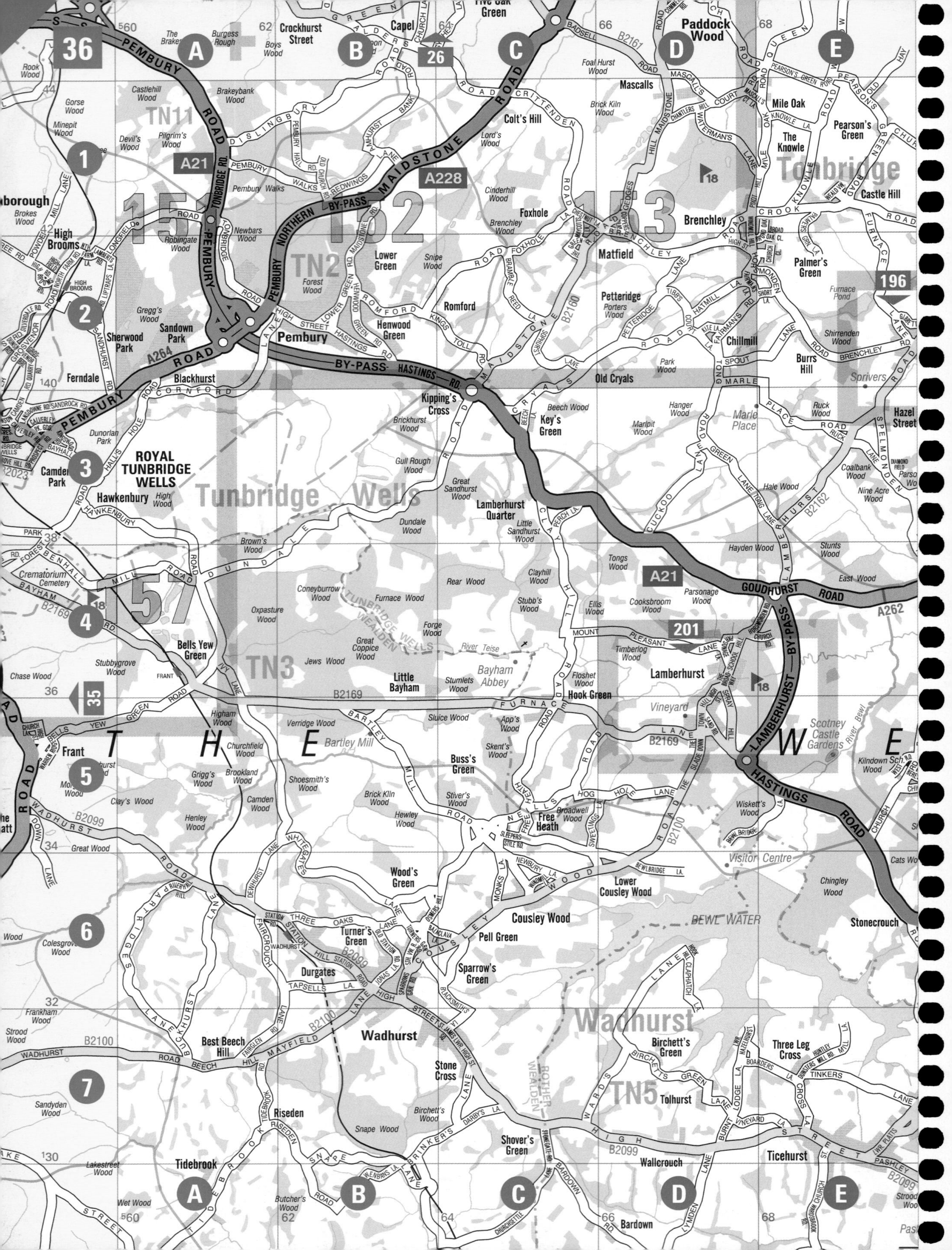

36
26
151
152
153
157
196
201
35
A
B
C
D
E
1
2
3
4
5
6
7
560
62
64
66
68
44
42
40
38
36
34
32
30
TN11
TN2
TN3
TN5
A21
A228
A264
A262
B2161
B2160
B2162
B2169
B2099
B2100
B2023
Crockhurst Street
Capel
Five Oak Green
Paddock Wood
The Brakes
Burgess Rough
Boys Wood
Rook Wood
Castlehill Wood
Brakeybank Wood
Gorse Wood
Minepit Wood
Devil's Wood
Pilgrim's Wood
Foal Hurst Wood
Mascalls
Brick Kiln Wood
Colt's Hill
Lord's Wood
Mile Oak
The Knowle
Pearson's Green
Tonbridge
Castle Hill
Cinderhill Wood
Foxhole
Brenchley Wood
Brenchley
Matfield
Pembury Walks
Newbars Wood
Robingate Wood
High Brooms
Brokes Wood
Lower Green
Snipe Wood
Forest Wood
Palmer's Green
Furnace Pond
Gregg's Wood
Sandown Park
Sherwood Park
Henwood Green
Romford
Petteridge
Porters Wood
Chillmill
Shirrenden Wood
Burrs Hill
Pembury
Ferndale
Blackhurst
Park Wood
Old Cryals
Sprivers
Kipping's Cross
Beech Wood
Key's Green
Hanger Wood
Marle Place
Ruck Wood
Hazel Street
Brickhurst Wood
Marlpit Wood
Dunorlan Park
ROYAL TUNBRIDGE WELLS
Camden Park
Gull Rough Wood
Coalbank Wood
Hawkenbury
High Wood
Tunbridge Wells
Great Sandhurst Wood
Lamberhurst Quarter
Hale Wood
Nine Acre Wood
Little Sandhurst Wood
Dundale Wood
Brown's Wood
Hayden Wood
Stunts Wood
Tongs Wood
Crematorium Cemetery
Clayhill Wood
Rear Wood
Coneyburrow Wood
East Wood
Furnace Wood
Stubb's Wood
Ellis Wood
Cooksbroom Wood
Parsonage Wood
Oxpasture Wood
Forge Wood
Great Coppice Wood
River Teise
Bells Yew Green
Stubbygrove Wood
Jews Wood
Bayham Abbey
Timberlog Wood
Lamberhurst
Chase Wood
Little Bayham
Stumlets Wood
Floshet Wood
Hook Green
Vineyard
Higham Wood
Verridge Wood
Sluice Wood
App's Wood
Scotney Castle Gardens
River Bewl
Frant
Bartley Mill
Skent's Wood
Kilndown Wood
Churchfield Wood
Grigg's Wood
Brookland Wood
Shoesmith's Wood
Buss's Green
Camden Wood
Brick Kiln Wood
Stiver's Wood
Wiskett's Wood
Clay's Wood
Hewley Wood
Free Heath
Broadwell Wood
Henley Wood
Great Wood
Visitor Centre
Wood's Green
Lower Cousley Wood
Chingley Wood
Cats Wood
Cousley Wood
BEWL WATER
Stonecrouch
Colesgrove Wood
Turner's Green
Pell Green
Durgates
Sparrow's Green
Frankham Wood
Wadhurst
Strood Wood
Best Beech Hill
Birchett's Green
Three Leg Cross
Stone Cross
Sandyden Wood
Riseden
Tolhurst
Birchett's Wood
Snape Wood
Shover's Green
Wallcrouch
Ticehurst
Tidebrook
Lakestreet Wood
Butcher's Wood
Wet Wood
Bardown
ROTHER WEALDEN
TUNBRIDGE WELLS WEALDEN
T H E
W E
PEMBURY ROAD
NORTHERN BY-PASS
MAIDSTONE ROAD
HASTINGS RD.
BY-PASS
GOUDHURST ROAD
LAMBERHURST BY-PASS
HASTINGS ROAD
FURNACE LANE
BELLS YEW GREEN ROAD
WADHURST ROAD
BEECH HILL
MAYFIELD LANE
HIGH STREET
COUSLEY WOOD
THREE OAKS LANE
HOG HOLE LANE
PLEASANT LANE
CRITTENDEN ROAD
DISLINGBURY ROAD
CROOK ROAD
FURNACE LANE
TINKERS LANE
PASHLEY

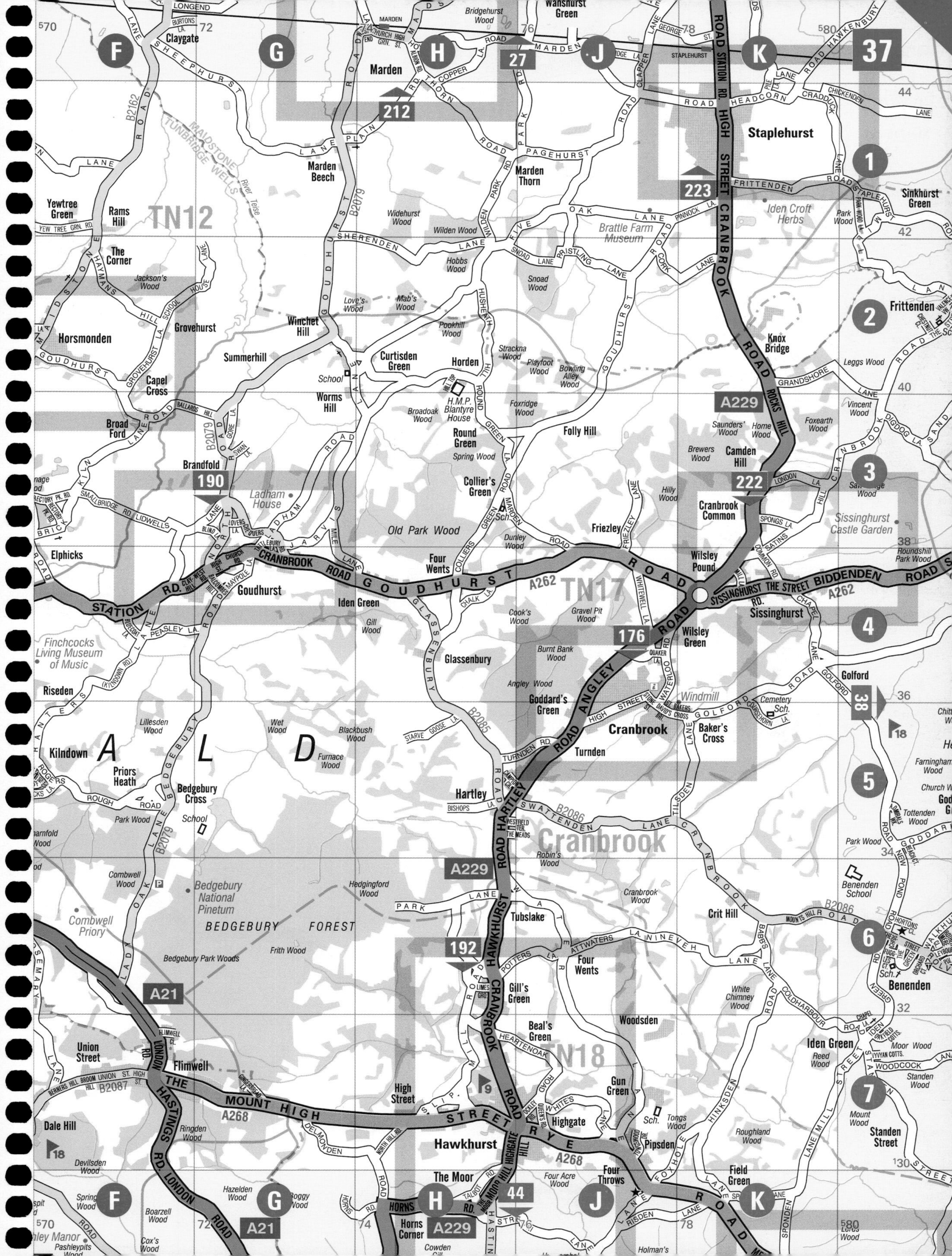

37
Claygate
Marden
Staplehurst
Frittenden
Sinkhurst Green
Iden Croft Herbs
Marden Beech
Marden Thorn
Yewtree Green
Rams Hill
TN12
The Corner
Widehurst Wood
Wilden Wood
Brattle Farm Museum
Hobbs Wood
Snoad Wood
Jackson's Wood
Horsmonden
Grovehurst
Winchet Hill
Love's Wood
Mab's Wood
Pookhill Wood
Knox Bridge
Summerhill
Curtisden Green
Horden
Strackna Wood
Playfoot Wood
Bowling Alley Wood
Leggs Wood
Capel Cross
School
Worms Hill
H.M.P. Blantyre House
Foxridge Wood
Broadoak Wood
Broad Ford
Round Green
Spring Wood
Folly Hill
Saunders' Wood
Home Wood
Vincent Wood
Foxearth Wood
Brewers Wood
Camden Hill
Brandfold
Collier's Green
Ladham House
Hilly Wood
Cranbrook Common
Sissinghurst Castle Garden
Old Park Wood
Friezley
Elphicks
Four Wents
Dunley Wood
Wilsley Pound
Roundshill Park Wood
Goudhurst
Iden Green
TN17
Sissinghurst
Gill Wood
Cook's Wood
Gravel Pit Wood
Wilsley Green
Finchcocks Living Museum of Music
Glassenbury
Burnt Bank Wood
Golford
Riseden
Angley Wood
Windmill
Goddard's Green
Cranbrook
Baker's Cross
Lillesden Wood
Wet Wood
Blackbush Wood
Kilndown
W E A L D
Furnace Wood
Turnden
Priors Heath
Bedgebury Cross
Hartley
Park Wood
School
Cranbrook
Robin's Wood
Tottenden Wood
Park Wood
Benenden School
Combwell Wood
Bedgebury National Pinetum
Hedgingford Wood
Cranbrook Wood
Combwell Priory
BEDGEBURY FOREST
Tubslake
Crit Hill
Frith Wood
Bedgebury Park Woods
Four Wents
Gill's Green
White Chimney Wood
Benenden
Union Street
Flimwell
Beal's Green
TN18
Woodsden
Iden Green
Moor Wood
Reed Wood
Standen Wood
High Street
Gun Green
Dale Hill
Ringden Wood
Highgate
Tongs Wood
Roughland Wood
Mount Wood
Standen Street
Hawkhurst
Pipsden
Devilsden Wood
The Moor
Four Throws
Field Green
Four Acre Wood
Hazelden Wood
Boggy Wood
Spring Wood
Boarzell Wood
Horns Corner
Cox's Wood
Cowden
A229
A262
A21
A268
B2079
B2086
B2085
B2087
B2162
190
212
223
222
176
192
27
44
38

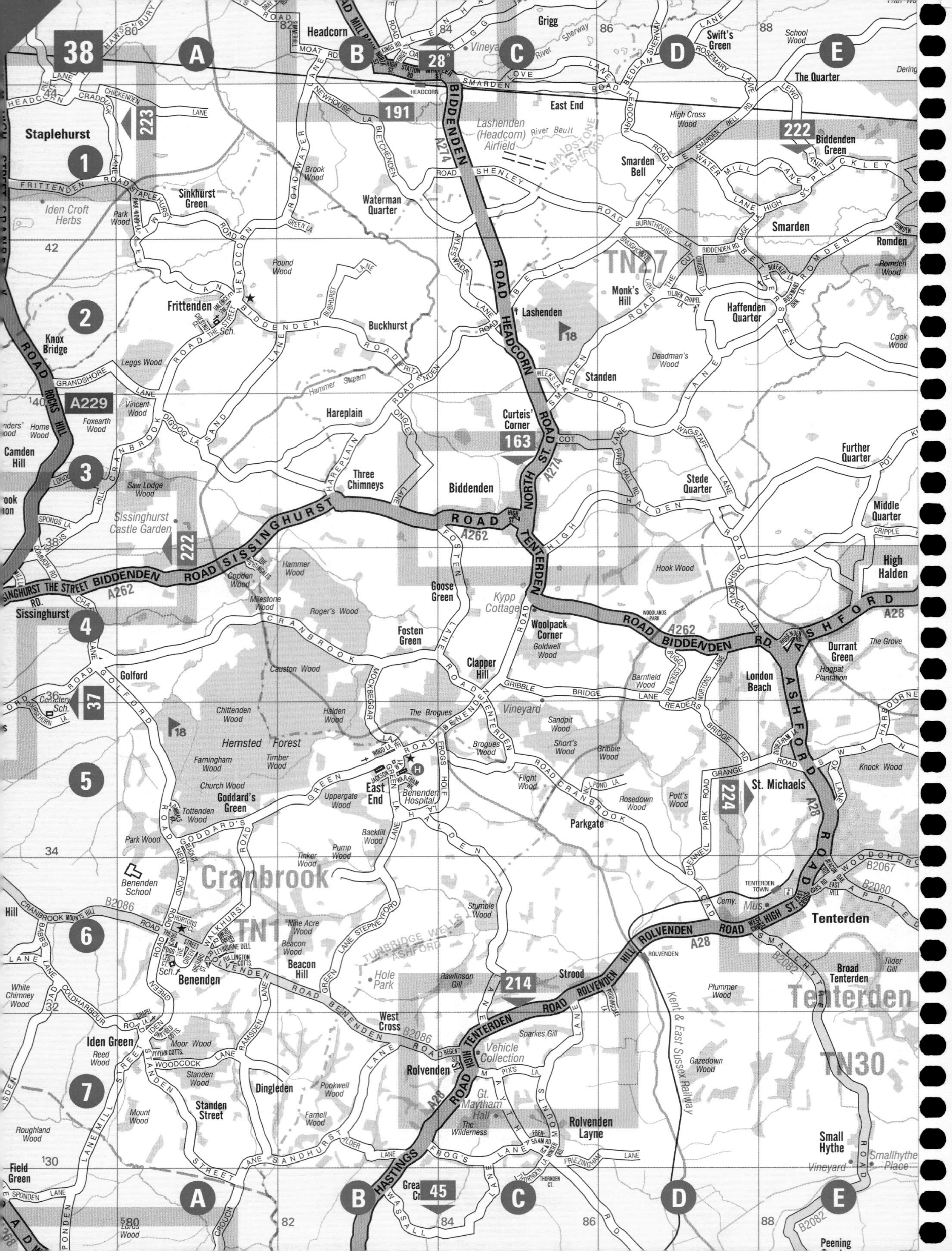
A
B
C
D
E
1
2
3
4
5
6
7
Headcorn
Grigg
Swift's Green
School Wood
The Quarter
East End
High Cross Wood
Lashenden (Headcorn) Airfield
River Beult
Smarden Bell
Biddenden Green
Staplehurst
Sinkhurst Green
Iden Croft Herbs
Park Wood
Waterman Quarter
Brook Wood
Smarden
Romden
Romden Wood
Pound Wood
Frittenden
Buckhurst
Lashenden
Monk's Hill
Haffenden Quarter
Knox Bridge
Leggs Wood
Deadman's Wood
Cook Wood
Standen
Hareplain
Vincent Wood
Foxearth Wood
Home Wood
Camden Hill
Curteis' Corner
Further Quarter
Saw Lodge Wood
Three Chimneys
Biddenden
Stede Quarter
Middle Quarter
Sissinghurst Castle Garden
Hammer Wood
Copden Wood
Hook Wood
High Halden
Sissinghurst
Milestone Wood
Roger's Wood
Goose Green
Kypp Cottage
Woolpack Corner
Goldwell Wood
Fosten Green
Durrant Green
The Grove
Hogpat Plantation
Golford
Causton Wood
Clapper Hill
Barnfield Wood
London Beach
Chittenden Wood
Halden Wood
The Brogues
Vineyard
Sandpit Wood
Hemsted Forest
Farningham Wood
Timber Wood
Brogues Wood
Short's Wood
Gribble Wood
Knock Wood
Church Wood
Goddard's Green
Tottenden Wood
East End
Benenden Hospital
Flight Wood
Rosedown Wood
Pott's Wood
St. Michaels
Parkgate
Park Wood
Uppergate Wood
Backtilt Wood
Pump Wood
Tinker Wood
Benenden School
Cranbrook
Stumble Wood
Tenterden
Nine Acre Wood
Beacon Wood
Beacon Hill
Hole Park
Broad Tenterden
Tilder Gill
Benenden
Rawlinson Gill
Strood
Plummer Wood
White Chimney Wood
West Cross
Sparkes Gill
Iden Green
Reed Wood
Moor Wood
Standen Wood
Dingleden
Vehicle Collection
Rolvenden
Pookwell Wood
Gazedown Wood
Standen Street
Mount Wood
Farnell Wood
Gt. Maytham Hall
The Wilderness
Rolvenden Layne
Roughland Wood
Small Hythe
Smallhythe Place
Field Green
Peening
Kent & East Sussex Railway
TN27
TN17
TN30
A274
A262
A229
A28
B2086
B2067
B2080
B2082
28
191
223
222
163
37
224
214
45

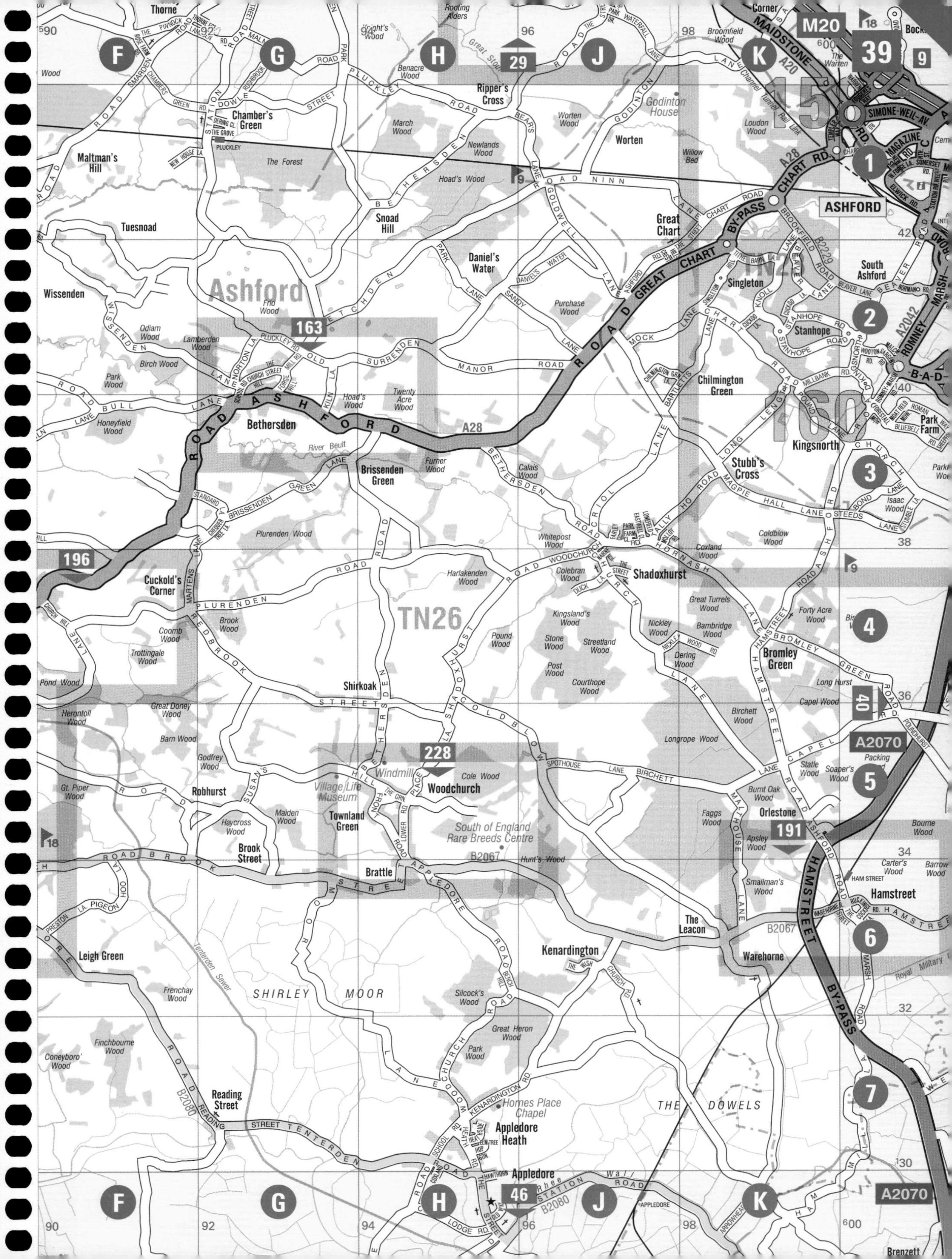

Thorne
Rooting Alders
Corner
M20
39
Wright's Wood
Broomfield Wood
MAIDSTONE
A20
The Warren
Benacre Wood
Ripper's Cross
Chamber's Green
Pluckley
March Wood
Godinton House
Worten Wood
Worten
Loudon Wood
SIMONE-WEIL-AV.
Maltman's Hill
The Forest
Newlands Wood
Hoad's Wood
Willow Bed
CHART RD.
ASHFORD
Tuesnoad
Snoad Hill
Great Chart
Daniel's Water
South Ashford
Singleton
Wissenden
Ashford
Frid Wood
Purchase Wood
Stanhope
Odiam Wood
Lamberden Wood
Birch Wood
Park Wood
Chilmington Green
Bethersden
Hoad's Wood
Twenty Acre Wood
Honeyfield Wood
Kingsnorth
Park Farm
River Beult
Brissenden Green
Furner Wood
Calais Wood
Stubb's Cross
Plurenden Wood
Whitepost Wood
Isaac Wood
Coldblow Wood
Coxland Wood
Cuckold's Corner
Harlakenden Wood
Colebran Wood
Shadoxhurst
TN26
Great Turrels Wood
Forty Acre Wood
Brook Wood
Coomb Wood
Kingsland's Wood
Nickley Wood
Bambridge Wood
Bromley Green
Trottingale Wood
Pound Wood
Stone Wood
Streetland Wood
Dering Wood
Post Wood
Courthope Wood
Long Hurst
Pond Wood
Shirkoak
Capel Wood
Herontoll Wood
Great Doney Wood
Birchett Wood
A2070
Barn Wood
Longrope Wood
Godfrey Wood
Windmill
Cole Wood
Statle Wood
Soaper's Wood
Packing
Gt. Piper Wood
Robhurst
Village Life Museum
Woodchurch
Burnt Oak Wood
Orlestone
Townland Green
Maiden Wood
Haycross Wood
Brook Street
South of England Rare Breeds Centre
Faggs Wood
Bourne Wood
B2067
Hunt's Wood
Apsley Wood
Carter's Wood
Barrow Wood
Brattle
Hamstreet
Smallman's Wood
The Leacon
B2067
Leigh Green
Kenardington
Warehorne
Royal Military
Tenterden Sewer
Frenchay Wood
SHIRLEY MOOR
Silcock's Wood
Great Heron Wood
Finchbourne Wood
Park Wood
Coneyboro' Wood
Reading Street
Homes Place Chapel
THE DOWELS
Appledore Heath
Appledore
A2070
Brenzett

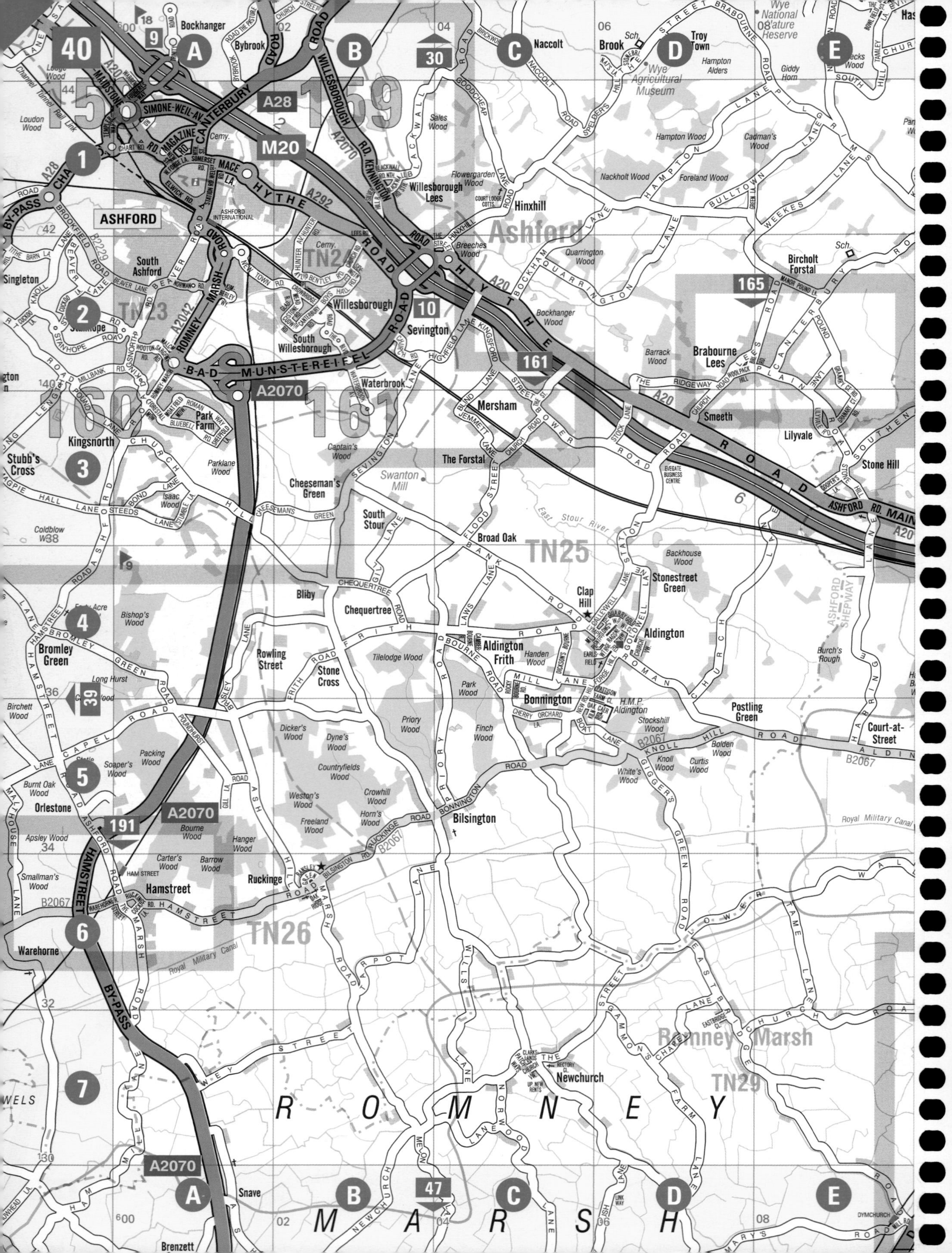
ASHFORD
Bockhanger
Bybrook
Naccolt
Brook
Troy Town
Wye National Nature Reserve
Hampton Alders
Wye Agricultural Museum
Giddy Horn
Loudon Wood
Sales Wood
Hampton Wood
Cadman's Wood
Flowergarden Wood
Nackholt Wood
Foreland Wood
Willesborough Lees
Hinxhill
Ashford
South Ashford
Singleton
Stanhope
Quarrington Wood
Breeches Wood
Bircholt Forstal
Willesborough
Sevington
South Willesborough
Bockhanger Wood
Barrack Wood
Brabourne Lees
Waterbrook
Mersham
Smeeth
Lilyvale
Kingsnorth
Park Farm
Stubb's Cross
Captain's Wood
Parklane Wood
The Forstal
Swanton Mill
Stone Hill
Cheeseman's Green
South Stour
Isaac Wood
Coldblow
Broad Oak
East Stour River
TN25
Backhouse Wood
Stonestreet Green
Clap Hill
Aldington
Bliby
Chequertree
Bishop's Wood
Bromley Green
Rowling Street
Aldington Frith
Tilelodge Wood
Handen Wood
Stone Cross
Long Hurst
Park Wood
Bonnington
H.M.P. Aldington
Postling Green
Burch's Rough
Birchett Wood
Dicker's Wood
Dyne's Wood
Priory Wood
Finch Wood
Stockshill Wood
Court-at-Street
Packing Wood
Soaper's Wood
Countryfields Wood
Knoll Wood
Curtis Wood
Bolden Wood
White's Wood
Burnt Oak Wood
Orlestone
Weston's Wood
Crowhill Wood
Freeland Wood
Horn's Wood
Bilsington
Royal Military Canal
Bourne Wood
Hanger Wood
Apsley Wood
Carter's Wood
Barrow Wood
Smallman's Wood
Hamstreet
Ruckinge
Warehorne
TN26
Romney Marsh
Newchurch
TN29
ROMNEY MARSH
Snave
Brenzett
Dymchurch
TN23
TN24
A20
A28
A2070
A292
A2042
B2067
B2229
M20
HYTHE ROAD
ASHFORD ROAD
BAD-MUNSTEREIFEL
159
160
161
165
191
30
39
47

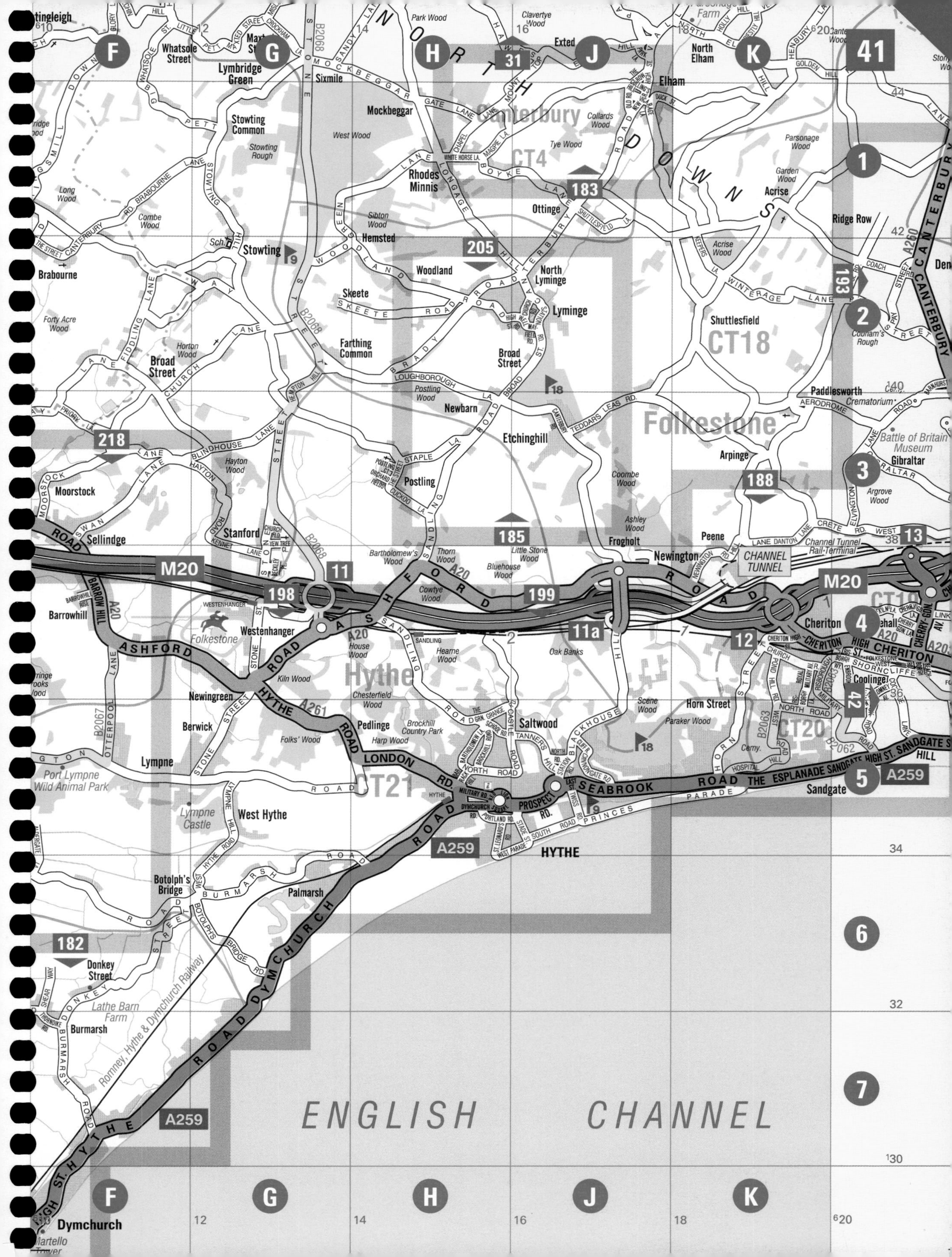

F
G
H
J
K
1
2
3
4
5
6
7
Whatsole Street
Lymbridge Green
Sixmile
Mockbeggar
Exted
North Elham
Elham
NORTH DOWNS
Canterbury
CT4
CT18
CT19
CT20
CT21
Stowting Common
Stowting Rough
West Wood
Rhodes Minnis
Tye Wood
Collards Wood
Parsonage Wood
Garden Wood
Acrise
Ridge Row
Long Wood
Combe Wood
Sibton Wood
Hemsted
Ottinge
Stowting
Brabourne
Woodland
North Lyminge
Lyminge
Acrise Wood
Skeete
Shuttlesfield
Cobham's Rough
Forty Acre Wood
Horton Wood
Broad Street
Farthing Common
Postling Wood
Newbarn
Paddlesworth
Crematorium
Folkestone
Battle of Britain Museum
Gibraltar
Etchinghill
Arpinge
Hayton Wood
Moorstock
Postling
Coombe Wood
Argrove Wood
Ashley Wood
Sellindge
Stanford
Peene
Frogholt
Newington
CHANNEL TUNNEL
Channel Tunnel Rail Terminal
Bartholomew's Wood
Thorn Wood
Little Stone Wood
Bluehouse Wood
Cowtye Wood
M20
A20
Barrowhill
Westenhanger
House Wood
Hearne Wood
Oak Banks
Cheriton
Folkestone
Hythe
Kiln Wood
Chesterfield Wood
Newingreen
Scene Wood
Horn Street
Paraker Wood
Cheriton
Shorncliffe
Cooling
Berwick
Pedlinge
Brockhill Country Park
Harp Wood
Folks' Wood
Saltwood
Lympne
Port Lympne Wild Animal Park
Sandgate
A259
A261
Lympne Castle
West Hythe
HYTHE
Botolph's Bridge
Palmarsh
Donkey Street
Lathe Barn Farm
Burmarsh
Romney, Hythe & Dymchurch Railway
ENGLISH CHANNEL
Dymchurch
Martello Tower
12
14
16
18
20
30
32
34
36
38
40
42
44
31
183
205
193
218
188
185
198
199
11
11a
12
13
182
42

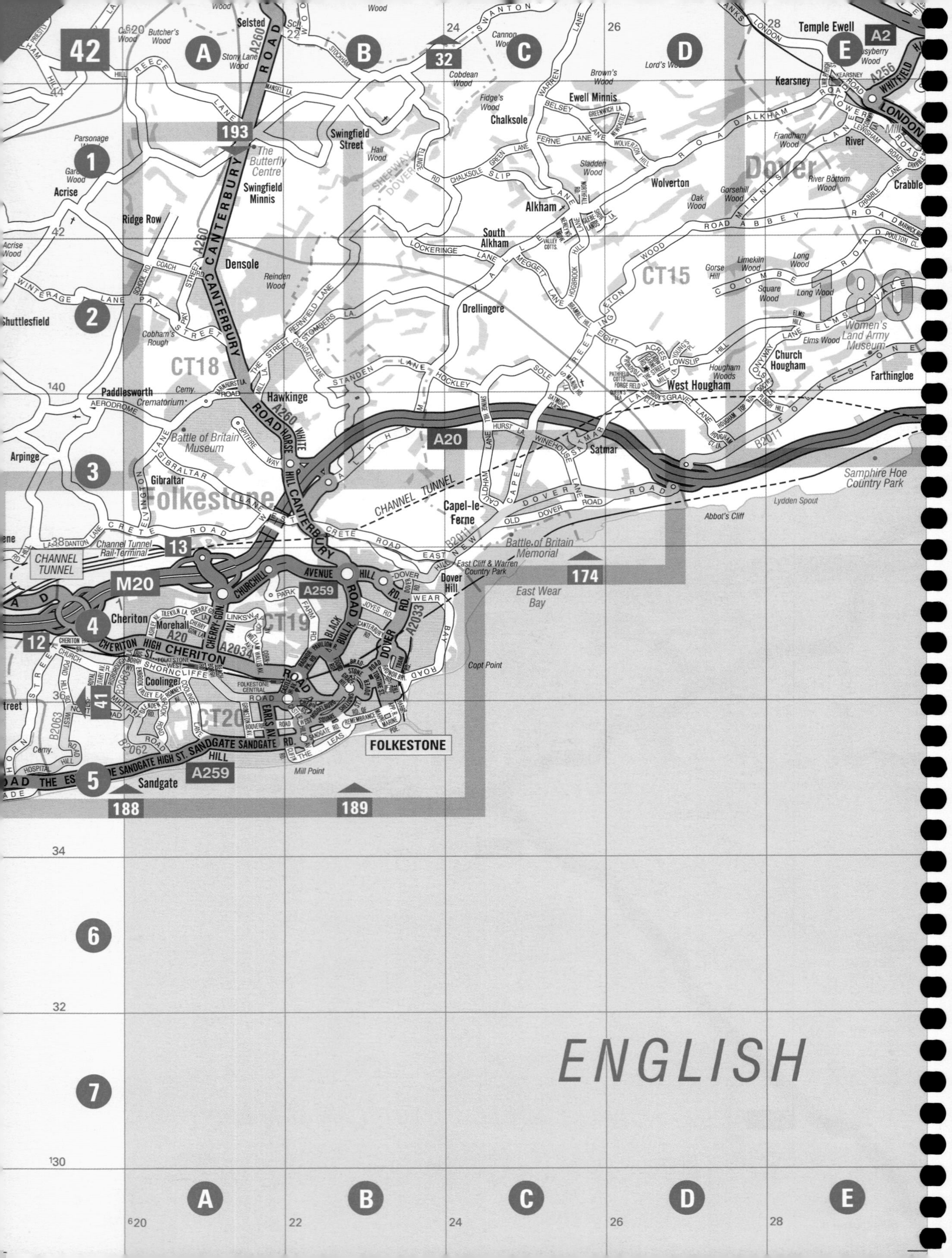
A
B
C
D
E
1
2
3
4
5
6
7
32
193
174
188
189
180
13
12
41
Selsted
Butcher's Wood
Stony Lane Wood
Temple Ewell
Kearsney
Cobdean Wood
Brown's Wood
Lord's Wood
Ewell Minnis
Fidge's Wood
Chalksole
Swingfield Street
Hall Wood
The Butterfly Centre
Swingfield Minnis
Parsonage Wood
Acrise
Ridge Row
Acrise Wood
Sladden Wood
Wolverton
Alkham
South Alkham
Oak Wood
Gorsehill Wood
Frandham Wood
River
Dover
Crabble
River Bottom Wood
Densole
Reinden Wood
Drellingore
CT15
Gorse Hill
Limekiln Wood
Long Wood
Square Wood
Long Wood
Shuttlesfield
Cobham's Rough
CT18
Elms Wood
Women's Land Army Museum
Church Hougham
West Hougham
Hougham Woods
Farthingloe
Paddlesworth
Crematorium
Hawkinge
Battle of Britain Museum
Arpinge
Gibraltar
Folkestone
Satmar
Samphire Hoe Country Park
Lydden Spout
Abbot's Cliff
Capel-le-Ferne
CHANNEL TUNNEL
Channel Tunnel Rail Terminal
Battle of Britain Memorial
East Cliff & Warren Country Park
Dover Hill
East Wear Bay
M20
A20
A259
A260
A2033
A2034
A256
A2
B2011
B2063
B2062
Cheriton
Morehall
CT19
Copt Point
Coolinge
CT20
FOLKESTONE
Mill Point
Sandgate
Cemy.
CANTERBURY ROAD
WHITE HORSE HILL
CHERITON HIGH STREET
SANDGATE HIGH ST.
SANDGATE HILL
CRETE ROAD
NEW DOVER ROAD
ALKHAM VALLEY ROAD
ABBEY ROAD
ENGLISH
620
22
24
26
28
140
42
38
36
34
32
130

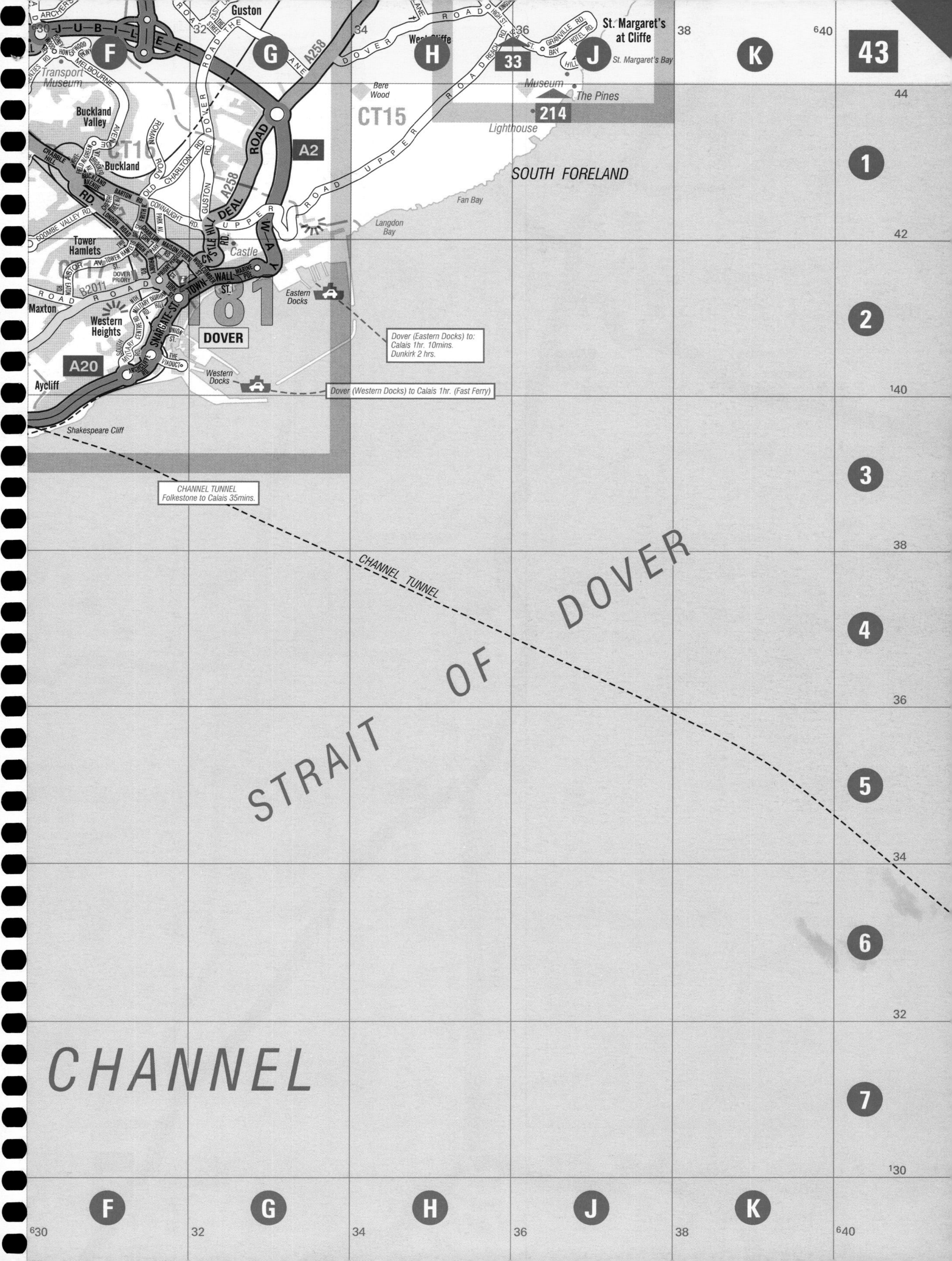

Guston
West Cliffe
St. Margaret's
at Cliffe
St. Margaret's Bay

Transport
Museum

Bere
Wood
Museum
The Pines
214

CT15

Buckland
Valley
CT16
Buckland
A2
A258
Lighthouse

Tower
Hamlets

SOUTH FORELAND

Fan Bay

Castle

Langdon
Bay

Maxton
DOVER
Eastern
Docks

Western
Heights

A20
Western
Docks

Aycliff

Dover (Eastern Docks) to:
Calais 1hr. 10mins.
Dunkirk 2 hrs.

Dover (Western Docks) to Calais 1hr. (Fast Ferry)

Shakespeare Cliff

CHANNEL TUNNEL
Folkestone to Calais 35mins.

CHANNEL TUNNEL

STRAIT   OF   DOVER

CHANNEL

44
1
42
2
140
3
38
4
36
5
34
6
32
7
130

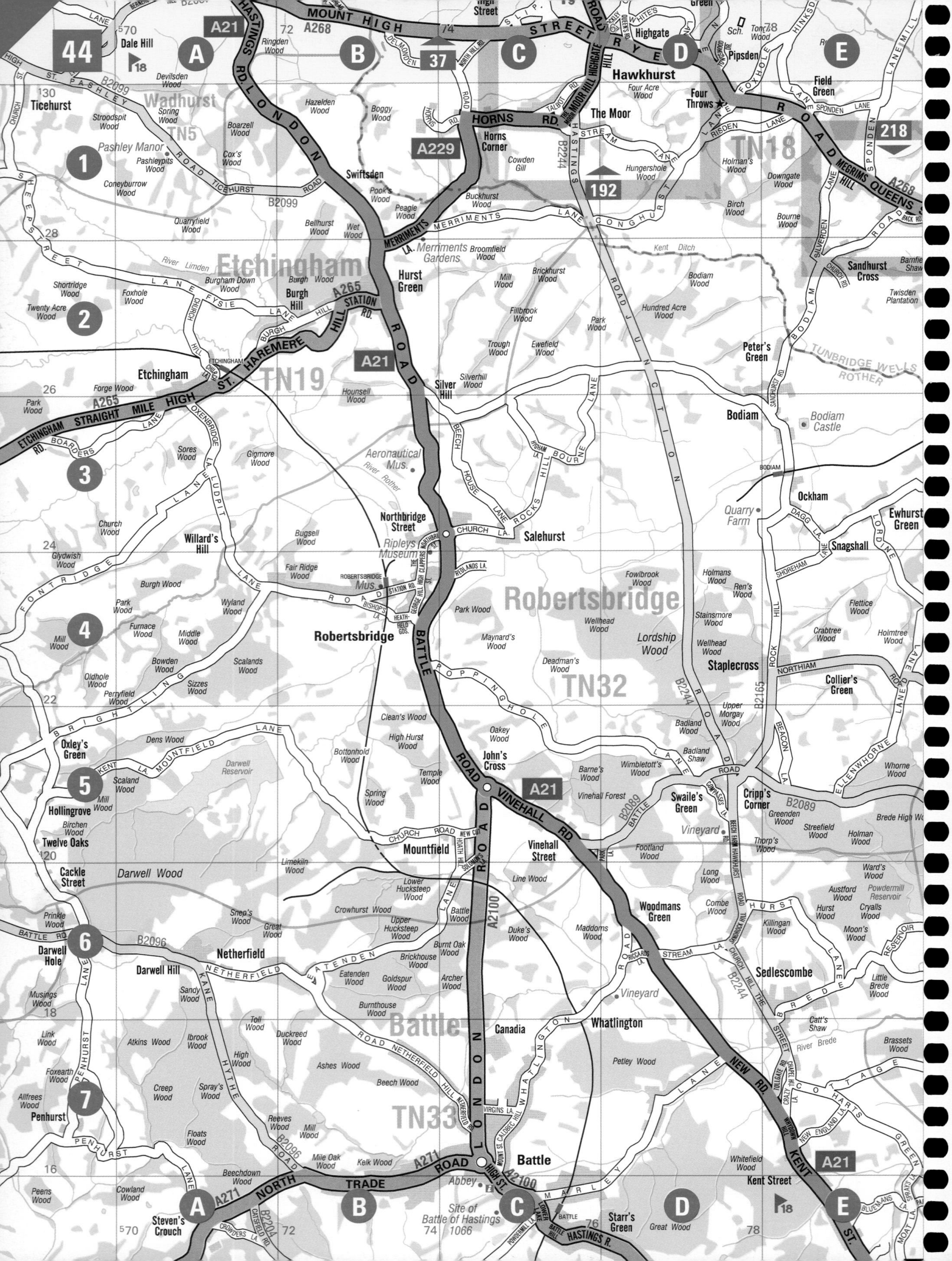

Ticehurst
Dale Hill
Wadhurst
TN5
Pashley Manor
Etchingham
Burgh Hill
Hurst Green
Swiftsden
Hawkhurst
Highgate
Pipsden
Four Throws
The Moor
Horns Corner
TN18
Sandhurst Cross
Merriments Gardens
TN19
Silver Hill
Bodiam
Bodiam Castle
Aeronautical Mus.
Northbridge Street
Ripleys Museum
Salehurst
Ockham
Ewhurst Green
Snagshall
Willard's Hill
Robertsbridge
Staplecross
TN32
Collier's Green
John's Cross
Oxley's Green
Hollingrove
Twelve Oaks
Cackle Street
Mountfield
Vinehall Street
Swaile's Green
Cripp's Corner
Woodmans Green
Darwell Hole
Netherfield
Darwell Hill
Sedlescombe
Whatlington
Canadia
Battle
TN33
Penhurst
Steven's Crouch
Abbey
Site of Battle of Hastings 1066
Starr's Green
Kent Street
A21
A268
A229
A265
A2100
A271
B2099
B2244
B2165
B2089
B2096
B2204
37
192
218

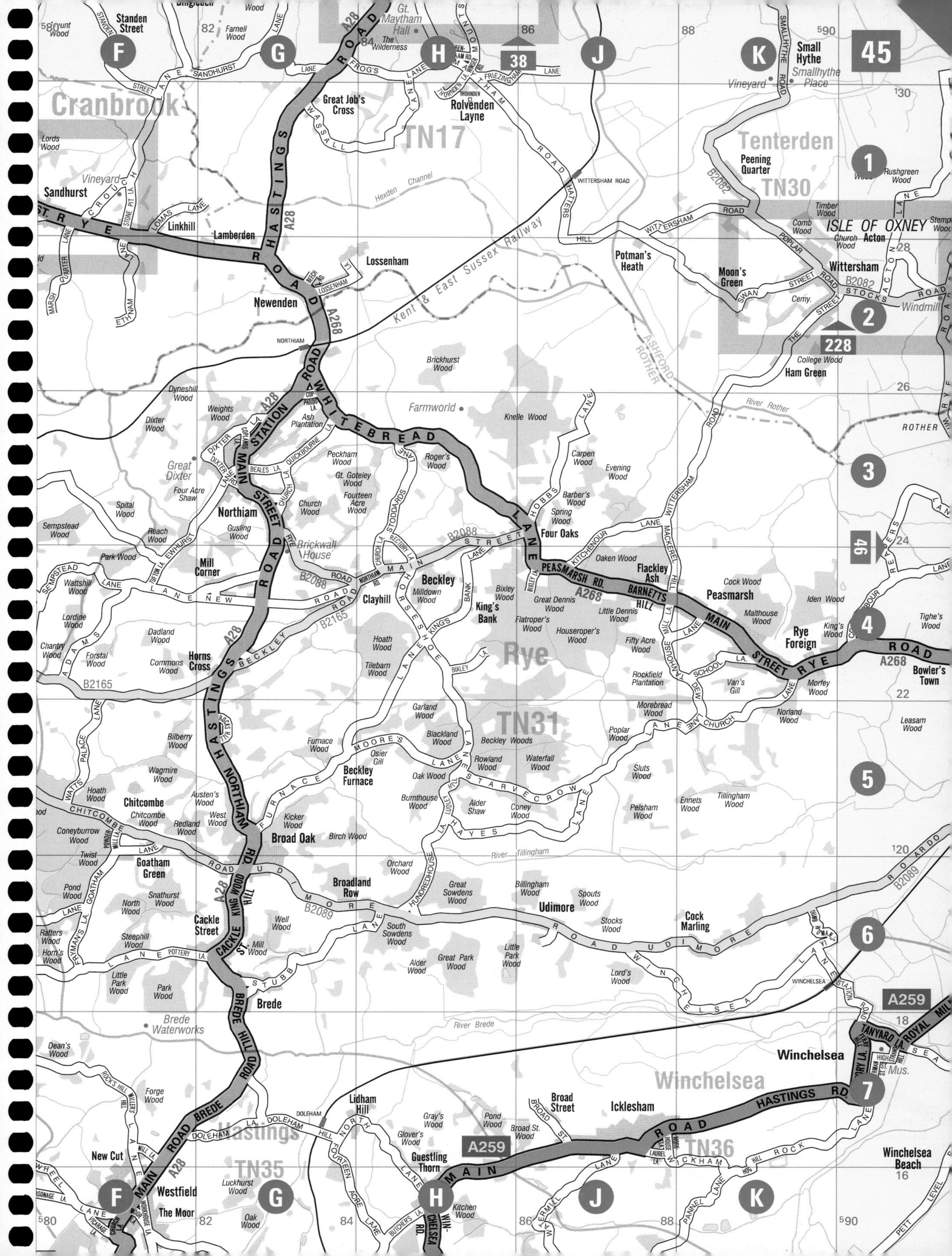

Cranbrook
Sandhurst
Standen Street
Vineyard
Linkhill
Lamberden
Newenden
Lossenham
Great Job's Cross
Rolvenden Layne
TN17
Gt. Maytham Hall
The Wilderness
38
Small Hythe
Smallhythe Place
Tenterden
Peening Quarter
TN30
Rushgreen Wood
ISLE OF OXNEY
Acton
Wittersham
Potman's Heath
Moon's Green
228
College Wood
Ham Green
Kent & East Sussex Railway
Hexden Channel
River Rother
Brickhurst Wood
Farmworld
Knelle Wood
Dyneshill Wood
Weights Wood
Dixter Wood
Great Dixter
Four Acre Shaw
Northiam
Brickwall House
Mill Corner
Beckley
Clayhill
King's Bank
Four Oaks
Flackley Ash
Peasmarsh
Rye Foreign
Rye
Bowler's Town
46
Horns Cross
Sempstead Wood
TN31
Beckley Woods
Beckley Furnace
Chitcombe
Broad Oak
Goatham Green
Broadland Row
Udimore
Cock Marling
Cackle Street
Brede
River Tillingham
River Brede
Brede Waterworks
Winchelsea
Icklesham
Broad Street
Lidham Hill
Guestling Thorn
New Cut
Westfield
The Moor
Hastings
TN35
TN36
Winchelsea Beach
A28
A268
A259
B2082
B2088
B2165
B2089
HASTINGS ROAD
WHITEBREAD LANE
PEASMARSH RD.
MAIN STREET
RYE ROAD
UDIMORE ROAD
HASTINGS RD.
MAIN ROAD
BREDE HILL

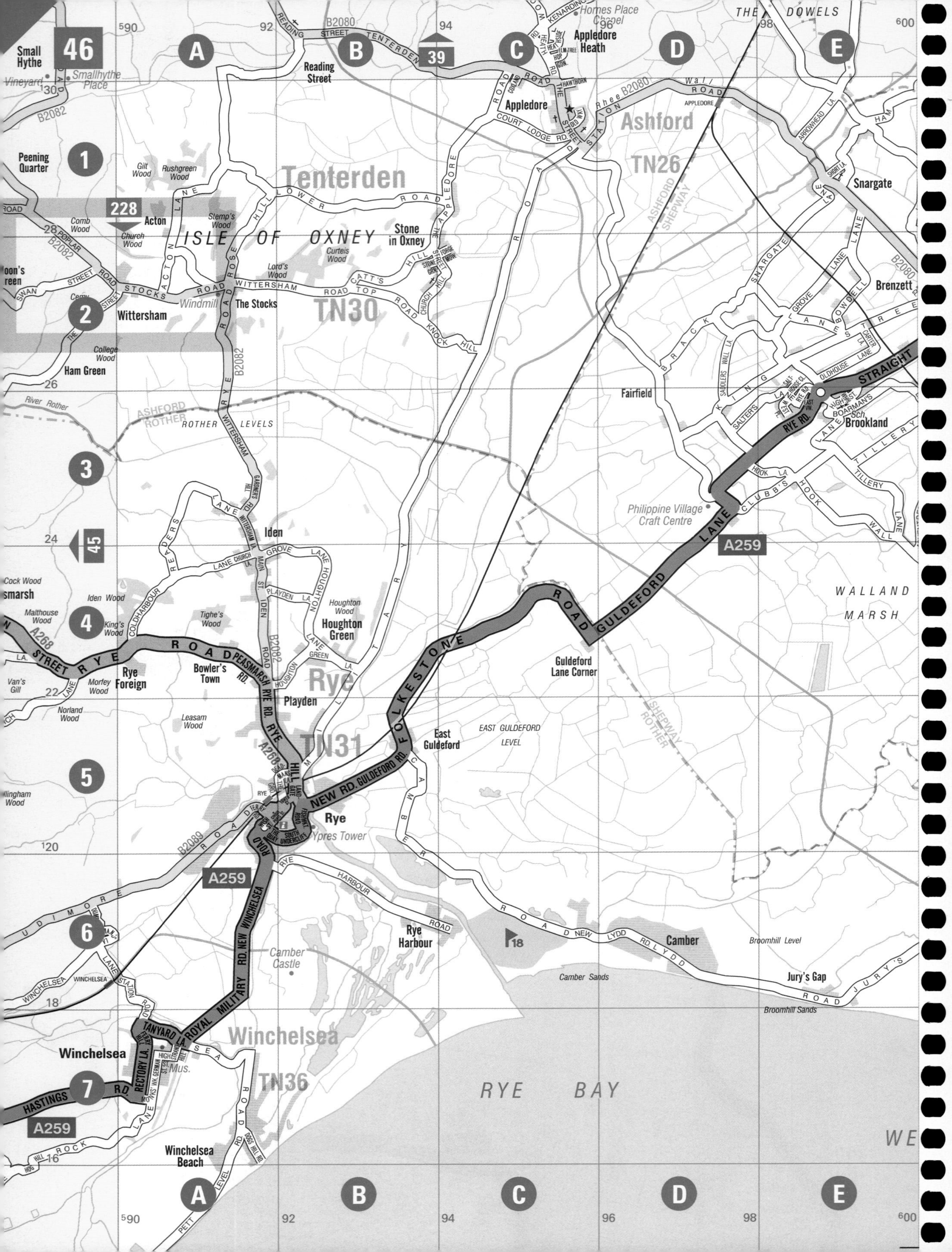
Small Hythe
Smallhythe Place
Vineyard
Reading Street
Appledore Heath
Homes Place Chapel
Appledore
Ashford
TN26
THE DOWELS
Peening Quarter
Gilt Wood
Rushgreen Wood
Tenterden
Snargate
Comb Wood
Acton
Stemp's Wood
Church Wood
ISLE OF OXNEY
Stone in Oxney
Curteis Wood
Lord's Wood
Brenzett
Wittersham
The Stocks
Windmill
TN30
College Wood
Ham Green
Fairfield
River Rother
ROTHER LEVELS
Brookland
Philippine Village Craft Centre
Iden
Cock Wood
Iden Wood
Malthouse Wood
King's Wood
Tighe's Wood
Houghton Wood
Houghton Green
WALLAND MARSH
Bowler's Town
Rye Foreign
Morfey Wood
Van's Gill
Norland Wood
Rye
Playden
Guldeford Lane Corner
Leasam Wood
TN31
East Guldeford
EAST GULDEFORD LEVEL
Rye
Ypres Tower
Rye Harbour
Camber Castle
Camber
Broomhill Level
Camber Sands
Jury's Gap
Broomhill Sands
Winchelsea
Winchelsea
Mus.
TN36
RYE BAY
Winchelsea Beach
A259
A268
B2082
B2080
B2089
228
39
45

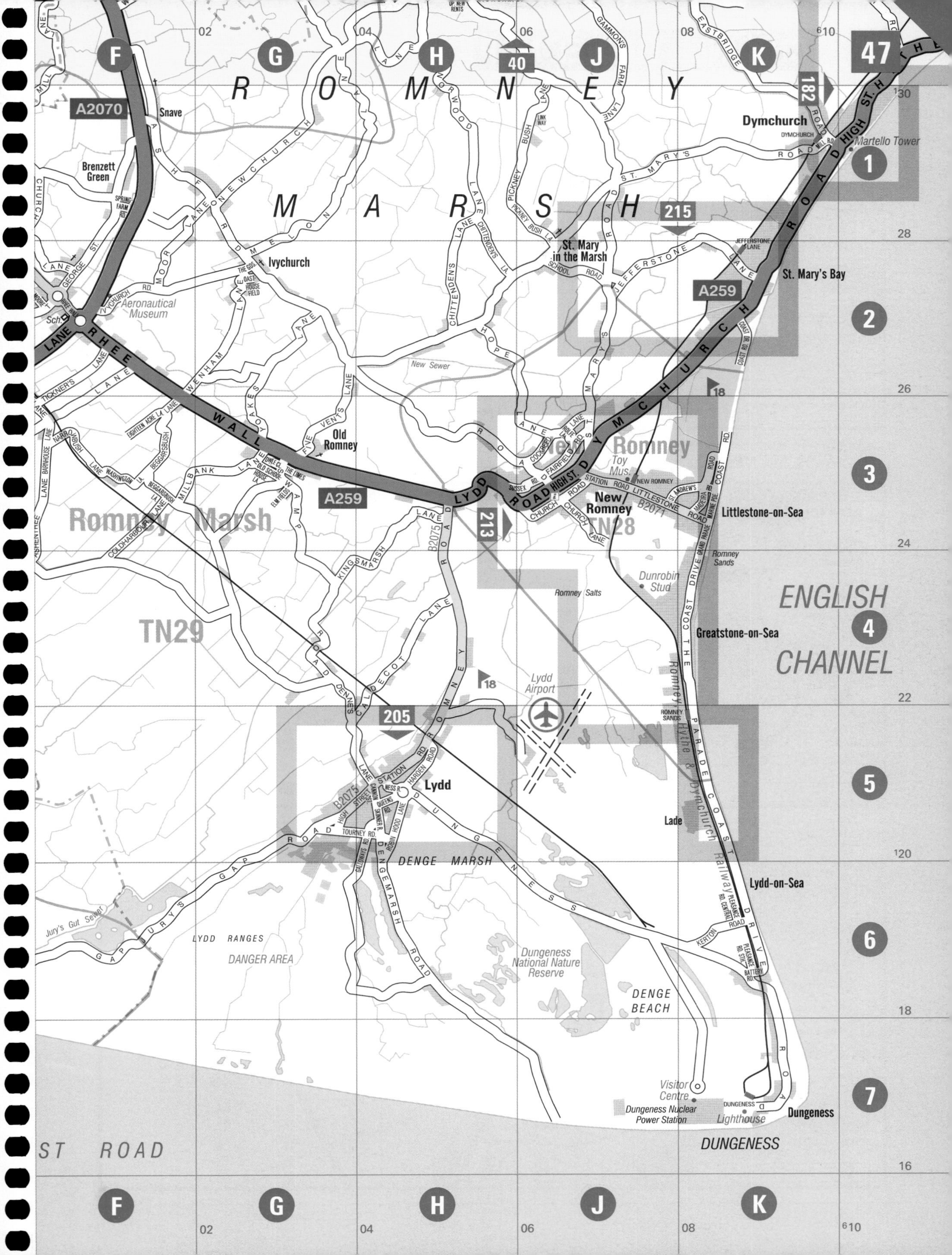

47
F
G
H
J
K
40
182
215
213
205
A2070
A259
ROMNEY MARSH
Snave
Brenzett Green
Ivychurch
Aeronautical Museum
Dymchurch
Martello Tower
St. Mary in the Marsh
St. Mary's Bay
Old Romney
New Romney
Toy Mus.
Littlestone-on-Sea
Romney Marsh
TN28
TN29
Romney Sands
Dunrobin Stud
Romney Salts
ENGLISH CHANNEL
Greatstone-on-Sea
Lydd Airport
Lydd
Lade
Romney, Hythe & Dymchurch Railway
DENGE MARSH
Lydd-on-Sea
LYDD RANGES
DANGER AREA
Jury's Gut Sewer
Dungeness National Nature Reserve
DENGE BEACH
Visitor Centre
Dungeness Nuclear Power Station
Lighthouse
Dungeness
DUNGENESS
New Sewer
RHEE WALL
DYMCHURCH ROAD
LYDD ROAD
ROMNEY ROAD
DUNGENESS ROAD
DENGEMARSH ROAD
JURY'S GAP ROAD
THE COAST DRIVE
PARADE
B2075
B2071
1
2
3
4
5
6
7
02
04
06
08
610
30
28
26
24
22
120
18
16

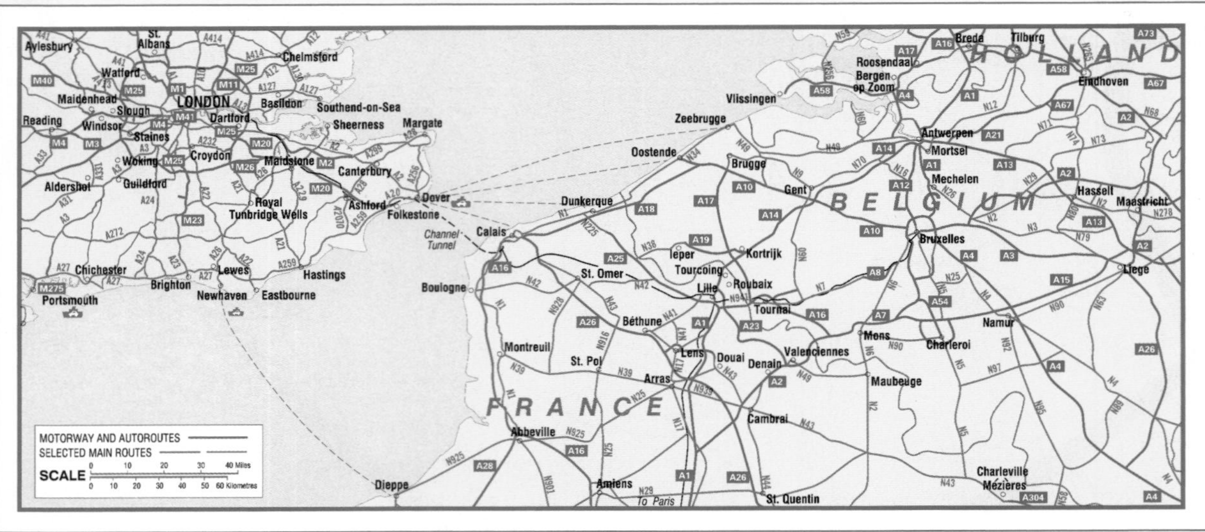

HOLLAND
BELGIUM
FRANCE
LONDON
Aylesbury
St. Albans
Chelmsford
Watford
Maidenhead
Slough
Southend-on-Sea
Basildon
Dartford
Sheerness
Margate
Reading
Windsor
Staines
Woking
Croydon
Guildford
Aldershot
Maidstone
Canterbury
Royal Tunbridge Wells
Ashford
Dover
Folkestone
Channel Tunnel
Chichester
Lewes
Hastings
Brighton
Newhaven
Eastbourne
Portsmouth
Vlissingen
Zeebrugge
Oostende
Brugge
Gent
Dunkerque
Calais
Boulogne
St. Omer
Ieper
Kortrijk
Tourcoing
Roubaix
Lille
Tournai
Béthune
Montreuil
St. Pol
Lens
Douai
Denain
Valenciennes
Mons
Charleroi
Namur
Arras
Cambrai
Maubeuge
Abbeville
Amiens
To Paris
St. Quentin
Dieppe
Charleville Mézières
Roosendaal
Bergen op Zoom
Breda
Tilburg
Eindhoven
Antwerpen
Mortsel
Mechelen
Hasselt
Maastricht
Bruxelles
Liège
MOTORWAY AND AUTOROUTES
SELECTED MAIN ROUTES
SCALE
0 10 20 30 40 Miles
0 10 20 30 40 50 60 Kilometres

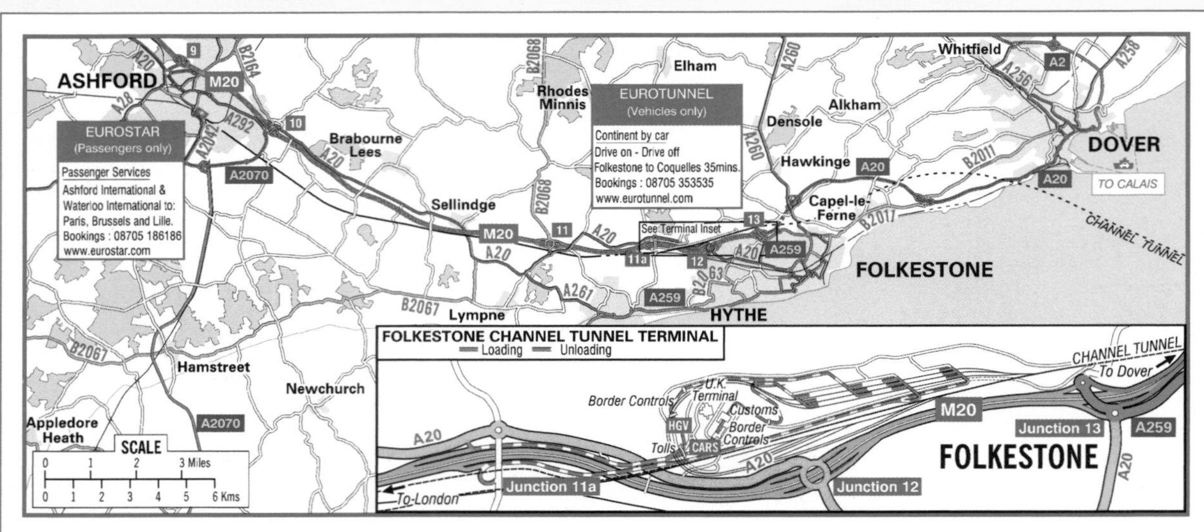

ASHFORD
EUROSTAR
(Passengers only)
Passenger Services
Ashford International & Waterloo International to: Paris, Brussels and Lille.
Bookings : 08705 186186
www.eurostar.com
EUROTUNNEL
(Vehicles only)
Continent by car
Drive on - Drive off
Folkestone to Coquelles 35mins.
Bookings : 08705 353535
www.eurotunnel.com
Brabourne Lees
Rhodes Minnis
Elham
Whitfield
Alkham
Densole
Hawkinge
DOVER
TO CALAIS
Capel-le-Ferne
CHANNEL TUNNEL
Sellindge
See Terminal Inset
FOLKESTONE
Lympne
HYTHE
Hamstreet
Newchurch
Appledore Heath
SCALE
0 1 2 3 Miles
0 1 2 3 4 5 6 Kms
FOLKESTONE CHANNEL TUNNEL TERMINAL
Loading
Unloading
CHANNEL TUNNEL
To Dover
U.K. Terminal
Border Controls
Customs
Border Controls
Tolls
HGV
CARS
Junction 13
Junction 11a
Junction 12
To London
FOLKESTONE

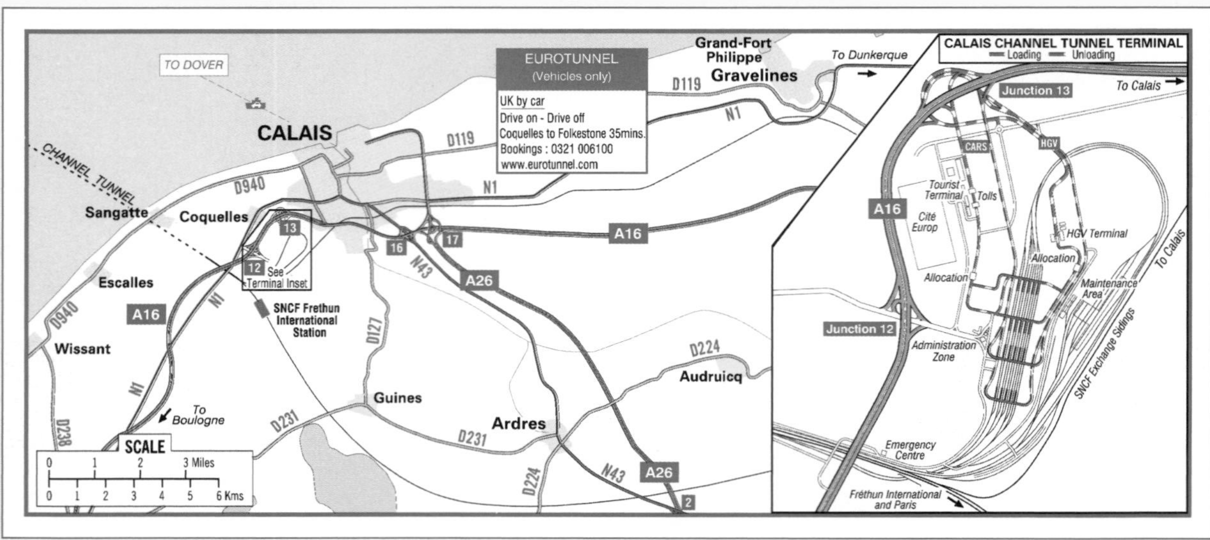

TO DOVER
EUROTUNNEL
(Vehicles only)
UK by car
Drive on - Drive off
Coquelles to Folkestone 35mins.
Bookings : 0321 006100
www.eurotunnel.com
Grand-Fort Philippe
Gravelines
To Dunkerque
CALAIS
CHANNEL TUNNEL
Sangatte
Coquelles
See Terminal Inset
Escalles
SNCF Frethun International Station
Wissant
Guines
Audruicq
Ardres
To Boulogne
SCALE
0 1 2 3 Miles
0 1 2 3 4 5 6 Kms
CALAIS CHANNEL TUNNEL TERMINAL
Loading
Unloading
Junction 13
To Calais
CARS
HGV
Tourist Terminal
Tolls
Cité Europ
HGV Terminal
Allocation
Allocation
Maintenance Area
Junction 12
Administration Zone
SNCF Exchange Sidings
Emergency Centre
Fréthun International and Paris

REFERENCE TO 3 INCHES TO 1 MILE STREET MAP SECTION

Motorway	M2
A Road	A2
Under Construction	
Proposed	
B Road	B2068
Dual Carriageway	
Tunnel	A299
One-Way Street Traffic flow on A Roads is also indicated by a heavy line on the driver's left	⇒ ⇒
Junction Names	SWANLEY INTERCHANGE
Restricted Access	
Pedestrianized Road	
Track & Footpath	
Residential Walkway	
Railway	Tunnel / Level Crossing
Stations:	
National Rail Network	⇋
Docklands Light Railway	DLR
Heritage Station	
Croydon Tramlink The boarding of Tramlink trams at stops may be limited to a single direction, indicated by the arrow	Tunnel / Stop
Local Authority Boundary	
Posttown & London Postal District Boundaries	
Postcode Boundary (within Posttown)	
Built-Up Area	HIGH STREET

Map Continuation For 3 Inches to 1 Mile Street Mapping (Red Pages)	110
Map Continuation To 1 Inch to 1 Mile Street Mapping (Blue Pages)	20
Airport	✈
Car Park (Selected)	P
Church or Chapel	†
Cycleway (Selected)	🚲
Fire Station	■
Hospital	H
House Numbers A & B Roads only	51 / 22 / 19 / 48
Information Centre	i
National Grid Reference	563
Park & Ride	North Station P+☐☐
Police Station	▲
Post Office	★
Toilets	
with facilities for the Disabled	▽
without facilities for the Disabled	▽
for the Disabled only	▽
Educational Establishment	▢
Hospital or Hospice	▢
Industrial Building	▢
Leisure or Recreational Facility	▢
Place of Interest	▢
Public Building	▢
Shopping Centre and Market	▢
Other Selected Buildings	▢

SCALE approx. 3 Inches (7.94 cm) to 1 Mile

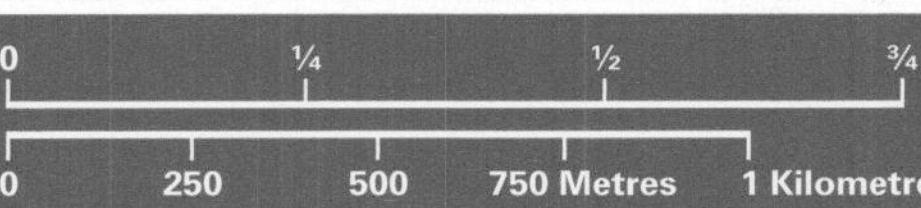

1:20,267 or 4.93 cm to 1km

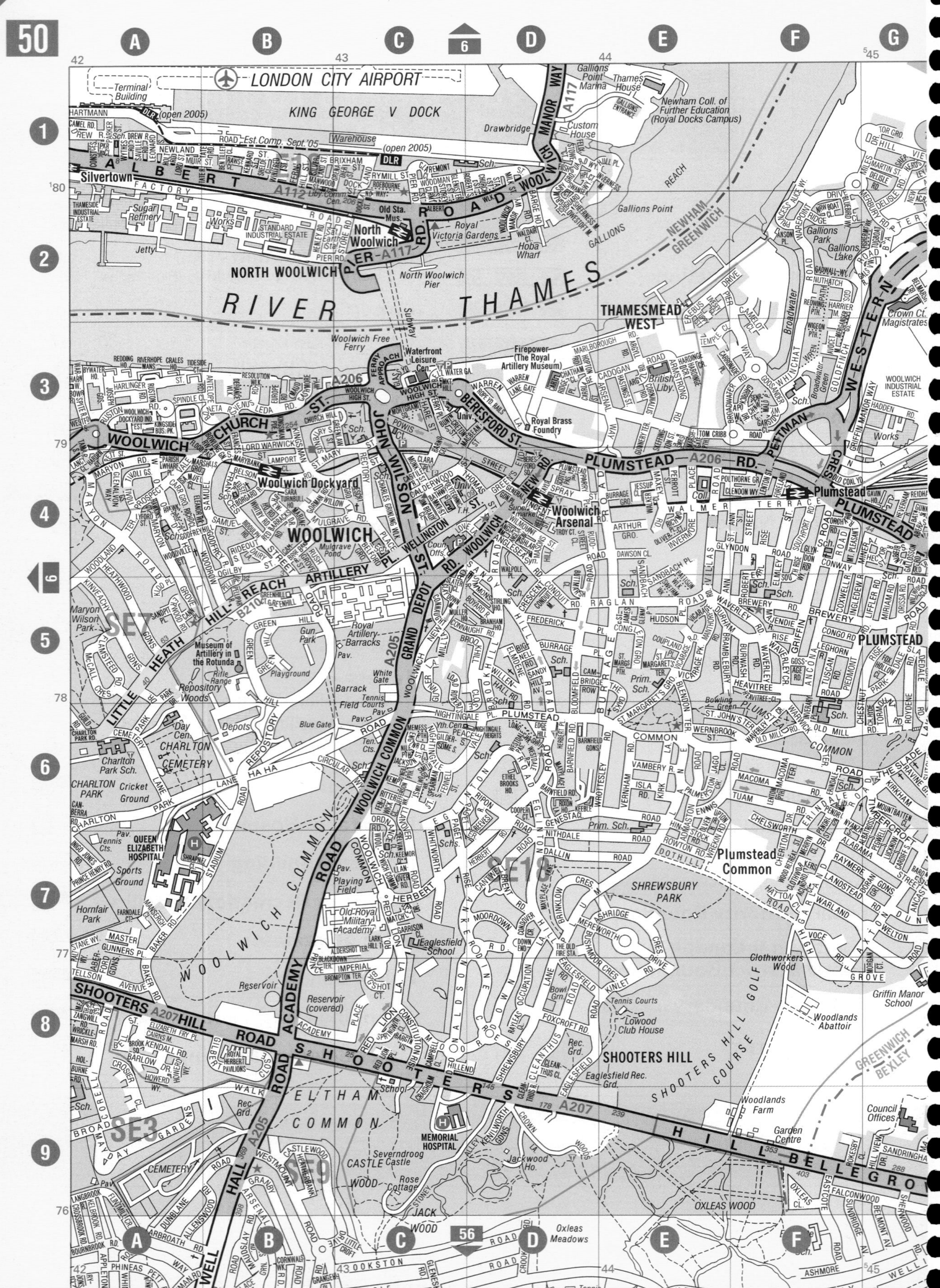
A
B
C
6
D
E
F
G
LONDON CITY AIRPORT
Terminal Building
KING GEORGE V DOCK
Gallions Point Marina
Thames House
Newham Coll. of Further Education (Royal Docks Campus)
Drawbridge
Custom House
Silvertown
ALBERT ROAD
WOOLWICH MANOR WAY
Sugar Refinery
STANDARD INDUSTRIAL ESTATE
THAMESIDE INDUSTRIAL ESTATE
North Woolwich
Old Sta. Mus.
Royal Victoria Gardens
Hoba Wharf
Gallions Point
GALLIONS REACH
NEWHAM
GREENWICH
NORTH WOOLWICH
North Woolwich Pier
RIVER THAMES
Subway
Woolwich Free Ferry
THAMESMEAD WEST
Firepower (The Royal Artillery Museum)
Waterfront Leisure Cen.
British Liby.
Royal Brass Foundry
Broadwater
Galllions Park
Gallions Lake
Crown Ct. Magistrates
WOOLWICH INDUSTRIAL ESTATE
Works
WOOLWICH CHURCH ST.
Woolwich Dockyard
WOOLWICH
BERESFORD ST.
PLUMSTEAD RD.
Plumstead
Woolwich Arsenal
WELLINGTON ST.
ARTILLERY PL.
GRAND DEPOT RD.
JOHN WILSON ST.
Mulgrave Pond
Maryon Wilson Park
SE7
HILL REACH
Museum of Artillery in the Rotunda
Rifle Range
Repository Woods
Gun Park
Royal Artillery Barracks
Playground
Barrack Field
Blue Gate
White Gate
PLUMSTEAD
SE18
WOOLWICH COMMON
PLUMSTEAD COMMON
Plumstead Common
SHREWSBURY PARK
Charlton Park Sch.
CHARLTON CEMETERY
CHARLTON PARK
Cricket Ground
QUEEN ELIZABETH HOSPITAL
Sports Ground
Hornfair Park
Old Royal Military Academy
Eaglesfield School
Reservoir
Reservoir (covered)
Clothworkers Wood
Griffin Manor School
Woodlands Abattoir
Lowood Club House
SHOOTERS HILL
SHOOTERS HILL GOLF COURSE
SHOOTERS HILL ROAD
A207
ELTHAM COMMON
Eaglesfield Rec. Grd.
MEMORIAL HOSPITAL
Severndroog Castle
CASTLE WOOD
Jackwood Ho.
Rose Cottage
JACK WOOD
OXLEAS WOOD
Oxleas Meadows
Woodlands Farm
Garden Centre
Council Offices
GREENWICH
BEXLEY
SE3
SE9
CEMETERY
BELLEGROVE
WELL HALL ROAD
56
1
2
3
4
5
6
7
8
9
42
43
44
45
80
79
78
77
76

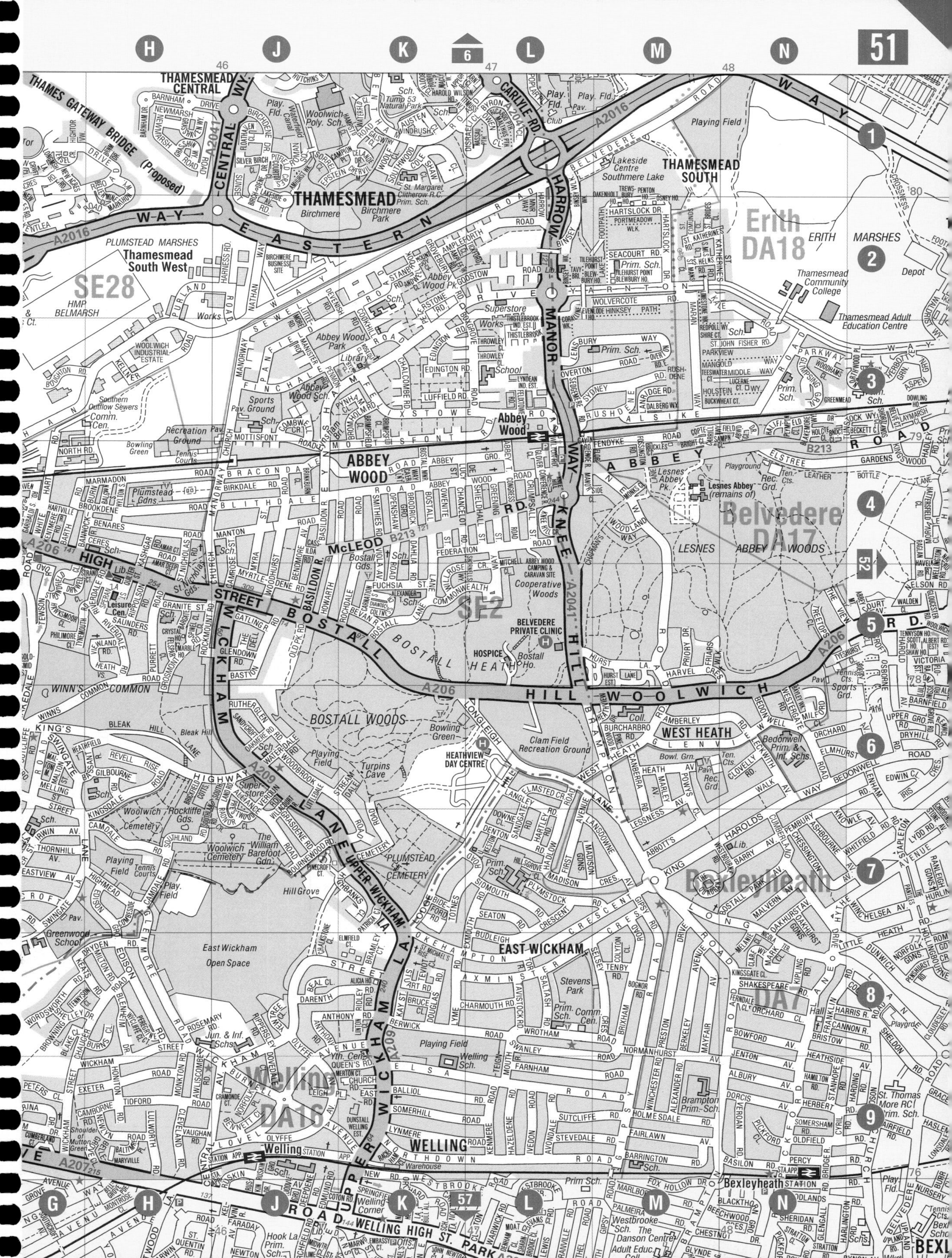
H
J
K
6
L
M
N
THAMESMEAD CENTRAL
THAMES GATEWAY BRIDGE (Proposed)
THAMESMEAD
Birchmere
Birchmere Park
THAMESMEAD SOUTH
Lakeside Centre
Southmere Lake
Erith DA18
ERITH MARSHES
PLUMSTEAD MARSHES
Thamesmead South West
SE28
HMP BELMARSH
WOOLWICH INDUSTRIAL ESTATE
Thamesmead Community College
Thamesmead Adult Education Centre
EASTERN WAY
A2016
A2041
HARROW MANOR WAY
Abbey Wood Park
Abbey Wood
ABBEY WOOD
ABBEY ROAD
Lesnes Abbey (remains of)
Belvedere DA17
LESNES ABBEY WOODS
52
HIGH STREET
BOSTALL HILL
A206
SE2
Cooperative Woods
BELVEDERE PRIVATE CLINIC
BOSTALL HEATH
KNEE HILL
WOOLWICH ROAD
WINN'S COMMON
BOSTALL WOODS
Bowling Green
HEATHVIEW DAY CENTRE
Clam Field Recreation Ground
WEST HEATH
Woolwich Cemetery
Rockliffe Gds.
Plumstead Cemetery
Hill Grove
WICKHAM LANE
A209
UPPER WICKHAM LANE
East Wickham Open Space
EAST WICKHAM
Stevens Park
Bexleyheath
DA7
Welling
DA16
WELLING
Welling Station
Bexleyheath Station
A207
G
H
J
K
57
L
M
N
46
47
48

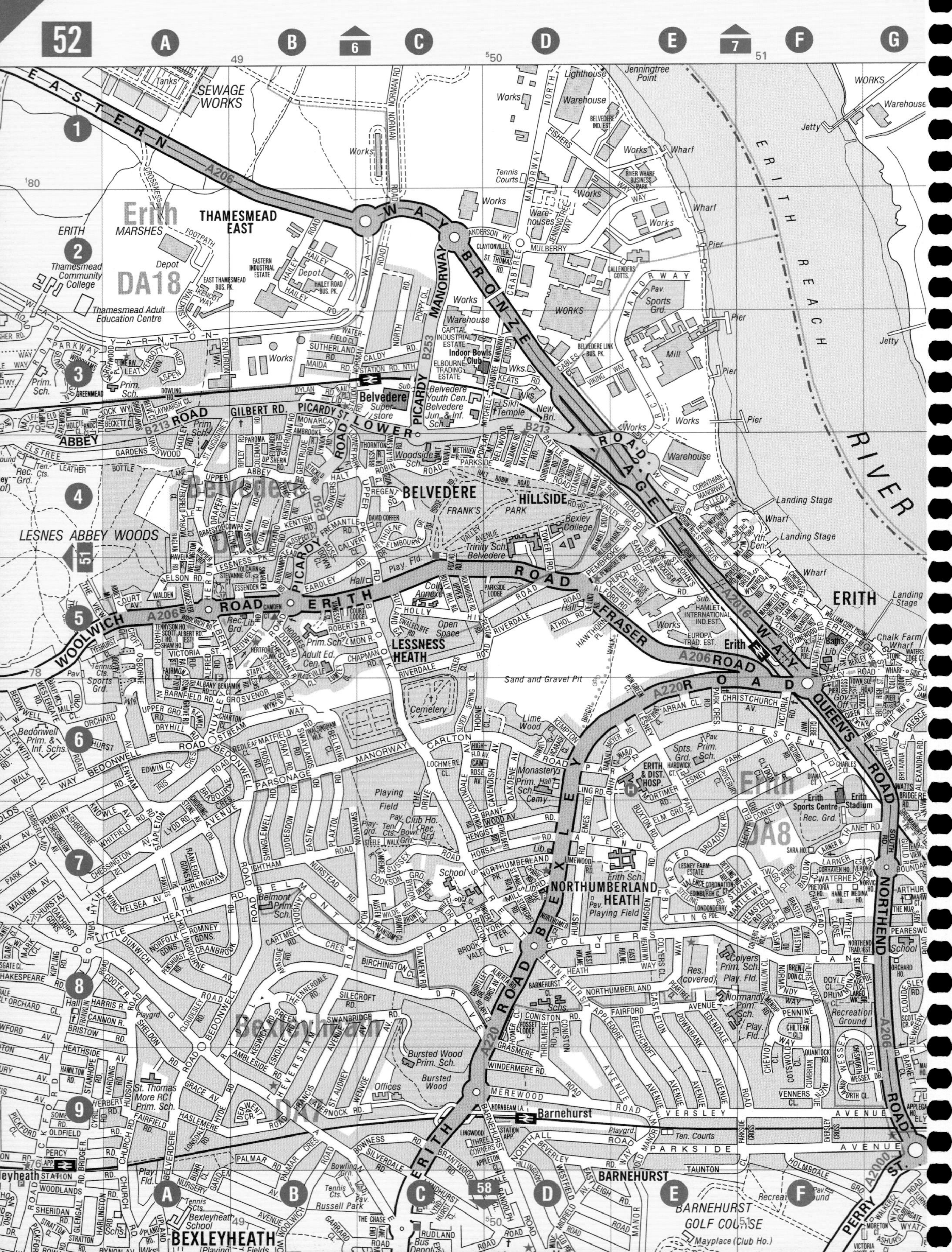
A
B
6
C
D
E
7
F
G
49
550
51
180
79
78
77
76
1
2
3
4
5
6
7
8
9
EASTERN WAY
A206
SEWAGE WORKS
Tanks
Erith MARSHES
ERITH
THAMESMEAD EAST
Thamesmead Community College
Thamesmead Adult Education Centre
DA18
Depot
EASTERN INDUSTRIAL ESTATE
HAILEY ROAD BUS. PK.
EAST THAMESMEAD BUS. PK.
Works
NORMAN RD.
Lighthouse
Jenningtree Point
Warehouse
BELVEDERE IND. EST.
Wharf
RIVER WHARF BUSINESS PARK
Tennis Courts
Wharf
Pier
Works
Mill
WORKS
Sports Grd.
BELVEDERE LINK BUS. PK.
ERITH REACH
RIVER
Jetty
WORKS
Warehouse
BRONZE WAY
MANORWAY
B253
PICARDY
CAPITAL INDUSTRIAL ESTATE
Indoor Bowls Club
ELBOURNE TRADING ESTATE
Belvedere Superstore
Belvedere
Belvedere Youth Cen.
Belvedere Jun. & Inf. Sch.
Sikh Temple
New Bri.
YARNTON WAY
GILBERT RD.
PICARDY ST.
LOWER ROAD
ABBEY ROAD
B213
GARDENS
BELVEDERE
HILLSIDE
FRANK'S PARK
Bexley College
Trinity Sch. Belvedere
Play. Fld.
Yth. Cen.
Landing Stage
Wharf
ERITH
Landing Stage
Chalk Farm Wharf
Baths
Lib.
LESNES ABBEY WOODS
51
ERITH ROAD
A206
WOOLWICH ROAD
Belvedere
Coll. Annexe
Open Space
LESSNESS HEATH
Adult Ed. Cen.
Prim. Sch.
Cemetery
FRASER ROAD
Works
HAMLET INTERNATIONAL IND. EST.
EUROPA TRAD. EST.
Erith
A2016
Sand and Gravel Pit
A220
ROAD
QUEEN'S ROAD
CHRISTCHURCH AV.
CRESCENT
Lime Wood
Bedonwell Prim. & Inf. Schs.
BEDONWELL
MANORWAY
PARSONAGE
Playing Field
Monastery Prim. Sch.
ERITH & DIST. HOSP.
Erith
DA8
Erith Sports Centre
Erith Stadium
Rec. Grd.
BEXLEY ROAD
Erith Sch.
NORTHUMBERLAND HEATH
Pav. Playing Field
Belmont Prim. Sch.
BELMONT ROAD
COLYERS LANE
Colyers Prim. Sch.
Res. (covered)
Normandy Prim. Sch.
Recreation Ground
NORTHEND ROAD
A206
School
Bexleyheath
Bursted Wood Prim. Sch.
Bursted Wood
Offices
St. Thomas More RC Prim. Sch.
DA7
Barnehurst
MEREWOOD
EVERSLEY AVENUE
PARKSIDE AVENUE
Ten. Courts
Playgrd.
BARNEHURST
BARNEHURST GOLF COURSE
Mayplace (Club Ho.)
Russell Park
Bexleyheath School
BEXLEYHEATH
Bus Depot
58
A2000
PERRY ST.
Bexleyheath STATION

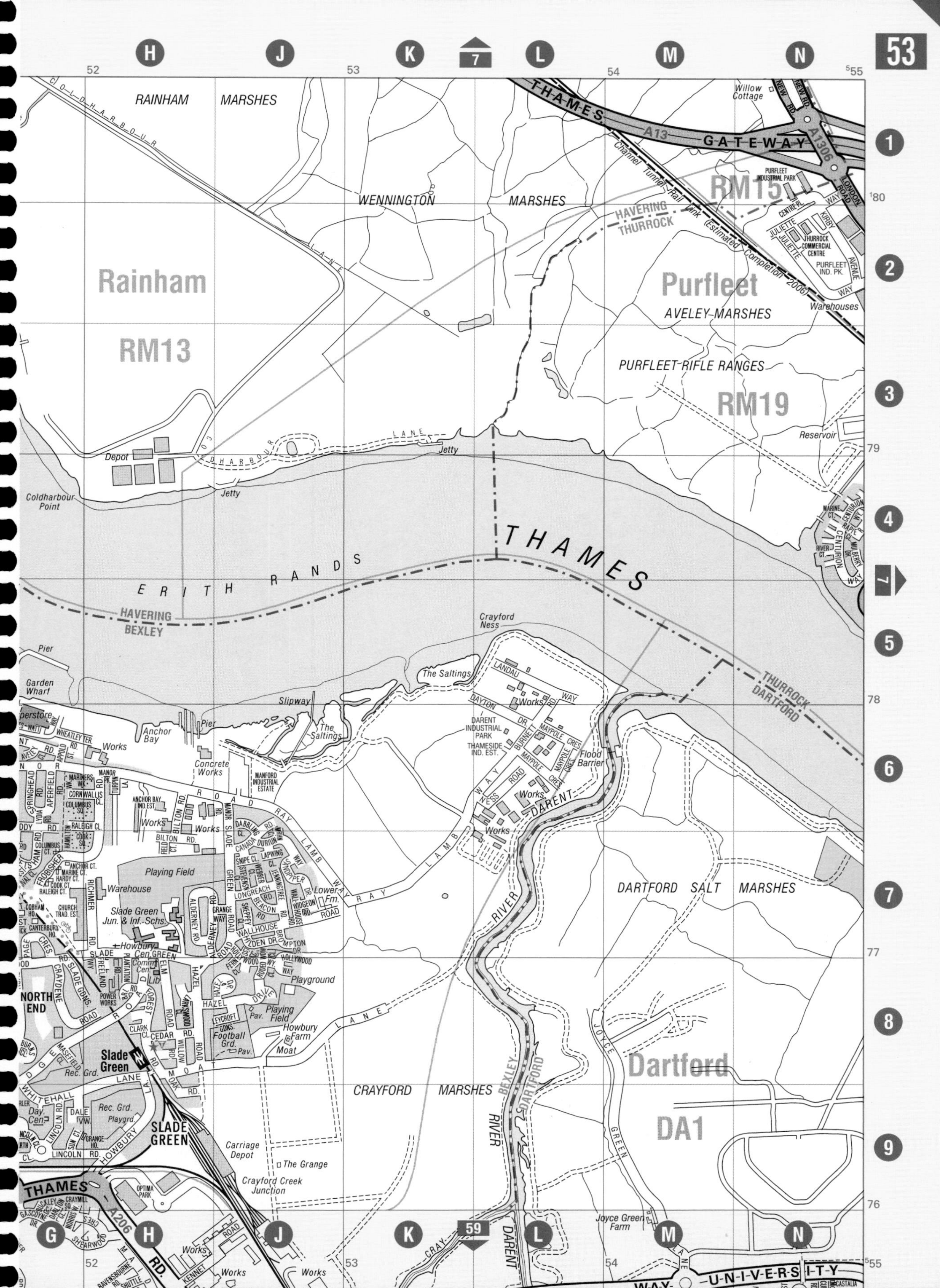

RAINHAM MARSHES
WENNINGTON MARSHES
Rainham
RM13
Purfleet
RM15
RM19
AVELEY MARSHES
PURFLEET RIFLE RANGES
THAMES
ERITH RANDS
HAVERING
BEXLEY
THURROCK
DARTFORD
Coldharbour Point
Crayford Ness
The Saltings
DARTFORD SALT MARSHES
CRAYFORD MARSHES
Dartford
DA1
SLADE GREEN
NORTH END
Slade Green
Flood Barrier
Carriage Depot
The Grange
Crayford Creek Junction
Joyce Green Farm
Howbury Farm
Moat
RIVER DARENT
UNIVERSITY WAY
THAMES GATEWAY
A13
A1306
A206

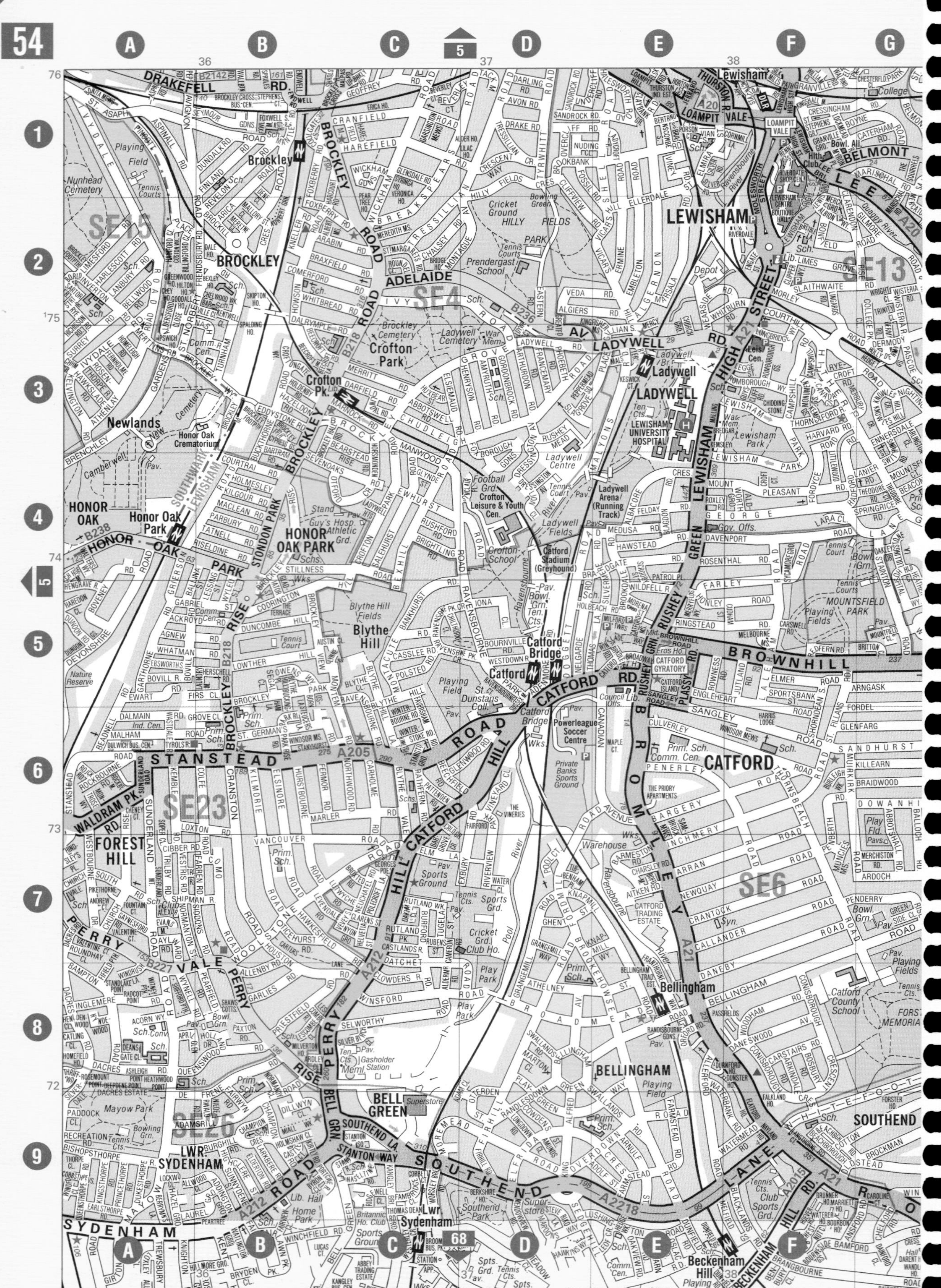
A
B
C
D
E
F
G
5
68
36
37
38
76
75
74
73
72
1
2
3
4
5
6
7
8
9
DRAKEFELL RD.
Brockley
BROCKLEY
BROCKLEY ROAD
Nunhead Cemetery
Playing Field
SE15
SE4
SE13
SE23
SE26
SE6
ADELAIDE AV.
Brockley Cemetery
Crofton Park
Ladywell Cemetery
Cricket Ground
HILLY FIELDS PARK
Prendergast School
LADYWELL RD.
Ladywell
LADYWELL
LEWISHAM UNIVERSITY HOSPITAL
Lewisham
LEWISHAM
LOAMPIT VALE
BELMONT
LEE
LEWISHAM HIGH STREET
RUSHEY GREEN
Lewisham Park
Crofton Pk.
Newlands
Honor Oak Crematorium
Cemetery
Camberwell
HONOR OAK
Honor Oak Park
HONOR OAK PARK
STONDON PARK
BROCKLEY RISE
Guy's Hosp. Athletic Grd.
Crofton Leisure & Youth Cen.
Ladywell Arena (Running Track)
Ladywell Fields
Catford Stadium (Greyhound)
Crofton School
Blythe Hill Fields
Blythe Hill
Catford
Catford Bridge
CATFORD RD.
CATFORD GYRATORY
BROWNHILL RD.
Powerleague Soccer Centre
Private Banks Sports Ground
CATFORD
MOUNTSFIELD PARK
STANSTEAD RD.
A205
A21
A212
A2218
CATFORD HILL
BROMLEY RD.
FOREST HILL
PERRY VALE
PERRY HILL
PERRY RISE
BELL GREEN
Superstore
Sports Ground
Cricket Grd. Club Ho.
Play Park
CATFORD TRADING ESTATE
Bellingham
BELLINGHAM
BROADMEAD
Playing Field
Catford County School
Mayow Park
LWR. SYDENHAM
Lwr. Sydenham
SOUTHEND LANE
SOUTHEND
SYDENHAM RD.
Beckenham Hill
BECKENHAM HILL RD.
Nature Reserve
Gasholder Station

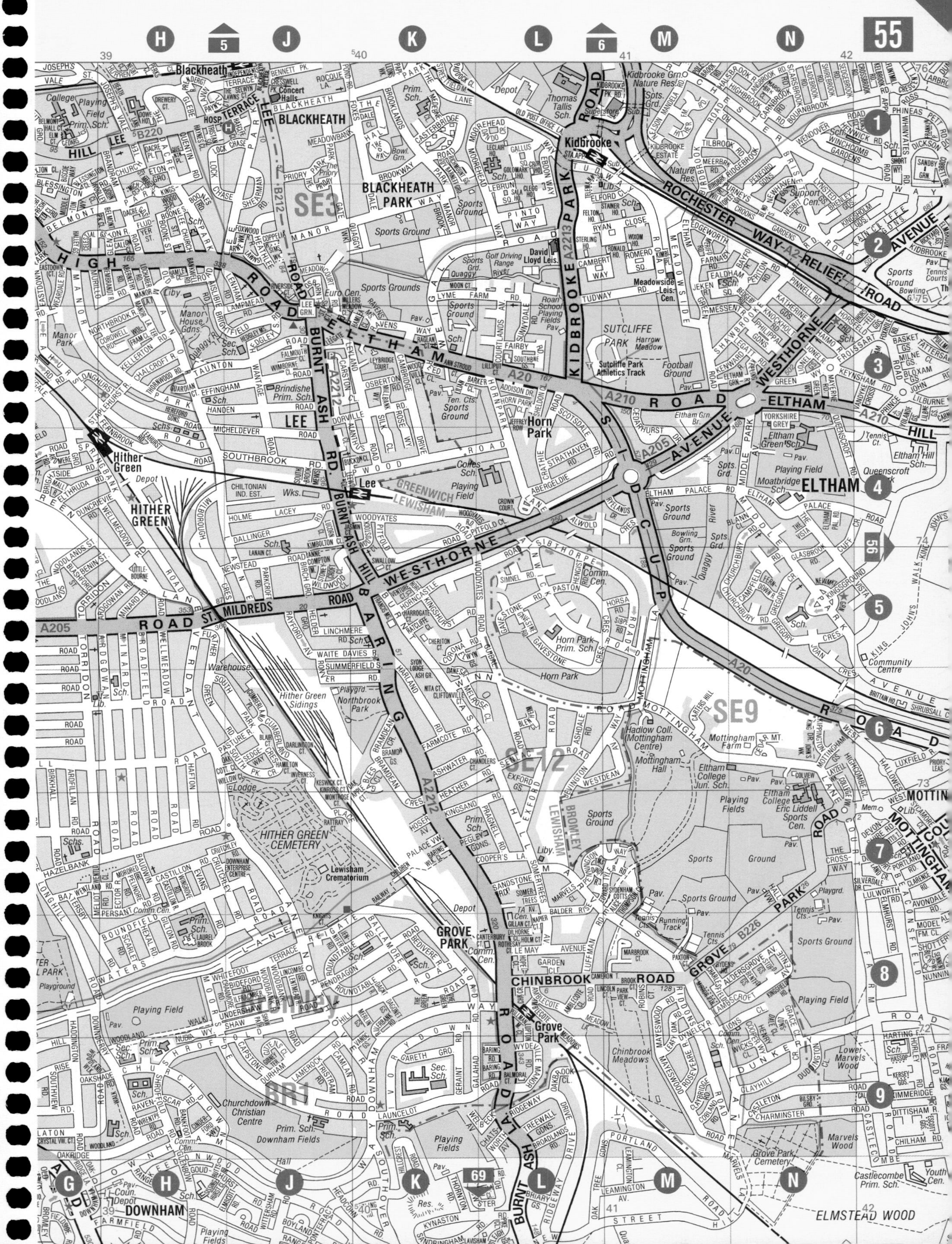
55
H
5
J
K
L
6
M
N
39
40
41
42
Blackheath
BLACKHEATH
BLACKHEATH PARK
SE3
Kidbrooke
Thomas Tallis Sch.
Kidbrooke Grn. Nature Res.
ROCHESTER WAY RELIEF ROAD
A2
KIDBROOKE PARK ROAD
A2213
HIGH ROAD
LEE ROAD
LEE
BURNT ASH RD.
A2212
ELTHAM ROAD
A20
A210
ROAD
ELTHAM
WESTHORNE AVENUE
A205
SIDCUP ROAD
SUTCLIFFE PARK
Sutcliffe Park Athletics Track
Football Ground
Sports Ground
Sports Grounds
Horn Park
Hither Green
HITHER GREEN
Lee
Manor Park
Manor House Gdns.
ST. MILDREDS ROAD
BARING ROAD
BURNT ASH HILL
HITHER GREEN CEMETERY
Lewisham Crematorium
Hither Green Sidings
Northbrook Park
SE12
SE9
Mottingham Farm
Mottingham Hall
Eltham College Jun. Sch.
Playing Fields
Eltham College
Eric Liddell Sports Cen.
GROVE PARK
Grove Park
CHINBROOK ROAD
Chinbrook Meadows
GROVE PARK ROAD
B226
Sports Ground
Playing Field
BROMLEY
LEWISHAM
BR1
Churchdown Christian Centre
Downham Fields
Lower Marvels Wood
Marvels Wood
Grove Park Cemetery
Castlecombe Prim. Sch.
ELMSTEAD WOOD
DOWNHAM
G
H
J
K
L
M
N
69
56
1
2
3
4
5
6
7
8
9
MOTTINGHAM
Community Centre
Queenscroft Park
Eltham Hill Sch.
Moatbridge Sch.
Eltham Green Sch.
Playing Field

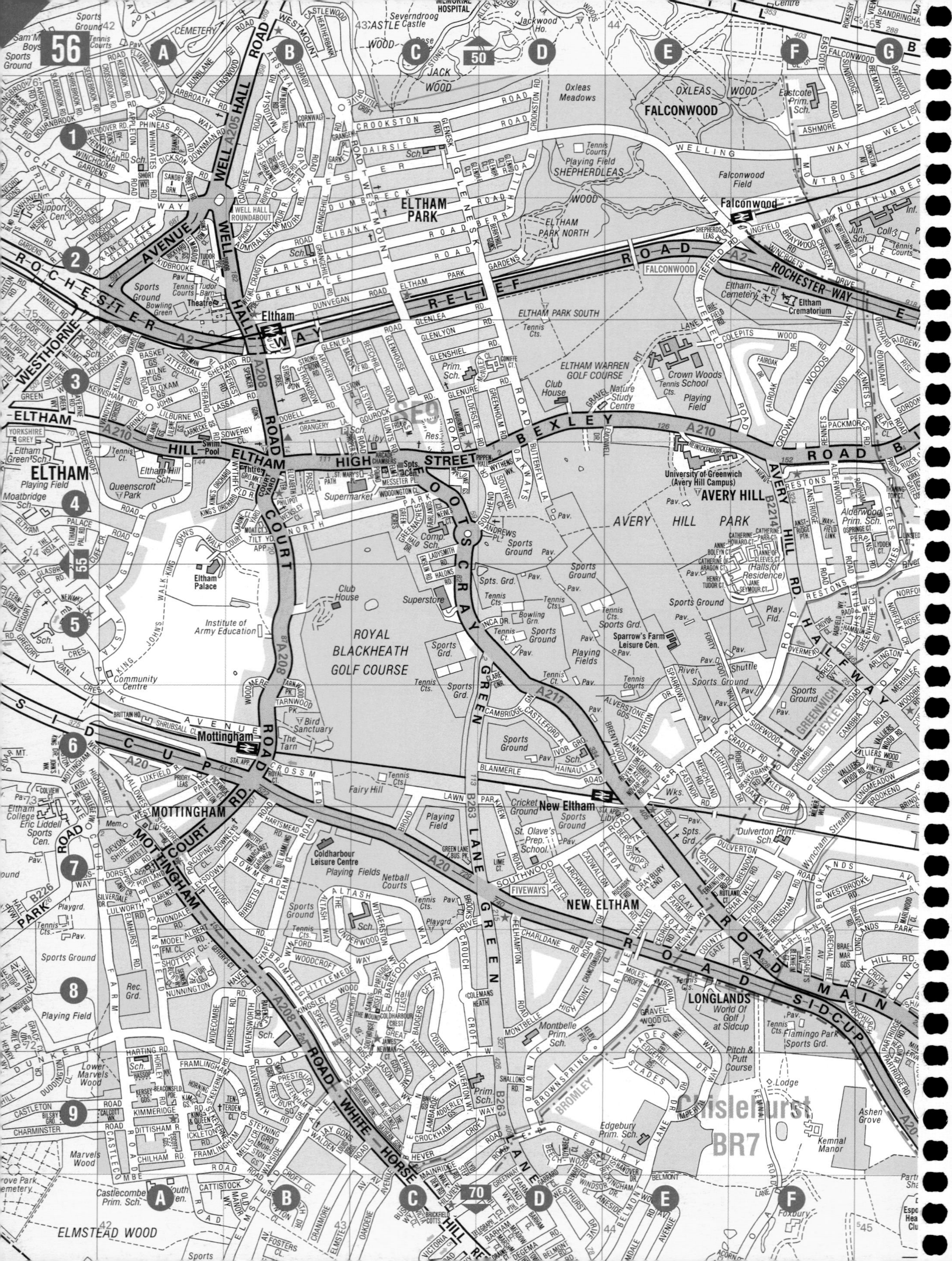
A
B
C
D
E
F
G
1
2
3
4
5
6
7
8
9
42
43
44
45
50
55
70
Sports Ground
Cemetery
Severndroog Castle
Castle Wood
Jack Wood
Jackwood Ho.
Oxleas Meadows
Oxleas Wood
Falconwood
Falconwood Field
Eastcote Prim. Sch.
Welling Way
Shepherdleas Wood
Eltham Park
Eltham Park North
Eltham Park South
Well Hall Roundabout
Well Hall Road
Rochester Way
Rochester Way Relief Road
Eltham
Eltham Cemetery
Eltham Crematorium
Eltham Warren Golf Course
Crown Woods School
Eltham High Street
Eltham Hill
Bexley Road
SE9
University of Greenwich (Avery Hill Campus)
Avery Hill
Avery Hill Park
Halls of Residence
Eltham Palace
Institute of Army Education
Royal Blackheath Golf Course
Court Road
Sidcup Road
Mottingham
Bird Sanctuary
Fairy Hill
New Eltham
Coldharbour Leisure Centre
Sparrow's Farm Leisure Cen.
Dulverton Prim. Sch.
Longlands
World Of Golf at Sidcup
Pitch & Putt Course
Flamingo Park Sports Grd.
Chislehurst BR7
Edgebury Prim. Sch.
Montbelle Prim. Sch.
Marvels Wood
Lower Marvels Wood
Castlecombe Prim. Sch.
Elmstead Wood
Eltham College
Eric Liddell Sports Cen.
Community Centre
Kemnal Manor
Ashen Grove
Foxbury
White Horse Road
Main Road
Halfway Street
Green Lane
Bexley
Greenwich
Bromley

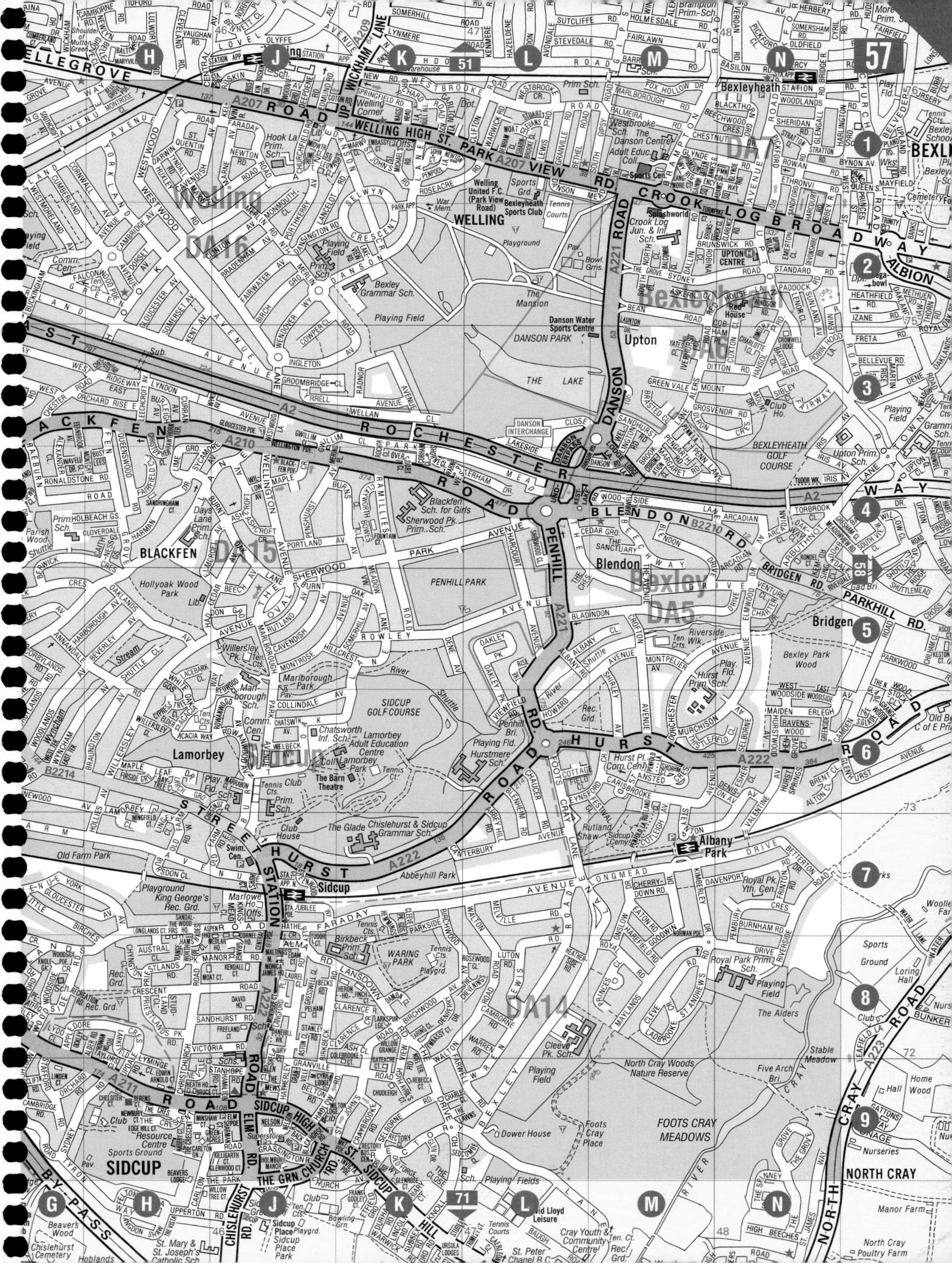

51
58
71
Welling
DA16
WELLING
Welling United F.C. (Park View Road)
Bexleyheath Sports Club
Bexleyheath Station
DA7
Bexleyheath
DA6
Upton
DANSON PARK
THE LAKE
The Mansion
Danson Water Sports Centre
Danson Interchange
Bexley Grammar Sch.
Playing Field
Crook Log Jun. & Inf. Sch.
Splashworld
Sports Cen.
Upton Centre
Red House
Bexleyheath Golf Course
Upton Prim. Sch.
BLACKFEN
DA15
Hollyoak Wood Park
Penhill Park
Blackfen Sch. for Girls
Sherwood Pk. Prim. Sch.
Blendon
Bexley
DA5
Bridgen
Bexley Park Wood
Hurst Prim. Sch.
Lamorbey
Sidcup
Sidcup Golf Course
Lamorbey Adult Education Centre
The Barn Theatre
Chatsworth Inf. Sch.
Hurstmere Sch.
Chislehurst & Sidcup Grammar Sch.
The Glade
Old Farm Park
Abbeyhill Park
Albany Park
Rutland Shaw
Sidcup
King George's Rec. Grd.
Birkbeck Prim. Sch.
Waring Park
Royal Park Prim. Sch.
Royal Pk. Yth. Cen.
DA14
Cleeve Pk. Sch.
North Cray Woods Nature Reserve
Foots Cray Meadows
Foots Cray Place
Five Arch Bri.
Stable Meadow
The Alders
Sports Ground
Loring Hall
Home Wood
NORTH CRAY
Manor Farm
North Cray Poultry Farm
SIDCUP
Sports Ground
Resource Centre
Beaver's Wood
Chislehurst Cemetery
Hoblands
Sidcup Place
St. Mary & St. Joseph's Catholic Sch.
Cray Youth & Community Centre
St. Peter Chanel R.C.
Dower House
A2
A207
A209
A210
A211
A221
A222
A223
B2210
B2214
ROCHESTER WAY
BLACKFEN ROAD
WELLING HIGH ST.
PARK VIEW RD
CROOK LOG
BROADWAY
DANSON ROAD
PENHILL RD.
HURST ROAD
SIDCUP HIGH ST.
STATION ROAD
BLENDON RD
BRIDGEN RD.
PARKHILL RD.
NORTH CRAY ROAD
SIDCUP BY-PASS

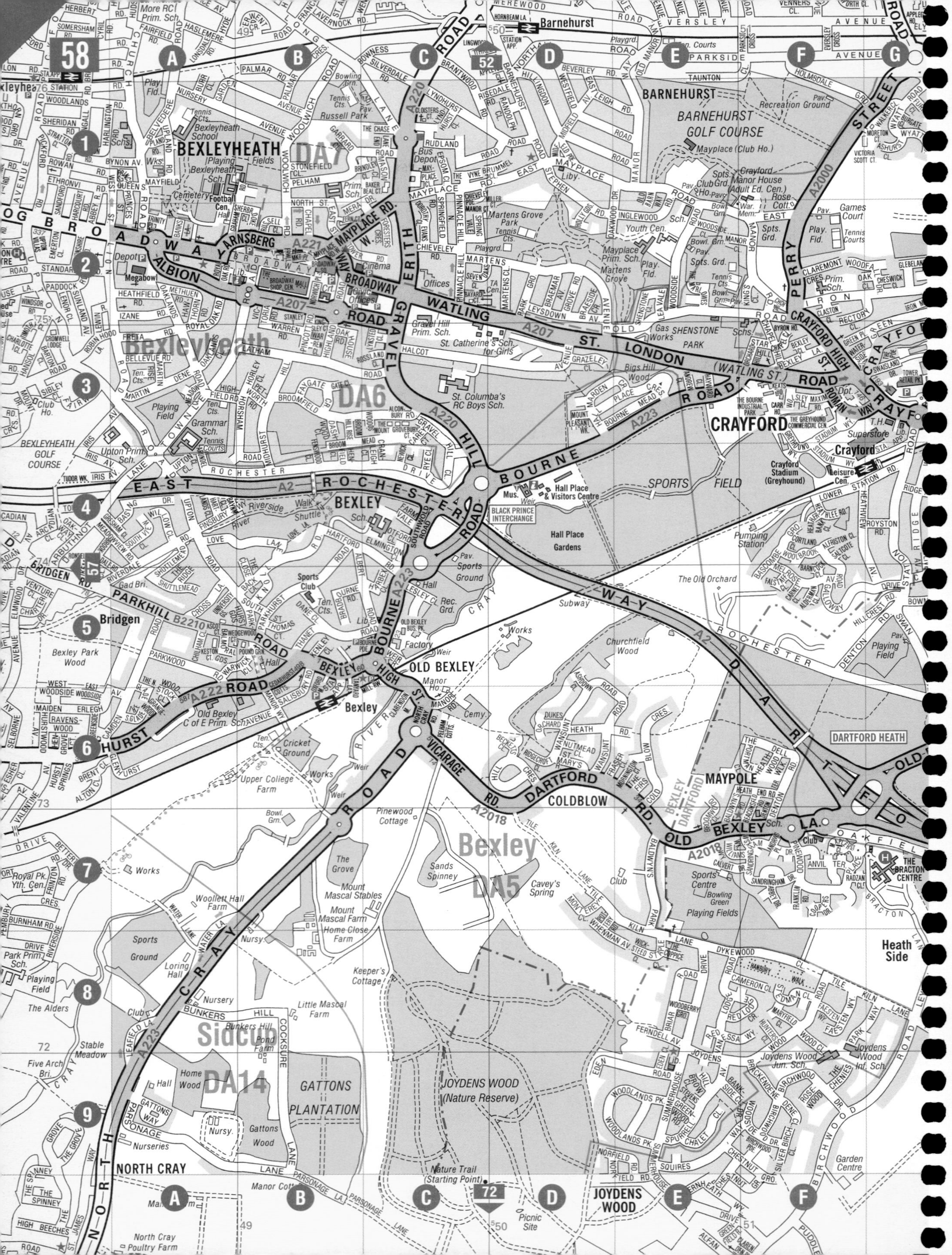
Barnehurst
BARNEHURST
BARNEHURST GOLF COURSE
Mayplace (Club Ho.)
Crayford Manor House (Adult Ed. Cen.)
Recreation Ground
BEXLEYHEATH
DA7
Bexleyheath School
Playing Fields
Russell Park
Bexleyheath
DA6
Martens Grove Park
Mayplace Prim. Sch.
Youth Cen.
Gravel Hill Prim. Sch.
St. Catherine's Sch. for Girls
St. Columba's RC Boys Sch.
Bigs Hill Wood
SHENSTONE PARK
CRAYFORD
THE BOURNE INDUSTRIAL PARK
Crayford
Crayford Stadium (Greyhound)
BEXLEYHEATH GOLF COURSE
Upton Prim. Sch.
Grammar Sch.
EAST ROCHESTER
BEXLEY
Hall Place & Visitors Centre
BLACK PRINCE INTERCHANGE
Hall Place Gardens
SPORTS FIELD
Pumping Station
The Old Orchard
Bridgen
Bexley Park Wood
OLD BEXLEY
Churchfield Wood
Old Bexley C of E Prim. Sch.
Bexley
Cricket Ground
Upper College Farm
DARTFORD HEATH
MAYPOLE
COLDBLOW
Pinewood Cottage
Bexley
DA5
Sands Spinney
Cavey's Spring
The Grove
Mount Mascal Stables
Mount Mascal Farm
Home Close Farm
Sports Centre
Bowling Green
Playing Fields
THE BRACTON CENTRE
Heath Side
Woollett Hall Farm
Sports Ground
Loring Hall
Keeper's Cottage
Little Mascal Farm
Royal Pk. Yth. Cen.
Park Prim. Sch.
Playing Field
The Alders
Stable Meadow
Five Arch Bri.
Sidcup
DA14
Home Wood
GATTONS PLANTATION
Gattons Wood
JOYDENS WOOD (Nature Reserve)
Joydens Wood Jun. Sch.
Joydens Wood Inf. Sch.
Garden Centre
NORTH CRAY
Nature Trail (Starting Point)
Picnic Site
JOYDENS WOOD
North Cray Poultry Farm
A2
A207
A220
A221
A222
A223
A2000
A2018
B2210
52
57
72

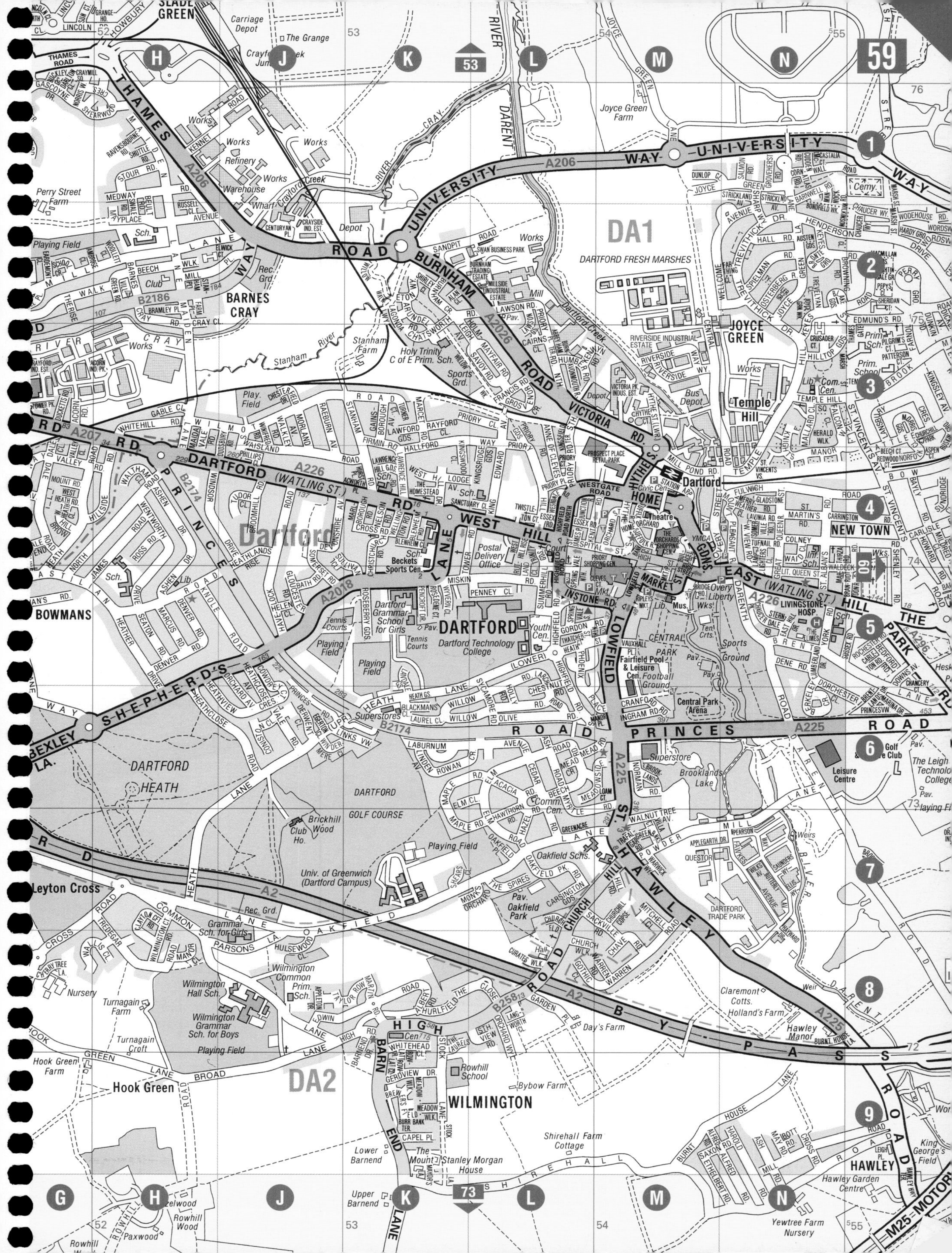

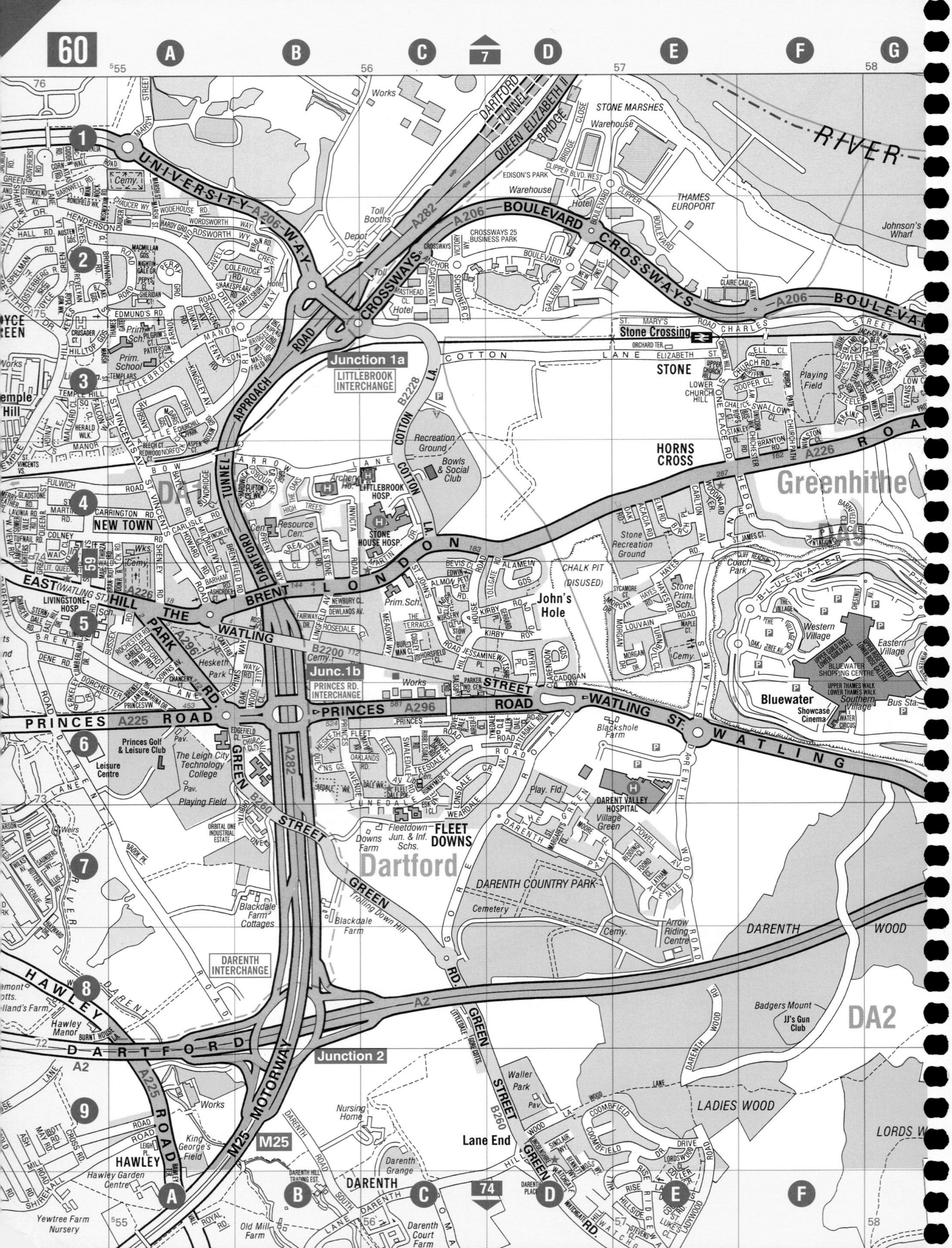
A
B
C
D
E
F
G
7
55
56
57
58
RIVER
STONE MARSHES
Warehouse
THAMES EUROPORT
Johnson's Wharf
EDISON'S PARK
CLIPPER BLVD. WEST
DARTFORD TUNNEL
QUEEN ELIZABETH II BRIDGE
UNIVERSITY WAY
A206
BOULEVARD
CROSSWAYS
A282
Toll Booths
Depot
CROSSWAYS 25 BUSINESS PARK
Hotel
Works
MARSH STREET
Cemy.
HENDERSON
WORDSWORTH WAY
WODEHOUSE RD.
COLERIDGE RD.
SHAKESPEARE RD.
EDMUND'S RD.
CRUSADER
HILLTOP GDS.
Prim. Sch.
Prim. School
TEMPLARS CT.
LITTLEBROOK MANOR WAY
KINGSLEY AV.
APPROACH ROAD
Junction 1a
LITTLEBROOK INTERCHANGE
B2228
COTTON LA.
COTTON LANE
ELIZABETH ST.
ST. MARY'S ROAD
CHARLES STREET
Stone Crossing
ORCHARD TER.
STONE
LOWER CHURCH HILL
Playing Field
CHURCH RD.
BELL CL.
COOPER CL.
SWALLOW CL.
CHURCH PATH
STONE PLACE RD.
HORNS CROSS
A226
ROAD
Greenhithe
Recreation Ground
Bowls & Social Club
Archery Ho.
LITTLEBROOK HOSP.
STONE HOUSE HOSP.
Resource Cen.
HIGH TREES
BOW ARROW LANE
Temple Hill
ST. VINCENTS AV.
FULWICH ROAD
CARRINGTON RD.
NEW TOWN
59
EAST HILL
(WATLING ST.)
LIVINGSTONE HOSP.
A226
TUNNEL
DARTFORD
BRENT
THE BRENT
LONDON
ST. JOHNS
Prim.Sch.
THE TERRACES
KIRBY RD.
John's Hole
CHALK PIT (DISUSED)
Stone Recreation Ground
HEDGE
CARLTON AV.
Stone Prim. Sch.
Cemy.
BLUEWATER
Western Village
Eastern Village
BLUEWATER SHOPPING CENTRE
UPPER GUILD HALL
LOWER GUILD HALL
UPPER THAMES WALK
LOWER THAMES WALK
UPPER ROSE GALLERY
LOWER ROSE GALLERY
Southern Village
Bluewater
Showcase Cinema
Bus Sta.
Coach Park
THE PARK
A296
WATLING STREET
Hesketh Park
PILGRIMS WAY
Junc.1b
PRINCES RD. INTERCHANGE
B2200
Cemy.
PRINCES ROAD
A225
A296
PARKER STREET
WATLING ST.
Blackshole Farm
Princes Golf & Leisure Club
Leisure Centre
The Leigh City Technology College
Pav.
Playing Field
GREEN
B260
ORBITAL ONE INDUSTRIAL ESTATE
FLEET
OAKLANDS RD.
LUNEDALE RD.
Fleetdown Jun. & Inf. Schs.
FLEET DOWNS
Downs Farm
Dartford
Play. Fld.
DARENT VALLEY HOSPITAL
Village Green
DARENTH RD.
DARENTH COUNTRY PARK
Cemetery
Cemy.
Arrow Riding Centre
DARENTH WOOD
Weirs
Blackdale Farm Cottages
Blackdale Farm
Trolling Down Hill
DARENTH INTERCHANGE
HAWLEY RD.
Hawley Manor
BURNT HOUSE LA.
DARTFORD RD
A2
Junction 2
M25 MOTORWAY
M25
Works
King George's Field
HAWLEY
Hawley Garden Centre
GORE RD.
GREEN STREET
B260
Waller Park
Pav.
Nursing Home
Darenth Grange
DARENTH
DARENTH HILL TRADING EST.
Lane End
LADIES WOOD
Badgers Mount
JJ's Gun Club
DA2
LORDS W
Yewtree Farm Nursery
Old Mill Farm
Darenth Court Farm
74
1
2
3
4
5
6
7
8
9

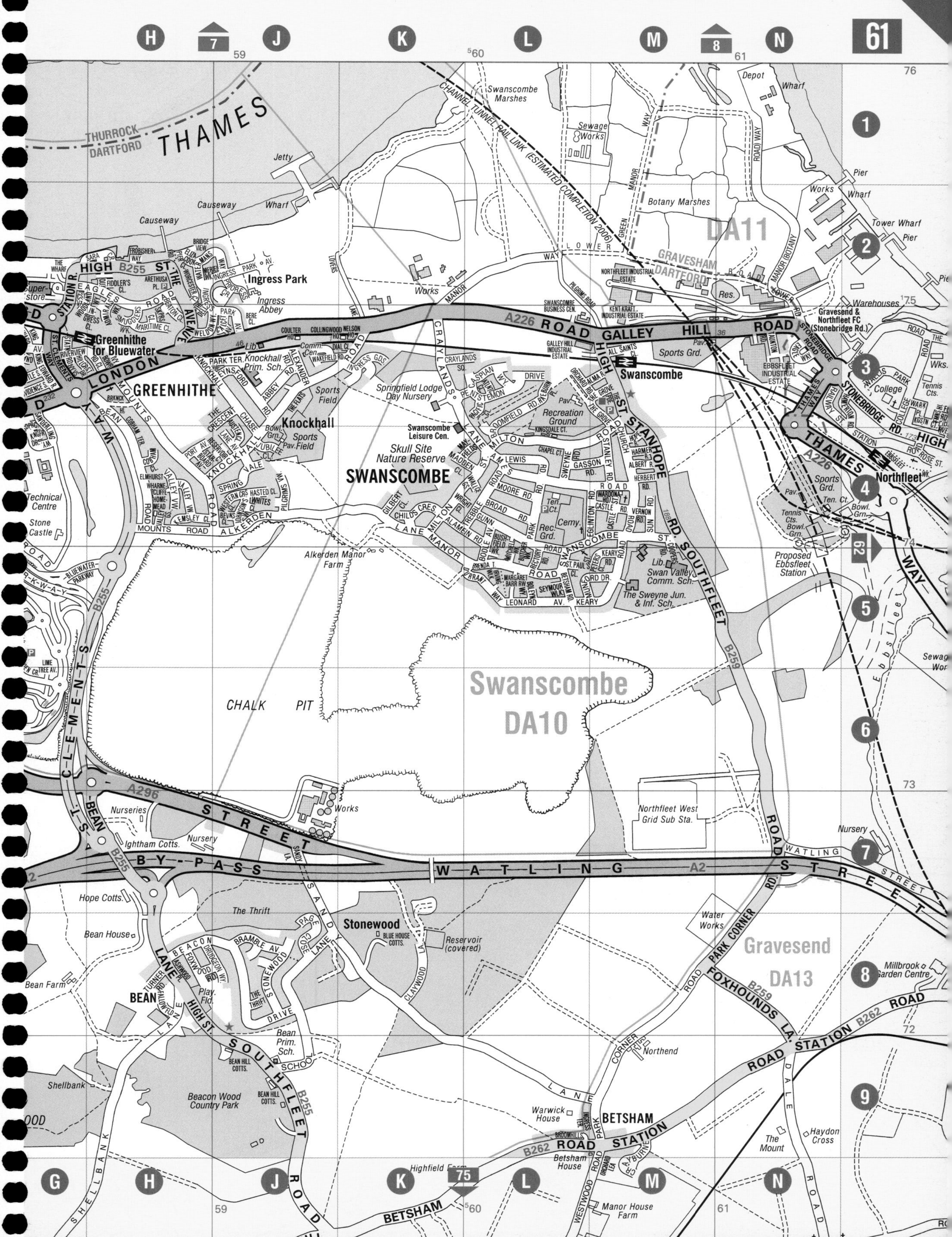
H
J
K
L
M
N
G
7
8
75
62
59
60
61
76
75
74
73
72
1
2
3
4
5
6
7
8
9
THAMES
THURROCK
DARTFORD
Jetty
Causeway
Wharf
Swanscombe Marshes
CHANNEL TUNNEL RAIL LINK (ESTIMATED COMPLETION 2006)
Sewage Works
Depot
Wharf
Botany Marshes
DA11
Pier
Works
Tower Wharf
Warehouses
GRAVESHAM
DARTFORD
NORTHFLEET INDUSTRIAL ESTATE
Res.
Ingress Park
Ingress Abbey
HIGH B255 ST.
Super-store
Greenhithe for Bluewater
GREENHITHE
LONDON
A226 ROAD GALLEY HILL ROAD
SWANSCOMBE BUSINESS CEN.
KENT KRAFT INDUSTRIAL ESTATE
GALLEY HILL INDUSTRIAL ESTATE
Swanscombe
Sports Grd.
EBBSFLEET INDUSTRIAL ESTATE
Gravesend & Northfleet FC (Stonebridge Rd.)
College
Tennis Cts.
THAMES
A226
Northfleet
Knockhall Prim. Sch.
Knockhall
Sports Field
Springfield Lodge Day Nursery
Swanscombe Leisure Cen.
Skull Site Nature Reserve
SWANSCOMBE
Recreation Ground
Technical Centre
Stone Castle
MOUNTS ROAD
ALKERDEN LANE
Alkerden Manor Farm
ST. STANHOPE
SOUTHFLEET RD.
Lib.
Swan Valley Comm. Sch.
The Sweyne Jun. & Inf. Sch.
Proposed Ebbsfleet Station
Sports Grd.
Ebbsfleet
Sewage Works
CHALK PIT
Swanscombe
DA10
B259
B255
ST. CLEMENTS WAY
Works
Northfleet West Grid Sub Sta.
Nurseries
Ightham Cotts.
Nursery
A296
BEAN STREET
BY-PASS
WATLING STREET
A2
Hope Cotts.
The Thrift
Stonewood
BLUE HOUSE COTTS.
Reservoir (covered)
Water Works
Gravesend
DA13
Bean House
Bean Farm
BEAN
Play. Fld.
Bean Prim. Sch.
BEAN HILL COTTS.
SOUTHFLEET ROAD
PARK CORNER RD.
FOXHOUNDS LA.
B262
STATION ROAD
Millbrook Garden Centre
Northend
Shellbank
Beacon Wood Country Park
SHELLBANK
Warwick House
BETSHAM
Betsham House
Highfield Farm
BETSHAM
WESTWOOD ROAD
Manor House Farm
DALE ROAD
The Mount
Haydon Cross

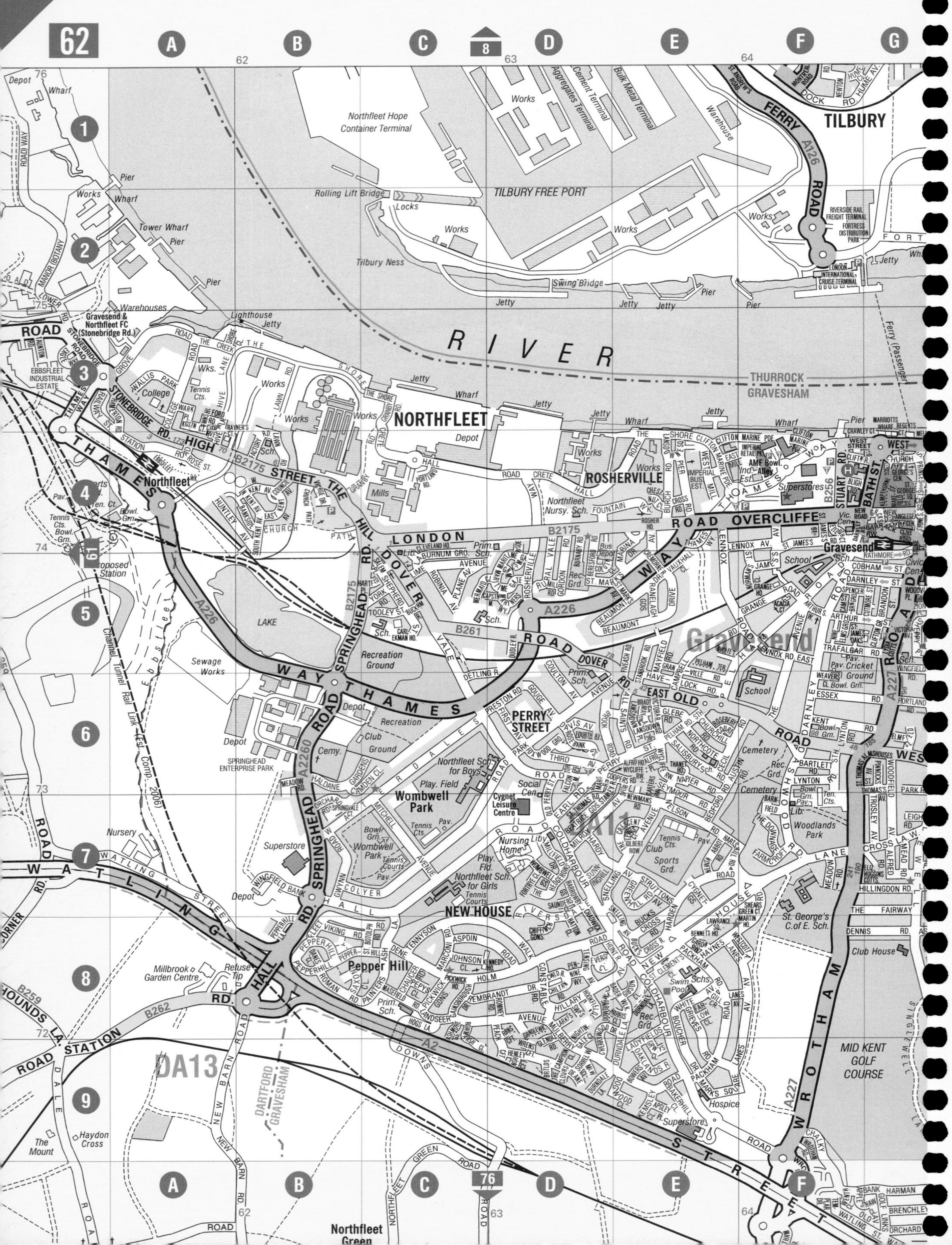

A
B
C
8
D
E
F
G
1
2
3
4
5
6
7
8
9
62
63
64
76
75
74
73
72
Northfleet Hope Container Terminal
Works
Aggregates Terminal
Cement Terminal
Bulk Metal Terminal
Warehouse
TILBURY
FERRY ROAD
A126
Rolling Lift Bridge
Locks
TILBURY FREE PORT
RIVERSIDE RAIL FREIGHT TERMINAL
FORTRESS DISTRIBUTION PARK
LONDON INTERNATIONAL CRUISE TERMINAL
Tilbury Ness
Swing Bridge
Jetty
Pier
Wharf
Tower Wharf
Warehouses
Depot
Lighthouse
RIVER
THURROCK
GRAVESHAM
Ferry (Passenger)
Gravesend & Northfleet FC (Stonebridge Rd.)
EBBSFLEET INDUSTRIAL ESTATE
STONEBRIDGE RD.
College
Tennis Cts.
NORTHFLEET
HIGH STREET
B2175
THE HILL
Northfleet
Mills
ROSHERVILLE
Northfleet Nursy. Sch.
LONDON ROAD
OVERCLIFFE
THAMES WAY
A226
Proposed Station
LAKE
Sewage Works
Channel Tunnel Rail Link (Est. Comp. 2006)
Ebbsfleet
DOVER RD.
SPRINGHEAD RD.
B261
Recreation Ground
Superstores
AMF Bowl. Alley
Gravesend
School
Gravesend
EAST
OLD ROAD
PERRY STREET
Prim. Sch.
Cemy.
Club Ground
Depot
SPRINGHEAD ENTERPRISE PARK
A2260
Northfleet Sch. for Boys
Play. Field
Wombwell Park
Cygnet Leisure Centre
Social Cen.
DA11
Nursing Home
Tennis Cts.
Club
Sports Grd.
Cemetery
Rec. Grd.
Woodlands Park
Nursery
Superstore
WATLING STREET
Northfleet Sch. for Girls
NEW HOUSE
St. George's C.of E. Sch.
Club House
Pepper Hill
Millbrook Garden Centre
Refuse Tip
HALL RD.
B262
B259
HOUNDS LA.
STATION ROAD
DA13
DARTFORD
GRAVESHAM
NEW BARN RD.
A2
Swim Pool
Hospice
Superstore
A227
WROTHAM
MID KENT GOLF COURSE
The Mount
Haydon Cross
Northfleet Green
SINGLEWELL
A
B
C
76
D
E
F

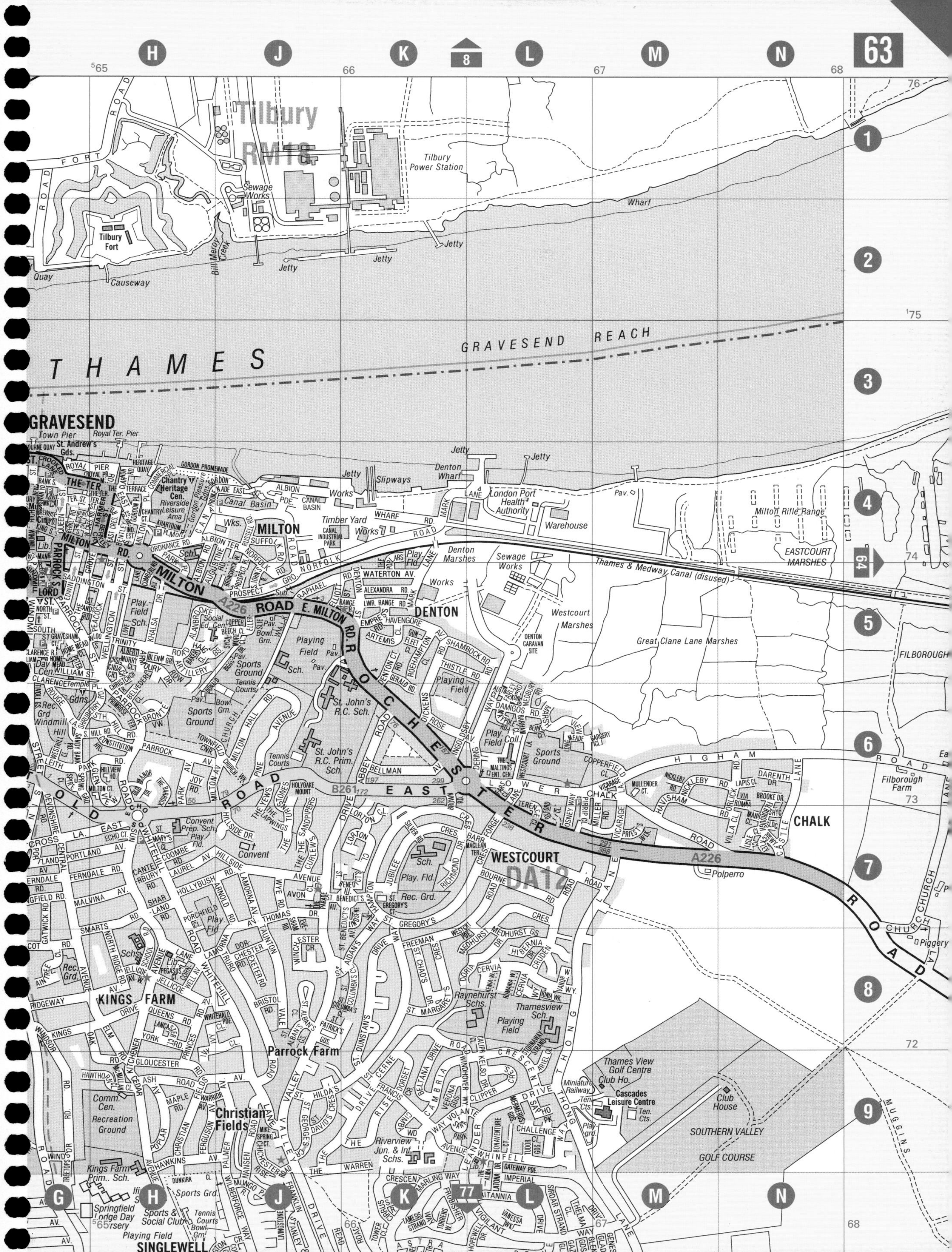
63
H
J
K
L
M
N
8
Tilbury
RM18
Tilbury Fort
Tilbury Power Station
Sewage Works
Wharf
Jetty
Quay
Causeway
Bill Meroy Creek
THAMES
GRAVESEND REACH
GRAVESEND
Town Pier
Royal Ter. Pier
St. Andrew's Gds.
Chantry Heritage Cen.
Riverside Leisure Area
Canal Basin
MILTON
Timber Yard
Works
Slipways
Denton Wharf
London Port Health Authority
Warehouse
Milton Rifle Range
EASTCOURT MARSHES
Denton Marshes
Thames & Medway Canal (disused)
64
DENTON
Westcourt Marshes
Great Clane Lane Marshes
FILBOROUGH
MILTON ROAD
A226
E. MILTON RD.
ROCHESTER ROAD
Playing Field
Sports Ground
St. John's R.C. Sch.
St. John's R.C. Prim. Sch.
DENTON CARAVAN SITE
HIGHAM ROAD
LOWER
CHALK
Filborough Farm
EAST
B261
WESTCOURT
DA12
Polperro
CHURCH LANE
Piggery
OLD ROAD EAST
Convent
KINGS FARM
Parrock Farm
Raynehurst Schs.
Thamesview Sch.
Thames View Golf Centre Club Ho.
Cascades Leisure Centre
Club House
SOUTHERN VALLEY GOLF COURSE
Christian Fields
Comm. Cen.
Recreation Ground
Riverview Jun. & Inf. Schs.
Kings Farm Prim. Sch.
Springfield Lodge Day Nursery
Sports & Social Club
Sports Grd.
Playing Field
SINGLEWELL
MUGGINS
77
G
1
2
3
4
5
6
7
8
9

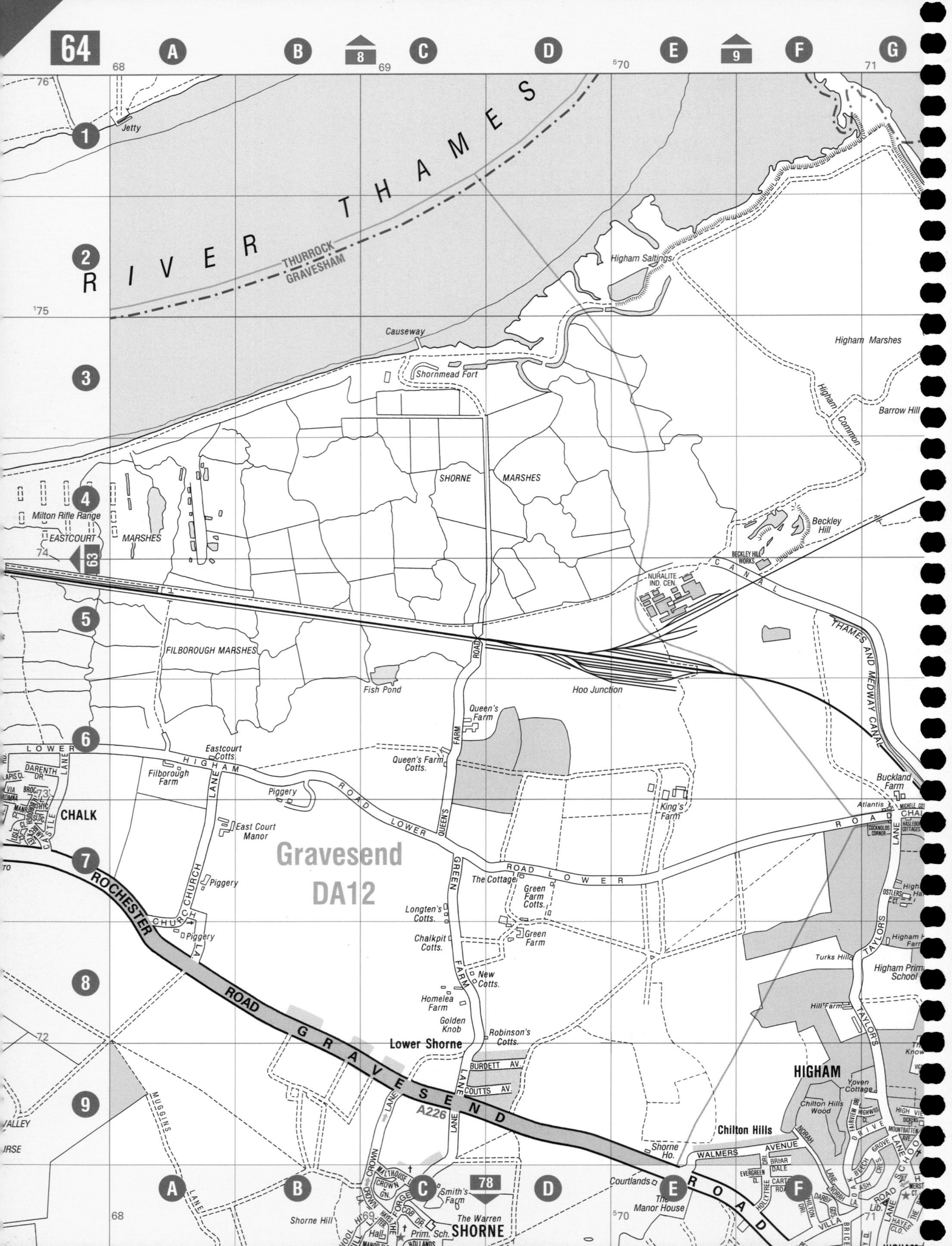

RIVER THAMES
THURROCK
GRAVESHAM
Jetty
Causeway
Shornmead Fort
Higham Saltings
Higham Marshes
Higham Common
Barrow Hill
SHORNE MARSHES
Beckley Hill
BECKLEY HILL WORKS
NURALITE IND. CEN.
CANAL
THAMES AND MEDWAY CANAL
Milton Rifle Range
EASTCOURT
MARSHES
FILBOROUGH MARSHES
Fish Pond
Hoo Junction
Queen's Farm
Queen's Farm Cotts.
Eastcourt Cotts.
Filborough Farm
Piggery
East Court Manor
LOWER HIGHAM ROAD
LOWER ROAD
QUEEN'S FARM ROAD
CHALK
Gravesend DA12
King's Farm
Buckland Farm
Atlantis
CUCKNOLDS CORNER
The Cottage
Green Farm Cotts.
Green Farm
Longten's Cotts.
Chalkpit Cotts.
New Cotts.
Homelea Farm
Golden Knob
Robinson's Cotts.
Lower Shorne
GREEN FARM LANE
CHURCH LANE
ROCHESTER ROAD
GRAVESEND ROAD
A226
BURDETT AV.
COUTTS AV.
MUGGINS LANE
Shorne Ho.
Chilton Hills
WALMERS AVENUE
Courtlands
The Manor House
Turks Hill
Higham Primary School
Hill Farm
TAYLORS LANE
HIGHAM
Yoven Cottage
Chilton Hills Wood
Smith's Farm
The Warren
SHORNE
Shorne Hill
Prim. Sch.
Lib.
8
9
63
78

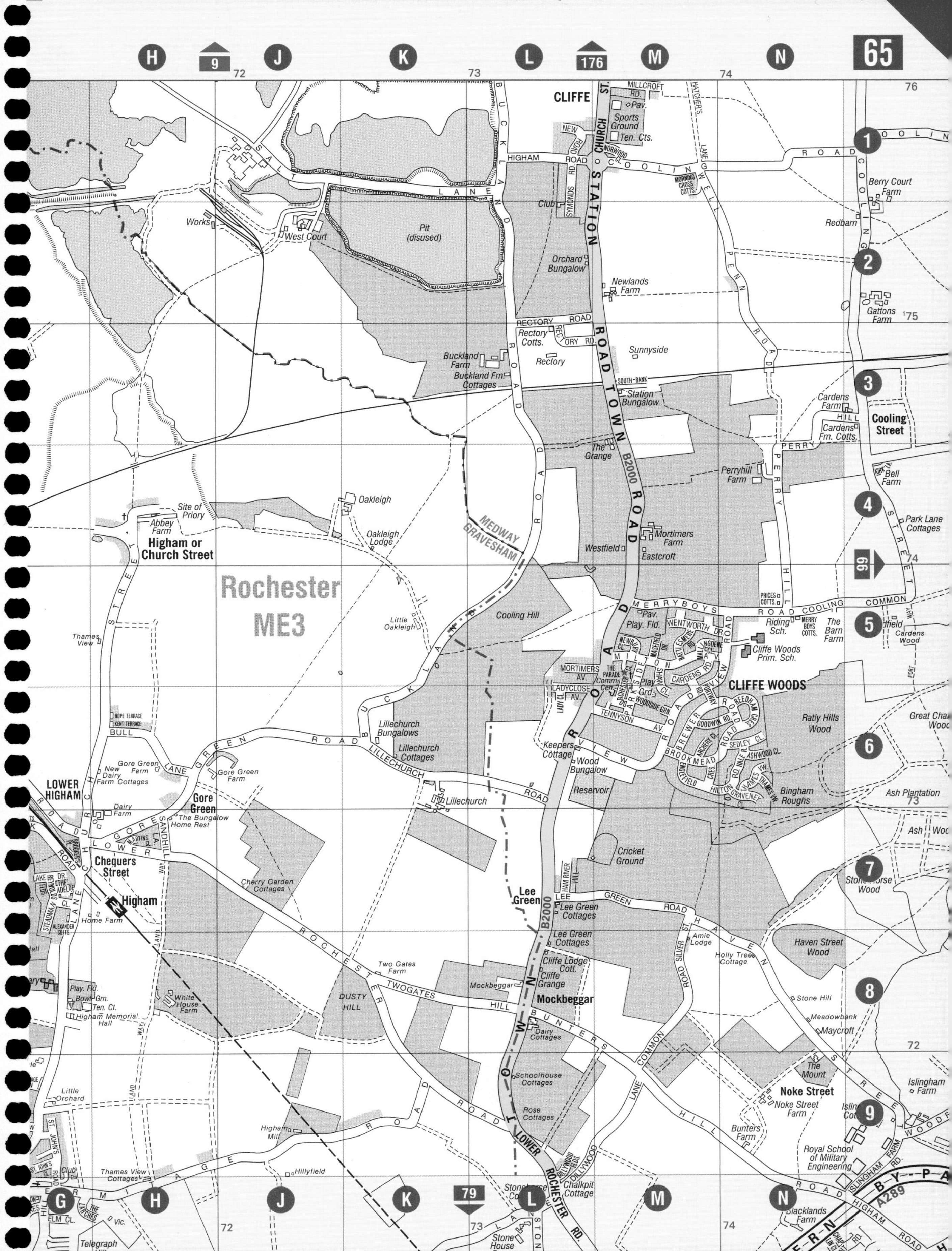
H
9
J
K
L
176
M
N
CLIFFE
Sports Ground
Higham or Church Street
Rochester ME3
Cooling Street
CLIFFE WOODS
LOWER HIGHAM
Gore Green
Chequers Street
Higham
Lee Green
Mockbeggar
Noke Street
MEDWAY
GRAVESHAM
99
79
G
H
J
K
L
M
N

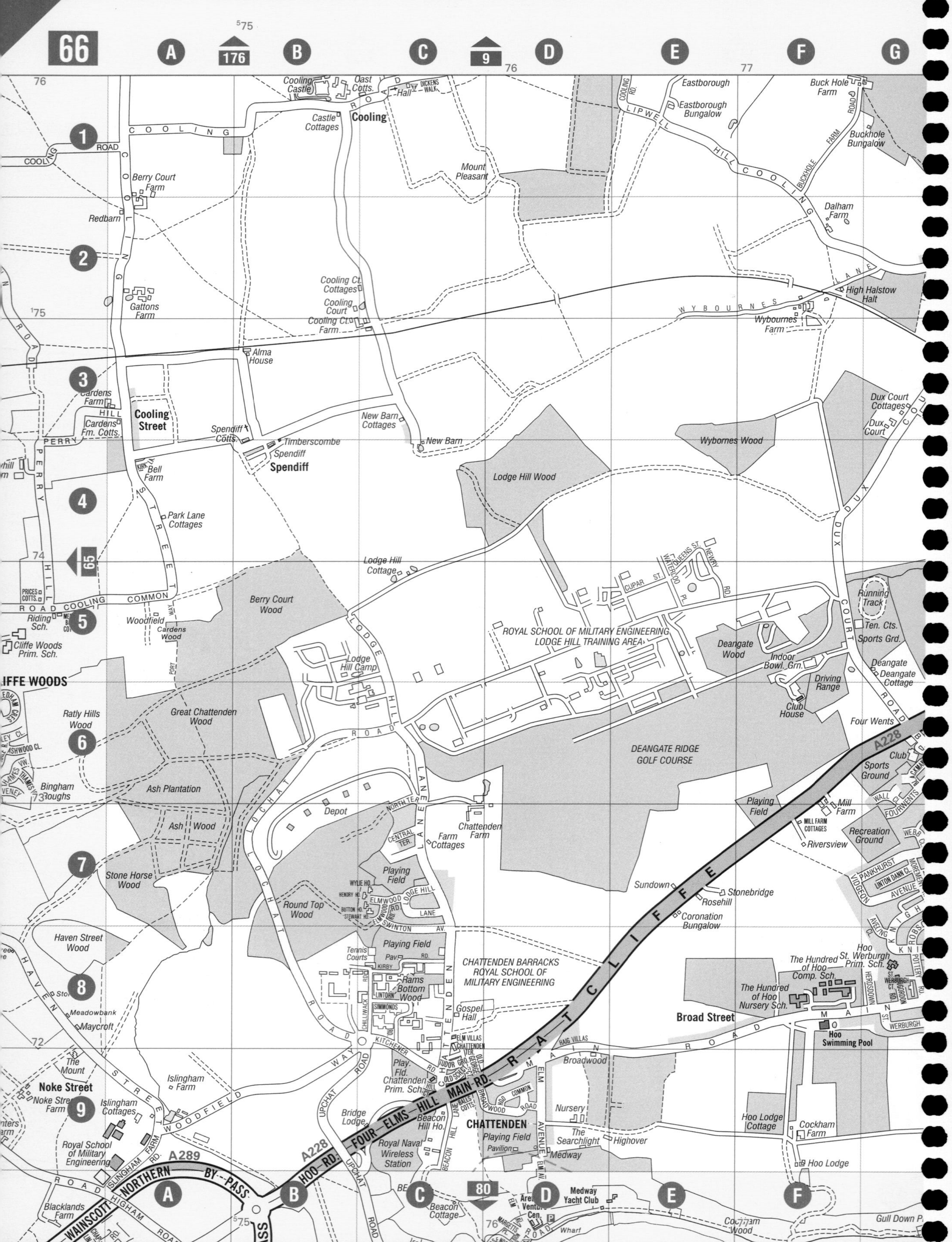
Cooling
Cooling Castle
Oast Cotts.
Castle Cottages
Eastborough
Eastborough Bungalow
Buck Hole Farm
Buckhole Bungalow
Berry Court Farm
Redbarn
Mount Pleasant
Dalham Farm
Gattons Farm
Cooling Ct. Cottages
Cooling Court
Cooling Ct. Farm
High Halstow Halt
Wybournes Farm
Alma House
Cardens Farm
Cooling Street
Cardens Fm. Cotts.
Spendiff Cotts.
Timberscombe
Spendiff
New Barn Cottages
New Barn
Dux Court Cottages
Dux Court
Wybornes Wood
Bell Farm
Lodge Hill Wood
Park Lane Cottages
Lodge Hill Cottage
Berry Court Wood
Woodfield
Cardens Wood
Riding Sch.
Cliffe Woods Prim. Sch.
ROYAL SCHOOL OF MILITARY ENGINEERING LODGE HILL TRAINING AREA
Running Track
Ten. Cts.
Sports Grd.
Deangate Wood
Indoor Bowl. Grn.
Deangate Cottage
Driving Range
Club House
Four Wents
Lodge Hill Camp
Ratly Hills Wood
Great Chattenden Wood
DEANGATE RIDGE GOLF COURSE
Sports Ground
Bingham Roughs
Ash Plantation
Depot
Playing Field
Mill Farm
Chattenden Farm
Farm Cottages
Recreation Ground
Riversview
Ash Wood
Stone Horse Wood
Round Top Wood
Sundown
Rosehill
Stonebridge
Coronation Bungalow
Haven Street Wood
Tennis Courts
CHATTENDEN BARRACKS ROYAL SCHOOL OF MILITARY ENGINEERING
Rams Bottom Wood
Hoo St. Werburgh Prim. Sch.
The Hundred of Hoo Comp. Sch.
The Hundred of Hoo Nursery Sch.
Broad Street
Hoo Swimming Pool
Gospel Hall
Meadowbank
Maycroft
Broadwood
The Mount
Noke Street
Islingham Farm
Noke Street Farm
Islingham Cottages
Chattenden Prim. Sch.
Nursery
Bridge Lodge
Beacon Hill Ho.
CHATTENDEN
Hoo Lodge Cottage
Cockham Farm
Royal School of Military Engineering
Royal Naval Wireless Station
The Searchlight
Highover
Medway
Hoo Lodge
Blacklands Farm
Beacon Cottage
Medway Yacht Club
Cockham Wood
Gull Down P
A228
A289
RATCLIFFE HIGHWAY
FOUR ELMS HILL
MAIN RD.
HOO RD.
NORTHERN BY-PASS
WAINSCOTT
HIGHAM ROAD
LODGE HILL
LOCHAT ROAD
UPCHAT ROAD
CHATTENDEN LANE
DUX COURT ROAD
PERRY HILL
COOLING STREET
COOLING COMMON
WYBOURNES LANE
LIPWELL HILL
MAIN ROAD
ROYAL SCHOOL OF MILITARY ENGINEERING
IFFE WOODS

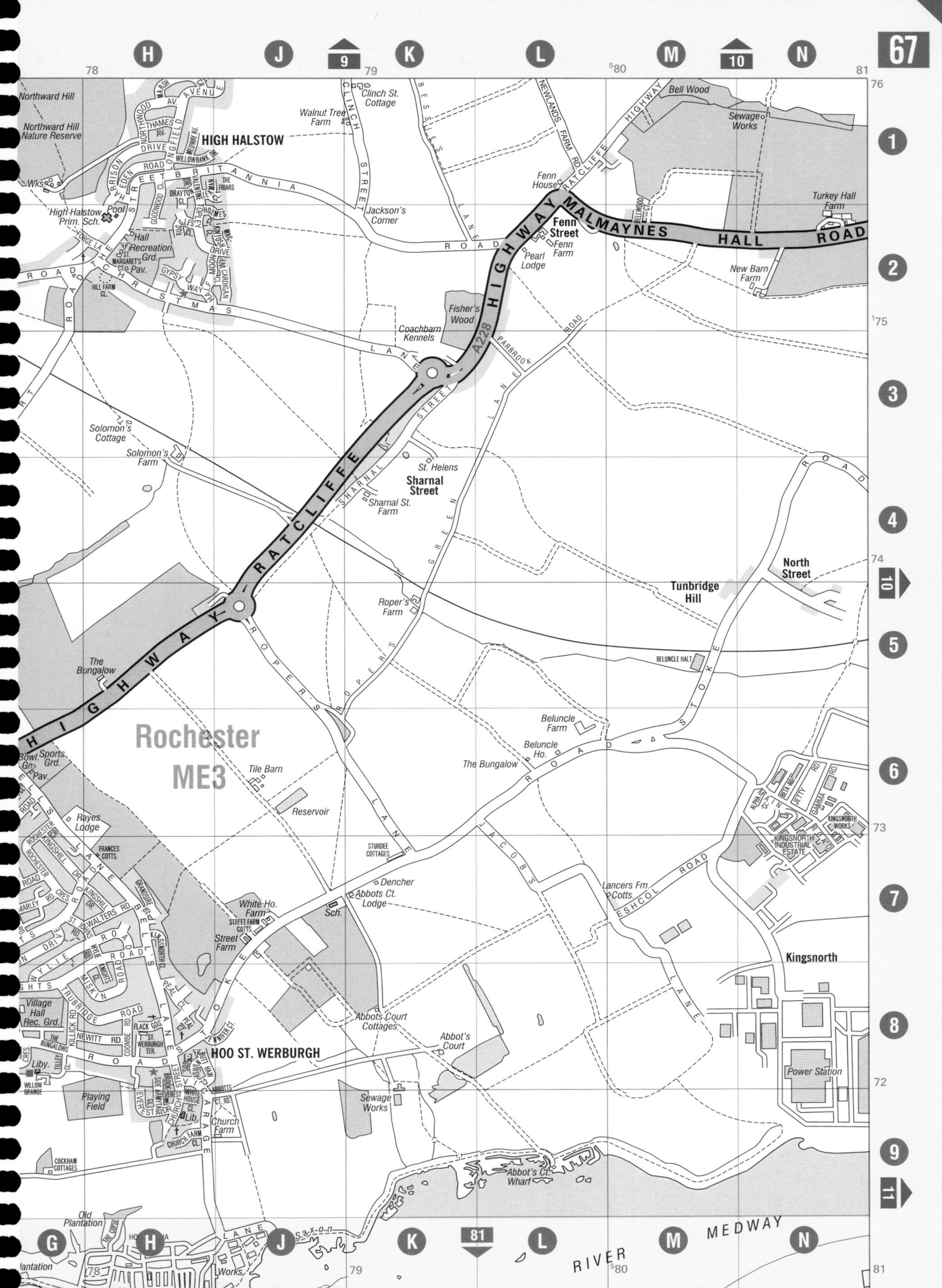

H
J
9
K
L
M
10
N
HIGH HALSTOW
Northward Hill
Northward Hill Nature Reserve
Walnut Tree Farm
Clinch St. Cottage
Bell Wood
Sewage Works
Fenn House
Fenn Street
Fenn Farm
Pearl Lodge
MALMAYNES HALL ROAD
Turkey Hall Farm
New Barn Farm
High Halstow Prim. Sch.
Hall Recreation Grd.
Jackson's Corner
Fisher's Wood
Coachbarn Kennels
A228
RATCLIFFE HIGHWAY
Solomon's Cottage
Solomon's Farm
St. Helens
Sharnal Street
Sharnal St. Farm
North Street
Tunbridge Hill
Roper's Farm
BELUNCLE HALT
The Bungalow
Beluncle Farm
Beluncle Ho.
Rochester ME3
Tile Barn
Reservoir
Rayes Lodge
STURDEE COTTAGES
Dencher
Abbots Ct. Lodge
Sch.
White Ho. Farm
Street Farm
Lancers Fm. Cotts.
KINGSNORTH INDUSTRIAL ESTATE
KINGSNORTH WORKS
Kingsnorth
Village Hall Rec. Grd.
Abbots Court Cottages
Abbot's Court
HOO ST. WERBURGH
Liby.
Playing Field
Sewage Works
Church Farm
Power Station
COCKHAM COTTAGES
Abbot's Ct. Wharf
Old Plantation
RIVER MEDWAY
81
11

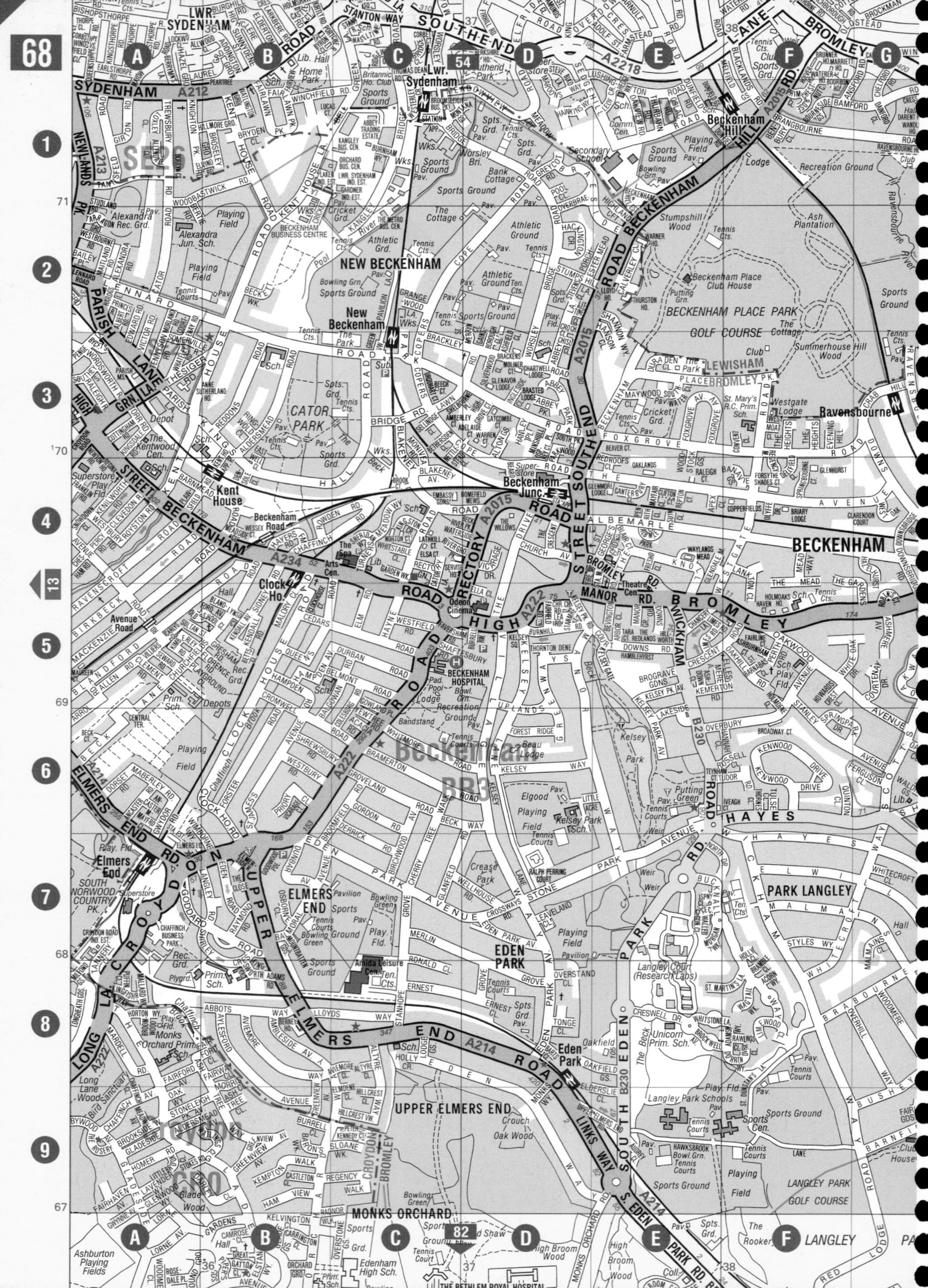
LWR SYDENHAM
SYDENHAM
A212
SOUTHEND
A2218
BROMLEY
54
Lwr. Sydenham
Beckenham Hill
SE26
NEWLANDS PK.
A213
Alexandra Rec. Grd.
Alexandra Jun. Sch.
Playing Field
BECKENHAM BUSINESS CENTRE
Athletic Grd.
Sports Ground
Worsley Bri.
Bank Cottage
The Cottage
Athletic Ground
Secondary School
Sports Ground
Playing Field
Recreation Ground
Ash Plantation
Stumpshill Wood
NEW BECKENHAM
New Beckenham
Bowling Grn. Sports Ground
Beckenham Place Club House
BECKENHAM PLACE PARK
GOLF COURSE
The Cottage
Summerhouse Hill Wood
LEWISHAM
BROMLEY
Sports Ground
Ravensbourne
PARISH LANE
CATOR PARK
Sports Grd.
The Kentwood Cen.
Superstore
Kent House
Beckenham Road
Beckenham Junc.
FOXGROVE ROAD
A2015
BECKENHAM ROAD
A234
Clock Ho.
The Spa
Arts Cen.
Odeon Cinema
HIGH STREET
A222
MANOR RD.
BROMLEY RD.
BECKENHAM
Avenue Road
BECKENHAM HOSPITAL
Recreation Ground
Beckenham BR3
Kelsey Park
Elgood Playing Field
Kelsey Park Sch.
HAYES ROAD
WICKHAM ROAD
B230
PARK LANGLEY
Playing Field
ELMERS END RD.
Elmers End
SOUTH NORWOOD COUNTRY PK.
CROYDON RD.
UPPER ELMERS END
ELMERS END
Sports Ground
Crease Park
EDEN PARK
Playing Field
Langley Court (Research Labs)
ELMERS END ROAD
A214
Eden Park
Monks Orchard Prim. Sch.
Long Lane Wood
UPPER ELMERS END
Crouch Oak Wood
Croydon CR0
Glade Wood
Langley Park Schools
Sports Ground
Sports Cen.
LANGLEY PARK GOLF COURSE
SOUTH EDEN PARK RD.
B230
LINKS WAY
MONKS ORCHARD
82
High Broom Wood
Ashburton Playing Fields
Edenham High Sch.
THE BETHLEM ROYAL HOSPITAL
LANGLEY
13
A B C D E F G
1 2 3 4 5 6 7 8 9
71 70 69 68 67
36 37 38

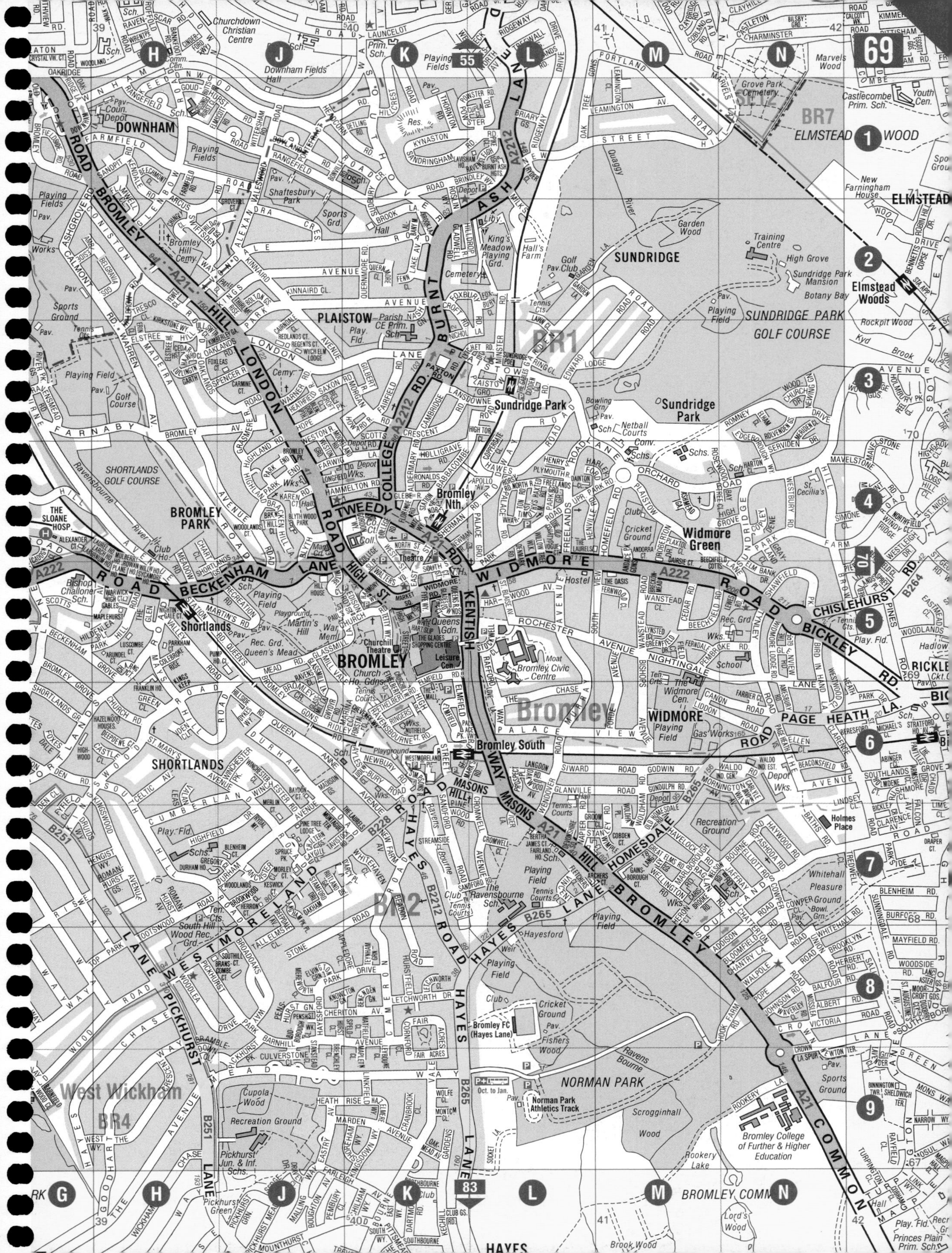
DOWNHAM
PLAISTOW
SUNDRIDGE
SUNDRIDGE PARK GOLF COURSE
Sundridge Park
Widmore Green
BROMLEY PARK
SHORTLANDS GOLF COURSE
BROMLEY
Bromley
WIDMORE
SHORTLANDS
NORMAN PARK
West Wickham
BR4
BR2
BR1
BR7
ELMSTEAD WOOD
ELMSTEAD
Elmstead Woods
Bromley South
Bromley Nth.
Shortlands
Sundridge Park
Bromley Civic Centre
Bromley College of Further & Higher Education
Norman Park Athletics Track
Bromley FC (Hayes Lane)
BROMLEY COMM
HAYES
55
83
70

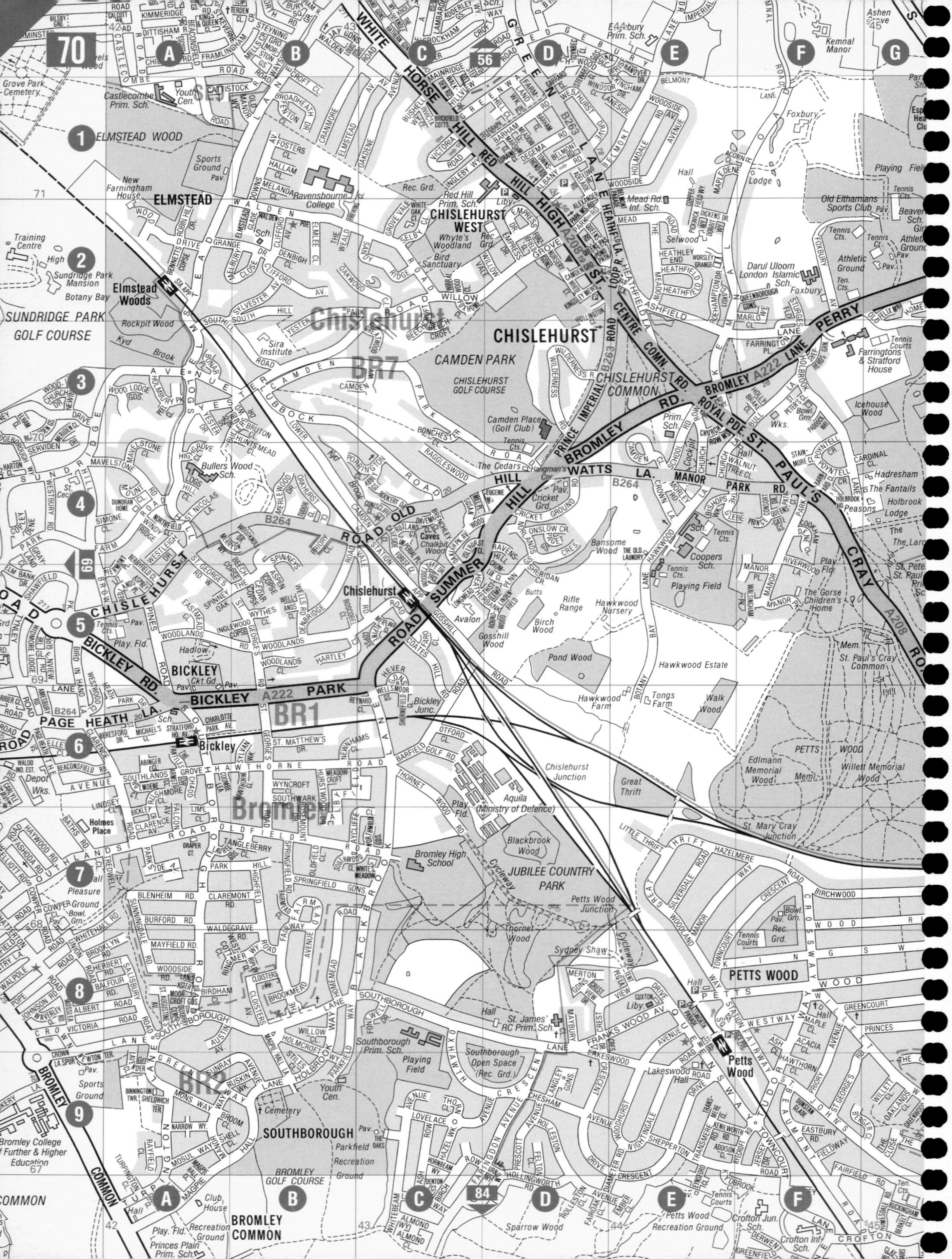

70
56
69
84
A
B
C
D
E
F
G
1
2
3
4
5
6
7
8
9
ELMSTEAD WOOD
ELMSTEAD
Grove Park Cemetery
Castlecombe Prim. Sch.
Youth Cen.
Sports Ground
New Farningham House
Training Centre
High
Sundridge Park Mansion
Botany Bay
SUNDRIDGE PARK GOLF COURSE
Elmstead Woods
Rockpit Wood
Kyd Brook
Ravensbourne College
Rec. Grd.
Red Hill Prim. Sch.
CHISLEHURST WEST
Whyte's Woodland
Bird Sanctuary
Chislehurst
CHISLEHURST
BR7
CAMDEN PARK
CHISLEHURST GOLF COURSE
Camden Place (Golf Club)
CHISLEHURST COMMON
Sira Institute
Mead Rd. Inf. Sch.
Selwood
Darul Uloom London Islamic Sch.
Foxbury
Kemnal Manor
Playing Field
Old Elthamians Sports Club
Athletic Ground
Farringtons & Stratford House
Icehouse Wood
Hadresham
The Fantails
Holbrook Lodge
Peasons
The Gorse Children's Home
St. Paul's Cray Common
Bullers Wood Sch.
Caves
Chalkpit Wood
Chislehurst
Bansome Wood
Coopers Sch.
Playing Field
Rifle Range
Hawkwood Nursery
Birch Wood
Gosshill Wood
Avalon
Pond Wood
Hawkwood Estate
Hawkwood Farm
Tongs Farm
Walk Wood
PETTS WOOD
Edlmann Memorial Wood
Willett Memorial Wood
Great Thrift
Chislehurst Junction
St. Mary Cray Junction
BICKLEY
Hadlow
Bickley
Bickley Junc.
BR1
Aquila (Ministry of Defence)
Blackbrook Wood
JUBILEE COUNTRY PARK
Bromley High School
Petts Wood Junction
Thornet Wood
Sydney Shaw
Bromley
Holmes Place
Pleasure Ground
PETTS WOOD
Petts Wood
Lakeswood Hall
St. James' RC Prim. Sch.
Southborough Prim. Sch.
Playing Field
Southborough Open Space (Rec. Grd.)
Youth Cen.
BR2
SOUTHBOROUGH
Cemetery
Parkfield Recreation Ground
BROMLEY GOLF COURSE
Sports Ground
Bromley College of Further & Higher Education
COMMON
Club House
BROMLEY COMMON
Recreation Ground
Princes Plain Prim. Sch.
Sparrow Wood
Petts Wood Recreation Ground
Crofton Jun. Sch.
Crofton Inf. Sch.
A208
A222
B263
B264
BICKLEY PARK
BICKLEY RD.
SUMMER HILL
BROMLEY RD.
PERRY LANE
ST. PAUL'S CRAY RD.
WHITE HORSE HILL
RED HILL
HIGH ST.

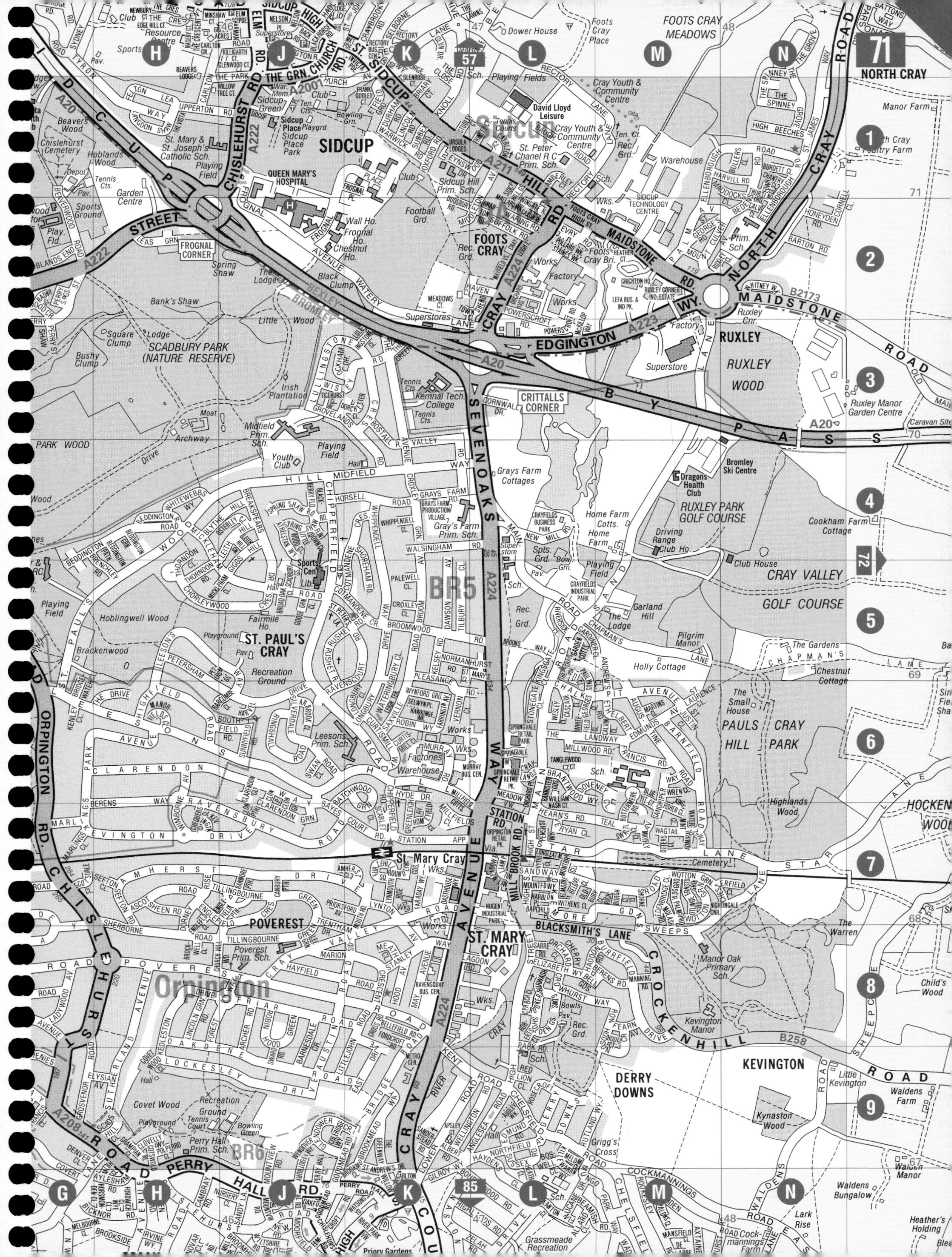

71
NORTH CRAY
FOOTS CRAY MEADOWS
Foots Cray Place
Dower House
57
Playing Fields
Cray Youth & Community Centre
David Lloyd Leisure
Manor Farm
North Cray Country Farm
HIGH BEECHES
THE SPINNEY
SIDCUP
Sidcup Green
Sidcup Place
Sidcup Place Park
QUEEN MARY'S HOSPITAL
St. Mary & St. Joseph's Catholic Sch.
Chislehurst Cemetery
Beavers Wood
Hoblands Wood
Sports Ground
Garden Centre
Playing Field
FROGNAL CORNER
Frognal Ho.
Chestnut Ho.
Wall Ho.
Football Grd.
St. Peter Chanel R C Prim. Sch.
Sidcup Hill Prim. Sch.
SIDCUP TECHNOLOGY CENTRE
Warehouse
FOOTS CRAY
Foots Cray Bri.
Works
Factory
RUXLEY CORNER IND. ESTATE
LEFA BUS. & IND PK.
Superstores
Superstore
RUXLEY
RUXLEY WOOD
Ruxley Cnr.
Ruxley Manor Garden Centre
Caravan Site
Bromley Ski Centre
Dragons Health Club
RUXLEY PARK GOLF COURSE
Driving Range
Club Ho.
Club House
CRAY VALLEY GOLF COURSE
Cookham Farm Cottage
72
Bank's Shaw
Spring Shaw
Square Clump
Bushy Clump
Lodge
Little Wood
SCADBURY PARK (NATURE RESERVE)
Irish Plantation
Moat
Archway
PARK WOOD
Midfield Prim. Sch.
Youth Club
Playing Field
Kemnal Tech. College
CRITTALLS CORNER
Grays Farm Cottages
Gray's Farm Prim. Sch.
GRAYS FARM PRODUCTION VILLAGE
CRAYFIELDS BUSINESS PARK
Home Farm Cotts.
Home Farm
CRAYFIELDS INDUSTRIAL PARK
Garland Hill
The Lodge
Pilgrim Manor
The Gardens
Holly Cottage
Chestnut Cottage
The Small House
PAULS CRAY HILL PARK
Highlands Wood
HOCKENDEN WOOD
BR5
Sports Cen.
Hoblingwell Wood
Brackenwood
Fairmile Ho.
ST. PAUL'S CRAY
Recreation Ground
Leesons Prim. Sch.
Factories
Warehouse
MURRAY BUS. CEN.
SPRINGVALE RETAIL PARK
ORPINGTON RETAIL PK.
St. Mary Cray
Cemetery
NUGENT INDUSTRIAL PARK
POVEREST
Poverest Prim. Sch.
ST. MARY CRAY
RAVENSQUAY BUS. CEN.
Orpington
Manor Oak Primary Sch.
Kevington Manor
KEVINGTON
Little Kevington
Waldens Farm
Kynaston Wood
Child's Wood
The Warren
DERRY DOWNS
Grigg's Cross
Covet Wood
Recreation Ground
Perry Hall Prim. Sch.
BR6
Walden Manor
Waldens Bungalow
Lark Rise
Cockmannings Farm
Heather's Holding
Grassmeade Recreation
Priory Gardens
85
SIDCUP BY PASS
CHISLEHURST RD.
MAIDSTONE RD.
NORTH CRAY ROAD
EDGINGTON WY.
MAIDSTONE ROAD
SEVENOAKS WAY
CRAY AVENUE
ORPINGTON RD.
CHISLEHURST ROAD
POVEREST ROAD
STAR LANE
CROCKENHILL ROAD
KEVINGTON ROAD
SHEEPCOTE LANE
PERRY HALL RD.
MAIN ROAD
CHAPMAN'S LANE
BLACKSMITH'S LANE
A20
A222
A224
A223
A211
A2001
A208
B2173
B258
H J K L M N
G H J K L M N
1 2 3 4 5 6 7 8 9

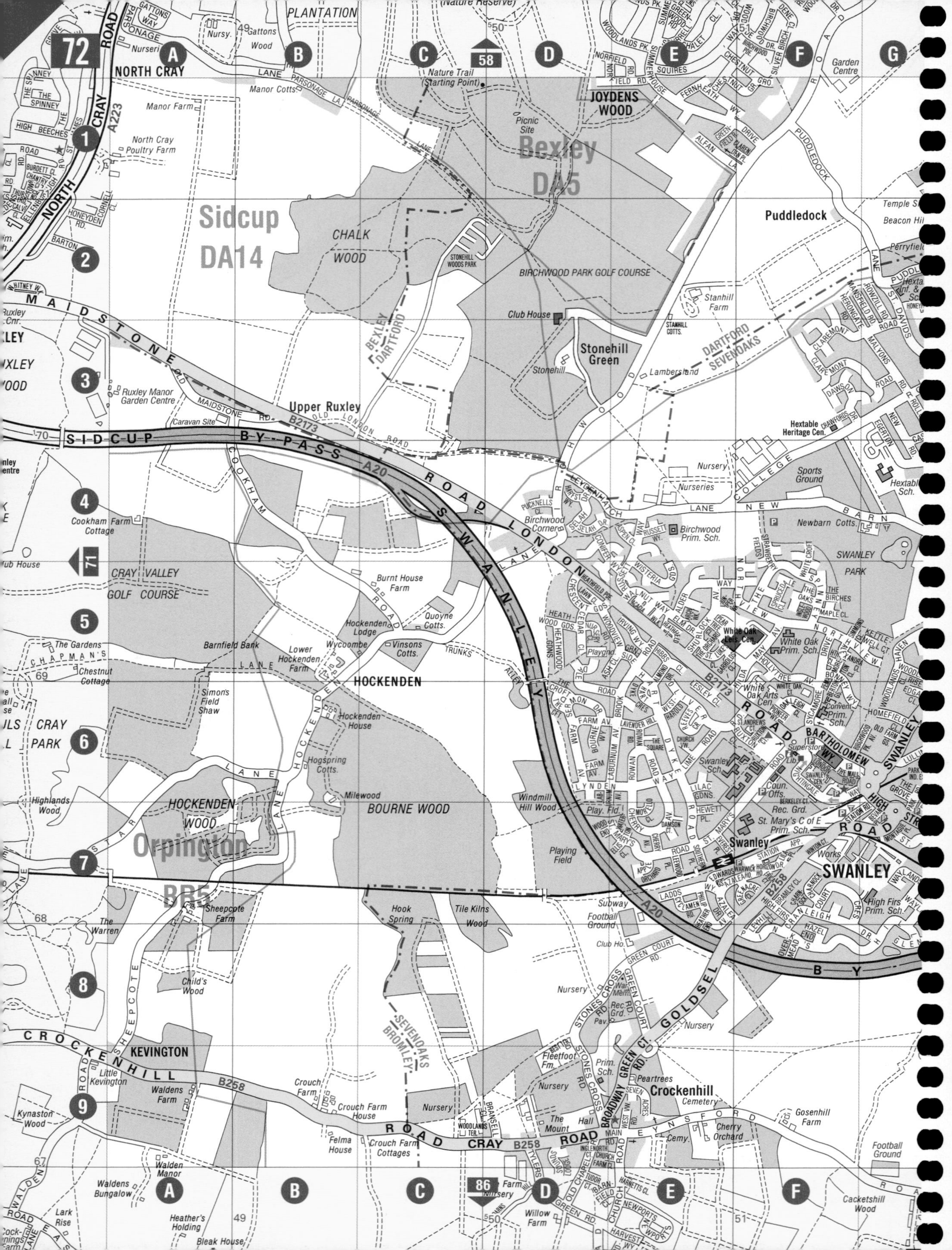

NORTH CRAY
PLANTATION
JOYDENS WOOD
Bexley DA5
Sidcup DA14
CHALK WOOD
BIRCHWOOD PARK GOLF COURSE
Club House
Stonehill Green
Puddledock
Upper Ruxley
SIDCUP-BY-PASS
MAIDSTONE ROAD
LONDON ROAD
SWANLEY BY-PASS
Hextable Heritage Cen.
Birchwood Corner
Birchwood Prim. Sch.
CRAY VALLEY GOLF COURSE
Burnt House Farm
Hockenden Lodge
HOCKENDEN
Hockenden House
White Oak Leis. Cen.
White Oak Prim. Sch.
SWANLEY PARK
Swanley Sch.
BOURNE WOOD
HOCKENDEN WOOD
Orpington BR5
Windmill Hill Wood
Playing Field
St. Mary's C of E Prim. Sch.
Swanley
SWANLEY
High Firs Prim. Sch.
Sheepcote Farm
Tile Kilns Wood
Hook Spring
Football Ground
Child's Wood
KEVINGTON
CROCKENHILL
B258
Crockenhill
Cemetery
Gosenhill Farm
Crouch Farm House
Crouch Farm Cottages
Waldens Farm
Kynaston Wood
Walden Manor
Waldens Bungalow
Lark Rise
Heather's Holding
Bleak House
Willow Farm
Cacketshill Wood
Football Ground

58
71
86

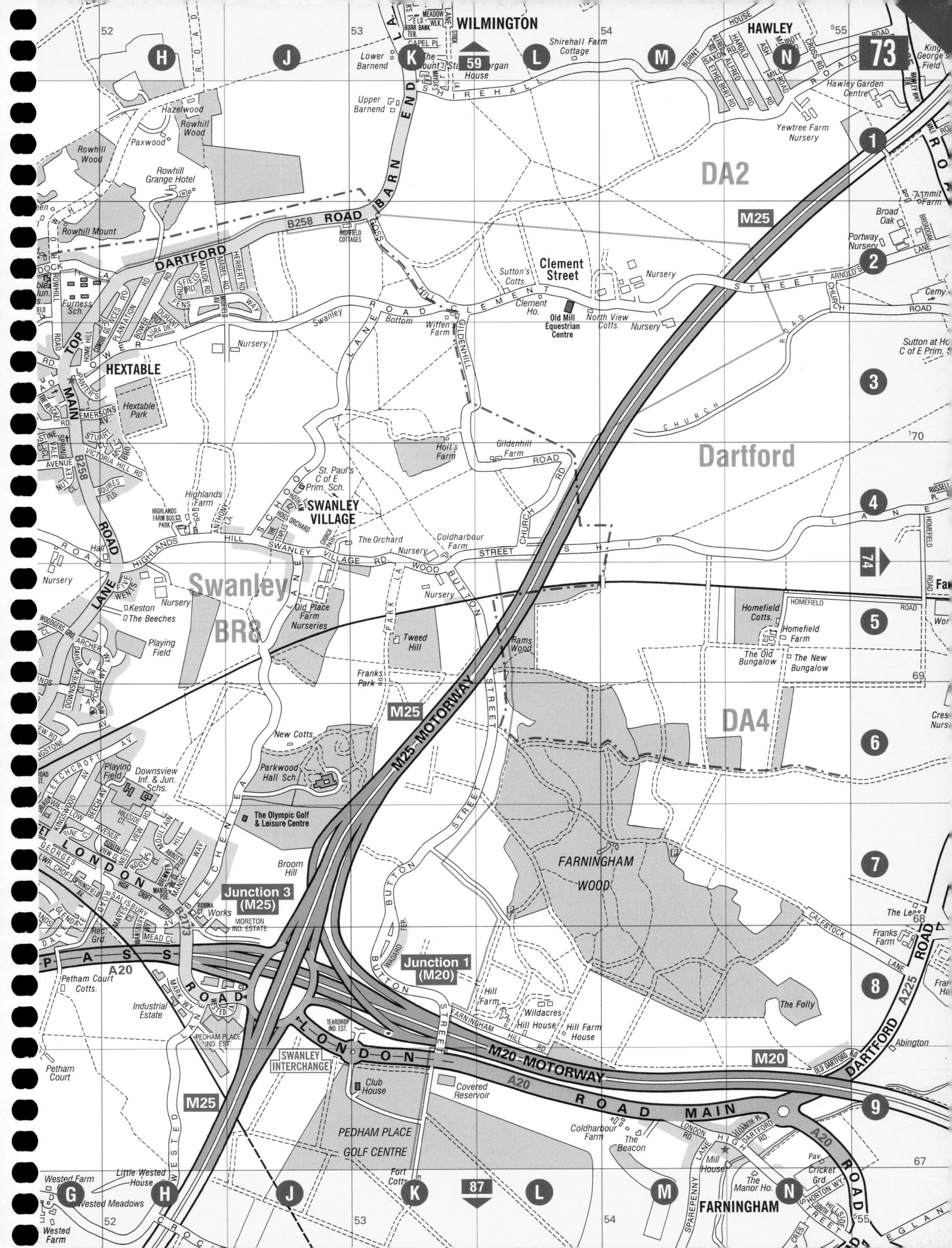
73
WILMINGTON
HAWLEY
59
Lower Barnend
Upper Barnend
The Mount
Stanmorgan House
Shirehall Farm Cottage
SHIREHALL
Hawley Garden Centre
Yewtree Farm Nursery
King George's Field
DA2
M25
Hazelwood
Rowhill Wood
Paxwood
Rowhill Grange Hotel
Rowhill Mount
B258 ROAD
BARN END LA.
DARTFORD
HIGHFIELD COTTAGES
Clement Street
Sutton's Cotts.
Clement Ho.
Old Mill Equestrian Centre
North View Cotts.
Nursery
CLEMENT STREET
Broad Oak
Portway Nursery
ARNOLD'S
CHURCH ROAD
Sutton at Hone C of E Prim. Sch.
Cemy.
Swanley Bottom
Wiffen's Farm
GILDENHILL
HEXTABLE
Furness Sch.
Hextable Park
TOP MAIN
LOWER
Holt's Farm
Gildenhill Farm
Dartford
St. Paul's C of E Prim. Sch.
SWANLEY VILLAGE
SCHOOL LANE
Highlands Farm
HIGHLANDS FARM BUS PARK
HIGHLANDS HILL
The Orchard
Coldharbour Farm
Nursery
SHIP LANE
74
SWANLEY VILLAGE RD.
WOOD STREET
Swanley
BR8
Keston
The Beeches
Playing Field
Old Place Farm Nurseries
Tweed Hill
Rams Wood
Homefield Cotts.
Homefield Farm
The Old Bungalow
The New Bungalow
HOMEFIELD ROAD
Franks Park
M25
M25-MOTORWAY
BUTTON STREET
DA4
New Cotts.
Parkwood Hall Sch.
Playing Field
Downsview Inf. & Jun. Schs.
The Olympic Golf & Leisure Centre
Broom Hill
LONDON
FARNINGHAM WOOD
Junction 3 (M25)
Works
MORETON IND. ESTATE
Junction 1 (M20)
B2173
BEECHENLEA LANE
CALFSTOCK LANE
The Lees
Franks Farm
A225 DARTFORD ROAD
Rec. Grd.
A20
Petham Court Cotts.
Industrial Estate
Hill Farm
Wildacres
Hill House
Hill Farm House
The Folly
Abington
TEARDROP IND. EST.
PEDHAM PLACE IND. EST.
SWANLEY INTERCHANGE
LONDON ROAD
M20-MOTORWAY
M20
A20 ROAD MAIN
Club House
Covered Reservoir
Petham Court
M25
PEDHAM PLACE GOLF CENTRE
Coldharbour Farm
The Beacon
Mill House
The Manor Ho.
Cricket Grd.
Pav.
FARNINGHAM
Wested Farm
Little Wested House
Wested Meadows
Wested Farm
Fort Cotts.
87
WESTED LANE
52
53
54
55
67
68
69
70
71
H
J
K
L
M
N
G
1
2
3
4
5
6
7
8
9

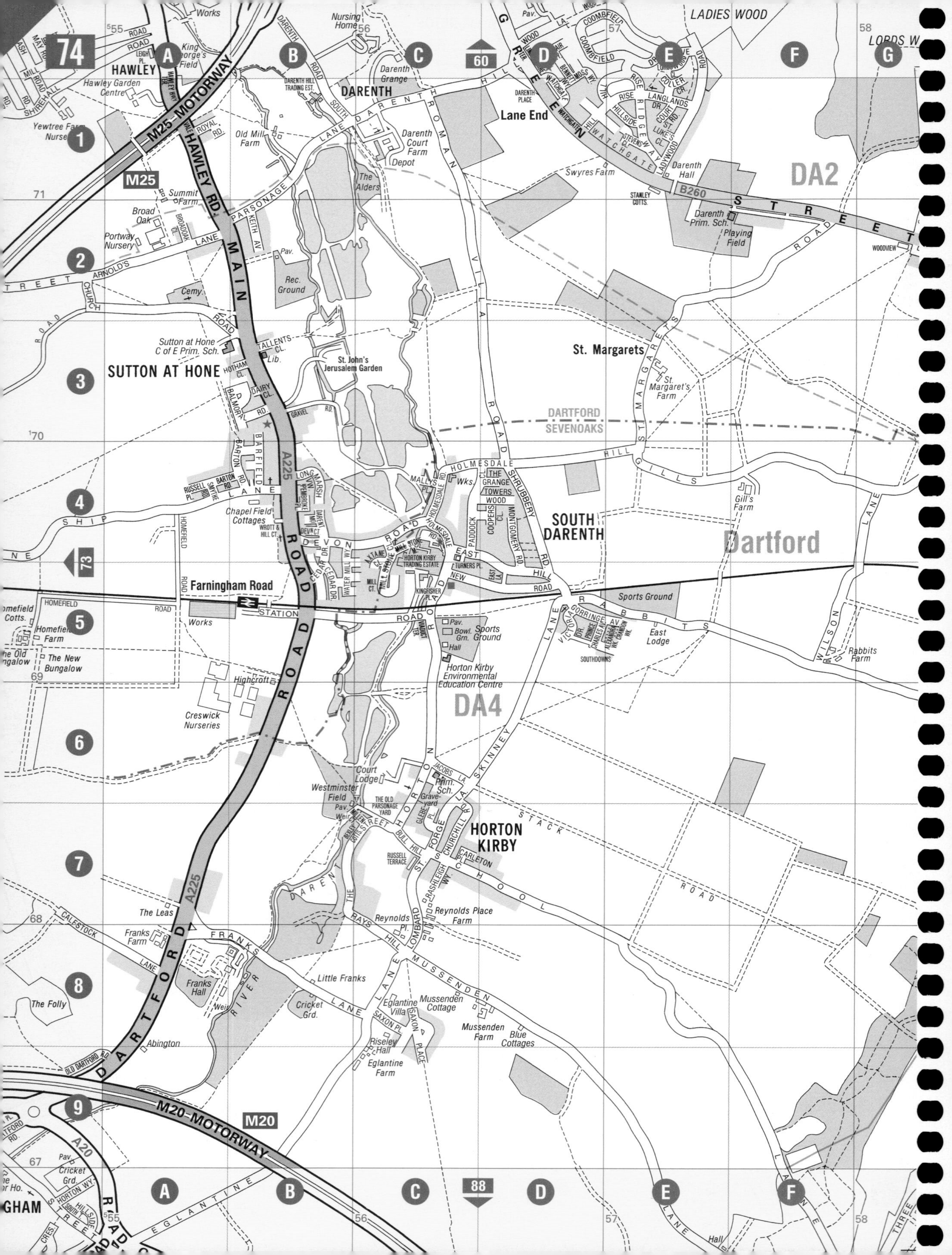

HAWLEY
Hawley Garden Centre
King George's Field
M25-MOTORWAY
M25
DARENTH
Darenth Grange
Darenth Court Farm
Old Mill Farm
Depot
The Alders
Lane End
LADIES WOOD
DA2
Darenth Hall
Swyres Farm
Darenth Prim. Sch.
Playing Field
Summit Farm
Broad Oak
Portway Nursery
Yewtree Farm Nursery
Rec. Ground
Cemy.
SUTTON AT HONE
Sutton at Hone C of E Prim. Sch.
Lib.
St. John's Jerusalem Garden
St. Margarets
St. Margaret's Farm
DARTFORD
SEVENOAKS
MAIN ROAD
A225
SOUTH DARENTH
Dartford
Gill's Farm
Chapel Field Cottages
Horton Kirby Trading Estate
Farningham Road
Sports Ground
East Lodge
Rabbits Farm
Homefield Farm
The New Bungalow
Works
Bowl. Grn.
Hall
Horton Kirby Environmental Education Centre
DA4
Highcroft
Creswick Nurseries
Court Lodge
Westminster Field
Prim. Sch.
Graveyard
HORTON KIRBY
The Leas
Franks Farm
Franks Hall
Reynolds Place Farm
Little Franks
Cricket Grd.
Eglantine Villa
Mussenden Cottage
Mussenden Farm
Blue Cottages
Riseley Hall
Eglantine Farm
The Folly
Abington
M20-MOTORWAY
M20
A20
Cricket Grd.
60
73
88

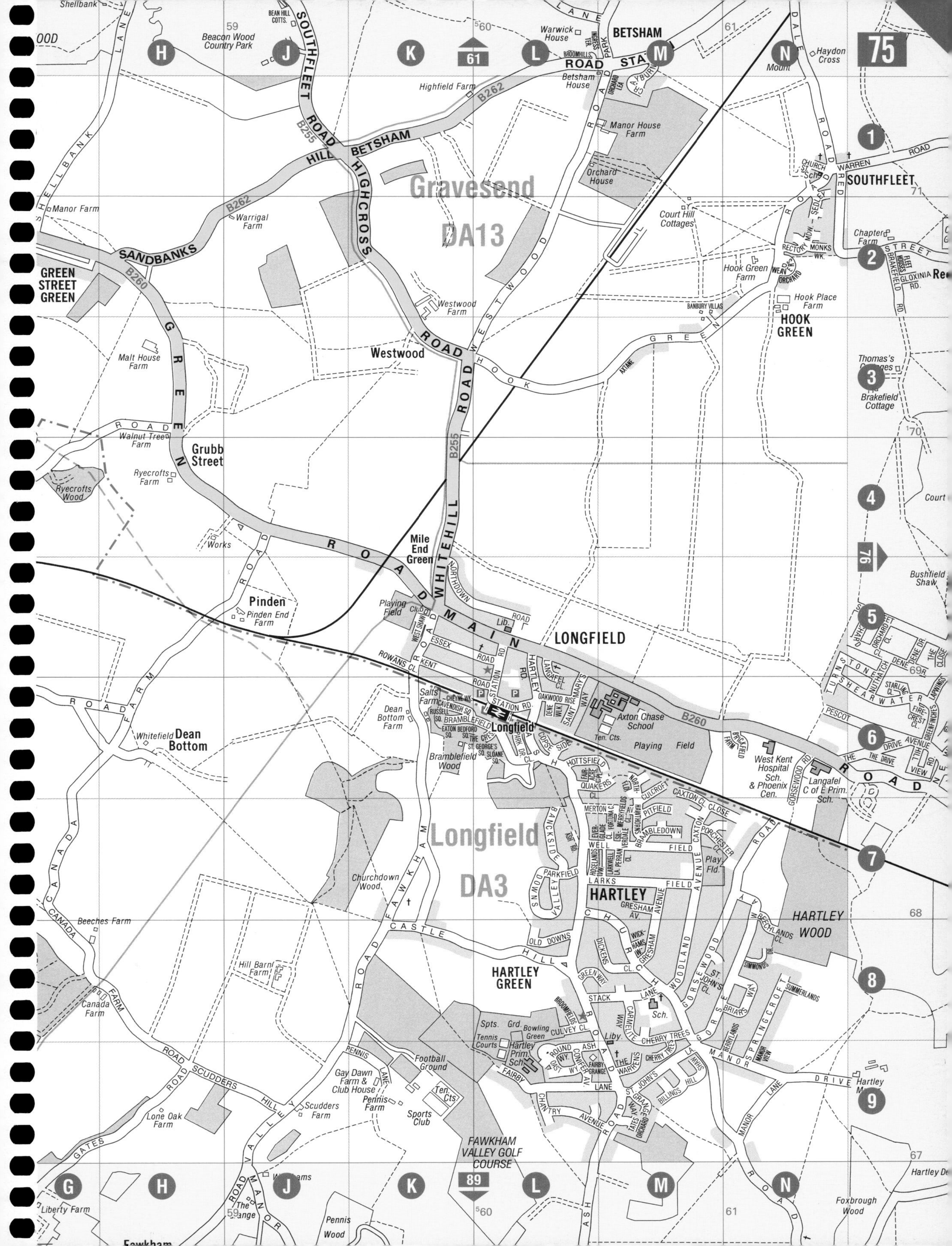
Gravesend
DA13
Longfield
DA3
BETSHAM
SOUTHFLEET
GREEN STREET GREEN
HOOK GREEN
Westwood
Grubb Street
Mile End Green
Pinden
LONGFIELD
Dean Bottom
HARTLEY
HARTLEY GREEN
HARTLEY WOOD
FAWKHAM VALLEY GOLF COURSE
Beacon Wood Country Park
Manor House Farm
Orchard House
Court Hill Cottages
Hook Green Farm
Hook Place Farm
Westwood Farm
Malt House Farm
Walnut Tree Farm
Ryecrofts Farm
Ryecrofts Wood
Pinden End Farm
Axton Chase School
Playing Field
West Kent Hospital Sch. & Phoenix Cen.
Langafel C of E Prim. Sch.
Bramblefield Wood
Churchdown Wood
Beeches Farm
Hill Barn Farm
Canada Farm
Lone Oak Farm
Scudders Farm
Gay Dawn Farm & Club House
Pennis Farm
Football Ground
Sports Club
Hartley Prim. Sch.
Thomas's Cottages
Brakefield Cottage
Bushfield Shaw
Foxbrough Wood
Haydon Cross
Chapter Farm
Warrigal Farm
Manor Farm
Highfield Farm
Betsham House
Warwick House
Liberty Farm
Pennis Wood
Longfield
B255
B262
B260
61
76
89

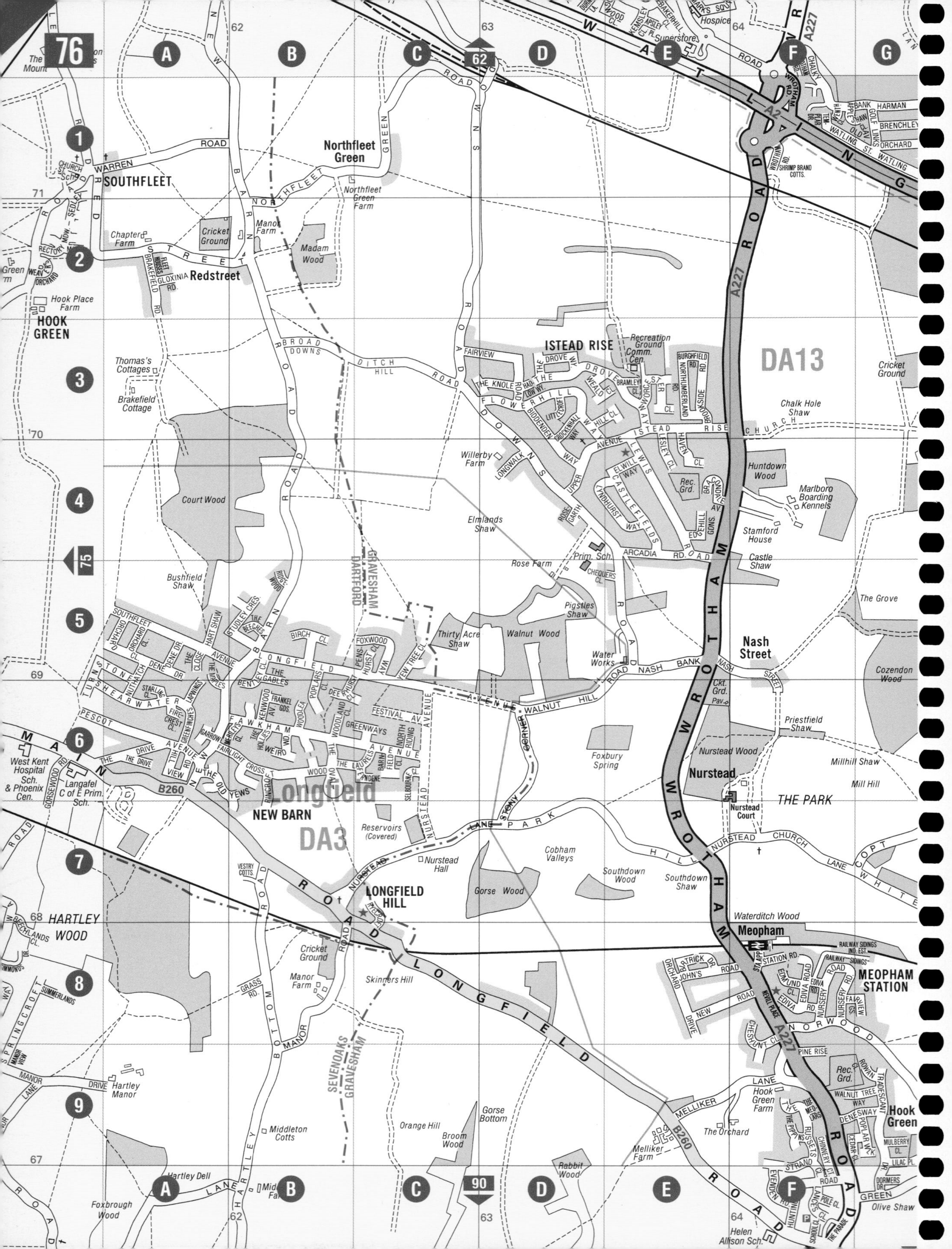
SOUTHFLEET
HOOK GREEN
Redstreet
Northfleet Green
ISTEAD RISE
DA13
Nash Street
Nurstead
THE PARK
Longfield
NEW BARN
DA3
LONGFIELD HILL
HARTLEY WOOD
Meopham
MEOPHAM STATION
Hook Green
WATLING STREET
A2
A227
WROTHAM ROAD
B260
LONGFIELD ROAD
Court Wood
Madam Wood
Walnut Wood
Gorse Wood
Huntdown Wood
Cozendon Wood
Nurstead Wood
Foxbury Spring
Cobham Valleys
Southdown Wood
Southdown Shaw
Waterditch Wood
Elmlands Shaw
Pigstyes Shaw
Thirty Acre Shaw
Bushfield Shaw
Castle Shaw
Priestfield Shaw
Millhill Shaw
Mill Hill
The Grove
Cricket Ground
Chalk Hole Shaw
Marlboro Boarding Kennels
Stamford House
Willerby Farm
Rose Farm
Water Works
Nurstead Court
Nurstead Hall
Reservoirs (Covered)
Skinners Hill
Manor Farm
Hartley Manor
Middleton Cotts
Orange Hill
Broom Wood
Gorse Bottom
Rabbit Wood
Melliker Farm
The Orchard
Hook Green Farm
Hartley Dell
Foxbrough Wood
Helen Allison Sch.
Olive Shaw
Chapter Farm
Hook Place Farm
Thomas's Cottages
Brakefield Cottage
Northfleet Green Farm
Manor Farm
West Kent Hospital Sch. & Phoenix Cen.
Langafel C of E Prim. Sch.
Prim. Sch.
Recreation Ground
Comm. Cen.
Superstore
Hospice
GRAVESHAM
DARTFORD
SEVENOAKS
62
63
64
71
70
69
68
67
75
90
A B C D E F G
1 2 3 4 5 6 7 8 9

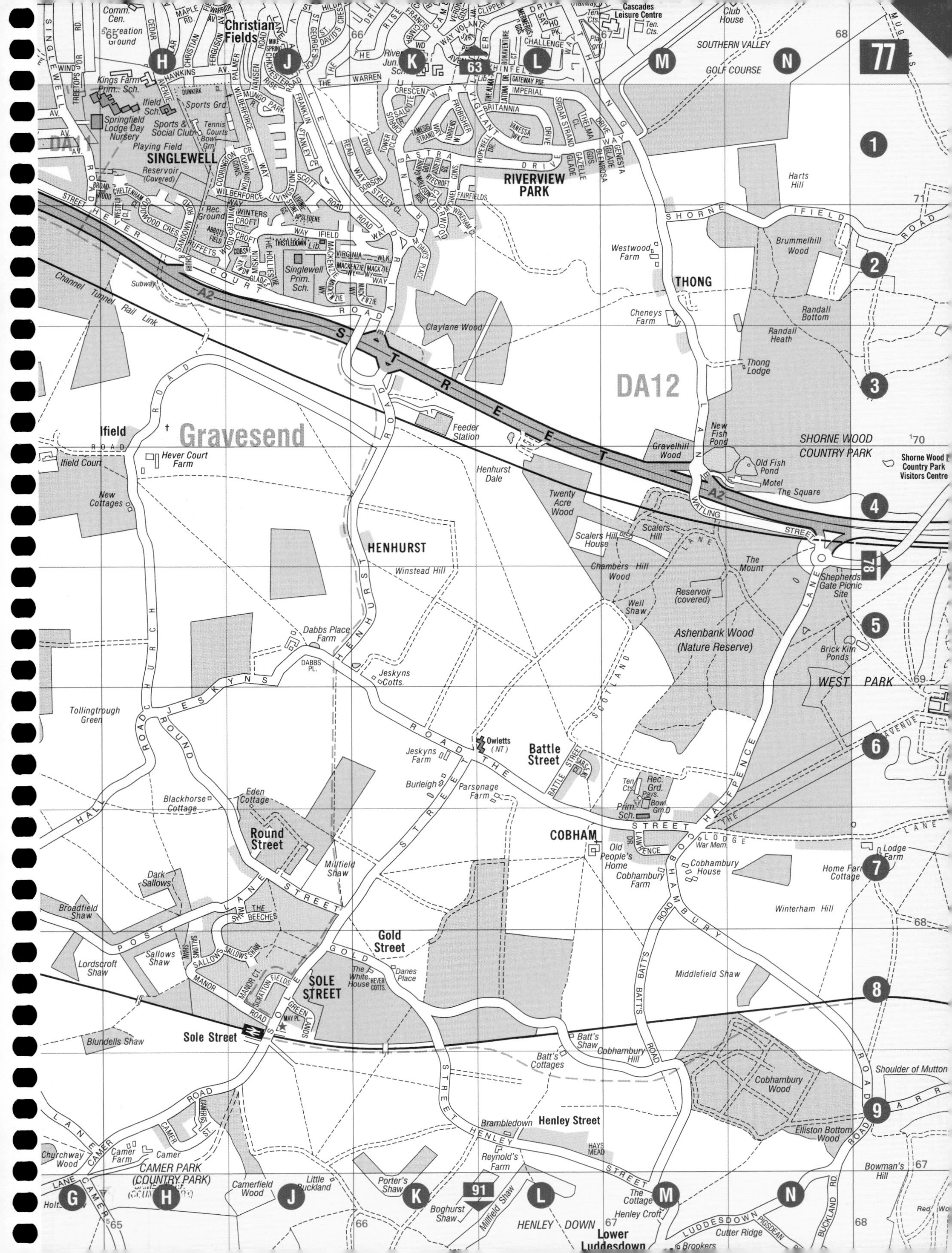

Christian Fields
Comm. Cen.
Recreation Ground
Cascades Leisure Centre
Club House
SOUTHERN VALLEY GOLF COURSE
H
J
K
L
M
N
63
Kings Farm Prim. Sch.
Ifield Sch.
Springfield Lodge Day Nursery
Sports Grd.
Sports & Social Club
Tennis Courts
Playing Field
SINGLEWELL
Reservoir (Covered)
DA11
RIVERVIEW PARK
Harts Hill
Rec. Ground
Singlewell Prim. Sch.
Subway
Channel Tunnel Rail Link
A2
WATLING STREET
SHORNE IFIELD ROAD
Westwood Farm
Brummelhill Wood
THONG
Cheneys Farm
Randall Bottom
Randall Heath
Thong Lodge
Claylane Wood
DA12
Gravesend
Ifield
Hever Court Farm
Ifield Court
Feeder Station
Henhurst Dale
New Fish Pond
Gravelhill Wood
Old Fish Pond
SHORNE WOOD COUNTRY PARK
Shorne Wood Country Park Visitors Centre
Motel
The Square
Twenty Acre Wood
New Cottages
Scalers Hill House
Scalers Hill
HENHURST
Winstead Hill
Chambers Hill Wood
The Mount
78
Shepherds Gate Picnic Site
Reservoir (covered)
Well Shaw
Ashenbank Wood (Nature Reserve)
Dabbs Place Farm
Brick Kiln Ponds
Jeskyns Cotts.
WEST PARK
Tollingtrough Green
Owletts (NT)
Battle Street
Jeskyns Farm
Burleigh
Parsonage Farm
Blackhorse Cottage
Eden Cottage
Rec. Grd.
Prim. Sch.
COBHAM
War Mem.
Lodge Farm
Home Farm Cottage
Round Street
Millfield Shaw
Old People's Home
Cobhambury Farm
Cobhambury House
Dark Sallows
Broadfield Shaw
THE BEECHES
Winterham Hill
Gold Street
Lordscroft Shaw
Sallows Shaw
Danes Place
The White House
SOLE STREET
Middlefield Shaw
Blundells Shaw
Sole Street
Batt's Shaw
Cobhambury Hill
Batt's Cottages
Cobhambury Wood
Shoulder of Mutton
Brambledown
Henley Street
Elliston Bottom Wood
Churchway Wood
Camer Farm
Camer
CAMER PARK (COUNTRY PARK)
Reynold's Farm
Camerfield Wood
Little Buckland
Porter's Shaw
91
Bowman's Hill
The Cottage
Henley Croft
Boghurst Shaw
Millfield Shaw
HENLEY DOWN
Lower Luddesdown
Cutter Ridge
Brookers
G
Holts

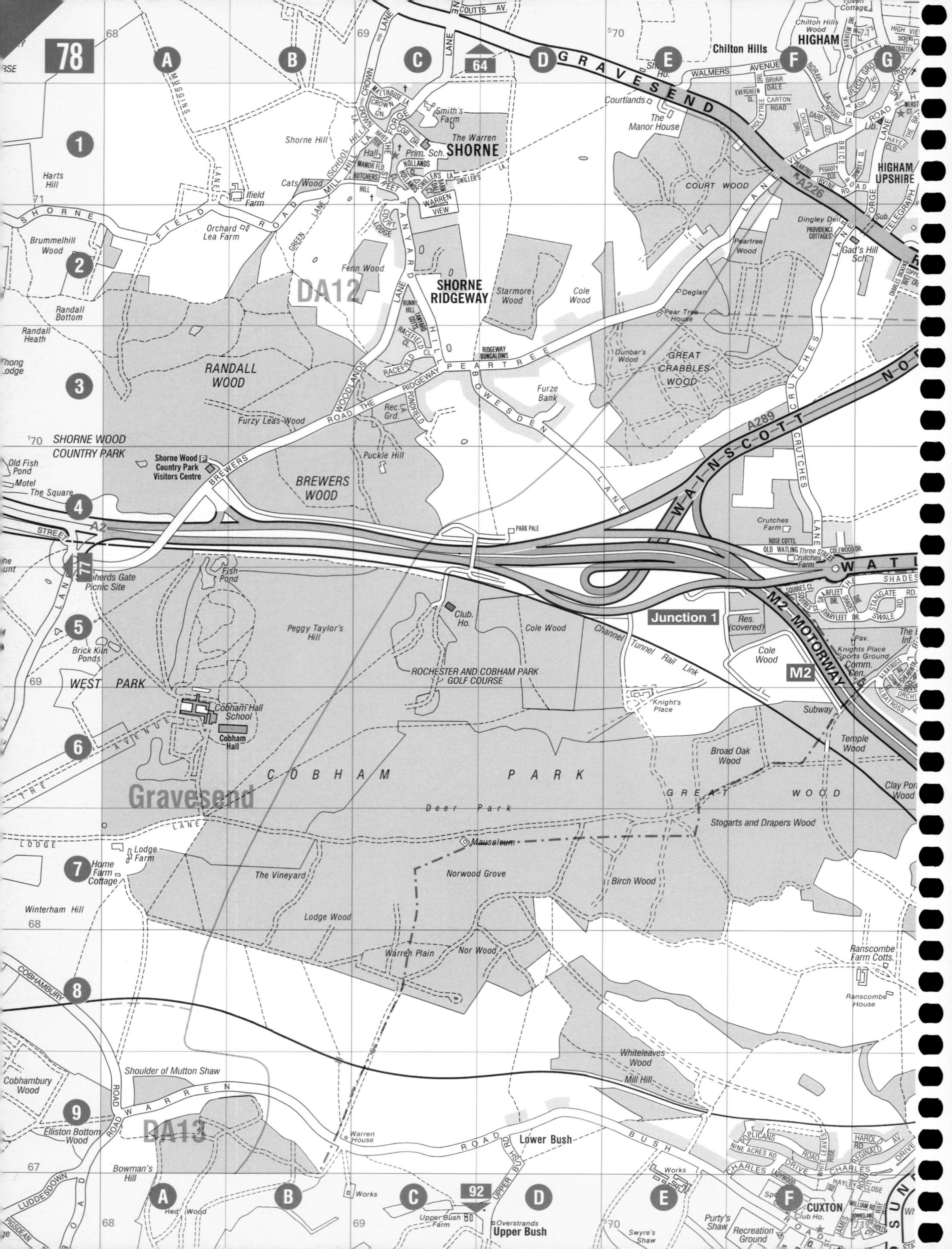
64
92
77
SHORNE
SHORNE RIDGEWAY
HIGHAM
HIGHAM UPSHIRE
Chilton Hills
DA12
DA13
Gravesend
RANDALL WOOD
BREWERS WOOD
SHORNE WOOD COUNTRY PARK
Shorne Wood Country Park Visitors Centre
WEST PARK
C O B H A M P A R K
Cobham Hall School
Cobham Hall
Deer Park
Mauseleum
GREAT CRABBLES WOOD
ROCHESTER AND COBHAM PARK GOLF COURSE
Junction 1
M2 MOTORWAY
M2
GRAVESEND ROAD
A226
A289
WAINSCOTT
A2
Channel Tunnel Rail Link
G R E A T W O O D
Stogarts and Drapers Wood
Lower Bush
Upper Bush
CUXTON
WARREN ROAD
BUSH ROAD
Shoulder of Mutton Shaw
Whiteleaves Wood
Mill Hill
Cobhambury Wood
Elliston Bottom Wood
Bowman's Hill
Winterham Hill
Home Farm Cottage
Lodge Farm
The Vineyard
Norwood Grove
Birch Wood
Lodge Wood
Warren Plain
Nor Wood
Peggy Taylor's Hill
Cole Wood
Knight's Place
Temple Wood
Broad Oak Wood
Ranscombe Farm Cotts.
Ranscombe House
Crutches Farm
Brick Kiln Ponds
Randall Bottom
Randall Heath
Harts Hill
Brummelhill Wood
Orchard Lea Farm
Ifield Farm
Cats Wood
Shorne Hill
Smith's Farm
The Warren
Fenn Wood
Starmore Wood
Cole Wood
Court Wood
Peartree Wood
Dingley Dell
Gad's Hill Sch.
Courtlands
The Manor House
Furze Bank
Puckle Hill
Furzy Leas Wood
Dunbar's Wood
Pear Tree House
Deglan
Clay Pond Wood
Subway
Knights Place Sports Ground
Res. (covered)
Club. Ho.
Fish Pond
Purty's Shaw
Recreation Ground
Swyre's Shaw
Upper Bush Farm
Overstrands
Warren House
Works

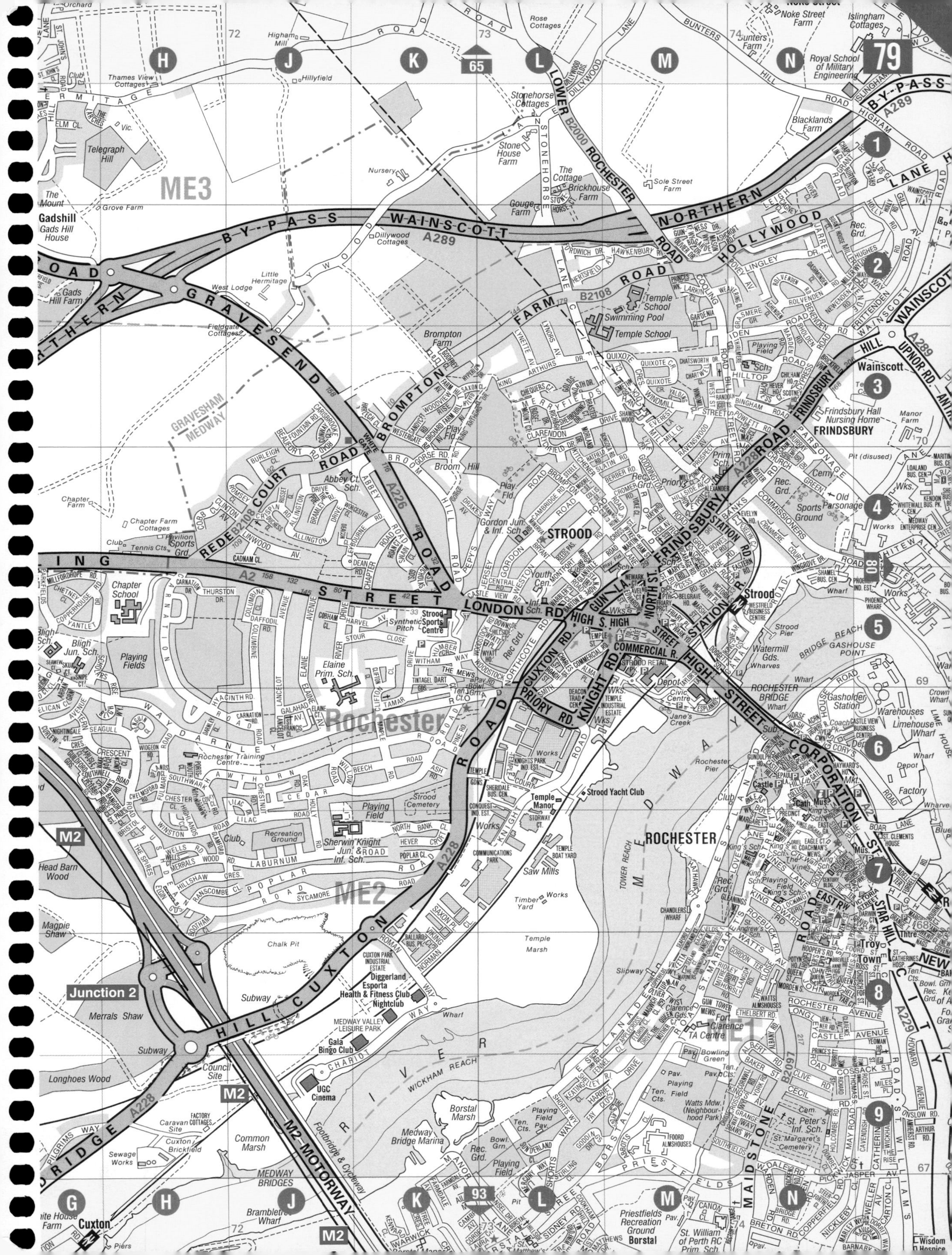
65
ME3
Gadshill
Gads Hill House
Telegraph Hill
The Mount
Grove Farm
Thames View Cottages
Higham Mill
Hillyfield
Rose Cottages
Noke Street Farm
Islingham Cottages
Bunters Farm
Royal School of Military Engineering
Stonehorse Cottages
Stone House Farm
The Cottage
Brickhouse Farm
Gouge Farm
Sole Street Farm
Blacklands Farm
Nursery
Dillywood Cottages
WAINSCOTT BY-PASS
NORTHERN BY-PASS
A289
LOWER ROCHESTER ROAD
B2000
HOLLYWOOD LANE
Little Hermitage
West Lodge
Gads Hill Farm
Fieldgate Cottages
GRAVESEND ROAD
FARM ROAD
B2108
Temple School
Swimming Pool
Brompton Farm
BROMPTON ROAD
GRAVESHAM
MEDWAY
Wainscott
Frindsbury Hall Nursing Home
FRINDSBURY
Manor Farm
Pit (disused)
Old Parsonage
Sports Ground
Chapter Farm
Chapter Farm Cottages
Pavilion
Sports Grd.
Tennis Cts.
Club
Abbey Ct. Sch.
COURT ROAD
A226
Broom Hill
Gordon Jun. & Inf. Sch.
STROOD
Youth Cen.
FRINDSBURY RD.
STATION RD.
Strood
A2
LONDON ROAD
Chapter School
Strood Sports Centre
Synthetic Pitch
Playing Fields
Elaine Prim. Sch.
Rochester
Rochester Training Centre
HIGH STREET
COMMERCIAL R.
STROOD RETAIL PK.
Depot
Civic Centre
Jane's Creek
Watermill Gds. Wharves
Strood Pier
GASHOUSE POINT
BRIDGE REACH
Wharf
ROCHESTER BRIDGE
Gasholder Station
Warehouses
Limehouse Wharf
Depot
Factory
CORPORATION ST.
Rochester Pier
MEDWAY
Strood Yacht Club
Temple Manor
Works
KNIGHTS PARK IND. EST.
CUXTON RD.
PRIORY RD.
KNIGHT RD.
Castle
Cath.
Mus.
King's Sch.
ROCHESTER
TOWER REACH
Saw Mills
Timber Yard
Temple Marsh
Playing Field
Strood Cemetery
Recreation Ground
Sherwin Knight Jun. & Inf. Sch.
M2
Head Barn Wood
ME2
Magpie Shaw
Chalk Pit
CUXTON ROAD
A228
Diggerland
Esporta Health & Fitness Club
Nightclub
Junction 2
Merrals Shaw
Subway
MEDWAY VALLEY LEISURE PARK
Gala Bingo Club
UGC Cinema
Wharf
RIVER
WICKHAM REACH
Longhoes Wood
Council Site
Caravan Site
Cuxton Brickfield
Sewage Works
Common Marsh
M2 MOTORWAY
Footbridge & Cycleway
Borstal Marsh
Medway Bridge Marina
MEDWAY BRIDGES
Brambletree Wharf
PILGRIMS WAY
BRIDGE
Cuxton
Piers
93
Rec. Grd.
Playing Field
Priestfields Recreation Ground
Borstal
St. William of Perth RC Prim. Sch.
ME1
Fort Clarence
TA Centre
Bowling Green
Playing Field
Watts Mdw. (Neighbourhood Park)
FOORD ALMSHOUSES
St. Peter's Inf. Sch.
St. Margaret's Cemetery
MAIDSTONE ROAD
B2097
Troy Town
Thtre
ROCHESTER AVENUE
CITY WAY
A229
Chandlers Wharf
Slipway
Wisdom Hospice
NEW ROAD
STAR HILL
EAST RW
H J K L M N G
1 2 3 4 5 6 7 8 9
72 73 74
70 69 68 67

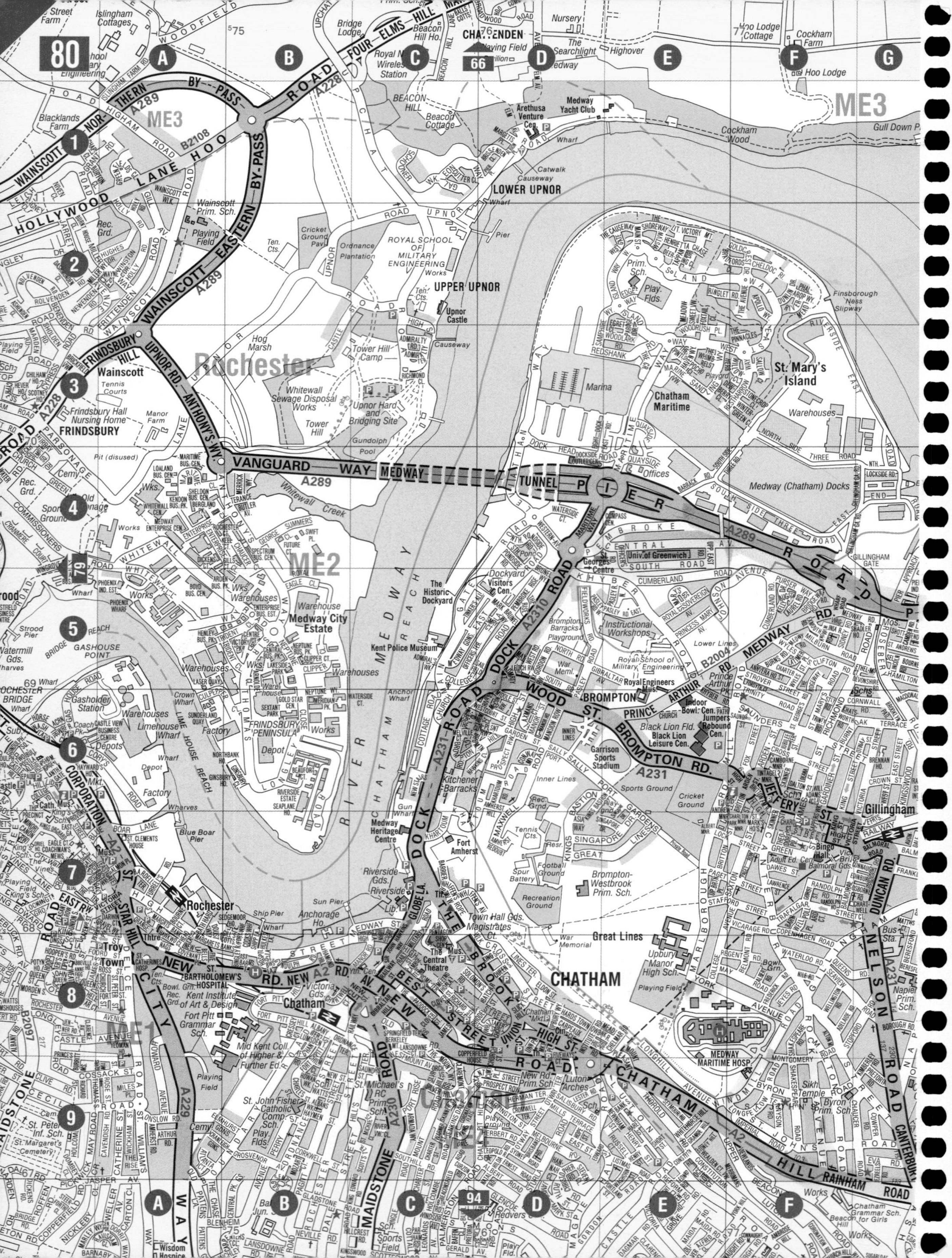

A
B
C
D
E
F
G
1
2
3
4
5
6
7
8
9
66
79
94
ME3
ME2
ME1
Rochester
CHATTENDEN
LOWER UPNOR
UPPER UPNOR
Upnor Castle
ROYAL SCHOOL OF MILITARY ENGINEERING
Wainscott
FRINDSBURY
Frindsbury Hall Nursing Home
Medway Yacht Club
Arethusa Venture Cen.
Cockham Wood
Gull Down Pt.
Hoo Lodge
Cockham Farm
Hoo Lodge Cottage
Highover
The Searchlight
Nursery
Beacon Hill
Beacon Cottage
Royal Naval Wireless Station
Bridge Lodge
Islingham Cottages
Blacklands Farm
Catwalk Causeway
Finsborough Ness Slipway
St. Mary's Island
Chatham Maritime
Marina
Warehouses
Medway (Chatham) Docks
Gillingham Gate
Univ. of Greenwich
St. George's Centre
The Historic Dockyard
Dockyard Visitors Cen.
Kent Police Museum
Medway City Estate
Frindsbury Peninsula
Whitewall Creek
Whitewall Sewage Disposal Works
Hog Marsh
Tower Hill Camp
Upnor Hard and Bridging Site
Tower Hill
Gundolph Pool
Limehouse Wharf
Limehouse Reach
Gasholder Station
Strood Pier
Gashouse Point
Bridge Reach
Rochester Bridge
Blue Boar Pier
River Medway
Chatham Reach
Medway Reach
Instructional Workshops
Royal School of Military Engineering
Royal Engineers Mus.
Brompton
Garrison Sports Stadium
Black Lion Leisure Cen.
Jumpers Rebound Cen.
Indoor Bowl. Cen.
Kitchener Barracks
Fort Amherst
Medway Heritage Centre
Brompton-Westbrook Prim. Sch.
Recreation Ground
Great Lines
Upbury Manor High Sch.
CHATHAM
Medway Maritime Hosp.
Gillingham
St. Bartholomew's Hospital
Kent Institute of Art & Design
Fort Pitt Grammar Sch.
Mid Kent Coll. of Higher & Further Ed.
St. John Fisher Catholic Comp. Sch.
Troy Town
Chatham
The Central Theatre
Town Hall Gds.
Luton Arches
Chatham Grammar Sch. for Girls
Sikh Temple
Byron Prim. Sch.
Napier Prim. Sch.
Wisdom Hospice
St. Margaret's Cemetery
Vanguard Way
Medway Tunnel
Pier Road
A289
A228
A2
A229
A230
A231
A2310
B2108
B2004
B2097
Wainscott Northern By-Pass
Wainscott Eastern By-Pass
Four Elms Hill
Hollywood Lane
Frindsbury Hill
Upnor Rd.
Anthony's Wy.
Dock Road
Wood St.
Brompton Rd.
Prince Arthur Rd.
Medway Rd.
New Rd.
Best Street
The Brook
High St.
Chatham Hill
Rainham Road
Nelson Road
Canterbury St.
Duncan Rd.
Maidstone Road
City Way
Star Hill
Corporation St.

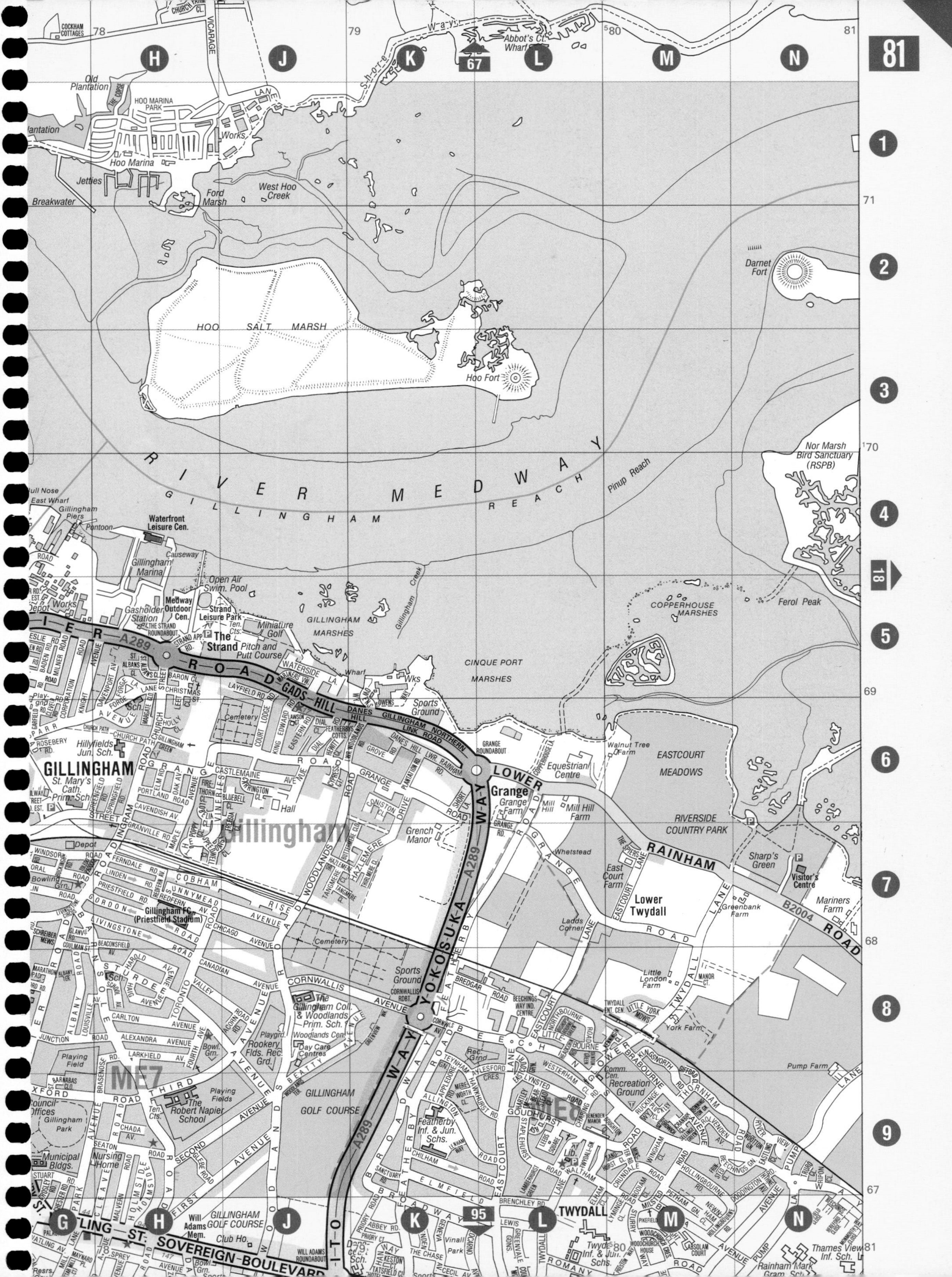
RIVER MEDWAY
GILLINGHAM REACH
HOO SALT MARSH
Hoo Fort
Darnet Fort
Hoo Marina
West Hoo Creek
Nor Marsh Bird Sanctuary (RSPB)
Pinup Reach
GILLINGHAM MARSHES
CINQUE PORT MARSHES
COPPERHOUSE MARSHES
Ferol Peak
EASTCOURT MEADOWS
RIVERSIDE COUNTRY PARK
GILLINGHAM
Gillingham
Lower Twydall
TWYDALL
Grange
GILLINGHAM GOLF COURSE
YOKOSUKA WAY
SOVEREIGN BOULEVARD
RAINHAM ROAD
B2004
A289
ME7
ME8
67
95
18

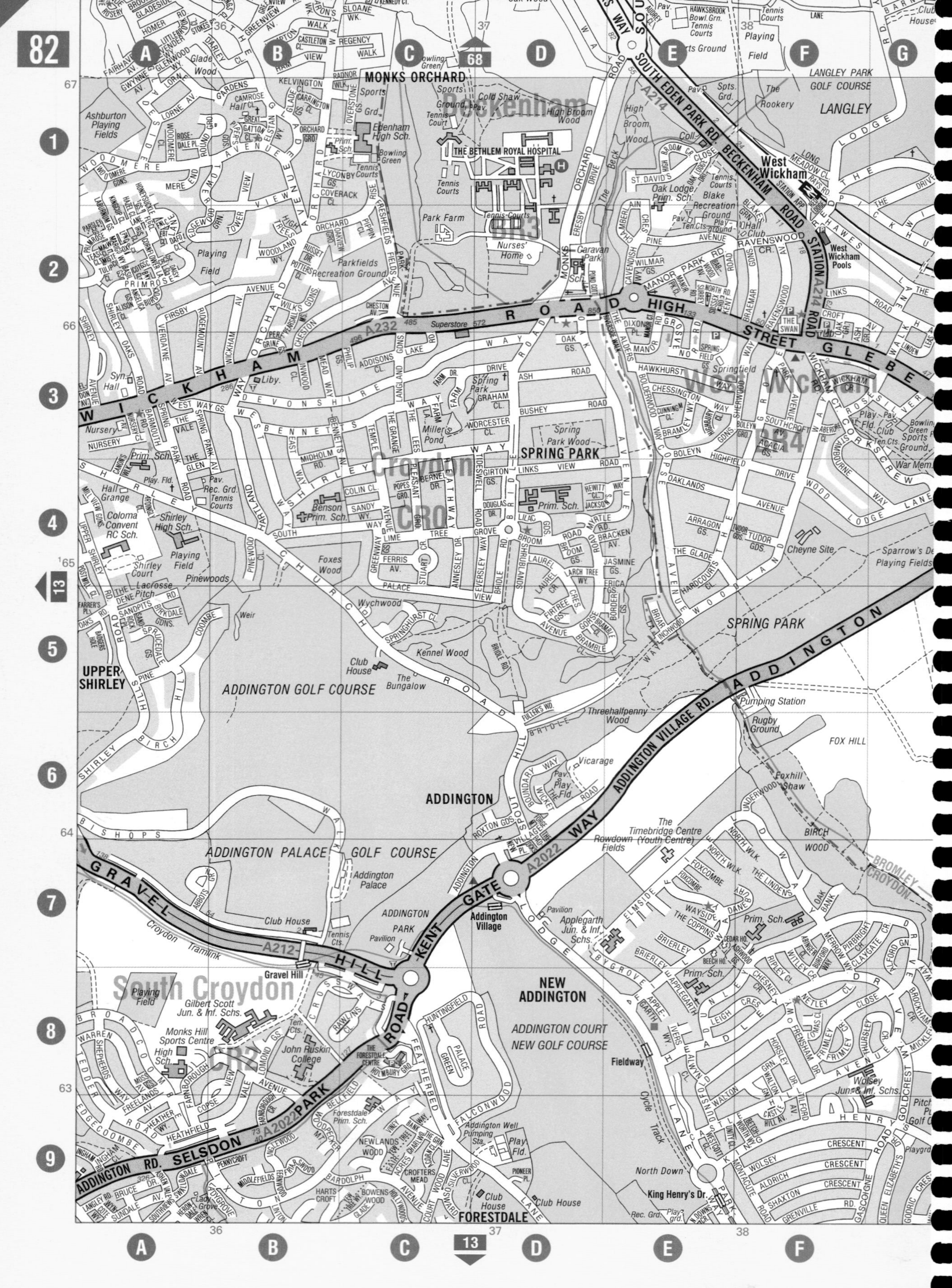

MONKS ORCHARD
Beckenham
THE BETHLEM ROYAL HOSPITAL
West Wickham
LANGLEY PARK GOLF COURSE
LANGLEY
WICKHAM ROAD
HIGH STREET
GLEBE WAY
SPRING PARK
Croydon
CR0
BR3
BR4
West Wickham
UPPER SHIRLEY
ADDINGTON GOLF COURSE
ADDINGTON
ADDINGTON PALACE GOLF COURSE
ADDINGTON VILLAGE RD.
A2022 WAY
GRAVEL HILL
KENT GATE
South Croydon
CR2
NEW ADDINGTON
ADDINGTON COURT NEW GOLF COURSE
SELSDON PARK RD.
FORESTDALE
FOX HILL
BIRCH WOOD
BROMLEY
CROYDON

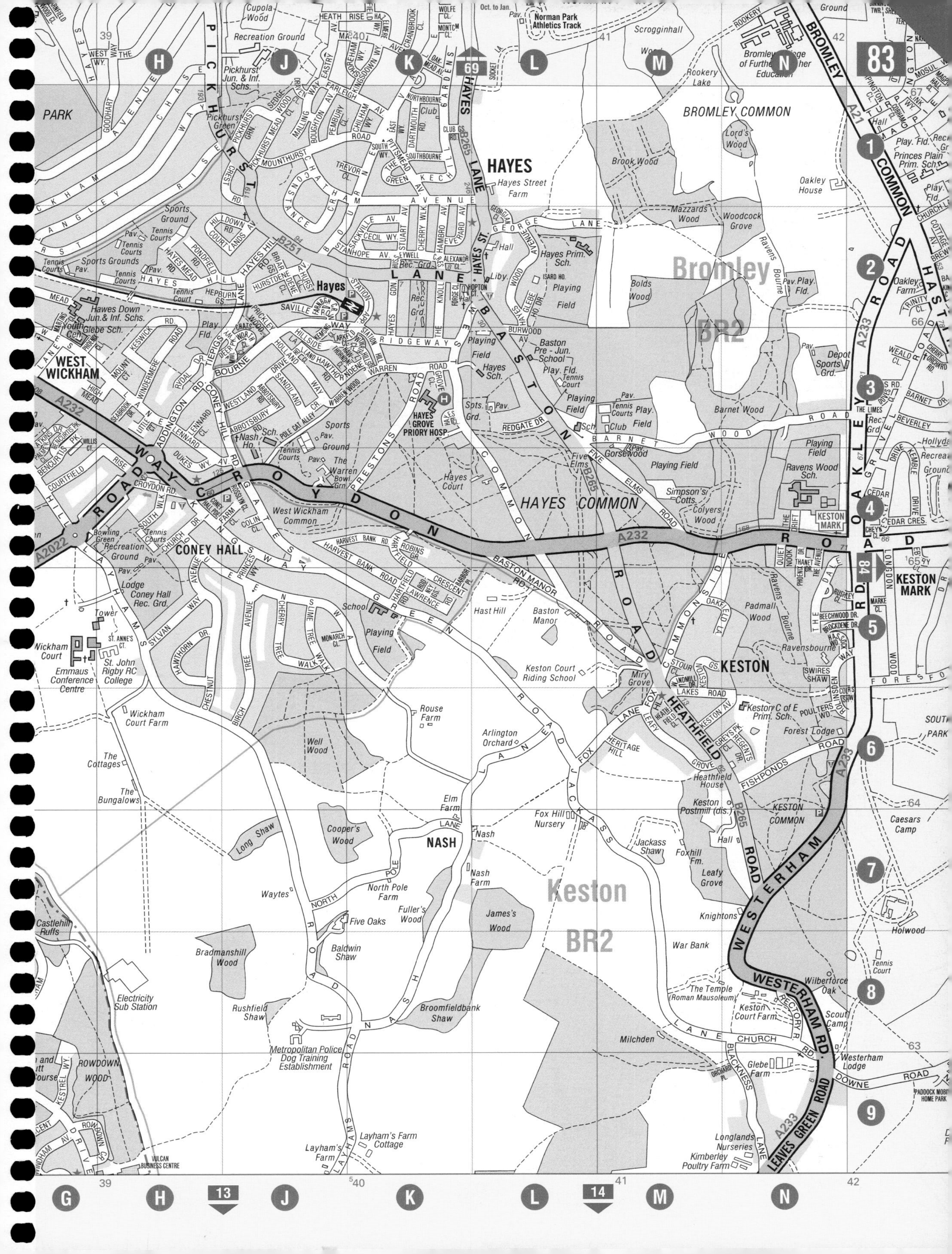
69
H
J
K
L
M
N
1
2
3
4
5
6
7
8
9
G
13
14
84
39
40
41
42
PARK
HAYES
WEST WICKHAM
CONEY HALL
KESTON
KESTON MARK
NASH
BROMLEY COMMON
HAYES COMMON
Bromley
BR2
Keston
BR2
Cupola Wood
Recreation Ground
Pickhurst Jun. & Inf. Schs.
Pickhurst Green
Norman Park Athletics Track
Scrogginhall Wood
Bromley College of Further & Higher Education
Rookery Lake
Lord's Wood
Brook Wood
Oakley House
Princes Plain Prim. Sch.
Hayes Street Farm
Mazzards Wood
Woodcock Grove
Ravens Bourne
Bolds Wood
Oakley Farm
Sports Ground
Tennis Courts
Sports Grounds
Hawes Down Jun.& Inf. Schs.
Glebe Sch.
Youth Cen.
Hayes
Play. Fld.
Hayes Prim. Sch.
Playing Field
Baston Pre - Jun. School
Hayes Sch.
Depot Sports Grd.
Barnet Wood
HAYES GROVE PRIORY HOSP.
Sports Ground
Nash Ho.
The Warren Bowl. Grn.
Gorsewood
Five Elms
Playing Field
Ravens Wood Sch.
Simpson's Cotts.
Colyers Wood
Hayes Court
West Wickham Common
Bowling Green
Recreation Ground
Lodge
Coney Hall Rec. Grd.
Tower
Wickham Court
Emmaus Conference Centre
St. John Rigby RC College
School
Playing Field
Hast Hill
Baston Manor
Keston Court Riding School
Miry Grove
Padmall Wood
Ravensbourne
Swires Shaw
Keston C of E Prim. Sch.
Forest Lodge
Wickham Court Farm
The Cottages
The Bungalows
Rouse Farm
Well Wood
Arlington Orchard
Heritage Hill
Heathfield House
Keston Postmill (dis.)
Keston Common
Caesars Camp
Elm Farm
Long Shaw
Cooper's Wood
Fox Hill Nursery
Nash
Jackass Shaw
Foxhill Fm.
Hall
Leafy Grove
Nash Farm
North Pole Farm
Waytes
Fuller's Wood
Five Oaks
James's Wood
Knightons
Holwood
Castlehill Ruffs
Bradmanshill Wood
Baldwin Shaw
War Bank
Tennis Court
Electricity Sub Station
Rushfield Shaw
Broomfieldbank Shaw
The Temple (Roman Mausoleum)
Wilberforce Oak
Keston Court Farm
Scout Camp
Metropolitan Police Dog Training Establishment
Milchden
Glebe Farm
Westerham Lodge
ROWDOWN WOOD
Layham's Farm
Layham's Farm Cottage
Longlands Nurseries
Kimberley Poultry Farm
VULCAN BUSINESS CENTRE
PADDOCK MOBILE HOME PARK
A21
A232
A2022
A233
B251
B265
CROYDON ROAD
WEST WICKHAM
HAYES LANE
PICKHURST LANE
BASTON ROAD
BARNET WOOD ROAD
FIVE ELMS ROAD
HEATHFIELD ROAD
COMMON ROAD
OAKLEY ROAD
BROMLEY COMMON
WESTERHAM ROAD
LEAVES GREEN ROAD
NASH LANE
JACKASS LANE
FOX LANE
LAYHAMS ROAD
GREEN WAY
BASTON MANOR ROAD
HARVEST BANK ROAD
NORTH POLE LANE
CHURCH LANE
DOWNE ROAD
FISHPONDS ROAD
LAKES ROAD
BLACKNESS LANE
RIDGEWAY
WARREN ROAD
GEORGE LANE
LONDON ROAD
FORESTDALE
KESTON PARK

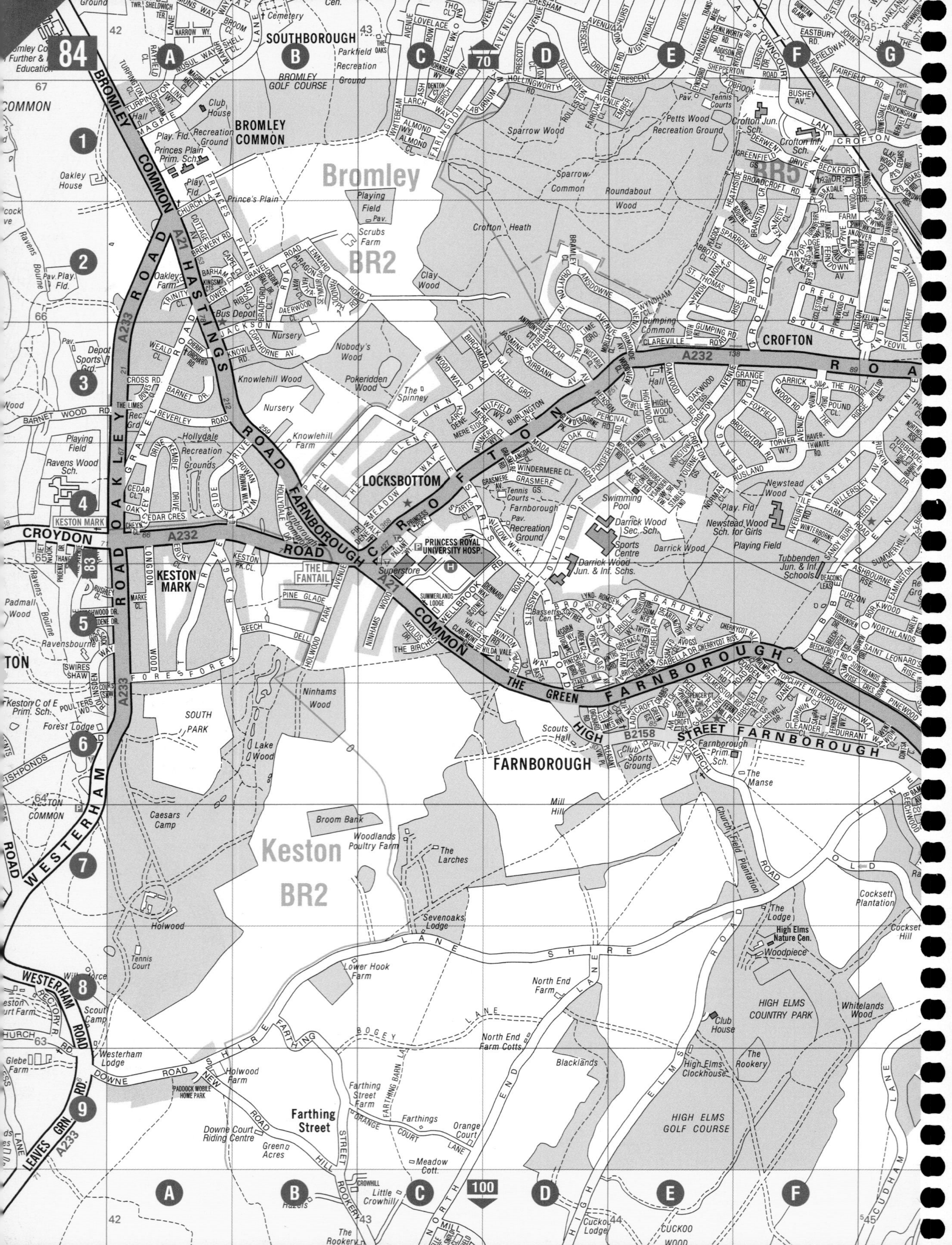
SOUTHBOROUGH
BROMLEY GOLF COURSE
BROMLEY COMMON
Bromley
BR2
BR5
Parkfield Recreation Ground
Sparrow Wood
Petts Wood Recreation Ground
Crofton Jun. Sch.
Crofton Inf. Sch.
Princes Plain Prim. Sch.
Play. Fld.
Recreation Ground
Oakley House
Prince's Plain
Playing Field
Scrubs Farm
Sparrow Common
Roundabout Wood
Crofton Heath
Clay Wood
Oakley Farm
Bus Depot
Nursery
Nobody's Wood
Gumping Common
CROFTON
Depot Sports Grd.
Knowlehill Wood
Pokeridden Wood
The Spinney
Knowlehill Farm
Hollydale Recreation Grounds
Playing Field
Ravens Wood Sch.
LOCKSBOTTOM
Swimming Pool
Darrick Wood Sec. Sch.
Sports Centre
Darrick Wood
Newstead Wood
Newstead Wood Sch. for Girls
Tubbenden Jun. & Inf. Schools
KESTON MARK
CROYDON ROAD
A232
A21
A233
PRINCESS ROYAL UNIVERSITY HOSP.
Superstore
THE FANTAIL
Farnborough Recreation Ground
Darrick Wood Jun. & Inf. Schs.
KESTON MARK
Padmall Wood
Ravensbourne
Keston C of E Prim. Sch.
Forest Lodge
SOUTH PARK
Ninhams Wood
Lake Wood
FARNBOROUGH COMMON
FARNBOROUGH HIGH STREET
B2158
Scouts Hall
Club Sports Ground
Farnborough Prim. Sch.
The Manse
FARNBOROUGH
KESTON COMMON
WESTERHAM ROAD
Caesars Camp
Broom Bank
Woodlands Poultry Farm
Mill Hill
Keston
BR2
The Larches
Church Field Plantation
Cocksett Plantation
Holwood
Sevenoaks Lodge
The Lodge
High Elms Nature Cen.
Woodpiece
Tennis Court
Lower Hook Farm
SHIRE LANE
North End Farm
HIGH ELMS COUNTRY PARK
Whitelands Wood
Scout Camp
Club House
North End Farm Cotts
Westerham Lodge
Holwood Farm
Blacklands
High Elms Clockhouse
The Rookery
Farthing Street Farm
Farthings
Orange Court
Farthing Street
Downe Court Riding Centre
Green Acres
Meadow Cott.
HIGH ELMS GOLF COURSE
Little Crowhill
The Rookery
Cuckoo Lodge
CUCKOO WOOD
70
100

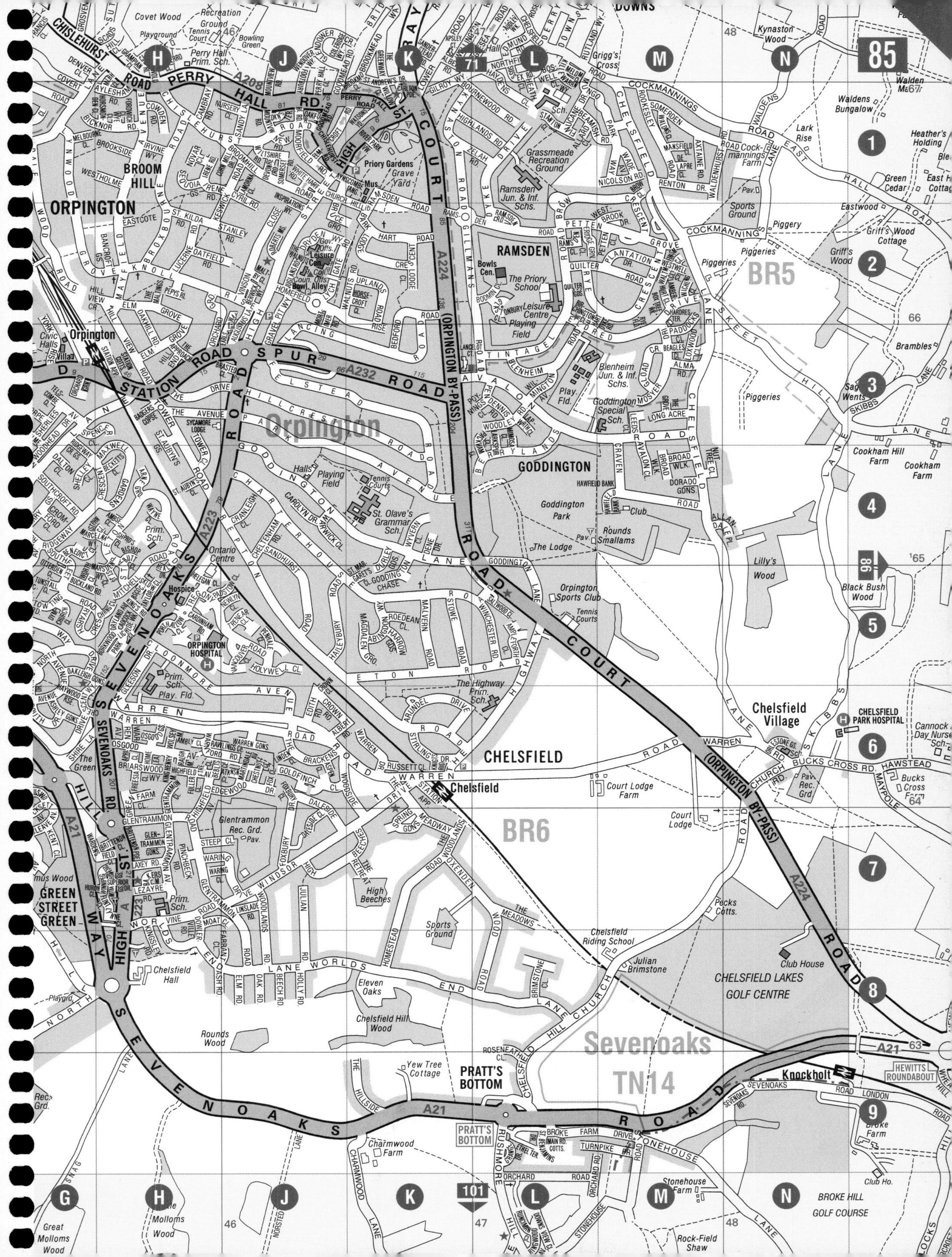
ORPINGTON
BROOM HILL
RAMSDEN
GODDINGTON
CHELSFIELD
Chelsfield Village
PRATT'S BOTTOM
GREEN STREET GREEN
Orpington
BR5
BR6
Sevenoaks
TN14
Priory Gardens
The Priory School
Leisure Centre
Goddington Park
St. Olave's Grammar Sch.
ORPINGTON HOSPITAL
CHELSFIELD PARK HOSPITAL
Glentrammon Rec. Grd.
Orpington Sports Club
Court Lodge Farm
CHELSFIELD LAKES GOLF CENTRE
Club House
Chelsfield Riding School
Chelsfield Hill Wood
Rounds Wood
Eleven Oaks
Knockholt
HEWITTS ROUNDABOUT
BROKE HILL GOLF COURSE
Lilly's Wood
Black Bush Wood
Cookham Hill Farm
Cookham Farm
Grassmeade Recreation Ground
Blenheim Jun. & Inf. Schs.
Goddington Special Sch.
Ramsden Jun. & Inf. Schs.
SEVENOAKS ROAD
SEVENOAKS WAY
COURT ROAD (ORPINGTON BY-PASS)
SPUR ROAD
PERRY HALL RD.
A21
A224
A223
A232
A208
71
101
99

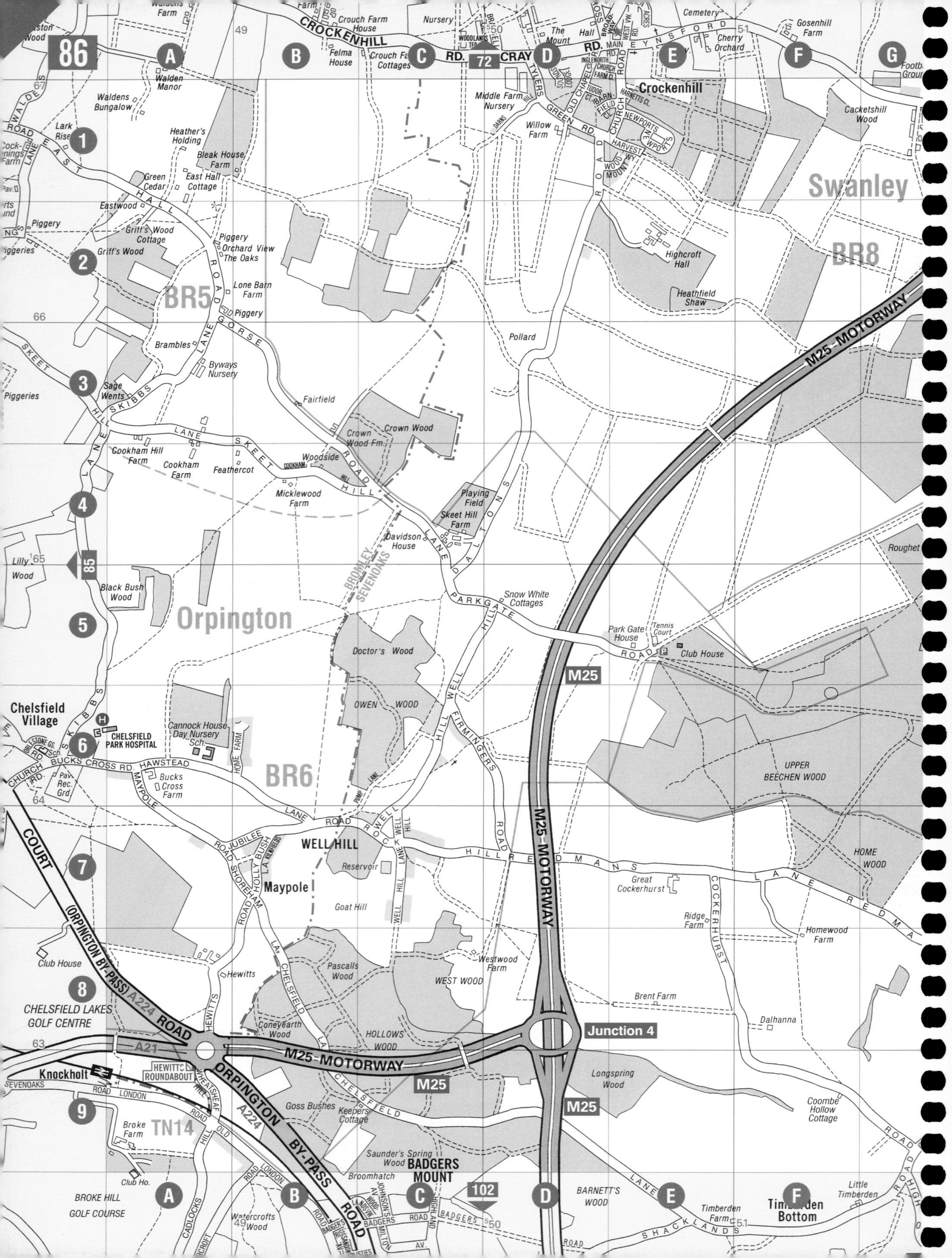

Crockenhill
Swanley
BR8
BR5
Orpington
BR6
TN14
Chelsfield Village
CHELSFIELD PARK HOSPITAL
WELL HILL
Maypole
Knockholt
BADGERS MOUNT
Junction 4
M25-MOTORWAY
M25
A224
A21
ORPINGTON BY-PASS
COURT (ORPINGTON BY-PASS) ROAD
CROCKENHILL RD.
CRAY RD.
EYNSFORD RD.
HEWITTS ROUNDABOUT
BROMLEY SEVENOAKS
Walden Manor
Waldens Bungalow
Lark Rise
Heather's Holding
Bleak House Farm
Green Cedar
East Hall Cottage
Eastwood
Griff's Wood Cottage
Griff's Wood
Piggery
Orchard View
The Oaks
Lone Barn Farm
Brambles
Byways Nursery
Sage Wents
Piggeries
Fairfield
Crown Wood Fm.
Crown Wood
Cookham Hill Farm
Cookham Farm
Feathercot
Woodside
Micklewood Farm
Playing Field
Skeet Hill Farm
Davidson House
Lilly Wood
Black Bush Wood
Snow White Cottages
Park Gate House
Tennis Court
Club House
Doctor's Wood
OWEN WOOD
Cannock House Day Nursery Sch.
Bucks Cross Farm
UPPER BEECHEN WOOD
HOME WOOD
Reservoir
Great Cockerhurst
Goat Hill
Ridge Farm
Homewood Farm
Westwood Farm
WEST WOOD
Pascalls Wood
Hewitts
Brent Farm
Dalhanna
Coneyearth Wood
HOLLOWS WOOD
Longspring Wood
Goss Bushes
Keepers Cottage
Coombe Hollow Cottage
Broke Farm
Saunder's Spring Wood
Broomhatch
Club Ho.
BROKE HILL GOLF COURSE
Watercrofts Wood
BARNETT'S WOOD
Timberden Farm
Timberden Bottom
Little Timberden
Club House
CHELSFIELD LAKES GOLF CENTRE
Crouch Farm House
Felma House
Crouch Farm Cottages
Nursery
The Mount
Hall
Cemetery
Gosenhill Farm
Cherry Orchard
Middle Farm Nursery
Willow Farm
Cacketshill Wood
Highcroft Hall
Heathfield Shaw
Pollard
Roughet
72
85
102

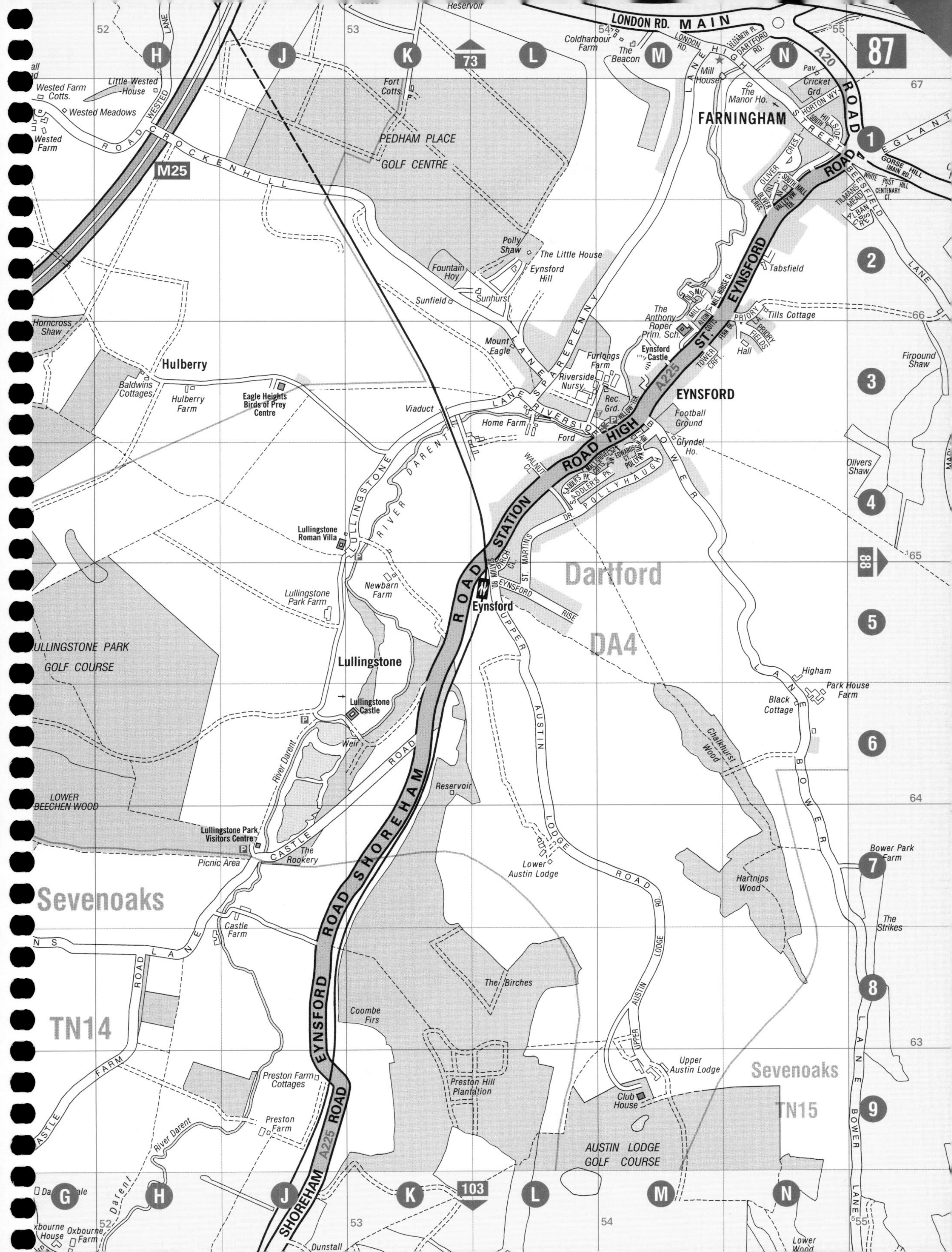
FARNINGHAM
EYNSFORD
Eynsford
Hulberry
Lullingstone
Dartford
DA4
Sevenoaks
TN14
TN15
M25
A20
A225
PEDHAM PLACE
GOLF CENTRE
LULLINGSTONE PARK
GOLF COURSE
AUSTIN LODGE
GOLF COURSE
Eagle Heights
Birds of Prey
Centre
Lullingstone
Roman Villa
Lullingstone
Castle
Lullingstone Park
Visitors Centre
Eynsford
Castle
The Anthony
Roper
Prim. Sch.
Club
House
73
88
103
52
53
54
55
67
66
65
64
63

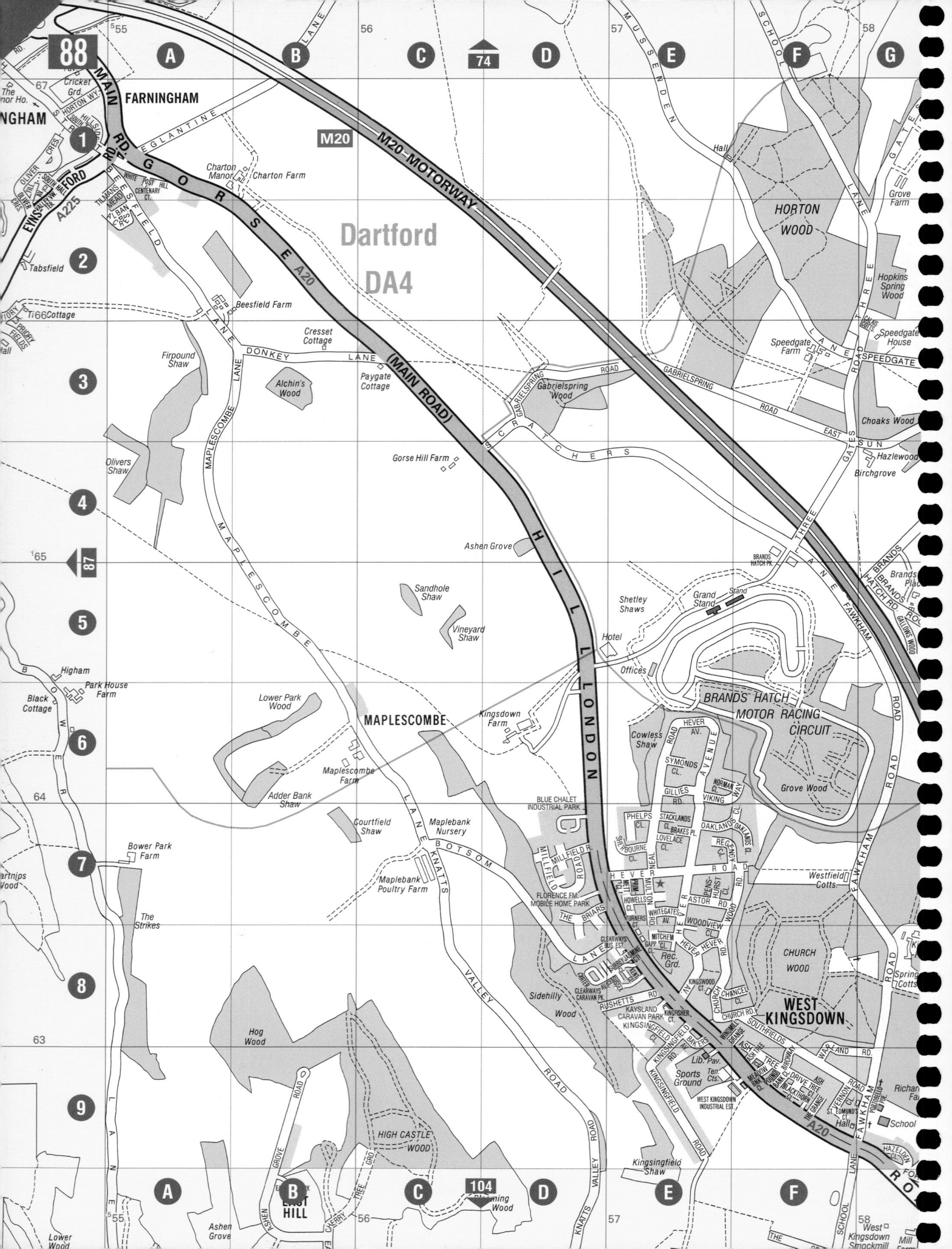

FARNINGHAM
M20
M20 MOTORWAY
Dartford
DA4
GORSE HILL (MAIN ROAD) A20
LONDON
HORTON WOOD
MAPLESCOMBE
BRANDS HATCH MOTOR RACING CIRCUIT
WEST KINGSDOWN
Charton Manor
Charton Farm
Beesfield Farm
Cresset Cottage
Paygate Cottage
Firpound Shaw
Alchin's Wood
Gabrielspring Wood
Olivers Shaw
Gorse Hill Farm
Ashen Grove
Sandhole Shaw
Vineyard Shaw
Lower Park Wood
Kingsdown Farm
Maplescombe Farm
Adder Bank Shaw
Courtfield Shaw
Maplebank Nursery
Maplebank Poultry Farm
Bower Park Farm
The Strikes
Hog Wood
HIGH CASTLE WOOD
Sidehilly Wood
Kingsingfield Shaw
Higham
Park House Farm
Black Cottage
Tabsfield
Speedgate Farm
Speedgate House
Hopkins Spring Wood
Grove Farm
Choaks Wood
Hazlewood
Birchgrove
Shetley Shaws
Grand Stand
Hotel
Offices
Cowless Shaw
Grove Wood
CHURCH WOOD
Westfield Cotts.
BLUE CHALET INDUSTRIAL PARK
FLORENCE FM. MOBILE HOME PARK
CLEARWAYS CARAVAN PK.
KAYSLAND CARAVAN PARK
Sports Ground
WEST KINGSDOWN INDUSTRIAL EST.
Rec. Grd.
EAST HILL
Ashen Grove
Lower Wood
A225
A20
74
87
104

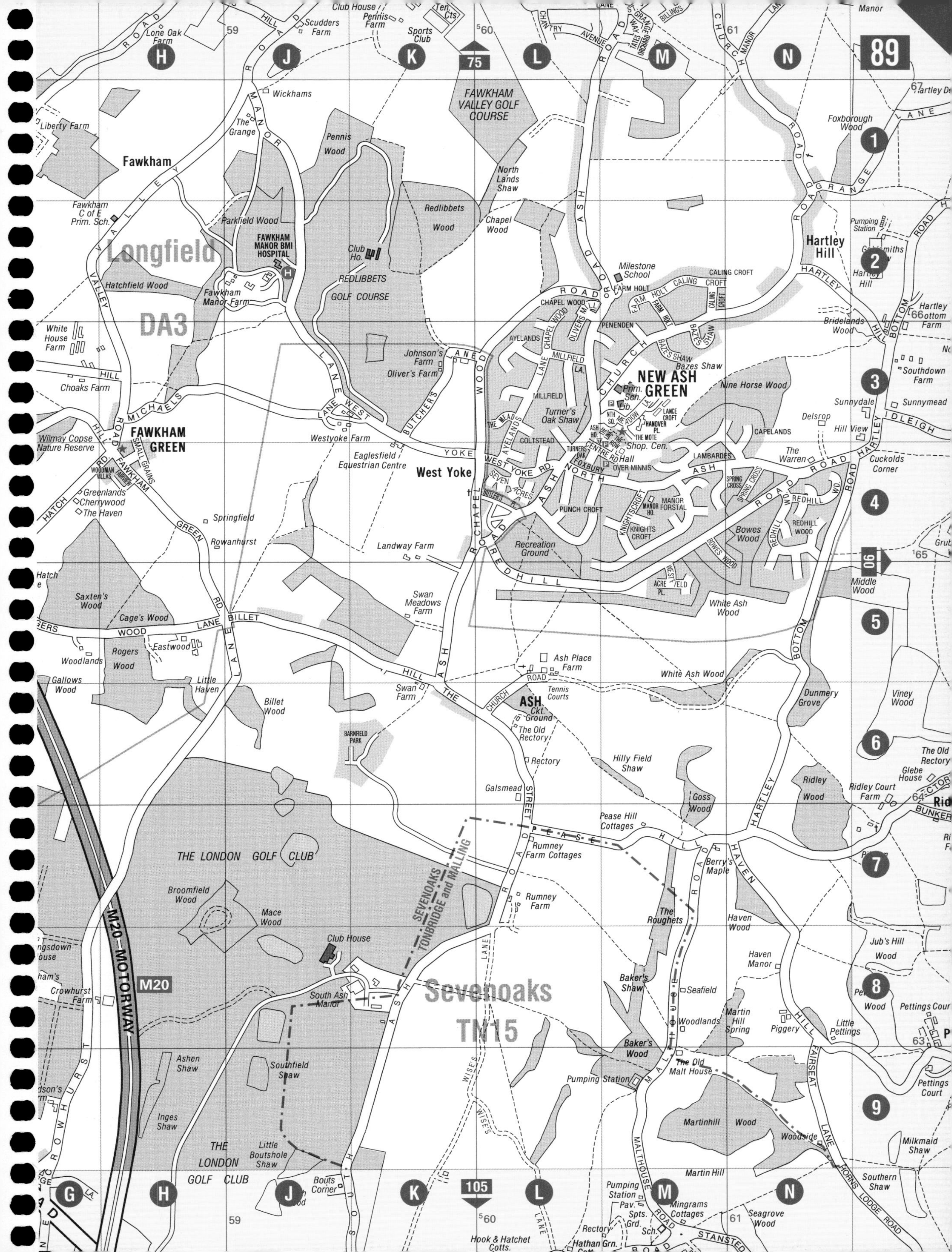

Longfield
DA3
Fawkham
FAWKHAM GREEN
West Yoke
NEW ASH GREEN
Hartley Hill
ASH
Sevenoaks
TN15
FAWKHAM VALLEY GOLF COURSE
REDLIBBETS GOLF COURSE
FAWKHAM MANOR BMI HOSPITAL
THE LONDON GOLF CLUB
Liberty Farm
Wickhams
The Grange
Pennis Wood
North Lands Shaw
Redlibbets Wood
Chapel Wood
Parkfield Wood
Fawkham C of E Prim. Sch.
Hatchfield Wood
Fawkham Manor Farm
Club Ho.
Milestone School
White House Farm
Johnson's Farm
Oliver's Farm
Choaks Farm
Westyoke Farm
Eaglesfield Equestrian Centre
Wilmay Copse Nature Reserve
Greenlands
Cherrywood
The Haven
Springfield
Rowanhurst
Landway Farm
Recreation Ground
Saxten's Wood
Cage's Wood
Swan Meadows Farm
White Ash Wood
Rogers Wood
Eastwood
Woodlands
Gallows Wood
Little Haven
Billet Wood
Swan Farm
Ash Place Farm
Tennis Courts
Ckt. Ground
The Old Rectory
Rectory
Hilly Field Shaw
Galsmead
Goss Wood
Pease Hill Cottages
Rumney Farm Cottages
Rumney Farm
Berry's Maple
The Roughets
Haven Wood
Haven Manor
Broomfield Wood
Mace Wood
Club House
South Ash Manor
Baker's Shaw
Seafield
Woodlands
Martin Hill Spring
Piggery
Little Pettings
Baker's Wood
The Old Malt House
Pumping Station
Martinhill Wood
Woodside
Martin Hill
Ashen Shaw
Southfield Shaw
Inges Shaw
Little Boutshole Shaw
Bouts Corner
Crowhurst Farm
Pumping Station
Mingrams Cottages
Seagrove Wood
Hook & Hatchet Cotts.
Foxborough Wood
Pumping Station
Hartley Hill
Bridelands Wood
Southdown Farm
Sunnydale
Sunnymead
Delsrop
Hill View
Capelands
The Warren
Cuckolds Corner
Bowes Wood
Redhill Wood
Middle Wood
Dunmery Grove
Viney Wood
Ridley Wood
Ridley Court Farm
Glebe House
The Old Rectory
Jub's Hill Wood
Pettings Court
Milkmaid Shaw
Southern Shaw
Nine Horse Wood
Bazes Shaw
Turner's Oak Shaw
Shop. Cen.
Hall
Prim. Sch.
Lib.
Club House
Pennis Farm
Scudders Farm
Sports Club
Lone Oak Farm
Ten. Cts.
BARNFIELD PARK
SEVENOAKS TONBRIDGE and MALLING
M20 MOTORWAY
M20
75
105
90
H J K L M N G
1 2 3 4 5 6 7 8 9
59 560 61 65 66 67 64 63

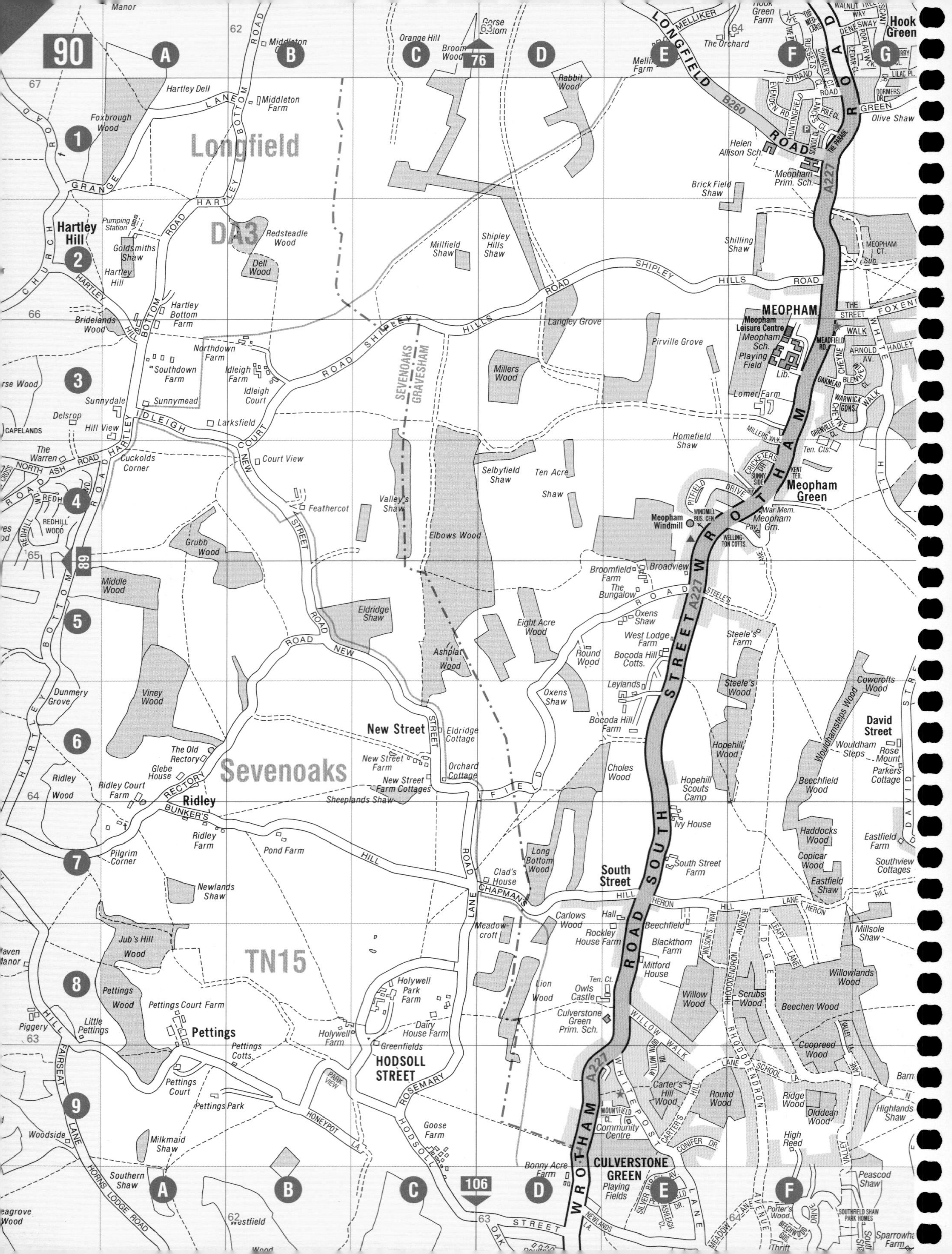
Longfield
DA3
Hartley Hill
Hartley Dell
Foxbrough Wood
Middleton Farm
Redsteadle Wood
Dell Wood
Goldsmiths Shaw
Hartley Bottom Farm
Bridelands Wood
Northdown Farm
Southdown Farm
Idleigh Farm
Idleigh Court
Sunnydale
Sunnymead
Larksfield
Delsrop
Hill View
Capelands
The Warren
Cuckolds Corner
Court View
Feathercot
Grubb Wood
Middle Wood
Viney Wood
Dunmery Grove
The Old Rectory
Glebe House
Ridley Court Farm
Ridley Wood
Ridley
Ridley Farm
Pond Farm
Pilgrim Corner
Newlands Shaw
Jub's Hill Wood
Pettings Wood
Pettings Court Farm
Little Pettings
Piggery
Pettings
Pettings Cotts.
Pettings Court
Pettings Park
Woodside
Milkmaid Shaw
Southern Shaw
Westfield
Sevenoaks
TN15
Eldridge Shaw
New Street
Eldridge Cottage
New Street Farm
New Street Farm Cottages
Orchard Cottage
Sheeplands Shaw
Holywell Park Farm
Dairy House Farm
Holywell Farm
Greenfields
HODSOLL STREET
Goose Farm
Orange Hill
Broom Wood
Gorse Bottom
Millfield Shaw
Shipley Hills Shaw
Valley's Shaw
Elbows Wood
Ashplat Wood
Selbyfield Shaw
Ten Acre Shaw
Eight Acre Wood
Round Wood
Langley Grove
Millers Wood
Rabbit Wood
SEVENOAKS
GRAVESHAM
Clad's House
Long Bottom Wood
Meadowcroft
Carlows Wood
Lion Wood
Bonny Acre Farm
Melliker Farm
The Orchard
Hook Green Farm
Hook Green
Helen Allison Sch.
Meopham Prim. Sch.
Brick Field Shaw
Shilling Shaw
Olive Shaw
MEOPHAM
Meopham Leisure Centre
Meopham Sch.
Playing Field
Lib.
Lomer Farm
Homefield Shaw
Pirville Grove
Meopham Green
Meopham Windmill
War Mem.
Meopham Pav.
Meopham Grn.
Broomfield Farm
The Bungalow
Broadview
Oxens Shaw
West Lodge Farm
Bocoda Hill Cotts.
Leylands
Bocoda Hill Farm
Steele's Farm
Steele's Wood
Hopehill Wood
Choles Wood
Hopehill Scouts Camp
Ivy House
South Street Farm
South Street
Hall
Beechfield
Rockley House Farm
Blackthorn Farm
Mitford House
Owls Castle
Culverstone Green Prim. Sch.
Willow Wood
Scrubs Wood
Carter's Hill Wood
Round Wood
Community Centre
CULVERSTONE GREEN
Playing Fields
Beechen Wood
Willowlands Wood
Coopreed Wood
Ridge Wood
Olddean Wood
Highlands Shaw
High Reed
Porter's Wood
Peascod Shaw
Southfield Shaw Park Homes
Sparrowhawk Farm
Thrift
Millsole Shaw
Cowcrofts Wood
Wouldhamsteps Wood
David Street
Wouldham Steps
Rose Mount
Parkers Cottage
Beechfield Wood
Haddocks Wood
Copicar Wood
Eastfield Shaw
Eastfield Farm
Southview Cottages
LONGFIELD ROAD
B260
A227
WROTHAM ROAD
SOUTH STREET ROAD
SHIPLEY HILLS ROAD
STEELE'S ROAD
HERON HILL LANE
CHAPMANS HILL
BUNKER'S HILL
RECTORY ROAD
NEW STREET ROAD
COURT ROAD
IDLEIGH ROAD
HARTLEY ROAD
HARTLEY BOTTOM ROAD
GRANGE LANE
CHURCH ROAD
NORTH ASH ROAD
FAIRSEAT LANE
HORNS LODGE ROAD
HODSOLL STREET
ROSEMARY LANE
HONEYPOT LA.
WILLOW WALK
SCHOOL LA.
RHODODENDRON AVENUE
CARTER'S HILL
CONIFER DR.
SILVER BIRCH AV.
NEWLANDS LA.
MEADOW AVENUE
76
89
106

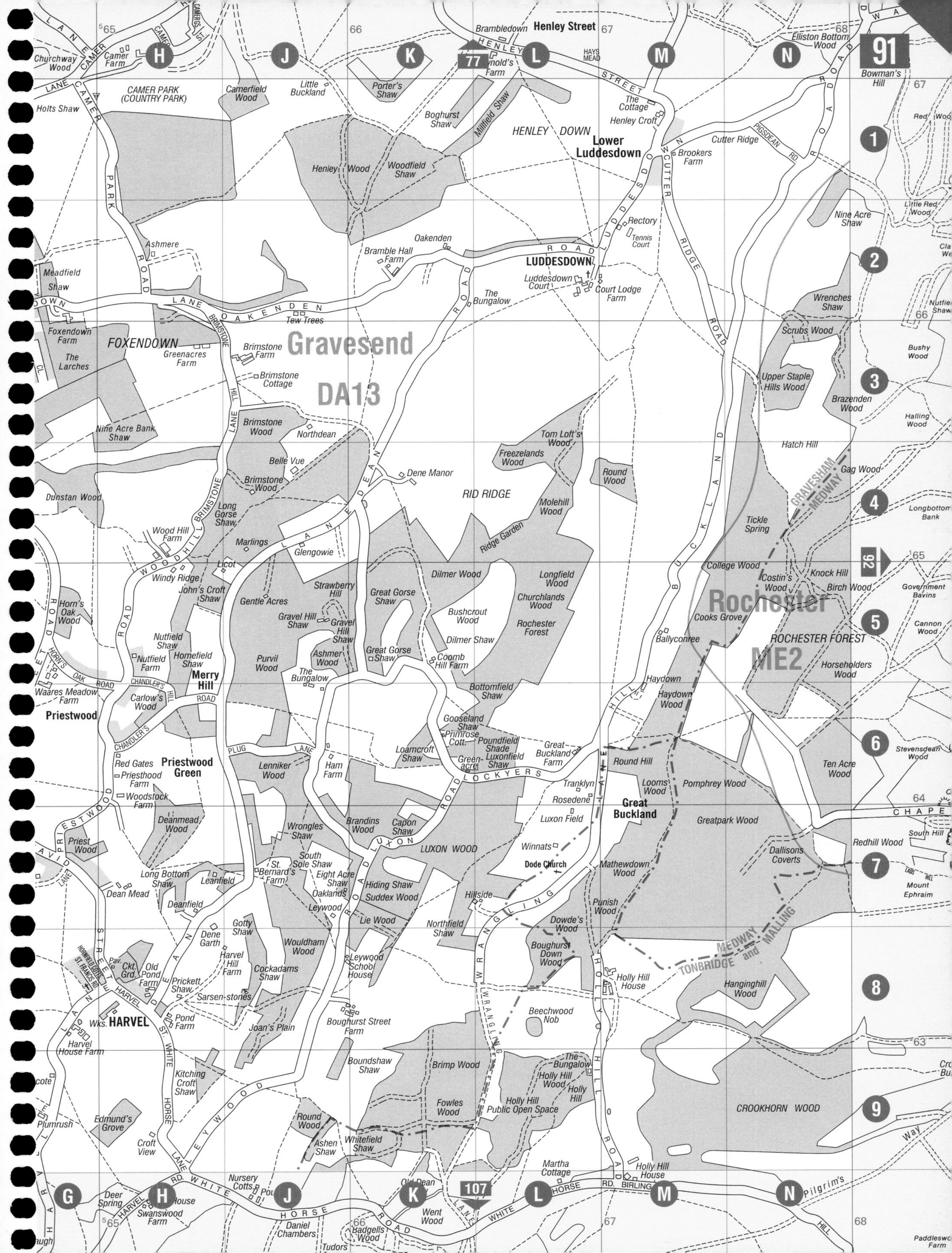

91
77
107
92
Henley Street
Brambledown
Churchway Wood
Camer Farm
CAMER PARK (COUNTRY PARK)
Camerfield Wood
Little Buckland
Porter's Shaw
Holts Shaw
Boghurst Shaw
Millfield Shaw
HENLEY DOWN
Lower Luddesdown
The Cottage
Henley Croft
Brookers Farm
Cutter Ridge
Elliston Bottom Wood
Bowman's Hill
Henley Wood
Woodfield Shaw
Nine Acre Shaw
Ashmere
Oakenden
Bramble Hall Farm
LUDDESDOWN
Rectory
Tennis Court
Luddesdown Court
Court Lodge Farm
The Bungalow
Meadfield Shaw
Tew Trees
Foxendown Farm
FOXENDOWN
The Larches
Greenacres Farm
Brimstone Farm
Brimstone Cottage
Gravesend
DA13
Wrenches Shaw
Scrubs Wood
Upper Staple Hills Wood
Brazenden Wood
Bushy Wood
Halling Wood
Hatch Hill
Nine Acre Bank Shaw
Brimstone Wood
Northdean
Belle Vue
Dene Manor
Tom Loft's Wood
Freezelands Wood
Round Wood
Gag Wood
Dunstan Wood
Long Gorse Shaw
RID RIDGE
Molehill Wood
Tickle Spring
Longbottom Bank
Wood Hill Farm
Marlings
Glengowie
Ridge Garden
GRAVESHAM
MEDWAY
Windy Ridge
Licot
Dilmer Wood
Longfield Wood
College Wood
Costin's Wood
Knock Hill
Birch Wood
Government Bavins
John's Croft Shaw
Gentle Acres
Strawberry Hill
Great Gorse Shaw
Churchlands Wood
Rochester
Horn's Oak Wood
Gravel Hill Shaw
Bushcrout Wood
Rochester Forest
Cooks Grove
Cannon Wood
Nutfield Shaw
Dilmer Shaw
Ballyconree
ROCHESTER FOREST
Nutfield Farm
Homefield Shaw
Purvil Wood
Ashmer Wood
Great Gorse Shaw
Coomb Hill Farm
ME2
Horseholders Wood
Merry Hill
Waares Meadow Farm
Carlow's Wood
The Bungalow
Bottomfield Shaw
Haydown
Haydown Wood
Priestwood
Gooseland Shaw
Primrose Cott.
Poundfield Shade
Luxonfield Shaw
Green-acre
Great Buckland Farm
Stevensdean Wood
Red Gates
Priestwood Green
Priesthood Farm
Lenniker Wood
Ham Farm
Loamcroft Shaw
Round Hill
Ten Acre Wood
Woodstock Farm
Tranklyn
Looms Wood
Pomphrey Wood
Rosedene
Great Buckland
Deanmead Wood
Wrongles Shaw
Brandins Wood
Capon Shaw
Luxon Field
Greatpark Wood
Priest Wood
LUXON WOOD
Winnats
Redhill Wood
South Hill
South Sole Shaw
St. Bernard's Farm
Dode Church
Mathewdown Wood
Dallisons Coverts
Long Bottom Shaw
Leanfield
Eight Acre Shaw
Hiding Shaw
Mount Ephraim
Dean Mead
Oaklands
Suddex Wood
Hillside
Punish Wood
Deanfield
Leywood
Lie Wood
Northfield Shaw
Dowde's Wood
Gotty Shaw
Dene Garth
Wouldham Wood
Boughurst Down Wood
Harvel Hill Farm
Leywood School House
TONBRIDGE and MALLING
Ckt. Grd.
Pav.
Old Pond Farm
Cockadams Shaw
Holly Hill House
Hanginghill Wood
Prickett Shaw
Sarsen-stones
Pond Farm
Boughurst Street Farm
Beechwood Nob
Wks.
HARVEL
Joan's Plain
Harvel House Farm
Boundshaw Shaw
Brimp Wood
The Bungalow
Holly Hill Wood
Kitching Croft Shaw
Holly Hill
Fowles Wood
Holly Hill Public Open Space
CROOKHORN WOOD
Edmund's Grove
Plumrush
Round Wood
Croft View
Ashen Shaw
Whitefield Shaw
Martha Cottage
Holly Hill House
Deer Spring
Nursery Cotts.
Old Dean
Pilgrim's Way
Swanswood Farm
Daniel Chambers
Went Wood
Badgells Wood
Tudors
Paddlesworth Farm
CAMER PARK ROAD
OAKENDEN LANE
BRIMSTONE HILL
WOODHILL LANE
HORN'S OAK ROAD
CHANDLER'S ROAD
PLUG LANE
DEAN LANE
LOCKYERS ROAD
LUXON ROAD
LEYWOOD ROAD
WHITE HORSE ROAD
BIRLING RD.
HOLLY HILL ROAD
WRANGLING LANE
BUCKLAND HILL
CUTTER RIDGE ROAD
LUDDESDOWN ROAD
HENLEY STREET
PIGSDEAN RD.
PRIESTWOOD ROAD
HARVEL ST.
ST. WHITE HORSE
1
2
3
4
5
6
7
8
9
G
H
J
K
L
M
N
65
66
67
68
64
63

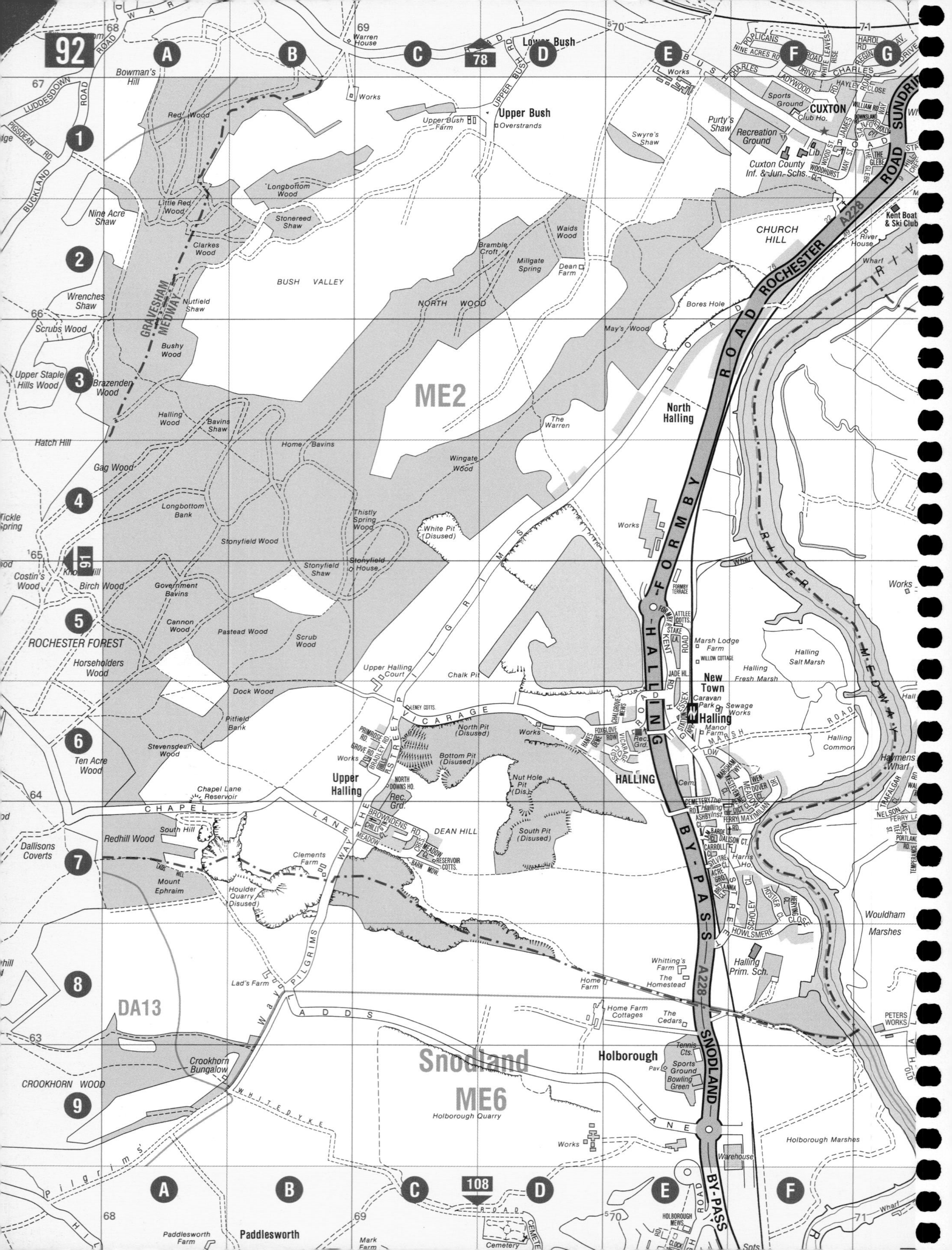

Lower Bush
Upper Bush
Upper Bush Farm
Overstrands
Works
Bowman's Hill
Red Wood
Longbottom Wood
Little Red Wood
Stonereed Shaw
Nine Acre Shaw
Clarkes Wood
Swyre's Shaw
Purty's Shaw
CUXTON
Sports Ground
Club Ho.
Recreation Ground
Cuxton County Inf. & Jun. Schs.
Kent Boat & Ski Club
River House
Wharf
CHURCH HILL
Waids Wood
Bramble Croft
Millgate Spring
Dean Farm
BUSH VALLEY
NORTH WOOD
Wrenches Shaw
Nutfield Shaw
Scrubs Wood
Bores Hole
May's Wood
GRAVESHAM
MEDWAY
Bushy Wood
Upper Staple Hills Wood
Brazenden Wood
ME2
North Halling
The Warren
Halling Wood
Bavins Shaw
Hatch Hill
Home Bavins
Wingate Wood
Gag Wood
Longbottom Bank
Thistly Spring Wood
White Pit (Disused)
Works
Tickle Spring
Stonyfield Wood
Stonyfield Shaw
Stonyfield House
Costin's Wood
Birch Wood
Government Bavins
Cannon Wood
Pastead Wood
Scrub Wood
ROCHESTER FOREST
Horseholders Wood
Upper Halling Court
Chalk Pit
Marsh Lodge Farm
Willow Cottage
Halling Salt Marsh
Halling Fresh Marsh
New Town
Caravan Park
Sewage Works
Halling
Manor Farm
Halling Common
Dock Wood
Pitfield Bank
North Pit (Disused)
Bottom Pit (Disused)
Works
Stevensdean Wood
Ten Acre Wood
Upper Halling
Rec. Grd.
Nut Hole Pit (Dis.)
HALLING
Haymens Wharf
Chapel Lane Reservoir
South Hill
Redhill Wood
DEAN HILL
South Pit (Disused)
Dallisons Coverts
Clements Farm
Mount Ephraim
Houlder Quarry (Disused)
Harris Ho.
Wouldham Marshes
Whitting's Farm
The Homestead
Halling Prim. Sch.
Home Farm
Lad's Farm
DA13
Home Farm Cottages
The Cedars
PETERS WORKS
Crookhorn Bungalow
Snodland
ME6
Holborough
Tennis Cts.
Sports Ground
Bowling Green
CROOKHORN WOOD
Holborough Quarry
Works
Holborough Marshes
Warehouse
Paddlesworth Farm
Paddlesworth
Mark Farm
Cemetery
HOLBOROUGH MEWS
ROCHESTER ROAD
FORMBY ROAD
HALLING BY-PASS
SNODLAND BY-PASS
A228
PILGRIMS WAY
CHAPEL LANE
VICARAGE ROAD
ADDS
WHITEDYKE
RIVER MEDWAY
CHARLES DRIVE
BUSH ROAD
LUDDESDOWN ROAD
BUCKLAND RD
PIGSDEAN RD
STATION RD
HIGH STREET
HOLBOROUGH LANE
78
91
108

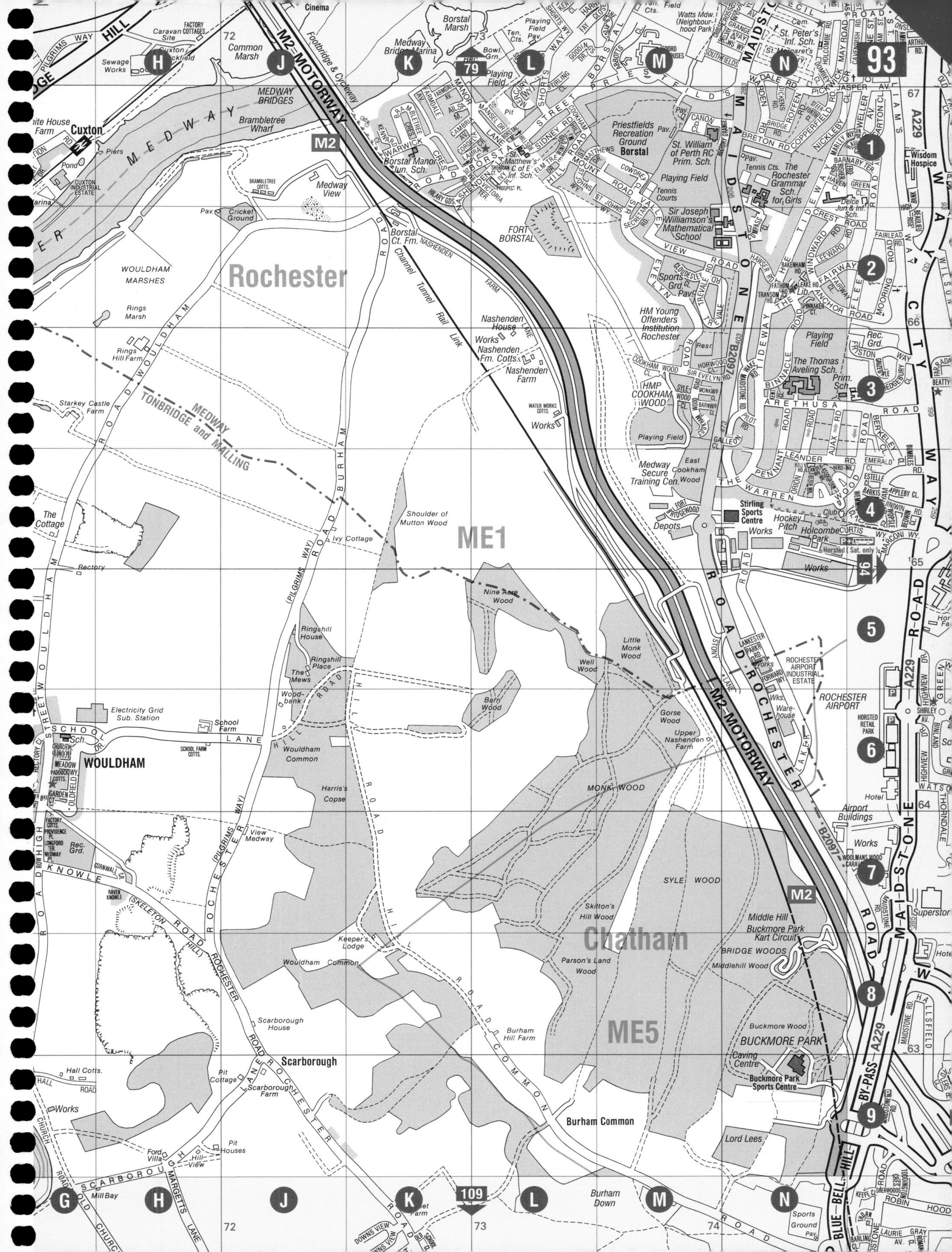

Rochester
Chatham
ME1
ME5
M2 MOTORWAY
WOULDHAM
Cuxton
Borstal
Scarborough
Burham Common
BUCKMORE PARK
ROCHESTER AIRPORT
MEDWAY BRIDGES
Brambletree Wharf
WOULDHAM MARSHES
Rings Marsh
Rings Hill Farm
Starkey Castle Farm
MEDWAY
TONBRIDGE and MALLING
FORT BORSTAL
Channel Tunnel Rail Link
Nashenden House
Nashenden Farm
HM Young Offenders Institution Rochester
HMP COOKHAM WOOD
Medway Secure Training Cen.
Stirling Sports Centre
Shoulder of Mutton Wood
Ivy Cottage
Nine Acre Wood
Little Monk Wood
Well Wood
Barn Wood
Gorse Wood
Upper Nashenden Farm
MONK WOOD
SYLE WOOD
Skilton's Hill Wood
Parson's Land Wood
Middle Hill Buckmore Park Kart Circuit
BRIDGE WOODS
Middlehill Wood
Buckmore Wood
Buckmore Park Sports Centre
Lord Lees
Burham Hill Farm
Burham Down
Keeper's Lodge
Wouldham Common
Harris's Copse
Ringshill House
Ringshill Place
Electricity Grid Sub. Station
School Farm
Scarborough House
Scarborough Farm
Pit Cottage
Pit Houses
Hall Cotts.
Mill Bay
Priestfields Recreation Ground
The Rochester Grammar Sch. for Girls
Sir Joseph Williamson's Mathematical School
The Thomas Aveling Sch.
Holcombe Park
Wisdom Hospice
MAIDSTONE ROAD
ROCHESTER ROAD
BLUE BELL HILL
BY-PASS
A229
B2097
CITY WAY
109
79
94
72
73
74
G H J K L M N
1 2 3 4 5 6 7 8 9

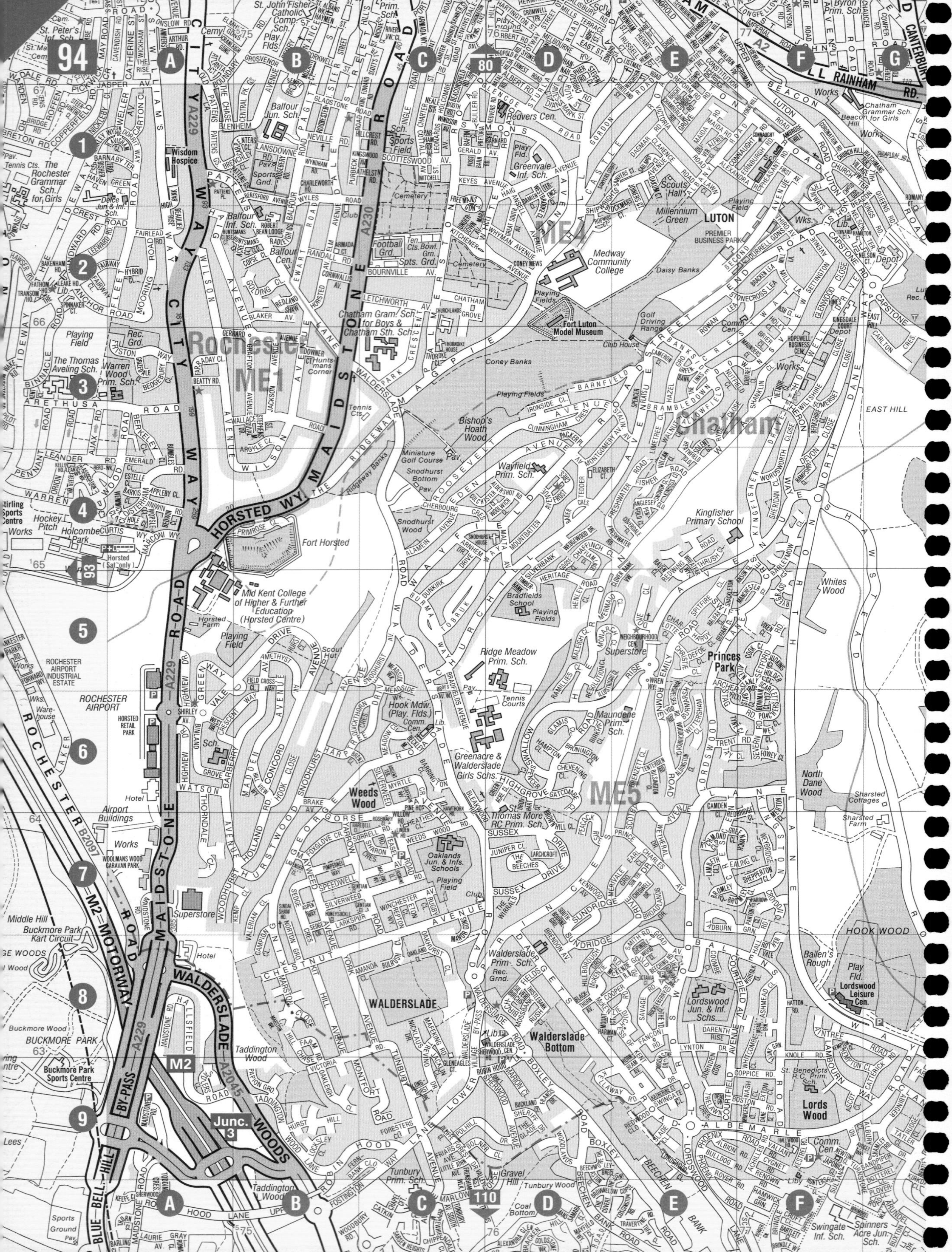

A
B
C
D
E
F
G
1
2
3
4
5
6
7
8
9
80
93
110
CITY WAY
A229
MAIDSTONE ROAD
A230
HORSTED WY.
CHATHAM HILL RAINHAM RD.
A2
CANTERBURY
Rochester
ME1
ME4
ME5
LUTON
Chatham
WALDERSLADE
Weeds Wood
Princes Park
Walderslade Bottom
St. Peter's Inf. Sch.
St. John Fisher Catholic Comp. Sch.
Byron Prim. Sch.
Chatham Grammar Sch. for Girls
Balfour Jun. Sch.
Balfour Inf. Sch.
Balfour Cen.
Wisdom Hospice
The Rochester Grammar Sch. for Girls
Delce Jun & Inf. Sch.
Redvers Cen.
Greenvale Inf. Sch.
Medway Community College
Millennium Green
Scouts Hall
PREMIER BUSINESS PARK
Daisy Banks
Golf Driving Range
Fort Luton Model Museum
Club House
Coney Banks
Chatham Gram. Sch. for Boys & Chatham Sth. Sch.
Huntsmans Corner
Football Grd.
Cemetery
The Thomas Aveling Sch.
Warren Wood Prim. Sch.
Rec. Grd.
Playing Field
Playing Fields
Bishop's Hoath Wood
Miniature Golf Course
Snodhurst Bottom
Ridgeway Banks
Snodhurst Wood
Fort Horsted
Wayfield Prim. Sch.
Kingfisher Primary School
Bradfields School
Ridge Meadow Prim. Sch.
Mid Kent College of Higher & Further Education (Horsted Centre)
Horsted Farm
Holcombe Park
Hockey Pitch
Stirling Sports Centre
Tennis Cts.
Scout Hut
ROCHESTER AIRPORT INDUSTRIAL ESTATE
ROCHESTER AIRPORT
HORSTED RETAIL PARK
Airport Buildings
Hotel
Works
WOOLMANS WOOD CARAVAN PARK
Superstore
Middle Hill
Buckmore Park Kart Circuit
BUCKMORE PARK
Buckmore Wood
Buckmore Park Sports Centre
M2 MOTORWAY
WALDERSLADE WOODS
A2045
Junc. 13
BY-PASS
BLUE BELL HILL
Taddington Wood
Tunbury Prim. Sch.
Tunbury Wood
Gravel Hill
Coal Bottom
Hook Mdw. (Play. Flds.)
Greenacre & Walderslade Girls Schs.
Thomas More RC Prim. Sch.
Oaklands Jun. & Infs. Schools
Walderslade Prim. Sch.
Maundene Prim. Sch.
Lordswood Jun. & Inf. Schs.
St. Benedicts R.C. Prim. Sch.
Lords Wood
Lordswood Leisure Cen.
Ballen's Rough
HOOK WOOD
North Dane Wood
Sharsted Cottages
Sharsted Farm
Whites Wood
EAST HILL
NORTH DANE WAY
Kingsdale Court Depot
Swingate Inf. Sch.
Spinners Acre Jun. Sch.
Sports Ground

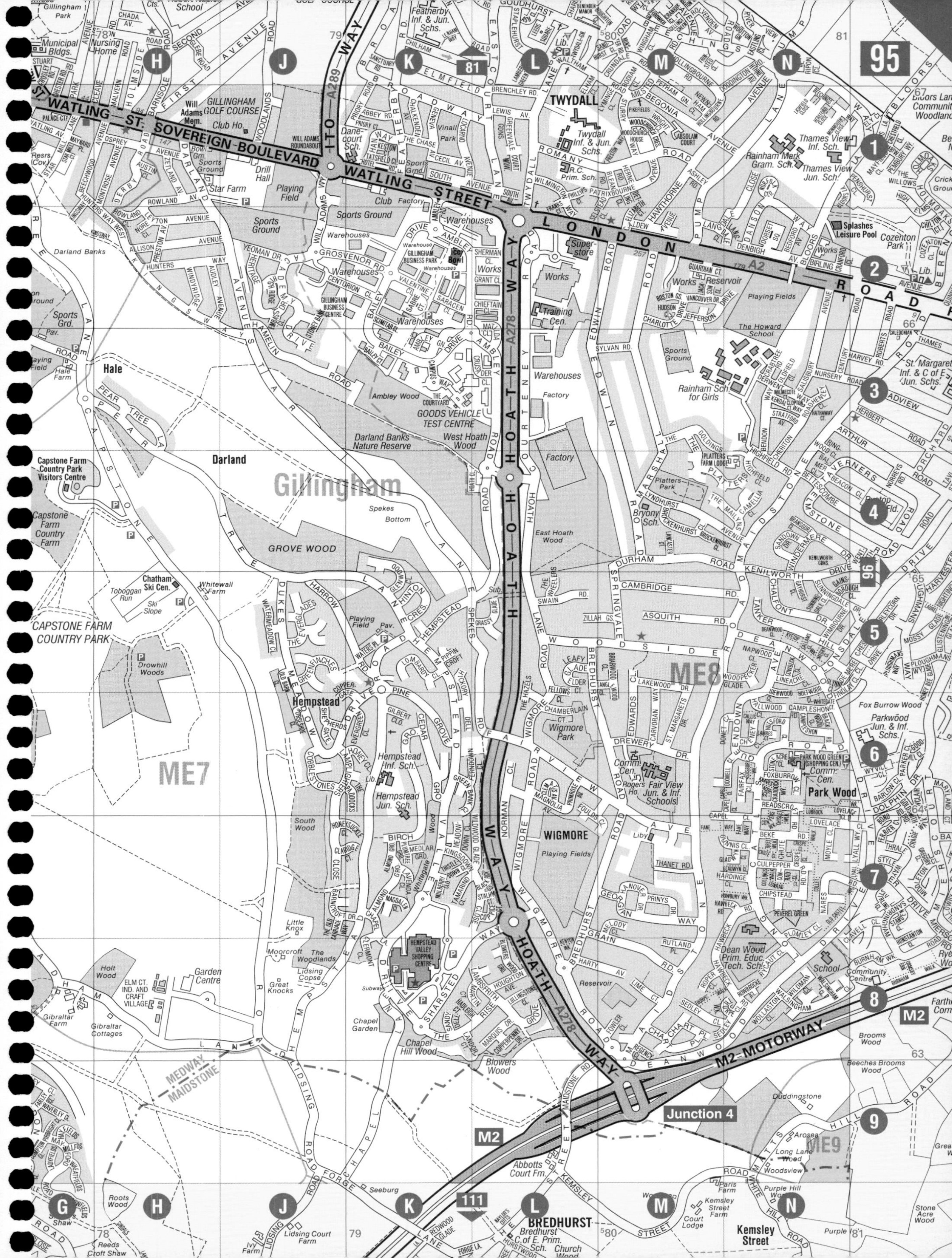

WATLING ST.
SOVEREIGN BOULEVARD
WATLING STREET
LONDON ROAD
A2
HOATH WAY
A278
A289
M2 MOTORWAY
M2
Junction 4
TWYDALL
Gillingham
Darland
Hale
Hempstead
WIGMORE
BREDHURST
Kemsley Street
ME7
ME8
ME9
GILLINGHAM GOLF COURSE
CAPSTONE FARM COUNTRY PARK
Capstone Farm Country Park Visitors Centre
Chatham Ski Cen.
Darland Banks Nature Reserve
GOODS VEHICLE TEST CENTRE
Ambley Wood
West Hoath Wood
East Hoath Wood
GROVE WOOD
Park Wood
Rainham Sch. for Girls
The Howard School
Rainham Mark Gram. Sch.
Thames View Inf. Sch.
Thames View Jun. Sch.
Splashes Leisure Pool
Twydall Inf. & Jun. Schs.
Hempstead Inf. Sch.
Hempstead Jun. Sch.
HEMPSTEAD VALLEY SHOPPING CENTRE
Fair View Jun. & Inf. Schools
Dean Wood Prim. Educ. Tech. Sch.
Parkwood Jun. & Inf. Schs.
Featherby Inf. & Jun. Schs.
Bredhurst C.of E. Prim. Sch.
Drowhill Woods
Holt Wood
Chapel Hill Wood
Blowers Wood
Gibraltar Farm
Lidsing Court Farm
Abbotts Court Fm.
Roots Wood
Garden Centre
81
111
96

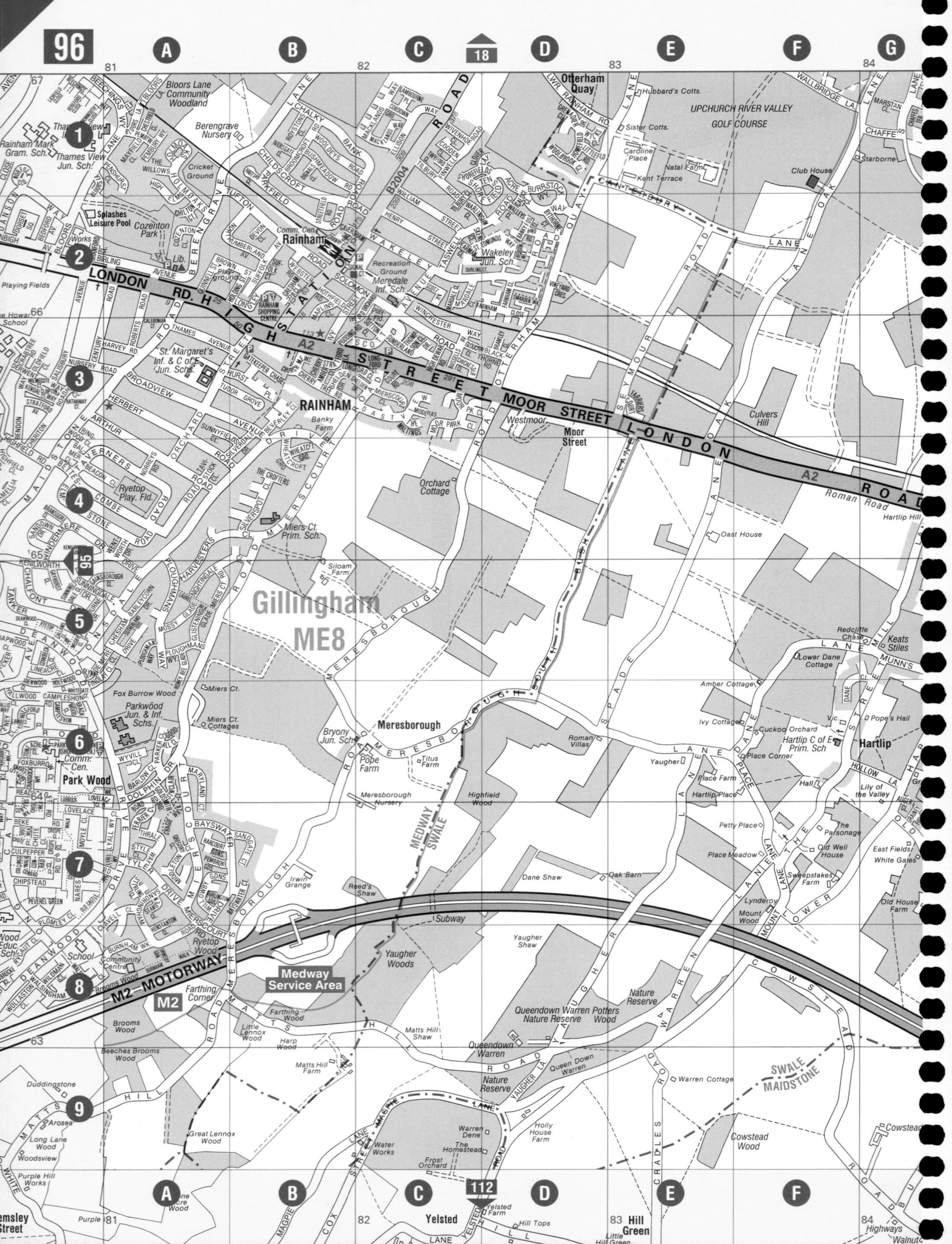

96
A
B
C
D
E
F
G
18
112
95
81
82
83
84
Gillingham
ME8
RAINHAM
Rainham
Otterham Quay
Moor Street
Hartlip
Park Wood
Meresborough
Yelsted
Hill Green
LONDON RD.
HIGH STREET
MOOR STREET
LONDON ROAD
A2
B2004
M2 MOTORWAY
M2
Medway Service Area
UPCHURCH RIVER VALLEY GOLF COURSE
Bloors Lane Community Woodland
Berengrave Nursery
Thames View Inf. Sch.
Thames View Jun. Sch.
Rainham Mark Gram. Sch.
Splashes Leisure Pool
Cozenton Park
Cricket Ground
Playing Fields
Recreation Ground
Meredale Inf. Sch.
Wakeley Jun. Sch.
St. Margaret's Inf. & C of E Jun. Schs.
Rainham Shopping Centre
Ryetop Play. Fld.
Miers Ct. Prim. Sch.
Miers Ct.
Miers Ct. Cottages
Fox Burrow Wood
Parkwood Jun. & Inf. Schs.
Comm. Cen.
Banky Farm
Siloam Farm
Orchard Cottage
Westmoor
Culvers Hill
Roman Road
Hartlip Hill
Oast House
Caroline Place
Kent Terrace
Natal Farm
Hubbard's Cotts.
Sister Cotts.
Club House
Starborne
Redcliffe Chase
Keats Stiles
Lower Dane Cottage
Amber Cottage
Ivy Cottage
Cuckoo Orchard
Hartlip C of E Prim. Sch
Pope's Hall
Place Corner
Place Farm
Hartlip Place
Yaugher
Lily of the Valley
Petty Place
The Parsonage
Old Well House
East Fields
White Gates
Place Meadow
Sweepstakes Farm
Lynderoy
Mount Wood
Old House Farm
Roman Villas
Bryony Jun. Sch.
Pope Farm
Titus Farm
Meresborough Nursery
Highfield Wood
MEDWAY SWALE
Irwin Grange
Reed's Shaw
Dane Shaw
Oak Barn
Subway
Yaugher Shaw
Yaugher Woods
Ryetop Wood
Community Centre
School
Wood Educ. Sch.
Brooms Wood
Farthing Corner
Farthing Wood
Little Lennox Wood
Harp Wood
Matts Hill Shaw
Matts Hill Farm
Beeches Brooms Wood
Queendown Warren Nature Reserve
Potters Wood
Nature Reserve
Queendown Warren
Queen Down Warren
Warren Cottage
SWALE
MAIDSTONE
Duddingstone
Arosea
Long Lane Wood
Woodsview
Purple Hill Works
Great Lennox Wood
Water Works
Warren Dene
The Homestead
Frost Orchard
Holly House Farm
Cowstead Wood
Cowstead
Yelsted Farm
Hill Tops
Little Hill Green
Highways
Walnut
Hemsley Street
Purple

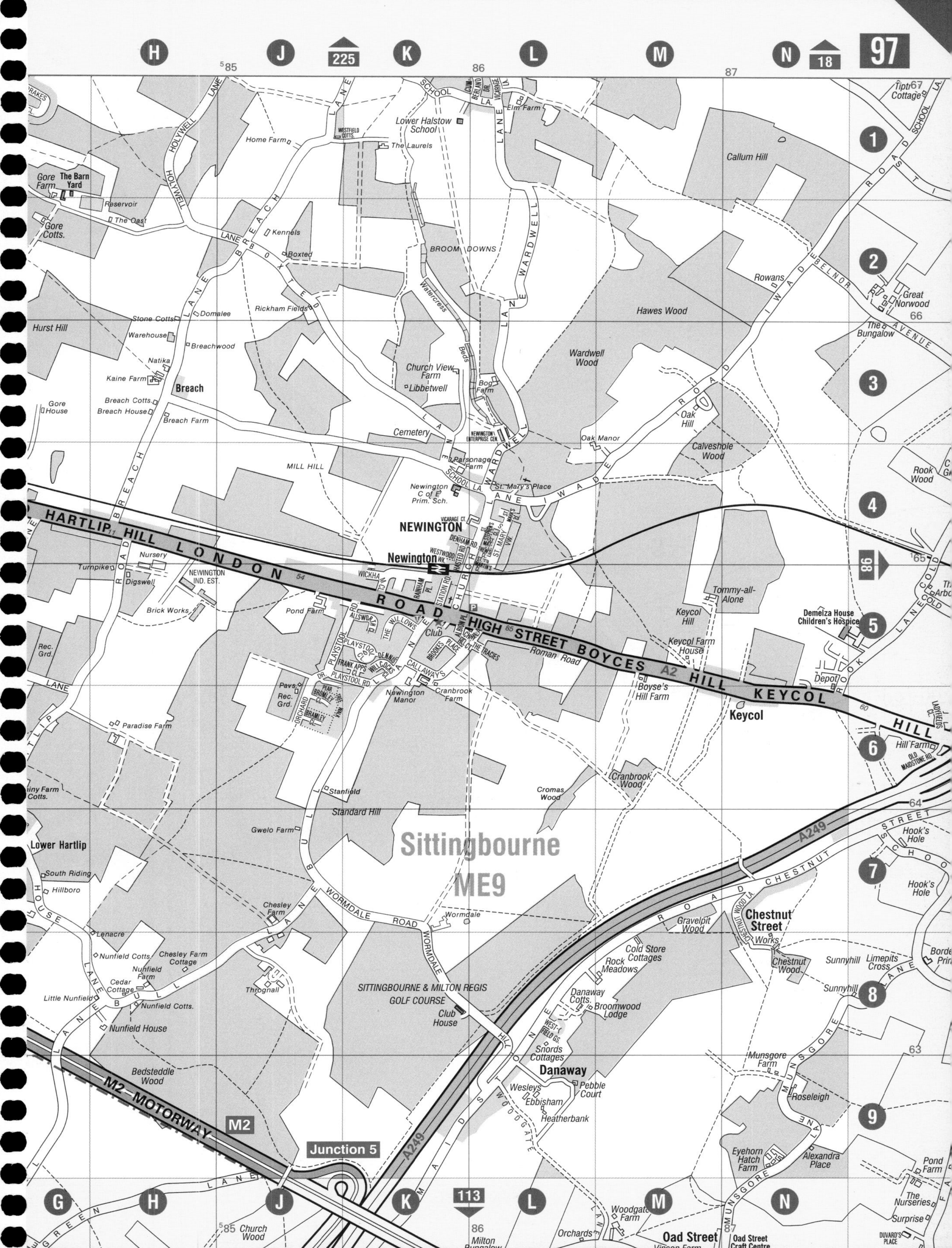

H
J
225
K
L
M
N
18
585
86
87
1
2
3
4
5
6
7
8
9
67
66
65
64
63
Tipti Cottage
SCHOOL LA.
SCHOOL LA.
CUMBERLAND DR.
VICARAGE LA.
Elm Farm
Lower Halstow School
WESTFIELD COTTS.
The Laurels
Home Farm
HOLYWELL LANE
Callum Hill
Gore Farm
The Barn Yard
Reservoir
The Oast
Gore Cotts.
Kennels
Boxted
BOXTED
BROOM DOWNS
WARDWELL LANE
Watercress Beds
Rowans
Great Norwood
BELNOR AVENUE
IWADE ROAD
The Bungalow
Hawes Wood
Stone Cotts
Domalee
Rickham Fields
Hurst Hill
Warehouse
Breachwood
Wardwell Wood
Church View Farm
Libbetwell
Bog Farm
Natika
Kaine Farm
Breach
Gore House
Breach Cotts.
Breach House
Breach Farm
Oak Hill
Cemetery
NEWINGTON ENTERPRISE CEN.
Oak Manor
Calveshole Wood
Rook Wood
MILL HILL
Parsonage Farm
Newington C of E Prim. Sch.
SCHOOL LA.
St. Mary's Place
IWADE LANE
BREACH LANE
HARTLIP HILL
LONDON ROAD
VICARAGE CT.
NEWINGTON
DENHAM RD.
ST. MARY'S VW.
Newington
Turnpike
Nursery
Digswell
NEWINGTON IND. EST.
WESTWOOD WK.
WICKHAM CL.
RAINHAM PL.
STATION RD.
HASTED RD.
CHURCH LA.
96
Tommy-all-Alone
Brick Works
Pond Farm
ALLSWORTH CL.
THE WILLOWS
P
HIGH STREET
Club
ALBION PL.
CHAPEL CT.
THE TRACIES
BROOKES PLACE
Roman Road
BOYCES HILL
A2
Keycol Hill
Keycol Farm House
Demelza House Children's Hospice
COLD LANE
Rec. Grd.
PLAYSTOOL RD.
PLAYSTOOL CL.
DENNIS WILLCOCKS CL.
FRANK APPS CL.
PLAYSTOOL RD.
CALLAWAYS LA.
Newington Manor
Cranbrook Farm
Boyse's Hill Farm
KEYCOL HILL
Keycol
Depot
LANE
Pavs. Rec. Grd.
ORCHARD DR.
PEAR TREE WLK.
BROMLEY CL.
BRAMLEY CL.
Paradise Farm
Hill Farm
OLD MAIDSTONE RD.
LADYFIELDS CL.
Cranbrook Wood
Cromas Wood
Stanfield
Standard Hill
Gwelo Farm
Lower Hartlip
Sittingbourne ME9
A249
STREET
CHESTNUT ROAD
Hook's Hole
South Riding
Hillboro
HOUSE LANE
Chesley Farm
WORMDALE ROAD
Wormdale
Lenacre
Chestnut Street
CHESTNUT WOOD LA.
Gravelpit Wood
Works
Nunfield Cotts.
Chesley Farm Cottage
Nunfield Farm
Cold Store Cottages
Rock Meadows
Chestnut Wood
Sunnyhill
Limepits Cross
LANE
Cedar Cottage
Thrognall
SITTINGBOURNE & MILTON REGIS GOLF COURSE
WORMDALE HILL
Sunnyhill
Little Nunfield
BULL LANE
Nunfield Cotts.
Club House
Danaway Cotts.
Broomwood Lodge
Nunfield House
WESTFIELD GS.
Snords Cottages
Munsgore Farm
MUNSGORE LANE
Bedsteddle Wood
Danaway
Wesleys
Pebble Court
Ebbisham
Roseleigh
Heatherbank
M2 MOTORWAY
M2
WOODGATE
Junction 5
Eyehorn Hatch Farm
Alexandra Place
Pond Farm
G
H
J
K
113
L
M
N
LANE
GREEN
585
Church Wood
86
Milton Bungalow
Orchards
Woodgate Farm
Oad Street
Vinson Farm
87
Oad Street Craft Centre
The Nurseries
Surprise
DUVARD'S PLACE

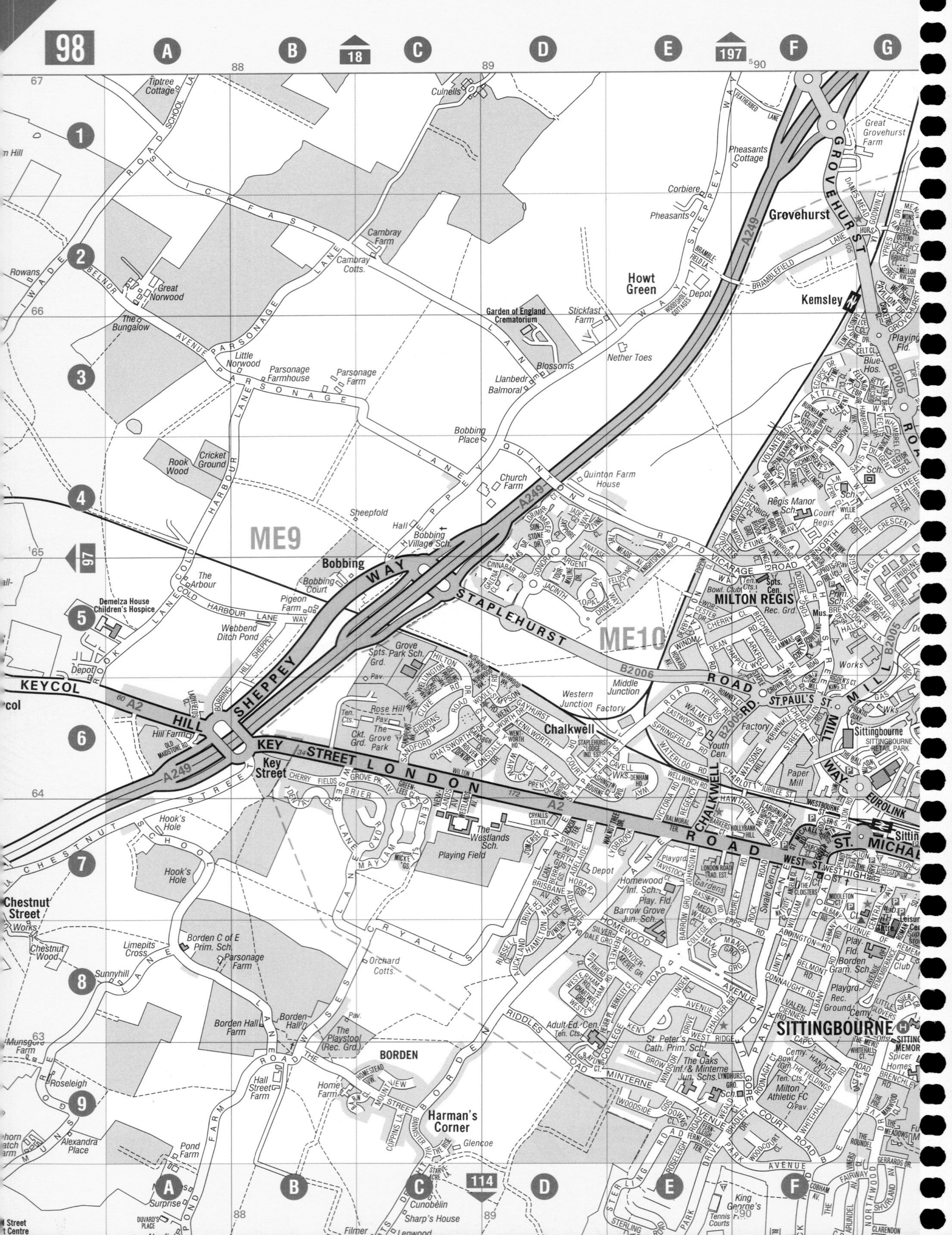

A
B
18
C
D
E
197
F
G
Tiptree Cottage
Culnells
Great Grovehurst Farm
Pheasants Cottage
Corbiere
Pheasants
Grovehurst
Cambray Farm
Cambray Cotts.
Rowans
Great Norwood
Howt Green
Depot
Kemsley
Garden of England Crematorium
Stickfast Farm
The Bungalow
Little Norwood
Parsonage Farmhouse
Parsonage Farm
Nether Toes
Blossoms
Llanbedr
Balmoral
Bobbing Place
Rook Wood
Cricket Ground
Church Farm
Quinton Farm House
Sheepfold
Hall
Bobbing Village Sch.
Regis Manor Sch.
Court Regis
ME9
Bobbing
Bobbing Court
The Arbour
Demelza House Children's Hospice
Pigeon Farm
Webbend Ditch Pond
MILTON REGIS
Rec. Grd.
ME10
Grove Park Sch.
Spts. Grd.
Middle Junction
Western Junction
Factory
Works
KEYCOL
HILL
SHEPPEY WAY
STAPLEHURST ROAD
Rose Hill
Ckt. Grd.
The Grove Park
Chalkwell
Sittingbourne
SITTINGBOURNE RETAIL PARK
Hill Farm
Key Street
Youth Cen.
Paper Mill
EUROLINK
LONDON ROAD
A2
A249
B2006
B2005
Hook's Hole
The Westlands Sch.
Playing Field
Depot
Homewood Inf. Sch.
Barrow Grove Jun. Sch.
Chestnut Street
Works
Chestnut Wood
Limepits Cross
Borden C of E Prim. Sch.
Parsonage Farm
Orchard Cotts.
Sunnyhill
Borden Hall Farm
Borden Hall
The Playstool (Rec. Grd.)
BORDEN
Adult Ed. Cen.
St. Peter's Cath. Prim. Sch.
The Oaks Inf. & Minterne Jun. Schs.
SITTINGBOURNE
Borden Gram. Sch.
Milton Athletic FC
Roseleigh
Hall Street Farm
Home Farm
Harman's Corner
Glencoe
Alexandra Place
Pond Farm
Surprise
Cunobelin
Sharp's House
Lenwood
Filmer
King George's Playing Field
Tennis Courts
A
B
114
C
D
E
F

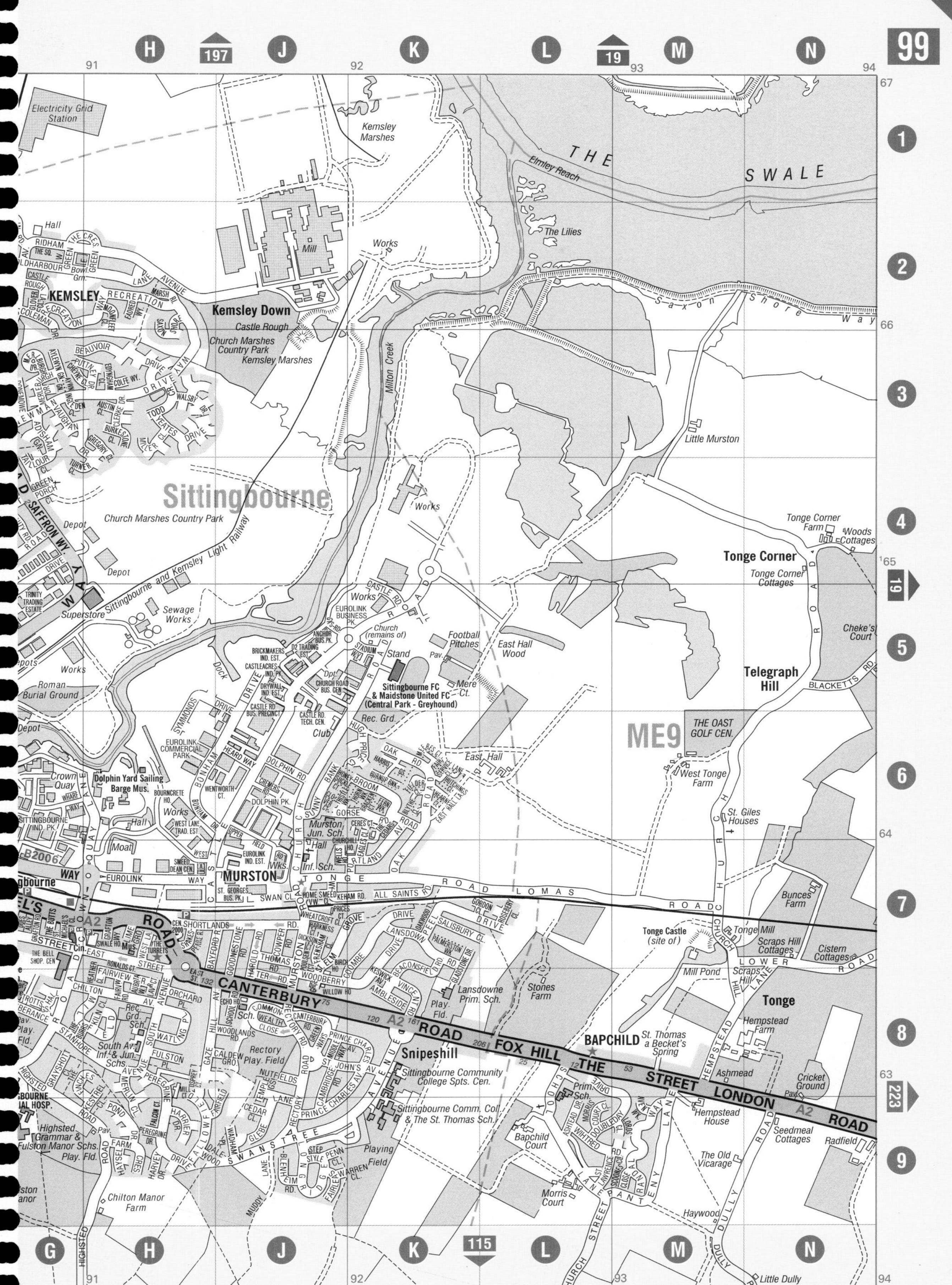
H
197
J
K
L
19
M
N
91
92
93
94
67
66
65
64
63
1
2
3
4
5
6
7
8
9
Electricity Grid Station
Kemsley Marshes
THE SWALE
Elmley Reach
The Lilies
Hall
Works
Mill
KEMSLEY
Kemsley Down
Castle Rough
Church Marshes Country Park
Kemsley Marshes
Saxon Shore Way
Milton Creek
Little Murston
Sittingbourne
Church Marshes Country Park
Sittingbourne and Kemsley Light Railway
Depot
Works
Tonge Corner Farm
Woods Cottages
Tonge Corner
Tonge Corner Cottages
Cheke's Court
Sewage Works
Superstore
TRINITY TRADING ESTATE
EUROLINK BUSINESS PK.
Church (remains of)
Football Pitches
East Hall Wood
Stand
Sittingbourne FC & Maidstone United FC (Central Park - Greyhound)
Telegraph Hill
BLACKETTS RD.
Roman Burial Ground
Depots
Depot
Dock
Rec. Grd.
Club
THE OAST GOLF CEN.
ME9
East Hall
West Tonge Farm
Crown Quay
Dolphin Yard Sailing Barge Mus.
EUROLINK COMMERCIAL PARK
SITTINGBOURNE IND. PK.
Works
Hall
Moat
Murston Jun. Sch.
Hall
Inf. Sch.
St. Giles Houses
B2006
WAY
EUROLINK WAY
MURSTON
TONGE ROAD
LOMAS ROAD
ALL SAINTS RD.
Bunces Farm
Tonge Castle (site of)
Tonge Mill
Scraps Hill Cottages
Cistern Cottages
LOWER ROAD
Mill Pond
Scraps Hill
Tonge
A2
CANTERBURY ROAD
FOX HILL
THE STREET
LONDON ROAD
Lansdowne Prim. Sch.
Stones Farm
Play. Fld.
Snipeshill
BAPCHILD
St. Thomas a Becket's Spring
Hempstead Farm
Ashmead
Cricket Ground
Sittingbourne Community College Spts. Cen.
Sittingbourne Comm. Coll. & The St. Thomas Sch.
Prim. Sch.
Hempstead House
Seedmeal Cottages
Radfield
Rectory Play. Field
South Av. Inf. & Jun. Schs.
Rec. Grd.
Sch.
Highsted Grammar & Fulston Manor Schs. Play. Fld.
Playing Field
Bapchild Court
The Old Vicarage
Morris Court
Haywood
Chilton Manor Farm
SWANSTREE AV.
HIGHSTED
CHURCH STREET
DULLY ROAD
Little Dully
Ashgores
G
115
223

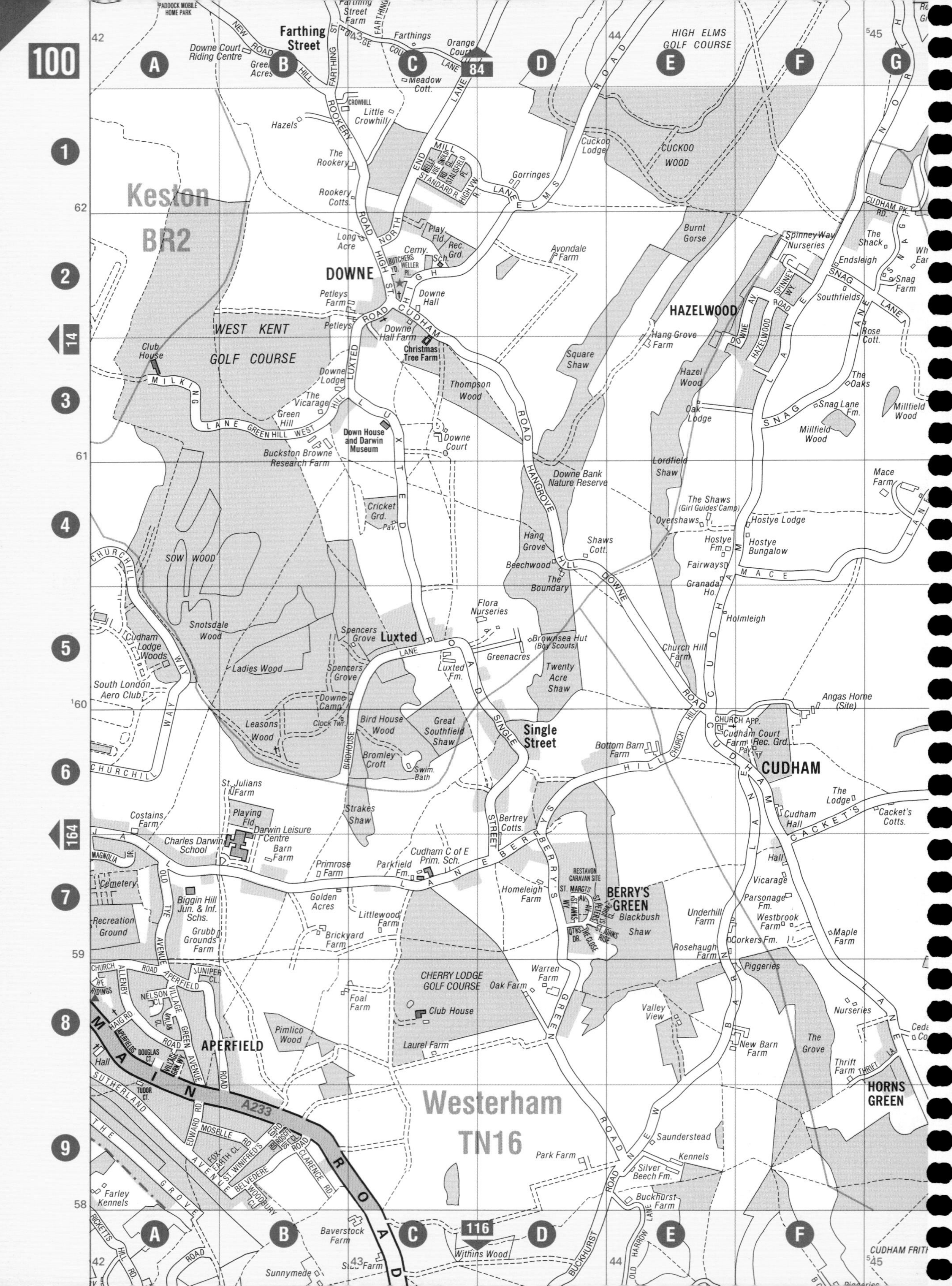

Farthing Street
Downe Court Riding Centre
HIGH ELMS GOLF COURSE
Keston
BR2
DOWNE
WEST KENT GOLF COURSE
Down House and Darwin Museum
HAZELWOOD
CUCKOO WOOD
Cuckoo Lodge
Burnt Gorse
Downe Bank Nature Reserve
SOW WOOD
Luxted
Single Street
CUDHAM
BERRY'S GREEN
APERFIELD
CHERRY LODGE GOLF COURSE
Westerham
TN16
HORNS GREEN
MAIN ROAD
A233
84
14
164
116

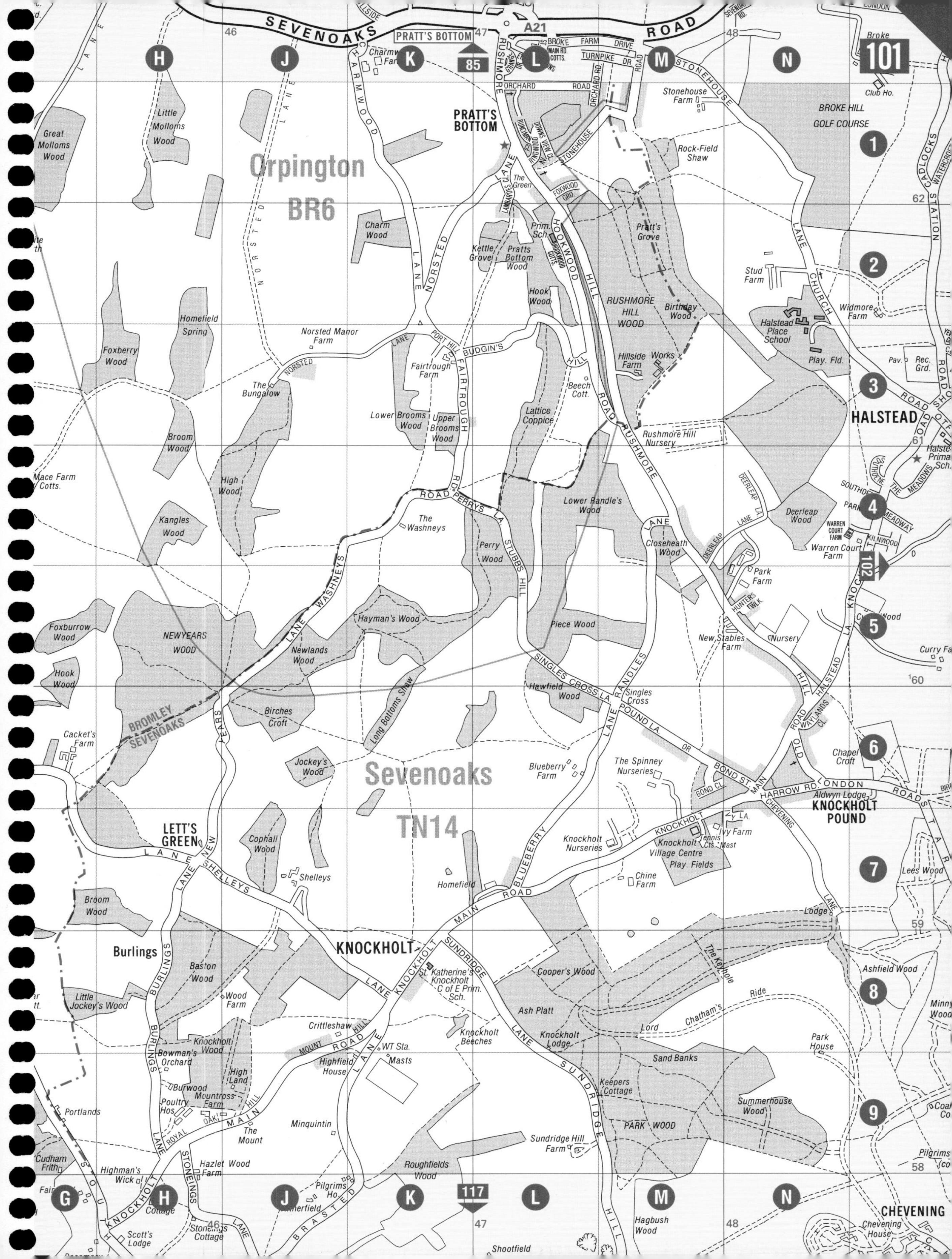
SEVENOAKS ROAD
A21
PRATT'S BOTTOM
85
117
102
Orpington
BR6
Sevenoaks
TN14
PRATT'S BOTTOM
HALSTEAD
KNOCKHOLT POUND
KNOCKHOLT
LETT'S GREEN
CHEVENING
Burlings
BROKE HILL GOLF COURSE
RUSHMORE HILL WOOD
NEWYEARS WOOD
Great Molloms Wood
Little Molloms Wood
Charm Wood
Foxberry Wood
Homefield Spring
Broom Wood
High Wood
Kangles Wood
Foxburrow Wood
Hook Wood
Norsted Manor Farm
The Bungalow
Fairtrough Farm
Lower Brooms Wood
Upper Brooms Wood
Kettle Grove
Pratts Bottom Wood
Hook Wood
Lattice Coppice
Beech Cott.
Lower Randle's Wood
Perry Wood
The Washneys
Hayman's Wood
Newlands Wood
Piece Wood
Hawfield Wood
Birches Croft
Long Bottoms Shaw
Jockey's Wood
Cophall Wood
Shelleys
Homefield
Blueberry Farm
The Spinney Nurseries
Knockholt Nurseries
Knockholt Village Centre
Play. Fields
Chine Farm
Ivy Farm
Tennis Cts.
Mast
Rock-Field Shaw
Pratt's Grove
Birthday Wood
Hillside Farm
Works
Rushmore Hill Nursery
Stonehouse Farm
Stud Farm
Halstead Place School
Play. Fld.
Widmore Farm
Rec. Grd.
Pav.
Club Ho.
Deerleap Wood
Warren Court Farm
Closeheath Wood
Park Farm
New Stables Farm
Nursery
Halstead Prim. Sch.
Chapel Croft
Aldwyn Lodge
Lees Wood
Lodge
Ashfield Wood
Curry Fa
Cacket's Farm
Mace Farm Cotts.
Broom Wood
Little Jockey's Wood
Baston Wood
Wood Farm
Knockholt Wood
Bowman's Orchard
High Land
Burwood
Mountross Farm
Poultry Hos.
Portlands
The Mount
Minquintin
Hazlet Wood Farm
Highman's Wick
Cudham Frith
Scott's Lodge
Stonings Cottage
Crittleshaw
Highfield House
WT Sta.
Masts
St. Katherine's Knockholt C of E Prim. Sch.
Knockholt Beeches
Cooper's Wood
Ash Platt
Knockholt Lodge
Sand Banks
Keepers Cottage
Summerhouse Wood
PARK WOOD
Sundridge Hill Farm
Roughfields Wood
Pilgrims Ho.
Hagbush Wood
Shootfield
Chevening House
Park House
Lord Chatham's Ride
The Keyhole
BROMLEY
SEVENOAKS
Prim. Sch.
The Green
SEVENOAKS ROAD
RUSHMORE HILL
ORCHARD ROAD
ORCHARD RD.
TURNPIKE DR.
BROKE FARM DRIVE
STONEHOUSE LANE
CHARMWOOD LANE
NORSTED LANE
FAIRTROUGH ROAD
PORT HILL
BUDGIN'S HILL
HOOKWOOD ROAD
PERRYS LA.
STUBBS HILL
WASHNEYS ROAD
LANE
SINGLES CROSS LA
POUND LA
RANDLES LANE
BOND ST.
BOND CL.
DEERLEAP LANE
HUNTERS WLK.
OLD ROAD
HALSTEAD HILL
KNOCKHOLT ROAD
LONDON ROAD
HARROW RD.
CHEVENING
MAIN ROAD
KNOCKHOLT LA.
BLUEBERRY LANE
SHELLEYS LANE
NEW YEARS LANE
LETT'S GREEN LANE
BURLINGS LANE
KNOCKHOLT ROAD
SUNDRIDGE LANE
SUNDRIDGE HILL
MOUNT ROAD
CRITTLESHAW HILL
ROYAL OAK HILL
STONEINGS LANE
BRASTED LANE
SOUTH
CHURCH ROAD
STATION ROAD
CADLOCKS
WAYLANDS CL.
KILNWOOD
MEADWAY
THE MEADOWS
SOUTHDENE
FOXWOOD GRO.
DOWNS VIEW CL.
46
47
48
62
61
60
59
58
G
H
J
K
L
M
N
1
2
3
4
5
6
7
8
9

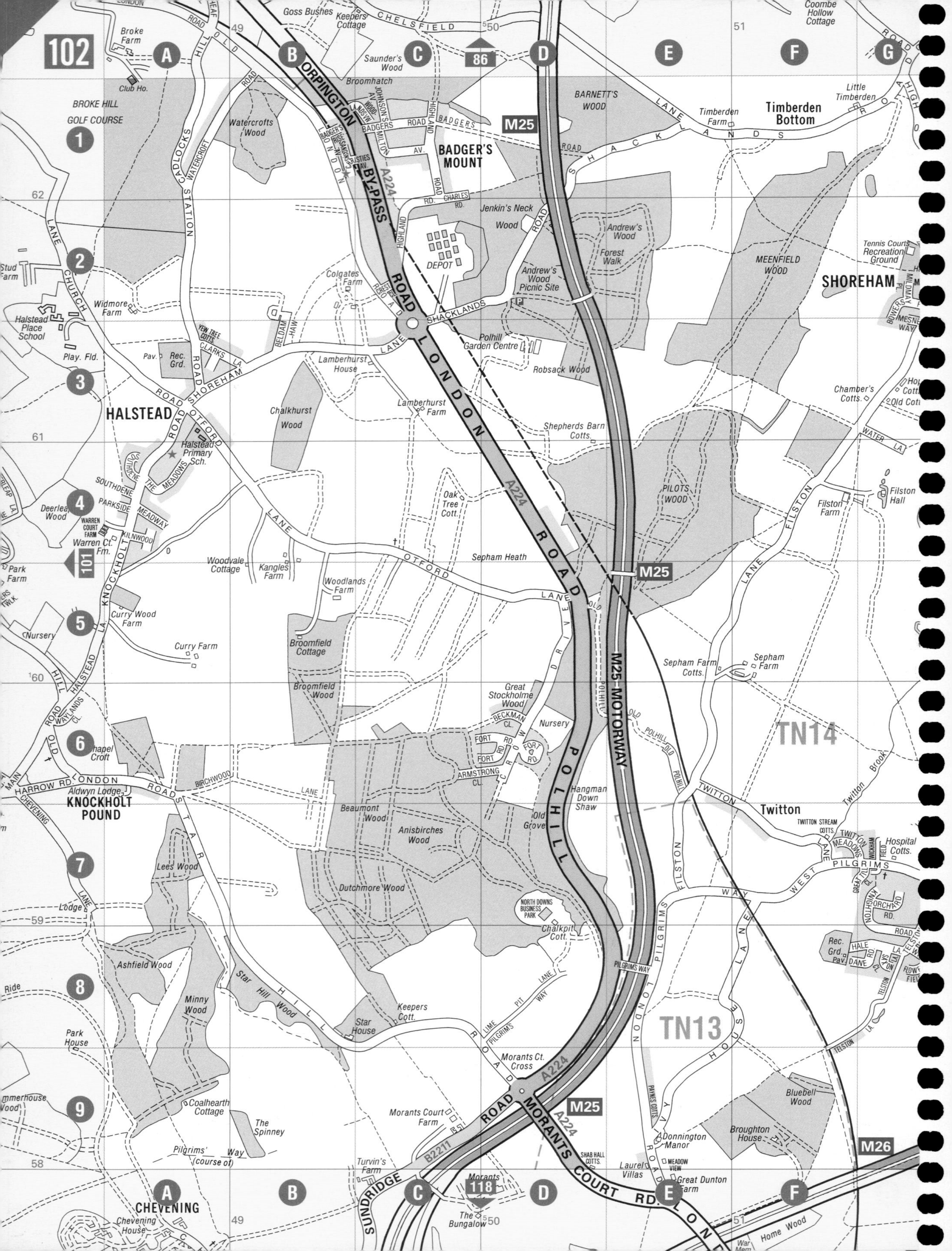

Broke Farm
Club Ho.
BROKE HILL
GOLF COURSE
Goss Bushes
Keepers Cottage
CHELSFIELD
Coombe Hollow Cottage
Saunder's Wood
86
Broomhatch
ORPINGTON BY-PASS
BADGERS ROAD
BADGER'S MOUNT
Watercrofts Wood
CADLOCKS
WATERCROFT
STATION
M25
BARNETT'S WOOD
SHACKLANDS
Timberden Farm
Timberden Bottom
Little Timberden
CHARLES RD.
HIGHLAND
Jenkin's Neck Wood
Andrew's Wood
Forest Walk
Andrew's Wood Picnic Site
DEPOT
Colgates Farm
MEENFIELD WOOD
Tennis Courts
Recreation Ground
SHOREHAM
Stud Farm
CHURCH LANE
Widmore Farm
Halstead Place School
Play. Fld.
YEW TREE COTTS.
CLARKS LA.
Pav.
Rec. Grd.
BELDAM HAW
SHACKLANDS
Polhill Garden Centre
Lamberhurst House
Robsack Wood
SHOREHAM ROAD
HALSTEAD
OTFORD ROAD
Chalkhurst Wood
Lamberhurst Farm
LONDON ROAD
Shepherds Barn Cotts.
Chamber's Cotts.
Old Cotts.
WATER LA.
Halstead Primary Sch.
THE MEADOWS
SOUTHDENE
PARKSIDE
MEADWAY
Deerleap Wood
Warren Court Farm
Warren Ct. Fm.
KILNWOOD
101
Oak Tree Cott.
A224
PILOTS WOOD
Filston Farm
Filston Hall
FILSTON LANE
Woodvale Cottage
Kangles Farm
OTFORD LANE
Sepham Heath
Woodlands Farm
Park Farm
Curry Wood Farm
Nursery
Curry Farm
Broomfield Cottage
Broomfield Wood
M25 MOTORWAY
Sepham Farm Cotts.
Sepham Farm
HALSTEAD LA.
KNOCKHOLT LA.
Great Stockholme Wood
BECKMAN CL.
Nursery
FORT RD.
ARMSTRONG CL.
CROW DRIVE
POLHILL
OLD POLHILL
TN14
Chapel Croft
HARROW RD.
LONDON ROAD
Aldwyn Lodge
KNOCKHOLT POUND
CHEVENING LANE
BIRCHWOOD
Beaumont Wood
Anisbirches Wood
Hangman Down Shaw
Old Grove
TWITTON
Twitton
Twitton Brook
TWITTON STREAM COTTS.
MEADOWS
Hospital Cotts.
PILGRIMS WAY WEST
Lees Wood
Dutchmore Wood
NORTH DOWNS BUSINESS PARK
Chalkpit Cott.
FILSTON
ORCHARD RD.
Lodge
Rec. Grd.
HALE RD.
DANE RD.
Ashfield Wood
Star Hill Wood
STAR HILL ROAD
PILGRIMS WAY
Ride
Minny Wood
Keepers Cott.
LIME PIT LANE
TN13
HOUSE LANE
Park House
Star House
Morants Ct. Cross
TELSTON LA.
Summerhouse
Coalhearth Cottage
The Spinney
Morants Court Farm
PAYNES COTTS.
Bluebell Wood
Broughton House
Donnington Manor
Pilgrims' Way (course of)
B2211
Turvin's Farm
MORANTS COURT RD.
SHAB HALL COTTS.
Laurel Villas
MEADOW VIEW
Great Dunton Farm
M26
SUNDRIDGE ROAD
118
The Bungalow
CHEVENING
Chevening House
Home Wood
War Mem.

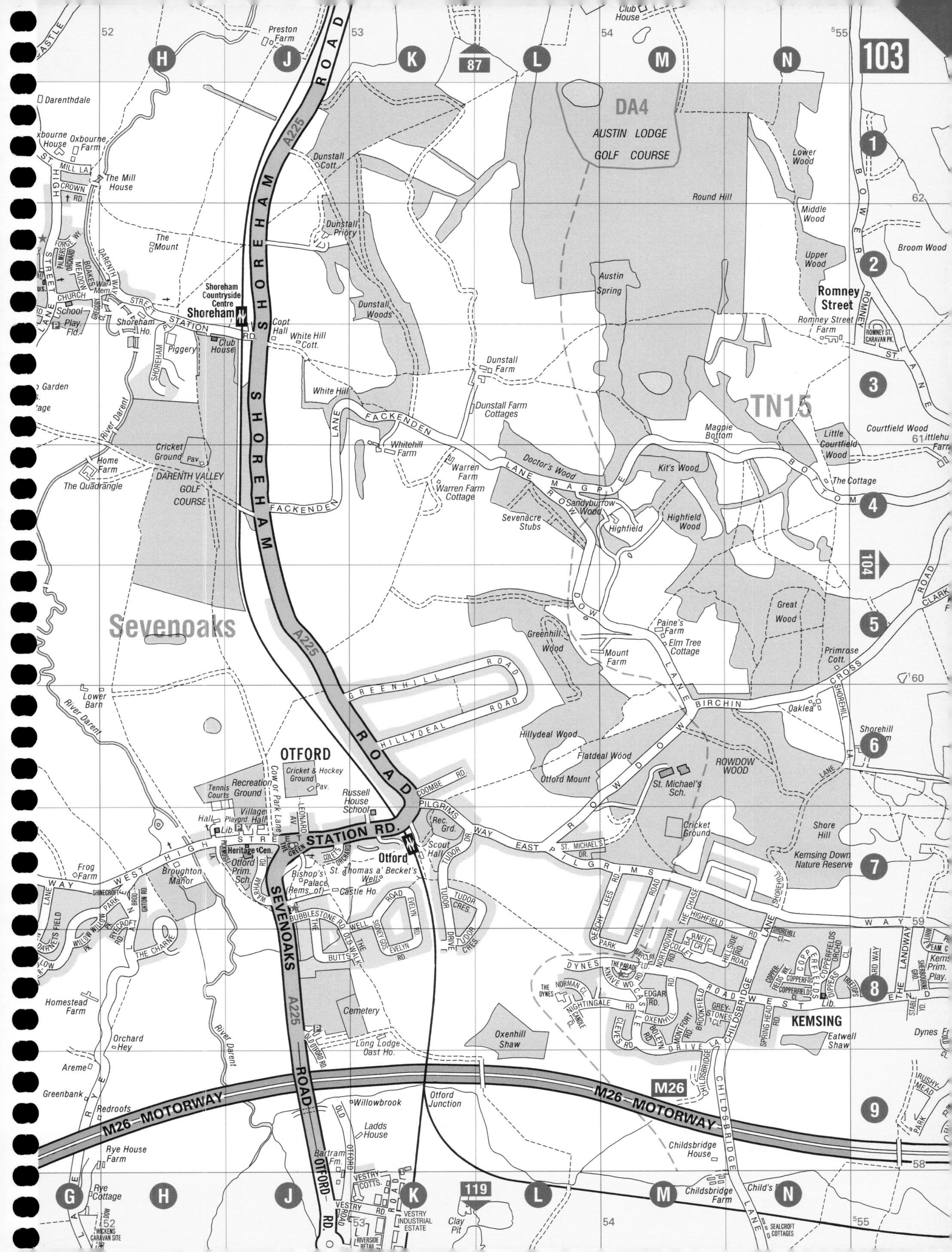
Preston Farm
Club House
DA4
AUSTIN LODGE GOLF COURSE
Darenthdale
Oxbourne Farm
The Mill House
Dunstall Cott.
Lower Wood
Round Hill
Middle Wood
Upper Wood
Broom Wood
Dunstall Priory
The Mount
Austin Spring
Romney Street
Romney Street Farm
ROMNEY ST. CARAVAN PK.
Shoreham Countryside Centre
Shoreham
Shoreham Ho.
Dunstall Woods
Copt Hall
White Hill Cott.
Piggery
Club House
Dunstall Farm
Dunstall Farm Cottages
White Hill
TN15
Magpie Bottom
Courtfield Wood
Little Courtfield Wood
River Darent
Cricket Ground
Pav.
Whitehill Farm
Warren Farm
Warren Farm Cottage
Doctor's Wood
Kit's Wood
The Cottage
Home Farm
The Quadrangle
DARENTH VALLEY GOLF COURSE
Sandyburrow Wood
Highfield
Highfield Wood
Sevenacre Stubs
SHOREHAM ROAD
A225
FACKENDEN LANE
MAGPIE BOTTOM
Sevenoaks
Great Wood
Greenhill Wood
Paine's Farm
Elm Tree Cottage
Mount Farm
Primrose Cott.
GREENHILL ROAD
HILLYDEAL ROAD
BIRCHIN CROSS
Oaklea
Lower Barn
Hillydeal Wood
Flatdeal Wood
Shorehill Farm
ROWDOW WOOD
OTFORD
Cricket & Hockey Ground
Recreation Ground
Tennis Courts
Otford Mount
St. Michael's Sch.
Russell House School
COOMBE RD.
PILGRIMS WAY EAST
Village Hall
Hall
Lib
Heritage Cen.
STATION RD.
Rec. Grd.
Scout Hall
Cricket Ground
Shore Hill
Otford
Frog Farm
Broughton Manor
Otford Prim. Sch.
Bishop's Palace (Rems. of)
St. Thomas a' Becket's Well
Castle Ho.
Kemsing Down Nature Reserve
HIGH STREET
WEST WAY
SEVENOAKS ROAD
PILGRIMS WAY
THE CHARNE
Homestead Farm
Cemetery
Oxenhill Shaw
KEMSING
Eatwell Shaw
Dynes
Orchard Hey
Long Lodge Oast Ho.
Areme
Greenbank
Redroofs
M26 MOTORWAY
M26
Otford Junction
Willowbrook
Ladds House
Childsbridge House
Childsbridge Farm
CHILDSBRIDGE LANE
Rye House Farm
Rye Cottage
Bartram Fm.
VESTRY COTTS.
VESTRY INDUSTRIAL ESTATE
Clay Pit
WICKENS CARAVAN SITE
SEALCROFT COTTAGES
OTFORD ROAD
87
104
119
G H J K L M N
1 2 3 4 5 6 7 8 9
52 53 54 55 58 59 60 61 62

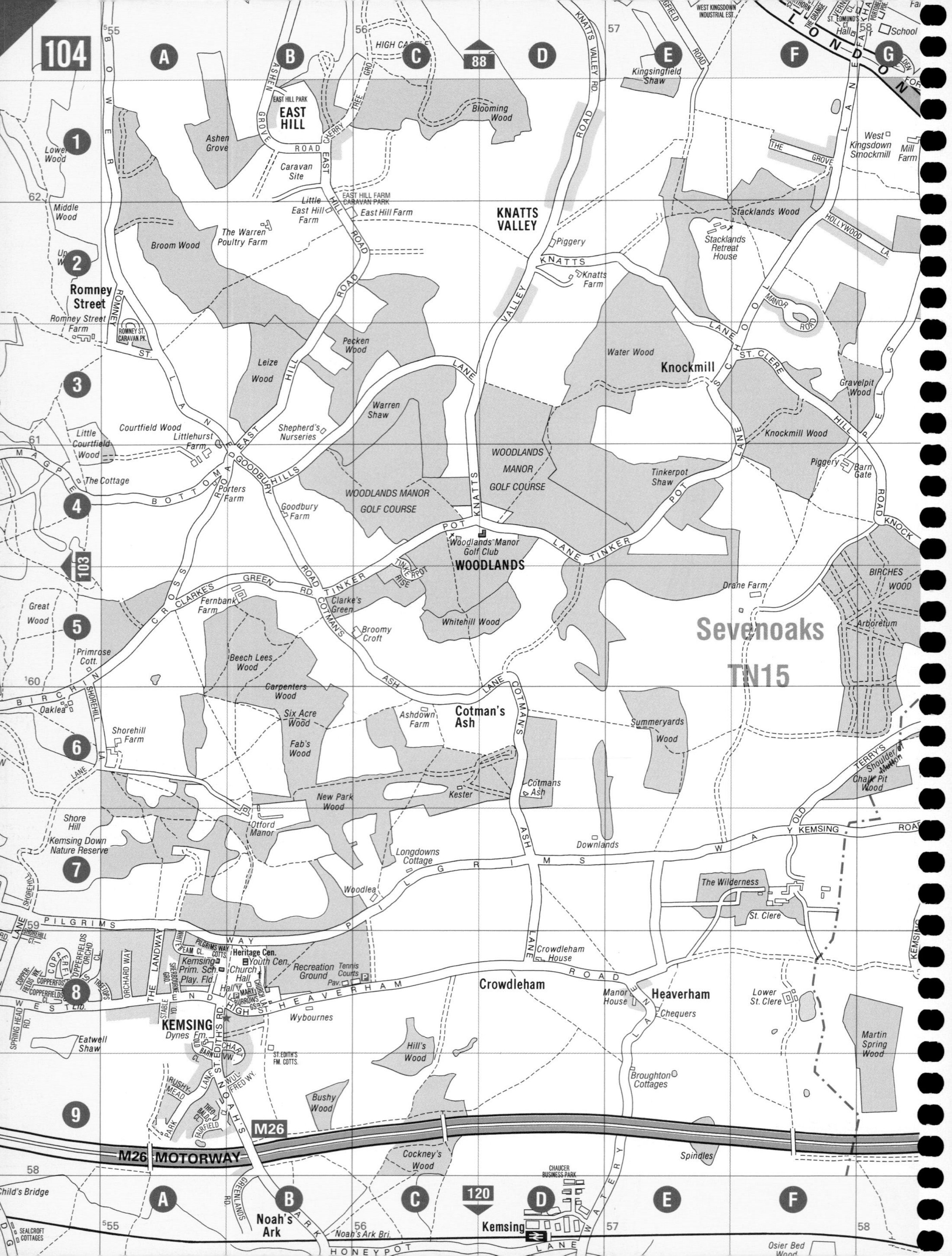
East Hill
Knatts Valley
Romney Street
Knockmill
Woodlands
Cotman's Ash
Sevenoaks
TN15
Crowdleham
Heaverham
Kemsing
Noah's Ark
M26 Motorway
Ashen Grove
Blooming Wood
Broom Wood
The Warren Poultry Farm
Caravan Site
Little East Hill Farm
East Hill Farm
Kingsingfield Shaw
West Kingsdown Smockmill
Mill Farm
Stacklands Wood
Stacklands Retreat House
Knatts Farm
Piggery
Water Wood
Pecken Wood
Leize Wood
Warren Shaw
Shepherd's Nurseries
Courtfield Wood
Littlehurst Farm
Little Courtfield Wood
The Cottage
Porters Farm
Goodbury Farm
Woodlands Manor Golf Course
Woodlands Manor Golf Club
Tinkerpot Shaw
Knockmill Wood
Gravelpit Wood
Barn Gate
Birches Wood
Arboretum
Drane Farm
Fernbank Farm
Clarke's Green
Broomy Croft
Whitehill Wood
Great Wood
Primrose Cott.
Beech Lees Wood
Carpenters Wood
Six Acre Wood
Fab's Wood
Ashdown Farm
Summeryards Wood
Oaklea
Shorehill Farm
New Park Wood
Kester
Cotmans Ash
Chalk Pit Wood
Shoulder of Mutton
Shore Hill
Kemsing Down Nature Reserve
Otford Manor
Longdowns Cottage
Downlands
Woodlea
The Wilderness
St. Clere
Heritage Cen.
Youth Cen.
Kemsing Prim. Sch.
Play. Fld.
Church Hall
Recreation Ground
Tennis Courts
Crowdleham House
Manor House
Chequers
Lower St. Clere
Wybournes
Eatwell Shaw
Dynes Fm.
St. Edith's Fm. Cotts.
Hill's Wood
Martin Spring Wood
Broughton Cottages
Bushy Wood
Cockney's Wood
Spindles
Child's Bridge
Sealcroft Cottages
Chaucer Business Park
Noah's Ark Bri.
Osier Bed Wood
Pilgrims Way
Knatts Valley Rd.
London Road
Honeypot Lane
Watery Lane
Heaverham Road
88
103
120

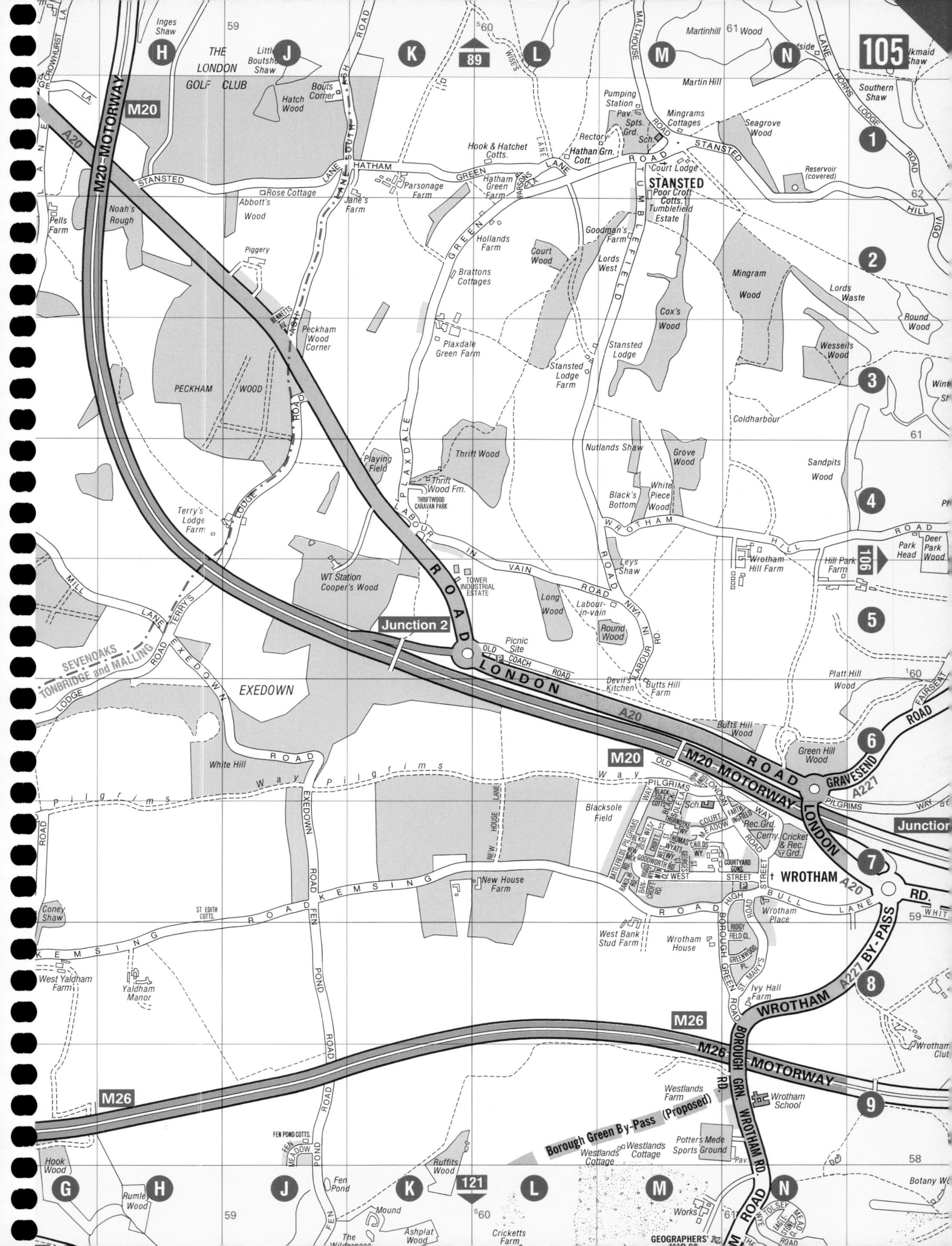

M20-MOTORWAY
M20
A20
THE LONDON GOLF CLUB
Inges Shaw
Hatch Wood
Bouts Corner
Little Boutshe Shaw
STANSTED
HATHAM GREEN LANE
Hook & Hatchet Cotts.
Rose Cottage
Parsonage Farm
Hatham Green Farm
Jane's Farm
Noah's Rough
Abbott's Wood
Pells Farm
Piggery
Peckham Wood Corner
PECKHAM WOOD
Martinhill Wood
Martin Hill
Pumping Station
Pav.
Spts. Grd.
Sch.
Rectory
Hathan Grn. Cott.
Mingrams Cottages
Seagrove Wood
Southern Shaw
Court Lodge
STANSTED
Poor Croft Cotts.
Tumblefield Estate
Reservoir (covered)
Hollands Farm
Brattons Cottages
Court Wood
Goodman's Farm
Lords West
Cox's Wood
Mingram Wood
Lords Waste
Round Wood
Wessels Wood
Plaxdale Green Farm
Stansted Lodge
Stansted Lodge Farm
Coldharbour
Thrift Wood
Thrift Wood Fm.
THRIFTWOOD CARAVAN PARK
Playing Field
Nutlands Shaw
Grove Wood
Black's Bottom
White Piece Wood
Sandpits Wood
Terry's Lodge Farm
WROTHAM HILL ROAD
Wrotham Hill Farm
Hill Park Farm
Park Head
Deer Park Wood
LABOUR IN VAIN ROAD
TOWER INDUSTRIAL ESTATE
WT Station Cooper's Wood
Long Wood
Leys Shaw
Labour-in-vain
Round Wood
Junction 2
Picnic Site
OLD COACH ROAD
LONDON ROAD
Devil's Kitchen
Butts Hill Farm
Platt Hill Wood
SEVENOAKS
TONBRIDGE and MALLING
EXEDOWN
EXEDOWN ROAD
White Hill ROAD
Butts Hill Wood
Green Hill Wood
GRAVESEND ROAD
A227
FAIRSEAT ROAD
Pilgrims Way
Blacksole Field
Sch.
Rec.Grd.
Cemy.
Cricket & Rec. Grd.
WROTHAM
New House Farm
NEW HOUSE LANE
KEMSING ROAD
ST. EDITH COTTS.
Coney Shaw
FEN POND ROAD
West Bank Stud Farm
Wrotham House
Wrotham Place
BULL LANE
HIGH STREET
BOROUGH GREEN ROAD
West Yaldham Farm
Yaldham Manor
Ivy Hall Farm
WROTHAM A227 BY-PASS
M26
M26-MOTORWAY
Westlands Farm
Wrotham School
Borough Green By-Pass (Proposed)
FEN POND COTTS.
FEN MEADOW
Buffits Wood
Westlands Cottage
Potters Mede Sports Ground
Hook Wood
Rumley Wood
Fen Pond
Mound
Ashplat Wood
Cricketts Farm
Works
Botany Wood
Wrotham Club
GEOGRAPHERS'
H J K L M N G
1 2 3 4 5 6 7 8 9
89 106 121
59 60 61 62 58

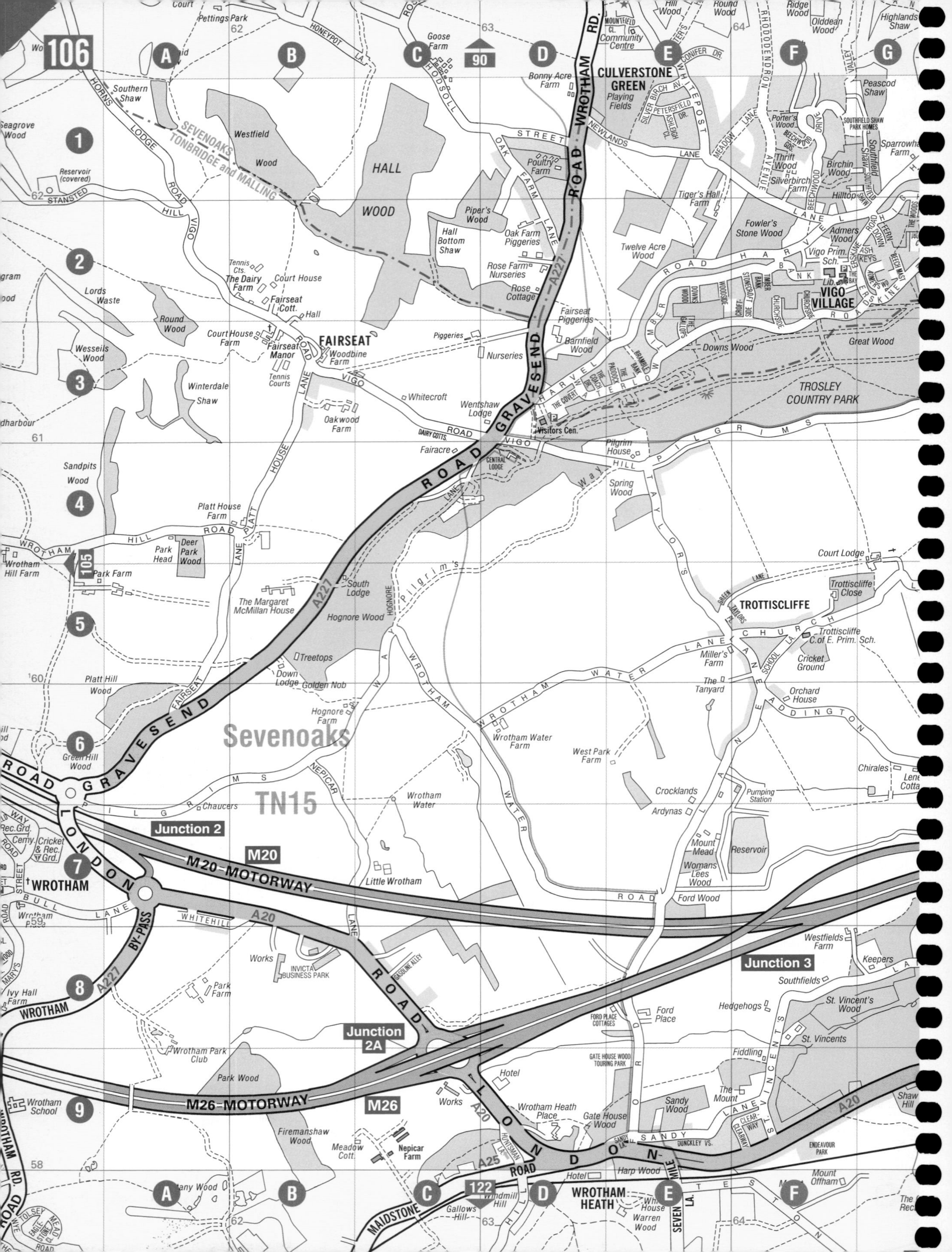
CULVERSTONE GREEN
FAIRSEAT
VIGO VILLAGE
TROSLEY COUNTRY PARK
TROTTISCLIFFE
WROTHAM
WROTHAM HEATH
Sevenoaks
TN15
HALL WOOD
Westfield Wood
Junction 2
Junction 2A
Junction 3
M20 MOTORWAY
M26 MOTORWAY
GRAVESEND ROAD
WROTHAM RD.
LONDON ROAD
Visitors Cen.
Vigo Prim. Sch.
Trottiscliffe C.of E. Prim. Sch.
INVICTA BUSINESS PARK
Wrotham School
Wrotham Park Club
Reservoir
Pumping Station
Little Wrotham
Wrotham Water Farm
Park Farm
Platt House Farm
The Margaret McMillan House
Hognore Wood
Court Lodge
Ford Place
Nepicar Farm

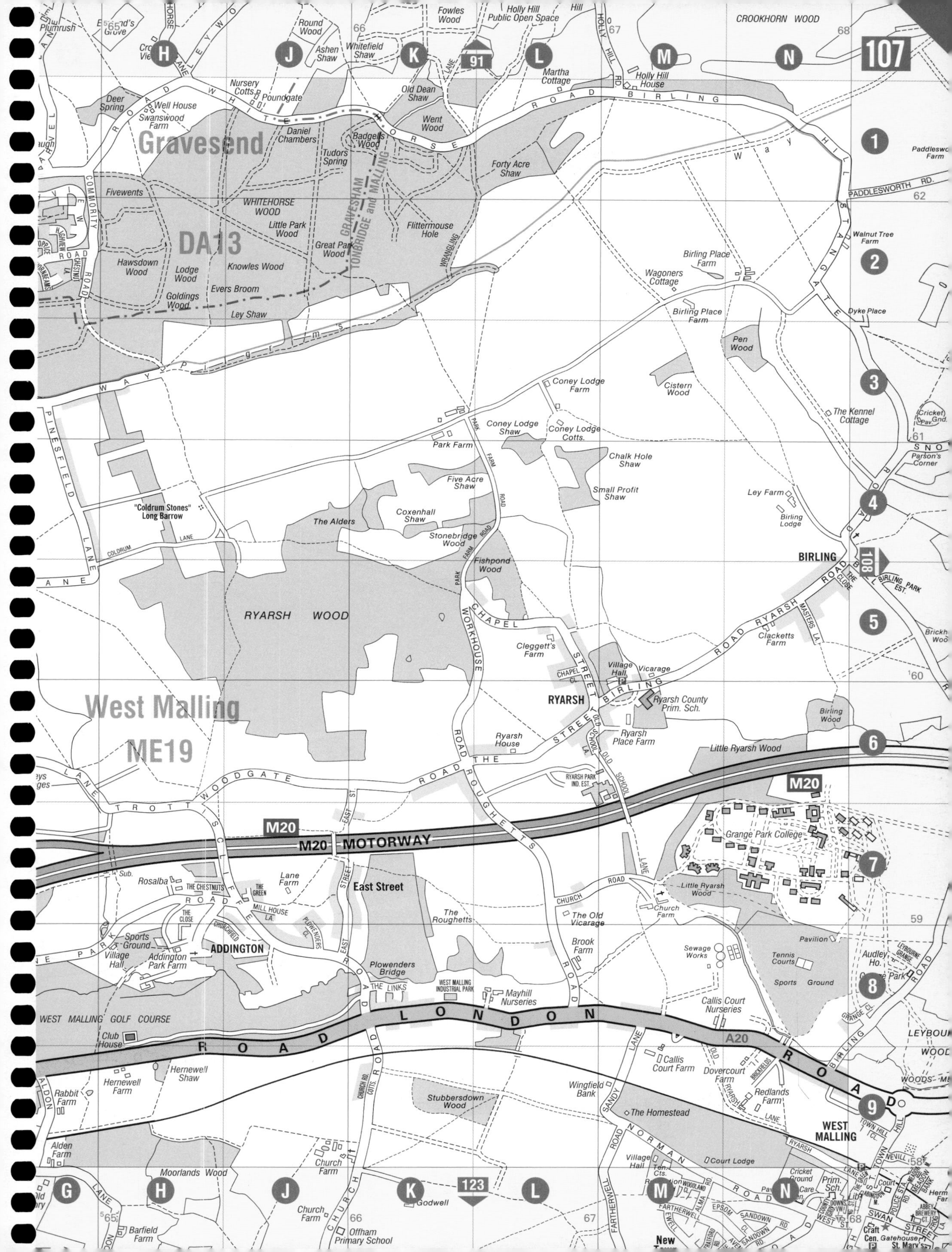

Gravesend
DA13
West Malling
ME19
Fowles Wood
Holly Hill Public Open Space
CROOKHORN WOOD
Round Wood
Ashen Shaw
Whitefield Shaw
91
Martha Cottage
Holly Hill House
Nursery Cotts.
Poundgate
Deer Spring
Well House
Swanswood Farm
Old Dean Shaw
Went Wood
Daniel Chambers
Badgells Wood
Tudors Spring
Forty Acre Shaw
PADDLESWORTH RD.
Paddlesworth Farm
Fivewents
WHITEHORSE WOOD
Little Park Wood
Flittermouse Hole
GRAVESHAM TONBRIDGE and MALLING
Great Park Wood
Walnut Tree Farm
Hawsdown Wood
Lodge Wood
Knowles Wood
Birling Place Farm
Wagoners Cottage
Evers Broom
Goldings Wood
Ley Shaw
Dyke Place
Pen Wood
Coney Lodge Farm
Cistern Wood
The Kennel Cottage
Cricket Gnd.
Pav.
Coney Lodge Shaw
Coney Lodge Cotts.
Park Farm
Chalk Hole Shaw
Parson's Corner
Five Acre Shaw
Small Profit Shaw
Ley Farm
Birling Lodge
"Coldrum Stones" Long Barrow
Coxenhall Shaw
The Alders
Stonebridge Wood
BIRLING
108
BIRLING PARK EST.
Fishpond Wood
RYARSH WOOD
Clacketts Farm
Brickh Woo
Cleggett's Farm
Village Hall
Vicarage
RYARSH
Ryarsh County Prim. Sch.
Birling Wood
Ryarsh House
Ryarsh Place Farm
Little Ryarsh Wood
RYARSH PARK IND. EST.
M20
M20 MOTORWAY
Grange Park College
Rosalba
THE CHESTNUTS
THE GREEN
Lane Farm
East Street
Little Ryarsh Wood
THE CLOSE
MILL HOUSE LA.
CHURCHFIELD
PLOWENDERS CL.
The Roughetts
The Old Vicarage
Church Farm
Sports Ground
ADDINGTON
Village Hall
Addington Park Farm
Brook Farm
Sewage Works
Pavilion
Tennis Courts
Audley Ho.
Sports Ground
Plowenders Bridge
THE LINKS
WEST MALLING INDUSTRIAL PARK
Mayhill Nurseries
Callis Court Nurseries
WEST MALLING GOLF COURSE
Club House
LONDON ROAD
A20
LEYBOURNE
Callis Court Farm
Dovercourt Farm
Redlands Farm
Hernewell Farm
Hernewell Shaw
Rabbit Farm
Stubbersdown Wood
Wingfield Bank
The Homestead
WEST MALLING
Alden Farm
Church Farm
Moorlands Wood
Village Hall
Court Lodge
Cricket Ground
Prim. Sch.
123
Godwell
Church Farm
Offham Primary School
Barfield Farm
New
Craft Cen.
Gatehouse
St. Mary's

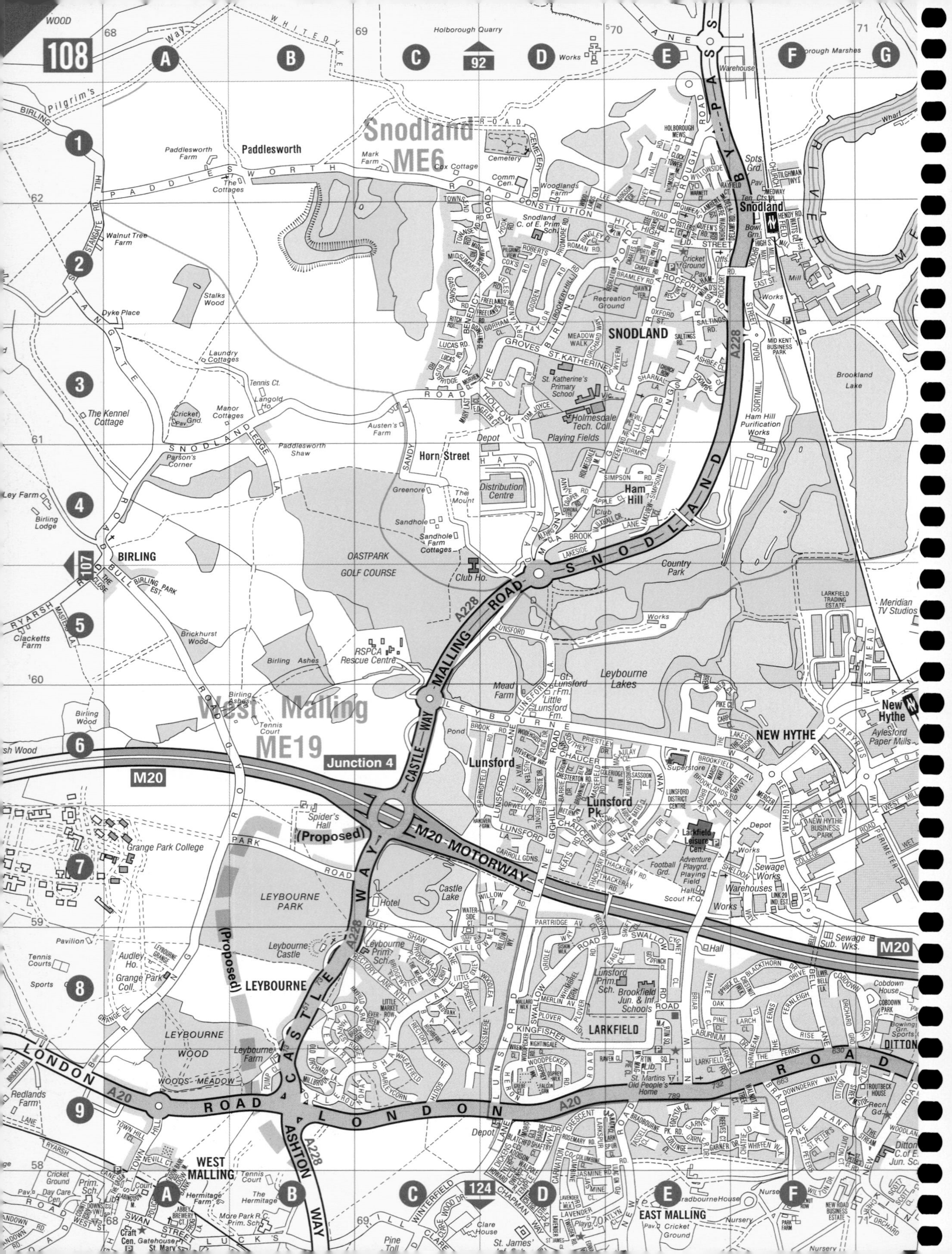
Holborough Quarry
92
Works
Warehouse
Snodland
ME6
Paddlesworth
Paddlesworth Farm
The Cottages
Mark Farm
Cox Cottage
Cemetery
Comm. Cen.
Woodlands Farm
Walnut Tree Farm
Stalks Wood
Dyke Place
Laundry Cottages
Tennis Ct.
Langold Ho.
Cricket Grnd.
Manor Cottages
The Kennel Cottage
Parson's Corner
Paddlesworth Shaw
Austen's Farm
Horn Street
Depot
Distribution Centre
Greenore
The Mount
Sandhole
Sandhole Farm Cottages
OASTPARK GOLF COURSE
Club Ho.
Ley Farm
Birling Lodge
BIRLING
107
Clacketts Farm
Brickhurst Wood
Birling Ashes
RSPCA Rescue Centre
Birling Wood
West Malling
ME19
Junction 4
M20
M20 MOTORWAY
Spider's Hall
(Proposed)
Grange Park College
LEYBOURNE PARK
Hotel
Castle Lake
Pavilion
Tennis Courts
Sports
Audley Ho.
Grange Park Coll.
Leybourne Castle
Leybourne Prim. Sch.
LEYBOURNE
LEYBOURNE WOOD
Leybourne Farm
WOODS MEADOW
Redlands Farm
A20
LONDON ROAD
A228
WEST MALLING
Cricket Ground
Prim. Sch.
Day Care Cen.
Tennis Court
The Hermitage
Hermitage Farm
More Park R.C. Prim. Sch.
Craft Cen.
124
Clare House
Pine Toll
St. James'
EAST MALLING
Nursery
SNODLAND
Recreation Ground
St. Katherine's Primary School
Holmesdale Tech. Coll.
Playing Fields
Ham Hill
Country Park
Leybourne Lakes
Mead Farm
Gt. Lunsford Fm.
Little Lunsford Fm.
Pond
Lunsford
Lunsford Pk.
Superstore
Lunsford District Centre
Larkfield Leisure Cen.
Adventure Playgrd.
Football Grd.
Playing Field
Scout H.Q.
NEW HYTHE
New Hythe
Aylesford Paper Mills
Sewage Works
Warehouses
Works
Depot
Sewage Sub. Wks.
Lunsford Prim. Sch.
Brookfield Jun. & Inf. Schools
LARKFIELD
St. Martins Old People's Home
Cobdown House
Cobdown Park
DITTON
Recn. Gd.
Ditton C. of E. Jun. Sc.
Snodland
Spts. Grd.
Pav.
Bowl. Grn.
Mill
MID KENT BUSINESS PARK
Ham Hill Purification Works
Brookland Lake
LARKFIELD TRADING ESTATE
Meridian TV Studios
RIVER MEDWAY
Wharf
NEW HYTHE BUSINESS PARK
Bradbourne House
Cricket Ground
NEW ROAD BUSINESS ESTATE
Junction 4
MALLING ROAD
SNODLAND BY-PASS
CASTLE WAY
ASHTON WAY

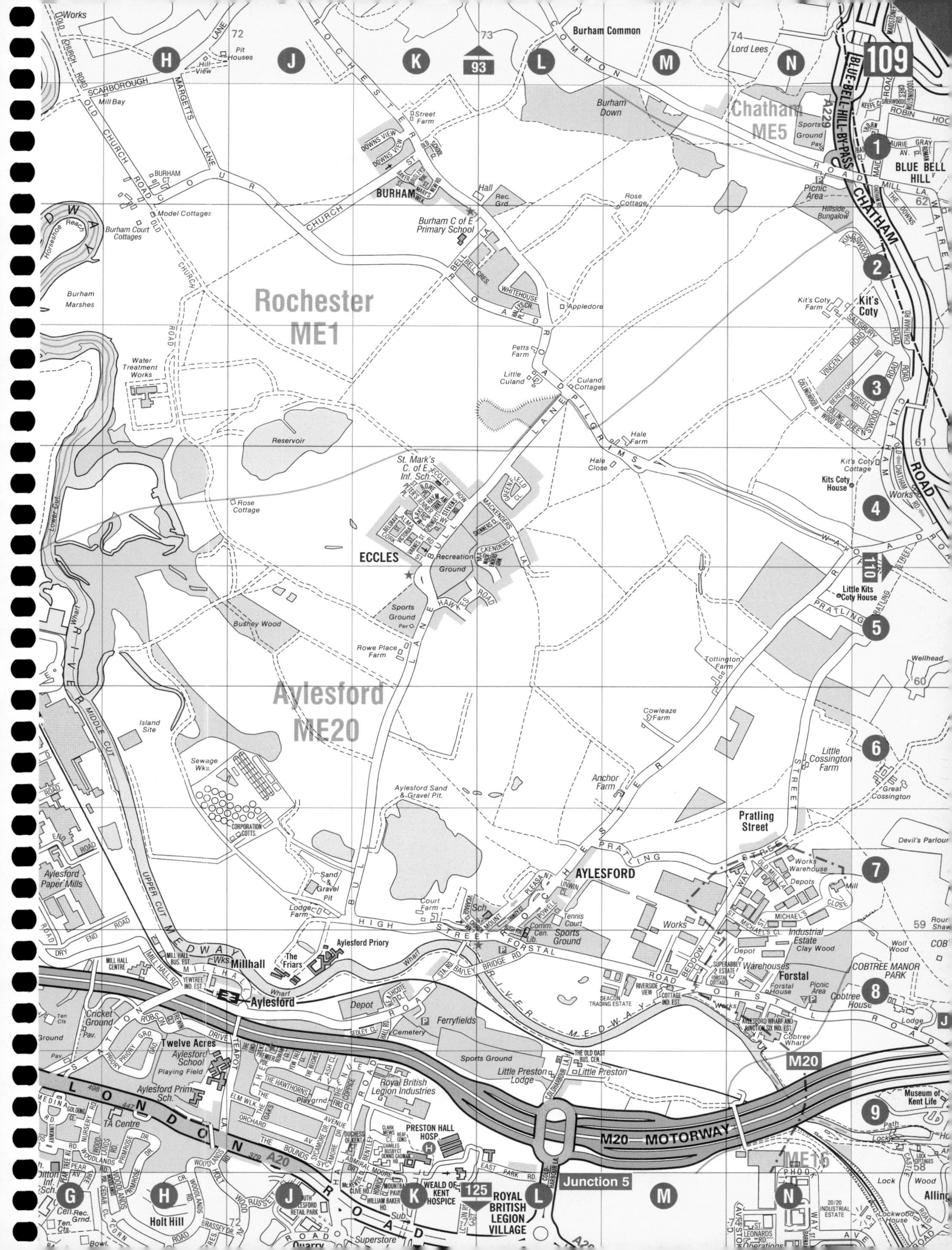

109
Burham Common
Lord Lees
Chatham ME5
Burham Down
BLUE BELL HILL
BURHAM
Burham C of E Primary School
Rochester ME1
Kit's Coty
Reservoir
St. Mark's C. of E. Inf. Sch.
ECCLES
Recreation Ground
Sports Ground
Bushey Wood
Rowe Place Farm
Aylesford ME20
Island Site
Sewage Wks.
Aylesford Sand & Gravel Pit.
Tottington Farm
Cowleaze Farm
Anchor Farm
Little Cossington Farm
Great Cossington
Pratling Street
AYLESFORD
Aylesford Paper Mills
Aylesford Priory
The Friars
Millhall
Forstal
COBTREE MANOR PARK
Cobtree House
Twelve Acres
Aylesford School
Aylesford Prim. Sch.
Royal British Legion Industries
PRESTON HALL HOSP.
WEALD OF KENT HOSPICE
ROYAL BRITISH LEGION VILLAGE
Junction 5
M20 MOTORWAY
M20
LONDON ROAD
A20
A229
Little Preston
Museum of Kent Life
Holt Hill
ME16
93
110
125

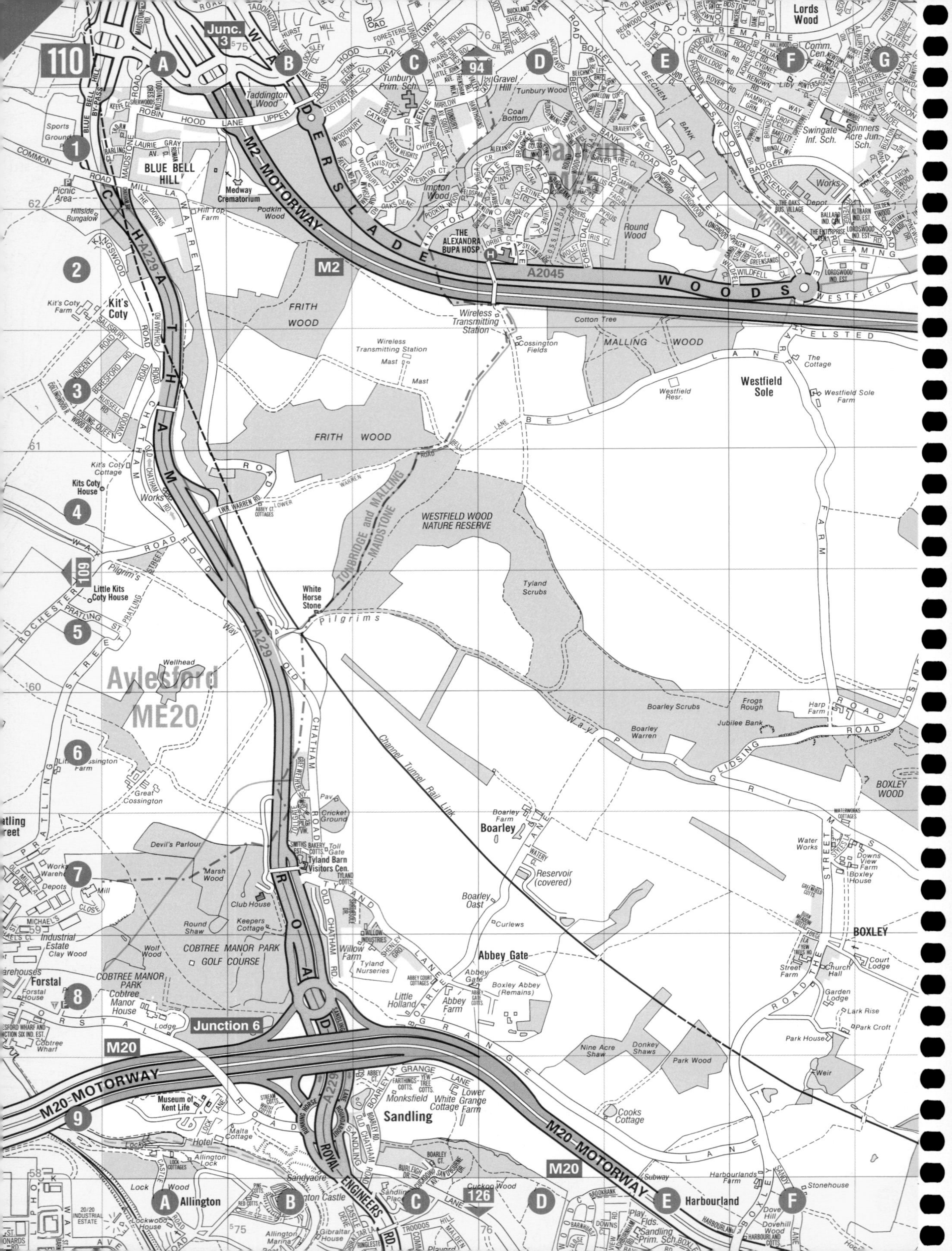
Junc. 3
Taddington Wood
Robin Hood Lane Upper
Sports Ground
Blue Bell Hill
Medway Crematorium
Common Road
Picnic Area
Hillside Bungalow
Hill Top Farm
Podkin Wood
M2 Motorway
Tunbury Prim. Sch.
Gravel Hill
Coal Bottom
Tunbury Wood
Chatham ME5
Impton Wood
The Alexandra Bupa Hosp.
Round Wood
Swingate Inf. Sch.
Spinners Acre Jun. Sch.
Lords Wood
Comm. Cen.
Works
Depot
The Oaks Bus. Village
Ballard Ind. Est.
Lordswood Ind. Est.
The Enterprise Cen.
Gleaming
Woods
Westfield
A2045
M2
Kit's Coty
Kit's Coty Farm
Frith Wood
Wireless Transmitting Station
Mast
Cossington Fields
Cotton Tree
Malling Wood
Hyelsted
Westfield Resr.
Westfield Sole
Westfield Sole Farm
The Cottage
Bell Lane
Chatham Road
Kit's Coty Cottage
Kits Coty House
Works
Lwr. Warren Rd.
Abbey Ct. Cottages
Westfield Wood Nature Reserve
Tonbridge and Malling
Maidstone
Pilgrim's Way
Little Kits Coty House
White Horse Stone
Tyland Scrubs
Aylesford ME20
Wellhead
Boarley Scrubs
Frogs Rough
Jubilee Bank
Harp Farm
Boarley Warren
Lidsing Road
Channel Tunnel Rail Link
Little Cossington Farm
Great Cossington
Boxley Wood
Pav.
Cricket Ground
Toll Gate
Tyland Barn Visitors Cen.
Boarley Farm
Boarley
Water Works
Downs View Farm
Boxley House
Devil's Parlour
Marsh Wood
Mill
Works
Depots
Reservoir (covered)
Boarley Oast
Curlews
Industrial Estate
Clay Wood
Club House
Round Shaw
Keepers Cottage
Wolf Wood
Cobtree Manor Park Golf Course
Willow Industries
Willow Farm
Tyland Nurseries
Abbey Gate
Boxley Abbey (Remains)
Abbey Farm
Little Holland
BOXLEY
Court Lodge
Church Hall
Street Farm
Garden Lodge
Lark Rise
Park Croft
Park House
Forstal
Forstal House
Cobtree Manor Park
Cobtree Manor House
Lodge
Junction 6
Cobtree Wharf
M20
M20 Motorway
Museum of Kent Life
Nine Acre Shaw
Donkey Shaws
Park Wood
Weir
Monksfield
White Cottage
White Grange Farm
Lower Grange Farm
Sandling
Cooks Cottage
Hotel
Malta Cottage
Allington Lock
Lock
Royal Engineers Rd.
Sandyacre
Subway
Harbourlands Farm
Stonehouse
Lock Wood
Allington
Cuckoo Wood
126
Harbourland
20/20 Industrial Estate
Lockwood House
Allington Marina
Gibraltar House
Play. Flds.
Sandling Prim. Sch.
Dove Hill
Dovehill Wood
109
94

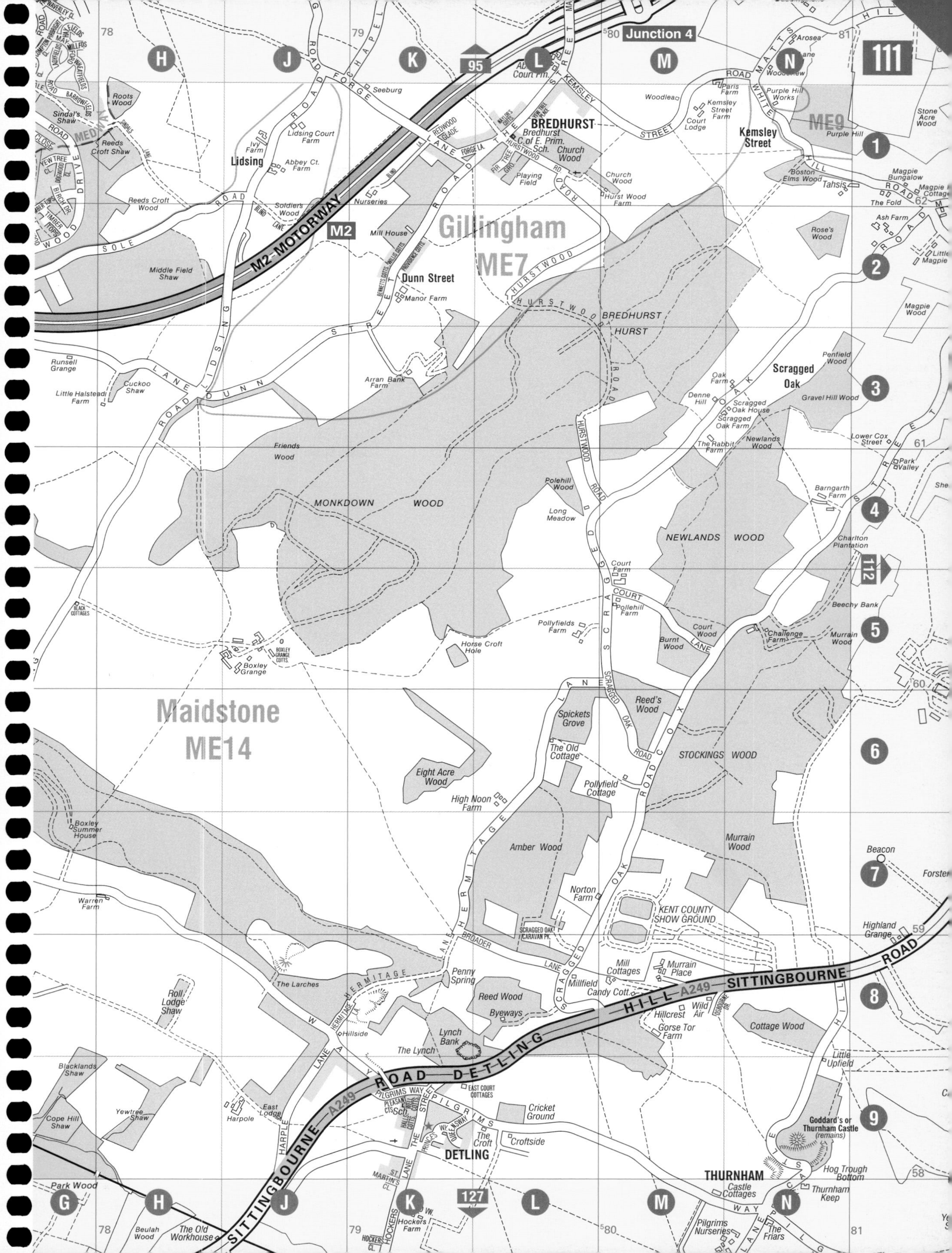

Junction 4
95
M2 MOTORWAY
M2
Gillingham
ME7
ME9
Maidstone
ME14
Lidsing
Bredhurst
Dunn Street
Kemsley Street
Scragged Oak
Detling
Thurnham
Roots Wood
Sindal's Shaw
Reeds Croft Shaw
Reeds Croft Wood
Middle Field Shaw
Lidsing Court Farm
Abbey Ct. Farm
Ivy Farm
Soldiers Wood
Nurseries
Mill House
Manor Farm
Seeburg
Church Wood
Playing Field
Church Wood
Hurst Wood Farm
Bredhurst C. of E. Prim. Sch.
Woodlea
Paris Farm
Kemsley Street Farm
Court Lodge
Purple Hill Works
Purple Hill
Arosea
Stone Acre Wood
Boston Elms Wood
Tahsis
Magpie Bungalow
The Fold
Ash Farm
Rose's Wood
Magpie Wood
Bredhurst Hurst
Runsell Grange
Little Halstead Farm
Cuckoo Shaw
Arran Bank Farm
Friends Wood
Monkdown Wood
Oak Farm
Denne Hill
Scragged Oak House
Scragged Oak Farm
The Rabbit Farm
Newlands Wood
Penfield Wood
Gravel Hill Wood
Lower Cox Street
Park Valley
Polehill Wood
Long Meadow
Barngarth Farm
Charlton Plantation
112
Court Farm
Pollyfields Farm
Pollehill Farm
Burnt Wood
Court Wood
Challenge Farm
Beechy Bank
Murrain Wood
Black Cottages
Boxley Grange
Boxley Grange Cotts.
Horse Croft Hole
Reed's Wood
Spickets Grove
The Old Cottage
Stockings Wood
Pollyfield Cottage
Eight Acre Wood
High Noon Farm
Amber Wood
Murrain Wood
Beacon
Boxley Summer House
Norton Farm
Kent County Show Ground
Scragged Oak Caravan Pk.
Highland Grange
Warren Farm
Roll Lodge Shaw
The Larches
Penny Spring
Reed Wood
Byeways
Mill Cottages
Murrain Place
Millfield
Candy Cott.
Hillcrest
Wild Air
Gorse Tor Farm
Cottage Wood
Hillside
Lynch Bank
The Lynch
Little Upfield
Sittingbourne Road
A249
Detling Hill
Blacklands Shaw
Cope Hill Shaw
Yewtree Shaw
East Lodge
Harpole
East Court Cottages
Cricket Ground
The Croft
Croftside
Goddard's or Thurnham Castle (remains)
Hog Trough Bottom
Thurnham Keep
Castle Cottages
Pilgrims Way
Pilgrims Nurseries
The Friars
Park Wood
Beulah Wood
The Old Workhouse
Hockers Farm
127
78
79
80
81
62
61
60
59
58

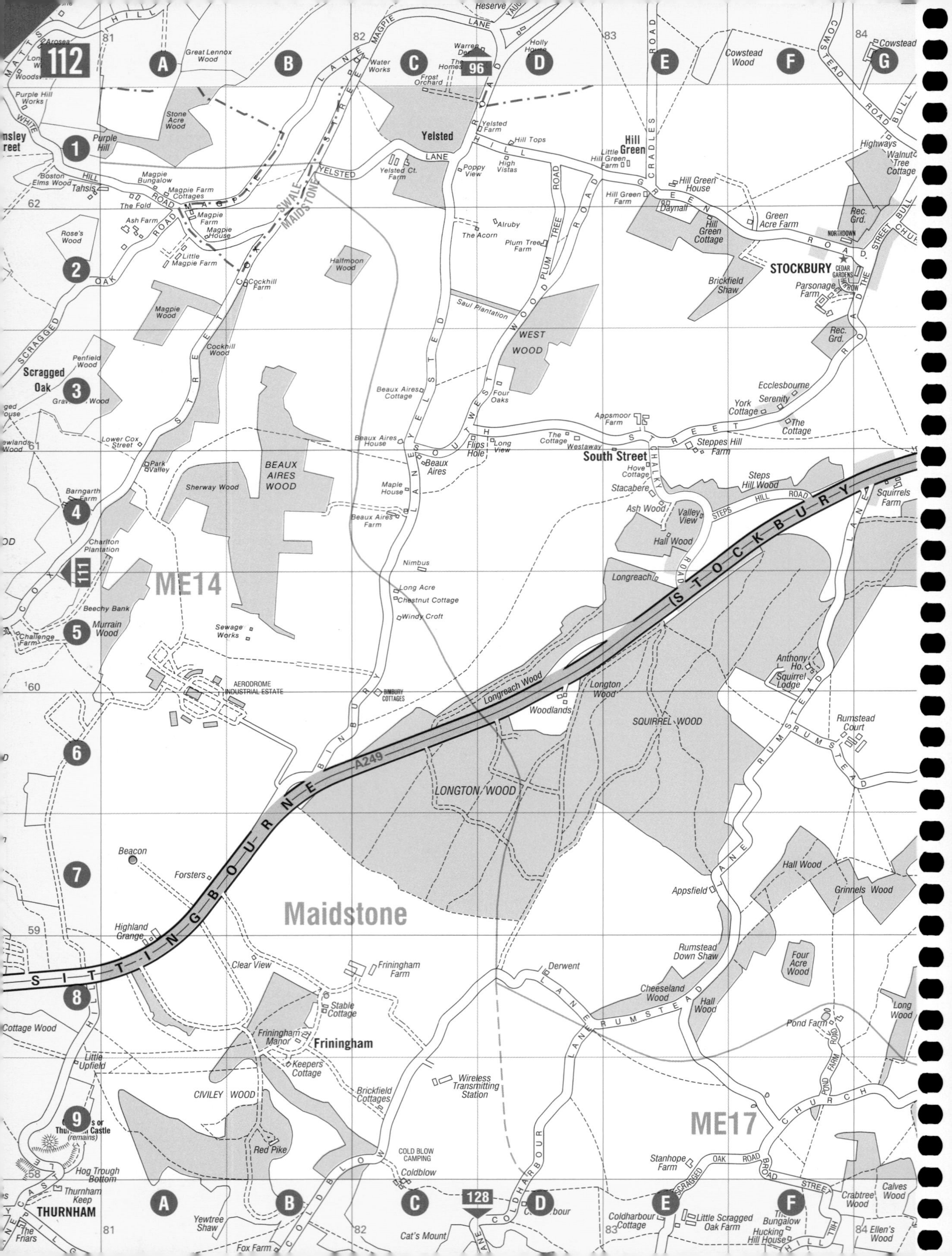

Great Lennox Wood
Water Works
Warren
96
Holly House
Cowstead Wood
Cowstead
Stone Acre Wood
Purple Hill
Purple Hill Works
Frost Orchard
Yelsted
Yelsted Farm
Hill Tops
Hill Green
Little Hill Green Farm
Highways
Walnut Tree Cottage
Boston Elms Wood
Tahsis
Magpie Bungalow
Magpie Farm Cottages
Yelsted Ct. Farm
Poppy View
High Vistas
Hill Green House
Hill Green Farm
Daynall
The Fold
Ash Farm
Magpie Farm
Magpie House
Little Magpie Farm
Rose's Wood
Alruby
The Acorn
Plum Tree Farm
Hill Green Cottage
Green Acre Farm
Rec. Grd.
NORTHDOWN
STOCKBURY
CEDAR GARDENS
Halfmoon Wood
Cockhill Farm
Brickfield Shaw
Parsonage Farm
Magpie Wood
Saul Plantation
WEST WOOD
Cockhill Wood
Penfield Wood
Scragged Oak
Beaux Aires Cottage
Four Oaks
Ecclesbourne
Serenity
York Cottage
Appsmoor Farm
The Cottage
Lower Cox Street
Beaux Aires House
Flips Hole
Long View
Westaway
South Street
Steppes Hill Farm
Park Valley
BEAUX AIRES WOOD
Sherway Wood
Beaux Aires
Maple House
Hove Cottage
Stacabere
Steps Hill Wood
Squirrels Farm
Barngarth Farm
Ash Wood
Valley View
Beaux Aires Farm
Charlton Plantation
Hall Wood
Nimbus
111
ME14
Longreach
Long Acre
Chestnut Cottage
Windy Croft
Beechy Bank
Murrain Wood
Challenge Farm
Sewage Works
Anthony Ho.
Squirrel Lodge
AERODROME INDUSTRIAL ESTATE
BIMBURY COTTAGES
Longreach Wood
Longton Wood
Woodlands
SQUIRREL WOOD
Rumstead Court
A249
LONGTON WOOD
Beacon
Forsters
Hall Wood
Grinnels Wood
Appsfield
Maidstone
Highland Grange
Rumstead Down Shaw
Four Acre Wood
Clear View
Friningham Farm
Derwent
Cheeseland Wood
Hall Wood
Long Wood
Stable Cottage
Pond Farm
Cottage Wood
Friningham Manor
Friningham
Little Upfield
Keepers Cottage
Wireless Transmitting Station
Brickfield Cottages
CIVILEY WOOD
ME17
Red Pike
COLD BLOW CAMPING
Coldblow
Stanhope Farm
Hog Trough Bottom
Thurnham Keep
THURNHAM
128
Calves Wood
Crabtree Wood
Little Scragged Oak Farm
Coldharbour Cottage
Yewtree Shaw
The Friars
Cat's Mount
The Bungalow
Hucking Hill House
Ellen's Wood
Fox Farm
STOCKBURY
SITTINGBOURNE
MAGPIE LANE
YELSTED LANE
YELSTED ROAD
HILL GREEN ROAD
CRADLES ROAD
PLUM TREE ROAD
WOOD STREET
SOUTH STREET
CHALKY ROAD
STEPS HILL ROAD
RUMSTEAD LANE
CHURCH ROAD
POND FARM ROAD
OAK ROAD
SCRAGGED OAK ROAD
BROAD STREET
COLDHARBOUR LANE
COLDBLOW
BIMBURY LANE
COX STREET
DETLING HILL

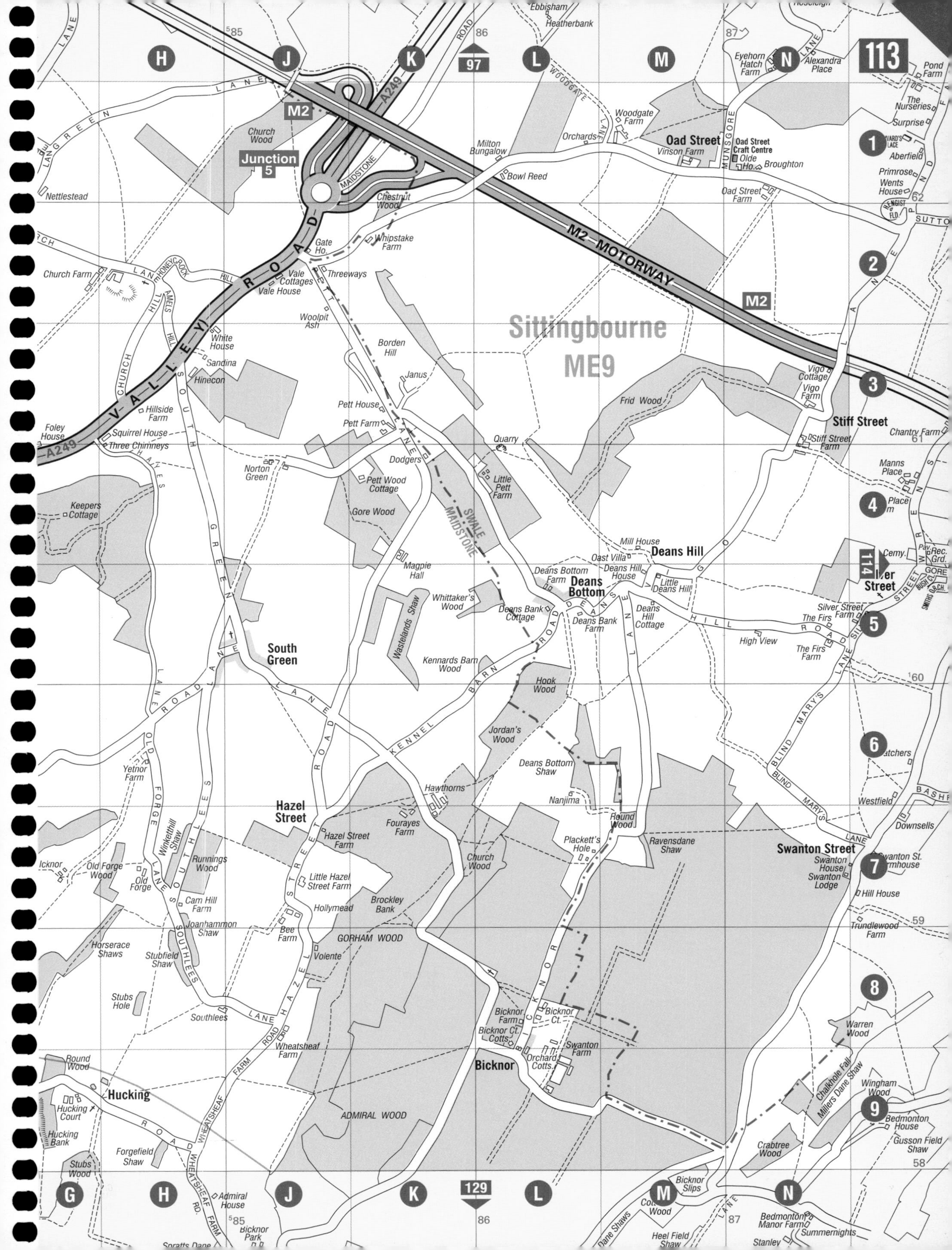
Sittingbourne
ME9
M2 MOTORWAY
M2
Junction 5
A249
VALLEY ROAD
Oad Street
Deans Hill
Deans Bottom
Stiff Street
South Green
Hazel Street
Swanton Street
Bicknor
Hucking
Church Wood
Chestnut Wood
Whipstake Farm
Gate Ho.
Threeways
Vale Cottages
Vale House
Woolpit Ash
Borden Hill
Janus
Pett House
Pett Farm
Dodgers
Pett Wood Cottage
Gore Wood
Little Pett Farm
Quarry
Frid Wood
Vigo Cottage
Vigo Farm
Stiff Street Farm
Chantry Farm
Manns Place
Mill House
Oast Villa
Deans Hill House
Little Deans Hill
Deans Bottom Farm
Deans Bank Cottage
Deans Bank Farm
Deans Hill Cottage
Silver Street Farm
The Firs
The Firs Farm
High View
Magpie Hall
Whittaker's Wood
Wastelands Shaw
Kennards Barn Wood
Hook Wood
Jordan's Wood
Deans Bottom Shaw
Nanjima
Round Wood
Plackett's Hole
Ravensdane Shaw
Hawthorns
Fourayes Farm
Hazel Street Farm
Little Hazel Street Farm
Church Wood
Brockley Bank
Hollymead
Bee Farm
GORHAM WOOD
Volente
Bicknor Farm
Bicknor Ct. Cotts.
Bicknor Ct.
Swanton Farm
Orchard Cotts.
ADMIRAL WOOD
Crabtree Wood
Bicknor Slips
Warren Wood
Chalkhole Fall
Millers Dane Shaw
Wingham Wood
Bedmonton House
Gusson Field Shaw
Bedmonton Manor Farm
Summernights
Stanley
Heel Field Shaw
Dane Shaws
Swanton St. Farmhouse
Swanton House
Swanton Lodge
Hill House
Trundlewood Farm
Downsells
Westfield
Hatchers
Milton Bungalow
Bowl Reed
Orchards
Woodgate Farm
Vinson Farm
Oad Street Craft Centre
Olde Ho.
Broughton
Oad Street Farm
Eyehorn Hatch Farm
Alexandra Place
Ebbisham
Heatherbank
Pond Farm
The Nurseries
Surprise
Aberfield
Primrose
Wents House
Nettlestead
Church Farm
White House
Sandina
Hinecon
Hillside Farm
Foley House
Squirrel House
Three Chimneys
Norton Green
Keepers Cottage
Yetnor Farm
Winketthill Shaw
Runnings Wood
Old Forge Wood
Old Forge
Cam Hill Farm
Joanhammon Shaw
Horserace Shaws
Stubfield Shaw
Stubs Hole
Southlees
Wheatsheaf Farm
Round Wood
Hucking Court
Hucking Bank
Forgefield Shaw
Stubs Wood
Admiral House
Bicknor Park
Sprats Dane
LANGREEN LANE
CHURCH HILL
HONEYCROCK HILL
AMELS HILL
SOUTH GREEN
HAYES LANE
PETT LANE
ROAD LANE
KENNEL BARN ROAD
DEANS HILL ROAD
VIGO LANE
SILVER STREET
BLIND MARY'S LANE
BICKNOR ROAD
HAZEL STREET ROAD
OLD FORGE LANE
SOUTHLEES LANE
WHEATSHEAF FARM RD.
HUCKING ROAD
WOODGATE LANE
MUNSGORE LANE
SWALE
MAIDSTONE
Cemy.
Rec. Grd.
97
114
129
585
86
87
62
61
160
59
58
H J K L M N G
1 2 3 4 5 6 7 8 9

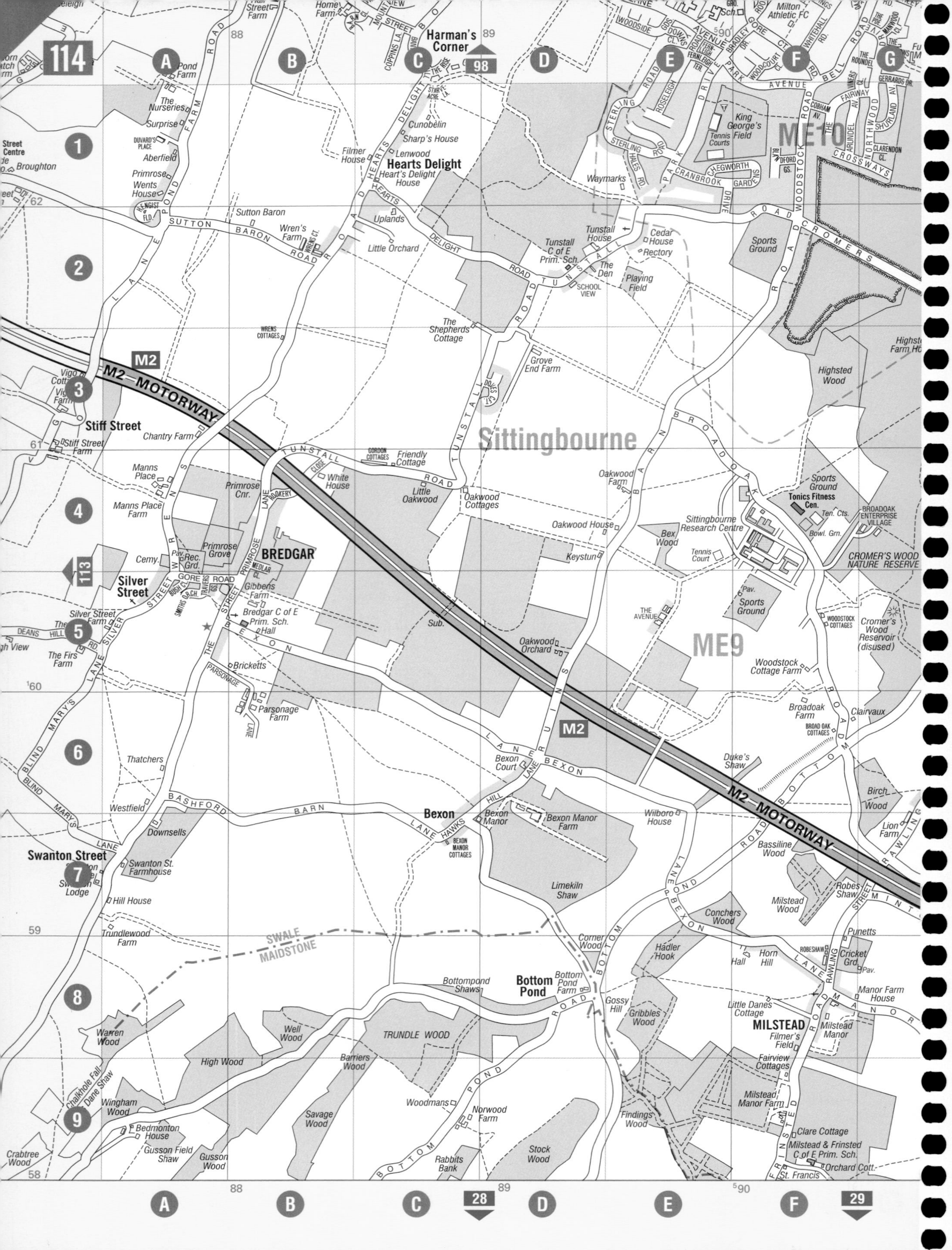
Harman's Corner
98
Hearts Delight
Sittingbourne
BREDGAR
Silver Street
Stiff Street
Swanton Street
Bexon
Bottom Pond
MILSTEAD
ME10
ME9
M2 MOTORWAY
Tunstall C of E Prim. Sch.
King George's Field
Sittingbourne Research Centre
Tonics Fitness Cen.
CROMER'S WOOD NATURE RESERVE
Highsted Wood
Cromer's Wood Reservoir (disused)
Bredgar C of E Prim. Sch.
TRUNDLE WOOD
High Wood
Savage Wood
Stock Wood
Findings Wood
Limekiln Shaw
Milstead & Frinsted C of E Prim. Sch.
SWALE
MAIDSTONE
113
28
29

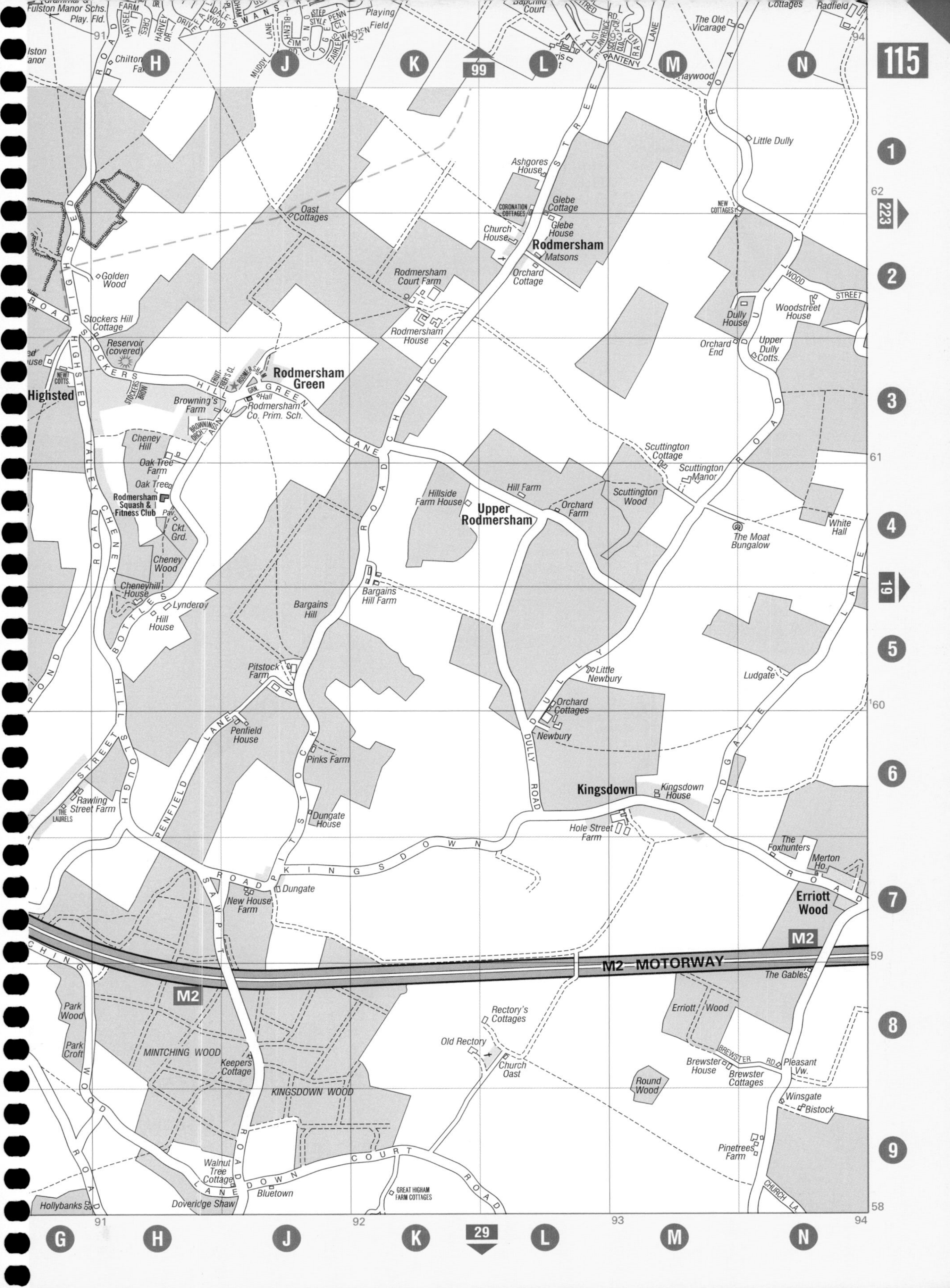
Rodmersham
Rodmersham Green
Upper Rodmersham
Highsted
Kingsdown
Erriott Wood
M2 MOTORWAY
M2
99
223
19
29
Little Dully
Ashgores House
Glebe Cottage
Glebe House
Coronation Cottages
Church House
Matsons
Orchard Cottage
Oast Cottages
Rodmersham Court Farm
Rodmersham House
Golden Wood
Stockers Hill Cottage
Reservoir (covered)
Browning's Farm
Rodmersham Co. Prim. Sch.
Cheney Hill
Oak Tree Farm
Oak Tree
Rodmersham Squash & Fitness Club
Ckt. Grd.
Cheney Wood
Cheneyhill House
Lyndery
Hill House
Bargains Hill
Bargains Hill Farm
Hillside Farm House
Hill Farm
Orchard Farm
Scuttington Wood
Scuttington Cottage
Scuttington Manor
The Moat Bungalow
White Hall
Dully House
Woodstreet House
Orchard End
Upper Dully Cotts.
Pitstock Farm
Penfield House
Pinks Farm
Dungate House
Rawling Street Farm
The Laurels
Little Newbury
Orchard Cottages
Newbury
Kingsdown House
Hole Street Farm
Ludgate
The Foxhunters
Merton Ho.
Dungate
New House Farm
The Gables
Erriott Wood
Rectory's Cottages
Old Rectory
Church Oast
Park Wood
Park Croft
MINTCHING WOOD
Keepers Cottage
KINGSDOWN WOOD
Brewster House
Brewster Cottages
Pleasant Vw.
Round Wood
Winsgate
Bistock
Pinetrees Farm
Walnut Tree Cottage
Bluetown
Doveridge Shaw
Hollybanks
Great Higham Farm Cottages
The Old Vicarage
Radfield
Haywood
Playing Field
Fulston Manor Schs. Play. Fld.
Chilton Fm
Bapchild Court
New Cottages
HIGHSTED ROAD
HIGHSTED VALLEY
CHENEY ROAD
STOCKERS HILL
RODMERSHAM GREEN
HILL LANE
CHURCH STREET
CHURCH ROAD
DULLY ROAD
DULLY LANE
WOOD STREET
LUDGATE LANE
KINGSDOWN ROAD
PITSTOCK ROAD
PENFIELD LANE
SLOUGH HILL
BOTTLES LANE
POND ROAD
RAWLING STREET
SAWPIT ROAD
COURT ROAD
DOWN COURT
LANE END
BREWSTER RD
CHURCH LA
PANTENY LANE
91
92
93
94
58
59
60
61
62
G
H
J
K
L
M
N
1
2
3
4
5
6
7
8
9

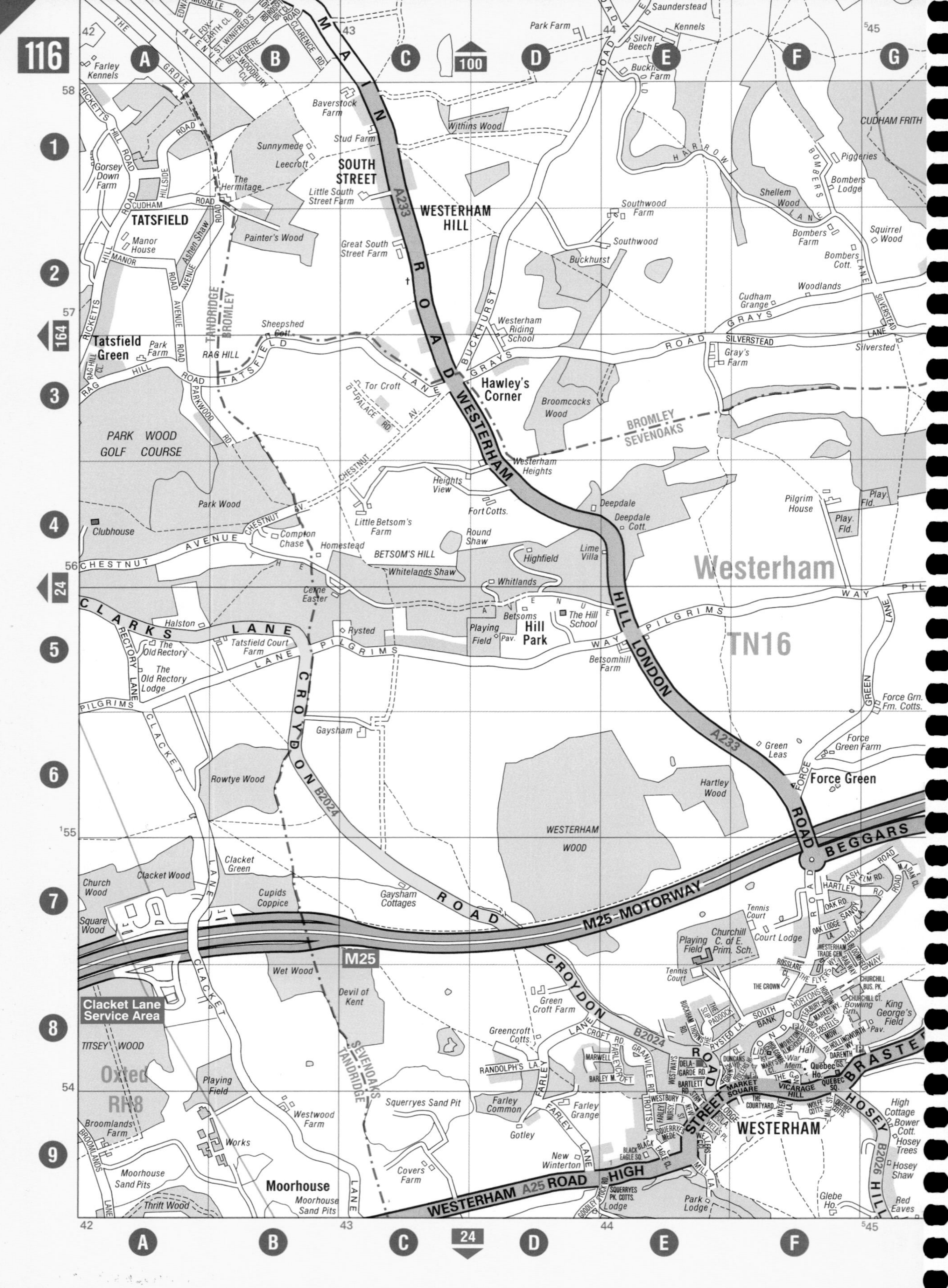
TATSFIELD
Tatsfield Green
SOUTH STREET
WESTERHAM HILL
Hawley's Corner
Westerham
TN16
Hill Park
Force Green
WESTERHAM
Oxted
RH8
Moorhouse
Clacket Lane Service Area
MAIN ROAD
WESTERHAM HILL
LONDON ROAD
M25-MOTORWAY
CROYDON ROAD
CLARKS LANE
PILGRIMS WAY
WESTERHAM ROAD
BEGGARS
CHESTNUT AVENUE
PARK WOOD GOLF COURSE
WESTERHAM WOOD
BROMLEY
SEVENOAKS
TANDRIDGE
CUDHAM FRITH
100
164
24

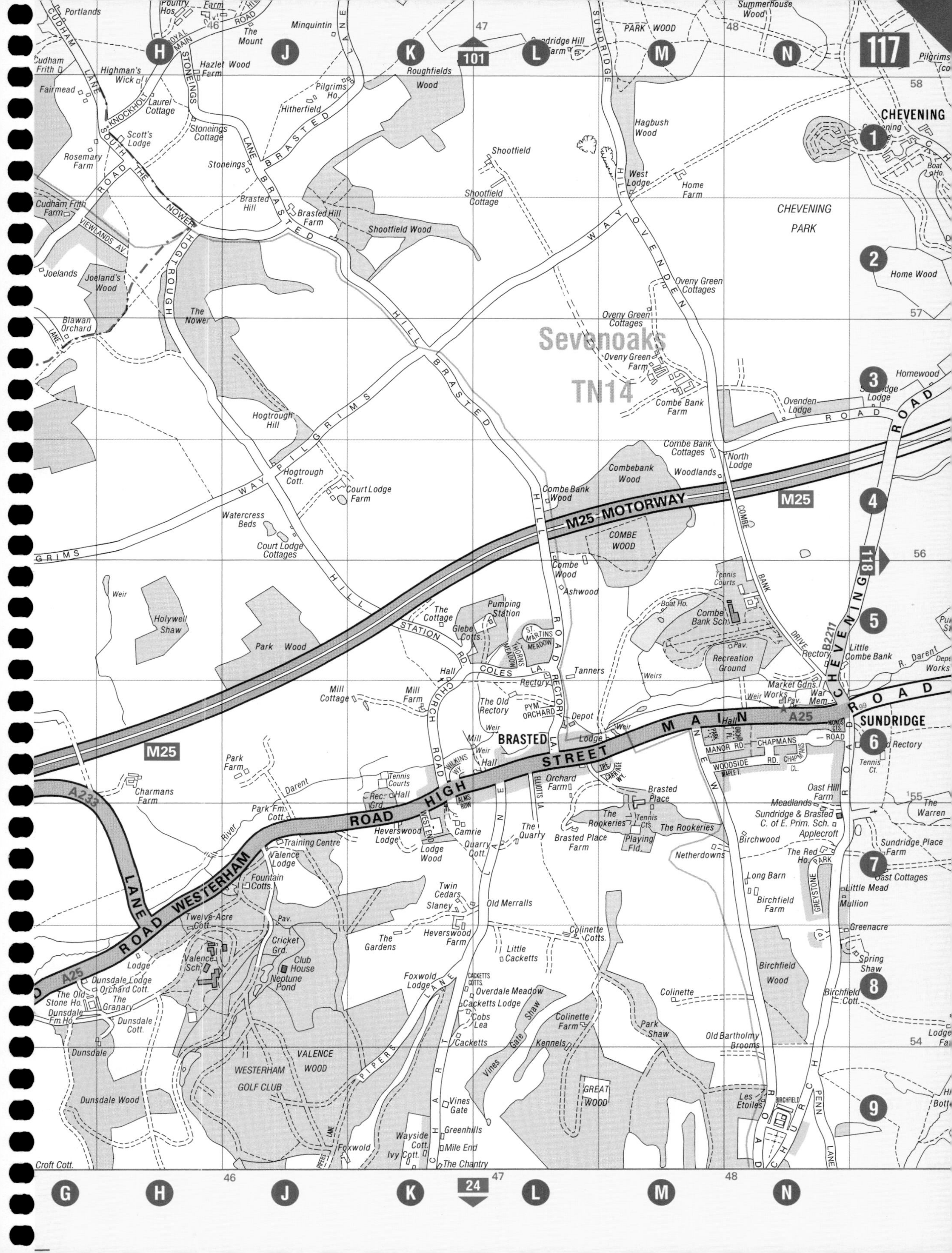

CHEVENING
CHEVENING PARK
Sevenoaks
TN14
BRASTED
SUNDRIDGE
M25 MOTORWAY
M25
A25
A233
B2211
MAIN ROAD
HIGH STREET
WESTERHAM ROAD
PILGRIMS WAY
BRASTED HILL
HOGTROUGH HILL
RECTORY LANE
CHURCH ROAD
STATION RD.
COLES LA.
OVENDEN ROAD
COMBE BANK DRIVE
CHEVENING ROAD
CHARTLANE
PIPERS LANE
CHURCH ROAD
PENN LANE
Hagbush Wood
Shootfield Wood
Combebank Wood
COMBE WOOD
Park Wood
Holywell Shaw
Joeland's Wood
The Nower
Roughfields Wood
Birchfield Wood
Dunsdale Wood
VALENCE WOOD
WESTERHAM GOLF CLUB
GREAT WOOD
Park Shaw
Home Wood
Combe Bank Sch.
Recreation Ground
Weir
R. Darent
101
24
118
G
H
J
K
L
M
N
1
2
3
4
5
6
7
8
9
46
47
48
54
55
56
57
58

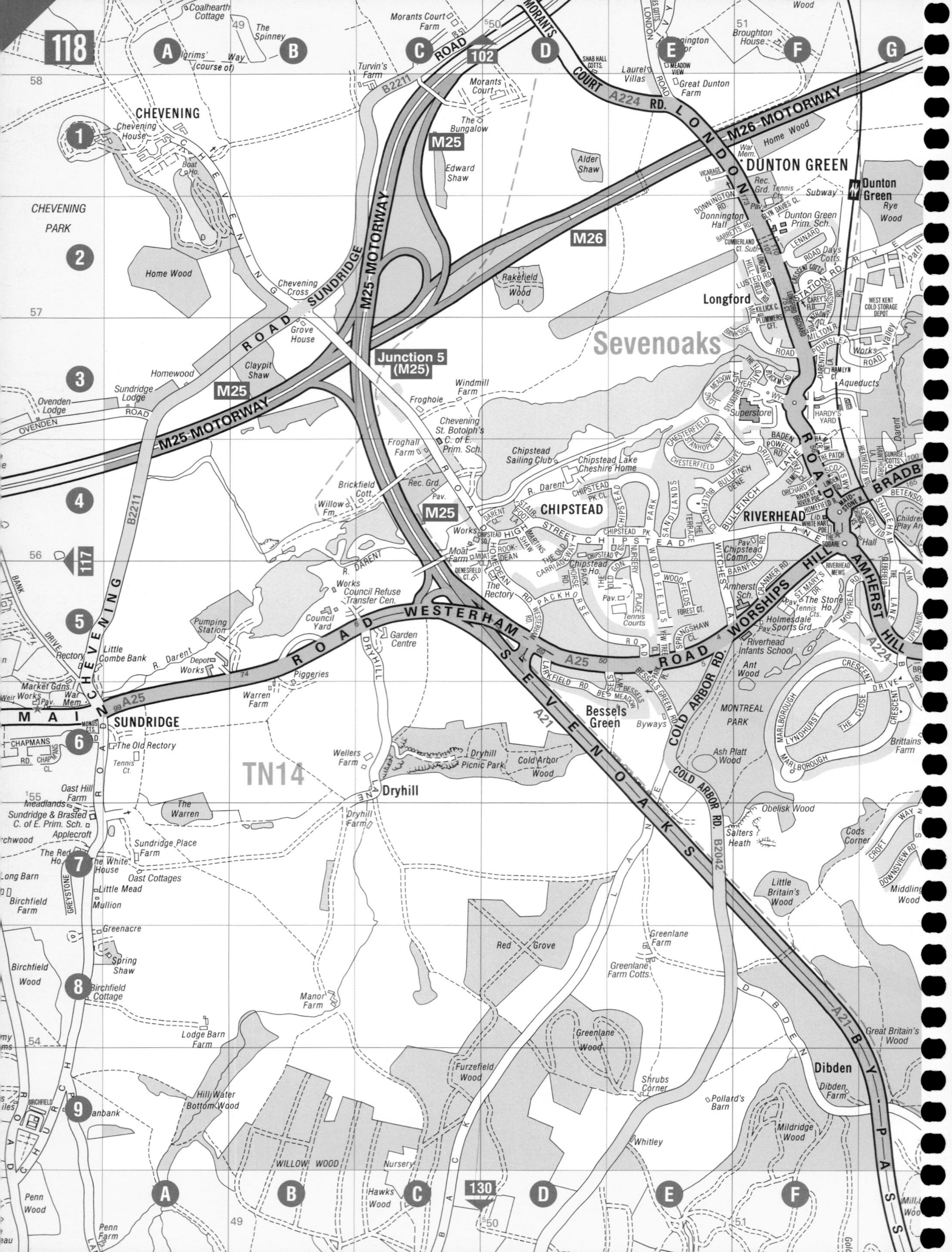
CHEVENING
Chevening House
CHEVENING PARK
Home Wood
Chevening Cross
Coalhearth Cottage
The Spinney
Pilgrims' Way (course of)
Morants Court Farm
Turvin's Farm
Morants Court
The Bungalow
Edward Shaw
Alder Shaw
Laurel Villas
Great Dunton Farm
Broughton House
DUNTON GREEN
Dunton Green
Home Wood
Rye Wood
Dunton Green Prim. Sch.
Donnington Hall
Longford
Sevenoaks
WEST KENT COLD STORAGE DEPOT
Aqueducts
Superstore
HARDY'S YARD
M26 MOTORWAY
M25 MOTORWAY
M25
M26
Junction 5 (M25)
SUNDRIDGE ROAD
Grove House
Claypit Shaw
Homewood
Sundridge Lodge
Ovenden Lodge
OVENDEN ROAD
Rakefield Wood
Windmill Farm
Froghole
Chevening St. Botolph's C. of E. Prim. Sch.
Froghall Farm
Rec. Grd.
Brickfield Cott.
Willow Fm.
Chipstead Sailing Club
Chipstead Lake Cheshire Home
R. Darent
CHIPSTEAD
RIVERHEAD
Chipstead Ho.
The Rectory
Moat Farm
Works
Council Refuse Transfer Cen.
Council Yard
Pumping Station
Garden Centre
Piggeries
Warren Farm
Little Combe Bank
Depot Works
Rectory
Market Gdns. Works
SUNDRIDGE
The Old Rectory
WESTERHAM ROAD
A25
SEVENOAKS
A21
LONDON ROAD
A224
Amherst Sch.
The Stone Ho.
Holmesdale Sports Grd.
Riverhead Infants School
WORSHIPS HILL
AMHERST HILL
Bessels Green
Byways
Ant Wood
MONTREAL PARK
Ash Platt Wood
Brittains Farm
COLD ARBOR RD.
Wellers Farm
Dryhill Picnic Park
Cold Arbor Wood
Dryhill
TN14
Oast Hill Farm
Meadlands
Sundridge & Brasted C. of E. Prim. Sch.
Applecroft
The Warren
Dryhill Farm
Obelisk Wood
Salters Heath
Cods Corner
Middling Wood
Little Britain's Wood
The Red Ho.
The White House
Sundridge Place Farm
Oast Cottages
Little Mead
Mullion
Long Barn
Birchfield Farm
Greenacre
Spring Shaw
Birchfield Wood
Birchfield Cottage
Red Grove
Greenlane Farm
Greenlane Farm Cotts.
Manor Farm
Lodge Barn Farm
Greenlane Wood
Furzefield Wood
Great Britain's Wood
Dibden
Dibden Farm
Shrubs Corner
Pollard's Barn
Mildridge Wood
Hill Water Bottom Wood
Whitley
WILLOW WOOD
Nursery
Hawks Wood
Penn Wood
Penn Farm
A21 BY-PASS
B2042
B2211
102
117
130

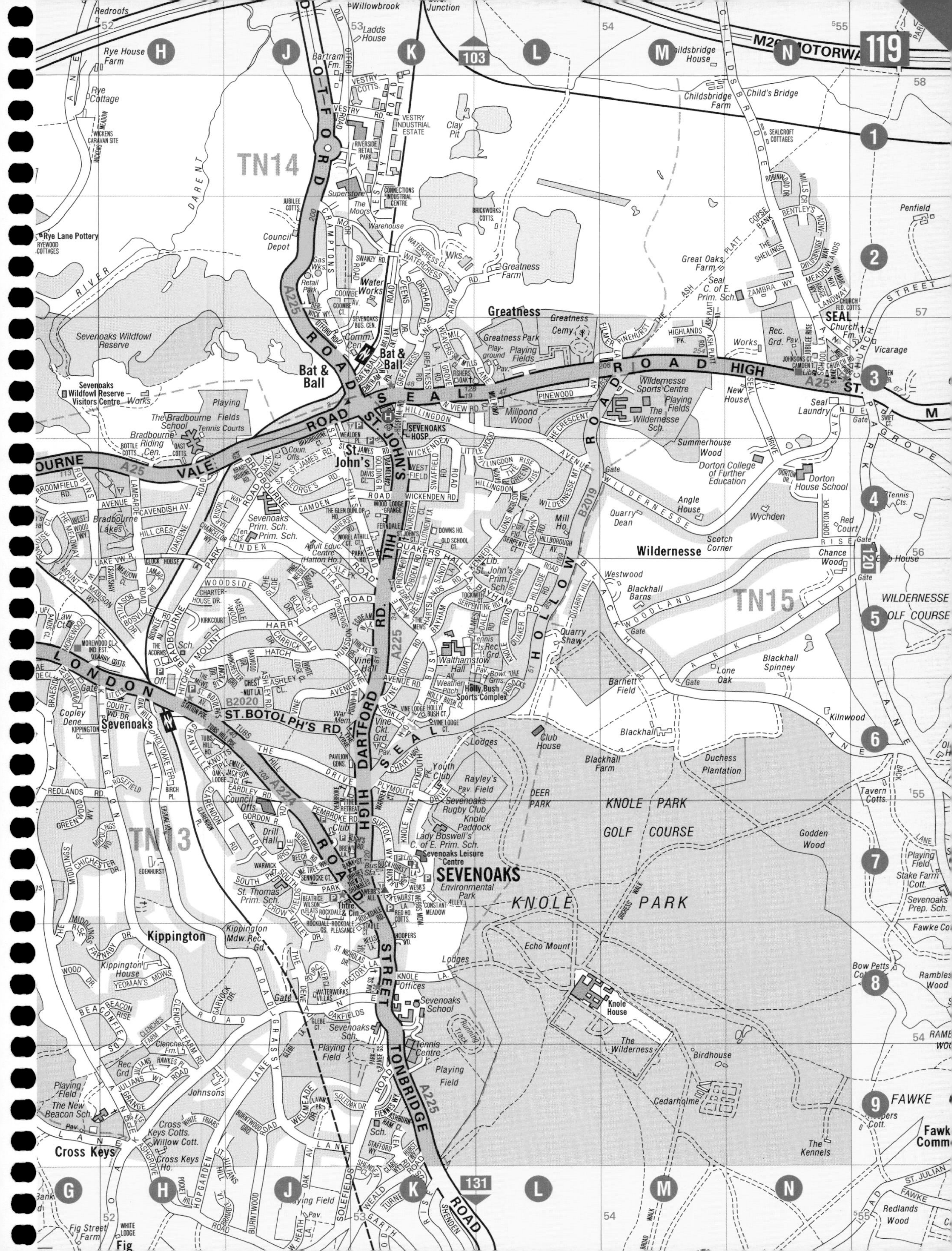

119
M26 MOTORWAY
103
120
131
TN14
TN13
TN15
Redroofs
Willowbrook
Ladds House
Junction
Rye House Farm
Bartram Fm.
Childsbridge House
Child's Bridge
Childsbridge Farm
Rye Cottage
Wickens Caravan Site
Vestry Cotts.
Vestry Industrial Estate
Riverside Retail Park
Clay Pit
Sealcroft Cottages
Superstore
Connections Industrial Centre
Jubilee Cotts.
The Moors
Brickworks Cotts.
Penfield
Rye Lane Pottery
Ryewood Cottages
Council Depot
Warehouse
Cramptons
Swanzy Rd.
Watercress Cl.
Watercress Dr.
Wks.
Greatness Farm
Great Oaks Farm
Seal C. of E. Prim. Sch.
Gas Wks.
Retail Park
Water Works
Orchard Cl.
Zambra Wy.
Meadowlands
Landway
Church Fld. Cotts.
River Darent
Greatness
Greatness Cemy.
Highlands Pk.
Ash Platt
Seal
Church Fm.
Vicarage
Sevenoaks Wildfowl Reserve
Comm. Cen.
Sevenoaks Bus. Cen.
Bat & Ball
Greatness Park
Playground
Playing Fields
Pinehurst
Works
Rec. Grd.
Sevenoaks Wildfowl Reserve Visitors Centre
Seal Road
High Street
Wilderness Sports Centre
Pinewood
Millpond Wood
New House
Seal Laundry
The Bradbourne School
Tennis Courts
Playing Fields
Bradbourne Riding Cen.
Hillingdon
Sevenoaks Hosp.
St. John's
The Wilderness Sch.
Summerhouse Wood
Vale Road
A25
Bradbourne
Wickenden Rd.
Little Wood
Dorton College of Further Education
Dorton House School
Hillingdon Rise
Wilderness Mt.
Broomfield Rd.
Avenue
Cavendish Av.
Lambarde
Bradbourne Lakes
St. George's Rd.
Camden
Angle House
Wychden
Tennis Cts.
Sevenoaks Prim. Sch.
Wood Lodge Grange
Quarry Dean
Mill Ho.
Red Court
Hill Crest
Linden
Adult Educ. Centre (Hatton Ho.)
Scotch Corner
Wilderness
Chance Wood
Quakers Hall La.
St. John's Prim. Sch.
Westwood
Blackhall Barns
Woodside
Charterhouse Dr.
Wilderness Golf Course
Kirkcourt
Harry
Harry Rd.
Woodland
Quarry Shaw
Law Ct.
Hatch
Bayham
Serpentine Rd.
Hollybush
Walthamstow Hall
Rec. Grd.
Blackhall Spinney
Barnett Field
Lone Oak
London Road
Vine Hall
Holly Bush Sports Complex
Copley Dene
Sevenoaks
St. Botolph's Rd.
B2020
Dartford Rd.
A225
Kilnwood
Blackhall
Blackhall Farm
Club House
Vine Ckt. Grd.
Lodges
Duchess Plantation
Redlands Rd.
Tubs Hill
The Hill Drive
Youth Club
Rayley's Pav. Field
Tavern Cotts.
Deer Park
Knole Park Golf Course
Council Offs.
Eardley Rd.
Plymouth
Sevenoaks Rugby Club
Knole Paddock
Godden Wood
Drill Hall
Lady Boswell's C. of E. Prim. Sch.
Sevenoaks Leisure Centre
Sevenoaks
Sevenoaks Environmental Park
Playing Field
Stake Farm Cott.
Chichester Dr.
Edenhurst
St. Thomas' Prim. Sch.
Knole Park
Sevenoaks Prep. Sch.
Fawke Co.
Kippington
Kippington Mdw. Rec. Gd.
Echo Mount
Kippington House
Yeoman's Mdws.
Lodges
Bow Petts Cott.
Ramblers Wood
Knole La.
Offices
Sevenoaks School
Knole House
Beacon Rise
Oakfields
Running Track
The Wilderness
Sevenoaks Sch.
Tennis Centre
Playing Field
Birdhouse
Johnsons
Cedarholme
Fawke
Fawke Common
The New Beacon Sch.
Cross Keys Cotts.
Willow Cott.
Cross Keys
Cross Keys Ho.
Tonbridge Road
The Kennels
Playing Field
Redlands Wood
Fig Street Farm
White Lodge
Fig

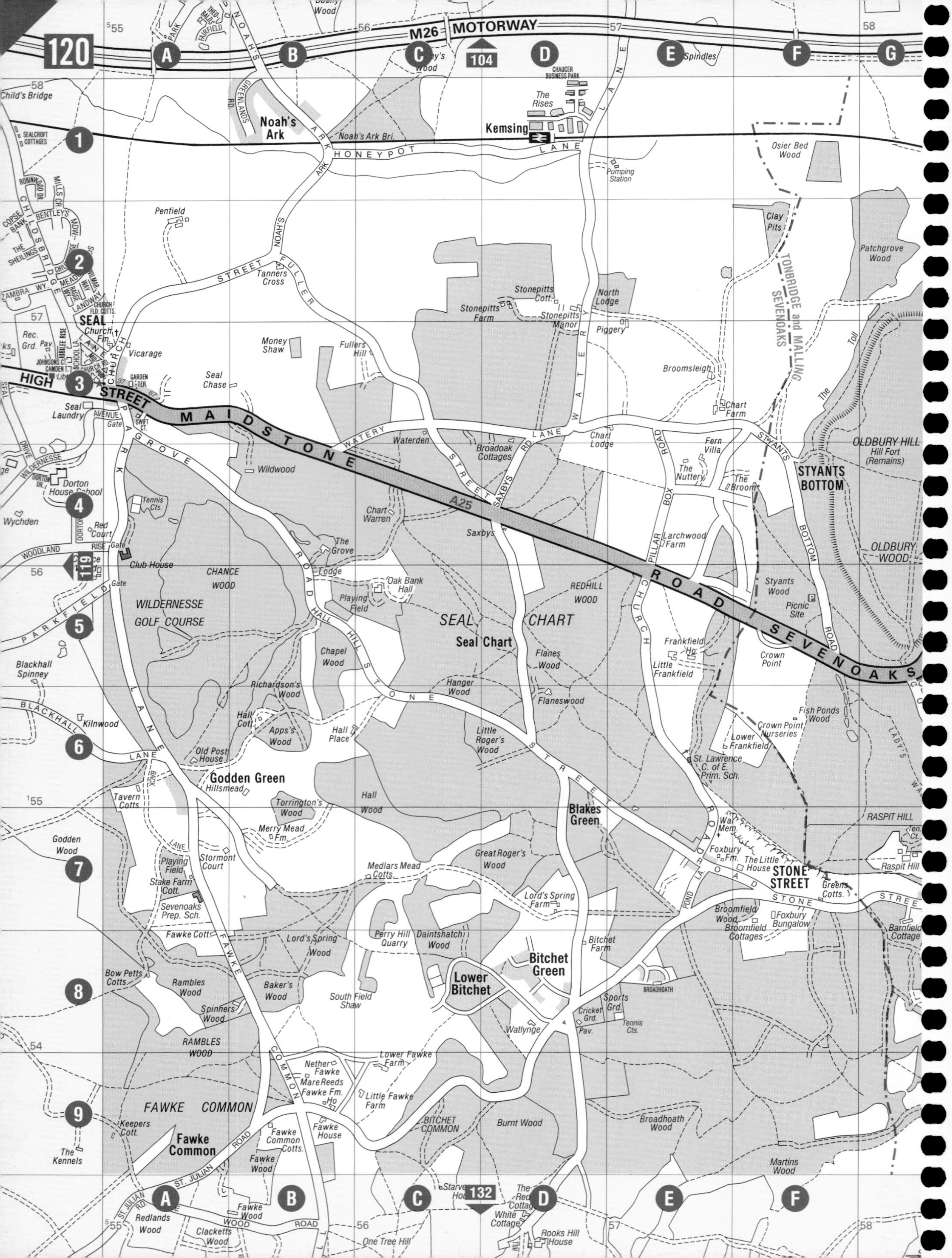

M26 MOTORWAY
104
Noah's Ark
Kemsing
Chaucer Business Park
The Rises
Noah's Ark Bri.
Honeypot Lane
Pumping Station
Osier Bed Wood
Child's Bridge
Sealcroft Cottages
Penfield
Tanners Cross
Clay Pits
Patchgrove Wood
Tonbridge and Malling Sevenoaks
Stonepitts Cott.
Stonepitts Farm
Stonepitts Manor
North Lodge
Piggery
SEAL
Church Fm.
Vicarage
Money Shaw
Fullers Hill
Seal Chase
Broomsleigh
High Street
Maidstone Road
Chart Farm
Seal Laundry
Waterden
Broadoak Cottages
Chart Lodge
Fern Villa
The Nuttery
The Broom
Styants Bottom
Oldbury Hill
Hill Fort (Remains)
Wildwood
Dorton House School
Chart Warren
A25
Saxbys
Larchwood Farm
Oldbury Wood
Wychden
Red Court
Tennis Cts.
The Grove
Lodge
Oak Bank Hall
Club House
119
Chance Wood
Redhill Wood
Styants Wood
Picnic Site
Wilderness Golf Course
Playing Field
Seal Chart
Sevenoaks Road
Crown Point
Blackhall Spinney
Chapel Wood
Frankfield Ho.
Little Frankfield
Flanes Wood
Richardson's Wood
Hanger Wood
Flaneswood
Fish Ponds Wood
Kilnwood
Hall Cott.
Apps's Wood
Hall Place
Little Roger's Wood
Crown Point Nurseries
Lower Frankfield
Old Post House
Godden Green
Hillsmead
St. Lawrence C. of E. Prim. Sch.
Tavern Cotts.
Torrington's Wood
Hall Wood
Blakes Green
Raspit Hill
Godden Wood
Merry Mead Fm.
War Mem.
Playing Field
Stormont Court
Great Roger's Wood
Foxbury Fm.
The Little House
Stone Street
Greens Cotts.
Raspit Hill
Medlars Mead Cotts.
Stake Farm Cott.
Lord's Spring Farm
Sevenoaks Prep. Sch.
Broomfield Wood
Foxbury Bungalow
Broomfield Cottages
Barnfield Cottage
Fawke Cott.
Lord's Spring Wood
Perry Hill Quarry
Daintshatch Wood
Bitchet Farm
Bitchet Green
Bow Petts Cotts
Rambles Wood
Baker's Wood
Lower Bitchet
Broadhoath
South Field Shaw
Sports Grd.
Cricket Grd.
Pav.
Tennis Cts.
Spinners Wood
Watlynge
Rambles Wood
Nether Fawke
Lower Fawke Farm
Mare Reeds
Fawke Fm. Ho
Little Fawke Farm
Fawke Common
Keepers Cott.
Fawke Common Cotts.
Fawke House
Bitchet Common
Burnt Wood
Broadhoath Wood
The Kennels
Fawke Common
Fawke Wood
Martins Wood
St. Julian Road
132
Redlands Wood
Fawke Wood
Clacketts Wood
Wood Road
One Tree Hill
White Cottage
Rooks Hill House

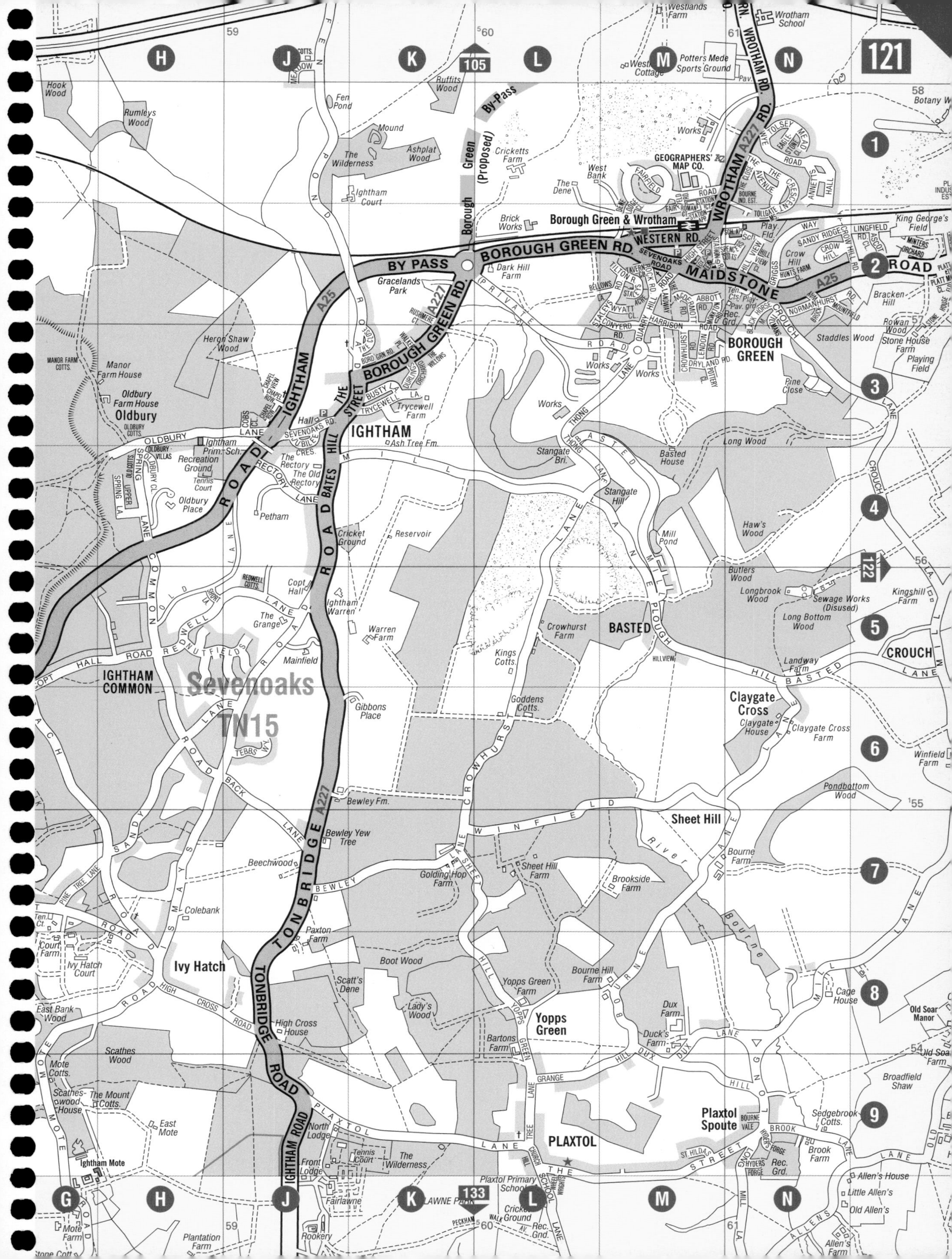

105
122
133
H
J
K
L
M
N
G
1
2
3
4
5
6
7
8
9
59
560
61
58
57
56
155
54
Hook Wood
Rumleys Wood
Fen Pond
Mound
The Wilderness
Ashplat Wood
Ightham Court
Ruffits Wood
By-Pass
Borough Green (Proposed)
Cricketts Farm
Westlands Farm
Wrotham School
West Cottage
Potters Mede Sports Ground
Pav.
Works
GEOGRAPHERS' MAP CO.
West Bank
The Dene
Brick Works
Borough Green & Wrotham
WROTHAM RD.
WROTHAM
A227 RD.
Botany W
TOLSEY MEAD
ROAD
THE AVENUE
THE CRESCENT
ANNETTS HALL
BOURNE IND. EST.
TOLLGATE
WESTERN RD.
BOROUGH GREEN RD.
BY PASS
A25
A227
Dark Hill Farm
Gracelands Park
PRIVATE ROAD
SEVENOAKS ROAD
MAIDSTONE
ROAD
SANDY RIDGE
Crow Hill
CROW HILL
LINGFIELD RD.
ASCOT CL.
King George's Field
Play. Fld.
WAY
HUNTS FARM CL.
GRIGGS
Bracken Hill
Rowan Wood
Staddles Wood
Stone House Farm
Playing Field
BOROUGH GREEN
HARRISON ROAD
CONYERD RD.
QUARRY HILL RD.
LENDON RD.
DRYLAND RD.
POTTERY
CROWHURST RD.
Rec. Grd.
Ten. Cts/Play Pav. grd.
CROUCH
NORMANHURST RD.
MOUNTFIELD
Pine Close
LANE
Works
THONG LANE
BASTED LANE
Stangate Bri.
Basted House
Long Wood
Stangate Hill
Mill Pond
Haw's Wood
CROUCH
Butlers Wood
Longbrook Wood
Sewage Works (Disused)
Kingshill Farm
Long Bottom Wood
MANOR FARM COTTS.
Manor Farm House
Heron Shaw Wood
Oldbury Farm House
Oldbury
OLDBURY COTTS.
OLDBURY LANE
Ightham Prim. Sch.
OLDBURY VILLAS
Recreation Ground
Tennis Court
Oldbury Place
SPRING LA.
UPPER SPRING
OLDBURY CL.
IGHTHAM
ROAD
CHAPEL ROW
CHAPEL VIEW
COBS CL.
Hall
SEVENOAKS RD.
JUBILEE CRES.
The Rectory
The Old Rectory
RECTORY LANE
Petham
BATES HILL
THE STREET
BOROUGH GREEN RD.
BUSTY LA.
TRYCEWELL LA.
Trycewell Farm
IGHTHAM
Ash Tree Fm.
MILL LANE
Cricket Ground
Reservoir
Copt Hall
REDWELL COTTS.
Ightham Warren
Warren Farm
Mainfield
The Grange
COMMON
OLD LANE
SHORT LA.
REDWELL
NUTFIELDS
OPT HALL ROAD
IGHTHAM COMMON
Sevenoaks
TN15
TEBBS WY.
Gibbons Place
Crowhurst Farm
Kings Cotts.
BASTED
PLOUGH
HILLVIEW
Goddens Cotts.
CROWHURST
Landway Farm
BASTED HILL
CROUCH
LANE
Claygate Cross
Claygate House
Claygate Cross Farm
Winfield Farm
Pondbottom Wood
BACK LANE
SANDY
Bewley Fm.
WINFIELD
Sheet Hill
Bewley Yew Tree
TONBRIDGE
A227
ROAD
Beechwood
BEWLEY
Golding Hop Farm
SHEET
Sheet Hill Farm
Brookside Farm
River
Bourne Farm
Bourne
PINE TREE LANE
ROAD
Colebank
Ten. Ct.
Court Farm
Ivy Hatch Court
Ivy Hatch
HIGH CROSS ROAD
Paxton Farm
Boot Wood
Scatt's Dene
Lady's Wood
Yopps Green Farm
Yopps Green
Bourne Hill Farm
Dux Farm
Duck's Farm
DUX LANE
DUX HILL
Cage House
Old Soar Manor
Old Soar Farm
Broadfield Shaw
East Bank Wood
Scathes Wood
High Cross House
Bartons Farm
YOPPS GREEN
GRANGE
Mote Cotts.
MOTE ROAD
Scathes-wood House
The Mount Cotts.
East Mote
North Lodge
PLAXTOL LANE
Ightham Mote
IGHTHAM ROAD
Front Lodge
Tennis Court
The Wilderness
Fairlawne
PLAXTOL
CHURCH HILL
TREE LANE
ST. HILDAS
THE STREET
Plaxtol Primary School
LAWNE PARK
Cricket Ground
Rec. Gnd.
PECKHAM AV.
SCHOOL LANE
Plaxtol Spoute
BOURNE VALE
HYDERS FORGE
Rec. Grd.
BROOK LANE
Sedgebrook Cotts.
Brook Farm
Allen's House
Little Allen's
Old Allen's
ALLENS
Allen's Farm
Mote Farm
Plantation Farm
Rookery
Stone Cott

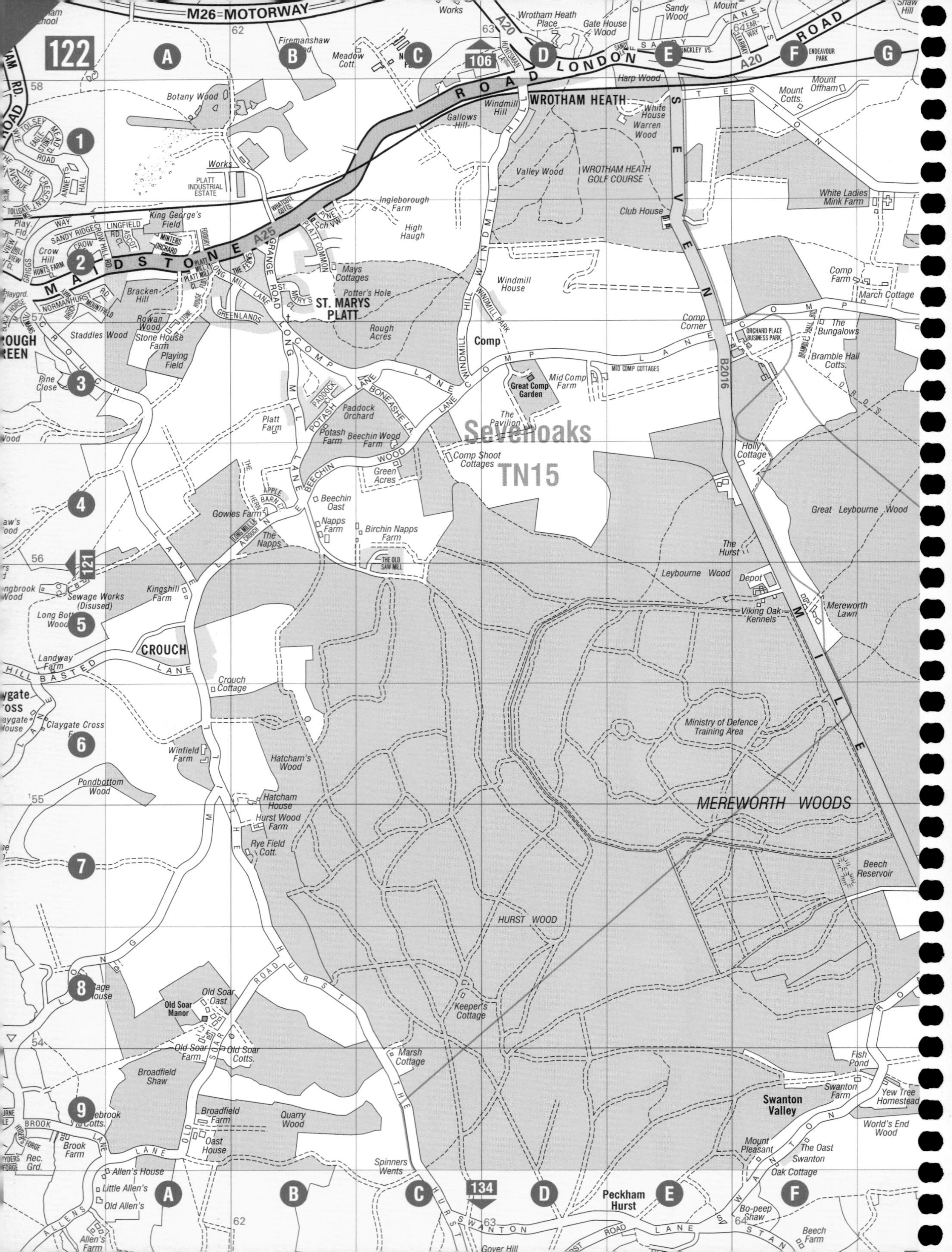
M26 MOTORWAY
Fireamanshaw Wood
Meadow Cott.
Works
Wrotham Heath Place
Gate House Wood
Sandy Wood
A20
LONDON ROAD
106
Harp Wood
Endeavour Park
Mount Offham
Mount Cotts.
Botany Wood
WROTHAM HEATH
Windmill Hill
Gallows Hill
White House
Warren Wood
Valley Wood
WROTHAM HEATH GOLF COURSE
Works
PLATT INDUSTRIAL ESTATE
Ingleborough Farm
High Haugh
Club House
White Ladies Mink Farm
King George's Field
MAIDSTONE ROAD
A25
Crow Hill
Bracken Hill
Mays Cottages
Potter's Hole
ST. MARYS PLATT
Windmill House
Comp Farm
March Cottage
Comp Corner
ORCHARD PLACE BUSINESS PARK
The Bungalows
Bramble Hall Cotts.
Staddles Wood
Rowan Wood
Stone House Farm
Playing Field
Rough Acres
Comp
COMP LANE
MID COMP COTTAGES
Mid Comp Farm
Great Comp Garden
B2016
Pine Close
Platt Farm
Paddock Orchard
Potash Farm
Beechin Wood Farm
The Pavilion
Sevenoaks
TN15
Comp Shoot Cottages
Green Acres
Holly Cottage
Beechin Oast
Napps Farm
Birchin Napps Farm
Gowles Farm
The Napps
THE OLD SAW MILL
Great Leybourne Wood
The Hurst
Leybourne Wood
Depot
121
Sewage Works (Disused)
Kingshill Farm
Long Bott Wood
Viking Oak Kennels
Mereworth Lawn
CROUCH
Landway Farm
BASTED LANE
Crouch Cottage
Claygate Cross
Ministry of Defence Training Area
Winfield Farm
Hatcham's Wood
Pondbottom Wood
MEREWORTH WOODS
Hatcham House
Hurst Wood Farm
Rye Field Cott.
Beech Reservoir
HURST WOOD
HURST ROAD
Old Soar Oast
Old Soar Manor
Keeper's Cottage
Old Soar Farm
Old Soar Cotts.
Marsh Cottage
Fish Pond
Broadfield Shaw
Swanton Farm
Yew Tree Homestead
Swanton Valley
Broadfield Farm
Quarry Wood
World's End Wood
Brook Farm
Oast House
Mount Pleasant
The Oast Swanton
Oak Cottage
Rec. Grd.
Allen's House
Little Allen's
Old Allen's
Spinners Wents
134
Peckham Hurst
Bo-peep Shaw
SWANTON LANE
Beech Farm
Allen's Farm
Gover Hill

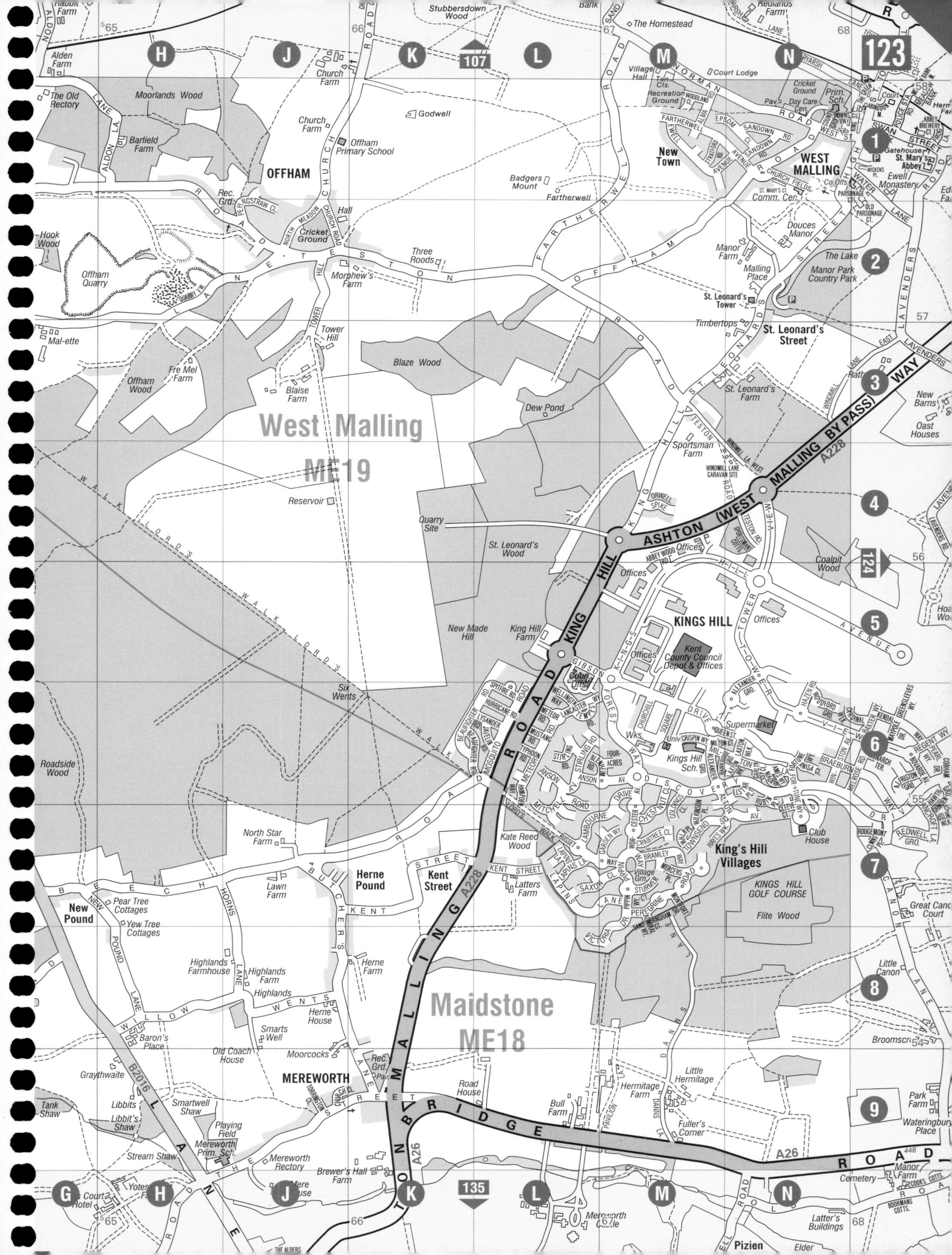

West Malling
ME19
Maidstone
ME18
OFFHAM
WEST MALLING
KINGS HILL
MEREWORTH
New Town
St. Leonard's Street
King's Hill Villages
Herne Pound
Kent Street
New Pound
KINGS HILL GOLF COURSE
Offham Quarry
Blaze Wood
St. Leonard's Wood
Manor Park Country Park
Kent County Council Depot & Offices
ASHTON (WEST MALLING BY PASS) WAY
TONBRIDGE ROAD
KING HILL
MALLING ROAD
107
124
135
A228
A26
B2016

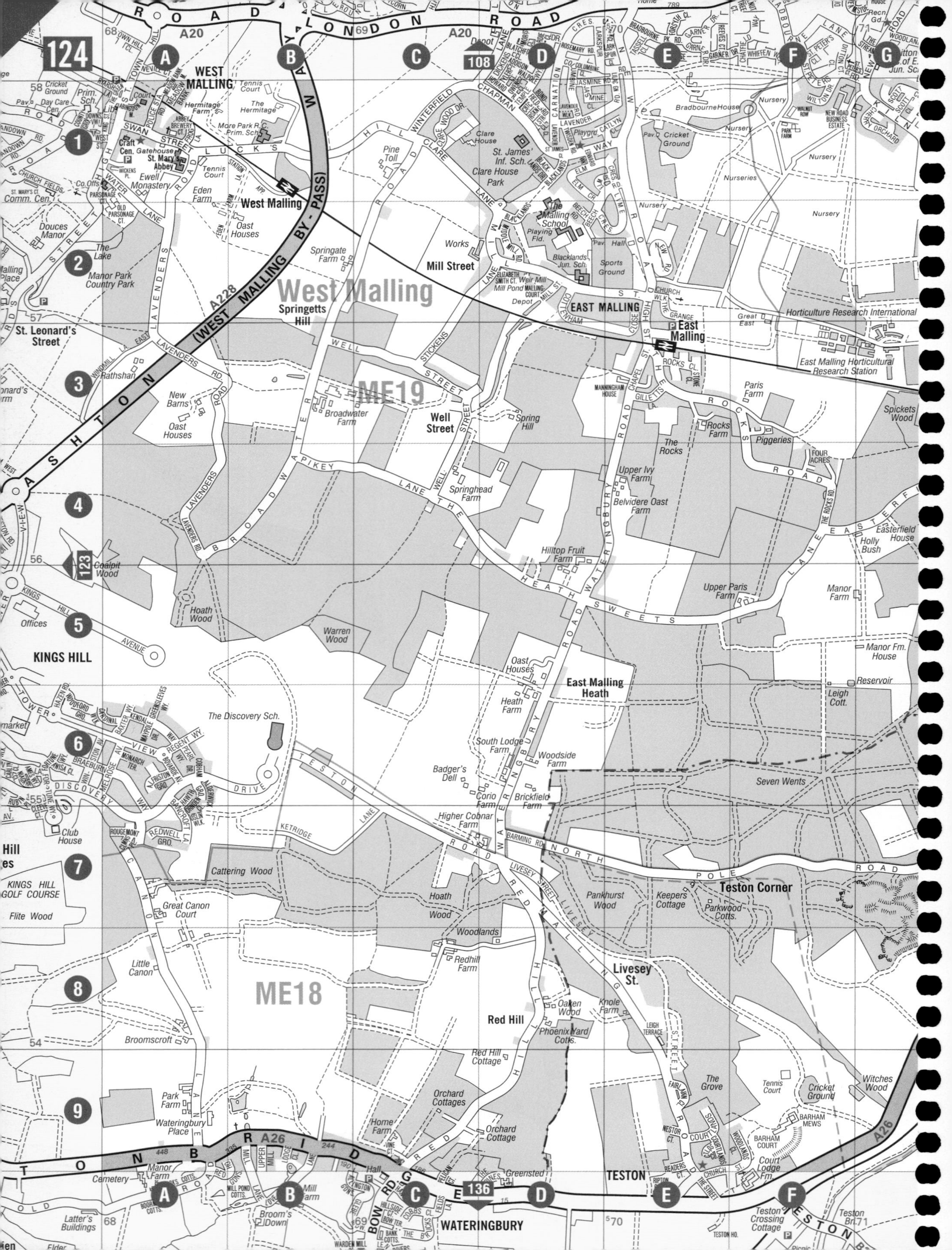
West Malling
WEST MALLING
ME19
ME18
EAST MALLING
East Malling
Mill Street
Well Street
St. Leonard's Street
Springetts Hill
KINGS HILL
East Malling Heath
Teston Corner
Livesey St.
Red Hill
TESTON
WATERINGBURY
LONDON ROAD
A20
ASHTON WAY
A228 (WEST MALLING BY-PASS)
TONBRIDGE ROAD
A26
Manor Park Country Park
Horticulture Research International
East Malling Horticultural Research Station
KINGS HILL GOLF COURSE
The Discovery Sch.
The Malling School
Blacklands Jun. Sch.
St. James' Inf. Sch.
Clare House Park
Springate Farm
Broadwater Farm
Springhead Farm
Hilltop Fruit Farm
Upper Paris Farm
Paris Farm
Rocks Farm
Upper Ivy Farm
Belvidere Oast Farm
Manor Farm
Heath Farm
South Lodge Farm
Woodside Farm
Corio Farm
Brickfield Farm
Higher Cobnar Farm
Great Canon Court
Cattering Wood
Hoath Wood
Warren Wood
Coalpit Wood
Pankhurst Wood
Keepers Cottage
Parkwood Cotts.
Seven Wents
Redhill Farm
Oaken Wood
Knole Farm
Phoenix Yard Cotts.
Broomscroft
Park Farm
Wateringbury Place
Little Canon
Orchard Cottages
Orchard Cottage
Home Farm
The Grove
Witches Wood
Spickets Wood
Easterfield House
Holly Bush
Leigh Cott.
Manor Fm. House
Reservoir
Cricket Ground
Teston Crossing Cottage
Teston Br.
123
108
136

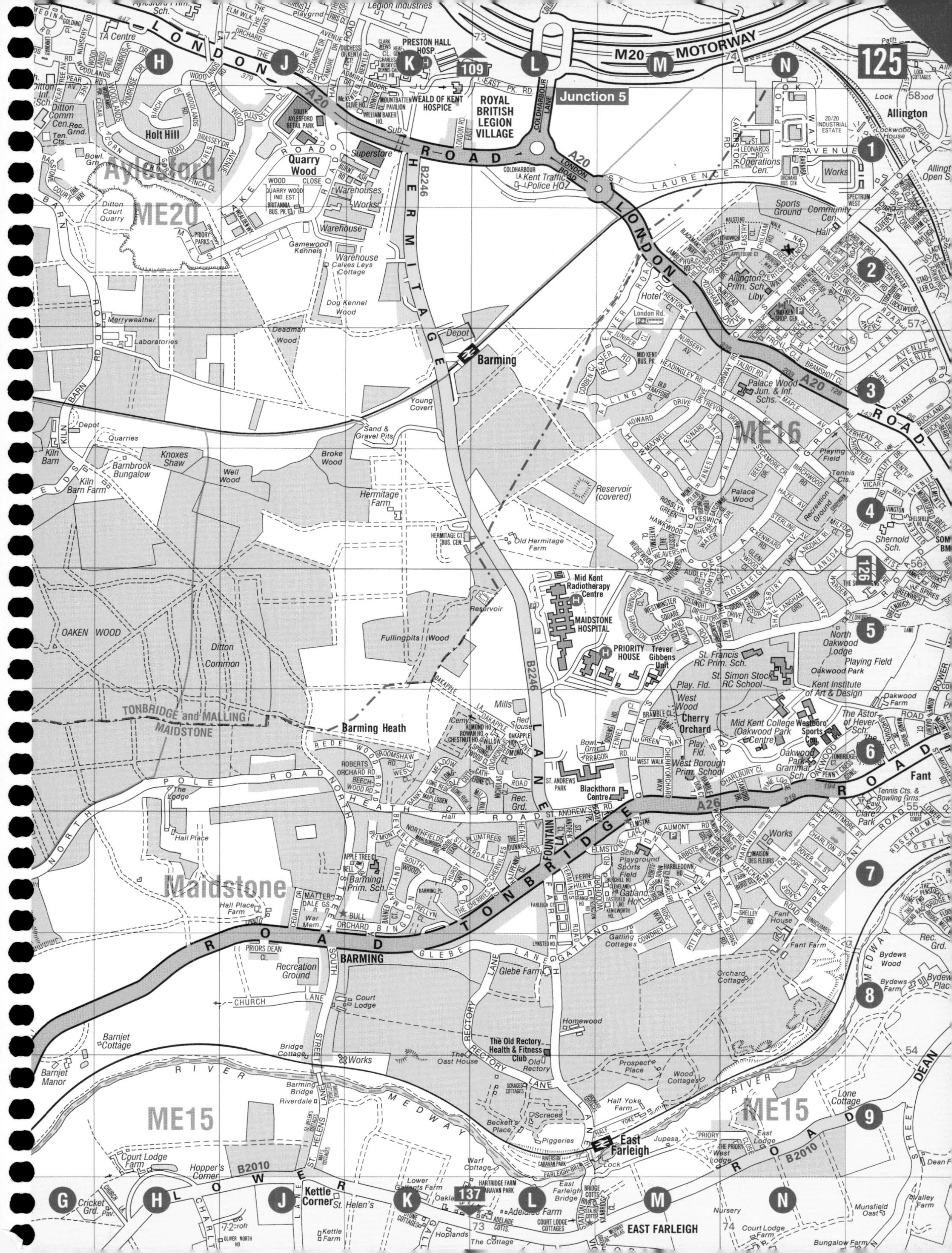

125
M20 MOTORWAY
Junction 5
LONDON ROAD
A20
ROYAL BRITISH LEGION VILLAGE
PRESTON HALL HOSP.
WEALD OF KENT HOSPICE
Superstore
Quarry Wood
Holt Hill
Aylesford
ME20
Ditton Court Quarry
Warehouses
Warehouse
Gamewood Kennels
Calves Leys Cottage
Dog Kennel Wood
HERMITAGE
B2246
Depot
Barming
Deadman Wood
Merryweather
Laboratories
Young Covert
Sand & Gravel Pits
Kiln Barn
Kiln Barn Farm
Quarries
Knoxes Shaw
Barnbrook Bungalow
Well Wood
Broke Wood
Hermitage Farm
Old Hermitage Farm
Reservoir (covered)
Allington
Lockwood House
20/20 INDUSTRIAL ESTATE
Operations Cen.
Works
Kent Traffic Police HQ
ST. LAURENCE AVENUE
Sports Ground
Community Cen.
Hall
Allington Prim. Sch.
Liby.
Hotel
Palace Wood Jun. & Inf. Schs.
ME16
Palace Wood
Playing Field
Tennis Cts.
Recreation Ground
Shernold Sch.
126
OAKEN WOOD
Ditton Common
Fullingpits Wood
Reservoir
Mid Kent Radiotherapy Centre
MAIDSTONE HOSPITAL
PRIORITY HOUSE
Trever Gibbens Unit
St. Francis RC Prim. Sch.
St. Simon Stock RC School
North Oakwood Lodge
Oakwood Park
Playing Field
Kent Institute of Art & Design
Oakwood Farm
The Astor of Hever Sch.
Mid Kent College (Oakwood Park Centre)
Westboro Sports Cen.
Oakwood Park Grammar Sch.
Fant
Tennis Cts. & Bowling Grns.
Clare Park
West Wood
Cherry Orchard
Play. Fld.
West Borough Prim. School
TONBRIDGE and MALLING
MAIDSTONE
Barming Heath
Mills
Red House
St. Andrews Park
Blackthorn Centre
Rec. Grd.
POLE ROAD
NORTH HEATH ROAD
TONBRIDGE ROAD
A26
The Lodge
Hall Place
Hall Place Farm
Maidstone
Barming Prim. Sch.
War Mem.
BULL
BARMING
Recreation Ground
Sports Field
Gatland Ho.
Gatling Cottages
Works
Fant House
Fant Farm
Orchard Cottage
Bydews Wood
Bydews Farm
Rec. Grd.
Glebe Farm
Court Lodge
CHURCH LANE
Barnjet Cottage
Barnjet Manor
Bridge Cottage
Works
Homewood
The Old Rectory Health & Fitness Club
The Oast House
Old Rectory
Prospect Place
Wood Cottages
RIVER MEDWAY
Barming Bridge
Riverdale
ME15
Half Yoke Farm
Beckett's Place
Scraces
Piggeries
East Farleigh
Jupesa
Lone Cottage
East Lodge
ME15
B2010
Court Lodge Farm
Hopper's Corner
LOWER ROAD
Kettle Corner
St. Helen's
Lower Gallants Farm
137
Adelaide Farm
East Farleigh Bridge
EAST FARLEIGH
Nursery
Court Lodge Farm
Munsfield Oast
Valley Farm
Bungalow Farm
Kettle Farm
Hoplands
The Cottage
Cricket Grd.
Dean Farm

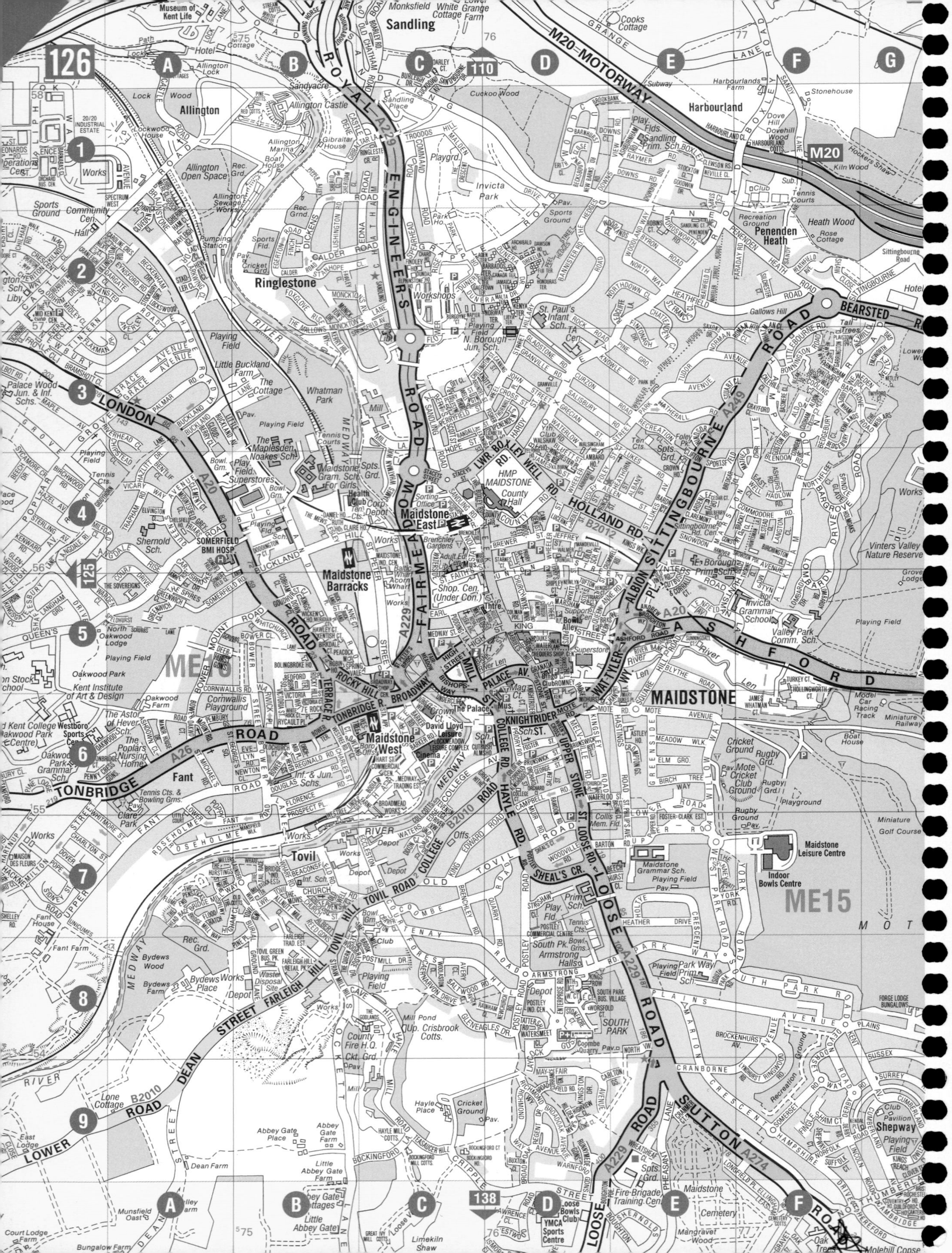

A
B
C
D
E
F
G
1
2
3
4
5
6
7
8
9
110
125
138
75
76
77
54
55
56
57
58
Museum of Kent Life
Sandling
Monksfield
White Cottage
Cooks Cottage
M20 MOTORWAY
Allington
Allington Lock
Allington Castle
Allington Marina
Allington Open Space
Sandling Place
Cuckoo Wood
Harbourland
Harbourlands Farm
Stonehouse
Dove Hill
M20
Kiln Wood
Invicta Park
Sports Ground
Penenden Heath
Heath Wood
Rose Cottage
Ringlestone
Sports Fld.
Cricket Grd.
Workshops
St. Paul's Infant Sch.
Gallows Hill
BEARSTED
Playing Field
Little Buckland Farm
The Cottage
Whatman Park
Playing Field
The Maplesden Noakes Sch.
Maidstone Gram. Sch. For Girls
HMP MAIDSTONE
County Hall
Maidstone East
HOLLAND RD.
SITTINGBOURNE ROAD
A249
A229
ENGINEERS
FAIRMEADOW
LONDON ROAD
A20
SOMERFIELD BMI HOSP.
Shernold Sch.
Maidstone Barracks
Superstores
Vinters Valley Nature Reserve
Invicta Grammar School
Valley Park Comm. Sch.
ASHFORD ROAD
Playing Field
Palace Wood Jun. & Inf. Schs.
North Oakwood Lodge
Playing Field
Oakwood Park
Kent Institute of Art & Design
ME16
Cornwallis Playground
Oakwood Farm
The Astor of Hever Sch.
Westboro Sports Cen.
The Poplars Nursing Home
Oakwood Park Grammar Sch.
Fant
TONBRIDGE ROAD
A26
Tennis Cts. & Bowling Grns.
Clare Park
ROCKY HILL
BROADWAY
Maidstone West
David Lloyd Leisure
Cinema
The Palace
KNIGHTRIDER
MAIDSTONE
Model Car Racing Track
Miniature Railway
Boat House
Cricket Ground
Rugby Grd.
Mote Cricket Club Ground
Playground
Rugby Ground
Miniature Golf Course
Maidstone Leisure Centre
Indoor Bowls Centre
Maidstone Grammar Sch.
Playing Field
ME15
Tovil
Works
Depot
LOOSE ROAD
A229
SHEAL'S CR.
Collis Mem. Fld.
Rec. Grd.
Bydews Wood
Bydews Farm
Bydews Place
Waste Disposal Site
Playing Field
Mill Pond
Up. Crisbrook Cotts.
County Fire H.Q.
Ckt. Grd.
South Pk. Armstrong Halls
Park Way Prim. Sch.
SOUTH PARK
Coombe Quarry
FORGE LODGE BUNGALOWS
Recreation Ground
Shepway
Playing Field
SUTTON ROAD
A274
B2010
LOWER ROAD
DEAN STREET
FARLEIGH HILL
Lone Cottage
East Lodge
Dean Farm
Abbey Gate Place
Abbey Gate Farm
Little Abbey Gate Farm
Abbey Gate Cottages
Little Abbey Gate
Hayle Place
Cricket Ground
Munsfield Oast
Court Lodge Farm
Bungalow Farm
Limekiln Shaw
Loose Bowls Club
YMCA Sports Centre
Fire Brigade Training Cen.
Spts. Grd.
Maidstone Cemetery
Mangravet Wood
Oak Trees
Molehill Copse

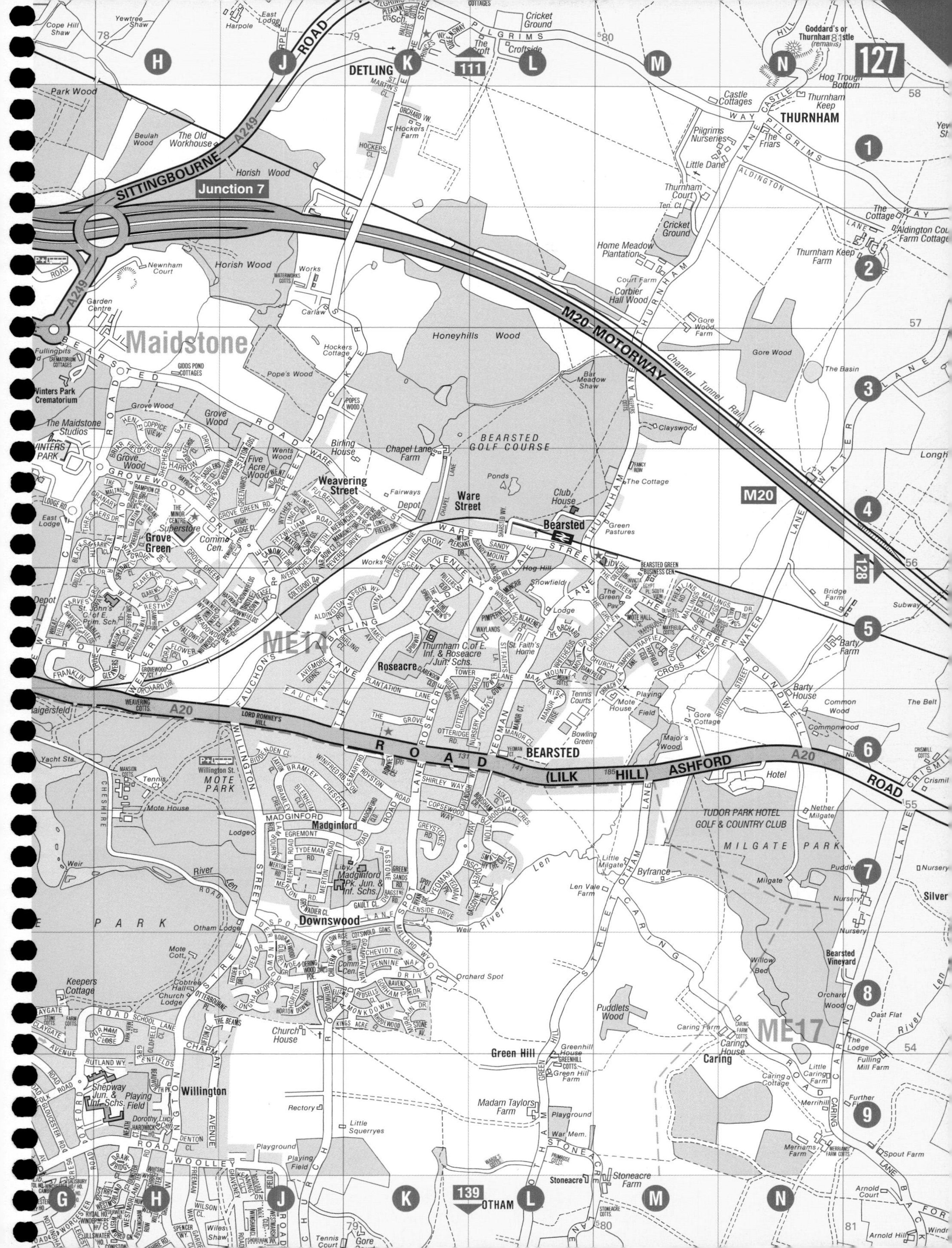
127
Detling
Thurnham
Goddard's or Thurnham Castle (remains)
Hog Trough Bottom
Thurnham Keep
Castle Cottages
Pilgrims Way
Cricket Ground
The Croft
Croftside
111
Harpole
East Lodge
Cope Hill Shaw
Yewtree Shaw
Park Wood
Beulah Wood
The Old Workhouse
Horish Wood
Sittingbourne Road
A249
Junction 7
M20 Motorway
Channel Tunnel Rail Link
Newnham Court
Garden Centre
Maidstone
Bearsted Road
Gidds Pond Cottages
Crematorium Cottages
Fullingpits
Winters Park Crematorium
The Maidstone Studios
Vinters Park
Grove Wood
Grove Green
Superstore
Comm. Cen.
Five Acre Wood
Wents Wood
Weavering Street
Ware Street
Bearsted
Bearsted Golf Course
Chapel Lane Farm
Birling House
Honeyhills Wood
Pope's Wood
Hockers Cottage
Hockers Farm
Carlaw
Works
Bar Meadow Shaw
Clayswood
Home Meadow Plantation
Court Farm
Corbier Hall Wood
Gore Wood Farm
Gore Wood
The Basin
Thurnham Court
Cricket Ground
Little Dane
Pilgrims Nurseries
The Friars
Aldington Way
The Cottage
Aldington Court Farm Cottages
Thurnham Keep Farm
Thurnham Lane
Water Lane
Green Pastures
Club House
Fairways
Depot
Hog Hill
Snowfield
Bearsted Green Business Cen.
Bridge Farm
Subway
Barty Farm
Barty House
Common Wood
Commonwood
The Belt
Roundwell
128
ME14
Roseacre
Thurnham C. of E. Inf. & Roseacre Jun. Schs.
St. Faith's Home
Tennis Courts
Mote House
Playing Field
Gore Cottage
Major's Wood
Bowling Green
Bearsted
A20
Ashford Road (Lilk Hill)
Lord Romney's Hill
Hotel
Tudor Park Hotel Golf & Country Club
Milgate Park
Nether Milgate
Milgate
Byfrance
Little Milgate
Len Vale Farm
Mote Park
Willington Street
Mote House
Yacht Sta.
Weir
River Len
Madginford
Madginford Pk. Jun. & Inf. Schs.
Downswood
Otham Lodge
Mote Cott.
Keepers Cottage
Cobtree Hall
Church Lodge
Orchard Spot
Caring Lane
Otham Street
Puddlets Wood
Willow Bed
Bearsted Vineyard
Orchard Wood
Oast Flat
ME17
Caring
Caring House
Caring Farm
Caring Cottage
Little Caring Farm
Merrihill
Fulling Mill Farm
The Lodge
Further Field
Green Hill
Greenhill House
Green Hill Farm
Madam Taylors Farm
Playground
War Mem.
Stoneacre
Stoneacre Farm
Stoneacre Lane
Merriams Farm
Spout Farm
Arnold Court
Arnold Hill
Back Lane
Church House
Rectory
Little Squerryes
Willington
Shepway Jun. & Inf. Schs.
Playing Field
Dorothy Lucy Cen.
Woolley Road
139
Otham
Tennis Court
Gore
Nursery
Puddle
Silver
Crismill
Longh
54
55
56
57
58
78
79
80
81
1
2
3
4
5
6
7
8
9
G
H
J
K
L
M
N

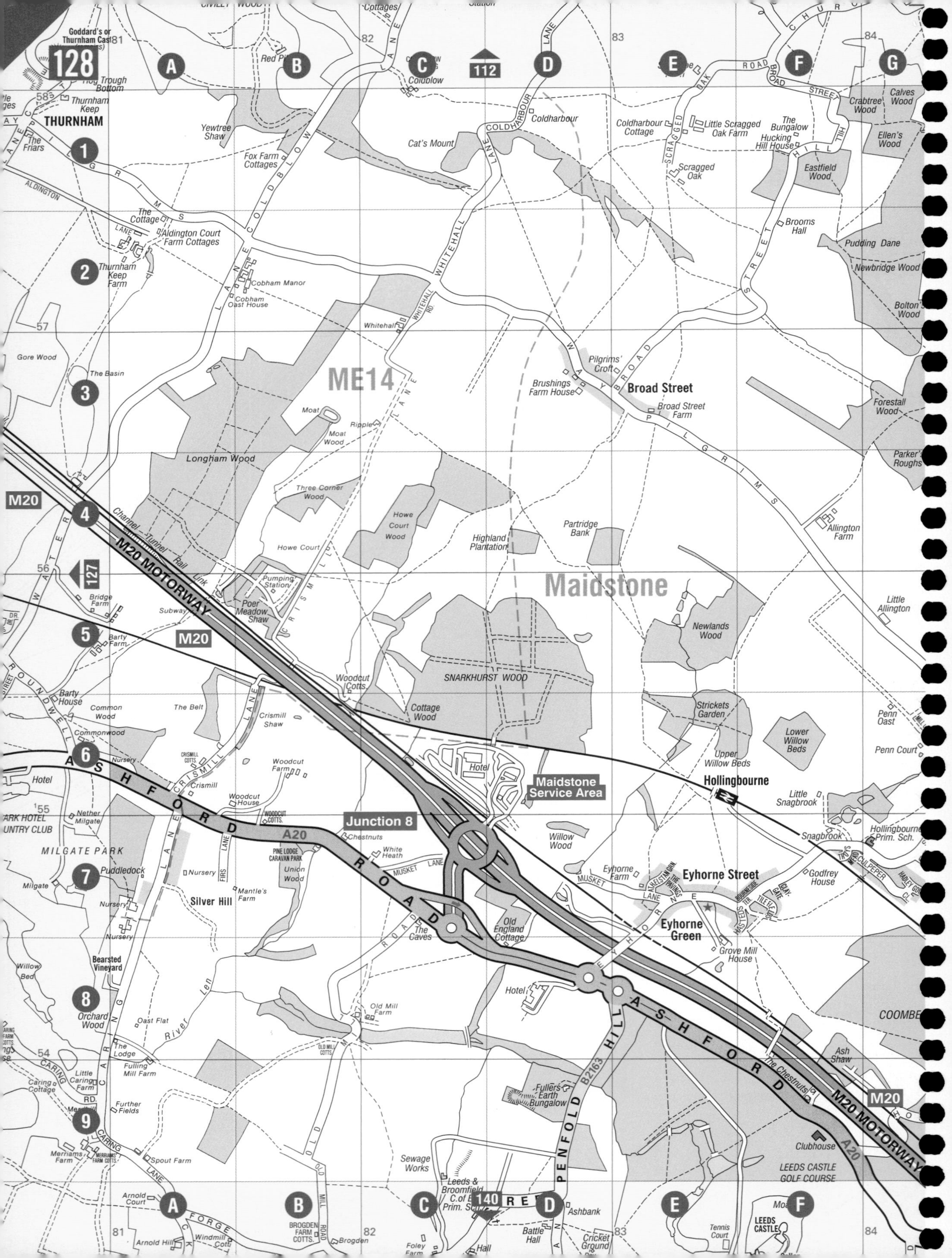
Goddard's or Thurnham Castle
Hog Trough Bottom
Thurnham Keep
THURNHAM
The Friars
Red Pi
Colddblow
112
Yewtree Shaw
Fox Farm Cottages
The Cottage
Aldington Court Farm Cottages
ALDINGTON
PILGRIMS
COLDBLOW
LANE
Coldharbour
COLDHARBOUR
Cat's Mount
Coldharbour Cottage
Little Scragged Oak Farm
The Bungalow
Hucking Hill House
Crabtree Wood
Calves Wood
Ellen's Wood
Scragged Oak
Eastfield Wood
SCRAGGED OAK ROAD
BROAD STREET
HILL
Brooms Hall
Pudding Dane
Newbridge Wood
Bolton's Wood
Thurnham Keep Farm
Cobham Manor
Cobham Oast House
WHITEHALL
Whitehall
WHITEHALL RD.
Gore Wood
The Basin
ME14
Moat
Ripple
Moat Wood
Pilgrims' Croft
Brushings Farm House
BROAD
Broad Street
Broad Street Farm
Forestall Wood
Parker's Roughs
Longham Wood
Three Corner Wood
Howe Court Wood
Howe Court
Highland Plantation
Partridge Bank
Allington Farm
M20
Channel Tunnel Rail Link
M20 MOTORWAY
127
Pumping Station
Poer Meadow Shaw
CRISMILL
Maidstone
Little Allington
Bridge Farm
Subway
Barty Farm
Newlands Wood
ROUNDWELL
Barty House
Common Wood
Commonwood
Woodcut Cotts.
SNARKHURST WOOD
The Belt
Crismill Shaw
Cottage Wood
Strickets Garden
Lower Willow Beds
Penn Oast
Penn Court
Upper Willow Beds
Nursery
CRISMILL COTTS.
Crismill
Woodcut Farm
Hotel
Maidstone Service Area
Hollingbourne
Little Snagbrook
Hotel
ASHFORD ROAD
Woodcut House
WOODCUT COTTS.
Junction 8
Nether Milgate
ARK HOTEL
UNTRY CLUB
MILGATE PARK
A20
Chestnuts
White Heath
PINE LODGE CARAVAN PARK
Union Wood
MUSKET LANE
Willow Wood
Eyhorne Farm
Eyhorne Street
Snagbrook
Hollingbourne Prim. Sch.
Godfrey House
CULPEPER
Puddledock
Milgate
Nursery
FIRS LANE
Mantle's Farm
Silver Hill
The Caves
Old England Cottage
Eyhorne Green
Grove Mill House
Bearsted Vineyard
Willow Bed
Orchard Wood
Oast Flat
River Len
Old Mill Farm
Hotel
COOMBE
The Lodge
Fulling Mill Farm
OLD MILL COTTS.
Ash Shaw
Little Caring Farm
Caring Cottage
CARING
RD.
Further Fields
Fullers Earth Bungalow
The Chestnuts
PENFOLD HILL
B2163
M20
Clubhouse
Merriams Farm
MERRIAMS FARM COTTS
Spout Farm
Sewage Works
LEEDS CASTLE GOLF COURSE
Arnold Court
Leeds & Broomfield C.of E. Prim. Sch.
140
Ashbank
Tennis Court
LEEDS CASTLE
Arnold Hill
FORGE
Windmill Cott.
BROGDEN FARM COTTS.
Brogden
OLD MILL ROAD
Foley Farm
Hall
Battle Hall
Cricket Ground
A B C D E F G
1 2 3 4 5 6 7 8 9
81 82 83 84
58 57 56 55 54

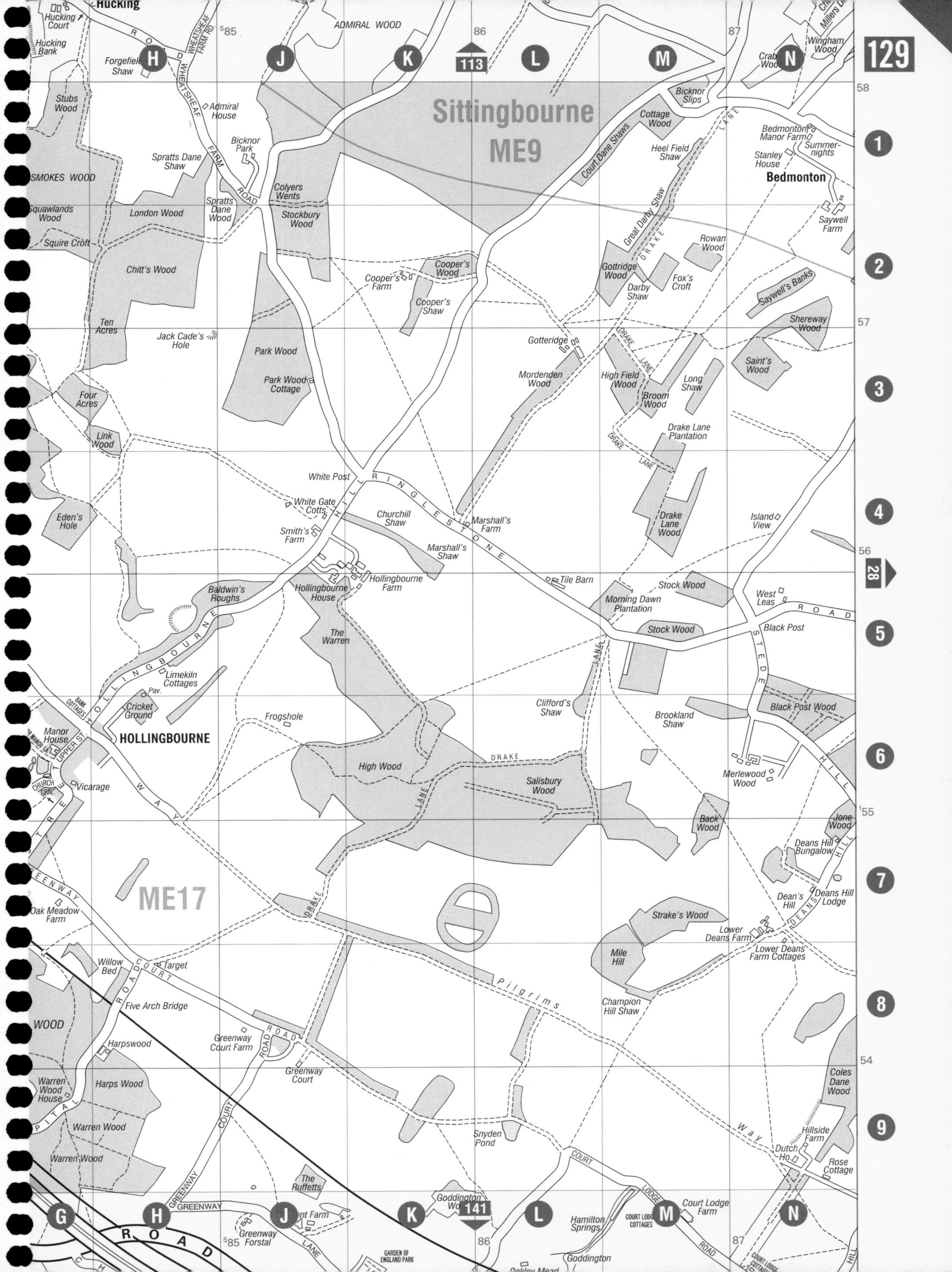
Hucking
Hucking Court
Hucking Bank
Forgefield Shaw
WHEATSHEAF FARM RD
ADMIRAL WOOD
86
85
87
113
H
J
K
L
M
N
Crab Wood
Wingham Wood
Millers
58
Sittingbourne
ME9
Stubs Wood
Admiral House
WHEATSHEAF FARM ROAD
Bicknor Park
Bicknor Slips
Cottage Wood
Court Dane Shaws
Bedmonton Manor Farm
Summer-nights
Stanley House
Bedmonton
1
Spratts Dane Shaw
SMOKES WOOD
Heel Field Shaw
LANE
Colyers Wents
Spratts Dane Wood
Squawlands Wood
London Wood
Stockbury Wood
Great Darby Shaw
DRAKE
Rowan Wood
Saywell Farm
Squire Croft
Chitt's Wood
Cooper's Wood
Cooper's Farm
Gottridge Wood
Fox's Croft
Darby Shaw
2
Saywell's Banks
Cooper's Shaw
Shereway Wood
Ten Acres
Jack Cade's Hole
57
Gotteridge
DRAKE LANE
Park Wood
Mordenden Wood
High Field Wood
Saint's Wood
Park Wood Cottage
Long Shaw
Broom Wood
3
Four Acres
Drake Lane Plantation
Link Wood
DRAKE LANE
White Post
RINGLESTONE
White Gate Cotts
HILL
Churchill Shaw
Marshall's Farm
Drake Lane Wood
Island View
4
Eden's Hole
Smith's Farm
Marshall's Shaw
56
28
Hollingbourne Farm
Tile Barn
Stock Wood
West Leas
Baldwin's Roughs
Hollingbourne House
Morning Dawn Plantation
ROAD
Black Post
Stock Wood
5
The Warren
HOLLINGBOURNE
LANE
STEDE
Limekiln Cottages
Pav.
Clifford's Shaw
BANK COTTAGES
Cricket Ground
Frogshole
Brookland Shaw
Black Post Wood
Manor House
HOLLINGBOURNE
UPPER ST
DRAKE
6
High Wood
Salisbury Wood
Merlewood Wood
HILL
CHURCH GRN.
Vicarage
WAY
LANE
55
Back Wood
Jone Wood
Deans Hill Bungalow
HILL
7
GREENWAY
ME17
DRAKE
Strake's Wood
Dean's Hill
Deans Hill Lodge
DEANS
Oak Meadow Farm
Lower Deans Farm
Lower Deans Farm Cottages
Willow Bed
COURT
ROAD
Target
Mile Hill
Pilgrims
Champion Hill Shaw
8
Five Arch Bridge
WOOD
ROAD
Greenway Court Farm
ROAD
Harpswood
54
Greenway Court
Coles Dane Wood
Warren Wood House
Harps Wood
COURT
Way
Hillside Farm
9
Warren Wood
Snyden Pond
COURT
Dutch Ho.
Rose Cottage
Warren Wood
GREENWAY
The Ruffetts
Goddington Wood
LODGE
G
H
J
K
L
M
N
141
GREENWAY
Court Lodge Farm
COURT LODGE COTTAGES
ROAD
Greenway Forstal
86
85
87
Hamilton Springs
LANE
GARDEN OF ENGLAND PARK
Goddington
ROAD
COURT LODGE COTTAGES

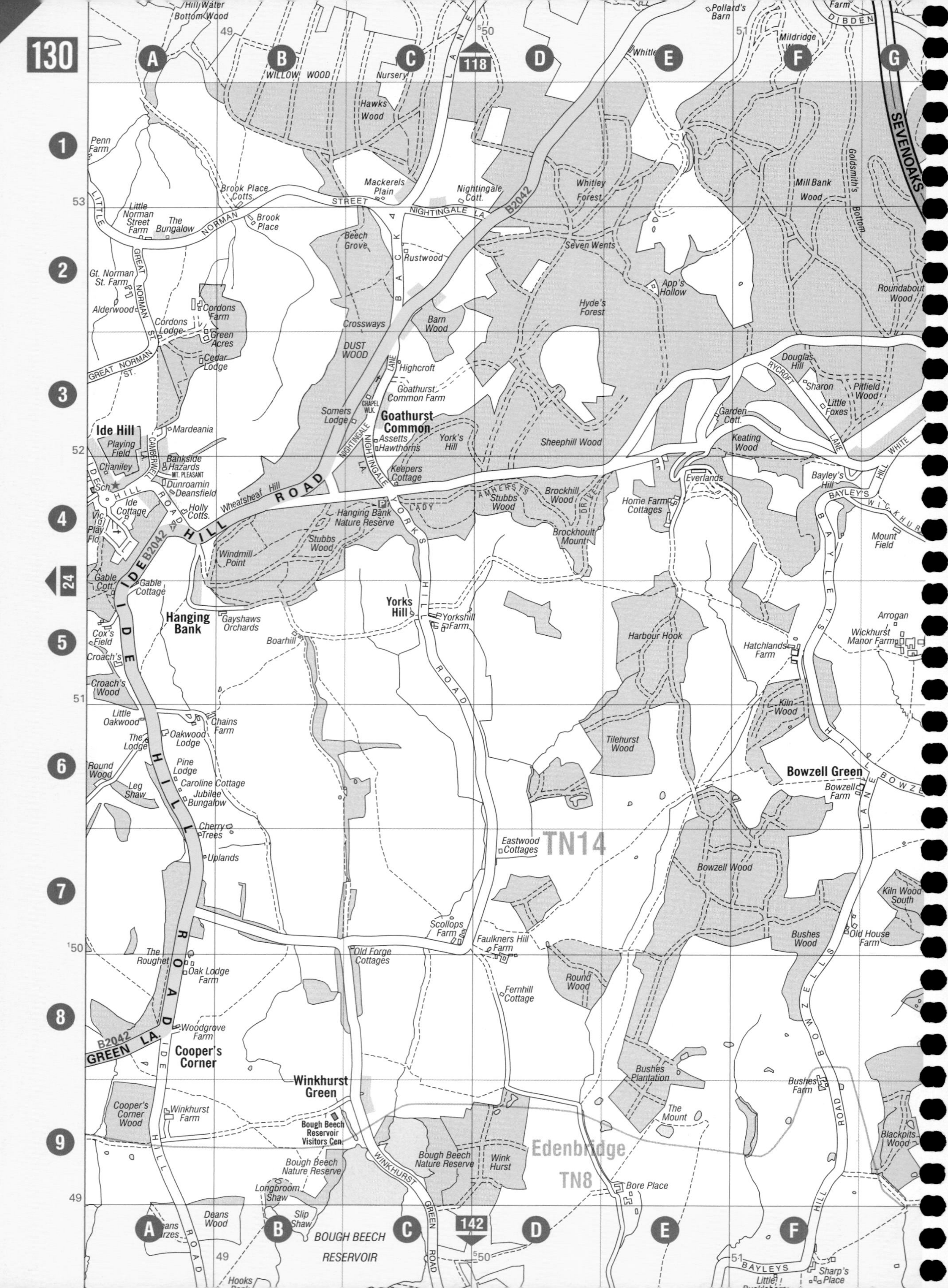

Hill Water Bottom Wood
Pollard's Barn
Farm
DIBDEN
Mildridge
Whitle
WILLOW WOOD
Nursery
118
Hawks Wood
SEVENOAKS
Penn Farm
Mackerels Plain
Nightingale Cott.
Whitley Forest
Mill Bank Wood
Goldsmith's Bottom
Brook Place Cotts
LITTLE NORMAN STREET
Little Norman Street Farm
The Bungalow
Brook Place
NIGHTINGALE LA.
B2042
Beech Grove
BACK LANE
Rustwood
Seven Wents
App's Hollow
Gt. Norman St. Farm
GREAT NORMAN ST.
Cordons Farm
Alderwood
Hyde's Forest
Roundabout Wood
Cordons Lodge
Green Acres
Crossways
Barn Wood
DUST WOOD
Cedar Lodge
Highcroft
Douglas Hill
RYCROFT
Sharon
Pitfield Wood
Goathurst Common Farm
Little Foxes
Somers Lodge
CHAPEL WLK.
Goathurst Common
Garden Cott.
Ide Hill
Mardeania
Assetts
Hawthorns
York's Hill
Sheephill Wood
Keating Wood
WHITE HILL
Playing Field
CAMBERWELL LA.
Bankside
Hazards
MT. PLEASANT
Chanlley
Keepers Cottage
Everlands
Bayley's Hill
BAYLEY'S
WICKHURST
Sch.
Dunroamin
Deansfield
Wheatsheaf Hill
ROAD
AMHERST'S
Stubbs Wood
Brockhill Wood
DRIVE
Home Farm Cottages
Ide Cottage
Holly Cotts.
LADY
Hanging Bank Nature Reserve
Vic.
Play Fld.
HILL
Brockhoult Mount
Mount Field
Windmill Point
Stubbs Wood
24
Gable Cott.
Gable Cottage
Arrogan
Hanging Bank
Gayshaws Orchards
Yorks Hill
Yorkshill Farm
Harbour Hook
Wickhurst Manor Farm
Cox's Field
Boarhill
Hatchlands Farm
Croach's
Croach's Wood
Kiln Wood
Little Oakwood
Chains Farm
Oakwood Lodge
The Lodge
Tilehurst Wood
Round Wood
Pine Lodge
Caroline Cottage
Bowzell Green
BOWZELL
Leg Shaw
Jubilee Bungalow
Bowzell Farm
Cherry Trees
Eastwood Cottages
TN14
Uplands
Bowzell Wood
Kiln Wood South
Scollops Farm
Faulkners Hill Farm
Bushes Wood
Old House Farm
The Roughet
Old Forge Cottages
Oak Lodge Farm
Round Wood
Fernhill Cottage
Woodgrove Farm
GREEN LA.
Cooper's Corner
Bushes Plantation
Bushes Farm
Winkhurst Green
The Mount
Cooper's Corner Wood
Winkhurst Farm
Bough Beech Reservoir Visitors Cen.
Blackpits Wood
Edenbridge
Bough Beech Nature Reserve
Wink Hurst
TN8
WINKHURST GREEN ROAD
Bore Place
Longbroom Shaw
Deans Wood
Slip Shaw
142
BOUGH BEECH RESERVOIR
BAYLEYS HILL
Sharp's Place
Hooks
A
B
C
D
E
F
G
1
2
3
4
5
6
7
8
9
49
50
51
52
53

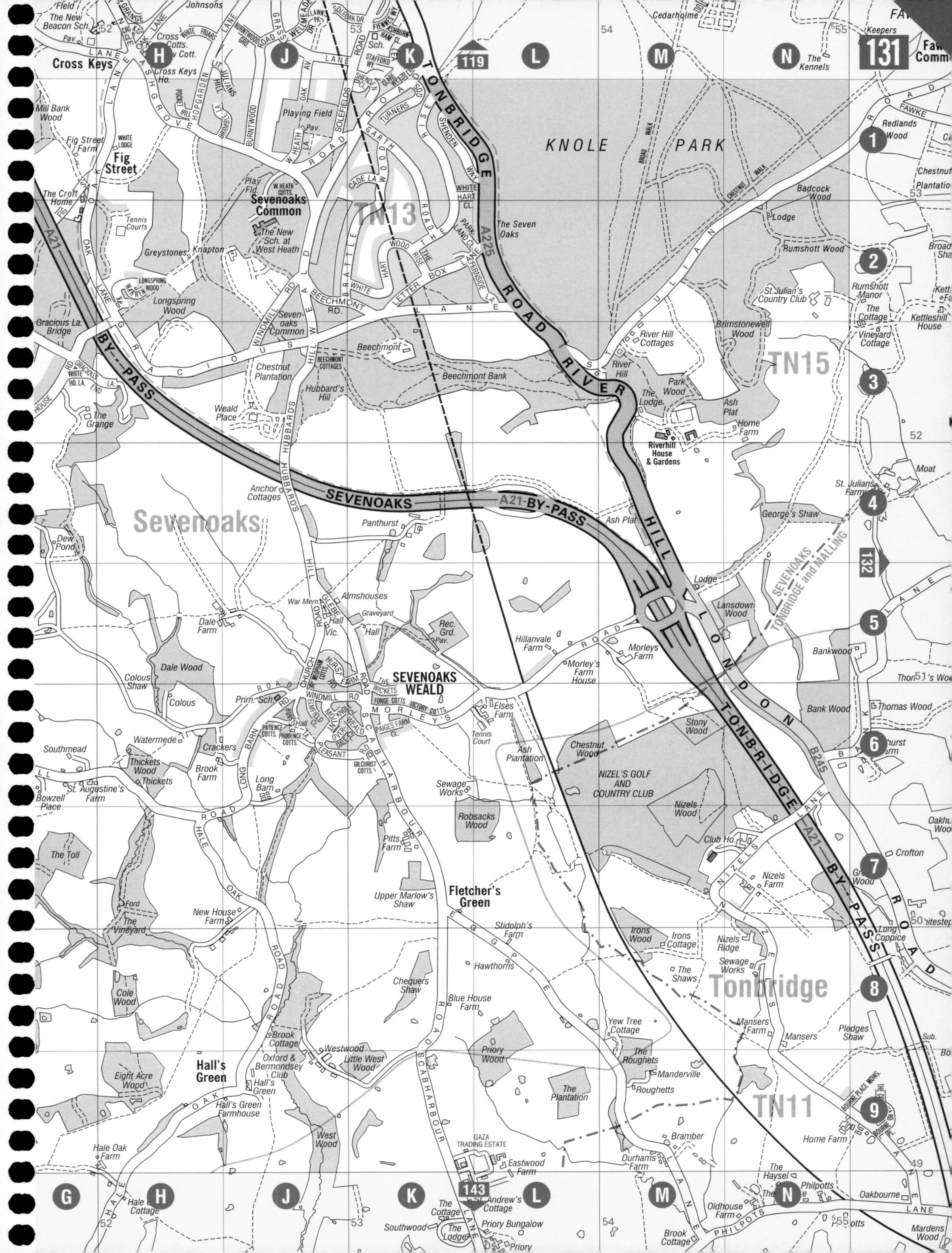
131
119
143
132
Cross Keys
The New Beacon Sch.
Field
Johnsons
Cross Cotts.
Cross Keys Ho.
Mill Bank Wood
Fig Street Farm
White Lodge
Fig Street
The Croft Home
Tennis Courts
Greystones
Knapton
Longspring Wood
Gracious La. Bridge
Sevenoaks Common
The New Sch. at West Heath
Play Fld.
W. Heath Cotts.
Playing Field
Pav.
TN13
TN15
TN11
Sevenoaks
Tonbridge
KNOLE PARK
Broad Walk
Chestnut Walk
Cedarholme
Keepers
The Kennels
Redlands Wood
Fawke Road
Chestnut Plantation
Badcock Wood
Lodge
Rumshott Wood
Rumshott Manor
The Cottage
Kettleshill House
St. Julian's Country Club
Vineyard Cottage
Brimstonewell Wood
River Hill Cottages
River Hill
Park Wood
The Lodge
Ash Plat
Home Farm
Riverhill House & Gardens
Moat
St. Julians Farm
George's Shaw
The Seven Oaks
TONBRIDGE ROAD
RIVER HILL
A225
A21
SEVENOAKS BY-PASS
A21 BY-PASS
LONDON ROAD
TONBRIDGE A21 BY-PASS
B245
SEVENOAKS TONBRIDGE and MALLING
Beechmont
Beechmont Cottages
Beechmont Bank
Chestnut Plantation
Hubbard's Hill
Weald Place
Gracious Lane
Letter Box Lane
Beechmont Rd.
Windmill Rd.
Weald
The Grange
Anchor Cottages
Panthurst
Ash Plat
Lodge
Lansdown Wood
Bankwood
Dew Pond
Dale Farm
Dale Wood
Colous Shaw
Colous
War Mem.
Almshouses
Graveyard
Hall
Vic.
Rec. Grd.
Hillanvale Farm
Morleys Farm
Morley's Farm House
SEVENOAKS WEALD
Prim. Sch.
The Wickets
Forge Cotts
Victory Cotts.
Elses Farm
Tennis Court
Ash Plantation
Chestnut Wood
Stony Wood
Bank Wood
Thomas Wood
NIZEL'S GOLF AND COUNTRY CLUB
Nizels Wood
Club Ho.
Nizels Farm
Crofton
Southmead
Watermede
Crackers
Thickets Wood
Thickets
Brook Farm
Long Barn
Patience Cotts.
Prudence Cotts.
Gilchrist Cotts.
Paiges Farm Cl.
St. Augustine's Farm
Bowzell Place
Sewage Works
Robsacks Wood
Pitts Farm
The Toll
Upper Marlow's Shaw
Fletcher's Green
New House Farm
Stidolph's Farm
Ford
The Vineyard
Irons Wood
Irons Cottage
Nizels Ridge
Sewage Works
The Shaws
Hawthorns
Chequers Shaw
Blue House Farm
Cole Wood
Yew Tree Cottage
Mansers Farm
Mansers
Pledges Shaw
Brook Cottage
Westwood
Little West Wood
Priory Wood
The Roughets
Manderville
Roughetts
Oxford & Bermondsey Club
Hall's Green
Hall's Green Farmhouse
Eight Acre Wood
The Plantation
Bourne Place Mdws.
Home Farm
West Wood
Bramber
Hale Oak Farm
Gaza Trading Estate
Eastwood Farm
Durhams Farm
The Haysel
Philpotts
Oakbourne
Hale Oak Road
Scabharbour Road
Egg Pie Lane
Oldhouse Farm
Brook Cottage
Philpots Lane
Mardens Wood
The Cottage
St. Andrew's Cottage
Priory Bungalow
Southwood
The Lodge
Priory
Hale Cottage
G
H
J
K
L
M
N
1
2
3
4
5
6
7
8
9
52
53
54
55
49
50
51

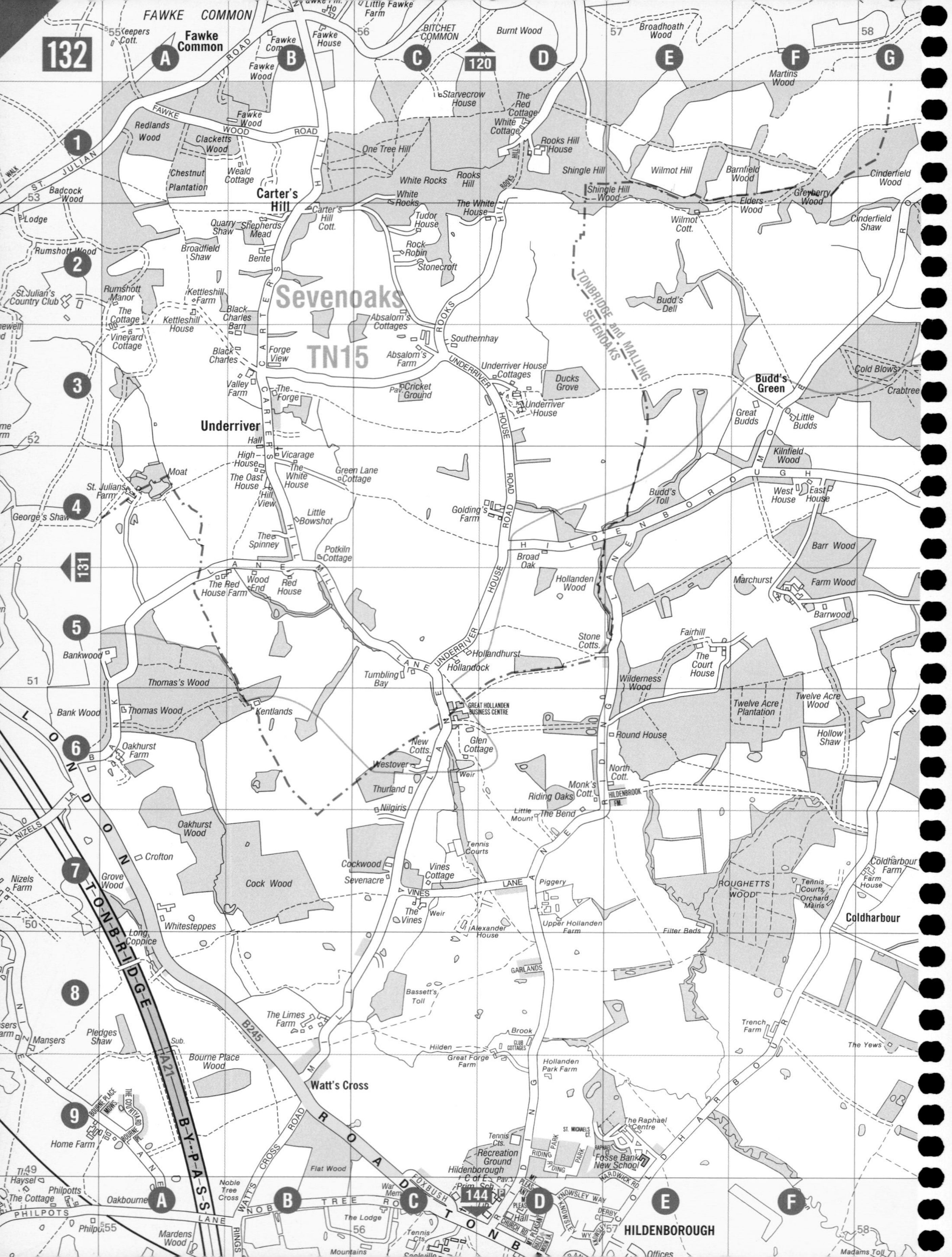
FAWKE COMMON
Fawke Common
Keepers Cott.
Fawke House
Fawke Wood
Little Fawke Farm
BITCHET COMMON
120
Burnt Wood
Broadhoath Wood
Martins Wood
Starvecrow House
The Red Cottage
White Cottage
Redlands Wood
Clacketts Wood
FAWKE WOOD ROAD
One Tree Hill
Rooks Hill House
Shingle Hill
Wilmot Hill
Barnfield Wood
Cinderfield Wood
ST. JULIAN
Chestnut Plantation
Weald Cottage
Carter's Hill
White Rocks
Rooks Hill
Shingle Hill Wood
Elders Wood
Greyberry Wood
Badcock Wood
Lodge
Quarry Shaw
Shepherds Mead
Carter's Hill Cott.
The White House
Tudor House
Wilmot Cott.
Cinderfield Shaw
Rumshott Wood
Broadfield Shaw
Bente
Rock Robin
Stonecroft
TONBRIDGE and MALLING
SEVENOAKS
St.Julian's Country Club
Rumshott Manor
Kettleshill Farm
Sevenoaks
Budd's Dell
The Cottage
Kettleshill House
Black Charles Barn
Absalom's Cottages
Vineyard Cottage
Southernhay
Black Charles
Forge View
TN15
Absalom's Farm
Underriver House Cottages
Ducks Grove
Cold Blows
Budd's Green
Crabtree
Valley Farm
The Forge
Cricket Ground
Underriver House
UNDERRIVER HOUSE ROAD
Great Budds
Little Budds
Underriver
Hall
High House
Vicarage
The White House
Green Lane Cottage
Kilnfield Wood
Moat
The Oast House
HILDENBOROUGH
West House
East House
St. Julians Farm
Hill View
Budd's Toll
George's Shaw
Little Bowshot
Golding's Farm
The Spinney
Broad Oak
Barr Wood
Potkiln Cottage
131
The Red House Farm
Wood End
Red House
Hollanden Wood
Marchurst
Farm Wood
Barrwood
Bankwood
Stone Cotts.
Fairhill
Hollandhurst
Hollandock
The Court House
Tumbling Bay
UNDERRIVER LANE
Wilderness Wood
Thomas's Wood
Bank Wood
Thomas Wood
Kentlands
GREAT HOLLANDEN BUSINESS CENTRE
Twelve Acre Plantation
Twelve Acre Wood
Round House
Hollow Shaw
Oakhurst Farm
New Cotts.
Glen Cottage
Westover
Weir
North Cott.
Thurland
Monk's Cott.
Riding Oaks
HILDENBROOK FM.
Nilgiris
Little Mount
The Bend
NIZELS LA
Oakhurst Wood
Crofton
Tennis Courts
Coldharbour Farm
Cockwood
Vines Cottage
Farm House
Nizels Farm
Grove Wood
Cock Wood
Sevenacre
VINES LANE
Piggery
ROUGHETTS WOOD
Tennis Courts
Orchard Mains
The Vines
Weir
Coldharbour
Whitesteppes
Alexander House
Upper Hollanden Farm
Filter Beds
Long Coppice
GARLANDS
TONBRIDGE BY-PASS
A21
Bassett's Toll
The Limes Farm
Mansers
Pledges Shaw
Sub.
Trench Farm
Brook
Hilden
CLUB COTTAGES
The Yews
Great Forge Farm
Bourne Place Wood
B245
Hollanden Park Farm
Watt's Cross
BOURNE PLACE MEWS
THE COWYARD
BOURNE PL
Home Farm
WATT'S CROSS ROAD
Tennis Cts.
ST. MICHAELS CT.
The Raphael Centre
Recreation Ground
RIDING PARK
Fosse Bank New School
Flat Wood
Hildenborough C of E Prim. Sch.
Haysel
Philpotts
The Cottage
Noble Tree Cross
War Mem
FOXBUSH
144
HARDWICK RD
Oakbourne
NOBLE TREE RD
KNOWSLEY WAY
DERBY CL
PHILPOTS LANE
The Lodge
Church Rd
Hall
HILDENBOROUGH
Mardens Wood
RINGS
Tennis Cts.
Offices
Mountains
Madams Court
LONDON ROAD
COLDHARBOUR
A B C D E F G
1 2 3 4 5 6 7 8 9
49 50 51 52 53
55 56 57 58

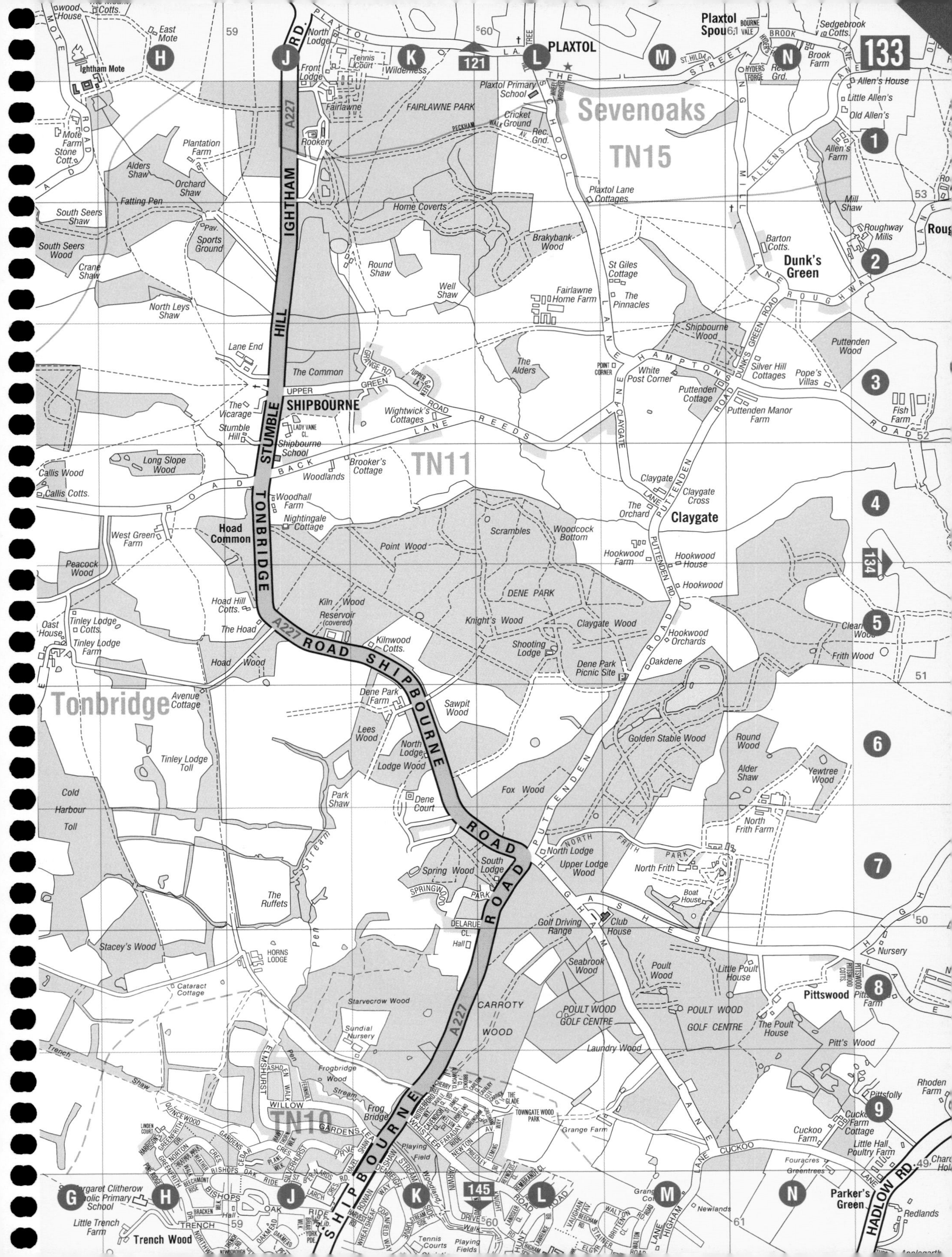

133
Ightham Mote
Mote Farm
Stone Cott.
Plantation Farm
Alders Shaw
Orchard Shaw
Fatting Pen
South Seers Shaw
South Seers Wood
Sports Ground
Crane Shaw
North Leys Shaw
Lane End
The Vicarage
Stumble Hill
Callis Wood
Callis Cotts.
Long Slope Wood
West Green Farm
Peacock Wood
Hoad Common
Hoad Hill Cotts.
Oast House
Tinley Lodge Cotts.
Tinley Lodge Farm
The Hoad
Hoad Wood
Tonbridge
Avenue Cottage
Tinley Lodge Toll
Cold Harbour Toll
The Ruffets
Stacey's Wood
Horns Lodge
Cataract Cottage
Trench Shaw
TN10
Margaret Clitherow Catholic Primary School
Little Trench Farm
Trench Wood
North Lodge
Front Lodge
Tennis Court
Wilderness
Fairlawne
FAIRLAWNE PARK
Rookery
The Common
SHIPBOURNE
Wightwick's Cottages
Shipbourne School
Woodlands
Brooker's Cottage
Woodhall Farm
Nightingale Cottage
Point Wood
Kiln Wood
Reservoir (covered)
Kilnwood Cotts.
Dene Park Farm
Lees Wood
North Lodge
Lodge Wood
Park Shaw
Dene Court
Spring Wood
South Lodge
Delarue Cl.
Hall
Starvecrow Wood
Sundial Nursery
Frogbridge Wood
Frog Bridge
Playing Field
Tennis Courts
Playing Fields
PLAXTOL
Plaxtol Primary School
Cricket Ground
Rec. Gnd.
Home Coverts
Round Shaw
Well Shaw
Brakybank Wood
Sevenoaks
TN15
Plaxtol Lane Cottages
St Giles Cottage
The Pinnacles
Fairlawne Home Farm
The Alders
White Post Corner
Puttenden Cottage
TN11
Scrambles
Woodcock Bottom
DENE PARK
Knight's Wood
Claygate Wood
Shooting Lodge
Dene Park Picnic Site
Sawpit Wood
Fox Wood
North Lodge
Upper Lodge Wood
Golf Driving Range
Club House
Seabrook Wood
CARROTY WOOD
POULT WOOD GOLF CENTRE
Laundry Wood
Towngate Wood Park
Grange Farm
Plaxtol Spout
Sedgebrook Cotts.
Brook Farm
Allen's House
Little Allen's
Old Allen's
Allen's Farm
Mill Shaw
Roughway Mills
Barton Cotts.
Dunk's Green
Shipbourne Wood
Silver Hill Cottages
Pope's Villas
Puttenden Wood
Puttenden Manor Farm
Fish Farm
Claygate
Claygate Cross
The Orchard
Hookwood Farm
Hookwood House
Hookwood
Hookwood Orchards
Oakdene
Frith Wood
Golden Stable Wood
Round Wood
Alder Shaw
Yewtree Wood
North Frith Farm
North Frith
Boat House
Poult Wood
Little Poult House
The Poult House
Pittswood
Pitt's Wood
Nursery
Rhoden Farm
Pittsfolly
Cuckoo Farm Cottage
Cuckoo Farm
Little Hall Poultry Farm
Fouracres
Greentrees
Newlands
Parker's Green
Redlands
A227
IGHTHAM HILL
STUMBLE HILL
TONBRIDGE ROAD
SHIPBOURNE ROAD
PUTTENDEN RD.
CLAYGATE LANE
HAMPTONS ROAD
REEDS LANE
BACK ROAD
ROUGHWAY LANE
HADLOW RD.
121
134
145
1
2
3
4
5
6
7
8
9
G
H
J
K
L
M
N
59
60
61
49
50
51
52
53

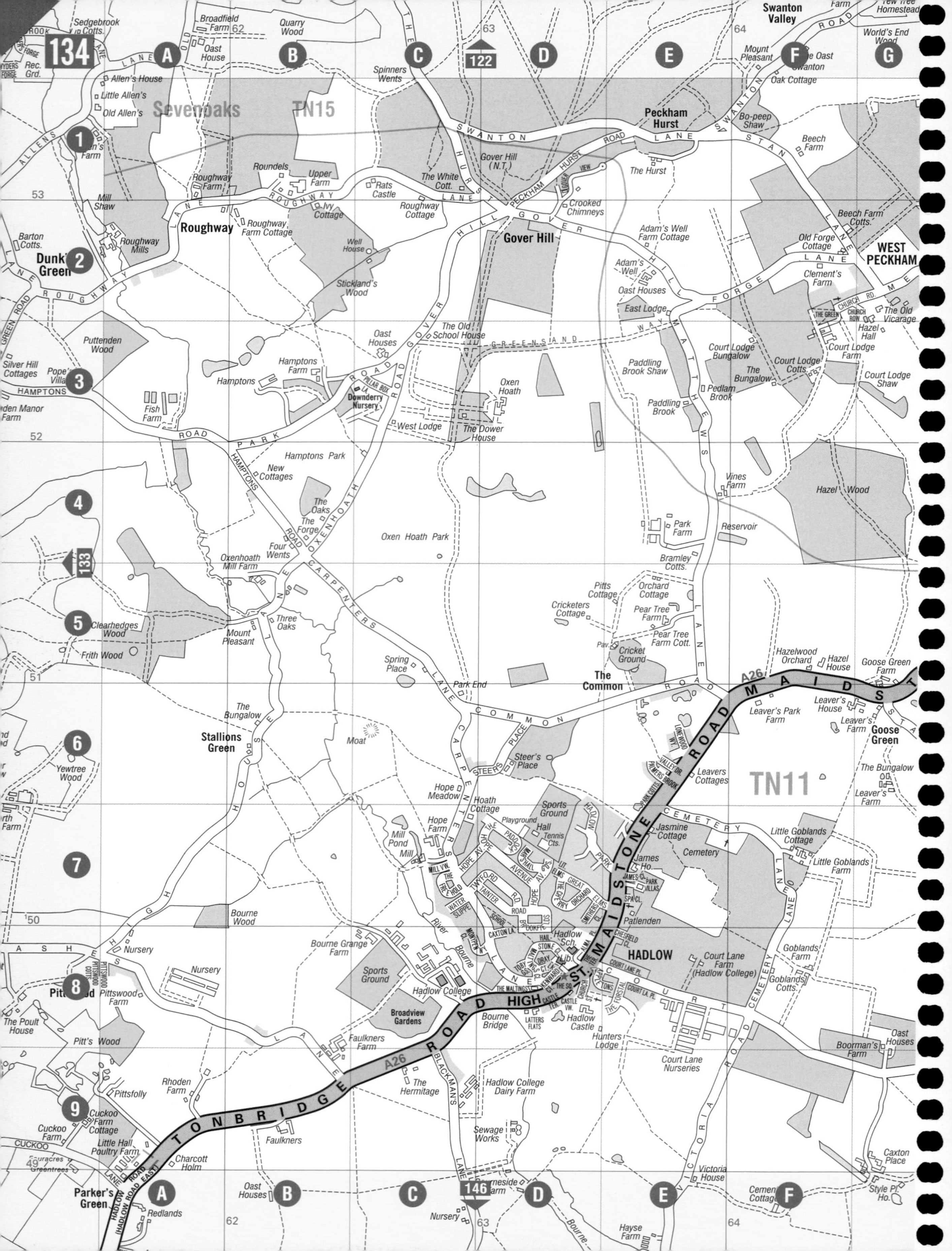

Sedgebrook Cotts.
Broadfield Farm
Quarry Wood
Oast House
122
Swanton Valley
Mount Pleasant
Oak Cottage
World's End Wood
A
B
C
D
E
F
G
Allen's House
Little Allen's
Old Allen's
Sevenoaks
TN15
Spinners Wents
Peckham Hurst
Bo-peep Shaw
Beech Farm
SWANTON LANE
Gover Hill (N.T.)
The Hurst
Roundels
Upper Farm
Roughway Farm
Rats Castle
The White Cott.
Mill Shaw
Ivy Cottage
Roughway Cottage
Crooked Chimneys
Beech Farm Cotts.
Barton Cotts.
Roughway
Roughway Farm Cottage
Roughway Mills
Gover Hill
Adam's Well Farm Cottage
Old Forge Cottage
WEST PECKHAM
Dunk's Green
Well House
Adam's Well
Oast Houses
Clement's Farm
Stickland's Wood
East Lodge
The Green
Church Row
The Old Vicarage
Hazel Hall
Puttenden Wood
Oast Houses
The Old School House
GREENSAND WAY
Court Lodge Bungalow
Court Lodge Cotts.
Court Lodge Farm
Silver Hill Cottages
Hamptons Farm
Paddling Brook Shaw
The Bungalow
Court Lodge Shaw
Hamptons
Pillar Box
Oxen Hoath
Pedlam Brook
Downderry Nursery
Fish Farm
Paddling Brook
West Lodge
The Dower House
Hamptons Park
New Cottages
Vines Farm
Hazel Wood
The Oaks
The Forge
Park Farm
Reservoir
Oxen Hoath Park
Four Wents
Bramley Cotts.
133
Oxenhoath Mill Farm
Pitts Cottage
Orchard Cottage
Cricketers Cottage
Pear Tree Farm
Clearhedges Wood
Three Oaks
Mount Pleasant
Pear Tree Farm Cott.
Frith Wood
Spring Place
Pav.
Cricket Ground
Hazelwood Orchard
Hazel House
Goose Green Farm
Park End
The Common
A26
MAIDSTONE ROAD
Leaver's Park Farm
Leaver's House
Leaver's Farm
Goose Green
The Bungalow
Stallions Green
Moat
Yewtree Wood
Steer's Place
Leavers Cottages
TN11
Leaver's Farm
Hope Meadow
Hoath Cottage
Sports Ground
Playground
Hall
Tennis Cts.
Hope Farm
Jasmine Cottage
CEMETERY LANE
Little Goblands Cottage
Mill Pond
Mill
Cemetery
James Ho.
Little Goblands Farm
Park Villas
Bourne Wood
Patlenden
Hadlow Sch.
Lib.
HADLOW
Court Lane Farm (Hadlow College)
Goblands Farm
Goblands Cotts.
Bourne Grange Farm
Nursery
Nursery
Sports Ground
River Bourne
Pittswood Farm
Hadlow College
The Maltings
Broadview Gardens
HIGH ST.
Bourne Bridge
Latters Flats
Hadlow Castle
The Poult House
Pitt's Wood
Faulkners Farm
Hunters Lodge
Oast Houses
Boorman's Farm
Court Lane Nurseries
Rhoden Farm
The Hermitage
Hadlow College Dairy Farm
Pittsfolly
Cuckoo Farm Cottage
TONBRIDGE ROAD
Cuckoo Farm
Little Hall Poultry Farm
Faulkners
Sewage Works
Charcott Holm
Caxton Place
Victoria House
Parker's Green
Oast Houses
146
Style Pl. Ho.
Redlands
Nursery
Hayse Farm
62
63
64
53
52
51
50
49
1
2
3
4
5
6
7
8
9

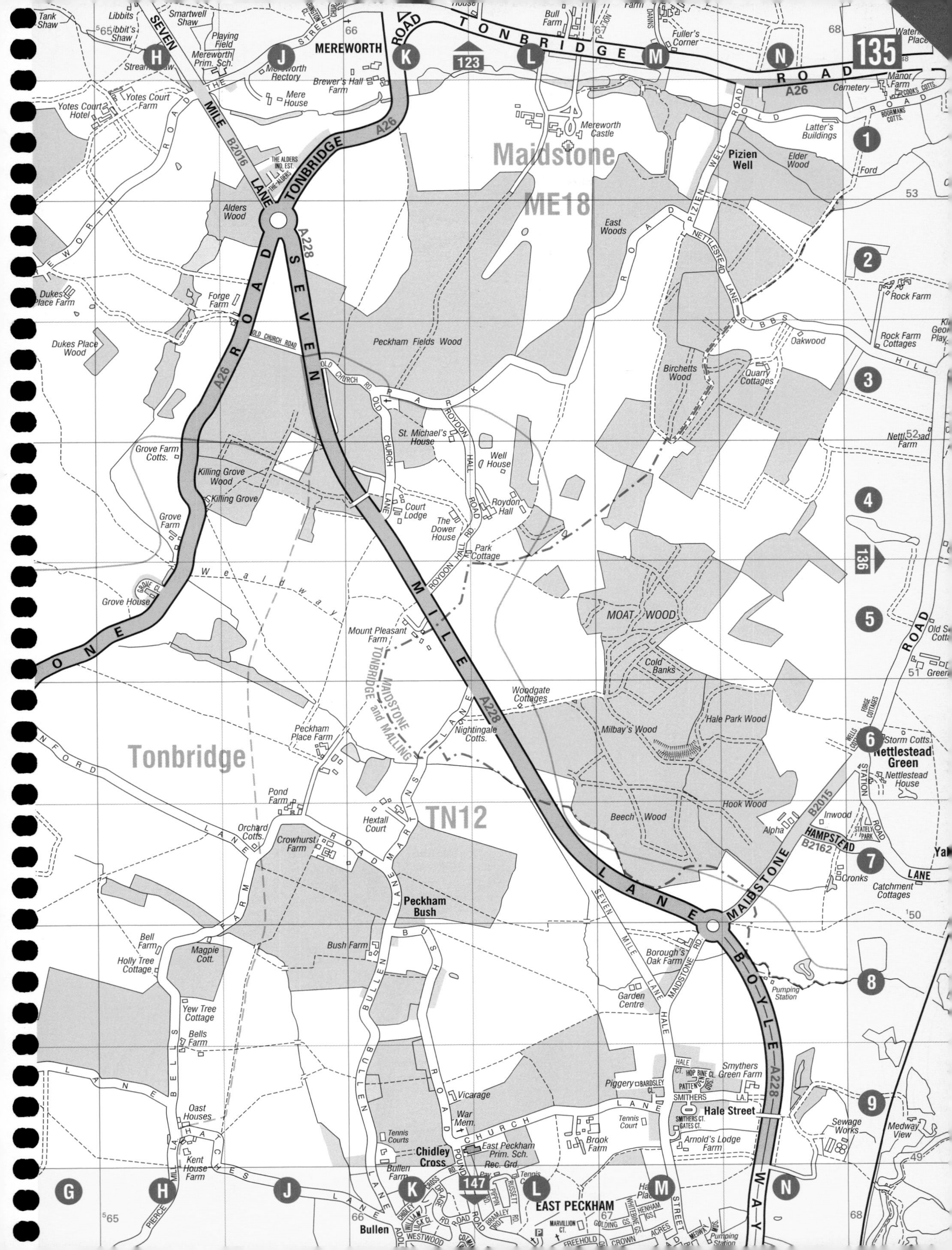

MEREWORTH
Maidstone
ME18
Tonbridge
TN12
TONBRIDGE ROAD
A26
SEVEN MILE LANE
A228
B2016
Mereworth Castle
Pizien Well
Peckham Fields Wood
MOAT WOOD
Nettlestead Green
Peckham Bush
Chidley Cross
EAST PECKHAM
Hale Street
Bullen
Wealdway
MAIDSTONE and MALLING
TONBRIDGE
B2015
B2162
123
136
147

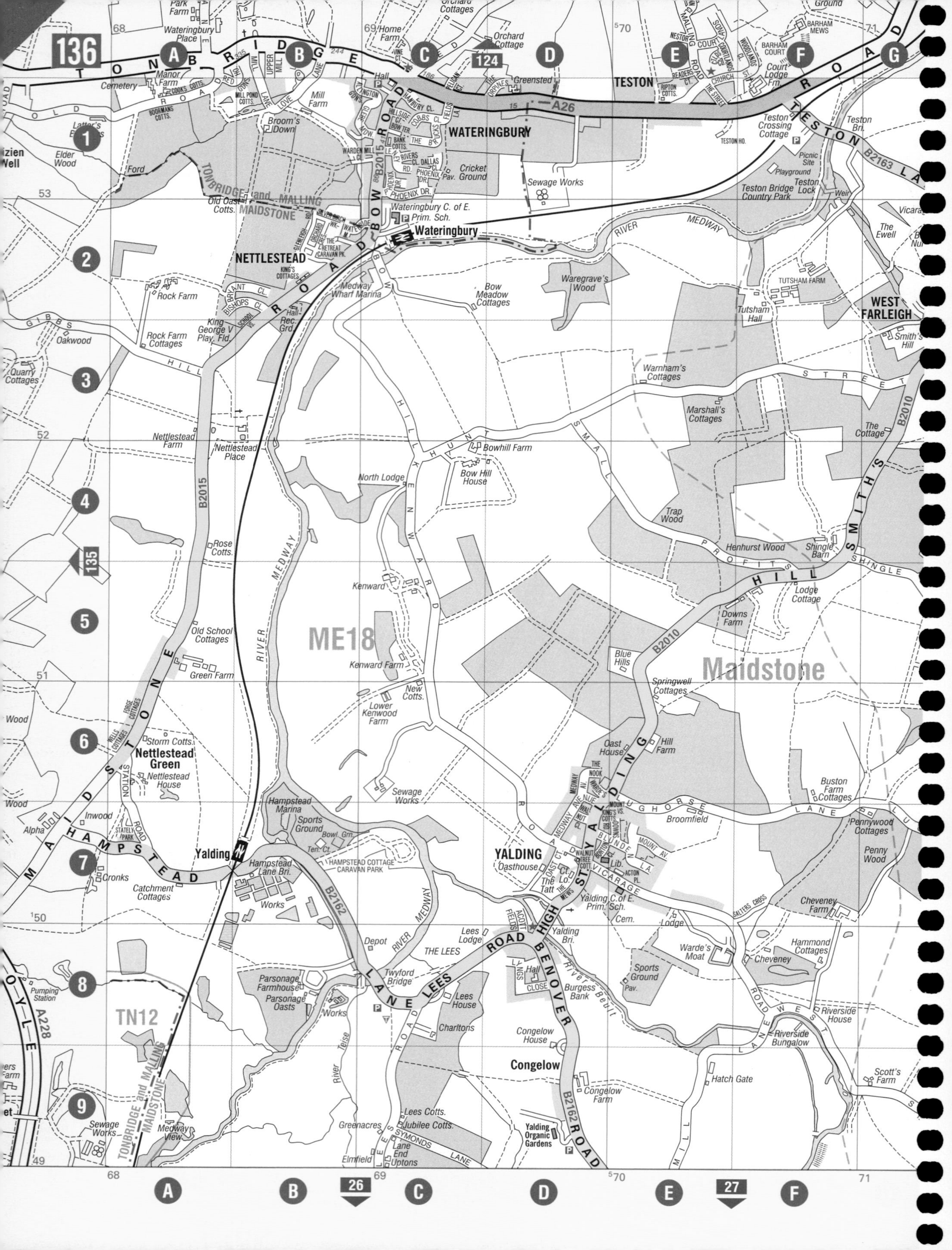
124
135
TONBRIDGE ROAD
A26
TESTON
WATERINGBURY
Wateringbury
NETTLESTEAD
WEST FARLEIGH
Nettlestead Green
YALDING
Yalding
Congelow
ME18
TN12
Maidstone
B2015
B2010
B2162
B2163
A228
RIVER MEDWAY
River Teise
River Beult
BOW ROAD
MAIDSTONE ROAD
HAMPSTEAD LANE
LEES ROAD
LANE LEES
BENOVER ROAD
HIGH STREET
VICARAGE
KENWARD ROAD
HUNT STREET
SMALL
PROFITS HILL
SMITH'S HILL
STREET
LUGHORSE LANE
WEST LANE
SYMONDS LANE
GIBBS HILL
STATION ROAD
SHINGLE BARN LANE
TESTON LANE
OLD ROAD
TONBRIDGE and MALLING
MAIDSTONE
Manor Farm
Cemetery
Latter's Barn
Elder Wood
Ford
Mill Farm
Broom's Down
Old Oast Cotts.
Cricket Ground
Sewage Works
Wateringbury C. of E. Prim. Sch.
Medway Wharf Marina
King's Cottages
Rock Farm
Rock Farm Cottages
King George V Play. Fld.
Rec. Grd.
Oakwood
Quarry Cottages
Bow Meadow Cottages
Waregrave's Wood
Teston Crossing Cottage
Teston Bridge Country Park
Teston Lock
Teston Bri.
Picnic Site
Playground
Weir
The Ewell
Tutsham Farm
Tutsham Hall
Smith's Hill
Warnham's Cottages
Marshall's Cottages
The Cottage
Nettlestead Farm
Nettlestead Place
Bowhill Farm
Bow Hill House
North Lodge
Trap Wood
Henhurst Wood
Shingle Barn
Lodge Cottage
Downs Farm
Rose Cotts.
Kenward
Kenward Farm
Old School Cottages
Green Farm
Blue Hills
Springwell Cottages
New Cotts.
Lower Kenwood Farm
Storm Cotts.
Nettlestead House
Oast House
Hill Farm
Sewage Works
Buston Farm Cottages
Broomfield
Pennywood Cottages
Penny Wood
Hampstead Marina
Sports Ground
Inwood
Alpha
Cronks
Catchment Cottages
Hampstead Lane Bri.
Hampstead Cottage Caravan Park
Works
Yalding Oasthouse
Yalding C. of E. Prim. Sch.
Cem.
Lodge
Cheveney Farm
Hammond Cottages
Cheveney
Warde's Moat
Sports Ground
Depot
THE LEES
Lees Lodge
Yalding Bri.
Twyford Bridge
Parsonage Farmhouse
Parsonage Oasts
Lees House
Charltons
Burgess Bank
Congelow House
Riverside House
Riverside Bungalow
Hatch Gate
Scott's Farm
Congelow Farm
Pumping Station
Sewage Works
Medway View
Greenacres
Lees Cotts.
Jubilee Cotts.
Lane End
Uptons
Elmfield
Yalding Organic Gardens
68
69
70
71
53
52
51
50
49
26
27

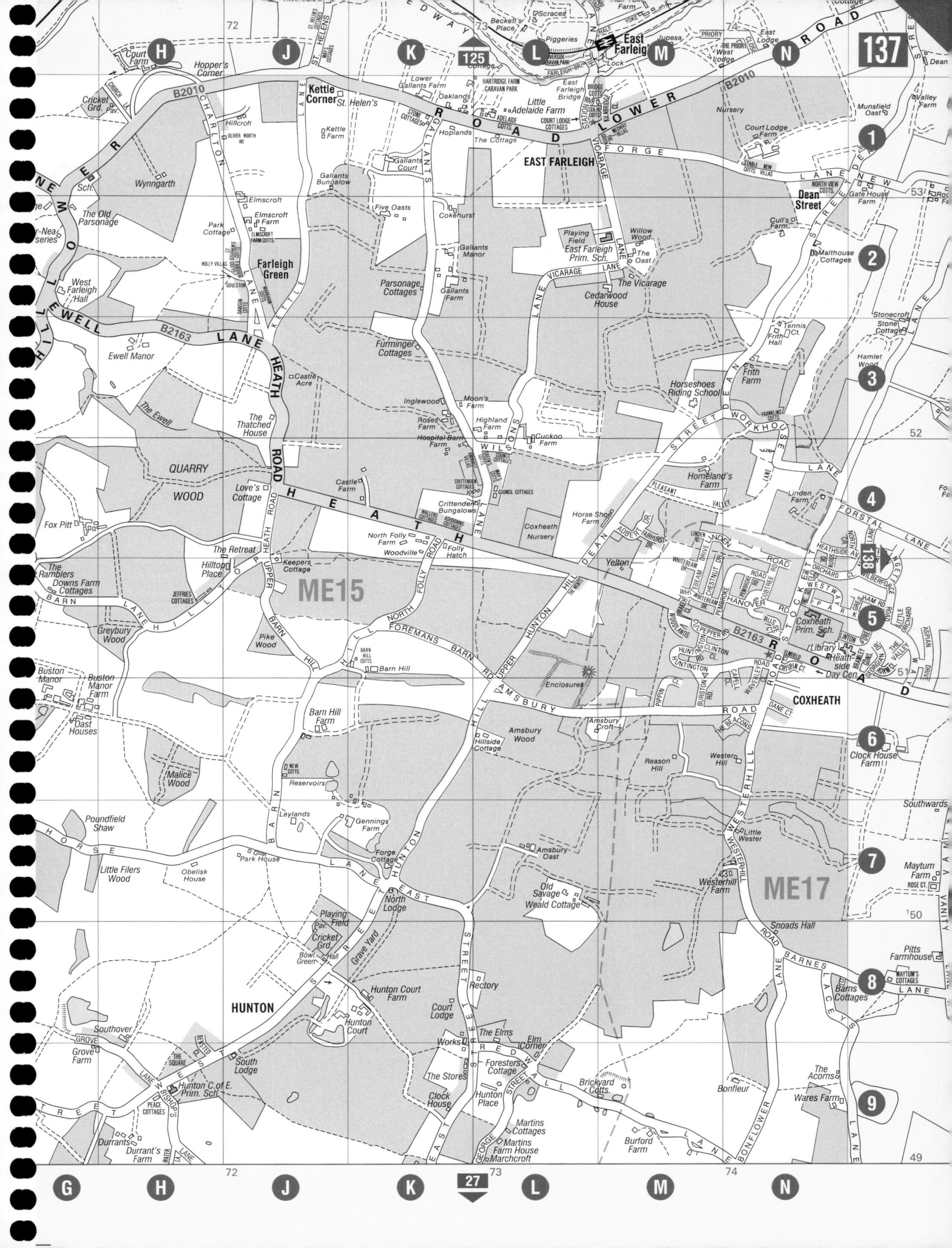

137
125
27
138
H
J
K
L
M
N
G
1
2
3
4
5
6
7
8
9
72
73
74
53
52
51
50
49
East Farleigh
EAST FARLEIGH
Dean Street
COXHEATH
HUNTON
ME15
ME17
B2010
B2163
LOWER ROAD
FORGE LANE
NEW LANE
DEAN STREET
VICARAGE LANE
GALLANTS LANE
KETTLE LANE
CHARLTON LANE
HEATH ROAD
EWELL LANE
WILSONS LANE
WORKHOUSE LANE
PLEASANT VALLEY
FORSTAL LANE
HUNTON HILL
UPPER HUNTON HILL
AMSBURY ROAD
FOREMANS BARN RD
NORTH FOLLY ROAD
BARN HILL
UPPER BARN HILL
BARN HILL
HILLTOP
HORSE LANE
EAST STREET
WEST STREET
REDWALL
GEORGE STREET
WESTERHILL ROAD
BARNES LANE
BONFLOWER LANE
LACEYS LANE
GROVE LANE
BISHOP'S LANE
Court Farm
Hopper's Corner
Cricket Grd.
Pav.
Kettle Corner
St. Helen's
Kettle Farm
Hillcroft
Wynngarth
Sch.
The Old Parsonage
Elmscroft
Elmscroft Farm
Park Cottage
Farleigh Green
West Farleigh Hall
Ewell Manor
The Ewell
The Thatched House
QUARRY WOOD
Love's Cottage
Fox Pitt
The Retreat
Hilltop Place
The Ramblers
Downs Farm Cottages
Greybury Wood
Pike Wood
Buston Manor
Buston Manor Farm
Oast Houses
Malice Wood
Poundfield Shaw
Little Filers Wood
Obelisk House
Park House
Southover
Grove Farm
South Lodge
Hunton C.of E. Prim. Sch.
Durrants
Durrant's Farm
Lower Gallants Farm
Oaklands
Hoplands
Gallants Court
Gallants Bungalow
Five Oasts
Cokehurst
Gallants Manor
Parsonage Cottages
Gallants Farm
Furminger Cottages
Castle Acre
Inglewood
Moon's Farm
Roses Farm
Hospital Barn Farm
Highland Farm
Cuckoo Farm
Castle Farm
Crittenden Bungalows
Council Cottages
Coxheath Nursery
North Folly Farm
Woodville
Folly Hatch
Keepers Cottage
Barn Hill
Barn Hill Farm
Reservoirs
Leylands
Gennings Farm
Forge Cottage
North Lodge
Playing Field
Cricket Grd.
Bowl. Green
Hall
Grave Yard
Hunton Court Farm
Hunton Court
Rectory
Court Lodge
Works
The Elms
Elm Corner
Foresters Cottage
The Stores
Clock House
Hunton Place
Martins Cottages
Martins Farm House
Marchcroft
Brickyard Cotts.
Burford Farm
Beckett's Place
Scraces
Piggeries
Jupesa
Lock
Little Adelaide Farm
East Farleigh Bridge
The Cottage
Playing Field
East Farleigh Prim. Sch.
Willow Wood
The Oast
The Vicarage
Cedarwood House
Horseshoes Riding School
Frith Farm
Frith Hall
Tennis Ct.
Homeland's Farm
Horse Shoe Farm
Yelton
Enclosures
Amsbury Croft
Amsbury Wood
Hillside Cottage
Reason Hill
Western Hill
Little Wester
Westerhill Farm
Amsbury Oast
Old Savage
Weald Cottage
Snoads Hall
Bonfleur
Nursery
Court Lodge Farm
Munsfield Oast
Valley Farm
Cull's Farm
Malthouse Cottages
Stonecroft
Stone Cottage
Hamlet Wood
Gate House Farm
Linden Farm
Coxheath Prim. Sch.
Library
Heath-side Day Cen.
Clock House Farm
Southwards
Maytum Farm
Pitts Farmhouse
Barns Cottages
The Acorns
Wares Farm
Dean

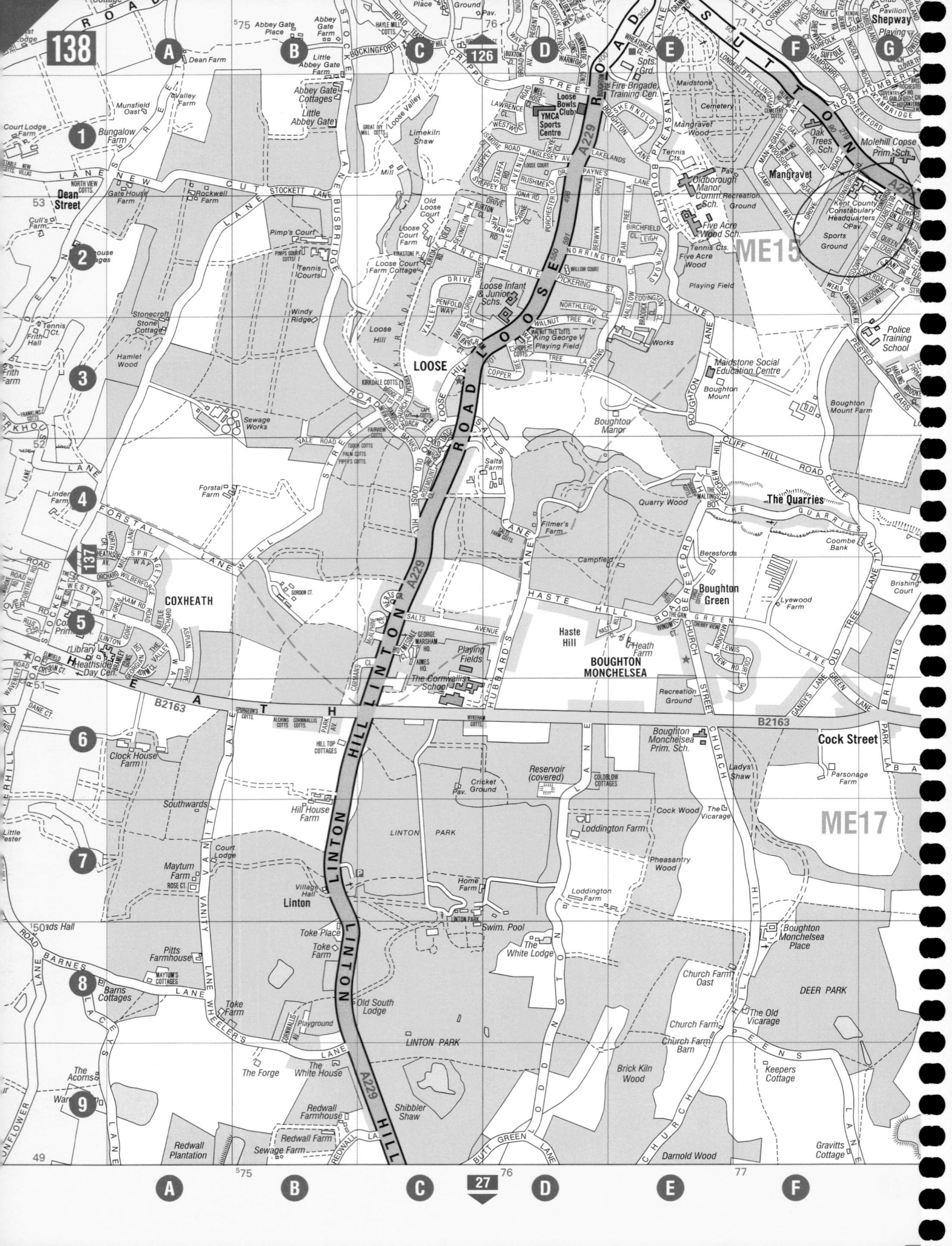
A
B
C
D
E
F
G
1
2
3
4
5
6
7
8
9
126
137
27
575
76
77
53
52
51
50
49
Abbey Gate Place
Abbey Gate Farm
Little Abbey Gate Farm
Abbey Gate Cottages
Little Abbey Gate
Dean Farm
Valley Farm
Munsfield Oast
Court Lodge Farm
Bungalow Farm
Dean Street
Gate House Farm
Rockwell Farm
Stockett Lane
New Cut
Bockingford
Cripple Street
Loose Valley
Limekiln Shaw
Loose Bowls Club
YMCA Sports Centre
Fire Brigade Training Cen.
Maidstone Cemetery
Mangravet Wood
Oak Trees Sch.
Mangravet
Molehill Copse Prim. Sch.
Shepway
Sutton Road
A274
A229
Loose Road
Oldborough Manor Comm. Sch.
Recreation Ground
Five Acre Wood Sch.
Five Acre Wood
Kent County Constabulary Headquarters
Sports Ground
ME15
Playing Field
Pimp's Court
Loose Court Farm
Loose Court Farm Cottage
Old Loose Court
Tennis Courts
Windy Ridge
Loose Hill
Loose Infant & Junior Schs.
King George V Playing Field
LOOSE
Works
Maidstone Social Education Centre
Boughton Mount
Boughton Mount Farm
Police Training School
Stonecroft Stone Cottage
Hamlet Wood
Frith Hall
Frith Farm
Sewage Works
Boughton Manor
Salts Farm
Forstal Farm
Linden Farm
Quarry Wood
The Quarries
Filmer's Farm
Coombe Bank
Beresfords
Campfield
Boughton Green
Lyewood Farm
Brishing Court
COXHEATH
Haste Hill
Heath Farm
BOUGHTON MONCHELSEA
Playing Fields
The Cornwallis School
Heathside Day Cen.
Library
B2163
Heath Road
Recreation Ground
Boughton Monchelsea Prim. Sch.
Cock Street
Parsonage Farm
Clock House Farm
Hill Top Cottages
Reservoir (covered)
Cricket Ground
Ladys Shaw
Southwards
Hill House Farm
Linton Park
Cock Wood
The Vicarage
Loddington Farm
ME17
Court Lodge
Maytum Farm
Pheasantry Wood
Village Hall
Linton
Home Farm
Linton Hill
Toke Place
Toke Farm
Swim. Pool
The White Lodge
Boughton Monchelsea Place
Pitts Farmhouse
Barns Cottages
Old South Lodge
Playground
Church Farm Oast
Deer Park
The Old Vicarage
Church Farm
Church Farm Barn
The Forge
The White House
Brick Kiln Wood
Keepers Cottage
The Acorns
Redwall Farmhouse
Shibbler Shaw
Redwall Farm
Sewage Farm
Redwall Plantation
Butt Green Lane
Darnold Wood
Gravitts Cottage

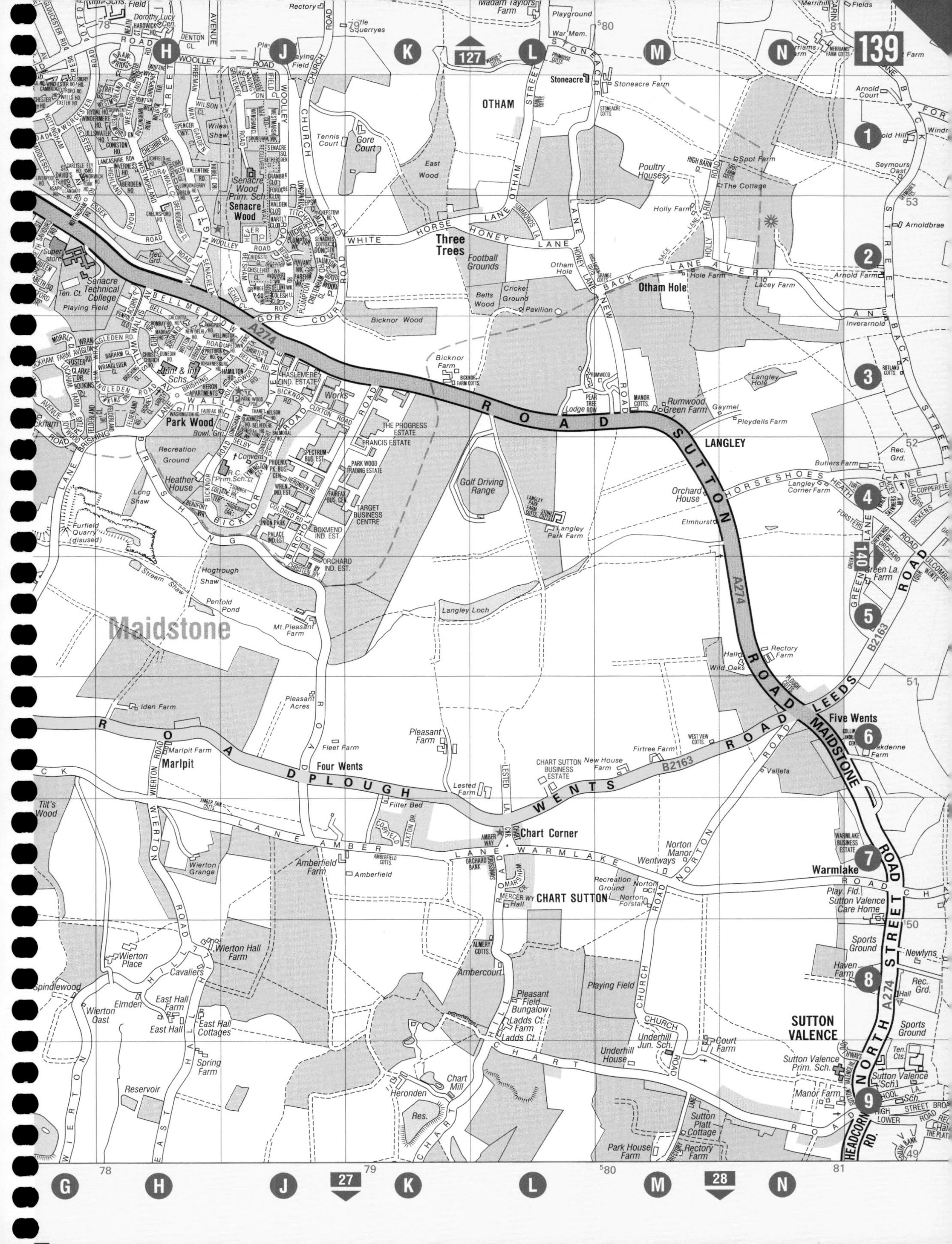

139
127
140
27
28
G
H
J
K
L
M
N
1
2
3
4
5
6
7
8
9
78
79
80
81
53
52
51
50
49
Maidstone
OTHAM
Stoneacre
Stoneacre Farm
Three Trees
Senacre Wood
Senacre Wood Prim. Sch.
Senacre Technical College
Playing Field
Park Wood
Recreation Ground
Heather House
Long Shaw
Furfield Quarry (disused)
Hogtrough Shaw
Penfold Pond
Mt.Pleasant Farm
Iden Farm
Marlpit
Marlpit Farm
Tilt's Wood
Four Wents
Fleet Farm
Pleasant Acres
Pleasant Farm
Lested Farm
Filter Bed
Chart Corner
CHART SUTTON
CHART SUTTON BUSINESS ESTATE
Amberfield Farm
Amberfield
Wierton Grange
Wierton Place
Wierton Hall Farm
Wierton Oast
Spindlewood
Cavaliers
Elmden
East Hall Farm
East Hall
East Hall Cottages
Spring Farm
Reservoir
Heronden
Res.
Chart Mill
Ambercourt
Pleasant Field Bungalow
Ladds Ct. Farm
Ladds Ct.
Playing Field
Underhill House
Underhill Jun. Sch.
Court Farm
Sutton Platt Cottage
Park House Farm
Rectory Farm
SUTTON VALENCE
Sutton Valence Prim. Sch.
Sutton Valence Sch.
Manor Farm
Sports Ground
Haven Farm
Newlyns
Rec. Grd.
Warmlake
Warmlake Business Estate
Sutton Valence Care Home
Wentways
Norton Manor
Norton Forstal
Recreation Ground
Valleta
Five Wents
Oakdenne Farm
Firtree Farm
New House Farm
Wild Oaks
Rectory Farm
Langley Loch
Langley Park Farm
Golf Driving Range
Elmhurst
Orchard House
LANGLEY
Langley Corner Farm
Butlers Farm
Green La. Farm
Pleydells Farm
Gaymel
Rumwood Green Farm
Lodge
Langley Hole
Rutland Cotts.
Inverarnold
Lacey Farm
Hole Farm
Otham Hole
Arnold Farm
Arnoldbrae
Seymours Oast
Arnold Court
Spot Farm
The Cottage
Poultry Houses
Holly Farm
Otham Hole
Football Grounds
Belts Wood
Cricket Ground
Pavilion
Bicknor Wood
Bicknor Farm
East Wood
Gore Court
Tennis Court
Playground
War Mem.
Madam Taylors Farm
Rectory
Little Squerryes
THE PROGRESS ESTATE
FRANCIS ESTATE
HASLEMERE IND. ESTATE
TARGET BUSINESS CENTRE
BOXMEND IND. EST.
ORCHARD IND. EST.
Works
A274
B2163
SUTTON ROAD
LEEDS ROAD
MAIDSTONE ROAD
NORTH STREET
WENTS ROAD
DPLOUGH ROAD
WARMLAKE ROAD
AMBER LANE
CHART ROAD
CHURCH ROAD
HONEY LANE
WHITE HORSE LANE
BACK LANE
AVERY LANE
HORSESHOES LANE
WOOLLEY ROAD
GORE COURT ROAD
BRISHING LANE
WIERTON ROAD
EAST HALL HILL
HEADCORN RD.

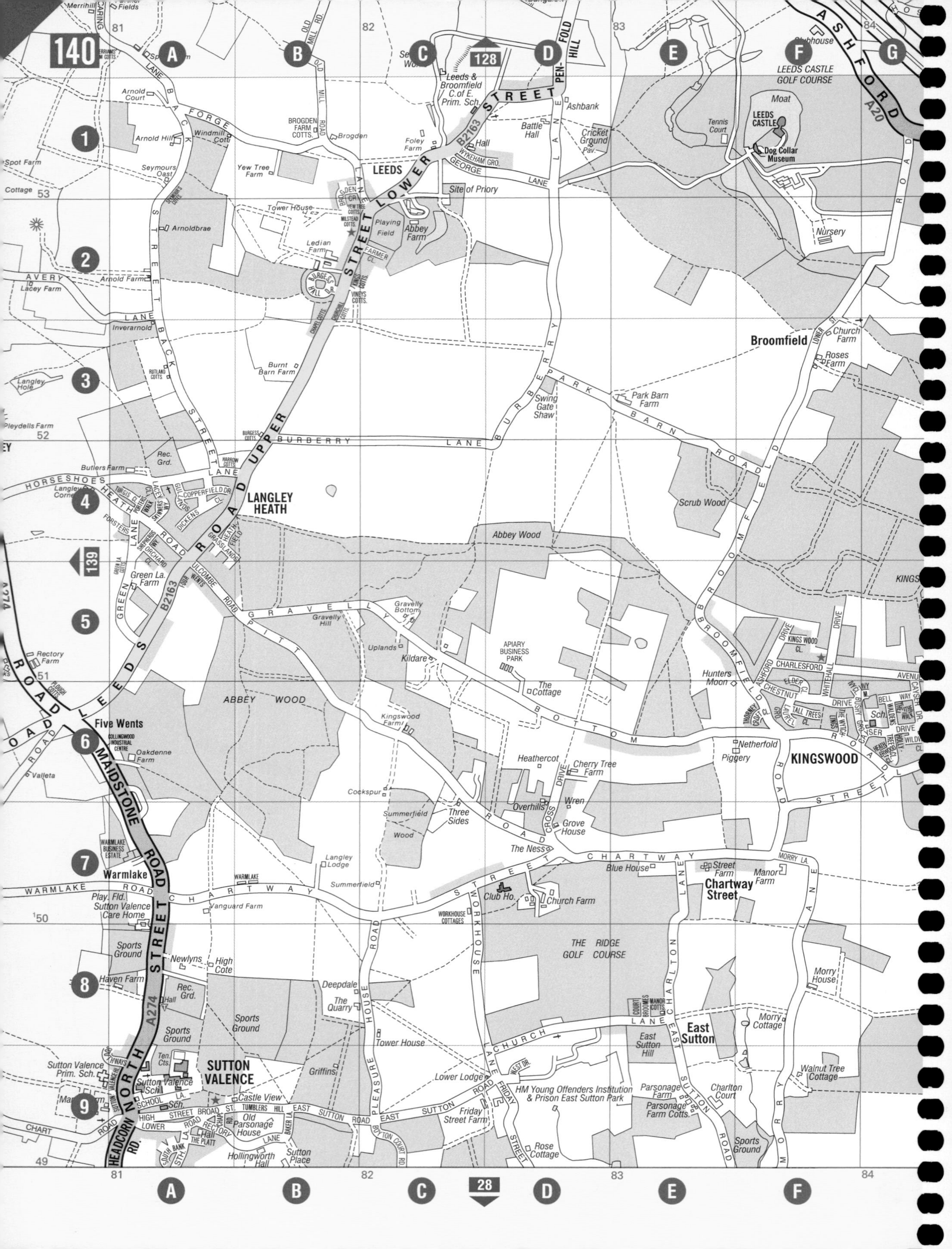

LEEDS
LANGLEY HEATH
Broomfield
KINGSWOOD
Chartway Street
East Sutton
SUTTON VALENCE
Five Wents
Warmlake
LEEDS CASTLE
LEEDS CASTLE GOLF COURSE
Dog Collar Museum
ABBEY WOOD
Abbey Wood
Scrub Wood
THE RIDGE GOLF COURSE
APIARY BUSINESS PARK
HM Young Offenders Institution & Prison East Sutton Park
LOWER STREET
UPPER STREET
ROAD
LEEDS ROAD
MAIDSTONE ROAD
NORTH STREET
ASHFORD ROAD
BROOMFIELD ROAD
BURBERRY LANE
PARK BARN ROAD
GRAVELLY BOTTOM ROAD
PITT ROAD
CHARTWAY STREET
WARMLAKE ROAD
WORKHOUSE ROAD
PLEASURE HOUSE ROAD
CHURCH LANE
EAST SUTTON ROAD
SUTTON ROAD
CHARLTON LANE
MORRY LANE
FORGE LANE
BACK STREET
AVERY LANE
HORSESHOES LANE
HEATH ROAD
PEN-FOLD HILL
GEORGE LANE

128
139
28

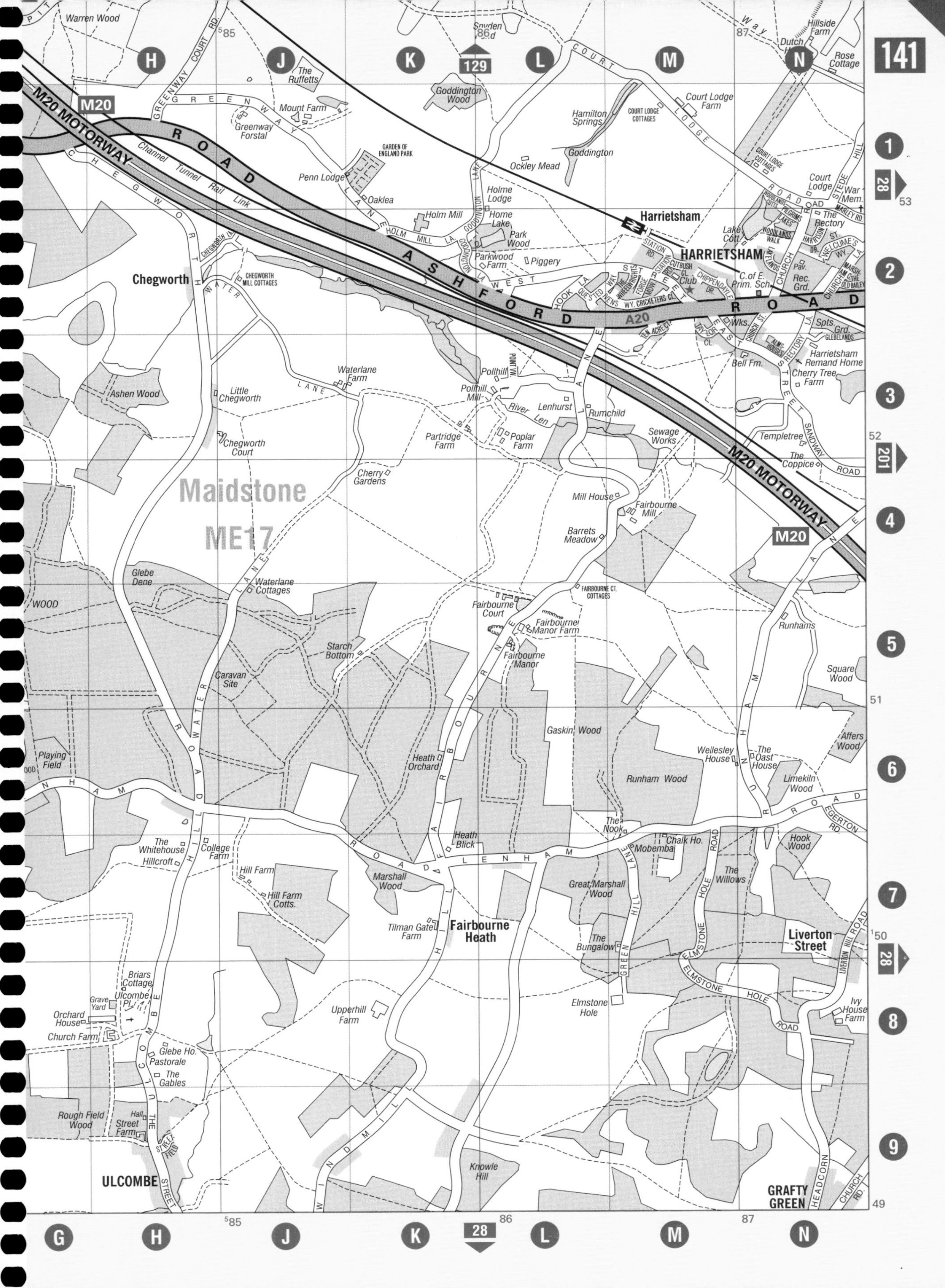

Warren Wood
The Ruffetts
Goddington Wood
Snyden Rd
Hillside Farm
Dutch
Rose Cottage
M20
M20 MOTORWAY
ASHFORD ROAD
Channel Tunnel Rail Link
Mount Farm
Greenway Forstal
GREENWAY
GREENWAY COURT RD.
GARDEN OF ENGLAND PARK
Penn Lodge
Oaklea
Holm Mill
HOLM MILL LA.
Holme Lodge
Home Lake
Park Wood
Parkwood Farm
Piggery
Ockley Mead
Goddington
Hamilton Springs
COURT LODGE COTTAGES
Court Lodge Farm
COURT LODGE
Court Lodge
War Mem.
Harrietsham
HARRIETSHAM
The Rectory
Lake Cott.
C.of E. Prim. Sch.
Par. Rec. Grd.
Club
Wks.
Bell Fm.
Spts. Grd.
Harrietsham Remand Home
Cherry Tree Farm
Chegworth
CHEGWORTH MILL COTTAGES
CHEGWORTH RD.
A20
Waterlane Farm
Pollhill
Pollhill Mill
River Len
Lenhurst
Rumchild
Little Chegworth
Ashen Wood
Chegworth Court
Partridge Farm
Poplar Farm
Sewage Works
Templetree
The Coppice
SANDWAY ROAD
Cherry Gardens
Maidstone
ME17
Mill House
Fairbourne Mill
Barrets Meadow
Glebe Dene
Waterlane Cottages
FAIRBOURNE CT. COTTAGES
Fairbourne Court
Fairbourne Manor Farm
Fairbourne Manor
Runhams
Starch Bottom
Caravan Site
WOOD
Square Wood
Gaskin Wood
Affers Wood
Playing Field
Heath Orchard
Wellesley House
The Oast House
Runham Wood
Limekiln Wood
FAIRBOURNE LANE
WATER LANE
EGERTON RD.
The Whitehouse
Hillcroft
College Farm
Heath Blick
The Nook
Chalk Ho.
Mobemba
Hook Wood
Hill Farm
Marshall Wood
Hill Farm Cotts.
Great Marshall Wood
The Willows
LENHAM ROAD
Tilman Gate Farm
Fairbourne Heath
The Bungalow
Liverton Street
LIVERTON HILL ROAD
ELMSTONE HOLE ROAD
Elmstone Hole
Upperhill Farm
Ivy House Farm
Briars Cottage
Ulcombe Pl.
Grave Yard
Orchard House
Church Farm
Glebe Ho.
Pastorale
The Gables
Rough Field Wood
Hall Street Farm
THE STREET
ULCOMBE
WINDMILL HILL
Knowle Hill
GRAFTY GREEN
HEADCORN ROAD
CHURCH RD.
G
H
J
K
L
M
N
1
2
3
4
5
6
7
8
9
129
28
201

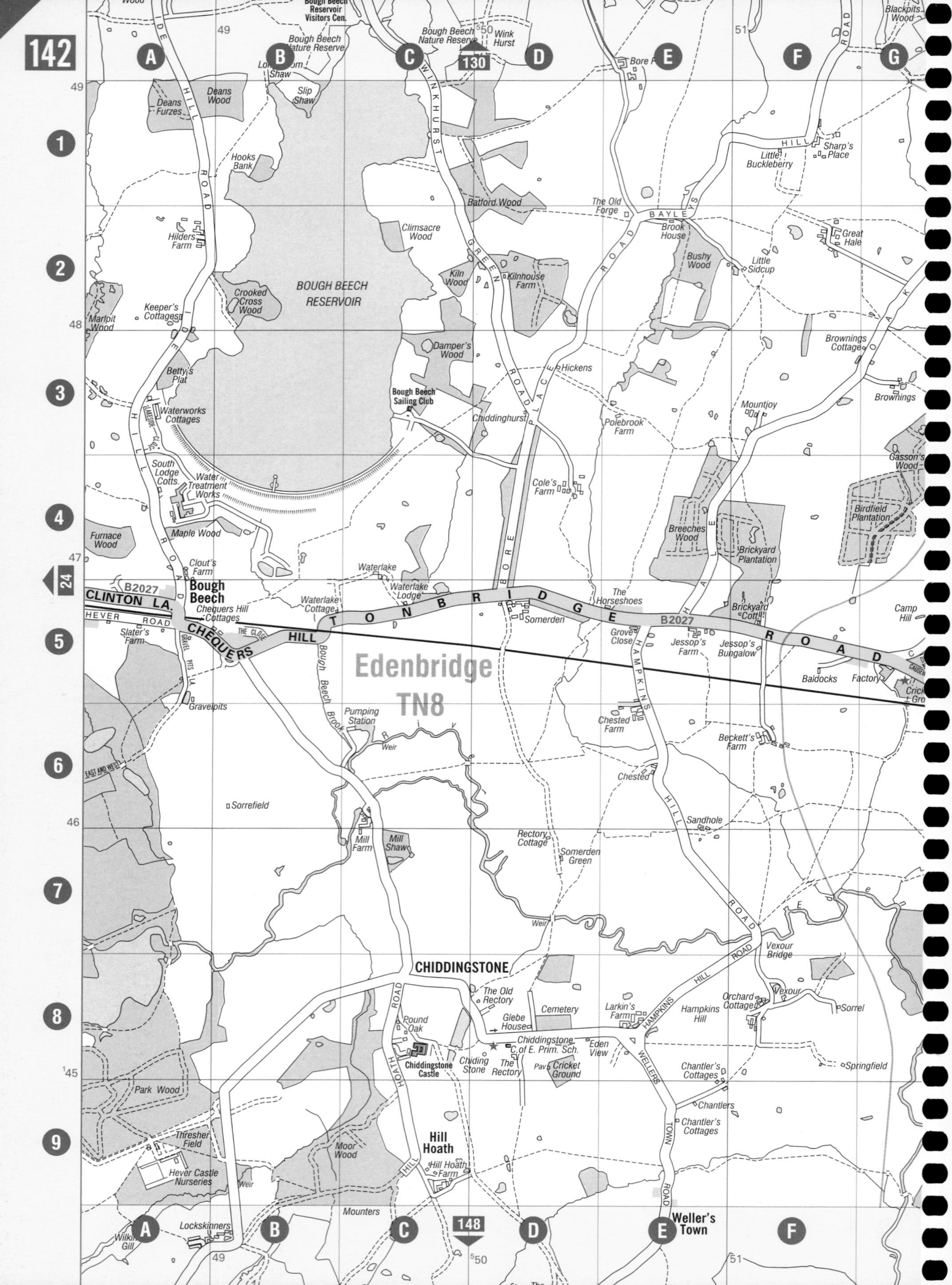
Bough Beech Reservoir Visitors Cen.
Bough Beech Nature Reserve
130
Wink Hurst
Deans Wood
Deans Furzes
Slip Shaw
Hooks Bank
Batford Wood
The Old Forge
Brook House
Bushy Wood
Little Sidcup
Great Hale
Little Buckleberry
Sharp's Place
Hilders Farm
Climsacre Wood
Kiln Wood
Kilnhouse Farm
BOUGH BEECH RESERVOIR
Crooked Cross Wood
Keeper's Cottages
Marlpit Wood
Damper's Wood
Hickens
Brownings Cottage
Brownings
Betty's Plat
Waterworks Cottages
Bough Beech Sailing Club
Chiddinghurst
Polebrook Farm
Mountjoy
Gasson's Wood
South Lodge Cotts.
Water Treatment Works
Cole's Farm
Birdfield Plantation
Furnace Wood
Maple Wood
Breeches Wood
Brickyard Plantation
Clout's Farm
Waterlake
Waterlake Lodge
Waterlake Cottage
24
B2027
Bough Beech
CLINTON LA.
HEVER ROAD
Chequers Hill Cottages
CHEQUERS HILL
TONBRIDGE ROAD
The Horseshoes
Somerden
Brickyard Cott.
Camp Hill
Slater's Farm
Grove Close
Jessop's Farm
Jessop's Bungalow
Baldocks
Factory
Edenbridge TN8
Gravelpits
Pumping Station
Chested Farm
Beckett's Farm
Weir
Chested
Sorrefield
Sandhole
Mill Farm
Mill Shaw
Rectory Cottage
Somerden Green
Vexour Bridge
CHIDDINGSTONE
The Old Rectory
Cemetery
Larkin's Farm
Orchard Cottage
Vexour
Sorrel
Hampkins Hill
Pound Oak
Glebe House
Chiddingstone C. of E. Prim. Sch.
Eden View
Chiddingstone Castle
Chiding Stone
The Rectory
Cricket Ground
Chantler's Cottages
Springfield
Park Wood
Chantlers
Hill Hoath
Thresher Field
Moor Wood
Hill Hoath Farm
Hever Castle Nurseries
Mounters
148
Weller's Town
Lockskinners
Wilkin Gill

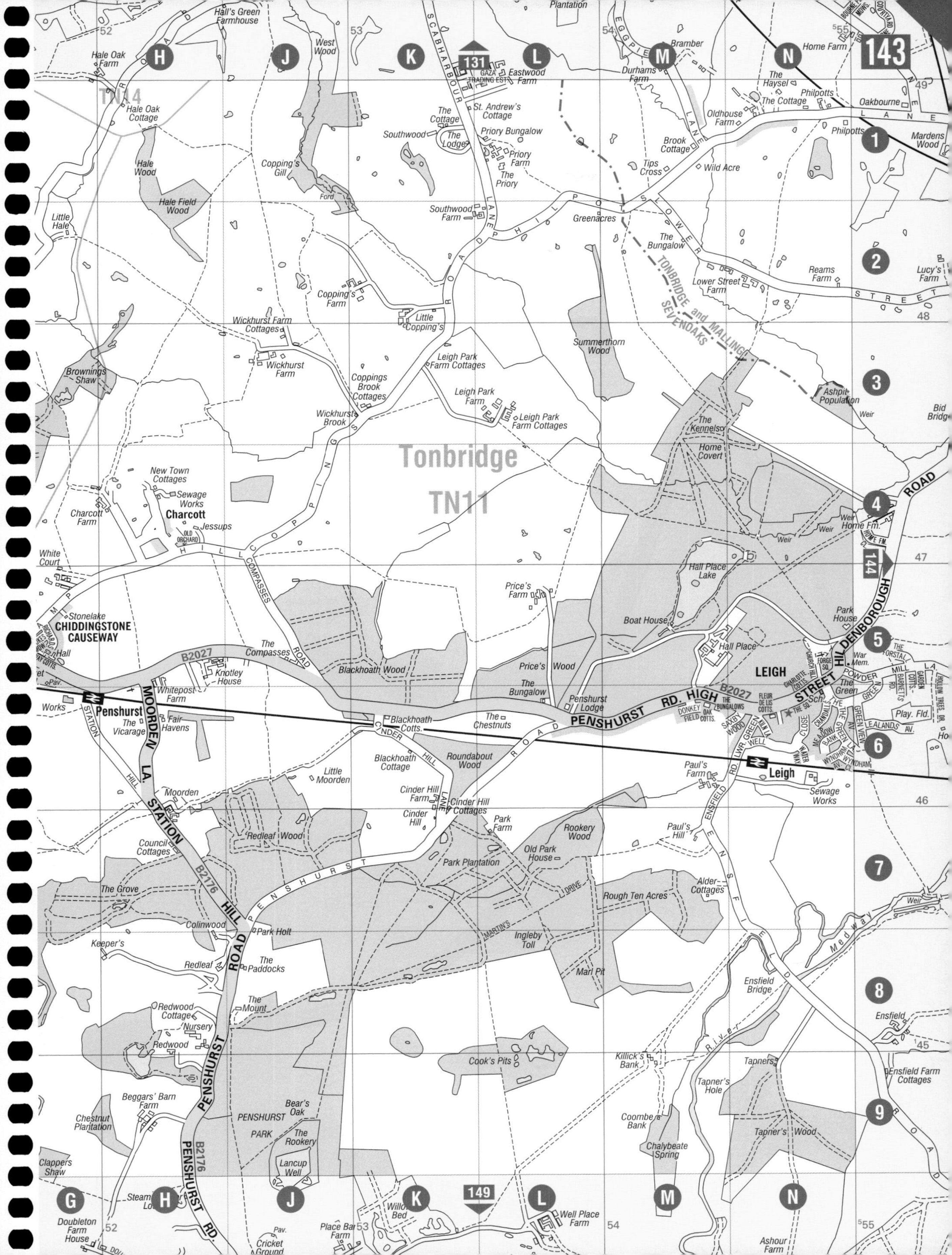

Tonbridge
TN11
TN14
CHIDDINGSTONE CAUSEWAY
LEIGH
Charcott
Penshurst
Leigh
Hall's Green Farmhouse
Hale Oak Farm
Hale Oak Cottage
Hale Wood
Hale Field Wood
Little Hale
West Wood
Copping's Gill
Ford
Plantation
Gaza Trading Est.
Eastwood Farm
The Cottage
St. Andrew's Cottage
Southwood
The Lodge
Priory Bungalow
Priory Farm
The Priory
Southwood Farm
Bramber
Durhams Farm
The Haysel
The Cottage
Philpotts
Home Farm
Oakbourne
Oldhouse Farm
Brook Cottage
Tips Cross
Wild Acre
Mardens Wood
Greenacres
The Bungalow
Lower Street Farm
Reams Farm
Lucy's Farm
Tonbridge and Malling
Sevenoaks
Copping's Farm
Little Copping's
Wickhurst Farm Cottages
Wickhurst Farm
Brownings Shaw
Leigh Park Farm Cottages
Coppings Brook Cottages
Leigh Park Farm
Leigh Park Farm Cottages
Wickhurst Brook
Summerthorn Wood
Ashpit Population
Weir
Bid Bridge
The Kennels
Home Covert
New Town Cottages
Sewage Works
Charcott Farm
Jessups
Old Orchard
White Court
Home Fm.
Hall Place Lake
Price's Farm
Boat House
Park House
Stonelake
Hall
The Compasses
Knotley House
Whitepost Farm
Works
Blackhoath Wood
Price's Wood
The Bungalow
Hall Place
War Mem.
Penshurst Lodge
The Vicarage
Fair Havens
Blackhoath Cotts.
The Chestnuts
Blackhoath Cottage
Little Moorden
Roundabout Wood
Paul's Farm
Sewage Works
Moorden
Cinder Hill Farm
Cinder Hill Cottages
Cinder Hill
Park Farm
Rookery Wood
Paul's Hill
Council Cottages
Redleaf Wood
Old Park House
Park Plantation
The Grove
Rough Ten Acres
Alder Cottages
Colinwood
Park Holt
Ingleby Toll
Keeper's
Redleaf
The Paddocks
Marl Pit
Enfield Bridge
Ensfield
The Mount
Redwood Cottage
Nursery
Redwood
Cook's Pits
Killick's Bank
Tapners
Tapner's Hole
Ensfield Farm Cottages
Beggars' Barn Farm
Chestnut Plantation
Bear's Oak
Penshurst Park
The Rookery
Coombe Bank
Tapner's Wood
Chalybeate Spring
Clappers Shaw
Lancup Well
Doubleton Farm House
Place Barn Farm
Cricket Ground
Well Place Farm
Ashour Farm
Medway
River
B2027
B2176
Penshurst Rd.
High Street
Hildenborough Road
Moorden La.
Station Hill
Penshurst Road
Coppings Road
Compasses Road
Cinder Hill Lane
Scabharbour Lane
Hill Road
Lower Street
Ensfield Road
Lwr Green Rd.
Powder Mill La.
Eggpie Lane
Martin's Drive
Penshurst Hill
Play. Fld.
Lealands Av.
Green View Av.
The Forstal
Charlotte Cotts.
Fleur de Lis Cotts.
Donkey Field
Oak Cotts.
The Bungalows
Saxby Wood
The Sq.
Sch.
The Green
131
144
149

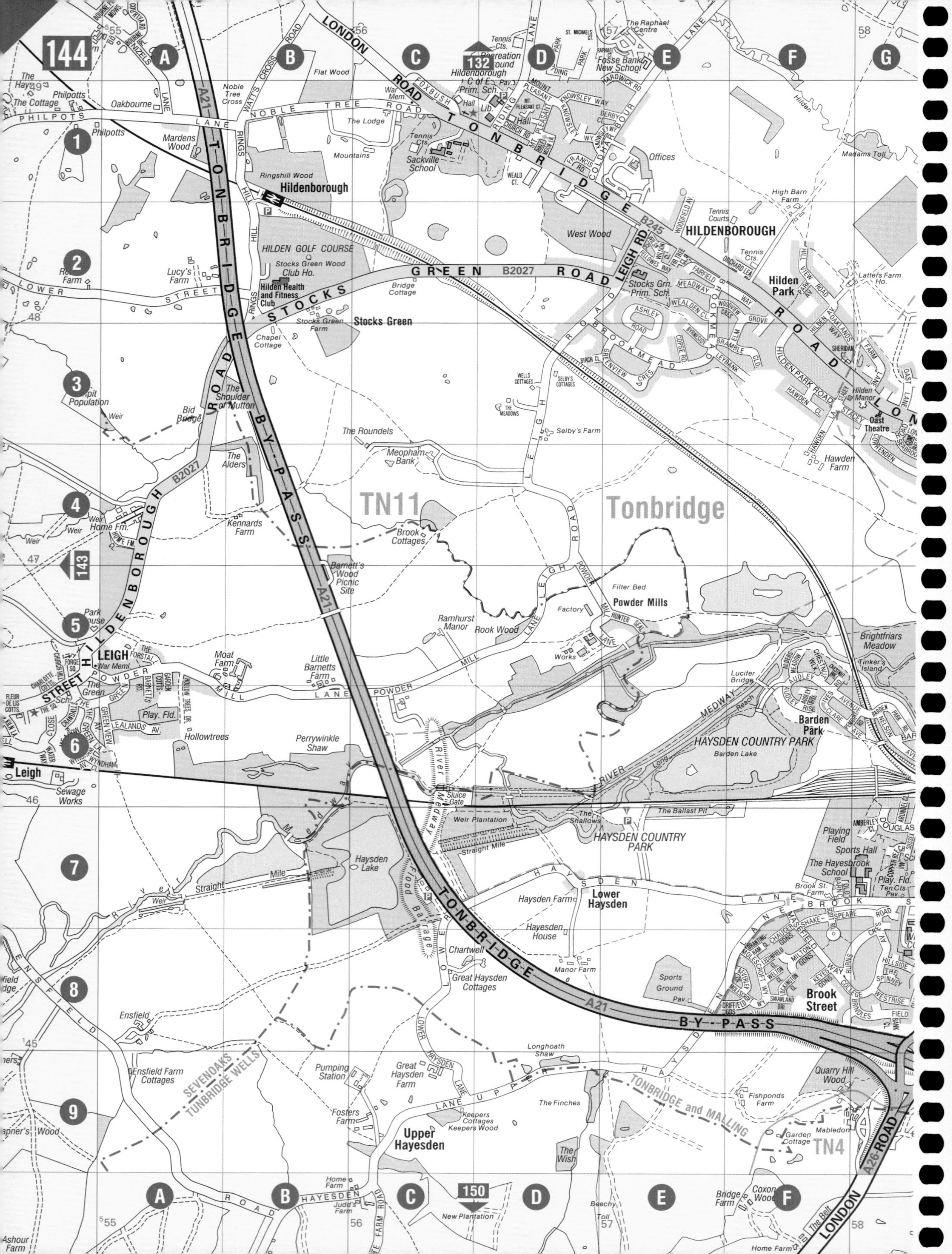

Hildenborough
HILDENBOROUGH
Stocks Green
Tonbridge
TN11
Powder Mills
LEIGH
Leigh
HAYSDEN COUNTRY PARK
Lower Haysden
Upper Hayesden
Brook Street
Barden Park
Hilden Park
TONBRIDGE BY-PASS
A21
B2027
B245
TONBRIDGE ROAD
LONDON ROAD
STOCKS GREEN ROAD
HILDENBOROUGH ROAD
LEIGH RD
POWDER MILL LANE
HAYSDEN LANE
UPPER HAYSDEN LANE
HILDEN GOLF COURSE
Sackville School
The Hayesbrook School
Fosse Bank New School
Stocks Grn. Prim. Sch.
Hilden Health and Fitness Club
Haysden Lake
Barden Lake
Weir Plantation
The Ballast Pit
Quarry Hill Wood
Sports Ground
SEVENOAKS
TUNBRIDGE WELLS
TONBRIDGE and MALLING
TN4
A26 ROAD
LONDON
132
143
150

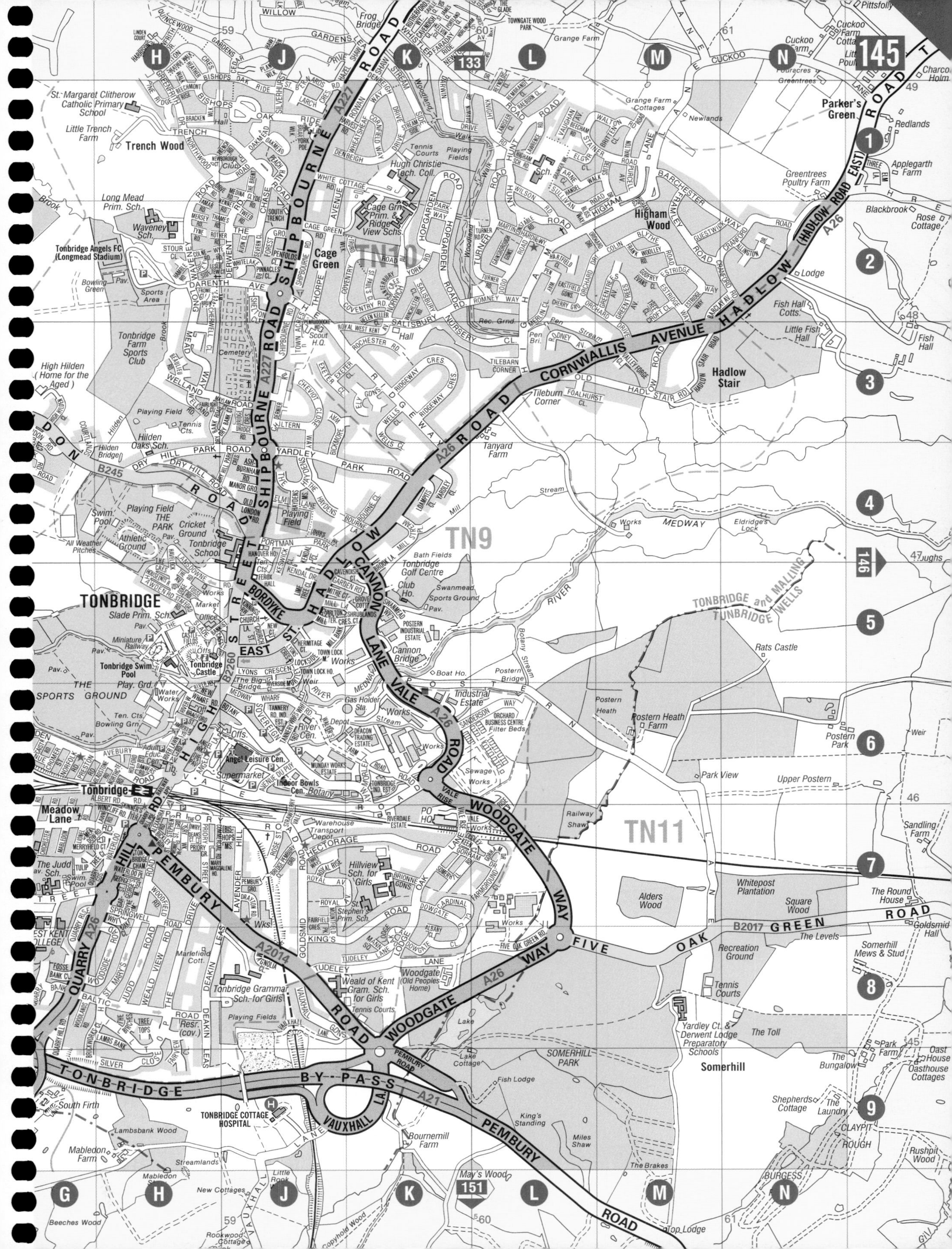
TONBRIDGE
TN10
TN9
TN11
Trench Wood
Little Trench Farm
St. Margaret Clitherow Catholic Primary School
Long Mead Prim. Sch.
Waveney Sch.
Tonbridge Angels FC (Longmead Stadium)
Bowling Green
Sports Area
Tonbridge Farm Sports Club
High Hilden (Home for the Aged)
Hilden Oaks Sch.
Cemetery
Cage Green
Cage Grn. Prim. & Ridge View Schs.
Hugh Christie Tech. Coll.
Tennis Courts
Playing Fields
Higham Wood
Parker's Green
Redlands
Applegarth Farm
Greentrees Poultry Farm
Blackbrook
Rose Cottage
Grange Farm
Grange Farm Cottages
Newlands
Cuckoo Farm
Fish Hall Cotts.
Little Fish Hall
Fish Hall
Hadlow Stair
Tileburn Corner
Tilebarn Corner
Tanyard Farm
Tonbridge Golf Centre
Swanmead Sports Ground
Bath Fields
Medway
Eldridge's Lock
River
Stream
Tonbridge School
Cricket Ground
Athletic Ground
Swim. Pool
Playing Field THE PARK
All Weather Pitches
Slade Prim. Sch.
Miniature Railway
Tonbridge Castle
Tonbridge Swim. Pool
THE SPORTS GROUND
Angel Leisure Cen.
Supermarket
Indoor Bowls Cen.
Tonbridge
Meadow Lane
The Judd Sch.
Hillview Sch. for Girls
St. Stephen's Prim. Sch.
Marlefield Cott.
Tonbridge Grammar Sch. for Girls
Weald of Kent Gram. Sch. for Girls
Woodgate (Old Peoples Home)
Playing Fields
Resr. (cov.)
Tonbridge Cottage Hospital
South Firth
Lambsbank Wood
Mabledon Farm
Mabledon
Streamlands
New Cottages
Beeches Wood
Rookwood Cottage
Copyhold Wood
Bournemill Farm
May's Wood
King's Standing
Fish Lodge
Miles Shaw
Somerhill Park
Somerhill
Yardley Ct. & Derwent Lodge Preparatory Schools
The Toll
Tennis Courts
Recreation Ground
Alders Wood
Whitepost Plantation
Square Wood
The Round House
Goldsmid Hall
Somerhill Mews & Stud
The Levels
Postern Heath
Postern Heath Farm
Postern Park
Park View
Upper Postern
Sandling Farm
Railway Shaw
Rats Castle
Industrial Estate
Sewage Works
Filter Beds
Cannon Bridge
Postern Bridge
Botany Stream
Boat Ho.
Gas Holder Sta.
Warehouse Transport Depot
Riverdale Estate
Park Farm
Oast House
Oasthouse Cottages
The Bungalow
Shepherds Cottage
The Laundry
Rushpit Wood
Claypit Rough
Burgess
The Brakes
Top Lodge
Lake Cottage
Lake
Pitts Folly
Charcoal Holm
Lodge
Weir
TONBRIDGE and MALLING
TUNBRIDGE WELLS
SHIPBOURNE ROAD
CORNWALLIS AVENUE
HADLOW ROAD
HADLOW ROAD EAST
HIGH STREET
WOODGATE WAY
PEMBURY ROAD
TONBRIDGE BY-PASS
FIVE OAK GREEN ROAD
QUARRY HILL
VAUXHALL LA.
CANNON LANE
VALE ROAD
DRY HILL PARK ROAD
YARDLEY PARK ROAD
A26
A227
A21
A2014
B2260
B245
B2017
G H J K L M N
1 2 3 4 5 6 7 8 9
59 60 61
45 46 47 48 49
133
146
151

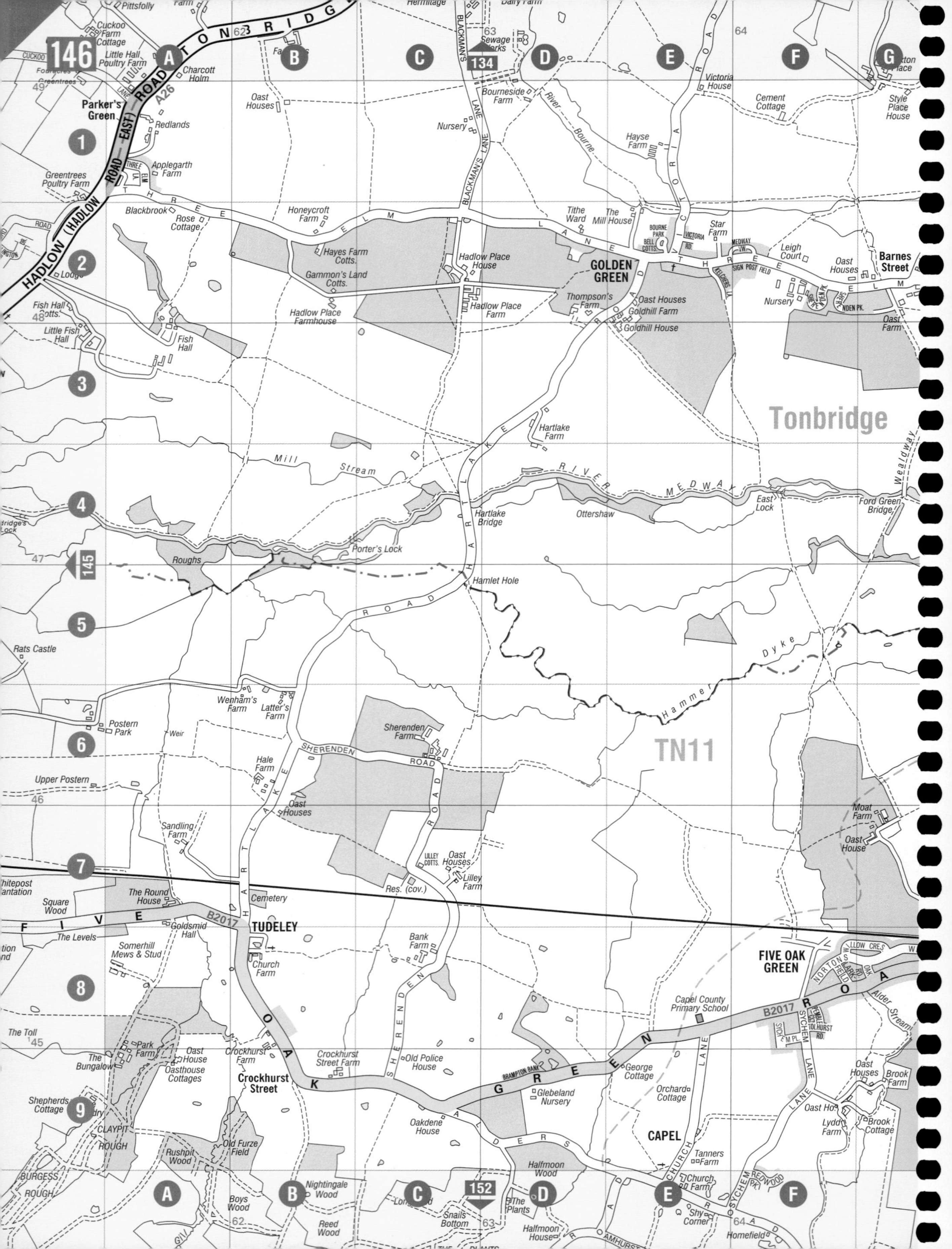
Pittsfolly
Cuckoo Farm Cottage
Little Hall Poultry Farm
Charcott Holm
TONBRIDGE ROAD
A26
Parker's Green
Redlands
Applegarth Farm
Greentrees Poultry Farm
HADLOW (HADLOW ROAD EAST)
Blackbrook
Rose Cottage
THREE ELM LANE
Honeycroft Farm
Hayes Farm Cotts.
Gammon's Land Cotts.
Hadlow Place Farmhouse
Hadlow Place House
Hadlow Place Farm
Oast Houses
Nursery
Sewage Works
134
Bourneside Farm
BLACKMAN'S LANE
River Bourne
Hayse Farm
Victoria House
VICTORIA ROAD
Cement Cottage
Style Place House
Tithe Ward
The Mill House
Star Farm
GOLDEN GREEN
Thompson's Farm
Oast Houses
Goldhill Farm
Goldhill House
Leigh Court
Oast Houses
Barnes Street
Nursery
Oast Farm
Tonbridge
Fish Hall Cotts.
Little Fish Hall
Fish Hall
Hartlake Farm
Mill Stream
RIVER MEDWAY
Hartlake Bridge
Ottershaw
East Lock
Ford Green Bridge
Wealdway
Roughs
Porter's Lock
145
Hamlet Hole
HARTLAKE ROAD
Rats Castle
Hammer Dyke
Wenham's Farm
Latter's Farm
Postern Park
Weir
Sherenden Farm
SHERENDEN ROAD
TN11
Hale Farm
Upper Postern
Oast Houses
Sandling Farm
Lilley Cotts.
Oast Houses
Lilley Farm
Moat Farm
Oast House
Whitepost Plantation
Square Wood
The Round House
Cemetery
Res. (cov.)
FIVE OAK GREEN ROAD
B2017
TUDELEY
Goldsmid Hall
The Levels
Somerhill Mews & Stud
Church Farm
Bank Farm
FIVE OAK GREEN
Capel County Primary School
The Toll
Park Farm
Oast House
Oasthouse Cottages
The Bungalow
Crockhurst Farm
Crockhurst Street
Crockhurst Street Farm
Old Police House
Brampton Bank
George Cottage
Orchard Cottage
Glebeland Nursery
Oast Houses
Brook Farm
Oast Ho.
Lydd Farm
Brook Cottage
Shepherds Cottage
Claypit Rough
Old Furze Field
Rushpit Wood
Oakdene House
ALDERS ROAD
CAPEL
CHURCH LANE
SYCHEM LANE
Tanners Farm
Church Farm
Halfmoon Wood
Burgess Rough
Boys Wood
Nightingale Wood
Reed Wood
152
Snails Bottom
The Plants
Halfmoon House
Shy Corner
Homefield
Alder Stream

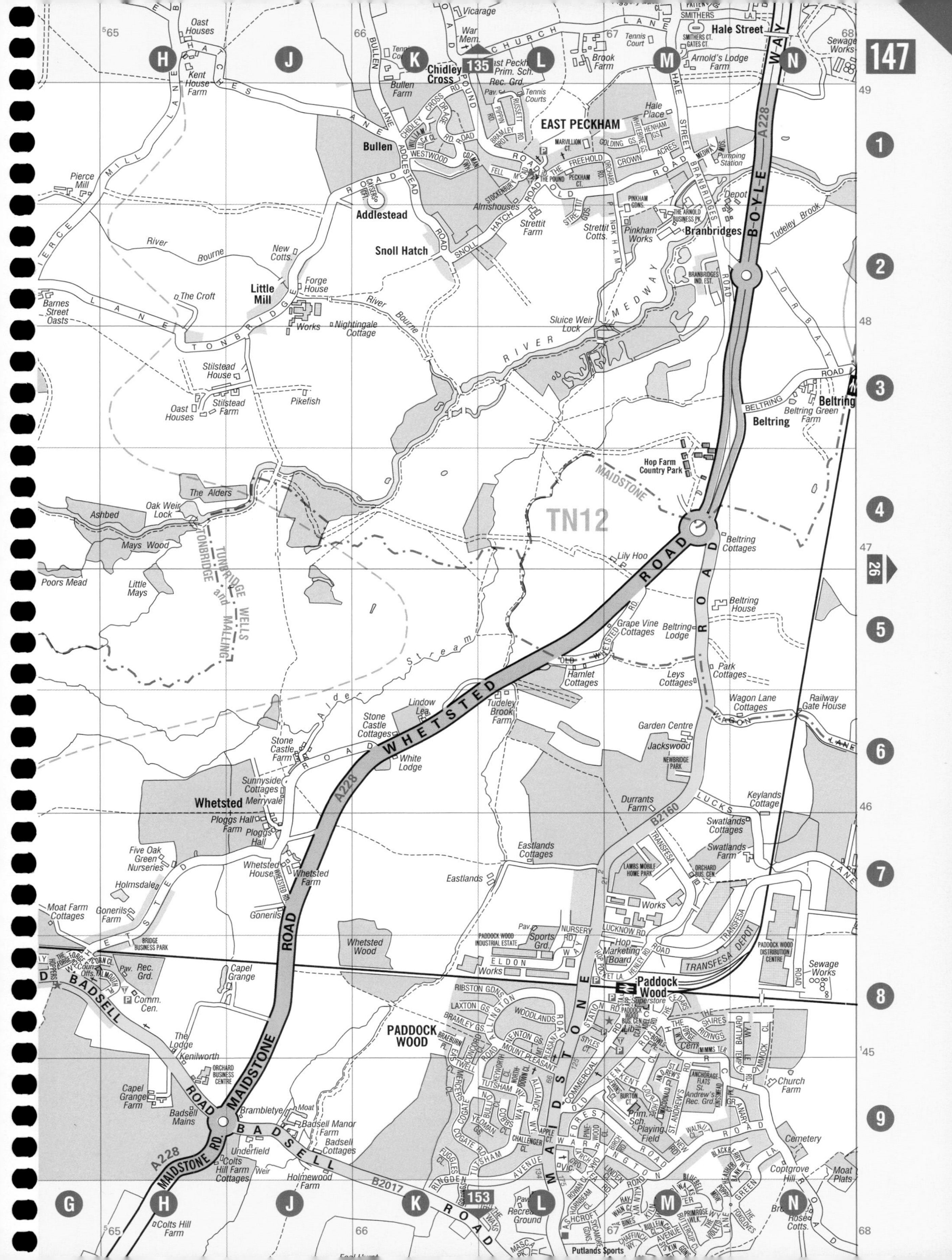
147
Hale Street
Vicarage
War Mem.
CHURCH LANE
Tennis Court
SMITHERS
Sewage Works
Oast Houses
Kent House Farm
Chidley Cross
135
East Peckham Prim. Sch.
Rec. Grd.
Brook Farm
Arnold's Lodge Farm
Bullen Farm
Tennis Courts
Hale Place
EAST PECKHAM
Bullen
ADDLESTEAD
Pumping Station
Pierce Mill
Addlestead
Almshouses
Strettit Farm
Strettit Cotts.
Pinkham Works
Branbridges
Depot
Tudeley Brook
River Bourne
New Cotts.
Snoll Hatch
BOYLE WAY
A228
The Croft
Little Mill
Forge House
Barnes Street Oasts
TONBRIDGE LANE
Works
Nightingale Cottage
Sluice Weir Lock
MEDWAY
RIVER
TORBAY ROAD
Stilstead House
Stilstead Farm
Oast Houses
Pikefish
BELTRING
Beltring
Beltring Green Farm
Hop Farm Country Park
MAIDSTONE
The Alders
Ashbed
Oak Weir Lock
TN12
Mays Wood
Beltring Cottages
Lily Hoo
TONBRIDGE and MALLING
TUNBRIDGE WELLS
Poors Mead
Little Mays
26
Beltring House
Grape Vine Cottages
Beltring Lodge
Alder Stream
Hamlet Cottages
Leys Cottages
Park Cottages
Lindow Lea
Tudeley Brook Farm
WHETSTED ROAD
Wagon Lane Cottages
Railway Gate House
Stone Castle Cottages
Stone Castle Farm
Garden Centre
Jackswood
White Lodge
Sunnyside Cottages
Whetsted
Merryvale
Durrants Farm
Keylands Cottage
B2160
Ploggs Hall Farm
Ploggs Hall
Swatlands Cottages
Eastlands Cottages
Swatlands Farm
Five Oak Green Nurseries
Whetsted House
Whetsted Farm
Eastlands
Holmsdale
Moat Farm Cottages
Gonerils Farm
Gonerils
Works
Whetsted Wood
Sports Grd.
Hop Marketing Board
TRANSFESA DEPOT
Capel Grange
Paddock Wood
Sewage Works
BADSELL
Rec. Grd.
Comm. Cen.
PADDOCK WOOD
MAIDSTONE ROAD
The Lodge
Kenilworth
Capel Grange Farm
Badsell Mains
Bramblety
Moat
Badsell Manor Farm
Badsell Cottages
Church Farm
Prim. Sch.
Playing Field
Cemetery
Underfield
Colts Hill Farm Cottages
Weir
Holmewood Farm
B2017
Coptgrove Hill
Moat Plats
153
Recreation Ground
Colts Hill Farm
Putlands Sports
G H J K L M N

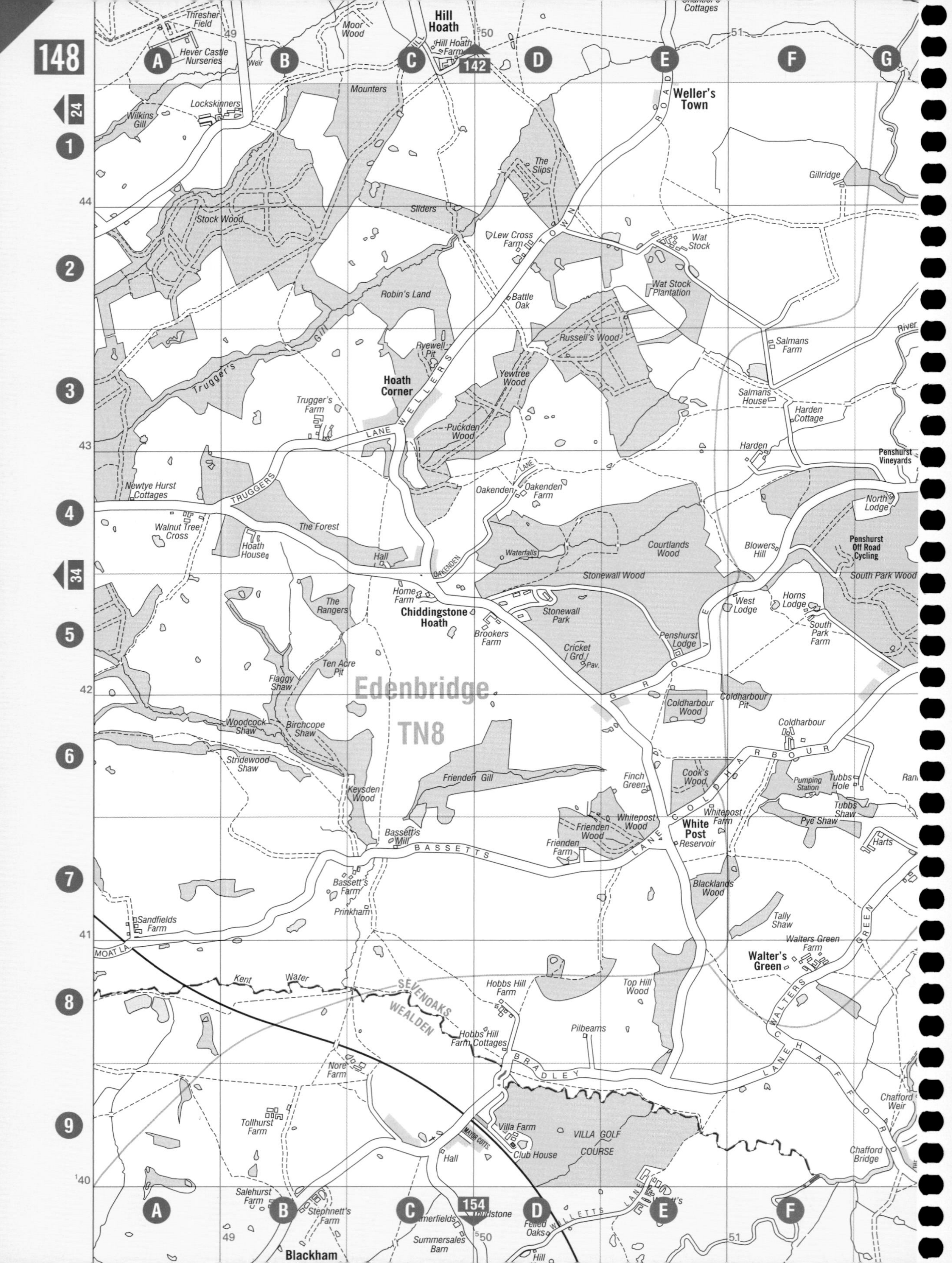
Hill Hoath
Hill Hoath Farm
142
Thresher Field
Hever Castle Nurseries
Moor Wood
Weir
Mounters
Lockskinners
Wilkins Gill
24
Weller's Town
The Slips
Gillridge
Stock Wood
Sliders
Lew Cross Farm
Wat Stock
Robin's Land
Battle Oak
Wat Stock Plantation
Russell's Wood
Salmans Farm
River
Ryewell Pit
Hoath Corner
Yewtree Wood
Salmans House
Harden Cottage
Trugger's Farm
Trugger's Gill
Puckden Wood
Harden
Penshurst Vineyards
Newtye Hurst Cottages
Oakenden
Oakenden Farm
North Lodge
Walnut Tree Cross
Hoath House
The Forest
Hall
Waterfalls
Courtlands Wood
Blowers Hill
Penshurst Off Road Cycling
South Park Wood
34
Stonewall Wood
Home Farm
The Rangers
Chiddingstone Hoath
Stonewall Park
West Lodge
Horns Lodge
Brookers Farm
South Park Farm
Penshurst Lodge
Cricket Grd.
Pav.
Ten Acre Pit
Flaggy Shaw
Edenbridge
TN8
Coldharbour Wood
Coldharbour Pit
Coldharbour
Woodcock Shaw
Birchcope Shaw
Stridewood Shaw
Friendén Gill
Finch Green
Cook's Wood
Pumping Station
Tubbs Hole
Keysden Wood
Whitepost Wood
Whitepost Farm
Tubbs Shaw
Friendén Wood
White Post
Pye Shaw
Bassett's Mill
Friendén Farm
Reservoir
Harts
Bassett's Farm
Blacklands Wood
Prinkham
Tally Shaw
Sandfields Farm
Walters Green Farm
Walter's Green
Moat La
Kent Water
Top Hill Wood
Hobbs Hill Farm
Sevenoaks
Wealden
Pilbeams
Hobbs Hill Farm Cottages
Nore Farm
Bradley Lane
Chafford Lane
Chafford Weir
Tollhurst Farm
Villa Farm
Villa Golf Course
Club House
Hall
Chafford Bridge
Salehurst Farm
Stephnett's Farm
154
Felled Oaks
Willetts Lane
Summersales Barn
Blackham
Hill
Weller's Road
Town Road
Weller's Lane
Truggers Lane
Oakenden Lane
Grove Road
Coldharbour Lane
Bassetts Lane
Walters Green
A B C D E F G
1 2 3 4 5 6 7 8 9
49 50 51
44 43 42 41 40

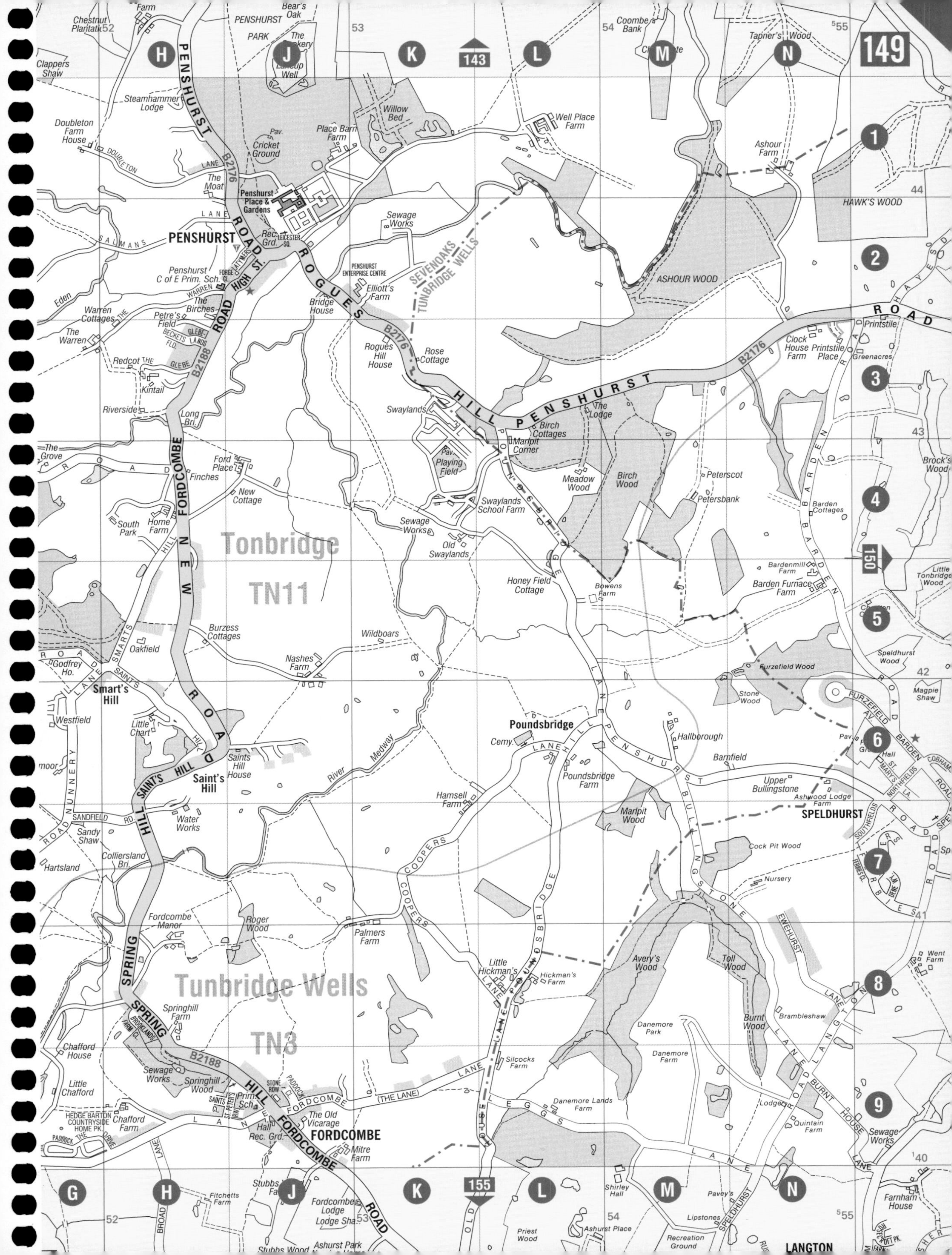
149
143
150
155
PENSHURST
PENSHURST PARK
Penshurst Place & Gardens
Tonbridge
TN11
Tunbridge Wells
TN3
SEVENOAKS
TUNBRIDGE WELLS
Poundsbridge
Smart's Hill
Saint's Hill
FORDCOMBE
SPELDHURST
LANGTON
ASHOUR WOOD
HAWK'S WOOD
PENSHURST ROAD
ROGUES HILL
PENSHURST ROAD
FORDCOMBE NEW ROAD
SAINT'S HILL
SPRING HILL
FORDCOMBE HILL
HIGH ST.
B2176
B2188
POUNDSBRIDGE LANE
POUNDSBRIDGE HILL
COOPERS LANE
OLD HOUSE LANE
EGGS LANE
BULLINGSTONE LANE
BARDEN ROAD
LANGTON ROAD
BURNT HOUSE LANE
HAYESDEN
NUNNERY ROAD
SANDFIELD RD
SMARTS HILL
SALMANS LANE
DOUBLETON LANE
RIVER MEDWAY
Chestnut Plantation
Clappers Shaw
Steamhammer Lodge
Doubleton Farm House
Cricket Ground
Place Barn Farm
Willow Bed
Well Place Farm
Ashour Farm
The Moat
Sewage Works
Rec. Grd.
Penshurst C of E Prim. Sch.
Penshurst Enterprise Centre
Elliott's Farm
Bridge House
The Birches
Warren Cottages
The Warren
Petre's Field
Redcot
Kintail
Riverside
Long Bri.
Rogues Hill House
Rose Cottage
Swaylands
Birch Cottages
The Lodge
Marlpit Corner
Playing Field
Clock House Farm
Printstile Place
Printstile
Greenacres
The Grove
Ford Place
Finches
New Cottage
Meadow Wood
Birch Wood
Peterscot
Petersbank
Brock's Wood
South Park
Home Farm
Swaylands School Farm
Old Swaylands
Barden Cottages
Bardenmill Farm
Barden Furnace Farm
Little Tonbridge Wood
Honey Field Cottage
Bowens Farm
Burzess Cottages
Oakfield
Wildboars
Nashes Farm
Speldhurst Wood
Furzefield Wood
Magpie Shaw
Godfrey Ho.
Westfield
Little Chart
Stone Wood
Hallborough
Cemy.
Barnfield
Saints Hill House
Poundsbridge Farm
Upper Bullingstone
Ashwood Lodge Farm
Hamsell Farm
Marlpit Wood
Water Works
Sandy Shaw
Colliersland Bri.
Hartsland
Cock Pit Wood
Nursery
Fordcombe Manor
Roger Wood
Palmers Farm
Little Hickman's
Hickman's Farm
Avery's Wood
Toll Wood
Went Farm
Springhill Farm
Brambleshaw
Chafford House
Danemore Park
Burnt Wood
Danemore Farm
Silcocks Farm
Little Chafford
Springhill Wood
Prim. Sch.
The Old Vicarage
Danemore Lands Farm
Lodge
Quintain Farm
Sewage Works
Hedge Barton Countryside Home Pk.
Chafford Farm
Hall
Rec. Grd.
Mitre Farm
Fitchetts Farm
Stubbs Farm
Fordcombe Lodge
Lodge Shaw
Shirley Hall
Pavey's
Farnham House
Priest Wood
Ashurst Place
Lipstones
Recreation Ground
Ashurst Park
Stubbs Wood
Tapner's Wood
Coombe Bank
Bear's Oak
The Rookery
Lancup Well
G
H
J
K
L
M
N
1
2
3
4
5
6
7
8
9
52
53
54
55
44
43
42
41
40

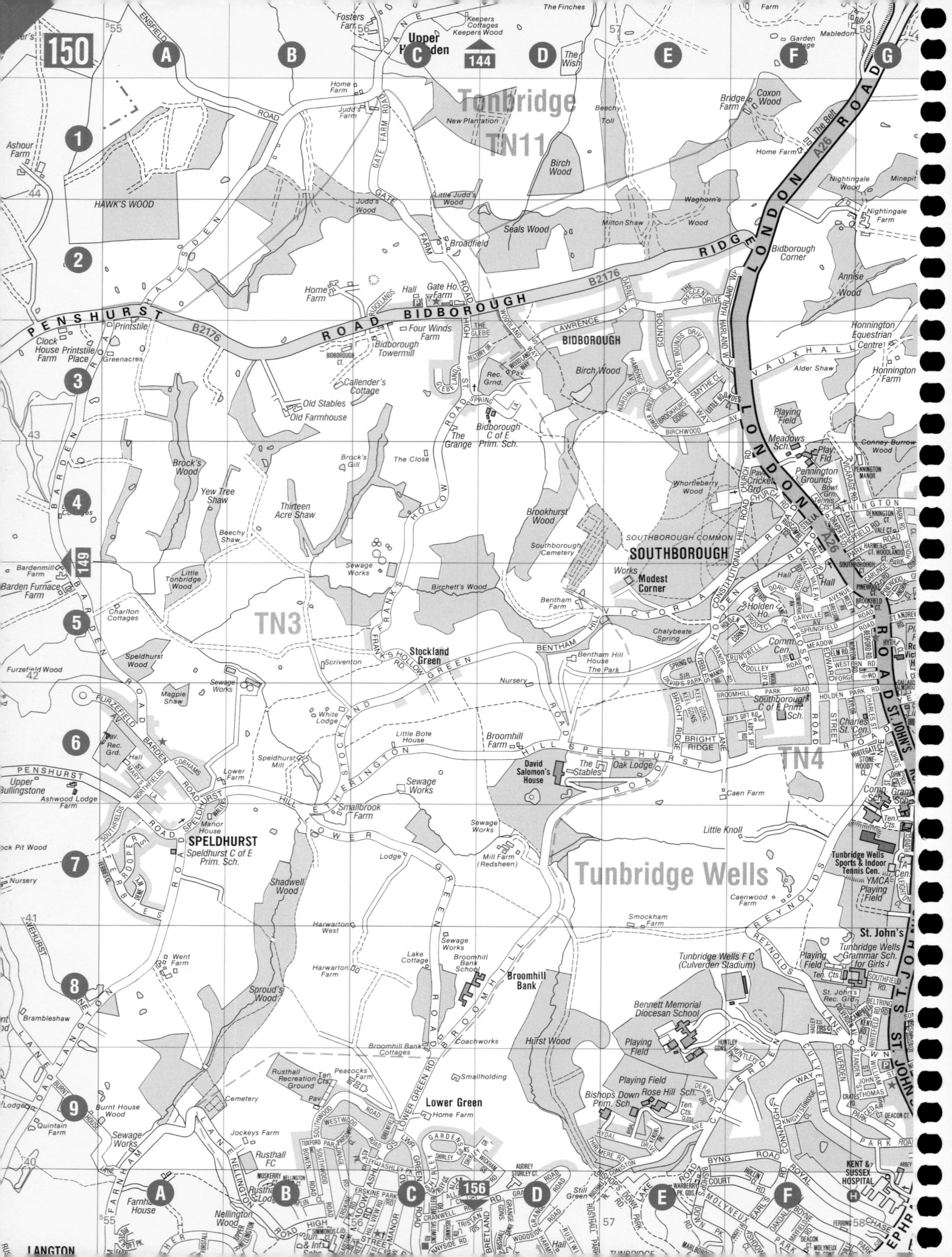

Tonbridge
TN11
TN3
TN4
Tunbridge Wells
SOUTHBOROUGH
BIDBOROUGH
SPELDHURST
Upper Hayesden
Stockland Green
Lower Green
Broomhill Bank
Modest Corner
Southborough Common
Hawk's Wood
Birch Wood
Seals Wood
Brock's Wood
Yew Tree Shaw
Thirteen Acre Shaw
Brookhurst Wood
Birchett's Wood
Speldhurst Wood
Shadwell Wood
Sproud's Wood
Hurst Wood
Little Knoll
PENSHURST ROAD
BIDBOROUGH RIDGE
B2176
LONDON ROAD
A26
ST. JOHN'S ROAD
David Salomon's House
Tunbridge Wells F C (Culverden Stadium)
Bennett Memorial Diocesan School
Kent & Sussex Hospital
Tunbridge Wells Sports & Indoor Tennis Cen.
Tunbridge Wells Grammar Sch. for Girls
Speldhurst C of E Prim. Sch.
Bidborough C of E Prim. Sch.
Southborough C of E Prim. Sch.
Bishops Down Prim. Sch.
Rose Hill Sch.
Rusthall Recreation Ground
Rusthall FC
LANGTON

144
149
156

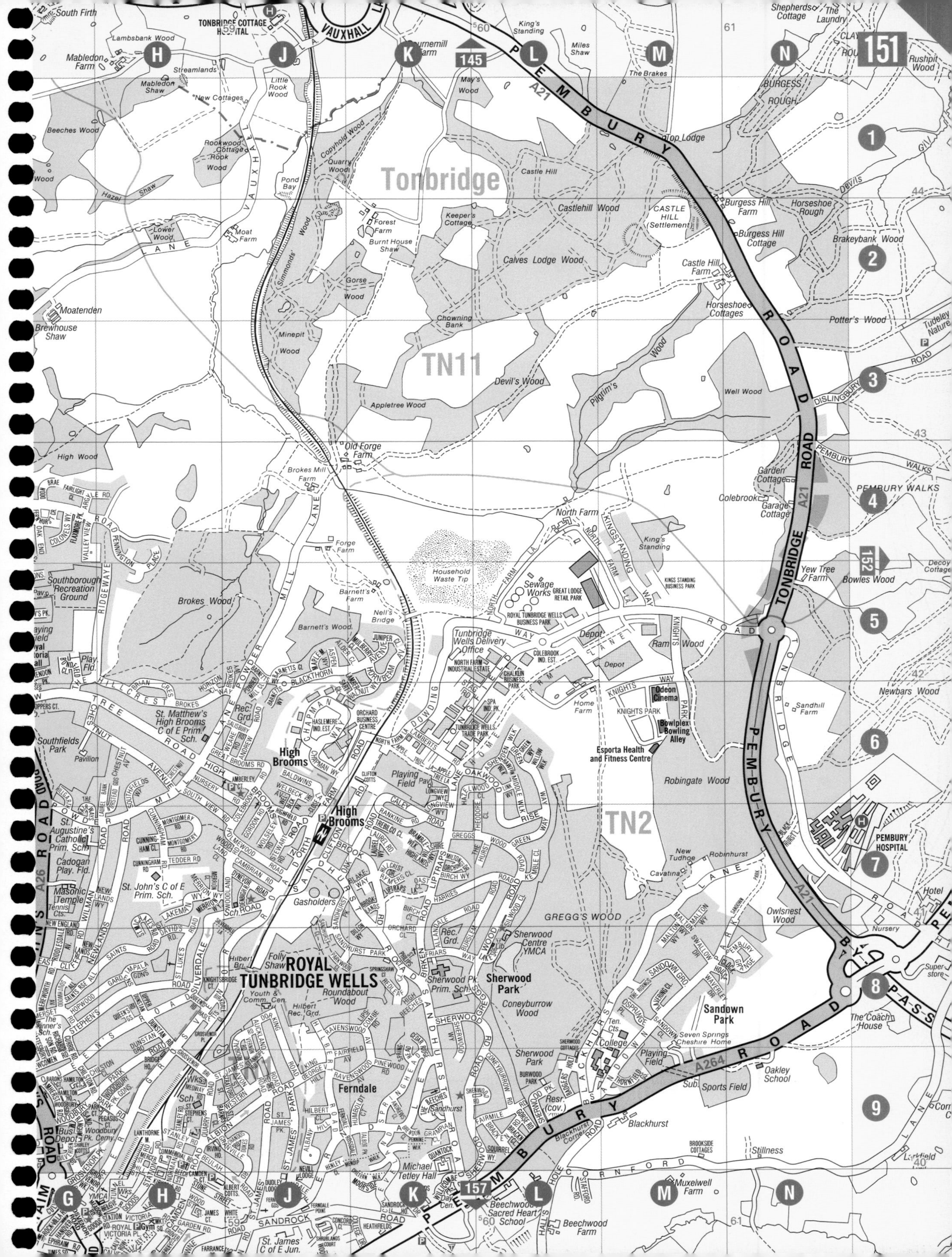

Tonbridge
TN11
TN2
ROYAL TUNBRIDGE WELLS
High Brooms
Ferndale
Sherwood Park
Sandown Park
PEMBURY ROAD
TONBRIDGE ROAD
A21
A26
A264
VAUXHALL LANE
MILL LANE
Castlehill Wood
Calves Lodge Wood
Devil's Wood
Appletree Wood
Brokes Wood
Household Waste Tip
Sewage Works
GREAT LODGE RETAIL PARK
ROYAL TUNBRIDGE WELLS BUSINESS PARK
Tunbridge Wells Delivery Office
NORTH FARM INDUSTRIAL ESTATE
Odeon Cinema
Bowlplex Bowling Alley
Esporta Health and Fitness Centre
Robingate Wood
PEMBURY HOSPITAL
Gregg's Wood
Sherwood Centre YMCA
Coneyburrow Wood
Roundabout Wood
Southborough Recreation Ground
St. Matthew's High Brooms C of E Prim. Sch.
St. John's C of E Prim. Sch.
Sherwood Pk. Prim. Sch.
Seven Springs Cheshire Home
Oakley School
Beechwood Sacred Heart School
Muxelwell Farm
145
152
157

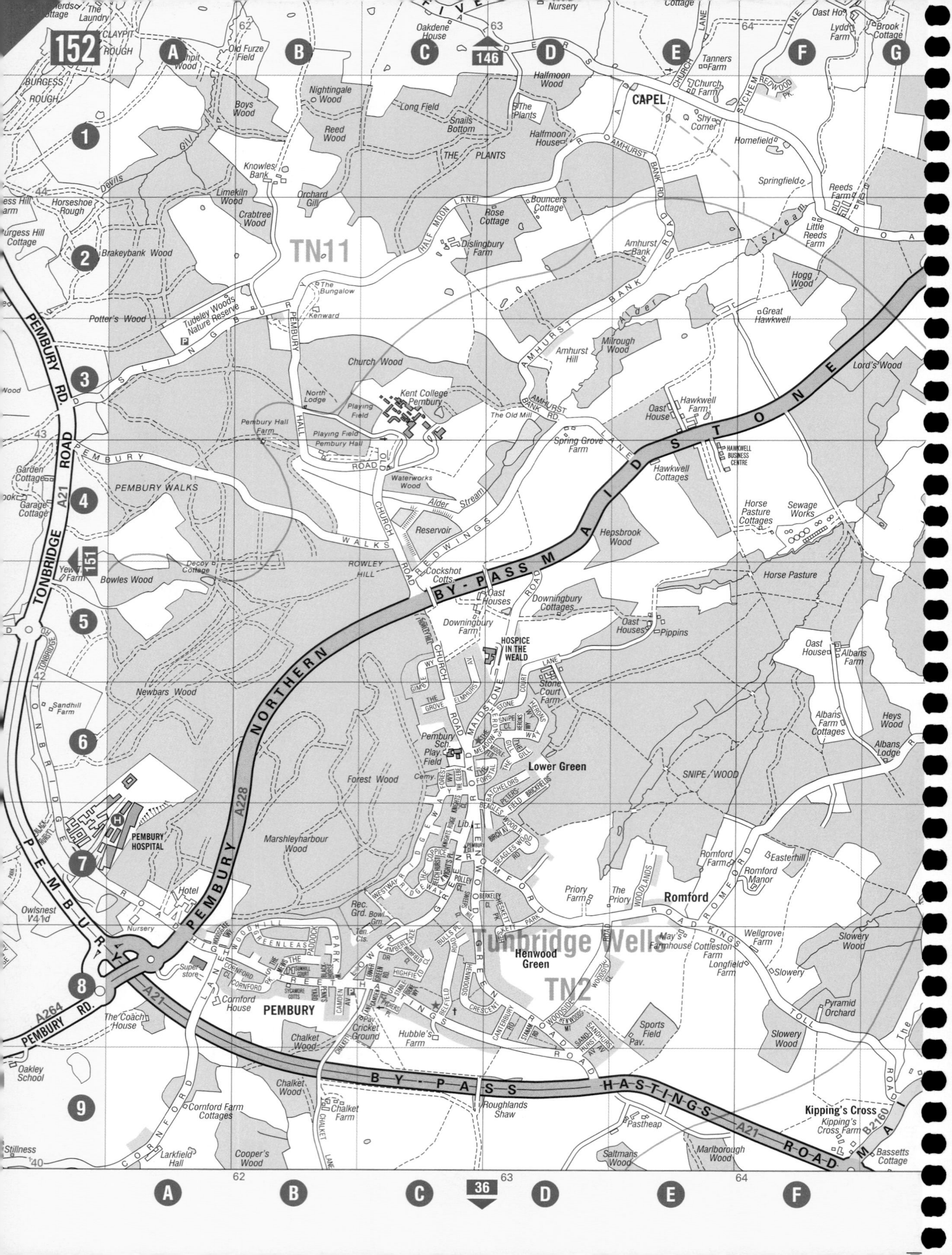

A
B
C
D
E
F
G
1
2
3
4
5
6
7
8
9
62
63
64
TN11
TN2
CAPEL
PEMBURY
Lower Green
Romford
Henwood Green
Kipping's Cross
Tunbridge Wells
PEMBURY HOSPITAL
HOSPICE IN THE WEALD
Kent College Pembury
HAWKWELL BUSINESS CENTRE
MAIDSTONE BY-PASS
NORTHERN BY-PASS
HASTINGS BY-PASS
TONBRIDGE ROAD
PEMBURY RD.
PEMBURY ROAD
A21
A228
A264
B2160
Tudeley Woods Nature Reserve
Potter's Wood
Church Wood
Bowles Wood
Newbars Wood
Forest Wood
Marshleyharbour Wood
Snipe Wood
Hepsbrook Wood
Milrough Wood
Lord's Wood
Hogg Wood
Heys Wood
Slowery Wood
Pyramid Orchard
Halfmoon Wood
Nightingale Wood
Reed Wood
Boys Wood
Limekiln Wood
Crabtree Wood
Brakeybank Wood
Pembury Walks
Horse Pasture
Sewage Works
Reservoir
Waterworks Wood
Chalket Wood
Chalket Farm
Cooper's Wood
Saltmans Wood
Marlborough Wood
Roughlands Shaw
Sports Field
Cricket Ground
Oakley School
Cornford Farm Cottages
Cornford House
Larkfield Hall
Stillness

146
151
36

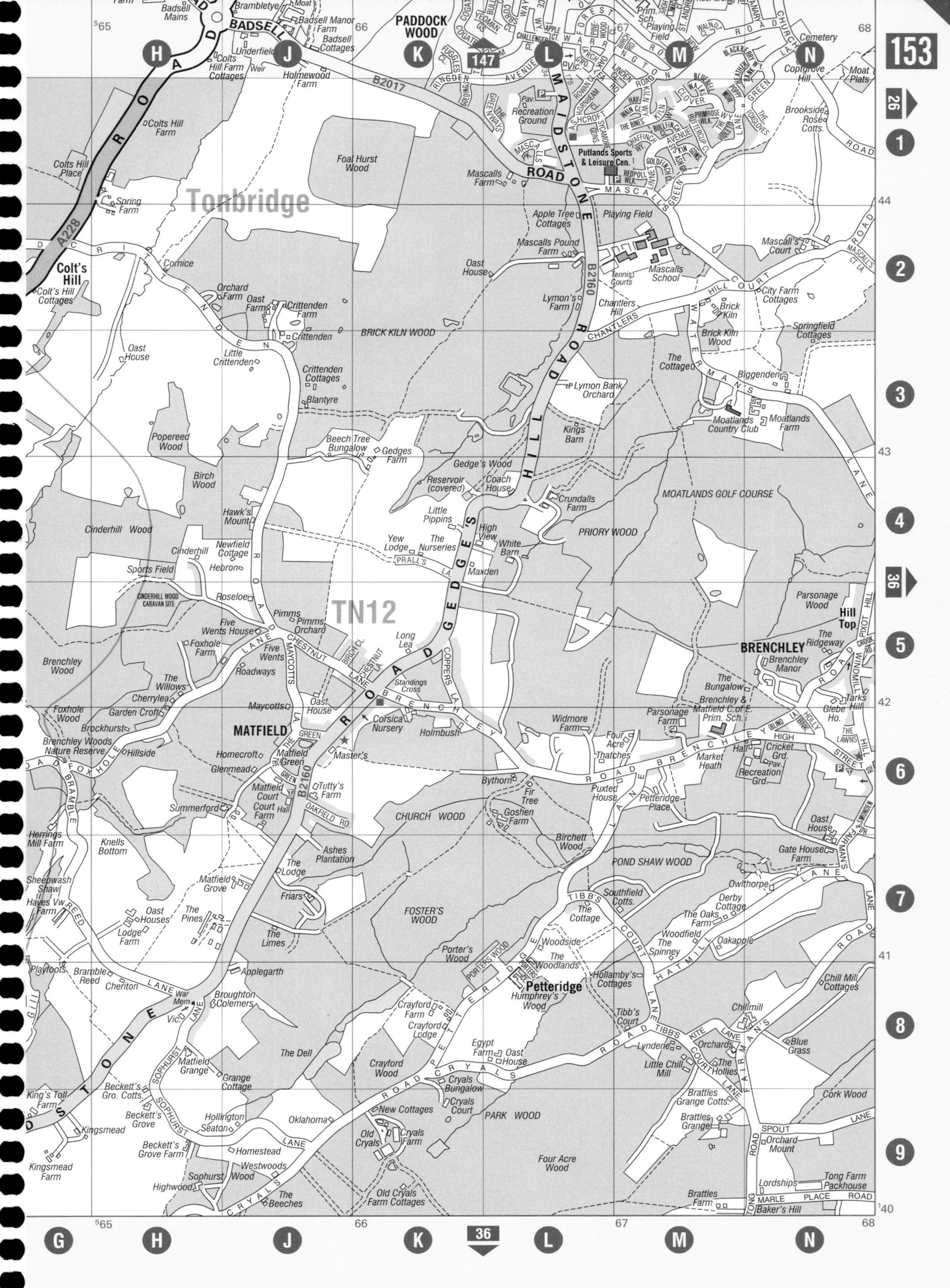

PADDOCK WOOD
147
BADSELL ROAD
Badsell Manor Farm
Badsell Cottages
Bramblety
Badsell Mains
Underfield
Colts Hill Farm Cottages
Holmewood Farm
B2017
Colts Hill Farm
Colts Hill Place
Spring Farm
Foal Hurst Wood
Tonbridge
A228
Colt's Hill
Colt's Hill Cottages
CRITTENDEN ROAD
Comice
Orchard Farm
Oast Farm
Crittenden Farm
Crittenden
Oast House
Little Crittenden
Crittenden Cottages
Blantyre
BRICK KILN WOOD
Popereed Wood
Birch Wood
Beech Tree Bungalow
Gedges Farm
Gedge's Wood
Reservoir (covered)
Coach House
Little Pippins
High View
Yew Lodge
The Nurseries
White Barn
PRALL'S LA.
Maxden
Cinderhill Wood
Hawk's Mount
Newfield Cottage
Cinderhill
Hebron
Sports Field
CINDERHILL WOOD CARAVAN SITE
Roseloe
TN12
Pimms
Pimms Orchard
Five Wents House
Foxhole Farm
Five Wents
Roadways
Long Lea
Standings Cross
Brenchley Wood
The Willows
Cherrylea
Garden Croft
Foxhole Wood
Brockhurst
Brenchley Woods Nature Reserve
Hillside
MATFIELD
Maycotts
Oast House
Corsica Nursery
Holmbush
Homecroft
Glenmead
Matfield Green
Master's
Matfield Court
Court Farm
Tutty's Farm
B2160
OAKFIELD RD.
Summerford
Herrings Mill Farm
Knells Bottom
Ashes Plantation
The Lodge
Friars
Sheepwash Shaw
Hayes Vw. Farm
Matfield Grove
Oast Houses
The Pines
Lodge Farm
The Limes
Playfoots
Bramble Reed
Cheriton
Applegarth
War Mem.
Broughton Colemers
Matfield Grange
Grange Cottage
The Dell
King's Toll Farm
Beckett's Gro. Cotts.
Beckett's Grove
Kingsmead
Kingsmead Farm
Hollington Seaton
Oklahoma
Beckett's Grove Farm
Homestead
Westwoods
Sophurst Wood
Highwood
The Beeches
Old Cryals Farm Cottages
CRYALS ROAD
MAIDSTONE ROAD
SOPHURST LANE
Recreation Ground
Putlands Sports & Leisure Cen.
Mascalls Farm
MASCALLS GREEN
Apple Tree Cottages
Playing Field
Mascalls Pound Farm
Oast House
Mascalls School
Tennis Courts
Lymon's Farm
Chantlers Hill
CHANTLERS HILL
B2160
Lymon Bank Orchard
Kings Barn
MAIDSTONE ROAD
Crundalls Farm
PRIORY WOOD
MOATLANDS GOLF COURSE
Moatlands Country Club
Moatlands Farm
The Cottage
Biggenden
WATERMAN'S LANE
Brick Kiln
Brick Kiln Wood
Springfield Cottages
City Farm Cottages
Mascall's Court
HILL COURT
Brookside Rose Cotts.
Copgrove Hill
Moat Plats
Cemetery
CHURCH ROAD
Parsonage Wood
Hill Top
BRENCHLEY
Brenchley Manor
The Ridgeway
The Bungalow
Brenchley & Matfield C. of E. Prim. Sch.
Parsonage Farm
Widmore Farm
Four Acre Thatches
Market Heath
Cricket Grd.
Recreation Grd.
Glebe Ho.
Tarks Hill
HIGH STREET
BRENCHLEY ROAD
Bythorn
Fir Tree
Goshen Farm
Puxted House
Petteridge Place
CHURCH WOOD
Birchett Wood
POND SHAW WOOD
Oast House
Gate House Farm
Owlthorpe
Southfield Cotts.
The Cottage
Derby Cottage
The Oaks Farm
Woodfield
The Spinney
Oakapple
FOSTER'S WOOD
Porter's Wood
Woodside
The Woodlands
Hollamby's Cottages
Petteridge
Humphrey's Wood
HATMILL LANE
TIBB'S COURT LANE
Tibb's Court
Chill Mill Cottages
Chillmill
Crayford Farm
Crayford Lodge
Egypt Farm
Oast House
Lynderie
Orchards
The Hollies
Little Chill Mill
Blue Grass
Crayford Wood
Cryals Bungalow
Cryals Court
PARK WOOD
Brattles Grange Cotts.
Brattles Grange
Cork Wood
New Cottages
Old Cryals
Cryals Farm
Four Acre Wood
SPOUT LANE
Orchard Mount
Lordships
Tong Farm Packhouse
Brattles Farm
MARLE PLACE ROAD
Baker's Hill
FAIRMAN'S LANE
26
36

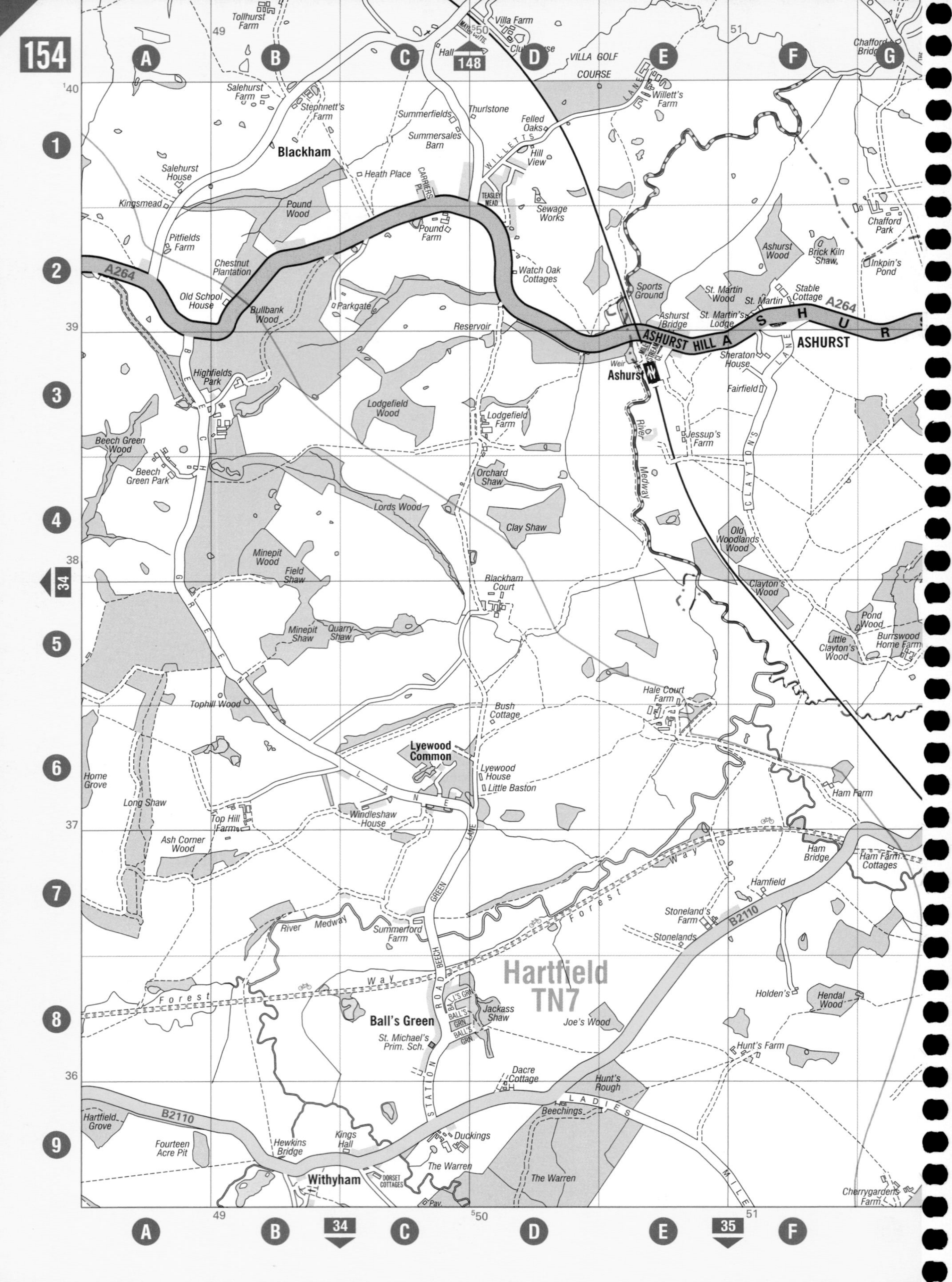
Tollhurst Farm
Villa Farm
Club House
VILLA GOLF COURSE
148
Hall
Chafford Bridge
Salehurst Farm
Stephnett's Farm
Summerfields
Thurlstone
Felled Oaks
Willett's Farm
Blackham
Summersales Barn
Hill View
Salehurst House
Heath Place
CARRIERS PL
WILLETTS LANE
TEASLEY MEAD
Sewage Works
Kingsmead
Pound Wood
Pound Farm
Pitfields Farm
Chafford Park
Ashurst Wood
Brick Kiln Shaw
Inkpin's Pond
A264
Chestnut Plantation
Watch Oak Cottages
Old School House
Bullbank Wood
Parkgate
Sports Ground
St. Martin Wood
St. Martin
Stable Cottage
Reservoir
Ashurst Bridge
St. Martin's Lodge
ASHURST HILL
ASHURST
Sheraton House
Weir
Ashurst
Highfields Park
Fairfield
Lodgefield Wood
Lodgefield Farm
River Medway
Jessup's Farm
Beech Green Wood
Beech Green Park
Orchard Shaw
CLAYTONS LANE
Lords Wood
Clay Shaw
Old Woodlands Wood
Minepit Wood
Field Shaw
34
Blackham Court
Clayton's Wood
Minepit Shaw
Quarry Shaw
Pond Wood
Little Clayton's Wood
Burrswood Home Farm
Hale Court Farm
Tophill Wood
Bush Cottage
Lyewood Common
Lyewood House
Little Baston
Home Grove
Long Shaw
Ham Farm
Top Hill Farm
Windleshaw House
Ash Corner Wood
Ham Bridge
Ham Farm Cottages
Forest Way
Hamfield
Stoneland's Farm
Stonelands
B2110
River Medway
Summerford Farm
Hartfield TN7
Holden's
Hendal Wood
BEECH GREEN LANE
Ball's Green
Jackass Shaw
Joe's Wood
St. Michael's Prim. Sch.
Hunt's Farm
Dacre Cottage
Hunt's Rough
STATION ROAD
LADIES MILE
Beechings
Hartfield Grove
Fourteen Acre Pit
Hewkins Bridge
Kings Hall
Duckings
The Warren
Withyham
DORSET COTTAGES
Pav.
Cherrygardens Farm
A B C D E F G
1 2 3 4 5 6 7 8 9
49 550 51
40 39 38 37 36
35

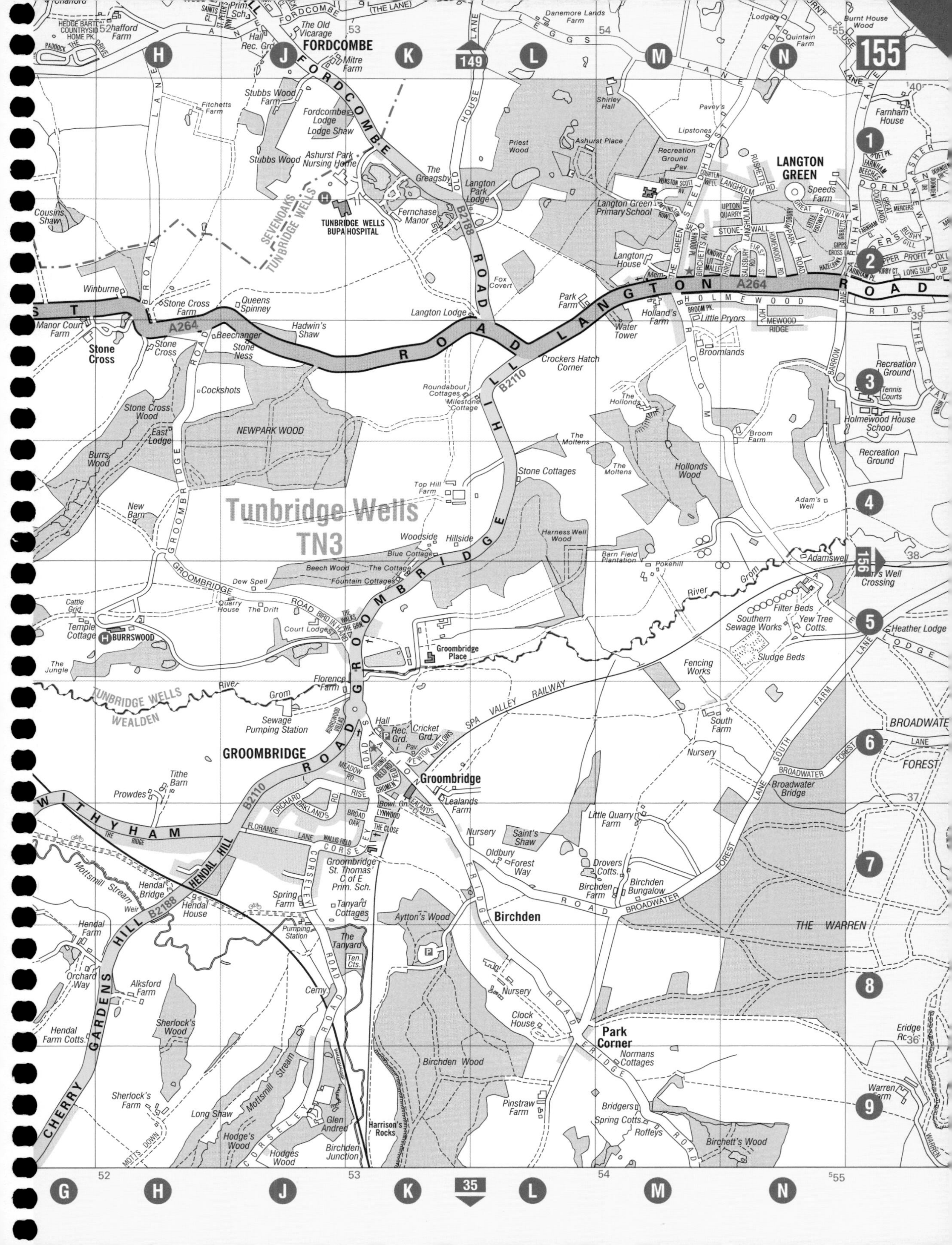

155
149
156
35
FORDCOMBE
Fordcombe
The Old Vicarage
Mitre Farm
Hall
Rec. Grd.
Prim. Sch.
(THE LANE)
Hedge Barton Countryside Home Pk.
Chafford Farm
Paddock
The Drive
Danemore Lands Farm
Leggs Lane
Lodge
Quintain Farm
Burnt House Wood
Burnt House Lane
Fitchetts Farm
Stubbs Wood Farm
Fordcombe Lodge
Lodge Shaw
Stubbs Wood
Ashurst Park Nursing Home
TUNBRIDGE WELLS BUPA HOSPITAL
Sevenoaks
Tunbridge Wells
Cousins Shaw
The Greagsby
Old House Lane
Langton Park Lodge
Fernchase Manor
B2188
Road
Priest Wood
Shirley Hall
Ashurst Place
Pavey's
Lipstones
Recreation Ground
Pav.
Farnham House
LANGTON GREEN
Speeds Farm
Langton Green Primary School
Winston Scott Av.
Langholm Rd.
Rushetts Rd.
Upton Quarry
Stone-Wall
Homewood Rd.
Lealands Av.
Birchetts Av.
Knowle Cl.
Salisbury Rd.
Great Footway
Little Footway
Gibbs Cross La.
Farnham Pl.
Kirby Ct.
Long Slip
Farnham Beeches
Courtlands
Great Bounds Dr.
Mercers
Bushy Gill
Upper Profit
Hazelbank
Langton House
Mem.
The Green
Fox Covert
Winburne
Stone Cross Farm
Queens Spinney
Manor Court Farm
Stone Cross
A264
Beechanger
Stone Ness
Hadwin's Shaw
Langton Lodge
Langton Road
Park Farm
Holland's Farm
Holmewood Ridge
Broom Pk.
Little Pryors
Mewood Ridge
Water Tower
Broomlands
Broom Lane
Barrow Lane
Crockers Hatch Corner
B2110
Cockshots
Roundabout Cottages
Milestone Cottage
Langton Hill
Recreation Ground
Tennis Courts
Holmewood House School
The Hollonds
Stone Cross Wood
East Lodge
NEWPARK WOOD
The Moltens
Broom Farm
Recreation Ground
Burrs Wood
Stone Cottages
Hollonds Wood
Top Hill Farm
Adam's Well
New Barn
Tunbridge Wells
TN3
Harness Well Wood
Groombridge Road
Woodside
Hillside
Blue Cottage
Beech Wood
The Cottage
Fountain Cottages
Barn Field Plantation
Pokehill
Adamswell
Adam's Well Crossing
Dew Spell
Quarry House
The Drift
River Grom
Cattle Grid
Temple Cottage
BURRSWOOD
Court Lodge
The Walks
The Grn.
Bird in Hand St.
Filter Beds
Southern Sewage Works
Yew Tree Cotts.
Heather Lodge
Lodge Lane
Groombridge Place
Sludge Beds
The Jungle
Fencing Works
Florence Farm
Spa Valley Railway
Tunbridge Wells
Wealden
Sewage Pumping Station
Burrswood Villas
South Farm
South Farm Lane
Broadwater Lane
GROOMBRIDGE
Hall
Rec. Grd.
Cricket Grd.
Pav.
Newton Willows
Nursery
Forest
Tithe Barn
Prowdes
Meadow Rd.
Station Rd.
Springfield Rd.
Groomen Field
Groombridge
Lealands Farm
Broadwater Bridge
Withyham Road
The Ridge
Orchard Rise
Oaklands
Broad Oak
Lynwood
Bowl. Gn.
The Close
Florance Lane
Wallis Field
Corseley Road
Little Quarry Farm
Saint's Shaw
Nursery
Oldbury
Forest Way
Drovers Cotts.
Groombridge St. Thomas' C of E Prim. Sch.
Hendal Bridge
Mottsmill Stream
Weir
Hendal Hill
B2188
Hendal House
Spring Farm
Tanyard Cottages
Birchden Farm
Birchden Bungalow
Broadwater Road
Forest Road
Eridge Road
Birchden
The Warren
Hendal Farm
Pumping Station
Aytton's Wood
The Tanyard
Ten. Cts.
Orchard Way
Alksford Farm
Cemy.
Nursery
Clock House
Sherlock's Wood
Park Corner
Normans Cottages
Eridge Rd.
Hendal Farm Cotts.
Birchden Wood
Cherry Gardens Hill
Sherlock's Farm
Long Shaw
Mottsmill Stream
Glen Andred
Harrison's Rocks
Pinstraw Farm
Bridgers
Spring Cotts.
Roffeys
Birchett's Wood
Warren Farm
Warren
Hodge's Wood
Hodges Wood
Motts Down
Birchden Junction
G H J K L M N
52 53 54 55
40 39 38 37 36
1 2 3 4 5 6 7 8 9

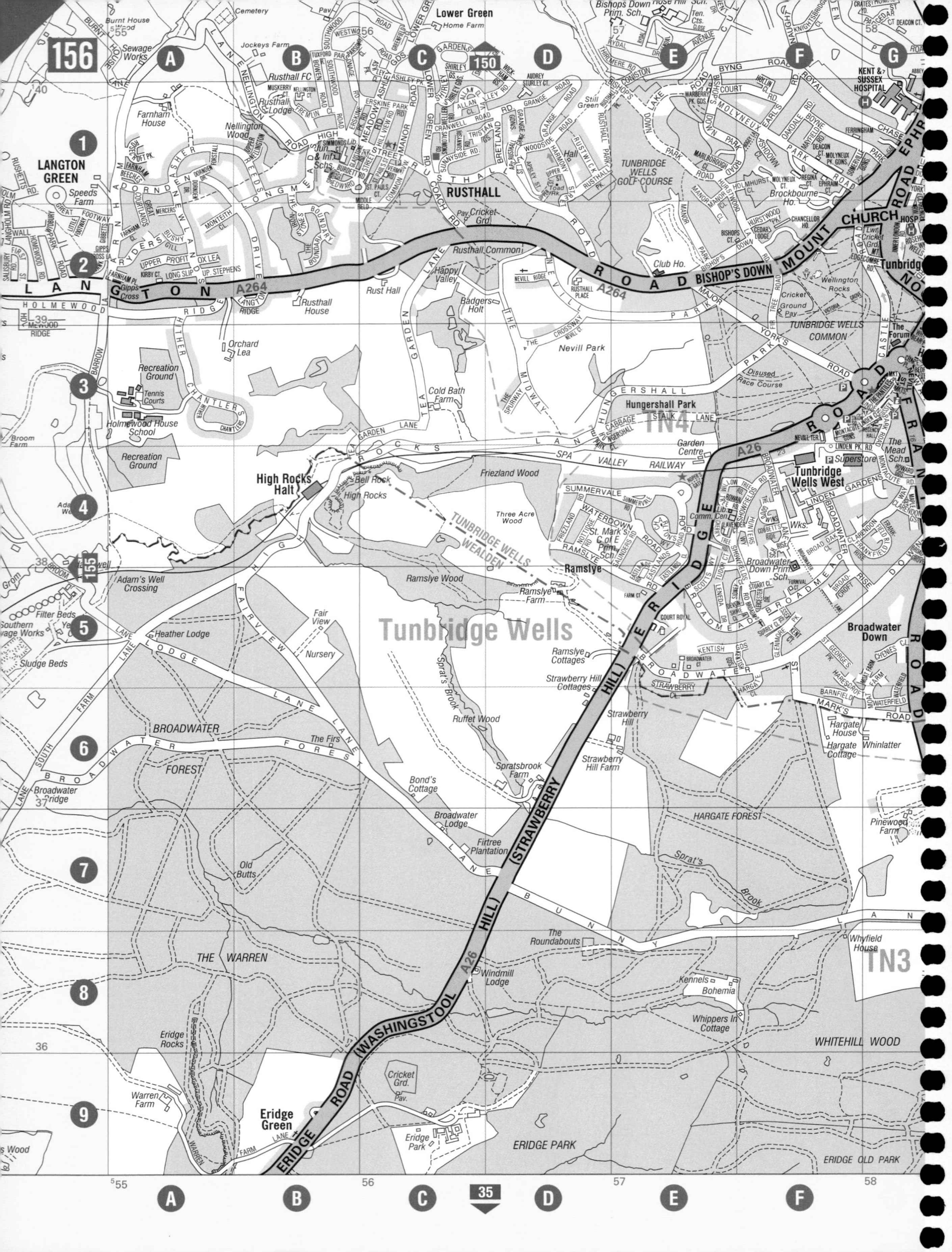
LANGTON GREEN
RUSTHALL
Lower Green
Tunbridge Wells
TN4
TN3
High Rocks Halt
Tunbridge Wells West
Broadwater Down
Ramslye
Hungershall Park
Nevill Park
TUNBRIDGE WELLS COMMON
TUNBRIDGE WELLS GOLF COURSE
KENT & SUSSEX HOSPITAL
BROADWATER FOREST
HARGATE FOREST
THE WARREN
WHITEHILL WOOD
ERIDGE PARK
ERIDGE OLD PARK
Eridge Green
Eridge Rocks
Warren Farm
Windmill Lodge
Bohemia
Whyfield House
LANGTON ROAD A264
BISHOP'S DOWN ROAD
MOUNT CHURCH ROAD
ERIDGE ROAD A26
ERIDGE ROAD (WASHINGSTOOL HILL) (STRAWBERRY HILL)
BUNNY LANE
SPA VALLEY RAILWAY
TUNBRIDGE WELLS WEALDEN
ROCKS LANE
HUNGERSHALL PARK
FAIRVIEW LANE
LODGE LANE
BROADWATER FOREST LANE
Holmewood House School
Recreation Ground
Rust Hall
Rusthall Common
Friezland Wood
Ramslye Wood
Ruffet Wood
Spratsbrook Farm
Strawberry Hill Farm
Fitree Plantation
Broadwater Lodge
Old Butts
Sludge Beds
Filter Beds
Adam's Well Crossing
A B C D E F G
1 2 3 4 5 6 7 8 9
150
155
35

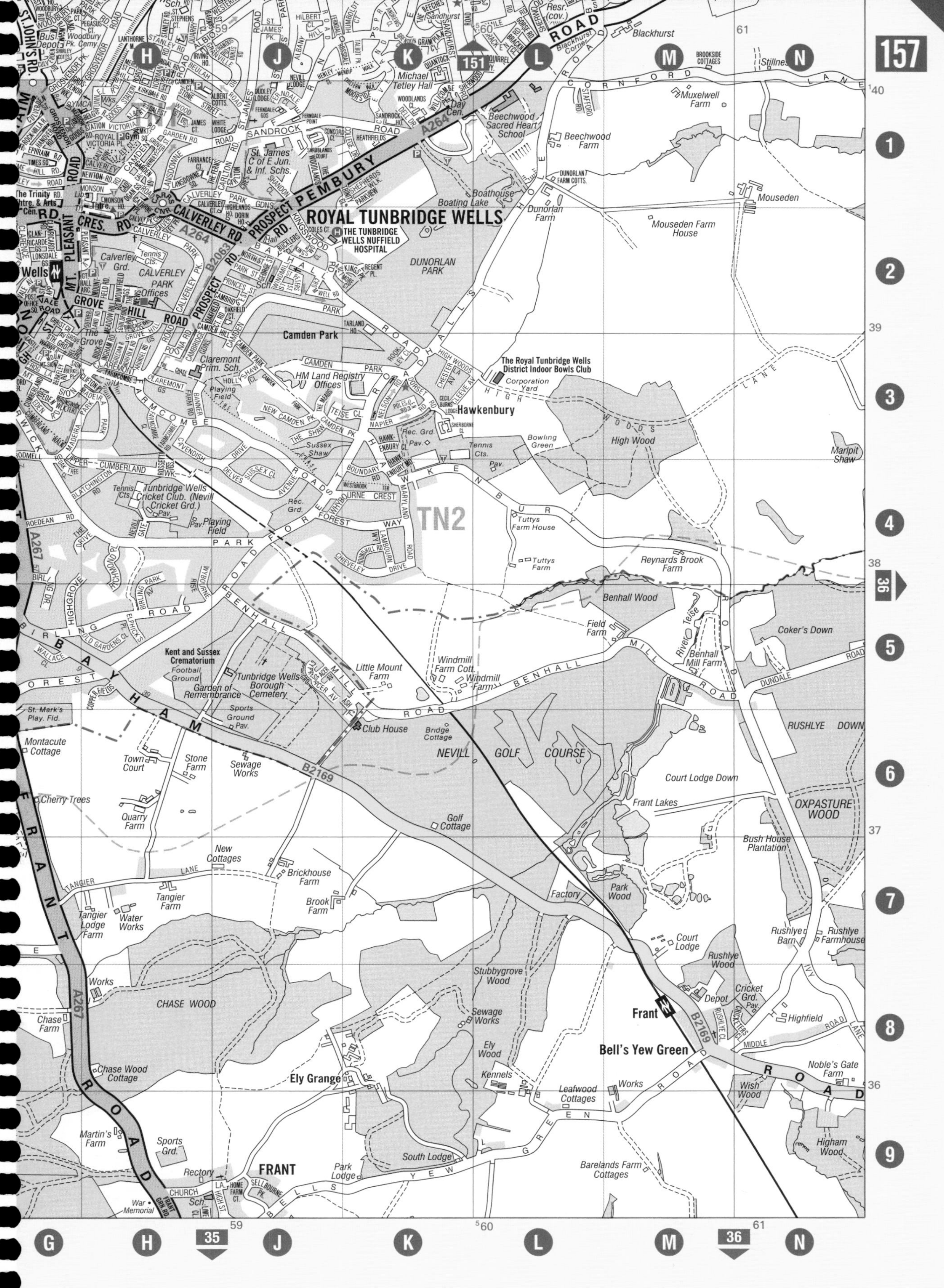
ROYAL TUNBRIDGE WELLS
THE TUNBRIDGE WELLS NUFFIELD HOSPITAL
DUNORLAN PARK
Camden Park
HM Land Registry Offices
Hawkenbury
The Royal Tunbridge Wells District Indoor Bowls Club
TN2
High Wood
Beechwood Sacred Heart School
Beechwood Farm
Mouseden
Mouseden Farm House
Muxelwell Farm
Blackhurst
Reynards Brook Farm
Benhall Wood
Coker's Down
Kent and Sussex Crematorium
Tunbridge Wells Borough Cemetery
Little Mount Farm
Club House
NEVILL GOLF COURSE
RUSHLYE DOWN
Court Lodge Down
Frant Lakes
OXPASTURE WOOD
Bush House Plantation
Park Wood
Stubbygrove Wood
CHASE WOOD
Frant
Bell's Yew Green
Ely Grange
FRANT
Higham Wood
Noble's Gate Farm
Highfield
Rushlye Farmhouse
Barelands Farm Cottages
Leafwood Cottages
Tangier Farm
Brickhouse Farm
Quarry Farm
Cherry Trees
Montacute Cottage
Chase Farm
Chase Wood Cottage
Martin's Farm
A264
A267
B2169
B2063
PEMBURY ROAD
FRANT ROAD
BAYHAM ROAD
BENHALL MILL ROAD
HAWKENBURY ROAD
FOREST ROAD
CALVERLEY RD.
GROVE HILL ROAD
CORNFORD LANE
BELLS YEW GREEN ROAD
MIDDLE ROAD
151
35
36

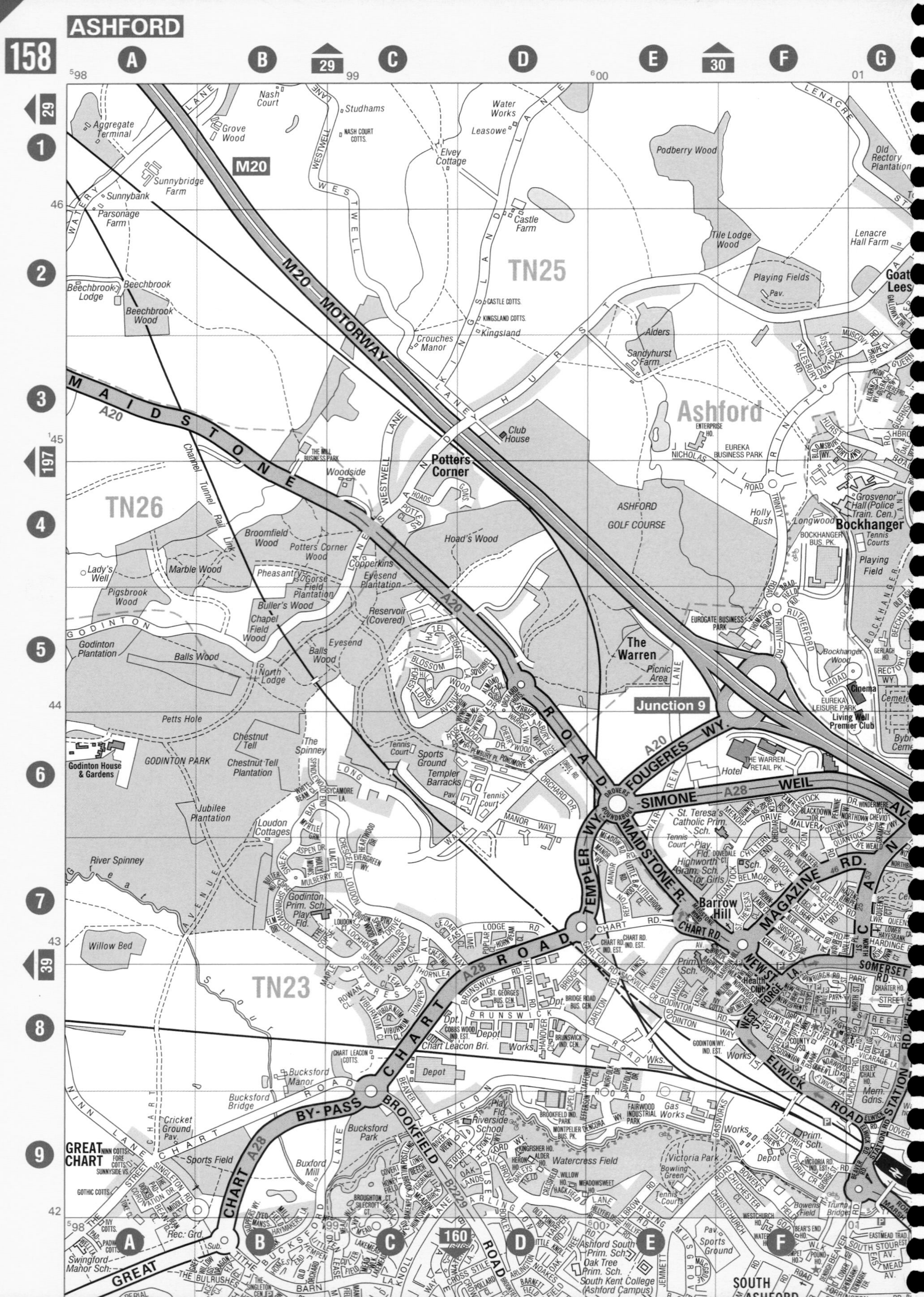
M20
M20 MOTORWAY
MAIDSTONE
A20
TN25
TN26
TN23
Ashford
Podberry Wood
Tile Lodge Wood
Playing Fields
Castle Farm
Kingsland
Crouches Manor
Potters Corner
Club House
Nash Court
Studhams
Grove Wood
Aggregate Terminal
Sunnybridge Farm
Sunnybank
Parsonage Farm
Beechbrook Lodge
Beechbrook
Beechbrook Wood
Elvey Cottage
Water Works
Leasowe
Alders
Sandyhurst Farm
Eureka Business Park
Enterprise Ho.
Holly Bush
Bockhanger
Grosvenor Hall (Police Train. Cen.)
Longwood
Old Rectory Plantation
Lenacre Hall Farm
Goat Lees
Ashford Golf Course
Hoad's Wood
Woodside
Broomfield Wood
Potters Corner Wood
Copperkins
Eyesend Plantation
Pheasantry
Gorse Field Plantation
Buller's Wood
Chapel Field Wood
Reservoir (Covered)
Marble Wood
Lady's Well
Pigsbrook Wood
Godinton Plantation
Balls Wood
North Lodge
Eyesend
Balls Wood
The Warren
Picnic Area
Junction 9
Eurogate Business Park
Bockhanger Wood
Cinema
Eureka Leisure Park
Living Well Premier Club
Petts Hole
Chestnut Tell
Chestnut Tell Plantation
The Spinney
Godinton House & Gardens
GODINTON PARK
Jubilee Plantation
Loudon Cottages
River Spinney
Willow Bed
Sports Ground
Templer Barracks
Tennis Court
The Warren Retail Pk.
Hotel
FOUGERES WY.
SIMONE WEIL AV.
MAIDSTONE RD.
TEMPLER WY.
MAGAZINE RD.
CHART ROAD
St. Teresa's Catholic Prim. Sch.
Highworth Gram. Sch. for Girls
Barrow Hill
Godinton Prim. Sch.
Chart Rd. Ind. Est.
St. Georges Bus. Cen.
Bridge Road Bus. Cen.
Cobbs Wood Ind. Est.
Chart Leacon Bri.
Depot
Works
Godinton Way Ind. Est.
Bucksford Manor
Bucksford Bridge
Cricket Ground
Sports Field
GREAT CHART
BY-PASS
BROOKFIELD
Bucksford Park
Buxford Mill
Riverside School
Watercress Field
Fairwood Industrial Park
Gas Works
Victoria Park
Bowling Green
Tennis Courts
Bowens Field
Trumper Bridge
Mem. Gdns.
ELWICK ROAD
STATION RD.
Swingford Manor Sch.
Rec. Grd.
Ashford South Prim. Sch.
Oak Tree Prim. Sch.
South Kent College (Ashford Campus)
Sports Ground
SOUTH ASHFORD

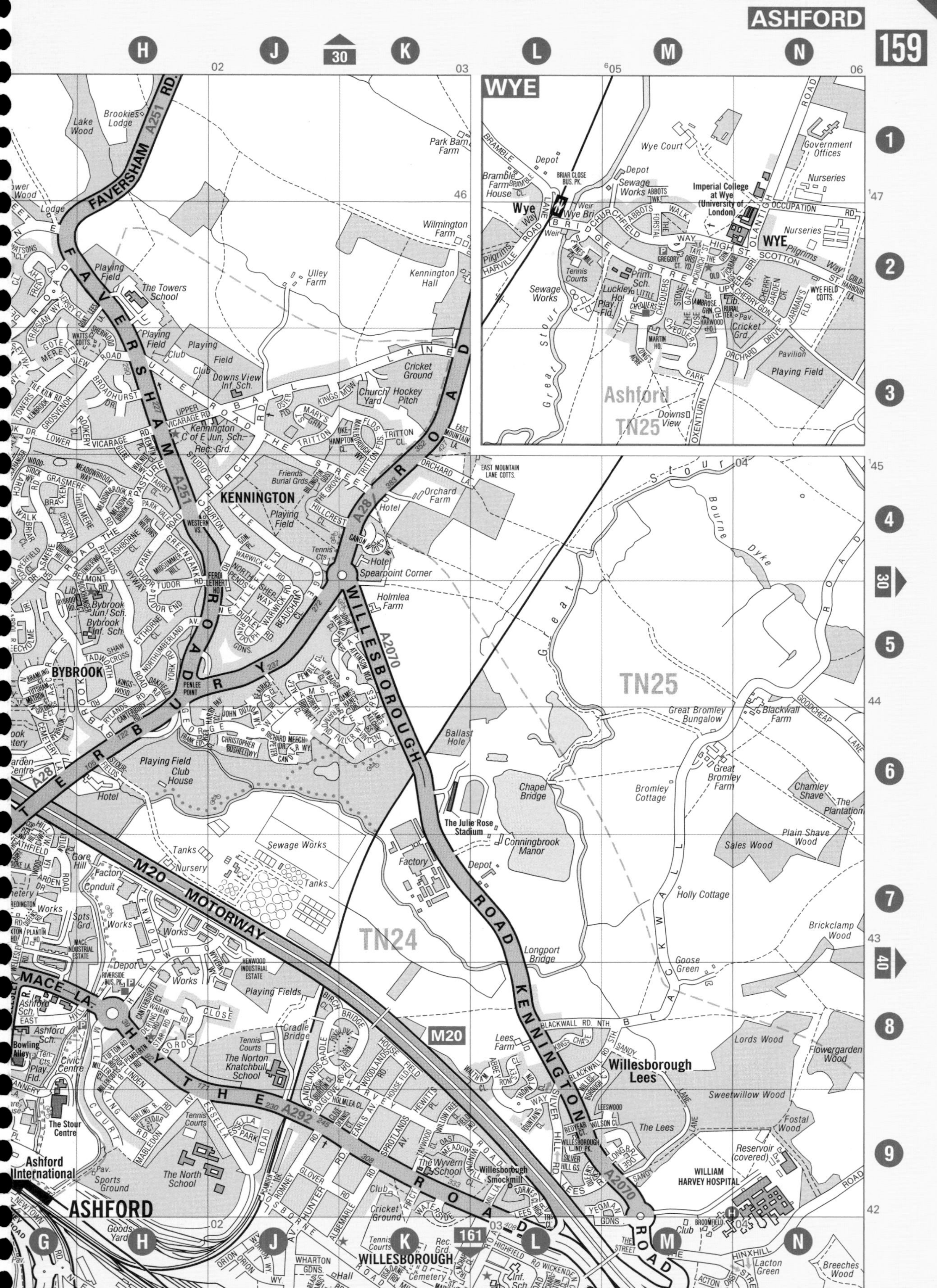
WYE
KENNINGTON
BYBROOK
ASHFORD
WILLESBOROUGH
Willesborough Lees
TN25
TN24
Ashford
Wye
Imperial College at Wye (University of London)
Great Stour
M20 MOTORWAY
FAVERSHAM RD.
KENNINGTON ROAD
WILLESBOROUGH ROAD
Spearpoint Corner
The Julie Rose Stadium
Conningbrook Manor
Chapel Bridge
Longport Bridge
Bourne Dyke
Great Bromley Bungalow
Blackwall Farm
Great Bromley Farm
Bromley Cottage
Holly Cottage
Sales Wood
Plain Shave Wood
Chamley Shave
The Plantation
Brickclamp Wood
Lords Wood
Flowergarden Wood
Sweetwillow Wood
Fostal Wood
The Lees
WILLIAM HARVEY HOSPITAL
Reservoir (covered)
Willesborough Smockmill
The Wyvern School
The Norton Knatchbull School
The North School
The Stour Centre
Ashford International
Sewage Works
Playing Fields
Ballast Hole
Holmlea Farm
Orchard Farm
Kennington Hall
Wilmington Farm
Park Barn Farm
Ulley Farm
Lake Wood
Brookies Lodge
The Towers School
Downs View Inf. Sch.
Bybrook Jun. Sch.
Bybrook Inf. Sch.
Friends Burial Grds.
Lacton Green
Breeches Wood
Wye Court
Government Offices
Nurseries
Cricket Ground
Hockey Pitch
Cricket Grd.
Playing Field
Downs View

30
40
161

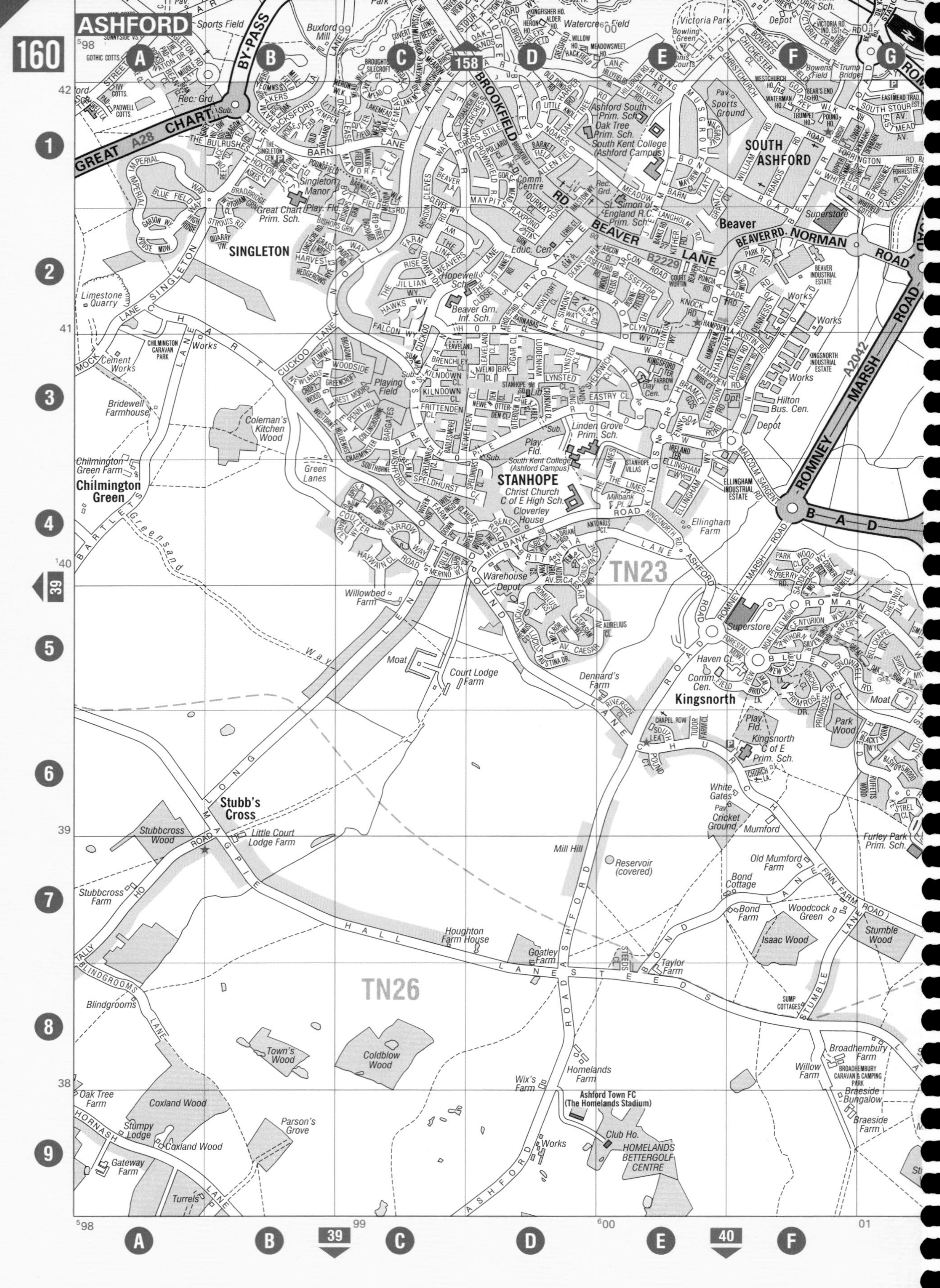
A
B
C
D
E
F
G
1
2
3
4
5
6
7
8
9
158
39
40
TN23
TN26
GREAT CHART
A28
BY-PASS
Sports Field
Buxford Mill
Watercress Field
Victoria Park
Bowling Green
Depot
Rec. Grd.
SINGLETON
Singleton Manor
Great Chart Prim. Sch.
Play. Fld.
Limestone Quarry
Cement Works
Works
Chilmington Caravan Park
Bridewell Farmhouse
Coleman's Kitchen Wood
Chilmington Green Farm
Chilmington Green
Green Lanes
BROOKFIELD
BEAVER LANE
B2229
Ashford South Prim. Sch.
Oak Tree Prim. Sch.
South Kent College (Ashford Campus)
SOUTH ASHFORD
Sports Ground
Comm. Centre
St. Simon of England R.C. Prim. Sch.
Educ. Cen.
Beaver
BEAVER RD.
NORMAN ROAD
Superstore
Beaver Industrial Estate
Kingsnorth Industrial Estate
Hopewell Sch.
Beaver Grn. Inf. Sch.
Playing Field
Day Cen.
Lib.
Linden Grove Prim. Sch.
Play. Fld.
STANHOPE
Christ Church C of E High Sch.
Cloverley House
Hilton Bus. Cen.
Ellingham Industrial Estate
Ellingham Farm
ROMNEY MARSH ROAD
A2042
Warehouse Depot
Willowbed Farm
Moat
Court Lodge Farm
Dennard's Farm
Haven Ct.
Comm. Cen.
Kingsnorth
Superstore
Play. Fld.
Kingsnorth C of E Prim. Sch.
Park Wood
Stubb's Cross
Stubbcross Wood
Little Court Lodge Farm
Stubbcross Farm
Mill Hill
Reservoir (covered)
White Gates
Cricket Ground
Mumford
Old Mumford Farm
Bond Cottage
Bond Farm
Woodcock Green
Isaac Wood
Stumble Wood
Furley Park Prim. Sch.
Houghton Farm House
Goatley Farm
Taylor Farm
Blindgrooms
Town's Wood
Coldblow Wood
Homelands Farm
Wix's Farm
Ashford Town FC (The Homelands Stadium)
Club Ho.
HOMELANDS BETTERGOLF CENTRE
Works
Oak Tree Farm
Coxland Wood
Stumpy Lodge
Gateway Farm
Turrels
Parson's Grove
Broadhembury Farm
Broadhembury Caravan & Camping Park
Willow Farm
Braeside Bungalow
Braeside Farm
Sump Cottages
HALL LANE
STEEDS LANE
ASHFORD ROAD
LONG LANE
MAGPIE HALL ROAD
BLINDGROOMS LANE
FINN FARM ROAD
STUMBLE LANE
598
99
600
01
42
41
140
39
38

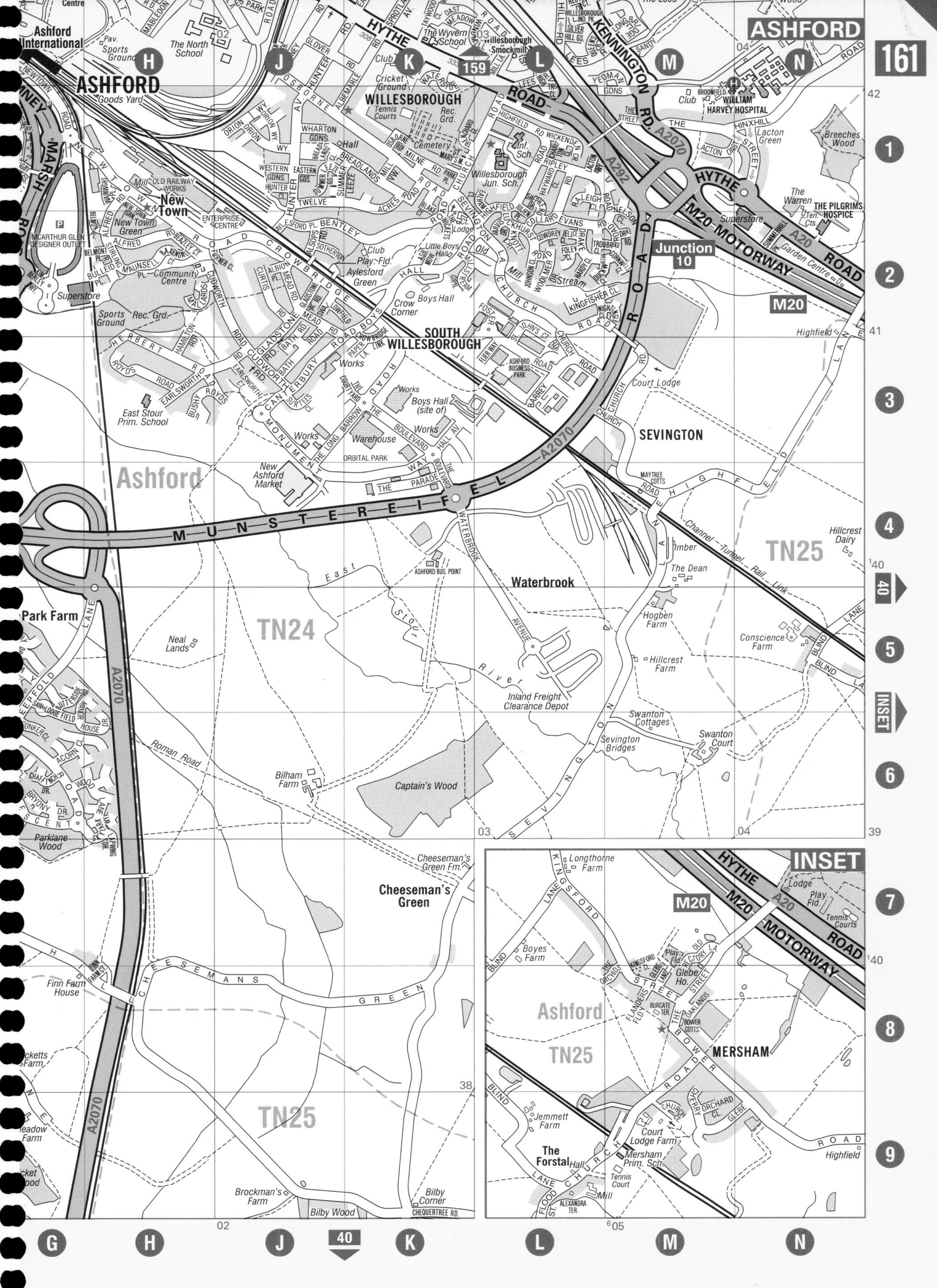

Ashford International
ASHFORD
Goods Yard
WILLESBOROUGH
New Town
SOUTH WILLESBOROUGH
SEVINGTON
Junction 10
M20 MOTORWAY
WILLIAM HARVEY HOSPITAL
Ashford
TN24
TN25
Waterbrook
Park Farm
Cheeseman's Green
Captain's Wood
Inland Freight Clearance Depot
MUNSTEREIFEL
A2070
INSET
MERSHAM
The Forstal

159
40
INSET

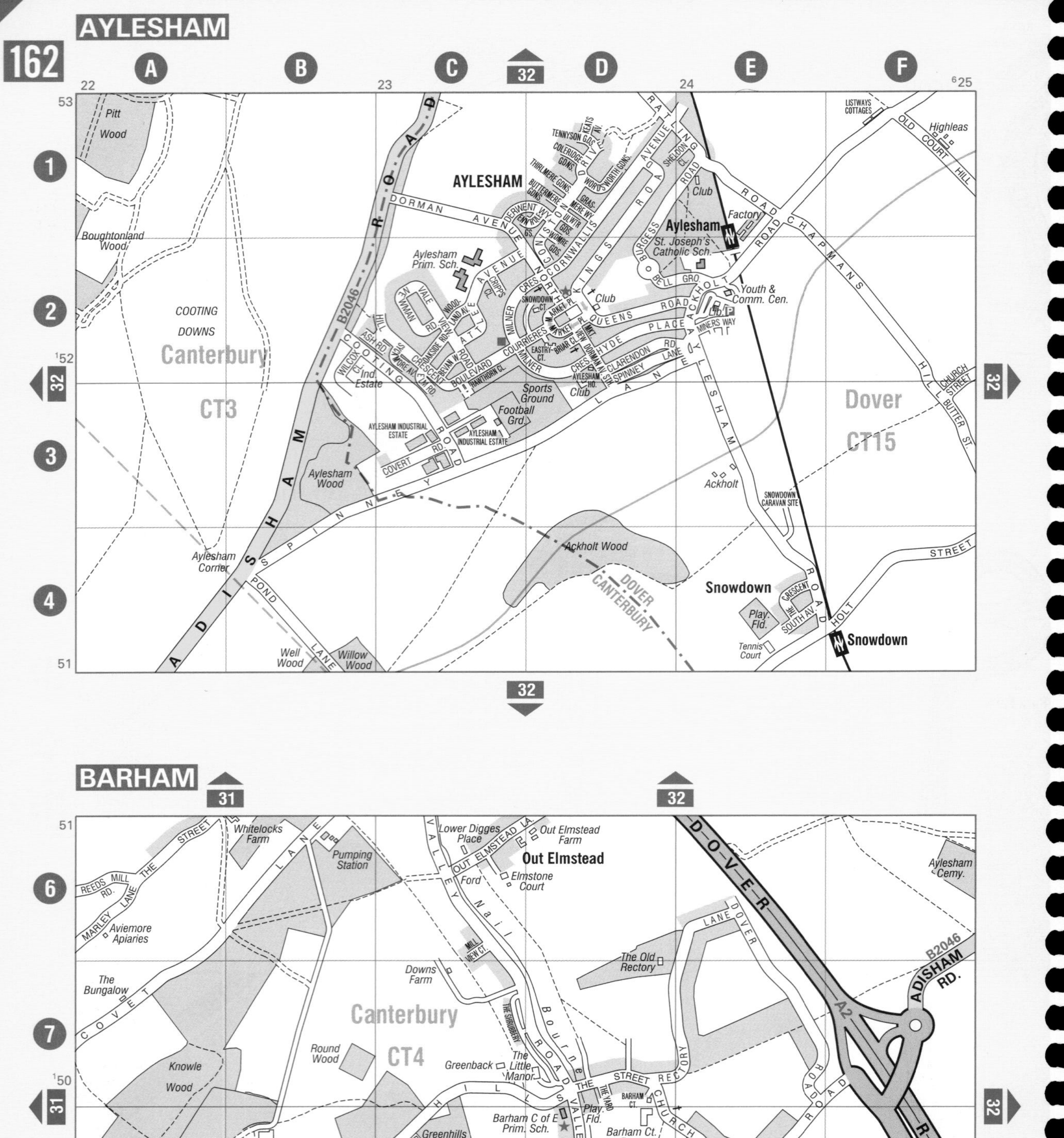
A
B
C
D
E
F
32
AYLESHAM
Pitt Wood
Boughtonland Wood
COOTING DOWNS
Canterbury
CT3
Aylesham Prim. Sch.
DORMAN AVENUE
ADISHAM ROAD
B2046
Ind. Estate
AYLESHAM INDUSTRIAL ESTATE
Sports Ground
Football Grd.
Club
COVERT RD
Aylesham Wood
SPINNEY LANE
Aylesham Corner
POND LANE
Well Wood
Willow Wood
Ackholt Wood
DOVER
CANTERBURY
Aylesham
St. Joseph's Catholic Sch.
Factory
Youth & Comm. Cen.
RATLING ROAD
CORNWALLIS
QUEENS ROAD
HYDE PLACE
AYLESHAM
Ackholt
SNOWDOWN CARAVAN SITE
Snowdown
Play. Fld.
Tennis Court
HOLT STREET
LISTWAYS COTTAGES
Highleas
OLD COURT HILL
CHAPMANS HILL
CHURCH STREET
BUTTER ST.
Dover
CT15
BARHAM
31
Whitelocks Farm
Pumping Station
Lower Digges Place
Out Elmstead Farm
Out Elmstead
Elmstone Court
REEDS MILL RD.
MARLEY LANE
Aviemore Apiaries
The Bungalow
COVET LANE
Knowle Wood
Long Ruffet Wood
Old Wood
Downs Farm
Canterbury
CT4
Round Wood
Greenback
The Little Manor
Greenhills Farm
Barham C of E Prim. Sch.
Play. Fld.
Barham Ct. Farm
Grave Yard
BARHAM
The Old Rectory
DOVER ROAD
A2
A260
B2046
ADISHAM RD.
Aylesham Cemy.
Gravel Castle
Derringstone
Sussex Farm
GREEN RAILWAY
Redgate Shaw
Cricket Grd.
RABBIT HOLE ROAD
SOUTH BARHAM RD
DERRINGSTONE HILL
MILL LA.

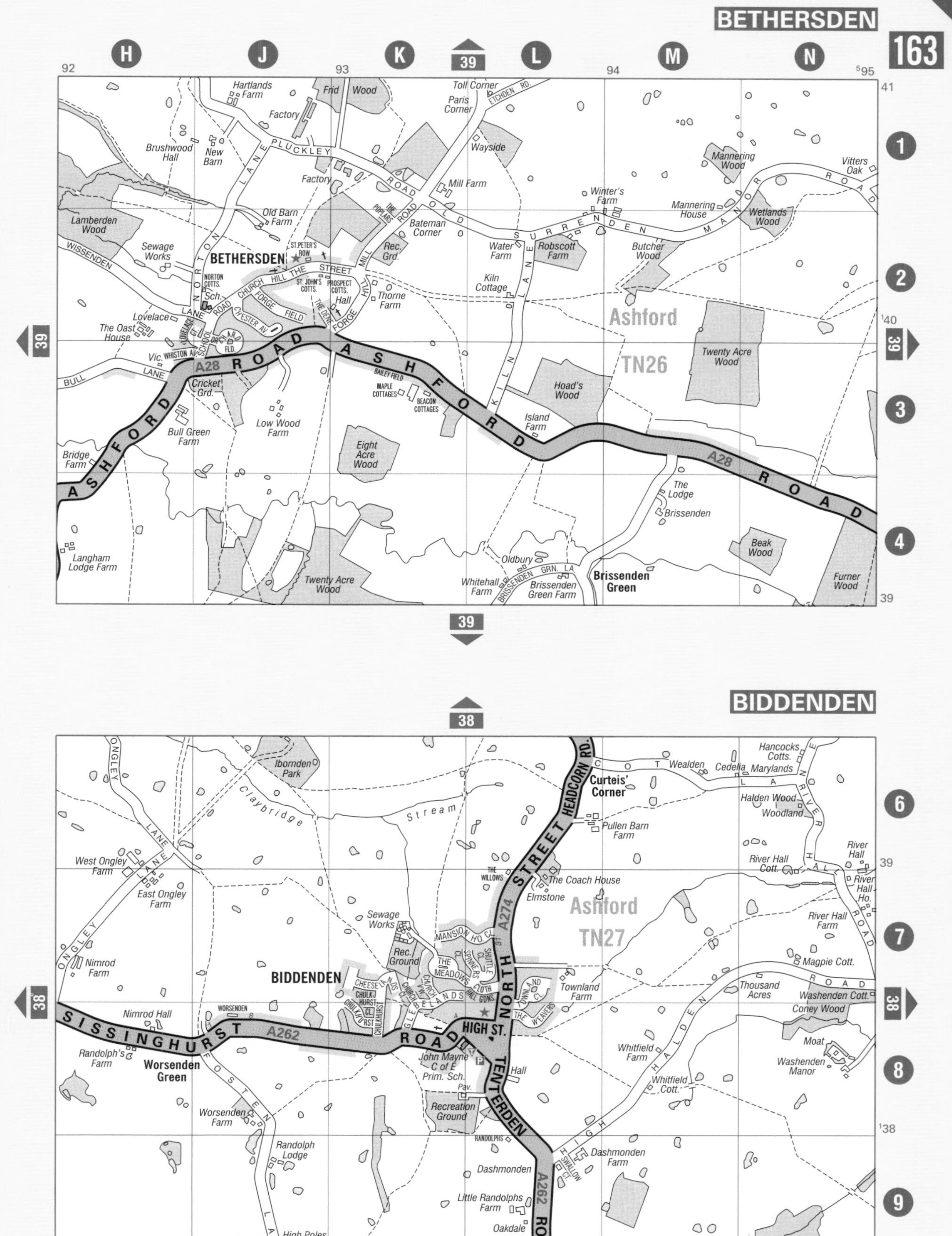
H
J
K
L
M
N
39
92
93
94
595
41
40
39
1
2
3
4
Hartlands Farm
Frid
Wood
Toll Corner
Paris Corner
ETCHDEN RD.
Factory
Brushwood Hall
New Barn
PLUCKLEY
Wayside
Manning Wood
Vitters Oak
Factory
ROAD
Mill Farm
Winter's Farm
Lamberden Wood
Old Barn Farm
THE POPLARS
OLD
Bateman Corner
Mannering House
Wetlands Wood
MANOR
ROAD
SURRENDEN
Sewage Works
WISSENDEN
BETHERSDEN
ST.PETER'S ROW
Rec. Grd.
MILL
Water Farm
Robscott Farm
Butcher Wood
THE STREET
CHURCH HILL
NORTON COTTS.
ST. JOHN'S COTTS.
PROSPECT COTTS.
Hall
Thorne Farm
Kiln Cottage
Sch.
FORGE
FIELD
NORTON
LANE
Lovelace
CHESTER AV.
THE DENE
FORGE
Ashford
The Oast House
LOVELACE CL.
SCHOOL
ORCHARD FLD.
Vic.
WHISTON AV.
A28
ROAD
ASHFORD
TN26
Twenty Acre Wood
BULL
LANE
Cricket Grd.
BAILEY FIELD
MAPLE COTTAGES
BEACON COTTAGES
KILN
Hoad's Wood
Island Farm
Bull Green Farm
Low Wood Farm
Eight Acre Wood
Bridge Farm
A28
ROAD
The Lodge
Brissenden
Langham Lodge Farm
Beak Wood
Oldbury
Twenty Acre Wood
Whitehall Farm
BRISSENDEN GRN. LA
Brissenden Green Farm
Brissenden Green
Furner Wood
BIDDENDEN
38
ONGLEY
Ibornden Park
Claybridge
HEADCORN RD.
COT
Wealden
Cedelia
Hancocks Cotts.
Marylands
Curteis' Corner
Stream
LANE
Halden Wood
Woodland
STREET
Pullen Barn Farm
West Ongley Farm
LANE
River Hall
RIVER
River Hall Cott.
HALL
River Hall Ho.
THE WILLOWS
The Coach House
East Ongley Farm
Elmstone
Ashford
TN27
Sewage Works
A274
MANSION HO. CL.
River Hall Farm
ROAD
Rec. Ground
THE MEADOWS
SPINNERS CL.
SHUTTLE CL.
NORTH
ST.
Nimrod Farm
BIDDENDEN
CHEESE
CHULKHURST
CHURCH
CLOTH HALL GDNS.
Magpie Cott.
ROAD
Townland Farm
TOWNLAND CL.
Thousand Acres
Washenden Cott.
Coney Wood
Nimrod Hall
WORSENDEN
THE WEAVERS
SISSINGHURST
A262
ROAD
HIGH ST.
HALDEN
Moat
Randolph's Farm
Worsenden Green
John Mayne C of E Prim. Sch.
P
Whitfield Farm
Washenden Manor
FOSTEN
Hall
TENTERDEN
Whitfield Cott.
Pav.
Recreation Ground
Worsenden Farm
HIGH
38
RANDOLPHS
Randolph Lodge
Dashmonden Farm
SWALLOW CL.
Dashmonden
A262
ROAD
Little Randolphs Farm
Oakdale
High Poles Farm
Goose Green
LANE
9
84
585
86
6
7
8
9

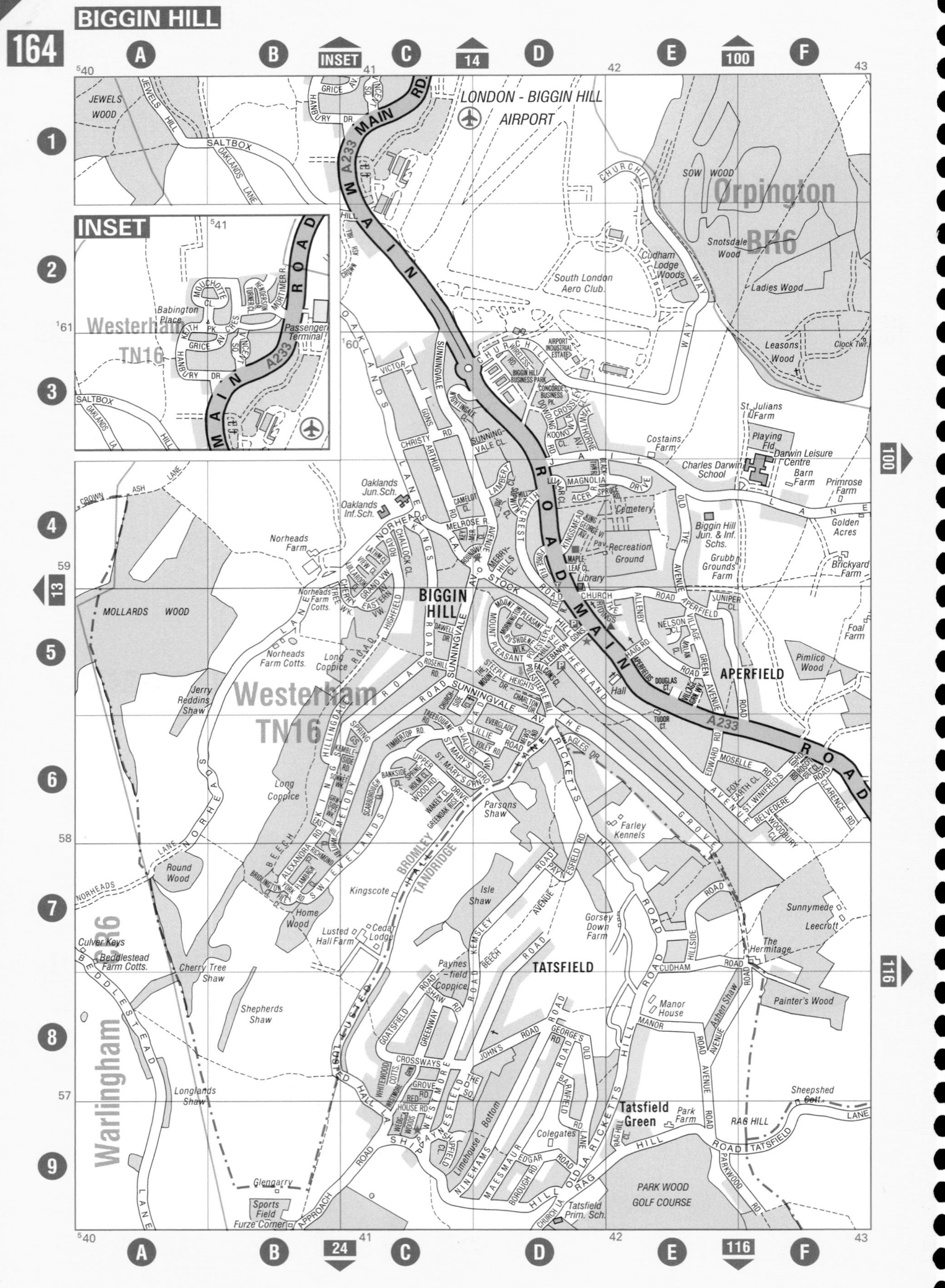

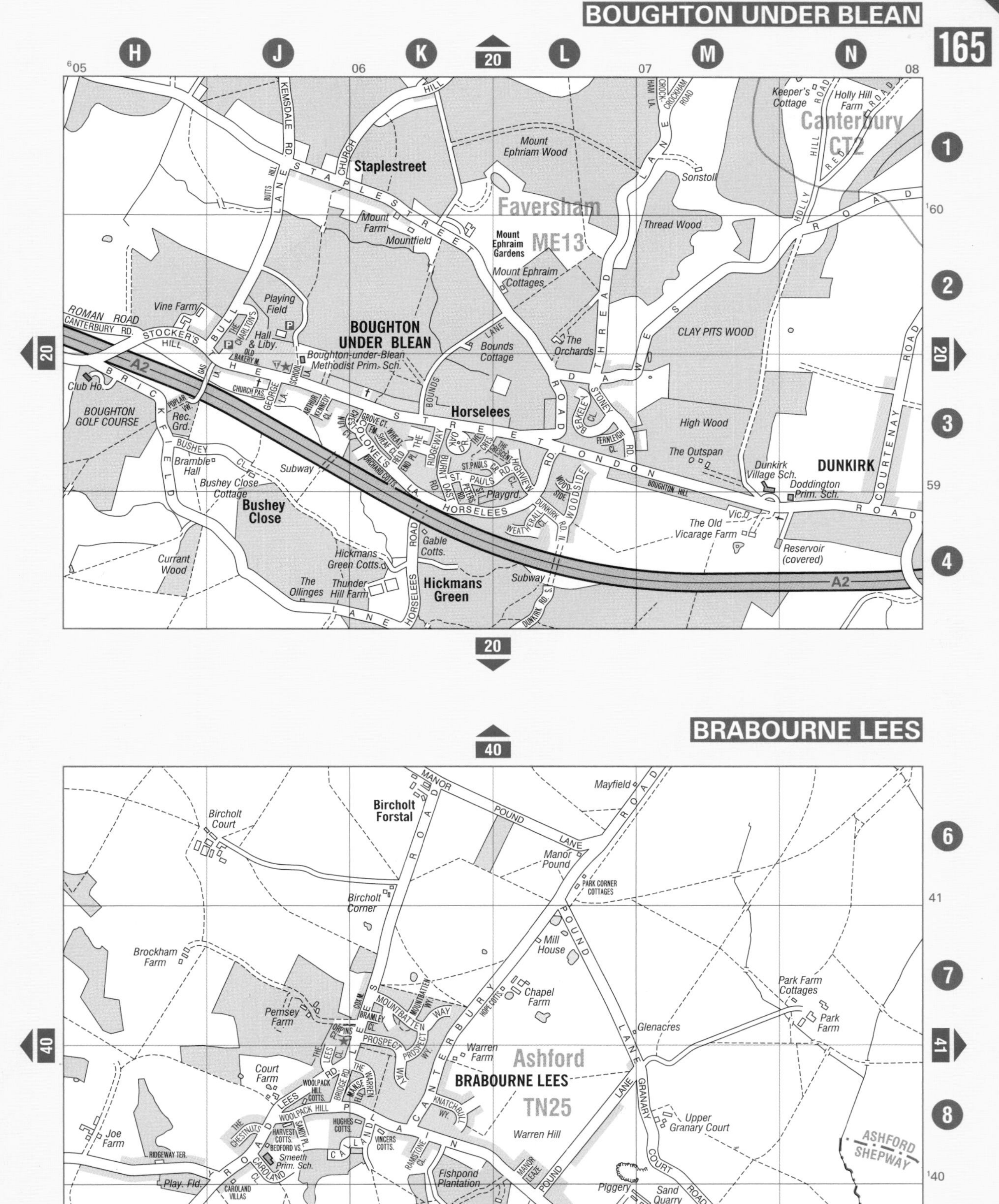
Staplestreet
Faversham
ME13
Mount Ephriam Wood
Sonstoll
Keeper's Cottage
Holly Hill Farm
Canterbury CT2
Mount Farm
Mountfield
Mount Ephraim Gardens
Mount Ephraim Cottages
Thread Wood
Vine Farm
Playing Field
Hall & Liby.
BOUGHTON UNDER BLEAN
Boughton-under-Blean Methodist Prim. Sch.
Bounds Cottage
The Orchards
CLAY PITS WOOD
Club Ho.
BOUGHTON GOLF COURSE
Rec. Grd.
Horselees
High Wood
The Outspan
Bramble Hall
Bushey Close Cottage
Bushey Close
Subway
Playgrd.
Dunkirk Village Sch.
DUNKIRK
Doddington Prim. Sch.
The Old Vicarage Farm
Reservoir (covered)
Currant Wood
Gable Cotts.
Hickmans Green Cotts.
The Ollinges
Thunder Hill Farm
Hickmans Green
A2
ROMAN ROAD
CANTERBURY RD.
STOCKER'S HILL
STAPLESTREET
LONDON ROAD
BOUGHTON HILL
HORSELEES RD.
DUNKIRK RD. N.
COURTENAY ROAD
HOLLY HILL
BRABOURNE LEES
Bircholt Court
Bircholt Forstal
Mayfield
Manor Pound
PARK CORNER COTTAGES
Bircholt Corner
Brockham Farm
Mill House
Chapel Farm
Park Farm Cottages
Park Farm
Pemsey Farm
Glenacres
Warren Farm
Ashford
BRABOURNE LEES
TN25
Court Farm
Joe Farm
Upper Granary Court
Warren Hill
ASHFORD
SHEPWAY
Smeeth Prim. Sch.
Play. Fld.
Fishpond Plantation
Piggery
Sand Quarry
Whin Croft
Little Granary Court
Oakleigh
Bog Farm
Pinehurst
Church Farm
The Rectory
Fishpond Wood
Southenay Farm
Smeeth
Scott's Hall Plantation
Lodge House
CHURCH GREEN COTTAGES
Church House
Lilyvale
The Firs
Coopers Wood
A20
MANOR POUND LANE
CANTERBURY ROAD
POUND LANE
GRANARY COURT ROAD
LILYVALE ROAD
CHURCH ROAD
SOUTHENAY LA.

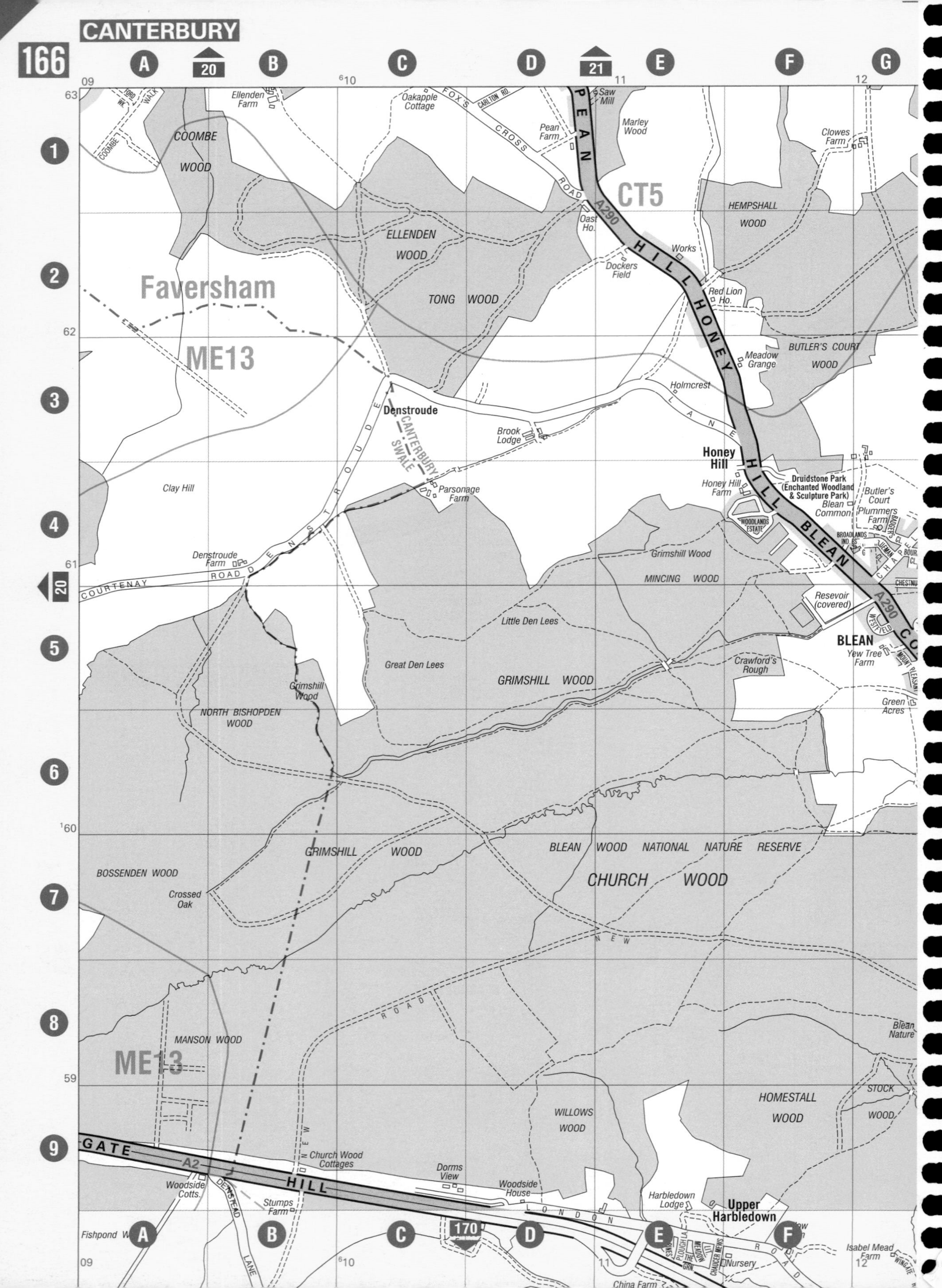
Ellenden Farm
Oakapple Cottage
FOX'S CROSS ROAD
CARLTON RD.
Saw Mill
Pean Farm
Marley Wood
Clowes Farm
COOMBE WOOD
CT5
PEAN HILL
A290
HEMPSHALL WOOD
Oast Ho.
ELLENDEN WOOD
Works
Dockers Field
Faversham
TONG WOOD
Red Lion Ho.
HONEY
ME13
Meadow Grange
BUTLER'S COURT WOOD
Holmcrest
LANE
Denstroude
CANTERBURY SWALE
Brook Lodge
Honey Hill
Clay Hill
Parsonage Farm
Honey Hill Farm
Druidstone Park (Enchanted Woodland & Sculpture Park)
Blean Common
Butler's Court
Plummers Farm
WOODLANDS ESTATE
BLEAN
DENSTROUDE
Grimshill Wood
Denstroude Farm
COURTENAY ROAD
MINCING WOOD
Resevoir (covered)
Little Den Lees
BLEAN
Yew Tree Farm
Great Den Lees
GRIMSHILL WOOD
Crawford's Rough
Grimshill Wood
NORTH BISHOPDEN WOOD
Green Acres
GRIMSHILL WOOD
BLEAN WOOD NATIONAL NATURE RESERVE
BOSSENDEN WOOD
CHURCH WOOD
Crossed Oak
NEW
ROAD
Blean Nature
MANSON WOOD
ME13
HOMESTALL WOOD
STOCK WOOD
WILLOWS WOOD
GATE HILL
A2
NEW
Church Wood Cottages
Dorms View
Woodside Cotts.
Woodside House
Stumps Farm
Harbledown Lodge
Upper Harbledown
LONDON ROAD
Fishpond
LANE
Isabel Mead Farm
Nursery
China Farm
A B C D E F G
1 2 3 4 5 6 7 8 9
09 610 11 12
63 62 61 160 59
20 21 170

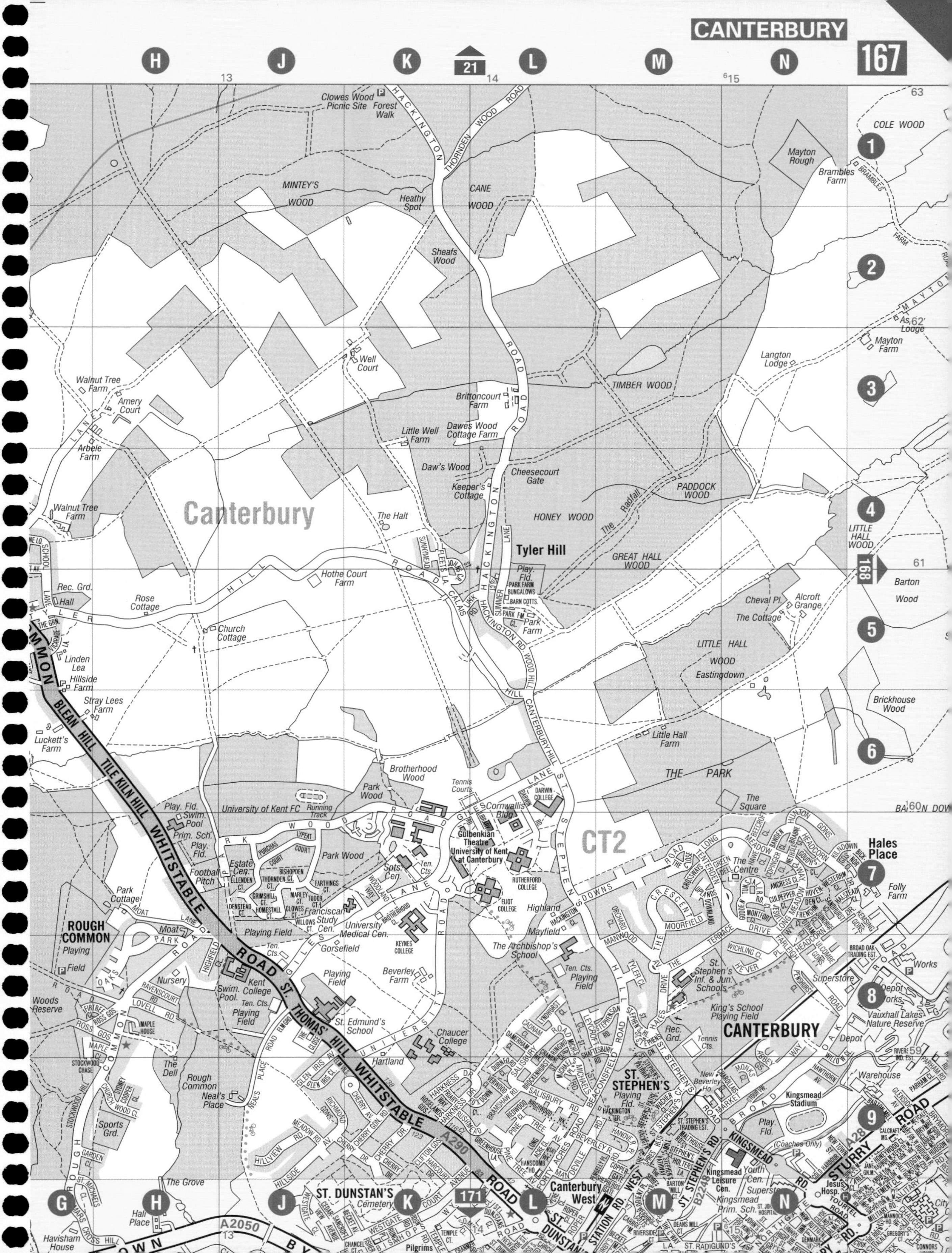
H
J
K
L
M
N
21
Clowes Wood Picnic Site
Forest Walk
MINTEY'S WOOD
Heathy Spot
CANE WOOD
COLE WOOD
Mayton Rough
Brambles Farm
Sheafs Wood
Well Court
Walnut Tree Farm
Amery Court
Brittoncourt Farm
TIMBER WOOD
Langton Lodge
Mayton Farm
Little Well Farm
Dawes Wood Cottage Farm
Arbele Farm
Daw's Wood
Cheesecourt Gate
Keeper's Cottage
PADDOCK WOOD
Canterbury
The Halt
HONEY WOOD
Walnut Tree Farm
Tyler Hill
GREAT HALL WOOD
LITTLE HALL WOOD
Hothe Court Farm
Rose Cottage
Rec. Grd.
Church Cottage
Park Farm
Cheval Pl.
The Cottage
Alcroft Grange
Barton Wood
Linden Lea
Hillside Farm
LITTLE HALL WOOD
Eastingdown
Stray Lees Farm
Brickhouse Wood
Luckett's Farm
Little Hall Farm
Brotherhood Wood
THE PARK
Park Wood
University of Kent FC
The Square
CT2
Hales Place
Gulbenkian Theatre
University of Kent at Canterbury
Cornwallis Bldg.
The Centre
Folly Farm
Park Wood
Football Pitch
Park Cottage
ROUGH COMMON
Franciscan Study Cen.
University Medical Cen.
Highland
Mayfield
The Archbishop's School
Playing Field
Gorsefield
Kent College
Beverley Farm
St. Stephen's Inf. & Jun. Schools
King's School Playing Field
Superstore
Works
Depot
Vauxhall Lakes Nature Reserve
Woods Reserve
Nursery
St. Edmund's School
Chaucer College
CANTERBURY
Rough Common
Neal's Place
Hartland
The Dell
ST. STEPHEN'S
Kingsmead Stadium
Warehouse
Sports Grd.
Kingsmead Leisure Cen.
The Grove
ST. DUNSTAN'S Cemetery
Canterbury West
Hall Place
Havisham House
Pilgrims
A290
A2050
A28
B2248
WHITSTABLE ROAD
ST. THOMAS' HILL
BLEAN HILL
TILE KILN HILL
HACKINGTON ROAD
THORNDEN WOOD ROAD
UNIVERSITY ROAD
STURRY ROAD
KINGSMEAD RD.
171
168
G
H
J
K
L
M
N
1
2
3
4
5
6
7
8
9

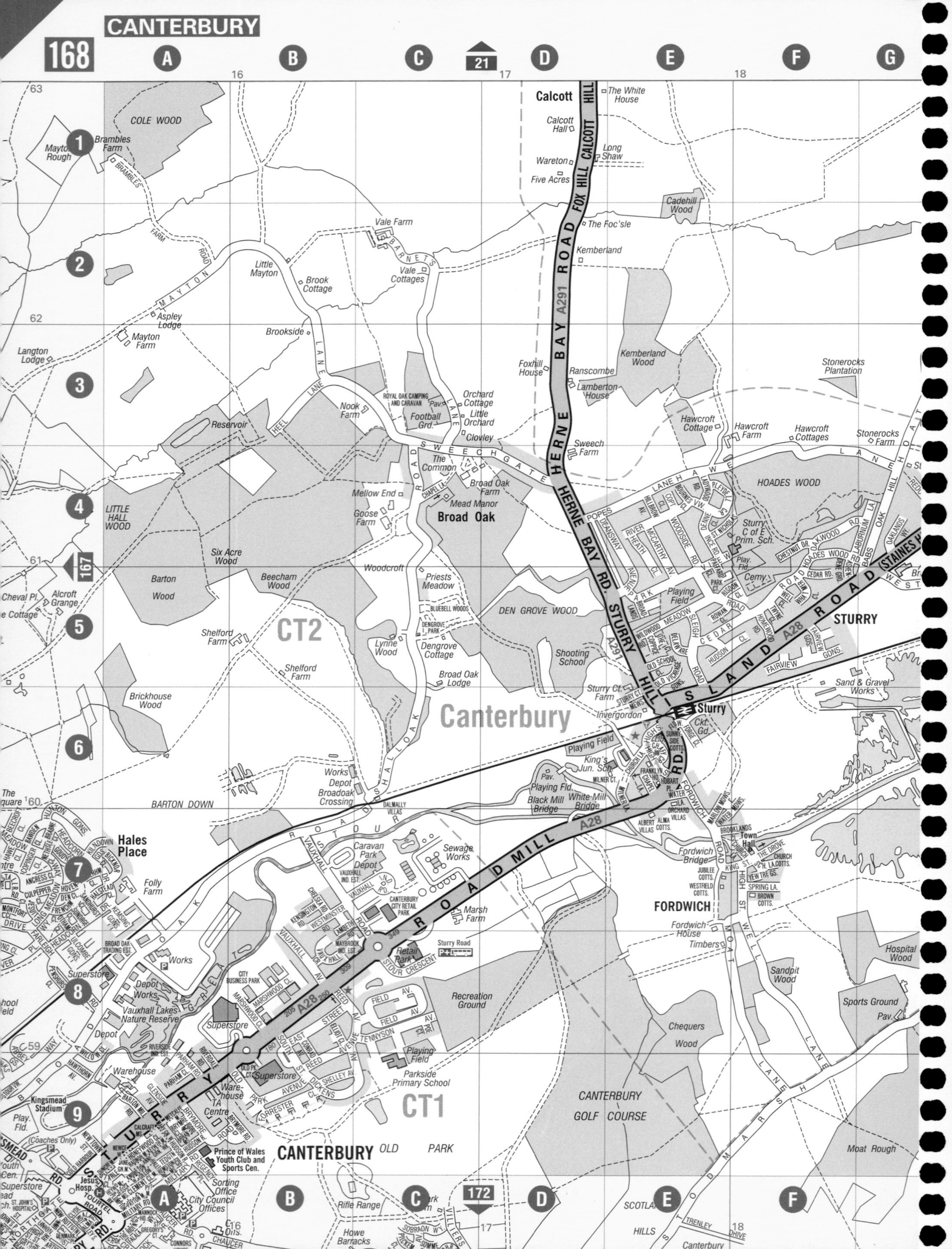
Calcott
The White House
Calcott Hall
Wareton
Long Shaw
Five Acres
FOX HILL
CALCOTT HILL
Cadehill Wood
The Foc'sle
Kemberland
HERNE BAY ROAD
A291
COLE WOOD
Brambles Farm
Mayton Rough
BRAMBLES
FARM ROAD
MAYTON
Vale Farm
BARNETS
Little Mayton
Brook Cottage
Vale Cottages
Aspley Lodge
Mayton Farm
Langton Lodge
Brookside
LANE
HEEL LANE
Foxhill House
Ranscombe
Lamberton House
Kemberland Wood
Stonerocks Plantation
Reservoir
Nook Farm
ROYAL OAK CAMPING AND CARAVAN
Pav.
Football Grd.
Orchard Cottage
Little Orchard
Clovley
Sweech Farm
Hawcroft Cottage
Hawcroft Farm
Hawcroft Cottages
Stonerocks Farm
SWEECHGATE
The Common
CHAPEL LA.
Broad Oak Farm
Mead Manor
Broad Oak
Mellow End
Goose Farm
HAWE LANE
HOADES WOOD
LITTLE HALL WOOD
Six Acre Wood
Barton Wood
Beecham Wood
Woodcroft
Priests Meadow
BLUEBELL WOODS
DENGROVE PARK
DEN GROVE WOOD
HERNE BAY RD.
STURRY HILL
POPES
DEANSWAY
RIVER HEATH
MCCARTHY AV.
WOODSIDE RD.
Sturry C of E Prim. Sch.
Play. Fld.
Cemy.
Playing Field
MEADOW
SLEIGH
CEDAR
HUDSON CL.
ISLAND ROAD
A28
FAIRVIEW
STURRY
STAINES HILL
Cheval Pl.
Alcroft Grange
Shelford Farm
CT2
Lynne Wood
Dengrove Cottage
Broad Oak Lodge
Shooting School
Sturry Ct. Farm
Invergordon
Sturry
Sand & Gravel Works
Brickhouse Wood
Canterbury
Playing Field
King's Jun. Sch.
Pav.
Playing Fld.
Black Mill Bridge
White Mill Bridge
Works
Depot
Broadoak Crossing
SHALLOAK
BARTON DOWN
Hales Place
DALMALLY VILLAS
STOUR
Caravan Park
Depot
Sewage Works
MILL ROAD
FORDWICH
ALBERT VILLAS
ALMA COTTS.
Town Hall
THE DROVE
Fordwich Bridge
KING ST.
HIGH ST.
SPRING LA.
BROWN COTTS.
FORDWICH
Fordwich House
Timbers
Folly Farm
VAUXHALL IND. EST.
CANTERBURY CITY RETAIL PARK
Marsh Farm
BROAD OAK TRADING EST.
Works
Retail Park
Sturry Road
STOUR CRESCENT
Superstore
Depot Works
Vauxhall Lakes Nature Reserve
CITY BUSINESS PARK
Recreation Ground
Sandpit Wood
Hospital Wood
Sports Ground
Pav.
Chequers Wood
Superstore
Depot
Warehouse
Superstore
Playing Field
Parkside Primary School
Kingsmead Stadium
Ware-house
TA Centre
CT1
CANTERBURY GOLF COURSE
MOAT LANE
MARSH LANE
Prince of Wales Youth Club and Sports Cen.
CANTERBURY
OLD PARK
Moat Rough
Superstore
Jesus Hosp.
Sorting Office
City Council Offices
Rifle Range
Howe Barracks
SCOTLAND HILLS
TRENLEY DRIVE
Canterbury

21
167
172

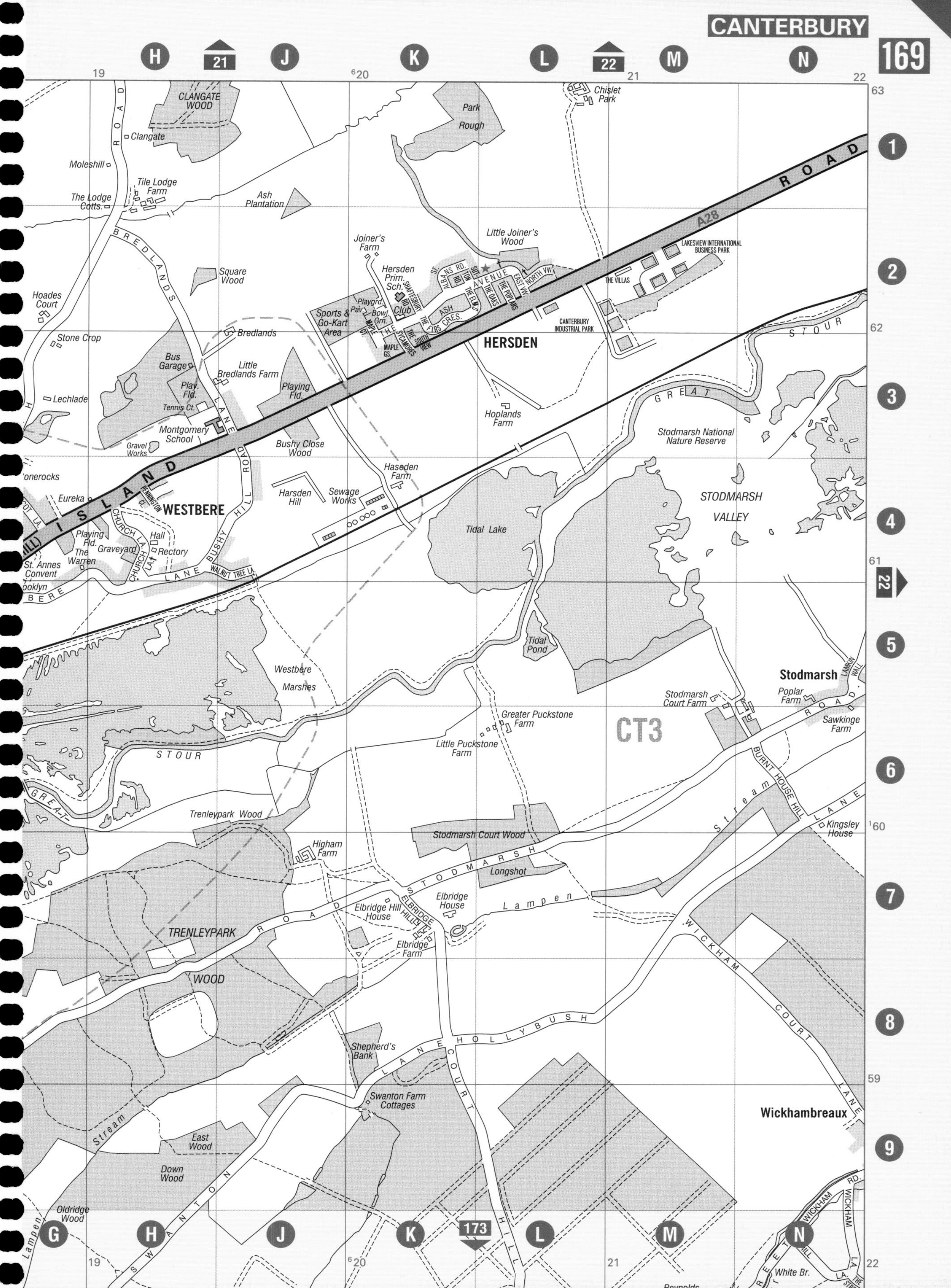

H 21 J K L 22 M N

CLANGATE WOOD
Clangate
Moleshill
Tile Lodge Farm
The Lodge Cotts.
Ash Plantation
Square Wood
Hoades Court
Stone Crop
Bredlands
Lechlade
Bus Garage
Little Bredlands Farm
Play. Fld.
Tennis Ct.
Gravel Works
Montgomery School
Bushy Close Wood

Park Rough
Chislet Park
Little Joiner's Wood
Joiner's Farm
Hersden Prim. Sch.
LAKESVIEW INTERNATIONAL BUSINESS PARK
THE ELMS
Playgrd. Bowl. Grn.
Club
Sports & Go-Kart Area
ASH CRES.
THE SOUTH VIEW
MAPLE GS.
THE SYCAMORES
THE VILLAS
CANTERBURY INDUSTRIAL PARK
HERSDEN

A28
ROAD
STOUR

Hoplands Farm
Stodmarsh National Nature Reserve
GREAT

ISLAND
Eureka
Westbere Marshes
PENNINGTON
WESTBERE
Harsden Hill
Sewage Works
Haseden Farm
Tidal Lake
STODMARSH VALLEY

Onerocks
Playing Fld.
The Warren
Hall
Graveyard
St. Annes Convent
Rectory
Brooklyn
WESTBERE
CHURCH LANE
BUSHY HILL ROAD
ASH LANE
WALNUT TREE LA.
22

Tidal Pond
Stodmarsh
Poplar Farm
Stodmarsh Court Farm
Sawkinge Farm

STOUR
GREAT
Trenleypark Wood
Greater Puckstone Farm
Little Puckstone Farm
CT3

Stodmarsh Court Wood
Kingsley House
BURNT HOUSE HILL LANE
LANWIN HILL

Higham Farm
Longshot
STODMARSH ROAD
Lampen
WICKHAM COURT LANE
Stream

TRENLEYPARK
Elbridge Hill House
Elbridge House
Elbridge Farm
ELBRIDGE HILL
Stream

WOOD
Shepherd's Bank
LANE
COURT
HOLLYBUSH LANE

Swanton Farm Cottages
Wickhambreaux

Stream
East Wood
SWANTON
Down Wood

Oldridge Wood
Lampen
White Br.
WICKHAM RD.
WICKHAM LA.
THE STREET
Reynolds

G H J K 173 L M N

1 2 3 4 5 6 7 8 9

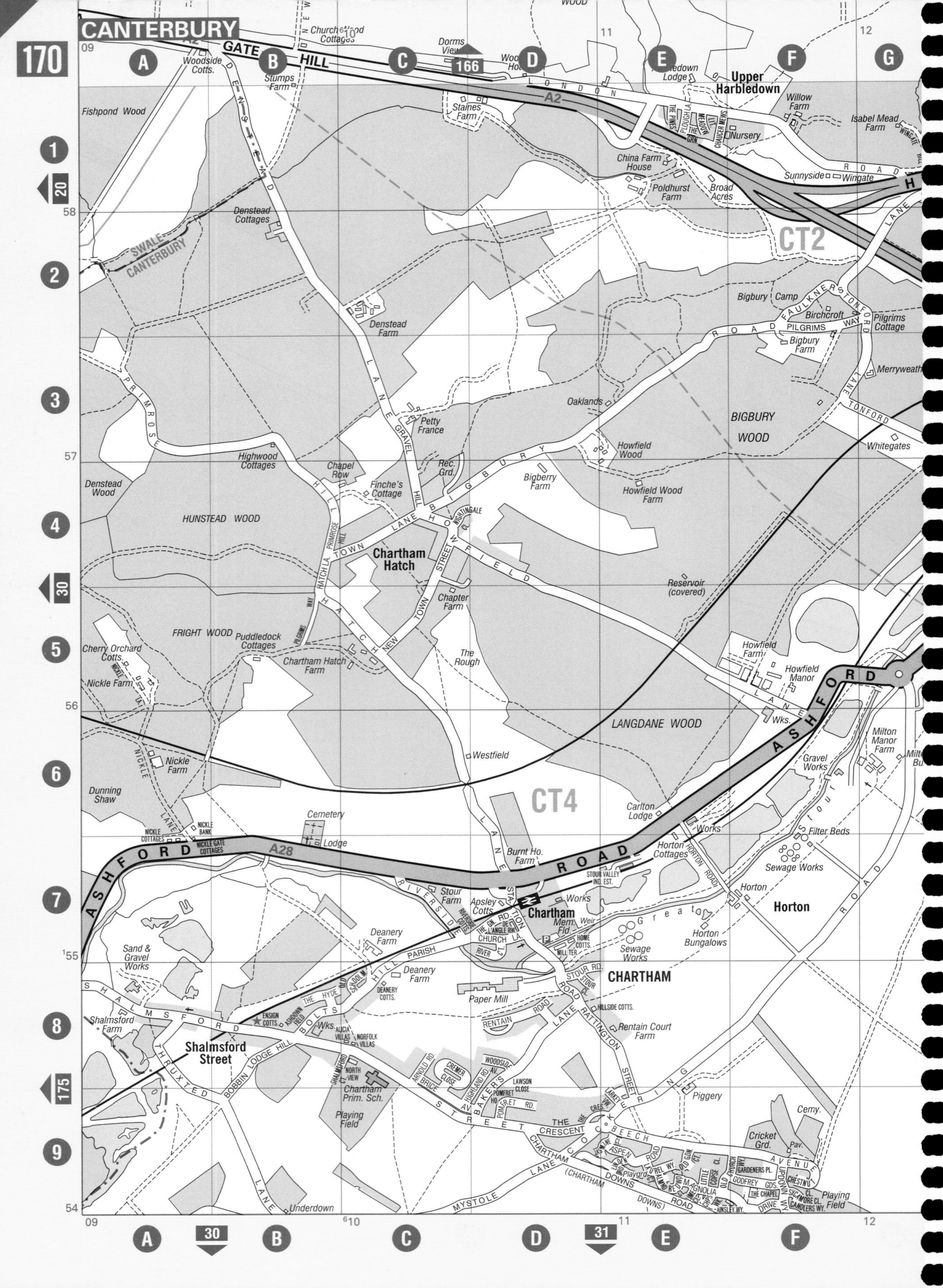
GATE HILL
A2
Church Wood Cottages
Dorms View
166
Woodside Cotts.
Stumps Farm
LONDON
Staines Farm
Harbledown Lodge
Upper Harbledown
Willow Farm
Isabel Mead Farm
Fishpond Wood
Nursery
China Farm House
Poldhurst Farm
Broad Acres
Sunnyside
Wingate
ROAD
20
Denstead Cottages
SWALE
CANTERBURY
CT2
Denstead Farm
Bigbury Camp
Birchcroft
PILGRIMS WAY
Pilgrims Cottage
Bigbury Farm
Merryweather
PRIMROSE
GRAVEL LANE
Petty France
Oaklands
BIGBURY WOOD
TONFORD
Whitegates
Highwood Cottages
Chapel Row
Rec. Grd.
Howfield Wood
Bigberry Farm
Denstead Wood
Finche's Cottage
Howfield Wood Farm
HUNSTEAD WOOD
BIGBURY
HOWFIELD
Chartham Hatch
TOWN STREET
Reservoir (covered)
30
Chapter Farm
FRIGHT WOOD
Puddledock Cottages
Cherry Orchard Cotts.
The Rough
Chartham Hatch Farm
Nickle Farm
Howfield Farm
Howfield Manor
ASHFORD ROAD
LANGDANE WOOD
Wks.
Westfield
Milton Manor Farm
Nickle Farm
Gravel Works
Dunning Shaw
CT4
Carlton Lodge
Cemetery
Lodge
Works
Filter Beds
Burnt Ho. Farm
Horton Cottages
Sewage Works
A28
Stour Farm
Apsley Cotts.
Chartham
Works
Horton
Weir
Great Stour
Deanery Farm
Horton Bungalows
Sand & Gravel Works
HILL PARISH
CHURCH LA.
Sewage Works
Deanery Farm
CHARTHAM
Paper Mill
SHALMSFORD
Shalmsford Farm
RENTAIN ROAD
Rentain Court Farm
Shalmsford Street
BOBBIN LODGE HILL
Chartham Prim. Sch.
Playing Field
RATTINGTON STREET
175
THRUXTED
Piggery
Cemy.
THE CRESCENT
BEECH AVENUE
Cricket Grd.
Pav.
MYSTOLE LANE
CHARTHAM DOWNS ROAD
Playing Field
Underdown
LANE
09
10
11
12
54
55
56
57
58
A
B
C
D
E
F
G
1
2
3
4
5
6
7
8
9
30
31

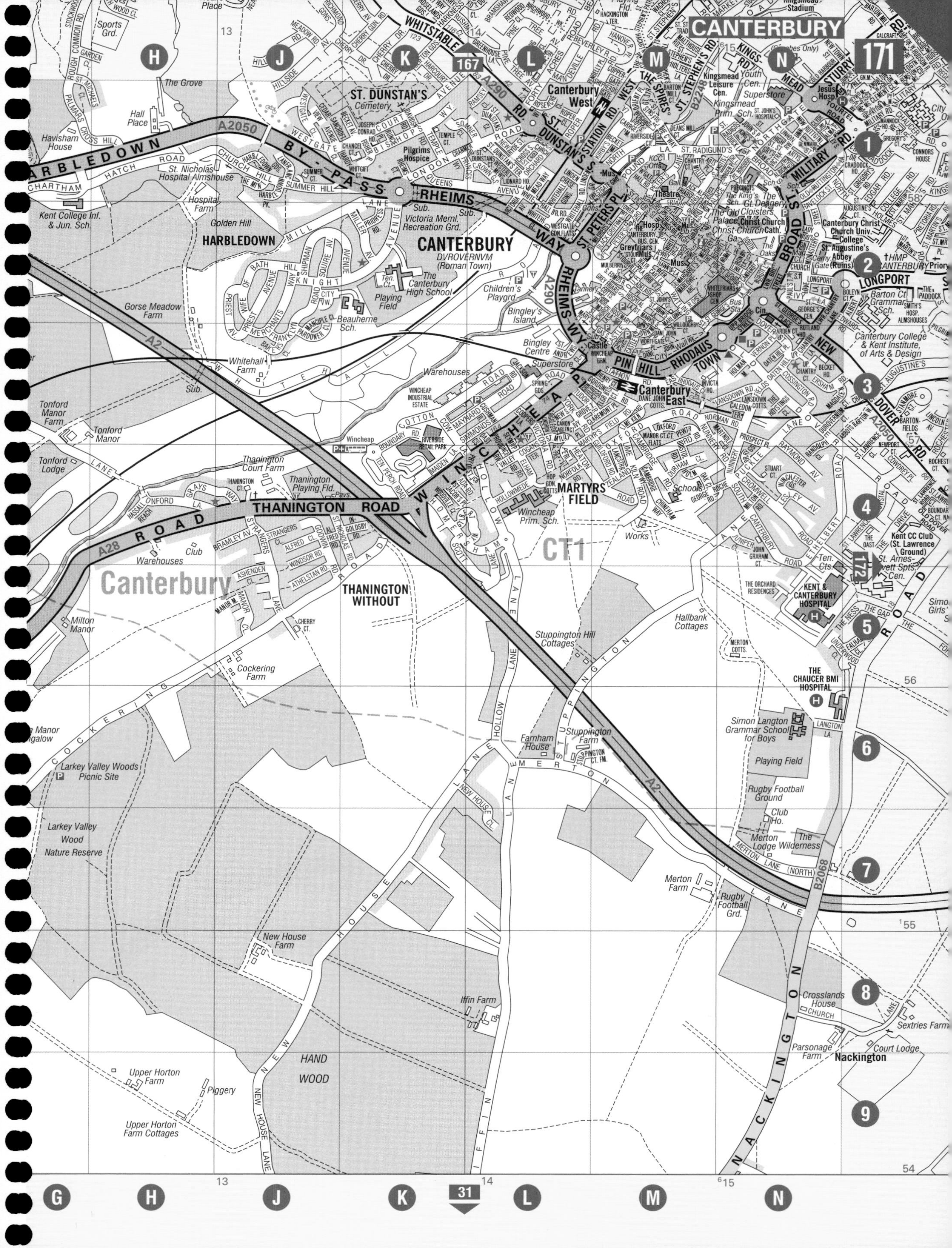

CANTERBURY
171
H
J
K
L
M
N
167
WHITSTABLE
Sports Grd.
The Grove
St. Dunstan's Cemetery
Canterbury West
Kingsmead Leisure Cen.
Kingsmead Prim. Sch.
Superstore
Jesus Hosp.
Hall Place
Havisham House
HARBLEDOWN BY-PASS
A2050
CHARTHAM
HATCH ROAD
St. Nicholas Hospital Almshouse
Pilgrims Hospice
RHEIMS WAY
Hospital Farm
Kent College Inf. & Jun. Sch.
Golden Hill
HARBLEDOWN
Victoria Meml. Recreation Grd.
CANTERBURY
DVROVERNVM (Roman Town)
The Canterbury High School
Playing Field
Beauherne Sch.
Children's Playgrd.
Bingley's Island
Bingley Centre
Superstore
Gorse Meadow Farm
Whitehall Farm
A2
A290
Theatre
The King's Sch.
The Deanery
The Old Palace
Christ Church Cath.
Cloisters
Christ Church Gate
Greyfriars
Mus.
Canterbury Christ Church Univ. College
St. Augustine's Abbey (Ruins)
HMP CANTERBURY
LONGPORT
Barton Ct. Grammar Sch.
Canterbury College & Kent Institute of Arts & Design
PIN HILL
RHODAUS TOWN
Canterbury East
Warehouses
WINCHEAP INDUSTRIAL ESTATE
RIVERSIDE RETAIL PARK
Wincheap
WINCHEAP
Tonford Manor Farm
Tonford Manor
Tonford Lodge
Thanington Court Farm
Thanington Playing Fld.
THANINGTON ROAD
A28 ROAD
Club
Warehouses
Canterbury
THANINGTON WITHOUT
Wincheap Prim. Sch.
MARTYRS FIELD
CT1
Schools
Works
Kent CC Club (St. Lawrence Ground)
172
KENT & CANTERBURY HOSPITAL
Milton Manor
Cockering Farm
Stuppington Hill Cottages
Hallbank Cottages
THE CHAUCER BMI HOSPITAL
Simon Langton Grammar School for Boys
Playing Field
Rugby Football Ground
Club Ho.
Merton Lodge
The Wilderness
COCKERING
Larkey Valley Woods Picnic Site
Larkey Valley Wood Nature Reserve
Farnham House
Stuppington Farm
MERTON LANE
MERTON LANE (NORTH)
Merton Farm
Rugby Football Grd.
B2068
New House Farm
Iffin Farm
HAND WOOD
Crosslands House
Sextries Farm
Court Lodge
Parsonage Farm
Nackington
NACKINGTON
Upper Horton Farm
Piggery
Upper Horton Farm Cottages
NEW HOUSE LANE
IFFIN LANE
13
14
15
54
55
56
57
1
2
3
4
5
6
7
8
9
G
H
J
K
L
M
N
31

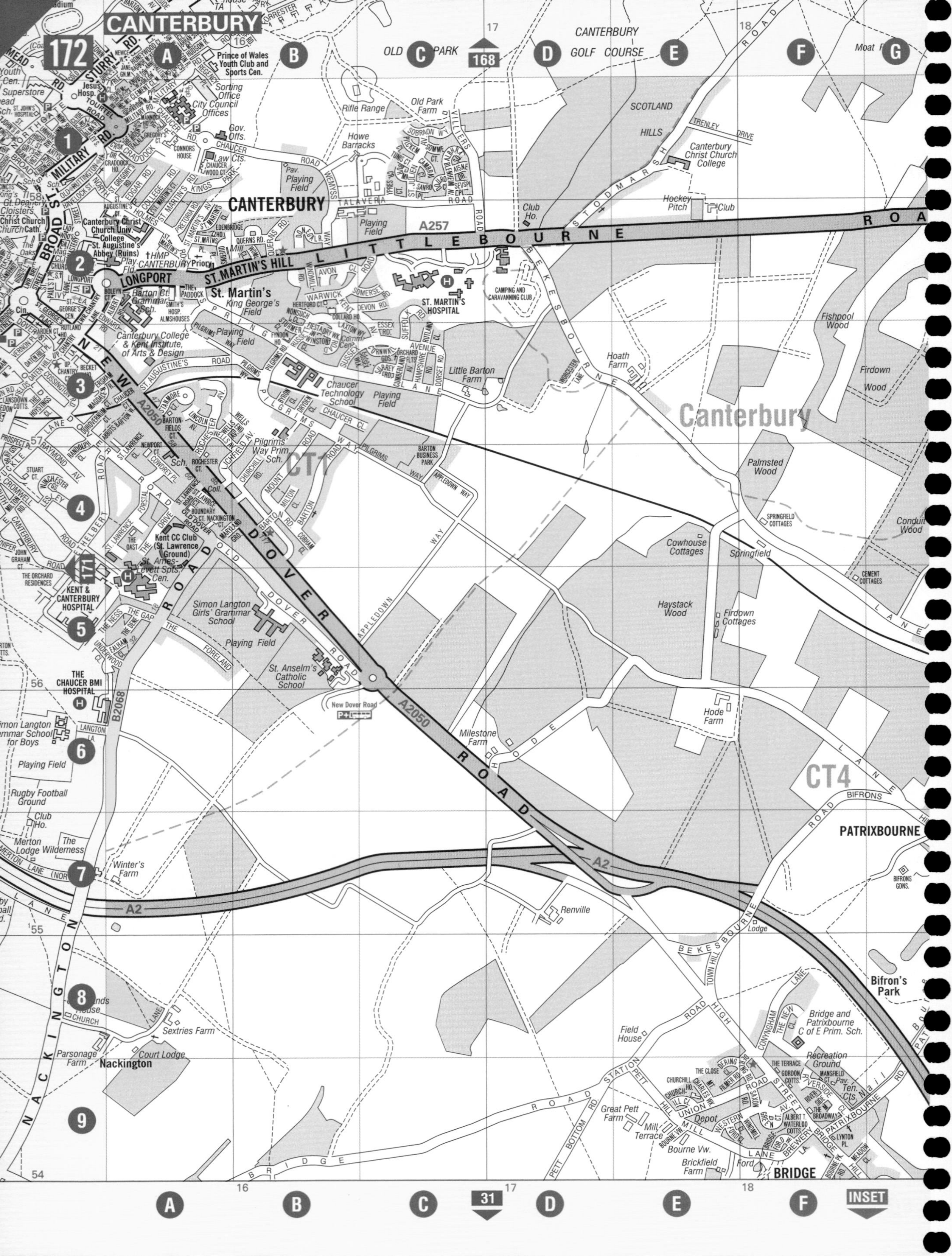
A
B
C
D
E
F
G
OLD PARK
168
CANTERBURY GOLF COURSE
Moat F
17
18
Prince of Wales Youth Club and Sports Cen.
Sorting Office
City Council Offices
Gov. Offs.
Law Cts.
Rifle Range
Old Park Farm
Howe Barracks
SCOTLAND HILLS
TRENLEY DRIVE
Canterbury Christ Church College
CANTERBURY
Pav. Playing Field
Playing Field
Hockey Pitch
Club
Club Ho.
A257
LITTLEBOURNE ROAD
ST. MARTIN'S HILL
LONGPORT
HMP CANTERBURY
Priory
St. Martin's King George's Field
ST. MARTIN'S HOSPITAL
CAMPING AND CARAVANNING CLUB
Canterbury Christ Church Univ. College
St. Augustine's Abbey (Ruins)
Christ Church Cath.
Barton Ct. Grammar Sch.
Canterbury College & Kent Institute of Arts & Design
Chaucer Technology School
Playing Field
Little Barton Farm
Hoath Farm
Fishpool Wood
Firdown Wood
Canterbury
Palmsted Wood
Pilgrims' Way Prim. Sch.
CT1
BARTON BUSINESS PARK
APPLEDOWN WAY
SPRINGFIELD COTTAGES
Conduit Wood
Cowhouse Cottages
Springfield
CEMENT COTTAGES
Kent CC Club (St. Lawrence Ground)
St. Anne's-Levett Spts. Cen.
KENT & CANTERBURY HOSPITAL
171
NEW DOVER ROAD
A2050
OLD DOVER ROAD
Simon Langton Girls' Grammar School
Playing Field
Haystack Wood
Firdown Cottages
St. Anselm's Catholic School
New Dover Road P+R
THE CHAUCER BMI HOSPITAL
B2068
Simon Langton Grammar School for Boys
Playing Field
Hode Farm
Milestone Farm
HODE LANE
CT4
BIFRONS ROAD
PATRIXBOURNE
Rugby Football Ground
Club Ho.
Merton Lodge
The Wilderness
Winter's Farm
MERTON LANE
A2
BIFRONS GDNS.
Renville
Lodge
BEKESBOURNE
TOWN HILL
Bifron's Park
NACKINGTON ROAD
Sextries Farm
Court Lodge
Parsonage Farm
Nackington
Field House
HIGH ROAD
Bridge and Patrixbourne C of E Prim. Sch.
Recreation Ground
STATION ROAD
PETT BOTTOM RD
Great Pett Farm
Mill Terrace
Depot
Bourne Vw.
Brickfield Farm
Ford
BRIDGE
BRIDGE ROAD
1
2
3
4
5
6
7
8
9
58
57
56
55
54
16

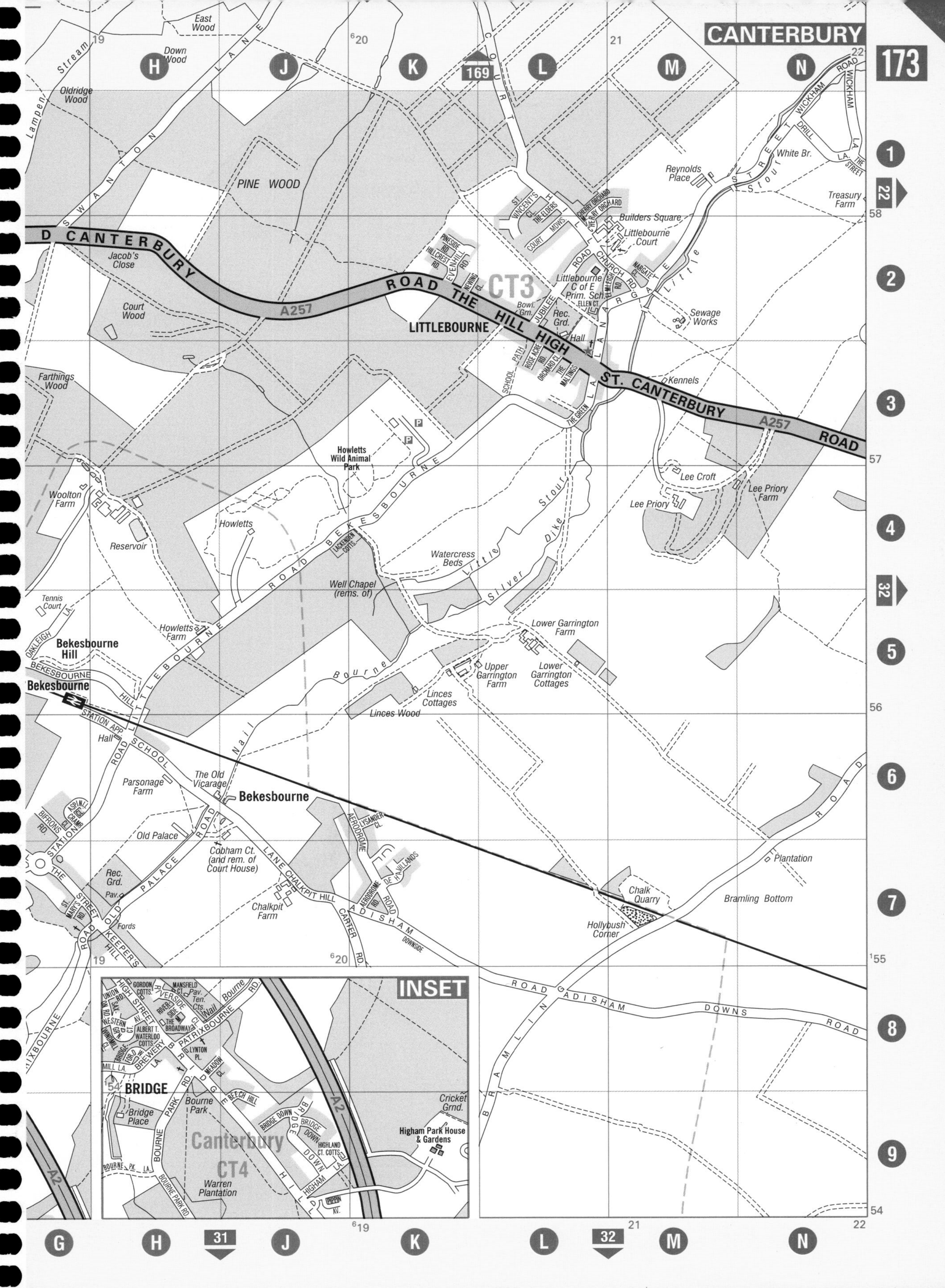
East Wood
Down Wood
Oldridge Wood
PINE WOOD
Jacob's Close
Court Wood
A257
LITTLEBOURNE
CT3
Farthings Wood
Howletts Wild Animal Park
Woolton Farm
Reservoir
Howletts
Watercress Beds
Well Chapel (rems. of)
Lower Garrington Farm
Howletts Farm
Bekesbourne Hill
Bekesbourne
Upper Garrington Farm
Lower Garrington Cottages
Linces Cottages
Linces Wood
Parsonage Farm
The Old Vicarage
Old Palace
Cobham Ct. (and rem. of Court House)
Rec. Grd.
Chalkpit Farm
Chalk Quarry
Hollybush Corner
Bramling Bottom
Plantation
Reynolds Place
White Br.
Treasury Farm
Builders Square
Littlebourne Court
Littlebourne C of E Prim. Sch.
Sewage Works
Kennels
Lee Croft
Lee Priory
Lee Priory Farm
CANTERBURY ROAD
THE HILL
HIGH ST.
BEKESBOURNE ROAD
LITTLEBOURNE ROAD
ADISHAM ROAD
ADISHAM DOWNS ROAD
BRAMLING ROAD
INSET
BRIDGE
Bridge Place
Bourne Park
Canterbury CT4
Warren Plantation
Higham Park House & Gardens
Cricket Grnd.
A2

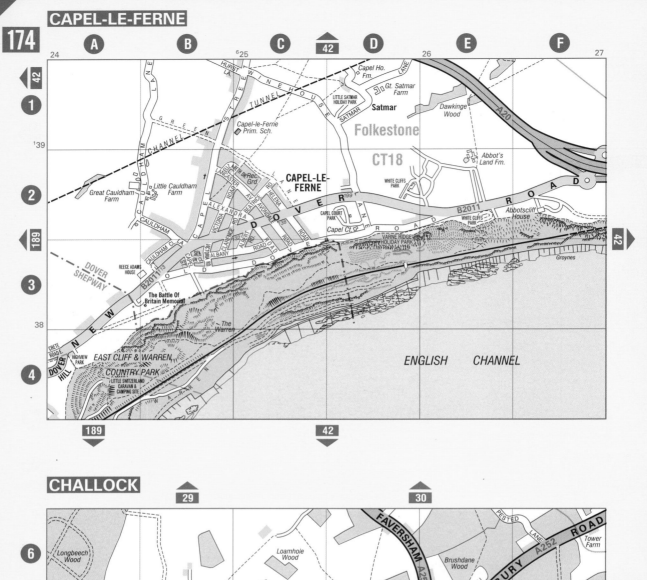

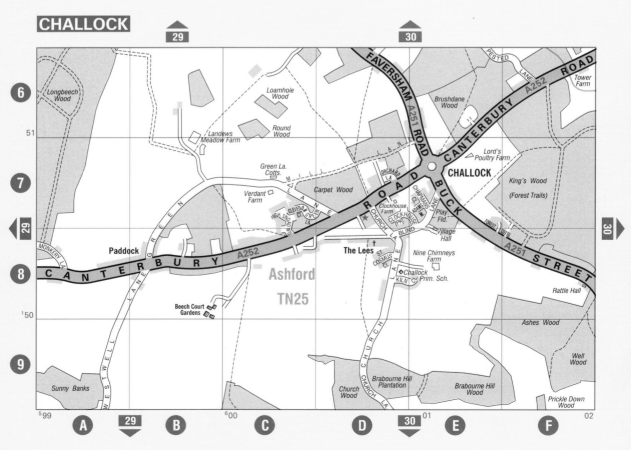

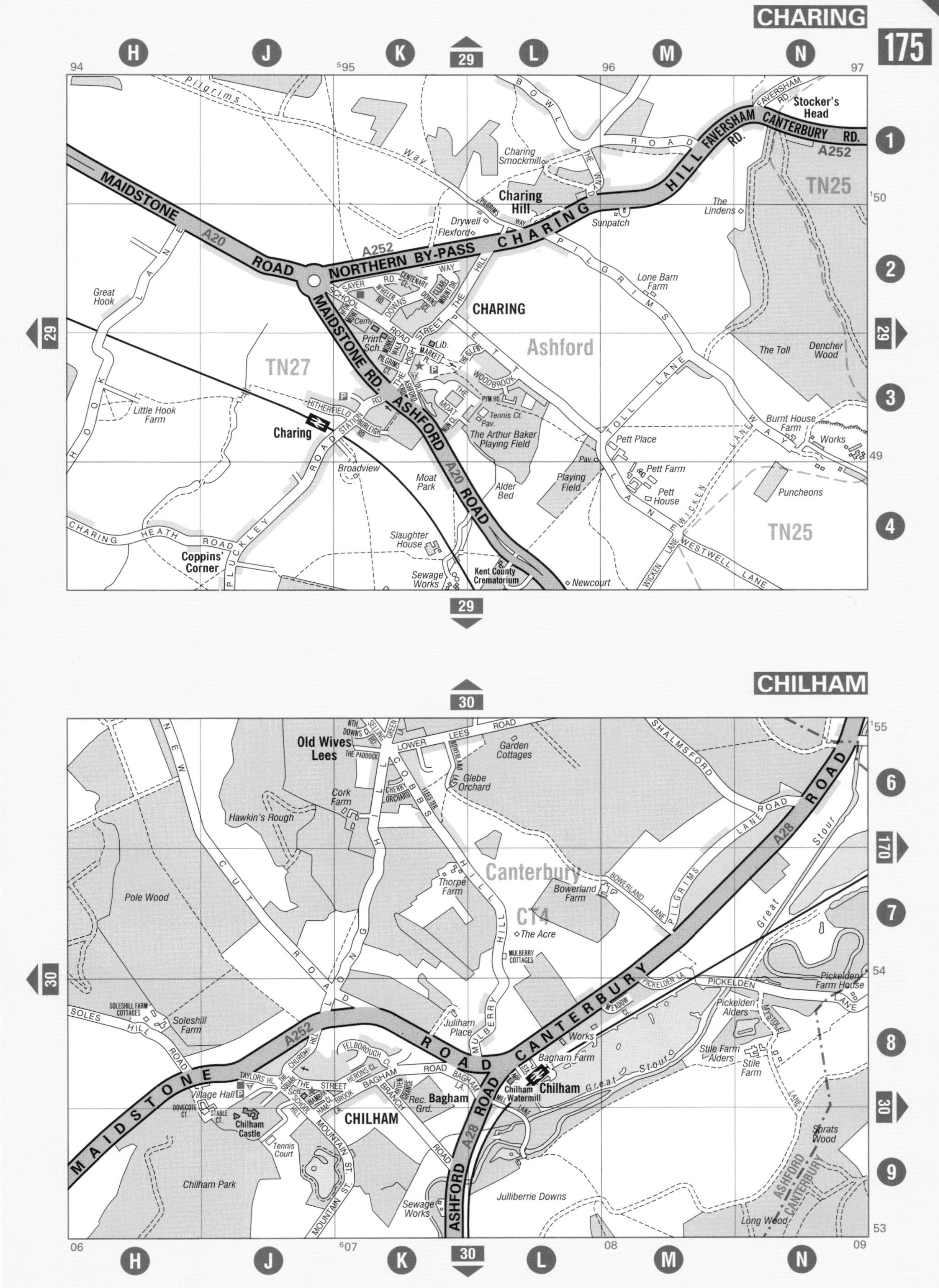

CHARING
175
H
J
K
L
M
N
29
94
95
96
97
1
2
3
4
50
49
Pilgrims Way
MAIDSTONE ROAD
A20
NORTHERN BY-PASS
A252
CHARING HILL
FAVERSHAM RD.
CANTERBURY RD.
FAVERSHAM RD.
Stocker's Head
BOWL ROAD
Charing Smockmill
Charing Hill
Drywell
Flexford
Sunpatch
The Lindens
TN25
Great Hook
HOOK LANE
SAYER RD.
WHEELER RD.
CENTENARY CL.
WAY
SCHOOL RD.
DOWNS
CHARING
Cemy.
Prim. Sch.
HIGH STREET
Lib.
MARKET PL.
THE GLEBE
PETT LANE
WOODBROOK
Ashford
TN27
MAIDSTONE RD.
ASHFORD RD.
HITHERFIELD RD.
PILGRIMS CT.
THE MOAT
PYM HO.
Tennis Ct.
Pav.
The Arthur Baker Playing Field
Little Hook Farm
Charing
STATION RD.
BURLEIGH RD.
Broadview
Moat Park
A20 ROAD
Alder Bed
Playing Field
Pav.
Lone Barn Farm
PILGRIMS WAY
TOLL LANE
The Toll
Dencher Wood
Burnt House Farm
Works
Pett Place
Pett Farm
Pett House
PETT LANE
WICKEN LANE
Puncheons
TN25
CHARING HEATH ROAD
PLUCKLEY ROAD
Coppins' Corner
Slaughter House
Sewage Works
Kent County Crematorium
Newcourt
WESTWELL LANE
CHILHAM
30
170
06
07
08
09
55
54
53
6
7
8
9
NEW CUT ROAD
NTH. DOWNS CL.
SELLING RD.
GREEN LA.
LOWER LEES ROAD
Old Wives Lees
THE PADDOCK
Garden Cottages
BOWERLAND
Glebe Orchard
CHERRY ORCHARD
COBBS HILL
LEES TER.
SHALMSFORD
Cork Farm
Hawkin's Rough
LONG HILL
Canterbury
Thorpe Farm
Bowerland Farm
BOWERLAND LANE
PILGRIMS LANE
LANE ROAD
A28 ROAD
Great Stour
Pole Wood
CT4
The Acre
MULBERRY COTTAGES
MULBERRY HILL
PICKELDEN LA.
PICKELDEN LANE
Pickelden Farm House
Pickelden Alders
MEADOW CL.
SOLESHILL FARM COTTAGES
Soleshill Farm
SOLES HILL ROAD
A252
Julliam Place
CANTERBURY ROAD
Works
Bagham Farm
Stile Farm Alders
Stile Farm
MAIDSTONE
TAYLORS HL.
CHURCH HILL
FELBOROUGH CL.
HERONS CL.
BAGHAM LA.
THE SQUARE
THE STREET
Sch.
HAMBROOK CL.
BAGHAM
BRANCH
Rec. Grd.
Bagham
Village Hall
DOVECOTE CT.
STABLE CT.
Chilham Castle
SCHOOL HILL
CHILHAM
MOUNTAIN ST.
Chilham Watermill
Chilham
Great Stour
MILL LANE
A28 ROAD
ASHFORD
Tennis Court
Chilham Park
Sewage Works
Julliberrie Downs
Sprats Wood
ASHFORD CANTERBURY
Long Wood

CLIFFE

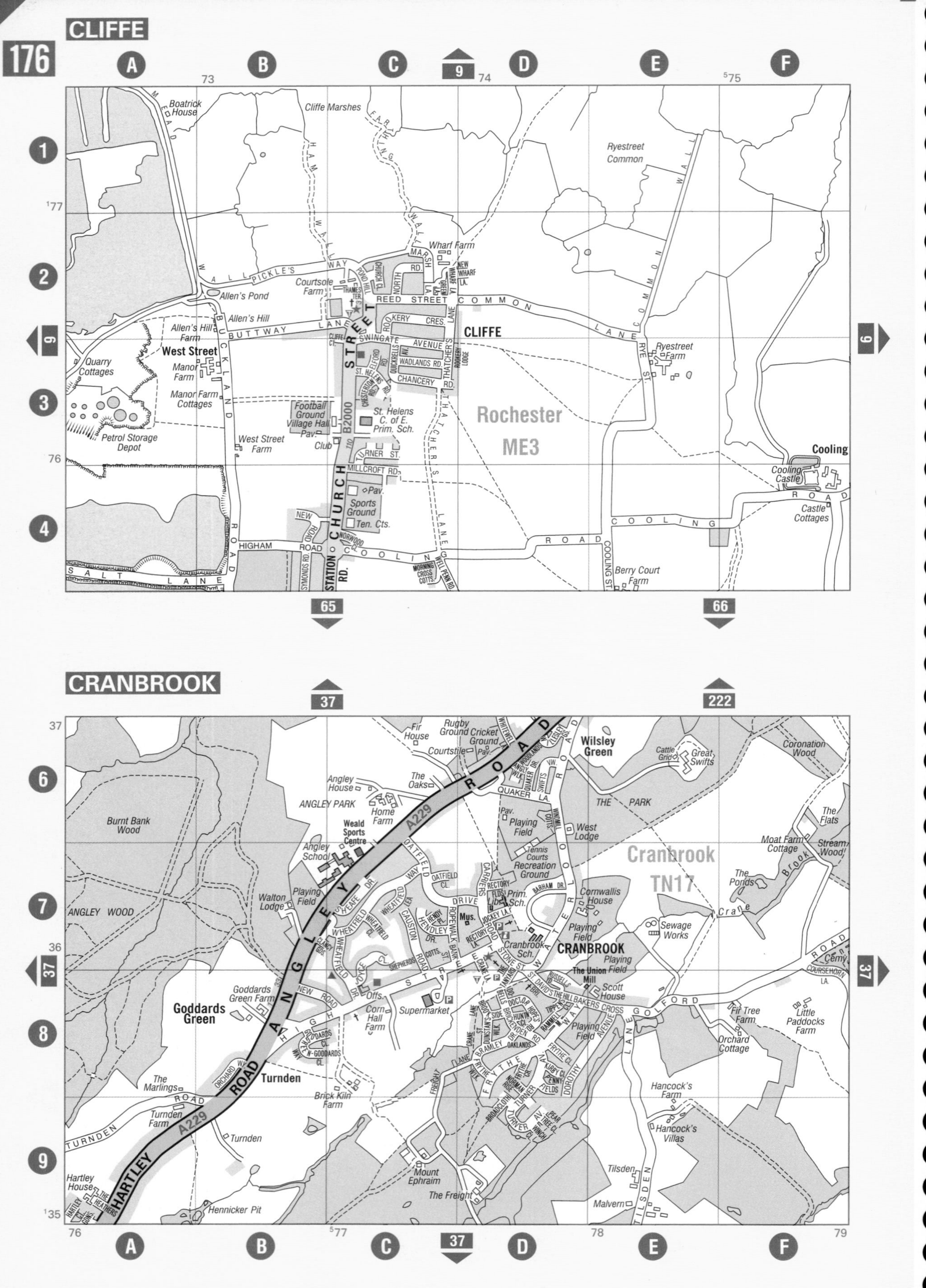

Map grid references (top section - CLIFFE)

A — B — C — **9** — D — E — F
73 — 74 — 575

1
177
2
9 — **9**
3
76
4

Boatrick House
Cliffe Marshes
Ryestreet Common
Wharf Farm
NEW WHARF LA.
Allen's Pond
Courtsole Farm
REED STREET
COMMON LANE
Allen's Hill
West Street
KERY CRES.
CLIFFE
Ryestreet Farm
BUTTWAY
Allen's Hill Farm
Quarry Cottages
Manor Farm
SWINGATE
AVENUE
WADLANDS RD.
CHANCERY
St. Helens C. of E. Prim. Sch.
Rochester ME3
Manor Farm Cottages
Football Ground Village Hall
Pav.
B2000
Club
Cooling
Cooling Castle
West Street Farm
URNER ST.
MILLCROFT RD.
Castle Cottages
Petrol Storage Depot
Pav.
Sports Ground
Ten. Cts.
COOLING ROAD
NEW
HIGHAM ROAD
STATION RD.
COOLING
Berry Court Farm
SALT LANE
SYMONDS RD.
NORWOOD RD.
MORNING CROSS COTTS.
WELL FROM RD.
COOLING ST.

65 — **66**

CRANBROOK

37 — **222**

37
6
7
36
37 — **37**
8
9
135

76 — 77 — **37** — 78 — 79
A — B — C — D — E — F

Fir House
Rugby Ground
Cricket Ground
WHITEHILL
Wilsley Green
Cattle Grid
Great Swifts
Coronation Wood
Courtstile
Pav.
The Oaks
Angley House
ANGLEY PARK
QUAKER LA.
SWIFTS
THE PARK
The Flats
Burnt Bank Wood
Home Farm
Weald Sports Centre
Pav.
Playing Field
West Lodge
Moat Farm Cottage
Stream Wood
Angley School
Playing Field
Tennis Courts Recreation Ground
Cranbrook TN17
The Ponds
Walton Lodge
OATFIELD CL.
Crane
ANGLEY WOOD
CARRIERS
BARHAM DR.
Prim. Sch.
Cornwallis House
Sewage Works
Cemy.
COURSEHORN LA.
WHEATFIELD
Mus.
Playing Field
Goddards Green Farm
NEW ROAD
HENDLEY
STONE ST.
CRANBROOK Sch.
Playing Field
Fir Tree Farm
Little Paddocks Farm
Goddards Green
A229 HIGH ROAD
Offs.
SHEPHERDS ROAD
The Union Mill
Scott House
Orchard Cottage
Corn Hall Farm
Supermarket
BAKERS CROSS
GOLFORD
The Marlings
Turnden
Brick Kiln Farm
BRAMLEY
FRITH
OAKLANDS
Playing Field
Hancock's Farm
TURNER
HARTLEY ROAD
Turnden Farm
A229
Turnden
Mount Ephraim
Hancock's Villas
Hartley House
HARTLEY
Hennicker Pit
The Freight
Tilsden
Malvern
TILSDEN

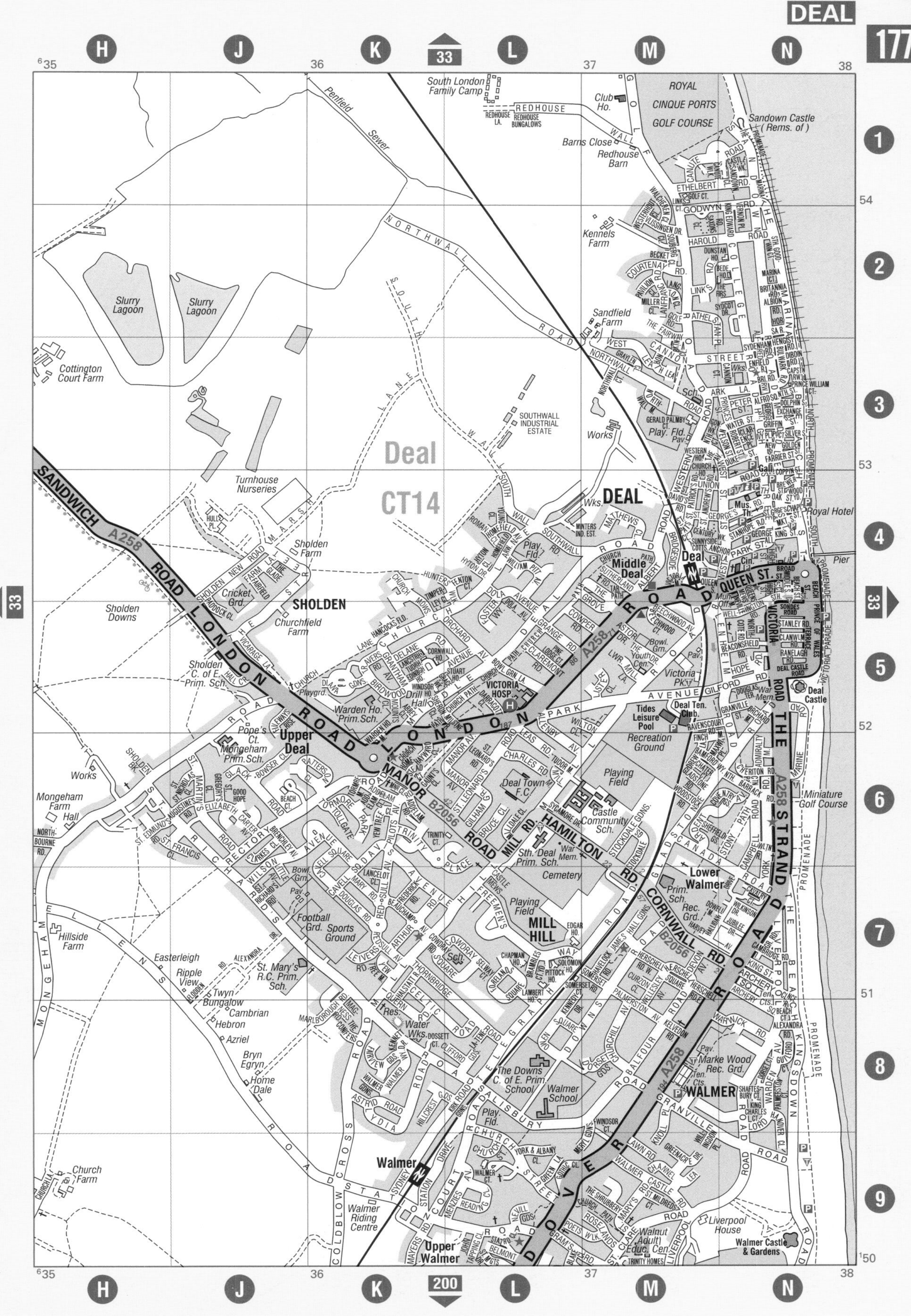
H
J
K
L
M
N
33
200
35
36
37
38
54
53
52
51
50
1
2
3
4
5
6
7
8
9
South London Family Camp
REDHOUSE
REDHOUSE BUNGALOWS
Club Ho.
ROYAL CINQUE PORTS GOLF COURSE
Sandown Castle (Rems. of)
Barns Close
Redhouse Barn
Penfield Sewer
Kennels Farm
NORTHWALL
Slurry Lagoon
Slurry Lagoon
Sandfield Farm
Cottington Court Farm
SOUTHWALL INDUSTRIAL ESTATE
Works
Deal
CT14
DEAL
Turnhouse Nurseries
SANDWICH ROAD
A258
LONDON ROAD
Sholden Farm
Cricket Grd.
SHOLDEN
Sholden Downs
Churchfield Farm
Sholden C. of E. Prim. Sch.
MINTERS IND. EST.
Middle Deal
Deal
QUEEN ST.
Royal Hotel
Pier
Play. Fld.
VICTORIA HOSP.
Warden Ho. Prim.Sch.
Drill Hall
Victoria Pk.
Tides Leisure Pool
Deal Ten. Club
Recreation Ground
War Mem.
Deal Castle
Pope's Ct.
Mongeham Prim.Sch.
Upper Deal
Works
Mongeham Farm
Hall
MANOR ROAD
B2056
Deal Town F.C.
Playing Field
Castle Community Sch.
HAMILTON RD.
Sth. Deal Prim. Sch.
War Mem.
Cemetery
MILL HILL
Miniature Golf Course
THE STRAND
Lower Walmer
Prim. Sch.
Rec. Grd.
CORNWALL RD.
Football Grd.
Sports Ground
Playing Field
Hillside Farm
Easterleigh
Ripple View
Twyn Bungalow
Cambrian
Hebron
Azriel
Bryn Egryn
Home Dale
St. Mary's R.C. Prim. Sch.
Res.
Water Wks.
The Downs C. of E. Prim. School
Walmer School
Marke Wood Rec. Grd.
WALMER
DOVER ROAD
Play. Fld.
Walmer
Church Farm
Walmer Riding Centre
Upper Walmer
Liverpool House
Walmer Castle & Gardens
Walnut Adult Educ. Cen.
MONGEHAM
PROMENADE
KINGSDOWN ROAD

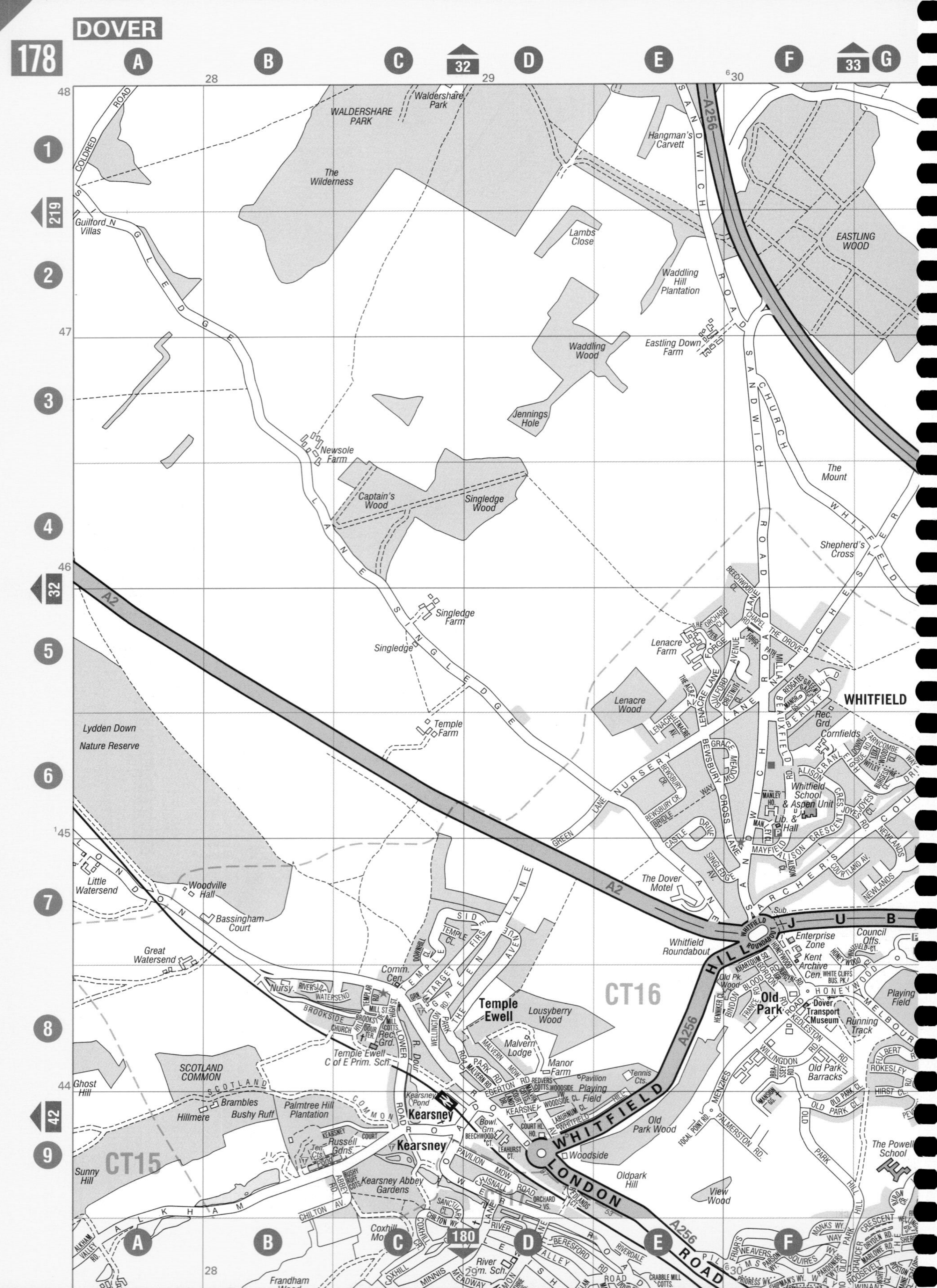
WALDERSHARE PARK
Waldershare Park
The Wilderness
Hangman's Carvett
Lambs Close
EASTLING WOOD
Waddling Hill Plantation
Eastling Down Farm
Waddling Wood
Jennings Hole
Newsole Farm
Captain's Wood
Singledge Wood
The Mount
Shepherd's Cross
Singledge Farm
Singledge
Lenacre Farm
Lenacre Wood
WHITFIELD
Temple Farm
Lydden Down Nature Reserve
Whitfield School & Aspen Unit
Little Watersend
Woodville Hall
Bassingham Court
The Dover Motel
Whitfield Roundabout
Enterprise Zone
Kent Archive Cen.
Council Offs.
Great Watersend
CT16
Temple Ewell
Lousyberry Wood
Old Park
Dover Transport Museum
Playing Field
Running Track
Temple Ewell C of E Prim. Sch.
Malvern Lodge
Manor Farm
Old Park Barracks
SCOTLAND COMMON
Ghost Hill
Hillmere
Brambles
Bushy Ruff
Palmtree Hill Plantation
Kearsney
Old Park Wood
Russell Gdns.
Kearsney Abbey Gardens
Woodside
Oldpark Hill
The Powell School
CT15
Sunny Hill
View Wood
Coxhill
River Prim. Sch.
Frandham Wood
A2
A256
LONDON ROAD
WHITFIELD HILL
SINGLEDGE LANE
SANDWICH ROAD
COLDRED ROAD

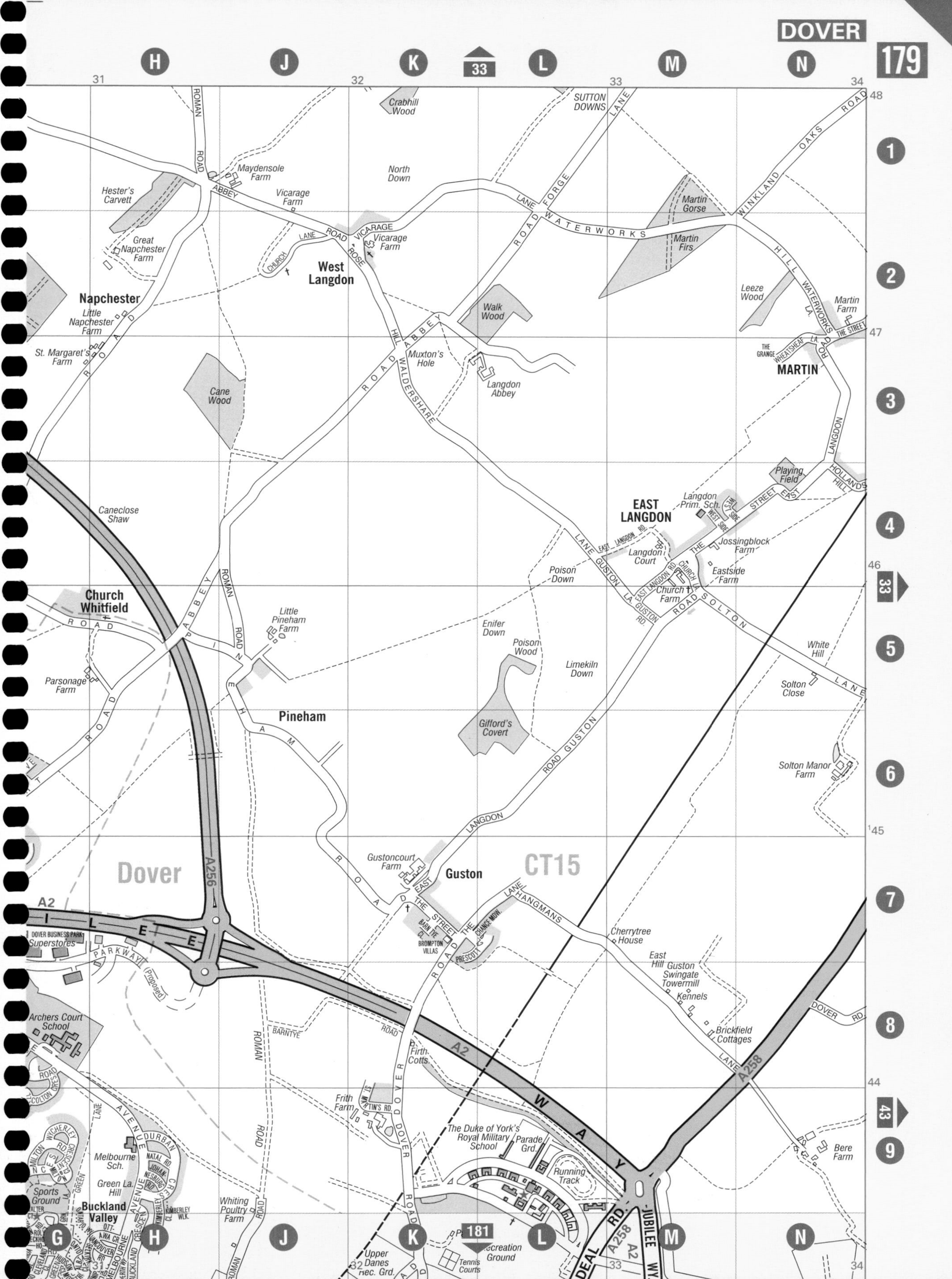
Crabhill Wood
SUTTON DOWNS
Maydensole Farm
North Down
Hester's Carvett
Vicarage Farm
Great Napchester Farm
West Langdon
Napchester
Little Napchester Farm
St. Margaret's Farm
Martin Gorse
Martin Firs
Leeze Wood
Martin Farm
MARTIN
Walk Wood
Muxton's Hole
Langdon Abbey
Cane Wood
Caneclose Shaw
Playing Field
Langdon Prim. Sch.
EAST LANGDON
Jossingblock Farm
Langdon Court
Eastside Farm
Church Farm
Poison Down
Church Whitfield
Little Pineham Farm
Enifer Down
Poison Wood
Limekiln Down
White Hill
Parsonage Farm
Solton Close
Pineham
Gifford's Covert
Solton Manor Farm
Gustoncourt Farm
Guston
CT15
Dover
Cherrytree House
East Hill
Guston Swingate Towermill
Kennels
Brickfield Cottages
Superstores
Archers Court School
Firth Cotts
Frith Farm
The Duke of York's Royal Military School
Parade Grd.
Running Track
Bere Farm
Melbourne Sch.
Green La. Hill
Sports Ground
Buckland Valley
Whiting Poultry Farm
Upper Danes Rec. Grd.
Tennis Courts
Recreation Ground

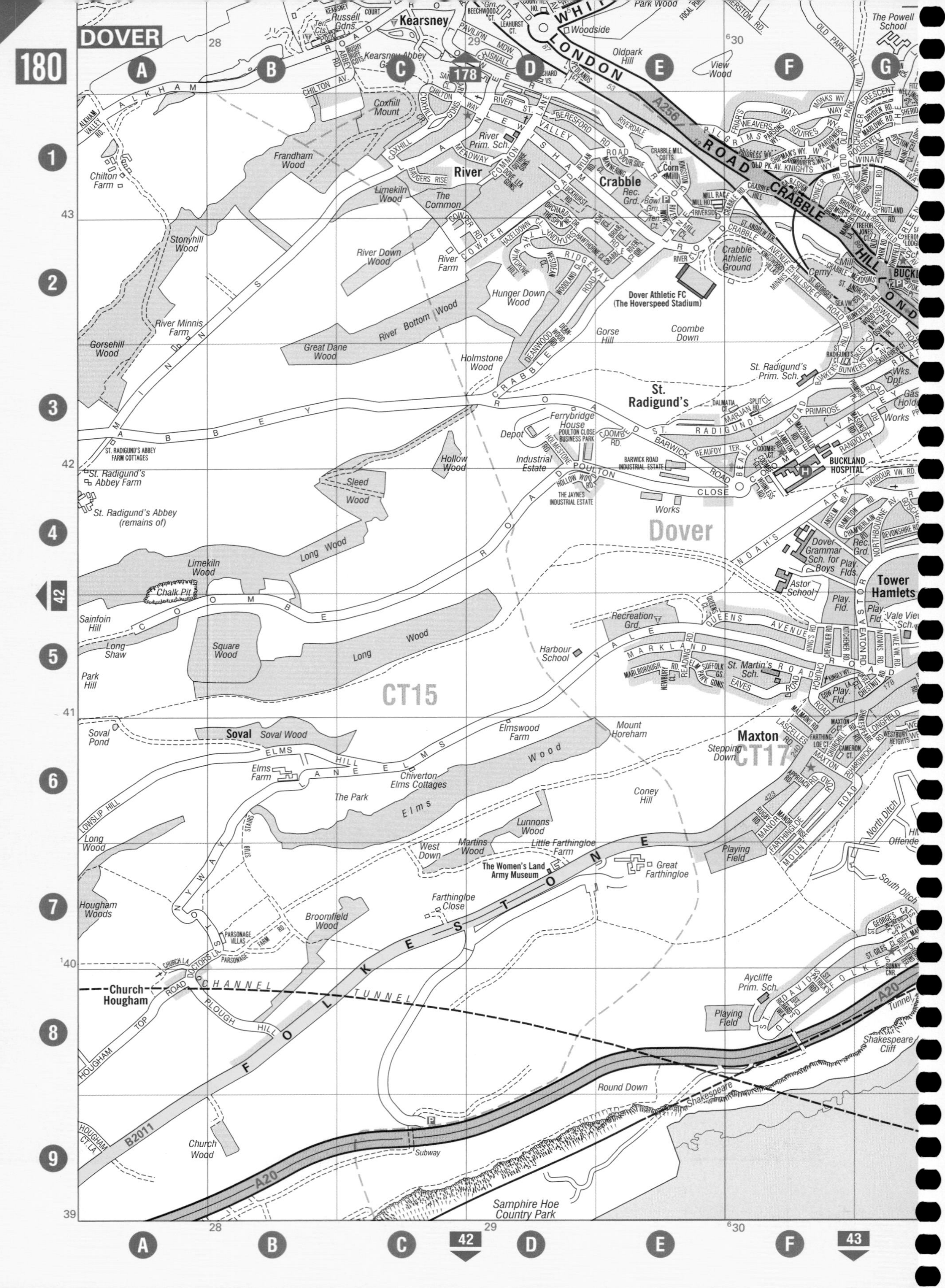
DOVER
180
178
Kearsney
Russell Gdns
Kearsney Abbey Gdns
Woodside
LONDON ROAD
Oldpark Hill
Park Wood
View Wood
The Powell School
Chilton Av.
Coxhill Mount
Alkham Valley Rd.
Chilton Farm
Frandham Wood
River
River Prim. Sch.
The Common
Limekiln Wood
Crabble
Crabble Rec. Grd.
Corn Mill
A256
Pilgrims Way
Crabble Hill
Crabble Road
Stonyhill Wood
River Down Wood
River Farm
Hunger Down Wood
Crabble Athletic Ground
Dover Athletic FC (The Hoverspeed Stadium)
Ridgeway
River Bottom Wood
Great Dane Wood
River Minnis Farm
Gorsehill Wood
Holmstone Wood
Gorse Hill
Coombe Down
Minnis Lane
St. Radigund's
St. Radigund's Prim. Sch.
Abbey Road
St. Radigund's Abbey Farm Cottages
St. Radigund's Abbey Farm
St. Radigund's Abbey (remains of)
Ferrybridge House
Depot
Industrial Estate
Poulton Close Business Park
Barwick Road Industrial Estate
The Jaynes Industrial Estate
Buckland Hospital
Hollow Wood
Sleed Wood
Long Wood
Limekiln Wood
Chalk Pit
Coombe
Dover
Dover Grammar Sch. for Boys
Astor School
Tower Hamlets
Sainfoin Hill
Long Shaw
Square Wood
Park Hill
Recreation Grd.
Queens Avenue
Harbour School
Markland Road
St. Martin's Sch.
CT15
Soval Pond
Soval
Soval Wood
Elmswood Farm
Mount Horeham
Maxton
CT17
Elms Farm
Chiverton Elms Cottages
Elms Hill
Elms Wood
The Park
Coney Hill
Stepping Down
Lowslip Hill
Long Wood
Lunnons Wood
West Down
Martins Wood
Little Farthingloe Farm
The Women's Land Army Museum
Great Farthingloe
Playing Field
Hougham Woods
Farthingloe Close
Broomfield Wood
Folkestone Road
Church Hougham
Channel Tunnel
Aycliffe Prim. Sch.
Playing Field
A20
Shakespeare Cliff
Round Down
Shakespeare
B2011
Church Wood
Subway
Samphire Hoe Country Park
28
29
30
39
40
41
42
43
A B C D E F G
1 2 3 4 5 6 7 8 9

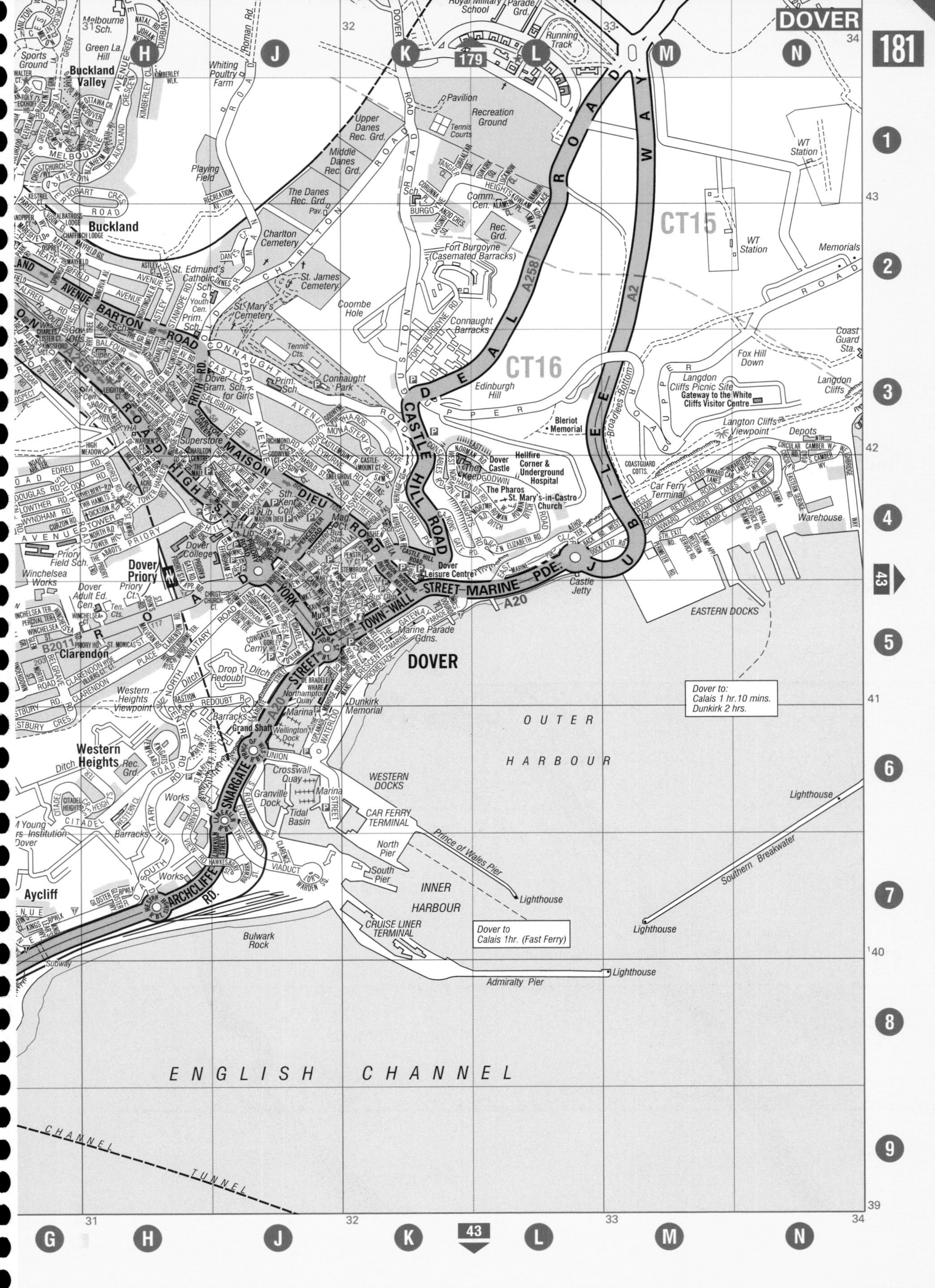
Royal Military School
Parade Grd.
Running Track
179
Melbourne Sch.
Green La. Hill
Sports Ground
Buckland Valley
Whiting Poultry Farm
Pavilion
Recreation Ground
Tennis Courts
Upper Danes Rec. Grd.
Middle Danes Rec. Grd.
The Danes Rec. Grd.
Playing Field
Buckland
Charlton Cemetery
St. Edmund's Catholic Sch.
St. James Cemetery
St. Mary's Cemetery
Comm. Cen.
Rec. Grd.
Fort Burgoyne (Casemated Barracks)
Connaught Barracks
Coombe Hole
Connaught Park
Edinburgh Hill
CT15
CT16
WT Station
Memorials
Coast Guard Sta.
Fox Hill Down
Langdon Cliffs Picnic Site
Gateway to the White Cliffs Visitor Centre
Langdon Cliffs
Langton Cliffs Viewpoint
Depots
Bleriot Memorial
Dover Castle
The Keep
Hellfire Corner & Underground Hospital
The Pharos
St. Mary's-in-Castro Church
Car Ferry Terminal
Warehouse
Dover Gram. Sch. for Girls
Superstore
Maison Dieu
Sth. Kent Coll.
Dover College
Dover Priory
Priory Field Sch.
Winchelsea Works
Dover Adult Ed. Cen.
Clarendon
Dover Leisure Centre
Castle Jetty
EASTERN DOCKS
DOVER
Drop Redoubt
Western Heights Viewpoint
Dunkirk Memorial
Dover to: Calais 1 hr.10 mins. Dunkirk 2 hrs.
OUTER HARBOUR
Western Heights
Grand Shaft
Wellington Dock
Crosswall Quay
Granville Dock
Tidal Basin
WESTERN DOCKS
CAR FERRY TERMINAL
North Pier
South Pier
Prince of Wales Pier
Lighthouse
INNER HARBOUR
Southern Breakwater
CRUISE LINER TERMINAL
Dover to Calais 1hr. (Fast Ferry)
Bulwark Rock
Admiralty Pier
Aycliff
ENGLISH CHANNEL
CHANNEL TUNNEL
DEAL ROAD
JUBILEE WAY
CASTLE HILL ROAD
MAISON DIEU ROAD
BARTON ROAD
HIGH ST.
YORK ST.
TOWN WALL STREET
MARINE PDE.
SNARGATE ST.
ARCHCLIFFE RD.
A2
A20
A256
A258
B2011
G H J K L M N
1 2 3 4 5 6 7 8 9
31 32 33 34
39 40 41 42 43
43

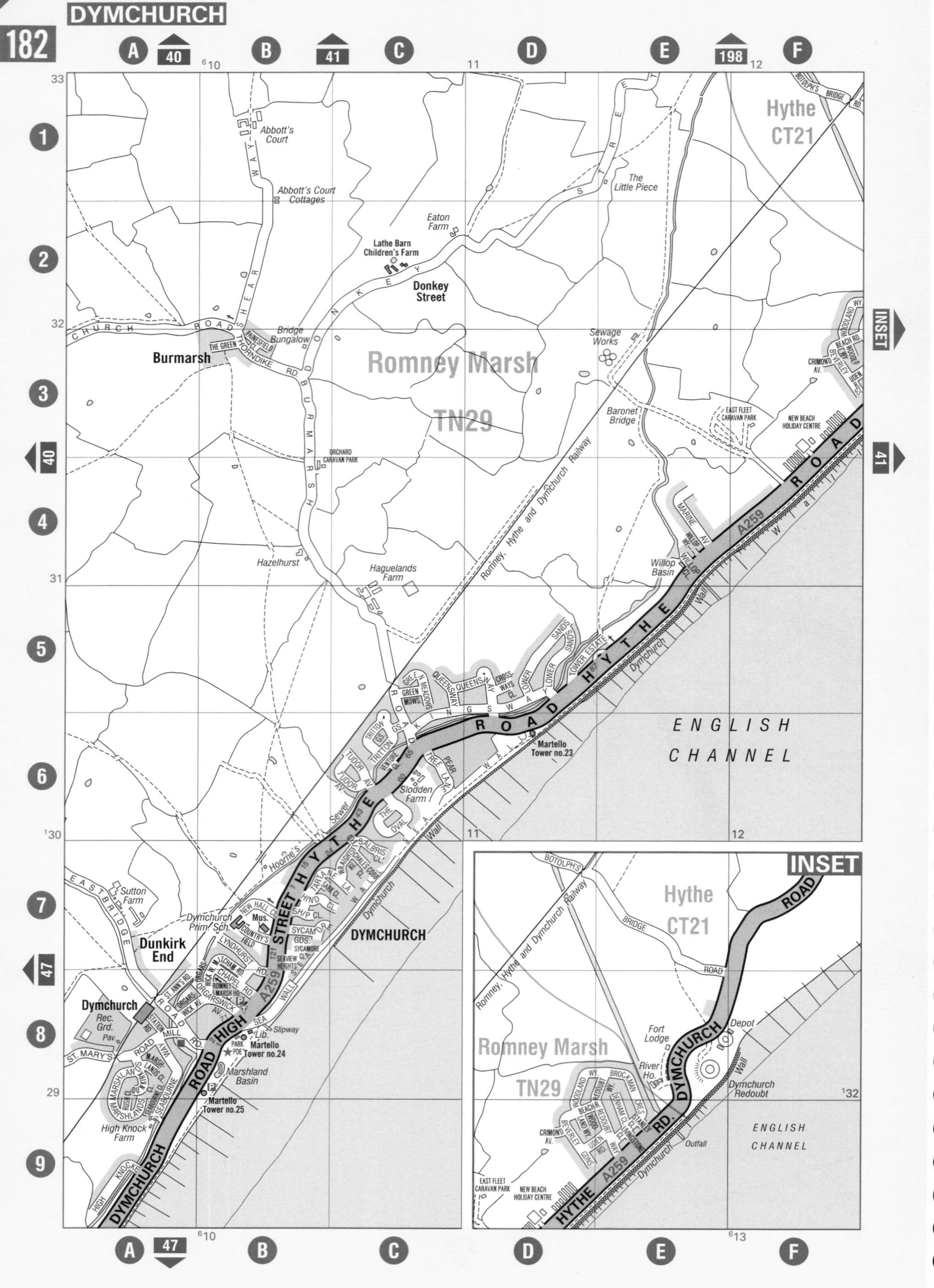

A · 40 · 6 10
B · 41
C · 11
D
E · 198 · 12
F

33

Hythe
CT21

1

The Little Piece

Abbott's Court

Abbott's Court Cottages

2

Eaton Farm

Lathe Barn Children's Farm

Donkey Street

32

Bridge Bungalow

Burmarsh

THE GREEN

CHURCH ROAD

SHEARWAY

THORNDIKE RD.

DUNGEFIELD

BURMARSH ROAD

KEELEY

Romney Marsh

TN29

Sewage Works

INSET

CRIMOND AV.

BEACH RD.
WOODLAND WY.
UDEN RD.
DENNANT RD.
BEVERLEY CL.

3

40

Baronet Bridge

East Fleet Caravan Park

New Beach Holiday Centre

ORCHARD CARAVAN PARK

31

Hazelhurst

Haguelands Farm

Romney, Hythe and Dymchurch Railway

MARINE AV.

WILLOP AV.

A259

Willop Basin

ROAD

WILLOP WALL

4

5

GREEN MEADOWS

QUEENSWAY

QUEENSWAY

KINGSWAY

GREEN MDWS.

CROSS WAYS

LOWER SANDS

LOWER SANDS

LOWER SANDS

TOWER ESTATE

ROAD HYTHE

ROAD HYTHE

Dymchurch

ENGLISH
CHANNEL

TRITON

TRITON

NEPTUNE

TUDOR AV.

OAK RD.

PEAR TREE LA.

Martello Tower no.23

6

30

Hoorne's Sewer

Sewer

HYTHE STREET

TUDOR

LYDOR

THE OVAL

ALBRIS CL.

MANSDINT.

CHARLES GDN.

Slodden Farm

SEA WALL

11

12

INSET

7

EASTBRIDGE

Sutton Farm

Dymchurch Prim. Sch.

NEW HALL CL.

Mus.

COUNTRY'S FIELD

LYNDHURST RD.

SCHM. RD.

HIND RD.

SHIP CL.

SYCAMORE GDS.

SYCAMORE CL.

SEAVIEW HEIGHTS

Dymchurch

DYMCHURCH

Romney, Hythe and Dymchurch Railway

BOTOLPH'S

BRIDGE

ROAD

Hythe
CT21

ROAD

Dunkirk End

ST. ANN'S RD.

NICK W. WY.

SCHM. RD.

CHAPEL RD.

ROMNEY HO.

G.MARSH HO.

GARSWICK RD.

NICK W. WY.

CHURCH RD.

A259

SEA WALL

7

47

8

Dymchurch
Rec. Grd.

Pav.

MILL RD.

ST. MARY'S

MARSH LANDS

RUSH CL.

LONGWOOD

LANDS CL.

MARSHLANDS

HIGH ROAD

MARSH RD.

ORGANS RD.

HIGH ROAD

HIGH STREET

Park
Pde.

Lib.

Martello Tower no.24

Slipway

Marshland Basin

Romney Marsh

TN29

Fort Lodge

River Ho.

WOODLAND WY.

BROCKMAN RD.

DENNANT RD.

DYMCHURCH RD.

SEA WALL

Depot

Dymchurch Redoubt

32

ENGLISH
CHANNEL

29

High Knock Farm

DYMCHURCH

HIGH KNOCK

Martello Tower no.25

9

CRIMOND AV.

BEACH RD.

WOODLAND WY.

UDEN RD.

DENNANT RD.

BEVERLEY GDNS.

A259

Dymchurch

HYTHE ROAD

Outfall

East Fleet Caravan Park

New Beach Holiday Centre

13

A · 47 · 6 10
B
C
D
E · 6 13
F

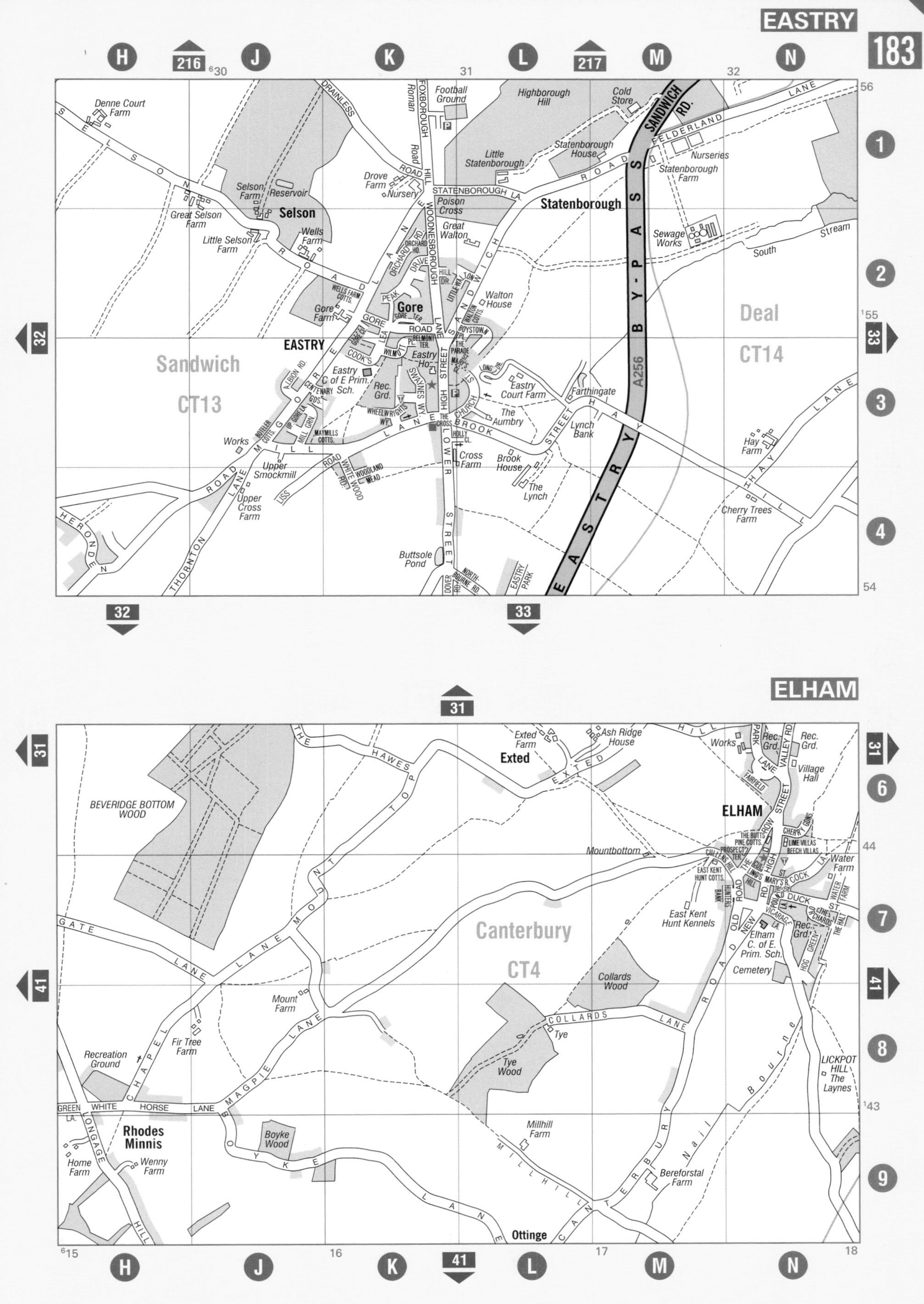
EASTRY
Selson
Gore
Statenborough
Sandwich CT13
Deal CT14
SANDWICH BY-PASS
EASTRY BY-PASS
A256
ELHAM
Exted
Elham
Canterbury CT4
Rhodes Minnis
Ottinge
BEVERIDGE BOTTOM WOOD
Collards Wood
Tye Wood
Boyke Wood

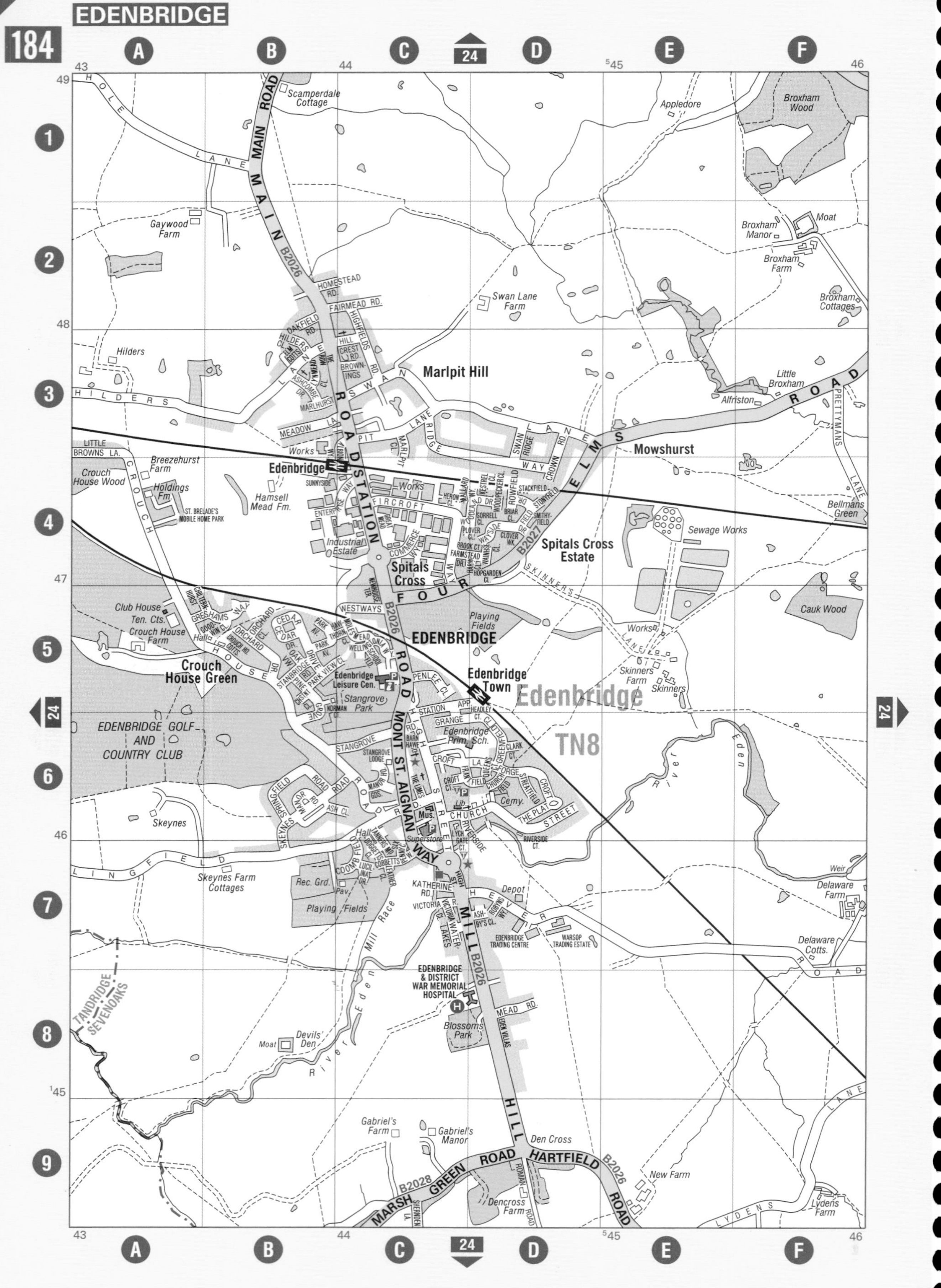
Scamperdale Cottage
Appledore
Broxham Wood
Gaywood Farm
Broxham Manor
Moat
Broxham Farm
Swan Lane Farm
Broxham Cottages
Hilders
Marlpit Hill
Little Broxham
Alfriston
Mowshurst
Edenbridge
Breezehurst Farm
Crouch House Wood
Holdings Fm.
Hamsell Mead Fm.
Industrial Estate
Spitals Cross Estate
Sewage Works
Bellmans Green
Spitals Cross
Club House
Crouch House Farm
EDENBRIDGE
Playing Fields
Cauk Wood
Crouch House Green
Edenbridge Leisure Cen.
Stangrove Park
Edenbridge Town
Edenbridge
TN8
Skinners Farm
Skinners
EDENBRIDGE GOLF AND COUNTRY CLUB
Edenbridge Prim. Sch.
Skeynes
Cemy.
Mus.
Superstore
Skeynes Farm Cottages
Rec. Grd.
Playing Fields
Depot
Delaware Farm
Weir
EDENBRIDGE TRADING CENTRE
WARSOP TRADING ESTATE
Delaware Cotts.
EDENBRIDGE & DISTRICT WAR MEMORIAL HOSPITAL
TANDRIDGE
SEVENOAKS
Blossoms Park
Devils' Den
Moat
Gabriel's Farm
Gabriel's Manor
Den Cross
New Farm
Dencross Farm
Lydens Farm
MAIN ROAD
STATION ROAD
MONT ST. AIGNAN WAY
MILL HILL
HIGH STREET
FOUR ELMS ROAD
HARTFIELD ROAD
MARSH GREEN ROAD
HILDERS LANE
HOLE LANE
CROUCH HOUSE ROAD
LINGFIELD ROAD
SWAN LANE
CHURCH STREET
STANGROVE ROAD
SPRINGFIELD ROAD
HEVER ROAD
SKINNER'S LANE
LYDENS LANE
B2026
B2027
B2028

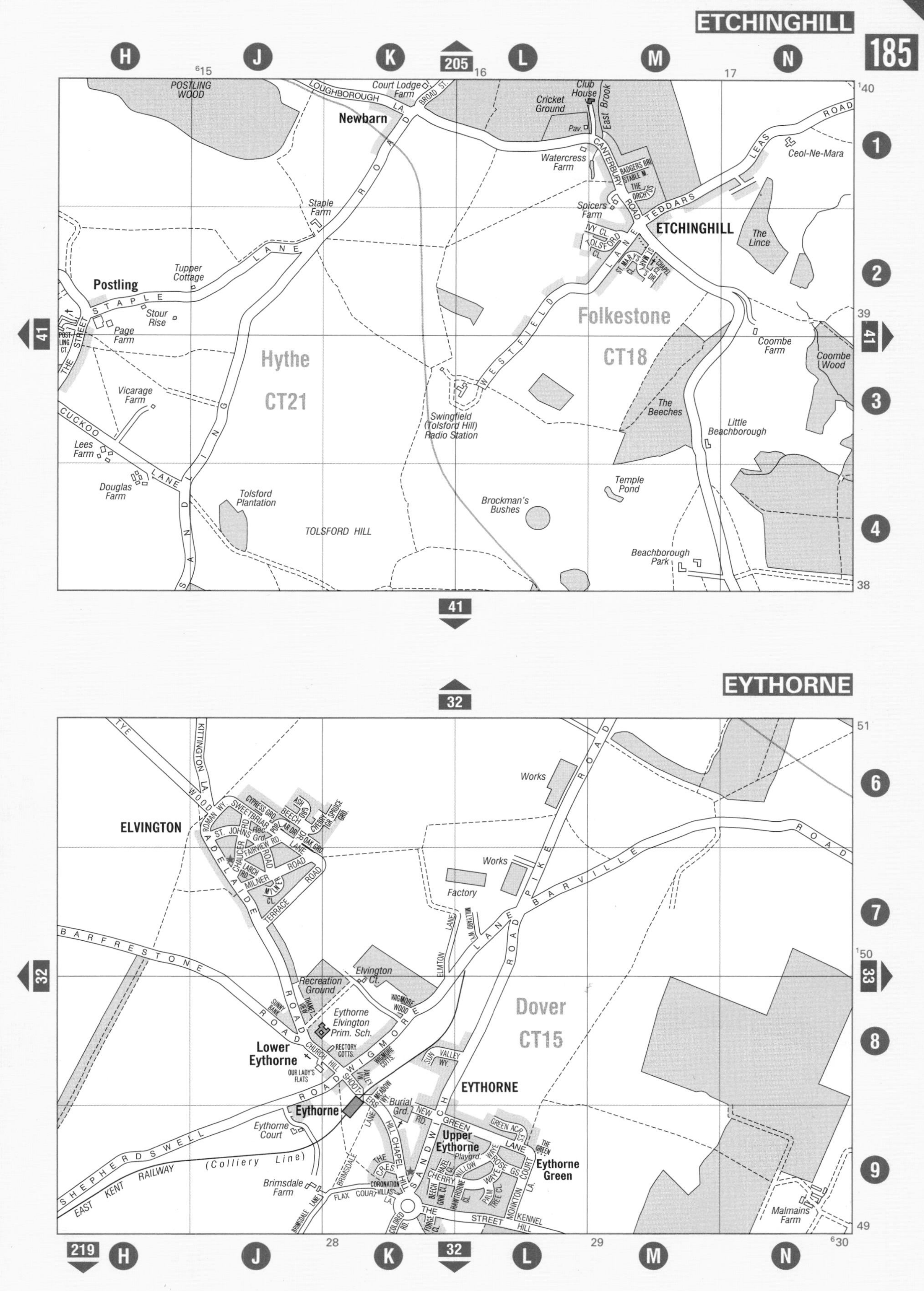

Map content — Etchinghill sheet (top):

POSTLING WOOD
Court Lodge Farm
Newbarn
LOUGHBOROUGH LA.
Club House
Cricket Ground
Pav.
Watercress Farm
Ceol-Ne-Mara
ETCHINGHILL
The Lince
Staple Farm
Spicers Farm
BADGERS DRI
STABLE M.
THE ORCHES
Tupper Cottage
Postling
Folkestone
CT18
Coombe Farm
Coombe Wood
Stour Rise
Page Farm
THE STREET
STAPLE
POSTLING CT.
Vicarage Farm
Hythe
CT21
The Beeches
Little Beachborough
CUCKOO
Lees Farm
Swingfield (Tolsford Hill) Radio Station
Temple Pond
Douglas Farm
LANE
Tolsford Plantation
Brockman's Bushes
Beachborough Park
TOLSFORD HILL

41   41   41

Map content — Eythorne sheet (bottom):

32   33

Works
ELVINGTON
TYE
KITTINGTON LA.
WOOD
ROMAN WY.
ADELAIDE
ST. JOHNS
CYPRESS GRO
SWEET BRIAR RD.
ASH GR.
BEECH
SPRUCE GRO.
OAK GRO.
CHAUCER
LARCH GRO.
FAIRVIEW ROAD
MILNER
ROAD
TERRACE
Works
Factory
BARFRESTONE
ROAD
Recreation Ground
SUNNY BANK
Elvington Ct.
WIGMORE WOOD
Eythorne Elvington Prim. Sch.
RECTORY COTTS.
Lower Eythorne
CHURCH HILL
OUR LADY'S FLATS
SHEPHERDSWELL
EAST KENT RAILWAY (Colliery Line)
Brimsdale Farm
Eythorne
Eythorne Court
BRIMSDALE RD.
CORONATION VILLAS
FLAX COURT
COLONELS RD.
DINSDALE LANE
SHOTTENDANE RD.
MILL ROAD
SANDY
Burial Grd.
NEW RD.
MEADOW
CHAPEL HILL
THE CYPRESSES
HILL
BEECH GRO.
HAZEL CL.
CHERRY
PALM
HAWTHORNE
WATER
TREE CL.
WILLOW
GREEN
GREEN ACR.
THE GREEN
WROSE
MONKTON GR.
KENNEL HILL
STREET
Upper Eythorne
Playgrd.
Eythorne Green
EYTHORNE
Dover
CT15
BARVILLE
PIKE ROAD
ELMTON LANE
DOWNTON LA.
VALLEY WY.
SUN
ROAD
Malmains Farm

BARFRESTONE

219   32

32   33

H J K L M N

205 16 17 40
39 38
51 50 49
28 29 30

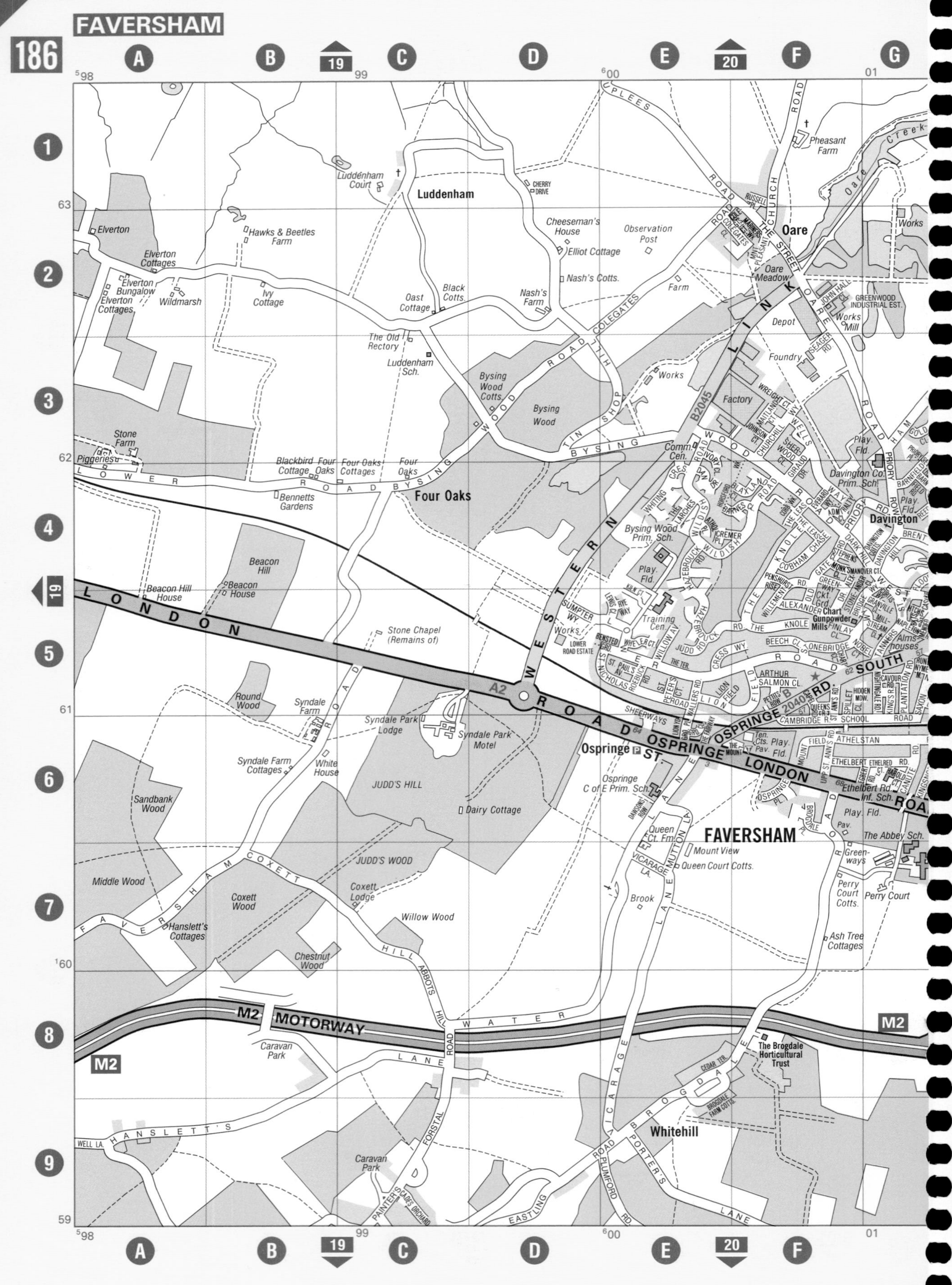
Luddenham
Luddenham Court
Elverton
Hawks & Beetles Farm
Cheeseman's House
Observation Post
Elliot Cottage
Nash's Cotts.
Oare
Oare Meadow
Pheasant Farm
Works
Elverton Cottages
Elverton Bungalow
Elverton Cottages
Wildmarsh
Ivy Cottage
Oast Cottage
Black Cotts.
Nash's Farm
Farm
Depot
GREENWOOD INDUSTRIAL EST.
Works Mill
The Old Rectory
Luddenham Sch.
Foundry
Works
Factory
Bysing Wood Cotts.
Bysing Wood
Stone Farm
Piggeries
Blackbird Cottage
Four Oaks
Four Oaks Cottages
Bennetts Gardens
Four Oaks
Comm. Cen.
Play. Fld.
Davington Co. Prim. Sch.
Davington
Bysing Wood Prim. Sch.
Beacon Hill
Beacon Hill House
Beacon House
Training Cen.
Chart Gunpowder Mills
Almshouses
Stone Chapel (Remains of)
Works
LOWER ROAD ESTATE
Round Wood
Syndale Farm
Syndale Park Lodge
Syndale Park Motel
Ospringe
Ospringe C of E Prim. Sch.
Syndale Farm Cottages
White House
JUDD'S HILL
Dairy Cottage
Sandbank Wood
Ethelbert Rd. Inf. Sch.
Play. Fld.
The Abbey Sch.
FAVERSHAM
Queen Ct. Fm.
Mount View
Queen Court Cotts.
Greenways
Perry Court Cotts.
Perry Court
Middle Wood
JUDD'S WOOD
Coxett Wood
Coxett Lodge
Willow Wood
Brook
Hanslett's Cottages
Ash Tree Cottages
Chestnut Wood
M2 MOTORWAY
Caravan Park
The Brogdale Horticultural Trust
BROGDALE FARM COTTS.
Whitehill
Caravan Park
LONDON ROAD
A2
WESTERN LINK
B2045
OSPRINGE ST.
OSPRINGE RD.
SOUTH RD.
UPLEES ROAD
THE STREET
CHURCH ROAD
COLEGATES ROAD
BYSING WOOD ROAD
LOWER ROAD
TIN SHOP HILL
PRIORY ROW
FAVERSHAM
COXETT HILL
ABBOTS HILL
WATER LANE
FORSTAL ROAD
HANSLETT'S LANE
WELL LA.
BROGDALE ROAD
VICARAGE LA.
MUTTON LANE
PORTER'S LANE
PLUMFORD RD.
EASTLING ROAD
M2
19
20

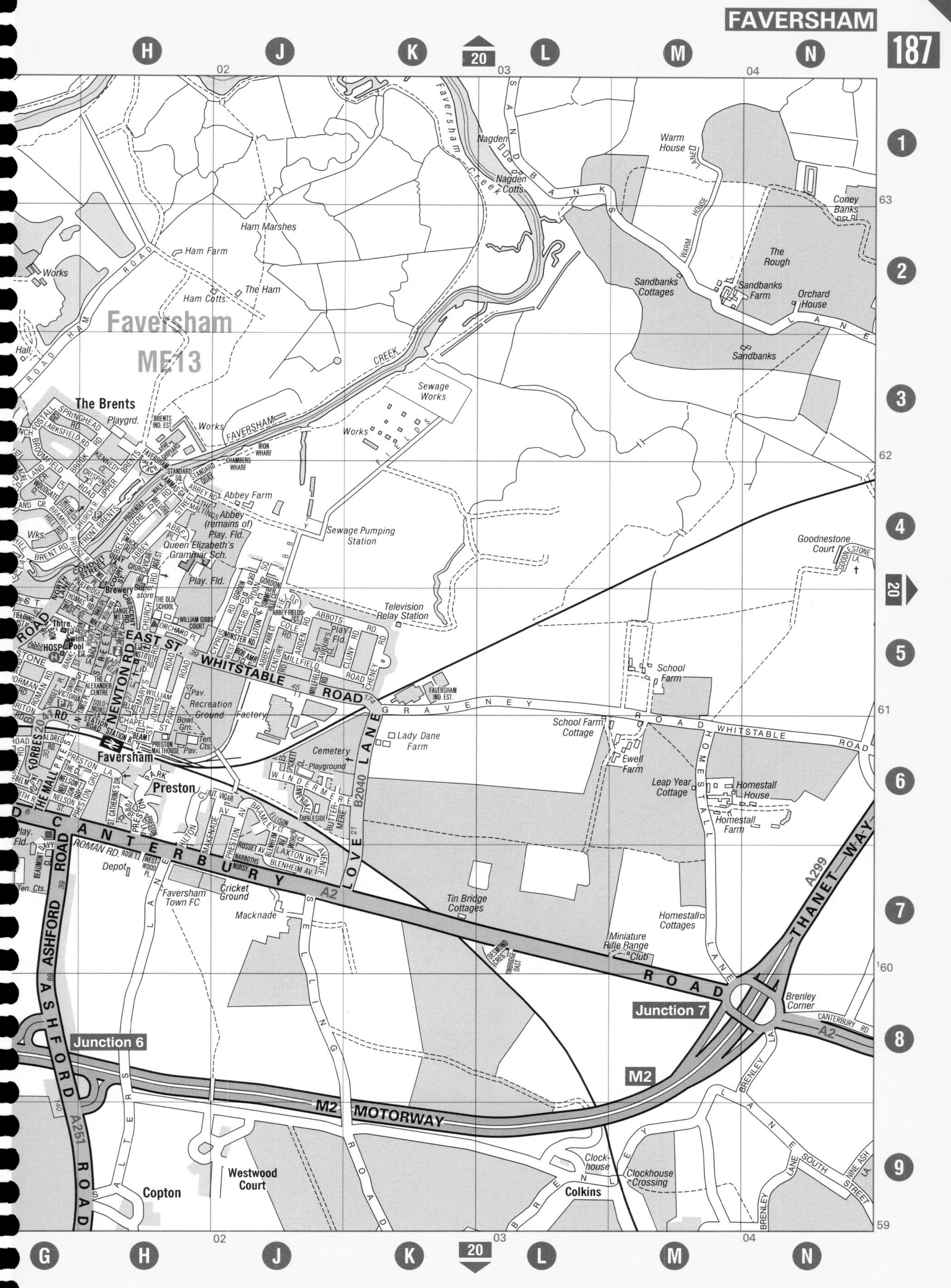
Faversham
ME13
The Brents
Ham Marshes
Ham Farm
The Ham
Ham Cotts.
Works
Nagden
Nagden Cotts.
Faversham Creek
SANDBANKS
Warm House
WARM HOUSE LANE
Coney Banks
The Rough
Sandbanks Cottages
Sandbanks Farm
Orchard House
Sandbanks
Sewage Works
Sewage Pumping Station
Abbey Farm
Abbey (remains of)
Play. Fld.
Queen Elizabeth's Grammar Sch.
Goodnestone Court
Television Relay Station
School Farm
School Farm Cottage
Ewell Farm
Leap Year Cottage
Homestall House
Homestall Farm
Homestall Cottages
Lady Dane Farm
Cemetery
Recreation Ground
Factory
FAVERSHAM IND. EST.
WHITSTABLE ROAD
GRAVENEY ROAD
EAST ST.
NEWTON RD.
Faversham
Preston
LOVE LANE
B2040
Tin Bridge Cottages
Miniature Rifle Range Club
CANTERBURY ROAD
A2
THANET WAY
A299
Junction 7
Brenley Corner
M2
M2 MOTORWAY
Junction 6
ASHFORD ROAD
A251
Faversham Town FC
Cricket Ground
Macknade
Depot
SALTERS LANE
SELLING ROAD
Westwood Court
Copton
Colkins
Clockhouse
Clockhouse Crossing
BRENLEY LANE
SOUTH STREET
NINE ASH LA.
H
J
K
L
M
N
G
1
2
3
4
5
6
7
8
9
02
03
04
20
59
60
61
62
63

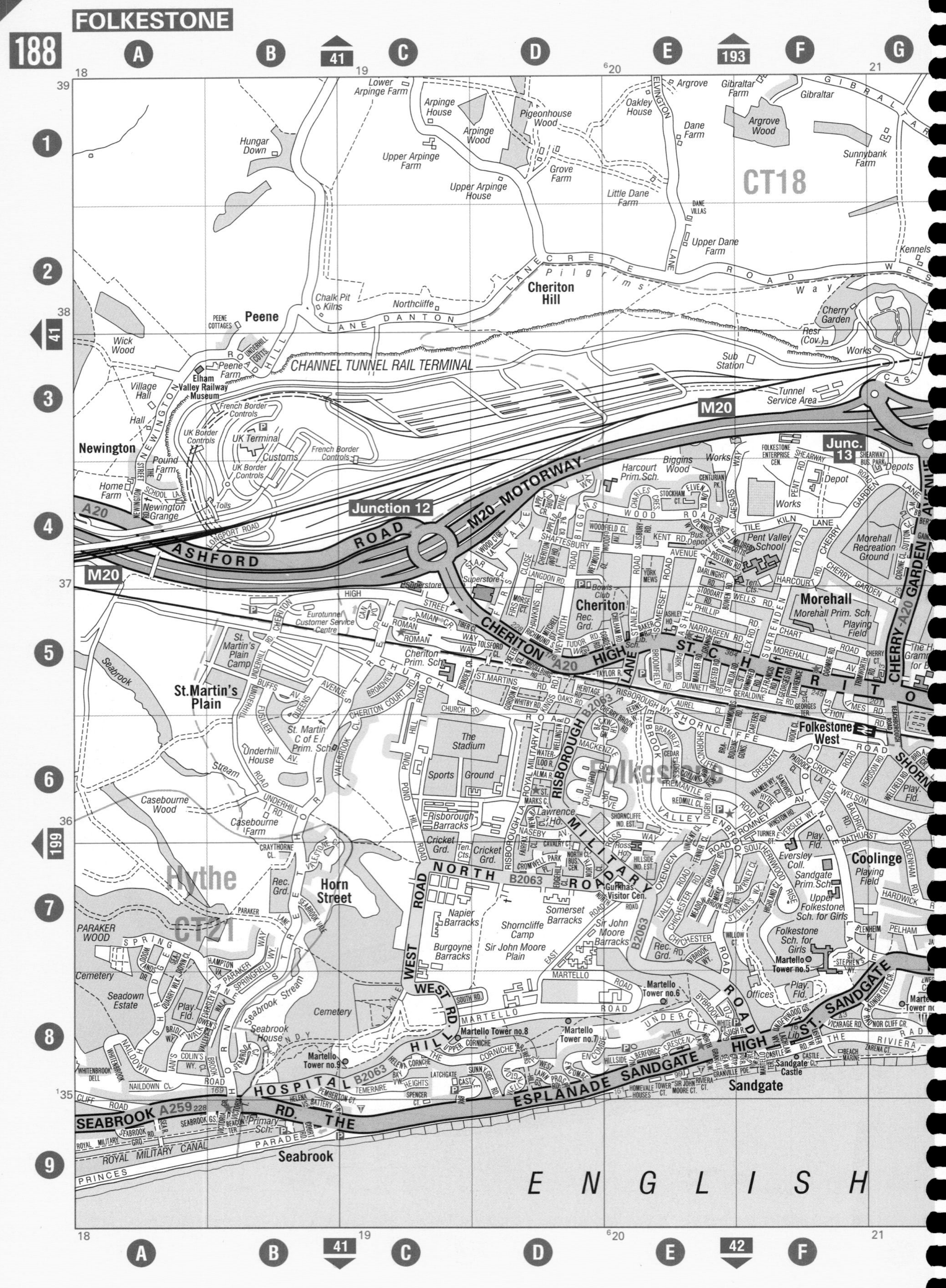

Place names and labels visible on the map include:

CT18

Hungar Down, Lower Arpinge Farm, Arpinge House, Arpinge Wood, Upper Arpinge Farm, Upper Arpinge House, Grove Farm, Pigeonhouse Wood, Argrove, Oakley House, Dane Farm, Little Dane Farm, Gibraltar Farm, Argrove Wood, Gibraltar, Sunnybank Farm, Dane Villas, Upper Dane Farm, Kennels

Peene, Peene Cottages, Chalk Pit Kilns, Northcliffe, Cheriton Hill, Cherry Garden, Resr (Cov.), Works

Wick Wood, Village Hall, Elham Valley Railway Museum, French Border Controls, CHANNEL TUNNEL RAIL TERMINAL, Sub Station, Tunnel Service Area, M20, Junc. 13

Newington, Home Farm, Pound Farm, Peene Farm, UK Border Controls, Customs, UK Terminal, French Border Controls, Folkestone Enterprise Cen., Harcourt Prim. Sch., Biggins Wood, Works, Centurian Pk., Depot, Depots, Shearway

Newington Grange, Tolls, Junction 12, Superstore, A20, ASHFORD ROAD, M20 MOTORWAY, Woodfield Cl., Shaftesbury, Kent Rd., Pent Valley School, Morehall Recreation Ground

M20, Eurotunnel Customer Service Centre, St. Martin's Plain Camp, Cheriton Prim. Sch., ROMAN WAY, CHERITON A20, Cheriton Rec. Grd., Bowls Club, York Mews, Morehall, Morehall Prim. Sch. Playing Field

Seabrook, St. Martin's Plain, Buffs Av., Queens Av., Fusilier Rd., St. Martin C of E Prim. Sch., Underhill House, RISBOROUGH B2063, ST CHERITO, Folkestone West, Heritage, Oaks Rd.

Casebourne Wood, Casebourne Farm, Craythorne Cl., Underhill Rd., The Stadium, Sports Ground, Risborough Barracks, Cricket Grd., Cavalry Park, Folkestone, MILITARY ROAD, Shorncliffe Ind. Est., Coolinge Playing Field, Eversley Coll., Sandgate Prim. Sch., Upper Folkestone Sch. for Girls

Hythe CT21, Paraker Wood, Horn Street, Rec. Grd., NORTH ROAD, B2063, Napier Barracks, Burgoyne Barracks, Somerset Barracks, Shorncliffe Camp, Sir John Moore Plain, Sir John Moore Barracks, Gurkhas Visitor Cen., Folkestone Sch. for Girls, Martello Tower no.5, Coolinge, Hardwick, Pelham, Blenheim

Cemetery, Seadown Estate, Play. Fld., Cemetery, Seabrook House, WEST HILL ROAD, WEST RD., Martello Tower no.9, Martello Tower no.8, Martello Tower no.7, Martello Tower no.6, SANDGATE HIGH ST., Sandgate Castle, Offices, Rec. Grd.

Whitenbrook Dell, HOSPITAL RD., THE STADE, Martello Tower no.9, B2063, Corniche, West Corniche, THE ESPLANADE, SANDGATE HIGH ST., Sandgate, The Riviera

Seabrook, A259, Seabrook, Primary Sch., ROYAL MILITARY CANAL, THE PARADE, Seabrook, Royal Military Canal, Princes

ENGLISH

41, 193, 41, 199, 41, 42

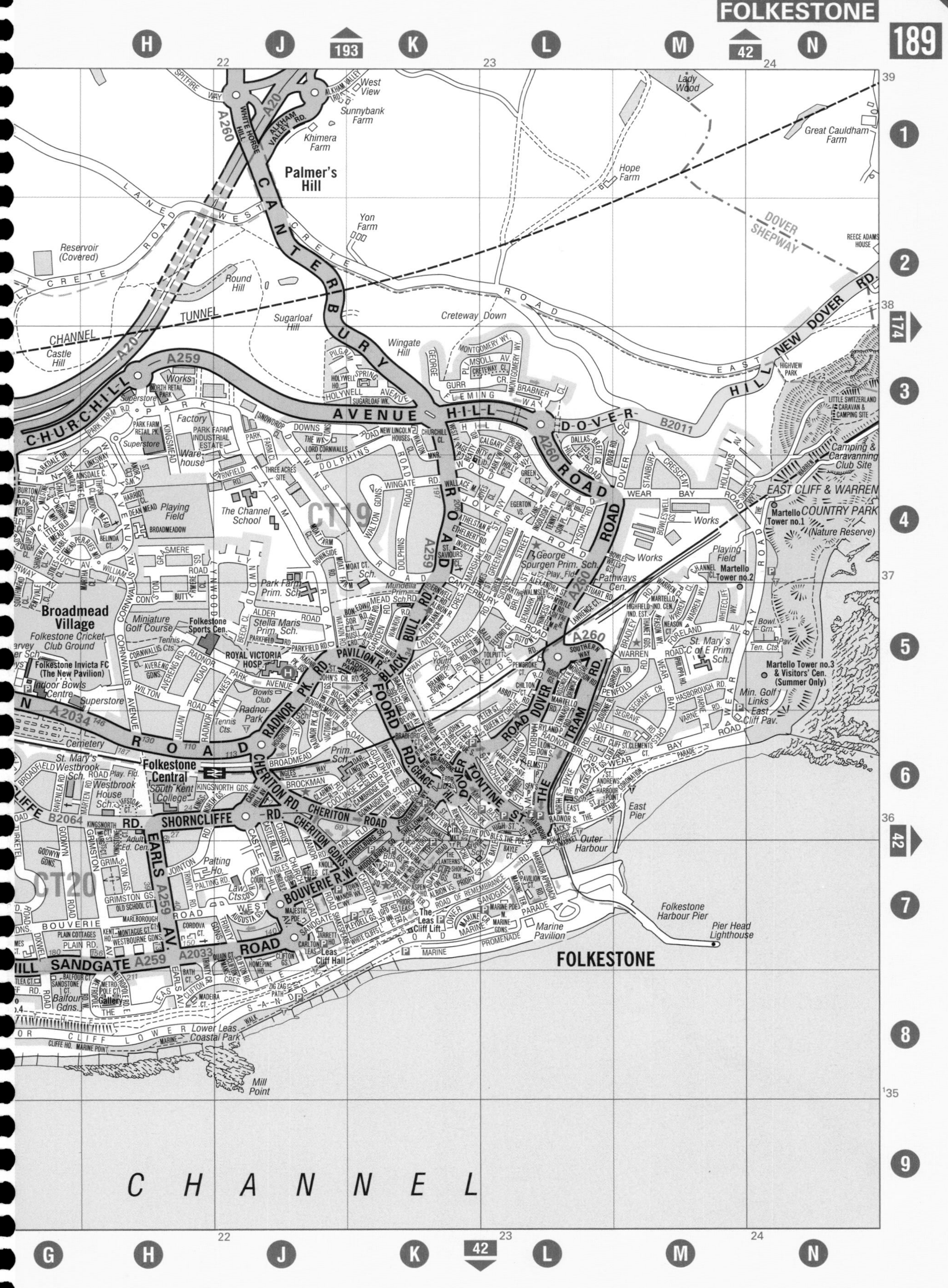
H
J
193
K
L
M
42
N
Lady Wood
West View
Sunnybank Farm
Khimera Farm
Palmer's Hill
Great Cauldham Farm
Hope Farm
Yon Farm
DOVER SHEPWAY
REECE ADAMS HOUSE
Reservoir (Covered)
Round Hill
Sugarloaf Hill
Creteway Down
Wingate Hill
Castle Hill
CHANNEL TUNNEL
CANTERBURY ROAD
CHURCHILL AVENUE
HILL ROAD
DOVER ROAD
NEW DOVER RD.
EAST CLIFF & WARREN COUNTRY PARK (Nature Reserve)
Camping & Caravanning Club Site
Martello Tower no.1
Martello Tower no.2
Martello Tower no.3 & Visitors' Cen. (Summer Only)
CT19
CT20
The Channel School
Playing Field
Broadmead Village
Folkestone Cricket Club Ground
Folkestone Invicta FC (The New Pavilion)
Indoor Bowls Centre
Superstore
Folkestone Sports Cen.
ROYAL VICTORIA HOSP.
Park Farm Prim. Sch.
Stella Maris Prim. Sch.
George Spurgen Prim. Sch.
Pathways Cen.
St. Mary's C of E Prim. Sch.
Min. Golf Links
East Cliff Pav.
Bowls Club
Radnor Park
Cemetery
St. Mary's Westbrook Sch.
Westbrook House Sch.
Folkestone Central
South Kent College
RADNOR PARK ROAD
CHERITON RD.
SHORNCLIFFE RD.
FOORD RD.
BOUVERIE R.W.
SANDGATE ROAD
TONTINE ST.
THE TRAM RD.
Outer Harbour
East Pier
Folkestone Harbour Pier
Pier Head Lighthouse
Marine Pavilion
Leas Cliff Lift
Leas Cliff Hall
FOLKESTONE
Lower Leas Coastal Park
Mill Point
C H A N N E L
G
H
J
K
42
L
M
N
1
2
3
4
5
6
7
8
9
174
42

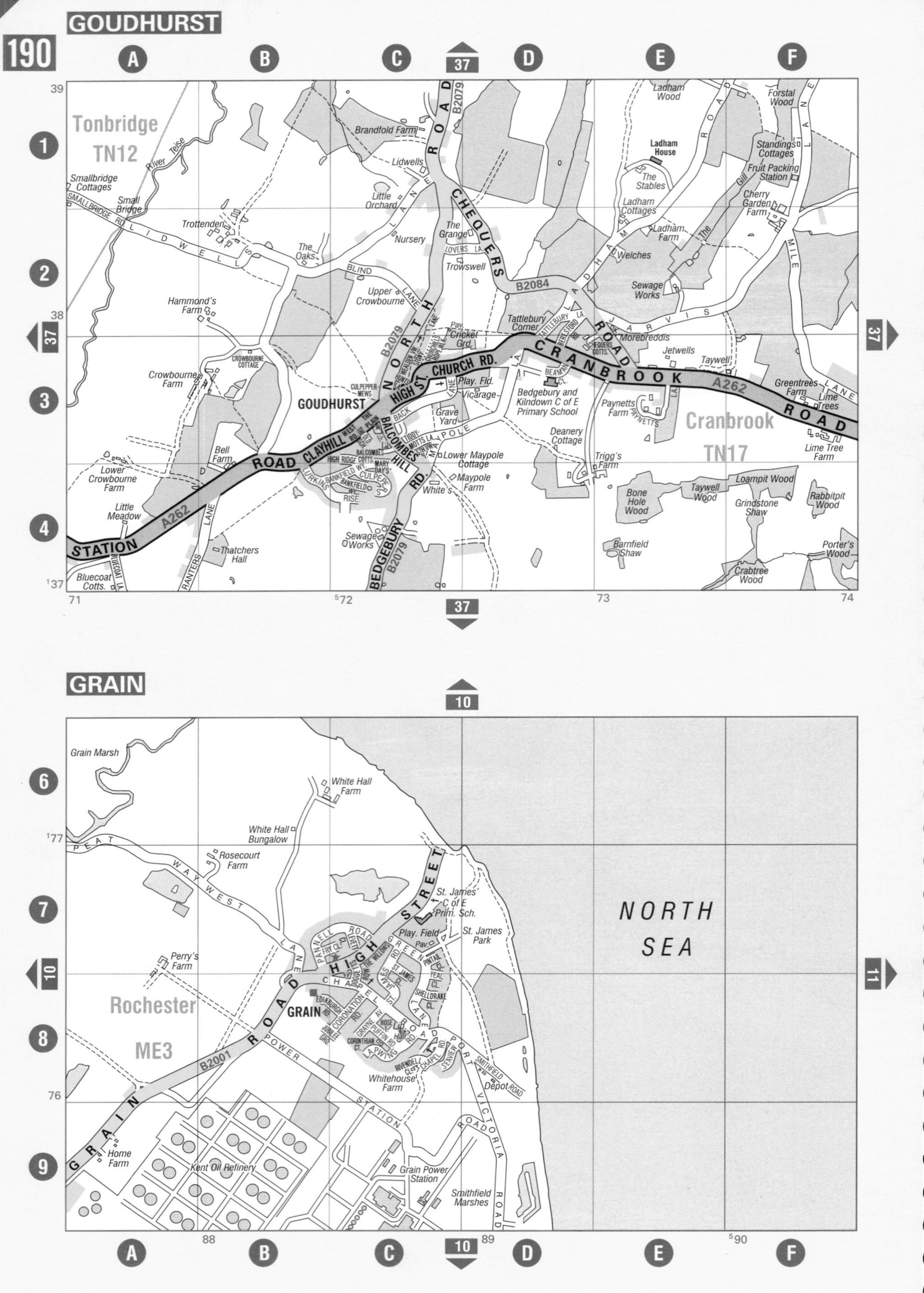

GOUDHURST

Tonbridge
TN12

Smallbridge Cottages

River Teise

Small Bridge

Trottenden

The Oaks

Brandfold Farm

Lidwells

Little Orchard

Nursery

The Grange

LOVERS LANE

Trowswell

Upper Crowbourne

Hammond's Farm

Crowbourne Cottage

Crowbourne Farm

CULPEPPER MEWS

GOUDHURST

Bell Farm

Lower Crowbourne Cottage

Little Meadow

STATION

Thatchers Hall

Bluecoat Cotts.

CLAYHILL

ROAD

A262

LURKINS

RANTERS LANE

HIGH ST

BALCOMBES HILL

BEDGEBURY RD.

B2079

CHEQUERS ROAD B2079

NORTH LANE

BLIND LANE

B2084

CHURCH RD.

Play. Fld.

Vicarage

Grave Yard

Cricket Grd.

Pav.

Tattlebury Corner

Morebreddis

Jetwells

Taywell

CRANBROOK ROAD A262

Bedgebury and Kilndown C of E Primary School

Deanery Cottage

Lower Maypole Cottage

White's

Maypole Farm

Trigg's Farm

Paynetts Farm

Greentrees Farm

Lime Trees

Cranbrook
TN17

Lime Tree Farm

Sewage Works

Ladham Wood

Ladham House

The Stables

Ladham Cottages

Ladham Farm

Welches

Sewage Works

Forstal Wood

Standings Cottages

Fruit Packing Station

Cherry Garden Farm

JARVIS LANE

MILE LANE

GILL LANE

Bone Hole Wood

Taywell Wood

Loampit Wood

Grindstone Shaw

Barnfield Shaw

Crabtree Wood

Rabbitpit Wood

Porter's Wood

Sewage Works

GRAIN

Grain Marsh

White Hall Farm

White Hall Bungalow

Rosecourt Farm

PEAT

WAY WEST LANE

Perry's Farm

Rochester
ME3

GRAIN ROAD B2001

Home Farm

Kent Oil Refinery

HIGH STREET

St. James' C of E Prim. Sch.

Play. Field

St. James Park

GRAIN

Whitehouse Farm

Grain Power Station

Smithfield Marshes

Smithfield

Depot Road

VICTORIA ROAD

NORTH SEA

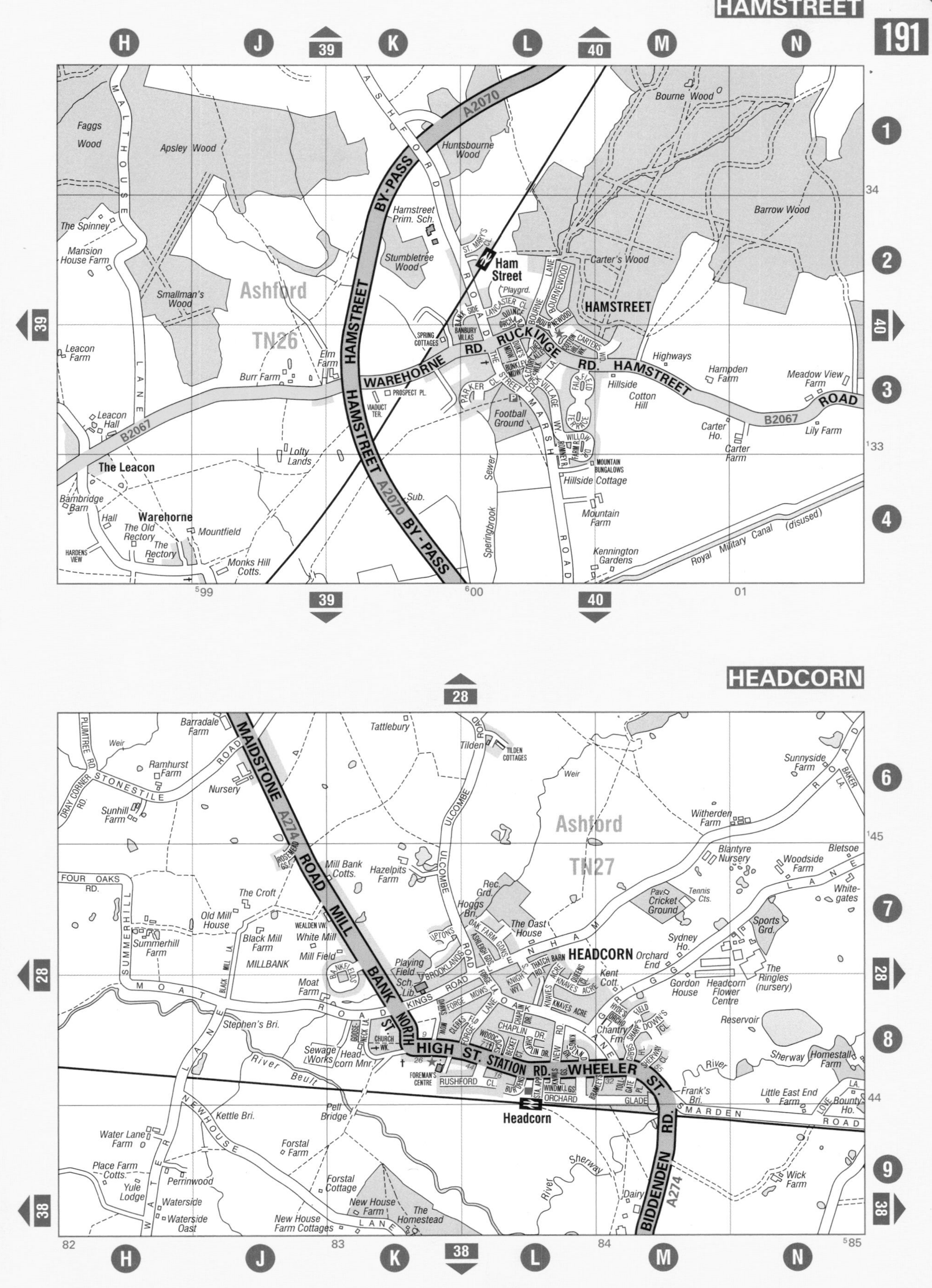
HAMSTREET
Faggs Wood
Apsley Wood
Huntsbourne Wood
Bourne Wood
Barrow Wood
The Spinney
Mansion House Farm
Hamstreet Prim. Sch.
Stumbletree Wood
Ham Street
Carter's Wood
Smallman's Wood
Ashford
TN26
HAMSTREET
Leacon Farm
Elm Farm
Burr Farm
Highways
Hampden Farm
Meadow View Farm
Hillside
Cotton Hill
Leacon Hall
Football Ground
Carter Ho.
Carter Farm
Lily Farm
The Leacon
Lofty Lands
Hillside Cottage
Bambridge Barn
Hall
Warehorne
The Old Rectory
The Rectory
Mountfield
Mountain Farm
Monks Hill Cotts.
Kennington Gardens
Royal Military Canal (disused)
HAMSTREET BY-PASS
A2070
B2067
WAREHORNE RD.
RUCKINGE RD.
HAMSTREET ROAD
Sewer
Speringbrook
HEADCORN
Barradale Farm
Tattlebury
Tilden
Ramhurst Farm
Nursery
Sunhill Farm
Sunnyside Farm
Witherden Farm
Ashford
TN27
Blantyre Nursery
Woodside Farm
Bletsoe
Mill Bank Cotts.
Hazelpits Farm
The Croft
Old Mill House
Rec. Grd.
Hoggs Bri.
Cricket Ground
Tennis Cts.
White-gates
Summerhill Farm
Black Mill Farm
White Mill
Mill Field
MILLBANK
The Oast House
HEADCORN
Orchard End
Sydney Ho.
Sports Grd.
Playing Field
Moat Farm
Kent Cott.
Gordon House
Headcorn Flower Centre
The Ringles (nursery)
Stephen's Bri.
Chantry Fm.
Reservoir
Sewage Works
Headcorn Mnr.
River Beult
Sherway
Homestall Farm
Headcorn
Frank's Bri.
Little East End Farm
Bounty Ho.
Kettle Bri.
Pell Bridge
Water Lane Farm
Forstal Farm
Place Farm Cotts.
Perrinwood
Yule Lodge
Forstal Cottage
Wick Farm
Waterside
Waterside Oast
New House Farm
The Homestead
New House Farm Cottages
Dairy
MAIDSTONE ROAD
MILL BANK
A274
HIGH ST.
STATION RD.
WHEELER ST.
BIDDENDEN RD.
MARDEN ROAD
MOAT ROAD
KINGS ROAD
STONESTILE ROAD
ULCOMBE ROAD
FOUR OAKS RD.
NEWHOUSE LANE
WATER LANE
SUMMERHILL

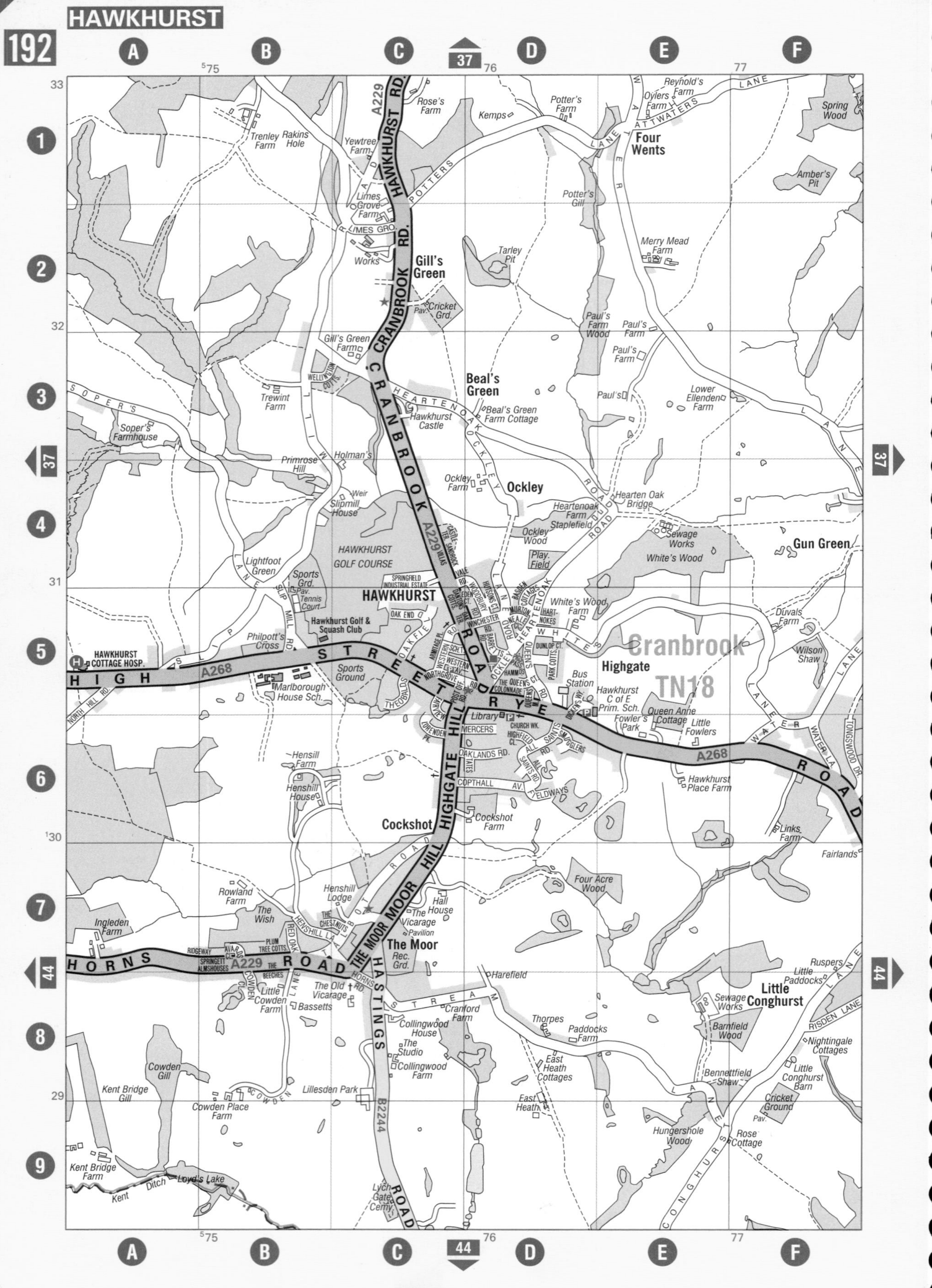
A
B
C
D
E
F
37
44
Trenley Farm
Rakins Hole
Yewtree Farm
Rose's Farm
Kemps
Potter's Farm
Reynold's Farm
Oylers Farm
Four Wents
Spring Wood
Amber's Pit
Potter's Gill
Limes Grove Farm
Works
Gill's Green
Tarley Pit
Merry Mead Farm
Cricket Grd.
Paul's Farm Wood
Paul's Farm
Gill's Green Farm
Beal's Green
Beal's Green Farm Cottage
Trewint Farm
Soper's Farmhouse
Hawkhurst Castle
Lower Ellenden Farm
Primrose Hill
Holman's
Ockley Farm
Ockley
Heartenoak Farm Staplefield
Hearten Oak Bridge
Slipmill House
Ockley Wood
Sewage Works
White's Wood
Gun Green
HAWKHURST GOLF COURSE
Lightfoot Green
Sports Grd.
Play. Field
HAWKHURST
Hawkhurst Golf & Squash Club
White's Wood Farm
Duvals Farm
HAWKHURST COTTAGE HOSP.
Philpott's Cross
Cranbrook
Highgate
Wilson Shaw
HIGH STREET
A268
Sports Ground
Marlborough House Sch.
Bus Station
Hawkhurst C of E Prim. Sch.
TN18
RYE ROAD
Library
Queen Anne Cottage
Fowler's Park
Little Fowlers
Hensill Farm
Henshill House
HIGHGATE HILL
Hawkhurst Place Farm
Cockshot
Cockshot Farm
Links Farm
Fairlands
Rowland Farm
Henshill Lodge
Hall House
Four Acre Wood
The Wish
The Vicarage
Ingleden Farm
The Moor
Rec. Grd.
HORNS ROAD
A229
THE MOOR
HASTINGS ROAD
B2244
Harefield
Ruspers
Little Paddocks
Little Conghurst
Little Cowden Farm
Bassetts
The Old Vicarage
Cranford Farm
Sewage Works
Thorpes
Paddocks Farm
Barnfield Wood
Collingwood House
The Studio
Collingwood Farm
East Heath Cottages
Nightingale Cottages
Cowden Gill
Bennettfield Shaw
Little Conghurst Barn
Kent Bridge Gill
Cowden Place Farm
Lillesden Park
East Heath
Cricket Ground
Hungershole Wood
Rose Cottage
Kent Bridge Farm
Loyd's Lake
Kent Ditch
Lych Gate Cemy.
CONGHURST LANE
RISDEN LANE

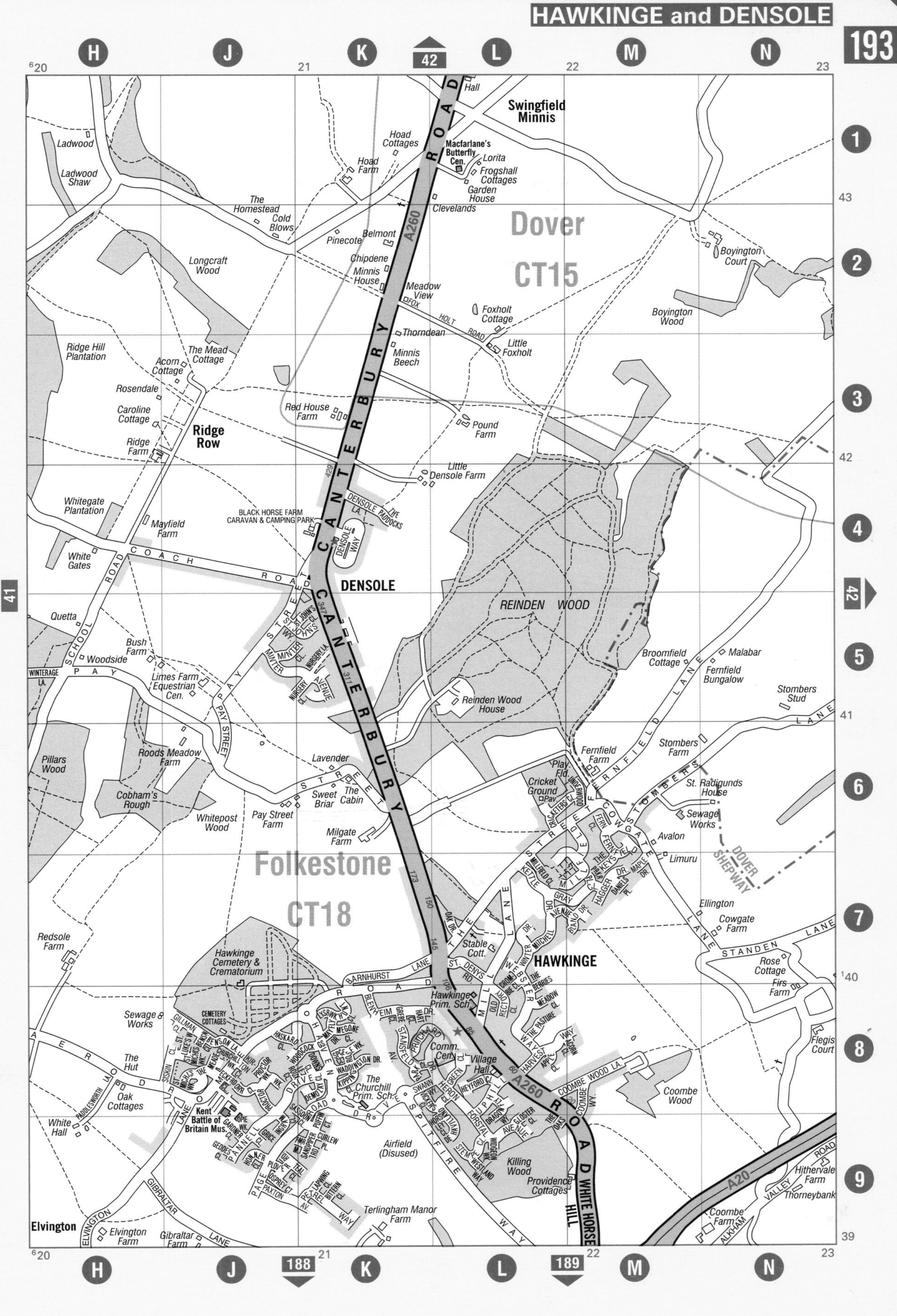

Swingfield Minnis

Dover CT15

Folkestone CT18

Hawkinge

Elvington

Ladwood
Ladwood Shaw
The Homestead
Cold Blows
Pinecote
Belmont
Longcraft Wood
Chipdene
Minnis House
Hoad Cottages
Hoad Farm
Hall
Macfarlane's Butterfly Cen.
Lorita
Frogshall Cottages
Garden House
Clevelands
Boyington Court
Meadow View
Thorndean
Minnis Beech
Foxholt Cottage
Little Foxholt
Boyington Wood
Ridge Hill Plantation
The Mead Cottage
Acorn Cottage
Rosendale
Caroline Cottage
Ridge Farm
Ridge Row
Red House Farm
Pound Farm
Little Densole Farm
Whitegate Plantation
Mayfield Farm
White Gates
Black Horse Farm Caravan & Camping Park
Densole Paddocks
The Densole La.
Densole Way
DENSOLE
REINDEN WOOD
Broomfield Cottage
Malabar
Fernfield Bungalow
Stombers Stud
Quetta
Bush Farm
Woodside
Limes Farm Equestrian Cen.
Reinden Wood House
Stombers Farm
Winterage La.
Pillars Wood
Roods Meadow Farm
Cobham's Rough
Whitepost Wood
Pay Street Farm
Lavender
Sweet Briar
The Cabin
Milgate Farm
Fernfield Farm
Play Fld.
Cricket Ground
Pav
St. Radigunds House
Sewage Works
Avalon
Limuru
Ellington
Cowgate Farm
Standen Lane
Rose Cottage
Firs Farm
Redsole Farm
Hawkinge Cemetery & Crematorium
Barnhurst Lane
Hawkinge Prim. Sch.
Stable Cott.
Flegis Court
Sewage & Works
Cemetery Cottages
The Hut
Oak Cottages
White Hall
Kent Battle of Britain Mus.
Comm. Cem.
Village Hall
The Churchill Prim. Sch.
Airfield (Disused)
Killing Wood
Providence Cottages
Coombe Wood La.
Coombe Wood
Elvington Farm
Gibraltar Farm
Terlingham Manor Farm
Coombe Farm
Hithervale Farm
Thorneybank

A260 CANTERBURY ROAD
COACH ROAD
SCHOOL ROAD
PAY STREET
SPITFIRE WAY
WHITE HORSE HILL
A20 VALLEY ROAD
DOVER SHEPWAY

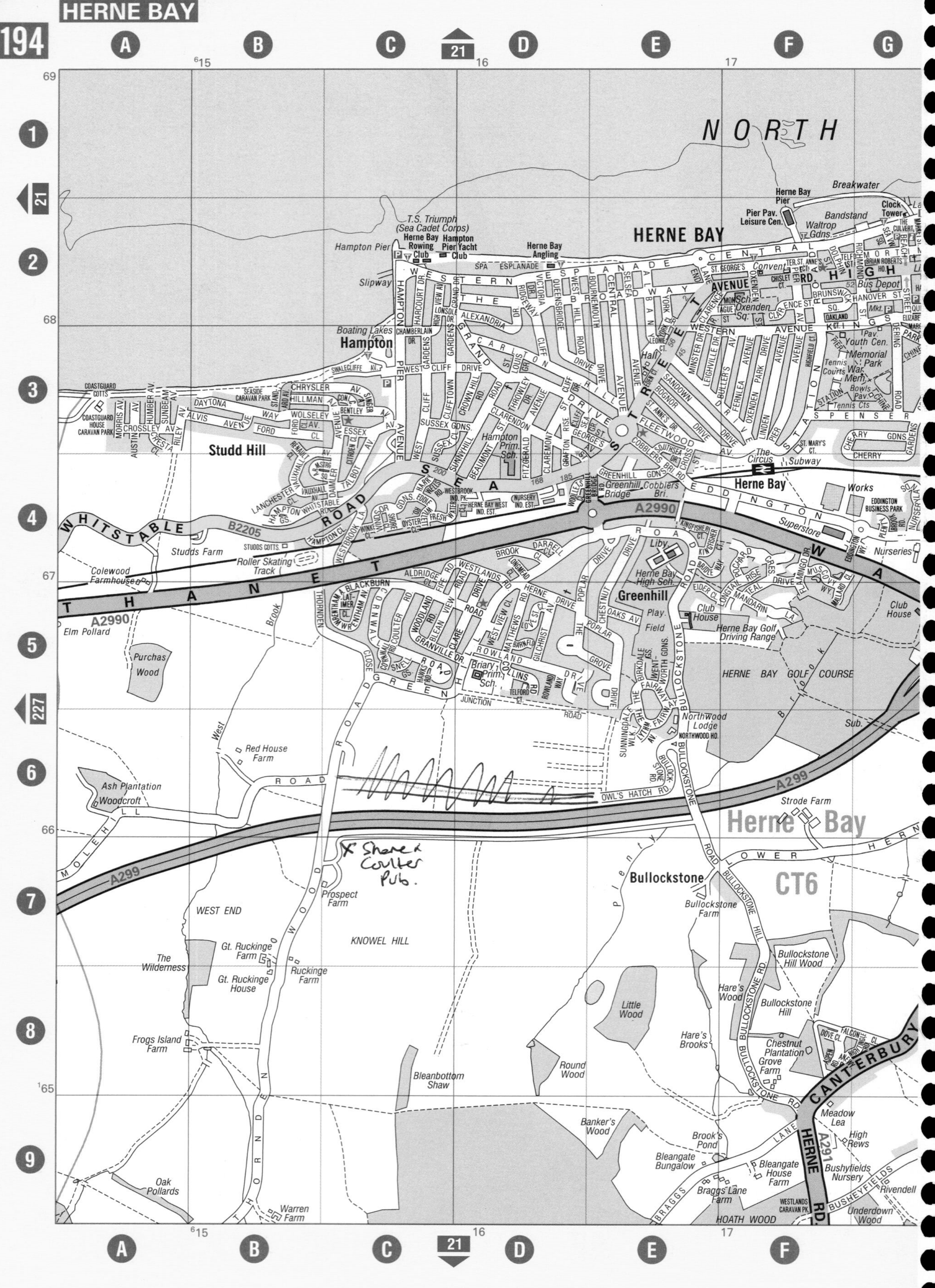
NORTH
HERNE BAY
Herne Bay Pier
Hampton
Studd Hill
Greenhill
Herne Bay
Bullockstone
CT6
THANET WAY
A2990
A299
WHITSTABLE ROAD
HERNE BAY GOLF COURSE
KNOWEL HILL
WEST END
Little Wood
Bleanbottom Shaw
Round Wood
Banker's Wood
Oak Pollards
Warren Farm
Prospect Farm
Red House Farm
Ash Plantation
Purchas Wood
Strode Farm
CANTERBURY RD.
HERNE RD.
A291
HOATH WOOD
X Shaner Coulter Pub.

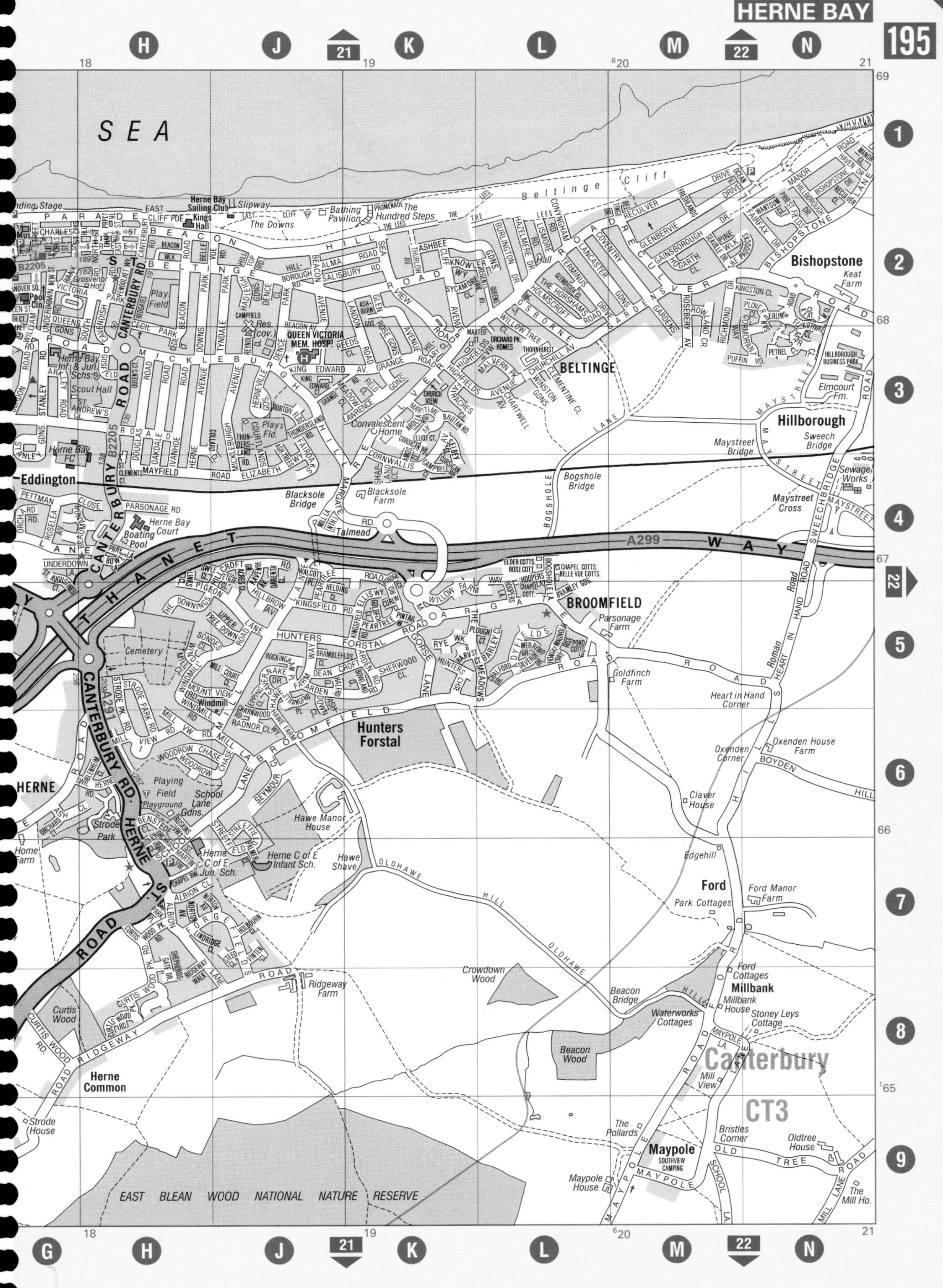
SEA
Herne Bay Sailing Club
Kings Hall
Slipway
Bathing Pavilion
The Hundred Steps
The Downs
Beltinge Cliff
Bishopstone
Keat Farm
BELTINGE
QUEEN VICTORIA MEM. HOSP.
Hillborough
Elmcourt Fm.
HILLBOROUGH BUSINESS PARK
Maystreet Bridge
Sweech Bridge
Sewage Works
Maystreet Cross
Bogshole Bridge
Blacksole Bridge
Blacksole Farm
Eddington
Herne Bay FC
Herne Bay Court
Boating Pool
Talmead
A299
THANET WAY
BROOMFIELD
Parsonage Farm
Goldfinch Farm
Heart in Hand Corner
Cemetery
Windmill
Hunters Forstal
Oxenden Corner
Oxenden House Farm
Claver House
HERNE
Playing Field
School Lane Gdns.
Strode Park
Hawe Manor House
Hawe Shave
Herne C of E Infant Sch.
Herne C of E Jun. Sch.
Home Farm
Edgehill
Ford
Ford Manor Farm
Park Cottages
Crowdown Wood
Ford Cottages
Millbank
Millbank House
Stoney Leys Cottage
Beacon Bridge
Waterworks Cottages
Ridgeway Farm
Curtis Wood
Beacon Wood
Canterbury
Mill View
CT3
Herne Common
Strode House
The Pollards
Bristles Corner
Oldtree House
Maypole
SOUTHVIEW CAMPING
Maypole House
The Mill Ho.
EAST BLEAN WOOD NATIONAL NATURE RESERVE

21
22
21
22

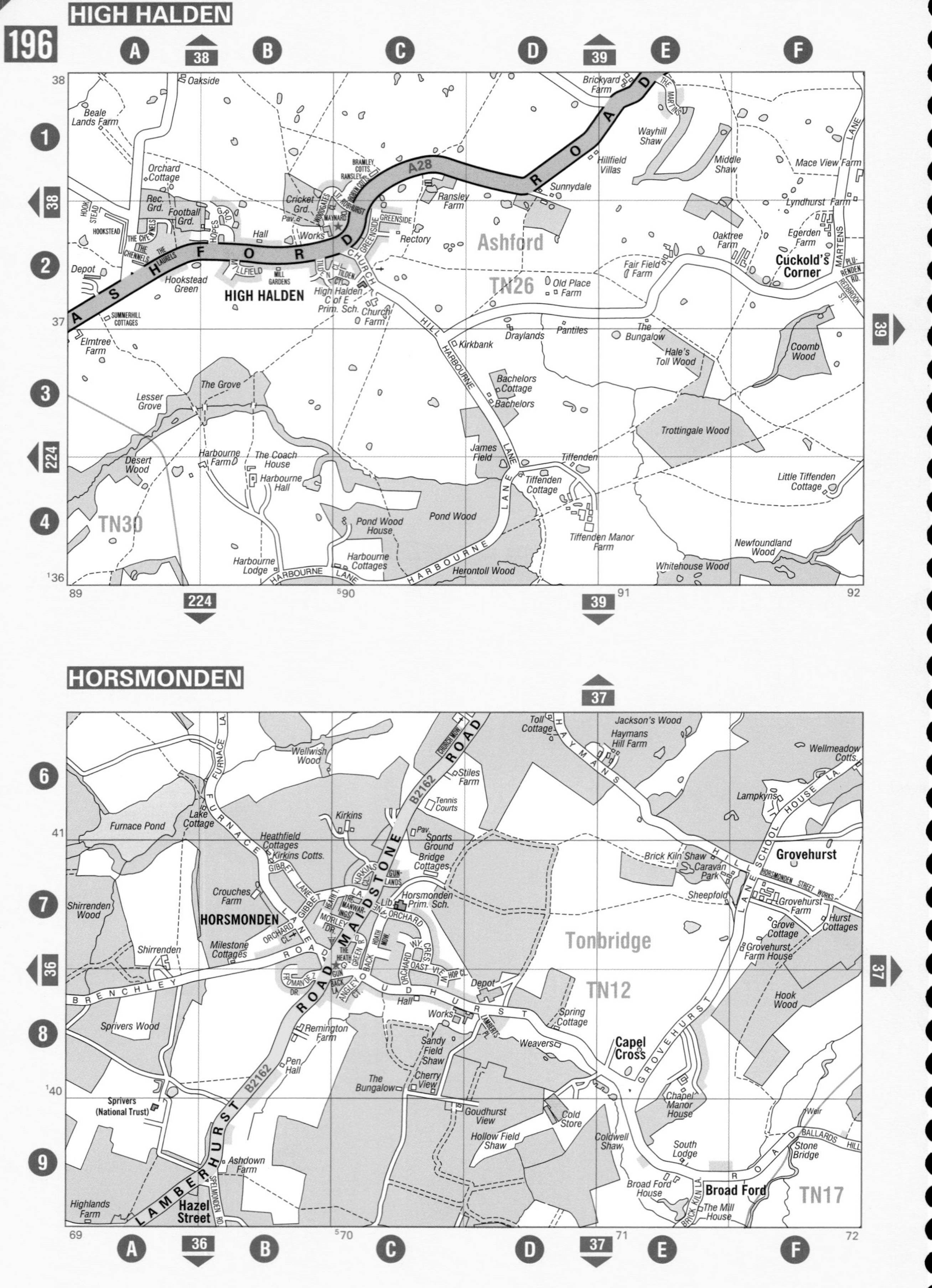

196
HIGH HALDEN
Oakside
Beale Lands Farm
Orchard Cottage
Rec. Grd.
Football Grd.
Cricket Grd.
Hookstead Green
HIGH HALDEN
High Halden C of E Prim. Sch.
Church Farm
Rectory
Works
Hall
Depot
Elmtree Farm
ASHFORD ROAD
A28
Brickyard Farm
Wayhill Shaw
Hillfield Villas
Sunnydale
Ransley Farm
Middle Shaw
Mace View Farm
Lyndhurst Farm
Oaktree Farm
Egerden Farm
Cuckold's Corner
Fair Field Farm
Old Place Farm
Ashford
TN26
Draylands
Pantiles
The Bungalow
Hale's Toll Wood
Coomb Wood
Kirkbank
Bachelors Cottage
Bachelors
Trottingale Wood
The Grove
Lesser Grove
Desert Wood
Harbourne Farm
The Coach House
Harbourne Hall
James Field
Tiffenden
Tiffenden Cottage
Little Tiffenden Cottage
Pond Wood House
Pond Wood
TN30
Tiffenden Manor Farm
Newfoundland Wood
Harbourne Lodge
Harbourne Cottages
Herontoll Wood
Whitehouse Wood
HARBOURNE LANE
HIGH HALDEN
HORSMONDEN
Toll Cottage
Jackson's Wood
Haymans Hill Farm
Wellwish Wood
Stiles Farm
Tennis Courts
Wellmeadow Cotts.
Lampkyns
Furnace Pond
Lake Cottage
Kirkins
Heathfield Cottages
Kirkins Cotts.
Sports Ground
Bridge Cottages
Brick Kiln Shaw
Caravan Park
Grovehurst
Crouches Farm
Horsmonden Prim. Sch.
Sheepfold
Grovehurst Farm
Shirrenden Wood
HORSMONDEN
Grove Cottage
Hurst Cottages
Tonbridge
Milestone Cottages
Shirrenden
Grovehurst Farm House
Hook Wood
Depot
TN12
BRENCHLEY ROAD
Hall
Works
Spring Cottage
Sprivers Wood
Remington Farm
Sandy Field Shaw
Weavers
Capel Cross
Pen Hall
The Bungalow
Cherry View
Sprivers (National Trust)
Goudhurst View
Cold Store
Chapel Manor House
Hollow Field Shaw
Coldwell Shaw
South Lodge
Stone Bridge
Ashdown Farm
Broad Ford House
Broad Ford
TN17
The Mill House
Highlands Farm
Hazel Street
LAMBERHURST ROAD
MAIDSTONE ROAD
B2162
GOUDHURST ROAD

HOTHFIELD

H J K L M N

29

Forstal Farm House
Little Chart Forstal
TN27
Coldham Wood
Oaks Wood
Coldham Alders
Great Stour
The Flookery
HOTHFIELD COMMON NATURE RESERVE
Hothfield Bogs
Foxenhill Toll
Picnic Site
Ash Court
Ripple Court
TN25
Ripple Cottage
Harven
MAIDSTONE ROAD
A20
WATERY LANE
Tollhill Wood
Orchard Cottage
Rooting Street Farm
Rooting Street
Cobb Cottage
Ashford
Hothfield Village Prim. Sch.
HOTHFIELD
Brownmill
Brownmill Bridge
Conyer Wood
Brownmill Spinney
WEST STREET
Turners
Rooting Alders
Hall Farm Cottages
Hall Farm
Mitchell Farm
Mitchell Plantation
Thanet Ter.
Hall
Park Lodge
Home Farm
PARK DR.
WATERFALL
Thanet House
Thanet Copse
TN26
The Larches
Egg Hole
Glebe Shaw
Fred's Spinney
Alder Beds
CHURCH LANE
THE STREET
Pump House
Waterfall
Alder Cotts
Alder House
Bert's Walk
Polla House
Mansion Copse
The Roundel
Ash Plantation
The Paddock
Paddocks Farm
Park Spinney
BETHERSDEN ROAD
GODINTON LANE
TN23

595 96 97 98
46 45 44

29 158 39

IWADE

18 19

Chetney Cottages
Willow Cottages
Willow Bank Ind. Est.
Marshbank
Raspberry Hill
RASPBERRY HILL LANE
Raspberry Hill Park
Speedway Training Track
OLD FERRY ROAD
SHEPPEY WAY
Sittingbourne
ME9
Ridham Cottage
Ridham Wall
Ridham
RIDHAM MARSHES
Warehouse
Fleet
Ridham Dock
Coldharbour Wall
Street Fm. Cotts.
Street Farm
Iwade Prim. Sch.
Church
SANDERLING
STANGATE
EVERGREEN CL.
MEADOW CL.
WOODPECKER
School Lane Farm
SCHOOL LANE
SPRINGVALE
Rec. Grd.
HELEN THOMPSON CL.
IWADE
COLESHALL COTTS.
MANSFIELD DR.
GROVEHURST
TEAL WY
PINTAIL
Coleshall
A249
COLDHARBOUR MARSHES
Coldharbour Fleet
Pond Farm
SHEPPEY WAY

H J K L M N

89 590 91 92
69 68 167

18 19 98 99

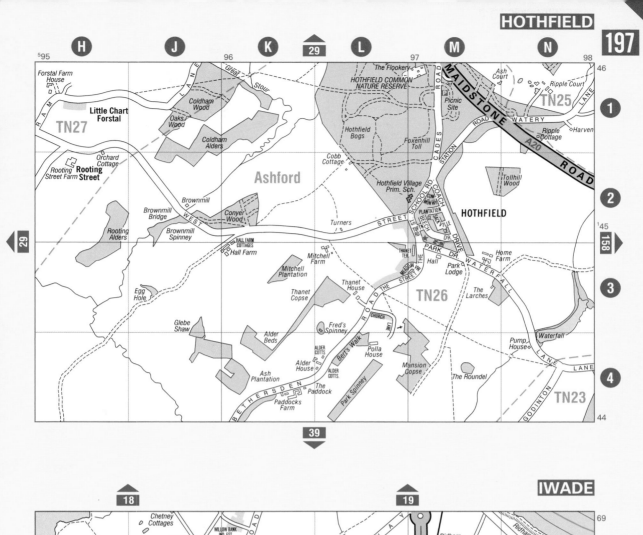

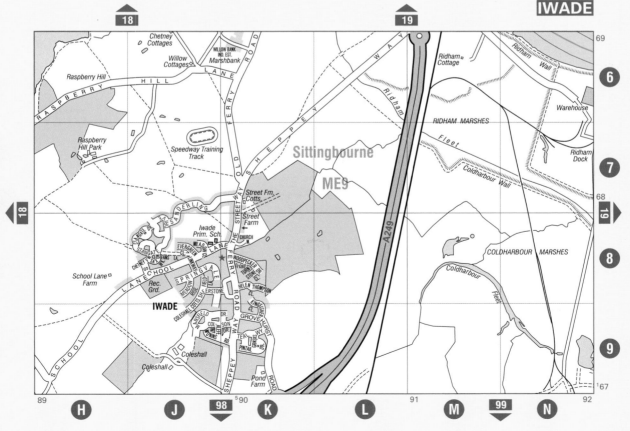

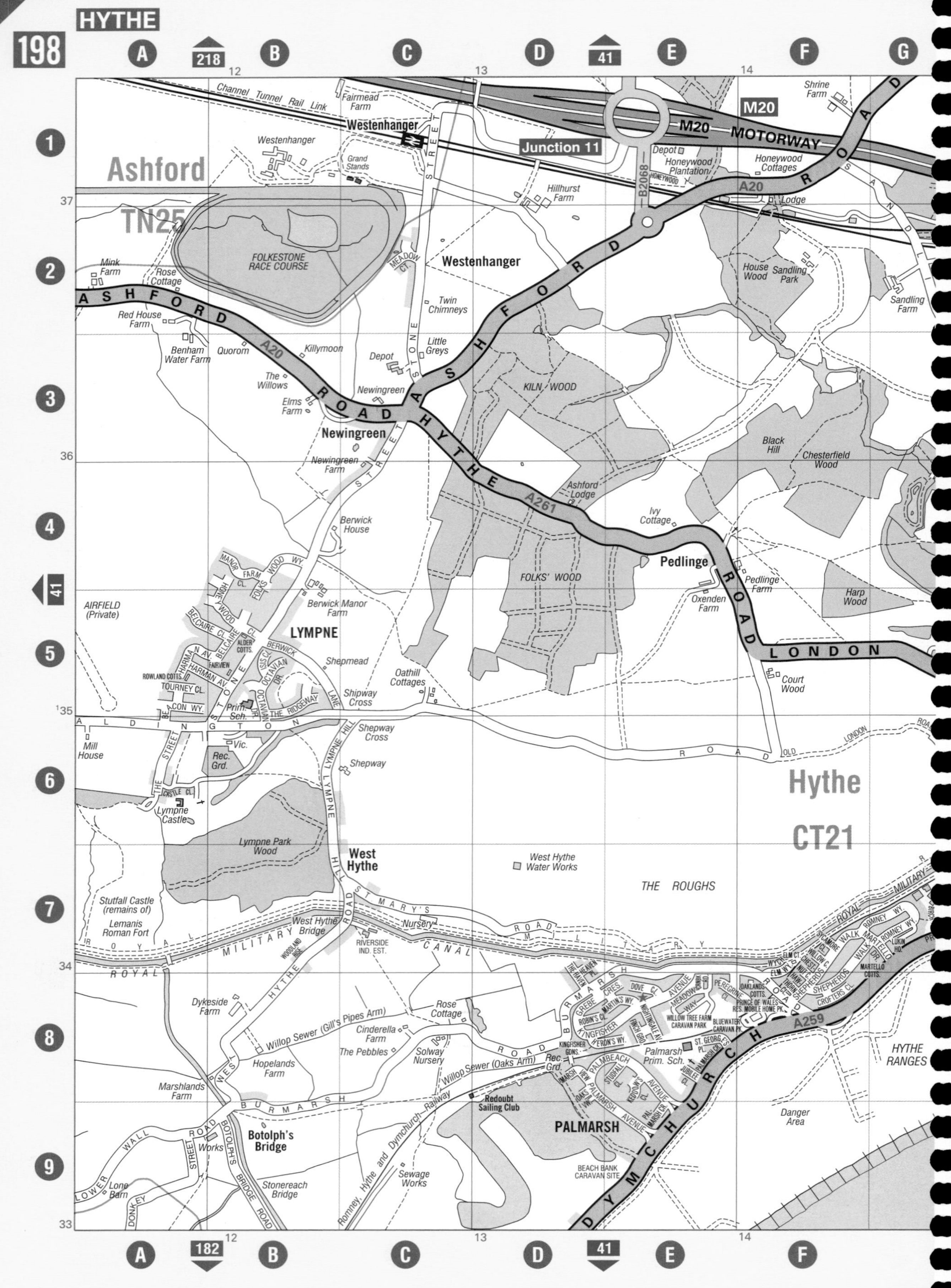

Channel Tunnel Rail Link
Fairmead Farm
Westenhanger
Grand Stands
Junction 11
M20
M20 MOTORWAY
Shrine Farm
Depot
Honeywood Plantation
Honeywood Cottages
Lodge
Hillhurst Farm
B2068
A20
Ashford
TN25
FOLKESTONE RACE COURSE
Mink Farm
Rose Cottage
Red House Farm
Benham Water Farm
Quorom
Killymoon
The Willows
Elms Farm
Depot
Newingreen
Twin Chimneys
Little Greys
MEADOW CT.
ASHFORD ROAD
HYTHE ROAD
A261
STONE STREET
KILN WOOD
House Wood
Sandling Park
Sandling Farm
SANDLING ROAD
Black Hill
Chesterfield Wood
Newingreen Farm
Ashford Lodge
Ivy Cottage
Berwick House
Pedlinge
Pedlinge Farm
Oxenden Farm
FOLKS' WOOD
Harp Wood
LONDON ROAD
Court Wood
AIRFIELD (Private)
MANOR FARM CL.
FOLKS WOOD WY.
Berwick Manor Farm
LYMPNE
BELCAIRE CL.
ALDER COTTS.
BERWICK
HARMAN AV.
ROWLAND COTTS.
TOURNEY CL.
BEACON WY.
Prim. Sch.
OCTAVIAN DR.
THE RIDGEWAY
Shepmead
Shipway Cross
Oathill Cottages
ALDINGTON ROAD
Mill House
Vic.
Rec. Grd.
Shepway Cross
Shepway
LYMPNE HILL
OLD LONDON ROAD
Hythe
CT21
CASTLE CL.
Lympne Castle
Lympne Park Wood
West Hythe
West Hythe Water Works
THE ROUGHS
Stutfall Castle (remains of)
Lemanis Roman Fort
ST MARY'S ROAD
Nursery
West Hythe Bridge
RIVERSIDE IND. EST.
WOODLAND RISE
ROYAL MILITARY CANAL
ROYAL MILITARY ROAD
Dykeside Farm
Rose Cottage
Willop Sewer (Gill's Pipes Arm)
Cinderella Farm
The Pebbles
Solway Nursery
Hopelands Farm
Willop Sewer (Oaks Arm)
Marshlands Farm
BURMARSH ROAD
Redoubt Sailing Club
Rec. Grd.
KINGFISHER GDNS.
PALMBEACH AVENUE
Palmarsh Prim. Sch.
ST. GEORGES PL.
JUBILEE
PALMARSH
BEACH BANK CARAVAN SITE
WILLOW TREE FARM CARAVAN PARK
BLUEWATER CARAVAN PK.
PRINCE OF WALES RES. MOBILE HOME PK.
OAKLANDS COTTS.
PEREGRINE CL.
DOVE CL.
GREBE CRES.
MEADOW WAY
A259
DYMCHURCH ROAD
ROMNEY WY.
MARTELLO DR.
LUKIN HO.
MARTELLO COTTS.
SHEPHERDS WALK
CROFTERS CL.
HYTHE RANGES
Danger Area
Botolph's Bridge
Works
WEST HYTHE ROAD
LOWER WALL ROAD
STREET ROAD
BOTOLPH'S BRIDGE ROAD
DONKEY
Lone Barn
Stonereach Bridge
Romney, Hythe and Dymchurch Railway
Sewage Works
A B C D E F G
1 2 3 4 5 6 7 8 9
12 13 14
37 36 35 34 33
218 41 182

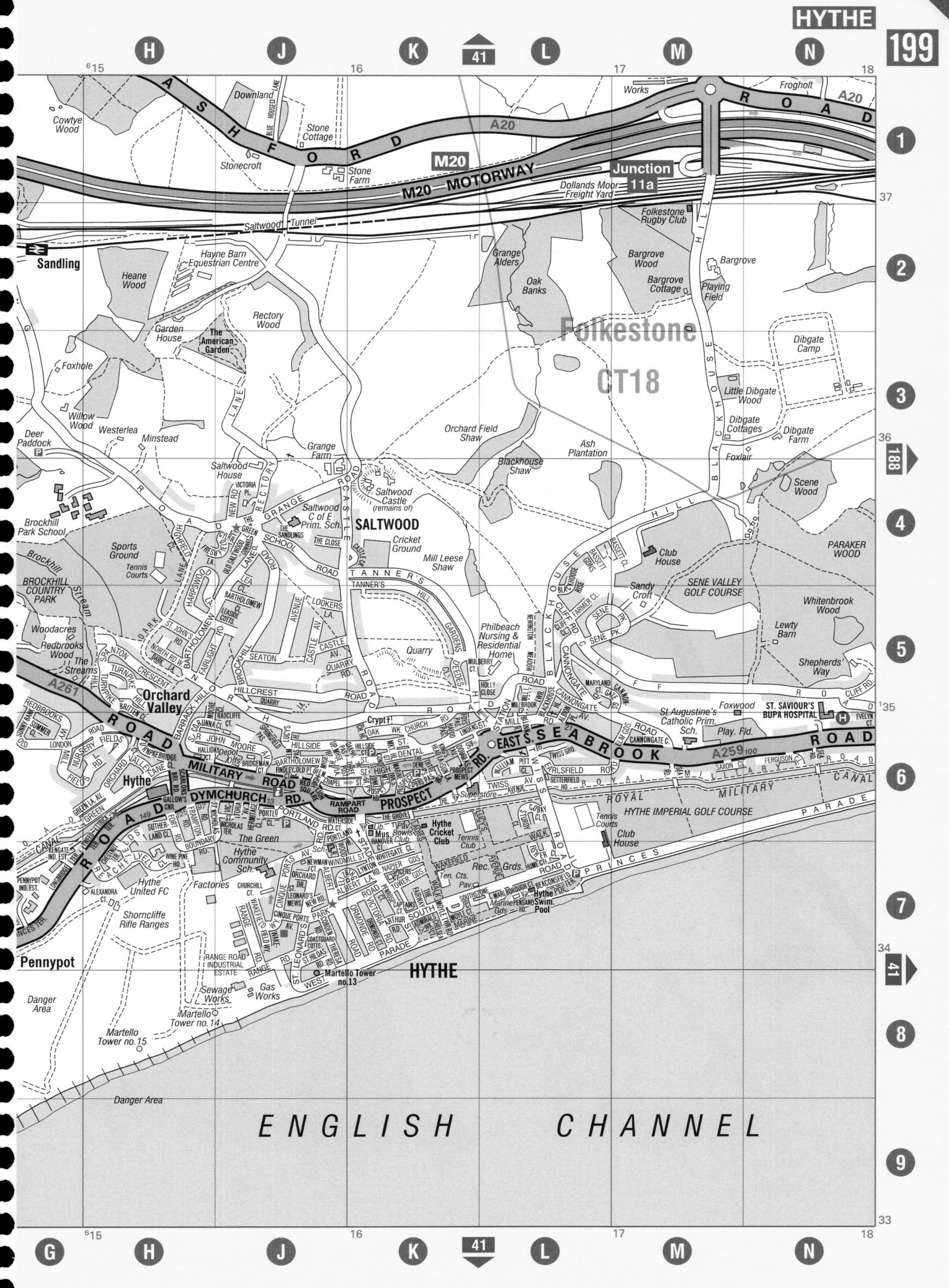
ASHFORD ROAD
A20
M20 MOTORWAY
Junction 11a
Dollands Moor Freight Yard
Saltwood Tunnel
Sandling
Folkestone
CT18
SALTWOOD
Saltwood Castle (remains of)
Orchard Valley
Hythe
SEABROOK ROAD
A259
A261
MILITARY ROAD
DYMCHURCH RD.
PROSPECT RD.
ROYAL MILITARY CANAL
HYTHE IMPERIAL GOLF COURSE
SENE VALLEY GOLF COURSE
PRINCES PARADE
HYTHE
Pennypot
Martello Tower no.13
Martello Tower no.14
Martello Tower no.15
Danger Area
ENGLISH CHANNEL
188
41

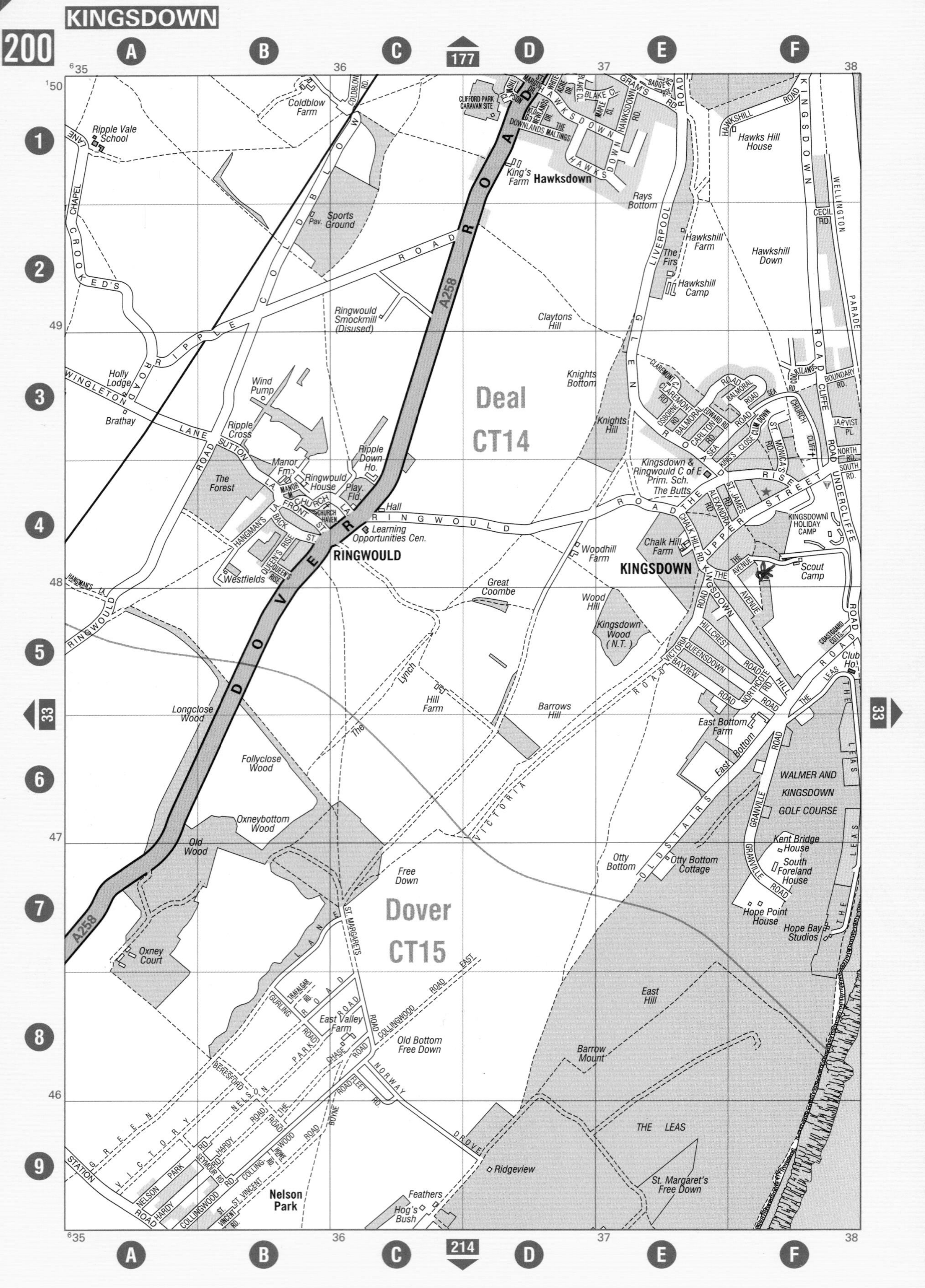
Deal CT14
Dover CT15
KINGSDOWN
RINGWOULD
Hawksdown
Nelson Park
Ripple Vale School
Coldblow Farm
Sports Ground
Ringwould Smockmill (Disused)
Holly Lodge
Brathay
Wind Pump
Ripple Cross
Manor Fm.
Ringwould House
The Forest
Ripple Down Ho.
Play. Fld.
Hall
Learning Opportunities Cen.
Westfields
King's Farm
Rays Bottom
The Firs
Hawkshill Farm
Hawkshill Camp
Hawks Hill House
Hawkshill Down
Claytons Hill
Knights Bottom
Knights Hill
Kingsdown & Ringwould C of E Prim. Sch.
The Butts
Chalk Hill Farm
Woodhill Farm
Great Coombe
Wood Hill
Kingsdown Wood (N.T.)
Kingsdown Holiday Camp
Scout Camp
Club Ho.
East Bottom Farm
Walmer and Kingsdown Golf Course
Kent Bridge House
South Foreland House
Hope Point House
Hope Bay Studios
Otty Bottom
Otty Bottom Cottage
Barrows Hill
Hill Farm
Longclose Wood
Follyclose Wood
Oxneybottom Wood
Old Wood
Free Down
Oxney Court
East Valley Farm
Old Bottom Free Down
East Hill
Barrow Mount
The Leas
St. Margaret's Free Down
Ridgeview
Feathers
Hog's Bush
Dover Road
A258
Ringwould Road
Ripple Road
Coldblow
Liverpool Road
Glen Road
Kingsdown Road
Upper Street
Victoria Road
Oldstairs Road
Granville Road
Victory Road
Green Lane
Station Road
Collingwood Road East
Norway Drove
St. Margarets Road
Clifford Park Caravan Site
Downlands
The Maltings
Hawksdown
Wingleton Lane
Crooked's Road
Chapel Lane
Sutton Lane
Hangman's Lane
Queen's Rise
Back St
Front St
Church Haven
Claremont Rd.
Osborne Rd.
Balmoral Rd.
Edward Rd.
Carlton Rd.
Sea Road
King's Close
Clim Down
St. Monica's Rd.
Church Cliff
Cliffe Road
Undercliffe Road
Jarvist Pl.
Boundary Rd.
Wellington Parade
Cecil Rd.
Alexandra Rd.
St. James Rd.
The Rise
Chalk Hill Rd.
The Avenue
Hillcrest
Queensdown Road
Bayview Road
Northcote Rd.
Coastguard Cotts.
The Leas
East Bottom
Trafalgar Rd.
Gurling Road
East Road
Chase
Nelson Park Road
Beresford
Hardy Rd.
Seymour Rd.
Colling-wood Rd.
Howe Rd.
Boyne Road
Fleet Rd.
St. Vincent Rd.
Collingwood
35
36
37
38
50
49
48
47
46
A B C D E F
1 2 3 4 5 6 7 8 9
177
214
33

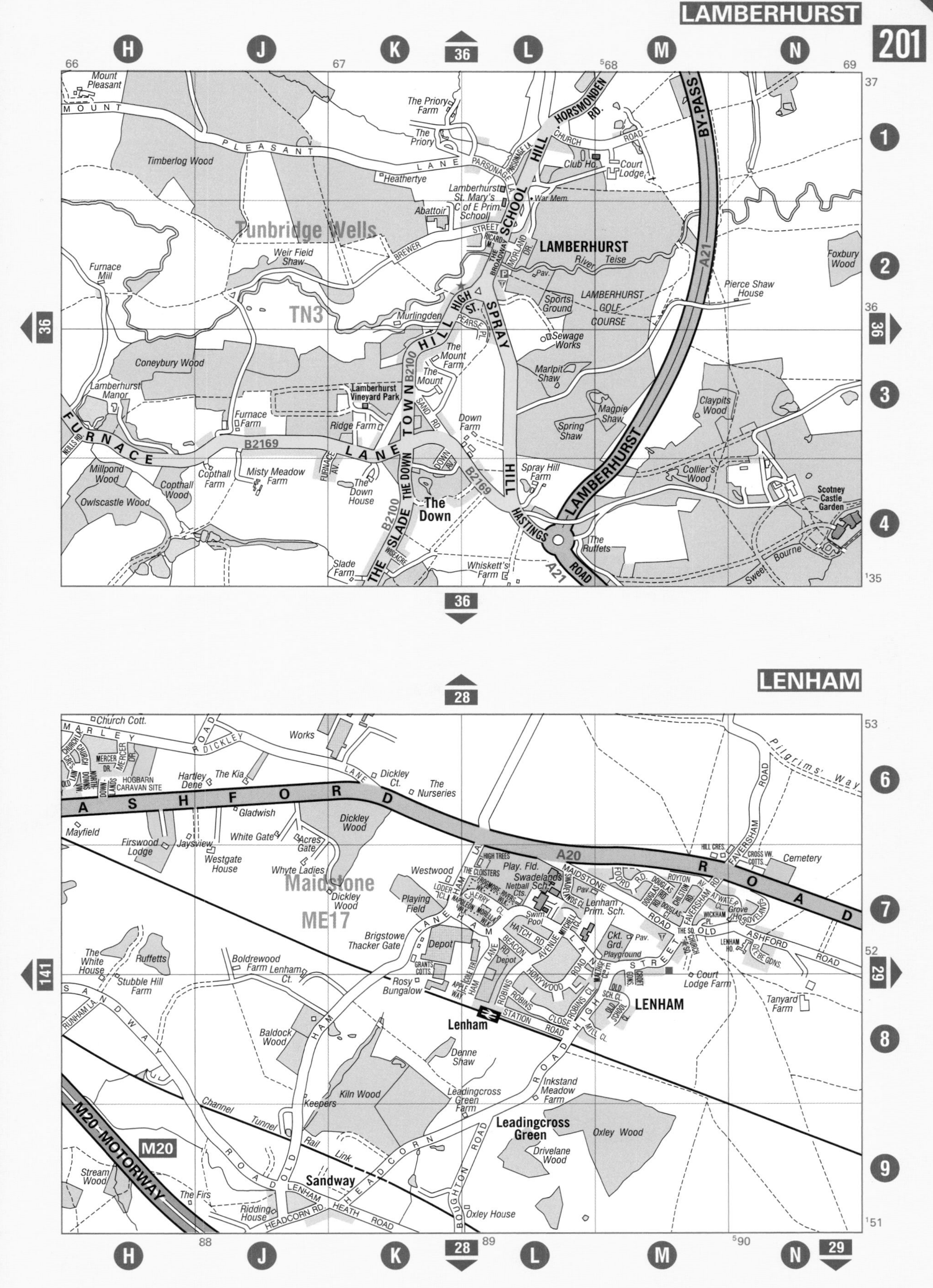
LAMBERHURST
Mount Pleasant
The Priory Farm
The Priory
Timberlog Wood
Heathertye
Lamberhurst St. Mary's C of E Prim. School
Abattoir
Tunbridge Wells
Weir Field Shaw
Furnace Mill
TN3
Murlingden
Club Ho.
Court Lodge
War Mem.
LAMBERHURST
River Teise
LAMBERHURST GOLF COURSE
Sports Ground
Sewage Works
Pierce Shaw House
Foxbury Wood
Coneybury Wood
Lamberhurst Manor
Lamberhurst Vineyard Park
The Mount Farm
The Mount
Marlpit Shaw
Magpie Shaw
Spring Shaw
Claypits Wood
Furnace Farm
Ridge Farm
Down Farm
Millpond Wood
Copthall Farm
Misty Meadow Farm
Copthall Wood
Owlscastle Wood
The Down House
The Down
Spray Hill Farm
Collier's Wood
Scotney Castle Garden
The Ruffets
Slade Farm
Whiskett's Farm
Sweet Bourne
A21
B2100
B2169
LENHAM
Church Cott.
Works
Hartley Dene
The Kia
Dickley Ct.
The Nurseries
HOGBARN CARAVAN SITE
Gladwish
Mayfield
Firswood Lodge
Jaysview
White Gate
Acres Gate
Dickley Wood
Westgate House
Whyte Ladies
Maidstone
Dickley Wood
ME17
Westwood
Playing Field
Play. Fld.
Swadelands Sch.
Lenham Prim. Sch.
Swim. Pool
Ckt. Grd.
Playground
Depot
Brigstowe
Thacker Gate
Cemetery
A20
The White House
Ruffetts
Boldrewood Farm
Lenham Ct.
Stubble Hill Farm
Rosy Bungalow
Court Lodge Farm
Tanyard Farm
Lenham
LENHAM
Baldock Wood
Denne Shaw
Kiln Wood
Keepers
Leadingcross Green Farm
Inkstand Meadow Farm
Leadingcross Green
Oxley Wood
Drivelane Wood
Channel Tunnel Rail Link
M20
M20-MOTORWAY
Stream Wood
Sandway
The Firs
Ridding House
Oxley House

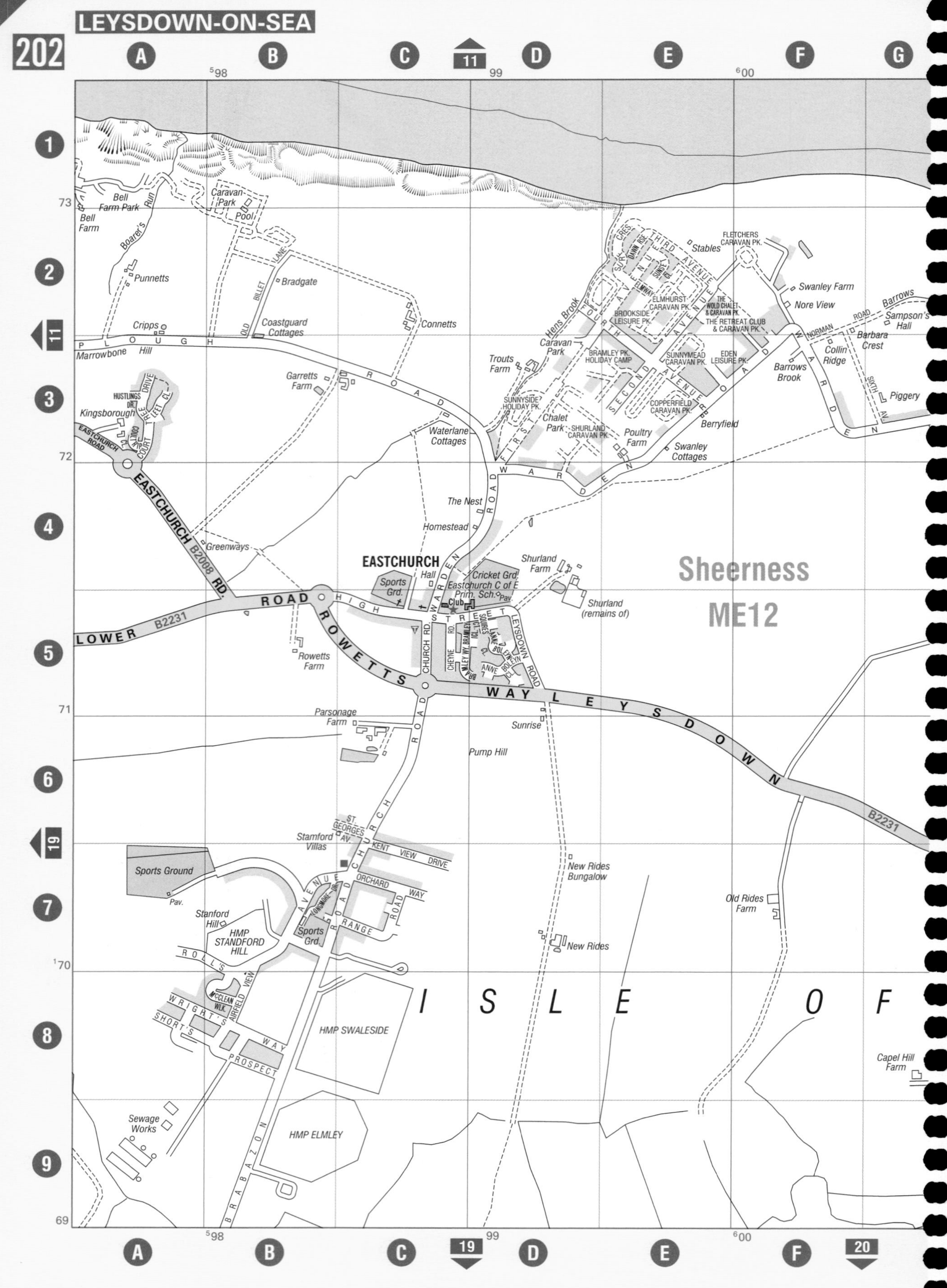
Bell Farm Park
Bell Farm
Boarer's Run
Caravan Park
Pool
Punnetts
Bradgate
Billet Lane
Cripps
Coastguard Cottages
Connetts
Plough
Marrowbone Hill
Road
Garretts Farm
Hustlings Dr.
Kingsborough
Tree Court
Eastchurch Road
Waterlane Cottages
Eastchurch B2008 Rd.
Greenways
The Nest
Homestead
EASTCHURCH
Sports Grd.
Hall
Cricket Grd.
Eastchurch C of E Prim. Sch.
Club
Pav.
Lower B2231 Road
High Street
Rowetts Way
Rowetts Farm
Church Rd.
Cheyne Rd.
Leysdown Road
Shurland Farm
Shurland (remains of)
Sheerness
ME12
Hens Brook
Stables
Fletchers Caravan Pk.
Third Avenue
Swanley Farm
Nore View
Elmhurst Caravan Pk.
Brookside Leisure Pk.
The Wold Chalet & Caravan Pk.
The Retreat Club & Caravan Pk.
Caravan Park
Trouts Farm
Bramley Pk. Holiday Camp
Sunnymead Caravan Pk.
Eden Leisure Pk.
Second Avenue
Copperfield Caravan Pk.
Sunnyside Holiday Pk.
Chalet Park
Shurland Caravan Pk.
First Avenue
Poultry Farm
Berryfield
Swanley Cottages
Warden Road
Barrows Brook
Norman Road
Barrows
Sampson's Hall
Barbara Crest
Collin Ridge
Sixth Av.
Piggery
Warden
Parsonage Farm
Sunrise
Leysdown
Pump Hill
B2231
St. Georges Av.
Stamford Villas
Kent View Drive
Church Road
Sports Ground
Pav.
Orchard Way
Stanford Hill
HMP Standford Hill
Range Road
Sports Grd.
Rolls
New Rides Bungalow
New Rides
Old Rides Farm
McClean Wlk.
Airfield View
Wright's Way
Short's Prospect
HMP SWALESIDE
ISLE OF
Capel Hill Farm
Sewage Works
HMP ELMLEY
Brabazon

11
19
20

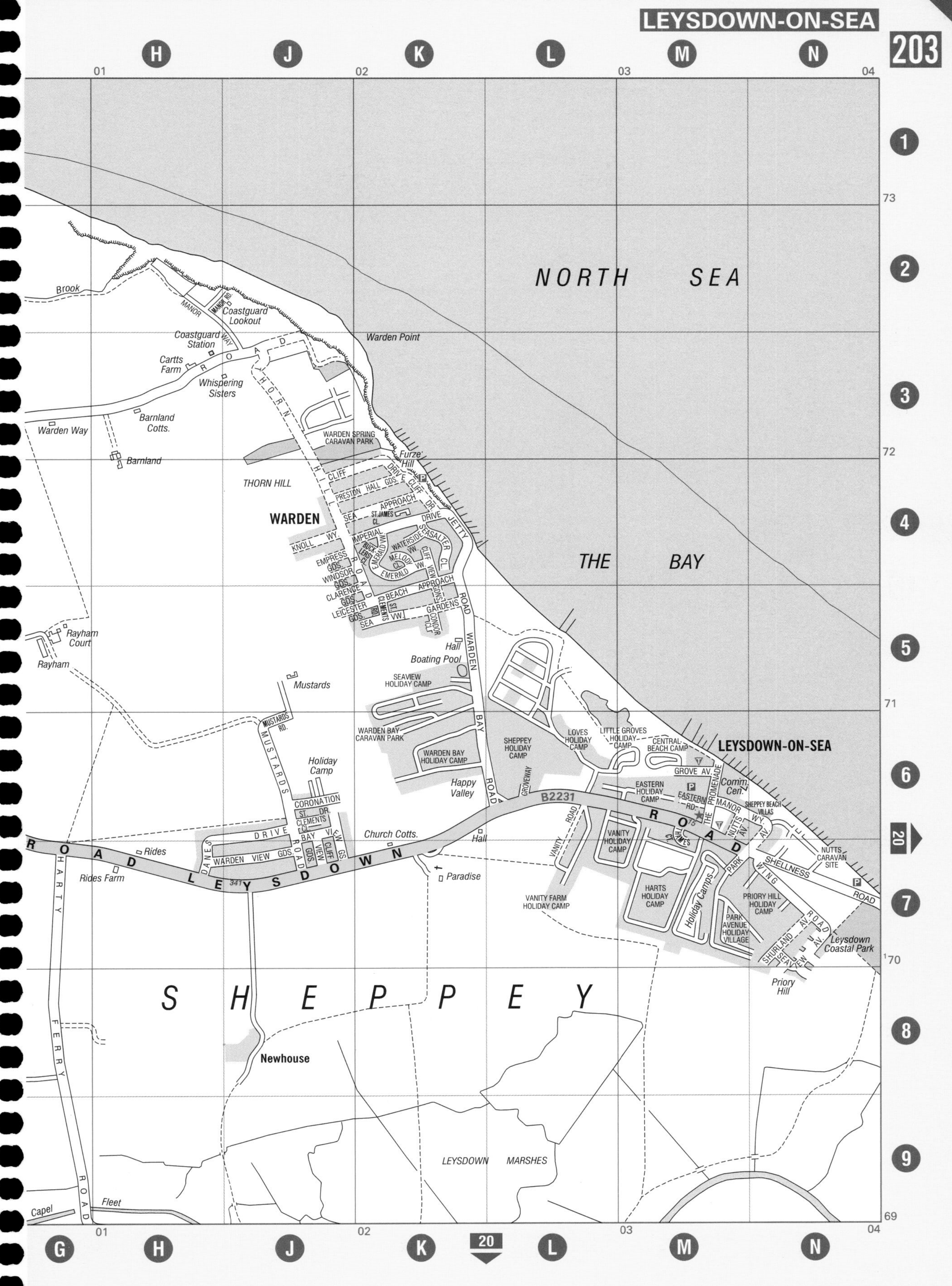

NORTH SEA

THE BAY

WARDEN

LEYSDOWN-ON-SEA

SHEPPEY

Brook

Coastguard Lookout
Coastguard Station
Cartts Farm
Whispering Sisters
Warden Point
Warden Way
Barnland Cotts.
Barnland

WARDEN SPRING CARAVAN PARK
Furze Hill
THORN HILL
CLIFF
PRESTON HALL GDS.
SEA WY.
ST. JAMES CL.
APPROACH
DRIVE
IMPERIAL
EMERALD GDS.
EMPRESS GDS.
WINDSOR GDS.
CLARENCE GDS.
LEICESTER GDS.
KNOLL WY.
MELDA VW.
EMERALD
CLIFF VIEW
CASALTER CL.
WATERSIDE
SEA VW.
CLEMENTS VW.
CLEMENTS RD.
BEACH GARDENS
CONOR PL.
CLIFF APPROACH
JETTY
WARDEN BAY ROAD

Rayham Court
Rayham

Mustards

Hall
Boating Pool
SEAVIEW HOLIDAY CAMP
WARDEN BAY CARAVAN PARK
WARDEN BAY HOLIDAY CAMP
Happy Valley

MUSTARDS RD.
Holiday Camp
CORONATION DR.
ST. CLEMENTS CL.
Church Cotts.
Hall
Paradise

SHEPPEY HOLIDAY CAMP
LOVES HOLIDAY CAMP
LITTLE GROVES HOLIDAY CAMP
CENTRAL BEACH CAMP
GROVE AV.
Comm. Cen.
EASTERN HOLIDAY CAMP
EASTERN RD.
THE PROMENADE
THE MANOR
Sheppey Beach Villas
B2231
GROVEWAY
VANITY ROAD
ST. JAMES
NUTTS AV.
SHELLNESS
NUTTS CARAVAN SITE
VANITY HOLIDAY CAMP
HARTS HOLIDAY CAMP
PARK AVENUE HOLIDAY VILLAGE
PRIORY HILL HOLIDAY CAMP
VANITY FARM HOLIDAY CAMP
Holiday Camps
SHURLAND AV.
SEAVIEW AV.
Priory Hill
Leysdown Coastal Park

ROAD
LEYSDOWN
WARDEN VIEW GDS.
DANES ROAD
BAY VW. GDS.
CLIFF VW. GDS.
341
DRIVE
Rides
Rides Farm
HARTY
FERRY ROAD

Newhouse

Capel
Fleet
LEYSDOWN MARSHES

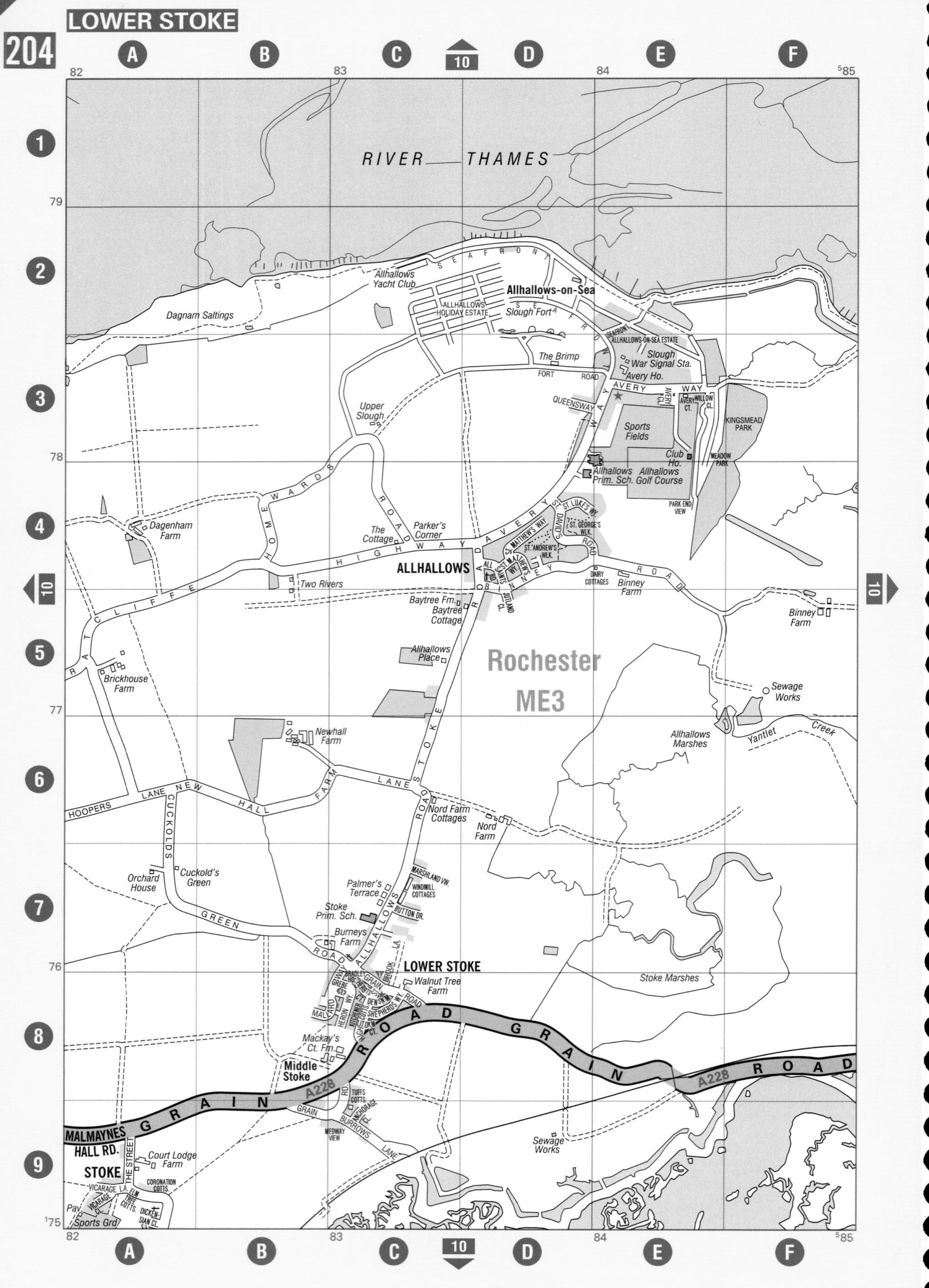

RIVER — THAMES

Allhallows Yacht Club

Dagnam Saltings

ALLHALLOWS HOLIDAY ESTATE

Allhallows-on-Sea

Slough Fort

The Brimp

Slough War Signal Sta.

Avery Ho.

ALLHALLOWS-ON-SEA ESTATE

AVERY

QUEENSWAY

Sports Fields

KINGSMEAD PARK

MEADOW PARK

Upper Slough

Club Ho.

Allhallows Prim. Sch.

Allhallows Golf Course

PARK END VIEW

Dagenham Farm

The Cottage

Parker's Corner

St. LUKE'S WY

St. DAVID'S

MATTHEW'S WAY

St. GEORGE'S WLK.

St. ANDREW'S WLK.

ALLHALLOWS

Two Rivers

Baytree Fm.

Baytree Cottage

DAIRY COTTAGES

Binney Farm

Rochester
ME3

Allhallows Place

Binney Farm

Brickhouse Farm

Newhall Farm

Allhallows Marshes

Yantlet Creek

Sewage Works

HOOPERS LANE

NEW HALL

CUCKOLDS GREEN

Orchard House

Cuckold's Green

Nord Farm Cottages

Nord Farm

Palmer's Terrace

MARSHLAND VW.

WINDMILL COTTAGES

BUTTON DR.

Stoke Prim. Sch.

Burneys Farm

BRICK LA.

LOWER STOKE

Walnut Tree Farm

Stoke Marshes

BRADLEY GRAIN

GREBE WY

DENS WY

SHEPHERDS WY

Mackay's Ct. Fm.

Middle Stoke

GRAIN ROAD

A228 ROAD

GRAIN

A228

RD

TUFFS COTTS

BURROWS

Sewage Works

MEDWAY VIEW

GRAIN LANE

MALMAYNES HALL RD.

THE STREET

Court Lodge Farm

STOKE

VICARAGE LA.

ELM

CORONATION COTTS

DICKEN SIAN CL.

Pav.

Sports Grd.

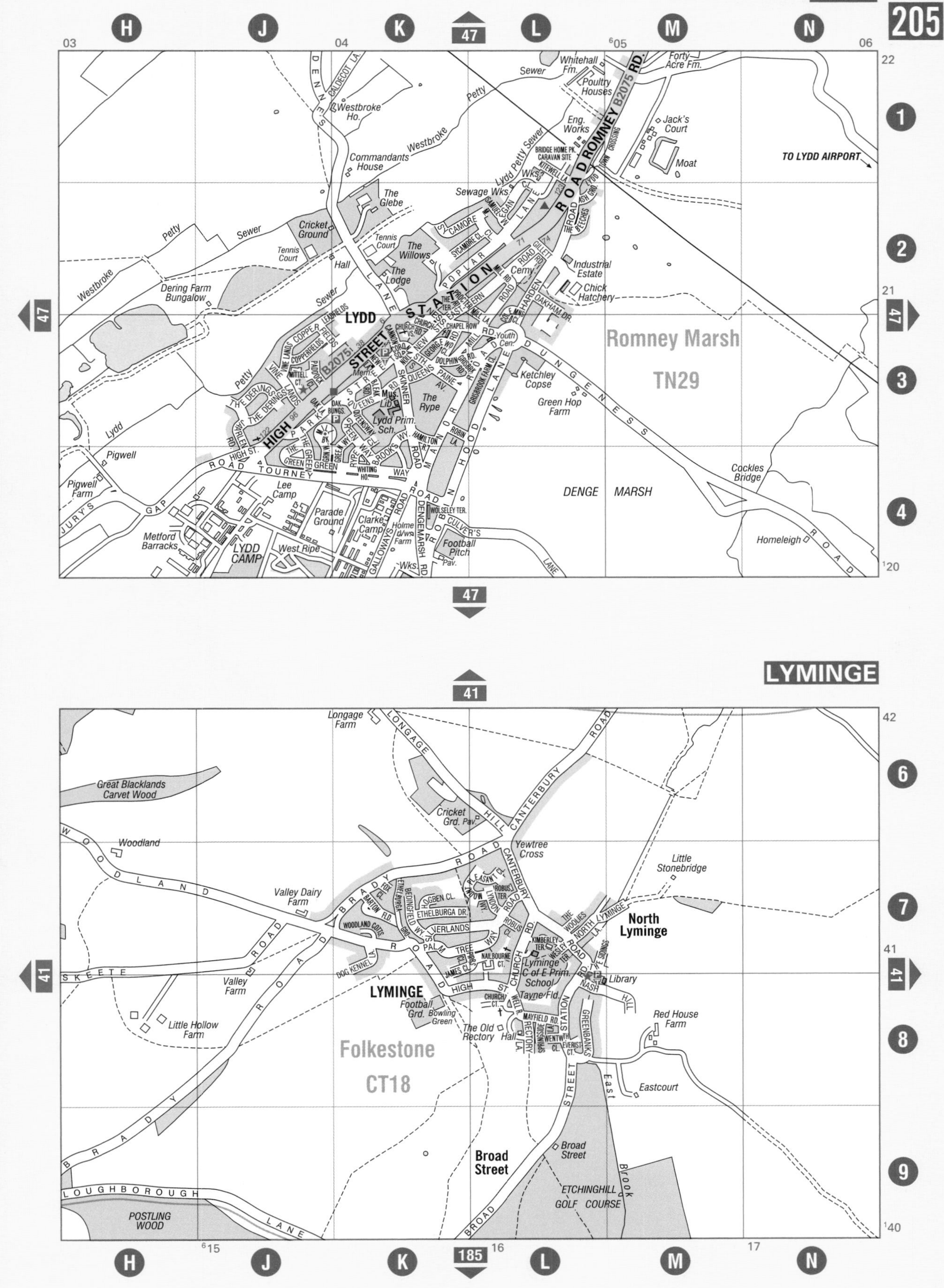
LYDD
Romney Marsh
TN29
DENGE MARSH
TO LYDD AIRPORT
Westbroke Ho.
Commandants House
The Glebe
Cricket Ground
The Willows
The Lodge
Dering Farm Bungalow
Pigwell Farm
Lee Camp
Parade Ground
Clarke Camp
Metford Barracks
LYDD CAMP
West Ripe
Football Pitch
Ketchley Copse
Green Hop Farm
Industrial Estate
Chick Hatchery
Cockles Bridge
Homeleigh
Jack's Court
Moat
Whitehall Fm.
Forty Acre Fm.
Poultry Houses
Eng. Works
Sewage Wks.
The Rype
Lydd Prim. Sch.
HIGH STREET
STATION ROAD
ROMNEY ROAD
DUNGENESS ROAD
TOURNEY ROAD
JURY'S GAP ROAD
LYMINGE
Folkestone
CT18
North Lyminge
LYMINGE
Broad Street
Longage Farm
Great Blacklands Carvet Wood
Cricket Grd.
Woodland
Valley Dairy Farm
Valley Farm
Little Hollow Farm
Yewtree Cross
Little Stonebridge
Lyminge C of E Prim. School
Tayne Fld.
Library
Red House Farm
The Old Rectory
Football Grd.
Eastcourt
ETCHINGHILL GOLF COURSE
POSTLING WOOD
WOODLAND ROAD
SKEETE ROAD
BRADY ROAD
CANTERBURY ROAD
LOUGHBOROUGH LANE
STATION ROAD
BROAD STREET

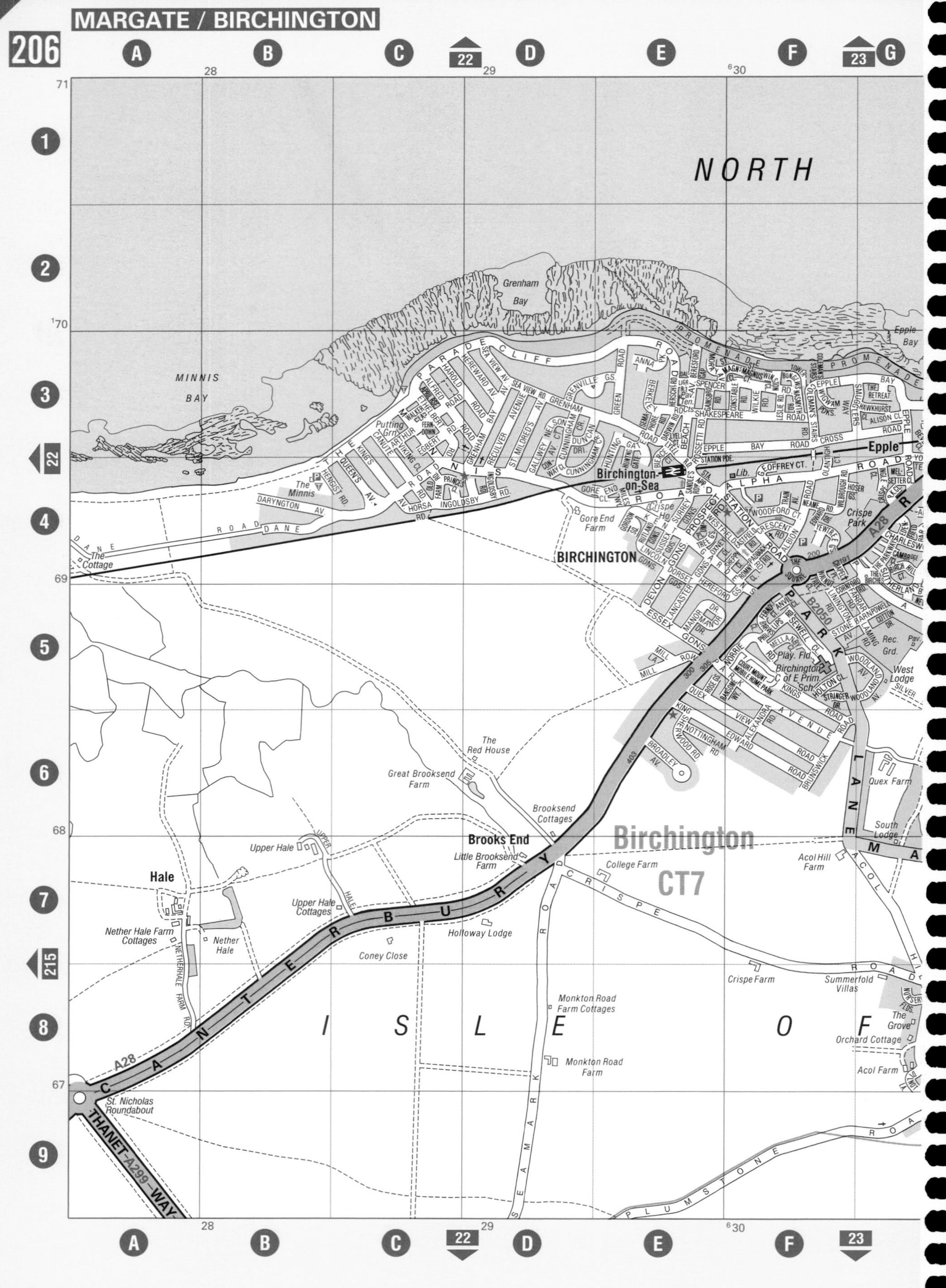
A
B
C
22
D
E
F
23
G
1
2
3
4
5
6
7
8
9
NORTH
Grenham Bay
MINNIS BAY
Epple Bay
PROMENADE
PARADE
CLIFF ROAD
Putting Grn
The Minnis
DARYNGTON AV.
DANE ROAD
The Cottage
Epple
Birchington-on-Sea
Lib.
ALPHA ROAD
Gore End Farm
Crispe Ho.
BIRCHINGTON
STATION ROAD
PARK LANE
B2050
Crispe Park
A28
Rec. Grd.
West Lodge
Play. Fld.
Birchington C of E Prim. Sch.
MILL ROW
The Red House
Great Brooksend Farm
Brooksend Cottages
Brooks End
Little Brooksend Farm
Upper Hale
Hale
Upper Hale Cottages
Nether Hale Farm Cottages
Nether Hale
NETHERHALE FARM RD.
Birchington
CT7
College Farm
CRISPE ROAD
Holloway Lodge
Coney Close
CANTERBURY ROAD
Quex Farm
South Lodge
Acol Hill Farm
Crispe Farm
Summerfold Villas
Monkton Road Farm Cottages
Monkton Road Farm
SEAMARK ROAD
ISLE OF
The Grove
Orchard Cottage
Acol Farm
St. Nicholas Roundabout
THANET WAY A299
PLUMSTONE ROAD
215
28
29
30
67
68
69
70
71

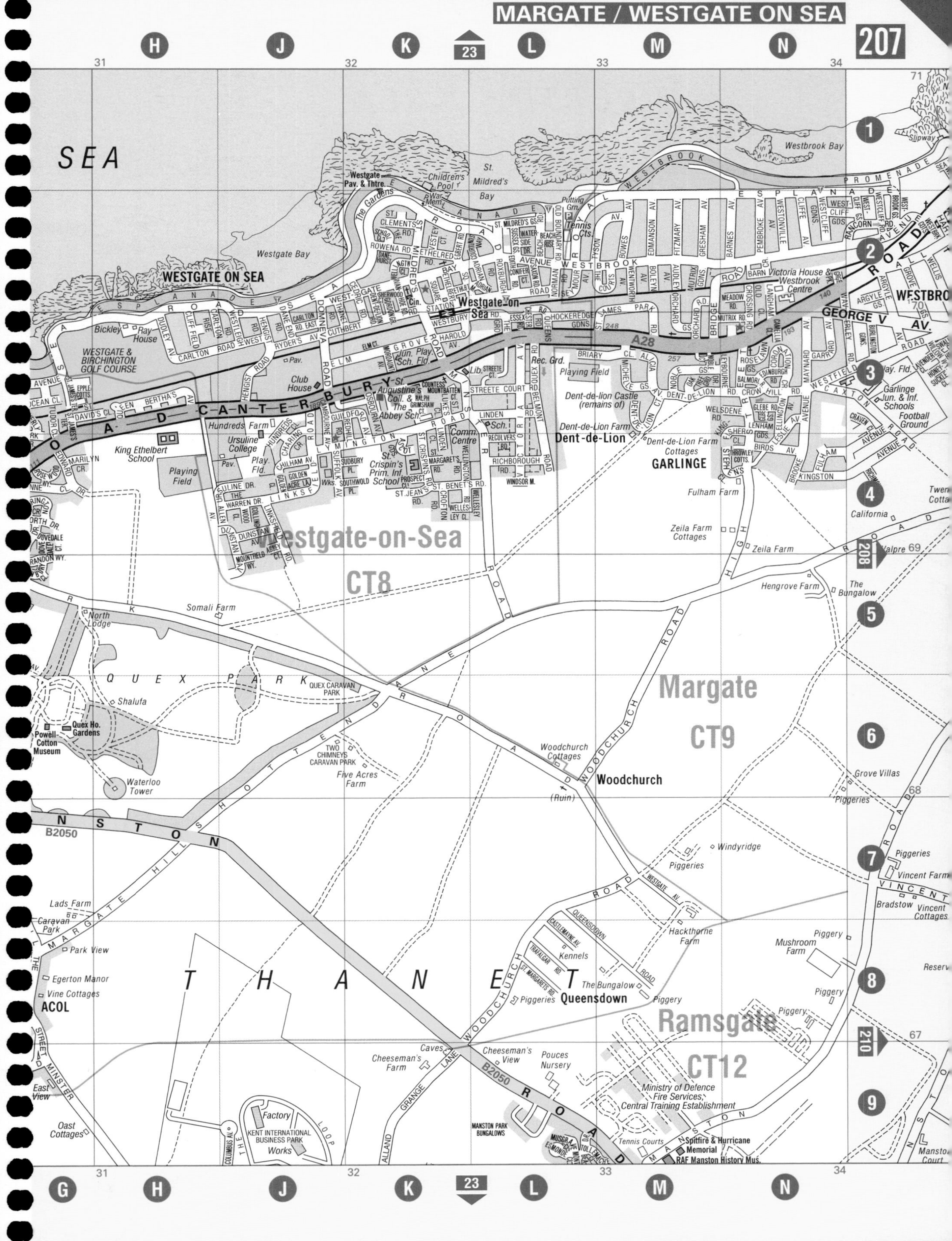
SEA
Westgate Bay
WESTGATE ON SEA
St. Mildred's Bay
Westbrook Bay
Westgate-on-Sea
CT8
QUEX PARK
Margate
CT9
Woodchurch
Dent-de-Lion
GARLINGE
THANET
Queensdown
Ramsgate
CT12
ACOL
WESTGATE & BIRCHINGTON GOLF COURSE
King Ethelbert School
Ursuline College
Westgate Pav. & Thtre.
Powell-Cotton Museum
Quex Ho. Gardens
Waterloo Tower
KENT INTERNATIONAL BUSINESS PARK
Ministry of Defence Fire Services, Central Training Establishment
Spitfire & Hurricane Memorial
RAF Manston History Mus.
A28
B2050
CANTERBURY ROAD
MANSTON ROAD
WOODCHURCH ROAD
George V Av.
208
210
23

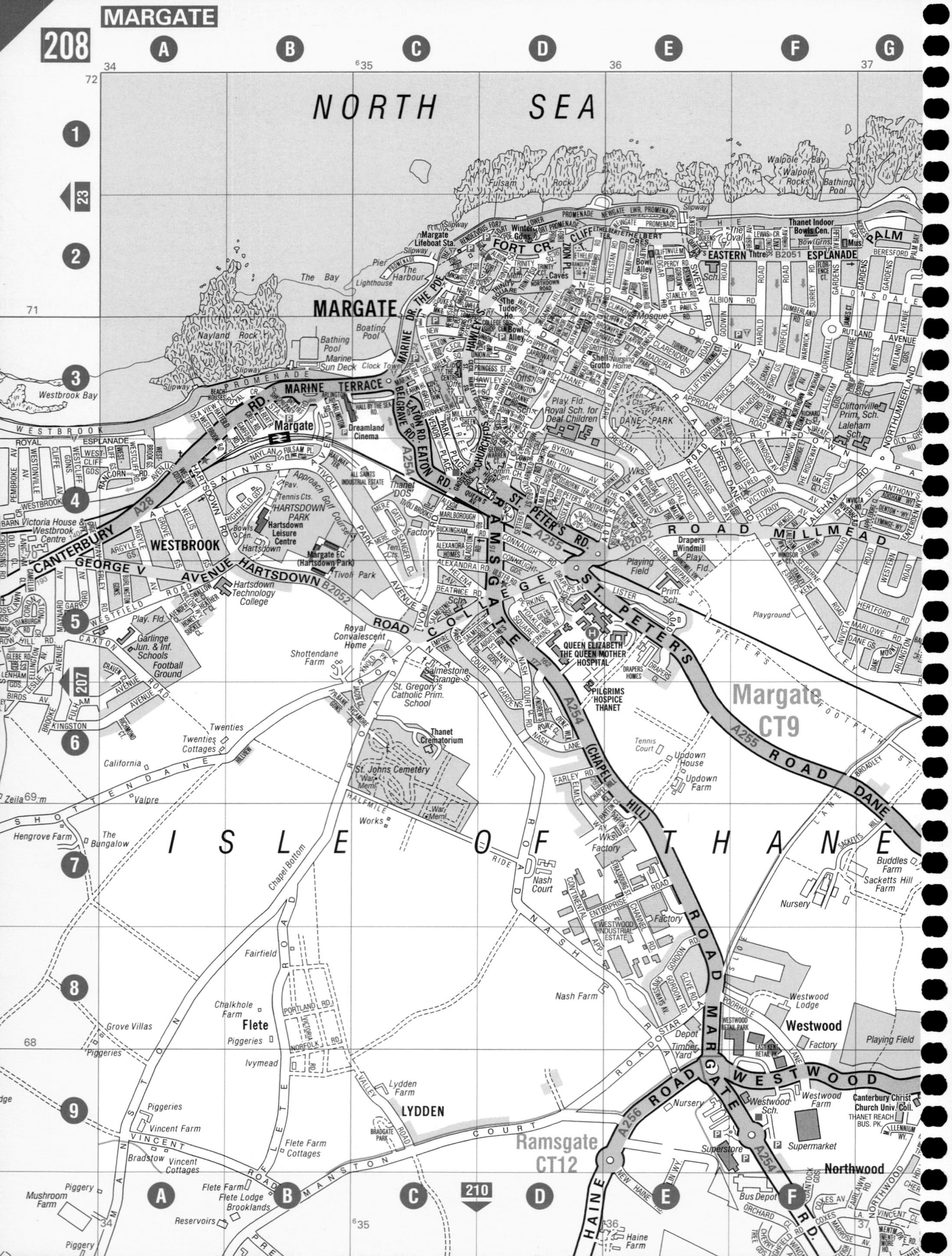
NORTH SEA
MARGATE
WESTBROOK
ISLE OF THANET
Margate CT9
Ramsgate CT12
Westbrook Bay
Nayland Rock
The Bay
Fulsam Rock
Walpole Bay
Walpole Rocks
Bathing Pool
Boating Pool
Marine Sun Deck
Clock Tower
Margate Lifeboat Sta.
The Harbour
Lighthouse
Pier
Winter Gdns.
Dreamland Cinema
Shell Grotto
Royal Sch. for Deaf Children
DANE PARK
Hartsdown Park
Hartsdown Leisure Centre
Margate FC (Hartsdown Park)
Tivoli Park
Hartsdown Technology College
Garlinge Jun. & Inf. Schools
Football Ground
Victoria House & Westbrook Centre
Royal Convalescent Home
Shottendane Farm
Salmestone Grange
St. Gregory's Catholic Prim. School
Thanet Crematorium
St. Johns Cemetery
QUEEN ELIZABETH THE QUEEN MOTHER HOSPITAL
PILGRIMS HOSPICE THANET
Drapers Windmill
Playing Field
Cliftonville Prim. Sch.
Laleham Sch.
Thanet Indoor Bowls Cen.
Updown House
Updown Farm
Buddles Farm
Sacketts Hill Farm
Nash Court
Westwood Industrial Estate
Nash Farm
Westwood
Westwood Lodge
Westwood Farm
Canterbury Christ Church Univ. Coll.
Thanet Reach Bus. Pk.
Supermarket
Superstore
Northwood
Bus Depot
Haine Farm
Flete
LYDDEN
Lydden Farm
Fairfield
Chalkhole Farm
Grove Villas
Ivymead
Piggeries
Vincent Farm
Bradstow
Vincent Cottages
Flete Farm Cottages
Flete Farm
Flete Lodge
Brooklands
Reservoirs
Mushroom Farm
Piggery
Twenties Cottages
California
Valpre
Zeila
Hengrove Farm
The Bungalow
CANTERBURY RD.
GEORGE V AVENUE
HARTSDOWN AVENUE
MARINE TERRACE
ROYAL ESPLANADE
EASTERN ESPLANADE
FORT CR.
RAMSGATE ROAD
COLLEGE ROAD
ST. PETER'S RD.
ST. PETER'S ROAD
DANE ROAD
MILLMEAD ROAD
MARGATE ROAD
WESTWOOD ROAD
MANSTON ROAD
MANSTON COURT ROAD
SHOTTENDANE ROAD
VINCENT ROAD
NASH ROAD
A28
A254
A255
A256
B2052
B2051
A B C D E F G
1 2 3 4 5 6 7 8 9
34 35 36 37
68 69 70 71 72
23
207
210

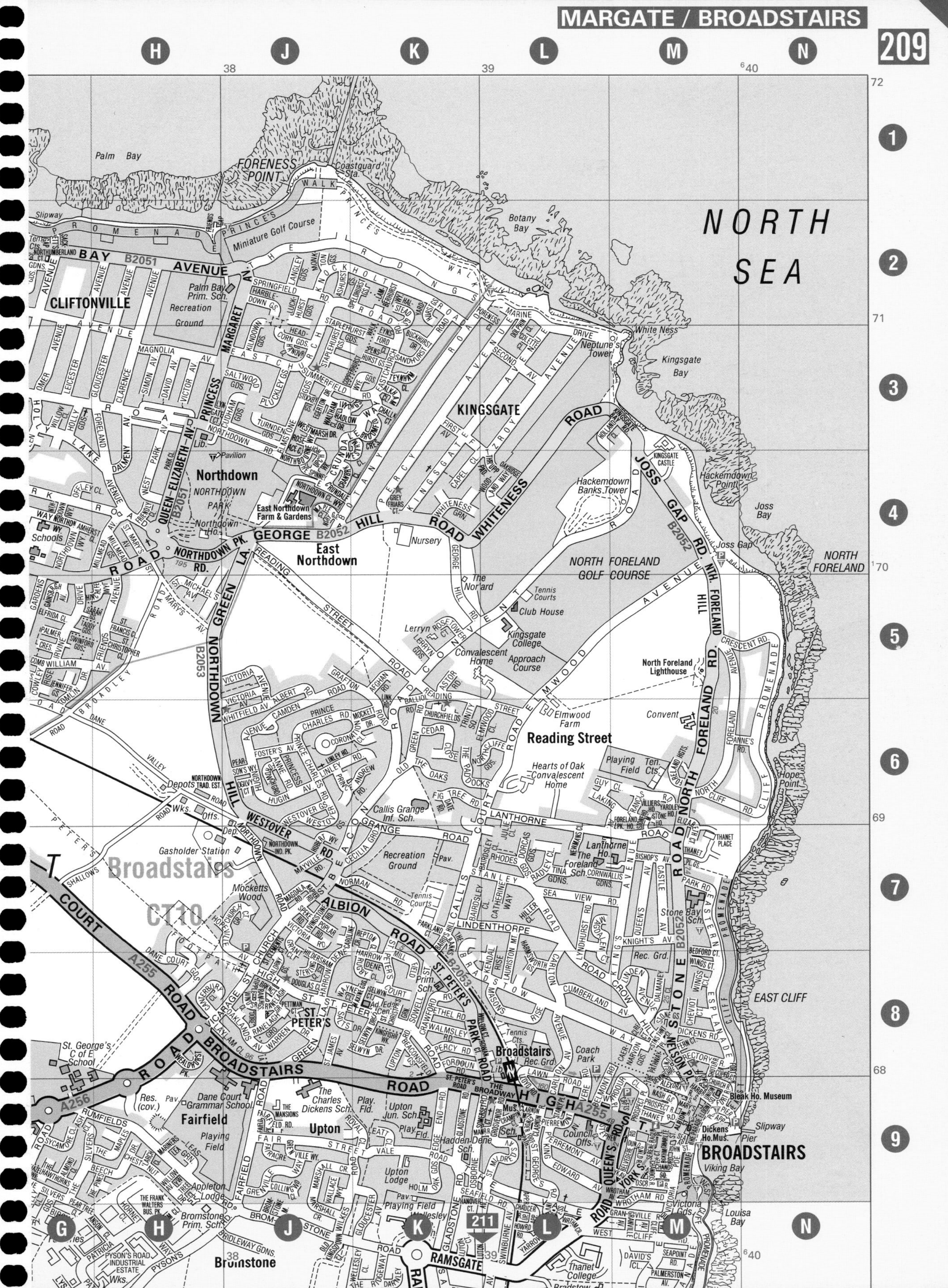
NORTH SEA
Palm Bay
FORENESS POINT
Coastguard Sta.
Botany Bay
White Ness
Neptune's Tower
Kingsgate Bay
CLIFTONVILLE
KINGSGATE
Hackemdown Point
Joss Bay
NORTH FORELAND
Northdown
East Northdown
NORTH FORELAND GOLF COURSE
Kingsgate College
North Foreland Lighthouse
Reading Street
Broadstairs
CT10
ST PETER'S
EAST CLIFF
BROADSTAIRS
Viking Bay
Louisa Bay
Fairfield
Upton
Bromstone
RAMSGATE

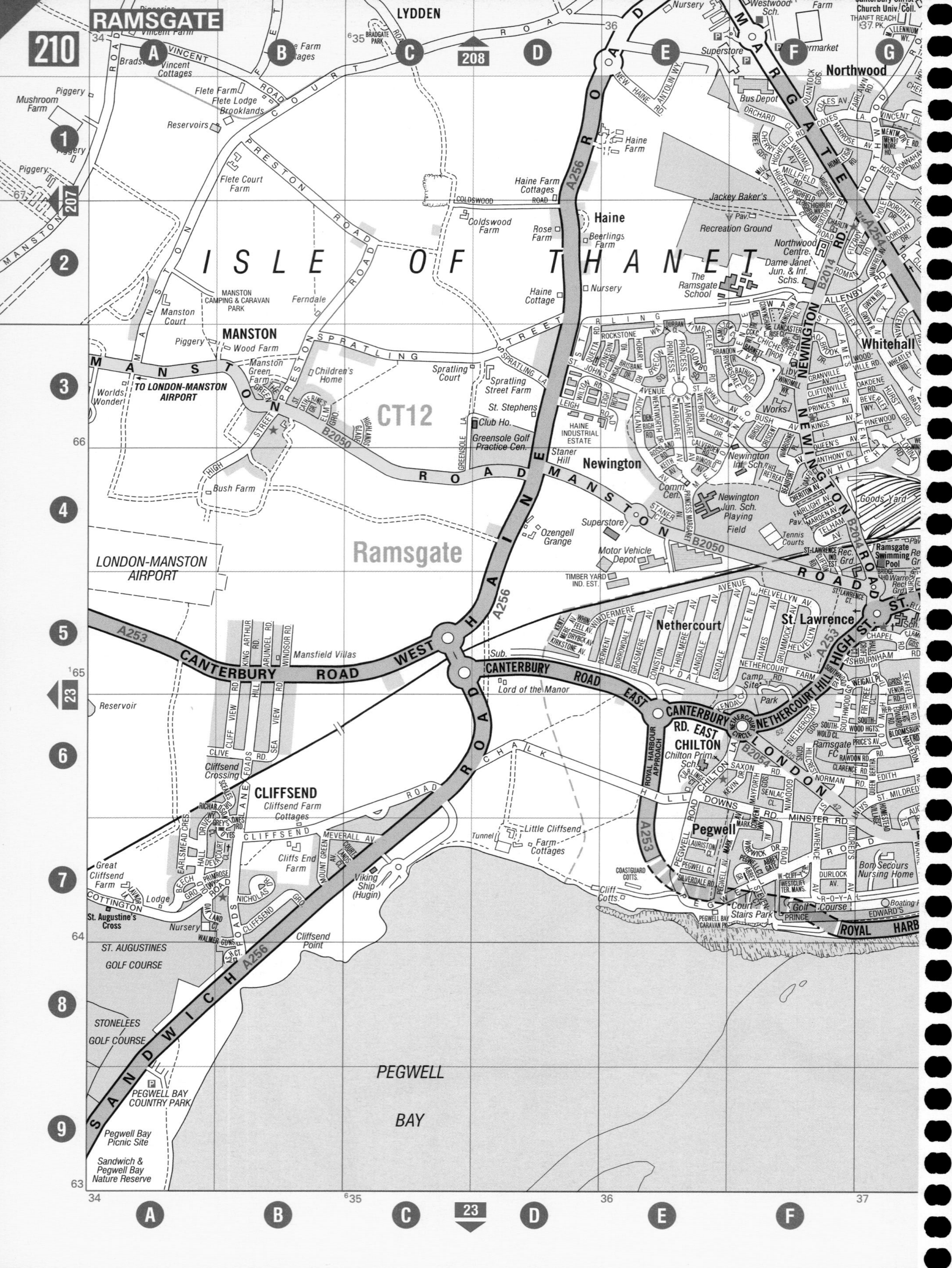
LYDDEN
ISLE OF THANET
MANSTON
CT12
Ramsgate
LONDON-MANSTON AIRPORT
TO LONDON-MANSTON AIRPORT
Haine
Newington
Northwood
Whitehall
Nethercourt
St. Lawrence
CHILTON
Pegwell
CLIFFSEND
PEGWELL BAY
ST. AUGUSTINES GOLF COURSE
STONELEES GOLF COURSE
PEGWELL BAY COUNTRY PARK
Pegwell Bay Picnic Site
Sandwich & Pegwell Bay Nature Reserve
Cliffsend Point
Viking Ship (Hugin)
Cliffs End Farm
Great Cliffsend Farm
St. Augustine's Cross
Mushroom Farm
Flete Farm
Flete Lodge
Brooklands
Reservoirs
Flete Court Farm
Vincent Cottages
Manston Court
MANSTON CAMPING & CARAVAN PARK
Ferndale
Coldswood Farm
Haine Farm Cottages
Haine Farm
Rose Farm
Beerlings Farm
Haine Cottage
Nursery
Spratling Court
Spratling Street Farm
St. Stephens
Club Ho.
Greensole Golf Practice Cen.
HAINE INDUSTRIAL ESTATE
Staner Hill
Ozengell Grange
Superstore
Motor Vehicle Depot
TIMBER YARD IND. EST.
Mansfield Villas
Lord of the Manor
Worlds Wonder
Children's Home
Bush Farm
Reservoir
Little Cliffsend Farm Cottages
Cliffsend Farm Cottages
Cliffsend Crossing
Jackey Baker's Recreation Ground
Northwood Centre
Dame Janet Jun. & Inf. Schs.
The Ramsgate School
Bus Depot
Newington Inf. Sch.
Newington Jun. Sch. Playing Field
Goods Yard
Ramsgate Swimming Pool
Camp. Site
Park
Chilton Prim. Sch.
Ramsgate FC
Bon Secours Nursing Home
Golf Course
Stairs Park
PEGWELL BAY CARAVAN PK.
COASTGUARD COTTS.
Cliff Cotts.
CANTERBURY ROAD WEST
CANTERBURY ROAD EAST
SANDWICH ROAD
HAINE ROAD
MANSTON ROAD
MANSTON COURT ROAD
PRESTON ROAD
SPRATLING STREET
CHALK HILL
NETHERCOURT HILL
HIGH ST.
LONDON RD.
MARGATE RD.
NEWINGTON RD.
ROYAL HARBOUR APPROACH
A256
A253
A254
B2050
B2014
B2054
208
207
23
A B C D E F G
1 2 3 4 5 6 7 8 9
34 35 36 37
63 64 65 66 67

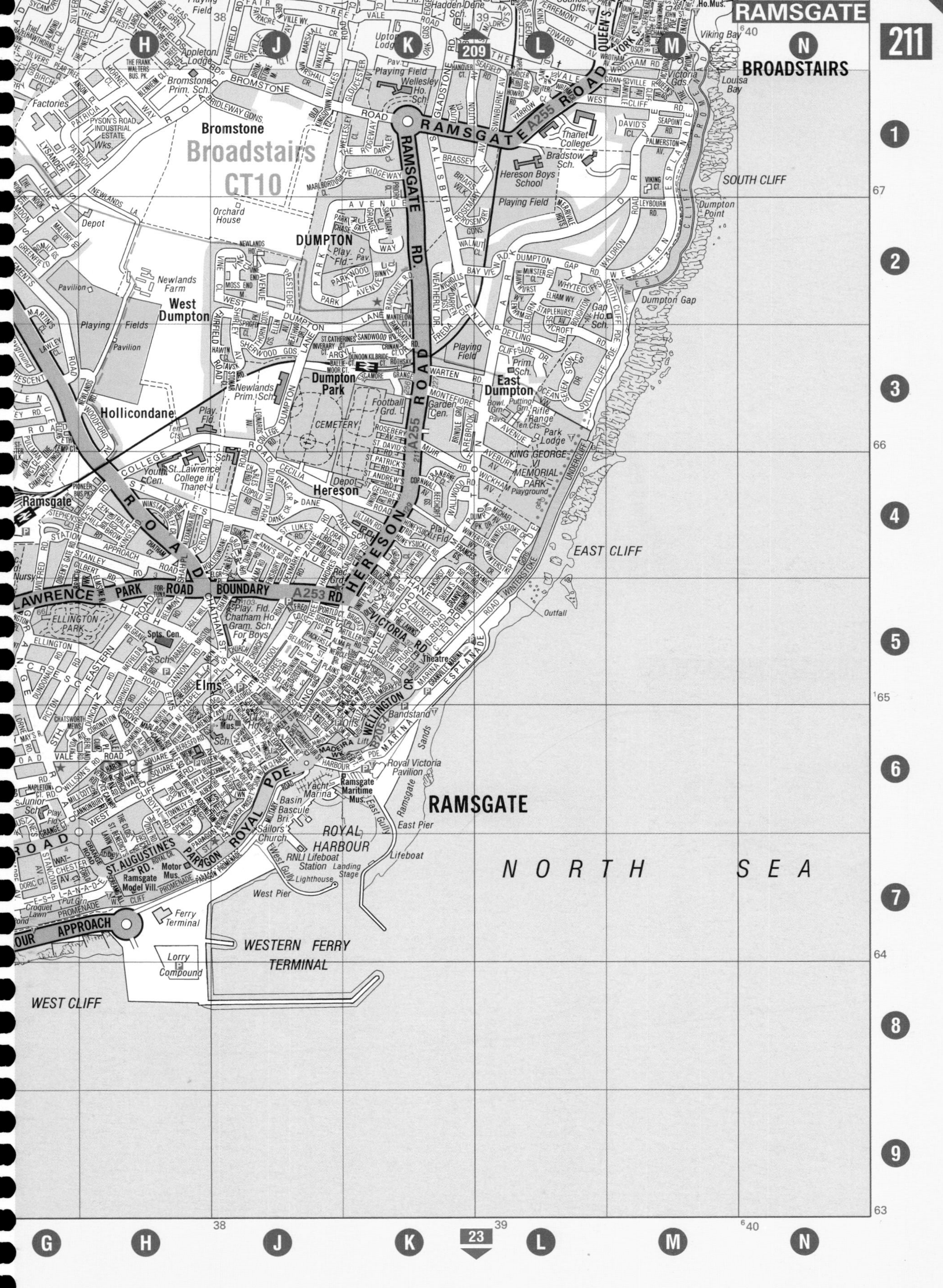
BROADSTAIRS
Bromstone
Broadstairs CT10
DUMPTON
West Dumpton
Hollicondane
Dumpton Park
East Dumpton
Hereson
Ramsgate
Elms
RAMSGATE
NORTH SEA
SOUTH CLIFF
EAST CLIFF
WEST CLIFF
ROYAL HARBOUR
WESTERN FERRY TERMINAL
Dumpton Point
Dumpton Gap
Louisa Bay
Viking Bay
Royal Victoria Pavilion
Ramsgate Maritime Mus.
East Pier
West Pier
Ferry Terminal
Lorry Compound
RAMSGATE ROAD
RAMSGATE RD.
HERESON ROAD
BOUNDARY RD.
LAWRENCE PARK ROAD
ROYAL PDE.
PARAGON
VICTORIA RD.
WELLINGTON CR.
A255
A253
B2054
209
23
G
H
J
K
L
M
N
1
2
3
4
5
6
7
8
9
38
39
40
63
64
65
66
67

MARDEN

A B C D E F

73 74 575 76

Little Pattenden
PATTENDEN LANE
Olivers
Depot
Nursery
Warehouse
Kent Air Ambulance Trust
Sports Ground
Works
WHEELBARROW PARK EST.
GUARDIAN INDUSTRIAL ESTATE
CREST INDUSTRIAL ESTATE
Marden
Church Farm
The Old Vicarage
RAILWAY COTTS.
Highfield House
Southons House
Cemetery
Bumpers Hall Cottages
Bridgehurst Wood
Reservoir
MAIDSTONE ROAD
B2079
HOWLAND COTTS.
Play. Fld.
Bridgehurst Farm
The Willows
MARDEN
Turkey Farmhouse
MEADES CL.
SOVEREIGNS WY.
BRAMLEY
WEST END
CHURCH GRN.
HIGH ST
HAFFENDEN CL.
WADES
BARNES WK.
MEADOW WY.
HOWLAND ROAD
SOUTH RD.
MOUNT FIELD PL.
Hall
Play. Fld.
Marden Prim. Sch.
BALLARD CL.
CHANTRY RD.
CHANTRY PL.
LIME CL.
Lib.
MAYNARDS
THE COCKPIT
SUTTON FORGE
SUTTON CT.
Rec. Grd.
CRANHAM SQ.
ROUNDEL
STELLA
ALBION RD.
ALBION COTT.
ALLENS
OAK TREE CL.
STANLEY ROAD
Sports Ground
Tennis Courts
The Howlands
Selby Farm
Stone Pit Farm
Holders Farm
Holders Cottages
Moatlands Farm
Little Mountain Farm
Depot
Gravelpit Farm Cottages
Westfield House
BROOKLYN VILLAS
Tonbridge
TN12
KON TIKI
THORN ROAD
COPPER LANE
Spring Grove
Lodge Farm
Branns
GOUDHURST ROAD
Roughlands Farm
Beechbridge Cotts.
Orchard Side
Poultry Farm Cottages
Poultry Farm
PLAIN ROAD
Cannon Farm
Longridge Farm
Beech Meadow Cottage
The Bungalows

$^{1}45$ 44

1 2 3 4

27 27 27 37 37 37

MINSTER (THANET)

22 23

MONKTON
Monkton C of E Prim. School
WILLETTS HILL
MONKTON STREET
MONKTON ROAD
Walters Hall
THE FOXHUNTER PARK
Playing Field
CHIPMANS WAY
Hoo
SHERIFFS COURT LANE
Sheriffs Court
Ramsgate
CT12
HOOVER CL.
PROSPECT GDNS.
PROSPECT ROAD
FAIRFIELD RD.
GREEN HILL GDNS.
ORCHARD CL.
BROCKMANS CL.
EDGAR RD.
FREEMAN'S RD.
ROSE GS.
KENTON GS.
The Freehold
AUGUSTINE RD.
EGBERT RD.
TOTHILL STREET
FOXBOROUGH LANE
BURGESS CL.
LAURENSFIELD
MINSTER
Eden Farm
The Orchards
THORNE RD.
TAYLOR RD.
MARY'S
MOLINEUX ROAD
ST MILDREDS RD.
HIGH STREET
Watchester Farm Cottages
Minster C of E Prim. School
Rec. Grd.
Watchester Farm
PETTS CRES.
GLEBE CT.
WATCHESTER LANE
STATION RD.
CHURCH ST
Abbey Green
Minster Mus. (Craft & Animal Cen.)
Fish Ponds
Minster Abbey
Lib.
BEDLAM CT. LA.
DURLOCK
Durlock
Durlock Farm
CHEESMANS CL.
Minster
MARSH FARM ROAD
Minster Stream

$^{1}65$ 64

6 7 8 9

29 $^{6}30$ 31

A B C D E F

22 23 22 23

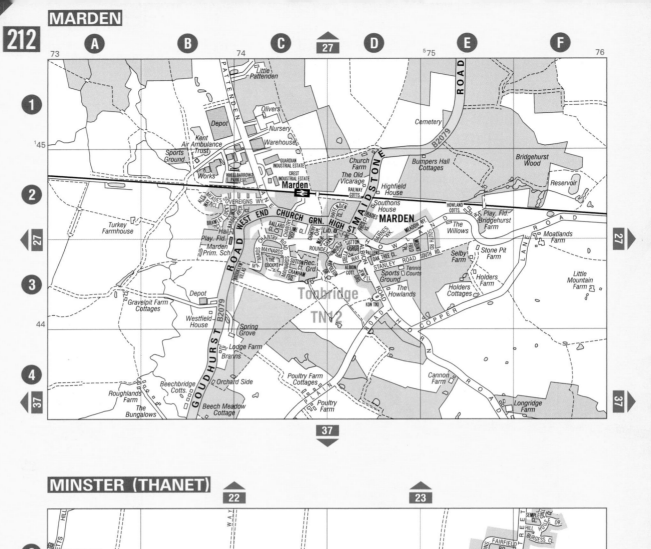

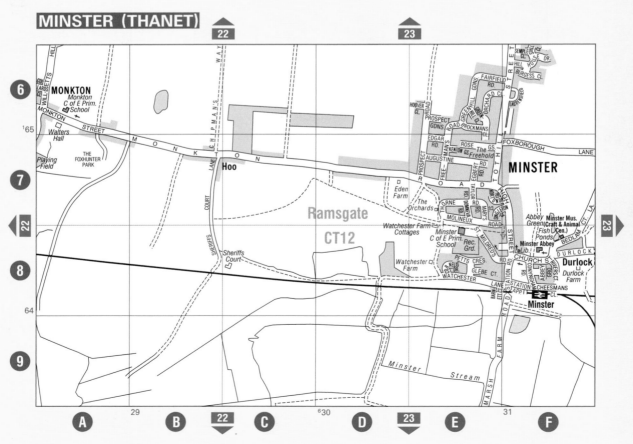

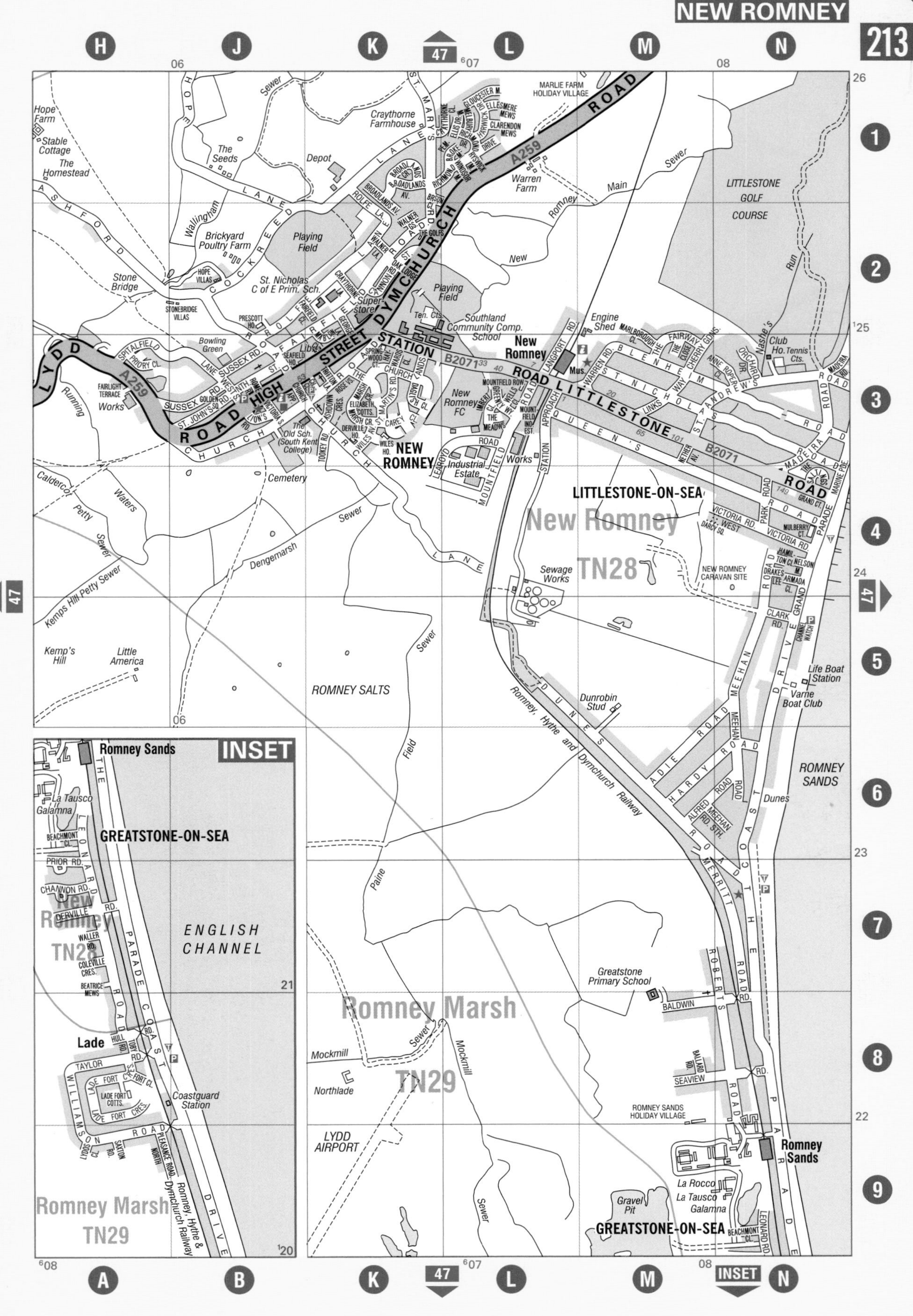
H
J
K
L
M
N
A
B
INSET
New Romney
TN28
Romney Marsh
TN29
LITTLESTONE-ON-SEA
GREATSTONE-ON-SEA
NEW ROMNEY
Romney Sands
ROMNEY SALTS
LITTLESTONE GOLF COURSE
ROMNEY SANDS
ENGLISH CHANNEL
LYDD AIRPORT
DYMCHURCH ROAD
HIGH STREET
LITTLESTONE ROAD
STATION ROAD
COAST DRIVE
GRAND PARADE
Romney, Hythe and Dymchurch Railway
Lade
Coastguard Station
Life Boat Station
Varne Boat Club
Dunrobin Stud
Sewage Works
New Romney Caravan Site
Greatstone Primary School
Romney Sands Holiday Village
Southland Community Comp. School
St. Nicholas C of E Prim. Sch.
Marlie Farm Holiday Village
Craythorne Farmhouse
Warren Farm
Hope Farm
Stable Cottage
The Homestead
Brickyard Poultry Farm
Stone Bridge
Kemp's Hill
Little America
Cemetery
Industrial Estate
New Romney FC
Engine Shed
Northlade
Gravel Pit
La Rocco
La Tausco
Galamna

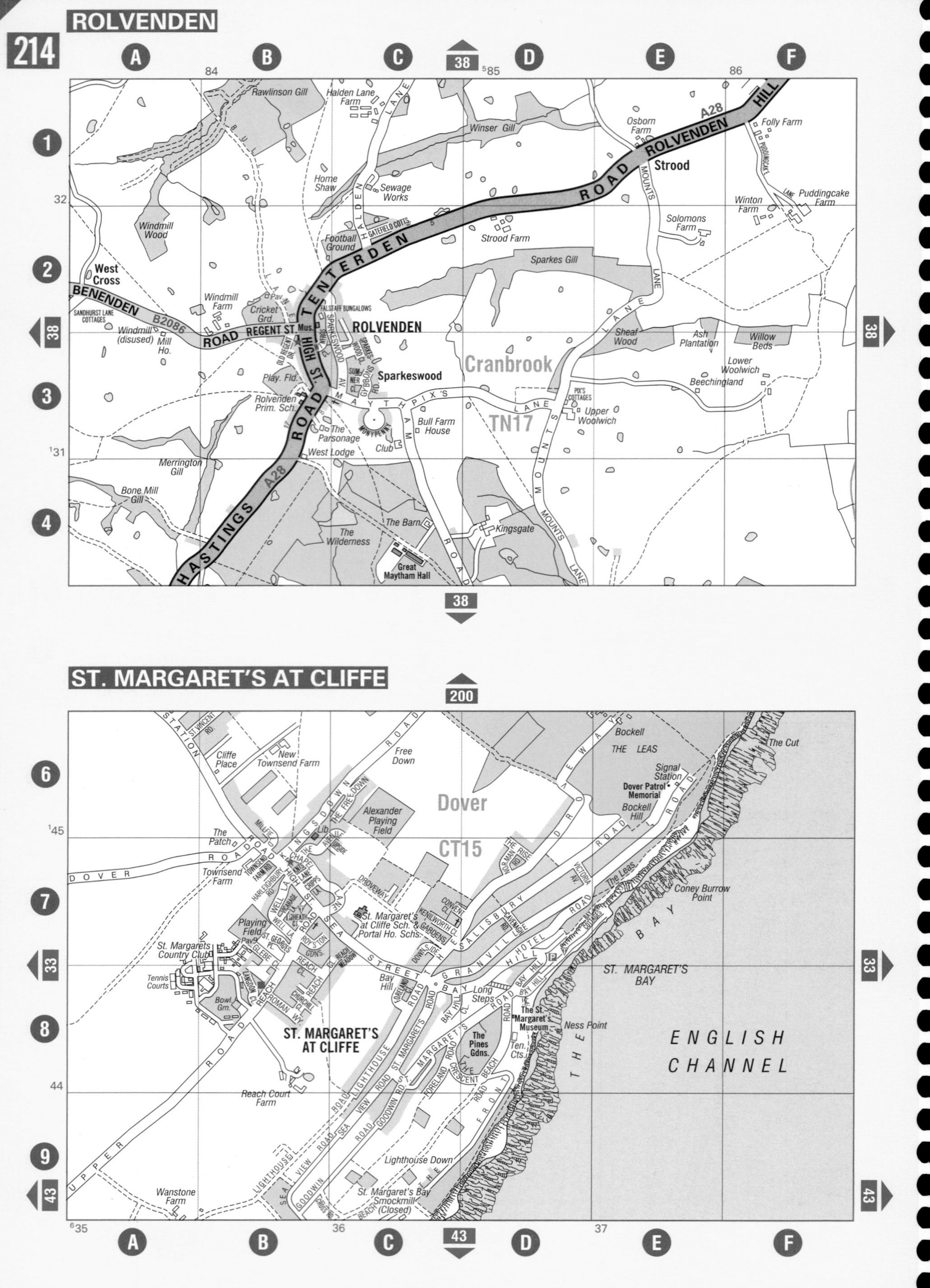
ROLVENDEN
Rawlinson Gill
Halden Lane Farm
Winser Gill
Osborn Farm
Folly Farm
ROLVENDEN HILL
A28
Strood
Home Shaw
Sewage Works
Puddingcake Farm
Winton Farm
Windmill Wood
Solomons Farm
Football Ground
Strood Farm
TENTERDEN ROAD
Sparkes Gill
West Cross
BENENDEN
Windmill Farm
Cricket Grd.
Pav.
FALSTAFF BUNGALOWS
SANDHURST LANE COTTAGES
B2086
Windmill (disused)
Mill Ho.
ROAD
REGENT ST.
Mus.
HIGH ST.
ROLVENDEN
Sheaf Wood
Ash Plantation
Willow Beds
Cranbrook
Lower Woolwich
Sparkeswood
Play. Fld.
Beechingland
MAYTHAM
PIX'S LANE
PIX'S COTTAGES
Rolvenden Prim. Sch.
Upper Woolwich
TN17
Bull Farm House
The Parsonage
MONYPENNY
Club
West Lodge
Merrington Gill
Bone Mill Gill
The Barn
Kingsgate
The Wilderness
HASTINGS ROAD
MOUNTS LANE
Great Maytham Hall
ST. MARGARET'S AT CLIFFE
STATION ROAD
Bockell
THE LEAS
The Cut
Cliffe Place
New Townsend Farm
Free Down
Signal Station
Dover Patrol Memorial
Dover
Alexander Playing Field
Bockell Hill
The Patch
KINGSDOWN ROAD
CT15
DOVER ROAD
Townsend Farm
DROVEWAY
The Leas
Coney Burrow Point
St. Margaret's at Cliffe Sch. & Portal Ho. Schs.
SALISBURY ROAD
Playing Field
BAY
St. Margarets Country Club
SEA STREET
GRANVILLE ROAD
HOTEL
Tennis Courts
Bay Hill
Long Steps
ST. MARGARET'S BAY
Bowl. Grn.
The St. Margaret's Museum
Ness Point
ST. MARGARET'S AT CLIFFE
The Pines Gdns.
ENGLISH CHANNEL
Ten. Cts.
Reach Court Farm
LIGHTHOUSE ROAD
SEA VIEW ROAD
GOODWIN ROAD
THE FRONT
Lighthouse Down
UPPER ROAD
Wanstone Farm
St. Margaret's Bay Smockmill (Closed)
A B C D E F
1 2 3 4 6 7 8 9
38 33 43 200

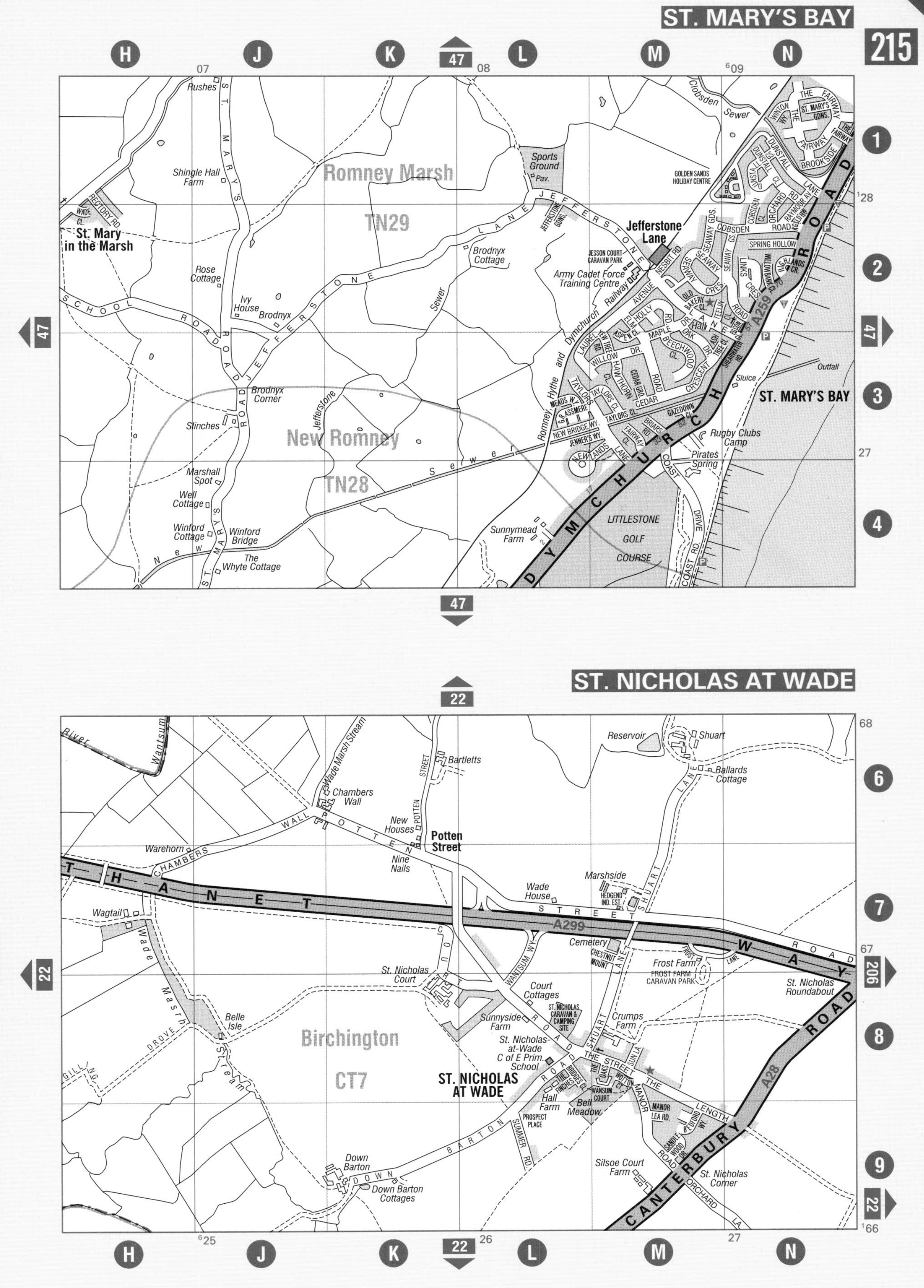
Romney Marsh
TN29
St. Mary in the Marsh
Shingle Hall Farm
Rushes
Rose Cottage
Ivy House
Brodnyx
Brodnyx Cottage
Sports Ground
Jefferstone Lane
Army Cadet Force Training Centre
Golden Sands Holiday Centre
Brodnyx Corner
Slinches
New Romney
TN28
Marshall Spot
Well Cottage
Winford Cottage
Winford Bridge
The Whyte Cottage
Sunnymead Farm
Littlestone Golf Course
Rugby Clubs Camp
Pirates Spring
Sluice
Outfall
ST. MARY'S BAY
Dymchurch Road
A259
ST. NICHOLAS AT WADE
Reservoir
Shuart
Ballards Cottage
Bartletts
Chambers Wall
New Houses
Potten Street
Nine Nails
Warehorn
Wagtail
Wade House
Marshside
Thanet Way
A299
Cemetery
Frost Farm
Frost Farm Caravan Park
St. Nicholas Roundabout
St. Nicholas Court
Court Cottages
Sunnyside Farm
Belle Isle
Birchington
CT7
St. Nicholas-at-Wade C of E Prim. School
ST. NICHOLAS AT WADE
Crumps Farm
Hall Farm
Bell Meadow
Down Barton
Down Barton Cottages
Silsoe Court Farm
St. Nicholas Corner
Canterbury Road
A28

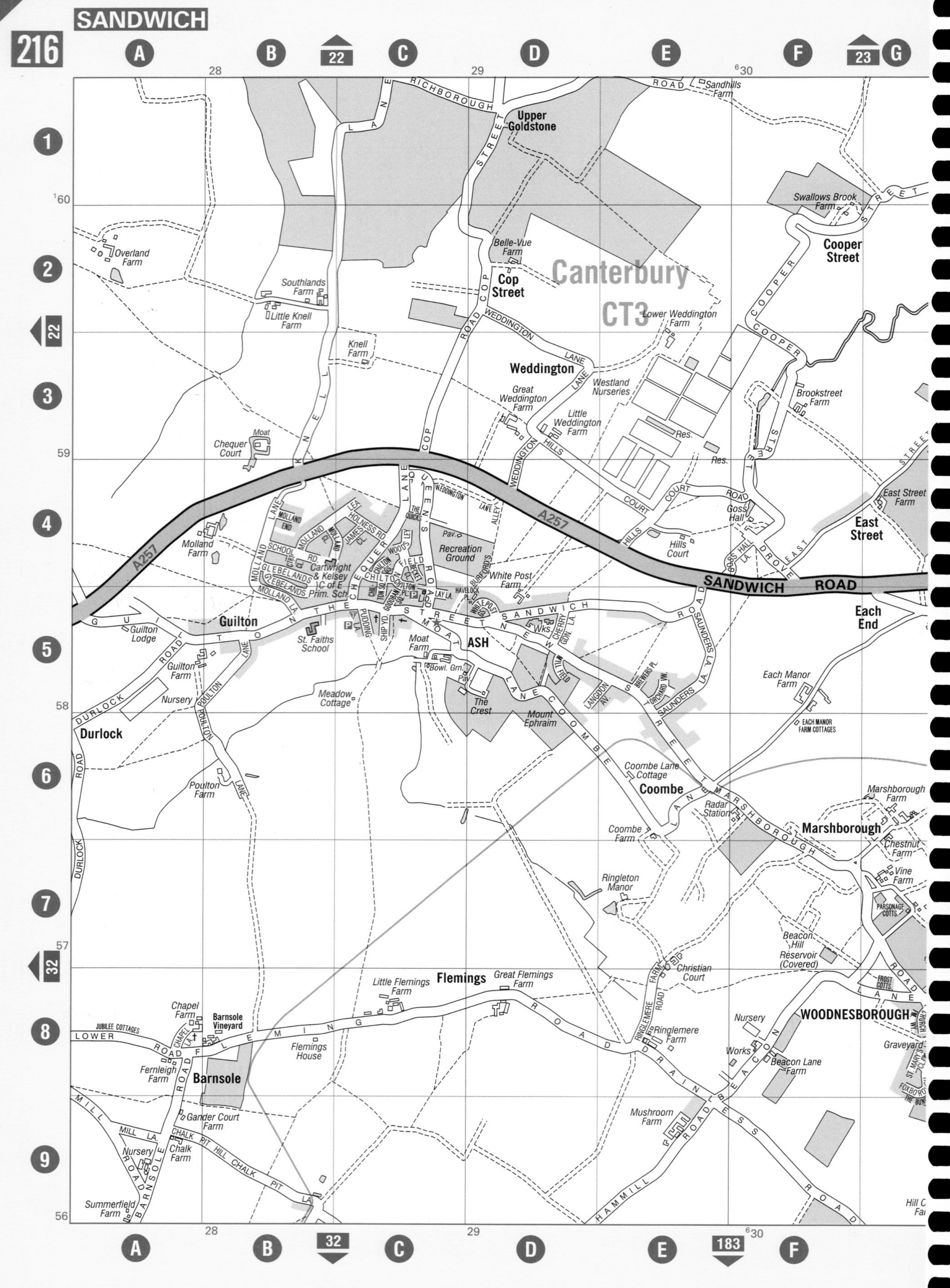
A
B
22
C
D
E
F
23
G
28
29
30
60
59
58
57
56
1
2
3
4
5
6
7
8
9
Upper Goldstone
RICHBOROUGH ROAD
Sandhills Farm
Swallows Brook Farm
Cooper Street
Overland Farm
Belle-Vue Farm
Canterbury CT3
Cop Street
Southlands Farm
Little Knell Farm
Lower Weddington Farm
Knell Farm
Weddington
Westland Nurseries
Great Weddington Farm
Little Weddington Farm
Brookstreet Farm
Chequer Court
Moat
Res.
A257
East Street Farm
East Street
Goss Hall
Hills Court
Molland Farm
Recreation Ground
Cartwright & Kelsey C of E Prim. Sch.
White Post Farm
SANDWICH ROAD
Each End
Guilton
Guilton Lodge
St. Faiths School
Moat Farm
ASH
Guilton Farm
Nursery
Meadow Cottage
Bowl. Grn.
The Crest
Mount Ephraim
Each Manor Farm
EACH MANOR FARM COTTAGES
Durlock
Poulton Farm
Coombe Lane Cottage
Coombe
Radar Station
Marshborough Farm
Marshborough
Coombe Farm
Chestnut Farm
Ringleton Manor
Vine Farm
PARSONAGE COTTS.
Beacon Hill Reservoir (Covered)
Christian Court
Little Flemings Farm
Flemings
Great Flemings Farm
Chapel Farm
Barnsole Vineyard
JUBILEE COTTAGES
LOWER ROAD
Nursery
WOODNESBOROUGH
Graveyard
Ringlemere Farm
Flemings House
Works
Beacon Lane Farm
Fernleigh Farm
Barnsole
Gander Court Farm
Mushroom Farm
Chalk Farm
Nursery
Summerfield Farm
Hill Court Farm
32
183

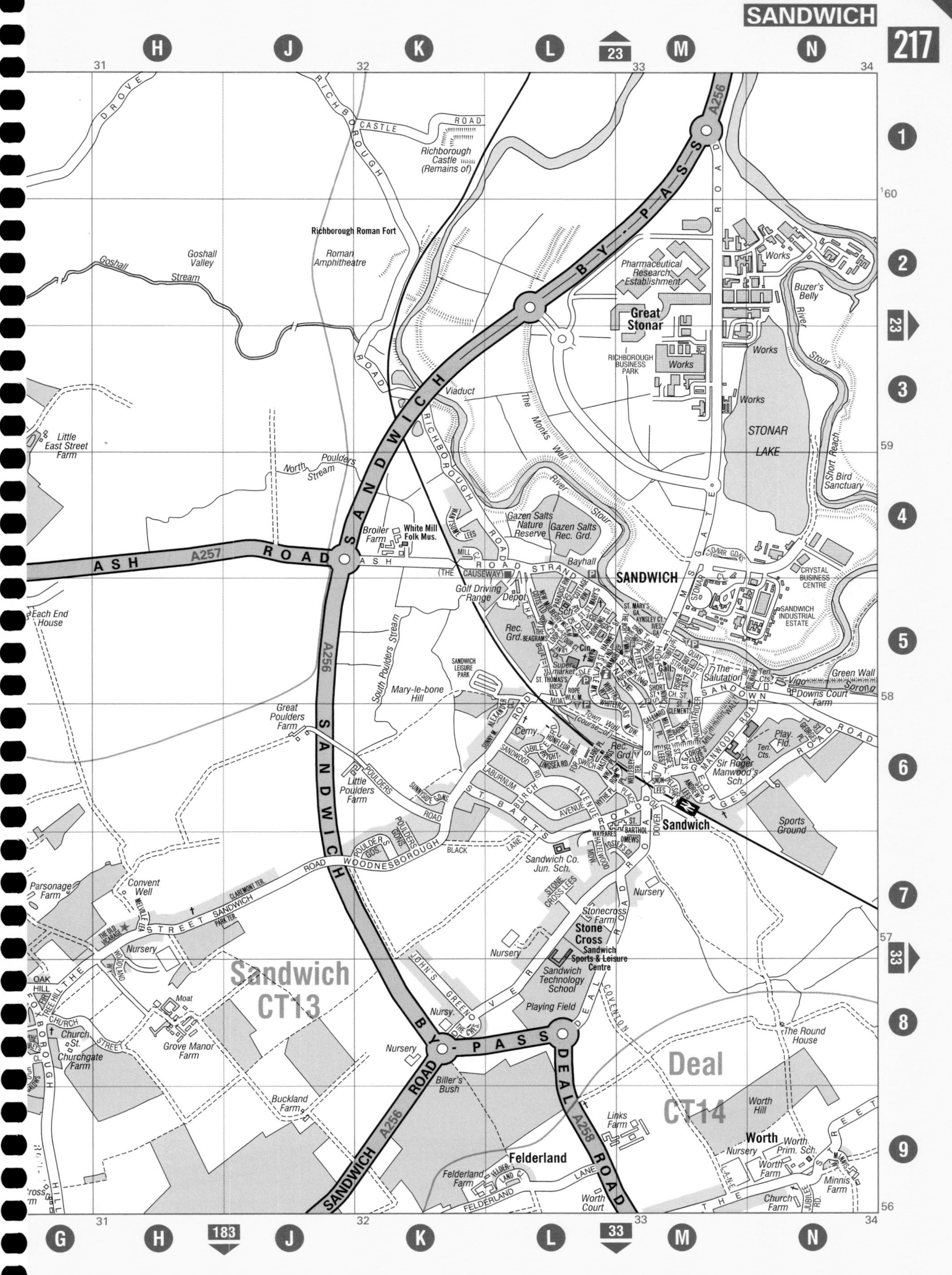
H
J
K
L
23
M
N
31
32
33
34
1
2
3
4
5
6
7
8
9
60
59
58
57
56
DROVE
RICHBOROUGH
CASTLE
ROAD
Richborough Castle (Remains of)
Richborough Roman Fort
Roman Amphitheatre
Goshall Valley
Goshall Stream
A256
BY-PASS
SANDWICH
Pharmaceutical Research Establishment
Works
Great Stonar
RICHBOROUGH BUSINESS PARK
Buzer's Belly
River Stour
Viaduct
The Monks Wall
STONAR LAKE
Short Reach
Bird Sanctuary
Little East Street Farm
North Poulders Stream
Broiler Farm
White Mill Folk Mus.
Gazen Salts Nature Reserve
Gazen Salts Rec. Grd.
ASH
A257
ROAD
(THE CAUSEWAY)
STRAND
Bayhall
SANDWICH
CRYSTAL BUSINESS CENTRE
SANDWICH INDUSTRIAL ESTATE
Each End House
Golf Driving Range
Depot
Rec. Grd.
Cin.
Supermarket
ST. THOMAS'S HOSP.
SANDWICH LEISURE PARK
South Poulders Stream
Mary-le-bone Hill
Gall.
The Salutation
Ten. Cts.
Vigo
Green Wall
Sprong
Downs Court Farm
SANDOWN
Great Poulders Farm
Cemy.
Rec. Grd.
Play. Fld.
Ten. Cts.
Sir Roger Manwood's Sch.
Little Poulders Farm
POULDERS
LABURNUM
AVENUE
ST. BARTS
Sandwich
Sports Ground
WOODNESBOROUGH
ROAD
BLACK
Sandwich Co. Jun. Sch.
Parsonage Farm
Convent Well
STREET
Nursery
Stonecross Farm
Stone Cross
Sandwich Sports & Leisure Centre
Sandwich Technology School
Sandwich CT13
Moat
Grove Manor Farm
Playing Field
The Round House
Church St.
Churchgate Farm
Nursery
Biller's Bush
Deal CT14
Worth Hill
Buckland Farm
Links Farm
A258
DEAL
ROAD
Felderland
Felderland Farm
FELDERLAND
LANE
Worth Court
Worth
Worth Prim. Sch.
Worth Farm
Minnis Farm
Church Farm
G
183
33

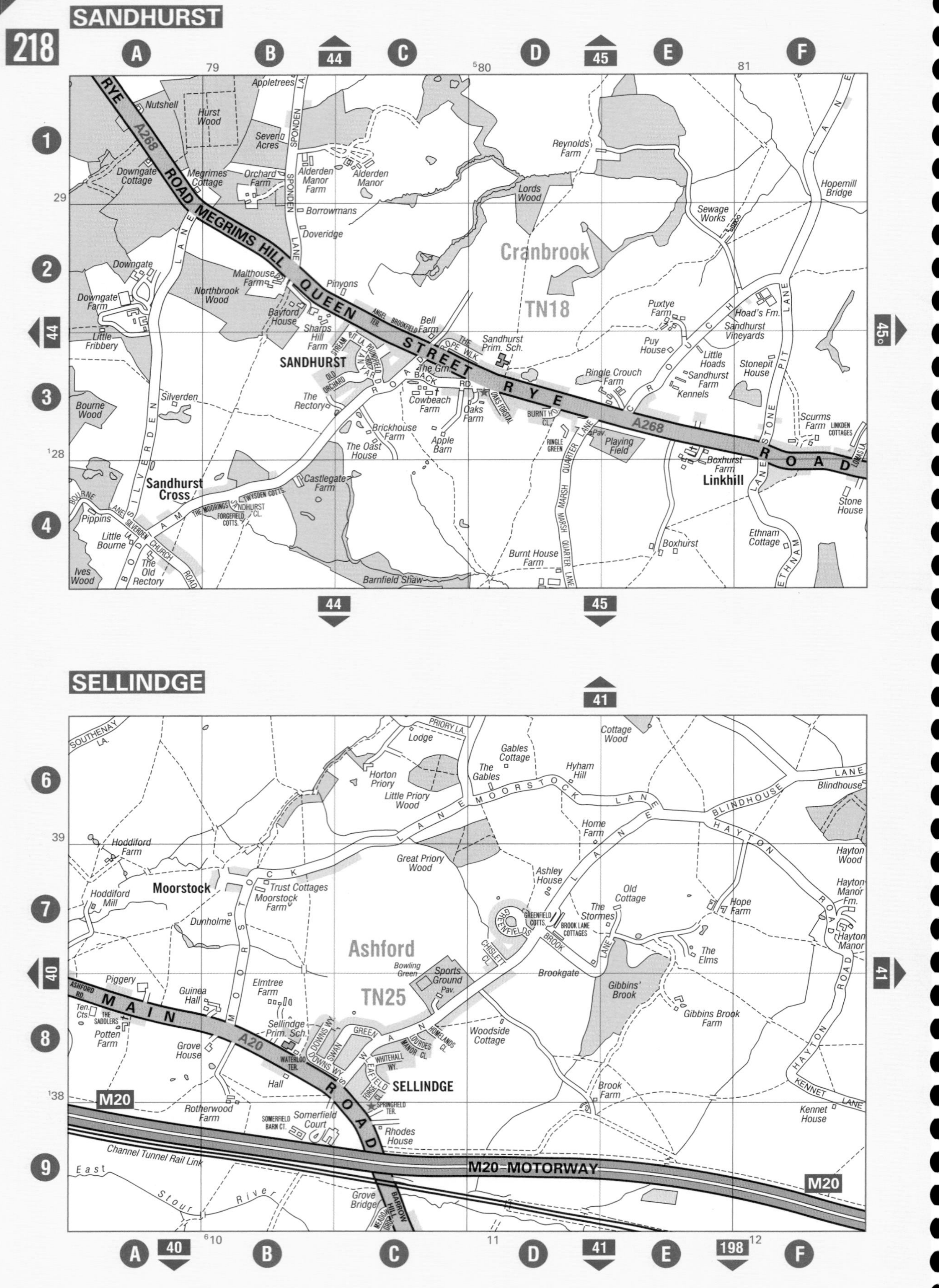
SANDHURST
A
B
C
D
E
F
44
45
79
580
81
29
128
1
2
3
4
Appletrees
Nutshell
Hurst Wood
Seven Acres
SPONDEN LANE
Alderden Manor Farm
Alderden Manor
Orchard Farm
Megrimes Cottage
Downgate Cottage
RYE ROAD
A268
MEGRIMS HILL
Borrowmans
Doveridge
Reynolds Farm
Lords Wood
Hopemill Bridge
Sewage Works
Cranbrook
TN18
Downgate
Downgate Farm
Northbrook Wood
Malthouse Farm
Pinyons
QUEEN STREET
Bayford House
Sharps Hill Farm
Bell Farm
ANGEL TER.
BROOKFIELD
ROPE WALK
Sandhurst Prim. Sch.
Puxtye Farm
Hoad's Fm.
Sandhurst Vineyards
Puy House
Little Hoads
Sandhurst Farm
Kennels
Stonepit House
RINGLE CROUCH
Ringle Crouch Farm
Little Fribbery
SANDHURST
OLD ORCHARD
The Grn.
BACK RD.
Cowbeach Farm
Oaks Farm
OAKS FORSTAL
BURNT HO. CL.
RYE ROAD
A268
Scurms Farm
LINKDEN COTTAGES
LOMAS LA.
Silverden
Bourne Wood
The Rectory
Brickhouse Farm
Apple Barn
RINGLE GREEN
Playing Field
Pav.
The Oast House
Boxhurst Farm
Linkhill
Stone House
Sandhurst Cross
Castlegate Farm
TWYSDEN COTTS.
THE MOORINGS
FORGEFIELD COTTS.
SANDHURST CL.
BOURNE LANE
Pippins
SILVERDEN LANE
Little Bourne
CHURCH ROAD
The Old Rectory
Ives Wood
BOURNE
MARSH QUARTER LANE
Boxhurst
Ethnam Cottage
ETHNAM LANE
STONE PIT LANE
Burnt House Farm
Barnfield Shaw
SELLINDGE
41
40
198
610
11
12
39
138
6
7
8
9
SOUTHENAY LA.
PRIORY LA.
Lodge
Cottage Wood
Gables Cottage
The Gables
Hyham Hill
Horton Priory
Little Priory Wood
MOORSTOCK LANE
BLINDHOUSE LANE
Blindhouse
Home Farm
HAYTON ROAD
Hoddiford Farm
Great Priory Wood
Hayton Wood
Ashley House
Hayton Manor Fm.
Hoddiford Mill
Moorstock
Trust Cottages
Moorstock Farm
Old Cottage
The Stormes
Hope Farm
Dunholme
GREENFIELD COTTS.
BROOK LANE COTTAGES
Hayton Manor
Ashford
GREENFIELDS
CHISLETT CL.
BROOK LANE
The Elms
Bowling Green
Sports Ground
Pav.
Brookgate
Piggery
Guinea Hall
Elmtree Farm
TN25
Gibbins' Brook
ASHFORD RD.
MAIN ROAD
A20
Ten. Cts.
THE SADDLERS
Gibbins Brook Farm
Potten Farm
Sellindge Prim. Sch.
DOWNS WY.
SWAN LANE
GREEN
HOMELANDS CL.
LOURDES CL.
MANOR CL.
WHITEHALL WY.
Woodside Cottage
Grove House
WATERLOO TER.
Hall
FORGE FIELD CL.
SELLINDGE
Brook Farm
KENNET LANE
M20
SPRINGFIELD TER.
Kennet House
Rotherwood Farm
SOMERFIELD BARN CT.
Somerfield Court
Rhodes House
Channel Tunnel Rail Link
M20 MOTORWAY
East Stour River
Grove Bridge
MEADOW GROVE
BARROW HILL

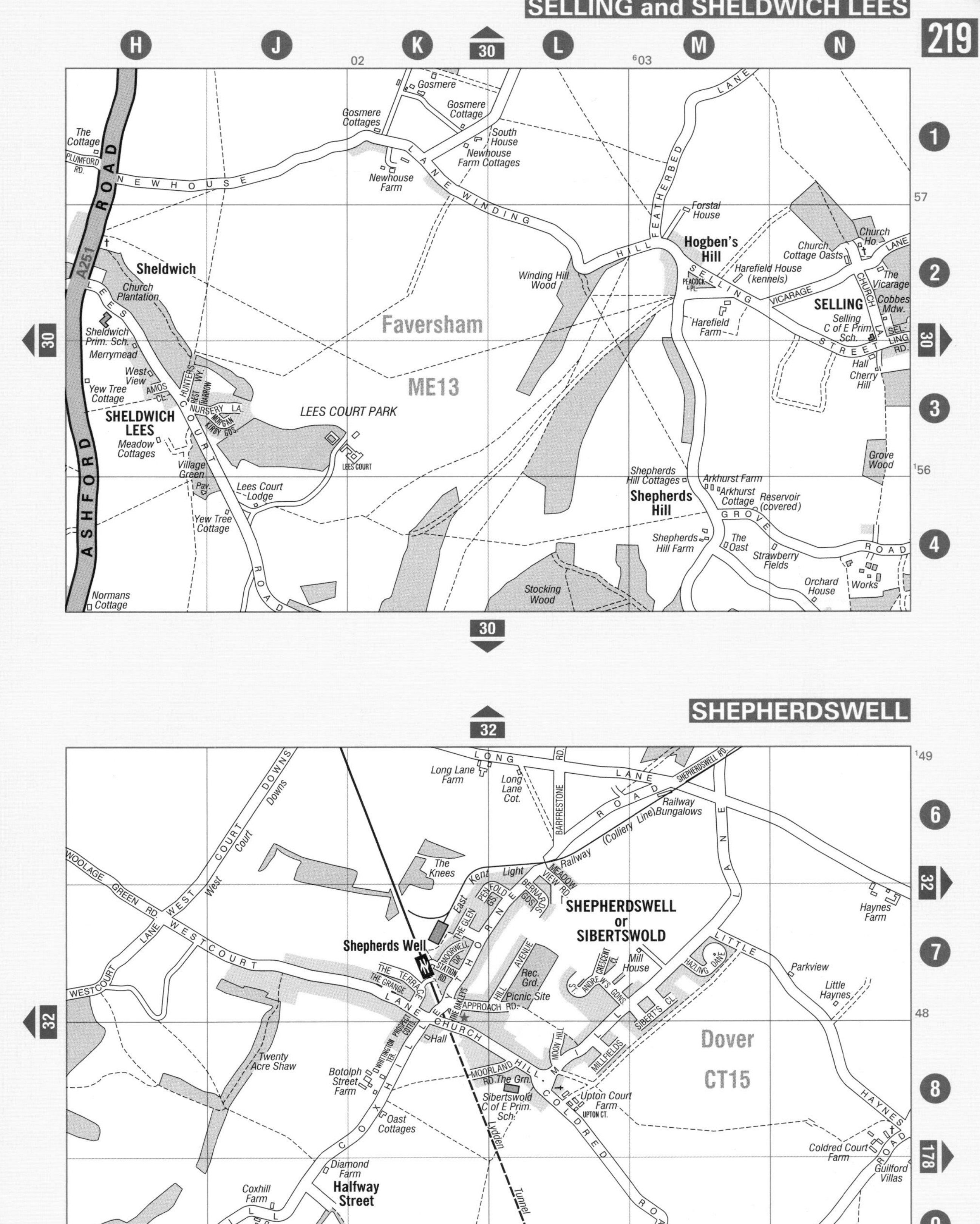
Sheldwich
Church Plantation
Sheldwich Prim. Sch.
Merrymead
West View
Yew Tree Cottage
AMOS CL.
SHELDWICH LEES
Meadow Cottages
Village Green
Pav.
Lees Court Lodge
Yew Tree Cottage
Normans Cottage
ASHFORD ROAD
A251
The Cottage
PLUMFORD RD.
NEWHOUSE LANE
Gosmere
Gosmere Cottages
Gosmere Cottage
South House
Newhouse Farm Cottages
Newhouse Farm
WINDING HILL
LEES COURT PARK
LEES COURT
Faversham
ME13
Winding Hill Wood
Stocking Wood
FEATHERBED LANE
Forstal House
Hogben's Hill
Harefield House (kennels)
PEACOCK PL.
Harefield Farm
Church Cottage Oasts
Church Ho.
The Vicarage
VICARAGE LANE
SELLING
Cobbes Mdw.
Selling C of E Prim. Sch.
SELLING STREET
CHURCH LA.
SELLING RD.
Hall
Cherry Hill
Grove Wood
Shepherds Hill Cottages
Arkhurst Farm
Arkhurst Cottage
Reservoir (covered)
Shepherds Hill
GROVE ROAD
Shepherds Hill Farm
The Oast
Strawberry Fields
Orchard House
Works
SHEPHERDSWELL
LONG LANE
Long Lane Farm
Long Lane Cot.
BARFRESTONE RD.
SHEPHERDSWELL RD.
Railway Bungalows
Railway (Colliery Line)
East Kent Light Railway
The Knees
WOOLAGE GREEN RD.
WEST COURT DOWNS
West Court Downs
WESTCOURT LANE
Shepherds Well
THE TERRACE
THE GRANGE
STATION RD.
MOORWELL DR.
THE GLEN
PENFOLD GS.
BERNARDS GDS.
MEADOW VIEW RD.
SHEPHERDSWELL or SIBERTSWOLD
AVENUE
Rec. Grd.
Picnic Site
APPROACH RD.
THE OAKLEYS
ST ANDREW'S GDS.
CRESCENT
Mill House
HAZLING DANE
LITTLE
SIBERT'S CL.
MILLFIELDS
MOON HILL
Dover
CT15
Parkview
Little Haynes
Haynes Farm
HAYNES LANE
CHURCH HILL
Hall
PROSPECT COTTS.
WHITTINGTON TER.
Twenty Acre Shaw
Botolph Street Farm
MOORLAND RD.
The Grn.
Sibertswold C of E Prim. Sch.
Upton Court Farm
UPTON CT.
COLDRED ROAD
Oast Cottages
Lydden Tunnel
Diamond Farm
Halfway Street
Coxhill Farm
COXHILL
Claysole Wood
UPTON WOOD RD.
COLDRED RD.
Coldred
Coldred Court Farm
Guilford Villas
CHURCH ROAD
Coldred Farm

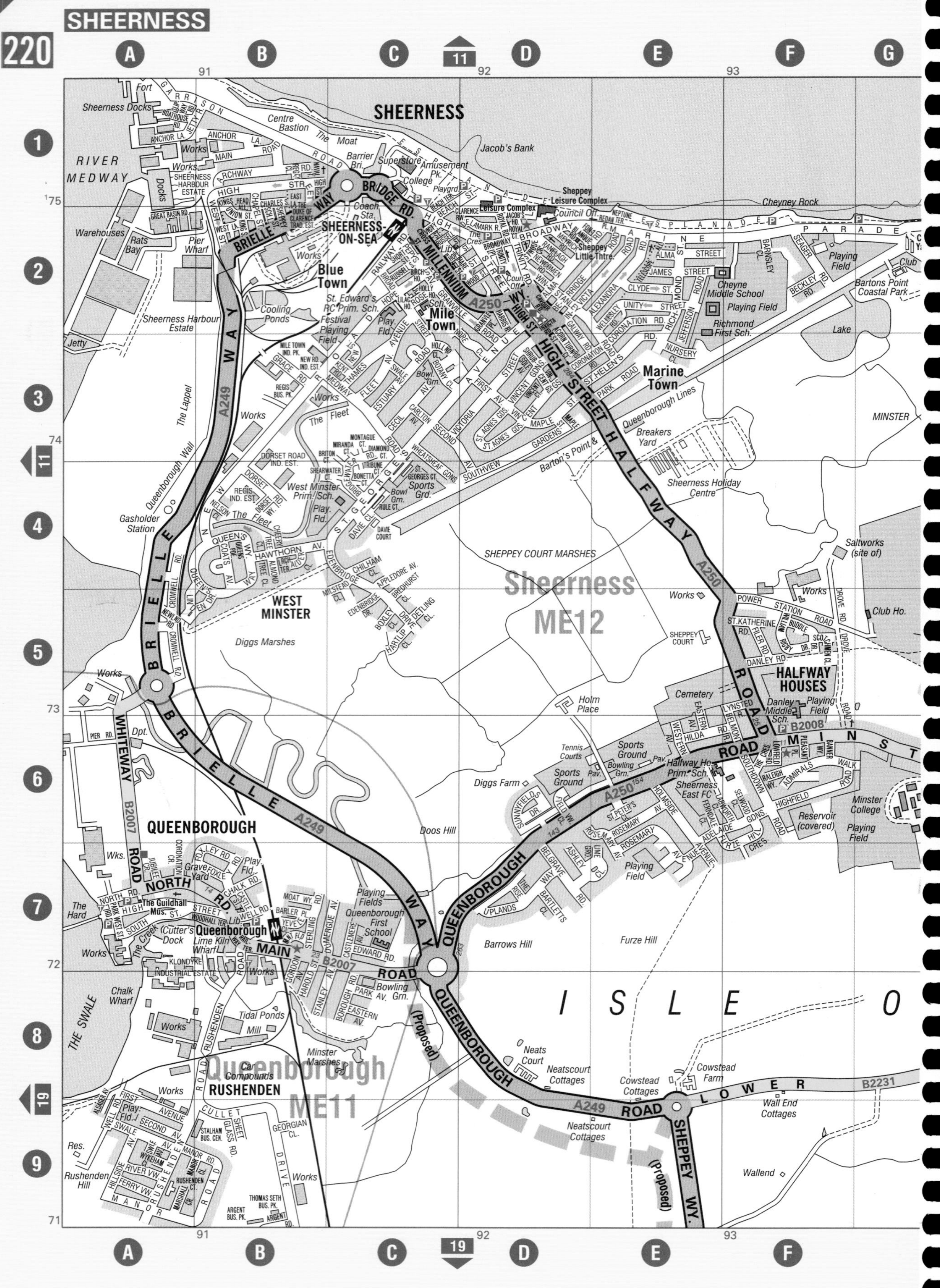
A
B
C
11
D
E
F
G
1
2
3
4
5
6
7
8
9
SHEERNESS
Sheerness Docks
Fort
GARRISON
Centre Bastion
The Moat
Barrier Bri.
Superstore
Amusement Pk.
College
Jacob's Bank
RIVER MEDWAY
Docks
SHEERNESS HARBOUR ESTATE
Warehouses
Rats Bay
Pier Wharf
ANCHOR LA.
Works
MAIN
ARCHWAY
HIGH
BRIELLE
WAY
BRIDGE RD.
Coach Sta.
SHEERNESS-ON-SEA
Blue Town
Cooling Ponds
St. Edward's RC Prim. Sch.
Festival Playing Field
Sheerness Harbour Estate
Jetty
Sheppey Leisure Complex
Leisure Complex
Council Off.
Cheyney Rock
ESPLANADE
MARINE PARADE
BROADWAY
Sheppey Little Thtre.
MILLENNIUM
A250
WY.
HIGH ST.
Mile Town
Lib.
Play. Fld.
ALMA
JAMES
STREET
CLYDE
UNITY
CORONATION RD.
Cheyne Middle School
Playing Field
Richmond First Sch.
Lake
BARNSLEY CL.
SEAGER
BECKLEY RD.
Bartons Point Coastal Park
Club
Marine Town
ST.HELEN'S
PARK ROAD
HIGH STREET
HALFWAY
Queenborough Lines
Barton's Point &
Breakers Yard
Sheerness Holiday Centre
MINSTER
The Lappel
A249
Works
REGIS BUS. PK.
The Fleet
DORSET ROAD IND. EST.
REGIS IND. EST.
West Minster Prim. Sch.
Sports Grd.
SOUTHVIEW
WHEATSHEAF GDNS.
Queenborough Wall
Gasholder Station
The Fleet
HAWTHORN AV.
EDENBRIDGE
CHILHAM CL.
APPLEDORE AV.
WEST MINSTER
SHEPPEY COURT MARSHES
Sheerness ME12
Works
POWER STATION ROAD
ST.KATHERINE RD.
Saltworks (site of)
Club Ho.
DROVE RD.
SHEPPEY COURT
Diggs Marshes
DANLEY RD.
HALFWAY HOUSES
Cemetery
Danley Middle Sch.
Playing Field
B2008
MINSTER
Holm Place
ROAD
Works
WHITEWAY
PIER RD.
Dpt.
Tennis Courts
Sports Ground
Pav.
Bowling Grn.
Sports Ground
Diggs Farm
Halfway Ho. Prim. Sch.
Sheerness East FC
SOUTHDOWN
ADMIRALS WALK
HIGHFIELD
Reservoir (covered)
Minster College
Playing Field
B2007
QUEENBOROUGH
Doos Hill
ROSEMARY
Playing Field
Wks.
NORTH RD.
Grave Yard
Play. Fld.
The Hard
The Guildhall Mus.
HIGH ST.
Playing Fields
Queenborough First School
QUEENBOROUGH
Barrows Hill
Furze Hill
Queenborough
Lime Kiln Wharf
(Cutter's Dock
The Creek
Works
MAIN
ROAD
B2007
EDWARD RD.
Bowling Grn.
KLONDYKE INDUSTRIAL ESTATE
ISLE O
Chalk Wharf
THE SWALE
Works
Tidal Ponds
Mill
(Proposed)
QUEENBOROUGH
Neats Court
Neatscourt Cottages
Cowstead Cottages
Cowstead Farm
LOWER
B2231
Minster Marshes
Car Compounds
Queenborough ME11
RUSHENDEN
Works
CULLET DRIVE
A249
ROAD
Wall End Cottages
Neatscourt Cottages
SHEPPEY WY.
Res.
Rushenden Hill
MANOR
STALHAM BUS. CEN.
GEORGIAN CL.
Works
(Proposed)
Wallend
THOMAS SETH BUS. PK.
ARGENT BUS. PK.
19
91
92
93
75
74
73
72
71

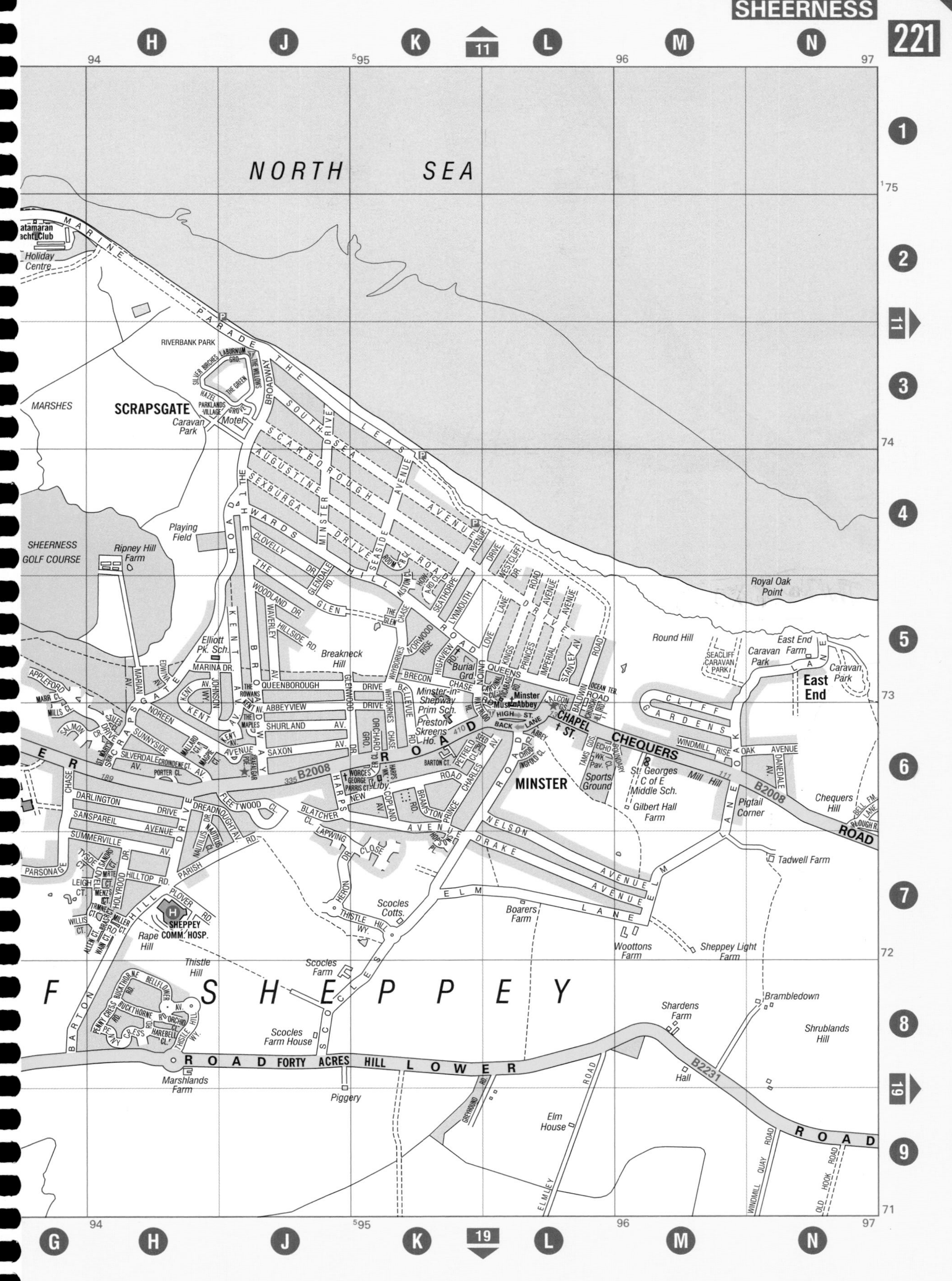
NORTH SEA
SCRAPSGATE
MARSHES
SHEERNESS GOLF COURSE
Ripney Hill Farm
Playing Field
Caravan Park
RIVERBANK PARK
Holiday Centre
Catamaran Yacht Club
MARINE PARADE
THE LEAS
Breakneck Hill
Elliott Pk. Sch.
Burial Grd.
Minster-in-Shepway Prim Sch.
Preston Skreens Ho.
Minster Abbey
Mus.
MINSTER
St. Georges C of E Middle Sch.
Sports Ground
Gilbert Hall Farm
Pigtail Corner
Chequers Hill
Round Hill
Royal Oak Point
SEACLIFF CARAVAN PARK
East End Farm
East End
Tadwell Farm
Boarers Farm
Scocles Cotts.
Woottons Farm
Sheppey Light Farm
Scocles Farm
Thistle Hill
Rape Hill
SHEPPEY COMM. HOSP.
Scocles Farm House
Marshlands Farm
Piggery
Shardens Farm
Brambledown
Shrublands Hill
Hall
Elm House
SHEPPEY
B2008
B2231
CHEQUERS ROAD
LOWER ROAD
FORTY ACRES HILL
ELM LANE
NELSON AVENUE
DRAKE AVENUE
CHAPEL ST.
HIGH ST.
BACK LANE
HALFWAY ROAD
MINSTER ROAD
SCOCLES ROAD
BARTON HILL DRIVE
PLOVER RD.
PARISH RD.
DARLINGTON DRIVE
SANSPAREIL AVENUE
SUMMERVILLE AV.
QUEENBOROUGH DRIVE
ABBEYVIEW DRIVE
SHURLAND AV.
SAXON AV.
SCARBOROUGH DRIVE
AUGUSTINE ROAD
SEXBURGA DRIVE
SOUTHSEA AVENUE
MINSTER DRIVE
SEASIDE AVENUE
BROADWAY
THE GLEN
HILLSIDE RD.
WAVERLEY AV.
WOODLAND DR.
CLOVELLY DR.
GLENDALE RD.
THE HILL
KENT AV.
WORDS ROAD
BRECON CHASE
HIGHVIEW RD.
LYNMOUTH
SEATHORPE
WESTCLIFF DR.
STANLEY AV.
IMPERIAL AV.
PRINCES AV.
KINGS
QUEENS
LOVE LANE
BALDWIN ROAD
WINDMILL RISE
CLIFF GARDENS
OAK LANE
DANEDALE
NEW RD.
CHARLES
PRINCE AVENUE
BRANSTON RD.
COPLAND AV.
ORCHARD GRO.
FLEETWOOD CL.
DREADNOUGHT AV.
BLATCHER CL.
LAPWING CL.
HERON DR.
THISTLE WY.
HILLTOP RD.
HOLYROOD
PARSONAGE CHASE
APPLEFORD
SALMON
SUNNYSIDE
NOREEN AV.
SILVERDALE AV.
PORTER CL.
MARINA DR.
EDWINA
MARIAN AV.
JOHNSON WY.
MALLARD CT.
MAGPIE CT.
TRAFALGAR PDE.
THE ROWANS
THE MAPLES
WHYBORNES CHASE
BELLEVUE RD.
GLENWOOD DR.
HARPS AV.
WORCES GEORGE PARRIS CT.
Liby.
BARTON CT.
PETFIELD CL.
HOPS CL.
INGFOLD CL.
ABBEY
ECHO WK.
BOUNDARY
TAMS GDS.
Pav.
OCEAN TER.
THE GREEN
LABURNUM GRO.
THE WILLOWS
SILVER BIRCHES
HAZEL GROVE
PARKLANDS VILLAGE
Motel
BUCKTHORNE RD.
BELLFLOWER AV.
ORCHID CL.
HAREBELL CL.
PENNY CRESS
THISTLE HILL WY.
GREYHOUND RD.
ELMLEY ROAD
WINDMILL QUAY ROAD
OLD HOOK ROAD
BELL FM LANE
PLOUGH RD.
Mill Hill
H J K L M N G
1 2 3 4 5 6 7 8 9
94 95 96 97 71 72 73 74 75
11 19

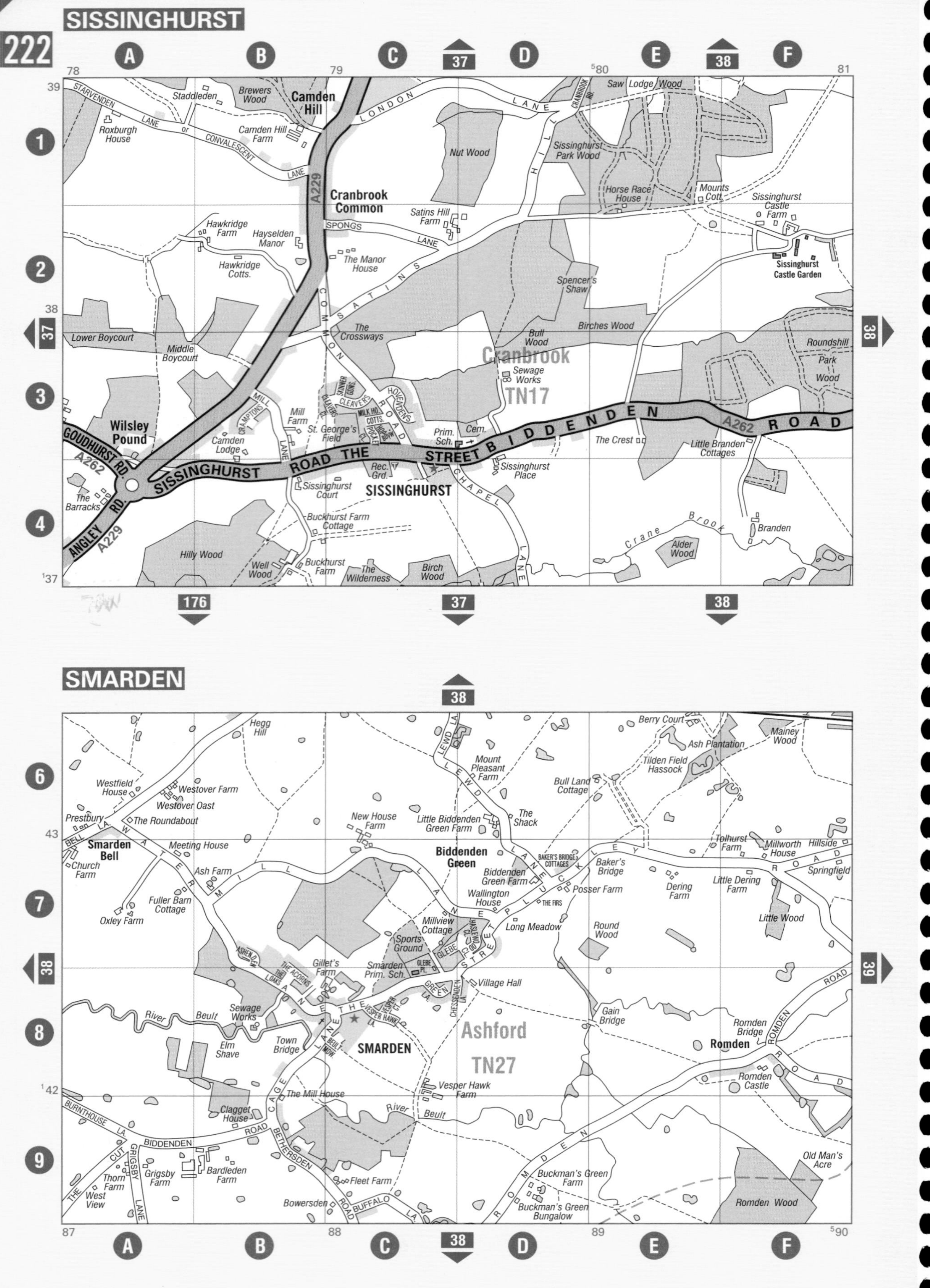
SISSINGHURST
Camden Hill
Cranbrook Common
Wilsley Pound
Cranbrook
TN17
SISSINGHURST ROAD
THE STREET
BIDDENDEN ROAD
Sissinghurst Castle Garden
SMARDEN
Smarden Bell
Biddenden Green
Ashford
TN27
Romden

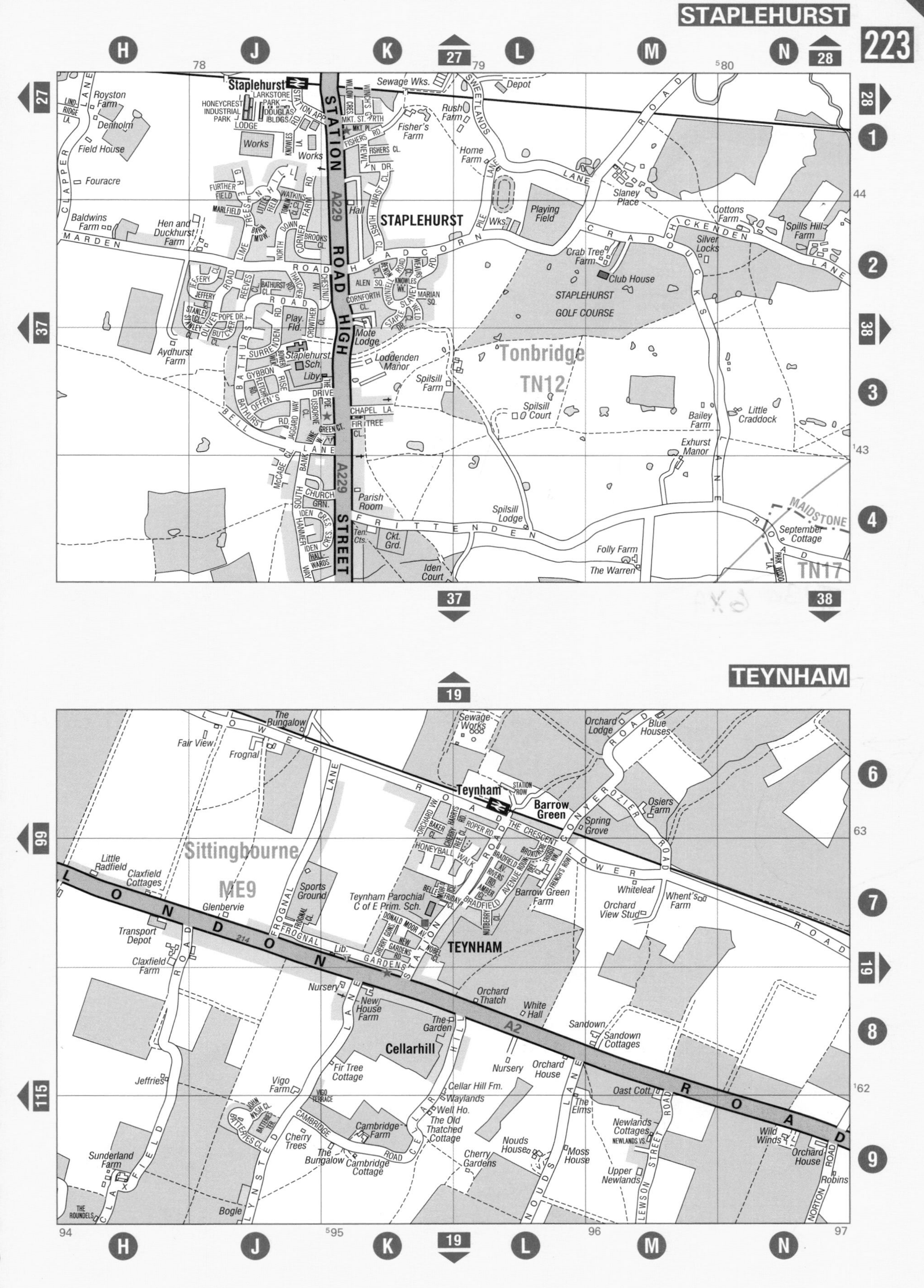

STAPLEHURST map

27 28

1

H 78 J K 27 79 L M 80 N 28

Lind Ridge La · Clapper Lane · Royston Farm · Larkstore Park · Staplehurst · Honeycrest Industrial Park · Lodge · Douglas Bldgs · Sewage Wks · Depot

Denholm · Works · Knowles La · Works · Fishers Cl · Fisher's Farm · Rush Farm · Home Farm · Sweetlands · Slaney Place · Cottons Farm · Spills Hill Farm

Field House · Fouracre · Further Field · Green Lane · Little Down · Watkins Rd · Hall · Staplehurst · Playing Field · Crad Corn Lane · Silver Locks · Ickenden Lane

44

Baldwins Farm · Marden · Hen and Duckhurst Farm · Marlfield · North · Corner Farm · Lime · Brooks Cl · Staplehurst · Crab Tree Farm · Club House · STAPLEHURST GOLF COURSE

2

Jeffery · Reeves · Bathurst Cl · Chestnut Rd · Alen Sq · Cornforth Cl · Knowles Wk · Marian Sq · Staple Slaney · Fonthill

Pope Dr · Stanley · Butch · Surrey Den · Play Fld · Staplehurst Sch · Mote Lodge · Loddenden Manor · Spilsill Farm · Tonbridge TN12

37 38

Aydhurst Farm · Bell · Bathurst · Gybbon · Offen's · The Drive · Usborne · Staplehurst Lib · The Pig · Green Ct · Chapel La · Fir Tree Cl · Spilsill Court · Bailey Farm · Little Craddock

3

Jaggard Rd · Lime Lane · McCabe · Bank · Hammer · Iden Grn · Church Grn · Gees Cres · A229 · Frittenden · Parish Room · Spilsill Lodge · Exhurst Manor

43

Mall · Wards · Way · Ckt Grd · Iden Court · Tent Cts · Folly Farm · The Warren · September Cottage · MAIDSTONE

4

Staple Street · A229 · TN17

37 38

TEYNHAM map

19

H 94 J 95 K 19 L M 96 N 97

The Bungalow · Lower Road · Fair View · Frognal · Sewage Works · Orchard Lodge · Blue Houses

Little Radfield · Claxfield Cottages · Sittingbourne ME9 · Sports Ground · Orchard Vw · Cherry · Teynham · Station Row · Barrow Green · Spring Grove · Osiers Farm

6

Glenbervie · Frognal · Teynham Parochial C of E Prim Sch · Bradfield · Avenue Road · Browning · Barrow Green Farm · Whiteleaf · Whent'sd Farm · Orchard View Stud

63

Transport Depot · Claxfield Farm · London Road · Frognal Gardens · Donald Moor Av · New Gardens Rd · Nobel · Lib · TEYNHAM

7

Jeffries · Nursery · New House Farm · The Garden · Orchard Thatch · White Hall · Sandown · Sandown Cottages

19

Vigo Farm · Fir Tree Cottage · Cellarhill · A2 · Nursery · Orchard House · Oast Cott · The Elms

8

Sunderland Farm · Claxfield · Lynsted Lane · Cambridge Road · Cambridge Farm · Well Ho · Waylands · The Old Thatched Cottage · Cherry Gardens · Nouds House · Moss House · Newlands Cottages · Wild Winds · Orchard House · Robins

62

The Roundels · Bogle · The Bungalow · Cambridge Cottage · Cherry Trees · Nouds Lane · Upper Newlands · Lewson Street Road · Norton

9

H J 19 K L M N

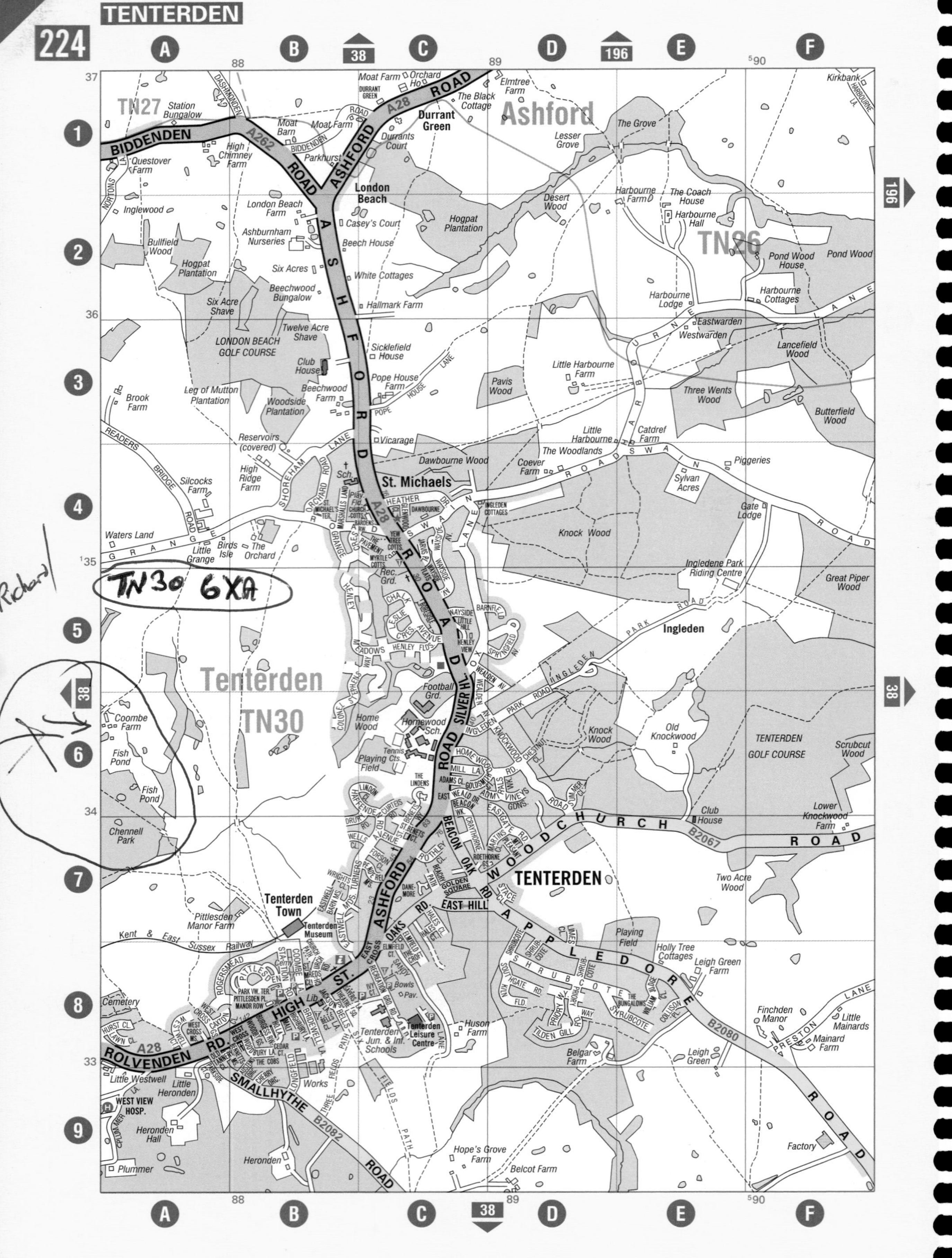
A
B
C
D
E
F
38
196
88
89
590
37
36
35
34
33
1
2
3
4
5
6
7
8
9
TN27
TN26
TN30
Ashford
Tenterden
TENTERDEN
St. Michaels
London Beach
Durrant Green
Ingleden
Tenterden Town
BIDDENDEN ROAD
ASHFORD ROAD
A28
A262
ROLVENDEN RD.
HIGH ST.
SMALLHYTHE ROAD
B2082
WOODCHURCH ROAD
B2067
APPLEDORE ROAD
B2080
Kent & East Sussex Railway
LONDON BEACH GOLF COURSE
TENTERDEN GOLF COURSE
Knock Wood
Hogpat Plantation
Dawbourne Wood
Pond Wood
Lancefield Wood
Three Wents Wood
Butterfield Wood
Great Piper Wood
Scrubcut Wood
Chennell Park
Coombe Farm
Fish Pond
Tenterden Museum
Homewood Sch.
Football Grd.
Tenterden Leisure Centre
Tenterden Jun. & Inf. Schools
WEST VIEW HOSP.
Heronden Hall
Plummer
Factory
TN30 6XA
Richard
A

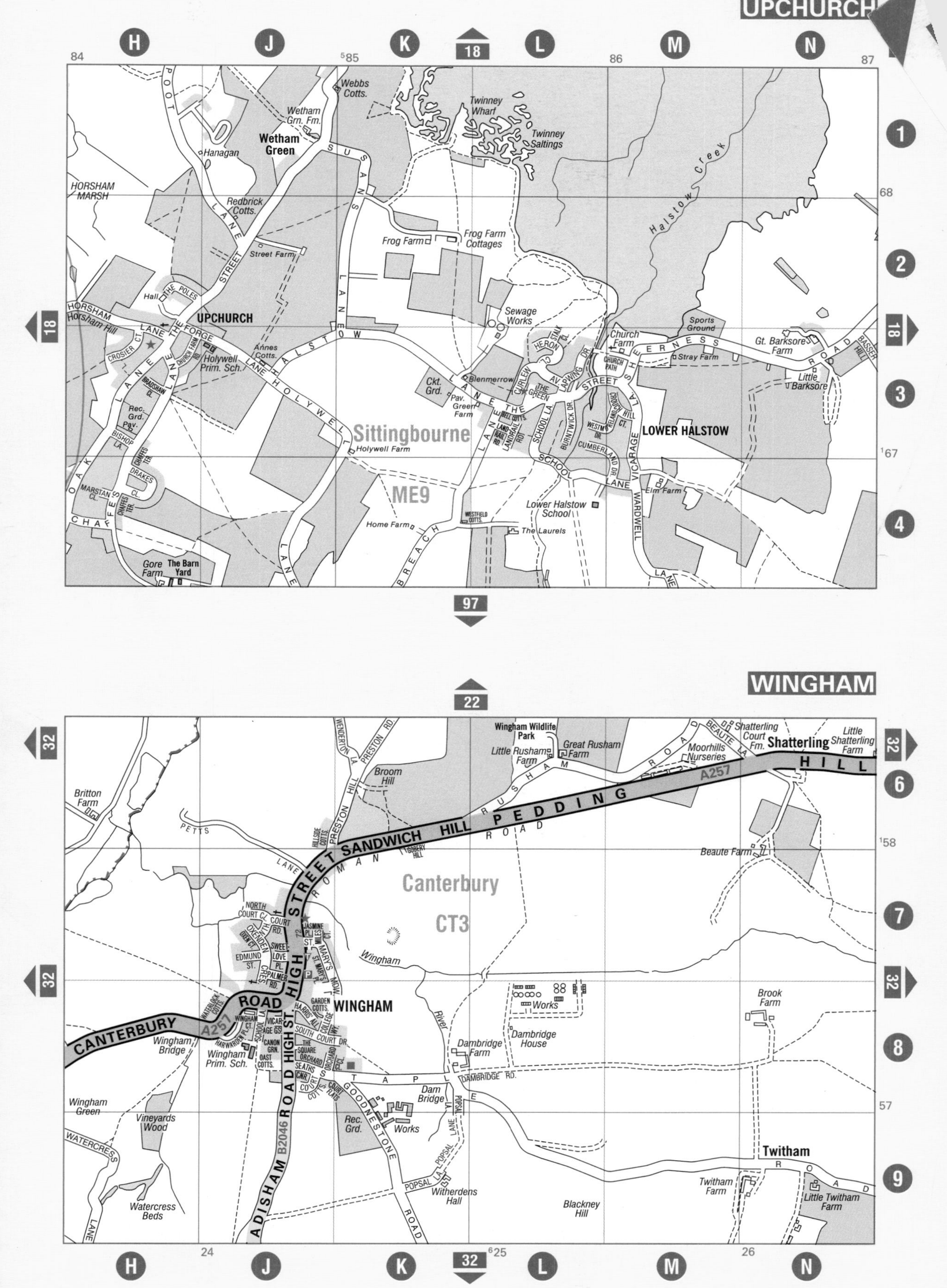

UPCHURCH
Wetham Green
Webbs Cotts.
Wetham Grn. Fm.
Hanagan
HORSHAM MARSH
Redbrick Cotts.
Street Farm
Twinney Wharf
Twinney Saltings
Halstow Creek
Frog Farm
Frog Farm Cottages
Sewage Works
Sports Ground
Church Farm
Gt. Barksore Farm
Stray Farm
Little Barksore
UPCHURCH
THE POLES
Hall
HORSHAM
Horsham Hill
THE FORGE
Holywell Prim. Sch.
Annes Cotts.
HALSTOW LANE
HOLYWELL LANE
Ckt. Grd.
Blenmerrow
Pav. Green Farm
Sittingbourne
Holywell Farm
ME9
LOWER HALSTOW
Lower Halstow School
Elm Farm
Home Farm
WESTFIELD COTTS.
The Laurels
Gore Farm
The Barn Yard
BREACH LANE
SCHOOL LANE
VICARAGE LA.
WARDWELL LANE
SHEERNESS ROAD
STREET
POOT LANE
CHAFFES LANE
Rec. Grd.
Pav.
BISHOP LA.
MARSTAN CL.
DRAKES CL.
WINGHAM
Wingham Wildlife Park
Little Rusham Farm
Great Rusham Farm
Moorhills Nurseries
Shatterling Court Fm.
Shatterling
Little Shatterling Farm
Britton Farm
Broom Hill
PRESTON HILL
PRESTON RD.
WENDERTON LA.
PEDDING HILL
RUSHAM ROAD
SANDWICH
A257
ROMAN ROAD
Beaute Farm
PETTS LANE
Canterbury
CT3
Wingham
HIGH STREET
HIGH ST.
NORTH COURT CL.
COURT RD.
EDMUND ST.
SWEETLOVE PL.
JASMINE PL.
ST. MARY'S MDW.
CANTERBURY ROAD
WINGHAM
Works
Brook Farm
Dambridge House
Dambridge Farm
DAMBRIDGE RD.
Wingham Bridge
Wingham Prim. Sch.
Wingham Green
Vineyards Wood
ADISHAM ROAD
B2046
STAPLE
Dam Bridge
POPSAL LANE
Rec. Grd.
GOODNESTONE ROAD
River
Witherdens Hall
Blackney Hill
Twitham
Twitham Farm
Little Twitham Farm
WATERCRESS LANE
Watercress Beds

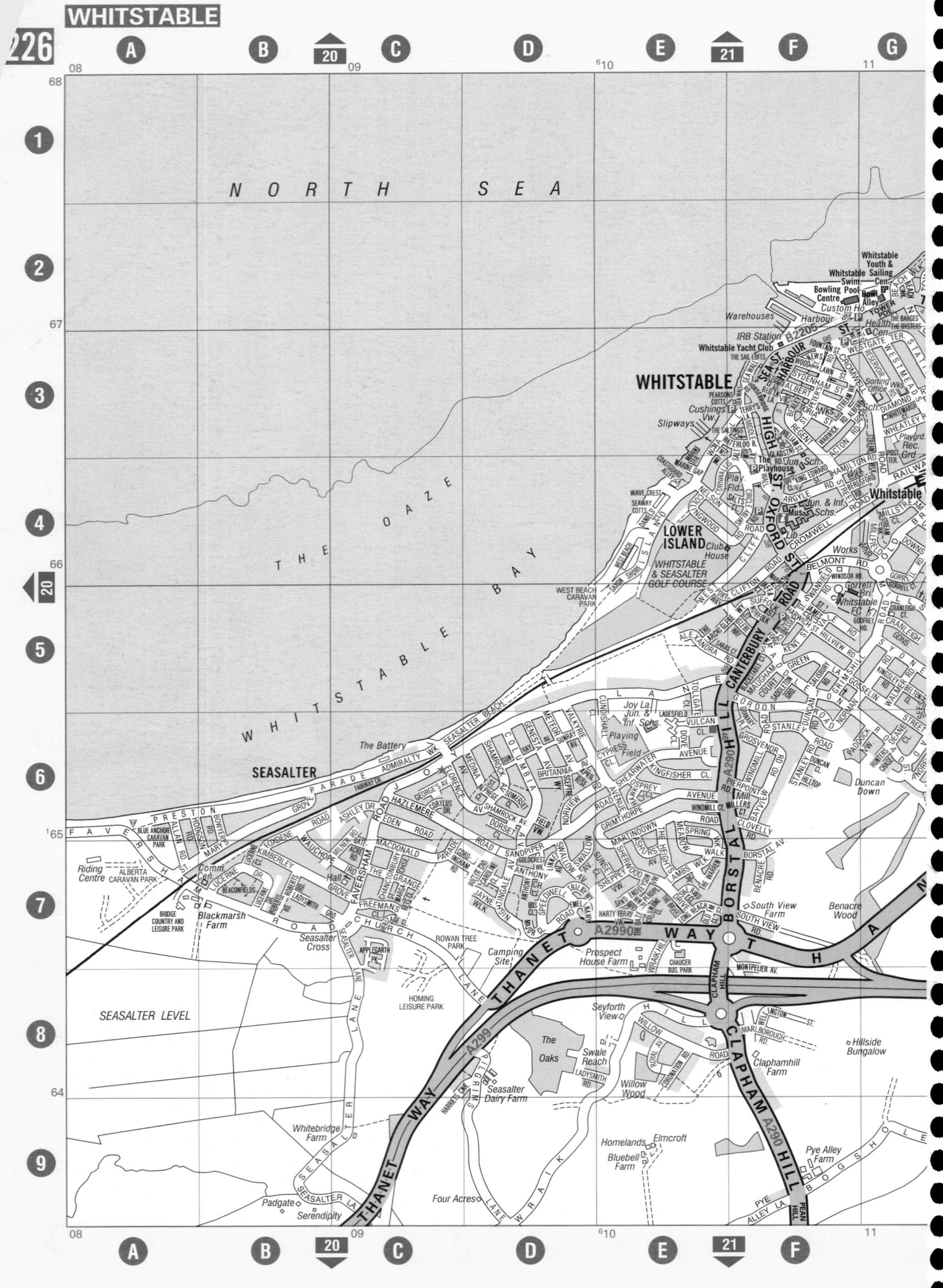
A
B
C
D
E
F
G
20
21
08
09
10
11
68
67
66
65
64
1
2
3
4
5
6
7
8
9
NORTH SEA
THE OAZE
WHITSTABLE BAY
WHITSTABLE
SEASALTER
LOWER ISLAND
Whitstable Youth & Sailing Cen.
Whitstable Swim. Pool
Bowling Centre
Bowl Alley
Custom Ho.
Harbour
Warehouses
IRB Station
Whitstable Yacht Club
B2205
HARBOUR ST.
Cushings Vw.
Slipways
The Playhouse
HIGH ST.
OXFORD ST.
Whitstable
WHITSTABLE & SEASALTER GOLF COURSE
Club House
WEST BEACH CARAVAN PARK
Gorrell Bri.
Whitstable FC
Works
CANTERBURY ROAD
The Battery
SEASALTER BEACH
FAVERSHAM ROAD
Joy La. Jun. & Inf. Schs.
Playing Field
Duncan Down
BORSTAL HILL
A290
Riding Centre
ALBERTA CARAVAN PARK
BLUE ANCHOR CARAVAN PARK
Comm. Cen.
BRIDGE COUNTRY AND LEISURE PARK
Blackmarsh Farm
Seasalter Cross
ROWAN TREE PARK
Camping Site
Prospect House Farm
CHAUCER BUS. PARK
South View Farm
Benacre Wood
THANET WAY
A2990
A299
HOMING LEISURE PARK
SEASALTER LEVEL
Seyforth View
The Oaks
Swale Reach
Willow Wood
Seasalter Dairy Farm
Claphamhill Farm
Hillside Bungalow
CLAPHAM HILL
Whitebridge Farm
Homelands
Elmcroft
Bluebell Farm
Pye Alley Farm
Four Acres
Padgate
Serendipity
SEASALTER LANE
PYE ALLEY LA.
BOGSHOLE LANE

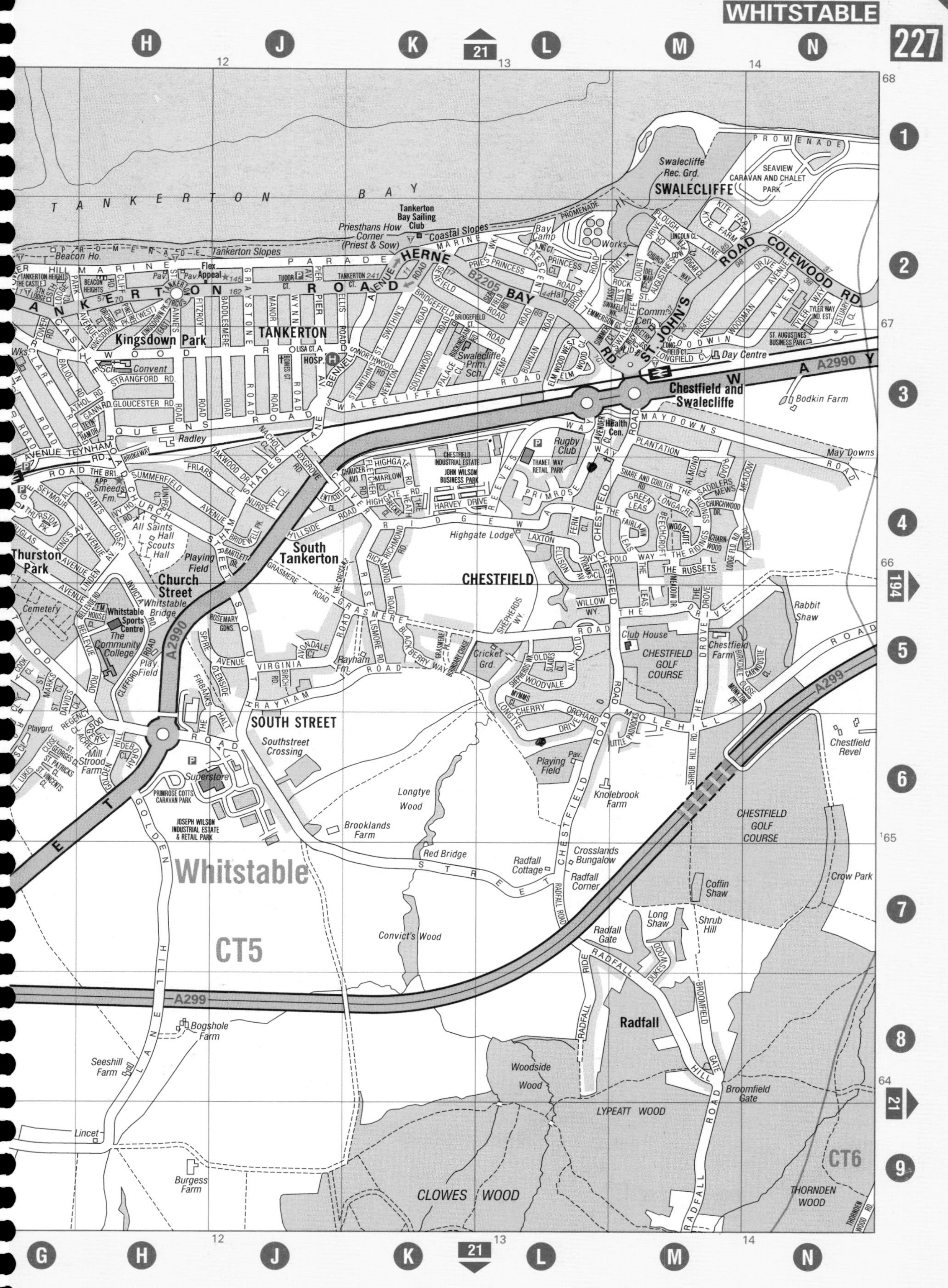
TANKERTON BAY
Tankerton Bay Sailing Club
Priesthans How Corner (Priest & Sow)
Coastal Slopes
Tankerton Slopes
Beacon Ho.
MARINE PARADE
Flex Appeal
TANKERTON ROAD
Kingsdown Park
TANKERTON
HERNE BAY ROAD
B2205
SWALECLIFFE
Swalecliffe Rec. Grd.
SEAVIEW CARAVAN AND CHALET PARK
PROMENADE
COLEWOOD RD
ST JOHN'S RD
Swalecliffe Prim. Sch.
Convent
QUEENS ROAD
Radley
SWALECLIFFE ROAD
Day Centre
Chestfield and Swalecliffe
A2990
Bodkin Farm
MAYDOWNS
May Downs
Rugby Club
Health Cen.
THANET WAY RETAIL PARK
CHESTFIELD INDUSTRIAL ESTATE
JOHN WILSON BUSINESS PARK
Highgate Lodge
South Tankerton
CHESTFIELD
Thurston Park
Church Street
Whitstable Bridge
Playing Field
All Saints Hall
Scouts Hall
Cemetery
Whitstable Sports Centre
The Community College
Club House
CHESTFIELD GOLF COURSE
Chestfield Farm
Rabbit Shaw
Cricket Grd.
Rayham Fm.
RAYHAM ROAD
SOUTH STREET
Southstreet Crossing
Superstore
PRIMROSE COTTS. CARAVAN PARK
JOSEPH WILSON INDUSTRIAL ESTATE & RETAIL PARK
Mill Strood Farm
Playing Field
Knolebrook Farm
Chestfield Revel
Longtye Wood
Brooklands Farm
Red Bridge
Radfall Cottage
Crosslands Bungalow
Radfall Corner
Coffin Shaw
Crow Park
Whitstable
CT5
Convict's Wood
Long Shaw
Shrub Hill
Radfall Gate
A299
Bogshole Farm
Radfall
Seeshill Farm
Woodside Wood
Broomfield Gate
LYPEATT WOOD
Lincet
Burgess Farm
CLOWES WOOD
THORNDEN WOOD
CT6

21
194
21

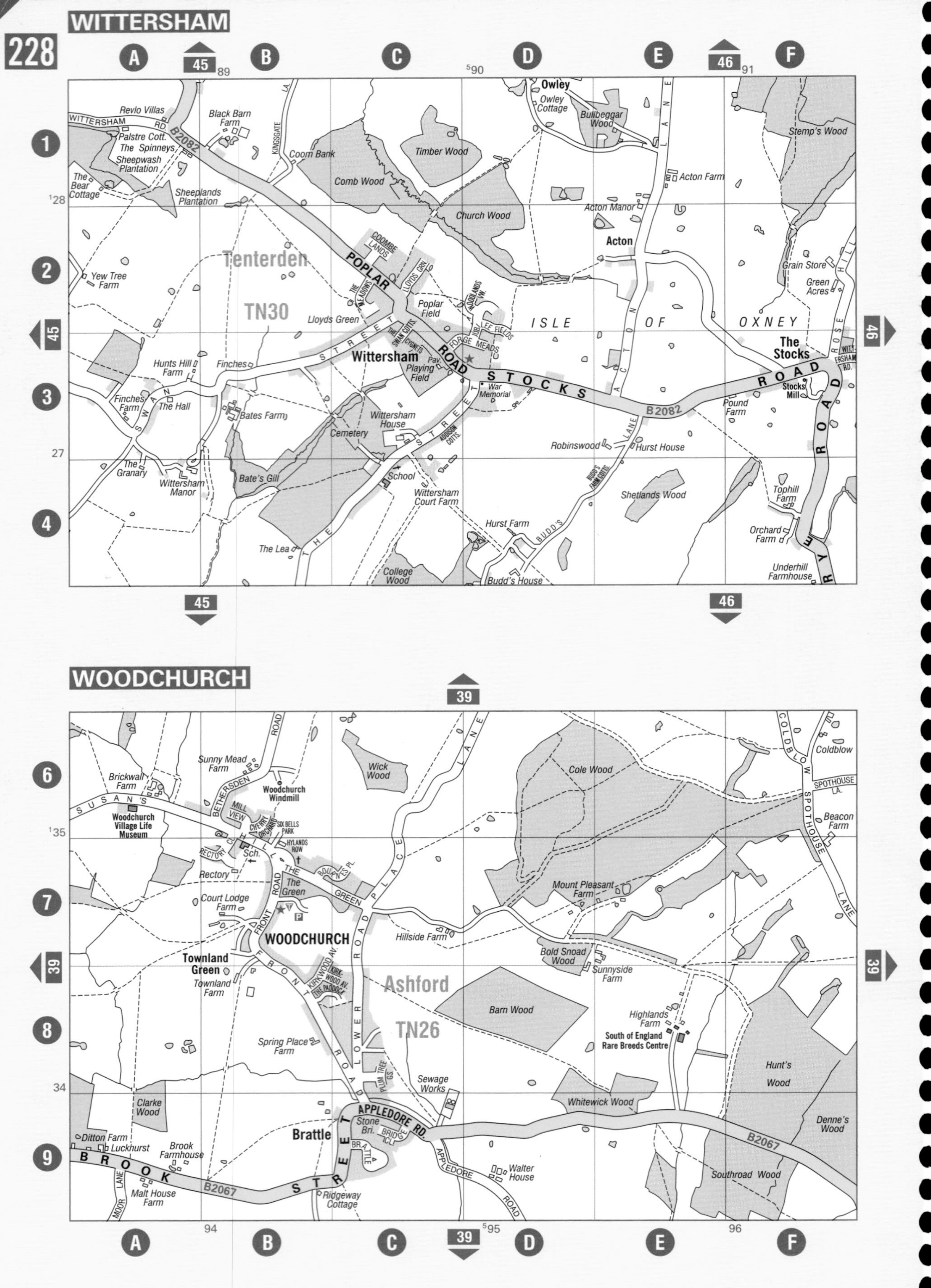

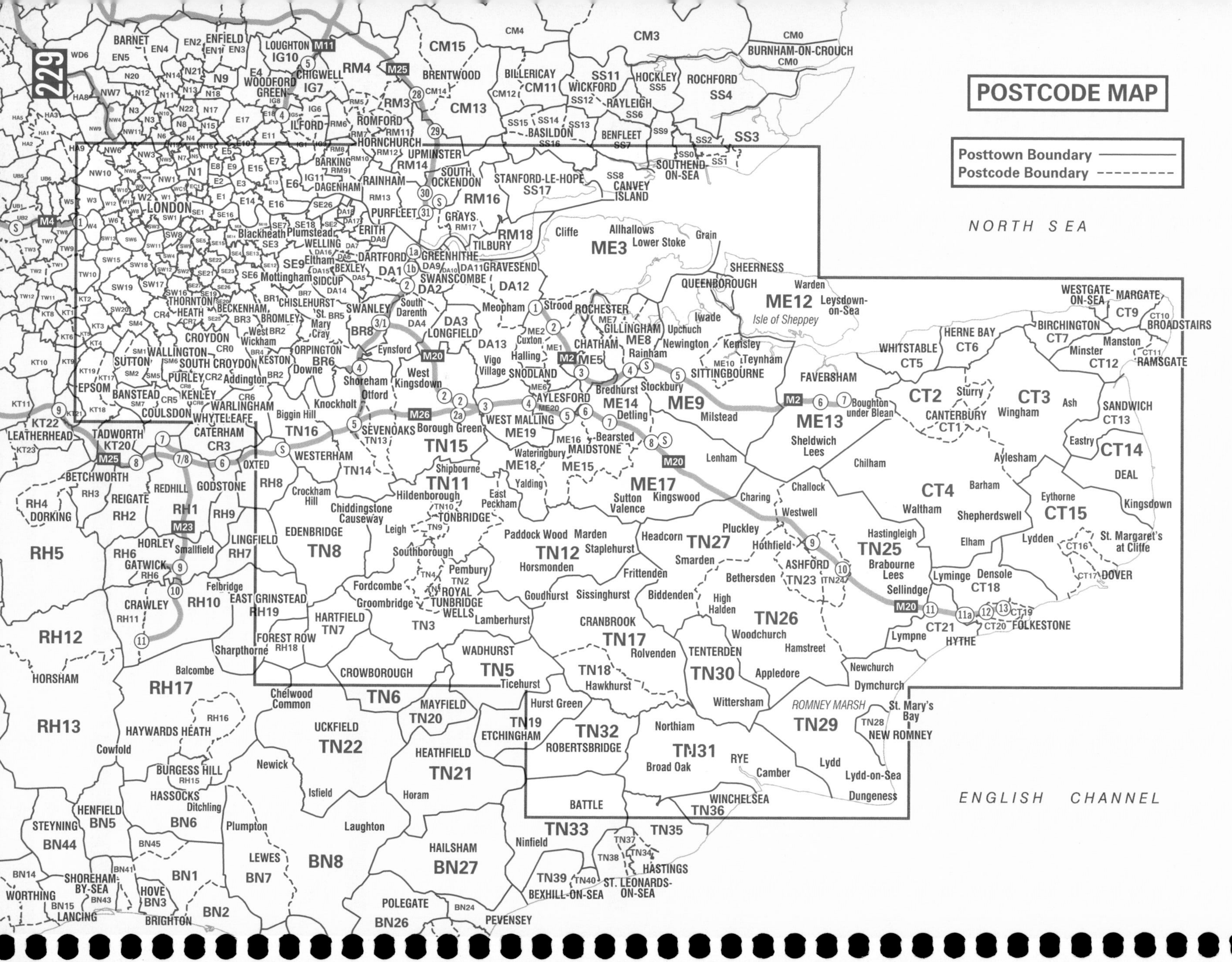

POSTCODE MAP

Posttown Boundary ————
Postcode Boundary - - - - - -

NORTH SEA

ENGLISH CHANNEL

INDEX

Including Streets, Places & Areas, Industrial Estates, Selected Flats & Walkways,
Junction Names, Stations and Selected Places of Interest.

HOW TO USE THIS INDEX

1. Each street name is followed by its Postcode District (or, if outside the London Postcode District, by its Locality), and then by its map reference; e.g. **Abbeyview Dr.** ME12: Minst . . . .6J **221** is in the ME12 Postcode District and the Minster Locality and is to be found in square 6J on page **221**. The page number is shown in bold type.

2. A strict alphabetical order is followed in which Av., Rd., St., etc. (though abbreviated) are read in full and as part of the street name; e.g. **Abbeyview Dr.** appears after **Abbey Trad. Est.** but before **Abbey Way.**

3. Streets and a selection of flats and walkways too small to be shown on the maps, appear in the index with the thoroughfare to which it is connected shown in brackets;
   e.g. **Ackerley Ct.** TN23: Ashf . . . . 3D **160** (off Stanhope Sq.)

4. Addresses that are in more than one part are referred to as not continuous.

5. Places and areas are shown in the index in BLUE TYPE and the map reference is to the actual map square in which the town centre or area is located and not to the place name shown on the map;
   e.g. **ABBEY GATE** 8C **110**

6. An example of a selected place of interest is 37 Gallery 5M **217**

7. Junction names are shown in the index in **BOLD TYPE**; e.g. **ANGEL** 2F **5**

8. An example of a station is **Bromley South Station (Rail)** . . . . 6K **69** (2A **14**). Included are Rail **(Rail)**, London Underground **(Tube)** Docklands Light Railway **(DLR)** and Croydon Tramlink **(CT)**.

9. Streets that appear on the 3 inches to 1 Mile Street Mapping red pages and 1 Inch to 1 Mile Street Mapping blue pages are given two references; e.g **Abbots Hill** ME13: Osp . . . . 8C **186** (7K **19**) is to be found in square 8C on page **186** on the 3 inches to 1 Mile Street Mapping and in square 7K on page **19** on the 1 inch to 1 Mile Street Mapping.

GENERAL ABBREVIATIONS

All. : Alley	**Cott.** : Cottage	**Ind.** : Industrial	**Pct.** : Precinct
App. : Approach	**Cotts.** : Cottages	**Info.** : Information	**Prom.** : Promenade
Arc. : Arcade	**Ct.** : Court	**Intl.** : International	**Quad.** : Quadrant
Av. : Avenue	**Cres.** : Crescent	**Junc.** : Junction	**Res.** : Residential
Bk. : Back	**Cft.** : Croft	**La.** : Lane	**Ri.** : Rise
Blvd. : Boulevard	**Dpt.** : Depot	**Lit.** : Little	**Rd.** : Road
Bri. : Bridge	**Dr.** : Drive	**Lwr.** : Lower	**Rdbt.** : Roundabout
B'way. : Broadway	**E.** : East	**Mnr.** : Manor	**Shop.** : Shopping
Bldg. : Building	**Emb.** : Embankment	**Mans.** : Mansions	**Sth.** : South
Bldgs. : Buildings	**Ent.** : Enterprise	**Mkt.** : Market	**Sq.** : Square
Bungs. : Bungalows	**Est.** : Estate	**Mdw.** : Meadow	**Sta.** : Station
Bus. : Business	**Ests.** : Estates	**Mdws.** : Meadows	**St.** : Street
Cvn. : Caravan	**Fld.** : Field	**M.** : Mews	**Ter.** : Terrace
C'way. : Causeway	**Flds.** : Fields	**Mt.** : Mount	**Twr.** : Tower
Cen. : Centre	**Gdn.** : Garden	**Mus.** : Museum	**Trad.** : Trading
Chu. : Church	**Gdns.** : Gardens	**Nth.** : North	**Up.** : Upper
Chyd. : Church Yard	**Gth.** : Garth	**No.** : Number	**Va.** : Vale
Circ. : Circle	**Ga.** : Gate	**Pal.** : Palace	**Vw.** : View
Cir. : Circus	**Gt.** : Great	**Pde.** : Parade	**Vs.** : Villas
Cl. : Close	**Grn.** : Green	**Pk.** : Park	**Vis.** : Visitors
Coll. : College	**Gro.** : Grove	**Pas.** : Passage	**Wlk.** : Walk
Comn. : Common	**Hgts.** : Heights	**Pav.** : Pavilion	**W.** : West
Cnr. : Corner	**Ho.** : House	**Pl.** : Place	**Yd.** : Yard

LOCALITY ABBREVIATIONS

Abb : **Abberton**	Bou Mo : **Boughton Monchelsea**	Coll S : **Collier Street**	Ewe M : **Ewell Minnis**
Acol : **Acol**	Bou B : **Boughton-under-Blean**	Cool : **Cooling**	Ewh G : **Ewhurst Green**
Acr : **Acrise**	Boxf : **Boxford**	Corr : **Corringham**	Eyns : **Eynsford**
Addtn : **Addington**	Boxl : **Boxley**	Coul : **Coulsdon**	Eyt : **Eythorne**
Adm : **Adisham**	Bra L : **Brabourne Lees**	Cous W : **Cousley Wood**	Farnb : **Farnborough**
Aldtn : **Aldington**	Bram : **Bramling**	Cowd : **Cowden**	Farn'm : **Farningham**
Alk : **Alkham**	Bras : **Brasted**	Cox : **Coxheath**	Fav : **Faversham**
Allh : **Allhallows**	Brede : **Brede**	Cran : **Cranbrook**	Fawk : **Fawkham**
Alltn : **Allington**	B'gar : **Bredgar**	Cray : **Crayford**	Fin : **Finglesham**
App : **Appledore**	B'hst : **Bredhurst**	Crock'n : **Crockenhill**	Five G : **Five Oak Green**
Ash : **Ash**	Brenc : **Brenchley**	Crock H : **Crockham Hill**	Flim : **Flimwell**
Ashf : **Ashford**	Bwood : **Brentwood**	Crowb : **Crowborough**	Fob : **Fobbing**
Ashy : **Ashley**	Bztt : **Brenzett**	C'hrst : **Crowhurst**	F'stone : **Folkestone**
Asht : **Ashtead**	Brid : **Bridge**	Croy : **Croydon**	Ford : **Fordcombe**
A'hst : **Ashurst**	Brig : **Brightling**	Crun : **Crundale**	F Row : **Forest Row**
A'hstw : **Ashurstwood**	B Oak : **Broad Oak**	Cud : **Cudham**	Four E : **Four Elms**
Avel : **Aveley**	B'stairs : **Broadstairs**	Cux : **Cuxton**	Frant : **Frant**
Aylfd : **Aylesford**	Brom : **Bromley**	Dag : **Dagenham**	Frin : **Frinsted**
Aysm : **Aylesham**	Brook : **Brook**	Dall : **Dallington**	Frit : **Frittenden**
Bad : **Badlesmere**	B'lnd : **Brookland**	Darg : **Dargate**	Gill : **Gillingham**
Bans : **Banstead**	Bkld : **Buckland**	Dart : **Dartford**	Godm : **Godmersham**
Bap : **Bapchild**	Bulp : **Bulphan**	Deal : **Deal**	Gold G : **Golden Green**
B'hm : **Barham**	Burh : **Burham**	D'sole : **Densole**	Good : **Goodnestone**
Bark : **Barking**	Burm : **Burmarsh**	Denst : **Denstroude**	Goud : **Goudhurst**
Barm : **Barming**	B'wsh : **Burwash**	Det : **Detling**	Graf G : **Grafty Green**
Bas : **Basildon**	Camb : **Camber**	Dit : **Ditton**	G'ney : **Graveney**
Batt : **Battle**	Cant : **Canterbury**	Dod : **Doddington**	Grav'nd : **Gravesend**
Bean : **Bean**	Can I : **Canvey Island**	Dor'land : **Dormansland**	Grays : **Grays**
Bear : **Bearsted**	Cap F : **Capel-le-Ferne**	Dover : **Dover**	Gt Cha : **Great Chart**
Beck'm : **Beckenham**	Cars : **Carshalton**	Downe : **Downe**	Gt Mon : **Great Mongeham**
Beckl : **Beckley**	Cat'm : **Caterham**	Drel : **Drellingore**	G'stne : **Greatstone**
Bek : **Bekesbourne**	Chad H : **Chadwell Heath**	Dung : **Dungeness**	Gt W : **Great Wakering**
Bell G : **Bell's Yew Green**	Chaf H : **Chafford Hundred**	Dunk : **Dunkirk**	G'hithe : **Greenhithe**
Belv : **Belvedere**	C'lck : **Challock**	Dun G : **Dunton Green**	Groom : **Groombridge**
Bendn : **Benenden**	Char'g : **Charing**	Dym : **Dymchurch**	Gues T : **Guestling Thorn**
Benf : **Benfleet**	Chart'm : **Chartham**	E Bra : **East Brabourne**	Gus : **Guston**
Beth : **Bethersden**	Cha H : **Chartham Hatch**	E'chu : **Eastchurch**	Hackl : **Hacklinge**
Bett : **Betteshanger**	Cha S : **Chart Sutton**	E Far : **East Farleigh**	Hdlw : **Hadlow**
Bex'y : **Bexley**	Chat'm : **Chatham**	E Grin : **East Grinstead**	Hall'g : **Halling**
Bexhth : **Bexleyheath**	C'den : **Chattenden**	E Guld : **East Guldeford**	Hals : **Halstead**
Bic : **Bicknor**	Chels : **Chelsfield**	E Lan : **East Langdon**	Ham : **Ham**
Bidb : **Bidborough**	Chel C : **Chelwood Common**	E'lng : **Eastling**	Hamm : **Hammerwood**
Bidd : **Biddenden**	Chel G : **Chelwood Gate**	E Mal : **East Malling**	Hams : **Hamstreet**
Big H : **Biggin Hill**	Chess : **Chessington**	E Peck : **East Peckham**	Harb : **Harbledown**
Bils : **Bilsington**	Chid : **Chiddingstone**	E'try : **Eastry**	H'shm : **Harrietsham**
Birch : **Birchington**	Chid H : **Chiddingstone Hoath**	E Stu : **East Studdal**	Hartf : **Hartfield**
Birl : **Birling**	Chil'm : **Chilham**	E Sut : **East Sutton**	Hart'y : **Hartley**
Bis : **Bishopsbourne**	Chill : **Chillenden**	E Til : **East Tilbury**	H'lip : **Hartlip**
Blkm : **Blackham**	Chilw : **Chilworth**	E'well : **Eastwell**	H'lgh : **Hastingleigh**
Blean : **Blean**	Chip : **Chipstead**	Eden : **Edenbridge**	Hawkh : **Hawkhurst**
Bluew : **Bluewater**	Chst : **Chislehurst**	Eger : **Egerton**	H'nge : **Hawkinge**
Bob : **Bobbing**	C'let : **Chislet**	Elham : **Elham**	H'crn : **Headcorn**
Bdm : **Bodiam**	Chu H : **Church Hougham**	Elms : **Elmsted**	Hpstd : **Hempstead**
Bods : **Bodsham**	Cliffe : **Cliffe**	Evtn : **Elvington**	H Bay : **Herne Bay**
Bon : **Bonnington**	Cli W : **Cliffe Woods**	Epp G : **Epping Green**	Hernh : **Hernhill**
B'den : **Borden**	C'snd : **Cliffsend**	Eps : **Epsom**	Hersd : **Hersden**
Bor G : **Borough Green**	Clift : **Cliftonville**	Eri G : **Eridge Green**	Hever : **Hever**
Bou A : **Boughton Aluph**	Cobh : **Cobham**	Erith : **Erith**	High'm : **Higham**
Bou L : **Boughton Lees**	Cold : **Coldred**	Etch'm : **Etchingham**	H Hald : **High Halden**
Bou Ma : **Boughton Malherbe**	Cole H : **Coleman's Hatch**	Etch'l : **Etchinghill**	H Hals : **High Halstow**

Hild : **Hildenborough**
Hin : **Hinxhill**
Hoath : **Hoath**
Holl : **Hollingbourne**
Hoo : **Hoo**
H'church : **Hornchurch**
Horn H : **Horndon-On-The-Hill**
Horsm : **Horsmonden**
Hors K : **Horsted Keynes**
Hort K : **Horton Kirby**
Hoth : **Hothfield**
Hou : **Hougham**
Hunt : **Hunton**
Hur G : **Hurst Green**
Hythe : **Hythe**
Ickh : **Ickham**
Ickl : **Icklesham**
Ide H : **Ide Hill**
Iden : **Iden**
Igh : **Ightham**
Ilf : **Ilford**
Isle G : **Isle of Grain**
Ist R : **Istead Rise**
Ivyc : **Ivychurch**
Ivy H : **Ivy Hatch**
Iwade : **Iwade**
Jar B : **Jarvis Brook**
Kems'g : **Kemsing**
Kems'y : **Kemsley**
Kena : **Kenardington**
Kenl : **Kenley**
Kenn : **Kennington**
Kes : **Keston**
Kiln : **Kilndown**
Kgdn : **Kingsdown**
Kgnt : **Kingsnorth**
Kgstn : **Kingston**
King T : **Kingston Upon Thames**
Kgswd : **Kingswood**
Knat : **Knatts Valley**
Knock : **Knockholt**
Ladd : **Laddingford**
Lain : **Laindon**
Lamb : **Lamberhurst**
Lang H : **Langdon Hills**
L'ly : **Langley**
Lang G : **Langton Green**
Lark : **Larkfield**
Leeds : **Leeds**
Leigh : **Leigh**
Lgh S : **Leigh-on-Sea**
Len : **Lenham**
Leyb : **Leybourne**
Ley S : **Leysdown-on-Sea**
Linf : **Linford**
Ling : **Lingfield**
Lint : **Linton**
L'brne : **Littlebourne**
L Char : **Little Chart**
L Mon : **Little Mongeham**
L'stne : **Littlestone**
Lon : **London**
Long : **Longfield**
Long H : **Longfield Hill**
Loose : **Loose**
Lwr Hal : **Lower Halstow**
Lwr Har : **Lower Hardres**
Lwr Sto : **Lower Stoke**
Lud'm : **Luddenham**
Lud'n : **Luddesdown**
Lydd : **Lydd**
Lyd'n : **Lydden**
Lye G : **Lye Green**
Lym'ge : **Lyminge**
Lymp : **Lympne**
Lyn : **Lynsted**
Maid : **Maidstone**
Mans : **Manston**
Mard : **Marden**
Mgte : **Margate**
Mark : **Markbeech**
Mark C : **Mark Cross**
Marsh G : **Marsh Green**
M'sde : **Marshside**
Mart : **Martin**
Mart M : **Martin Mill**
Mat : **Matfield**
Mayf : **Mayfield**
Med E : **Medway City Estate**
Meop : **Meopham**
Mere : **Mereworth**
Mers : **Mersham**
Mils : **Milstead**
Minst : **Minster**
Mitc : **Mitcham**
Mol : **Molash**
M Hor : **Monks Horton**
Monk'n : **Monkton**
Mord : **Morden**
Mount : **Mountfield**
Neth : **Netherfield**
New A : **New Ash Green**
Newchu : **Newchurch**
N'den : **Newenden**
N'grn : **Newingreen**
N'tn : **Newington**
N Mald : **New Malden**
Newn : **Newnham**
New R : **New Romney**
Non : **Nonington**
Nflt : **Northfleet**
Nflt G : **Northfleet Green**
N'thiam : **Northiam**
N Ock : **North Ockendon**
N Stif : **North Stifford**
Nut : **Nutley**
Oare : **Oare**
Off : **Offham**
Old R : **Old Romney**
Old L : **Old Wives Lees**
Orp : **Orpington**
Ors : **Orsett**
Osp : **Ospringe**
Otf : **Otford**
Otham : **Otham**
O'den : **Otterden**
O'nge : **Ottinge**
Oxt : **Oxted**
P'wth : **Paddlesworth**
Pad W : **Paddock Wood**
Peas : **Peasmarsh**
Peene : **Peene**
Pem : **Pembury**
Pen H : **Penenden Heath**
P'hrst : **Penhurst**
Pens : **Penshurst**
P'hm : **Petham**
Pett : **Pett**
Pet W : **Petts Wood**
Plax : **Plaxtol**
Play : **Playden**
P'ley : **Pluckley**
Post : **Postling**
Prat B : **Pratts Bottom**
Pres : **Preston**
Purf : **Purfleet**
Purl : **Purley**
Queen : **Queenborough**
Rain : **Rainham**
Ram : **Ramsgate**
Rec : **Reculver**
R Min : **Rhodes Minnis**
Rich : **Richmond**
R'wld : **Ringwould**
Ripp : **Ripple**
Riv : **Riverhead**
Rob : **Robertsbridge**
Roch : **Rochester**
Rod : **Rodmersham**
Rolv : **Rolvenden**
Rolv L : **Rolvenden Layne**
Roth : **Rotherfield**
R Comn : **Rough Common**
Rough : **Roughway**
Ruck : **Ruckinge**
Rush G : **Rush Green**
R'hall : **Rusthall**
Rya : **Ryarsh**
Rye : **Rye**
Rye F : **Rye Foreign**
Salt : **Saltwood**
S'gte : **Sandgate**
Sandh : **Sandhurst**
S'lng : **Sandling**
S'wy : **Sandway**
S'wch : **Sandwich**
Seal : **Seal**
Seas : **Seasalter**
Sed : **Sedlescombe**
S'ndge : **Sellindge**
Sell'g : **Selling**
S'oaks : **Sevenoaks**
Svgtn : **Sevington**
Shad : **Shadoxhurst**
Sharp : **Sharpthorne**
Shtng : **Shatterling**
S'ness : **Sheerness**
Shel : **Sheldwich**
S'wll : **Shepherdswell**
S'brne : **Shipbourne**
Shoe : **Shoeburyness**
Shol : **Sholden**
S'ham : **Shoreham**
Shorne : **Shorne**
Shortl : **Shortlands**
Sidc : **Sidcup**
Siss : **Sissinghurst**
Sit : **Sittingbourne**
Smar : **Smarden**
Sme : **Smeeth**
Snar : **Snargate**
Snod : **Snodland**
Sole S : **Sole Street**
S'bgh : **Southborough**
S Croy : **South Croydon**
S Dar : **South Darenth**
Sth S : **Southend-on-Sea**
Sflt : **Southfleet**
S Ock : **South Ockendon**
Speld : **Speldhurst**
Stal : **Stalisfield**
Stanf : **Stanford**
Stan H : **Stanford-le-Hope**
Stans : **Stansted**
S'le : **Staple**
S'cross : **Staplecross**
S'hrst : **Staplehurst**
S Min : **Stelling Minnis**
St Marg : **St Margarets-at-Cliffe**
St M Cry : **St Mary Cray**
St M Hoo : **St Mary Hoo**
St M Mar : **St Mary in the Marsh**
St M Bay : **St Marys Bay**
St Mic : **St Michaels**
St N : **St Nicholas at Wade**
S'bry : **Stockbury**
Ston C E : **Stone-cum-Ebony**
St'gate : **Stonegate**
Stow : **Stowting**
St P : **St Pauls Cray**
Strood : **Strood**
Stu X : **Stubbs Cross**
Sturry : **Sturry**
Sund : **Sundridge**
Surb : **Surbiton**
Sutt : **Sutton**
Sut V : **Sutton Valence**
Swanl : **Swanley**
Swans : **Swanscombe**
S'fld : **Swingfield**
Tad : **Tadworth**
Tats : **Tatsfield**
Temp E : **Temple Ewell**
Tent : **Tenterden**
Tstn : **Teston**
Tey : **Teynham**
Thor H : **Thornton Heath**
T Oaks : **Three Oaks**
Throw : **Throwley**
T'hm : **Thurnham**
Tice : **Ticehurst**
Tide : **Tidebrook**
Tilb : **Tilbury**
Tilm : **Tilmanstone**
Tonb : **Tonbridge**
Tonge : **Tonge**
Town R : **Town Row**
Tros : **Trottiscliffe**
Tude : **Tudeley**
Tun W : **Tunbridge Wells**
T'stall : **Tunstall**
T Hill : **Tyler Hill**
Udim : **Udimore**
Ulc : **Ulcombe**
Under : **Underriver**
Upc : **Upchurch**
Upm : **Upminster**
Upnor : **Upnor**
Up Harb : **Upper Harbledown**
Up Hard : **Upper Hardres**
Up Hart : **Upper Hartfield**
Ups : **Upstreet**
Van : **Vange**
Wadh : **Wadhurst**
Wain : **Wainscott**
W'share : **Waldershare**
Wall : **Wallington**
Walm : **Walmer**
Walt : **Waltham**
Ward : **Warden**
W'hrne : **Warehorne**
Warl : **Warlingham**
War S : **Warren Street**
W'bury : **Wateringbury**
Weald : **Weald**
Weav : **Weavering**
Well : **Welling**
Wemb : **Wembley**
Wenn : **Wennington**
W Bra : **West Brabourne**
Wclf S : **Westcliff-on-Sea**
Wnhgr : **Westenhanger**
Westrm : **Westerham**
W Far : **West Farleigh**
W'fld : **Westfield**
Wgte S : **Westgate-on-Sea**
W Hou : **West Hougham**
W Hyt : **West Hythe**
W King : **West Kingsdown**
W Lan : **West Langdon**
W Mal : **West Malling**
W Peck : **West Peckham**
W Thur : **West Thurrock**
W Til : **West Tilbury**
Westw : **Westwell**
W W'ck : **West Wickham**
What : **Whatlington**
Whitf : **Whitfield**
Whits : **Whitstable**
Whyt : **Whyteleafe**
Wich : **Wichling**
Wickh : **Wickhambreaux**
W'boro : **Willesborough**
Winch : **Winchelsea**
Wing : **Wingham**
Withy : **Withyham**
Witter : **Wittersham**
Wold : **Woldingham**
Wom : **Womenswold**
Wdchu : **Woodchurch**
Wdboro : **Woodnesborough**
Woot : **Wootton**
Wor Pk : **Worcester Park**
Worm : **Wormshill**
Worth : **Worth**
Woul : **Wouldham**
Wro : **Wrotham**
Wych C : **Wych Cross**
Wye : **Wye**
Yald : **Yalding**

37 Gallery 5M **217**
20/20 Ind. Est. ME16: Alltn 1N **125**

A

Abbeville Ho. ME1: Roch 8N **79**
Abbeville Rd. SW4 6E **4**
Abbey Brewery Ct. ME19: W Mal 1A **124**
Abbey Cl. CT14: Deal 5K **177**
ME12: Minst 6L **221**
Abbey Cotts. ME14: S'lng 9C **110**
Abbey Ct. CT8: Wgte S 4J **207**
TN4: Tun W 9G **151**
Abbey Ct. Cotts. ME5: Aylfd 4B **110**
ME14: S'lng 8C **110**
Abbey Cres. DA17: Belv 4B **52**
Abbey Dr. DA5: Bex'y 7F **58**
Abbey Flds. ME13: Fav 5J **187**
(not continuous)
Abbey Flds. Ct. ME13: Fav 5J **187**
Abbey Gdns. BR7: Chst 4C **70**
CT2: Cant 9N **167**
ABBEY GATE 8C **110**
Abbey Ga. CT11: Ram 7F **210**
Abbey Ga. Cotts. ME14: S'lng 8C **110**
Abbey Gro. CT11: Ram 7F **210**
CT12: Minst 8F **212**
SE2 4K **51**
Abbey Hill Rd. DA15: Sidc 7L **57**
Abbey La. BR3: Beck'm 3D **68**
E15 2K **5**
Abbey Mt. DA17: Belv 5A **52**
Abbey Pk. BR3: Beck'm 3D **68**
Abbey Pl. DA1: Dart 3L **59**
ME13: Fav 4H **187**
Abbey Rd. CT15: Ashy, W Lan 1H **179** (6F **33**)
CT15: Dover 3A **180** (1D **42**)
CT15: W Lan, Whitf 5H **179** (6F **33**)
CT16: Temp E 9C **178**
CT17: Dover 3A **180** (1E **42**)
DA7: Bexhth 2N **57**
DA9: G'hithe 3J **61**
DA12: Grav'nd 6K **63** (7D **8**)
DA17: Belv 4M **51** (4D **6**)
E15 2K **5**
IG11: Bark 1B **6**
ME2: Strood 4K **79**
ME8: Gill 1K **95**
ME13: Fav 4H **187**
NW6 1C **4**
NW8 2C **4**
NW10 2A **4**
SE2 4D **6**
Abbey St. ME13: Fav 4H **187**
SE1 4G **5**
Abbey Ter. SE2 4L **51**
Abbey Trad. Est. SE26 1C **68**
Abbeyview Dr. ME12: Minst 6J **221**
Abbey Way TN24: W'boro 8L **159**
ABBEY WOOD 4L **51** (4D **6**)
Abbey Wood Camping & Cvn. Site SE2 4L **51**
Abbey Wood Rd. ME19: W Mal 4M **123**
SE2 4K **51**
Abbey Wood Station (Rail) 3L **51** (4D **6**)
Abbots Barton Wlk. CT1: Cant 3A **172**
Abbotsbury Rd. BR2: Shortl 3J **83**
SM4: Mord 3C **12**
Abbots Cl. BR5: Farnb 2E **84**
Abbots Fld. DA12: Grav'nd 2H **77**
ME16: Maid 7M **125**
Abbots Grn. CR0: Croy 7A **82**
Abbotshall Rd. SE6 6G **54**
Abbot's Hill CT11: Ram 6J **211**
Abbots Hill ME13: Osp 8C **186** (7K **19**)
Abbots Pl. CT1: Cant 1M **171**
Abbots Rd. ME13: Fav 5J **187**
Abbots, The CT17: Dover 4H **181**
Abbots Wlk. TN25: Wye 2M **159**
Abbotswell Rd. SE4 3C **54**
Abbots Wood CT4: B'hm 5J **31**
Abbotswood Cl. DA17: Belv 3N **51**
Abbott Rd. CT20: F'stone 5L **189**
E14 3K **5**
(not continuous)
TN15: Bor G 2M **121**
Abbotts Cl. BR8: Swanl 7H **73**
ME1: Roch 9M **79**
Abbotts Ct. Rd. ME3: Hoo 9J **67**
Abbotts Dr. SS17: Stan H 2E **8**
Abbotts Rd. SM3: Sutt 4C **12**
Abbott's Wlk. DA7: Bexhth 7M **51**
Abbs Cross La. RM12: H'church 1G **7**
ABC Cinema
Canterbury 2N **171**
Chatham 8D **80**
Aberconway Rd. SM4: Mord 2C **12**
Abercorn Pl. NW8 2D **4**
Aberdare Cl. BR4: W W'ck 3F **82**
Aberdeen Cl. CT3: Ups 5B **22**
Aberdeen Ho. ME15: Maid 1H **139**
Aberdeen Rd. CR0: Croy 4G **13**
NW10 1A **4**
Aberford Gdns. SE18 8A **50**
Abergeldie Rd. SE12 4L **55**
Abernethy Rd. SE13 2H **55**
Abery St. SE18 4G **50**
Abigail Cres. ME5: Chat'm 1D **110**
Abingdon Gro. CT3: Ups 5B **22**
Abingdon Lodge *BR1: Brom* *4J* ***69***
(off Beckenham La.)
Abingdon M. ME19: W Mal 1A **124**
Abingdon Rd. ME16: Barm 7K **125**
Abingdon Way BR6: Chels 5K **85**
Abinger Cl. BR1: Brom 6A **70**
CR0: Croy 7F **82**
Abinger Dr. ME5: Chat'm 9G **94**
Aboyne Rd. SW17 7D **4**
Absolam Ct. ME8: Gill 1M **95**
Acacia Cl. BR5: Pet W 8F **70**
Acacia Ct. DA11: Grav'nd 5F **62**
Acacia Dr. SS1: Sth S 1F **11**
Acacia Gdns. BR4: W W'ck 3F **82**
Acacia Rd. BR3: Beck'm 6C **68**
DA1: Dart 6L **59**
DA9: G'hithe 4E **60**
Acacia Ter. ME10: Sit 7D **98**
Acacia Wlk. BR8: Swanl 5E **72**
Acacia Way DA15: Sidc 6H **57**
Acadamy Dr. ME7: Gill 2J **95**
Academy Pl. SE18 8B **50**
Academy Rd. SE18 8B **50** (5B **6**)
Acer Av. TN2: Tun W 5J **157**
Acer Rd. TN16: Big H 4D **164**
Achilles Rd. ME5: Chat'm 9F **94**
Ackerley Ct. *TN23: Ashf* *3D* ***160***
(off Stanhope Sq.)
Ackholt Rd. CT3: Aysm 2E **162** (3C **32**)
Ackroyd Rd. SE23 5A **54**
Acland Cl. SE18 7F **50**
ACOL 8G **207** (3F **23**)
Acol Hill CT7: Acol 7G **206** (3F **23**)
Acorn Cl. BR7: Chst 1E **70**
CT18: H'nge 8M **193**
TN12: Five G 8G **147**

Acorn Cl.—Allen Rd.

Acorn Cl. TN23: Kgnt 6G 161
Acorn Gro. ME20: Dit 1H 125
Acorn Ind. Pk. DA1: Cray 3H 59
Acorn Pl. ME15: Maid 2H 139
Acorn Rd. DA1: Cray 3G 59
ME7: Gill 8J 81
Acorns, The TN13: S'oaks 5H 119
TN27: Smar 8B 222
Acorn St. ME12: S'ness 3D 220
Acorn Way BR3: Beck'm 8F 68
BR6: Farnb 5D 84
SE23 8A 54
Acorn Wharf Rd. ME1: Roch 6N 79
Acott Flds. ME18: Yald 7D 136
Acre Cl. ME1: Roch 2B 94
Acre Gro. ME2: Hall'g 7E 92
Acre La. SM5: Cars 4E 12
SM6: Wall 4E 12
SW2 6F 5
Acre, The CT16: Whitf 5E 178
ACRISE 1K 41
ACTON
Ealing 3A 4
Wittersham 2E 228 (2A 46)
Acton Central Station (Rail) 3A 4
ACTON GREEN 4A 4
Acton La. NW10 2A 4
TN30: Witter 3E 228 (2A 46)
W4 4A 4
(Chiswick High Rd.)
W4 4A 4
(Winchester St.)
Acton Main Line Station (Rail) 3A 4
Acton Pl. ME18: Yald 7E 136
Acton Rd. CT5: Whits 3F 226
Acton Town Station (Tube) 4A 4
Acworth Ho. *SE18* *6D 50*
(off Barnfield Rd.)
Acworth Pl. DA1: Dart 4K 59
Adam Cl. ME17: Cox 5A 138
SE6 9C 54
Adams Cl. TN30: Tent 6C 224
Adams La. TN31: N'thiam 4F 45
Adamson Way BR3: Beck'm 8F 68
Adamsrill Rd. SE26 9A 54
Adams Rd. BR3: Beck'm 8B 68
Adams Sq. DA6: Bexhth 1N 57
Ada Rd. CT1: Cant 4K 171
Adbert Dr. ME15: E Far 4M 137
Adcock Wlk. BR6: Orp 5H 85
Addelam Cl. CT14: Deal 6K 177
Addelam Rd. CT14: Deal 6K 177
Adderley Gdns. SE9 9C 56
ADDINGTON
Croydon 6D 82 (4J 13)
West Malling 7J 107 (7C 16)
Addington Gro. SE26 9B 54
Addington La. ME19: Tros 6F 106 (7C 16)
Addington Pl. CT11: Ram 6J 211
Addington Rd. BR4: W W'ck 5F 82 (4K 13)
CR2: S Croy 9A 82 (6H 13)
CT9: Mgte 3D 208
ME10: Sit 8F 98
Addington Sq. CT9: Mgte 3D 208
Addington St. CT9: Mgte 3D 208
CT11: Ram 6H 211
Addington Village Rd. CR0: Croy 7C 82 (4J 13)
(not continuous)
Addington Village Stop (CT) 7D 82 (5J 13)
ADDISCOMBE 3H 13
Addiscombe Gdns. CT9: Mgte 4D 208
Addiscombe Gro. CR0: Croy 4G 13
Addiscombe Rd. CR0: Croy 4G 13
CT9: Mgte 4E 208 (1J 23)
Addiscombe Stop (CT) 3H 13
Addison Cl. BR5: Pet W 9E 70
ME19: E Mal 9D 108
Addison Cotts. TN30: Witter 3C 228
Addison Cres. W14 4C 4
Addison Dr. SE12 3L 55
Addison Rd. BR2: Shortl 8M 69
W14 4C 4
Addisons Cl. CR0: Croy 3C 82
ADDLESTEAD 2K 147 (5D 26)
Addlestead Rd. TN12: E Peck 1K 147 (5D 26)
Adelaide Av. SE4 2C 54 (6J 5)
Adelaide Cotts. ME15: E Far 1L 137
Adelaide Ct. BR3: Beck'm 3C 68
Adelaide Dr. ME10: Sit 7D 98
Adelaide Gdns. CT11: Ram 6J 211
ME12: Minst 6E 220
Adelaide Pl. CT1: Cant 2M 171
Adelaide Rd. BR7: Chst 1D 70
CT15: Evtn, Eyt 7J 185 (4D 32)
ME7: Gill 8F 80
NW3 1D 4
Adelaide, The ME3: High'm 7G 65
Adenmore Rd. SE6 5D 54
Aden Ter. ME14: Maid 2C 126
Adie Rd. TN28: G'stne 6M 213
ADISHAM 2B 32
Adisham Downs Rd. CT3: Adm 2A 32
CT3: Bek 8L 173 (2A 32)
CT4: Bek 8L 173
Adisham Dr. ME16: Alltn 2M 125
Adisham Grn. ME10: Kems'y 3G 99
Adisham Rd. CT3: Aysm 4A 162 (4B 32)
CT3: Wing,Good, Aysm 9J 225 (2B 32)
CT4: Aysm, B'hm 7F 162 (4B 32)
CT4: Bek 7K 173 (2A 32)
Adisham Station (Rail) 3B 32
Adisham Way CT9: Mgte 4G 208
Admaston Rd. SE18 7E 50
Admers Wood DA13: Meop 2G 106
Admiral Cl. BR5: St P 7M 71
Admiral Moore Dr. ME20: Aylfd 9K 109
Admiral Seymour Rd. SE9 2B 56
Admirals Wlk. CT21: Hythe 7K 199
DA9: G'hithe 3H 61
Admiral's Wlk. ME4: Chat'm 5C 80
Admirals Wlk. ME5: Chat'm 8E 94
ME12: Minst 6F 220
TN17: Bendn 5A 38
TN30: Tent 7D 224
Admiralty Cl. ME13: Fav 4F 186
Admiralty M. CT14: Walm 6N 177
Admiralty Rd. ME2: Upnor 3C 80
Admiralty Ter. ME2: Upnor 3C 80
ME7: Gill 5D 80
Admiralty Wlk. CT5: Whits 6C 226
Admiral Way ME19: W Mal 7M 123
Adolf St. SE6 9E 54
Adrian M. CT8: Wgte S 2L 207
Adrian Sq. CT8: Wgte S 2L 207
Adrian St. CT17: Dover 5J 181
Adventure Kingdom *5L 69*
(off Stockwell Cl.)
Aerodrome Ind. Est. ME14: Det 5B 112
Aerodrome Rd. CT4: Bek 6K 173
CT18: H'nge, P'wth 8H 193 (3K 41)
Aeronautical Mus.
Ivychurch 2F 47
Robertsbridge 3B 44
Afghan Rd. CT10: B'stairs 5K 209
ME4: Chat'm 8B 80
Agar Gro. NW1 1E 4
Agaton Rd. SE9 7E 56
Agester La. CT4: Woot 6A 32
Agincourt Rd. NW3 1D 4
Agnew Rd. SE23 5A 54
Ailsa M. ME1: Roch 1K 93
Aimes Ho. ME15: Loose 5C 138
Ainsdale Cl. BR6: Orp 2F 84
CT19: F'stone 4H 189
Ainsley Way CT4: Chart'm 9E 170
Aintree Cl. DA12: Grav'nd 8G 63
Aintree Ho. *ME15: Maid* *2J 139*
(off Epsom Cl.)
Aintree Rd. ME5: Chat'm 8F 94
Airedale Cl. CT9: Mgte 4E 208
DA2: Dart 6C 60
Aireys, The CT13: Wdboro 8G 217
Airfield Vw. ME12: E'chu 8B 202
Airfield Way RM13: H'church 1G 7
Airport Ind. Est. TN16: Big H 3D 164
Aisher Way TN13: Riv 3F 118
Aislibie Rd. SE12 2H 55
Aisne Dr. CT1: Cant 1C 172
Aitken Rd. SE6 7E 54
Ajax Rd. ME1: Roch 3N 93
Akehurst La. TN13: S'oaks 7K 119
Akerman Rd. SW9 5F 5
Alabama St. SE18 7F 50
Alamein Av. ME5: Chat'm 4C 94
Alamein Cl. CT15: Gus 2L 181
Alamein Gdns. DA2: Dart 5D 60
Alamein Rd. DA10: Swans 4K 61
Alanbrooke DA12: Grav'nd 5H 63
Alan Cl. DA1: Dart 2K 59
Alanthus Cl. SE12 4K 55
Albacore Cres. SE13 4E 54
Alban Cres. DA4: Farn'm 2A 88
Albany Cl. DA5: Bex'y 5L 57
TN9: Tonb 8K 145
Albany Dr. CT6: H Bay 2E 194
Albany Hill TN2: Tun W 9J 151
Albany Ho. *CT17: Dover* *5J 181*
(off Albany Pl.)
Albany M. BR1: Brom 2K 69
Albany Park Station (Rail) 7M 57 (7D 6)
Albany Pl. CT17: Dover 5J 181
Albany Rd. BR7: Chst 1D 70 (1B 14)
CT18: Cap F 3B 174
DA5: Bex'y 5L 57
DA17: Belv 6A 52
ME1: Roch 8N 79
ME4: Chat'm 1E 94
ME7: Gill 8G 81
ME10: Sit 7F 98 (5F 19)
SE5 5G 5
Albany St. ME14: Maid 4E 126
NW1 2E 4
Albany Ter. ME4: Chat'm 8B 80 (3H 17)
ME7: Gill 8G 81
Albatross Av. ME2: Strood 5G 78
Albatross Lodge CT16: Dover 2G 181
Albatross St. SE18 7G 50
Albemarle Pk. BR3: Beck'm 4E 68
Albemarle Rd. BR3: Beck'm 4E 68 (2J 13)
ME5: Chat'm 9E 94 (5J 17)
TN24: W'boro 1J 161
Alberta Cvn. Pk. CT5: Seas 7A 226
Alberta Cl. CT16: Dover 1G 181
Alberta Rd. DA8: Erith 8D 52
Albert Bri. SW3 5D 4
SW11 5D 4
Albert Bri. Rd. SW11 5D 4
Albert Costain Ct. *CT20: F'stone* *6K 189*
(off Foord Rd.)
Albert Cotts. TN1: Tun W 1J 157
Albert Ct. CT5: Whits 3F 226
CT11: Ram *6J 211*
(off York St.)
Albert Emb. SE1 4F 5
Albert Ho. *SE28* *2E 50*
(off Erebus Dr.)
Albert La. CT21: Hythe 7J 199
Albert Mnr. ME7: Gill 7E 80
Albert M. SE4 2B 54
Albert Murray Cl. DA12: Grav'nd 5H 63
Albert Pl. ME2: Strood 5M 79
ME14: Maid 2J 27
Albert Reed Gdns. ME15: Maid 7B 126
Albert Rd. BR2: Shortl 8N 69
BR5: St M Cry 9K 71
BR6: Chels 6J 85
CT1: Cant 2A 172
CT9: Mgte 3B 208
CT10: B'stairs 5J 209
CT11: Ram 5K 211
CT14: Deal 4M 177 (3J 33)
CT16: Dover 3J 181
CT19: F'stone 5K 189
CT21: Hythe 7J 199
DA2: Dart 8K 59
DA5: Bex'y 4B 58
DA10: Swans 4M 61
DA17: Belv 5A 52 (4E 6)
Albert Rd. E16 1A 50 (3B 6)
ME1: Roch 8N 79
ME4: Chat'm 9D 80
ME7: Gill 8F 80
SE9 8A 56
SE20 2A 68
TN9: Tonb 6H 145
TN24: Ashf 7F 158
Albert Rd. Est. DA17: Belv 5A 52
Albert St. CT5: Whits 3F 226
CT11: Ram 6H 211
ME14: Maid 3C 126
TN1: Tun W 1H 157
Albert Ter. CT4: Brid 8H 173
CT9: Mgte 3C 208
NW1 2E 4
Albert Vs. CT2: Sturry 7E 168
Albert Wlk. E16 2C 50
Albion Cl. CT6: H Bay 7H 195
Albion Cott. TN12: Mard 3D 212
Albion Dr. E8 1H 5
Albion Hill CT11: Ram 6J 211
Albion Ho. *E16* *1D 50*
(off Church St.)
Albion La. CT6: H Bay 7H 195 (4K 21)
Albion M. CT11: Ram 6J 211
Albion M. Rd. CT20: F'stone 7K 189
Albion Pde. DA12: Grav'nd 4J 63
Albion Pl. CT1: Cant 1N 171
CT9: Mgte 2D 208
CT11: Ram 6J 211
ME2: Upnor 1D 80
ME9: N'tn 5K 97
ME12: S'ness *2D 220*
(off Millennium Way)
ME13: Fav 5G 187
ME14: Maid 5D 126
TN24: Ashf 2J 161
Albion Rd. CT7: Birch 4F 206
CT9: Clift 2E 208
CT10: B'stairs 7J 209 (2K 23)
CT11: Ram 5K 211
CT13: E'try 3J 183
CT14: Deal 2N 177
CT19: F'stone 5K 189
CT21: Hythe 6L 199
DA6: Bexhth 2A 58 (6E 6)
DA12: Grav'nd 5H 63
ME5: Chat'm 9E 94
N16 1G 5
TN1: Tun W 9H 151
TN12: Mard 3D 212 (7H 27)
Albion Row *TN1: Tun W* *9J 151*
(off Albion Rd.)
Albion St. CT10: B'stairs 9M 209 (3K 23)
Albion Ter. DA12: Grav'nd 4H 63
ME10: Sit 5G 98
Albion Vs. CT20: F'stone 7K 189
Albion Way SE13 2F 54
TN8: Eden 3C 184
Albuhera Sq. CT1: Cant 1C 172
Albury Av. DA7: Bexhth 9N 51
Albury Cl. ME5: Chat'm 9G 94
Albyfield BR1: Brom 7B 70
Alchins Cotts. ME17: Lint 6B 138
Alconbury DA6: Bexhth 3C 58
Alder Cl. ME12: S'ness 4B 220
TN4: S'bgh 5J 151
Alder Cotts. CT21: Lymp 5B 198
TN26: Hoth 4L 197
(not continuous)
Aldergate La. CT21: W Hyt 5F 41
Alder Ho. SE4 1D 54
TN23: Ashf 9D 158
Alder La. TN17: Rolv 7B 38
Alderman Cl. DA1: Cray 5F 58
Aldermary Rd. BR1: Brom 4K 69
Aldermoor Rd. SE6 8C 54
Alderney Gdns. CT10: B'stairs 8J 209
Alderney Rd. DA8: Erith 7H 53
Alderney Way TN24: Kenn 3G 158
Alder Rd. CT19: F'stone 5J 189
DA14: Sidc 8H 57
Aldersbrook Rd. E11 1A 6
E12 1A 6
Aldersford Cl. SE4 3A 54
Aldersgate St. EC1 3G 5
Aldersgrove Av. SE9 8N 55
Aldershot Rd. ME5: Chat'm 4D 94
Aldershot Ter. SE18 7C 50
Alders Ind. Est., The ME18: Mere 1J 135
Aldersmead Av. CR0: Croy 9A 68
Alders Mdw. TN9: Tonb 5F 144
Aldersmead Rd. BR3: Beck'm 3B 68
Alders Rd. TN11: Tude 9C 146 (7B 26)
TN12: Five G 9C 146 (7B 26)
Alders, The BR4: W W'ck 2E 82
ME18: Mere 1J 135
Alder Way BR8: Swanl 5E 72
Alderwick Gro. ME19: W Mal 6A 124
Alderwood Rd. SE9 4F 56
ALDGATE 3G 5
Aldgate Station (Tube) 3G 5
Aldgate East Station (Tube) 3G 5
ALDINGTON 4D 40
Aldington Cl. ME5: Chat'm 6E 94
ALDINGTON FIRTH 4C 40
Aldington La. ME14: T'hm 1N 127
Aldington Rd. CT21: Lymp 6A 198 (5E 40)
ME14: Bear 5J 127
ALDON 1C 26
Aldon Cl. ME14: Maid 3F 126
Aldon Ct. ME14: Maid 3F 126
Aldon La. ME19: Off 9G 107 (7C 16)
Aldred Rd. ME13: Fav 6G 187
Aldrich Cres. CR0: Croy 9F 82
Aldridge Cl. CT6: H Bay 4C 194
Aldrington Rd. SW16 1E 12
Aldwick Cl. SE9 8F 56
Aldworth Gro. SE13 4F 54
Aldwych WC2 3F 5
Aldwych Cl. TN10: Tonb 9K 133
Aldwych Station (Tube) 3F 5
Alec Pemble Cl. TN24: Kenn 5J 159
Alefe Way ME9: Iwade 9J 197
Alen Sq. TN12: S'hrst 2K 223
Alers Rd. DA6: Bexhth 3M 57
Alexander Cen., The ME13: Fav 5H 187
Alexander Cl. BR2: Shortl 2K 83
CT13: S'wch 6L 217
DA15: Sidc 3G 57
ME13: Fav 4F 186
Alexander Cotts. ME3: High'm 7G 65
Alexander Ct. BR3: Beck'm 4G 69
ME2: Strood 4M 79
Alexander Dr. ME13: Fav 5F 186
Alexander Evans M. SE23 7A 54
Alexander Gro. ME19: W Mal 6M 123
(Discovery Dr.)
ME19: W Mal 6N 123
(Tower Vw.)
Alexander Rd. BR7: Chst 2D 70
DA7: Bexhth 9M 51
DA9: G'hithe 3J 61
Alexander Ter. SE2 5K 51
Alexandra Av. ME7: Gill 8H 81
W4 5A 4
Alexandra Cl. BR8: Swanl 5F 72
ME10: Sit 4F 98
Alexandra Ct. CT21: Hythe 7H 199
Alexandra Cres. BR1: Brom 2J 69
Alexandra Dr. CT6: H Bay 2D 194
CT14: Deal 7J 177
KT5: Surb 3A 12
Alexandra Gdns. CT20: F'stone 7K 189
Alexandra Glen ME5: Chat'm 1D 110
Alexandra Homes CT9: Mgte 4C 208
Alexandra Pl. CT17: Dover 3H 181
Alexandra Rd. CT5: Whits 5E 226
CT7: Birch 6F 206
CT9: Mgte 5C 208
CT10: B'stairs 9M 209
CT11: Ram 4H 211
CT14: Kgdn 4E 200
CT14: Walm 8N 177
CT18: Cap F 2B 174
DA8: Erith 6G 52
DA12: Grav'nd 5K 63
KT17: Eps 6A 12
ME4: Chat'm 1E 94
ME12: S'ness 2E 220
SE26 2A 68
SW19 1C 12
TN9: Tonb 7H 145
TN16: Big H 7B 164
Alexandra St. CT19: F'stone 4L 189
ME14: Maid 3C 126
SS1: Sth S 1E 10
Alexandra Ter. CT9: Mgte 4C 208
TN25: Mers 9L 161
Alexandra Wlk. DA4: S Dar 5E 74
Alex Hughes Cl. ME6: Snod 4D 108
Alfan La. DA2: Dart 1E 72
Alford Grn. CR0: Croy 7G 82
Alford Rd. DA8: Erith 5D 52
Alfred Cl. CT1: Cant 4J 171
ME4: Chat'm 1E 94
Alfred Cotts. CT11: Ram 5J 211
Alfred Ho. DA11: Nflt 6E 62
Alfred Pl. DA11: Nflt 6E 62
Alfred Rd. CT1: Cant 4J 171
CT7: Birch 3C 206
CT9: Mgte 4F 208
CT16: Dover 2G 181
DA2: Dart 9M 59
DA11: Grav'nd 7G 62
DA17: Belv 5A 52
TN24: Ashf 2H 161
TN28: G'stne 6M 213
Alfred Row CT14: Deal 3N 177
Alfred Sq. CT14: Deal 3N 177
Alfreds Way IG11: Bark 2C 6
Alfriston Cl. DA1: Cray 4F 58
Alfriston Gro. ME19: W Mal 6A 124
Algernon Rd. SE13 2E 54
Algiers Rd. SE13 2D 54
Alice Bright La. TN6: Crowb 7F 35
Alice Thompson Cl. SE12 7M 55
Alicia Av. CT9: Mgte 3M 207
Alicia Ho. DA16: Well 8K 51
Alicia Vs. CT4: Chart'm 8C 170
Alison Cl. CR0: Croy 2A 82
CT7: Birch 3G 206
CT16: Whitf 7F 178
Alison Cres. CT16: Whitf 6F 178
Alkali Row *CT9: Mgte* *2C 208*
(off King St.)
Alkerden La. DA9: G'hithe, Swans 4J 61 (6K 7)
DA10: G'hithe, Swans 4J 61 (6K 7)
ALKHAM 1C 42
Alkham Cl. CT9: Clift 3K 209
Alkham Rd. CT15: Temp E 1A 180 (1D 42)
CT16: Temp E 1A 180
ME14: Maid 5F 126
Alkham Twr. *BR5: St M Cry* *7L 71*
(off Bapchild Pl.)
Alkham Valley Rd. CT15: Alk, Drel 1A 180 (3B 42)
CT18: Drel, F'stone, H'nge 1J 189 (3B 42)
(not continuous)
Allan Cl. TN4: R'hall 1C 156
Allandale Pl. BR6: Chels 4M 85
Allandale Rd. TN2: Tun W 8K 151
Alland Grange La. CT12: Mans 3G 23
Allan Rd. CT5: Seas 6A 226
Allard Cl. BR5: Orp 1L 85
Allen Av. CT8: Wgte S 4J 207
Allenby Av. CT14: Deal 5L 177
Allenby Rd. CT12: Ram 2F 210 (3J 23)
SE23 8B 54
TN16: Big H 5E 164
Allenby Wlk. ME10: Sit 6C 98
Allen Cl. ME5: Chat'm 5F 94
Allen Ct. ME12: Minst 7H 221
Allendale Cl. DA2: Dart 6D 60
SE26 1A 68
Allendale St. CT19: F'stone 5K 189
Allen Fld. TN23: Ashf 1D 160
Allen Rd. BR3: Beck'm 5A 68

Allens—Arran Grn.

Allens TN12: Mard .3D 212
Allens La. TN15: Plax .1N 133 (3A 26)
Allen St. ME14: Maid .4D 126
Allenswood Rd. SE9 .1A 56
Allerford Rd. SE6 .8E 54
Alleyn Pk. SE21 .7G 5
Alley, The TN26: Hams .3L 191
ALLHALLOWS .4D 204 (5B 10)
Allhallows Holiday Est. ME3: Allh .2C 204
ALLHALLOWS-ON-SEA .2D 204 (4C 10)
Allhallows-on-Sea Est. ME3: Allh .3E 204
Allhallows Rd. ME3: Allh, Lwr Sto . .7C 204 (5B 10)
Alliance Rd. CT11: Ram .6K 211
SE18 .6J 51
Alliance Way TN12: Pad W .9L 147
ALLINGTON .1A 126 (1H 27)
Allington Cl. DA12: Grav'nd .6L 63
Allington Dr. ME2: Strood .4J 79
TN10: Tonb .2N 145
Allington Gdns. ME18: W'bury .1B 136
Allington Rd. BR6: Orp .3F 84
ME8: Gill .9K 81
TN12: Pad W .8L 147
Allington Way ME16: Alltn .3M 125
Allison Av. ME7: Gill .2H 95
Allnutt Mill Cl. ME15: Maid .7B 126
Allotment La. TN13: S'oaks .4K 119
All Saints' Av. CT9: Mgte .4A 208 (1H 23)
All Saints Church .6D 126
All Saints Cl. CT5: Whits .4G 227
DA10: Swans .3M 61
All Saints Ind. Est. CT9: Mgte .4C 208
All Saints La. CT1: Cant .2M 171
All Saints Ri. TN4: Tun W .8G 151
All Saints Rd. DA11: Nflt .6E 62
ME3: Allh .4D 204
ME10: Sit .7K 99
SM1: Sutt .4C 12
TN4: Tun W .8G 151
TN18: Hawkh .6D 192
All Saints Station (DLR) .3J 5
All Saints Vw. ME13: G'ney .5C 20
Allsop Pl. NW1 .2D 4
All Souls Av. NW10 .2B 4
Allsworth Cl. ME9: N'tn .5K 97
Allwood Cl. SE26 .9A 54
Alma Cotts. CT2: Sturry .7E 168
Alma Pl. CT1: Cant .1N 171
CT11: Ram .5J 211
ME2: Strood .5L 79
TN11: Hdlw .8D 134
Alma Rd. BR5: Orp .3M 85
CT6: H Bay .2J 195
CT9: Mgte .4D 208
CT11: Ram .4J 211
CT20: F'stone .6D 188
DA10: Swans .3M 61
DA14: Sidc .8J 57 (7D 6)
ME12: S'ness .2D 220
ME19: W Mal .1M 123
ME20: Burh .4K 109
SM5: Cars .4D 12
Alma St. CT1: Cant .1N 171
ME12: S'ness .2E 220
Alma St. Pas. ME12: S'ness .2E 220
(off Richmond St.)
Alma, The DA12: Grav'nd .1L 77
Almery Cotts. ME17: Cha S .8L 139
Almond Cl. BR2: Shortl .1C 84
CT5: Whits .4M 227
CT10: B'stairs .9G 209
TN25: Ashf .5D 158
Almond Ct. CT4: Chart'm .9E 170
Almond Dr. BR8: Swanl .5E 72
Almond Gro. ME7: Hpstd .7K 95
Almond Ho. ME16: Barm .6L 125
Almond Rd. DA2: Dart .5C 60
Almonds, The ME14: Bear .5K 127
Almond Tree Cl. ME12: S'ness .4B 220
Almond Way BR2: Shortl .1C 84
Almon Pl. ME1: Roch .7A 80
Almshouse Rd. ME13: Throw .3K 29
Almshouses ME17: H'shm .3N 141
Alms Row TN16: Bras .6K 117
Alnwick Ct. DA2: Dart .4B 60
(off Osbourne Rd.)
Alnwick Rd. SE12 .4L 55
Alpha Cl. ME3: Hoo .6N 67
Alpha Rd. CT7: Birch .4F 206 (2F 23)
CT11: Ram .6H 211
Alpine Copse BR1: Brom .5C 70
Alsager Av. ME11: Queen .9A 220
Alsike Rd. SE2 .3M 51
Alsops Rd. TN24: W'boro .2J 161
Alston Cl. ME12: Minst .5K 221
Altash Way SE9 .7B 56
Altbarn Ind. Est. ME5: Chat'm .2G 110
Alton Av. ME19: W Mal .6M 123
Alton Cl. DA5: Bex'y .6N 57
Alton Cotts. DA4: Eyns .2M 87
Alton Gdns. BR3: Beck'm .3D 68
Alton M. ME7: Gill .8F 80
Altyre Cl. BR3: Beck'm .8C 68
Altyre Way BR3: Beck'm .8C 68
Alverstone Gdns. SE9 .6E 56
Alvis Av. CT6: H Bay .3B 194
Alwold Cres. SE12 .4L 55
Alwyn Ct. CR0: Croy .8E 82
Amadeus Ho. BR1: Brom .6L 69
(off Elmfield Rd.)
Amadeus Nightclub .8K 79
Amage Rd. TN25: Wye .6D 30
Amanda Cl. ME5: Chat'm .8C 94
Amar Ct. SE18 .4H 51
Amar Deep Ct. SE18 .5H 51
Amber Cl. ME9: Tey .7L 223
Amberfield Cotts. ME17: Cha S .7K 139
Amber Grn. Cotts. ME17: Cha S .7H 139
Amber La. ME17: Cha S .7J 139 (4K 27)
Amberleaze Dr. TN2: Pem .8C 152
Amberley Cl. BR6: Chels .6H 85
TN9: Tonb .7G 144
Amberley Ct. BR3: Beck'm .3C 68
DA14: Sidc .1L 71
Amberley Ct. TN4: Tun W .6J 151
Amberley Rd. SE2 .6M 51
Amber Ri. ME10: Sit .4D 98
Amber Way ME17: Cha S .7L 139
Amberwood Ri. KT3: N Mald .3A 12
Amblecote Cl. SE12 .8L 55
Amblecote Mdws. SE12 .8L 55
Amblecote Rd. SE12 .8L 55
Ambleside BR1: Brom .2G 69
ME10: Sit .8K 99
ME13: Fav .6J 187
Ambleside Av. BR3: Beck'm .8B 68 (3J 13)
SW16 .1E 12
Ambleside Rd. DA7: Bexhth .9B 52
Ambley Grn. ME8: Gill .3K 95
Ambley Rd. ME8: Gill .2K 95 (3K 17)
Ambrooke Rd. DA17: Belv .3B 52
Ambrose Cl. BR6: Orp .4H 85
DA1: Cray .2G 59
Ambrose Hill ME5: Chat'm .1F 94
Amels Hill ME9: S'bry .2H 113
American Garden, The .3H 199
Ames Av. ME14: Bear .5K 127
Amesbury Rd. BR1: Brom .6N 69
Ames Rd. DA10: Swans .4L 61
Ames Way ME19: W Mal .6N 123
Amethyst Av. ME5: Chat'm .5B 94
AMF Bowling
Ashford .8G 159
Chatham .8C 80
Gravesend .4F 62
Lewisham .1F 54
Maidstone .5D 126
Margate .3D 208
Whitstable .2G 226
Amherst Cl. BR5: St M Cry .7J 71
CT9: Mgte .4G 209
ME16: Maid .5A 126
Amherst Dr. BR5: St M Cry .7H 71
Amherst Hill ME7: Gill .6D 80
TN13: Riv .5G 118 (2F 25)
Amherst Redoubt ME7: Gill .7D 80
Amherst Rd. ME1: Roch .9A 80
TN4: Tun W .9G 151
TN13: S'oaks .4J 119
Amhurst Bank Rd. TN2: Pem .3D 152 (1B 36)
TN11: Five G .1E 152 (1B 36)
Amhurst Rd. E8 .1H 5
N16 .1G 5
Amhurst Vs. ME15: E Far .4K 137
Amhurst Wlk. SE28 .1J 51
Amida Leisure Cen. .8C 68
Amos Cl. CT6: H Bay .4K 195
ME13: Shel .3H 219
Ampere Way CR0: Croy .3F 13
Ampere Way Stop (CT) .3F 13
Ampleforth Cl. BR6: Chels .5L 85
Ampleforth Rd. SE2 .2K 51
Amsbury Rd. ME15: Cox .6L 137 (4G 27)
ME17: Cox .6L 137 (4G 27)
Amwell St. EC1 .2F 5
Amyruth Rd. SE4 .3D 54
Anatase Cl. ME10: Sit .4D 98
Ancaster M. BR3: Beck'm .6A 68
Ancaster Rd. BR3: Beck'm .6A 68
Ancaster St. SE18 .7G 50
Anchorage Cl. ME3: Lwr Sto .9C 204
Anchorage Flats TN12: Pad W .9M 147
Anchor Bay Ind. Est. DA8: Erith .6H 53
Anchor Blvd. DA2: Dart .2C 60
Anchor Bus. Pk. ME10: Sit .5J 99
Anchor Ct. DA8: Erith .7G 53
Anchor Hill CT9: Mgte .3D 208
Anchor La. CT14: Deal .4M 177
ME12: S'ness .1A 220
(not continuous)
Anchor Rd. ME1: Roch .2N 93
Ancona Rd. SE18 .5F 50
Ancress Cl. CT2: Cant .7N 167
Andace Pk. Gdns. BR1: Brom .5M 69
Anderson Way DA17: Belv .2C 52
Andorra Ct. BR1: Brom .4M 69
Andover Rd. BR6: Orp .2F 84
Andover Wlk. ME15: Maid .2J 139
Andreck Ct. BR3: Beck'm .5F 68
(off Crescent Rd.)
Andrew Broughton Way ME14: Maid .5E 126
Andrew Cl. DA1: Cray .3E 58
Andrew Ct. SE23 .7A 54
Andrew Mnr. ME7: Gill .6E 80
Andrew Rd. TN4: Tun W .6J 151
Andrew's Cl. BR5: St P .5M 71
Andrews Cl. TN2: Tun W .9K 151
Andrews Pl. DA5: Bex'y .7F 58
SE9 .4D 56
Andrews Wlk. ME10: Sit .6C 98
Andringham Lodge BR1: Brom .4L 69
(off Palace Gro.)
Andwell Cl. SE2 .2K 51
Anemone Way CT6: H Bay .8F 194
ANERLEY .2H 13
Anerley Cl. ME16: Alltn .2A 126
Anerley Hill SE19 .1G 13
Anerley Rd. SE19 .1H 13
SE20 .1H 13
Anerley Station (Rail) .1H 13
ANGEL .2F 5
Angel Hill SM1: Sutt .4C 12
Angelica Gdns. CR0: Croy .2A 82
Angel Indoor Bowls Cen. .6J 145
Angel La. E15 .1K 5
TN9: Tonb .6H 145
Angel Leisure Cen. .6J 145
Angel Station (Tube) .2F 5
Angel Ter. TN18: Sandh .2C 218
Angel Wlk. TN9: Tonb .6H 145
Anglesea Av. SE18 .4D 50
Anglesea Cen. DA11: Grav'nd .4G 62
Anglesea M. SE18 .4D 50
Anglesea Pl. DA11: Grav'nd .4G 62
(off New Rd.)
Anglesea Rd. BR5: St M Cry .9L 71
SE18 .4D 50
Anglesey Av. ME15: Maid .2D 138
Anglesey Cl. ME5: Chat'm .4E 94
Angley Ct. TN12: Horsm .8C 196
Angley Rd. TN17: Cran, Siss .4A 222 (4J 37)
Angley Wlk. TN17: Cran .6D 176
Angus Dr. TN24: Kenn .3G 158
Anisa Cl. ME19: W Mal .6N 123
Ankerdine Cres. SE18 .7D 50
Annandale Rd. DA15: Sidc .5G 57
Anna Pk. CT7: Birch .3E 206
Anne Boleyn Cl. ME12: E'chu .5D 202
Anne Boleyn Ct. SE9 .4E 56
Anne Cl. CT7: Birch .4G 206
Anne Compton M. SE12 .5J 55
Anne Figg Ct. ME1: Roch .8N 79
Anne Grn. Wlk. CT1: Cant .9A 168
Anne of Cleeves Ct. SE9 .4F 56
Anne of Cleves Rd. DA1: Dart .3L 59
Anne Roper Cl. TN28: L'stne .3N 213
Annesley Dr. CR0: Croy .4C 82
Anne's Rd. CT10: B'stairs .6M 209
Anne Sutherland Ho. BR3: Beck'm .3B 68
Annetts Hall TN15: Bor G .1N 121
Annie Rd. ME6: Snod .4D 108
Ann's Rd. CT11: Ram .4J 211
Ann St. SE18 .5E 50
(not continuous)
Ann Stroud Ct. SE12 .3K 55
Annvera Ho. ME7: Gill .5F 80
ANSDORE .5F 31
Ansell Av. ME4: Chat'm .1D 94
Anselm Cl. ME10: Sit .7F 98
Anselm Rd. CT17: Dover .4F 180
Ansford Rd. BR1: Brom .1F 68
Anson Av. ME19: W Mal .6L 123
Anson Cl. CT10: B'stairs .1H 211
ME5: Chat'm .5F 94
Anson Pl. SE28 .2F 50
Anson Rd. NW2 .1B 4
Anstee Rd. CT17: Dover .3H 181
Anstridge Path SE9 .4F 56
Anstridge Rd. SE9 .4F 56
Antelope Rd. SE18 .3B 50
Anthony Cl. CT12: Ram .4F 210
TN13: Dun G .3F 118
Anthony Cres. CT5: Whits .7D 226
Anthony La. BR8: Swanl .4H 73
Anthony Rd. DA16: Well .8J 51
Anthony's Way ME2: Strood, Med E . . .3A 80 (1H 17)
Antolin Way CT12: Ram .1E 210
Antonius Ct. TN23: Ashf .4D 160
Anvil Cl. CT7: Birch .5F 206
ANVIL GREEN .5F 31
Anvil Grn. Farm Rd. CT4: Walt .5F 31
Anvil Grn. Rd. CT4: Walt .5F 31
Anvil Ter. DA5: Bex'y .7F 58
Anzio Cres. CT15: Gus .2K 181
APERFIELD .5E 164 (7B 14)
Aperfield Rd. DA8: Erith .6G 53
TN16: Big H .5E 164
Aperfields TN16: Big H .5E 164
Apex Cl. BR3: Beck'm .4E 68
Apiary Bus. Pk. ME17: Kgswd .5D 140
Apollo Av. BR1: Brom .4L 69
Apollo Way DA8: Erith .4E 52
ME4: Chat'm .2F 80
SE28 .3F 50
Apple Barn Ct. TN15: Bor G .4B 122
Appleby Cl. ME1: Roch .4A 94
Apple Cl. CT18: H'nge .8L 193
ME6: Snod .4D 108
Apple Ct. TN12: Pad W .9L 147
Applecross Cl. ME1: Roch .8M 79
APPLEDORE .1C 46
Appledore Av. DA7: Bexhth .8D 52
ME12: S'ness .4C 220
Appledore Cl. BR2: Shortl .8J 69
CT9: Mgte .4G 208
Appledore Ct. ME16: Alltn .2N 125
Appledore Cres. CT19: F'stone .4D 188
DA14: Sidc .8G 57
APPLEDORE HEATH .7H 39
Appledore Rd. ME8: Gill .9K 81
TN26: App .1C 46
TN26: Wdchu .9C 228 (6H 39)
TN30: Ston C E, App .1C 46
TN30: Tent .8D 224 (6E 38)
Appledore Station (Rail) .1D 46
Appledown Way CT1: Cant .4C 172
Appleford Dr. ME12: Minst .5G 221
Applegarth CR0: Croy .8E 82
(not continuous)
Applegarth Dr. DA1: Dart .7M 59
Applegarth Ho. DA8: Erith .9G 52
Applegarth Pk. CT5: Seas .7C 226
Applegarth Rd. SE28 .1K 51
Apple Orchard BR8: Swanl .7E 72
Appleshaw Cl. DA11: Grav'nd .1F 76
Appleton Cl. DA7: Bexhth .9D 52
Appleton Dr. DA2: Dart .8J 59
Appleton Rd. SE9 .1A 56
Appletons TN11: Hdlw .8D 134
Apple Tree Cl. ME16: Barm .7K 125
Apple Tree La. TN2: Tun W .6K 151
(not continuous)
Appold St. DA8: Erith .6G 53
Approach Rd. CT9: Mgte .3E 208 (1J 23)
CT10: B'stairs .9L 209
CT15: S'wll .7K 219
CT17: Dover .6F 180
SW20 .2B 12
TN16: Tats .9B 164 (1A 24)
Approach, The BR6: Orp .3H 85
April Cl. BR6: Chels .6H 85
April Glen SE23 .8A 54
April Ri. CT5: Whits .6D 226
CT7: Birch .3C 206
Apsledene DA12: Grav'nd .2J 77
Apsley Ct. BR5: St M Cry .9K 71
CT11: Ram .5J 211
(off Plains of Waterloo)
Apsley St. TN23: Ashf .8F 158
Arabin Rd. SE4 .2B 54
Aragon Cl. BR2: Shortl .2B 84
TN23: Ashf .2C 160
Arbor Cl. BR3: Beck'm .5E 68
Arbroath Rd. SE9 .1A 56
Arbrook Cl. BR5: St P .6J 71
Arbuthnot La. DA5: Bex'y .4N 57 (6E 6)
Arcade Chambers SE9 .4C 56
Arcade, The SE9 .4C 56
(off High St.)
Arcadian Av. DA5: Bex'y .4N 57
Arcadian Cl. DA5: Bex'y .4N 57
Arcadian Rd. DA5: Bex'y .4N 57
Arcadia Rd. DA13: Ist R .4E 76 (2B 16)
Archbishops' Palace, The .6C 126
Archcliffe Rd. CT17: Dover .7H 181 (2F 43)
Archer Rd. BR5: St M Cry .8J 71
CT19: F'stone .5K 189
ME5: Chat'm .5E 94
Archers Ct. BR2: Shortl .7L 69
Archer's Ct. Rd. CT16: Whitf .7F 178 (7F 33)
Archer Way BR8: Swanl .5G 73
Archery Cl. ME3: Cli W .6M 65
Archery Rd. SE9 .3B 56
Archery Sq. CT14: Walm .7N 177 (4J 33)
(not continuous)
Arches Vw. ME4: Chat'm .8E 80
(off Hillside Rd.)
Archibald Ho. ME14: Maid .2D 126
ARCHWAY .1E 4
Archway Ct. ME2: Strood .4M 79
(off Frindsbury Rd.)
Archway Rd. CT11: Ram .6J 211
ME12: S'ness .1B 220
Archway Station (Tube) .1E 4
Arcon Cl. TN23: Ashf .2E 160
Arcon Rd. TN23: Ashf .2E 160
Arcus Rd. BR1: Brom .2H 69
Arden Bus. Pk. ME2: Med E .5A 80
Arden Ct. CT1: Cant .3N 171
Arden Dr. TN24: Ashf .7G 159
Arden Grange CT4: Chil'm .8K 175
Arden Gro. BR6: Farnb .5D 84
Ardenlee Dr. ME14: Maid .4E 126
Arden Rd. CT6: H Bay .5J 195
ME13: Fav .5J 187
Arden St. ME7: Gill .6F 80
Ardent Av. CT14: Walm .6M 177
Arden Theatre .5G 187
Ardfillan Rd. SE6 .6G 55
Ardgowan Rd. SE6 .5H 55
Ardingly Cl. CR0: Croy .4A 82
Ardley Cl. SE6 .8B 54
Ardmere Rd. SE13 .4G 55
Ardoch Rd. SE6 .7G 54
Arena Stop (CT) .3H 13
Arethusa Pl. DA9: G'hithe .2H 61
Arethusa Rd. ME1: Roch .3N 93 (4H 17)
Arethusa Venture Cen. .1D 80
Argali Ho. DA18: Erith .3N 51
(off Kale Rd.)
Argent Bus. Pk. ME11: Queen .9B 220
Argent St. RM17: Grays .5A 8
Argent Ter. ME5: Chat'm .6C 94
Argent Way ME10: Sit .5D 98
Argles Cl. DA9: G'hithe .3G 60
Argyle Av. CT9: Mgte .4A 208
Argyle Cen, The CT11: Ram .6J 211
(off York St.)
Argyle Cl. ME1: Roch .3B 94
Argyle Gdns. CT9: Mgte .4A 208
Argyle Rd. CT5: Whits .4F 226
TN4: S'bgh .4G 151
TN13: S'oaks .7J 119
Argyll Dr. CT11: Ram .3J 211
Argyll Rd. SE18 .3E 50
Arica Rd. SE4 .2B 54
Ariel Cl. DA12: Grav'nd .9L 63
Arisdale Av. RM15: S Ock .2K 7
Arkindale Rd. SE6 .8F 54
Ark La. CT14: Deal .3M 177
Arkley Rd. CT6: H Bay .3G 195
Arklow Sq. CT11: Ram .5K 211
Arkwright Rd. CR2: S Croy .5G 13
NW3 .1D 4
Arlington TN23: Ashf .9D 158
Arlington Cl. DA15: Sidc .5G 56
SE13 .3G 54
Arlington Gdns. CT9: Mgte .5G 208
Arlington Ho. CT9: Mgte .3B 208
Arlington Sq. CT9: Mgte .3B 208
Arlott Cl. ME14: Maid .3C 126
Armada Cl. TN28: L'stne .4N 213
Armada Ct. ME4: Chat'm .2B 94
Armada Way ME4: Chat'm .9C 80
Armitage Pl. TN18: Hawkh .5C 192
Armourer's Wlk. CT16: Dover .1F 180
Armoury Dr. DA12: Grav'nd .5H 63
Armoury Way SW18 .6C 4
Armstrong Cl. BR1: Brom .6A 70
TN14: Hals .6C 102
Armstrong Rd. ME15: Maid .8D 126
SE18 .3E 50
Armstrong Sq. CT6: H Bay .4B 194
Armytage Cl. ME3: Hoo .9H 67
Arne Cl. TN10: Tonb .1L 145
Arne Gro. BR6: Orp .4H 85
Arne Wlk. SE3 .2J 55
Arngask Rd. SE6 .5G 54
Arnhem Dr. CR0: Croy .6K 13
ME5: Chat'm .4C 94
Arnold Av. DA13: Meop .3G 90
Arnold Bus. Pk., The TN12: E Peck .2M 147
Arnolde Cl. ME2: Med E .5B 80
Arnold Rd. CT4: Chart'm .8C 170
CT9: Mgte .4D 208
DA12: Grav'nd .7J 63
Arnold's La. DA4: S at H .2N 73 (1H 15)
Arnott Cl. SE28 .1L 51
Arnsberg Way DA7: Bexhth .2B 58 (6E 6)
Arnside Rd. DA7: Bexhth .8B 52
Arnulf St. SE6 .9E 54
Arolla Rd. CT6: H Bay .3K 195
ARPINGE .3K 41
Arragon Gdns. BR4: W W'ck .4E 82
Arran Cl. DA8: Erith .6E 52
Arran Grn. ME2: Strood .6G 79

Arran M.—Aylesford Priory

Arran M. CT1: Cant 9A 168
Arran Rd. ME15: Maid 2D 138
SE6 7E 54
Arrol Rd. BR3: Beck'm 6A 68
Arrowhead La. TN26: Snar 1E 46
Arsenal F.C. (Highbury) 1F 5
Arsenal Rd. SE9 9B 50
Arsenal Station (Tube) 1F 5
Arsenal Way SE18 3E 50
Artemis Cl. DA12: Grav'nd 5K 63
Arterial Rd. RM15: Purf 4H 7
RM16: N Stif 4K 7
RM20: W Thur 4K 7
SS17: Horn H 2E 8
Arthurdon Rd. SE4 3D 54
Arthur Gro. SE18 4E 50
Arthur Kennedy Cl. ME13: Bou B 3J 165
Arthur Rd. CT7: Birch 3C 206
CT9: Mgte 2E 208
CT14: Deal 7K 177
CT21: Hythe 7K 199
ME1: Roch 9A 80
ME8: Gill 3N 95
SW19 1C 12
TN16: Big H 3C 164
Arthur Salmon Cl. ME13: Fav 5F 186
Arthur St. CT19: F'stone 5L 189
DA8: Erith 7G 52
DA11: Grav'nd 5F 62
ME10: Sit 7F 98
Arthur St. W. DA11: Grav'nd 5F 62
Artillery Gdns. CT1: Cant 1N 171
Artillery Ho. *CT1: Cant* *1N 171*
(off Victoria Row)
SE18 *5C 50*
(off Connaught M.)
Artillery Pl. SE18 5B 50 (4B 6)
Artillery Rd. CT11: Ram 5K 211
Artillery Row DA12: Grav'nd 5H 63
Artillery St. CT1: Cant 1N 171
Artington Cl. BR6: Farnb 5E 84
Arundel Av. ME10: Sit 1F 114
Arundel Cl. DA6: Bexhth 4A 58
ME5: Chat'm 1G 110
TN9: Tonb 7G 144
Arundel Ct. BR2: Shortl 5H 69
Arundel Dr. BR6: Chels 6K 85
Arundel Rd. CT9: Mgte 3F 208
CT12: C'snd 5B 210
DA1: Dart 2K 59
TN1: Tun W 3H 157
Arundel St. ME14: Maid 3C 126
Ascot Cl. ME5: Chat'm 9F 94
TN15: Bor G 2A 122
Ascot Ct. DA5: Bex'y 5A 58
Ascot Gdns. CT8: Wgte S 4K 207
Ascot Ho. *ME15: Maid* *2J 139*
(off Epsom Cl.)
Ascot Rd. BR5: St M Cry 7H 71
DA12: Grav'nd 8G 63
ASH
Canterbury 6L 89 (4K 15)
Sevenoaks 5C 216 (7E 22)
Ashbee Cl. ME6: Snod 3E 108
Ashbee Gdns. CT6: H Bay 2K 195
Ashborne Cl. TN24: Kenn 4H 159
Ashbourne Av. DA7: Bexhth 7N 51
Ashbourne Ri. BR6: Orp 5F 84
Ashburn Gdns. CT6: H Bay 2K 195
Ashburnham Cl. TN13: S'oaks 9K 119
Ashburnham Ct. BR3: Beck'm 5F 68
Ashburnham Rd. CT11: Ram 5F 210
DA17: Belv 4D 52
ME14: Pen H 1E 126
SW10 5D 4
TN10: Tonb 4J 145
Ashburton Cl. TN24: W'boro 8J 159
Ashburton Rd. CR0: Croy 3H 13
Ashby Cl. ME2: Hall'g 7E 92
Ash By-Pass CT3: Ash 7D 22
Ashby's Cl. TN8: Eden 7D 184
Ash Cl. BR5: Pet W 8F 70
BR8: Swanl 5D 72
CT6: H Bay 6G 195
CT10: B'stairs 9G 209
CT17: Dover 2E 180
DA14: Sidc 8K 57
ME5: Chat'm 2F 94
ME8: Gill 9L 81
ME20: Aylfd 9J 109
TN2: Tun W 5K 157
TN8: Eden 6B 184
TN23: Ashf 8C 158
Ashcombe Dr. TN8: Eden 3B 184
Ash Coombe Vineyard 7E 22
Ash Ct. CT12: C'snd 8B 210
Ash Cres. CT3: Hersd 2K 169
ME3: High'm 1G 78
Ashcroft Av. DA15: Sidc 4J 57
Ashcroft Ct. DA1: Dart 5A 60
Ashcroft Cres. DA15: Sidc 4J 57
Ashcroft Rd. ME3: Wain 2M 79
TN12: Pad W 1L 153
Ashdale Rd. SE12 6L 55
Ashden Wlk. TN10: Tonb 9J 133
Ashdown Cl. BR3: Beck'm 5E 68
CT6: H Bay 5J 195
DA5: Bex'y 5D 58
ME16: Maid 6A 126
TN4: Tun W 1F 156
Ashdown Ct. TN24: Ashf 7G 158
Ashdown Cres. TN28: New R 3K 213
Ashdown Fld. CT4: Chart'm 8B 170
Ashdown Forest Cen., The 6B 34
Ashdown Llama Farm 7B 34
Ashdown Rd. ME9: Wich 2F 29
ME17: Len, Wich 2F 29
Ashdowns Cotts. ME15: E Far 4K 137
Ashenbank Wood (Nature Reserve) 5M 77
Ashenden TN27: Smar 7B 222
Ashenden Cl. CT1: Cant 5J 171
ME2: Wain 2N 79
Ashendene Gro. CT2: Sturry 4F 168
Ashenden Wlk. TN2: Tun W 6L 151
Ashen Dr. DA1: Dart 4H 59
Ashenfield Rd. CT4: Walt 7E 30
TN25: H'igh, Wye 7E 30
Ashen Gro. Rd. TN15: Knat 1B 104
Ashen Tree La. CT16: Dover 4K 181
Ashentree La. TN29: Old R 3F 47
Ashen Va. CR2: S Croy 9A 82
Asher Reeds TN3: Lang G 1A 156
Ashes La. TN11: Hdlw 7M 133 (4A 26)
Ashfield Cl. BR3: Beck'm 3D 68
Ashfield La. BR7: Chst 2D 70
(not continuous)
ASHFORD 8F 158 (1A 40)
Ashford Bus. Pk. TN24: Svgtn 3L 161
Ashford Bus. Point TN24: Ashf 4K 161
Ashford Dr. ME17: Kgswd 5F 140
Ashford International
Station (Rail) 9G 158 (1A 40)
Ashford Rd. CT1: Cant, Chart'm 6F 170 (2E 30)
CT4: Cant, Chart'm 7A 170 (2E 30)
CT4: Chil'm, Godm 9K 175 (4D 30)
CT18: N'tn, Peene 4A 188 (4J 41)
CT21: N'grn, Post, Salt, S'lng,
3C 198 (4F 41)
CT21: Post, Salt 1H 199 (4F 41)
CT21: Wnhgr 3C 198 (4F 41)
ME13: Bad, Shel 4H 219 (3A 30)
ME13: Fav, Shel 7G 187 (7A 20)
ME14: Maid, Weav, Bear 5E 126 (2J 27)
ME17: H'shm, Holl, Leeds, Len
7A 128 (2A 28)
(not continuous)
TN23: Ashf, Gt Cha 4E 160 (2J 39)
TN25: S'ndge 2A 198 (4F 41)
(Barrow Hill)
TN25: S'ndge 8A 218
(Stone hill)
TN26: Beth, Gt Cha 4H 163 (3G 39)
TN26: Beth, H Hald 1C 196 (4E 38)
TN26: Hams 1K 191 (5K 39)
TN26: Kgnt, Shad 9D 160 (3K 39)
TN27: Char'g 3K 175 (5H 29)
TN28: New R 1H 213 (1F 47)
TN29: Bztt, Ivyc, Old R 1F 47
TN30: St Mic, Tent 2B 224 (4E 38)
TN30: Tent 7C 224
Ashford Town F.C.
(Homelands Stadium, The) 9D 160
Ash Gro. BR4: W W'ck 3F 82
CT15: Evtn 6J 185
ME16: Alltn 3N 125
SE12 6K 55
Ashgrove TN25: Ashf 5D 158
Ash Gro. TN29: Lydd 2L 205
Ashgrove Rd. BR1: Brom 2G 69 (1K 13)
TN13: S'oaks 9H 119 (3G 25)
Ash Hill TN26: Ruck 5A 40
Ash Ho. DA3: New A 3L 89
Ashington Cl. ME10: Sit 6D 98
Ash Keys DA13: Meop 2G 106
Ash La. TN15: Ash, W King 3J 105 (6K 15)
Ashlar Pl. SE18 4D 50
Ashleigh Cl. DA13: Meop 1E 106
Ashleigh Gdns. TN27: H'crn 7L 191
Ashleigh Point SE23 8A 54
ASHLEY 5F 33
Ashley Av. CT19: F'stone 5E 188 (4A 42)
KT18: Eps 6A 12
Ashley Cl. CT12: Ram 2F 210
ME12: Minst 7D 220
TN13: S'oaks 6J 119
Ashley Dr. CT5: Seas 6C 226
Ashley Gdns. BR6: Orp 6G 85
TN4: R'hall 1C 156 (2J 35)
Ashley Ho. CT19: F'stone 5E 188
Ashley Mill Cotts. *CT19: F'stone* *4E 188*
(off Ashley Av.)
Ashley Pk. TN4: R'hall 9C 150
Ashley Pk. Cl. TN4: R'hall 9C 150
Ashley Rd. KT18: Eps 6A 12
ME8: Gill 1M 95
TN11: Hild 2E 144
TN13: S'oaks 6J 119
Ashmead Cl. ME5: Chat'm 8F 94
Ashmead Ga. BR1: Brom 4M 69
Ash Mdw. TN24: W'boro 2K 161
Ashmere Av. BR3: Beck'm 5G 68
Ashmore Gdns. DA11: Nflt 8C 62
Ashmore Gro. DA16: Well 1F 56
Ashmore La. BR2: Kes 6A 14
Ash Platt Rd. TN15: Seal 3M 119
(not continuous)
Ash Platt, The TN15: Seal 2M 119
Ashridge Cres. SE18 7E 50
Ash Rd. BR6: Chels 8H 85
CR0: Croy 3D 82
CT3: Ash, S'wch 4H 217 (7F 23)
CT3: Aysm 2B 162
CT13: S'wch 4K 217
DA1: Dart 6L 59
DA2: Dart 9N 59
DA3: Hart'y, Long, New A 6L 75 (2A 16)
DA12: Grav'nd 9H 63
ME2: Strood 6K 79
TN15: Ash, New A 5K 89 (4K 15)
TN16: Westrm 7F 116
Ash Row BR2: Shortl 1C 84
Ashtead Dr. ME9: Bap 9L 99
ASHTEAD PARK 7A 12
Ashton Cl. CT14: Gt Mon 4H 33
Ashton Way ME19: W Mal 9B 108 (1D 26)
Ashtree Cl. BR6: Farnb 5D 84
Ash Tree Cl. CR0: Croy 9B 68
CT7: Birch *4G 206*
(off Parkway, The)
TN15: W King 9F 88
TN29: St M Bay 3M 215
Ash Tree Ct. TN15: W King 9F 88
Ash Tree Dr. TN15: W King 8F 88
Ashtree Ho. *ME10: Sit* *8J 99*
(off Woodberry Dr.)
Ash Tree La. ME5: Chat'm 1G 94 (3J 17)
Ash Tree Rd. CT19: F'stone 5L 189
Ash Trees CT6: H Bay 3J 195
Ash Tree Way CR0: Croy 8A 68
ASHURST 3E 154 (3F 35)
Ashurst Av. CT5: Whits 7E 226
Ashurst Cl. DA1: Cray 1G 58
Ashurst Gdns. CT9: Clift 2J 209
Ashurst Hill TN3: A'hst 3E 154 (3F 35)
Ashurst Rd. ME14: Maid 4F 126
TN3: A'hst, Ford 2F 154 (3F 35)
Ashurst Station (Rail) 3E 154 (3F 35)
ASHURSTWOOD 4A 34
Ashwater Rd. SE12 6K 55
Ashwood Cl. ME3: Cli W 6N 65
Ashwood Gdns. CR0: Croy 7F 82
Ashwood Pl. DA2: Bean 8H 61
Ashworth Av. *TN15: W King* *8D 88*
(off London Rd.)
Askern Cl. DA6: Bexhth 2M 57
Askes Ct. TN23: Ashf 1B 160
Askew Rd. W12 4A 4
Aspdin Rd. DA11: Nflt 8C 62
Aspen Cl. BR6: Chels 6J 85
BR8: Swanl 4E 72
TN29: St M Bay 3M 215
Aspen Copse BR1: Brom 5B 70
Aspen Ct. DA1: Dart 4A 60
Aspen Dr. TN23: Ashf 6D 158
Aspen Grn. DA18: Erith 3A 52
Aspen Ho. CT20: F'stone 7K 189
DA15: Sidc 8J 57
Aspen Rd. CT4: Chart'm 9E 170
CT6: H Bay 8F 194
Aspen Way E14 3J 5
ME5: Chat'm 7B 94
TN4: S'bgh 5J 151
Aspian Dr. ME17: Cox 5A 138
Aspinall Cl. CT4: Brid 6G 173
Aspinall Rd. SE4 1A 54
(not continuous)
Aspley St. TN4: R'hall 1D 156
Asprey Pl. BR1: Brom 5A 70
Asquith Rd. ME8: Gill 5M 95
Assembly Hall Theatre, The 1H 157
Association Wlk. ME1: Roch 4N 93
Astley Av. CT16: Dover 2H 181
Astley Ct. CT16: Dover 2H 181
Astley Ho. ME15: Maid 6E 126
Astley St. ME14: Maid 5D 126
Aston Cl. DA14: Sidc 8J 57
ME5: Chat'm 9D 94
Astor Av. CT17: Dover 5G 180 (2F 43)
Astor Dr. CT14: Deal 5M 177
Astor Rd. CT10: B'stairs 5K 209
TN15: W King 7E 88
Astor Theatre Arts Cen., The 4N 177
Astra Dr. DA12: Grav'nd 1K 77
Astrid Rd. CT14: Walm 8K 177
Athelney St. SE6 8D 54
Athelstan Grn. ME17: Holl 7E 128
Athelstan Pl. CT14: Deal 2M 177
Athelstan Rd. CT1: Cant 5J 171
CT9: Mgte 2E 208
CT19: F'stone 4K 189
ME4: Chat'm 1C 94
ME13: Fav 6F 186
Athelstan Way BR5: St P 4J 71
Athenlay Rd. SE15 3A 54
Athill Ct. TN13: S'oaks 4K 119
Athol Pl. ME13: Fav 4E 186
Athol Rd. CT5: Whits 3H 227
DA8: Erith 5D 52
TN23: Ashf 2D 160
Athol Ter. CT16: Dover 4L 181
Atkins Dr. BR4: W W'ck 3G 83
Atkinson Cl. BR6: Chels 6J 85
Atkinson Wlk. TN24: Kenn 5K 159
Atkins Rd. SW12 7E 4
Atlanta Ct. ME4: Chat'm 9A 80
Atlantic Cl. DA10: Swans 3L 61
Atlas Rd. DA1: Dart 1N 59
Atterbury Cl. TN16: Westrm 8F 116
Attlee Av. CT3: Aysm 2C 162
Attlee Cotts. ME2: Hall'g 5E 92
Attlee Dr. DA1: Dart 3A 60 (6H 7)
Attlee Way ME10: Sit 3F 98
Attwaters La. TN18: Hawkh 1E 192 (6J 37)
Atwater Ct. ME17: Len 7M 201
Aubretia Wlk. ME10: Sit 8H 99
Auckland Av. CT12: Ram 3E 210
Auckland Cres. CT16: Dover 1H 181
Auckland Dr. ME10: Sit 8D 98
Auckland Rd. SE19 2G 13
TN1: Tun W 8J 151
Auden Rd. ME20: Lark 7E 108
Audley Av. CT9: Mgte 2M 207
ME7: Gill 2H 95
TN9: Tonb 5F 144
Audley Ct. ME16: Alltn 5M 125
Audley Ri. TN9: Tonb 6F 144
Audley Rd. CT20: F'stone 6F 188
Audley Wlk. BR5: St M Cry 9L 71
Audrey Cl. BR3: Beck'm 9E 68
Audrey Sturley Ct. TN4: R'hall 9D 150
Auger Cl. ME9: H'lip 6G 96
Augusta Cl. ME7: Gill 5F 80
Augusta Gdns. CT20: F'stone 7J 189
Augusta Pl. CT11: Ram 5K 211
Augusta Rd. CT11: Ram 5K 211
Augustine Rd. BR5: St P 6M 71
CT12: Minst 7E 212
DA12: Grav'nd 5H 63
(not continuous)
ME12: Minst 4J 221
Augustus La. BR6: Orp 3J 85
Augustus Rd. SW19 7C 4
Augustus Wlk. TN23: Ashf 4D 160
Aultmore Ct. TN2: Tun W 2J 157
Aurelius Cl. TN23: Ashf 5E 160
Austell Mnr. *ME7: Gill* *6F 80*
(off Skinner St.)
Austen Cl. DA9: G'hithe 4J 61
SE28 1K 51
Austen Gdns. DA1: Dart 2N 59
Austen Rd. DA8: Erith 7C 52
Austens Orchard TN30: Tent 9B 224
Austen Way ME20: Lark 6D 108
Austin Av. BR2: Shortl 8A 70
CT6: H Bay 3A 194
Austin Cl. ME5: Chat'm 1H 95
ME10: Kems'y 3H 99
SE23 5B 54
Austin Rd. BR5: St M Cry 9J 71
DA11: Nflt 6E 62
TN23: Ashf 3F 160
Austins La. CT13: S'wch 5M 217
Austral Cl. DA15: Sidc 8H 57
Autumn Glade ME5: Chat'm 2G 110
Avalon Cl. BR6: Chels 4M 85
Avalon Rd. BR6: Chels 3K 85
Avard Gdns. BR6: Farnb 5E 84
Avards Cl. TN18: Hawkh 7B 192
Avebury Av. CT11: Ram 4L 211
TN9: Tonb 6H 145
Avebury Rd. BR6: Orp 4F 84
AVELEY 3J 7
Aveley By-Pass RM15: Avel 3J 7
Aveley Cl. DA8: Erith 6G 53
Aveley Rd. RM14: Upm 1H 7
Aveling Cl. ME3: Hoo 7G 66
Aveling Ct. ME2: Strood 5M 79
Avent Wlk. ME9: Bap 9M 99
Avenue Du Puy TN9: Tonb 6J 145
Avenue Gdns. CT9: Clift 3G 208
Avenue of Remembrance
ME10: Sit 8F 98 (5F 19)
Avenue Rd. CT6: H Bay 2F 194 (2J 21)
CT11: Ram 5K 211
CT16: Dover 3H 181
DA7: Bexhth 1N 57 (6E 6)
DA8: Erith 7D 52
DA17: Belv, Erith 4D 52
KT18: Eps 6A 12
NW3 2D 4
NW8 1D 4
SE20 4A 68
SM2: Sutt 5C 12
TN13: S'oaks 6K 119
TN16: Tats 8F 164
Avenue Road Station (CT) 5A 68 (2H 13)
Avenue, The BR1: Brom 6N 69
BR2: Kes 5N 83
BR3: Beck'm 4E 68
(not continuous)
BR4: W W'ck 1H 83 (3K 13)
BR5: St P 3K 71
BR6: Orp 3H 85
CT3: Hersd 3K 169
CT9: Mgte 4E 208
CT14: Deal 3M 177
CT14: Kgdn 4E 200
CT15: St Marg 7B 214
CT16: Temp E 8C 178
CT21: Hythe 6K 199
DA5: Bex'y 5M 57
DA9: G'hithe 2H 61 (6K 7)
DA11: Grav'nd 6F 62
DA12: Cobh 7N 77
KT4: Wor Pk 4A 12
ME4: Chat'm 2F 80
ME9: T'stall 5E 114
ME20: Aylfd 9J 109
NW6 2B 4
SW4 6E 4
TN9: Tonb 5H 145
TN15: Bor G 1N 121
TN16: Westrm 4B 116
W4 4A 4
Avenue Theatre 8G 98
Averenches Rd. ME14: Weav 4J 127
Averenches Rd. Sth. ME14: Weav 5J 127
Avereng Gdns. CT19: F'stone 5H 189
Avereng Rd. CT19: F'stone 5H 189
Avery Cl. ME3: Allh 3E 204
ME15: Maid 8C 126
Avery Ct. ME3: Allh 3E 204
AVERY HILL 4F 56 (6C 6)
Avery Hill Rd. SE9 4F 56 (6C 6)
Avery La. ME15: Otham 2N 139 (3A 28)
ME17: Otham 2N 139
Avery Way ME3: Allh 4D 204 (5B 10)
Aviemore Cl. BR3: Beck'm 8C 68
Aviemore Gdns. ME14: Bear 5J 127
Aviemore Way BR3: Beck'm 8B 68
Avignon Rd. SE4 1A 54 (6H 5)
Avington Cl. ME15: Maid 8C 126
Avocet M. SE28 3F 50
Avocet Wlk. ME5: Chat'm 9F 94
Avon Cl. CT1: Cant 2B 172
DA12: Grav'nd 7J 63
TN10: Tonb 2J 145
Avondale Ct. CT5: Whits 5J 227
Avondale Pl. *ME3: Lwr Sto* *8C 204*
(off High St.)
Avondale Rd. CT18: Cap F 2C 174
DA16: Well 9L 51
ME7: Gill 7G 80
SE9 7A 56
Avonmouth Rd. DA1: Dart 3L 59
Avon Rd. SE4 1D 54
Avonstowe Cl. BR6: Farnb 4E 84
Avon St. TN1: Tun W 9J 151
Avontar Rd. RM15: S Ock 2K 7
Awliscombe Rd. DA16: Well 9H 51
Axminster Cres. DA16: Well 8L 51
Axtaine Rd. BR5: St M Cry 1M 85
Axtane DA13: Sflt 3M 75
Axtane Cl. DA4: S Dar 4C 74
AYCLIFF 7G 180 (2F 43)
Aycliffe Cl. BR1: Brom 7B 70
Ayelands DA3: New A 3L 89
Ayelands La. DA3: New A 4L 89
Aylesbury Rd. BR2: Shortl 6K 69
TN25: Kenn 3F 158
AYLESFORD 7L 109 (7G 17)
Aylesford Av. BR3: Beck'm 8B 68
Aylesford Cres. ME8: Gill 8L 81
Aylesford Pl. TN24: Ashf 2B 40
TN24: W'boro 2J 161 (2B 40)
Aylesford Priory 8J 109

Aylesford Station (Rail)—Barton Rd.

Aylesford Station (Rail) 8J 109 (7G 17)
Aylesford Wharf And Junction Six Ind. Est.
ME20: Aylfd 8N 109
AYLESHAM 2D 162 (3B 32)
Aylesham Ho. CT3: Aysm 2D 162
Aylesham Ind. Est. CT3: Aysm 3C 162
(not continuous)
Aylesham Rd. BR6: Orp 1H 85
CT3: Aysm 2E 162
CT15: Aysm 2E 162 (3C 32)
Aylesham Station (Rail) 1E 162 (3C 32)
Aylewade La. TN27: Frit 2C 38
Aylewyn Grn. ME10: Kems'y 3G 99
Aylward Rd. SE23 . . . . .7A 54
Aynscombe Angle BR6: Orp 1J 85
Aynsley Ct. CT13: S'wch 5M 217
Ayton Rd. CT11: Ram 6G 211
Azalea Dr. BR8: Swanl 7E 72

B

Babbacombe Rd. BR1: Brom 4K 69
Babb's La. TN17: Bendn 6K 37
Babs Oak Hill CT2: Sturry 4G 168 (6K 21)
Babylon La. ME17: Cha S 6K 27
TN12: Sut V 6K 27
Backfields ME1: Roch 8M 79
Back La. DA5: Bex'y 5B 58
ME12: Minst 6L 221 (7H 11)
ME13: Fav 5H 187
ME15: Otham 2M 139
ME17: Bou Mo, Cha S 6G 138 (4J 27)
TN11: S'brne 4J 133 (4K 25)
TN12: Horsm 7C 196
TN14: Ide H 2C 130 (3E 24)
TN15: Igh, ...6J 121 (2K 25)
TN15: S'oaks 6A 120
TN17: Goud 3C 190
Back Rd. DA14: Sidc 9J 57
TN18: Sandh 3C 218 (1E 44)
Back Rd. W. CT16: Dover 4L 181
Back St. CT14: R'wld 4B 200
CT19: F'stone 6L 189
ME17: Leeds 1A 140 (3A 28)
Baddlesmere Rd. CT5: Whits 2J 227
Baden Powell Ho. DA17: Belv 3B 52
(off Ambrooke Rd.)
Baden Powell Rd. TN13: Riv 3F 118
Baden Rd. ME7: Gill 5G 81
Bader Cres. ME5: Chat'm 4D 94
Bader Wlk. DA11: Nflt 8E 62
Badger Rd. ME5: Chat'm 1F 110
Badgers Bri. CT18: Etch'l 1M 185 (3J 41)
Badgers Cl. CT2: Blean 4G 166
Badgers Copse BR6: Orp 3H 85
Badgers Cft. SE9 . . . . .8C 56
Badgers Hole CR0: Croy 5A 82
Badgers Holt TN2: Tun W 9L 151
BADGER'S MOUNT 1B 102 (5E 14)
Badgers Oak TN23: Ashf 1B 160
Badgers Ri. CT14: Walm 1E 200
CT17: Dover 1C 180
Badger's Ri. TN14: Hals 1B 102
Badgers Rd. TN14: Hals, S'ham 1C 102
(not continuous)
BADLESMERE 2A 30
Badlesmere Cl. TN23: Ashf 3C 160
Badlow Cl. DA8: Erith 7F 52
Bad Munstereifel Rd. TN23: Ashf 4F 160 (2A 40)
TN24: Ashf, Svgtn, W'boro 4F 160 (2A 40)
Badsell Rd. TN12: Five G, Pad W 8G 147 (7C 26)
Baffin Cl. ME4: Chat'm 1C 94
BAGHAM 8L 175 (3E 30)
Bagham La. CT4: Chil'm 8K 175 (3D 30)
Bagham Rd. CT4: Chil'm 8K 175 (3D 30)
Bagshill Rd. ME13: Throw 2K 29
Bagshot Ct. SE18 . . . . .8C 50
Bailey Bri. Rd. ME20: Aylfd 8K 109
Bailey Ct. ME8: Gill 3K 95
Bailey Dr. ME8: Gill 2K 95 (3K 17)
Bailey Fld. TN26: Beth 3K 163
Bailey Pl. SE26 . . . . .2A 68
Baileys Fld. TN23: Ashf 9D 158
Baird's Hill CT10: B'stairs 7K 209 (2K 23)
Bairdsley Cl. CT10: B'stairs 7K 209
(not continuous)
Bakenham Ho. ME1: Roch 2N 93
Baker Beal Ct. DA7: Bexhth 1C 58
Baker Cl. ME9: Tey 6K 223
Bakerhill Cl. DA11: Nflt 9E 62
Baker La. ME17: Sut V 9B 140 (5A 28)
TN27: H'crn 6N 191 (7C 28)
Baker Rd. CT19: F'stone 5E 188
SE18 . . . . .7A 50
Bakers Av. TN15: W King 8E 88
Baker's Bri. Cotts. TN27: Smar 7D 222
Bakers Cl. CT2: Cant 3J 171
BAKER'S CROSS 5K 37
Bakers Cross TN17: Cran 8D 176 (5K 37)
Baker's La. CT4: Chart'm 9D 170 (2F 31)
Bakers La. RH7: Ling 1A 34
Bakers M. BR6: Chels 7H 85
BAKER STREET 3B 8
BAKER STREET 2D 4
Baker St. ME1: Burh 1K 109
ME1: Roch 9N 79
NW1 . . . . .2D 4
RM16: Ors 3B 8
W1 . . . . .3D 4
Baker Street Station (Tube) 2D 4
Bakers Wlk. ME1: Roch 6N 79
Bakery Cotts. ME14: S'lng 7B 110
Balaam St. E13 . . . . .2A 6
Balaclava La. TN5: Wadh 6B 36
Balas Dr. ME10: Sit .5D 98
Balcaskie Rd. SE9 . . . . .3B 56
Balcomb Cres. CT9: Mgte 5G 209
Balcombe Cl. DA6: Bexhth 2M 57
Balcombe La. RH17: Sharp, Hors K 7A 34
RH19: Sharp 7A 34
Balcombes Cotts. TN17: Goud 3C 190
Balcombes Hill TN17: Goud 3C 190 (4G 37)
Balder Ri. SE12 . . . . .7L 55
Baldric Rd. CT20: F'stone 6F 188
Baldwin Rd. ME12: Minst 6L 221 (7H 11)
TN28: G'stne 8M 213
Baldwins La. TN4: Tun W 6J 151
Baldwin Ter. CT19: F'stone 5L 189
Baldwyn's Pk. DA5: Bex'y 7E 58 (7F 7)
Baldwyn's Rd. DA5: Bex'y 7E 58
Balfour Ct. CT20: F'stone 8G 189
Balfour Rd. BR2: Shortl 8N 69
CT14: Walm 8M 177
CT16: Dover 3H 181
ME4: Chat'm 2B 94
Balgowan Rd. BR3: Beck'm 6B 68
Balgowan St. SE18 .4H 51
BALHAM 7E 4
Balham High Rd. SW12 . . . . .7E 4
SW17 . . . . .7E 4
Balham Hill SW12 . . . . .7E 4
Balham Station (Rail & Tube) 7E 4
Baliol Rd. CT5: Whits 3G 227
Ballamore Rd. BR1: Brom 8K 55
Ballard Bus. Pk. ME2: Strood 8K 79
Ballard Cl. TN12: Mard 2C 212
Ballard Ind. Cen. ME5: Chat'm 2F 110
Ballard Rd. TN28: G'stne 8M 213
Ballards Hill TN17: Goud 9F 196 (3F 37)
Ballards Rd. RM10: Dag 2E 6
Ballards Way CR0: Croy 5H 13
CR2: S Croy 5H 13
Ballard Way TN12: Pad W 8N 147
Ballens Rd. ME5: Chat'm 8E 94
Balliemoor Ct. CT11: Ram 3J 211
Ballina St. SE23 . . . . .5A 54
Balliol Rd. CT10: B'stairs 5K 209 (2K 23)
DA16: Well 9K 51
Ball La. TN24: Kenn 3J 159
(not continuous)
TN25: Kenn 7B 30
Balloch Rd. SE6 . . . . .6G 54
Balls Cotts. ME3: C'den 9C 66
BALL'S GREEN 8C 154 (4E 34)
Ball's Grn. TN7: Withy 8C 154
Balls Pond Rd. N1 . . . . .1G 5
Balmer Cl. ME8: Gill .4N 95
Balmoral Av. BR3: Beck'm 7B 68
Balmoral Ct. BR3: Beck'm 4F 68
(off Avenue, The)
SE12 . . . . .9L 55
Balmoral Gdns. DA5: Bex'y 5A 58
Balmoral Ho. ME15: Maid 3J 139
Balmoral Pl. CT11: Ram 5K 211
Balmoral Rd. CT9: Mgte 3N 207
CT14: Kgdn 3E 200
DA4: S at H 3B 74
E7 . . . . .1A 6
ME7: Gill .7F 80 (2J 17)
Balmoral Ter. ME10: Sit 7E 98
BALSTONIA 1E 8
Baltic Rd. TN9: Tonb 8G 145
Baltimore Pl. DA16: Well 9H 51
Bamford Rd. BR1: Brom 1F 68
Bamford Way CT14: Deal 6M 177
Bampton Rd. SE23 . . . . .8A 54
Banavie Gdns. BR3: Beck'm 4F 68
Banbury Vs. DA13: Sflt 2M 75
TN26: Hams 3L 191
Banckside DA3: Hart'y 7L 75
Bancroft Gdns. BR6: Orp 2H 85
Bancroft La. ME19: W Mal 6A 124
Bancroft Rd. TN15: Wro 7M 105
BANDONHILL 4E 12
Bangor Rd. ME2: Strood 6H 79
Bank Cotts. ME17: Holl 6G 129
Bank Ct. DA1: Dart .4M 59
Bankfields TN27: H'crn 7K 191
Bankfield Way TN17: Goud 4C 190
Bankfoot Rd. BR1: Brom 9H 55
Bankhurst Rd. SE6 . . . . .5C 54
Bank La. TN11: Hild 6A 132 (4H 25)
TN15: Under 5A 132 (4H 25)
Bank Rd. TN25: Mers 4C 40
Banks Cotts. ME18: W'bury 1C 136
Bankside DA11: Nflt .4B 62
ME5: Chat'm 3E 94
TN13: Dun G 3E 118
Bank Side TN26: Hams 2K 191
Bankside Cl. DA5: Bex'y 9E 58
TN16: Big H 6C 164
Banks La. DA6: Bexhth 2A 58
Banks Rd. ME2: Strood 4N 79 (2H 17)
TN23: Ashf 2E 160
Bank Station (Tube & DLR) 3G 5
Banks, The CT10: B'stairs 7K 209
Bank St. CT6: H Bay 2G 195
CT21: Hythe 6K 199
DA12: Grav'nd 4G 63
ME4: Chat'm 9E 80
ME13: Fav 5G 187
ME14: Maid 5C 126
TN9: Tonb 5H 145
TN13: S'oaks 7J 119
TN17: Cran 7C 176
TN23: Ashf 8F 158
Bankwell Rd. SE13 . . . . .2H 55
Banky Flds. Cl. ME8: Rain 2D 96
Banky Mdw. ME16: Barm 6K 125
Banner Farm Rd. TN2: Tun W 3H 157
Banner Way ME12: Minst 6F 220
Banning St. ME2: Strood 4M 79
Bannister Gdns. BR5: St P 6L 71
Bannister Hill ME9: B'den 9C 98 (5E 18)
Bannister Rd. ME14: Pen H 2D 126
Bannockburn Rd. SE18 . . . . .4G 51
BANSTEAD 7C 12
Banstead Rd. CR8: Purl 6F 13
KT17: Eps 6B 12
SM5: Cars 5D 12
SM7: Bans 6B 12
Banstead Rd. Sth. SM2: Sutt 6D 12
Banstead Station (Rail) 6C 12
Banwell Rd. DA5: Bex'y 4M 57
BAPCHILD 9L 99 (5G 19)
Bapchild Pl. BR5: St M Cry 7L 71
Barbados Ter. ME14: Maid 2D 126
Barberry Av. ME5: Chat'm 6A 94
Barbers Almshouses CT11: Ram 6H 211
(off Elms Av.)
Barbican Station (Rail & Tube) 3F 5
Barcham Ct. ME15: Maid 3C 138
Barchester Way TN10: Tonb 1M 145
Barclay Av. TN10: Tonb 2M 145
Barclay Fld. TN15: Kems'g 8M 103
Barclay Rd. CR0: Croy 4G 13
Barcombe Cl. BR5: St P 6H 71
Bardell Ter. ME1: Roch 7A 80 (2H 17)
Barden Ct. ME14: Maid 4E 126
BARDEN PARK 6F 144 (6J 25)
Barden Pk. Rd. TN9: Tonb 6G 144
Barden Rd. TN3: Bidb, Speld 4N 149 (1H 35)
TN9: Tonb 6G 144
Bardens Row TN30: St Mic 4C 224
Barden St. SE18 . . . . .7G 50
Bardolph Av. CR0: Croy 9B 82
BARDOWN 7D 36
Bardown Rd. TN5: Tice, St'gate 7C 36
Bardsley Cl. TN12: E Peck 9M 135
Barfield DA4: S at H .3B 74
Barfield Rd. BR1: Brom 6C 70
Barfleur Manor ME7: Gill 6D 80
(off Middle St.)
Barfreston Cl. ME15: Maid 7C 126
BARFRESTONE 4D 32
Barfrestone Rd. CT15: Eyt 6L 219 (5D 32)
Bargate Cl. SE18 . . . . .5H 51
Bargates TN23: Ashf 3C 160
Barge Ho. Rd. E16 . . . . .2D 50
Bargery Rd. SE6 . . . . .6E 54
Barges, The CT5: Whits 2G 226
Bargrove Cres. SE6 . . . . .7C 54
Bargrove Rd. ME14: Maid 3F 126
BARHAM .8D 162 (4A 32)
Barham Cl. BR2: Shortl 2A 84
BR7: Chst 1D 70
DA12: Grav'nd 6L 63
ME15: Maid 3H 139
Barham Ct. CT4: B'hm 7D 162
ME18: Tstn 9F 124
Barham Dr. TN17: Cran 7D 176
Barham M. ME18: Tstn 9F 124
Barham Rd. BR7: Chst 1D 70
DA1: Dart 5A 60
Barham's Mill Rd. TN27: Eger 6D 28
Baring Cl. SE12 . . . . .7K 55
Baring Rd. SE12 . . . . .5K 55 (7A 6)
Barker Rd. ME16: Maid 6C 126
Barkers Ct. ME10: Sit 7E 98
Bark Hart Rd. BR6: Orp 2K 85
BARKING 1C 6
Barking Northern Relief Rd. IG11: Bark 1B 6
Barking Rd. E6 . . . . .2A 6
E13 . . . . .2K 5
Barking Station (Rail & Tube) 1C 6
Barkis Cl. ME1: Roch 4A 94
Barlby Rd. W10 . . . . .3B 4
Barler Pl. ME11: Queen 7B 220
Barley Cl. CT15: Mart M 6H 33
Barleycorn ME19: Leyb 9C 108
Barleycorn Dr. ME8: Gill 5A 96
Barley Ct. CT6: H Bay 5L 195
Barleyfields ME14: Weav 5G 127
Barleymow Cl. ME5: Chat'm 5F 94
Barley Way TN23: Kgnt 4C 160
Barling Cl. ME5: Chat'm 1A 110
Barlings Ho. SE4 . . . . .2A 54
(off Frendsbury Rd.)
Barlow Cl. ME8: Gill .6A 96
Barlow Dr. SE18 . . . . .8A 50
Barmeston Rd. SE6 . . . . .7E 54
BARMING .7K 125 (2G 27)
BARMING HEATH 6K 125 (2G 27)
Barming Pl. ME16: Barm 7K 125
Barming Rd. ME18: E Mal 7D 124
Barming Station (Rail) 3L 125 (1G 27)
Barmouth Rd. CR0: Croy 3A 82
Barnaby Ter. ME1: Roch 1N 93
Barnard Cl. BR7: Chst 4F 70
SE18 . . . . .4C 50
Barnard Ct. DA2: Dart 4B 60
(off Clifton Wlk.)
ME4: Chat'm 1D 94
Barnberry Cl. TN23: Ashf 1C 160
Barn Cl. CT3: Hoath .4A 22
CT5: Seas 5E 20
ME9: B'den 9B 98
Barn Cotts. CT2: T Hill 5L 167
Barn Cres. CT9: Mgte 2N 207
Barncroft Cl. ME14: Weav 5J 127
Barncroft Dr. ME7: Hpstd 7J 95
Barndale Ct. DA12: Shorne 1C 78
Barned Ct. ME16: Barm 7K 125
BARNEHURST 1D 58 (6F 7)
Barnehurst Av. DA7: Bexhth 8D 52
DA8: Bexhth, Erith 8D 52
Barnehurst Cl. DA8: Erith 8D 52
Barnehurst Rd. DA7: Bexhth 9D 52 (5F 7)
Barnehurst Station (Rail) 9D 52 (5F 7)
Barn End Dr. DA2: Dart 9K 59
Barn End La. DA2: Dart, Swanl 1K 73 (1G 15)
BARNES 5A 4
Barnes Av. CT9: Mgte 2N 207
Barnes Bridge Station (Rail) 5A 4
Barnes Ct. CT1: Cant 4K 171
(off St Jacob's Pl.)
BARNES CRAY 2H 59 (6G 7)
Barnes Cray Rd. DA1: Cray 2H 59
Barnesdale Cres. BR5: St M Cry 9J 71
Barnesende Ct. CT13: S'wch 6M 217
Barnes High St. SW13 . . . . .5A 4
Barnes La. ME17: Lint 8N 137 (5H 27)
SW20 . . . . .2B 12
Barnes Station (Rail) .6B 4
BARNES STREET 2G 146 (5C 26)
Barnes Wlk. TN12: Mard 2D 212
Barnet Dr. BR2: Shortl 3A 84
Barnet's La. CT2: B Oak 2C 168
Barnett Cl. DA8: Erith 9G 52
Barnett Ct. CT12: Minst 8E 212
CT12: Ram 3F 210
Barnett Fld. TN23: Ashf 1D 160
Barnetts Cl. TN4: S'bgh 5J 151
Barnetts Hill TN31: Peas 4J 45
Barnetts Rd. TN11: Leigh 5A 144
Barnetts Way TN4: S'bgh 5J 151
Barnet Wood Rd. BR2: Shortl 3M 83
Barnfield CT6: H Bay 5D 194
DA11: Grav'nd 7F 62
ME5: Chat'm 3D 94
TN2: Tun W 6F 156
TN30: St Mic 5C 224
Barnfield Cl. BR8: Crock'n 1D 86
DA3: Long 6C 76
DA9: G'hithe 4F 60
Barnfield Cres. TN15: Kems'g 8M 103
Barnfield Gdns. SE18 .6D 50
Barnfield Pk. La. TN27: Char'g 6G 29
Barnfield Rd. BR5: St P 6M 71
CT19: F'stone 4J 189
DA17: Belv 6A 52
ME13: Fav 4G 186
SE18 . . . . .6D 50
(not continuous)
TN13: Riv 5F 118
TN16: Tats 8D 164
Barnfield Wood Cl. BR3: Beck'm 9G 69
Barnfield Wood Rd. BR3: Beck'm 9G 68
Barnham Dr. SE28 . . . . .1H 51
(not continuous)
Barn Hawe TN8: Eden 6C 184
Barn Hill ME15: Hunt 7J 137 (4G 27)
Barnhill Av. BR2: Shortl 8J 69
Barn Hill Cotts. ME15: Hunt 5K 137
Barnhouse La. TN29: Ivyc 3F 47
Barnhurst La. CT18: H'nge 7K 193 (2A 42)
Barnhurst Rd. ME14: Pen H 1D 126
Barn Mdw. ME2: Hall'g 7C 92
TN12: S'hrst 2J 223
Barnmead Rd. BR3: Beck'm 4A 68
Barnock Cl. DA1: Cray 5F 58
Barn Platt TN23: Ashf 1E 160
BARNSBURY 1F 5
Barnsbury Rd. N1 . . . . .2F 5
Barns Cl. ME13: Fav .4E 186
Barnsley Cl. ME12: S'ness 2F 220
BARNSOLE .8B 216 (1D 32)
Barnsole Rd. CT3: S'le 9A 216 (1D 32)
ME7: Gill 7G 81 (2J 17)
Barnsole Vineyard 8B 216
Barnstable La. SE13 .2F 54
Barnstaple Ho. SE12 .3J 55
(off Taunton Rd.)
Barn St. ME3: St M Hoo 5A 10
Barn Theatre, The 6J 57
Barn Tye Cl. CT15: Gus 7K 179
Barntye Rd. CT15: Gus 8J 179
Barnwell Pl. ME7: Gill 7F 80
Barnwell Rd. DA1: Dart 1N 59
Barnwood Cl. ME1: Roch 3M 93
Barn Yard, The 4H 225
Baron Cl. ME7: Gill 5H 81
ME14: Weav 4J 127
Barons Ct. TN4: Tun W 9G 151
Barons Court Station (Tube) 4C 4
Baron's Wlk. CR0: Croy 9B 68
Barrack Hill CT21: Hythe 6H 199 (5H 41)
Barrack Rd. ME4: Chat'm 4E 80
Barrack Row DA11: Grav'nd 4G 62
Barrack Arch Cl. TN12: Mard 2B 212
Barretts Rd. TN13: Dun G 2E 118
TN18: Hawkh 5D 192
Barrey Rd. TN24: Svgtn 3L 161
Barrie Dr. ME20: Lark 6D 108
Barrier Rd. ME4: Chat'm 7C 80
Barrington Cl. ME5: Chat'm 6C 94
Barrington Cres. CT7: Birch 4G 206
Barrington Rd. DA7: Bexhth 9M 51
Barrington Vs. SE18 .8C 50
Barrow Ct. SE6 . . . . .6J 55
(off Cumberland Pl.)
Barrowfields ME5: Chat'm 1G 111
BARROW GREEN 6L 223 (5H 19)
Barrow Gro. ME10: Sit 8E 98
BARROWHILL 4F 41
BARROW HILL 7E 158
Barrow Hill TN23: Ashf 8F 158
TN25: S'ndge 9C 218 (4F 41)
Barrow Hill Cotts. TN23: Ashf 7E 158
Barrow Hill Pl. TN23: Ashf 7E 158
Barrow Hill Ri. TN25: S'ndge 4F 41
Barrow Hill Ter. TN23: Ashf 7F 158
(off Barrow Hill Pl.)
Barrow La. TN3: Lang G 3N 155
Barrows Cl. CT7: Birch 5F 206
Barr Rd. DA12: Grav'nd 7L 63
Barry Av. DA7: Bexhth 7N 51
Barry Cl. BR6: Orp 4G 84
Barry Rd. SE22 . . . . .6H 5
Bartholomew Cl. CT21: Hythe 5J 199
Bartholomew La. CT21: Hythe 5H 199 (5H 41)
Bartholomew St. CT16: Dover 3H 181
CT21: Hythe 6J 199
Bartholomew Way BR8: Swanl 6F 72 (2F 15)
Barth Rd. SE18 . . . . .4G 51
(not continuous)
Bartlets La. TN23: Gt Cha 4A 160 (3J 39)
Bartlett Cl. ME5: Chat'm 1F 110
Bartlett Dr. CT5: Whits 4J 227
Bartlett Rd. DA11: Grav'nd 6F 62
TN16: Westrm 8E 116
Bartletts Cl. ME12: Minst 7D 220
Bartley Mill 5B 36
Bartley Mill Rd. TN3: Lamb, Wadh 5B 36
TN5: Wadh, Cous W 5B 36
Barton Cl. DA6: Bexhth 3N 57
Barton Ct. ME12: Minst 6K 221
Barton Fld. CT18: Lym'ge 7K 205
Bartonfields Ct. CT1: Cant 3A 172
Barton Hill Dr. ME12: Minst 8G 221 (1G 19)
Barton Mill Ct. CT2: Cant 1M 171
Barton Mill Rd. CT1: Cant 9A 168
Barton Path CT16: Dover 2H 181
Barton Rd. CT1: Cant 4B 172
CT16: Dover 2H 181 (1F 43)

Barton Rd.—Beechin Wood La.

Barton Rd. DA4: S at H .4B 74
DA14: Sidc .2N 71
ME2: Strood .5L 79
ME15: Maid .7D 126 (2J 27)
Bartons Bus. Pk. CT1: Cant .4C 172
Bartons Point Coastal Pk. .2G 220 (6G 11)
Barton Vw. Ter. CT17: Dover .3H 181
Bartram Rd. SE4 .3B 54
Barts Cl. BR3: Beck'm .8D 68
Barville Cl. SE4 .2B 54
Barville Rd. CT15: Eyt .7L 185 (4E 32)
Barwick Rd. CT17: Dover .3E 180 (1E 42)
Barwick Rd. Ind. Est. CT17: Dover .3E 180
Barwood Av. BR4: W W'ck .2E 82
Bascombe Gro. DA1: Bex'y, Cray .5F 58
Basden Cotts. TN18: Hawkh .5D 192
Bashford Barn La. ME9: B'gar .6A 114 (7D 18)
Basi Cl. ME2: Strood .3N 79
Basildon Rd. SE2 .5J 51 (4D 6)
Basil Gdns. CR0: Croy .2A 82
Basilon Rd. DA7: Bexhth .9N 51
Basing Cl. ME15: Maid .6E 126
Basing Dr. DA5: Bex'y .4A 58
Baskerville TN24: Ashf .7F 158
Basket Gdns. SE9 .3A 56
Basmere Cl. ME14: Maid .3F 126
Bassant Rd. SE18 .6H 51
Basser Hill ME9: Lwr Hal .3N 225
Bassett Cl. CT21: Hythe .4M 199
Bassett Gdns. CT21: Hythe .4L 199
Bassett Rd. ME10: Sit .7E 98
Bassett's Cl. BR6: Farnb .5D 84
Bassetts La. TN8: Chid H .7C 148 (2E 34)
Bassett's Way BR6: Farnb .5D 84
Bastable Av. IG11: Bark .2C 6
BASTED .5M 121 (2A 26)
Basted La. TN15: Bor G .5N 121 (1A 26)
Basted Mill TN15: Bor G .3L 121
Bastion Rd. CT17: Dover .5H 181
SE2 .5J 51
Baston Mnr. Rd. BR2: Shortl .4L 83
Baston Rd. BR2: Shortl .2L 83 (3A 14)
BAT & BALL .3K 119 (1G 25)
Bat & Ball Ent. Cen. TN14: S'oaks .3K 119
Bat & Ball Rd. TN14: S'oaks .3K 119
Bat & Ball Station (Rail) .3K 119 (1G 25)
Batchelors TN2: Pem .6D 152
Batchelor St. ME4: Chat'm .8D 80
Batchwood Grn. BR5: St P .6J 71
Bates Cl. CT3: S'le .1D 32
ME20: Lark .7E 108
Bates Hill TN15: Igh .4J 121 (1K 25)
Bateson St. SE18 .4G 50
Bath Ct. CT20: F'stone .8H 189
Bath Hard ME1: Roch .7A 80
Bathhurst Cl. TN12: S'hrst .2J 223
Bath Pl. CT9: Mgte .2D 208
Bath Rd. CT9: Mgte .3D 208 (1H 23)
DA1: Dart .5J 59
TN24: Ashf .3J 161
W4 .4A 4
Baths Rd. BR2: Shortl .7N 69
Bath St. DA11: Grav'nd .4G 62 (6C 8)
EC1 .2G 5
Bathurst Cl. CT12: Ram .3F 210
Bathurst Rd. CT20: F'stone .6F 188
TN12: S'hrst .3J 223
Bathway SE18 .4C 50
Batteries Cl. ME9: Lyn .9J 223
Batteries Ter. ME9: Lyn .9J 223
Battersby Rd. SE6 .7G 55
BATTERSEA .5E 4
Battersea Bri. SW3 .5D 4
SW11 .5D 4
Battersea Bri. Rd. SW11 .5D 4
Battersea Pk. .5D 4
Battersea Pk. Rd. SW8 .5D 4
SW11 .5D 4
Battersea Park Station (Rail) .5E 4
Battersea Ri. SW11 .6D 4
Battery Point CT20: Hythe .9B 188
Battery Rd. SE28 .2G 50
TN29: Lydd .6K 47
BATTLE .7C 44
Battle Abbey .7C 44
Battlefields Rd. TN15: Wro .7M 105 (7A 16)
Battle Hill TN33: Batt .7C 44
Battle La. TN12: Mard .6H 27
Battle of Britain Flats CT17: Dover .5J 181
(off York St.)
Battle of Britain Memorial, The .3B 174 (3C 42)
Battle of Hastings, Site of (1066) .7C 44
Battle Rd. DA8: Erith .4D 52 (4F 7)
DA17: Belv, Erith .4D 52 (4F 7)
TN21: Dall .6A 44
TN32: Rob, Mount .4B 44
TN32: What, S'cross .5D 44
TN33: Dall, Neth .6A 44
Battlesmere Rd. ME3: Cli W .5M 65
Battle Station (Rail) .7C 44
BATTLE STREET .6L 77
Battle St. DA12: Cobh .6L 77
Batt's Rd. DA12: Cobh, Lud'n .8M 77
DA13: Lud'n .3D 16
Baudwin Rd. SE6 .7H 55
Baugh Rd. DA14: Sidc .1L 71
Bawden Cl. CT2: Cant .7N 167
Baxendale Ct. TN24: Ashf .2H 161
Baxter Way ME19: W Mal .6A 124
Bayard Ct. DA6: Bexhth .2C 58
Bay Cotts. CT15: St Marg .7D 214
Baydon Cl. BR2: Shortl .6J 69
Baye La. CT3: Ickh .7B 22
Bayfield ME13: Osp .7K 19
Bayfield Ho. SE4 .2A 54
(off Coston Wlk.)
Bayfield Rd. SE9 .2N 55
BAYFORD .2C 18
Bayford Rd. ME10: Sit .7H 99
Bayhall Rd. TN2: Tun W .2J 157 (3K 35)
Bayham Abbey .4C 36
Bayham Rd. TN2: Tun W .5H 157 (4K 35)
TN3: Bell G .5H 157 (4K 35)
TN3: Tun W .5H 157 (4K 35)
Bayham Rd. TN13: S'oaks .5K 119 (2G 25)
Bayham St. NW1 .2E 4
Bay Hill CT15: St Marg .8C 214 (7J 33)
Bay Hill Cl. CT15: St Marg .8C 214
Bayle Ct. CT20: F'stone .7L 189
Bayle St. CT20: F'stone .6L 189
Bayle, The CT20: F'stone .7L 189
BAYLEY'S HILL .3F 25
Bayley's Hill TN14: S'oaks, Weald .4F 130 (4F 25)
Bayleys Hill Rd. TN8: Chid .2E 142
Bayley Wlk. SE2 .6N 51
Bayly Rd. DA1: Dart .4A 60
Bay Mus., The .7J 33
Baynham Cl. DA5: Bex'y .4A 58
BAYSWATER .3D 4
Bayswater Dr. ME8: Rain .7A 96
Bayswater Rd. W11 .3C 4
Bayswater Station (Tube) .3C 4
Bay, The DA13: Meop .2F 106
Bay Tree Cl. BR1: Brom .4N 69
Baytree Cl. DA15: Sidc .6H 57
BAY VIEW .1A 20
Bay Vw. CT20: S'gte .8C 188
Bay Vw. Gdns. ME12: Ley S .6J 203
Bay Vw. Hgts. CT7: Birch .3C 206
(off Ethelbert Rd.)
Bayview Rd. CT5: Whits .6F 226
Bay Vw. Rd. CT10: B'stairs .2L 211
Bayview Rd. CT14: Kgdn .5E 200
Baywell ME19: Leyb .8C 108
Bazes Shaw DA3: New A .3M 89
(not continuous)
Beach All. CT5: Whits .3F 226
(off Island Wall)
Beachamwell Dr. ME19: W Mal .7A 124
(off Rougemont)
Beach App. ME12: Ward .5K 203 (1B 20)
Beach Av. CT7: Birch .3E 206 (2E 22)
Beach Bank Cvn. Site CT21: Hythe .9D 198
Beachborough Rd. BR1: Brom .9F 54
CT19: F'stone .5G 188 (4A 42)
Beach Ct. CT14: Deal .6J 177
CT14: Walm .8N 177
TN17: Bendn .5A 38
Beach Ho's. CT9: Mgte .3A 208
Beach Marine CT20: S'gte .8F 188
Beachmont Cl. TN28: G'stne .6H 213
Beach Ride CT8: Wgte S .2L 207
Beach Rd. CT8: Wgte S .2L 207
CT15: St Marg .9C 214
TN29: Dym .9D 182
Beach St. CT6: H Bay .2G 194
CT14: Deal .3N 177 (3J 33)
CT20: F'stone .7L 189
ME12: S'ness .2C 220
Beach Ter. ME12: S'ness .2C 220
Beach, The CT14: Walm .7N 177 (4J 33)
Beach Wlk. CT5: Whits .2G 226
Beachy Path TN30: Tent .7C 224
Beacon Av. CT6: H Bay .2J 195
Beacon Cl. ME8: Gill .4N 95
Beacon Cotts. TN26: Beth .3K 163
Beacon Dr. DA2: Bean .8H 61
Beaconfields CT5: Seas .7B 226
TN13: S'oaks .8G 119
Beacon Hgts. CT5: Whits .2H 227
BEACON HILL .6B 38
Beacon Hill CT6: H Bay .2H 195 (2K 21)
CT14: L Mon .4G 33
ME5: Chat'm .1F 94
Beacon Hill La. ME3: C'den .9C 66
Beacon La. CT13: Wdboro .8F 216 (1F 33)
TN32: S'cross .5E 44
Beacon Oak Rd. TN30: Tent .7C 224 (6E 38)
Beacon Ri. TN13: S'oaks .8H 119
Beacon Rd. CT6: H Bay .2H 195
CT10: B'stairs .7J 209 (2K 23)
DA8: Erith .7J 53
ME5: Chat'm .1F 94
ME17: Len .7L 201
SE13 .4G 54
TN6: Crowb .7F 35
Beaconsfield Av. CT16: Dover .3H 181
ME7: Gill .7H 81
Beaconsfield Gdns. CT10: B'stairs .8K 209
Beaconsfield Pde. SE9 .9A 56
Beaconsfield Rd. BR1: Brom .6N 69
CT2: Cant .9L 167 (7H 21)
CT14: Deal .5N 177
CT16: Dover .3H 181
DA5: Bex'y .7F 58
ME4: Chat'm .1C 94
ME10: Sit .7K 99
ME15: Maid .7B 126
RH17: Chel G .7A 34
SE9 .7A 56
W4 .4A 4
Beaconsfield Ter. CT21: Hythe .7L 199
Beacons, The ME17: Cox .6N 137
Beacon Ter. CT21: Hythe .9B 188
Beacon Wlk. CT6: H Bay .2H 195
TN30: Tent .6C 224
Beacon Way CT21: Lymp .5A 198
Beacon Wood Country Pk. .9H 61 (1K 15)
Beadnell Rd. SE23 .6A 54
Beadon Rd. BR2: Shortl .7K 69
W6 .4B 4
Beagles Cl. BR5: Orp .3M 85
Beagles Wood Rd. TN2: Pem .7D 152
(not continuous)
Beagrams, The CT13: S'wch .5L 217
Beal Cl. DA16: Well .8J 51
Beales La. TN31: N'thiam .3G 45
BEAL'S GREEN .3D 192 (7H 37)
Beaman Cl. TN17: Goud .3D 190
Beamish Rd. BR5: Orp .1L 85
Beamont Cl. CT12: Mans .9L 207
Beams, The ME15: Maid .8J 127
BEAN .8J 61 (7K 7)
Bean Cl. TN23: Gt Cha .9A 158
Beane Cft. DA12: Grav'nd .6L 63
Beaney's La. CT4: Chil'm .2B 30
Bean Hill Cotts. DA2: Bean .9J 61
(not continuous)
Bean La. DA2: Bean .7H 61 (7K 7)
Bean Rd. DA6: Bexhth .2M 57
DA9: G'hithe .3H 61
Beanshaw SE9: Chst .9C 56
Bear's End Ho. TN23: Ashf .1F 160
Bear's La. TN26: Beth .1J 39
Beaside Cl. ME8: Gill .9L 81
BEARSTED .5M 127 (2A 28)
Bearsted Grn. Bus. Cen. ME14: Bear .4M 127
Bearsted Ri. SE4 .3C 54
Bearsted Rd. ME14: Maid, Weav .2F 126 (1J 27)
Bearsted Station (Rail) .4L 127 (1K 27)
Bearsted Ter. BR3: Beck'm .4D 68
Bearsted Vineyard .8N 127 (2A 28)
Beaton Cl. DA9: G'hithe .3H 61
Beatrice Gdns. DA11: Nflt .7D 62
Beatrice Hills Cl. TN24: Kenn .5J 159
Beatrice M. TN28: G'stne .7H 213
Beatrice Rd. CT9: Mgte .5C 208 (2H 23)
CT18: Cap F .2C 174
Beatrice Wilson Flats TN13: S'oaks .7J 119
Beatty Av. ME7: Gill .9J 81
Beatty Cl. CT19: F'stone .3L 189
Beatty Rd. CT19: F'stone .3K 189
ME1: Roch .3A 94
Beauchamp Av. CT14: Deal .7K 177
Beauchamp Cl. TN24: Kenn .5J 159
Beauchamp Pl. SW3 .4D 4
Beauchamps La. CT15: Non .3C 32
Beaufighter Rd. ME19: W Mal .6K 123
Beaufort Av. CT12: Ram .4F 210
Beaufort Ct. ME2: Med E .6B 80
Beaufort Rd. ME2: Strood .3J 79
Beaufort St. SW3 .5D 4
Beaufort Wlk. ME15: Maid .4H 139
Beaufoy Rd. CT17: Dover .3F 180
Beaufoy Ter. CT17: Dover .3E 180
Beaulieu Ri. ME1: Roch .2A 94
Beaulieu Rd. TN10: Tonb .3H 145
Beaulieu Wlk. ME16: Alltn .2N 125
Beaumanor CT6: H Bay .4H 195
Beaumanor Gdns. SE9 .9C 56
Beaumont Davy Cl. ME13: Fav .7G 187
Beaumont Dr. DA11: Nflt .5D 62
Beaumont Rd. BR5: Pet W .9F 70
ME16: Maid .7M 125
SW19 .7C 4
Beaumont St. CT6: H Bay .4D 194
Beaumont Ter. ME13: Fav .6H 187
SE13 .5H 55
(off Wellmeadow Rd.)
Beaute La. CT3: Shtng .6M 225 (7C 22)
Beauvoir Dr. ME10: Kems'y .3H 99
Beauworth Pk. ME15: Maid .9H 127
Beauxfield CT16: Whitf .5F 178
BEAVER .2E 160
Beaverbank Rd. SE9 .6F 56
Beaver Ct. BR3: Beck'm .3E 68
TN23: Ashf .2E 160
Beaver Ind. Est. TN23: Ashf .2F 160
Beaver La. TN23: Ashf .1C 160 (2K 39)
(Brookfield Rd.)
TN23: Ashf .8C 158
(Leacon Rd.)
Beaver Rd. ME16: Alltn .3M 125
TN23: Ashf .2F 160 (2A 40)
Beavers Lodge DA14: Sidc .9H 57
Beaverwood Rd. BR7: Chst .1G 71
Beazley Ct. TN24: Ashf .2H 161
Bebbington Rd. SE18 .4G 50
Beblets Cl. BR6: Chels .6H 85
Beck Ct. BR3: Beck'm .6A 68
BECKENHAM .4D 68 (2J 13)
Beckenham Bus. Cen. BR3: Beck'm .2B 68
Beckenham Dr. ME16: Alltn .2A 126
Beckenham Gro. BR2: Shortl .5G 69
Beckenham Hill Est. BR3: Beck'm .1E 68
Beckenham Hill Rd. BR3: Beck'm .2E 68 (1J 13)
SE6 .2E 68 (1K 13)
Beckenham Hill Station (Rail) .1F 68 (1J 13)
Beckenham Junction Station
(Rail & CT) .4D 68 (2J 13)
Beckenham La. BR2: Shortl .5H 69 (2K 13)
Beckenham Pk. ME8: Rain .3B 18
Beckenham Pl. Pk. BR3: Beck'm .3E 68
Beckenham Rd. BR3: Beck'm .4A 68 (2J 13)
BR4: W W'ck .1E 82 (3K 13)
Beckenham Road Station (CT) .4B 68 (2J 13)
Beckenham Theatre Cen., The .5E 68
Becket Av. CT2: Cant .1K 171
Becket Cl. CT3: Ash .4C 216
CT5: Whits .4K 227
CT14: Deal .2M 177
Becket Ct. TN9: Tonb .7H 145
(off Alexandra Rd.)
TN27: H'crn .8L 191
Becket Ho. CT1: Cant .3N 171
Becket M. CT2: Cant .1M 171
Beckets Cl. TN25: H'lgh .7E 30
Beckets Fld. TN11: Pens .3H 149
Beckets Sports Cen. .4K 59
Beckets Wood CT3: Ups .5B 22
Beckett Cl. DA17: Belv .3A 52
Becketts Cl. BR6: Orp .4H 85
DA5: Bex'y .6D 58
Beckett St. ME13: Fav .5G 186
Beckett Wlk. BR3: Beck'm .2B 68
Beckford Dr. BR5: Orp .1F 84
Beck La. BR3: Beck'm .6A 68
BECKLEY .4H 45
Beckley Cl. DA12: Grav'nd .7N 63
BECKLEY FURNACE .5G 45
Beckley Hill Works ME3: High'm .4F 64
Beckley M. ME5: Chat'm .6C 94
Beckley Pl. TN25: Stanf .4G 41
Beckley Rd. ME12: S'ness .2F 220
TN31: N'thiam, Bkld .4G 45
Beckman Cl. TN14: Hals .6D 102
Beck River Pk. BR3: Beck'm .4D 68
Becksbourne Cl. ME14: Pen H .1D 126
Becks Rd. DA14: Sidc .8J 57
BECKTON .3B 6
Beckton Park Station (DLR) .3B 6
Beckton Rd. E16 .3K 5
Beckton Station (DLR) .3B 6
Beck Way BR3: Beck'm .6C 68
Beckwith Grn. CT20: F'stone .6D 188
Beckworth Pl. ME16: Maid .6M 125
BECONTREE .1E 6
Becontree Av. RM8: Dag .1D 6
Becontree Station (Tube) .1D 6
Becton Pl. DA8: Erith .7C 52
Bedale Wlk. DA2: Dart .6B 60
BEDDINGTON .4F 13
BEDDINGTON CORNER .3E 12
Beddington Farm Rd. CR0: Croy .3F 13
Beddington Grn. BR5: St P .4H 71
Beddington La. CR0: Croy .3E 12
Beddington Lane Station (CT) .3E 12
Beddington Path BR5: St P .4H 71
Beddington Rd. BR5: St P .5G 71
Beddlestead La. CR6: Warl .7A 164 (7K 13)
Beddow Way ME20: Aylfd .8M 109 (7G 17)
Bede Ho. CT14: Deal .2N 177
Bedens Rd. DA14: Sidc .2N 71
Bedford Av. ME8: Rain .2N 95
Bedford Ct. CT10: B'stairs .8M 209
Bedford Hill SW12 .7E 4
SW16 .7E 4
Bedford M. SE6 .7E 54
BEDFORD PARK .4A 4
Bedford Pl. ME16: Maid .5B 126
Bedford Rd. BR6: Orp .3K 85
DA1: Dart .5A 60
DA11: Nflt .7E 62
DA15: Sidc .8G 57
SW4 .6F 5
TN4: S'bgh .5G 150
Bedford Sq. CT12: Ram .2F 210
(off Stirling Way)
DA3: Long .6K 75
WC1 .3E 4
Bedford Ter. TN1: Tun W .3G 156
Bedford Vs. TN25: Sme .8J 165
Bedford Way CT7: St N .9M 215
Bedgebury Cl. ME1: Roch .3A 94
ME14: Maid .3F 126
BEDGEBURY CROSS .5F 37
Bedgebury National Pinetum .6G 37
Bedgebury Rd. SE9 .2N 55
TN17: Goud .4C 190 (5F 37)
Bedingfield Way CT18: Lym'ge .7K 205
Bedivere Rd. BR1: Brom .8K 55
Bedlam Ct. La. CT12: Minst .8F 212 (4F 23)
Bedlam La. TN27: Smar, Eger .7D 28
Bedlington Sq. ME13: Fav .5H 187
BEDMONTON .1N 129 (1D 28)
Bedonwell Rd.
DA7: Belv, Bexhth, Erith .6A 52 (5E 6)
DA17: Belv .6N 51 (5E 6)
SE2 .6N 51
Bedson Wlk. ME8: Rain .2D 96
Bedwell Rd. DA17: Belv .5B 52
Bedwin Cl. ME1: Roch .4A 94
Beecham Rd. TN10: Tonb .1L 145
Beech Av. BR8: Swanl .7G 73
CT4: Chart'm .9E 170
DA15: Sidc .5J 57
TN16: Tats .7D 164
Beech Cl. CT19: F'stone .5J 189
ME13: Fav .5F 186
Beech Copse BR1: Brom .4B 70
Beech Ct. BR1: Brom .4J 69
(off Blyth Rd.)
BR3: Beck'm .3C 68
DA1: Dart .4A 60
Beech Court Gardens .8B 174 (5K 29)
Beechcroft BR7: Chst .3C 70
CT5: Whits .4M 227
Beechcroft Av. DA7: Bexhth .8E 52
Beechcroft Cl. BR6: Orp .5F 84
Beechcroft Gdns. CT11: Ram .4K 211
Beechcroft Rd. BR6: Orp .5F 84
Beech Dell BR2: Kes .5B 84
Beech Dr. CT10: B'stairs .9H 209
CT15: Evtn .6J 185
ME16: Alltn .4N 125
TN26: Hoth .2M 197
Beechen Bank Rd. ME5: Chat'm .9D 94
Beechenlea La. BR8: Swanl .7H 73 (2G 15)
Beechen Pl. SE23 .7A 54
Beeches Av. SM5: Cars .5D 12
Beeches, The BR8: Swanl .3G 73
DA3: Long .5B 76
DA13: Sole S .7J 77
ME5: Chat'm .7D 94
ME20: Aylfd .9J 109
TN2: Tun W .9K 151
TN18: Hawkh .7B 192
TN29: Lydd .2L 205
Beech Farm Rd. CR6: Warl .7K 13
TN32: S'cross .5D 44
Beechfield Cotts. BR1: Brom .4M 69
Beechfield Rd. BR1: Brom .5M 69
DA8: Erith .7F 52
SE6 .6C 54
Beech Grn. Cl. CT15: Eyt .9K 185
Beech Grn. La. TN7: Withy .3A 154
Beech Grn. Rd. TN7: Withy .3E 34
Beech Gro. CT12: C'snd .7A 210
CT16: Dover .1G 180
ME3: High'm .1F 78
Beech Haven Ct. DA1: Cray .3E 58
(off London Rd.)
Beech Hill CT4: Brid .9J 173
TN5: Wadh .7A 36
Beech Ho. CR0: Croy .7C 82
Beech Ho. La. TN32: Rob .3C 44
Beech Hurst TN2: Pem .7C 152
Beech Hurst Cl. ME15: Maid .7E 126
Beechill Rd. SE9 .3C 56
Beechin Bank Rd. ME5: Chat'm .5J 17
Beeching Rd. ME5: Chat'm .8E 94
Beechings Grn. ME8: Gill .9M 81
Beechings Way ME8: Gill, Rain .8L 81 (3K 17)
Beechings Way Ind. Cen. ME8: Gill .8L 81
Beeching Way RH19: E Grin .3A 34
Beechin Wood La. TN15: Bor G .4B 122 (1B 26)

Beechlands Cl.—Bickley Station (Rail)

Beechlands Cl. DA3: Hart'y 8N 75
Beech La. TN12: Mat 3C 36
Beech Mast DA13: Meop 2G 106
Beechmont Cl. BR1: Brom 1H 69
Beechmont Cotts. TN13: Weald 3J 131
Beechmont Ri. TN10: Tonb 1H 145
Beechmont Rd. TN13: S'oaks 2J 131 (3G 25)
Beechmore Dr. ME5: Chat'm 9D 94
Beecholme Dr. TN24: Kenn 5G 158
Beech Rd. BR6: Chels 8J 85
DA1: Dart 6L 59
ME2: Strood 6K 79
ME18: Mere 7G 123
ME19: E Mal 2D 124
TN13: S'oaks 7J 119
TN15: Mere 2C 26
TN16: Big H 7B 164
TN18: N'den 2G 45
Beech St. EC2 3G 5
TN1: Tun W 1H 157
Beech Vs. CT4: Elham 6N 183
Beech Wlk. DA1: Cray 2H 59
Beechway DA5: Bex'y 4M 57
Beechwood Av. BR6: Chels 6G 84
CT14: Deal 5M 177
ME5: Chat'm 1G 95
ME10: Sit 5F 98
Beechwood Cl. CT16: Whitf 4F 178
TN29: St M Bay 3M 215
Beechwood Ct. CT14: Deal 5M 177
CT16: Dover 9D 178
Beechwood Cres. DA7: Bexhth 1M 57
Beechwood Dr. BR2: Kes 5N 83
DA13: Meop 2F 106
Beechwood Gdns. DA13: Meop 1F 106
Beechwood Ri. BR7: Chst 9D 56
Beechwood Rd. ME16: Barm 6K 125
Beechy Lees Rd. TN14: Otf 8L 103
Beecroft Cl. CT2: Cant 7N 167
Beecroft La. SE4 3B 54
Beecroft M. SE4 3B 54
Beecroft Rd. SE4 3B 54
Beeken Dene BR6: Farnb 5E 84
Beer Cart La. CT1: Cant 2M 171
Beesfield La. DA4: Farn'm 1A 88 (3H 15)
Beeston Ct. DA2: Dart 4B 60
(off Hardwick Cres.)
Beggarsbush La. TN29: Old R 3F 47
BEGGAR'S HILL 5A 12
Beggars La. TN16: Westrm 7F 116 (2C 24)
Begonia Av. ME8: Gill 1M 95
Beke Rd. ME8: Gill 7N 95
BEKESBOURNE 6G 173 (2K 31)
BEKESBOURNE HILL 5G 173 (1K 31)
Bekesbourne Hill CT4: Bek 5G 173 (1K 31)
Bekesbourne La. CT1: Cant 2D 172
CT3: Cant 2D 172 (1J 31)
CT3: L'brne 4J 173 (1K 31)
CT4: Bek 2D 172 (1J 31)
Bekesbourne Rd. CT4: Brid 8E 172 (2J 31)
Bekesbourne Station (Rail) 5G 173 (1K 31)
Bekesbourne Twr. BR5: Orp 2M 85
(off Wichling Cl.)
Belcaire Cl. CT21: Lymp 5A 198
Belcroft Cl. BR1: Brom 3J 69
Beldam Haw TN14: Hals 3B 102
Belfast Ho. ME15: Maid 1H 139
Belfield Rd. TN2: Pem 8C 152
Belford Gro. SE18 4C 50
Belgrave Cl. BR5: St M Cry 7L 71
CT11: Ram 5H 211
Belgrave Ho. ME2: Strood 5M 79
Belgrave Pl. SW1 4E 4
Belgrave Rd. CT9: Mgte 3C 208 (1H 23)
CT17: Dover 5G 181
ME12: Minst 7D 220
SW1 4E 4
TN1: Tun W 1H 157
Belgrave Sq. SW1 4E 4
Belgrave St. ME20: Burh 4K 109
Belgrave Walk Station (CT) 2D 12
BELGRAVIA 4E 4
Belgravia Gdns. BR1: Brom 2H 69
Belgrove TN1: Tun W 3G 157
Belhus Woods Country Pk. 2J 7
Belinda Ct. CT19: F'stone 4H 189
Bell Chapel Cl. TN23: Kgnt 5G 160
Bell Cl. DA9: G'hithe 3F 60
Bell Cotts. ME9: Lwr Hal 3L 225
TN11: Gold G 2E 146
Bell Cres. ME1: Burh 2K 109
Bellefield Rd. BR5: St M Cry 8K 71
Belle Friday Cl. ME9: Tey 7K 223
Bellegrove Cl. DA16: Well 9H 51
Bellegrove Pde. DA16: Well 1H 57
Bellegrove Rd. DA16: Well 9F 50 (5C 6)
Bellermine Cl. SE28 1H 51
Bellevue Av. CT11: Ram 5K 211
Belle Vue Cotts. CT6: H Bay 4L 195
Belle Vue Rd. BR6: Downe 1C 100
Bellevue Rd. CT5: Whits 5H 227
Belle Vue Rd. CT6: H Bay 2H 195
Bellevue Rd. CT11: Ram 5K 211 (4K 23)
DA6: Bexhth 3A 58
ME12: Minst 5K 221
SW17 7D 4
Bellevue St. CT20: F'stone 6K 189
Bell Farm Gdns. ME16: Barm 7K 125
Bell Farm La. ME12: Minst 6N 221 (7J 11)
Bellfield CR0: Croy 9B 82
Bellflower Av. ME12: Minst 8H 221
Bell Gdns. BR5: St M Cry 8L 71
BELL GREEN 9B 54 (7J 5)
Bell Grn. SE26 9C 54 (1J 13)
Bell Grn. La. SE26 1C 68 (1J 13)
Bell Gro. CT3: Aysm 2D 162
Bellgrove Ct. ME5: Chat'm 2D 110
BELLINGHAM 8D 54 (7J 5)
Bellingham Grn. SE6 8D 54
Bellingham Rd. SE6 8E 54 (7K 5)
Bellingham Station (Rail) 8E 54 (7J 5)
Bellingham Trad. Est. SE6 8E 54
Bellingham Way ME20: Lark 6F 108
Bell Inn Rd. CT21: Hythe 6L 199
Bell La. CT13: S'wch 5M 217
ME1: Burh 2K 109 (6G 17)
ME14: Bear 4K 127
ME14: Boxl 3C 110 (6J 17)
ME20: Dit 8F 108
ME20: Lark 8F 108
TN12: S'hrst 3J 223
TN27: Bidd, Smar 7A 222 (2C 38)
Bellman Av. DA12: Grav'nd 6K 63
Bellmeadow ME15: Maid 2H 139
Bellows La. TN15: Bor G 2L 121
Bellring Cl. DA17: Belv 6B 52
Bell Rd. ME10: Sit 9F 98 (5F 19)
ME15: Maid 2H 139
Bells Cl. TN30: Tent 8B 224
Bells Farm Rd. TN11: E Peck 9H 135 (5C 26)
TN12: E Peck 9H 135 (5C 26)
Bells Hill Rd. SS16: Van 1F 9
Bell Shop. Cen., The ME10: Sit 7G 99
Bell's La. ME3: Hoo 6G 66 (7J 9)
Bells La. TN30: Tent 8B 224
Bell St. SE18 8A 50
BELL'S YEW GREEN 8M 157 (4A 36)
Bells Yew Grn. Rd.
TN3: Frant, Bell G 9J 157 (5K 35)
Bell Water Ga. SE18 3C 50
Bell Way ME17: Kgswd 6G 140
Bellwood Ct. ME3: St M Hoo 2M 67
Bellwood Rd. SE15 2A 54
Belmarsh Rd. SE28 2G 50
BELMONT 5C 12
Belmont 1K 29
Belmont CT14: Walm 9L 177
Belmont Av. DA16: Well 9G 50
Belmont Cl. ME16: Barm 7K 125
Belmont Ct. CT11: Ram 5H 211
(off Park Rd.)
Belmont Gro. SE13 1G 54
Belmont Hall Ct. SE13 1G 55
Belmont Hill SE13 1F 54 (6K 5)
Belmont La. BR7: Chst 1D 70
(not continuous)
Belmont Pde. BR7: Chst 1E 70
Belmont Pk. SE13 2G 55
Belmont Pk. Cl. SE13 2H 55
Belmont Pl. TN24: Ashf 2H 161
(not continuous)
Belmont Ri. SM2: Sutt 5C 12
Belmont Rd. BR3: Beck'm 5A 68
BR7: Chst 1D 70
CT5: Whits 4F 226 (3F 21)
CT8: Wgte S 3L 207
CT10: B'stairs 9L 209
CT11: Ram 5H 211
DA8: Erith 7B 52 (5E 6)
ME7: Gill 8F 80
ME10: Sit 8F 98
ME12: Minst 6F 220
ME13: Fav 6G 187
TN24: Kenn 4H 159
Belmont Station (Rail) 5C 12
Belmont St. CT11: Ram 5J 211
Belmont Ter. CT13: E'try 3K 183
Belmore Pk. TN24: Ashf 7F 158
Belnor Av. ME9: Bob 2N 97
Belsey La. CT15: Ewe M 1C 42
Belsize Av. NW3 1D 4
Belsize Pk. NW3 1D 4
Belsize Park Station (Tube) 1D 4
Belsize Rd. NW6 2C 4
Belson Rd. SE18 4B 50
Beltana Dr. DA12: Grav'nd 9K 63
BELTINGE 2L 195 (2K 21)
Beltinge Dr. CT6: H Bay 2M 195
Beltinge Rd. CT6: H Bay 2H 195 (2K 21)
Belton Cl. CT5: Whits 5G 226
Belton Gdns. SS9: Lgh S 1B 10
Belton Rd. DA14: Sidc 9J 57
Belton Way E. SS9: Lgh S 1B 10
Belton Way W. SS9: Lgh S 1B 10
BELTRING 3N 147 (6D 26)
Beltring Rd. TN4: Tun W 8G 150
TN12: Pad W 3N 147 (6D 26)
Beltring Station (Rail) 3N 147 (6D 26)
Beltwood Rd. DA17: Belv 4D 52
Beluncle Halt ME3: Hoo 5M 67
BELVEDERE 3B 52 (4E 6)
Belvedere Cl. DA12: Grav'nd 6H 63
ME13: Fav 4H 187
Belvedere Ct. DA17: Belv 3A 52
Belvedere Ho. ME15: Maid 3J 139
Belvedere Ind. Est. DA17: Belv 1D 52
Belvedere Link Bus. Pk. DA8: Erith 3D 52
Belvedere Rd. CT10: B'stairs 9M 209
DA7: Bexhth 1A 58 (6E 6)
ME13: Fav 4H 187
SE2 1L 51
TN16: Big H 6F 164
Belvedere Station (Rail) 3C 52 (4E 6)
Belvoir Cl. SE9 8A 56
Benacre Rd. CT5: Whits 7F 226
Benares Rd. SE18 4H 51
Benbury Cl. BR1: Brom 1F 68
Bench Hill TN26: Kena 6H 39
Bench St. CT16: Dover 5J 181
Bencurtis Pk. BR4: W W'ck 4G 83
Benden Cl. TN12: S'hrst 2K 223
Benden Ho. SE13 3F 54
(off Monument Gdns.)
Bendish Point SE28 2E 50
(off Erebus Dr.)
Bendmore Av. SE2 5J 51
Bendon Way ME8: Gill 3N 95
Benedict Cl. BR6: Orp 4G 85
DA17: Belv 3N 51
ME2: Hall'g 7F 92
BENENDEN 6A 38
Benenden Grn. BR2: Shortl 8K 69
Benenden Mnr. ME8: Gill 3M 95
Benenden Rd. ME2: Wain 2N 79
TN17: Bendn,Rolv 2A 214 (6B 38)
TN27: Bendn, Bidd 5C 38
Benfleet for Canvey Island Station (Rail) 1J 9
Benfleet Rd. SS7: Benf 1K 9
Bengal Rd. CT12: Ram 3E 210
Benhall Mill Rd. TN2: Tun W 5J 157 (4K 35)
TN3: Tun W 5L 157 (4K 35)
Benhill Av. SM1: Sutt 4D 12
Benhill Rd. SM1: Sutt 4D 12
BENHILTON 4D 12
Benin St. SE13 5G 55
Benjamin Ct. DA17: Belv 6A 52
Ben Jonson Rd. E1 3J 5
Bennells Av. CT5: Whits 3J 227 (3G 21)
Bennett Cl. DA16: Well 9J 51
Bennett Ho. DA11: Nflt 8E 62
Bennett Pk. SE3 1J 55
Bennetts Av. CR0: Croy 3B 82
TN15: W King 3J 105
Bennett's Castle La. RM8: Dag 1D 6
Bennetts Copse BR7: Chst 2A 70
Bennetts Cotts. ME7: B'hst 2K 111
Bennetts M. TN30: Tent 8B 224
Bennetts Way CR0: Croy 3B 82
Bennett Way DA2: Dart 9D 60
BENOVER 5F 27
Benover Rd. ME18: Yald 8D 136 (5E 26)
Bensham La. CR0: Croy 3F 13
CR7: Thor H 3F 13
Benson Cl. CT18: H'nge 8J 193
Benson La. CT18: H'nge 8J 193
Bensted TN23: Ashf 4D 160
Bensted Cl. ME15: Hunt 8H 137
Benstede Cl. CT6: H Bay 6H 195
Bensted Gro. ME13: Fav 5E 186
Bentfield Gdns. SE9 8N 55
Bentham Hill TN3: S'bgh 5D 150 (1J 35)
Bentham Rd. SE28 1K 51 (3D 6)
Bentham Sq. ME12: S'ness 1B 220
(off Charles St.)
Ben Tillet Cl. E16 1B 50
Bentley Av. CT6: H Bay 3C 194
Bentley Cl. DA3: Long 6B 76
ME5: Chat'm 9G 94
ME20: Aylfd 9K 109
Bentley Rd. TN24: W'boro 2J 161 (2B 40)
Bentley's Mdw. TN15: Seal 2N 119
Bentley St. DA12: Grav'nd 4H 63
Bentley St. Ind. Est. DA12: Grav'nd 4H 63
Bentlif Cl. ME16: Maid 4A 126
Berber Rd. ME2: Strood 4M 79
Bercta Rd. SE9 7E 56
Bere Cl. DA9: G'hithe 3J 61
Berengrave La. ME8: Rain 2A 96 (3A 18)
Berens Ct. DA14: Sidc 9H 57
Berens Rd. BR5: St M Cry 8M 71
Berens Way BR7: Chst 6H 71
Beresford Av. HA0: Wemb 2A 4
ME1: Roch 1B 94
Beresford Cl. TN17: Kiln 5E 36
Beresford Dr. BR1: Brom 6A 70
Beresford Gap CT7: Birch 3E 206
Beresford Gdns. CT9: Clift 2G 208
Beresford Hill ME17: Bou Mo 5E 138 (4J 27)
Beresford Rd. CT5: Whits 4F 226
CT11: Ram 6H 211
CT15: St Marg 8B 200
CT17: Dover 1D 180
DA11: Nflt 5D 62
ME7: Gill 8G 80
ME20: Aylfd 3N 109
TN17: Goud 3D 190
Beresford Sq. SE18 4D 50
Beresford St. SE18 3D 50 (4B 6)
Berger Cl. BR5: Pet W 9F 70
Bergland Pk. ME2: Med E 4A 80
Berkeley Av. DA7: Bexhth 8M 51
Berkeley Cl. BR5: Pet W 1G 84
CT19: F'stone 4G 189
ME1: Roch 3A 94
ME13: Dunk 3L 165
TN2: Pem 7D 152
Berkeley Ct. BR8: Swanl 6F 72
ME10: Sit 8E 98
Berkeley Cres. DA1: Dart 6N 59
Berkeley Mt. ME4: Chat'm 8C 80
Berkeley Pl. TN1: Tun W 3G 157
Berkeley Rd. CT7: Birch 3E 206
TN1: Tun W 3G 157
Berkeley St. W1 3E 4
Berkhampstead Rd. DA17: Belv 5B 52
Berkley Cres. DA12: Grav'nd 4H 63
Berkley Rd. DA12: Grav'nd 4G 63
Berkshire Cl. ME5: Chat'm 3F 94
Berkshire Ho. SE6 9D 54
BERMONDSEY 4H 5
Bermondsey Station (Tube) 4H 5
Bermondsey St. SE1 3G 5
Bernards Gdns. CT15: S'wll 7L 219
Bernard St. DA12: Grav'nd 4G 63
WC1 2F 5
Bernel Dr. CR0: Croy 4C 82
Berners Hill TN5: Flim 7F 37
Berney Ho. BR3: Beck'm 8B 68
Berridge Rd. ME12: S'ness 2D 220
Berries, The CT18: H'nge 7L 193
BERRYFIELD 7K 11
Berryfield Cl. BR1: Brom 4A 70
Berryhill SE9 2D 56
Berryhill Gdns. SE9 2D 56
BERRYLANDS 3A 12
Berrylands BR6: Chels 4L 85
DA3: Hart'y 9N 75
Berrylands Station (Rail) 2A 12
Berryman's La. SE26 9A 54
BERRY'S GREEN 7D 100 (7B 14)
Berry's Grn. Rd. TN16: Big H 7D 100 (7B 14)
Berry's Hill TN16: Big H 7D 100 (7B 14)
Berry St. ME10: Sit 7G 98
(off St Michael's Rd.)
ME10: Sit 7G 98
(High St.)
Bertha Hollamby Ct. DA14: Sidc 1L 71
(off Sidcup Hill)
Bertha James Ct. BR2: Shortl 7L 69
Bertie Rd. SE26 2A 68
Bertrand St. SE13 1E 54
BERWICK 5G 41
Berwick Cres. DA15: Sidc 5G 57
Berwick La. CT21: Lymp 5B 198
Berwick Pond RM14: Rain 2H 7
Berwick Pond Rd. RM13: Rain 2H 7
Berwick Rd. DA16: Well 8K 51
Berwick Way BR6: Orp 2J 85
TN14: S'oaks 2J 119
Berwyn Gro. ME15: Maid 2D 138
Beryl Ho. SE18 5H 51
(off Spinel Cl.)
Besant Ct. SE28 1K 51
(off Titmuss Av.)
BESSELS GREEN 6E 118 (2F 25)
Bessels Grn. Rd. TN13: Riv 5E 118 (2F 25)
Bessels Mdw. TN13: Riv 6E 118
Bessels Way TN13: Riv 6D 118
Bessie's La. ME3: H Hals 1K 67
Bessingham Wlk. SE4 2A 54
(off Aldersford Cl.)
Besson St. SE14 5H 5
BEST BEECH HILL 7A 36
Best La. CT1: Cant 2M 171
Best St. ME4: Chat'm 8C 80 (3H 17)
Best Ter. BR8: Crock'n 9D 72
Beta Rd. ME3: Hoo 6N 67
Betchworth Way CR0: Croy 9F 82
Betenson Av. TN13: S'oaks 4G 118
Bethel Rd. DA16: Well 1L 57
TN13: S'oaks 5K 119
BETHERSDEN 2J 163 (2G 39)
Bethersden Cl. BR3: Beck'm 3C 68
Bethersden Ct. ME15: Maid 1J 139
Bethersden Rd. TN26: Beth, Hoth 1H 39
(Hothfield)
TN26: Beth, Shad 3H 39
(Shadoxhurst)
TN26: Hoth 4K197 (1H 39)
TN26: Smar, Beth 9B 222 (2D 38)
TN26: Wdchu 6B 228 (5H 39)
TN27: Smar 9B 222 (2D 38)
BETHNAL GREEN 2H 5
Bethnal Grn. Rd. E2 2G 5
Bethnal Green Station (Rail) 2H 5
Bethnal Green Station (Tube) 2H 5
Betjeman Cl. ME20: Lark 7D 108
Betony Cl. CR0: Croy 2A 82
Betony Gdns. ME14: Weav 4J 127
BETSHAM 9M 61 (1A 16)
Betsham Rd. DA8: Erith 7G 53
DA10: Swans 5L 61
DA13: Sflt 1K 75 (1K 15)
ME15: Maid 2J 139
Betterton Dr. DA14: Sidc 7N 57
Bettescombe Rd. ME8: Gill 4N 95
BETTESHANGER 3G 33
Betts Cl. BR3: Beck'm 5B 68
Betty Shelvey Ct. CT14: Deal 5M 177
(off Finch M.)
Beulah Hill SE19 1F 13
Beulah Rd. CR7: Thor H 2G 13
TN1: Tun W 9H 151
Beult Mdw. TN27: Smar 8C 222
Beult Rd. DA1: Cray 2H 59
Bevan Pl. BR8: Swanl 7G 72
Bevan Rd. SE2 5K 51
Bevans Cl. DA9: G'hithe 4J 61
Bevan Way CT3: Aysm 2C 162
Bevercote Wlk. DA17: Belv 6A 52
(off Osborne Rd.)
Beverley Av. DA15: Sidc 5H 57
Beverley Cl. ME8: Gill 3B 96
Beverley Ct. SE4 1C 54
(not continuous)
Beverley Cres. TN9: Tonb 8F 144
Beverley Gdns. TN29: Dym 9D 182
Beverley Ho. BR1: Brom 1G 68
(off Brangbourne Rd.)
Beverley Rd. BR2: Shortl 3A 84
CR3: Whyt 7G 13
CT2: Cant 9L 167
DA7: Bexhth 9D 52
ME16: Barm 7K 125
RM9: Dag 1E 6
Beverley Way CT12: Ram 3G 210
KT3: N Mald 2A 12
SW20 2A 12
Beverly Cl. CT7: Birch 3G 207
Bevington Rd. BR3: Beck'm 5E 68
Bevis Cl. DA2: Dart 5C 60
Bewlbridge La. TN3: Lamb 5D 36
TN5: Lamb 6D 36
Bewley La. TN15: Plax 7J 121 (2K 25)
Bewl Water Visitor Centre 6D 36
Bewsbury Cres. CT16: Whitf 6E 178
Bewsbury Cross La.
CT16: Whitf 6E 178 (7E 32)
Bexhill Rd. SE4 4C 54
BEXLEY 5C 58 (7E 6)
Bexley Cl. DA1: Cray 3F 58
Bexley Cotts. DA4: Hort K 7B 74
BEXLEYHEATH 2A 58 (6E 6)
Bexleyheath Sports Club 1L 57
Bexleyheath Station (Rail) 9N 51 (5E 6)
Bexley High St. DA5: Bex'y 5B 58 (7E 6)
Bexley Ho. SE4 2B 54
Bexley La. DA1: Cray 3F 58
DA14: Sidc 9L 57 (1D 14)
Bexley Lawn Tennis & Squash Club 5B 58
Bexley Mus. 4D 58
Bexley Rd. DA8: Erith 7D 52 (5F 7)
SE9 3D 56 (6B 6)
Bexley Station (Rail) 6B 58 (7E 6)
Bexley St. CT5: Whits 3F 226
BEXON 7C 114 (7E 18)
Bexon La. ME9: B'gar 5B 114 (6E 18)
Bexon Mnr. Cotts. ME9: B'gar 7C 114
Beynon Rd. SM5: Cars 4D 12
Bhutan Rd. CT6: H Bay 3K 195
BICKLEY 6A 70 (2B 14)
Bickley Cres. BR1: Brom 7A 70
Bickley Pk. Rd. BR1: Brom 6A 70 (2B 14)
Bickley Rd. BR1: Brom 5N 69 (2A 14)
TN9: Tonb 7H 145
Bickley Station (Rail) 6A 70 (2B 14)

Bickmore Way—Bluemans La.

Bickmore Way TN9: Tonb 4J 145
BICKNOR 8L 113 (7D 18)
Bicknor Cl. CT2: Cant 7A 168
Bicknor Farm Cotts. ME17: L'ly 3K 139
Bicknor La. ME9: Bic, B'gar 8L 113 (7D 18)
Bicknor Rd. BR6: Orp 1G 85
ME15: Maid 3J 139
BIDBOROUGH 2C 150 (1J 35)
Bidborough Cl. BR2: Shortl 8J 69
Bidborough Ct. TN3: Bidb 3B 150
Bidborough Ridge TN3: Bidb 2C 150 (1J 35)
TN4: Bidb 2C 150 (1J 35)
BIDDENDEN 8L 163 (3C 38)
Biddenden Cl. *CT9: Mgte 4G 208*
(off Denton Way)
ME15: Bear 6J 127
BIDDENDEN GREEN 7C 222 (1E 38)
Biddenden Rd. TN17: Frit 2A 38
TN17: Siss 3D 222 (4K 37)
TN26: St Mic 1B 224 (4E 38)
TN27: H'crn, Frit 9M 191 (1C 38)
TN27: Smar 9A 222 (2D 38)
TN27: St Mic 4D 38
TN30: St Mic 1A 224 (4D 38)
Biddenden Vineyard 5C 38
Biddenden Way DA13: Ist R 3D 76
SE9 9C 56
Biddulph Ho. SE18 4B 50
Bideford Rd. BR1: Brom 8J 55
DA16: Well 7K 51
Bierce Ct. CT7: Birch 4E 206
Bifrons Gdns. CT4: Brid 7G 172
Bifrons Hill CT4: Brid 6F 172 (2K 31)
BIFRON'S PK. 8G 172
Bifrons Rd. CT4: Brid 6G 173
Bigbury Rd. CT2: Harb 4C 170 (1F 31)
CT4: Cha H 4C 170 (1F 31)
BIGGIN HILL 5D 164 (7A 14)
BIGGIN HILL AIRPORT 1D 164 (6B 14)
Biggin Hill Bus. Pk. TN16: Big H 3D 164
Biggin La. RM16: Grays 5C 8
Biggin St. CT16: Dover 4J 181
(not continuous)
Biggins Wood Rd. CT19: F'stone 4D 188
Biggleswade Pas. CT1: Cant 3L 171
Bignell Rd. SE18 5D 50
Big Pett TN25: Elms, Stow 1F 41
Bilberry Cl. ME14: Weav 4H 127
Billet Hill TN15: Ash 5J 89 (4K 15)
Billet La. SS17: Stan H 2E 8
Bill Hamling Cl. SE9 7B 56
Billingford Cl. SE4 2A 54
Billings Hill Shaw DA3: Hart'y 9M 75
Billington Gdns. TN24: Kenn 4J 159
Bills Hill CT4: Elham 6J 31
Bill St. Rd. ME2: Strood 3N 79 (1G 17)
Bilsby Gro. SE9 9N 55
BILSINGTON 5C 40
Bilsington Cl. ME5: Chat'm 6E 94
Bilsington Rd. TN26: Ruck 6B 40
BILTING 5C 30
Bilting La. TN25: Godm 5C 30
Bilton Rd. DA8: Erith 7H 53
Bilton Sq. CT9: Mgte 3C 208
Binbury Cotts. ME14: Det 5C 112
Binbury La. ME9: S'bry 6B 112 (7A 18)
ME14: Det 6B 112 (7A 18)
Bindon Blood Rd. CT16: Dover 8F 178
Bines, The TN12: Pad W 1M 153
Bingham Rd. CR0: Croy 3H 13
ME2: Strood 3N 79
Bingley Rd. ME1: Roch 8B 80
ME6: Snod 2D 108
Binland Gro. ME5: Chat'm 6A 94
Binnacle Rd. ME1: Roch 3N 93
Binney Rd. ME3: Allh 4D 204
Binnie Cl. CT10: B'stairs 2K 211
Binnington Twr. BR2: Shortl 9A 70
Binsey Wlk. SE2 2L 51
(not continuous)
Birbetts Rd. SE9 7B 56
Bircham Path *SE4 2A 54*
(off Aldersford Cl.)
Birchanger Rd. SE25 3H 13
Birch Cl. CT10: B'stairs 1G 211
DA3: Long 5B 76
DA4: Eyns 5L 87
TN2: Tun W 7K 151
TN11: Hild 3D 144
TN12: Mat 5J 153
TN13: S'oaks 5J 119
TN24: W'boro 8J 159
Birch Ct. CT4: B'hm 8D 162
Birch Cres. ME20: Aylfd 1H 125
BIRCHDEN 7L 155 (4G 35)
Birchdene Dr. SE28 1J 51
Birch Dr. ME5: Chat'm 1G 111
Birches, The *BR2: Shortl 7J 69*
(off Durham Av.)
BR6: Farnb 5C 84
BR8: Swanl 5F 72
CT7: Birch 4G 206
TN9: Tonb 8H 145
Birchett TN23: Ashf 9C 158
Birchett La. TN26: W'hrne, Hams 5J 39
Birchetts Av. TN3: Lang G 2M 155
BIRCHETT'S GREEN 7D 36
Birchetts Grn. La. TN5: Tice 7D 36
Birchfield TN14: Sund 9N 117
Birchfield Cl. ME15: Maid 2E 138
Birchfields ME5: Chat'm 8D 94
BIRCHGROVE 7A 34
Birch Gro. DA16: Well 2J 57
ME7: Hpstd 7K 95
SE12 5J 55
Birchgrove La. RH17: Hors K 7A 34
Birch Gro. Rd. RH17: Hors K 7A 34
Birch Hill CR0: Croy 6A 82
Birch Hill Ct. CT7: Birch 4G 206
Birch Ho. ME10: Sit 7J 99
ME12: S'ness 2C 220
ME16: Barm 6L 125
(off Springwood Rd.)
Birchin Cross Rd. TN15: Knat 6M 103 (7H 15)
BIRCHINGTON 4F 206 (2E 22)
Birchington Cl. BR5: Orp 2L 85
DA7: Bexhth 8C 52
ME14: Maid 4F 126
Birchington-on-Sea Station (Rail) 4E 206 (2E 22)
Birchmead BR6: Farnb 3C 84
Birchmere Bus. Site SE28 2J 51
BIRCHOLT FORSTAL 6K 165 (2E 40)
Bircholt Rd. ME15: Maid 4J 139
Birch Pl. DA9: G'hithe 4E 60
TN13: S'oaks 6H 119
Birch Rd. CT5: Whits 5J 227
TN12: Pad W 9M 147
Birch Row BR2: Shortl 1C 84
Birch Tree Av. BR4: W W'ck 6J 83
Birch Tree Way ME15: Maid 6E 126
Birch Wlk. DA8: Erith 6D 52
Birch Way CT21: Hythe 7G 198
TN2: Tun W 7K 151
Birchway TN15: W King 9F 88
Birchwood Av. BR3: Beck'm 7C 68
DA14: Sidc 7K 57
TN4: S'bgh 3E 150
Birchwood Dr. DA2: Dart 9F 58
Birchwood La. TN14: Dun G 6A 102
Birchwood Pde. DA2: Dart 9F 58
Birchwood Pk. Av. BR8: Swanl 6F 72
Birchwood Ri. CT17: Dover 5H 181
Birchwood Rd. BR5: Pet W 7F 70
BR8: Swanl 4D 72 (2F 15)
DA2: Dart 9F 58 (2F 15)
ME16: Alltn 4N 125
Birchwood Wlk. CT2: Cant 9L 167
Birdbrook Rd. SE3 2M 55
Birdcage Wlk. TN1: Tun W 2H 157
Birdham Cl. BR1: Brom 8A 70
Birdhouse La. BR6: Downe 3F 164
Bird in Hand La. BR1: Brom 5N 69
Bird in Hand St. TN3: Groom 5J 155 (4G 35)
Birds Av. CT9: Mgte 4N 207
Birds Birds Birds 5H 187
(off Limes Pl.)
Birdwood Av. CT14: Deal 5K 177
Birkbeck Rd. BR3: Beck'm 5A 68
DA14: Sidc 8J 57
W3 3A 4
Birkbeck Station (CT) 2H 13
Birkdale TN1: Tun W 8H 151
Birkdale Cl. BR6: Orp 1F 84
CT5: Whits 5M 227
Birkdale Ct. ME16: Maid 5B 126
Birkdale Dr. CT19: F'stone 4G 189
Birkdale Gdns. CR0: Croy 5A 82
CT6: H Bay 5E 194
Birkdale Rd. SE2 4J 51
Birken Rd. TN2: Tun W 8K 151 (2K 35)
Birkhall Cl. ME5: Chat'm 6D 94
Birkhall Rd. SE6 6G 55
BIRLING 5A 108 (6E 16)
Birling Av. ME8: Rain 2N 95 (3A 18)
ME14: Bear 5J 127
Birling Cl. ME14: Bear 5J 127
Birling Dr. TN2: Tun W 4G 157
Birling Hill DA13: Meop, Birl 1M 107 (5D 16)
ME6: Birl 1M 107
Birling Pk. Av. TN2: Tun W 5H 157
Birling Pk. Est. ME19: Birl 5A 108
Birling Rd. DA8: Erith 7E 52
ME6: Snod 3D 108 (6E 16)
ME19: Birl, Rya 6M 107 (7D 16)
ME19: Leyb 9N 107 (7E 16)
TN2: Tun W 5G 157 (4K 35)
TN24: Ashf 8H 159
Birnam Sq. ME16: Maid 5B 126
Birtrick Dr. DA13: Meop 8E 76
Biscoe Way SE13 1G 55
Bishop Butt Cl. BR6: Orp 4H 85
Bishop Ct. *ME10: Sit 6F 98*
(off High St.)
Bishopden Ct. CT2: Cant 7J 167
Bishop La. ME9: Upc 3H 225
Bishops Av. BR1: Brom 5M 69
Bishop's Av. CT10: B'stairs 7M 209
BISHOPSBOURNE 3K 31
Bishopsbourne Grn. ME8: Gill 8L 81
Bishop's Bri. W2 3C 4
Bishops Cl. ME18: W'bury 2A 136
Bishop's Cl. SE9 7E 56
Bishops Ct. DA9: G'hithe 3F 60
Bishop's Ct. TN4: Tun W 2E 156
Bishop's Down TN4: Tun W 2E 156 (3J 35)
Bishop's Down Pk. Rd. TN4: Tun W 1E 156
Bishop's Down Rd. TN4: Tun W 2E 156
Bishopsford Rd. SM4: Mord 3D 12
Bishopsgate EC2 3G 5
Bishops Grn. *BR1: Brom 4L 69*
(off Up. Park Rd.)
TN23: Ashf 2B 160
Bishop's La. ME15: Hunt 9H 137 (5F 27)
Bishops La. TN17: Cran 5H 37
Bishop's La. TN32: Rob 4B 44
Bishops M. TN9: Tonb 7J 145
Bishops Oak Ride TN10: Tonb 9H 133
Bishopsthorpe Rd. SE26 9A 54
BISHOPSTONE 2N 195 (2A 22)
Bishopstone Dr. CT6: H Bay 1N 195
Bishopstone La. CT6: H Bay 2N 195 (2A 22)
Bishops Wlk. BR7: Chst 4E 70
CR0: Croy 6A 82
ME1: Roch 7N 79
Bishops Way CT2: Cant 1K 171
Bishop's Way E2 2H 5
Bishopsway ME14: Maid 5C 126
Bishopswood TN23: Kgnt 6G 160
BITCHET GREEN 8D 120 (2J 25)
Bittern Cl. CT18: H'nge 9K 193
Bixley La. TN31: Beckl 4J 45
(Four Oaks)
TN31: Beckl 4H 45
(King's Bank, not continuous)
Blackberry Fld. BR5: St P 4J 71
Blackberry La. RH7: Ling 1A 34
Blackberry Rd. RH7: Ling 2A 34
Blackberry Way CT5: Whits 5K 227
Blackberry WayTN12: Pad W 9M 147
Blackbird Hill NW9 1A 4
Blackbrook La. BR1: Brom 7C 70 (3B 14)
BR2: Shortl 8B 70 (3B 14)
Black Bull Rd. CT19: F'stone 5K 189 (4B 42)
Blackburn Rd. CT6: H Bay 5C 194
Black Bush La. SS17: Horn H 2C 8
Black Cotts. ME14: Boxl 5G 111
Blackdon Hill TN3: Epp G 6H 35
Blackdown Dr. TN24: Ashf 6F 158
Blackdown Ter. SE18 8B 50
Black Eagle Cl. TN16: Westrm 9E 116
Black Eagle Sq. TN16: Westrm 9E 116
Blacketts Rd. ME9: Tonge 5N 99 (4G 19)
BLACKFEN 5J 57 (6D 6)
Blackfen Pde. DA15: Sidc 4J 57
Blackfen Rd. DA15: Sidc 3G 57 (6C 6)
Blackfriars Bri. EC4 3F 5
SE1 3F 5
Blackfriars Clearly Gallery, The 1M 171
Blackfriars Rd. SE1 3F 5
Blackfriars Station (Rail & Tube) 3F 5
Blackfriars St. CT1: Cant 1M 171
Black Griffin La. CT1: Cant 2M 171
Blackhall La. TN15: S'oaks 5L 119 (2H 25)
BLACKHAM 1B 154 (3E 34)
BLACKHEATH 5K 5
Blackheath Concert Halls 1J 55
Blackheath Hill SE10 5K 5
BLACKHEATH PARK 2K 55 (6A 6)
Blackheath Pk. SE3 1J 55
Blackheath Rd. SE10 5J 5
Blackheath Station (Rail) 1J 55 (5K 5)
Blackheath Village SE3 1J 55 (5K 5)
BLACK HILL 7D 34
Black Hill CT14: Ripp 4H 33
Black Horse Farm Cvn. & Camping Pk.
CT18: Acr 4J 193
Blackhorse La. CR0: Croy 3H 13
Blackhorse Lane Station (CT) 3H 13
Blackhorse M. TN2: Pem 8B 152
Black Horse M. TN15: Bor G 3N 121
Blackhorse Rd. DA14: Sidc 9J 57
Blackhouse Hill CT18: N'tn 4M 199 (5J 41)
CT21: Hythe, N'tn 5L 199 (5J 41)
Blackhouse Ri. CT21: Hythe 5L 199
BLACKHURST 2A 36
Blackhurst La. TN2: Pem 7N 151
TN2: Tun W 9L 151
Blacklands ME19: E Mal 2D 124
(not continuous)
Blacklands Dr. ME19: E Mal 1D 124
Blacklands Rd. SE6 9F 54
Black La. CT13: S'wch 7K 217
Black Lion Leisure Cen. 6E 80
Blackman Cl. ME3: Hoo 6G 66
Blackmans Cl. DA1: Dart 6K 59
Blackman's La. CR6: Warl 6K 13
TN11: Hdlw 9C 134 (5B 26)
Blackmanstone Way ME16: Alltn 2M 125
Blackmead TN13: Riv 3F 118
Black Mill La. TN27: H'crn 8J 191
Blackness La. BR2: Kes 9N 83 (5A 14)
Blackness Rd. TN6: Crowb 7F 35
BLACK PRINCE INTERCHANGE 4C 58 (6E 6)
Black Robin La. CT4: Kgstn 4A 32
Black Rock Gdns. ME7: Hpstd 7L 95
Blackshaw Rd. SW17 1D 12
Blackshots La. RM16: Grays 3B 8
Blacksmith Dr. ME14: Weav 4G 127
Blacksmith's La.
BR5: St M Cry 8L 71 (2D 14)
TN5: Wadh 6C 36
Blacksole Cotts. TN15: Wro 6M 105
Blacksole La. TN15: Wro 7M 105
Blacksole Rd. TN15: Wro 7M 105
Blackstable Ct. CT5: Whits 5F 226
Blackstock Rd. N4 1F 5
N5 1F 5
Blackthorn Av. ME5: Chat'm 8D 94
TN4: S'bgh 5J 151
Blackthorn Cen. ME16: Maid 6L 125
Blackthorn Cl. TN15: W King 9F 88
Blackthorn Dr. ME20: Lark 8F 108
Blackthorne Rd. ME8: Rain 3D 96
Blackthorn Gro. DA7: Bexhth 1N 57
Blackthorn Rd. TN16: Big H 4D 164
Blackthorn Way TN23: Kgnt 6G 160
BLACKWALL 3K 5
Blackwall La. SE10 4K 5
Blackwall Rd. TN24: Hin 8M 159
TN25: Brook, Hin 8M 159 (1B 40)
Blackwall Rd. Nth.
TN24: W'boro 8L 159 (1B 40)
Blackwall Rd. Sth.
TN24: W'boro 8L 159 (1B 40)
Blackwall Station (DLR) 3K 5
Blackwall Tunnel Northern App. E3 2K 5
E14 3K 5
Blackwall Tunnel Southern App. SE10 4K 5
Blackwell Hollow RH19: E Grin 3A 34
Blackwell Rd. RH19: E Grin 3A 34
BLADBEAN 6K 31
Bladindon Dr. DA5: Bex'y 5L 57
Blagdon Rd. SE13 4E 54
Blair Cl. DA15: Sidc 3G 56
Blair Ct. BR3: Beck'm 4E 68
SE6 6J 55
Blair Dr. TN13: S'oaks 5J 119
Blake Cl. CT14: Walm 1D 200
DA16: Well 8G 51
Blake Ct. TN24: W'boro 1K 161
Blake Dr. ME20: Lark 6D 108
Blake Gdns. DA1: Dart 2N 59
Blakemore Way DA17: Belv 3N 51
Blakeney Av. BR3: Beck'm 4C 68
Blakeney Cl. ME14: Bear 5L 127
Blakeney Rd. BR3: Beck'm 3C 68 (1J 13)
Blaker Av. ME1: Roch 2B 94
BLAKES GREEN 7D 120
Blake's Grn. BR4: W W'ck 2F 82
Blakeway TN2: Tun W 7K 151
Blanchard Cl. SE9 8A 56
Bland Dr. CT18: H'nge 7M 193
Blandford Av. BR3: Beck'm 5B 68
Blandford Gdns. ME10: Sit 1F 114
Blandford Rd. BR3: Beck'm 5A 68
Bland St. SE9 2N 55
Blanmerle Rd. SE9 6D 56
Blann Cl. SE9 4N 55
Blashford St. SE13 5G 55
Blatcher Cl. ME12: Minst 6J 221
Blatchford Cl. ME19: E Mal 9D 108
Blatchington Rd. TN2: Tun W 4G 157
Blaxland Cl. ME13: Fav 4F 186
Bleak Hill La. SE18 6H 51
Bleak House CT10: B'stairs 9M 209
Bleak House Mus. 9M 209 (2K 23)
Bleak Rd. TN29: Lydd 3K 205
Bleakwood Rd. ME5: Chat'm 6C 94
BLEAN 5G 166 (6G 21)
Blean Comn. CT2: Blean 4F 166 (6F 21)
Blean Hill CT2: Blean 6G 167 (6G 21)
Blean Rd. ME8: Gill 1M 95
Blean Sq. ME14: Maid 3F 126
Blean Vw. Rd. CT6: H Bay 5C 194
Blean Wood National Nature Reserve 7D 166
BLENDON 4M 57 (6D 6)
Blendon Dr. DA5: Bex'y 4M 57
Blendon Path BR1: Brom 3J 69
Blendon Rd. DA5: Bex'y 4M 57 (6D 6)
ME14: Maid 4F 126
Blendon Ter. SE18 5E 50
Blenheim Av. CT1: Cant 1C 172
ME4: Chat'm 1A 94
ME13: Fav 7J 187
Blenheim Cl. CT6: H Bay 6H 195
CT10: B'stairs 1H 211
DA1: Dart 4K 59
DA13: Meop 3F 90
ME15: Bear 6J 127
SE12 6L 55
Blenheim Ct. BR2: Shortl 7J 69
DA14: Sidc 8F 56
Blenheim Dr. CT16: Dover 1H 181
CT18: H'nge 8K 193
DA16: Well 8H 51
Blenheim Gro. DA12: Grav'nd 5H 63
Blenheim Pl. CT20: F'stone 7F 188
Blenheim Rd. BR1: Brom 7A 70
BR6: Orp 3L 85
CT14: Deal 5N 177
DA1: Dart 4K 59
DA15: Sidc 6L 57
ME10: Sit 9J 99
ME19: W Mal 6L 123
TN28: L'stne 3M 213
Bleriot Memorial 3L 181
Blessington Cl. SE13 1G 55
Blessington Rd. SE13 1G 55
Bletchenden Rd. TN27: H'crn 1B 38
Bletchinglye La. TN6: Town R 7J 35
Blewbury Ho. SE2 2L 51
(Tavy Bri.)
SE2 2M 51
(Tilehurst Point)
BLIBY 4B 40
Bligh Rd. DA11: Grav'nd 4F 62
Bligh's Mdw. *TN13: S'oaks 7K 119*
(off High St.)
Bligh's Rd. TN13: S'oaks 7K 119
Bligh Way ME2: Strood 5G 78 (2F 17)
Blindgrooms La. TN26: Shad 8A 160
Blindhouse La. TN25: M Hor 6E 218 (3G 41)
Blind La. ME7: B'hst 1K 111
ME14: B'hst 2J 111
TN12: Brenc 6N 153
TN17: Goud 2C 190 (3G 37)
TN25: C'lck 8D 174 (4A 30)
TN25: Mers 7L 161 (3C 40)
Blind Mary's La. ME9: B'gar 6N 113 (6D 18)
Bliss Way TN10: Tonb 2L 145
Blithdale Rd. SE2 4J 51
Blockmakers Ct. ME4: Chat'm 2D 94
Bloemfontein Rd. W12 3B 4
BLOODDEN 3B 32
Bloomfield Rd. BR2: Shortl 8N 69
SE18 6D 50
Bloomfield Ter. TN16: Westrm 7F 116
BLOOMSBURY 3F 5
Bloomsbury Rd. CT11: Ram 6G 210
Bloomsbury St. WC1 3E 4
Bloomsbury Wlk. *ME14: Maid 5D 126*
(off Wyatt St.)
Bloomsbury Way TN24: Kenn 3F 158
Bloors La. ME8: Rain 2N 95 (3A 18)
(London Rd.)
ME8: Rain 1A 96 (3A 18)
(Lwr. Rainham Rd.)
Bloors Wharf Rd. ME8: Rain 3A 18
Blossom La. TN25: Ashf 5C 158
Blowers Wood Gro. ME7: Hpstd 8L 95
Bloxam Gdns. SE9 3A 56
Blue Anchor Cvn. Pk. CT5: Seas 6A 226
Blue Anchor La. RM18: W Til 4D 8
Bluebell Cl. BR6: Farnb 3E 84
ME7: Gill 6J 81
TN23: Kgnt 5F 160
BLUE BELL HILL 1A 110 (6H 17)
Blue Bell Hill By-Pass
ME5: Chat'm 1N 109 (6H 17)
ME20: Aylfd 6H 17
Bluebell Rd. TN23: Kgnt 5F 160 (3A 40)
Bluebell Walks TN12: Pad W 9M 147
Bluebell Woods CT2: B Oak 5C 168
Blueberry La. TN14: Knock 7L 101 (7D 14)
Bluebird Way SE28 2F 50
Blue Boar La. ME1: Roch 7N 79
Blue Chalet Ind. Pk. TN15: W King 6D 88
Bluecoat La. TN17: Goud 4A 190 (4F 37)
Blue Fld. TN23: Ashf 1A 160
Bluefields M. *CT5: Whits 7E 226*
(off Old Farm Cl.)
Blue Ho. Cotts. DA2: Bean 8K 61
Blue Ho. La. CT21: Salt 1J 199
Bluehouse La. RH8: Oxt 3A 24
Blue Line La. TN24: Ashf 7F 158
Bluemans La. TN33: Sed 7E 44

Blue Town—Bradstone St.

BLUE TOWN
Milstead 7F 19
Sheerness 2B 220 (6F 11)
Bluett St. ME14: Maid 3D 126
BLUEWATER 6F 60 (7J 7)
Bluewater Cvn. Pk. CT21: Hythe 8E 198
Bluewater Parkway
DA9: Bluew, G'hithe 5F 60 (7J 7)
Bluewater Shop. Cen. DA9: Bluew 5F 60
Blunden La. ME18: Yald 7D 136
Blunts Rd. SE9 ....3C 56
Blyth Ct. BR1: Brom 4J 69
(off Blyth Rd.)
Blythe Cl. ME10: Sit 6K 99
SE6 ....5C 54
Blythe Ct. CT21: Hythe 6L 199
(off Prospect Rd.)
BLYTHE HILL 5C 54
Blythe Hill BR5: St P 4H 71
SE6 ....5C 54
Blythe Hill La. SE6 ....5C 54
Blythe Hill Pl. SE23 ....5B 54
Blythe Rd. ME15: Maid 5E 126
Blythe Va. SE6 ....6C 54
Blyth Hill Pl. SE23 ....5B 54
(off Brockley Pk.)
Blyth Rd. BR1: Brom 4J 69
Blyth Wood Pk. BR1: Brom 4J 69
Boakes Mdw. TN14: S'ham 2G 103
Boarders La. TN5: Tice 7D 36
TN19: Etch'm 3A 44
BOARLEY 7D 110 (7J 17)
Boarley Ct. ME14: Maid 9C 110
Boarley La. ME14: S'lng 9C 110 (7J 17)
Boarley Rd. ME14: S'lng 9C 110
Boarman's La. TN29: B'lnd 3E 46
BOARSHEAD 6G 35
Boathouse Rd. ME12: S'ness 1A 220
Boat La. TN25: Aldtn 5C 40
BOBBING 5B 98 (4E 18)
Bobbing Hill ME9: Bob 6A 98 (4D 18)
Bobbin Lodge Hill CT4: Chart'm 9B 170 (2E 30)
Bob Hope Theatre, The 4B 56
Bockham La. TN25: W Bra 2C 40
BOCKHANGER 4G 159 (7A 30)
Bockhanger Bus. Pk. TN25: Kenn 4F 158
Bockhanger Ct. TN24: Kenn 5H 159
Bockhanger La. TN24: Kenn 5G 158
(not continuous)
Bockingford Ct. ME15: Maid 9C 126
Bockingford Ho. ME15: Maid 9C 126
Bockingford La. ME15: Maid 9C 126 (3H 27)
Bockingford Mill Cotts. ME15: Maid 9C 126
Bodenham Rd. CT20: F'stone 7G 188
BODIAM 3D 44
Bodiam Castle 3E 44
Bodiam Cl. ME8: Gill 9M 81
Bodiam Ct. ME16: Maid 6C 126
Bodiam Rd. TN18: Sandh 4A 218 (2E 44)
Bodiam Station (Rail) 3E 44
Bodkins Cl. ME15: Maid 3G 139
Bodle Av. DA10: Swans 5L 61
Bodmin Cl. BR5: Orp 2L 85
BODSHAM 7F 31
Bodsham Cres. ME15: Bear 6L 127
Boevey Path DA17: Belv 5A 52
Bogarde Dr. ME3: Wain 2M 79
Bogey La. BR6: Downe 8C 84
TN4: Tun W 1F 156
Bogle La. ME9: Lyn 6H 19
Bognor Dr. CT6: H Bay 3E 194
Bognor Rd. DA16: Well 8M 51
Bogshole La. CT5: Whits 9F 226 (5F 21)
CT6: H Bay 4L 195
(not continuous)
Bolderwood Way BR4: W W'ck 3E 82
Boley Hill ME1: Roch 6N 79 (2H 17)
Boleyn Av. CT9: Mgte 2M 207
Boleyn Ct. CT1: Cant 2A 172
Boleyn Gdns. BR4: W W'ck 3E 82
Boleyn Gro. BR4: W W'ck 3F 82
Boleyn Rd. N16 ....1G 5
TN15: Kems'g 8M 103
Boleyn Way DA10: Swans 5L 61
Bolingbroke Gro. SW11 ....6D 4
Bolingbroke Ho. ME16: Maid 5B 126
Bollo La. W3 ....4A 4
W4 ....4A 4
Bolner Cl. ME5: Chat'm 9C 94
Bolters La. SM7: Bans 6C 12
Bolton Gdns. BR1: Brom 2J 69
Bolton Rd. CT19: F'stone 5K 189
Bolton St. CT11: Ram 4H 211
W1 ....3E 4
Bolts Hill CT4: Chart'm 8B 170 (2E 30)
Bombay Ho. ME15: Maid 3H 139
Bombers La. TN16: Westrm 1F 116
Bonar Pl. BR7: Chst 3A 70
Bonaventure Ct. DA12: Grav'nd 9L 63
Bonchester Cl. BR7: Chst 3C 70
Bond Cl. TN14: Knock 6M 101
Bondfield Cl. TN4: S'bgh 5G 151
Bondfield Rd. ME19: E Mal 1D 124
Bondfield Wlk. DA1: Dart 2N 59
Bond La. TN23: Kgnt 7E 160 (3A 40)
Bond Rd. ME8: Gill 7A 96
TN23: Ashf 1E 160
Bond St. TN14: Knock 6M 101
Bond Street Station (Tube) 3E 4
Boneashe La. TN15: Bor G 3C 122 (1B 26)
Boneta Rd. SE18 ....3B 50
Bonetta Ct. ME12: S'ness 4C 220
Bonfield Rd. SE13 ....2F 54
Bonflower La. ME17: Lint 9N 137 (5H 27)
Bonham Dr. ME10: Sit 6H 99
Bonita M. SE4 ....1A 54
Bonner Rd. E2 ....2H 5
Bonners All. CT5: Whits 3F 226
(off Middle Wall)
Bonney Way BR8: Swanl 5F 72
BONNINGTON 4C 40
Bonnington Grn. ME8: Gill 9M 81
Bonnington Rd. ME14: Maid 3F 126
TN25: Bils, Bon 5C 40
Bonny Bush Hill CT4: Bis, Kgstn 3K 31
Bonsor Rd. CT19: F'stone 5K 189
Bonville Rd. BR1: Brom 1J 69
Boones Rd. SE13 ....2H 55
Boone St. SE13 ....2H 55
Boormans Cotts. ME18: W'bury 1A 136
Bootham Cl. ME2: Strood 7H 79
Booth Cl. SE28 ....1K 51
Booth Pl. CT9: Mgte 2D 208
Booth Rd. ME4: Chat'm 1C 94
BORDEN 9C 98 (5E 18)
Borden La. ME9: B'den 9C 98 (5E 18)
ME10: Sit 9C 98 (5E 18)
Border Gdns. CR0: Croy 5E 82
Bordyke TN9: Tonb 5J 145 (6K 25)
Bore Pl. Rd. TN8: Chid 4D 142
Boresisle TN30: St Mic 5C 224
Borgard Rd. SE18 ....4B 50
Borkwood Pk. BR6: Orp 5H 85
Borkwood Way BR6: Orp 5G 84
Borland Cl. DA9: G'hithe 3G 60
Borland Rd. SE15 ....2A 54
Bornefields TN23: Ashf 2E 160
BOROUGH GREEN 2M 121 (1A 26)
Borough Green & Wrotham
Station (Rail) 2M 121 (1A 26)
Borough Grn. Rd. TN15:Bor G, Igh 3K 121 (1K 25)
(not continuous)
TN15: Wro 8M 105 (7A 16)
Borough High St. SE1 ....4G 5
Borough Rd. ME7: Gill 8G 80
ME11: Queen 8C 220
SE1 ....4F 5
TN16: Tats 9D 164
Borough Station (Tube) 4G 5
BOROUGH, THE 4G 5
Borough, The CT1: Cant 1N 171
Borrowdale Av. CT11: Ram 5E 210
BORSTAL 1L 93 (3G 17)
Borstal Av. CT5: Whits 7F 226
Borstal Hill CT5: Whits 7F 226 (4F 21)
Borstal Hill Smockmill 6F 226
(off Millers Ct.)
Borstal M. ME1: Roch 1L 93
Borstal Rd. ME1: Roch 9M 79 (3G 17)
Borstal St. ME1: Roch 1L 93 (3G 17)
Borton Cl. ME18: Yald 7D 136
Bosbury Rd. SE6 ....8F 54
Boscobel Cl. BR1: Brom 5B 70
Bosco Cl. BR6: Orp 5H 85
Boscombe Rd. CT19: F'stone 5J 189
Bosney Banks CT15: Lyd'n 7D 32
BOSSINGHAM 5H 31
Bossingham Rd. CT4: S Min 5H 31
BOSSINGTON 2B 32
Bossington Rd. CT3: Adm 2B 32
Bostall Hill SE2 ....5J 51 (4D 6)
Bostall La. SE2 ....4K 51
Bostall Mnr. Way SE2 ....4K 51
Bostall Pk. Av. DA7: Bexhth 7N 51
Bostall Rd. BR5: St P 3K 71
Boston Cl. CT16: Dover 1G 180
Boston Gdns. ME8: Gill 2M 95
Boston Rd. ME5: Chat'm 9F 94
Bosville Av. TN13: S'oaks 5H 119
Bosville Dr. TN13: S'oaks 5H 119
Bosville Rd. TN13: S'oaks 5H 119
Boswell Cl. BR5: Orp 9L 71
Bosworth Ho. DA8: Erith 5F 52
(off Saltford Cl.)
Botany TN9: Tonb 6J 145
Botany Bay La. BR7: Chst 6E 70
Botany Cl. ME12: S'ness 3C 220
Botany Rd. CT10: B'stairs 4J 209 (1K 23)
DA11: Nflt 2N 61
Boteler Cotts. CT13: E'try 3J 183
BOTOLPH'S BRIDGE 9B 198 (6G 41)
Botolph's Bri. Rd. CT21: W Hyt 9B 198 (6G 41)
Botsom La. TN15: Farn'm, W King 7C 88 (5J 15)
Bottle Cotts. TN13: S'oaks 4H 119
Bottlescrew Hill ME17: Bou Mo 4E 138 (4J 27)
Bottles La. ME9: Rod 5H 115 (6F 19)
BOTTOM POND 8D 114 (7E 18)
Bottom Pond Rd.
ME9: B'gar, Mils, Rod, Worm 9C 114 (1E 28)
Bott Rd. DA2: Dart 9N 59
Boucher Dr. DA11: Nflt 8E 62
BOUGH BEECH 5A 142 (6E 24)
Bough Beech Nature Reserve 9B 130
Bough Beech Reservoir 2B 142
Bough Beech Reservoir Vis. Cen. 9B 130
Bough Beech Rd. TN8: Four E 5D 24
Bough Beech Sailing Club 3C 142
BOUGHTON ALUPH 5B 30
Boughton Av. BR2: Shortl 1J 83
CT10: B'stairs 2L 211
Boughton Cl. ME8: Gill 9M 81
BOUGHTON CORNER 5C 30
BOUGHTON GREEN 5E 138 (4J 27)
Boughton Hill ME13: Dunk 3M 165
Boughton La. ME15: Maid 1E 138 (3J 27)
ME17: Maid 1E 138
BOUGHTON LEES 6B 30
BOUGHTON MALHERBE 5E 28
BOUGHTON MONCHELSEA 5E 138 (4J 27)
Boughton Pde. ME15: Maid 1D 138
Boughton Rd. ME17: S'wy 9K 201 (5E 28)
SE28 ....3G 51
BOUGHTON UNDER BLEAN 3J 165 (7C 20)
Boulevard Courrieres CT3: Aysm 2C 162
Boulevard, The TN24: Ashf 3K 161 (2B 40)
Boulogne Ct. CT20: F'stone 6L 189
(off Harbour Way)
Boundary Chase CT5: Whits 5K 227
Boundary Cl. ME12: Minst 6M 221
Boundary Ct. CT1: Cant 4A 172
Boundary Ho. DA11: Nflt 6E 62
(off Victoria Rd.)
Boundary Rd. CT1: Cant 4K 171
CT11: Ram 5J 211 (4K 23)
CT14: Kgdn 3F 200
CT21: Hythe 7H 199
DA15: Sidc 3G 56
E13 ....2A 6
Boundary Rd. ME4: Chat'm 9A 80
NW8 ....2C 4
SM5: Wall 5E 12
TN2: Tun W 4K 157
Boundary St. DA8: Erith 7G 52
Boundary, The TN3: Lang G 2B 156
Boundary Way CR0: Croy 6D 82
Boundfield Rd. SE6 ....8H 55
Bounds La. ME13: Bou B, Hernh 3K 165
Bounds Oak Way TN4: S'bgh 3E 150
Bounds, The ME20: Aylfd 9J 109
Bourbon Ho. SE6 ....1F 68
Bourchier Cl. TN13: S'oaks 8J 119
Bourg-de-Peage Av. RH19: E Grin 3A 34
Bournbrook Rd. SE3 ....1N 55
Bourncrete Ho. ME10: Sit 6H 99
Bourne Cl. ME1: Roch 7A 80
TN9: Tonb 4K 145
Bourne Gro. ME10: Sit 6D 98
Bourne Ind. Est. TN15: Bor G 1N 121
Bourne Ind. Pk., The DA1: Cray 5G 59
Bourne La. TN9: Tonb 4K 145
TN15: Plax 8M 121 (2A 26)
TN18: Sandh 4A 218
TN26: Hams 2L 191
TN32: Rob 3C 44
Bourne Lodge Cl. CT2: Blean 4G 166
Bourne Mead DA5: Bex'y 3D 58
Bournemouth Dr. CT6: H Bay 2E 194
Bournemouth Gdns. CT19: F'stone 5J 189
Bournemouth Rd. CT19: F'stone 5J 189
Bourne Pde. DA5: Bex'y 5C 58
BOURNE PARK 9J 173
Bourne Pk. TN11: Gold G 2E 146
Bourne Pk. La. CT4: Brid 9H 173
Bourne Pk. Rd. CT4: Brid, Bis 9H 173 (3K 31)
Bourne Pl. TN11: Hild 9A 132
Bourne Pl. Mdws. TN11: Hild 9N 131
Bourne Rd. BR2: Shortl 7N 69
DA1: Cray 4D 58
DA5: Bex'y, Dart 5C 58 (7E 6)
DA12: Grav'nd 7L 63
TN25: Bils, Aldtn 4C 40
Bournes Cl. CT2: Sturry 4E 168
BOURNES GREEN 1F 11
Bournes Grn. Chase SS1: Sth S 1F 11
SS3: Shoe 1F 11
Bournes Hill CT4: Elham 6K 31
Bourneside Gdns. SE6 ....1F 68
Bourneside Ter. ME17: Holl 7F 128
Bournes Pl. TN26: Wdchu 7B 228
Bourne Va. BR2: Shortl 2J 83
TN15: Plax 9N 121
Bourne Vw. CT4: Brid 9E 172
Bourne Way BR2: Shortl 3J 83 (4K 13)
BR8: Swanl 6D 72
Bournewood TN26: Hams 2L 191
Bournewood Cl. ME15: Bear 8J 127
Bournewood Rd. BR5: Orp 1K 85
SE18 ....7J 51
Bournville Av. ME4: Chat'm 2C 94
Bournville Rd. SE6 ....5D 54
Boutique Hall SE13 ....2F 54
Bouverie Pl. CT20: F'stone 7K 189
Bouverie Rd. W. CT20: F'stone 7G 189 (5A 42)
Bouverie Sq. CT20: F'stone 7K 189
Bovarde Av. ME19: W Mal 6A 124
Boveney Rd. SE23 ....5A 54
Bovill Rd. SE23 ....5A 54
BOW 2J 5
Bow Arrow La. DA1: Dart 4A 60
(not continuous)
Bowater Rd. SE18 ....3A 50
Bow Church Station (DLR) 2J 5
BOW COMMON 3J 5
Bow Comn. La. E3 ....2J 5
Bowdell La. TN29: B'lnd, Bztt, Snar 2E 46
Bowden Cres. CT20: F'stone 5C 188
Bowen Rd. CT19: F'stone 5E 188
TN4: R'hall 9B 150
Bowen's Fld. TN23: Ashf 9F 158
Bowens Wood CR0: Croy 9C 82
Bower Cl. ME16: Maid 5B 126
Bower Cotts. TN25: Mers 8M 161
Bower Grn. ME5: Chat'm 1F 110
Bowerland La. CT4: Chil'm 7M 175
CT4: Old L 6K 175
RH7: Ling 7A 24
Bower La. DA4: Eyns 3M 87 (4H 15)
ME16: Maid 6B 126
TN15: Eyns 3M 87 (4H 15)
TN15: Knat 1A 104 (4H 15)
Bower Mt. Rd. ME16: Maid 6A 126 (2H 27)
Bower Pl. ME16: Maid 6B 126
Bower Rd. BR8: Swanl 3H 73
TN25: Mers, Sme 8M 161 (3C 40)
Bowers Av. DA11: Nflt 9E 62
Bowers Rd. TN14: S'ham 2G 102
Bower St. ME16: Maid 5B 126
Bower Ter. ME16: Maid 6B 126
Bower Wlk. TN12: S'hrst 3J 223
Bowes Av. CT9: Mgte 2M 207
Bowes Cl. DA15: Sidc 4K 57
Bowes Ct. CT5: Whits 3J 227
DA2: Dart 4B 60
(off Osbourne Rd.)
Bowesden La. DA12: Shorne 3C 78
ME2: Grav'nd 3C 78
Bowes La. CT6: H Bay 4H 195
Bowes Rd. ME2: Strood 4M 79
Bowes Wood DA3: New A 4M 89
Bowford Av. DA7: Bexhth 8N 51
Bow Hill CT4: S Min 5H 31
CT4: Up Hard 4H 31
ME18: W'bury 2C 136 (3E 26)
BOW INTERCHANGE 2K 5
Bowland Cl. CT6: H Bay 5K 195
BOWLER'S TOWN 4A 46
Bowles Outdoor Cen. 6H 35
Bowles Wells Gdns. CT19: F'stone 4M 189
(not continuous)
Bowley La. ME17: S'wy, Bou Ma 5E 28
Bowl Fld. TN25: H'lgh 7E 30
Bowl Grn. La. CT14: Deal 5L 177
Bowling Grn. Row SE18 ....3B 50
Bowling Grn. Ter. CT17: Dover 5J 181
Bowling St. CT13: S'wch 5L 217
Bowlplex Bowling Alley
Tunbridge Wells 6M 151
Bowl Rd. TN27: Char'g 1L 175 (4H 29)
Bowls Pl. TN12: Pad W 8M 147
Bowman Cl. ME5: Chat'm 6F 94
BOWMANS 5H 59
Bowman's Rd. DA1: Dart 5G 58
Bowmead SE9 ....7B 56
Bown Cl. RM18: Tilb 1G 62
Bowness Rd. DA7: Bexhth 9C 52
SE6 ....5E 54
Bow Rd. E3 ....2J 5
ME18: W'bury 2C 136 (3E 26)
Bow Road Station (Tube) 2J 5
Bowser Cl. CT14: Deal 6J 177
Bow St. WC2 ....3F 5
Bow Ter. ME18: W'bury 1C 136
Bowyer Pl. SE5 ....5G 5
Bowyer Rd. CT5: Seas 6B 226
BOWZELL GREEN 6G 130
Bowzell Rd. TN14: Weald 6G 130 (4F 25)
Bowzells La. TN8: Chid, Weald 6F 25
TN14: Chid, Weald 8F 130 (6F 25)
Boxgrove Rd. SE2 ....3L 51
Box La. ME13: Osp 7K 19
BOXLEY 8F 110 (7J 17)
Boxley TN23: Ashf 1D 160
Boxley Cl. ME12: S'ness 5C 220
ME14: Pen H 1E 126
Boxley Grange Cotts. ME14: Boxl 5J 111
Boxley Rd. ME5: Chat'm 9D 94 (5J 17)
(Robin Hood La.)
ME5: Chat'm 5J 17
(Beechin Bank Rd.)
ME14: Maid, Pen H, Boxl 3D 126 (1J 27)
Boxmend Ind. Est. ME15: Maid 4J 139
Boxted La. ME9: N'tn, Upc 2J 97 (3C 18)
Box Tree Wlk. BR5: Orp 2M 85
Boyard Rd. SE18 ....5D 50
Boyces Hill ME9: N'tn 5L 97 (4D 18)
Boy Ct. Rd. TN27: Ulc 6C 28
Boyd Bus. Cen. ME2: Med E 5A 80
BOYDEN GATE 3B 22
Boyden Ga. Hill CT3: C'let 3A 22
Boyden Hill CT3: Hoath, C'let 6N 195 (3A 22)
Boyes La. CT3: Good 2C 32
Boyke La. CT4: O'nge, R Min 9J 183 (1H 41)
Boyland Rd. BR1: Brom 1J 69
Boyle Way TN12: E Peck 8N 135 (5D 26)
Boyne Pk. TN4: Tun W 1F 156
Boyne Rd. CT15: St Marg 9C 200
SE13 ....1F 54
Boys Hall Rd. TN24: Ashf, W'boro 2K 161 (2B 40)
Boystown Pl. CT13: E'try 2L 183
Boyton Ct. Rd. ME17: Sut V 9C 140 (5B 28)
Brabazon Rd. ME12: E'chu 9B 202
Brabner Cl. CT19: F'stone 3L 189
BRABOURNE 2F 41
Brabourne Av. ME8: Gill 8M 81
Brabourne Cl. CT2: Cant 7N 167
Brabourne Cres. DA7: Bexhth 6A 52
Brabourne Gdns. CT20: F'stone 6E 188
Brabourne La. TN25: Stow 1F 41
BRABOURNE LEES 8J 165 (2D 40)
Brabourne Ri. BR3: Beck'm 8F 68
Brabourne Rd. TN25: Wye 7D 30
Bracken Av. CR0: Croy 4D 82
Bracken Cl. TN2: Tun W 9L 151
TN24: Kenn 4G 159
Bracken Ct. CT10: B'stairs 8J 209
ME10: Sit 6K 99
Brackendene DA5: Dart 9F 58
Bracken Hill ME5: Chat'm 1D 110
Bracken Hill Cl. BR1: Brom 4J 69
Bracken Hill La. BR1: Brom 4J 69
Bracken Lea ME5: Chat'm 2F 94
Bracken Rd. TN2: Tun W 9L 151
Brackens BR3: Beck'm 3D 68
Brackens, The BR6: Chels 6J 85
Bracken Wlk. TN10: Tonb 1H 145
Brack La. TN29: Snar, B'lnd 2D 46
Brackley Cl. ME14: Maid 4F 126
Brackley Rd. BR3: Beck'm 3C 68
Brackwood Cl. ME8: Gill 6N 95
Bracondale Av. DA13: Ist R 4E 76
Bracondale Rd. SE2 ....4J 51
Bracton La. DA5: Bex'y 7G 58
Bradbourne Ct. TN13: S'oaks 4J 119
Bradbourne La. ME20: Dit 9F 108
Bradbourne Pk. Rd. ME19: E Mal 9E 108
TN13: S'oaks 5H 119 (2G 25)
Bradbourne Rd. DA5: Bex'y 5B 58
TN13: S'oaks 4J 119 (1G 25)
Bradbourne Va. Rd. TN13: S'oaks 4G 118 (1F 25)
Bradbridge Grn. TN23: Ashf 1B 160
Bradbury Ct. DA11: Nflt 6E 62
Braddick Cl. ME15: Maid 3E 138
Bradenham Av. DA16: Well 2J 57
Bradfield Av. ME9: Tey 7L 223
Bradfield Rd. TN25: Ashf 5F 158
Bradfields Av. ME5: Chat'm 5C 94
Bradfields Av. W. ME5: Chat'm 5C 94
Bradford Cl. BR2: Shortl 2B 84
Bradford Ct. CT20: F'stone 6K 189
(off Foord Rd.)
Bradfords Cl. ME4: Chat'm 2E 80
Bradford St. TN9: Tonb 6H 145
Bradgate Pk. CT9: Mgte 9C 208
Bradgate Rd. SE6 ....4E 54
Bradley Dr. ME10: Sit 9F 98 (5F 19)
Bradley Ho. ME3: Lwr Sto 8C 204
Bradley La. TN3: Blkm, Pens 8D 148 (2F 35)
Bradley Rd. CT12: Ram 3G 210
CT19: F'stone 5M 189
ME2: Hall'g 6C 92
Bradshaw Cl. ME9: Upc 3H 225
Bradstone Av. CT19: F'stone 5K 189
Bradstone New Rd. CT20: F'stone 6K 189
Bradstone Rd. CT20: F'stone 6K 189
(not continuous)
Bradstone St. CT20: F'stone 4B 42

Broadhurst Dr.—Buckmans Grn. La.

Broadhurst Dr. TN24: Kenn 3H 159
Broadhurst Gdns. NW6 1C 4
Broadlands CT2: Sturry 5E 168
Broadlands Av. TN28: New R 1K 213
Broadlands Cres. TN28: New R 1K 213
Broadlands Dr. ME5: Chat'm 7E 94
Broadlands Ind. Est. CT2: Blean 4F 166
Broadlands Rd. BR1: Brom 9L 55
Broad La. CT14: Fin 3G 33
DA2: Dart 9H 59 (1G 15)
TN3: A'hst, Ford 2H 155 (3G 35)
Broad Lawn SE9 7C 56
Broadley Av. CT7: Birch 6E 206
Broadley Rd. CT10: Mgte 6G 208
Broadmead SE6 8D 54
TN2: Tun W 5E 156
TN23: Ashf 3C 160
Broadmead Av. TN2: Tun W 5F 156
Broadmeadow CT19: F'stone 4H 189
Broadmead Rd. CT19: F'stone 6J 189
BROADMEAD VILLAGE 4G 189 (4A 42)
Broadmead Works ME16: Maid 6C 126
BROAD OAK
Ashford 3C 40
Canterbury 4C 168 (6J 21)
Rye 5G 45
Broadoak ME19: Leyb 8B 108
Broad Oak TN3: Groom 7K 155
TN12: Brenc 2E 36
Broadoak Av. ME15: Maid 9D 126
Broad Oak Cl. BR5: St P 5J 71
Broadoak Cl. DA4: S at H 2A 74
Broad Oak Cl. TN2: Tun W 4F 156
TN12: Brenc 1E 36
Broad Oak Cotts. ME9: Mils 6F 114
Broadoak Ent. Village ME9: Sit 4G 114
Broad Oak Rd. CT2: Cant 9N 167 (7H 21)
Broadoak Rd. DA8: Erith 7E 52
ME9: Mils, Sit 3E 114 (6E 18)
Broadoaks Way BR2: Shortl 8J 69
Broad Oak Trad. Est. CT2: Cant 8A 168
Broad Rd. DA10: Swans 4L 61
Broad Sanctuary SW1 4E 4
Broadsole La. CT15: W Hou 2D 42
BROADSTAIRS 9M 209 (3K 23)
Broadstairs Mus., Arts & Media Cen. 8M 209
(off Crow Hill)
Broadstairs Rd. CT10: B'stairs 8H 209 (2K 23)
Broadstairs Station (Rail) 8L 209 (2K 23)
BROADSTONE 6D 28
BROAD STREET
Ashford 2F 41
Folkestone 9L 205 (2J 41)
Maidstone 3E 128 (1B 28)
Rochester 8E 66 (7J 9)
Winchelsea 7J 45
Broad St. CT1: Cant 2N 171 (7H 21)
CT9: Mgte 2C 208
CT11: Ram 5J 211 (4K 23)
CT14: Deal 4N 177 (3J 33)
CT18: Lym'ge 1K 185 (2J 41)
ME12: S'ness 2C 220
ME17: Sut V 9A 140 (5A 28)
RM10: Dag 1E 6
TN36: Ickl 7J 45
Broad St. Hill ME17: Holl 3E 128 (1B 28)
BROAD TENTERDEN 6E 38
Broadview CT20: F'stone 5C 188
TN17: Siss 3C 222
Broadview Av. ME8: Gill 3A 96
Broadview Gardens 8C 134 (5B 26)
Broadviews CT21: Hythe 7L 199
(off South Rd.)
Broad Wlk. BR6: Chels 4M 85
SE3 9A 50 (5A 6)
TN15: S'oaks 1M 131
Broadwater Ct. TN2: Tun W 5E 156
BROADWATER DOWN 4F 156 (4J 35)
Broadwater Down TN2: Tun W 5E 156 (4J 35)
Broadwater Forest La.
TN3: Groom, Tun W 7M 155
Broadwater Forest Rd. TN3: Groom, Tun W 4H 35
Broadwater Gdns. BR6: Farnb 5D 84
Broadwater La. TN2: Tun W 4F 156
Broadwater Ri. TN2: Tun W 4F 156
Broadwater Rd. ME19: W Mal 4A 124 (1E 26)
SE28 3F 50 (4C 6)
Broadway BR8: Crock'n 9D 72 (3F 15)
CT4: P'hm 4G 31
DA6: Bexhth 2N 57 (6E 6)
(not continuous)
E15 1K 5
KT6: Surb 3A 12
ME8: Gill 9K 81
ME12: S'ness 2D 220 (6G 11)
ME16: Maid 6C 126 (2H 27)
RM13: Rain 2G 7
SS9: Lgh S 1C 10
Broadway Ct. BR3: Beck'm 6F 68
Broadway Ho. BR1: Brom 1G 69
(off Bromley Rd.)
Broadway Mkt. E8 2H 5
Broadway Shop. Cen. DA6: Bexhth 2B 58
ME16: Maid 5C 126
Broadway Sq. DA6: Bexhth 2B 58
Broadway, The CT4: Brid 8H 173
CT6: H Bay 2D 194 (2J 21)
CT10: B'stairs 9L 209 (2K 23)
CT11: Ram 6H 211
ME12: Minst 4J 221 (6H 11)
RM12: H'church 1G 7
SM3: Sutt 5C 12
SS1: Sth S 1F 11
SW19 1C 12
TN3: Lamb 2L 201 (4D 36)
TN6: Crowb 7F 35
TN11: Hdlw 8D 134
(off High St.)
Broadway Theatre, The 5E 54
Broadway W. SS9: Lgh S 1B 10
Broadwood DA11: Grav'nd 1G 77
Broadwood Rd. ME3: C'den 9C 66
Brockbank Cl. ME5: Chat'm 1D 110
Brockdene Dr. BR2: Kes 5N 83
Brockenhurst Av. ME15: Maid 8E 126
Brockenhurst Cl. CT2: Cant 9L 167
ME8: Gill 4M 95
Brockenhurst Rd. CT11: Ram 4K 211
Brockham Cres. CR0: Croy 8G 82
Brockhill Country Pk. 4G 198 (5H 41)
Brockhill Rd. CT21: Hythe 5J 199 (5H 41)
Brockill Cres. SE4 2B 54
Brocklebank Ho. E16 1C 50
(off Glenister St.)
BROCKLEY 2A 54 (6J 5)
Brockley Cross SE4 1B 54
Brockley Cross Bus. Cen. SE4 1B 54
Brockley Footpath SE4 3B 54
(not continuous)
Brockley Gro. SE4 3C 54 (6J 5)
Brockley Hall Rd. SE4 3B 54
Brockley M. SE4 3B 54
Brockley Pk. SE23 5B 54
Brockley Ri. SE23 6B 54 (7J 5)
Brockley Rd. CT9: Mgte 3D 208
SE4 1C 54 (6J 5)
Brockley Station (Rail) 1B 54 (6J 5)
Brockley Vw. SE23 5B 54
Brockley Way SE4 3A 54
Brockman Cres. TN29: Dym 8E 182
Brockman Ri. BR1: Brom 9G 54
Brockman Rd. CT20: F'stone 6J 189
Brockmans Cl. CT12: Minst 6E 212
Brockway TN15: Bor G 2N 121
Brockwell Av. BR3: Beck'm 8E 68
Brockwell Cl. BR5: St M Cry 8H 71
Brodrick Gro. SE2 4K 51
Brogdale Farm Cotts. ME13: Osp 9E 186
Brogdale Horticultural Trust, The 8F 186 (7A 20)
Brogdale Pl. ME13: Osp 6F 186
Brogdale Rd. ME13: Osp 9E 186 (7A 20)
Brogden Cres. ME17: Leeds 1B 140
Brogden Farm Cotts. ME17: Leeds 1B 140
Brograve Gdns. BR3: Beck'm 5E 68
Broke Farm Dr. BR6: Prat B 9L 85
Brokes Way TN4: S'bgh 6H 151
Brome Rd. SE9 1B 56
Bromhedge SE9 8B 56
Bromholm Rd. SE2 3K 51
BROMLEY
Bow 2J 5
Shortlands 5K 69 (2A 14)
Bromley Av. BR1: Brom 3H 69
Bromley-by-Bow Station (Tube) 2J 5
Bromley Cl. ME5: Chat'm 7E 94
(not continuous)
ME9: N'tn 6J 97
BROMLEY COMMON 2A 84 (3B 14)
Bromley Comn. BR2: Shortl 7M 69 (2A 14)
Bromley Cres. BR2: Shortl 6J 69
Bromley F.C. (Hayes Lane) 8L 69
Bromley Gdns. BR2: Shortl 6J 69
BROMLEY GREEN 4K 39
Bromley Grn. Rd. TN26: Shad 4K 39
Bromley Gro. BR2: Shortl 5G 69
Bromley Hill BR1: Brom 2H 69 (1K 13)
Bromley Indoor Bowls Cen. 2L 85
Bromley Ind. Cen. BR1: Brom 6N 69
Bromley La. BR7: Chst 3E 70 (1C 14)
Bromley Mus. 1K 85 (3D 14)
Bromley North Station (Rail) 4K 69 (2A 14)
BROMLEY PARK 4H 69
Bromley Pk. BR1: Brom 4J 69
Bromley Rd. BR1: Brom 1F 68 (7J 5)
BR2: Shortl 4E 68 (2J 13)
BR3: Beck'm 4E 68 (2J 13)
BR7: Chst 4D 70 (2B 14)
SE6 6E 54 (7J 5)
Bromley Ski Cen. 4N 71
Bromley South Station (Rail) 6K 69 (2A 14)
Bromley Valley Gymnastics Cen. 4J 71
BELGRAVIA 4D 4
BROMPTON
Gillingham 6D 80 (2J 17)
Knightsbridge 3B 4
Brompton Cl. ME4: Chat'm 6C 80
Brompton Dr. DA8: Erith 7J 53
Brompton Farm Rd. ME2: Strood 3K 79 (1G 17)
Brompton Hill ME4: Chat'm 6C 80
Brompton La. ME2: Strood 4L 79
Brompton Rd. ME7: Gill 6E 80 (2J 17)
SW3 4D 4
Brompton Ter. SE18 8B 50
Brompton Vs. CT15: Gus 7K 179
BROMSTONE 1J 211 (3K 23)
Bromstone M. CT10: B'stairs 1J 211
Bromstone Rd. CT10: B'stairs 1J 211 (3K 23)
BRONDESBURY 1C 4
BRONDESBURY PARK 1B 4
Brondesbury Pk. NW2 1B 4
NW6 1B 4
Brondesbury Park Station (Rail) 2C 4
Brondesbury Rd. NW6 2C 4
Brondesbury Station (Rail) 1C 4
Bronington Cl. ME5: Chat'm 6D 94
Bronte Cl. DA8: Erith 7C 52
ME20: Lark 7D 108
Bronte Gro. DA1: Dart 2N 59
Bronte Vw. DA12: Grav'nd 6H 63
Bronze Age Way DA8: Erith 2C 52 (4F 7)
DA17: Belv 2C 52 (4F 7)
Brookbank ME14: Pen H 1D 126
Brookbank Rd. SE13 1D 54
Brook Cl. CT6: H Bay 4D 194
CT21: Hythe 8B 188
Brook Ct. BR3: Beck'm 4C 68
SE12 8M 55
TN8: Eden 4C 184
Brookdale Rd. DA5: Bex'y 4N 57
SE6 5E 54
(not continuous)
Brookdene Rd. SE18 4G 51
Brooke Av. CT9: Mgte 4N 207
Brooke Dr. DA12: Grav'nd 6N 63
Brookehowse Rd. SE6 7D 54
Brookend Rd. DA15: Sidc 6G 56
Brooker Cl. ME15: Maid 3G 138
Brooke Rd. TN24: Ashf 7F 158
Brooker's Pl. ME3: High'm 7G 65
Brookes Pl. ME9: N'tn 5K 97
Brookfield TN8: Four E 5D 24
TN15: Kems'g 8M 103
TN18: Sandh 2C 218
Brookfield Av. CT16: Dover 2G 180 (1F 43)
ME20: Lark 6E 108
Brookfield Ct. TN4: S'bgh 5G 150
TN23: Ashf 1D 160
Brookfield Ind. Pk. TN23: Ashf 9D 158
Brookfield Pl. CT16: Dover 2G 180
Brookfield Rd. CT16: Dover 1F 180
TN23: Ashf 9C 158 (1K 39)
Brookfields TN11: Hdlw 8D 134
BROOK GREEN 4B 4
Brookhill Cl. SE18 5D 50
Brookhill Rd. SE18 6D 50
Brookhurst Gdns. TN4: S'bgh 3E 150
BROOKLAND 3E 46
Brooklands DA1: Dart 6M 59
TN2: Tun W 7K 151
TN27: H'crn 7K 191
Brooklands Av. DA15: Sidc 7F 56
Brooklands Cl. CT2: Cant 7E 168
Brooklands Farm Cl. TN3: Ford 8H 149
Brooklands Pk. SE3 1K 55
Brooklands Rd. ME20: Lark 6E 108
Brooklands Way RH19: E Grin 3A 34
Brook La. BR1: Brom 2K 69
CT6: H Bay, Rec 2A 22
DA5: Bex'y, Bexhth 4M 57
ME3: Lwr Sto 8C 204
ME6: Snod 4D 108
TN9: Tonb 5K 145
TN15: Plax 9N 121 (3A 26)
TN25: S'ndge 7D 218
Brook La. Cotts. TN25: S'ndge 7D 218
Brooklyn Paddock ME7: Gill 6G 80
Brooklyn Rd. BR2: Shortl 8N 69
Brooklyn Vs. TN12: Mard 3C 212
Brookmead TN11: Hild 3D 144
Brookmead Av. BR1: Brom 8B 70
Brookmead Cl. BR5: St M Cry 1K 85
Brookmead Rd. ME3: Cli W 6M 65
Brookmead Way BR5: St M Cry 9K 71
Brookmill Rd. SE8 5J 5
Brook Pk. DA1: Dart 7A 60
Brook Pl. TN14: Ide H, Sund 3E 24
Brook Rd. BR8: Swanl 6E 72
CT5: Whits 2L 227
DA11: Nflt 6D 62
ME13: Fav 4G 187
ME20: Lark 6C 108
TN2: Tun W 7J 151
Brooks Cl. SE9 7C 56
TN10: Tonb 9K 133
TN12: S'hrst 2J 223
BROOKS END 7D 206 (3E 22)
Brookside BR6: Orp 1H 85
CT16: Temp E 8B 178
(not continuous)
ME3: Hoo 8H 67
TN17: Cran 8D 176
TN29: Dym 1N 215
Brookside Cotts. TN2: Tun W 9M 151
Brookside Leisure Pk. ME12: E'chu 2E 202
Brookside Rd. DA13: Ist R 3E 76
Brookside Way CR0: Croy 9A 68
Brooks Pl. ME14: Maid 5D 126
Brook Sq. SE18 8A 50
BROOK STREET
Ashford 6G 39
Tonbridge 8F 144 (7J 25)
Brook St. CT13: E'try 3L 183 (2F 33)
DA8: Erith 5C 52 (5E 6)
DA17: Belv, Erith 5C 52 (4E 6)
ME6: Snod 2F 108 (6F 17)
TN9: Tonb 7F 144 (7K 25)
TN26: Wdchu 9A 228 (5F 39)
Brooks Way BR5: St P 5L 71
TN29: Lydd 4K 205
Brook, The ME4: Chat'm 7C 80 (2H 17)
Brook Theatre, The 7C 80
Brook Va. DA8: Erith 8C 52
Brookway SE3 1K 55
Brook Wood TN25: Brook 1D 40
Brookwood Cl. BR2: Shortl 7J 69
Broom Av. BR5: St P 5K 71
Broom Cl. BR2: Shortl 9A 70
Broomcroft Rd. ME8: Rain 1B 96
BROOMFIELD
Herne Bay 5L 195 (3A 22)
Maidstone 3F 140 (3B 28)
Broomfield TN24: W'boro 1M 161
Broomfield Cres. CT9: Clift 3K 209
Broomfield Ga. CT5: Whits 8M 227
Broomfield Rd. BR3: Beck'm 6B 68
CT6: H Bay 6J 195 (3K 21)
CT19: F'stone 5E 188
DA6: Bexhth 3B 58
DA10: Swans 4L 61
ME13: Fav 3G 187
ME17: Kgswd, Leeds 5E 140 (4B 28)
TN13: S'oaks 4G 119
Broomfields DA3: Hart'y 8L 75
Broom Gdns. CR0: Croy 4D 82
BROOM HILL 1H 85
Broom Hill TN5: Flim 7F 37
BROOMHILL BANK 8D 150
Broomhill Pk. Rd. TN4: S'bgh 6E 150
Broom Hill Ri. DA6: Bexhth 3B 58
Broomhill Rd. BR6: Orp 1J 85
DA1: Dart 4J 59
Broom Hill Rd. ME2: Strood 4K 79
Broomhill Rd. TN3: S'bgh, Tun W 8C 150 (2J 35)
Broomhills DA13: Sflt 9L 61
Broom La. TN3: Lang G, Tun W 2M 155 (3H 35)
Broomleigh BR1: Brom 4K 69
(off Tweedy Rd.)
Broom Mead DA6: Bexhth 4B 58
Broom Pk. TN3: Lang G 2M 155
Broom Rd. CR0: Croy 4D 82
ME10: Sit 6K 99
Broomshaw Rd. ME16: Barm 6K 125
Broomsleigh Bus. Pk. SE26 1C 68
Broom St. ME13: G'ney 5C 20
Broomwood Cl. CR0: Croy 8A 68
DA5: Bex'y 7E 58
Broomwood Rd. BR5: St P 5K 71
SW11 6D 4
Broseley Gro. SE26 1B 68
Brotherhood Cl. CT2: Cant 7K 167
Brougham Ct. DA2: Dart 4B 60
(off Hardwick Cres.)
Broughton Ct. TN23: Ashf 9C 158
Broughton Rd. BR6: Orp 3F 84
TN14: Otf 7H 103
Brow Cl. BR5: Orp 1M 85
Brow Cres. BR5: Orp 2L 85
Brown Cotts. CT2: Cant 7F 168
Browndens Rd. ME2: Hall'g 7C 92
Brownelow Copse ME5: Chat'm 1D 110
Brownhill Cl. ME5: Chat'm 7D 94
Brownhill Rd. SE6 5E 54 (7K 5)
Browning Cl. DA16: Well 8G 51
ME20: Lark 6D 108
Browning Pl. CT19: F'stone 4L 189
Browning Rd. DA1: Dart 2N 59
E12 1B 6
Brownings TN8: Eden 3C 184
Brownings Orchard ME9: Rod 3H 115
Brown Rd. DA12: Grav'nd 6K 63
Browns La. TN8: Eden 6B 24
Brownspring Dr. SE9 9D 56
Brown St. ME8: Rain 2A 96
ME13: G'ney 5C 20
Brownswood Rd. N4 1G 5
Broxbourne Rd. BR6: Orp 2H 85
Broxhall Rd. CT4: Up Hard 4H 31
Broxted Rd. SE6 7C 54
Bruce Cl. CT14: Deal 6L 177
DA16: Well 8K 51
Bruce Ct. DA15: Sidc 9H 57
Bruce Dr. CR2: S Croy 9A 82
Bruce Gro. BR6: Orp 2J 85
Brucks, The ME18: W'bury 1C 136
Bruges Ct. ME10: Kems'y 2G 98
Brummel Cl. DA7: Bexhth 1D 58
Brunel Cl. RM18: Tilb 1G 62
Brunel Rd. SE16 4H 5
Brunel Way ME4: Chat'm 5D 80
Brunger's Wlk. TN10: Tonb 2H 145
Brunner Ho. SE6 9F 54
Brunswick Cl. DA6: Bexhth 2M 57
Brunswick Ct. CT11: Ram 5J 211
(off Hardres St.)
Brunswick Fld. ME9: Tey 4J 19
Brunswick Gdns. CT16: Dover 1G 180
Brunswick Ind. Cen. TN23: Ashf 8D 158
Brunswick Rd. CT7: Birch 6F 206
DA6: Bexhth 2M 57
TN23: Ashf 8D 158
Brunswick Sq. CT6: H Bay 2F 194
Brunswick St. CT11: Ram 5J 211
ME15: Maid 6D 126
Brunswick St. E. ME15: Maid 6D 126
Brunswick Ter. TN1: Tun W 3G 157
Brunswick Wlk. DA12: Grav'nd 5J 63
(not continuous)
Bruton Cl. BR7: Chst 3B 70
Bruton St. W1 3E 4
Bryant Cl. ME18: W'bury 2A 136
Bryant Rd. ME2: Strood 4L 79
Bryant St. ME4: Chat'm 9D 80
Bryden Cl. SE26 1B 68
Brymore Cl. CT1: Cant 9A 168
Brymore Rd. CT1: Cant 9A 168
Bryony Dr. TN23: Kgnt 6G 161
Bubblestone Rd. TN14: Otf 7J 103
Bubhurst La. TN17: Frit 2B 38
Buckden Cl. SE12 4K 55
Buckham Thorns Rd. TN16: Westrm 8E 116
Buckhold Rd. SW18 6C 4
Buckhole Farm Rd. ME3: H Hals 1F 66 (6J 9)
BUCKHURST 2B 38
Buckhurst Av. TN13: S'oaks 7K 119
Buckhurst Dr. CT9: Clift 3K 209
Buckhurst La. TN5: Wadh 7A 36
TN13: S'oaks 7K 119
Buckhurst Rd. TN16: Westrm 3C 116 (1B 24)
Buckingham Av. DA16: Well 2G 57
Buckingham Cl. BR5: Pet W 1G 84
Buckingham Dr. BR7: Chst 9E 56
Buckingham Hill Rd. SS17: Ors, Stan H 3D 8
Buckingham La. SE23 5B 54
Buckingham Palace 4E 4
Buckingham Pal. Rd. SW1 4E 4
Buckingham Rd. CT5: Whits 3K 227
CT9: Mgte 4C 208
CT10: B'stairs 9M 209
DA11: Nflt 5C 62
ME7: Gill 7G 81
TN1: Tun W 3H 157
Buckingham Row ME15: Maid 1H 139
BUCKLAND 2G 180 (1F 43)
Buckland Av. CT16: Dover 2G 180
CT17: Dover 1F 43
Buckland Cl. ME5: Chat'm 9D 94
Buckland Cres. NW3 1D 4
Buckland Hill ME16: Maid 4B 126 (1H 27)
Buckland La. CT3: S'le, Good 2D 32
ME16: Alltn 3A 126
(not continuous)
Buckland Pl. ME16: Maid 5B 126
(not continuous)
Buckland Rd. BR6: Orp 5G 85
DA13: Meop, Lud'n 5M 91 (4D 16)
ME3: Cliffe 2B 176
ME3: High'm 6K 65 (7G 9)
ME16: Alltn, Maid 4B 126
Buckland Ter. CT17: Dover 3H 181
BUCKLAND VALLEY 1G 181 (1F 43)
Buckler Gdns. SE9 8B 56
Bucklers Cl. ME12: Ward 4K 203
TN2: Tun W 2J 157
Buckles Ct. DA17: Belv 4M 51
Buckley Cl. DA1: Cray 9G 53
Buckmans Grn. La. TN27: Smar 2E 38

Buckmore Pk.—Cambrian Cotts.

Buckmore Pk. 8N 93
Buckmore Pk. Kart Circuit 8N 93
Buckmore Pk. Sports Cen. 9N 93
Bucknall Way BR3: Beck'm 7F 68
Bucks Cross Rd. BR6: Chels 6N 85 (4E 14)
DA11: Nflt 8E 62
Bucksford La. TN23: Ashf 1B 160
Buck St. TN25: C'lck 7E 174 (4A 30)
Buckthorn Cl. CT14: Deal 3M 177
Buckthorne Rd. ME12: Minst 8H 221
SE4 3B 54
Buckthorn Ho. DA15: Sidc 8H 57
(off Longlands Rd.)
Buckwheat Ct. DA18: Erith 3M 51
Buddle Dr. ME12: Minst 5F 220
BUDDS 3J 25
Budd's Farm Cotts. TN30: Witter 4E 228
BUDD'S GREEN 3F 132
Budd's La. TN30: Witter 4D 228
Budgin's Hill BR6: Prat B 3L 101 (6D 14)
Budleigh Cres. DA16: Well 8L 51
Buenos Ayres CT9: Mgte 3B 208
Buffalo La. TN27: Smar 9C 222 (2E 38)
Buffs Av. CT20: F'stone 5B 188
Buffs Regimental Mus. 2M 171
Bugglesden Rd. TN27: St Mic 4D 38
TN30: St Mic 4D 38
Bug Hill CR3: Wold 7H 13
Buglehorn Cotts. ME15: Otham 2L 139
Bugsby's Way SE7 4K 5
SE10 4K 5
Bugsy's Ten Pin Bowling 2E 208
Bullace La. DA1: Dart 4M 59
Bull All. DA16: Well 1K 57
Bullbanks Rd. DA17: Belv 4D 52
Bulldog Rd. ME5: Chat'm 9E 94
Bulleid Pl. TN24: Ashf 2H 161
BULLEN 1K 147
Bullen La. TN12: E Peck 8K 135 (5D 26)
Buller Gro. CT5: Seas 7D 226
Buller Rd. ME4: Chat'm 1C 94
Buller's Av. CT6: H Bay 3E 194
Bullers Cl. DA14: Sidc 1N 71
Bullers Wood Dr. BR7: Chst 3B 70
Bullfields ME6: Snod 2E 108
Bullfinch Cl. TN12: Pad W 1M 153
TN13: Riv 4E 118
Bullfinch Dene TN13: Riv 4E 118
Bullfinch La. TN13: Riv 4E 118 (1F 25)
Bull Hill DA4: Hort K 7C 74
ME17: Len 5F 29
Bullingstone La.
TN3: Pens, Speld 7M 149 (2H 35)
Bullion Cl. TN12: Pad W 9L 147
Bullivant Cl. DA9: G'hithe 3G 60
Bull La. BR7: Chst 3F 70
ME1: Roch 6N 79
ME3: High'm 6H 65 (7F 9)
ME9: N'tn 8H 97 (5C 18)
ME9: S'bry 2G 112 (5C 18)
ME13: Bou B 2J 165 (7C 20)
ME20: Aylfd, Burh 7K 109 (7G 17)
TN15: Wro 7N 105 (7A 16)
TN17: Rolv 1B 214
TN26: Beth 3H 163 (3F 39)
BULLOCKSTONE 7E 194
Bullockstone Hill CT6: H Bay 7F 194
Bullockstone Rd. CT6: H Bay 6E 194 (3J 21)
Bull Orchard ME16: Barm 7J 125
Bull Rd. ME19: Birl 5A 108 (6E 16)
Bulls Cotts. CT21: Hythe 7J 199
(off St Leonard's Rd.)
Bulls Head Yd. DA1: Dart 4M 59
(off High St.)
Bulls Pas. CT21: Hythe 6K 199
(off Dental St.)
Bulls Pl. TN2: Pem 8C 152
Bulltown La. TN25: W Bra 1D 40
Bull Yd. DA12: Grav'nd 4G 63
(off Crooked La.)
BULPHAN 1B 8
Bulphan By-Pass RM14: Bulp 1C 8
Bulrush Cl. ME5: Chat'm 8C 94
Bulrushes, The TN23: Ashf 1A 160
Bulwark Rd. CT14: Deal 3N 177
Bulwark St. CT17: Dover 7J 181
Bulwark, The CT13: S'wch 5N 217
Bumbles Cl. ME1: Roch 4A 94
Bunce Ct. Rd. ME13: O'den 3G 29
ME17: O'den 3G 29
Bungalows, The CT13: Wdboro 9G 216
ME3: Hoo 8G 67
TN11: Leigh 6M 143
TN30: Tent 9E 224
Bunhill Row EC1 2G 5
Bunkers Hill CT4: Woot, Elham 7K 31
Bunker's Hill CT17: Dover 2F 180
Bunkers Hill DA14: Sidc 8A 58 (7E 6)
DA17: Belv 4B 52
Bunker's Hill TN15: Ash 7A 90 (5A 16)
Bunkers Hill Av. CT17: Dover 3F 180
Bunkers Hill Rd. CT17: Dover 3F 180
Bunkley Mdw. TN26: Hams 3L 191
Bunny Hill DA12: Shorne 2C 78
Bunny La. TN3: Tun W 7D 156 (4J 35)
Bunters Hill Rd. ME3: Cli W, Wain 8L 65 (7G 9)
Bunton St. SE18 3C 50
Burberry La. ME17: Leeds 3B 140 (3B 28)
Burcharbro Rd. SE2 6M 51
Burch Av. CT13: S'wch 6L 217
Burch Rd. DA11: Nflt 4E 62
Burdens TN27: H'crn 8L 191
Burdett Av. DA12: Shorne 9C 64
Burdett Cl. DA14: Sidc 1N 71
Burdett Rd. E3 2J 5
E14 2J 5
TN4: R'hall 1B 156
Burdock Cl. CR0: Croy 2A 82
Burdon La. SM2: Sutt 5C 12
Burford Rd. BR1: Brom 7A 70
SE6 7C 54
Burford's All. CT3: Ash 4D 216
Burford Way CR0: Croy 7F 82
Burgate CT1: Cant 2N 171
Burgate Cl. DA1: Cray 1G 58
Burgate La. CT1: Cant 2N 171
Burgate Ter. TN25: Mers 8M 161
Burges Rd. E6 1B 6
Burgess Cl. CT12: Minst 6F 212
CT16: Whitf 6G 178
Burgess Cotts. ME17: Leeds 3B 140
Burgess Grn. CT14: Hackl 3H 33
Burgess Hall Dr. ME17: Leeds 2B 140
Burgess Pk. 5G 5
Burgess Rd. CT3: Aysm 2D 162
ME2: Strood 5M 79
Burgess Row TN30: Tent 8B 224
Burghclere Dr. ME16: Maid 7M 125
Burghfield Rd. DA13: Ist R 3E 76
BURGH HEATH 7B 12
Burgh Heath Rd. KT17: Eps 6A 12
BURGH HILL 2B 44
Burgh Hill TN19: Etch'm 2A 44
Burghill Rd. SE26 9B 54
Burghley Rd. SW19 1C 12
Burgoyne Ct. ME14: Maid 2C 126
Burgoyne Gro. CT16: Dover 8F 178
Burgoyne Hgts. CT15: Gus 2K 181
BURHAM 1K 109 (5G 17)
BURHAM COMMON 9L 93 (5G 17)
BURHAM COURT 6F 17
Burham Ct. ME1: Burh 1H 109
Burham Crematorium CT4: B'hm 5A 32
Burham Rd. ME1: Woul 4J 93
Burial Ground La. ME15: Maid 7B 126 (2H 27)
Burkestone Cl. ME10: Kems'y 3H 99
Burleigh Av. DA15: Sidc 3H 57
Burleigh Cl. ME2: Strood 4J 79
Burleigh Dr. ME14: Maid 9C 110
Burleigh Rd. TN27: Char'g 3K 175
Burleigh Wlk. SE6 6F 54
Burley Rd. ME10: Sit 7F 98
BURLINGS 8H 101
Burlings La. TN14: Knock 8H 101 (7C 14)
Burlington Cl. BR6: Farnb 3D 84
Burlington Dr. CT6: H Bay 2L 195
Burlington Gdns. CT9: Mgte 5A 208
ME8: Rain 7A 96
Burlington La. W4 5A 4
Burlington Rd. KT3: N Mald 2A 12
Burlington Rd. W. KT3: N Mald 2B 12
Burma Cres. CT1: Cant 1C 172
Burman Cl. DA2: Dart 5C 60
BURMARSH 3B 182 (7F 41)
Burmarsh Cl. ME5: Chat'm 6E 94
Burmarsh Rd. CT21: Hythe 9B 198 (6G 41)
TN29: Dym 3B 182 (7F 41)
Burma Way ME5: Chat'm 5C 94
Burnaby Rd. DA11: Nflt 5D 62
Burnan Rd. CT5: Whits 3L 227
Burnell Av. DA16: Well 9J 51
Burnett Rd. DA8: Erith 6L 53
Burnham Cl. ME10: Sit 3F 98
Burnham Cres. DA1: Dart 2K 59
Burnham Rd. DA1: Dart 2K 59 (6G 7)
DA14: Sidc 7N 57
ME1: Woul 4G 17
Burnham Ter. DA1: Dart 3L 59
Burnham Trad. Est. DA1: Dart 2L 59
Burnham Wlk. ME8: Rain 8A 96
(not continuous)
Burnham Way SE26 1C 68
Burnhill Rd. BR3: Beck'm 5D 68
Burn Mdw. Cotts. ME14: Boxl 7F 110
Burns Av. DA15: Sidc 4K 57
Burns Cl. DA8: Erith 8G 53
DA16: Well 8H 51
Burns Cres. TN9: Tonb 8F 144
Burns Rd. ME7: Gill 5F 80
ME16: Maid 7N 125
Burnt Ash Hgts. BR1: Brom 1L 69
Burnt Ash Hill SE12 4J 55 (6K 5)
(not continuous)
Burnt Ash La. BR1: Brom 3K 69 (1A 14)
Burnt Ash Rd. ME20: Aylfd 1J 125
SE12 3J 55 (6K 5)
Burnt Ho. Cl. ME2: Wain 2N 79
TN18: Sandh 3D 218
Burnt Ho. Hill CT3: Sturry 6N 169 (6A 22)
Burnt Ho. La. DA2: Dart 9M 59
(not continuous)
TN3: Lang G 9N 149 (2H 35)
Burnthouse La. TN27: Smar 9A 222 (1D 38)
Burnt Lodge La. TN5: Tice 7D 36
Burnt Mill Rd. TN27: Eger 5F 29
Burnt Oak La. DA15: Sidc 4J 57
Burnt Oak Ter. ME7: Gill 6F 80
Burnt Oast Rd. ME13: Bou B 3K 165
Burntwick Dr. ME9: Lwr Hal 3L 225
Burntwood Gro. TN13: S'oaks 9J 119
Burntwood La. SW17 7D 4
Burntwood Rd. TN13: S'oaks 1J 131
Burnup Bank ME10: Sit 6K 99
Burrage Gro. SE18 4E 50
Burrage Pl. SE18 5D 50
Burrage Rd. SE18 6E 50 (4C 6)
Burr Bank Ter. DA2: Dart 9K 59
Burr Cl. DA7: Bexhth 1A 58
Burrell Cl. CR0: Croy 9B 68
Burrell Row BR3: Beck'm 5D 68
Burrfield Dr. BR5: St M Cry 8M 71
Burritt M. ME1: Roch 9N 79
Burrow Rd. CT19: F'stone 5L 189
Burrows La. ME3: Lwr Sto 9C 204 (6B 10)
BURRS HILL 2E 36
Burrs, The ME10: Sit 8G 99
Burrstock Way ME8: Rain 1D 96
BURRSWOOD 4F 35
Burrswood Vs. TN3: Groom 6J 155
Bursdon Cl. DA15: Sidc 7H 57
Bursill Cres. CT12: Ram 3F 210
Burslem Rd. TN2: Tun W 8K 151
Bursted Hill CT4: Up Hard 4H 31
Burston Rd. ME17: Cox 6M 137
Burton Cl. CT19: F'stone 4G 189
ME3: Wain 1N 79
Burton Ct. TN12: Pad W 9M 147
Burton Flds. CT6: H Bay 3J 195
Burton Rd. TN24: Kenn 4J 159
Burtons La. TN12: Coll S 7F 27
Burwash Ct. BR5: St M Cry 8L 71
Burwash Rd. SE18 5F 50
Burwood Av. BR2: Shortl 3L 83
Burwood Pk. TN2: Tun W 9L 151
Busbridge Rd. ME6: Snod 3C 108
ME15: Loose 2B 138 (3H 27)
Bush Av. CT12: Ram 3F 210
Bush Cl. ME9: B'gar 5A 114
Bushell Way BR7: Chst 1C 70
Bushey Av. BR5: Pet W 1F 84
BUSHEY CLOSE 4J 165
Bushey Cl. ME13: Bou B 3H 165
Bushey Ct. DA8: Erith 8H 53
(off Hazel Rd.)
Busheyfields Rd. CT6: H Bay 9F 194 (4J 21)
BUSHEY MEAD 2B 12
Bushey Rd. CR0: Croy 3D 82
SW20 2B 12
Bushey Way BR3: Beck'm 9G 68
Bushfield Wlk. DA10: Swans 4L 61
Bushmeadow Rd. ME8: Rain 1B 96
Bushmoor Cres. SE18 7D 50
Bush Rd. ME2: Cux 9E 78 (3E 16)
SE8 4H 5
TN12: E Peck 8K 135 (5D 26)
Bush Row ME20: Aylfd 7L 109
Bushy Gill TN3: Lang G 2A 156
Bushy Gro. ME17: Kgswd 6F 140
Bushy Hill Rd. CT2: Sturry 4H 169 (6K 21)
Bushy Lees DA15: Sidc 4H 57
Bushy Royds TN24: Ashf 3H 161
Bushy Ruff Cotts. CT16: Temp E 9C 178
BUSS'S GREEN 5C 36
Busty La. TN15: Igh 3K 121
Butcher Cl. TN12: S'hrst 3J 223
Butcherfield La. TN7: Hartf 4C 34
Butcher Row E1 3H 5
Butchers Hill DA12: Shorne 1C 78
Butchers La. CT15: Non 4D 32
Butcher's La. ME18: Mere 7J 123 (2C 26)
TN15: Ash, Hart'y 3K 89 (4K 15)
TN35: Gues T 7H 45
Butchers Yd. BR6: Downe 2C 100
(off High St.)
Butcher Wlk. DA10: Swans 5L 61
Butchery La. CT1: Cant 2M 171
Butchery, The CT13: S'wch 5M 217
Butler's Hill ME13: Hernh, Darg 6D 20
Butler's Pl. TN15: New A 4L 89
Buttercup Cl. TN12: Pad W 1M 153
Butterfly La. SE9 4D 56
Butterly Av. DA1: Dart 7N 59
Buttermere ME13: Fav 6J 187
Buttermere Cl. CT19: F'stone 5H 189
ME7: Gill 7J 81
Buttermere Gdns. CT3: Aysm 1D 162
Buttermere Rd. BR5: St P 7M 71
Butternut Copse TN23: Ashf 7B 158
Butterside Rd. TN23: Kgnt 5G 161
Butter St. CT15: Non 3F 162 (4C 32)
Butterwell Hill TN8: Cowd 2D 34
Butt Fld. Rd. TN23: Ashf 1C 160
Butt Grn. La. ME17: Lint 9C 138 (5H 27)
Butt Haw Cl. ME3: Hoo 8H 67
Buttmarsh Cl. SE18 5D 50
Button Dr. ME3: Lwr Sto 7C 204
Button Ho. ME3: C'den 7B 66
Button La. ME15: Bear 7L 127
Button St. BR8: Swanl 5K 73 (2G 15)
Butts Ct. CT4: Lwr Har 3H 31
Butts Hill ME13: Bou B 1J 165 (6C 20)
Butts Ho. CT1: Cant 1N 171
(off Artillery St.)
Butts La. SS17: Stan H 2E 8
BUTTSOLE 2F 33
Butts Rd. BR1: Brom 1H 69
Butts, The CT4: Elham 6N 183
CT13: S'wch 5L 217
ME10: Sit 7G 99
TN14: Otf 7J 103
Buttway La. ME3: Cliffe 2B 176 (5G 9)
Buxton Cl. ME5: Chat'm 1G 110
ME15: Maid 9D 126
Buxton La. CR3: Cat'm 7G 13
Buxton Rd. CT12: Ram 2F 210
DA8: Erith 7E 52
BYBROOK 5H 159 (7A 30)
Bybrook Ct. TN24: Kenn 6G 159
Bybrook Fld. CT20: S'gte 8E 188
Bybrook Rd. TN24: Kenn 6H 159 (7A 30)
Bybrook Way CT20: S'gte 7E 188
Bychurch Pl. ME15: Maid 6D 126
Bycliffe Ter. DA11: Grav'nd 5E 62
Bycroft St. SE20 3A 68
Bygrove CR0: Croy 7E 82
Bylands Cl. SE2 3K 51
Byllan Rd. CT17: Dover 1D 180
Byng Rd. TN4: Tun W 9E 150
Bynon Av. DA7: Bexhth 1A 58
Byrneside TN11: Hild 3E 144
Byron Av. CT9: Mgte 4D 208
Byron Cl. CT1: Cant 3B 172
SE26 9B 54
SE28 1L 51
Byron Cres. CT16: Dover 9G 178
Byron Dr. DA8: Erith 7C 52
Byron Ho. DA1: Cray 3F 58
Byron Rd. DA1: Dart 2B 60
ME7: Gill 9F 80
ME14: Pen H 2E 126
Bysing Wood Rd. ME13: Fav 3D 186 (5A 20)
ME13: Lud'm, Fav 4C 186 (6K 19)
Bythorne Ct. ME8: Rain 2D 96
Bywater Ho. SE18 3A 50
Bywood Av. CR0: Croy 9A 68

C

Cabbage Stalk La. TN4: Tun W 3E 156
Cables Cl. DA17: Erith 3D 52
Cable St. E1 3H 5
Cacket's La. TN14: Cud 6F 100 (7C 14)
Cacketts Cotts. TN16: Bras 8L 117
CACKLE STREET
Robertsbridge 6A 44
Rye 6G 45
Cackle St. TN31: Brede 6G 45
Cade La. TN13: S'oaks 1K 131
Cade Rd. TN23: Ashf 2F 160
Cades Orchard ME13: Osp 9C 186
Cades Rd. TN26: Hoth 1M 197 (7J 29)
Cadlocks Hill TN14: Hals 1A 102 (5E 14)
Cadnam Cl. CT2: Cant 8L 167
ME2: Strood 4J 79
Cadogan Av. DA2: Dart 5D 60
Cadogan Cl. BR3: Beck'm 4G 69
Cadogan Gdns. TN1: Tun W 1H 157
Cadogan Rd. SE18 3E 50
Cadogan Ter. E9 1J 5
Cadwallon Rd. SE9 7D 56
Caerleon Cl. DA14: Sidc 1L 71
Caerleon Ter. SE2 4K 51
Caernarvon Dr. ME15: Maid 8C 126
Caernarvon Gdns. CT10: B'stairs 8M 209
Caesar Av. TN23: Ashf 4D 160
Caesars Way CT19: F'stone 4E 188
CAGE GREEN 2J 145 (5K 25)
Cage Grn. Rd. TN10: Tonb 2J 145
Cage La. TN27: Smar 9B 222 (1D 38)
Cagney Cl. ME3: Wain 2N 79
Cairndale Cl. BR1: Brom 3J 69
Cairns Cl. DA1: Dart 3L 59
Cairns M. SE18 8A 50
Cairo New Rd. CR0: Croy 4G 13
Caister Rd. TN9: Tonb 6G 145
Caithness Gdns. DA15: Sidc 4H 57
Calais Cotts. DA3: Fawk 3G 88
Calais Hill CT2: T Hill 5K 167 (6G 21)
CALCOTT 1D 168 (5J 21)
Calcott Hill CT3: Sturry 1D 168 (5J 21)
Calcott Wlk. SE9 9A 56
Calcraft M. CT1: Cant 9A 168
Calcroft Av. DA9: G'hithe 3J 61
Calcutta Ho. ME15: Maid 3H 139
Calcutta Rd. RM18: Tilb 5C 8
Caldbec Hill TN33: Batt 7C 44
Caldecote Cl. ME8: Rain 2D 96
Caldecot La. TN29: Lydd 1K 205 (4H 47)
Calder Rd. ME14: Maid 2B 126
Calderwood DA12: Grav'nd 1K 77
Calderwood St. SE18 4C 50
(not continuous)
Caldew Av. ME8: Gill 2M 95
Caldew Gro. ME10: Sit 8J 99
Caldy Rd. DA17: Belv 3C 52
Caledonian Ct. ME8: Gill 3A 96
Caledonian Rd. N1 2F 5
N7 1F 5
Caledonian Road
& Barnsbury Station (Rail) 1F 5
Caledonian Road Station (Tube) 1F 5
Caledon Ter. CT1: Cant 3N 171
Calehill Cl. ME14: Maid 3F 126
Calehill Rd. TN27: L Char 6H 29
Caley Rd. TN2: Tun W 6K 151
Calfstock La. DA4: Farn'm 7N 73
Calgary Cres. CT19: F'stone 3L 189
Calgary Ter. CT16: Dover 1G 181
(off Alberta Cl.)
Caling Cft. DA3: New A 2M 89
(not continuous)
Caliph Cl. DA12: Grav'nd 8L 63
Callaghan Cl. SE13 2H 55
Callams Cl. ME8: Gill 5N 95
Calland TN25: Sme 8J 165
Callander Rd. SE6 7E 54
Callaways La. ME9: N'tn 5K 97 (4C 18)
Callenders Cotts. DA17: Erith 2E 52
Calleywell La. TN25: Aldtn 4D 40
Callis Ct. Rd. CT10: B'stairs 7K 209 (2K 23)
Callis Way ME8: Gill 6N 95
Calmont Rd. BR1: Brom 2G 69 (1K 13)
Calonne Rd. SW19 1B 12
Calshot Ct. DA2: Dart 4B 60
(off Osbourne Rd.)
Calthorpe St. WC1 2F 5
Calton Av. SE21 6G 5
Calverden Rd. CT12: Ram 3E 210
Calverley Cl. BR3: Beck'm 2E 68
Calverley Ct. TN1: Tun W 1H 157
Calverley Pk. TN1: Tun W 2H 157
Calverley Pk. Cres. TN1: Tun W 2H 157
Calverley Pk. Gdns. TN1: Tun W 1H 157 (3K 35)
Calverley Rd. TN1: Tun W 1H 157 (3K 35)
(not continuous)
Calverley Row TN1: Tun W 1H 157
Calverley St. TN1: Tun W 1H 157
Calvert Cl. DA14: Sidc 2N 71
DA17: Belv 4B 52
Calvert Dr. DA5: Bex'y 7E 58
Calvin Cl. BR5: St P 6M 71
CAMBER 6D 46
Camberbourne Rd. TN25: Mers 4C 40
Camber Castle 6B 46
Camber Rd. TN31: E Guld, Camb 5B 46
Cambert Way SE3 2L 55
CAMBERWELL 5G 5
Camberwell Chu. St. SE5 5G 5
CAMBERWELL GREEN 5G 5
Camberwell Grn. SE5 5G 5
Camberwell La. TN14: Ide H 3A 130
Camberwell New Rd. SE5 5F 5
Camberwell Rd. SE5 5G 5
Camborne Mnr. ME7: Gill 6F 80
Camborne Rd. DA14: Sidc 8L 57
DA16: Well 9G 51
Cambourne Av. CT8: Wgte S 3J 207
Cambrai Ct. CT1: Cant 1C 172
Cambray Rd. BR6: Orp 1H 85
Cambria Av. ME1: Roch 1K 93
Cambria Cl. DA15: Sidc 6F 56
Cambria Cres. DA12: Grav'nd 9K 63
Cambria Ho. DA8: Erith 7F 52
(off Larner Rd.)
Cambrian Cotts. CT11: Ram 6H 211

Cambrian Gro.—Castle Cl.

Cambrian Gro. DA11: Grav'nd .5F 62
Cambrian Rd. TN4: Tun W .7J 151
Cambridge Av. CT13: S'wch .1J 33
DA16: Well .2H 57
Cambridge Barracks Rd. SE18 .4B 50
Cambridge Cl. CT7: Birch .4G 206
Cambridge Cres. ME15: Maid .1G 138
Cambridge Dr. SE12 .3K 55
Cambridge Gdns. CT20: F'stone .6K 189
TN2: Tun W .3H 157
W10 .2C 4
Cambridge Grn. SE9 .6D 56
Cambridge Heath Rd. E1 .2H 5
E2 .2H 5
Cambridge Heath Station (Rail) .2H 5
Cambridge Ho. ME15: Maid .1G 139
Cambridge Rd. BR1: Brom .3K 69
CT1: Cant .3M 171
CT14: Walm .7N 177
CT17: Dover .6J 181
DA14: Sidc .9G 57
KT1: King T .2A 12
ME2: Strood .4L 79
ME8: Gill .5M 95
ME9: Lyn .9J 223 (6H 19)
ME10: Sit .8J 99
ME13: Fav .6F 186
SS0: Wclf S .1D 10
SW11 .5D 4
Cambridge Row SE18 .5D 50
Cambridge St. TN2: Tun W .2J 157
Cambridge Ter. CT9: Mgte .4F 208
CT16: Dover .5K 181
CT20: F'stone .6L 189
ME4: Chat'm .8C 80
Cambridge Way CT1: Cant .4M 171
Camdale Rd. SE18 .7H 51
Camden Av. TN2: Pem .8B 152
Camden Cl. BR7: Chst .4E 70
DA11: Nflt .6B 62
ME5: Chat'm .6E 94
Camden Ct. DA17: Belv .5B 52
TN1: Tun W .1H 157
TN2: Pem .8C 152
Camden Cres. CT16: Dover .5K 181
Camden Gro. BR7: Chst .2D 70
Camden High St. NW1 .2E 4
CAMDEN HILL .1B 222 (3K 37)
Camden Hill TN2: Tun W .2H 157
CAMDEN PARK .3J 157 (3K 35)
Camden Pk. TN2: Tun W .3J 157
(not continuous)
Camden Pk. Rd. BR7: Chst .3B 70
NW1 .1E 4
Camden Rd. CT10: B'stairs .6J 209
CT11: Ram .6J 211
DA5: Bex'y .6N 57
ME7: Gill .5G 80
N7 .1F 5
NW1 .1E 4
TN1: Tun W .1H 157 (3K 35)
TN13: S'oaks .4J 119
Camden Road Station (Rail) .1E 4
Camden Sq. CT11: Ram .5J 211
Camden St. ME14: Maid .4D 126
NW1 .1E 4
Camden Ter. TN15: Seal .3N 119
TN24: W'boro .9J 159
CAMDEN TOWN .2E 4
Camden Town Station (Tube) .1E 4
Camden Way BR7: Chst .3B 70
Camellia Cl. CT9: Mgte .3N 207
ME8: Gill .4N 95
Camelot Cl. SE28 .2F 50
TN16: Big H .4C 164
Camel Rd. E16 .1A 50
CAMER .3C 16
Camer Gdns. DA13: Meop .9H 77
Cameron Cl. DA5: Bex'y .8F 58
ME5: Chat'm .3E 94
Cameron Ct. CT17: Dover .6F 180
Cameron Rd. BR2: Shortl .8K 69
SE6 .7C 54
Camerons TN18: Hawkh .5D 192
(off Heartenoak Rd.)
Cameron Ter. SE12 .8L 55
Camer Pk. (Country Pk.) .1H 91 (3C 16)
Camer Pk. Rd. DA13: Meop .1G 91 (3C 16)
Camer Rd.
DA13: Meop, Sole S .9G 77 (3C 16)
Camer St. DA13: Meop .9H 77
Camlan Rd. BR1: Brom .9J 55
Camomile Dr. ME14: Weav .4J 127
Campbell Cl. CT6: H Bay .4K 195
SE18 .8C 50
Campbell Rd. CT14: Walm .6N 177
DA11: Grav'nd .6E 62
E3 .2J 5
ME15: Maid .6D 126
TN4: Tun W .8G 150
Campden Hill Rd. W8 .3C 4
Camperdown Mnr. ME7: Gill .6D 80
(off River St.)
Campfield CT6: H Bay .2J 195
Campfield Rd. SE9 .5N 55
SS3: Shoe .1G 11
Camp Hill TN11: Chid .5G 142 (6F 25)
Camping and Caravanning Club
CT3: Cant .2D 172
Campion Cl. DA11: Nflt .9D 62
ME5: Chat'm .8B 94
Campion Cres. TN17: Cran .5H 37
Campion Pl. SE28 .1J 51
Campleshon Rd. ME8: Gill .6N 95
Campshill Pl. SE13 .3F 54
Campshill Rd. SE13 .3F 54
Campus Way ME8: Gill .3K 95
Camp Way ME15: Maid .1F 138
Camrose Av. DA8: Erith .6C 52
Camrose Cl. CR0: Croy .1B 82
Camrose St. SE2 .5J 51
Canada Cl. CT19: F'stone .5C 188
Canada Farm Rd. DA2: Dart .7G 75
DA3: Fawk .7G 75 (3K 15)
Canada Farm Rd. DA4: S Dar .7G 75 (2K 15)
Canada Gdns. SE13 .3F 54
Canada Rd. CT14: Walm .6M 177
DA8: Erith .7J 53
Canada Ter. ME14: Maid .2D 126
Canada Water Station (Tube) .4H 5
CANADIA .7C 44
Canadian Av. ME7: Gill .8H 81 (3K 17)
SE6 .6E 54 (7J 5)
Canal Basin DA12: Grav'nd .4J 63
CANAL BRIDGE .5H 5
Canal Ind. Pk. DA12: Grav'nd .4J 63
Canal Rd. DA12: Grav'nd .4H 63 (6C 8)
ME2: Strood .5N 79
ME3: High'm .5E 64 (7F 9)
Canary Wharf Station (DLR) .3J 5
Canary Wharf Station (Tube) .3J 5
Canberra Gdns. ME10: Sit .7D 98
Canberra Rd. DA7: Bexhth .6M 51
SE7 .6A 50 (5A 6)
Canbury Path BR5: St M Cry .7J 71
Candlers Way CT4: Chart'm .9F 170
Canfield Gdns. NW6 .1C 4
Canham Rd. SE25 .2G 13
CANN HALL .1K 5
Cann Hall Rd. E11 .1K 5
Canning St. ME14: Maid .3D 126
CANNING TOWN .3K 5
CANNING TOWN .3K 5
Canning Town Station (Rail, DLR & Tube) .3K 5
Cannizaro Rd. SW19 .1B 12
Cannonbury Rd. CT11: Ram .6H 211
Cannongate Av. CT21: Hythe .5L 199
Cannongate Cl. CT21: Hythe .6M 199
Cannongate Gdns. CT21: Hythe .5M 199
Cannongate Rd. CT21: Hythe .5L 199 (5J 41)
Cannon La. ME18: W'bury .2E 26
TN9: Tonb .5K 145 (6K 25)
Cannon Pl. SE7 .5A 50
Cannon Rd. CT11: Ram .5H 211
DA7: Bexhth .8N 51
Cannon St. CT14: Deal .3M 177
CT16: Dover .5J 181
EC4 .3G 5
TN28: New R .2K 213
TN29: Lydd .3K 205 (5H 47)
Cannon St. Rd. E1 .3H 5
Cannon Street Station (Rail & Tube) .3G 5
Cannon Wlk. DA12: Grav'nd .5H 63
(off Albert Murray Cl.)
Canon Appleton Ct. CT1: Cant .3L 171
CANONBURY .1G 5
Canonbury Pk. Nth. N1 .1G 5
Canonbury Rd. N1 .1F 5
Canonbury Station (Rail) .1G 5
Canon Cl. ME1: Roch .1M 93
Canon Grn. CT3: Wing .8J 225
Canon La. ME18: W'bury .7A 124
Canon Rd. BR1: Brom .6M 69
Canons Ga. Rd. CT16: Dover .4K 181
Canon's Wlk. CR0: Croy .4A 82
Canon Woods Way TN24: Kenn .4K 159
Cansiron La. RH19: A'hstw .4B 34
TN8: Cowd .3C 34
CANTERBURY .2M 171 (1H 31)
Canterbury Av. DA15: Sidc .7K 57
Canterbury Bus. Cen., The CT1: Cant .2M 171
Canterbury Castle .3M 171
Canterbury Christ Church University College
Canterbury Campus .2N 171
Westwood Campus .9G 208
Canterbury City F.C.
(Kingsmead Stadium) .9N 167
Canterbury City Retail Pk. CT1: Cant .7C 168
Canterbury Cl. BR3: Beck'm .4E 68
CT10: B'stairs .8H 209
CT19: F'stone .5L 189
(off Canterbury Rd.)
DA1: Dart .5A 60
Canterbury Ct. SE12 .8L 55
TN24: Ashf .8H 159
Canterbury Cres. TN10: Tonb .2K 145
Canterbury East Station (Rail) .3M 171 (1H 31)
Canterbury Environment Cen. CT1: Cant .1M 171
(off St Alphege La.)
Canterbury Hill CT2: T Hill .6L 167 (6H 21)
Canterbury Ho. DA8: Erith .7G 53
ME15: Maid .1G 138
Canterbury Ind. Pk. CT3: Hersd .2L 169
Canterbury La. CT1: Cant .2N 171
ME8: Rain .1E 96 (3B 18)
TN25: H'lgh .7E 30
Canterbury Rd. CR0: Croy .3F 13
CT3: L'brne .2G 173 (1K 31)
(Swanton La.)
CT3: L'brne, Bram, Wing .3M 173 (1A 32)
(Lanargate St.)
CT3: Wing .8H 225
CT4: B'hm, Woot .5A 32
CT4: Chart'm, Chil'm .8L 175 (3D 30)
CT4: Mol .8A 174 (4K 29)
CT4: O'nge, Elham .9L 183 (2J 41)
CT5: Whits .5F 226 (4F 21)
CT6: H Bay .5H 195 (4J 21)
(Herne Rd.)
CT6: H Bay .4H 195 (3J 21)
(Thanet Way)
CT6: H Bay .8F 195 (4J 21)
(Bullockstone Rd.)
CT6: Sturry .5J 21
(Hicks Forstall Rd.)
CT7: St N .9M 215
CT7: St N, Birch .8A 206 (4D 22)
CT8: Birch, Wgte S .3J 207 (2F 23)
CT9: Mgte .3M 207 (2G 23)
CT15: Lyd'n .7D 32
CT15: S'fld .4K 193
CT18: D'sole, H'nge .4K 193 (2A 42)
CT18: Etch'l .1M 185 (3J 41)
CT18: Lym'ge, O'nge .6L 205 (2J 41)
CT19: H'nge .2J 189 (3B 42)
DA12: Grav'nd .7H 63
ME10: Sit .8J 99 (5F 19)
(not continuous)
Canterbury Rd. ME13: Bou B .8N 187 (7C 20)
ME13: Fav .6H 187 (6A 20)
TN2: Pem .8D 152
TN24: Ashf .3J 161 (2B 40)
(Monument Way)
TN24: Ashf .7G 158 (1A 40)
(North St.)
TN24: Kenn .6H 159 (1A 40)
(Rylands Rd.)
TN25: Bra L, E Bra .8K 165 (2E 40)
(Brabourne Lees)
TN25: Bra L, Stow .2F 41
(Brabourne)
TN25: C'lck, Char'g .8A 174 (4J 29)
TN25: Char'g,C'lck .1N 175 (4J 29)
TN25: Kenn, Bou A, Wye .7F 158 (1A 40)
TN27: Char'g .1N 175
Canterbury Rd. E. CT11: Ram .4H 23
CT12: Ram .5D 210 (4H 23)
Canterbury Rd. W. CT12: C'snd .5A 210 (4H 23)
Canterbury St. ME7: Gill .7F 80 (2J 17)
Canterbury Tales
Vis. Attraction, The (Mus.) .2M 171
Canterbury West Station (Rail) .1M 171 (7H 21)
Cantwell Rd. SE18 .7D 50
Canute Rd. CT7: Birch .3C 206
CT14: Deal .1M 177
ME13: Fav .6G 186
Canute Wlk. CT14: Deal .1M 177
CANVEY ISLAND .2K 9
Canvey Rd. SS8: Can I .2J 9
CANVEY VILLAGE .2K 9
Canvey Way SS8: Can I .1J 9
Cape Cotts. ME15: Loose .3C 138
CAPEL .9E 146 (7B 26)
Capelands DA3: New A .3N 89
Capel Cl. BR2: Shortl .2A 84
CT10: B'stairs .4K 209
ME8: Gill .7M 95
TN23: Ashf .9D 158
Capel Ct. Pk. CT18: Cap F .2C 174
CAPEL CROSS .8E 196 (2F 37)
Capell Cl. ME17: Cox .5N 137
CAPEL-LE-FERNE .2C 174 (3C 42)
Capel Pl. DA2: Dart .9K 59
Capel Rd. CT4: P'hm .4F 31
E7 .1A 6
E12 .1A 6
ME10: Sit .8F 98
ME13: Fav .5F 186
TN26: Hams .5K 39
Capel St. CT15: Hou .3C 42
CT18: Cap F .2B 174 (3C 42)
(Cauldham La.)
CT18: Cap F .3B 174 (3C 42)
(Sea Vw. Cl.)
Capel Ter. SS1: Sth S .1E 10
Capetown Ho. ME15: Maid .3J 139
Capital Ind. Est. DA17: Belv .3C 52
Capstan Ct. DA2: Dart .2C 60
Capstan M. DA11: Nflt .5D 62
Capstan Row CT14: Deal .3N 177
CAPSTONE .4J 17
Capstone Farm Country Pk. .5G 95 (4J 17)
Capstone Farm Country Pk. Vis. Cen. .4G 94
Capstone Rd. BR1: Brom .9J 55
ME5: Chat'm, Hals .2F 94 (3J 17)
ME7: Chat'm, Gill .3G 95 (3J 17)
Captain's Cl. ME17: Sut V .5A 28
Captains Ct. CT21: Hythe .7K 199
Captain Webb Memorial .5K 181
(off Marine Pde)
Cardens Rd. ME3: Cli W .5M 65
Cardiff St. SE18 .7G 50
Cardigan Cl. ME3: H Hals .2J 67
Cardinal Cl. BR7: Chst .4F 70
ME12: Minst .5L 221
TN9: Tonb .7K 145
Cardinal Wlk. ME19: W Mal .6N 123
Cardine Cl. ME10: Sit .4F 98
Cardinham Rd. BR6: Chels .5H 85
Carey Cl. TN28: New R .3K 213
Carey Ct. DA6: Bexhth .3C 58
Carey Ho. CT1: Cant .3M 171
(off Station Rd. E.)
Carey's Fld. TN13: Dun G .2F 118
Carholme Rd. SE23 .6C 54
CARING .8N 127 (2A 28)
Caring Farm Cotts. ME17: Leeds .8N 127
Caring La. ME14: Bear .9N 127 (2A 28)
ME17: Leeds, Bear .9N 127 (2A 28)
Caring Rd. ME15: Leeds .7M 127 (2A 28)
ME17: Leeds .2A 28
Carisbrooke Av. DA5: Bex'y .6M 57
Carisbrooke Ct. DA2: Dart .4B 60
(off Osbourne Rd.)
Carisbrooke Dr. ME16: Maid .4A 126
Carisbrooke Rd. BR2: Shortl .7M 69
ME2: Strood .3J 79
Carl Ekman Ho. DA11: Nflt .5C 62
Carleton Pl. DA4: Hort K .7C 74
Carleton Rd. DA1: Dart .5A 60
Carlisle Cl. ME2: Strood .6G 79
Carlisle Ho. ME15: Maid .1G 139
Carlisle Rd. DA1: Dart .4A 60
Carlsden Cl. CT17: Dover .1F 180
Carlton Av. CT10: B'stairs .8L 209
CT11: Ram .6H 211
DA9: G'hithe .4E 60
ME7: Gill .8H 81
ME12: S'ness .3C 220
Carlton Cinema .2K 207
Carlton Cl. ME19: W Mal .6N 123
TN10: Tonb .9K 133
Carlton Cres. ME5: Chat'm .3G 94
TN1: Tun W .1J 157
Carlton Gdns. ME15: Maid .9D 126
Carlton Grn. DA14: Sidc .9H 57
Carlton Hill CT6: H Bay .3D 194
Carlton Leas CT20: F'stone .7J 189
Carlton Mans. CT9: Clift .2E 208
Carlton Pde. BR6: St M Cry .1K 85
TN13: S'oaks .4K 119
Carlton Ri. CT8: Wgte S .3H 207
Carlton Rd. CR2: S Croy .5G 13
CT5: Whits .1D 166
CT14: Kgdn .3E 200
DA8: Erith .6C 52 (5E 6)
DA14: Sidc .1H 71
DA16: Well .1K 57
TN1: Tun W .1J 157
TN23: Ashf .7E 158
Carlton Rd. E. CT8: Wgte S .3J 207
Carlton Rd. W. CT8: Wgte S .3H 207
Carlton Va. NW6 .2C 4
Carlyle Av. BR1: Brom .6N 69
Carlyle Rd. SE28 .1L 51 (3D 6)
Carlys Cl. BR3: Beck'm .5A 68
Carman's Cl. ME15: Loose .6B 138
Carmel Ct. CT7: Birch .3E 206
(off Gainsborough Rd.)
Carmelite Way DA3: Hart'y .8M 75
Carmichael Rd. SE25 .2H 13
Carmine Ct. BR1: Brom .3J 69
Carnatation Cl. ME19: E Mal .9E 108
Carnation Cres. ME19: E Mal .1D 124
Carnation Dr. ME2: Strood .5H 79
Carnation Rd. ME2: Strood .5H 79
Carnation St. SE2 .5K 51
Carn Brea CT9: Mgte .3D 208
Carnbrook Rd. SE3 .1N 55
Carnecke Gdns. SE9 .3A 56
Carnet Cl. DA1: Cray .5F 58
Carnoustie Cl. CT5: Whits .5N 227
Caroland Cl. TN25: Sme .8J 165
Caroland Vs. TN25: Sme .9J 165
Caroline Cl. CT5: Whits .7D 226
Caroline Ct. SE6 .9G 54
Caroline Cres. CT10: B'stairs .7J 209
ME16: Alltn .2A 126
Caroline Sq. CT9: Mgte .2D 208
Carolyn Dr. BR6: Chels .4J 85
Carp Cl. ME20: Lark .6E 108
Carpeaux Cl. ME4: Chat'm .8D 80
Carpenters Arms Path SE9 .4B 56
Carpenters Cl. ME1: Roch .1B 94
Carpenters La. TN11: Hdlw .5B 134 (4B 26)
Carpenter's Rd. E15 .1J 5
Carpinus Cl. ME5: Chat'm .1E 110
Carrack Ho. DA8: Erith .5F 52
(off Saltford Cl.)
Carr Gro. SE18 .4A 50
Carr Ho. DA1: Cray .3F 58
Carriage M. CT2: Cant .1M 171
Carriage St. SE18 .3D 50
Carriage Way, The TN16: Bras .6M 117
Carrick Cl. TN10: Tonb .9L 133
Carrick Dr. TN13: S'oaks .5J 119
Carriers Pl. TN3: Blkm .1C 154
Carriers Rd. TN17: Cran .7D 176
Carrill Way DA17: Belv .3M 51
Carrington Cl. CR0: Croy .1B 82
ME7: Gill .6J 81
Carrington Rd. DA1: Dart .4N 59
Carroll Cl. ME2: Hall'g .7E 92
Carroll Gdns. ME20: Lark .7D 108
Carronade Pl. SE28 .3F 50
Carroway's Pl. CT9: Mgte .3D 208
Carrs Cnr. TN1: Tun W .1H 157
CARSHALTON .4E 12
CARSHALTON BEECHES .5D 12
Carshalton Beeches Station (Rail) .5D 12
CARSHALTON ON THE HILL .5D 12
Carshalton Pk. Rd. SM5: Cars .5D 12
Carshalton Rd. CR4: Mitc .3E 12
SM1: Sutt .4D 12
SM5: Cars .4D 12
SM7: Bans .6D 12
Carshalton Station (Rail) .4D 12
Carsington Gdns. DA1: Dart .7L 59
Carstairs Rd. SE6 .8F 54
Carston Cl. SE12 .3J 55
Carswell Rd. SE6 .5F 54
Carter Av. TN15: W King .8D 88
Carter La. TN29: B'lnd .2E 46
Carter Rd. CT4: Bek .7J 173 (2A 32)
CARTER'S HILL .1B 132 (3H 25)
Carter's Hill TN15: Under .3B 132 (4H 25)
Carters Hill Cl. SE9 .6M 55
Carter's Hill La. DA13: Meop .9E 90
Carters La. SE23 .7B 54
Carters Rd. CT20: F'stone .6F 188
Carters Row DA11: Nflt .6E 62
Carters Wood TN26: Hams .3L 191
Cartmel Rd. DA7: Bexhth .8B 52
Carton Cl. ME1: Roch .1A 94
Carton Rd. ME3: High'm .1F 78
Cartridge Pl. SE18 .3D 50
Cartwright Cl. CT3: Ash .4B 216
Carville Av. TN4: S'bgh .5F 150
Carvoran Way ME8: Gill .6M 95
Cascade Cl. BR5: St P .6L 71
Cascades Leisure Cen. .9M 63
Caslocke St. ME13: Fav .5G 186
Caspian Way DA10: Swans .3L 61
Cassilda Rd. SE2 .4J 51
Cassino Sq. CT15: Gus .2K 181
Cassland Rd. E9 .1H 5
Casslee Rd. SE6 .5C 54
Casstine Cl. BR8: Swanl .3G 72
Castalia Cotts. CT14: Walm .7N 177
(off Cambridge Rd.)
Castalia Ct. DA1: Dart .1N 59
CASTELNAU .5B 4
Castelnau SW13 .5B 4
Casterbridge Rd. SE3 .1K 55
Castile Rd. SE18 .4C 50
Castillon Rd. SE6 .7H 55
Castlands Rd. SE6 .7C 54
Castleacres Ind. Pk. ME10: Sit .5J 99
Castle Av. CT10: B'stairs .7M 209
CT16: Dover .3J 181
CT21: Hythe .5J 199
ME1: Roch .8N 79
Castle Bay CT20: S'gte .8C 188
Castle Cl. BR2: Shortl .6H 69
CT20: S'gte .8F 188
CT21: Lymp .6A 198

Castlecombe Rd.—Chapel Rd.

Castlecombe Rd. SE9 9A 56
Castle Cotts. TN25: Westw 2D 158
Castle Ct. SE26 9B 54
Castle Cres. CT21: Salt 4K 199
Castle Dean ME14: Maid 1B 126
Castle Dr. CT16: Whitf 7E 178
TN15: Kems'g 8M 103
Castle Farm Rd. TN14: S'ham 9G 87 (5F 15)
Castlefields DA13: Ist R 4E 76
TN7: Hartf 5E 34
TN9: Tonb 5H 145
Castle Fine Arts Studio 4K 181
(off Castle St.)
Castleford Av. SE9 6D 56
CASTLE HILL 1E 36
Castle Hill CT19: F'stone 3G 188
DA3: Fawk, Hart'y 8K 75 (3K 15)
ME1: Roch 6N 79
ME14: T'hm 1N 127 (7A 18)
Castle Hill Av. CR0: Croy 9E 82
CT20: F'stone 6J 189 (4B 42)
Castle Hill Court 6N 79
(off Castle Hill)
Castle Hill Pas. CT20: F'stone 6J 189
Castle Hill Rd. CT16: Dover 3K 181 (2G 43)
Castle La. DA12: Grav'nd 7N 63 (7D 8)
Castlemaine Av. ME7: Gill 6J 81
Castle Mayne Av. CT7: Wdchu 8L 207
Castlemere Av. ME11: Queen 7C 220
Castle M. CT14: Deal 7L 177
Castlemount Ct. CT16: Dover 4K 181
Castlemount Rd. CT16: Dover 3J 181
Castle Point Transport Mus. 2A 10
Castle Rd. CR5: Chip 7D 12
CT5: Whits 3G 227 (3F 21)
CT13: S'wch 1K 217
CT20: S'gte 8F 188
CT21: Hythe, Salt 4J 199 (5H 41)
DA4: Eyns 7J 87 (5G 15)
DA10: Swans 4M 61
ME4: Chat'm 1D 94 (3J 17)
ME10: Sit 7H 99 (4F 19)
ME16: Alltn 2N 125 (1H 27)
TN4: Tun W 3G 156
Castle Rd. Bus. Pct. ME10: Sit 5J 99
Castle Rd. Technical Cen. ME10: Sit 6J 99
Castle Rough La. ME10: Kems'y 2G 99
Castle Row CT1: Cant 3M 171
Castle St. CT1: Cant 3M 171
CT16: Dover 5J 181
DA9: G'hithe 3G 60
DA10: Swans 4M 61
ME1: Woul 7G 92
ME2: Upnor 3B 80 (1H 17)
ME11: Queen 7B 220
TN1: Tun W 3G 157
TN4: S'bgh 4F 150
TN9: Tonb 5H 145
TN24: Ashf 8F 158
Castle Ter. TN11: Hdlw 8D 134
TN18: Hawkh 4C 192
Castle, The CT5: Whits 2G 227
Castleton Av. DA7: Bexhth 8E 52
Castleton Cl. CR0: Croy 9B 68
Castleton Rd. SE9 9N 55
Castle Vw. TN11: Hdlw 8D 134
Castle Vw. Bus. Cen. ME1: Roch 6A 80
Castleview Ct. CT17: Dover 3G 180
Castle Vw. Rd. ME2: Strood 5K 79
Castle Wlk. CT14: Deal 1N 177
Castle Way ME19: Leyb 9B 108 (7E 16)
Castlewood Dr. SE9 9B 50
Catamaran Yacht Club 2G 220
Caterbury Rd. CT18: Acr, S'fld 2A 42
Caterfield La. RH7: Ling 6A 24
RH8: Oxt 6A 24
Caterham Rd. SE13 1G 54
CATFORD 5E 54 (7J 5)
Catford Bridge Station (Rail) 5D 54 (7J 5)
Catford B'way. SE6 5E 54
CATFORD GYRATORY 5E 54 (7J 5)
Catford Hill SE6 6C 54 (7J 5)
Catford Island SE6 5E 54
Catford M. SE6 5E 54
Catford Rd. SE6 5D 54 (7J 5)
Catford Stadium (Greyhound) 4D 54
Catford Station (Rail) 5D 54 (7J 5)
Catford Trad. Est. SE6 7E 54
Cathall Rd. E11 1K 5
Cathcart Dr. BR6: Orp 3G 84
Catherine Cl. ME16: Barm 6L 125
Catherine Howard Ct. SE9 4F 56
Catherine of Aragon Ct. SE9 4E 56
Catherine Parr Ct. SE9 4E 56
Catherine Pl. TN1: Tun W 1H 157
Catherine St. ME1: Roch 9A 80 (3H 17)
Catherine Way CT10: B'stairs 7L 209
Catkin Cl. ME5: Chat'm 1C 110
Catling Cl. SE23 8A 54
Catlyn Cl. ME19: E Mal 1E 124
Cator La. BR3: Beck'm 4C 68
Cator Rd. SE26 2A 68
Catsfield Rd. TN33: Batt 7A 44
Catsole Hill CT3: Good 2C 32
Cat St. TN7: Cole H, Up Hart 5C 34
Catterick Rd. ME5: Chat'm 9G 94
Cattistock Rd. SE9 1A 70
Cattle Mkt. CT13: S'wch 5L 217
Catts Hill TN6: Town R, Mark C 7C 35
Catt's Hill TN30: Ston C E 2B 46
Catt's Wood Rd. CT4: Up Hard, Lwr Har 4H 31
Cauldham Cl. CT18: Cap F 3B 174
Cauldham La. CT18: Cap F 2B 174 (3C 43)
Caulfield Rd. SS3: Shoe 1G 11
Caulkers Ho. ME4: Chat'm 1E 94
(off Shipwrights Av.)
Causeway Cotts. TN11: Chid 5G 142
Causeway, The CT1: Cant 1M 171 (7H 21)
CT13: S'wch 4K 217
ME4: Chat'm 2E 80
Causton Rd. TN17: Cran 7C 176
Cavalry Cl. TN10: Tonb 9L 133
Cavalry Ct. CT14: Walm 7N 177
CT20: F'stone 7D 188
Cave Hill ME15: Maid 8B 126 (2H 27)
Cave La. CT3: Good 2C 32
Cavell Cres. DA1: Dart 2A 60
Cavell Sq. CT14: Deal 7K 177
Cavell Way ME10: Sit 6E 98
Cavenagh Rd. CT15: St Marg 7D 214
Cavendish Av. DA8: Erith 6D 52
DA15: Sidc 5J 57
DA16: Well 1H 57
ME7: Gill 6H 81
TN13: S'oaks 4H 119
Cavendish Cl. TN10: Tonb 9K 133
Cavendish Ct. CT6: H Bay 2H 195
(off Cavendish Rd.)
TN9: Tonb 5J 145
Cavendish Dr. TN2: Tun W 3H 157
Cavendish Gdns. SS0: Wclf S 1C 10
Cavendish Pl. CT11: Ram 6J 211
Cavendish Rd. CT6: H Bay 3H 195
NW6 1C 4
SW12 6E 4
Cavendish Sq. DA3: Long 6K 75
W1 3E 4
Cavendish St. CT11: Ram 5J 211
ME1: Roch 9A 80
Cavendish Way BR4: W W'ck 2E 82
ME15: Bear 6K 127
Caversham Cl. ME8: Rain 2B 96
Caveside Cl. BR7: Chst 4C 70
Cavour Rd. ME12: S'ness 2D 220
ME13: Fav 5G 186
Caxton Cl. DA3: Hart'y 6M 75
TN30: Tent 8A 224
Caxton Ho. TN24: Ashf 7G 159
Caxton La. TN11: Hdlw 8D 134
Caxton Rd. CT9: Mgte 3N 207
Caygill Cl. BR2: Shortl 7J 69
Cayser Dr. ME17: Kgswd 6G 140
Caysers Cft. TN12: E Peck 1K 147
Cazeneuve St. ME1: Roch 7N 79
Cazenove Rd. N16 1G 5
Cecil Av. ME2: Strood 4M 79
ME8: Gill 1K 95
ME12: S'ness 3C 220
Cecil Burns Lodge TN2: Tun W 3K 157
Cecil Ct. CT6: H Bay 3H 195
TN24: Ashf 7F 158
Cecilia Gro. CT10: B'stairs 7K 209
Cecilia Rd. CT11: Ram 4J 211
Cecil Pk. CT6: H Bay 2H 195
Cecil Rd. CT14: Walm 2F 200
DA11: Grav'nd 6E 62
ME1: Roch 9N 79 (3H 17)
Cecil Sq. CT9: Mgte 3C 208
Cecil St. CT9: Mgte 3C 208 (1H 23)
Cecil Way BR2: Shortl 2K 83
Cedar Av. DA12: Grav'nd 9H 63
DA15: Sidc 5J 57
Cedar Cl. BR2: Shortl 4A 84
BR8: Swanl 5D 72
CT7: Birch 4G 206
(off Parkway, The)
CT9: Mgte 4F 208
CT10: B'stairs 6K 209
DA13: Meop 9F 76
ME10: Sit 9J 99
ME20: Dit 1H 125
TN23: Ashf 7C 158
Cedar Copse BR1: Brom 5B 70
Cedar Ct. CT20: F'stone 6E 188
ME14: Maid 4E 126
TN4: Tun W 9G 150
TN30: Tent 8B 224
Cedar Cres. BR2: Shortl 4A 84
TN10: Tonb 9J 133
TN29: St M Bay 3M 215
Cedar Dr. DA4: S Dar 5B 74 (2H 15)
ME16: Barm 7J 125
TN8: Eden 5B 184
Cedar Gdns. ME9: S'bry 2F 112
Cedar Gro. DA5: Bex'y 4M 57
ME7: Hpstd 6K 95
Cedar Ho. ME12: S'ness 2C 220
(off Russell St.)
Cedarhurst BR1: Brom 3H 69
Cedarhurst Cotts. DA5: Bex'y 5B 58
Cedarhurst Dr. SE9 3M 55
Cedar Lodge TN4: Tun W 2F 156
Cedar Mt. SE9 6N 55
Cedar Ridge TN2: Tun W 8K 151
Cedar Rd. BR1: Brom 5M 69
CT2: Sturry 5E 168
DA1: Dart 6L 59
DA8: Erith 8H 53
ME2: Strood 6J 79
SM2: Sutt 5D 12
Cedars Av. CR4: Mitc 2E 12
Cedars Cl. SE13 1G 55
Cedars Rd. BR3: Beck'm 5B 68
SW4 6E 4
W4 4A 4
Cedars, The ME10: Sit 6K 99
TN12: Pad W 8M 147
Cedar Ter. CT16: Dover 1H 181
(off Selkirk Rd.)
ME13: Osp 8E 186
Cedar Ter. Rd. TN13: S'oaks 5K 119
Cedarview CT2: Cant 1J 171
Cedric Rd. CT8: Wgte S 2K 207
SE9 8E 56
Celandine Dr. SE28 1K 51
Celestial Gdns. SE13 2G 55
Celestine Cl. ME5: Chat'm 1D 110
Celia Av. TN15: W King 8E 88
(off London Rd.)
CELLARHILL 8K 223 (5H 19)
Cellar Hill ME9: Lyn 9K 223 (6H 19)
Celt Cl. ME10: Kems'y 3G 98
Celtic Av. BR2: Shortl 6H 69
Celtic Rd. CT14: Deal 7K 177
Cement Cotts. CT4: Bek 5F 172
Cemetery Cotts. CT18: H'nge 8J 193
ME15: Maid 1F 138
Cemetery La. SE7 6A 50
Cemetery La. TN11: Hdlw 7E 134 (4B 26)
TN24: Kenn 6G 159
Cemetery Rd. ME2: Hall'g 7E 92
ME6: Snod 1D 108
SE2 7K 51
Centenary Cl. TN27: Char'g 2K 175
Centenary Ct. DA4: Farn'm 1A 88
Centenary Gdns. CT13: E'try 3J 183
Central Av. CT6: H Bay 2E 194 (3J 21)
DA12: Grav'nd 7G 63
DA16: Well 9H 51 (5C 6)
ME4: Chat'm 4E 80
ME10: Sit 8G 98
SS2: Sth S 1E 10
Central Beach Camp ME12: Ley S 6M 203
Central Bus. Pk. ME2: Med E 5B 80
Central Hill SE19 1G 13
Central Lodge TN15: Wro 4D 106
Central Pde. CR0: Croy 5K 13
CT6: H Bay 2J 21
DA15: Sidc 8J 57
ME1: Roch 1A 94
SE20 3A 68
(off High St.)
Central Pk. 5K 99
Central Park Arena 6M 59
Central Pk. Gdns. ME4: Chat'm 1B 94
Central Pk. Rd. E6 2A 6
Central Rd. CT11: Ram 4H 211
DA1: Dart 2M 59
KT4: Wor Pk 4B 12
ME2: Strood 5L 79
ME20: Lark 7F 108
SM4: Mord 3C 12
Central Service Rd. CT16: Dover 4N 181
Central St. EC1 2G 5
Central Ter. BR3: Beck'm 6A 68
ME3: C'den 7C 66
Central Theatre, The 8C 80
Central Wall Rd. SS8: Can I 1K 9
Central Way SE28 1J 51 (3D 6)
Centre 2000 ME10: Sit 7H 99
Centre Comn. Rd. BR7: Chst 2E 70 (1C 14)
Centre Ct. ME2: Med E 5B 80
Centre Rd. CT17: Dover 6H 181 (2F 43)
DA3: New A 4L 89
E7 1A 6
E11 1A 6
Centre, The CT9: Mgte 3C 208
CT12: Ram 3E 210
Centurian Pk. CT19: F'stone 4E 188
Centurion Cl. ME8: Gill 2J 95
Centurion Wlk. TN23: Kgnt 5F 160
Centurion Way DA18: Erith 3A 52
RM19: Purf 4N 53
Centuryan Pl. DA1: Cray 2J 59
Century Building ME1: Roch 7N 79
Century Rd. ME8: Gill 3N 95
ME13: Fav 5J 187
Century Wlk. CT14: Deal 4M 177
Ceres Ct. ME10: Sit 6K 99
Ceres Rd. SE18 4H 51
Cerne Rd. DA12: Grav'nd 9K 63
Cervia Way DA12: Grav'nd 8L 63
Chada Av. ME7: Gill 9H 81
Chadd Dr. BR1: Brom 6A 70
Chadwell By-Pass RM16: Grays 4C 8
Chadwell Rd. RM17: Grays 4B 8
CHADWELL ST MARY 4C 8
Chadwick Cl. DA11: Nflt 7D 62
Chaffe's La. ME9: Upc 4H 225 (3C 18)
Chaffes Ter. ME9: Upc 4H 225
(not continuous)
Chaffinch Av. CR0: Croy 9A 68
Chaffinch Bus. Pk. BR3: Beck'm 6A 68
Chaffinch Cl. CR0: Croy 8A 68
ME5: Chat'm 4D 94
Chaffinch Dr. TN23: Kgnt 6G 161
Chaffinch Lodge CT16: Dover 2G 181
Chaffinch Rd. BR3: Beck'm 4B 68
Chaffinch Way TN12: Pad W 1M 153
CHAFFORD HUNDRED 4K 7
Chafford Hundred Station (Rail) 4K 7
Chafford La. TN3: Ford 8F 148 (2F 35)
Chafy Cres. CT2: Sturry 6E 168
CHAINHURST 6G 27
Chain, The CT13: S'wch 6M 217
Chalcombe Rd. SE2 3K 51
Chalcroft Rd. CT20: F'stone 7E 188
SE13 3H 55
Chaldon Way CR5: Coul 7F 13
Chalet Cl. DA5: Bex'y 9E 58
Chalfont Dr. ME8: Gill 5N 95
Chalford Dr. CT6: H Bay 5L 195
Chalgrove M. ME2: Hall'g 6E 92
Chalice Way DA9: G'hithe 3E 60
CHALK 6L 63 (7D 8)
Chalk Av. TN30: St Mic 5C 224
Chalk Cl. CT19: F'stone 4G 189
Chalkenden Av. ME8: Gill 1K 95
CHALKER'S CORNER 6A 4
Chalket La. TN2: Pem 9B 152
CHALK FARM 1D 4
Chalk Farm Rd. NW1 1E 4
Chalk Farm Station (Tube) 1D 4
Chalk Hill CT11: Ram 6D 210
CT12: C'snd, Ram 6D 210
Chalk Hill Rd. CT14: Kgdn 4E 200 (5J 33)
Chalk La. TN17: Cran 4H 37
Chalklin Bus. Pk. TN2: Tun W 5L 151
Chalk Pit Av. BR5: St P 6L 71
Chalk Pit Hill CT3: S'le 9A 216 (1D 32)
Chalkpit Hill CT4: Bek 7J 173 (2K 31)
Chalk Pit Hill ME4: Chat'm 9D 80
Chalk Pit La. CT3: S'le 9B 216
CT13: S'le 1E 32
Chalk Pit Rd. KT18: Eps 7A 12
Chalk Pit Way SM1: Sutt 5D 12
Chalk Rd. DA12: Grav'nd 6M 63 (7D 8)
ME3: High'm 7G 64 (7F 9)
ME11: Queen 7B 220
Chalksole Grn. La. CT15: Alk 1C 42
CHALKSTONE 1C 42
Chalkstone Cl. DA16: Well 8J 51
CHALKWELL
Sittingbourne 6D 98 (4E 18)
Westcliff-on-Sea 1C 10
Chalkwell Av. SS0: Wclf S 1C 10
Chalkwell Esplanade SS0: Can I 1C 10
Chalkwell Rd. ME10: Sit 7E 98 (4E 18)
Chalkwell Station (Rail) 1C 10
Chalky Bank DA11: Grav'nd 9F 62
Chalky Bank Rd. ME8: Rain 1B 96
Chalky Rd. ME9: S'bry 4E 112 (6B 18)
Challenge Cl. DA12: Grav'nd 9L 63
Challenger Cl. ME10: Sit 4F 98
TN12: Pad W 9L 147
CHALLOCK 7D 174 (4A 30)
Challock Cl. TN16: Big H 4C 164
Challock Ct. CT9: Clift 3K 209
Challock Wlk. ME14: Maid 3F 126
Chalsey Rd. SE4 2C 54
Chamberlain Av. ME16: Maid 7M 125
Chamberlain Cl. SE28 3F 50
Chamberlain Ct. ME8: Gill 6L 95
Chamberlain Cres. BR4: W W'ck 2E 82
Chamberlain Dr. CT6: H Bay 3C 194
Chamberlain Rd. CT17: Dover 4F 180
ME4: Chat'm 1E 94
Chamberlayne Rd. NW10 2B 4
Chambers Cl. DA9: G'hithe 3G 60
CHAMBER'S GREEN 1G 39
Chambers Grn. Rd. TN27: P'ley 7F 29
Chambers La. NW10 1B 4
Chambers Wall CT7: St N 7H 215 (3C 22)
Chambers Wharf ME13: Fav 4J 187
Champion Cres. SE26 9B 54
Champion Pk. SE5 5G 5
Champion Rd. SE26 9B 54
Chancel Cl. TN15: W King 8E 88
Chancel Ct. CT2: Cant 1K 171
Chancellor Ho. TN4: Tun W 2F 156
Chancellor Rd. SS1: Sth S 1E 10
Chancellor Way TN13: S'oaks 4H 119
Chancelot Rd. SE2 4K 51
Chance Mdw. CT15: Gus 7L 179
Chancery Ct. DA1: Dart 5A 60
Chancery La. BR3: Beck'm 5E 68
ME15: Maid 6E 126
WC2 3F 5
Chancery Lane Station (Tube) 3F 5
Chancery Rd. ME3: Cliffe 3C 176
Chanctonbury Chase CT5: Seas 7C 226
Chanctonbury Cl. SE9 8D 56
CHANDLERS CORNER 2G 7
Chandlers Ct. SE12 6L 55
Chandlers Dr. DA8: Erith 4E 52
Chandler's Hill DA13: Meop 5H 91
Chandler's Rd. DA13: Meop 6H 91 (4C 16)
Chandlers Wharf ME1: Roch 7M 79
Chandos Rd. CT10: B'stairs 9M 209
TN1: Tun W 9J 151
Chandos Sq. CT10: B'stairs 9M 209
Channel Cl. CT19: F'stone 4M 189
Channel Lea CT14: Walm 9M 177
Channel Rd. CT9: Mgte 7E 208
Channel Tunnel Rail Terminal 3B 188 (4K 41)
Channel Vw. CT19: F'stone 6L 189
(off North St.)
Channel Vw. Ct. CT11: Ram 5K 211
(off Granville Marina)
Channel Vw. Rd. CT17: Dover 6H 181
Channel Watch TN28: G'stne 5N 213
Channon Rd. TN28: G'stne 7H 213
Chantlers Hill TN12: Pad W 3L 153 (1D 36)
Chantlers Mead TN8: Cowd 2D 34
Chantry Av. DA3: Hart'y 9L 75
Chantry Cl. DA14: Sidc 1N 71
Chantry Ct. CT1: Cant 1M 171
DA12: Grav'nd 4H 63
Chantry Heritage Cen. 4H 63
Chantry La. BR2: Shortl 8N 69
Chantry Pk. CT7: St N 4C 22
Chantry Pl. TN12: Mard 2C 212
Chantry Rd. TN12: Mard 2C 212
Chapel Cl. CT18: Etch'l 2M 185
DA1: Cray 3F 58
ME19: Rya 5L 107
Chapel Cott. CT6: H Bay 5L 195
Chapel Cotts. CT6: H Bay 4L 195
ME17: Leeds 3B 140
Chapel Ct. DA10: Swans 4L 61
Chapel Farm Rd. SE9 8B 56
Chapel Hill CT9: Mgte 6D 208
CT15: Eyt 9K 185 (5E 32)
DA1: Cray 3F 58
TN33: Sed 7E 44
Chapel Hill Cl. CT9: Mgte 6D 208
Chapel La. CT2: B Oak 4C 168
CT2: Blean 4G 166
CT2: Sturry 6E 168
CT3: S'le 8A 216
CT4: R Min 8H 183 (1H 41)
CT14: Ripp 2A 200 (5H 33)
CT15: Ashy 5F 33
CT15: St Marg 7B 214
CT16: Dover 5J 181
(off York St.)
ME2: Hall'g 7A 92 (5E 16)
ME7: Hpstd 7K 95 (5K 17)
ME7: Hpstd 9K 95
ME14: Bear 4K 127
TN12: S'hrst 3K 223
TN17: Bendn 7A 38
TN17: Siss 4D 222 (4K 37)
TN27: Eger 6E 28
TN29: Newchu, Burm 7D 40
Chapel M. TN24: Ashf 8G 158
(off North St.)
Chapel Pl. CT7: Birch 4F 206
CT11: Ram 5H 211
CT17: Dover 5J 181
TN1: Tun W 3G 156
Chapel Pl. La. CT11: Ram 5H 211
Chapel Rd. CT11: Ram 5G 210
CT14: Tilm 4F 33
CT16: Whitf 5F 178 (7E 32)
Chapel Rd. DA7: Bexhth 2B 58

Chapel Rd.—Chesney Cres.

Chapel Rd. IG1: Ilf 1B 6
ME3: Isle G 8C 190 (5E 10)
ME6: Snod 2E 108
ME17: Sut V 9A 140
RH8: Oxt 3A 24
SE27 1G 13
TN25: Hoth 6J 29
TN29: Dym 8B 182
Chapel Row CT6: H Bay 7H 195
TN15: Igh 3J 121
TN23: Kgnt 6E 160
TN29: Lydd 3K 205
Chapel St. CT6: H Bay 2H 195
CT14: Deal 4N 177
CT21: Hythe 6J 199
ME12: Minst 6L 221 (7H 11)
ME12: S'ness 1B 220
ME13: Fav 6H 187
ME19: E Mal 3E 124 (1F 27)
ME19: Rya 5L 107 (6D 16)
NW1 3D 4
Chapel, The CT4: Chart'm 9F 170
Chapel Vw. TN15: Igh 3J 121
Chapel Wlk. DA5: Bex'y 7F 58
(off Maplehurst Cl.)
TN14: Ide H 3C 130
Chapel Wood DA3: New A 2L 89
(not continuous)
Chapel Wood Rd. DA3: Hart'y 4L 89
TN15: Ash, S'le (4L 89) 4A 16
Chapel Woods TN27: Char'g 4J 29
Chaplin Cl. ME3: Wain 1N 79
Chaplin Dr. TN27: H'crn 8L 191
Chaplins Wlk. CT4: Chart'm 9E 170
Chapman Av. ME15: Maid 8H 127
Chapman Ho. CT14: Deal 7L 177
Chapman Rd. DA17: Belv 5B 52
E9 1J 5
Chapmans Cl. TN14: Sund 6N 117
TN25: C'lck 7E 174
Chapmans Hill CT3: Aysm 1E 162 (3C 32)
CT15: Aysm, Non 1E 162
CT15: Non 3C 32
Chapman's Hill DA13: Meop 7D 90 (5B 16)
Chapman's La. BR5: St P 5M 71
(not continuous)
SE2 4L 51
Chapmans Rd. TN14: Sund 6N 117
Chapman Way ME19: E Mal 1D 124 (1E 26)
TN2: Tun W 6J 151
Chappell Way ME10: Sit 5E 98
Chapter Rd. ME2: Strood 5K 79
NW2 1B 4
Charcoal La. CT4: Elham 6J 31
CHARCOTT 4H 143 (6G 25)
Chard Ct. ME7: Gill 7F 80
Chard Ho. ME14: Maid 2C 126
CHARING 3K 175 (5H 29)
Charing Cl. BR6: Orp 5H 85
CT12: Ram 4G 211
Charing Ct. BR2: Shortl 5H 69
Charing Cres. CT8: Wgte S 4J 207
Charing Cross Rd. WC2 3E 4
Charing Cross Station (Rail & Tube) 3F 5
CHARING HEATH 5G 29
Charing Heath Rd.
TN27: Char'g 4H 175 (5G 29)
(Egerton Rd.)
TN27: Char'g 5G 29
(Maidstone Rd.)
CHARING HILL 2L 175 (4H 29)
Charing Hill TN27: Char'g 2L 175 (5H 29)
Charing Rd. ME8: Gill 9L 81
Charing Station (Rail) 3J 175 (5H 29)
Chariot Way ME2: Strood 9J 79
Charlbury Cl. ME16: Maid 6N 125
Charldane Rd. SE9 8D 56
Charlecote Ct. ME8: Gill 3N 95
(off Derwent Way)
Charles Busby Ct. ME20: Aylfd 9K 109
Charles Cl. DA14: Sidc 9K 57
ME6: Snod 2E 108
Charles Cobb Cl. TN29: Dym 7C 182
Charles Ct. DA8: Erith 6F 52
Charles Cres. CT19: F'stone 4E 188
Charles Dickens Av. ME3: High'm 2G 78
Charles Dickens Cen., The 7A 80 (2H 17)
Charles Drayson Ct. ME13: Fav 5J 187
(off Gordon Sq.)
Charles Dr. ME2: Cux 9F 78
Charlesfield SE9 8M 55
Charlesford Av. ME17: Kgswd 5F 140
Charles Grinling Wlk. SE18 4C 50
Charles Ho. CT14: Deal 7L 177
(off Freemen's Way)
Charles Lister Ct. CT17: Dover 3G 181
Charles Rd. CT11: Ram 4J 211
CT14: Deal 6L 177
TN14: Hals 1C 102
Charles St. CT6: H Bay 2G 195
DA9: G'hithe 3E 60
ME2: Strood 5L 79
ME4: Chat'm 9B 80
ME12: S'ness 1B 220
ME16: Maid 6B 126
TN4: S'bgh 6G 150
Charleston Ct. CT10: B'stairs 1M 211
(off W. Cliff Rd.)
Charlesworth Dr. CT7: Birch 4G 206 (2F 23)
Charleworth Ho. ME4: Chat'm 1B 94
Charlieville Rd. DA8: Erith 7D 52
Charlock Cl. ME16: Alltn 1A 126
Charlotte Cl. DA6: Bexhth 3N 57
ME5: Chat'm 5E 94
Charlotte Cotts. TN11: Leigh 5N 143
Charlotte Ct. CT11: Ram 6J 211
Charlotte Dr. ME8: Gill 2M 95
Charlotte Pk. Av. BR1: Brom 6A 70
Charlotte Pl. CT9: Mgte 4D 208
Charlotte Sq. CT9: Mgte 3D 208
Charlotte St. CT10: B'stairs 9M 209
CT20: F'stone 6L 189
ME10: Sit 6F 98
CHARLTON 5A 6
Charlton Arc. CT16: Dover 4H 181
(off High St.)
Charlton Athletic F.C. (Valley, The) 4A 6
Charlton Av. CT16: Dover 3H 181
Charlton Cen. CT16: Dover 3H 181
Charlton Chu. La. SE7 4A 6
Charlton Cl. CT12: Ram 2F 210
TN24: W'boro 1L 161
Charlton Dr. TN16: Big H 5D 164
Charlton Grn. CT16: Dover 3H 181 (1F 43)
Charlton La. ME15: W Far 1H 137 (3F 27)
ME17: E Sut 8E 140 (5B 28)
Charlton Mnr. ME7: Gill 7F 80
Charlton Pk. La. SE7 6A 50 (5A 6)
Charlton Pk. Rd. SE7 6A 50 (5A 6)
Charlton Rd. SE3 5A 6
SE7 5A 6
Charlton Station (Rail) 4A 6
Charltons, The ME13: Bou B 2J 165
Charlton St. ME16: Maid 7N 125
Charlton's Way TN4: Tun W 4E 156
Charlton Ter. TN9: Tonb 5J 145
Charlton Way SE10 5K 5
Charlwood CR0: Croy 9C 82
Charminster TN23: Ashf 3C 160
Charminster Rd. SE9 9N 55
Charmouth Rd. DA16: Well 8L 51
Charmwood La. BR6: Prat B 9K 85 (5D 14)
Charne, The TN14: Otf 8H 103
Charnock BR8: Swanl 7F 72
(not continuous)
Charnwood CT5: Whits 4M 227
Charnwood Rd. CT6: H Bay 6J 195
Charollais Cl. CT2: Cant 9N 167
Charsley Rd. SE6 7E 54
Chart Av. TN23: Ashf, Gt Cha 9A 158
Chart Cl. BR2: Shortl 4H 69
ME13: Fav 5F 186
CHART CORNER 7L 139 (4K 27)
Chart Cnr. ME17: Cha S 7L 139
Charter Dr. DA5: Bex'y 5N 57
Charter Ho. CT16: Dover 5K 181
(off Camden Cres.)
TN24: Ashf 8G 158
Charterhouse Dr. TN13: S'oaks 5H 119
Charterhouse Rd. BR6: Chels 4J 85
Charterhouse St. EC1 3F 5
Charter St. ME4: Chat'm 1C 94
ME7: Gill 5F 80
Chart Gunpowder Mills 5F 186 (6A 20)
CHARTHAM 7D 170 (2F 31)
Chartham Downs CT4: Chart'm 9D 170
Chartham Downs Rd.
CT4: Chart'm, P'hm 9D 170 (2F 31)
CHARTHAM HATCH 4C 170 (1F 31)
Chartham Hatch Rd. CT2: Harb 1G 171 (7G 21)
Chartham Station (Rail) 7D 170 (2F 31)
Chartham Ter. CT11: Ram 7H 211
(off St Augustines Rd.)
CHART HILL 5K 27
Chart Hill Rd.
ME17: Bou Mo, Cha S 9K 139 (6K 27)
Chart La. TN16: Bras, Westrm 9K 117 (4D 24)
Chart Leacon Cotts. TN23: Gt Cha 8C 158
Charton Cl. DA17: Belv 6A 52
Chart Pl. ME8: Gill 8M 95
Chart Rd. CT19: F'stone 5F 188
ME17: Cha S, Sut V 9L 139 (5K 27)
TN23: Ashf 2A 160 (2K 39)
(Singleton)
TN23: Ashf, Gt Cha 9A 158 (1K 39)
(Great Chart)
TN24: Ashf 7E 158
Chart Rd. Ind. Est. TN23: Ashf 7E 158
CHART SUTTON 7L 139 (4K 27)
Chart Sutton Bus. Est. ME17: Cha S 6L 139
Chart Vw. TN15: Kems'g 8B 104
Chartway TN13: S'oaks 6K 119
CHARTWAY STREET 7E 140
Chartway St.
ME17: Sut V, E Sut, Kgswd 7A 140 (4A 28)
Chartwell 4C 24
Chartwell Av. CT6: H Bay 3L 195
Chartwell Cl. ME2: Strood 3M 79
SE9 7F 56
Chartwell Ct. ME4: Chat'm 8B 80
ME7: Gill 7G 80
Chartwell Dr. BR6: Farnb 6F 84
Chartwell Gro. ME10: Sit 8D 98
Chartwell Lodge BR3: Beck'm 3D 68
Chase Rd. NW10 2A 4
Chase Sq. DA11: Grav'nd 4G 62
Chase, The BR1: Brom 6L 69
CT11: Ram 3K 211
(off Montefiore Av.)
CT15: St Marg 9B 200
DA7: Bexhth 1C 58
ME4: Chat'm 1A 94
ME8: Gill 1K 95
TN2: Tun W 3H 157
(not continuous)
TN10: Tonb 2J 145
TN15: Kems'g 7M 103
Chastilian Rd. DA1: Dart 5G 58
Chater Ct. CT14: Deal 6M 177
Chatfield Way ME19: E Mal 9F 108
CHATHAM 8C 80 (3H 17)
Chatham Av. BR2: Shortl 1J 83
Chatham Cl. SE18 3D 50
Chatham Ct. CT11: Ram 4H 211
Chatham Gro. ME4: Chat'm 2C 94
Chatham Hill ME5: Chat'm 9E 80 (3J 17)
ME7: Chat'm 9E 80 (3J 17)
Chatham Hill Rd. TN14: S'oaks 3K 119
CHATHAM MARITIME 3E 80 (2J 17)
Chatham Pl. CT11: Ram 5J 211
Chatham Rd. ME5: Aylfd 1A 110
ME14: S'lng 6H 17
ME20: Aylfd 2A 110 (6H 17)
Chatham Ski Cen. 5H 95
Chatham Station (Rail) 8B 80 (3H 17)
Chatham St. CT11: Ram 5H 211 (4J 23)
Chatsworth Av. BR1: Brom 9L 55
DA15: Sidc 6J 57
Chatsworth Cl. BR4: W W'ck 3J 83
Chatsworth Dr. ME2: Strood 3M 79
ME10: Sit 6C 98
Chatsworth Ho. BR2: Shortl 7K 69
(off Westmoreland Rd.)
Chatsworth M. CT11: Ram 6G 211
Chatsworth Pde. BR5: Pet W 8E 70
Chatsworth Rd. DA1: Dart 3K 59
E5 1H 5
ME7: Gill 6F 80
NW2 1B 4
CHATTENDEN 9C 66 (7H 9)
Chattenden Ct. ME14: Pen H 2E 126
Chattenden La. ME3: C'den 9C 66 (7H 9)
Chattenden Ter. ME3: C'den 8C 66
Chatterton Rd. BR2: Shortl 7N 69
Chaucer Av. CT5: Whits 4K 227
Chaucer Bus. Pk. CT5: Whits 7E 226
TN15: Kems'g 9D 104
Chaucer Cl. CT1: Cant 3B 172
ME2: Med E 4B 80
ME15: Maid 1H 139
Chaucer Ct. CT1: Cant 3A 172
Chaucer Cres. CT16: Dover 1G 180
Chaucer Gdns. TN9: Tonb 8F 144
Chaucer M. CT2: Up Harb 1E 170
Chaucer Pk. DA1: Dart 5N 59
Chaucer Rd. CT1: Cant 1A 172
CT10: B'stairs 1L 211
CT15: Evtn 7J 185
DA11: Nflt 8C 62
DA15: Sidc 6L 57
DA16: Well 8G 51
ME7: Gill 9G 80
ME10: Sit 8E 98
Chaucer Way DA1: Dart 2A 60
(not continuous)
ME20: Lark 6D 108
Chaucer Wood Ho. CT1: Cant 1A 172
Chaundrye Cl. SE9 4B 56
Chave Rd. DA2: Dart 8M 59
CHEAM 5C 12
Cheam Comn. Rd. KT4: Wor Pk 4B 12
Cheam Rd. KT17: Eps 5B 12
SM1: Sutt 5C 12
SM2: Sutt 5B 12
Cheam Station (Rail) 5C 12
CHEAM VILLAGE 5C 12
Cheddar Cl. TN24: Ashf 6F 158
Cheeselands TN27: Bidd 7K 163
CHEESEMAN'S GREEN 7K 161 (3B 40)
Cheeseman's Grn. TN24: Mers 8H 161
TN25: Mers 3A 40
Cheesmans Cl. CT12: Minst 8F 212
Chegwell Dr. ME5: Chat'm 7E 94
CHEGWORTH 2H 141 (3C 28)
Chegworth Gdns. ME10: Sit 1E 114
Chegworth La. ME17: H'shm 2H 141
Chegworth Mill Cotts. ME17: H'shm 2J 141
Chegworth Rd. ME17: H'shm 1H 141 (3C 28)
Cheldoc Ri. ME4: Chat'm 2F 80
Chelford Rd. BR1: Brom 1G 68
Chelmar Rd. ME4: Chat'm 8E 80
Chelmsford Ho. ME15: Maid 2H 139
Chelmsford Rd. ME2: Strood 6H 79
CHELSEA 4D 4
Chelsea Bri. SW1 5E 4
SW8 5E 4
Chelsea Bri. Rd. SW1 4E 4
Chelsea Ct. BR1: Brom 6A 70
(off Holmdene Ct.)
CT21: Hythe 7K 199
Chelsea Emb. SW3 5D 4
Chelsea F.C. (Stamford Bridge) 5C 4
Chelsea Rd. CT1: Cant 7B 168
CHELSFIELD 6K 85 (4D 14)
Chelsfield Hill BR6: Chels 9L 85 (5D 14)
Chelsfield Ho. ME16: Maid 4A 126
Chelsfield La. BR5: Orp 1M 85 (3D 14)
BR6: Chels 3D 14
(Goddington)
BR6: Chels 5E 14
(Maypole)
BR6: Orp 8B 86
(Badgers Mount)
BR6: Orp, Chels 3M 85
(Chelsfield Village)
TN14: Hals, S'ham 8B 86 (5E 14)
Chelsfield Rd. BR5: St M Cry 9L 71 (3D 14)
Chelsfield Station (Rail) 6K 85 (4D 14)
CHELSFIELD VILLAGE 6N 85 (4E 14)
CHELSHAM 7J 13
Chelsham Comn. Rd. CR6: Warl 7J 13
Chelsham Ct. Rd. CR6: Warl 7K 13
Chelsham Rd. CR6: Warl 7J 13
Chelsiter Ct. DA14: Sidc 9H 57
Chelsworth Dr. SE18 6F 50
Cheltenham Cl. DA12: Grav'nd 1H 77
ME15: Maid 2J 139
Cheltenham Gdns. E6 2B 6
Cheltenham Rd. BR6: Chels 4J 85
SE15 3A 54 (6H 5)
CHELWOOD COMMON 7A 34
CHELWOOD GATE 7A 34
Chelwood Ga. Rd. RH17: Chel G 7B 34
Chelwood Wlk. SE4 2B 54
Cheney Cl. ME8: Gill 6N 95
Cheney Ct. SE23 6A 54
Cheney Hill ME9: Rod 4H 115 (6F 19)
Cheney Rd. ME13: Fav 5K 187
Chenies Cl. TN2: Tun W 5G 156
Chenies St. WC1 3E 4
Chenies, The BR6: Pet W 9G 70
DA2: Dart 9F 58
Chennell Pk. Rd. TN30: Tent, St Mic 6D 38
Chennels, The TN26: H Hald 2A 196
(not continuous)
Chepstow Ho. ME15: Maid 2J 139
Chepstow Rd. CR0: Croy 4G 13
W2 3C 4
Chepstow Vs. W11 3C 4
Chequer La. CT3: Ash 5C 216 (7E 22)
Chequers Cl. BR5: St P 7H 71
DA13: Ist R 5D 76
Chequers Cl. ME5: Chat'm 2D 110
Chequers Cotts. TN17: Goud 3D 190
Chequers Ct. ME2: Strood 3L 79
Chequers Hill CT4: P'hm 4G 31
ME9: Dod 1G 29
TN8: Chid 5A 142 (6E 24)
Chequers La. RM9: Dag 2E 6
Chequers Orchard CT4: P'hm 4G 31
Chequers Pde. SE9 4B 56
(off Eltham High St.)
Chequers Pk. TN25: Wye 3M 159
Chequers Rd. ME12: Minst 6M 221 (7J 11)
TN17: Goud 1C 190 (3G 37)
Chequers Shop. Cen. ME15: Maid 5D 126
CHEQUERS STREET 7H 65
CHEQUERTREE 4B 40
Chequer Tree La. TN26: Beth 3G 39
Chequertree Rd. TN25: Bils, Mers 9K 161 (4B 40)
Cherbourg Cres. ME5: Chat'm 4C 94
CHERITON 5E 188 (4A 42)
Cheriton Av. BR2: Shortl 8J 69
CT12: Ram 4F 210
Cheriton Ct. SE12 5K 55
Cheriton Ct. Rd. CT20: F'stone 5C 188
Cheriton Dr. SE18 7F 50
Cheriton Gdns. CT20: F'stone 6J 189 (5B 42)
Cheriton High St. CT18: F'stone 5B 188
CT19: F'stone 5D 188 (4K 41)
CHERITON HILL 2D 188
Cheriton Pl. CT14: Walm 6N 177
CT20: F'stone 7K 189
Cheriton Rd. CT14: Walm 6N 177
CT19: F'stone 5F 188 (4A 42)
CT20: F'stone 6J 189
ME8: Gill 4N 95
Cheriton Way ME16: Alltn 2N 125
(not continuous)
Cheriton Wood Ho. CT19: F'stone 4D 188
Cherries, The ME16: Barm 7K 125
Cherry Amber Cl. ME8: Rain 3B 96
Cherry Av. BR8: Swanl 7E 72
CT2: Cant 9K 167
Cherry Brook Rd. CT20: F'stone 5E 188
Cherry Cl. ME10: Sit 5E 98
ME17: Len 7L 201
Cherrycot Hill BR6: Farnb 5E 84
Cherrycot Ri. BR6: Farnb 5E 84
Cherry Ct. CT1: Cant 5J 171
CT19: F'stone 5G 188
TN23: Ashf 9F 158
Cherrydown Rd. DA14: Sidc 7M 57
Cherry Dr. CT2: Cant 9J 167
ME13: Lud'm 1D 186
Cherry Flds. ME10: Sit 6B 98
Cherryfields TN17: Bendn 6A 38
Cherry Gdn. Av. CT19: F'stone 5G 188 (4A 42)
Cherry Garden Cres. TN25: Wye 2N 159
Cherry Gdn. La. CT3: Ash 5D 216
CT19: F'stone 4F 188 (4A 42)
TN25: Wye 2N 159
Cherry Gdn. Rd. CT2: Cant 9K 167
Cherry Gdns. CT4: Elham 6N 183
CT6: H Bay 3F 194
CT10: B'stairs 1G 210
ME9: Tey 7K 223
TN28: L'stne 3M 213
Cherry Gdns. Hill TN3: Groom 9G 155 (5F 35)
TN6: Groom 5F 35
Cherry Glebe TN25: Mers 9M 161
Cherry Gro. CT15: Evtn 6J 185
TN10: Tonb 2L 145
Cherry Hill Ct. ME9: N'tn 5K 97
Cherry La. CT14: Gt Mon 4H 33
CHERRY ORCHARD 6M 125
Cherry Orchard CT3: L'brne 2L 173
CT4: Old L 6K 175
CT5: Whits 5L 227
ME20: Dit 1G 124
TN26: Wdchu 6B 228
TN30: Tent 9B 224
Cherry Orchard Cl. BR5: St M Cry 8L 71
Cherry Orchard La. TN25: Aldtn 5C 40
Cherry Orchard M. CT3: L'brne 1L 173
Cherry Orchard Rd. BR2: Shortl 3A 84
CR0: Croy 4G 13
Cherry Orchard, The TN11: Hdlw 7D 134
Cherry Orchard Way ME16: Maid 6M 125
Cherry Tree Av. CT16: Dover 3H 181 (1F 43)
Cherry Tree Cl. ME9: Tey 7K 223
ME12: S'ness 4B 220
Cherry Tree Gdns. CT12: Ram 1F 210
Cherry Tree Gro. TN15: Knat 1B 104
Cherry Tree La. DA2: Dart 8G 59
RM13: Rain 2F 7
Cherry Tree Rd. ME8: Rain 3B 96
TN2: Tun W 4E 156
TN10: Tonb 9K 133
TN27: Char'g 5G 29
Cherry Trees DA3: Hart'y 8M 75
Cherry Tree Wlk. BR3: Beck'm 7C 68
BR4: W W'ck 5J 83
TN16: Big H 5C 164
Cherry Vw. ME17: Bou Mo 5E 138
Cherry Wlk. BR2: Shortl 2K 83
Cherry Waye CT15: Eyt 9K 185
Cherrywood Dr. DA11: Nflt 9D 62
Cherrywood Ri. TN25: Ashf 6D 158
Cherville La. CT3: Ickh 1B 32
Chervilles ME16: Barm 7L 125
Chervil M. SE28 1K 51
Cherwell Cl. TN10: Tonb 2H 145
Chesfield Cl. TN11: Hdlw 8E 134
Chesham Av. BR5: Pet W 9D 70
Chesham Dr. ME8: Gill 5A 96
Chesham Pl. SW1 4E 4
Chesham Rd. SE20 4A 68
Cheshire Rd. ME15: Maid 6H 127
(Mansion Cotts.)
ME15: Maid 1H 139
(Willington St.)
Cheshire St. E2 2H 5
Cheshunt Cl. DA13: Meop 8F 76
Cheshunt Rd. DA17: Belv 5B 52
Chesney Cres. CR0: Croy 8F 82

Church La.—Clermont Cl.

Church La. TN25: Aldtn, S'ndge 4D **40**
TN25: Bou L 6B **30**
TN25: C'lck 7D **174** (4A **30**)
TN25: M Hor 2F **41**
TN26: Hoth 3L **197**
TN26: Shad 4J **39**
TN28: New R 3K **213** (3J **47**)
TN29: Bztt 1F **47**
TN31: Beckl 4H **45**
TN31: Iden 4A **46**
TN31: N'thiam 3G **45**
TN31: Peas 5K **45**
TN35: W'fld 7F **45**
Church Manorway DA8: Erith 4E **52**
SE2 . . . . 5J **51**
Church Marshes Country Pk. 3J **99**
Church Mdw. TN12: Horsm 6C **196**
Church Mdws. CT14: Deal 4K **177**
Church M. ME8: Rain 3B **96**
ME9: Iwade 8K **197**
Church Path BR8: Swanl 4J **73**
CT14: Deal 6K **177**
(not continuous)
CT14: Walm 9M **177**
DA9: G'hithe 3F **60**
(not continuous)
DA11: Nflt 4B **62**
ME2: Strood 5M **79**
ME7: Gill 6G **81**
(Church St.)
ME7: Gill 6E **80**
(Prince Arthur Rd.)
ME9: Lwr Hal 3M **225**
TN30: Tent 8B **224**
Church Pl. CT16: Dover 4J **181**
ME1: Woul 6G **93**
Church Ri. SE23 . . . . 7A **54**
Church Rd. BR2: Kes 8N **83** (5A **14**)
BR2: Shortl 5K **69** (2A **14**)
(Glassmill La.)
BR2: Shortl 6H **69**
(Shortlands Rd.)
BR6: Chels 8L **85** (5D **14**)
BR6: Farnb 6E **84** (4C **14**)
BR8: Crock'n 1E **86** (3F **15**)
(Crockenhill)
BR8: Swanl 4L **73** (2G **15**)
(Swanley Village)
CR4: Mitc 2D **12**
CT3: Hoath 4A **22**
CT3: L'brne 2L **173** (1A **32**)
CT4: Mol 3B **30**
CT9: Mgte 4D **208**
CT10: B'stairs 9M **209**
CT11: Ram 5J **211**
CT15: Cold 9N **219** (6D **32**)
CT17: Dover 5F **180**
CT18: Lym'ge 8L **205** (2J **41**)
CT20: F'stone 5C **188** (4K **41**)
CT21: Hythe 6K **199**
DA3: Hart'y, New A 8M **75** (3A **16**)
DA3: New A, Hart'y 3M **89** (4A **16**)
DA4: S at H 2N **73** (1H **15**)
(not continuous)
DA7: Bexhth 9A **52** (6E **6**)
DA8: Erith 5E **52**
DA9: G'hithe 3F **60**
DA10: Swans 4M **61**
DA12: Grav'nd 2H **77**
DA13: Cobh 6H **77** (2C **16**)
DA13: Cobh, Grav'nd 3F **76**
DA14: Sidc 9J **57**
DA16: Well 9K **51**
E12 . . . . 1B **6**
KT4: Wor Pk 3A **12**
KT17: Eps 6A **12**
ME9: Tonge 7M **99** (4G **19**)
ME10: Sit 7J **99** (4F **19**)
ME12: E'chu 1K **19**
ME13: Fav 5H **187**
(East St.)
ME13: Fav 4H **187**
(Up. Brents)
ME13: Oare 2F **186** (5A **20**)
ME13: Stal 4J **29**
ME15: Maid 7B **126** (2H **27**)
ME15: Otham, Bear 1J **139** (3K **27**)
ME17: Cha S 8M **139** (5A **28**)
ME17: Graf G, Bou Ma 9N **141** (5D **28**)
ME17: H'shm 2N **141** (3D **28**)
ME17: Holl 9F **112** (7B **18**)
ME18: W Peck 2F **134** (3C **26**)
ME19: Off 1J **123** (1C **26**)
ME19: Rya 7L **107**
NW10 . . . . 1A **4**
RH7: Ling 1A **34**
RM14: Bulp 1B **8**
(not continuous)
RM18: W Til 5D **8**
SE19 . . . . 2G **13**
SS17: Corr 2F **9**
SW13 . . . . 5A **4**
SW19 . . . . 2D **12**
(Merton)
SW19 . . . . 1C **12**
(Wimbledon)
TN1: Tun W 2F **156** (3K **35**)
TN2: Pem 5C **152**
TN3: Lamb 1L **201** (4E **36**)
TN4: S'bgh 4F **150** (1J **35**)
TN5: Flim 5E **36**
TN6: Crowb 7F **35**
TN6: Roth 7H **35**
TN11: Hild 1D **144**
TN12: Pad W 8M **147** (7D **26**)
TN14: Hals 2N **101** (6E **14**)
TN14: Sund 9N **117** (3E **24**)
TN14: Weald 5J **131** (4G **25**)
TN15: Ash 6L **89** (4A **16**)
TN15: Ivy H, Seal 5E **120** (2J **25**)
TN15: W King 8E **88**
TN16: Big H 5D **164**
TN16: Bras 6K **117** (2D **24**)
TN17: Goud 3C **190** (4G **37**)
Church Rd. TN17: Kiln 5E **36**
TN18: Sandh 4A **218** (2E **44**)
TN23: Ashf 9G **158**
TN24: Kenn 4J **159** (7B **30**)
TN24: Svgtn 2L **161** (2B **40**)
(Nightingale Cl., not continuous)
TN24: W'boro 1K **161** (2B **40**)
(Bentley Rd.)
TN25: H'lgh 7E **30**
TN25: Mers 9L **161** (3C **40**)
TN25: Sme 9H **165** (3D **40**)
TN26: Kena 6J **39**
TN27: Char'g 4H **29**
TN28: New R 3J **213** (3J **47**)
TN29: Burm 3A **182** (7E **40**)
TN29: Lydd 3K **205**
TN30: Tent 8B **224**
TN32: Mount 5B **44**
TN32: Rob 3C **44**
Church Rd. Bus. Cen. ME10: Sit 5J **99**
Church Rd. Cotts. ME19: Off 9K **107**
Church Row BR7: Chst 4E **70**
ME6: Snod 3E **108**
ME18: W Peck 2F **134**
Church Row M. BR7: Chst 3E **70**
Churchsettle La. TN5: Wadh 7C **36**
Churchside DA13: Meop 2F **106**
(not continuous)
Churchside Cl. TN16: Big H 5C **164**
Church Sq. CT10: B'stairs 9M **209**
ME17: Len 7M **201**
CHURCH STREET
Rochester 4H 227
Whitstable 4H 65 (6F 9)
Church St. CT1: Cant 2N **171**
CT2: Cant 1L **171**
CT5: Whits 4H **227** (3F **21**)
CT9: Mgte 4D **208**
CT10: B'stairs 7J **209** (2K **23**)
CT12: Minst 8F **212** (4F **23**)
CT13: E'try 3L **183**
CT13: S'wch 5M **217**
CT13: Wdboro 8G **217**
CT14: Walm 9L **177**
CT15: Non 2F **162** (3C **32**)
CT16: Dover 5J **181**
CT20: F'stone 7K **189**
DA11: Grav'nd 4G **62**
DA13: Sflt 1N **75**
E16 . . . . 1D **50**
KT17: Eps 6A **12**
ME1: Burh 2J **109** (6G **17**)
ME1: Roch 8A **80**
ME3: Cliffe 4C **176** (6G **9**)
ME3: High'm 7G **65** (7F **9**)
ME3: Hoo 9H **67** (7K **9**)
ME4: Chat'm 8D **80**
(not continuous)
ME7: Gill 6H **81** (2K **17**)
ME9: Rod 3K **115** (6G **19**)
ME10: Sit 7F **98**
(Dover St.)
ME10: Sit 6F **98**
(St Paul's St.)
ME13: Fav 4H **187**
ME14: Maid 5D **126**
ME15: Loose 3C **138** (3H **27**)
ME15: Maid 7B **126**
ME17: Bou Mo 5E **138** (4J **27**)
ME17: H'shm 3N **141** (3D **28**)
ME18: Tstn 1E **136**
TN5: Tice 7E **36**
TN8: Cowd 2D **34**
TN8: Eden 6C **184**
TN9: Tonb 5J **145**
TN11: Hdlw 8D **134**
TN14: S'ham 2G **103** (6F **15**)
TN15: Seal 3A **120** (1H **25**)
TN25: Wye 2M **159** (6C **30**)
Church St. St Mary's CT13: S'wch 5L **217**
Church Street Station (CT) 4G 13
Church Ter. ME5: Chat'm 1F **94**
SE13 . . . . 1H **55**
Church Trad. Est. DA8: Erith 7G **53**
Church Va. SE23 . . . . 7A **54**
Church Vw. BR8: Swanl 6E **72**
CT6: H Bay 3K **195**
TN25: Aldtn 4D **40**
TN27: Bidd 7K **163**
TN29: Newchu 7C **40**
Church Vs. TN13: Riv 4F **118**
TN29: Lydd 3K **205**
Church Wlk. *CT4: Elham 7N 183*
(off Pound La.)
DA2: Dart 8L **59**
DA4: Eyns 4M **87**
DA12: Grav'nd 6J **63**
(not continuous)
ME19: E Mal 2E **124**
ME20: Aylfd 7K **109**
TN18: Hawkh 6D **192**
TN27: H'crn 8K **191**
Church Way CR2: S Croy 5G **13**
CT5: Whits 2M **227**
(not continuous)
CHURCH WHITFIELD 5G 179 (7F 33)
Chu. Whitfield Rd. CT15: Whitf 3F **178**
CT16: Whitf 3F **178** (6F **33**)
Church Wood Cl. CT2: R Comn 9H **167**
Churchwood Dr. CT5: Whits 4M **227**
Church Yd. TN23: Ashf 8F **158**
Churchyard Pas. *TN23: Ashf 8F 158*
(off Tufton St.)
Churn La. TN12: Pad W, Horsm 1E **36**
Chute Cl. ME8: Gill 7N **95**
Chyngton Cl. DA15: Sidc 8H **57**
Cibber Rd. SE23 . . . . 7A **54**
Cimba Wood DA12: Grav'nd 9K **63**
Cinder Footpath CT10: B'stairs 9L **209**
Cinderford Way BR1: Brom 9H **55**
CINDER HILL 6G 25
Cinder Hill La. TN11: Leigh 6K **143** (6G **25**)
Cinderhill Wood Cvn. Site TN12: Mat 5H **153**
Cineworld Cinema 5G 158
Cinnabar Cl. ME5: Chat'm 1D **110**
Cinnabar Dr. ME10: Sit 5D **98**
Cinque Ports Av. CT21: Hythe 7J **199**
Cinque Ports St. TN31: Rye 5A **46**
Circular Rd. CT14: Fin 3G **33**
CT16: Dover 3N **181**
Circular Way SE18 . . . . 6B **50**
Circus Rd. NW8 . . . . 2D **4**
Cirrus Cres. DA12: Grav'nd 1K **77**
Citadel Cres. CT17: Dover 6G **181**
Citadel Hgts. CT17: Dover 6G **181**
Citadel Rd. CT17: Dover 6G **181**
Citroen Cl. CT6: H Bay 3C **194**
CITY AIRPORT 1B 50 (3B 6)
City Bus. Pk. CT1: Cant 8B **168**
CITY OF LONDON 3G 5
City Rd. EC1 . . . . 2F **5**
City Thameslink Station (Rail) 3F 5
City Vw. CT2: Cant 2J **171**
City Way ME1: Roch 8A **80** (3H **17**)
Civic Sq. RM18: Tilb 5C **8**
Civic Way *TN1: Tun W 2H 157*
(off Crescent Rd.)
Clacket La. TN16: Westrm 6A **116** (2B **24**)
Clackhams La. TN6: Jar B 7G **35**
Clacton Rd. E6 . . . . 2A **6**
Claire C'way. DA2: Dart 2E **60**
Claire Ct. CT10: B'stairs 8M **209**
Claire Ho. ME16: Maid 4B **126**
Clairville Point *SE23 . . . . 8A 54*
(off Dacres Rd.)
Clancy Gdns. TN17: Cran 7B **176**
Clandon Rd. ME5: Chat'm 9G **94** (5J **17**)
Clanricarde Gdns. TN1: Tun W 2G **157**
Clanricarde Rd. TN1: Tun W 2G **157**
Clanwilliam Rd. CT14: Deal 5N **177**
CLAPHAM 6E 4
CLAPHAM COMMON 6E **4**
Clapham Comn. Nth. Side SW4 . . . . 6E **4**
Clapham Comn. Sth. Side SW4 . . . . 6E **4**
Clapham Common Station (Tube) 6E 4
Clapham Comn. W. Side SW4 . . . . 6D **4**
Clapham High St. SW4 . . . . 6E **4**
Clapham High Street Station (Rail) 6E 4
Clapham Hill
CT5: Whits 8E **226** (4F **21**)
CLAPHAM JUNCTION 6D 4
Clapham Junction Station (Rail) 6D 4
Clapham North Station (Tube) 6F 5
CLAPHAM PARK 6E 4
Clapham Pk. Rd. SW4 . . . . 6E **4**
Clapham Rd. SW9 . . . . 6F **5**
Clapham South Station (Tube) 6E 4
Claphatch La. TN5: Wadh 6D **36**
CLAP HILL 4C 40
CLAPPER HILL 4C 38
Clapper Hill CT4: Walt 6G **31**
Clapper La. TN12: S'hrst 1H **223** (7J **27**)
Clappers, The TN32: Rob 4B **44**
CLAPTON PARK 1H 5
Clapton Station (Rail) 1H 5
Clara Pl. SE18 . . . . 4C **50**
Clare Av. TN9: Tonb 6F **144**
Clare Cnr. SE9 . . . . 5D **56**
Clare Dr. CT6: H Bay 5C **194**
Clare La. ME19: E Mal 1C **124** (1E **26**)
Claremont Av. KT3: N Mald 3B **12**
Claremont Cl. BR6: Farnb 5C **84**
CT14: Kgdn 3E **200**
E16 . . . . 1C **50**
Claremont Cres. DA1: Cray 2F **58**
Claremont Gdns. CT11: Ram 5G **210**
TN2: Tun W 3H **157**
Claremont Pl. CT1: Cant 3M **171**
CT11: Ram 4J **211**
DA11: Grav'nd 5G 62
(off Arthur St.)
ME4: Chat'm 9D **80**
Claremont Rd. BR1: Brom 7A **70**
BR8: Swanl 3F **72**
CT14: Deal 5L **177**
CT14: Kgdn 3E **200**
CT20: F'stone 6J **189**
ME14: Maid 4E **126**
TN1: Tun W 3H **157**
Claremont St. CT6: H Bay 4D **194**
E16 . . . . 2C **50**
Claremont Ter. CT13: Wdboro 7J **217**
Claremont Way ME4: Chat'm 9C **80** (3H **17**)
Clarence Av. BR1: Brom 7A **70**
CT9: Clift 3H **209**
KT3: N Mald 2A **12**
ME1: Roch 8N **79**
Clarence Ct. ME14: Weav 5H **127**
Clarence Cres. DA14: Sidc 8K **57**
Clarence Gdns. ME12: Ward 5J **203**
Clarence La. SW15 . . . . 6A **4**
Clarence Pl. CT14: Deal 3N **177**
CT17: Dover 7J **181**
DA12: Grav'nd 5G **63**
Clarence Rd. BR1: Brom 6N **69**
CT6: H Bay 2E **194**
CT11: Ram 6F **210**
CT14: Walm 7N **177** (4J **33**)
CT18: Cap F 3B **174**
DA6: Bexhth 2N **57**
DA14: Sidc 8K **57**
ME4: Chat'm 1E **94**
RM17: Grays 4A **8**
SE9 . . . . 7A **56**
TN1: Tun W 2G **157**
TN16: Big H 6F **164**
Clarence Row DA12: Grav'nd 5G **63**
ME12: S'ness 2D **220**
TN1: Tun W 2G **156**
Clarence St. CT6: H Bay 2F **194**
CT20: F'stone 6K **189**
Clarenden Pl. DA2: Dart 1F **72**
CLARENDON 5G 181
Clarendon Cl. BR5: St P 6J **71**
ME10: Sit 1G **114**
ME14: Bear 5K **127**
Clarendon Ct. *BR3: Beck'm 4E 68*
(off Blair Ct.)
Clarendon Ct. BR3: Beck'm 4G **68**
(West Oak)
Clarendon Dr. ME2: Strood 3L **79**
Clarendon Gdns. CT11: Ram 6H **211**
(not continuous)
DA2: Dart 5D **60**
TN2: Tun W 4G **156**
Clarendon Grn. BR5: St P 7J **71**
Clarendon Gro. BR5: St P 7J **71**
Clarendon M. CT10: B'stairs 9L **209**
DA5: Bex'y 6C **58**
TN28: New R 1L **213**
Clarendon Path BR5: St P 7J **71**
(not continuous)
Clarendon Pl. CT17: Dover 5G **181**
ME14: Maid 5D 126
(off King St.)
TN13: S'oaks 7H **119**
Clarendon Ri. SE13 . . . . 2F **54**
Clarendon Rd. CT3: Aysm 2D **162**
CT9: Mgte 3E **208**
CT10: B'stairs 9L **209**
CT17: Dover 5H **181**
DA12: Grav'nd 4H **63**
TN13: S'oaks 6H **119**
W11 . . . . 3C **4**
Clarendon St. CT6: H Bay 3D **194**
CT17: Dover 5G **181**
Clarendon Way BR5: St P 6J **71**
BR7: Chst 6H **71**
TN2: Tun W 4F **156**
Clarens St. SE6 . . . . 7C **54**
Clare Rd. CT5: Whits 3G **227**
Clareville Rd. BR5: Farnb 3E **84**
Clare Way DA7: Bexhth 8N **51**
TN13: S'oaks 1K **131**
Clare Wood Dr. ME19: E Mal 1C **124**
Claridge Ct. ME7: Hpstd 7J **95**
Claridge M. *CT21: Hythe 6J 199*
(off Chapel St.)
Clark Cl. DA8: Erith 8H **53**
Clarke Cres. TN24: Kenn 5J **159**
Clarkes Cl. CT14: Deal 6J **177**
Clarke's Grn. Rd. TN15: Knat 5A **104** (6H **15**)
Clark M. ME20: Aylfd 9K **109**
Clark Rd. TN28: G'stne 5N **213**
Clarkslands TN29: Newchu 7C **40**
Clarks La. CR6: Warl, Westrm 2A **24**
TN14: Hals 3A **102**
TN16: Tats 5A **116** (2A **24**)
Claston Cl. DA1: Cray 2F **58**
Claudius Gro. TN23: Ashf 4D **160**
Clavadel Rd. TN12: Pad W 8M **147**
Clavell Cl. ME8: Gill 7A **96**
Clavering Ho. *SE13 . . . . 2G 55*
(off Blessington Rd.)
Claverton St. SW1 . . . . 4E **4**
Claxfield Rd. ME9: Lyn, Tey 9H **223** (6H **19**)
Claxton Path *SE4 . . . . 2A 54*
(off Coston Wlk.)
Claybank Gro. SE13 . . . . 1E **54**
Claybridge Rd. SE12 . . . . 9M **55**
Claydown M. SE18 . . . . 5C **50**
Clay Farm Rd. SE9 . . . . 7E **56**
CLAYGATE
Marden 7F 27
Tonbridge 4M 133 (4A 26)
Claygate ME15: Maid 8G **126**
ME17: Holl 7F **128**
TN23: Ashf 4C **160**
Claygate Cres. CR0: Croy 7F **82**
CLAYGATE CROSS 6N 121 (2A 26)
Claygate La. TN11: S'brne 3M **133** (3A **26**)
Claygate Rd. ME18: Ladd 6E **26**
TN12: Coll S 6E **26**
CLAYHILL 4H 45
Clayhill TN17: Goud 3B **190** (4F **37**)
Clayhill Cres. SE9 . . . . 9N **55**
Clay Hill Rd. TN3: Lamb 3C **36**
Clayton Cft. Rd. DA2: Dart 7H **59**
Clayton's La. TN3: A'hst 4F **154**
Claytonville Ter. DA17: Belv 2D **52**
Clay Tye Rd. RM14: Upm 1K **7**
Claywood Cl. BR6: Orp 1G **84**
Claywood La. DA2: Bean 8K **61**
Clayworth Cl. DA15: Sidc 4K **57**
Cleanthus Cl. SE18 . . . . 8D **50**
Cleanthus Rd. SE18 . . . . 9D **50**
(not continuous)
Clearmount Dr. TN27: Char'g 2K **175**
Clearway ME19: Addtn 9F **106**
Clearways Bus. Est. TN15: W King 8E **88**
Clearways Cvn. Pk. TN15: W King 8D **88**
Cleave Av. BR6: Chels 7G **85**
Cleaver La. CT11: Ram 5J **211**
Cleave Rd. ME7: Gill 1H **95**
Cleavers TN17: Siss 3C **222**
Cleavers Cl. TN17: Siss 3C **222**
Cleavesland ME18: Ladd 5E **26**
Cleeve Av. TN2: Tun W 3K **157**
Cleeve Ct. ME19: W Mal 7N **123**
Cleeve Pk. Gdns. DA14: Sidc 7K **57**
Cleeves Vw. *DA1: Dart 4L 59*
(off Priory Pl.)
Clegg Ho. SE3 . . . . 2L **55**
Clematis Av. ME8: Gill 6L **95**
Clemens Pl. ME19: W Mal 7A **124**
Clement Cl. CT1: Cant 1A **172**
ME10: Sit 3F **98**
Clement Ct. ME16: Maid 4A **126**
Clementine Cl. CT6: H Bay 3L **195**
Clement Rd. BR3: Beck'm 5A **68**
Clement's Rd. CT12: Ram 2G **210**
CLEMENT STREET 2L 73
Clement St. BR8: Swanl, Dart 2L **73** (1G **15**)
DA4: S at H, Swanl 2L **73**
Clenches Farm La. TN13: S'oaks 8H **119**
Clenches Farm Rd. TN13: S'oaks 8H **119**
Clendon Way SE18 . . . . 4F **50**
Clerke Dr. ME10: Kems'y 3H **99**
CLERKENWELL 2F 5
Clerkenwell Rd. EC1 . . . . 2F **5**
Clerks Fld. TN27: H'crn 8K **191**
Clermont Cl. ME7: Hpstd 8K **95**

Clevedon Ct.—Collingwood Cl.

Clevedon Ct. TN25: C'lck .7C 174
Clevedon Rd. SE20 .4A 68
Cleve Hill ME13: G'ney .5C 20
Cleveland TN2: Tun W .1K 157
Cleveland Cl. CT16: Dover .1G 181
Cleveland Ho. DA11: Nflt .4C 62
ME16: Maid .7M 125
Cleveland Rd. DA16: Well .9H 51
ME7: Gill .6G 81
Cleveland St. W1 .2E 4
Cleve Rd. DA14: Sidc .8M 57
NW6 .1C 4
Cleves Ct. DA1: Dart .5M 59
Cleves Rd. TN15: Kems'g .8M 103
Cleves Way TN23: Ashf .1C 160
Clewer Ho. *SE2* .*2M 51*
(off Wolvercote Rd.)
Clewson Ri. ME14: Pen H .1E 126
Cley Ho. SE4 .2A 54
Cliff Av. CT6: H Bay .2K 195
Cliff Cl. CT21: Hythe .5L 199
Cliff Dr. CT6: H Bay .3D 194
ME12: Ward .4J 203
CLIFFE .2C 176 (5G 9)
Cliffe Av. CT9: Mgte .2N 207
Cliffe Ct. ME3: Cliffe .2C 176
Cliffe Ho. CT20: F'stone .8G 189
Cliffe Rd. CT14: Kgdn .3F 200 (5J 33)
ME2: Strood .2L 79 (1G 17)
CLIFFE WOODS .5M 65 (7G 9)
Cliff Fld. CT8: Wgte S .3H 207
Cliff Gdns. ME12: Minst .6M 221
SS9: Lgh S .1C 10
Cliff Hill ME17: Bou Mo .4F 138 (4J 27)
Cliff Hill Rd. ME17: Bou Mo .4F 138 (4J 27)
Clifford Av. BR7: Chst .2B 70
SW14 .5A 4
(not continuous)
Clifford Gdns. CT14: Deal .8L 177
Clifford Ho. *BR3: Beck'm* .*2E 68*
(off Calverley Cl.)
Clifford Pk. Cvn. Site CT14: Walm .1D 200
Clifford Rd. CT5: Whits .5H 227
SE25 .2H 13
Cliff Pde. SS9: Lgh S .1C 10
Cliff Prom. CT10: B'stairs .6N 209
Cliff Reach DA9: Bluew .4F 60
Cliff Rd. CT5: Whits .2H 227
CT7: Birch .3D 206 (2E 22)
CT10: B'stairs .6M 209
CT20: F'stone .8G 188
CT21: Hythe .5L 199 (5J 41)
Cliff Sea Gro. CT6: H Bay .3D 194
CLIFFSEND .7B 210 (4H 23)
Cliffsend Gro. CT12: C'snd .7B 210
Cliffsend Rd. CT12: C'snd .7B 210 (4H 23)
Cliffside Dr. CT10: B'stairs .3L 211
Cliffstone Ct. CT20: F'stone .6H 189
Cliff St. CT11: Ram .6J 211
Cliff Ter. CT9: Mgte .2D 208 (1H 23)
Clifftown Gdns. CT6: H Bay .3C 194
Clifftown Pde. SS1: Sth S .1D 10
Cliff Vw. Gdns. ME12: Ley S .7J 203
ME12: Ward .4K 203
Cliff Vw. Rd. CT12: C'snd .6B 210
Cliffview Rd. SE13 .1D 54
Clifton Cl. BR6: Farnb .6E 84
ME2: Strood .6K 79
ME14: Maid .4E 126
Clifton Cotts. TN2: Tun W .6K 151
Clifton Ct. BR3: Beck'm .4E 68
Clifton Cres. CT20: F'stone .8H 189
Clifton Gdns. CT2: Cant .9K 167
CT9: Mgte .2D 208
CT20: F'stone .7J 189
W9 .2D 4
Clifton Gro. DA11: Grav'nd .5G 62
Clifton Lawn CT11: Ram .7H 211
Clifton Mans. CT20: F'stone .7J 189
Clifton Marine Pde.
DA11: Nflt, Grav'nd .4E 62 (6B 8)
(not continuous)
Clifton Pl. CT9: Mgte .2E 208
TN1: Tun W .3H 157
Clifton Rd. CT5: Whits .5F 226
CT9: Mgte .3E 208
(not continuous)
CT11: Ram .4F 210
CT20: F'stone .7J 189 (5B 42)
DA11: Grav'nd .4F 62
DA14: Sidc .9G 57
DA16: Well .1L 57
ME7: Gill .5F 80
TN2: Tun W .7J 151
Clifton St. CT9: Mgte .2D 208
CLIFTONVILLE .3G 208 (1J 23)
Cliftonville Av. CT9: Mgte .3E 208
CT12: Ram .3F 210
Cliftonville Ct. *CT9: Clift* .*2E 208*
(off Edgar Rd.)
SE12 .6K 55
Cliftonville M. CT9: Clift .2E 208
Clifton Wlk. DA2: Dart .4B 60
Clim Down CT14: Kgdn .3F 200
Clinch St. ME3: H Hals .1K 67 (5K 9)
Clinton Av. DA16: Well .2J 57
ME2: Strood .4H 79
Clinton Cl. ME17: Cox .5M 137
Clinton La. TN8: Chid, Four E .5A 142 (6D 24)
Clints La. CT4: Woot .5B 32
Clipper Blvd. DA2: Dart .1E 60
Clipper Blvd. W. DA2: Dart .1D 60
Clipper Cl. ME2: Med E .5B 80
Clipper Ct. ME2: Med E .5B 80
Clipper Cres. DA12: Grav'nd .9L 63
Clipper Way SE13 .2F 54
Clive Av. DA1: Cray .4G 58
Cliveden Cl. ME16: Alltn .2A 126
Clive Dennis Ct. TN24: W'boro .9J 159
Cliveden Pl. SW1 .4E 4
Clive Ho. ME20: Aylfd .1K 125
Clive Rd. CT9: Mgte .8E 208
CT12: C'snd .6B 210
DA11: Grav'nd .4G 62
Clive Rd. DA17: Belv .4B 52
ME1: Roch .9N 79
ME10: Sit .6C 98
CLOCK HOUSE .6E 12
Clockhouse TN2: Tun W .8M 151
TN23: Ashf .9C 158
Clockhouse Ct. BR3: Beck'm .5B 68
Clockhouse La. RM16: Chad H .4A 8
(not continuous)
Clock Ho. La. TN13: S'oaks .5H 119
(not continuous)
Clockhouse Pk. TN25: C'lck .7D 174
Clock Ho. Rd. BR3: Beck'm .6B 68 (2J 13)
Clock House Station (Rail) .4B 68 (2J 13)
Clock Twr. M. ME6: Snod .1E 108
Cloisterham Rd. ME1: Roch .4A 94
Cloisters Av. BR2: Shortl .8B 70
Cloisters Ct. DA7: Bexhth .1C 58
Cloisters, The *CT1: Cant* .*1M 171*
(off King St.)
CT11: Ram .6H 211
DA1: Dart .*4M 59*
(off Orchard St.)
ME10: Sit .7F 98
ME17: Len .7L 201
Cloonmore Av. BR6: Chels .5H 85
Clopton Ct. ME8: Gill .3N 95
Close, The BR3: Beck'm .7B 68
BR5: Pet W .9G 70
CT2: Cant .7M 167
(Downs Rd.)
CT2: Cant .8J 167
(St Thomas' Hill)
CT4: Brid .9E 172
CT15: Lyd'n .7D 32
CT19: F'stone .*3K 189*
(off Fleming Way)
CT21: Salt .4J 199
DA2: Dart .8K 59
DA3: Long .5A 76
DA5: Bex'y .4B 58
DA14: Sidc .9K 57
ME1: Roch .6N 79
ME13: Fav .6G 187
ME19: Addtn .7H 107
ME19: Birl .5N 107
TN3: Groom .7K 155
TN4: Tun W .6J 151
TN8: Chid .5B 142
TN13: S'oaks .6F 118
TN15: Bor G .1N 121
TN15: Igh .3K 121
TN16: Big H .7D 100
TN23: Ashf .2D 160
TN25: Wye .2M 159
Cloth Hall Gdns. TN27: Bidd .7L 163
Clothworkers Rd. SE18 .7F 50
Cloudberry Cl. ME16: Alltn .3A 126
Cloudesley Cl. ME1: Roch .2M 93
Cloudesley Rd. DA7: Bexhth .8A 52
DA8: Erith .8G 52
Clovelly Dr. ME12: Minst .4J 221
Clovelly Rd. CT5: Whits .6F 226
DA7: Bexhth .6N 51
Clovelly Way BR6: St M Cry .9H 71
Clover Bank Vw. ME5: Chat'm .5E 94
Clover Ct. ME10: Sit .6J 99
Cloverdale Gdns. DA15: Sidc .4H 57
Clover Lay ME8: Rain .1C 96
Clover Ri. CT5: Whits .4K 227
Clovers, The DA11: Nflt .9D 62
Clover St. ME4: Chat'm .8C 80
(not continuous)
Clover Ter. ME15: Maid .9G 126
Clover Wlk. TN8: Eden .4D 184
Clover Way TN12: Pad W .1M 153
Clowders Rd. SE6 .8C 54
Clowes Ct. CT2: Cant .7J 167
Clubb's La. TN29: B'lnd .3D 46
Club Cotts. TN11: Hild .8D 132
Club Gdns. Rd. BR2: Shortl .1K 83
Cluny Rd. ME13: Fav .5K 187
Clyde Rd. TN10: Tonb .1J 145
Clydesdale Ho. *DA18: Erith* .*2N 51*
(off Kale Rd.)
Clyde St. CT1: Cant .1N 171
ME12: S'ness .2E 220
Clydon Cl. DA8: Erith .6F 52
Clynton Way TN23: Ashf .2E 160
C.M. Booth Collection
of Historic Vehicles .2B 214 (7C 38)
Coach & Horses Pas. *TN2: Tun W* .*3G 156*
(off Market St.)
Coach Dr. TN26: Hoth .2M 197 (7J 29)
Coach Dr., The DA13: Meop .3D 106
Coach Ho. M. SE23 .4A 54
Coachman's M. ME1: Roch .7N 79
Coach Rd.
CT18: Acr, D'sole .4H 193 (2A 42)
ME17: Bou Ma .5E 28
TN4: R'hall .1C 156 (3J 35)
TN15: Igh, Ivy H .6G 120 (2K 25)
TN27: Eger .5E 28
Coalhouse Fort .5E 8
Coalpit La. ME9: Frin .1F 29
Coast Dr. TN28: G'stne .6N 213 (4K 47)
TN29: G'stne, Lydd .8H 213 (5K 47)
TN29: St M Bay .4M 215 (2K 47)
Coastguard Alley CT5: Whits .4E 226
Coastguard Cotts. CT6: H Bay .3A 194
CT11: Ram .7E 210
CT14: Kgdn .5F 200
CT16: Dover .4M 181
CT21: Hythe .7J 199
ME3: Isle G .*8C 190*
(off Chapel Rd.)
Coastguard Ho. Cvn. Pk. CT6: H Bay .3A 194
Coast Rd. TN28: L'stne .4M 215 (3K 47)
TN29: L'stne .4M 215 (2K 47)
Coates Hill Rd. BR1: Brom .5C 70
Coats Av. ME12: S'ness .4B 220
Cobay Cl. CT21: Hythe .6L 199
COBBARN .5H 35
Cobb Cl. ME2: Strood .4H 79
Cobb Ct. *CT9: Mgte* .*2D 208*
(off Cobbs Pl.)
Cobbett Cl. ME19: E Mal .1D 124
Cobbett Rd. SE9 .1A 56
Cobbett's Ride TN2: Tun W .4F 156
Cobbetts Way TN8: Eden .7C 184
Cobblers Bri. Rd. CT6: H Bay .3E 194 (3J 21)
Cobblestones ME7: Hpstd .6J 95
Cobbs Cl. ME18: W'bury .1C 136
TN12: Pad W .9L 147
Cobbs Hill CT4: Old L .6K 175 (2D 30)
Cobbs M. CT20: F'stone .7J 189
Cobbs Pas. CT21: Hythe .6K 199
Cobbs Pl. CT9: Mgte .2D 208
Cobbsthorpe Vs. SE26 .9A 54
Cobbs Wood Ind. Est. TN23: Ashf .8C 158
Cobb Wlk. ME13: Fav .4F 186
Cobden Ct. BR2: Shortl .7M 69
Cobden Pl. CT1: Cant .1N 171
Cobden Rd. BR6: Farnb .5F 84
CT19: F'stone .5E 188
CT21: Hythe .7J 199
ME4: Chat'm .1E 94
TN13: S'oaks .5K 119
Cobdown Cl. ME20: Dit .8F 108
Cobdown Gro. ME8: Rain .1C 96
Cobdown Pk. ME20: Dit .8G 108
Cob Dr. DA12: Shorne .1C 78
Cobfield ME17: Cha S .7K 139
COBHAM .7M 77 (2D 16)
Cobham Av. ME10: Sit .1F 114
Cobhambury Rd. DA12: Cobh .7M 77 (2D 16)
DA13: Lud'n .8N 77 (2D 16)
Cobham Chase ME13: Fav .4F 186
Cobham Cl. BR2: Shortl .1A 84
CT1: Cant .4B 172
DA9: G'hithe .4H 61
DA15: Sidc .4K 57
ME2: Strood .5J 79
ME16: Maid .5B 126
Cobham Dr. ME19: W Mal .6A 124
Cobham Hall .6A 78 (2E 16)
Cobham Ho. DA8: Erith .7G 53
Cobham Pl. DA6: Bexhth .3M 57
Cobham Ri. ME7: Gill .7H 81
Cobhams TN3: Speld .6A 150
Cobham St. DA11: Grav'nd .5F 62
Cobham Ter. DA9: G'hithe .3H 61
DA11: Nflt .*6E 62*
(off Southfleet Rd.)
Cobland Rd. SE12 .9M 55
Coborn Rd. E3 .2J 5
Cobs Cl. TN15: Igh .3J 121
Cobsden Cl. TN29: St M Bay .2N 215
Cobsdene DA12: Grav'nd .2J 77
Cobsden Rd. TN29: St M Bay .2N 215
Cobs, The TN30: Tent .8B 224
Cobtree Cl. ME5: Chat'm .3F 94
Cobtree Mnr. Pk. ME14: S'lng .8A 110
Cobtree Rd. ME17: Cox .5N 137
Cockerhurst Rd. TN14: S'ham .7E 86 (5F 15)
Cockering Rd. CT1: Cant .6G 171 (1G 31)
CT4: Chart'm, Cant .9D 170 (2F 31)
(not continuous)
Cockham Cotts. ME3: Hoo .9G 67
Cock La. CT4: Elham .7N 183
TN26: Hams .3L 191 (6A 40)
Cockmannings La. BR5: St M Cry .2M 85 (3D 14)
Cockmannings Rd. BR5: St M Cry .1M 85 (3D 14)
COCK MARLING .6K 45
Cockpit, The TN12: Mard .3C 212
Cockreed La. TN28: New R .2J 213 (3J 47)
Cocksett Av. BR6: Chels .7G 84
COCKSHOT .6C 192
COCK STREET .6G 138 (4J 27)
Cocksure La. DA14: Sidc .8B 58 (7E 6)
Codrington Cres. DA12: Grav'nd .1H 77
Codrington Gdns. DA12: Grav'nd .1J 77
(not continuous)
Codrington Hill SE23 .5B 54
Codrington Rd. CT11: Ram .5H 211
Cogans Ter. CT1: Cant .4L 171
Cogate Rd. TN12: Pad W .9K 147
Coggan Ho. *CT1: Cant* .*3M 171*
(off Station Rd. E.)
Colburn Rd. CT10: B'stairs .2L 211
Colchester Cl. ME5: Chat'm .4C 94
Cold Arbor Rd. TN13: Riv .6E 118 (2F 25)
COLDBLOW .6D 58 (7F 7)
Coldblow CT14: Walm .2B 200 (5H 33)
TN26: Wdchu .6F 228
Cold Blow Camping ME14: T'hm .9C 112
Coldblow Cotts. ME17: Lint .6D 138
Cold Blow Cres. DA5: Bex'y .6E 58
Coldblow La. ME9: T'hm .2B 128 (1A 28)
ME14: T'hm .2B 128 (1A 28)
Coldblow Rd. TN26: Wdchu .5H 39
Coldbridge La. ME17: Bou Ma .6D 28
TN27: Eger .6D 28
COLDHARBOUR .7F 132 (4K 25)
COLD HARBOUR .4D 18
Cold Harbour CT1: Cant .9N 167
Coldharbour Crest SE9 .8C 56
Coldharbour La. CT4: Bis .3K 31
Cold Harbour La. ME9: Bob .5A 98 (4D 18)
Coldharbour La. ME10: Kems'y .2G 98
ME14: T'hm .1D 128
ME17: T'hm .1D 128 (7B 18)
ME20: Aylfd .1L 125
(not continuous)
RM19: Rain .3H 53
SE5 .6G 5
SW9 .6F 5
TN11: Hild .1D 144 (5J 25)
TN25: Wye .2N 159 (6D 30)
TN29: Old R .3F 47
TN31: Rye F, Iden .4A 46
Coldharbour Leisure Cen. .7B 56
Coldharbour Rd. DA11: Nflt .7D 62 (7B 8)
Cold Harbour Rd. ME13: O'den .3G 29
ME17: O'den .3G 29
Coldharbour Rd. TN8: Chid H .6E 148 (2F 35)
TN11: Chid H, Pens .6E 148 (2F 35)
TN17: Bendn .6K 37
COLDRED .9M 219 (6D 32)
Coldred Hill CT15: Cold, Lyd'n .7D 32
Coldred Rd. CT15: Cold, S'wll .8L 219 (6D 32)
CT15: Eyt, W'share .1A 178 (6D 32)
ME15: Maid .4J 139
Coldrum La. ME19: Tros .4H 107
Coldrum Stones Long Barrow .4H 107 (6C 16)
Coldswood Rd. CT12: Ram .1C 210
Colebeck St. DA8: Erith .6G 52
Colebrooke Ct. DA14: Sidc .8K 57
Colebrooke Ri. BR2: Shortl .5H 69
Colebrook Ind. Est. TN2: Tun W .5L 151
Colebrook Rd. TN4: Tun W .7J 151
Cole Cl. SE28 .1K 51
Colegate Dr. ME14: Bear .5M 127
Colegates Cl. ME13: Oare .2E 186
Colegates Ct. ME13: Oare .2F 186
Colegates Rd. ME13: Oare .2E 186 (5A 20)
Coleman Cres. CT12: Ram .2G 210
Coleman Dr. ME10: Kems'y .2G 99
Coleman Rd. DA17: Belv .4B 52
Colemans Cl. TN29: Lydd .3L 205
COLEMAN'S HATCH .6C 34
Colemans Hatch Rd.
RH18: Cole H, Wych C .6B 34
Coleman's Hatch Rd. TN7: Cole H .6B 34
Colemans Heath SE9 .8C 56
Coleman's Stairs CT7: Birch .3F 206
Coleman's Stairs Rd. CT7: Birch .3F 206
Coleman's Yd. CT11: Ram .6J 211
Colepits Wood Rd. SE9 .3F 56
Coleridge Cl. ME20: Lark .6D 108
Coleridge Gdns. CT3: Aysm .1D 162
Coleridge Rd. DA1: Dart .2B 60
Coleridge Way BR6: St M Cry .9J 71
Cole Rd. ME13: Fav .5J 187
Colesburg Rd. BR3: Beck'm .6C 68
Coles Ct. TN2: Tun W .2J 157
Coleshall Cotts. ME9: Iwade .9J 197
Coleshill Cl. ME15: Maid .2J 139
Coles La. TN16: Bras .5L 117 (2D 24)
Cole Ter. ME17: Len .8L 201
Colets Orchard TN14: Otf .7J 103
Colette Cl. CT10: B'stairs .3L 209
Coleville Cres. TN28: G'stne .7H 213
Colewood Dr. ME2: Roch .4F 78
Colewood Rd. CT5: Whits .2N 227 (3H 21)
Colfe & Hatcliffe Glebe *SE13* .*3E 54*
(off Lewisham High St.)
Colfe Rd. SE23 .6B 54
Colfe Way ME10: Kems'y .3H 99
Colin Blythe Rd. TN10: Tonb .2M 145
Colin Cl. BR4: W W'ck .4J 83
CR0: Croy .4C 82
DA2: Dart .4B 60
Colin's Way CT21: Hythe .8A 188
COLKINS .9L 187 (7B 20)
Collard Cl. CT6: H Bay .3J 195
Collard Ho. CT1: Cant .2B 172
Collard Rd. TN24: W'boro .2L 161
Collards Cl. CT12: Monk'n .6A 212
Collards La. CT4: Elham .8L 183
College Av. ME7: Gill .8E 80
ME15: Maid .6C 126
TN9: Tonb .8F 144
College Cotts. ME15: Maid .7C 126
College Ct. ME15: Maid .6D 126
TN23: Ashf .8G 158
College Cres. NW3 .1D 4
College Dr. TN2: Tun W .1K 157
College La. RH19: E Grin .3A 34
COLLEGE PARK .2B 4
College Pk. Cl. SE13 .2G 54
College Rd. BR1: Brom .4K 69 (2A 14)
BR8: Swanl .4F 72 (2F 15)
CT1: Cant .2A 172
CT9: Mgte .5C 208 (2H 23)
CT11: Ram .4H 211 (4J 23)
CT14: Deal .2N 177 (3J 33)
DA11: Nflt .3A 62
KT17: Eps .6A 12
ME4: Chat'm .5C 80
ME10: Sit .9D 98 (5E 18)
ME15: Maid .6D 126 (2H 27)
ME20: Lark .7F 108
SE19 .7G 5
SE21 .7G 5
College Row *CT17: Dover* .*5G 180*
(off Elms Va. Rd.)
College Slip BR1: Brom .4K 69
College Sq. *CT9: Mgte* .*3D 208*
(off Union Row)
College Sq. Shop. Cen. CT9: Mgte .3D 208
College St. NW1 .1E 4
College Vw. SE9 .6N 55
College Wlk. *CT9: Mgte* .*3D 208*
(off Union Row)
ME15: Maid .6D 126
College Way CT3: Wing .8J 225
College Yd. ME1: Roch .6N 79
Coller Cres. DA2: Dart .1E 74
Collet Rd. TN15: Kems'g .8M 103
Collett Cl. TN25: Elms .7F 31
Collet Wlk. ME8: Gill .7N 95
Collie Dr. TN23: Kgnt .4C 160
COLLIER'S GREEN
Cranbrook .3H 37
Staplecross .4E 44
Colliers Grn. Rd. TN17: Cran, Siss .4H 37
Colliers Shaw BR2: Kes .6N 83
COLLIER STREET .7F 27
Colliers Water La. CR7: Thor H .2F 13
COLLIER'S WOOD .1D 12
COLLIERS WOOD .1D 12
Colliers Wood Station (Tube) .1D 12
Collindale Av. DA8: Erith .7C 52
DA15: Sidc .6J 57
Collingbourne TN23: Ashf .3C 160
Collinge Cl. ME19: E Mal .9E 108
Collings Wlk. ME8: Gill .7N 95
Collington Cl. DA11: Nflt .5D 62
Collington Ter. ME15: Maid .4H 139
Collingwood Cl. CT8: Wgte S .4J 207
CT10: B'stairs .9J 209

Cyril Lodge—Denham Ho.

Cyril Lodge DA14: Sidc .9J 57
Cyril Rd. BR6: Orp .1J 85
DA7: Bexhth .9N 51

D

Dabbling Cl. DA8: Erith .6J 53
Dabbs Pl. DA13: Cobh .5J 77
Dacre Gdns. SE13 .2H 55
Dacre Pk. SE13 .1H 55
Dacre Pl. SE13 .1H 55
Dacres Rd. SE23 .7A 54
Daerwood Cl. BR2: Shortl .2B 84
Daffodil Cl. CR0: Croy .2A 82
Daffodil Rd. ME2: Strood .5J 79
DAGENHAM .1E 6
Dagenham & Redbridge F.C. .1E 6
Dagenham Av. RM9: Dag .2E 6
(not continuous)
Dagenham Dock Station (Rail) .2E 6
Dagenham East Station (Tube) .1F 7
Dagenham Heathway Station (Tube) .1E 6
Dagenham Rd. RM7: Rush G .1F 7
RM10: Dag .1F 7
RM13: Rain .1F 7
Dagg La. TN32: Ewh G .3E 44
Daglish Cl. TN28: New R .3K 213
Dagmar Rd. ME4: Chat'm .1E 94
Dagonet Gdns. BR1: Brom .8K 55
Dagonet Rd. BR1: Brom .8K 55
Dahlia Dr. BR8: Swanl .5G 73
Dahlia Rd. SE2 .4K 51
Daiglen Dr. RM15: S Ock .3K 7
Daimler Av. CT6: H Bay .4C 194
Dainford Cl. BR1: Brom .1G 68
Dainton Cl. BR1: Brom .4L 69
Dairsie Ct. BR1: Brom .4M 69
Dairsie Rd. SE9 .1C 56
Dairy Cl. BR1: Brom .3L 69
DA4: S at H .3B 74
Dairy Cotts. ME3: Allh .4E 204
TN15: Stans .3C 106
Dairy La. SE18 .4B 50
TN8: Eden .4B 24
TN12: Mard .6G 27
Daisy Cl. CR0: Croy .2A 82
Dalberg Way SE2 .3M 51
Dalby Rd. CT9: Mgte .2E 208
Dalby Sq. CT9: Clift .2E 208
Dale Cl. DA1: Cray .4G 59
SE3 .1K 55
Dale End DA1: Cray .4G 59
DALE HILL .7F 37
Dale Ho. SE4 .2B 54
Dale Rd. BR8: Swanl .5D 72
DA1: Cray .4G 59
DA13: Sflt .9N 61 (1A 16)
ME1: Roch .9N 79
Daleside BR6: Chels .6J 85
Daleside Cl. BR6: Chels .7J 85
Dale St. ME4: Chat'm .1B 94
TN1: Tun W .1H 157
Dale, The BR2: Kes .5N 83
Dale Vw. DA8: Erith .9G 53
Dale Wlk. DA2: Dart .6C 60
TN24: Kenn .3G 158
Dalewood ME10: Sit .9H 99
Dale Wood Rd. BR6: Orp .1G 84
Dalison Ct. ME2: Hall'g .7E 92
Dallas-Brett Cres. CT19: F'stone .3L 189
Dallinger Rd. CT7: Birch .3E 206
SE12 .4J 55
Dalling Rd. W6 .4B 4
Dallin Rd. DA6: Bexhth .2M 57
SE18 .7D 50
Dalmain Rd. SE23 .6A 54
Dalmally Vs. CT2: B Oak .6C 168
Dalmaney Cl. CT10: B'stairs .8M 209
Dalmatia Ct. CT17: Dover .3E 180
Dalmeny Av. CT9: Mgte .4H 209
Dalmeny Rd. DA8: Erith .8C 52
Dalmeny Ter. CT21: Hythe .6H 199
(off Dymchurch Rd.)
Dalrymple Rd. SE4 .2B 54
DALSTON .1G 5
Dalston Kingsland Station (Rail) .1G 5
Dalston La. E8 .1G 5
Dalton Cl. BR6: Orp .4G 85
Dalton Ct. CT11: Ram .5J 211
(off Belmont St.)
Daltons Rd. BR6: Crock'n, Orp .4C 86 (4F 15)
BR8: Crock'n .4C 86 (4F 15)
Dalton St. ME7: Gill .6F 80
Dambridge Rd. CT3: Wing .8K 225
Damerham Cl. CT2: Cant .8L 167
Dames Rd. E7 .1A 6
Damien Cl. ME4: Chat'm .1D 94
Damigos Rd. DA12: Grav'nd .6L 63
Damon Cl. DA14: Sidc .8K 57
Damson Ct. BR8: Swanl .7E 72
DANAWAY .9L 97 (5D 18)
Dando Cres. SE3 .1L 55
Dan Dr. ME13: Fav .4E 186
Danebury CR0: Croy .7F 82
Daneby Rd. SE6 .8E 54
Dane Cl. BR6: Farnb .6F 84
DA5: Bex'y .5B 58
ME5: Chat'm .9F 94
ME9: H'lip .6F 96
Dane Ct. ME17: Cox .6N 137
Dane Ct. Gdns. CT10: B'stairs .8H 209
Dane Ct. Rd. CT10: .6G 208 (2J 23)
Dane Cres. CT11: Ram .4J 211
Danecroft Ct. CT1: Cant .1M 171
(off King St.)
Danecroft Ho. CT1: Cant .1M 171
(off King St.)
Danedale Av. ME12: Minst .6N 221
Dane End Rd. CT8: Wgte S .3J 207
Danefield Ct. ME14: Bear .5L 127
Dane Gdns. CT9: Mgte .5F 208
DANEGATE .5J 35
Dane Hill CT9: Mgte .2D 208
Dane Hill Gro. CT9: Mgte .3D 208
Dane Hill Rd. CT4: Elham .6J 31
Dane Hill Row CT9: Mgte .3D 208
Danehill Wlk. DA14: Sidc .8J 57
Danehurst CT8: Wgte S .2K 207
Dane John Cotts. CT1: Cant .3M 171
Dane John Ct. CT1: Cant .3M 171
Dane John M. CT1: Cant .3M 171
Dane John Wlk. CT1: Cant .3M 171
Dane La. CT17: Dover .5H 181
ME9: H'lip .6F 96 (4B 18)
Danemore TN30: Tent .7C 224
Dane Mt. CT9: Mgte .5G 208
Dane Pk. Rd. CT9: Mgte .3D 208
CT11: Ram .4J 211
Dane Rd. CT7: Birch .4A 206
CT9: Mgte .3D 208 (1H 23)
CT11: Ram .4J 211
TN14: Otf .8F 102
Danes Cl. DA11: Nflt .8B 62
Danescombe SE12 .6K 55
Danes Ct. CT16: Dover .2J 181
(not continuous)
Danes Dr. ME12: Ley S .7H 203
Danes Hill ME7: Gill .6K 81 (2K 17)
(not continuous)
Danes Mead ME10: Kems'y .1F 98
Danesmead Ter. CT9: Mgte .3D 208
DANE STREET .3C 30
Daneswood Av. SE6 .8F 54
Dane Valley Rd. CT9: Mgte .4F 208
(not continuous)
CT10: B'stairs .6H 209
Dane Vs. CT18: H'nge .2E 188
Daniel Ho. ME16: Maid .4B 126
Daniels Ct. CT5: Whits .4E 226
Daniels Pl. CT18: H'nge .7M 193
DANIEL'S WATER .2H 39
Daniel's Water TN26: Gt Cha .2J 39
Danley Rd. ME12: Minst .5F 220
Danns La. ME18: W'bury, W Mal .9M 123 (3D 26)
Dansington Rd. DA16: Well .2J 57
Danson Cres. DA16: Well .1K 57
DANSON INTERCHANGE .3M 57 (6D 6)
Danson La. DA16: Well .2K 57 (6D 6)
Danson Mead DA16: Well .1L 57
Danson Rd. DA5: Bex'y, Bexhth .4L 57
DA6: Bexhth .3M 57 (6D 6)
Danson Underpass DA15: Sidc .4L 57
Danson Water Sports Cen. .2L 57
Danson Way ME8: Rain .2N 95
Danton La. CT18: Peene .2C 188 (3K 41)
Dantons Cotts. TN18: Hawkh .5C 192
Danvers Rd. TN9: Tonb .6H 145
Darby Gdns. ME3: High'm .1F 78
Darby Pl. CT20: F'stone .6K 189
Darby Rd. CT20: F'stone .6K 189
Darby's La. TN5: Wadh .7C 36
D'Arcy Pl. BR2: Shortl .7K 69
Darcy Sq. TN28: L'stne .4M 213
Darent Cl. TN13: Riv .4D 118
DARENTH .1C 74 (1J 15)
Darenth Av. TN10: Tonb .2H 145
Darenth Cl. CT6: H Bay .4J 195
Darenth Country Pk. .7D 60
Darenth Dr. DA12: Grav'nd .6N 63
Darenth Gdns. TN16: Westrm .8F 116
Darenth Hill DA2: Dart .1C 74 (1H 15)
Darenth Hill Trad. Est. DA2: Dart .1B 74
DARENTH INTERCHANGE .8B 60 (7H 7)
Darenth La. TN13: Dun G .3F 118
Darent Ho. BR1: Brom .1G 68
Darenth Park Av. DA2: Dart .7D 60
Darenth Pl. DA2: Dart .1D 74
Darenth Ri. ME5: Chat'm .8E 94
Darenth Rd. DA1: Dart .5N 59 (7H 7)
DA2: Dart .1H 15
DA16: Well .8J 51
Darenth Rd. Sth. DA2: Dart .9B 60
Darenth Way TN14: S'ham .2H 103
Darenth Wood Rd. DA2: Dart .6E 60 (7J 7)
(not continuous)
Darent Ind. Pk. DA8: Erith .6L 53
Darent Mead DA4: S at H .4B 74
Darfield Rd. SE4 .3C 54
DARGATE .6D 20
Dargate Cl. ME16: Alltn .2A 126
Dargate Rd. CT2: Denst .6E 20
CT5: Seas .5E 20
ME13: Darg .6E 20
Dargets Rd. ME5: Chat'm .8D 94 (5J 17)
Dark Hill ME13: Fav .4F 186 (6A 20)
Dark La. CT21: Hythe .5H 199
DARLAND .4J 95 (4K 17)
Darland Av. ME7: Gill .1H 95 (3K 17)
Darland Banks Nature Reserve .3K 95
Darley Cl. CR0: Croy .9B 68
Darlinghurst Rd. CT19: F'stone .4E 188
Darling Rd. SE4 .1D 54
Darlington Ct. SE6 .6J 55
Darlington Dr. ME12: Minst .6G 221
Darlington St. CT20: F'stone .6K 189
Darlton Cl. DA1: Cray .1G 59
Darman La. ME18: Ladd .6E 26
TN12: Pad W .6E 26
Darnets Fld. TN14: Otf .8G 103
Darnley Cl. CT10: B'stairs .1K 211
CT20: F'stone .7F 188
ME2: Strood .6H 79
Darnley Ct. DA11: Grav'nd .5F 62
(off Darnley Rd.)
Darnley Dr. TN4: Bidb .2E 150
Darnley Rd. DA11: Grav'nd .6F 62 (7C 8)
(not continuous)
E9 .1H 5
ME2: Strood .6H 79 (2F 17)
Darnley St. DA11: Grav'nd .5F 62
Darns Hill BR8: Crock'n .1D 86
Darracott Cl. CT14: Deal .5L 177
Darrell Cl. CT6: H Bay .4D 194
Darren Gdns. CT10: B'stairs .2K 211
Darrick Wood Rd. BR6: Orp .3F 84
Darrick Wood School Sports Cen. .4E 84
Darrick Wood School Swimming Pool .4E 84
Dart Cl. ME2: Strood .5K 79
DARTFORD .4M 59 (6H 7)
Dartford Borough Mus. .5M 59 (7H 7)
Dartford By-Pass DA1: Bex'y .5E 58 (7F 7)
DA2: Bean, Dart .9N 59 (7F 7)
DA5: Bex'y, Dart .5E 58 (7F 7)
DARTFORD HEATH .6G 58 (7F 7)
Dartford Rd. DA1: Dart .4H 59 (6G 7)
DA4: Farn'm, Hort K, S Dar .9N 73 (3H 15)
DA5: Bex'y .6D 58 (7F 7)
TN13: S'oaks .6K 119 (2G 25)
Dartford Station (Rail) .4M 59 (6H 7)
Dartford Trade Pk. DA1: Dart .7M 59
Dartford Tunnel DA1: Dart .1D 60
Dartford Tunnel App. Rd. DA1: Dart .5B 60
Dartmouth Hill SE10 .5K 5
DARTMOUTH PARK .1E 4
Dartmouth Pk. Hill NW5 .1E 4
Dartmouth Rd. BR2: Shortl .1K 83
SE23 .7H 5
SE26 .7H 5
DARWELL HILL .6A 44
DARWELL HOLE .6A 44
Darwin Cl. BR6: Farnb .6F 84
Darwin College
University of Cambridge .6L 167
Darwin Ct. ME1: Roch .7A 80
Darwin Dr. TN10: Tonb .1K 145
Darwin Leisure Cen. .3F 164
Darwin Rd. CT2: Cant .6L 167
CT7: Birch .3E 206
DA16: Well .1H 57
Daryngton Av. CT7: Birch .4B 206
Dashmonden Cl. ME2: Wain .2N 79
Dashmonden La.
TN27: Bidd, H Hald, St M Cry .1A 224(4D 38)
Dashwood Cl. DA6: Bexhth .3B 58
Dashwood Rd. DA11: Grav'nd .6F 62 (7C 8)
Datchet Rd. SE6 .7C 54
Daubeney Rd. E5 .1J 5
Davema Cl. BR7: Chst .4C 70
Davenport Av. ME7: Gill .5H 81
Davenport Rd. DA14: Sidc .7N 57
SE6 .4E 54
David Av. CT9: Clift .3H 209
David Coffer Ct. DA17: Belv .4C 52
David Evans World of Silk .3F 58
(off Bourne Rd.)
David Ho. DA15: Sidc .8J 57
David Lloyd Leisure
Maidstone .6C 126
Kidbrooke .2L 55
Sidcup .1L 71
David Salomon's House .6D 150
David's Cl. CT10: B'stairs .1M 211
Davidson Rd. CR0: Croy .3G 13
CT2: Cant .1K 171
DAVID STREET .6G 90 (4C 16)
David St. DA13: Meop .7G 90 (5C 16)
Davie Cl. ME12: S'ness .4C 220
Davie Ct. ME12: S'ness .4C 220
DAVINGTON .4G 186 (6A 20)
Davington Cotts. ME13: Fav .4G 186
Davington Hill ME13: Fav .4G 186 (6A 20)
Davis Av. CT14: Deal .6K 177
DA11: Nflt .6D 62
Davis Cl. TN13: S'oaks .4K 119
Davy Ct. ME1: Roch .7N 79
Davy's Pl. DA12: Grav'nd .2K 77
Dawbourne TN30: St Mic .4C 224
Dawell Dr. TN16: Big H .5C 164
Dawes Cl. DA9: G'hithe .3F 60
Dawes Rd. CT2: Denst .3L 165 (7D 20)
ME13: Dunk .3L 165 (7D 20)
SW6 .5C 4
Dawes St. ME7: Gill .7F 80
Dawks Mdw. TN27: H'crn .8K 191
Dawn Ri. ME12: E'chu .2E 202
Dawn Ter. ME6: Snod .2E 108
Dawson Av. BR5: St P .5K 71
Dawson Cl. SE18 .4E 50
Dawson Cotts. ME15: W Far .2J 137
Dawson Dr. BR8: Swanl .3F 72
Dawson Ho. ME14: Maid .2D 126
Dawson Rd. CT19: F'stone .5K 189
Dawsons Row ME13: Osp .6E 186
Day at The Wells .3G 156
(off Linden Pk. Rd.)
Days La. DA15: Sidc .5G 56
Daytona Way CT6: H Bay .3B 194
Dayton Dr. DA8: Erith .5L 53
Dayton Rd. ME13: Bad .2A 30
Deacon Cl. ME2: Strood .4J 79
Deacon Ct. TN4: Tun W .9G 150
(Culverden Pk. Rd.)
TN4: Tun W .1F 156
(Molyneux Pk. Rd.)
Deacons Leas BR6: Orp .5F 84
Deacon Trad. Cen. ME2: Strood .6L 79
Deacon Trad. Est. ME20: Aylfd .8M 109
TN9: Tonb .6K 145
Deadmans La. TN31: Rye .5B 46
Deakin Leas TN9: Tonb .8H 145
Deakins Ter. BR6: Orp .1J 85
DEAL .4N 177 (3J 33)
Deal Castle .5N 177 (4J 33)
Deal Castle Rd. CT14: Deal .5N 177 (3J 33)
Deal Library Gallery .4N 177
(off Broad St.)
Deal Maritime & Local History Mus. .4N 177
Deal Pier .4N 177
Deal Rd. CT13: S'wch .8L 217 (1G 33)
CT14: Worth .8L 217 (1G 33)
CT15: Dover, Gus .3K 181 (1G 43)
CT16: Dover, Gus .3K 181 (1G 43)
Deal Station (Rail) .4M 177 (3J 33)
Deal Tennis Club .5M 177
Deana Ct. ME7: Gill .6F 80
DEAN BOTTOM .6H 75 (2K 15)
Dean Ct. CT1: Cant .1N 171
Dean Cft. CT6: H Bay .5J 195
Deane Cl. CT5: Whits .6G 226
Deanery Cotts. CT4: Chart'm .8C 170
Deanery Rd. TN8: Crock H .4C 24
Dean Farm La. CT3: Wing .2C 32
Dean Hill CT4: Elms .6G 31
Dean La. DA13: Meop .8H 91 (5C 16)
Dean Mead CT19: F'stone .4H 189
Dean Rd. DA13: Meop, Lud'n .4K 91 (4D 16)
ME2: Strood .4K 79
ME10: Sit .5E 98
DEANS BOTTOM .5L 113 (6D 18)
Deans Ct. TN9: Tonb .7H 145
Deans Ga. Cl. SE23 .8A 54
DEANS HILL .4M 113 (6D 18)
Deans Hill ME17: H'shm .7N 129 (2D 28)
Deans Hill Rd. ME9: B'gar .5L 113 (6D 18)
Deans Mill Ct. CT2: Cant .1M 171
DEAN STREET .1N 137 (3H 27)
Dean St. ME15: E Far .4L 137 (4G 27)
W1 .3E 4
Dean's Wlk. TN23: Ashf .2D 160
Deansway Av. CT2: Sturry .4D 168
Deanwood Cl. ME8: Gill .5N 95
Deanwood Dr. ME8: Gill .9M 95 (5A 18)
Deanwood Rd. CT17: Dover .2D 180
De Beauvoir Rd. N1 .1G 5
DE BEAUVOIR TOWN .2G 5
Deborah Cl. CT5: Whits .6H 227
Debrabant Cl. DA8: Erith .6E 52
De Bradelei Wharf CT17: Dover .5J 181
De Burgh Hill CT17: Dover .3H 181
De Burgh St. CT17: Dover .4H 181
Decimus Pl. TN1: Tun W .1H 157
(off Calverley Pk. Gdns.)
Decoy Hill Rd. ME3: H Hals .5K 9
Deedes Cl. CT21: Hythe .5K 199
Deepdale Av. BR2: Shortl .7J 69
Deepdene Ct. BR2: Shortl .6H 69
Deepdene Point SE23 .8A 54
Deepdene Rd. DA16: Well .1J 57
Deerhurst Cl. DA3: Long .6B 76
Deerhurst Gdns. ME16: Maid .5A 126
Deering Cl. ME4: Chat'm .2E 80
Deerleap La. TN14: Knock .4N 101
Deer Pk. Way BR4: W W'ck .3J 83
Deerson La. CT3: Pres .7C 22
DEERTON STREET .5J 19
Defiance Wlk. SE18 .3B 50
Defiant Cl. ME5: Chat'm .5E 94
Defoe Cl. DA8: Erith .8F 52
ME5: Chat'm .5E 94
De Frene Rd. SE26 .9A 54
Degema Rd. BR7: Chst .1D 70
De Havilland Cl. CT18: H'nge .9L 193
De Havillands CT4: Bek .7K 173
Deirdre Chapman Ho. DA10: Swans .4L 61
(off Craylands La.)
Delacourt Cl. CT12: C'snd .7A 210
Delagarde Rd. TN16: Westrm .8E 116
Delamark Rd. ME12: S'ness .2D 220
Delamere Gdns. ME6: Snod .2E 108
Delamere Rd. ME6: Snod .2F 108
Delancey St. NW1 .2E 4
Delane Rd. CT14: Deal .5K 177
De L'angle Row CT4: Chart'm .7D 170
De Lapre Cl. BR5: St M Cry .1M 85
Delarue Cl. TN11: Tonb .7K 133
Delaware Cl. CT2: Sturry .5E 168
Delaware Rd. SS3: Shoe .1G 11
Delce Rd. ME1: Roch .8A 80 (3H 17)
Delfside CT13: S'wch .6M 217
Delf St. CT13: S'wch .5L 217 (7G 23)
Delisle Rd. SE28 .2G 50
(not continuous)
Delius Dr. TN10: Tonb .1M 145
Dell Dr. TN2: Tun W .1K 157
Dellfield Cl. BR3: Beck'm .4F 68
Dell, The DA5: Bex'y .6F 58
DA9: G'hithe .3H 61
SE2 .5J 51
Delmar Cl. CT5: Whits .2M 227
Delmonden Rd. TN18: Hawkh .7G 37
De Luci Rd. DA8: Erith .5D 52
De Lucy St. SE2 .4K 51
Delvan Cl. SE18 .7C 50
Delves Av. TN2: Tun W .4J 157
De Mere Cl. ME8: Gill .5N 95
Demesne Rd. SM6: Wall .4E 12
Demozay Cl. CT18: H'nge .8K 193
Denbeigh Dr. TN10: Tonb .1J 145
Denberry Dr. DA14: Sidc .8K 57
Denbigh Av. ME8: Rain .2N 95
Denbigh Cl. BR7: Chst .2B 70
ME10: Sit .4F 98
Denbigh Pl. TN23: Ashf .1F 160
Denbigh Rd. CT12: Ram .3E 210
TN4: Tun W .7J 151
Denbridge Rd. BR1: Brom .5B 70
Dence Cl. CT6: H Bay .2J 195
Dence Pk. CT6: H Bay .3J 195
Den Cl. BR3: Beck'm .6G 69
Dencora Way TN23: Ashf .9E 158
Dene Av. DA15: Sidc .5K 57
Dene Cl. BR2: Shortl .2J 83
DA2: Dart .9F 58
SE4 .1B 54
Dene Dr. BR6: Chels .4K 85
DA3: Long .5A 76
Dene Holm Rd. DA11: Nflt .8C 62
Dene Lodge Cl. TN15: Bor G .2M 121
Dene Rd. DA1: Dart .5N 59
KT21: Asht .7A 12
Denesfield Ct. TN13: Riv .5C 118
Denesway DA13: Meop .9F 76
Dene, The CR0: Croy .5A 82
CT1: Cant .5A 172
CT21: Hythe .6K 199
TN13: S'oaks .8J 119
TN26: Beth .2J 163
Dene Wlk. CT9: Mgte .6D 208
DA3: Long .6L 75
Dene Way TN3: Speld .7A 150
Dengemarsh Rd. TN29: Lydd .4K 205 (5H 47)
Dengrove Pk. CT2: B Oak .5C 168
Denham Cl. DA16: Well .1L 57
TN29: Dym .8E 182
Denham Ho. ME10: Sit .6E 98

Denham Rd.—Down House & Darwin Mus.

Denham Rd. ME9: N'tn 4K **97**
Denison M. ME3: Lwr Sto 8C **204**
Deniston Av. DA5: Bex'y 6N **57**
Den La. ME18: Coll S 6F **27**
Denmark Hill SE5 5G **5**
Denmark Hill Station (Rail) 5G 5
Denmark Pl. CT1: Cant 1N **171**
Denmark Rd. BR1: Brom 4L **69**
CT11: Ram 4J **211**
Denmark St. CT19: F'stone 5L **189**
Denmark Ter. TN23: Ashf 1G **160**
Dennard Way BR6: Farnb 5D **84**
Denne Cl. CT2: Sturry 4E **168**
DENNE HILL 5B 32
Denne Mnr. La. CT4: Chil'm 3C **30**
Denne's La. TN29: Lydd 1J **205** (4G **47**)
Dennes Mill Cl. TN25: Wye 2L **159**
Denness Rd. TN23: Ashf 2F **160**
Dennett Rd. CR0: Croy 3F **13**
Dennettsland Rd. TN8: Crock H 4C **24**
Denning Av. CR0: Croy 4F **13**
Dennington Ct. TN4: S'bgh 4G **150**
Dennis Cadman Ho. ME20: Aylfd 9K **109**
Dennises La. RM14: Upm 2J **7**
RM15: S Ock 2K **7**
Dennis Rd. DA11: Grav'nd 8F **62**
RM15: S Ock 2K **7**
Dennis Way CT19: F'stone 4E **188**
Dennis Willcocks Cl. ME9: N'tn 5K **97**
DENNY BOTTOM 3J 35
Denny Ct. *DA2: Dart 4B 60*
(off Bow Arrow La.)
Den Rd. BR2: Shortl 6G **69**
Densham Rd. E15 2K **5**
DENSOLE 4K 193 (2A 42)
Densole Cl. BR3: Beck'm 4B **68**
Densole La. CT18: D'sole 4K **193**
Densole Way CT18: D'sole 4K **193**
Denstead Ct. CT2: Cant 7J **167**
Denstead La. CT4: Cha H, Dunk 9B **166** (7E **20**)
Denstead Wlk. ME15: Maid 2J **139**
DENSTROUDE 3C 166 (6F 21)
Denstroude La. CT2: Denst 4B **166** (6E **20**)
Dental Cl. ME10: Sit 6B **98**
Dental St. CT21: Hythe 6K **199**
DENT-DE-LION 3L 207
Dent-de-Lion Ct. CT9: Mgte 3M **207**
Dent-de-Lion Rd. CT8: Wgte S 2K **207**
CT9: Mgte 3M **207**
DENTON
Canterbury 6A 32
Gravesend 5K 63 (7D 8)
Denton Cvn. Site DA12: Grav'nd 5L **63**
Denton Cl. ME15: Maid 9H **127**
Denton Ct. BR2: Shortl 1C **84**
Denton Ct. Rd. DA12: Grav'nd 5K **63**
Denton Grn. ME8: Gill 8L **81**
Denton Rd. DA1: Dart 5F **58** (7F **7**)
DA5: Bex'y 7F **58**
DA16: Well 7L **51**
Denton St. DA12: Grav'nd 5K **63**
Denton Ter. DA5: Bex'y 7F **58**
Denton Way CT9: Mgte 4G **208**
Denver Cl. BR6: Pet W 9G **71**
Denver Rd. DA1: Dart 5H **59**
Denwood SE23 8A **54**
Denwood St. CT4: Crun 5D **30**
TN25: Crun 5D **30**
Denzil Rd. NW10 1A **4**
DEPTFORD 5J 5
Deptford Bri. SE8 5J **5**
Deptford Bridge Station (DLR) 5J 5
Deptford B'way. SE8 5J **5**
Deptford Chu. St. SE8 5J **5**
Deptford High St. SE8 5J **5**
Deptford Station (Rail) 5J 5
Derby Cl. ME10: Sit 5E **98**
TN11: Hiid 1E **144**
Derby Rd. CR0: Croy 3F **13**
ME5: Chat'm 1H **95**
ME15: Maid 9F **126**
RM17: Grays 5A **8**
Dereham Ho. *SE4 2A 54*
(off Frendsbury Rd.)
Dering Cl. CT4: Brid 9E **172**
TN27: P'ley 1G **39**
Dering Rd. CT4: Brid 8H **173**
CT6: H Bay 3G **194**
TN24: Ashf 8H **159**
Derings, The TN29: Lydd 3J **205**
Dering Way DA12: Grav'nd 6L **63**
Deringwood Dr. ME15: Bear 8J **127** (2K **27**)
Deringwood Pde. ME15: Bear 8J **127**
Dermody Gdns. SE13 3G **54**
Dermody Rd. SE13 3G **54**
Dernier Rd. TN10: Tonb 3J **145**
Derrick Rd. BR3: Beck'm 6C **68**
DERRINGSTONE 9D 162 (5A 32)
Derringstone Downs CT4: B'hm 9D **162** (5A **32**)
Derringstone Hill CT4: B'hm 9D **162** (5A **32**)
Derringstone St. CT4: B'hm 9D **162** (5A **32**)
DERRY DOWNS 9L 71 (3D 14)
Derry Downs BR5: St M Cry 9L **71**
Derville Ho. TN28: New R 3K **213**
Derville Rd. TN28: G'stne 7H **213**
Derwent Av. CT11: Ram 5E **210**
Derwent Cl. DA1: Dart 6J **59**
Derwent Cres. DA7: Bexhth 9B **52**
Derwent Dr. BR5: Pet W 1F **84**
TN4: Tun W 9E **150**
Derwent Ho. ME15: Maid 1H **139**
Derwent Rd. TN10: Tonb 2J **145**
Derwent Way CT3: Aysm 1C **162**
ME8: Gill 3N **95**
Desmond Cres. ME13: Fav 7L **187**
D'este Rd. CT11: Ram 5K **211**
Detillens La. RH8: Oxt 3A **24**
DETLING 9K 111 (7K 17)
Detling Av. CT10: B'stairs 3L **211**
Detling Cl. ME8: Gill 1M **95**
ME12: S'ness 5C **220**
Detling Hill ME14: Det 9L **111** (7K **17**)
Detling Rd. BR1: Brom 1K **69**
DA8: Erith 7E **52**
Detling Rd. DA11: Nflt 6C **62**
Devas St. E3 2J **5**
Devenish Rd. SE2 2J **51**
Deveroux Cl. BR3: Beck'm 8F **68**
DEVIL'S DEN 6A 28
Devon Av. CT14: Walm 7M **177**
Devon Cl. ME5: Chat'm 4F **94**
ME8: Rain 2B **96**
Devon Ct. DA4: S at H 4B **74**
Devon Gdns. CT7: Birch 5E **206** (2E **22**)
Devon Rd. CT1: Cant 2C **172**
CT19: F'stone 6K **189**
DA4: S Dar, S at H 4B **74** (2H **15**)
ME15: Maid 8F **126**
Devonshire Av. DA1: Dart 4J **59**
Devonshire Cl. TN2: Tun W 5E **156**
Devonshire Gdns. CT9: Clift 3F **208**
Devonshire Ho. Bus. Cen. *BR2: Shortl 7L 69*
(off Devonshire Sq.)
Devonshire Rd. BR6: Orp 1J **85**
CT17: Dover 4G **180**
DA6: Bexhth 2N **57**
DA12: Grav'nd 6G **63**
ME7: Gill 5G **80**
RM17: Grays 4A **8**
SE9 7A **56**
SE23 5A **54** (7H **5**)
Devonshire Road Nature Reserve 5A 54
Devonshire Sq. BR2: Shortl 7L **69**
Devonshire Ter. CT10: B'stairs 8M **209**
Devonshire Way CR0: Croy 3B **82**
Devons Rd. E3 3J **5**
Devons Road Station (DLR) 2J 5
Dewberry Cl. ME4: Chat'm 3E **80**
Dewhurst La. TN5: Wadh 6A **36**
Dewlands Av. DA2: Dart 5B **60**
Dew La. TN31: Peas 4K **45**
Dexter Cl. TN25: Kenn 2G **159**
Dexter Ho. *DA18: Erith 3N 51*
(off Kale Rd.)
Dhekelia Cl. ME14: Maid 2D **126**
Dial Cl. DA9: G'hithe 3J **61**
ME7: Gill 6J **81**
Dial Rd. ME7: Gill 6J **81**
Diameter Rd. BR5: Pet W 1D **84**
Diamond Ct. ME12: S'ness 3C **220**
Diamond Fld. TN12: Horsm 3E **36**
Diamond Rd. CT5: Whits 3G **226**
Diana Ct. DA8: Erith 6F **52**
Diana Gdns. CT14: Deal 5K **177**
Diana Rd. ME4: Chat'm 1D **94**
Dianthus Cl. SE2 5K **51**
DIBDEN 9F 118 (3F 25)
Dibden La. TN14: Ide H, S'oaks 8F **118** (2F **25**)
Dibdin Rd. CT14: Deal 3N **177**
Dickens Av. CT1: Cant 9B **168**
DA1: Dart 2A **60**
Dickens Cl. DA3: Hart'y 8M **75**
DA8: Erith 7C **52**
ME17: L'ly 4A **140**
Dickens Ct. ME2: Med E 4A **80**
ME3: High'm 9G **64**
Dickens Dr. BR7: Chst 2E **70**
ME19: E Mal 9D **108**
Dickens House Mus. 9M 209 (3K 23)
Dickensian Cl. ME3: Lwr Sto 9A **204**
Dickens Rd. CT10: B'stairs 8M **209**
DA12: Grav'nd 6K **63**
ME1: Roch 1N **93**
ME14: Maid 2B **126**
Dickens Wlk. *CT10: B'stairs 9M 209*
(off Eldon Pl.)
ME3: Cool 1C **66**
Dickens Way TN18: Hawkh 5D **192**
Dickerage La. KT3: N Mald 2A **12**
Dickerage Rd. KT1: King T 2A **12**
Dickley La. ME17: Len 6J **201** (3E **28**)
Dickson Ct. ME10: Sit 7J **99**
Dickson Rd. CT17: Dover 4H **181**
SE9 1A **56**
Dickson's Bourne TN25: Aldtn 4C **40**
Dieu Stone La. CT16: Dover 4J **181**
Digby Rd. CT20: F'stone 6E **188**
Digdog La. TN17: Frit 3A **38**
Diggerland 8K 79
Dignals Cl. ME8: Rain 1B **96**
Dilhorne Cl. SE12 8L **55**
Diligent Dr. ME10: Sit 4G **98**
Dillon Way TN2: Tun W 8K **151**
Dillwyn Cl. SE26 9B **54**
Dillywood Flds. ME3: Strood 9L **65**
Dillywood La. ME3: High'm, Strood 1L **79** (1G **17**)
Dilnot La. CT7: Acol 8G **206**
Dimmock Cl. TN12: Pad W 9N **147**
DINGLEDEN 7A 38
Dippers Cl. TN15: Kems'g 8N **103**
Discovery Dr. ME19: W Mal 6M **123** (2D **26**)
Discovery Rd. ME15: Bear 7L **127**
Discovery Wlk. CT1: Cant 3B **172**
Dislingbury Rd. TN11: Five G, Tude 3N **151** (1A **36**)
Disraeli Cl. ME15: Maid 3H **139**
SE28 1L **51**
Dittisham Rd. SE9 9A **56**
DITTON 9G 108 (7F 17)
Ditton Ct. Cl. ME20: Dit 9F **108**
Ditton Pl. ME20: Dit 9F **108**
Ditton Rd. DA6: Bexhth 3M **57**
Dixon Cl. ME15: Maid 7C **126**
Dixon Pl. BR4: W W'ck 2E **82**
Dixter La. TN31: N'thiam 3G **45**
Dixter Rd. TN31: N'thiam 3G **45**
Dixwell Cl. ME8: Gill 6N **95**
Dixwell Rd. CT20: F'stone 7G **189**
Dobbie Cl. ME10: Sit 5F **98**
Dobell Rd. SE9 3B **56**
Dobells TN17: Cran 8D **176**
Dobson Rd. DA12: Grav'nd 1K **77**
Dock Exit Rd. CT16: Dover 4L **181**
Dock Head Rd. ME4: Chat'm 3D **80**
DOCKLANDS 3B 6
Dockland St. E16 1C **50**
(not continuous)
Dock Rd. ME4: Chat'm 7C **80** (2H **17**)
RM17: Grays 5B **8**
Dock Rd. RM18: Tilb 1F **62** (5B **8**)
Dockside Outlet Cen. ME4: Chat'm 3D **80**
Dock St. E1 3H **5**
Doctor Hope's Rd. TN17: Cran 8D **176**
Doctor's La. CT15: Chu H 8A **180** (2D **42**)
DODDINGTON 1G 29
Doddington Ct. ME16: Maid 4B **126**
Doddington Rd. ME8: Gill 9N **81**
Dodd Rd. TN10: Tonb 2L **145**
Dodds La. CT16: Dover 1F **180**
Dode Church 7L 91
Doebury Wlk. *SE18 6J 51*
(off Prestwood Cl.)
Does All. ME10: Sit 7G **99**
Doesgate La. RM14: Bulp 1C **8**
Dog Collar Mus. 1F 140
Doggerel Acre CT5: Whits 6H **227**
Doggett Rd. SE6 5D **54**
Doggetts Cl. TN8: Eden 7C **184**
Doggetts Row ME3: Isle G 8C **190**
Doggett's Sq. ME2: Strood 5M **79**
Doghurst La. CR5: Chip 7D **12**
Dog Kennel Hill SE22 6G **5**
Dog Kennel La. CT18: Lym'ge 7K **205**
Dogs Hill Rd. TN36: Winch 7A **46**
Dogwood Cl. DA11: Nflt 9E **62**
ME5: Chat'm 1G **111**
Dola Av. CT14: Deal 4L **177**
(not continuous)
Doleham Hill TN35: W'fld, Gues T 7G **45**
Doleham La. TN35: W'fld 7G **45**
Doleham Station (Rail) 7G 45
DOLLIS HILL 1B 4
Dollis Hill La. NW2 1A **4**
Dollis Hill Station (Tube) 1B 4
Dolphin Cl. CT10: B'stairs 3L **209**
Dolphin Dr. ME8: Gill 6A **96** (4A **18**)
Dolphin Ho. *CT16: Dover 5K 181*
(off Market Sq.)
Dolphin La. CT16: Dover 5K **181**
Dolphin Pk. ME10: Sit 6J **99**
Dolphin Pas. CT16: Dover 5K **181**
Dolphin Pl. CT16: Dover 5K **181**
Dolphin Rd. ME10: Sit 6J **99** (4F **19**)
TN29: Lydd 3K **205**
Dolphins Rd. CT19: F'stone 4J **189**
Dolphin St. CT6: H Bay 2F **194**
CT14: Deal 3N **177**
Dolphin Yard Sailing Barge Mus. 6H 99 (4F 19)
Dolphin Yd., The *DA12: Grav'nd 4G 63*
(off Queen St.)
Dombey Cl. ME1: Roch 9N **79**
ME3: High'm 1G **78**
Domneva Rd. CT8: Wgte S 3J **207** (2F **23**)
CT12: Minst 7E **212**
Domonic Dr. SE9 9D **56**
Donald Biggs Dr. DA12: Grav'nd 6H **63**
Donald Moor Av. ME9: Tey 7K **223**
Donaldson Rd. SE18 9E **50**
Doncaster Cl. ME15: Maid 2J **139**
Donegal Rd. CT1: Cant 2B **172**
Donemowe Dr. ME10: Kems'y 3G **99**
Donet Cl. ME8: Gill 6N **95**
Dongola Rd. ME2: Strood 3M **79**
Donkey Fld. TN11: Leigh 6M **143**
Donkey La. CT3: Adm 3B **32**
DA4: Farn'm 3B **88** (4H **15**)
DONKEY STREET 2C 182 (6F 41)
Donkey St. CT21: Burm 9A **198**
TN29: Burm 3B **182** (6F **41**)
Donnahay Rd. CT12: Ram 1G **210**
Donnington Ct. *DA2: Dart 4B 60*
(off Bow Arrow La.)
Donnington Rd. NW10 1B **4**
TN13: Dun G 2E **118**
Donnithorne Ho. *CT6: H Bay 2F 194*
(off Brunswick Sq.)
Doon Brae TN4: S'bgh 4G **151**
Dorado Gdns. BR6: Chels 4M **85**
Doran Gro. SE18 7G **50**
Dorcas Gdns. CT10: B'stairs 7L **209**
Dorchester Av. DA5: Bex'y 6M **57**
Dorchester Cl. BR5: St P 3K **71**
DA1: Dart 5N **59**
ME3: Cli W 6M **65**
Dorchester Gro. W4 4A **4**
Dorchester Rd. DA12: Grav'nd 8J **63**
Dorcis Av. DA7: Bexhth 9N **51**
Doria Dr. DA12: Grav'nd 8K **63**
Doric Av. TN4: S'bgh 5F **150**
Doric Cl. TN4: S'bgh 5F **150**
Doric Ct. CT11: Ram 7G **211**
Dorin Ho. TN1: Tun W 2J **157**
Doris Av. DA8: Erith 8D **52**
Dorking Rd. KT18: Eps 7C **12**
TN1: Tun W 8J **151**
Dorman Av. Nth. CT3: Aysm 1C **162** (3B **32**)
Dorman Av. Sth. CT3: Aysm 2D **162** (3B **32**)
DORMANSLAND 1A 34
DORMANS PARK 2A 34
Dormans Rd. RH7: Dor'land 1A **34**
Dormans Station (Rail) 2A 34
Dormers Dr. DA13: Meop 1G **90**
Dornden Dr. TN3: Lang G 1A **156**
Dornden Gdns. ME5: Chat'm 9E **94**
Dorney Ri. BR5: St M Cry 7H **71**
Dorothy Av. TN17: Cran 8D **176**
Dorothy Dr. CT12: Ram 2G **210**
Dorothy Evans Cl. DA7: Bexhth 2C **58**
Dorrington Way BR3: Beck'm 8F **68**
Dorrit Way BR7: Chst 2E **70**
ME1: Roch 1A **94**
Dorryn Ct. SE26 1A **68**
Dorset Av. DA16: Well 2H **57**
Dorset Cl. CT5: Whits 6D **226**
Dorset Cotts. TN7: Withy 9C **154**
Dorset Ct. CT14: Walm 8N **177**
Dorset Cres. DA12: Grav'nd 9K **63**
Dorset Gdns. CT7: Birch 4E **206**
CT14: Walm 8M **177**
Dorset Pl. ME13: Fav 5G **187**
Dorset Rd. BR3: Beck'm 6A **68**
CT1: Cant 3C **172**
ME12: S'ness 4B **220**
Dorset Rd. SE9 7A **56**
SW19 2C **12**
TN2: Tun W 3K **157**
Dorset Rd. Ind. Est. ME12: S'ness 3B **220**
Dorset Sq. ME8: Rain 2N **95**
Dorset St. TN13: S'oaks 7K **119**
Dorset Way ME15: Maid 8F **126**
Dorton Dr. TN15: Seal 4N **119**
(not continuous)
Dorville Rd. SE12 3J **55**
Dossett Ct. CT14: Deal 8K **177**
Dothill Rd. SE18 7E **50**
Dotterel Cl. ME5: Chat'm 9G **94**
Doubleday Dr. ME9: Bap 9L **99**
Doubleton La. TN11: Pens 1H **149**
Douglas Av. CT5: Whits 4G **227**
CT21: Hythe 6K **199**
Douglas Bldgs. TN12: S'hrst 1J **223**
Douglas Cl. CT10: B'stairs 8J **209**
Douglas Ct. ME17: Len 7M **201**
TN16: Big H 5E **164**
Douglas Dr. CR0: Croy 4D **82**
Douglas Rd. CT6: H Bay 3H **195**
CT14: Deal 7K **177**
CT17: Dover 4G **181**
DA16: Well 8K **51**
ME16: Maid 6B **126** (2H **27**)
ME17: Len 7M **201**
TN9: Tonb 7G **144**
Douglas Ter. CT14: Deal 5N **177**
Douro Cl. CT1: Cant 1C **172**
Douro Pl. CT16: Dover 5K **181**
Dour Side CT17: Dover 1E **180**
Dour St. CT16: Dover 4J **181**
Dour Ter. CT16: Temp E 8C **178**
Doust Way ME1: Roch 7A **80**
Dove Cl. CT5: Whits 6E **226**
CT6: H Bay 8F **194**
CT21: Hythe 8E **198**
ME5: Chat'm 5E **94**
TN23: Kgnt 6G **160**
Dovecote Ct. CT4: Chil'm 8H **175**
Dovedale CT7: Birch 4G **207**
Dovedale Cl. DA16: Well 9J **51**
Dove Dale Ct. CT7: Birch 4G **207**
Dovedale Ct. TN24: Ashf 7F **158**
Dovedale Rd. DA2: Dart 6C **60**
Dove Lea Gdns. CT17: Dover 1D **180**
Doveney Cl. BR5: St P 6L **71**
DOVER 4J 181 (2F 43)
Dover Athletic F.C.
(Hoverspeed Stadium, The) 2E 180
Dover Bus. Pk. CT16: Whitf 7G **179**
Dover Castle 4L 181 (2G 43)
DOVER HILL 4C 42
Dover Hill CT19: F'stone 3L **189** (4B **42**)
Dover Ho. Rd. SW15 6B **4**
Dover Leisure Cen. 4K 181
Dover Mus. & Bronze Age Boat Gallery 5J 181
Dove Rd. TN10: Tonb 1H **145**
Dover Patrol Memorial 6E 214
Dover Pl. TN23: Ashf 9G **158**
Dover Priory Station (Rail) 4H 181 (2F 43)
Dover Rd. CT4: B'hm 6E **162** (4A **32**)
(not continuous)
CT4: Wom, S'wll, Cold 5B **32**
CT13: E'try 4K **183** (3F **33**)
CT13: S'wch 8K **217** (1G **33**)
CT14: R'wld 5B **200** (6H **33**)
CT14: Tilm, E'try 4F **33**
CT14: Walm 9L **177** (6H **33**)
CT15: Gus 1K **181** (1G **43**)
CT15: St Marg 7A **214** (7H **33**)
CT20: F'stone 6K **189** (4B **42**)
DA11: Nflt 5C **62** (7B **8**)
Dover Rd. E. DA11: Grav'nd 5D **62** (7B **8**)
DOVERS CORNER 2G **7**
Dover St. CT1: Cant 2N **171**
ME10: Sit 7F **98**
(not continuous)
ME16: Maid 7N **125**
Dover Transport Mus. 8F 178 (7F 33)
Dovervelt Rd. SS8: Can I 1K **9**
Dover Western
Heights Viewpoint 5H 181 (2F 43)
Doves Cl. BR2: Shortl 3A **84**
Doves Cft. ME9: T'stall 3D **114**
Dowanhill Rd. SE6 6G **54**
Dowding Rd. TN16: Big H 3D **164**
Dowding Wlk. DA11: Nflt 8D **62**
Dowding Way TN2: Tun W 6K **151**
Dowe Ho. SE3 1H **55**
Dowell M. CT14: Walm 7M **177**
Dower Ho. Cres. TN4: S'bgh 3E **150**
Dowgate Cl. TN9: Tonb 7K **145**
Dowle Cl. TN29: Old R 3G **47**
Dowlerville Rd. BR6: Chels 7H **85**
Dowle St. TN27: P'ley 1G **39**
Dowling Cl. ME6: Snod 3C **108**
Dowling Ho. DA17: Belv 3A **52**
Downage, The DA11: Grav'nd 7F **62**
Down Av. TN3: Lamb 4K **201**
Downbank Av. DA7: Bexhth 8E **52**
Down Barton Rd. CT7: St N 9K **215** (3C **22**)
Down Ct. TN23: Ashf 4C **160**
Down Ct. Rd. ME9: Dod 9J **115** (7F **19**)
Downderry Nursery 3C 134
Downderry Rd. BR1: Brom 8G **55**
Downderry Way ME20: Dit 9F **108**
DOWNE 2C 100 (6B 14)
Downe Av. TN14: Cud 3F **100**
Downe Bank Nature Reserve 4D 100
Downe Cl. DA16: Well 7L **51**
Down End SE18 7D **50**
Downer Ct. ME1: Roch 3B **94**
Downe Rd. BR2: Kes 9N **83** (5B **14**)
TN14: Cud 4E **100** (6C **14**)
DOWNHAM 1G 69 (1K 13)
Downham Ent. Cen. SE6 7J **55**
Downham La. BR1: Brom 1G **69**
Downham Rd. N1 1G **5**
Downham Way BR1: Brom 1G **69** (1K **13**)
Downhill Cl. CT16: Temp E 7C **178**
Down House and Darwin Mus. 3C 100 (6B 14)

Eurogate Bus. Pk.—Felday Rd.

Eurogate Bus. Pk. TN24: Ashf . . . 5E 158
Eurolink Bus. Pk. ME10: Sit . . . 5J 99
Eurolink Commercial Pk. ME10: Sit . . . 6H 99
Eurolink Ind. Est. ME10: Sit . . . 7J 99
Eurolink Way ME10: Sit . . . 7G 98 (4F 19)
Europa Trad. Est. DA8: Erith . . . 5E 52
Europe Rd. SE18 . . . 3B 50
Eustace Pl. SE18 . . . 4B 50
Euston Rd. NW1 . . . 2E 4
Euston Square Station (Tube) . . . 2E 4
Euston Station (Rail & Tube) . . . 2E 4
EUSTON UNDERPASS . . . 2E 4
Evans Cl. DA9: G'hithe . . . 3G 60
Evans Rd. SE6 . . . 7H 55
TN24: W'boro . . . 2L 161
Eva Rd. ME7: Gill . . . 9G 80
Evegate Bus. Cen. TN25: Sme . . . 3D 40
Evelina Rd. SE15 . . . 6H 5
Evelings All. *CT5: Whits* . . . *3F 226*
(off Middle Wall)
Evelyn Cl. ME2: Strood . . . 4N 79
Evelyn Ct. CT21: Hythe . . . 6N 199
Evelyn Ho. ME2: Strood . . . 4N 79
Evelyn Rd. ME16: Maid . . . 6B 126
TN14: Otf . . . 7K 103
Evelyn St. SE8 . . . 4J 5
Evenden Rd. DA13: Meop . . . 1F 90
Evenhill Rd. CT3: L'brne . . . 2K 173
Evening Hill BR3: Beck'm . . . 3F 68
Evenlode Ho. SE2 . . . 2L 51
Everard Av. BR2: Shortl . . . 2K 83
Everard Way ME13: Fav . . . 4F 186
Everest Cl. DA11: Nflt . . . 8D 62
Everest Dr. ME3: Hoo . . . 9H 67
Everest La. ME2: Strood . . . 3M 79
Everest M. ME3: Hoo . . . 9H 67
Everest Pl. BR8: Swanl . . . 7E 72
Everest Rd. SE9 . . . 3B 56
Everett Wlk. *DA17: Belv* . . . *5A 52*
(off Osborne Rd.)
Everglade TN16: Big H . . . 6D 164
Everglade Cl. DA3: Hart'y . . . 7L 75
Everglades, The ME7: Hpstd . . . 5J 95
Evergreen Cl.
ME3: High'm . . . 1F 78
ME7: Hpstd . . . 6K 95
ME9: Iwade . . . 8J 197
ME19: Leyb . . . 8C 108
Evergreen Way TN23: Ashf . . . 7C 158
Evering Rd. E5 . . . 1H 5
N16 . . . 1G 5
Everist Ct. CT18: Lym'ge . . . 8L 205
Eversholt St. NW1 . . . 2E 4
Eversley Av. DA7: Bexhth . . . 9E 52
Eversley Cl. ME16: Alltn . . . 2N 125
Eversley Cross DA7: Bexhth . . . 9F 52
Eversley Rd. CT21: Hythe . . . 8B 188
Eversley Way CR0: Croy . . . 5D 82
CT20: F'stone . . . 6F 188
Evesham Rd. DA12: Grav'nd . . . 7J 63
EVINGTON . . . 7F 31
Evington Pk. TN25: H'lgh . . . 7E 30
Evison Cl. CT16: Dover . . . 2G 181
Evry Rd. DA14: Sidc . . . 2L 71
Ewart Rd. ME4: Chat'm . . . 2B 94
SE23 . . . 5A 54
Ewehurst La. TN3: Speld . . . 8N 149
EWELL . . . 5A 12
Ewell Av. ME19: W Mal . . . 1M 123
Ewell By-Pass KT17: Eps . . . 5B 12
Ewell East Station (Rail) . . . 5B 12
Ewell La. ME15: W Far . . . 2G 137 (3F 27)
EWELL MINNIS . . . 1C 42
Ewell Rd. SM3: Sutt . . . 5B 12
Ewell West Station (Rail) . . . 5A 12
EWHURST GREEN . . . 3E 44
Ewhurst La. TN31: N'thiam . . . 4F 45
Ewhurst Rd. SE4 . . . 4C 54
Ewins Cl. TN12: Pad W . . . 9M 147
Exbury Rd. SE6 . . . 7D 54
ExCeL . . . 3A 6
Exchange St. CT14: Deal . . . 3N 177
Exedown Rd. TN15: Wro . . . 5H 105 (6K 15)
Exeter Cl. CT19: F'stone . . . 5D 188
TN10: Tonb . . . 3J 145
Exeter Ho. ME15: Maid . . . 1G 139
Exeter Rd. DA12: Grav'nd . . . 8J 63
DA16: Well . . . 9H 51
Exeter Wlk. ME1: Roch . . . 4N 93
Exford Gdns. SE12 . . . 6L 55
Exford Rd. SE12 . . . 7L 55
Exhibition Rd. SW7 . . . 4D 4
Exmoor Ri. TN24: Ashf . . . 6F 158
Exmouth Rd. DA16: Well . . . 8L 51
ME7: Gill . . . 5F 80
EXTED . . . 6L 183 (7J 31)
Exted Hill CT4: Elham . . . 6L 183 (7J 31)
Exton Cl. ME5: Chat'm . . . 9F 94
Exton Gdns. ME14: Weav . . . 4J 127
Eyebright Cl. CR0: Croy . . . 2A 82
EYHORNE GREEN . . . 7E 128
EYHORNE STREET . . . 7E 128 (2B 28)
Eyhorne St. ME17: Holl . . . 8E 128 (2B 28)
EYNSFORD . . . 3M 87 (4H 15)
Eynsford Castle . . . 3M 87 (4H 15)
Eynsford Cl. BR5: Pet W . . . 1E 84
CT9: Clift . . . 3K 209
Eynsford Cres. DA5: Bex'y . . . 6L 57
Eynsford Ri. DA4: Eyns . . . 5L 87
Eynsford Rd.
BR8: Crock'n . . . 9E 72 (3F 15)
DA4: Eyns, Farn'm . . . 2N 87 (3H 15)
DA9: G'hithe . . . 3J 61
ME16: Alltn . . . 2A 126
TN14: Eyns, S'ham . . . 8J 87 (5G 15)
Eynsford Station (Rail) . . . 5L 87 (4G 15)
Eynsham Dr. SE2 . . . 4J 51 (4D 6)
Eynswood Dr. DA14: Sidc . . . 1K 71
EYTHORNE . . . 9K 185 (5E 32)
Eythorne Cl. TN24: Kenn . . . 5H 159
EYTHORNE GREEN . . . 9L 185
Eythorne Rd. CT15: S'wll . . . 7K 219 (5C 32)
Eythorne Station
East Kent Railway . . . 9K 185 (5D 32)

F

Fackenden La. TN14: S'ham . . . 4J 103 (6G 15)
Factory Cotts. ME1: Woul . . . 7G 93
ME2: Cux . . . 9H 79
Factory Rd. DA11: Nflt . . . 4B 62
E16 . . . 1A 50 (4B 6)
Faesten Way DA5: Bex'y . . . 8F 58
Fagus Cl. ME5: Chat'm . . . 1E 110
Fairacre CT10: B'stairs . . . 9J 209
Fairacre Pl. DA3: Hart'y . . . 6L 75
Fair Acres BR2: Shortl . . . 8K 69
CR0: Croy . . . 9C 82
Fairacres Cl. CT6: H Bay . . . 3K 195
Fairbank Av. BR6: Farnb . . . 3D 84
Fairbourne Ct. Cotts. ME17: H'shm . . . 5L 141
FAIRBOURNE HEATH . . . 7K 141 (4C 28)
Fairbourne La. ME17: H'shm . . . 6K 141 (4C 28)
Fairby Grange DA3: Hart'y . . . 9L 75
Fairby La. DA3: Hart'y . . . 9L 75
Fairby Rd. SE12 . . . 3L 55
Fairchildes Rd. CR6: Warl . . . 6K 13
FAIR CROSS . . . 1C 6
Faircrouch La. TN5: Wadh . . . 6A 36
Fairfax Bus. Cen. ME15: Maid . . . 4J 139
Fairfax Cl. CT20: F'stone . . . 7D 188
ME8: Gill . . . 6N 95
Fairfax Dr. CT6: H Bay . . . 2N 195
Fairfax Ho. ME15: Maid . . . 3H 139
FAIRFIELD
Broadstairs . . . 9H 209
Romney Marsh . . . 3D 46
Fairfield CT4: Elham . . . 6N 183
CT14: Shol . . . 4J 177
Fairfield Av. TN2: Tun W . . . 9J 151
Fairfield Cl. DA15: Sidc . . . 4H 57
TN15: Kems'g . . . 9A 104
TN28: New R . . . 2K 213
Fairfield Cres. TN9: Tonb . . . 7J 145
Fairfield Pk. CT10: B'stairs . . . 9J 209
Fairfield Pool & Leisure Cen. . . . 5M 59
Fairfield Rd. BR1: Brom . . . 3K 69
BR3: Beck'm . . . 5D 68
BR5: Pet W . . . 9F 70
CR0: Croy . . . 4G 13
CT10: B'stairs . . . 9J 209 (3K 23)
CT11: Ram . . . 2J 211
CT12: Minst . . . 6E 212
DA7: Bexhth . . . 9A 52
E3 . . . 2J 5
TN15: Bor G . . . 1M 121
TN28: New R . . . 3J 213 (3J 47)
Fairfields DA12: Grav'nd . . . 1K 77
Fairfield St. SW18 . . . 6C 4
Fairfield Ter. TN26: Hams . . . 3L 191
Fairfield Way TN11: Hild . . . 2E 144
Fairford SE6 . . . 6D 54
Fairford Av. CR0: Croy . . . 8A 68
DA7: Bexhth . . . 8E 52
Fairford Cl. CR0: Croy . . . 8B 68
Fairglen Rd. TN5: Wadh . . . 7A 36
Fairhaven Av. CR0: Croy . . . 9A 68
Fairhurst Dr. ME15: E Far . . . 4M 137
Fairings, The *TN30: Tent* . . . *7C 224*
(off Ashford Rd.)
Fairland Ho. BR2: Shortl . . . 7L 69
Fairlands Ct. SE9 . . . 4C 56
Fairlawn CT5: Whits . . . 4M 227
Fairlawn Av. DA7: Bexhth . . . 9M 51
Fairlawn Cl. ME18: Tstn . . . 9E 124
Fairlawn Pk. SE26 . . . 1B 68
Fairlawn Rd. CT12: Ram . . . 1F 210
Fairlead Rd. ME1: Roch . . . 2A 94
Fairleas ME10: Sit . . . 9J 99
Fairlight Av. CT12: Ram . . . 4F 210
Fairlight Cl. TN4: S'bgh . . . 4G 151
Fairlight Ct. TN10: Tonb . . . 3H 145
Fairlight Cross DA3: Long . . . 6A 76
Fairlight Rd. CT21: Hythe . . . 5H 199
Fairlight Ter. TN28: New R . . . 3H 213
Fairline Ct. BR3: Beck'm . . . 5F 68
Fairman's La. TN12: Brenc . . . 7N 153 (2D 36)
Fairman's Rd. TN12: Brenc . . . 8N 153 (2D 36)
Fairmead BR1: Brom . . . 7B 70
Fairmead Cl. BR1: Brom . . . 7B 70
Fairmeadow ME14: Maid . . . 5C 126 (1H 27)
Fairmead Rd. TN8: Eden . . . 2C 184
Fairmile Rd. TN2: Tun W . . . 9L 151
Fairmont Cl. DA17: Belv . . . 5A 52
Fairoak Cl. BR5: Pet W . . . 1D 84
Fairoak Dr. SE9 . . . 3F 56
Fairoaks CT6: H Bay . . . 3J 195
FAIRSEAT . . . 3B 106 (6B 16)
Fairseat La. TN15: Ash, Stans . . . 9N 89 (5A 16)
TN15: Wro . . . 6A 106 (6A 16)
Fairservice Cl. ME10: Sit . . . 6K 99
Fair St. CT10: B'stairs . . . 9J 209
Fairtrough Rd. BR6: Prat B . . . 3K 101 (6D 14)
Fairview CT21: Lymp . . . 5B 198
DA3: Fawk . . . 4H 89
DA8: Erith . . . 7G 52
TN18: Hawkh . . . 5C 192
Fairview Av. ME8: Hpstd, Gill . . . 6L 95 (4K 17)
Fairview Cl. CT9: Mgte . . . 3E 208
SE26 . . . 1B 68
TN9: Tonb . . . 9H 145
Fairview Cotts. ME15: Loose . . . 3C 138
ME15: W Far . . . 2J 137
Fairview Dr. BR6: Orp . . . 5F 84
ME3: High'm . . . 9F 64
Fairview Gdns. CT2: Sturry . . . 5F 168
CT14: Walm . . . 8K 177
DA13: Meop . . . 8F 76
Fairview La. TN3: Tun W . . . 5B 156 (4H 35)
Fairview Rd. CT15: Evtn . . . 7J 185
DA13: Ist R . . . 3C 76
ME10: Sit . . . 8H 99
Fairwater Av. DA16: Well . . . 2J 57
Fairway BR5: Pet W . . . 8F 70 (3C 14)
DA6: Bexhth . . . 3N 57
RM16: Grays . . . 3A 8
Fairway Av. CT19: F'stone . . . 4G 188
Fairway Cl. CR0: Croy . . . 8B 68
Fairway Cl. ME1: Roch . . . 2N 93
TN29: St M Bay . . . 3M 215
Fairway Cres. CT5: Seas . . . 6C 226
Fairway Dr. DA2: Dart . . . 5B 60
Fairway Gdns. BR3: Beck'm . . . 9G 68
Fairways, The TN4: S'bgh . . . 6G 151
Fairway, The BR1: Brom . . . 8B 70
CT6: H Bay . . . 5E 194
CT14: Deal . . . 2M 177
CT21: Hythe . . . 7K 199
DA11: Grav'nd . . . 7F 62
ME1: Roch . . . 2N 93
ME10: Sit . . . 1F 114
ME13: Fav . . . 6E 186
TN28: L'stne . . . 3M 213
TN29: Dym . . . 1N 215
Fairwood Ind. Est. TN23: Ashf . . . 9E 158
Fairwyn Rd. SE26 . . . 9B 54
Falala Way CT1: Cant . . . 1A 172
Falcon Av. BR1: Brom . . . 7A 70
Falcon Cl. CT6: H Bay . . . 8F 194
DA1: Dart . . . 3N 59
Falcon Ct. ME10: Sit . . . 9H 99
Falcon Gdns. ME12: Minst . . . 5L 221
Falcon Grn. ME20: Lark . . . 9D 108
Falcon M. DA11: Nflt . . . 6D 62
Falcon Rd. SW11 . . . 5D 4
Falcons Cl. TN16: Big H . . . 5D 164
Falcon Way TN23: Ashf . . . 2C 160
FALCONWOOD . . . 2H 57 (6C 6)
FALCONWOOD . . . 2F 56 (6C 6)
Falconwood Av. DA16: Well . . . 9F 50
Falconwood Pde. DA16: Well . . . 2G 57
Falconwood Rd. CR0: Croy . . . 9C 82
Falconwood Station (Rail) . . . 2F 56 (6C 6)
Falkland Ho. SE6 . . . 9F 54
Falkland Pl. ME5: Chat'm . . . 1B 110
Fallowfield DA2: Bean . . . 8H 61
ME5: Chat'm . . . 3E 94
ME10: Sit . . . 9H 99
Fallowfield Cl. ME14: Weav . . . 5H 127
Falmouth Cl. SE12 . . . 3J 55
Falmouth Pl. TN12: Five G . . . 8H 147
Falstaff Bungs. TN17: Rolv . . . 2B 214
Falstaff Cl. DA1: Cray . . . 5F 58
Fambridge Cl. SE26 . . . 9C 54
Fanconi Rd. ME5: Chat'm . . . 8E 94
Fancy Row ME14: Bear . . . 4M 127
Fane Way ME8: Gill . . . 7M 95
(not continuous)
Fanshawe Av. IG11: Bark . . . 1C 6
Fans La. ME9: Iwade . . . 8J 197
FANT . . . 6A 126 (2H 27)
FANTAIL, THE . . . 4B 84 (4B 14)
Fan, The CT16: Dover . . . 4N 181
Fant La. ME16: Maid . . . 7M 125 (2G 27)
Faraday Av. DA14: Sidc . . . 7J 57 (7D 6)
Faraday Ride TN10: Tonb . . . 9K 133
Faraday Rd. DA16: Well . . . 1J 57
ME14: Pen H . . . 2F 126
Faraday Way BR5: St M Cry . . . 7K 71
Fareham Wlk. ME15: Maid . . . 2J 139
Faringdon Av. BR2: Shortl . . . 1C 84
Farington Cl. ME16: Maid . . . 5M 125
FARLEIGH . . . 6J 13
Farleigh Av. BR2: Shortl . . . 1J 83
Farleigh Bri. ME16: E Far . . . 9L 125
Farleigh Ct. ME16: Maid . . . 7L 125
Farleigh Ct. Rd. CR6: Warl . . . 6J 13
FARLEIGH GREEN . . . 2J 137 (3G 27)
Farleigh Hill ME15: Maid . . . 8B 126 (2H 27)
Farleigh Hill Retail Pk. ME15: Maid . . . 8B 126
Farleigh La. ME16: Maid . . . 7L 125 (2G 27)
Farleigh Rd. CR6: Warl . . . 7H 13
CT2: Cant . . . 8N 167
Farleigh Trad. Est. ME15: Maid . . . 7B 126
Farley Cl. ME5: Chat'm . . . 9G 94
TN26: Shad . . . 3J 39
Farleycroft TN16: Westrm . . . 8E 116
Farley La. TN16: Westrm . . . 8D 116 (3B 24)
Farley Nursery TN16: Westrm . . . 9E 116
Farley Rd. CR2: S Croy . . . 5H 13
CT9: Mgte . . . 6D 208
DA12: Grav'nd . . . 6L 63
SE6 . . . 5E 54
Farlow Cl. DA11: Nflt . . . 8E 62
Farm Av. BR8: Swanl . . . 6D 72
Farm Cl. BR4: W W'ck . . . 4J 83
TN23: Ashf . . . 2C 160
Farmcombe Cl. TN2: Tun W . . . 3H 157
Farmcombe La. TN2: Tun W . . . 3H 157
Farmcombe Rd. TN2: Tun W . . . 3H 157
Farmcote Rd. SE12 . . . 6K 55
Farm Cotts. ME15: Maid . . . 8G 127
Farm Ct. CT15: Non . . . 3D 32
TN4: Tun W . . . 5E 156
Farm Cres. ME10: Sit . . . 9H 99
Farmcroft DA11: Grav'nd . . . 7F 62
Farmdale Av. ME1: Roch . . . 1K 93
Farm Dr. CR0: Croy . . . 3C 82
Farmer Cl. CT21: Hythe . . . 5L 199
ME17: Leeds . . . 2C 140
Farmfield Rd. BR1: Brom . . . 1H 69
Farmground Cl. TN9: Tonb . . . 7L 145
Farm Hill Av. ME2: Strood . . . 3K 79
Farm Holt DA3: New A . . . 2M 89
(not continuous)
Farmhouse Cl. CT4: B'hm . . . 9D 162
Farm Ho. Cl. CT5: Whits . . . 5H 227
Farming World . . . 7C 20
Farmland Wlk. BR7: Chst . . . 1D 70
Farm La. CR0: Croy . . . 3C 82
CT14: Shol . . . 4J 177
KT18: Eps . . . 7A 12
KT21: Asht . . . 7A 12
TN10: Tonb . . . 3G 144
Farm Pl. DA1: Cray . . . 2H 59
Farm Rd. ME5: Chat'm . . . 8B 94
SM4: Mord . . . 3C 12
TN14: S'oaks . . . 2K 119
TN26: Hams . . . 3L 191
Farmstead Dr. TN8: Eden . . . 4C 184
Farmstead Rd. SE6 . . . 9E 54
Farm Va. DA5: Bex'y . . . 4C 58
Farmworld . . . 3H 45
Farnaby Dr. TN13: S'oaks . . . 8G 119
Farnaby Rd. BR1: Brom . . . 3G 69 (2K 13)
BR2: Shortl . . . 3G 69
SE9 . . . 2M 55
FARNBOROUGH . . . 6E 84 (4C 14)
Farnborough Av. CR2: S Croy . . . 9A 82
Farnborough Cl. ME16: Maid . . . 7N 125
Farnborough Comn. BR6: Farnb . . . 4B 84 (4B 14)
Farnborough Cres. BR2: Shortl . . . 2J 83
CR2: S Croy . . . 9B 82
Farnborough Hill BR6: Farnb, Chels . . . 6F 84 (4C 14)
Farnborough Way
BR6: Farnb, Chels . . . 6E 84 (4C 14)
Farncombe Way CT16: Whitf . . . 6G 178
Farndale Ct. SE18 . . . 7A 50
Farne Cl. ME15: Maid . . . 2D 138
Farnham Beeches TN3: Lang G . . . 1A 156
Farnham Cl. ME8: Rain . . . 2D 96
TN3: Lang G . . . 2A 156
Farnham La. TN3: Lang G . . . 2A 156 (3H 35)
TN4: R'hall . . . 2A 156 (3H 35)
Farnham Pl. TN3: Lang G . . . 2A 156
Farnham Rd. DA16: Well . . . 9L 51
FARNINGHAM . . . 1N 87 (3H 15)
Farningham Cl. ME14: Maid . . . 3F 126
Farningham Hill Rd. DA4: Farn'm . . . 8K 73
Farningham Road Station (Rail) . . . 5B 74 (2H 15)
Farnol Rd. DA1: Dart . . . 3A 60
Faro Cl. BR1: Brom . . . 5C 70
Farquhar Rd. SE19 . . . 1G 13
Farraday Cl. ME1: Roch . . . 3A 94
Farrance Ct. TN1: Tun W . . . 1H 157
Farrant Cl. BR6: Chels . . . 8J 85
Farrar Rd. CT7: Birch . . . 5F 206
Farren Rd. SE23 . . . 7B 54
Farrer's Pl. CR0: Croy . . . 5A 82
Farrers Wlk. TN23: Kgnt . . . 5F 160
Farrier Cl. BR1: Brom . . . 6N 69
ME14: Weav . . . 4H 127
TN25: Ashf . . . 5D 158
Farriers Cl. DA12: Grav'nd . . . 6L 63
Farriers Ct. ME8: Rain . . . 3E 96
Farrier St. CT14: Deal . . . 3N 177
Farringdon Rd. EC1 . . . 2F 5
Farringdon Station (Rail & Tube) . . . 3F 5
Farrington Av. BR5: St P . . . 6K 71
Farrington Pl. BR7: Chst . . . 3F 70
Farrow Ct. TN23: Ashf . . . 3E 160
Fartherwell Av. ME19: W Mal . . . 1M 123
Fartherwell Rd. ME19: W Mal . . . 2L 123 (1D 26)
Farthing Barn La. BR6: Downe . . . 9C 84
Farthing Cl. DA1: Dart . . . 2N 59
FARTHING COMMON . . . 2H 41
Farthingfield TN15: Wro . . . 7N 105
FARTHING GREEN . . . 6A 28
FARTHINGLOE . . . 2E 42
Farthingloe Ct. CT17: Dover . . . 6F 180
Farthingloe Rd. CT17: Dover . . . 7F 180
Farthings Cotts. ME14: S'ing . . . 9C 110
Farthings Ct. CT2: Cant . . . 7J 167
FARTHING STREET . . . 9B 84 (5B 14)
Farthing St. BR6: Downe . . . 8B 84 (5B 14)
Farthing Wall ME3: Cliffe . . . 1C 176
Farwell Rd. DA14: Sidc . . . 9K 57
Farwig La. BR1: Brom . . . 4J 69
Fashoda Rd. BR2: Shortl . . . 7N 69
Fathom Ho. ME1: Roch . . . 2N 93
Fauchon's Cl. ME14: Bear . . . 6J 127
Fauchon's La. ME14: Bear . . . 6J 127
Faulkners La. CT2: Harb . . . 2F 170 (1F 31)
Faussett Hill CT4: Lwr Har . . . 3H 31
Faustina Dr. TN23: Ashf . . . 5D 160
FAVERSHAM . . . 5H 187 (6A 20)
Faversham Ind. Est. ME13: Fav . . . 5K 187
Faversham Reach ME13: Fav . . . 3H 187
Faversham Rd. BR3: Beck'm . . . 5C 68
CT5: Seas . . . 6A 226 (4D 20)
ME9: Newn . . . 1H 29
ME9: Wich . . . 7N 201 (3E 28)
ME13: Char'g, Throw . . . 1N 175 (4J 29)
ME13: Osp . . . 7A 186 (7J 19)
ME17: Len . . . 7M 201 (3F 29)
SE6 . . . 5C 54
SM4: Mord . . . 3C 12
TN24: Kenn . . . 2H 159 (7A 30)
TN25: Bou A, Bou L . . . 1H 159 (6A 30)
TN25: Bou L, C'lck . . . 4B 30
TN25: C'lck . . . 6D 174 (3A 30)
TN25: Kenn . . . 2H 159 (7A 30)
TN27: Char'g . . . 1M 175 (4J 29)
Faversham Station (Rail) . . . 6H 187 (6A 20)
Faversham Swimming Pool . . . 5G 187
FAWKE COMMON . . . 9B 120 (3H 25)
Fawke Comn.
TN15: Under, S'oaks . . . 8A 120 (2H 25)
Fawkes Av. DA1: Dart . . . 7N 59
Fawke Wood Rd. TN15: Under . . . 1A 132 (3H 25)
FAWKHAM . . . 1H 89 (3K 15)
Fawkham Av. DA3: Long . . . 6B 76
FAWKHAM GREEN . . . 4H 89 (4K 15)
Fawkham Grn. Rd. DA3: Ash, Fawk . . . 4H 89 (4K 15)
Fawkham Rd. DA3: Fawk . . . 5F 88 (4J 15)
(West Kingsdown)
DA3: Fawk, Long . . . 7K 75 (2K 15)
(Longfield)
TN15: W King . . . 9G 88 (4J 15)
Fawley Cl. ME14: Maid . . . 2B 126
Fay Cl. ME1: Roch . . . 9L 79
Faygate Cres. DA6: Bexhth . . . 3B 58
Featherbed La. CR0: Croy . . . 8C 82
CR2: Croy . . . 5J 13
CR6: Warl . . . 6K 13
ME9: Bob . . . 1F 98
ME13: Sell'g . . . 2M 219 (1B 30)
Featherby Rd. ME8: Gill . . . 1K 95 (1K 95)
(Twydall, not continuous)
ME8: Gill . . . 8K 81 (2K 17)
(Grange)
Featherbys Cotts. ME7: Gill . . . 6J 81
Federation Rd. SE2 . . . 4K 51
Feenan Highway RM18: Tilb . . . 5C 8
Felborough Cl. CT4: Chil'm . . . 8K 175
Felday Rd. SE13 . . . 4E 54

Felderland—Ford Wlk.

FELDERLAND .9L 217 (2G 33)
Felderland Cl. CT14: Worth .9L 217
ME15: Maid .3G 139
Felderland Dr. ME15: Maid .3H 139
Felderland La. CT14: Worth .1M 183 (2F 33)
Felderland Rd. ME15: Maid .3H 139
Feldspar Cl. ME10: Sit .5E 98
Felhampton Rd. SE9 .7D 56
Felix Mnr. BR7: Chst .2G 70
Felixstowe Ct. E16 .1D 50
Felixstowe Rd. SE2 .3K 51
Fell Mead TN12: E Peck .1L 147
Fellowes Way TN11: Hild .2E 144
Fellows Cl. ME8: Gill .5L 95
Felspar Cl. SE18 .5H 51
Felstead Rd. BR6: Chels .3J 85
Felton Cl. BR5: Pet W .9D 70
Felton Ho. SE3 .2L 55
Felton Lea DA14: Sidc .1H 71
Fenchurch Street Station (Rail) .3G 5
Fendyke Rd. DA17: Belv .4M 51
Fen Gro. DA15: Sidc .3H 57
Fen La. RM14: Bulp .1B 8
(Bulphan)
RM14: Bulp, N Ock .1K 7
(North Ockendon)
RM16: Ors .2B 8
Fen Mdw. TN15: Igh .9J 105
Fenn Cl. BR1: Brom .2K 69
Fennel Cl. CR0: Croy .2A 82
ME1: Roch .9L 79
ME16: Maid .6M 125
Fennell St. SE18 .6C 50
Fenner Cl. CT20: F'stone .7E 188
Fenner Rd. RM16: Chad H .4K 7
FENN STREET .2L 67 (6K 9)
Fenoulhet Way CT6: H Bay .2H 195
Fen Pond Cotts. TN15: Igh .9J 105
Fen Pond Rd. TN15: Igh .9J 105
TN15: Wro .7J 105
Fens Way BR8: Swanl .2H 73
Fenswood Cl. DA6: Bexhth .4B 58
Fentiman Rd. SW8 .5F 5
Fenton Cl. BR7: Chst .1B 70
Fenton Ct. CT14: Deal .4L 177
Fenwick Cl. SE18 .6C 50
Ferbies TN3: Speld .7A 150
Ferbies Cl. TN3: Speld .7A 150
Ferby Ct. *DA14: Sidc* .9H 57
(off Main Rd.)
SE9 .8F 56
(off Main Rd.)
Ferdi Lethert Ho. TN24: Kenn .5J 159
Ferdinand Ter. *TN3: Groom* .6K 155
(off Corseley Rd.)
Ferguson Av. DA12: Grav'nd .9H 63
Ferguson Cl. BR2: Shortl .6G 68
CT21: Hythe .6N 199
Ferholt TN10: Tonb .9J 133
Fermor Rd. SE23 .6B 54
TN6: Crowb .7F 35
Fern Bank DA4: Eyns .3N 87
Fernbank Cl. ME5: Chat'm .9B 94
Fern Bank Cres. CT19: F'stone .5K 189
Fernbrook Av. DA15: Sidc .3G 57
Fernbrook Cres. *SE13* .4H 55
(off Leahurst Rd.)
Fernbrook Rd. SE13 .3H 55
Fern Cl. CT5: Whits .4L 227
CT18: H'nge .6M 193
DA8: Erith .8J 53
Fern Ct. CT10: B'stairs .8M 209
DA7: Bexhth .2B 58
FERNDALE .9J 151 (2K 35)
Ferndale BR1: Brom .5M 69
TN2: Tun W .1J 157
TN13: S'oaks .4K 119
Ferndale Cl. DA7: Bexhth .8N 51
ME12: Minst .6E 220
TN2: Tun W .1J 157
Ferndale Ct. CT7: Birch .5F 206
Ferndale Gdns. TN2: Tun W .1J 157
Ferndale Point TN2: Tun W .1J 157
Ferndale Rd. DA12: Grav'nd .7G 63
ME7: Gill .7H 81
Ferndale Way BR6: Farnb .6F 84
Ferndell Av. DA5: Bex'y .8E 58
Ferndene DA3: Long .6C 76
Ferndown CT7: Birch .3C 206
Fern Down DA13: Meop .2G 106
Ferndown Av. BR6: Orp .2F 84
Ferndown Cl. ME7: Hpstd .6K 95
Ferndown Rd. SE9 .5N 55
Ferne La. CT15: Alk .1C 42
Ferne Way CT20: F'stone .5E 188
Fernfield CT18: H'nge .6M 193
Fernfield La. CT18: H'nge .6M 193 (2B 42)
Fernhead Rd. W9 .2C 4
Fernheath Way DA2: Dart .1E 72
Fern Hill Pl. BR6: Farnb .6E 84
Fernhill Rd. ME16: Maid .7L 125
Fernhill St. E16 .1B 50
Fernholme Rd. SE15 .3A 54
Fernhurst Cres. TN4: S'bgh .4G 151
Fernlea Av. CT6: H Bay .3F 194
Fernlea Rd. SW12 .7E 4
Fernleigh ME10: Sit .9E 98
Fernleigh Cl. ME13: Dunk .3L 165
Fernleigh Ri. ME20: Dit .8F 108
Fernleigh Ter. ME10: Sit .9E 98
Fernside La. TN13: S'oaks .2L 131
Ferns, The ME20: Lark .9F 108
TN1: Tun W .1J 157
TN15: Bor G .2B 122
Fern Wlk. ME10: Sit .6K 99
Fernwood CR0: Croy .9B 82
Fernwood Cl. BR1: Brom .5M 69
Ferox Hall TN9: Tonb .5J 145
Ferrier Cl. ME8: Gill .7A 96
Ferringham TN4: Tun W .1F 156
Ferris Av. CR0: Croy .4C 82
Ferry App. SE18 .3C 50
Ferry Hill TN36: Winch .7A 46
Ferry La. ME1: Woul .7G 92
Ferry La. RM13: Rain .3F 7
Ferry Pl. SE18 .3C 50
Ferry Rd. ME2: Hall'g .7E 92
ME9: Iwade .8K 197 (3F 19)
RM18: Tilb .1F 62 (6C 8)
SS7: Benf .1J 9
TN31: Rye .5A 46
Ferry Vw. ME11: Queen .9A 220
Festival Av. DA3: Long .6C 76
Festival Cl. DA5: Bex'y .6M 57
DA8: Erith .7G 52
Fetter La. EC4 .3F 5
Ffinch Cl. ME20: Dit .1H 125
FICKLESHOLE .6K 13
Fiddler's Cl. DA9: G'hithe .2H 61
Fiddling La. TN25: M Hor .2F 41
Field Av. CT1: Cant .8C 168
Field Cl. BR1: Brom .5M 69
ME5: Chat'm .5B 94
Field Dr. TN8: Eden .4D 184
Field End TN24: W'boro .9K 159
Fld. End Pl. ME13: Bou B .3K 165
Fielder Cl. ME10: Sit .6K 99
FIELD GREEN .1E 44
Fielding Dr. ME20: Lark .7E 108
Fieldings, The ME10: Sit .9F 98
Fielding St. ME13: Fav .5G 187
Field Mill Rd. TN27: Eger .5F 29
Fieldside Cl. BR6: Farnb .5E 84
Fieldside Rd. BR1: Brom .1G 69
Fields La. ME18: W'bury .1C 136
Fieldspar Cl. ME5: Chat'm .1C 110
Field Vw. CT5: Whits .6D 226
TN23: Kgnt .5E 160
Field Vw. Cl. ME12: Minst .6D 220
Fieldway BR5: Pet W .9F 70
CR0: Croy .8E 82 (5J 13)
Field Way CT2: Sturry .6E 168
Fieldways TN18: Hawkh .6D 192
Fieldway Station (CT) .8E 82 (5J 13)
Fieldworks Rd. ME7: Gill .5D 80
Fiennes Way TN13: S'oaks .9K 119
Fiesta Wlk. CT1: Cant .3B 172
Fife Rd. CT6: H Bay .5C 194
SW14 .6A 4
Fifield Path SE23 .8A 54
Fifth Av. CT9: Clift .2F 208
Fifth Way HA9: Wemb .1A 4
FIG STREET .1H 131
Fig St. TN14: S'oaks .2G 131
Fig Tree Rd. CT10: B'stairs .6K 209
Fiji Ter. ME14: Maid .2D 126
Filborough Way DA12: Grav'nd .7N 63
Filer Rd. ME12: Minst .5F 220
Filey Cl. TN16: Big H .7B 164
Filmer La. TN14: S'oaks .3M 119
Filmer Rd. CT4: Brid .9E 172
Film Terrace Fitness Cen. .4C 56
Filston La. TN13: Otf .2F 102
TN14: Otf, S'ham .4F 102 (7F 15)
Filston Rd. DA8: Erith .5D 52
Finborough Rd. SW10 .4C 4
Finchale Rd. SE2 .3J 51
Finchcocks Living Mus. of Music .4F 37
Finch Ct. DA14: Sidc .8K 57
ME14: Maid .2B 126
Finches, The CT7: St N .8L 215
ME10: Sit .8G 99
Finch Gro. CT21: Hythe .8E 198
Finchley Cl. DA1: Dart .4A 60
Finchley Rd. NW2 .1C 4
NW3 .1C 4
NW8 .2D 4
Finchley Road & Frognal Station (Rail) .1D 4
Finchley Road Station (Tube) .1D 4
Finch M. CT14: Deal .6M 177
Findlay Cl. ME8: Gill .6N 95
Findley Cl. CT21: Hythe .6J 199
Findley Ho. ME14: Maid .2C 126
FINGLESHAM .3G 33
Finglesham Cl. BR5: Orp .2M 85
Finglesham Ct. ME15: Maid .9F 126
Finland Rd. SE4 .1B 54
Finlay Cl. ME13: Fav .5F 186
Finn Farm Ct. TN23: Kgnt .8H 161
Finn Farm Rd. TN23: Kgnt .7F 160
FINSBURY .2F 5
Finsbury Ct. *CT11: Ram* .4J 211
(off Finsbury Rd.)
FINSBURY PARK .1F 5
Finsbury Park Station (Rail & Tube) .1F 5
Finsbury Rd. CT11: Ram .4J 211
Finsbury Way DA5: Bex'y .4A 58
Fintonagh Dr. ME14: Pen H .2E 126
Finucane Dr. BR5: Orp .1L 85
Finwell Rd. ME8: Rain .1C 96
Firbank Gdns. CT9: Mgte .6B 208
Firbanks CT5: Whits .5H 227
Fir Ct. TN24: W'boro .9K 159
Fircroft Way TN8: Eden .4C 184
Fir Dene BR6: Farnb .4B 84
Firecrest Cl. DA3: Long .6A 76
Firepower (Royal Artillery Mus., The) .3D 50
Fire Sta. M. BR3: Beck'm .4D 68
Firethorn Cl. ME7: Gill .6H 81
Firhill Rd. SE6 .9D 54
Firmin Av. ME15: Maid .3G 138
Firmingers Rd. BR6: Orp .6C 86 (4E 14)
Firmin Rd. DA1: Dart .3K 59
Firsby Av. CR0: Croy .2A 82
Firs Cl. CT19: F'stone .5D 188
ME20: Aylfd .9J 109
SE23 .5B 54
Firs Ct. TN4: Tun W .8F 150
Firside Gro. DA15: Sidc .6H 57
Firs La. CT19: F'stone .5D 188
ME17: Holl .7A 128
Firs Rd. CT4: Wom .4B 32
First Av. CT9: Clift .2F 208
CT10: B'stairs .3K 209
DA7: Bexhth .7L 51
DA11: Nflt .6D 62
ME4: Chat'm .1F 94
ME7: Gill .1H 95
First Av. ME11: Queen .8A 220
ME12: E'chu .3D 202
(not continuous)
ME12: S'ness .3D 220
SS0: Wclf S .1C 10
SS17: Stan H .2E 8
Firs, The CT3: Hersd .2K 169
CT14: Deal .2N 177
DA5: Bex'y .6E 58
DA15: Sidc .7H 57
TN27: Smar .7D 222
First St. TN3: Lang G .2N 155
First Way HA9: Wemb .1A 4
Fir Tree Cl. BR6: Chels .6H 85
Firtree Cl. CT2: R Comn .8G 167
Fir Tree Cl. CT11: Ram .6G 210
TN11: Hild .2E 144
TN12: S'hrst .3K 223
Firtree Gdns. CR0: Croy .5D 82
Fir Tree Gro. ME5: Chat'm .1G 110
ME7: B'hst .1L 111
Fir Tree Hill CT4: S Min .6J 31
CT13: Wdboro .8G 217 (1F 33)
Fir Tree Rd. KT17: Eps .7B 12
SM7: Bans .6B 12
TN4: Tun W .3F 156
Fisher Cl. CT21: Hythe .7L 199
Fishermans Wlk. SE28 .2G 50
Fishermens Hill DA11: Nflt .3A 62
Fisher Rd. CT2: Cant .1K 171
ME5: Chat'm .4E 94
Fishers Cl. TN12: S'hrst .1K 223
Fishers La. CT4: S Min .6J 31
Fishers Oak TN14: S'oaks .3K 119
Fishers Rd. TN12: S'hrst .1K 223
Fisher St. CT13: S'wch .5M 217
ME14: Maid .3D 126
Fisher St. Rd. ME13: Bad, Mol .2A 30
Fishers Way DA17: Belv .1D 52
Fishguard Way E16 .1D 50
(not continuous)
Fishmarket CT19: F'stone .6L 189
Fishmarket Rd. TN31: Rye .5B 46
Fishmonger's La. CT16: Dover .5K 181
Fishponds Rd. BR2: Kes .6N 83 (4A 14)
Fitness First Health Club
Ashford .8F 158
Lewisham .1F 54
Fitzgerald Av. CT6: H Bay .4D 194
Fitzjohn's Av. NW3 .1D 4
Fitzmary Av. CT9: Mgte .2M 207
Fitzroy Av. CT9: Mgte .4F 208
CT10: B'stairs .3K 209
CT12: Ram .2F 210
Fitzroy Ct. *DA1: Dart* .6B 60
(off Churchill Cl.)
Fitzroy Rd. CT5: Whits .2H 227
Fitzwalter Ct. CT16: Dover .9G 178
Fitzwilliam Rd. ME14: Weav .4J 127
Fiveash Rd. DA11: Grav'nd .5E 62
Five Bells La. ME1: Roch .8A 80
Five Elms Rd. BR2: Shortl .4L 83 (4A 14)
Five Flds. La. TN8: Four E .6D 24
FIVE OAK GREEN .8G 147 (7C 26)
Five Oak Grn. Rd. TN11: Tonb .8L 145 (7A 26)
TN11: Tude .8L 145 (7A 26)
TN12: Five G .8L 145 (7A 26)
Five Oak La. TN12: S'hrst .1J 37
Five Vents La. TN29: Old R .3G 47
FIVEWAYS .7D 56 (7B 6)
FIVEWAYS CORNER
CROYDON .4F 13
Fiveways Ct. ME4: Chat'm .8D 80
Fiveways Ri. CT14: Deal .5J 177
FIVE WENTS .6N 139 (4A 28)
Five Wents BR8: Swanl .5H 73
Flack Gdns. ME3: Hoo .8H 67
FLACKLEY ASH .4J 45
Flag Cl. CR0: Croy .2A 82
Flamborough Cl. TN16: Big H .7B 164
Flamingo Cl. ME5: Chat'm .4D 94
Flamingo Dr. CT6: H Bay .5F 194
Flamsteed Rd. SE7 .5A 50
Flanders Cl. ME10: Kems'y .2G 98
Flanders Fld. TN25: Mers .8M 161
Flatford Ho. SE6 .9F 54
Flats, The DA9: G'hithe .3J 61
Flax Ct. La. CT15: Eyt .9K 185
Flaxlands La. CT4: P'hm .4F 31
Flaxman Ct. *DA17: Belv* .5B 52
(off Hoddesdon Rd.)
Flaxman Dr. ME16: Alltn .3N 125
Flaxmans Ct. ME7: Gill .6D 80
Flaxmore Pk. TN4: S'bgh .4G 151
Flaxpond Rd. TN23: Ashf .2D 160
Flaxton Rd. SE18 .8F 50
Fleet Av. DA2: Dart .6C 60
ME12: S'ness .3C 220
Fleetdale Pde. DA2: Dart .6C 60
FLEET DOWNS .6C 60 (7J 7)
Fleet Ho's. DA13: Sflt .2A 76
Fleet Rd. CT15: St Marg .8C 200
DA2: Dart .6B 60
DA11: Nflt .8B 62
ME1: Roch .2A 94
NW3 .1D 4
Fleets La. CT2: T Hill .4K 167
Fleet St. EC4 .3F 5
Fleetwood Av. CT6: H Bay .3E 194 (3J 21)
Fleetwood Cl. ME12: Minst .6J 221
Fleming Rd. CT3: S'le .8B 216 (1E 32)
CT13: Wdboro .8B 216 (1E 32)
RM16: Chaf H .4K 7
FLEMINGS .8C 216 (1E 32)
Fleming Way CT19: F'stone .3K 189
TN10: Tonb .9L 133
Fletcher Rd. CT5: Whits .4K 227
TN12: S'hrst .3J 223
Fletchers Cvn. Pk. ME12: E'chu .2E 202
Fletchers Cl. BR2: Shortl .7L 69
FLETCHER'S GREEN .7K 131 (4G 25)
Fletchers Way *CT14: Deal* .5K 177
(off Church La.)
FLETE .8B 208
Flete Rd. CT9: Mgte .9B 208 (3H 23)
Fleur De Lis Cotts. TN11: Leigh .6N 143
Fleur de Lis Heritage Cen. .5H 187
(off Preston St.)
Flex Appeal .2H 227
Flicks Cinema .4N 177
FLIMWELL .7F 37
Flimwell TN23: Ashf .3B 160
Flimwell Bird Pk. .7G 37
Flimwell Cl. BR1: Brom .1H 69
TN5: Flim .7F 37
Flint Cl. BR6: Chels .7H 85
ME10: Kems'y .3F 98
Flint Down Cl. BR5: St P .4J 71
Flint Grn. ME5: Chat'm .9F 94
Flint La. ME17: Len .3E 28
Flintmill Cres. SE3 .9A 50
(not continuous)
Floathaven Cl. SE28 .1J 51
Floats, The TN13: Riv .3F 118
Flodden Rd. CT14: Deal .7J 177
Flood Hatch ME15: Maid .7A 126
Flood La. ME13: Fav .4G 186
(not continuous)
Flood Pas. SE18 .3A 50
Flood St. TN25: Mers .9L 161 (3C 40)
Florance La. TN3: Groom .7J 155
Flora Rd. CT11: Ram .4J 211
Flora St. DA17: Belv .5A 52
Florence Av. CT5: Whits .6C 226
Florence Ct. CT9: Clift .2F 208
Florence Farm Mobile Home Pk.
TN15: W King .7D 88
Florence Rd. BR1: Brom .4K 69
BR3: Beck'm .5B 68
CT11: Ram .6H 211
ME16: Maid .6B 126
SE2 .4M 51
SE14 .5J 5
Florence St. ME2: Strood .4M 79
Florida Cl. CT16: Dover .1G 180
Florida Ct. *BR2: Shortl* .7J 69
(off Westmoreland Rd.)
Florin Dr. ME1: Roch .8M 79
Flowerfield TN14: Otf .8G 102
Flowerhill Way DA13: Ist R .3D 76
Flower Ri. ME14: Maid .3C 126
Floyd Cl. TN4: Tun W .7G 150
Fludyer St. SE13 .2H 55
Flume End ME15: Maid .7A 126
Flyers Way, The TN16: Westrm .8F 116
Flying Horse La. CT16: Dover .5K 181
Foads Hill CT12: C'snd .6B 210 (4H 23)
Foads La. CT12: C'snd .8B 210 (4H 23)
Foalhurst Cl. TN10: Tonb .3L 145
FOBBING .1F 9
Fobbing Rd. SS17: Corr .2F 9
Focal Point Rd. CT16: Dover .9E 178
Fodbury Ct. *CT8: Wgte S* .2K 207
(off Ethelbert Sq.)
Foksville Rd. SS8: Can I .2A 10
Foley Cl. TN24: W'boro .2L 161
Foley Ct. *DA1: Dart* .6B 60
(off Churchill Cl.)
Foley Rd. TN16: Big H .6D 164
Foley St. ME14: Maid .4D 126
FOLKESTONE .7K 189 (4B 42)
Folkestone Central Station (Rail) .6H 189 (4A 42)
Folkestone Ho. *ME15: Maid* .2J 139
(off Fontwell Cl.)
Folkestone Invicta F.C.
(New Pavilion Stadium, The .5G 189
Folkestone Library, Mus.
& Sassoon Gallery .6K 189
(off Grace Hill)
Folkestone Race Course .2B 198 (4G 41)
Folkestone Rd. CT15: Chu H .8B 180 (3E 42)
CT17: Dover .8B 180 (3E 42)
TN31: E Guld .5B 46
Folkestone Sports Cen. .5H 189
Folkestone West Station (Rail) .6F 188 (4A 42)
Folkestone Ent. Cen. CT19: F'stone .3F 188
Folks Wood Way CT21: Lymp .5B 198
FOLLY HILL .3J 37
Folly Rd. CT20: F'stone .5L 189
Fonblanque Rd. ME12: S'ness .2D 220
Fontridge La. TN19: Etch'm .4A 44
Fontwell Cl. ME15: Maid .2J 139
Fontwell Dr. BR2: Shortl .8C 70
Foord Almshouses ME1: Roch .9M 79
Foord Cl. DA2: Dart .7E 60
Foord Rd. CT19: F'stone .5K 189 (4B 42)
CT20: F'stone .5K 189
ME17: Len .7M 201
Foord Rd. Sth. CT20: F'stone .6K 189
Foord St. ME1: Roch .8N 79
Footbury Hill Rd. BR6: St M Cry .9J 71
FOOTS CRAY .2L 71 (1D 14)
Foots Cray High St. DA14: Sidc .2L 71
Foots Cray La. DA14: Sidc .6L 57 (7D 6)
Footscray Rd. SE9 .4C 56 (6B 6)
Forbes Rd. ME13: Fav .6G 187 (6A 20)
FORCE GREEN .6F 116 (2C 24)
Force Grn. La. TN16: Westrm .6F 116 (2C 24)
FORD .7M 195 (4A 22)
Ford Cl. CT4: Brid .9E 172
CT6: H Bay .3B 194
FORDCOMBE .9J 149 (2G 35)
Fordcombe Cl. ME15: Maid .1E 139
Fordcombe La. TN3: Ford .9J 149 (2G 35)
Fordcombe Rd. TN3: Ford .9J 149 (2G 35)
TN11: Pens .4H 149 (1G 35)
Fordcroft Rd. BR5: St M Cry .8K 71
Forde Av. BR1: Brom .6M 69
Fordel Rd. SE6 .6F 54
Ford Hills CT3: Hoath, H Bay .8M 195 (4A 22)
Fordingbridge Cl. ME16: Alltn .4M 125
Ford La. ME19: Wro .9E 106 (7B 16)
RM13: Rain .1F 7
Fordmill Rd. SE6 .7D 54
Fordoun Rd. CT10: B'stairs .8K 209
Ford Pl. Cotts. TN15: Wro .8E 106
Ford Rd. DA11: Nflt .3A 62
Ford Wlk. CT5: Seas .1A 166 (5E 20)

Ford Way—Frittenden Rd.

Ford Way TN23: Ashf 9D 158
FORDWICH 7F 168 (7K 21)
Fordwich Cl. BR6: Orp 1H 85
ME16: Alltn 2M 125
Fordwich Dr. ME2: Strood 2L 79
Fordwich Grn. ME8: Gill 9M 81
Fordwich Gro. CT10: B'stairs 6J 209
Fordwich Pl. CT13: S'wch 6L 217
Fordwich Rd. CT2: Cant 6E 168 (6J 21)
Fordwich Town Hall 7F 168 (7K 21)
Fordyce Rd. SE13 4F 54
Fore Cotts. TN23: Gt Cha 9A 158
Foreland Av. CT9: Mgte 3H 209 (1J 23)
CT19: F'stone 5M 189
Foreland Ct. CT11: Ram 7H 211
CT15: St Marg 8C 214
Foreland Hgts. CT10: B'stairs 6M 209
Foreland Pk. Ho. CT10: B'stairs 6M 209
Foreland Rd. CT15: St Marg 8C 214
Forelands Sq. CT14: Deal 7L 177
Foreland St. SE18 4F 50
Foreland, The CT1: Cant 5A 172
Foremans Barn Rd.
ME15: Hunt 5K 137 (4G 27)
Foreman's Cen. TN27: H'crn 8K 191
Foreman's Wlk. TN27: H'crn 8K 191
(off High St.)
Foreness Cl. CT10: B'stairs 2L 209
Forestall Mdw. TN23: Kgnt 5F 160 (3A 40)
Forest Av. TN25: Ashf 5C 158
Forest Cl. BR7: Chst 4C 70
Forest Cotts. TN25: C'lck 7E 174
FORESTDALE 9C 82 (5J 13)
Forestdale Cen., The CR0: Croy 8C 82
Forestdale Rd. ME5: Chat'm 2D 110
Forest Dr. BR2: Kes 5A 84
E12 1A 6
ME5: Chat'm 9C 94
Foresters Cl. ME5: Chat'm 9C 94
Foresters Cres. DA7: Bexhth 2C 58
Foresters Dr. SM6: Wall 5E 12
Forester's Way CT20: F'stone 6K 189
FOREST GATE 1A 6
Forest Gate Station (Rail) 1A 6
Forest Gro. TN10: Tonb 2J 145
FOREST HILL 7H 5
Forest Hill ME15: Maid 8C 126
Forest Hill Rd. SE22 6H 5
SE23 6H 5
Forest Hill Station (Rail) 7H 5
Forest La. E7 1K 5
E15 1K 5
Forest Ridge BR2: Kes 5A 84
BR3: Beck'm 6D 68
Forest Rd. DA8: Erith 8H 53
SM3: Sutt 3C 12
TN2: Tun W 5G 157 (4K 35)
TN12: Pad W 9L 147
FOREST ROW 5B 34
Forest Way BR5: St M Cry 8H 71
DA15: Sidc 5F 56
ME19: W Mal 6M 123 (2D 26)
TN2: Pem 6C 152
TN2: Tun W 4J 157
Forge Cl. BR2: Shortl 2K 83
CT2: Sturry 6E 168
CT15: Eyt 9K 185
ME13: Fav 6H 187
TN11: Pens 2J 149
TN12: Five G 8G 147
TN25: S'ndge 8C 218
Forge Cotts. ME14: Bear 5M 127
(off Green, The)
ME17: Bou Mo 5E 138
ME18: W'bury 6A 136
TN14: Weald 6K 131
Forge Cft. TN8: Eden 6D 184
Forge Fld. CT15: W Hou 2D 42
TN16: Big H 4D 164
TN26: Beth 2J 163
Forgefield Cotts. TN18: Sandh 4B 218
Forgefields CT6: H Bay 7H 195
Forge Hill TN25: Aldtn 4D 40
TN26: Beth 2K 163 (2G 39)
Forge La. CT3: C'let 4B 22
CT5: Whits 5F 226
CT11: Ram 5G 210
(off Chapel Rd.)
CT15: Sutt 1L 179 (6G 33)
CT16: Whitf 5E 178 (7E 32)
DA4: Hort K 7C 74 (2J 15)
DA12: Grav'nd 7L 63
DA12: Shorne 1C 78 (1E 16)
ME3: H Hals 2G 67
ME3: High'm 2G 78 (1F 17)
ME7: Gill 6H 81
ME7: Gill, B'hst 9J 95 (5K 17)
ME9: Upc 3H 225 (3C 18)
ME14: Boxl 7F 110
ME15: E Far 1M 137 (3G 27)
ME17: Bou Mo 5K 27
ME17: Leeds 1A 140 (3A 28)
ME17: Wich 2F 29
ME18: Coll S 6F 27
ME18: W Peck 2E 134
TN11: W Peck 3C 26
TN15: W King 1G 104
TN23: Ashf 8F 158 (1A 40)
TN27: Eger 6E 28
TN27: H'crn 8L 191 (7B 28)
Forge Lodge Bungs. ME15: Maid 8G 126
Forge Mdw. ME17: H'shm 2M 141
TN30: Ston C E 2C 46
Forge Mdws. TN27: H'crn 8K 191
Forge Meads TN30: Witter 3C 228
Forge M. CR0: Croy 6D 82
Forge Path CT16: Whitf 5F 178
Forge Rd. ME10: Sit 5F 98
TN3: Groom, Epp G 5G 35
TN4: S'bgh 5F 150
Forge Sq. TN11: Leigh 5N 143
Forge, The TN12: Five G 8G 147
Forge Way TN12: Pad W 8M 147
TN14: S'ham 2G 103
Formation, The E16 2D 50
(off Woolwich Mnr. Way)
Formby Rd. ME2: Hall'g 5E 92 (4F 17)
Formby Ter. ME2: Hall'g 5E 92
Forrester Cl. CT1: Cant 9B 168
Forrester Pl. TN23: Ashf 1G 160
Forsham La. ME17: Cha S 6K 27
Forson Cl. TN30: Tent 7C 224
FORSTAL 8N 109 (7H 17)
Forstal Cl. BR2: Shortl 6K 69
Forstal Cotts. ME20: Aylfd 8M 109
Forstall TN3: Lang G 1A 156
Forstal La. ME17: Cox 4A 138 (4H 27)
Forstall, The TN11: Leigh 5A 144
Forstal Rd. CT4: Wom 4B 32
ME14: S'lng 8M 109 (7G 17)
ME20: Aylfd 8L 109 (7G 17)
TN27: Eger 6E 28
FORSTAL, THE 9L 161 (3C 40)
Forstal, The CT3: Pres 6C 22
TN2: Pem 6C 152
TN3: Epp G 5H 35
TN11: Hdlw 8E 134
TN25: Wye 2M 159
Forster Ho. BR1: Brom 9G 54
Forster Rd. BR3: Beck'm 6B 68
Forsters ME17: L'ly 4A 140
Forsyth Cl. ME19: E Mal 9E 108
Forsyth Ct. ME7: Gill 5F 80
Forsythe Shades Ct. BR3: Beck'm 4F 68
Fort Amherst 7C 80 (2J 17)
Fort Bridgewood ME1: Roch 4M 93
Fort Cl. TN29: G'stne 8H 213
Fort Cres. CT9: Mgte 2D 208 (1H 23)
Fortess Rd. NW5 1E 4
Fort Gardens 4H 63
Fort Hill CT9: Mgte 2C 208 (1H 23)
Fort Lwr. Prom. CT9: Mgte 2D 208
Fort Luton Model Mus. 2D 94 (3J 17)
Fort Mt. CT9: Mgte 2D 208
Fort Pde. CT9: Mgte 2D 208
Fort Paragon CT9: Mgte 2D 208
Fort Pitt Hill ME4: Chat'm 8B 80 (3H 17)
Fort Pitt St. ME4: Chat'm 9B 80
Fort Prom. CT9: Mgte 2D 208
Fortress Distribution Pk. RM18: Tilb 2F 62
Fort Rd. CT9: Mgte 2C 208
CT10: B'stairs 8M 209
(not continuous)
CT21: Hythe 6H 199
RM18: Tilb, W Til 2G 62 (6C 8)
TN14: Hals 6D 102
Fortrye Cl. DA11: Nflt 7D 62
Fort St. ME1: Roch 8A 80
Fortuna Cl. DA3: Hart'y 7M 75
Fortuna Ct. CT11: Ram 5H 211
FORTUNE GREEN 1C 4
Fortune Grn. NW6 1C 4
Fortune Wlk. SE28 3F 50
(off Broadwater Rd.)
Fortune Way ME19: W Mal 6N 123
Forty Acres Hill ME12: Minst 8J 221
Forty Acres Rd. CT2: Cant 1L 171 (7H 21)
Forty Foot Way SE9 5E 56
Forty La. HA9: Wemb 1A 4
Forum, The 3G 156
Forum, The ME10: Sit 7G 98
(not continuous)
Forum Way TN23: Kgnt 4C 160
Forward Way ME1: Roch 5N 93
Fosse Bank Cl. TN9: Tonb 8G 145
Fosse Rd. TN9: Tonb 5H 145
Fosset Lodge DA7: Bexhth 8D 52
Fossil Rd. SE13 1D 54
Fossington Rd. DA17: Belv 4M 51
FOSTALL 6D 20
Fostall Grn. TN23: Ashf 2D 160
Fostall Rd. ME13: Fav 3G 187
FOSTEN GREEN 4B 38
Fosten La. TN27: Bidd 8J 163 (3C 38)
Foster Clarke Dr. ME15: Maid 3G 139
Foster Clark Est. ME15: Maid 7E 126
Foster Rd. TN24: Svgtn 2L 161
Foster's Av. CT10: B'stairs 6J 209
Fosters Cl. BR7: Chst 1B 70
CT19: F'stone 4E 188
Foster's Ct. CT13: S'wch 7L 217
Foster St. ME15: Maid 6D 126
Foster Way CT14: Deal 5L 177
Fostington Way ME5: Chat'm 1B 110 (5H 17)
(not continuous)
Fougeres Way TN24: Ashf 6E 158 (1A 40)
Foulds Cl. ME8: Gill 6L 95
Foundry Wharf ME1: Roch 8B 80
Fountain Ct. DA4: Eyns 3M 87
DA15: Sidc 4K 57
SE23 7A 54
Fountain Dr. SE19 1G 13
Fountain La. ME16: Maid 7L 125 (2G 27)
Fountain Pas. ME12: S'ness 2B 220
(off West St.)
Fountain Rd. ME2: Strood 3J 79
Fountains Cl. TN24: W'boro 9L 159
Fountain St. CT5: Whits 3F 226
ME10: Sit 7F 98
Fountain Wlk. DA11: Nflt 4D 62
Four Acres ME19: E Mal 4F 124
FOUR ELMS 5D 24
Four Elms Hill ME3: C'den 9C 66 (1H 17)
Four Elms Rd. TN8: Eden, Four E 5C 184 (6C 24)
Four Horse Shoes Pk. ME13: G'ney 6C 20
FOUR OAKS
Faversham 4C 186 (5K 19)
Rye 3J 45
Four Oaks Rd. TN12: Sut V 7A 28
TN27: H'crn 7H 191 (7A 28)
Fourteen Acre La.
TN35: Gues T, T Oaks 7G 45
Fourth Av. DA11: Nflt 6D 62
E12 1B 6
ME7: Gill 8H 81
ME12: E'chu 2D 202
FOUR THROWS 1D 44
Fourth Way HA9: Wemb 1A 4
FOUR WENTS
ME17 6J 139
TN17 4H 37
TN18 1E 192 (6J 37)
Four Wents ME17: L'ly 5A 140
Fourwents Rd. ME3: Hoo 7G 66
Fowey Cl. ME5: Chat'm 6F 94
Fowler Cl. ME8: Gill 8M 95
Fowlers Cl. DA14: Sidc 1N 71
Foxberry Rd. SE4 1B 54
Foxberry Wlk. DA11: Nflt 8C 62
Foxborough Cl. CT13: Wdboro 8G 216
Foxborough Gdns. SE4 3D 54
Foxborough Hill CT13: Wdboro 8G 217 (1F 33)
Foxborough La. CT12: Minst 7F 212 (4F 23)
Foxburrow Cl. ME8: Gill 6N 95
Foxbury DA3: New A 4L 89
TN15: Bor G 2A 122
Foxbury Av. BR7: Chst 2F 70
Foxbury Cl. BR1: Brom 2L 69
BR6: Chels 6J 85
Foxbury Dr. BR6: Chels 7J 85
Foxbury Rd. BR1: Brom 2K 69
Foxbush TN11: Hild 1C 144
Fox Cl. BR6: Chels 6J 85
CT18: Lym'ge 7K 205
Foxcombe CR0: Croy 7E 82
(not continuous)
Foxcroft Rd. SE18 8D 50
Foxden Dr. ME15: Bear 8J 127
Foxdene Rd. CT5: Seas 7B 226
Foxdown Cl. CT2: Cant 9L 167
Foxearth Cl. TN16: Big H 6E 164
FOXENDOWN 3C 16
Foxendown La. DA13: Meop 2G 90 (3C 16)
Foxes Dale BR2: Shortl 6G 69
SE3 1K 55
Foxfield Rd. BR6: Orp 3F 84
Foxglove Cl. TN8: Eden 4D 184
(off Wayside Dr.)
Foxglove Cres. ME5: Chat'm 7B 94
Foxglove Grn. TN24: W'boro 8J 159
Foxglove Ri. ME14: Maid 2B 126
Foxglove Rd. TN24: W'boro 9J 159
Foxglove Row ME2: Hall'g 6D 92
Foxgloves, The TN12: Pad W 1N 153
Foxgrove ME10: Sit 4F 98
Foxgrove Av. BR3: Beck'm 3E 68
Foxgrove Rd. BR3: Beck'm 3E 68
CT5: Whits 4J 227
Fox Hill BR2: Kes 6M 83
CT3: Sturry 2D 168
ME9: Bap 8L 99 (5G 19)
FOXHOLE 1C 36
Foxhole La. TN12: Mat 6G 153 (2C 36)
TN18: Hawkh 1D 44
Foxhole Rd. SE9 3A 56
Fox Hollow Cl. SE18 5G 50
Fox Hollow Dr. DA7: Bexhth 1M 57
Fox Holt Rd. CT15: S'fld 2K 193
Foxhome Cl. BR7: Chst 2C 70
Foxhounds La. DA13: Sflt 8N 61 (7A 8)
Fox Ho. Rd. DA17: Belv 5C 52
(not continuous)
Foxhunter Pk., The CT12: Monk'n 7A 212
Fox La. BR2: Kes 6L 83 (4A 14)
Fox Lea TN15: Bor G 2M 121
Foxleas Ct. BR1: Brom 3H 69
Foxley Hill Rd. CR8: Purl 6F 13
Foxley La. CR8: Purl 6E 12
Foxley Rd. ME11: Queen 7B 220
SW9 5F 5
Fox's Cross Hill CT5: Seas 5E 20
Fox's Cross Rd. CT5: Whits 1C 166 (5E 20)
Fox St. ME7: Gill 6F 80
Foxtail Cl. ME4: Chat'm 2E 80
Foxton Ho. E16 2C 50
(off Albert Rd.)
Fox Way CT4: B'hm 8D 162
Foxwell M. SE4 1B 54
Foxwell St. SE4 1B 54
Foxwood Gro. BR6: Prat B 1L 101
DA11: Nflt 6D 62
Foxwood Rd. DA2: Bean 8H 61
SE3 2J 55
Foxwood Way DA3: Long 5C 76
Foyle Dr. RM15: S Ock 3K 7
Foys Pas. CT21: Hythe 6K 199
Framley Rd. TN10: Tonb 1M 145
Framlingham Cres. SE9 9A 56
Frampton Rd. CT21: Hythe 6H 199
Francemary Rd. SE4 3D 54
France Rd. CT16: Dover 8F 178
Frances Cotts. ME3: Hoo 7H 67
Frances Gdns. CT11: Ram 4H 211
Frances St. SE18 3B 50 (4B 6)
Francis Av. CT13: S'wch 1J 33
DA7: Bexhth 9B 52
Franciscan Way CT1: Cant 2M 171
(off Water La.)
Francis Dr. ME5: Chat'm 9D 94
Francis Est. ME15: Maid 4K 139
Francis La. ME15: Maid 3J 139
Francis M. SE12 5K 55
Francis Rd. BR5: St P 6M 71
CT10: B'stairs 6M 209
DA1: Dart 3L 59
E10 1K 5
TN11: Hild 1D 144
TN23: Ashf 1F 160
Frank Apps Cl. ME9: N'tn 5K 97
Frank Edinger Cl. TN24: Kenn 6H 159
Frankfield Ri. TN2: Tun W 4G 156
Frank Godley Ct. DA14: Sidc 1K 71
Franklin Dr. ME14: Weav 5G 127
Franklin Ho. BR2: Shortl 6H 69
Franklin Pas. SE9 1A 56
Franklin Rd. DA5: Bex'y 7F 58
DA7: Bexhth 8N 51
DA12: Grav'nd 1J 77
ME7: Gill 7G 80
SE20 4A 68
Franklins Cotts. ME15: E Far 3N 137
Franklyn Ho. CT2: Sturry 6E 168
Franklyn Rd. CT2: Cant 3J 171
Franks Ct. ME8: Gill 1L 95
Frank's Hollow Rd.
TN3: Bidb, Tun W 5C 150 (1J 35)
Franks La. DA4: Hort K 8A 74 (3H 15)
Franks Wood Av. BR5: Pet W 8D 70 (3B 14)
Frank Walters Bus. Pk., The
CT10: B'stairs 9H 209
Frank Woolley Rd. TN10: Tonb 2M 145
FRANT 9J 157 (5K 35)
Frant Fld. TN8: Eden 6C 184
Frant Grn. Rd. TN3: Frant 9H 157
Franthorne Way SE6 7E 54
Frant Rd. CR7: Thor H 3F 13
TN2: Tun W 3G 156 (3K 35)
TN3: Frant, Tun W 6G 157 (3K 35)
Frant Station (Rail) 8M 157 (4A 36)
Fraser Cl. DA5: Bex'y 6D 58
Fraser Rd. DA8: Erith 5E 52 (4F 7)
Freathy La. TN25: Kenn 2G 159
Freda Cl. CT10: B'stairs 3K 211
Frederick Pl. SE18 5D 50
Frederick Rd. CT14: Deal 7K 177
ME7: Gill 8F 80
Frederick St. ME10: Sit 7F 98
Freedown, The CT15: St Marg 6C 214
FREE HEATH 5C 36
Free Heath Rd. TN3: Lamb 5C 36
TN5: Lamb 5C 36
Freehold, The TN11: Hdlw 7C 134
TN12: E Peck 1L 147
Freeland Ct. DA15: Sidc 8J 57
Freelands Av. CR2: S Croy 9A 82
Freelands Gro. BR1: Brom 4L 69
Freelands Rd. BR1: Brom 4L 69 (2A 14)
ME6: Snod 2D 108
Freeland Way DA8: Erith 8H 53
Freeman Rd. DA12: Grav'nd 8K 63
Freeman's Cl. CT5: Seas 7C 226
Freemans Gdns. ME4: Chat'm 1C 94
Freeman's Rd. CT12: Minst 7E 212
Freeman's Way CT14: Deal 7L 177
Freeman Way ME15: Maid 9H 127
Freemasons Rd. E16 3A 6
Freesia Cl. BR6: Chels 6H 85
ME7: Gill 6J 81
Freight La. TN17: Cran 8C 176
Fremantle Rd. CT20: F'stone 6E 188
DA17: Belv 4B 52
Fremlin Cl. TN4: R'hall 1B 156
Fremlins Rd. ME14: Bear 5M 127
Frencham Cl. CT2: Cant 7N 167
French's Row ME9: Tey 7L 223
FRENCH STREET 3C 24
French St. TN16: Westrm 3C 24
Frendsbury Rd. SE4 2B 54 (6H 5)
Frensham Cl. ME10: Sit 7J 99
Frensham Dr. CR0: Croy 8F 82
Frensham Rd. SE9 7F 56
TN17: Rolv L 7C 38
Frensham Wlk. ME5: Chat'm 9C 94
Fresham Ho. BR2: Shortl 6J 69
(off Durham Rd.)
Freshfield Cl. SE13 2G 55
Freshfield La. CT21: Salt 4H 199
Freshfields CR0: Croy 2C 82
Freshland Rd. ME16: Maid 5M 125
Freshlands CT6: H Bay 1M 195
Freshwater Cl. CT6: H Bay 4C 194
Freshwater Rd. ME5: Chat'm 4D 94
Freshwood Cl. BR3: Beck'm 4E 68
Freta Rd. DA6: Bexhth 3A 58
Frewing Cl. BR7: Chst 2B 70
Friar Rd. BR5: St M Cry 8J 71
Friars Av. ME5: Chat'm 9C 94
Friars Cl. CT5: Whits 4H 227
Friars Ct. ME14: Maid 5D 126
FRIAR'S GATE 6E 34
Friars M. SE9 3C 56
Friars Pl. La. W3 3A 4
Friars, The 8J 109 (7G 17)
Friars, The CT1: Cant 2M 171
ME3: H Hals 1J 67
Friars Wlk. SE2 5M 51
Friar's Way CT16: Dover 1F 180
Friars Way TN2: Tun W 8K 151
Friarswood CR0: Croy 9B 82
Friary Pl. ME2: Strood 5M 79
Friary Pct. ME2: Strood 5M 79
Friary Rd. W3 3A 4
Friary Way CT2: Cant 9K 167
Friday Rd. DA8: Erith 5E 52
Friday St. ME17: E Sut 9D 140 (5B 28)
Friendly Cl. CT9: Mgte 4H 209
Friends Av. CT9: Mgte 5H 209
Friend's Gap CT9: Clift 2H 209
Friesian Way TN24: Kenn 3G 159
Friezeland Rd. TN4: Tun W 4D 156
Friezingham La. TN17: Rolv L 7C 38
FRIEZLEY 3J 37
Friezley La. TN17: Cran 3J 37
Frimley Cl. CR0: Croy 8F 82
Frimley Ct. DA14: Sidc 1L 71
Frimley Cres. CR0: Croy 8F 82
FRINDSBURY 3N 79 (1H 17)
Frindsbury Hill ME2: Strood 3N 79 (1H 17)
Frindsbury Rd. ME2: Strood 4M 79 (2G 17)
FRININGHAM 8B 112 (7A 18)
Frinstead Wlk. ME16: Alltn 2N 125
FRINSTED 1E 28
Frinsted Cl. ME8: Gill 9M 81
Frinsted Gro. BR5: St M Cry 7M 71
Frinsted Rd. DA8: Erith 7E 52
ME9: Mils 9F 114 (1F 29)
Frinton Rd. DA14: Sidc 7N 57
Friston Way ME1: Roch 3A 94
Friswell Pl. DA6: Bexhth 2B 58
Frith Rd. CT16: Dover 3H 181 (1F 43)
TN25: Bils 4B 40
Frithwood Cl. ME15: Bear 8J 127
FRITTENDEN 2A 38
Frittenden Cl. TN23: Ashf 3C 160
Frittenden Rd. ME2: Wain 2A 80
TN12: S'hrst 4K 223 (1K 37)

Frittenden Rd.—Gilroy Way

Frittenden Rd. TN27: Bidd 2B 38
Frizlands La. RM10: Dag 1E 6
Frobisher Cl. ME10: Sit 5F 98
Frobisher Gdns. ME1: Roch 1N 93
Frobisher Rd. DA8: Erith 7G 53
Frobisher Way DA9: G'hithe 2H 61
DA12: Grav'nd 1K 77
FROGHAM 4C 32
FROGHOLE 4C 24
Froghole La. TN8: Westrm 4C 24
FROGHOLT 3J 41
Frog La. CT4: Bis 3K 31
ME19: W Mal 1A 124
TN1: Tun W 3G 157
Frogmore Wlk. ME17: Len 7L 201
Frognal NW3 1D 4
Frognal Av. DA14: Sidc 1J 71 (1D 14)
Frognal Cl. ME9: Tey 7J 223
FROGNAL CORNER 2H 71 (1C 14)
Frognal Gdns. ME9: Tey 7J 223
Frognal La. ME9: Tey 7J 223 (5H 19)
NW3 1C 4
Frognal Pl. DA14: Sidc 2J 71
Frogs Hole La. TN17: Bendn 5C 38
Frog's La. TN17: Rolv, Rolv L 7C 38
Froissart Rd. SE9 3N 55
Fromandez Dr. TN12: Horsm 8B 196
Frome Ct. TN10: Tonb 2H 145
Front Brents ME13: Fav 4H 187
Front La. RM14: Upm 1J 7
Front Rd. TN26: Wdchu 7B 228 (5H 39)
Front St. CT14: R'wld 4B 200 (5H 33)
Front, The CT15: St Marg 9C 214
Frost Cotts. CT13: Wdboro 8G 216
Frost Cres. ME5: Chat'm 4D 94
Frost La. CT7: St N 7M 215
Froyle Cl. ME16: Alltn 3N 125
Fruiterer's Cl. ME9: Rod 3H 115
Fry Cl. ME3: Isle G 7B 190
Fryman's La. TN31: Brede 6F 45
Frythe Cl. TN17: Cran 8D 176
Frythe Cres. TN17: Cran 8D 176
Frythe Wlk. TN17: Cran 8D 176
Frythe Way TN17: Cran 8D 176
Fuchsia St. SE2 5K 51
Fuggles Cl. TN12: Pad W 9K 147
Fuggles Ct. TN17: Bendn 6A 38
Fulbert Dr. ME14: Weav 4J 127
Fulbert Rd. CT16: Dover 8G 178
FULHAM 5C 4
Fulham Av. CT9: Mgte 4N 207
FULHAM BROADWAY 5C 4
Fulham Broadway Station (Tube) 5C 4
Fulham F.C. (Craven Cottage) 5B 4
Fulham High St. SW6 5C 4
Fulham Pal. Rd. SW6 5B 4
W6 4B 4
Fulham Rd. SW3 5C 4
SW6 5C 4
SW10 5C 4
Fuller Cl. BR6: Chels 6H 85
Fullers Cl. ME14: Bear 5K 127
Fullers Hill TN16: Westrm 8F 116
Fuller St. TN15: Seal 2B 120 (1H 25)
Fuller's Wood CR0: Croy 6D 82
Fulmar Cl. CT6: H Bay 2N 195
Fulmar M. CT18: H'nge 9K 193
Fulmar Rd. ME2: Strood 6H 79
Fulsam Pl. CT9: Mgte 4B 208
Fulston Pl. ME10: Sit 8H 99
Fulwich Rd. DA1: Dart 4N 59
FUNTON 3D 18
Furfield Cl. ME15: Maid 3H 139
Furnace Av. TN3: Lamb 4J 201
Furnace La. TN3: Lamb 3H 201 (5C 36)
TN12: Brenc, Horsm 6B 196 (1E 36)
TN31: B Oak 5G 45
Furner Cl. DA1: Cray 1G 58
Furness Rd. SM4: Mord 3C 12
Furnival Ct. TN2: Tun W 5F 156
Furrells Rd. ME1: Roch 7A 80
Further Fld. TN12: S'hrst 1J 223
Further Grn. Rd. SE6 7H 55
FURTHER QUARTER 3E 38
Furtherwick Rd. SS8: Can I 2K 9
FURZEDOWN 1E 12
Furzefield Av. TN3: Speld 6A 150
Furzefield Cl. BR7: Chst 2D 70
Furze Hill Cres. ME12: Minst 7F 220
Furzehill Sq. BR5: St M Cry 7K 71
Fusilier Av. CT20: F'stone 5B 188
Future Ct. ME2: Med E 4B 80
Fyfe Way BR1: Brom 5K 69
Fyfield Cl. BR2: Shortl 7G 69
Fyndon Ho. CT1: Cant 3B 172
Fysie La. TN19: Etch'm 2A 44

G

Gable Cl. DA1: Cray 3H 59
Gable Cotts. ME15: Otham 1L 139
Gables Cl. SE12 6K 55
Gables, The BR1: Brom 3L 69
DA3: Long 5B 76
Gabriel Gdns. DA12: Grav'nd 1K 77
Gabriel's Hill ME15: Maid 5D 126
Gabrielspring Rd. DA3: Fawk 3D 88 (4J 15)
Gabrielspring Rd. E.
DA3: Fawk, Hort K 3E 88 (4J 15)
Gabriel St. SE23 5A 54
Gadby Rd. ME10: Sit 6D 98
GADSHILL 2G 78 (1F 17)
Gads Hill ME7: Gill 5J 81 (2K 17)
Gadwall Way SE28 2F 50
Gagetown Ter. ME14: Maid 2C 126
Gaggs Hill CT15: Ashy, W'share 5F 33
Gainsborough Av. CT9: Mgte 5G 209
DA1: Dart 3K 59
Gainsborough Cl. BR3: Beck'm 3D 68
CT19: F'stone 4G 188
ME8: Gill 5N 95
ME10: Sit 6C 98
Gainsborough Ct. BR2: Shortl 7M 69
Gainsborough Dr. CT6: H Bay 2M 195
DA11: Nflt 8C 62
ME16: Maid 5M 125
Gainsborough Gdns. TN10: Tonb 2L 145
Gainsborough Rd. CT7: Birch 3E 206
Gainsborough Sq. DA6: Bexhth 1M 57
Gaitskell Rd. SE9 6E 56
Gala Bingo
Dover 4J 181
(off Biggin St.)
Medway Valley Leisure Pk. 8J 79
Gillingham 7F 80
Maidstone 5D 126
Galahad Av. ME2: Strood 6J 79
Galahad Rd. BR1: Brom 9K 55
Galena Cl. ME5: Chat'm 1D 110
ME10: Sit 5D 98
Galena Ho. SE18 5H 51
(off Grosmont Rd.)
Gale St. RM9: Dag 1D 6
Gallants La. ME15: E Far 1K 137 (3G 27)
Gallards Almshouses TN4: S'bgh 5G 150
Galleon Blvd. DA2: Dart 2D 60
Galleon Cl. DA8: Erith 4E 52
ME1: Roch 3N 93
Galleon M. DA11: Nflt 5D 62
Galleon Way ME2: Upnor 1C 80
Gallery Rd. SE21 7G 5
Galley Hill Ind. Est. DA10: Swans 3L 61
Galley Hill Rd. DA10: Nflt 3M 61 (6A 8)
DA11: Nflt 3M 61 (6A 8)
Galliard St. CT13: S'wch 6M 217
Gallions Entrance E16 1E 50
Gallions Reach Station (DLR) 3C 6
Gallions Vw. Rd. SE28 2G 50
Gallipot Hill TN7: Up Hart, Hartf 5D 34
GALLIPOT STREET 5D 34
Gallops, The DA13: Meop 3E 106
Gallosson Rd. SE18 4G 50
Galloway Dr. DA1: Cray 1F 58
TN25: Kenn 2G 158
Galloways Rd. TN29: Lydd 4K 205
Gallow's Cnr. CT21: Hythe 6H 199
Gallows Wood DA3: Fawk 5G 88
Gallus Sq. SE3 1L 55
Gallwey Av. CT7: Birch 4D 206
Galpins Rd. CR7: Thor H 2F 13
Galsworthy Cl. SE28 1K 51
Galsworthy Rd. KT2: King T 2A 12
Galway Rd. ME12: S'ness 2D 220
Gamma Rd. ME3: Hoo 6N 67
Gammon's Farm La. TN29: Newchu 7D 40
Gander Grn. La. SM1: Sutt 4C 12
SM3: Sutt 4C 12
Gandy's La. ME17: Bou Mo 6F 138 (4J 27)
Gange M. ME13: Fav 5H 187
Gann Rd. CT5: Whits 3H 227
Ganyes Pk. Rd. RM14: Upm 1H 7
Gaol La. CT17: Dover 5J 181
(off Queen St.)
Gapp Cl. TN15: W King 8E 88
Gap Rd. SW19 1C 12
Gap, The CT1: Cant 5A 172
CT2: Blean 4G 166
Garden Av. DA7: Bexhth 1A 58
Garden Cl. CT2: R Comn 9G 167
ME15: Maid 1H 139
SE12 8L 55
TN16: Westrm 4D 24
Garden Cotts. BR5: St P 5L 71
CT3: Wing 8J 225
TN11: Leigh 5A 144
Garden Ct. ME1: Woul 6G 93
TN13: S'oaks 4L 119
(off Garden Rd.)
Gardeners Pl. CT4: Chart'm 9F 170
Gardeners Quay CT13: S'wch 5M 217
(off Up. Strand St.)
Gardenia Cl. ME2: Strood 2M 79
Garden La. BR1: Brom 2L 69
Garden of England Crematorium ME9: Bob 4E 18
Gdn. of England Pk. ME17: H'shm 1K 141
Garden Pl. DA2: Dart 8L 59
TN24: Kenn 4J 159
Garden Rd. BR1: Brom 1L 69
CT19: F'stone 5K 189
TN1: Tun W 1H 157
TN9: Tonb 5J 145
TN13: S'oaks 4L 119
Garden Row DA11: Nflt 8E 62
Gardens, The BR3: Beck'm 4F 68
ME17: Cox 5N 137
(not continuous)
TN29: Ivyc 2G 47
Garden St. ME7: Gill 6D 80
TN1: Tun W 1H 157
Garden Ter. TN15: Seal 3A 120
Garden Wlk. BR3: Beck'm 4C 68
CT14: Deal 3M 177
Garden Way ME19: W Mal 7M 123
Gardiner Cl. BR5: St P 5L 71
Gardiner St. ME7: Gill 6F 80
Gardner Cl. CT18: H'nge 9J 193
Gardner Ind. Est. SE26 1C 68
Gardner's Hill TN31: Iden 3A 46
Gardyne M. TN9: Tonb 7H 145
Gareth Gro. BR1: Brom 9K 55
Garfield Pl. ME13: Fav 5H 187
Garfield Rd. CT9: Mgte 3B 208
ME7: Gill 6G 81
Gargery Cl. DA12: Grav'nd 6M 63
Garibaldi St. SE18 4G 51
Garland Rd. SE18 7F 50
Garlands TN11: Hild 8D 132
Garlies Rd. SE23 8B 54
GARLINGE 3N 207 (2G 23)
Garlinge CT9: Mgte 3N 207
GARLINGE GREEN 3F 31
Garlinge Grn. Rd. CT4: P'hm, Chart'm 3F 31
Garlinge Rd. TN4: S'bgh 5G 150
Garner Dr. ME19: E Mal 9E 108
Garnet St. E1 3H 5
Garnett Cl. SE9 1B 56
Garrad's Rd. SW16 7E 4
Garrard Av. CT9: Mgte 3N 207
Garrard Cl. BR7: Chst 1D 70
DA7: Bexhth 1B 58
Garratt La. SW17 7D 4
SW18 6C 4
Garratts La. SM7: Bans 7C 12
Garrick Dr. SE28 3F 50
Garrick St. DA11: Grav'nd 4G 62
Garrington Cl. ME14: Maid 3F 126
Garrison Cl. SE18 7C 50
Garrison Rd. ME12: S'ness 1A 220
Garrison Sports Stadium 6D 80
Garrolds Cl. BR8: Swanl 5E 72
Garrow DA3: Long 6A 76
Garside Cl. SE28 3F 50
Garsington M. SE4 1C 54
Garthorne Rd. SE23 5A 54
Garth Rd. SM4: Mord 3B 12
TN13: S'oaks 1K 131
Garton Way TN23: Ashf 2A 160
Garvock Dr. TN13: S'oaks 8H 119
Gascoigne Rd. CR0: Croy 9F 82 (5K 13)
IG11: Bark 2C 6
Gascoyne Dr. DA1: Cray 1G 59
Gascoyne Pl. ME15: Bear 7L 127
Gascoyne Rd. E9 1H 5
Gas Ho. Rd. ME1: Roch 6N 79
Gas La. ME13: Bou B 3H 165
Gasoline All. TN15: Wro 8C 106
Gas Pas. CT1: Cant 3M 171
Gas Rd. ME10: Sit 5J 99
(Eurolink Bus. Pk.)
ME10: Sit 6G 98
(Mill Way)
Gasson Rd. DA10: Swans 4L 61
Gassons Rd. ME6: Snod 2C 108
Gas St. CT1: Cant 3M 171
Gasworks La. TN23: Ashf 9F 158
(not continuous)
Gatcombe Cl. ME5: Chat'm 6D 94
ME16: Alltn 4M 125
Gatcombe Ct. BR3: Beck'm 3D 68
Gateacre Ct. DA14: Sidc 9K 57
Gateacre Rd. CT5: Seas 7C 226
Gate Farm Rd. TN3: Bidb 1C 150 (7J 25)
Gatefield Cotts. TN17: Rolv 2C 214
Gatefield La. ME13: Fav 5H 187
(not continuous)
Gate Hill CT2: Dunk 9A 166 (7E 20)
ME13: Dunk 9A 166 (7E 20)
Gate Ho. Wood Touring Pk. TN15: Wro 9D 106
Gatekeeper Chase ME8: Rain 3B 96
Gate La. CT4: R Min 7H 183 (1H 41)
Gateley Ho. SE4 2A 54
(off Coston Wlk.)
Gate Quays CT9: Mgte 3C 208
(off Marine Gdns.)
Gates Ct. TN12: E Peck 9M 135
Gates Grn. Rd. BR2: Kes 4J 83 (4A 14)
BR4: W W'ck, Brom 4J 83 (4K 13)
Gateway Ct. CT11: Ram 5K 211
(off Victoria Pde.)
Gateway Pde. DA12: Grav'nd 9L 63
Gateway, The CT16: Dover 5K 181
Gateway to the White Cliffs Vis. Cen. 3M 181
Gatland La. ME16: Maid 8L 125 (2G 27)
Gatling Rd. SE2 5J 51
Gattons Way DA14: Sidc 9A 58
Gatwick Rd. DA12: Grav'nd 8G 63
Gault Cl. ME15: Bear 7K 127
Gaunt's Cl. CT14: Deal 6K 177
Gavestone Cres. SE12 5L 55
Gavestone Rd. SE12 5L 55
Gavin Ho. SE18 4G 50
Gayhurst Cl. ME8: Gill 5N 95
Gayhurst Dr. ME10: Sit 6D 98
Gaynesford Rd. SE23 7A 54
Gayton Rd. SE2 3L 51
Gaza Trad. Est. TN11: Hild 9L 131
Gazedown Ct. TN29: St M Bay 3M 215
Gaze Hill Av. ME10: Sit 8H 99
Gazelle Glade DA12: Grav'nd 1L 77
Gazen Salts Nature Reserve 4L 217
Gean Cl. ME5: Chat'm 1D 110
Geddes Cl. CT18: H'nge 9J 193
Geddes Pl. DA6: Bexhth 2B 58
(off Arnsberga Way)
Geddinge La. CT4: Woot 6B 32
Gedge's Hill TN12: Mat 5K 153 (1D 36)
Geffery's Ct. SE9 8A 56
Gellatly Rd. SE14 5H 5
General Gordon Pl. SE18 4D 50
General Wolfe Rd. SE10 5K 5
Genesta Av. CT5: Whits 6D 226
Genesta Cl. ME10: Sit 4F 98
Genesta Glade DA12: Grav'nd 1M 77
Genesta Rd. SE18 6D 50
SS0: Wclf S 1D 10
Geneva Av. ME8: Gill 1K 95
Gentian Cl. ME5: Chat'm 7B 94
(not continuous)
ME14: Weav 4H 127
Geoffrey Ct. CT7: Birch 4F 206
Geoffrey Rd. SE4 1C 54
Geographers' A-Z Map Co. 1M 121
George All. CT14: Deal 4N 177
George V Av. CT9: Mgte 3N 207 (1H 23)
George Cooper Ho. CT20: F'stone 7J 189
(off Leas, The)
George Gurr Cres. CT19: F'stone 3K 189
George Hill TN32: Rob 4B 44
George Hill Rd. CT10: B'stairs 4J 209 (1K 23)
George La. BR2: Shortl 2L 83
CT20: F'stone 7K 189
ME1: Roch 6N 79
ME13: Bou B 3J 165
ME17: Leeds 1C 140 (3B 28)
SE13 4E 54
TN28: New R 2K 213
George Marsham Ho. ME15: Loose 5C 138
George Pk. CT9: Mgte 2N 207
George Parris Ct. ME12: Minst 6K 221
George Roche Rd. CT1: Cant 4M 171
Georges Av. CT5: Whits 6C 226
Georges Cl. BR5: St P 6L 71
Georges House Gallery 6L 189
(off Old High St.)
George's Rd. TN16: Tats 8D 164
George St. CT11: Ram 5J 211
CT14: Deal 3N 177
CT17: Dover 3G 181
ME10: Sit 8J 99
ME15: Hunt 9L 137 (5G 27)
ME15: Maid 6D 126
TN2: Tun W 2J 157
TN9: Tonb 7H 145
TN12: S'hrst 7J 27
TN23: Ashf 9F 158
TN29: Bztt 2F 47
W1 3D 4
George Street Station (CT) 4G 13
George Summers Cl. ME2: Med E 4B 80
George Warren Ct. CT9: Mgte 4D 208
George Williams Way TN24: Kenn 6H 159
George Wood Cl. TN29: Lydd 3K 205
Georgian Cl. BR2: Shortl 2L 83
ME11: Queen 9B 220
Georgian Dr. ME17: Cox 5A 138
Georgian Way ME8: Gill 7M 95
Geraint Rd. BR1: Brom 9K 55
Gerald Av. ME4: Chat'm 1C 94
Geraldine Rd. CT19: F'stone 5F 188
Gerald Palmby Ct. CT14: Deal 3M 177
Gerald Rd. DA12: Grav'nd 5K 63
Gerda Rd. SE9 7E 56
Gerdview Dr. DA2: Dart 9K 59
Gerlach Ho. TN24: Kenn 5G 158
German St. TN36: Winch 7A 46
Gerpins La. RM14: Upm 2H 7
Gerrard Av. ME1: Roch 3A 94
Gerrards Dr. ME10: Sit 9G 98
Gertrude Rd. DA17: Belv 4B 52
Ghent St. SE6 7D 54
Gibbet La. TN12: Horsm 7B 196
Gibbett La. TN12: Horsm 2E 36
Gibbetts TN3: Lang G 2N 155
Gibbon Rd. SE15 5H 5
Gibbons Rd. ME10: Sit 6C 98
Gibbs Brook La. RH8: Oxt 5A 24
Gibbs Hill ME18: W'bury 3N 135 (3D 26)
TN27: H'crn 8M 191
Gibbs Ho. BR1: Brom 4J 69
(off Longfield)
Gibney Ter. BR1: Brom 9J 55
GIBRALTAR 3A 42
Gibraltar Av. ME7: Gill 5D 80
Gibraltar Hill ME4: Chat'm 8C 80 (3H 17)
Gibraltar La. CT18: H'nge 9H 193 (3A 42)
ME14: Maid 1B 126
Gibraltar Sq. CT15: Gus 1K 181
Gibson Cl. DA11: Nflt 8E 62
Gibson Dr. ME19: W Mal 5L 123 (2D 26)
Gibson St. ME10: Sit 7F 98
Gidds Pond Cotts. ME14: Weav 3H 127
Giddyhorn La. ME16: Maid 5N 125
Gideon Cl. DA17: Belv 4C 52
Gifford Cl. ME8: Gill 8M 81
Giffords Cross Rd. SS17: Corr 2F 9
Gigger's Grn. Rd. TN25: Aldtn 5D 40
Gighill Rd. ME20: Lark 7D 108 (7E 16)
Giggs Hill BR5: St P 5J 71
Gilbert Cl. DA10: Swans 4K 61
ME7: Hpstd 6K 95
SE18 8B 50
Gilbert Pl. CT20: S'gte 8E 188
Gilbert Rd. BR1: Brom 3K 69
CT11: Ram 4H 211
DA17: Belv 3B 52 (4E 6)
TN24: Ashf 8F 158
Gilbert Row DA11: Nflt 7E 62
Gilbert Ter. ME14: Maid 2C 126
Gilbert Way CT1: Cant 4K 171
Gilbourne Rd. SE18 6H 51
Gilchrist Av. CT6: H Bay 5D 194
Gilchrist Cotts. TN14: Weald 6K 131
Gildenhill Rd. BR8: Swanl 3K 73 (1G 15)
Gildersome St. SE18 6C 50
Gildrage Hill CT4: S Min 6H 31
Giles Gdns. CT9: Mgte 5D 208
Giles La. CT2: Cant 8J 167 (7G 21)
Giles Young Ct. ME10: Sit 6F 98
(off High St.)
Gilford Rd. CT14: Deal 5M 177 (3J 33)
Gilham Gro. CT14: Deal 6L 177
Gillan Ct. SE12 8L 55
Gill Av. ME2: Wain 1A 80
Gill Cres. DA11: Nflt 8E 62
Gillespie Rd. N5 1F 5
Gillett Rd. TN29: Lydd 2L 205
Gilletts La. ME19: E Mal 3E 124
Gillian St. SE13 3E 54
Gillies Rd. TN15: W King 6E 88
Gilling Drove CT7: St N 8H 215
GILLINGHAM 7F 80 (2J 17)
Gillingham Bus. Cen. ME8: Gill 2J 95
Gillingham Bus. Pk. ME8: Gill 2K 95
Gillingham F.C.
(Priestfield Stadium) 7H 81 (2K 17)
Gillingham Ga. ME7: Chat'm 4G 80
Gillingham Ga. Rd. ME4: Chat'm 4F 80
Gillingham Grn. ME7: Gill 6H 81
Gillingham Northern Link Rd. ME7: Gill 6K 81
Gillingham Rd. ME7: Gill 8F 80 (2J 17)
Gillingham Station (Rail) 7G 80 (2J 17)
Gill La. TN24: Mers 4B 40
TN25: Mers 4B 40
TN26: Ruck 5A 40
Gillman Cl. CT18: H'nge 8J 193
Gillmans Rd. BR5: Orp 2K 85
Gillon M. CT1: Cant 1A 172
Gill's Cotts. ME1: Roch 8B 80
Gills Ct. ME2: Med E 4B 80
GILL'S GREEN 2C 192 (6H 37)
Gills Rd. DA2: Dart 4E 74 (2J 15)
DA4: S Dar 4E 74 (2J 15)
Gill, The TN2: Pem 6D 152
Gilmore Rd. SE13 2G 54
Gilroy Way BR5: Orp 1K 85

Gilton Rd.—Gorse Rd.

Gilton Rd. SE6 8H 55
Giltspur St. EC4 3F 5
Gimble Way TN2: Pem 6C 152
Gingerbread La. TN18: Flim 7G 37
Ginsbury Cl. ME2: Med E 6B 80
Ginsbury Ho. ME2: Med E 6A 80
Gipps Cross La. TN3: Lang G 2N 155
Gipsy Hill SE19 1G 13
Gipsy Hill Station (Rail) 1G 13
Gipsy Rd. DA16: Well 7M 51
SE27 1G 13
Giraud Dr. ME13: Fav 4F 186
Girton Gdns. CR0: Croy 4D 82
Girton Rd. SE26 1A 68
Gittens Cl. BR1: Brom 9J 55
Glack Rd. CT14: Deal 6J 177
Glade Gdns. CR0: Croy 1B 82
Gladeside CR0: Croy 9A 68
Glades Pl. BR1: Brom 5K 69
Glades Shop. Cen., The BR1: Brom 5K 69
Glades, The DA12: Grav'nd 2J 77
Gladeswood Rd. DA17: Belv 4C 52
Glade, The BR1: Brom 5N 69
BR4: W W'ck 4E 82
CR0: Croy 1B 82 (3H 13)
CT14: Shol 4J 177
ME5: Chat'm 9D 94
TN10: Tonb 9L 133
TN13: S'oaks 5J 119
Gladiator St. SE23 5B 54
Gladstone Rd. BR6: Farnb 6E 84
CT5: Whits 3F 226
CT9: Mgte 4C 208
CT10: B'stairs 1K 211 (3K 23)
CT14: Deal, Walm 6M 177
CT19: F'stone 5L 189
DA1: Dart 4N 59
ME4: Chat'm 1B 94
ME14: Pen H 3D 126
TN4: R'hall 1B 156
TN9: Tonb 6H 145
TN24: Ashf 3J 161 (2B 40)
Gladwell Rd. BR1: Brom 2K 69
Gladwyn Cl. ME8: Gill 7N 95
(not continuous)
Glamford Rd. ME2: Strood 7H 79
Glamis Cl. ME5: Chat'm 6D 94
Glanfield Rd. BR3: Beck'm 7C 68
Glanville Rd. BR2: Shortl 6L 69
ME2: Strood 5L 79
ME7: Gill 7G 81
Glasbrook Rd. SE9 5N 55
Glasford St. SW17 1D 12
Glasgow Ho. ME15: Maid 1H 139
(off Lancaster Rd.)
GLASSENBURY 4H 37
Glassenbury Rd. TN17: Cran, Goud 4H 37
Glassmill La. BR2: Shortl 5J 69 (2K 13)
(not continuous)
Glass Yd. SE18 3C 50
Glastonbury Cl. BR5: Orp 2L 85
Glastonbury Ho. SE12 3J 55
(off Wantage Rd.)
Gleaming Wood Dr. ME5: Chat'm 2F 110 (6J 17)
Gleaners Cl. ME14: Weav 5H 127
Gleanings M. ME1: Roch 7N 79
Glebe Cl. CT15: St Marg 7B 214
TN27: Smar 7C 222
Glebe Cotts. ME13: E'lng 1J 29
Glebe Ct. CT12: Minst 8E 212
SE3 1H 55
(off Glebe, The)
TN13: S'oaks 8J 119
Glebefield, The TN13: Riv 5G 118
Glebe Gdns. CT9: Mgte 3N 207
ME17: Len 7N 201
Glebe Ho. Dr. BR2: Shortl 2L 83
Glebeland TN25: Mers 8M 161
TN27: Eger 6F 29
Glebelands CT3: Ash 4B 216
CT15: Alk 1C 42
(not continuous)
DA1: Cray 2G 58
ME17: H'shm 3N 141
TN3: Bidb 3C 150
TN11: Pens 3H 149
TN27: Bidd 8K 163
Glebe La. ME10: Sit 9J 99
ME16: Maid 8K 125 (2G 27)
TN13: S'oaks 9J 119
Glebe Mdw. ME18: W'bury 1C 136
Glebe Pl. DA4: Hort K 7C 74
TN27: Smar 7C 222
Glebe Rd. BR1: Brom 4K 69
CT9: Mgte 3N 207
DA11: Grav'nd 6E 62
ME7: Gill 9H 81
TN14: Weald 5J 131 (4G 25)
Glebe, The BR7: Chst 4E 70
ME2: Cux 1G 92
SE3 1H 55
TN2: Pem 6C 152
TN3: Bidb 3C 150
TN11: Pens 3H 149
TN27: Char'g 3K 175
Glebe Way BR4: W W'ck 3F 82 (4K 13)
CT5: Whits 5F 226
DA8: Erith 6F 52
TN24: Kenn 3H 159
Gleeson Dr. BR6: Chels 6H 85
Glenalvon Way SE18 4A 50
Glen Av. CT6: H Bay 2K 195
Glenavon Ho. CT10: B'stairs 6M 209
(off Francis Rd.)
Glenavon Lodge BR3: Beck'm 3D 68
Glenbarr Cl. SE9 1D 56
Glenbervie Dr. CT6: H Bay 2M 195
Glenbow Rd. BR1: Brom 2H 69
Glenbrook Cl. CT6: H Bay 2L 195
Glenbrook Gro. ME10: Sit 4F 98
Glencoe Rd. CT9: Mgte 4E 208
ME4: Chat'm 1D 94
Glen Ct. DA15: Sidc 9J 57
Glendale BR8: Swanl 7G 73
Glendale Cl. SE9 1C 56
Glendale M. BR3: Beck'm 4E 68
Glendale Rd. DA8: Erith 4D 52
DA11: Nflt 9D 62
ME12: Minst 5J 221
Glendower Cres. BR6: St M Cry 9J 71
Glendown Rd. SE2 5J 51
Glen Dunlop Ho., The TN13: S'oaks 4J 119
Gleneagles Cl. BR6: Orp 2F 84
Gleneagles Ct. ME5: Chat'm 9C 94
Gleneagles Dr. ME15: Maid 8C 126
Gleneagles Grn. BR6: Orp 2F 84
Glenesk Rd. SE9 1C 56
Glenfarg Rd. SE6 6F 54
Glenfield Rd. CT16: Dover 1G 180
Glengall Rd. DA7: Bexhth 1N 57
Glen Gro. CT17: Dover 5G 181
Glenhead Cl. SE9 1D 56
Glen Ho. E16 1C 50
(off Storey St.)
Glenhouse Rd. SE9 3C 56
Glenhurst BR3: Beck'm 4F 68
Glenhurst Av. DA5: Bex'y 6A 58
Glen Iris Av. CT2: Cant 9J 167
Glen Iris Cl. CT2: Cant 9J 167
Glenister St. E16 1C 50
Glenlea Rd. SE9 3B 56
Glenleigh Rd. ME18: W'bury 2B 136
Glenlyon Rd. SE9 3C 56
Glenmore Lodge BR3: Beck'm 4E 68
Glenmore Pk. TN2: Tun W 5F 156
Glenmore Rd. DA16: Well 7H 51
Glenmount Path SE18 5E 50
Glen Rd. CT14: Kgdn 3E 200 (5J 33)
Glenrosa Gdns. DA12: Grav'nd 1L 77
Glenrose Ct. DA14: Sidc 1K 71
Glensdale Rd. SE4 1C 54
Glenshiel Rd. SE9 3C 56
Glenside CT5: Whits 5J 227
Glenside Av. CT1: Cant 9A 168
Glen, The BR2: Shortl 5H 69
BR6: Farnb 4B 84
CR0: Croy 4A 82
CT3: Ups 5B 22
CT15: S'wll 7K 219
ME12: Minst 4J 221
(not continuous)
Glenthorne Rd. W6 4B 4
Glenton Rd. SE13 2H 55
Glentrammon Av. BR6: Chels 7H 85
Glentrammon Cl. BR6: Chels 6H 85
Glentrammon Gdns. BR6: Chels 7H 85
Glentrammon Rd. BR6: Chels 7H 85
Glenure Rd. SE9 3C 56
Glen Vw. DA12: Grav'nd 6H 63
Glenview SE2 6M 51
Glenview Rd. BR1: Brom 5N 69
Glen Wlk. CT5: Seas 5E 20
Glenwood Cl. ME5: Chat'm 2F 94
ME7: Hpstd 5K 95
ME16: Alltn 4N 125
TN30: St Mic 4C 224
Glenwood Ct. DA14: Sidc 9J 57
Glenwood Dr. ME12: Minst 5J 221
Glenwood Rd. SE6 6C 54
Glenwood Way CR0: Croy 9A 68
Glimpsing Grn. DA18: Erith 3N 51
Glistening Glade ME8: Rain 5A 96
Gload Cres. BR5: Orp 3M 85
Globe La. ME4: Chat'm 7C 80
(not continuous)
Globe Rd. E1 2H 5
E2 2H 5
GLOBE TOWN 2H 5
Glory La. TN25: H'lgh 7F 31
Gloster Cl. CT18: H'nge 9L 193
Gloster Ropewalk CT17: Dover 7H 181
Gloster Way CT17: Dover 7H 181
Gloucester Av. CT9: Clift 3H 209
CT10: B'stairs 1K 211
DA15: Sidc 7G 57
DA16: Well 2H 57
NW1 2E 4
Gloucester Cl. ME8: Rain 3C 96
Gloucester M. TN28: New R 1L 213
Gloucester Pde. DA15: Sidc 3J 57
Gloucester Pl. CT20: F'stone 6K 189
NW1 2D 4
W1 3D 4
Gloucester Rd. CT5: Whits 3H 227
DA1: Dart 5J 59
DA12: Grav'nd 9H 63
DA17: Belv 5A 52
KT1: King T 2A 12
ME15: Maid 9G 127
SW7 4D 4
Gloucester Road Station (Tube) 4D 4
Gloucester Ter. W2 3C 4
Glover Cl. ME10: Kems'y 2G 99
SE2 4L 51
Glover Rd. TN24: W'boro 9J 159
Glovers Cres. ME10: Sit 8G 98
Glovers Mill ME1: Roch 9A 80
Gloxinia Rd. DA13: Sflt 2A 76
Glyn Davies Cl. TN13: Dun G 2F 118
Glyndebourne Pk. BR6: Farnb 3D 84
Glynde Rd. DA7: Bexhth 1M 57
Glynde St. SE4 4C 54
Glyndon Rd. SE18 4E 50
(not continuous)
Glyn Dr. DA14: Sidc 9K 57
Glynne Cl. ME8: Gill 5N 95
Goad Av. ME5: Chat'm 8E 94
Goals Football Training Cen. 1A 58
GOATHAM GREEN 6F 45
Goatham La. TN31: B Oak 6F 45
GOATHURST COMMON 3C 130 (3E 24)
GOAT LEES 2G 158
Goat Lees La. TN24: Kenn 2H 159
Goat Rd. CR4: Mitc 3E 12
Goatsfield Rd. TN16: Tats 8C 164
Gobery Hill CT3: Wing 7K 225
Goddard Rd. BR3: Beck'm 7A 68 (2H 13)
Goddard's Castle 9N 111
Goddards Cl. TN17: Cran 8B 176
(not continuous)
GODDARDS GREEN 8B 176 (5J 37)
GODDARD'S GREEN 5A 38
Goddard's Grn. Rd. TN17: Bendn 5A 38
GODDEN GREEN 6A 120 (2H 25)
Godden Rd. CT2: Cant 7N 167
ME6: Snod 2D 108
Goddings Dr. ME1: Roch 9L 79
GODDINGTON 3M 85 (4D 14)
Goddington Chase BR6: Chels 5K 85
Goddington La. BR6: Chels 4J 85 (4D 14)
ME17: H'shm 2K 141 (3D 28)
Goddington Rd. ME2: Strood 4M 79
Godfrey Cl. ME2: Strood 3K 79
Godfrey Evans Cl. TN10: Tonb 2M 145
Godfrey Gdns. CT4: Chart'm 9F 170
Godfrey Hill SE18 4A 50
Godfrey Ho. CT5: Whits 5G 226
Godfrey Rd. SE18 4B 50
Godfrey Wlk. TN23: Ashf 1F 160
Godington La. TN23: Gt Cha 4N 197
TN26: Ashf, Hoth 5A 158
Godinton House & Gardens 6A 158 (1K 39)
Godinton La. TN23: Gt Cha, Ashf 1J 39
TN26: Hoth 1J 39
Godinton Rd. TN23: Ashf 8F 158
(Apsley St.)
TN23: Ashf 8E 158
(Sackville Cres.)
Godinton Way TN23: Ashf 8E 158
Godinton Way Ind. Est. TN23: Ashf 8E 158
Godlands, The ME15: Maid 8C 126
GODMERSHAM 4D 30
Godmersham Pk. 4D 30
Godric Cres. CR0: Croy 9G 82
Godstone Rd. CR8: Kenl 6F 13
CR8: Purl 6F 13
Godstow Rd. SE2 2K 51
Godwin Cl. ME10: Kems'y 2G 98
Godwin Rd. BR2: Shortl 6M 69
CT1: Cant 4J 171
CT9: Clift 3E 208
CT16: Dover 4L 181
Godwyne Cl. CT16: Dover 4J 181
Godwyne Ct. CT16: Dover 3J 181
Godwyne Path CT16: Dover 3J 181
Godwyne Rd. CT16: Dover 4J 181
Godwyn Gdns. CT20: F'stone 7G 189
Godwyn Rd. CT14: Deal 2M 177 (2J 33)
CT20: F'stone 6G 189
Goffers Rd. SE3 5K 5
GOGWAY 6G 31
Goldcrest Dr. ME4: Chat'm 2F 80
Goldcrest Wlk. CT5: Whits 7D 226
Goldcrest Way CR0: Croy 9G 82 (5K 13)
Golden Acre La. CT8: Wgte S 4J 207
Golden Cl. CT8: Wgte S 4J 207
GOLDEN GREEN 2E 146 (5B 26)
Golden Hill CT4: Acr 7K 31
CT5: Whits 6H 227 (4F 21)
(not continuous)
Golden La. EC1 2G 5
Golden Sands Holiday Cen.
TN29: St M Bay 1M 215
Golden Sq. TN28: New R 3J 213
TN30: Tent 7C 224
Golden St. CT14: Deal 3N 177
Golden Wood Cl. ME5: Chat'm 2G 110
Goldfinch Cl. BR6: Chels 6J 85
CT6: H Bay 5K 195
ME13: Fav 3G 186
ME20: Lark 8E 108
TN12: Pad W 1M 153
Goldfinch Rd. SE28 3F 50
Goldhawk Rd. W6 4A 4
W12 4A 4
Goldhawk Road Station (Tube) 4B 4
Gold Hill TN25: Westw 6K 29
Golding Cl. ME1: Roch 2B 94
ME20: Dit 9G 109
Golding Gdns. TN12: E Peck 1M 147
Golding Rd. TN13: S'oaks 4K 119
Goldings TN12: Pad W 1K 153
Goldings Cl. ME19: W Mal 7M 123
Goldings Ct. TN24: Kenn 6G 159
Goldings, The ME8: Gill 3M 95
Goldmark Ho. SE3 1L 55
Goldsel Rd.
BR8: Crock'n, Swanl 8E 72 (3F 15)
Goldsmid Rd. TN9: Tonb 8J 145 (7K 25)
Goldsmid St. SE18 5G 51
Goldsmith Ct. TN30: Tent 6C 224
Goldsmith Rd. ME8: Gill 6A 96
W3 3A 4
Goldsmith's Row E2 2H 5
Gold Star Cen. ME2: Med E 6B 80
Goldstone Drove CT3: Ash 6E 22
Goldstone Wlk. ME5: Chat'm 1D 110
GOLD STREET 8K 77
Gold St. DA12: Sole S, Lud'n 8J 77 (3D 16)
DA13: Lud'n 8J 77
Goldsworth Dr. ME2: Strood 3L 79
Goldthorne Cl. ME14: Maid 4F 126
Goldups La. CT4: Chil'm 2C 30
Goldwell Cl. TN25: Aldtn 4D 40
Goldwell La. TN25: Aldtn 4D 40
TN26: Beth, Gt Cha 1J 39
Golf Ct. CT14: Deal 1M 177
Golf Ho. Rd. RH8: Oxt 3A 24
Golf Links Av. DA11: Grav'nd 1G 76
GOLFORD 4A 38
Golford Rd. TN17: Cran 8E 176
TN17: Cran, Siss 5K 37
TN17: Siss, Bendn 4K 37
Golf Rd. BR1: Brom 6C 70
CT14: Deal 1M 177 (2J 33)
Golfs, The TN28: New R 2K 213
GOLGOTHA 5D 32
Gooch Cl. ME16: Alltn 1A 126
Goodall Cl. ME8: Gill 6A 96
Goodall Ho. SE4 2A 54
Goodban Sq. CT3: Ash 5C 216
Goodbury Rd. TN15: Knat 4B 104
Goodcheap La. TN25: Hin 5N 159 (7C 30)
Goodfellow Way CT16: Dover 4J 181
Goodge St. W1 3E 4
Goodge Street Station (Tube) 3E 4
Goodhart Way BR4: W W'ck 1H 83
Good Hope CT14: Deal 6J 177
GOODLEY STOCK 3B 24
Goodley Stock Rd. TN8: Crock H, Westrm 4B 24
TN16: Crock H, Westrm 4B 24
GOODMAYES 1D 6
Goodmayes La. IG3: Ilf 1D 6
Goodmead Rd. BR6: Orp 1J 85
GOODNESTONE
Canterbury 2C 32
Faversham 6C 20
Goodnestone Hill CT3: Good 2C 32
Goodnestone La. ME13: Fav 4N 187 (6C 20)
Goodnestone Pk. 2C 32
Goodnestone Rd. CT3: Wing 8K 225
CT3: Wing, Good 1C 32
ME10: Sit 7J 99
Goods Sta. Rd. TN1: Tun W 1G 157
Goods Way NW1 2F 5
Goodwin Av. CT5: Whits 3M 227
Goodwin Cl. TN8: Eden 5B 184
Goodwin Dr. DA14: Sidc 8M 57
ME14: Pen H 1E 126
Goodwin Rd. CT11: Ram 6F 210
CT15: St Marg 9B 214
(not continuous)
ME3: Cli W 6M 65
Goodwins, The TN2: Tun W 4F 156
Goodwood Cl. ME3: H Hals 2H 67
ME15: Maid 2J 139
Goodwood Cres. DA12: Grav'nd 1H 77
Goodwood Pde. BR3: Beck'm 7B 68
Goodworth Rd. TN15: Wro 7M 105
Goosander Way SE28 3F 50
Gooseberry Hall La. CT3: Chill 3D 32
Goose Cl. ME5: Chat'm 4D 94
Goosefields ME13: G'ney 5C 20
GOOSE GREEN
Ashford 9K 163 (4C 38)
Tonbridge 6G 134 (4C 26)
Goose Grn. Cl. BR5: St P 5J 71
Gooseneck La. TN27: H'crn 8K 191
Gordon Av. ME11: Queen 8B 220
Gordonbrock Rd. SE4 3D 54
Gordon Cl. ME10: Sit 7K 99
TN24: Ashf 8H 159
Gordon Cotts. CT4: Brid 8H 173
ME9: B'gar 4C 114
Gordon Ct. ME15: Loose 5B 138
Gordon Gro. CT8: Wgte S 2K 207
Gordon Ho. Rd. NW5 1E 4
Gordon Pl. DA12: Grav'nd 4H 63
Gordon Prom. DA12: Grav'nd 4H 63
Gordon Prom. E. DA12: Grav'nd 4H 63
Gordon Rd. BR3: Beck'm 6C 68
CT1: Cant 3M 171
CT5: Whits 5F 226
CT6: H Bay 3G 195
CT9: Clift 2E 208
CT9: Mgte 8E 208
CT11: Ram 4H 211
CT16: Dover 8F 178
CT20: F'stone 5D 188
DA1: Dart 5L 59
DA11: Nflt 5D 62
DA15: Sidc 3G 56
DA17: Belv 4D 52
ME2: Strood 4L 79
ME3: Hoo 8G 66
ME4: Chat'm 1D 94
ME4: Gill 5D 80
ME7: Gill 7H 81
ME13: Fav 4J 187
SM5: Cars 5D 12
SS17: Corr, Stan H 2E 8
TN4: Tun W 7J 151
TN13: S'oaks 7J 119
Gordon Sq. CT7: Birch 4E 206
ME13: Fav 5J 187
WC1 2E 4
Gordon Ter. ME1: Roch 8N 79
Gordon Way BR1: Brom 4K 69
GORE 2K 183 (2F 33)
Gore Cl. CT13: E'try 3K 183
Gore Cotts. DA2: Dart 8C 60
Gore Ct. Rd. ME10: Sit 9F 98 (5F 19)
ME15: Maid 3K 27
ME15: Otham 3J 139
Gore End Cl. CT7: Birch 4D 206
GORE GREEN 6H 65
Gore Grn. La. ME3: High'm 7H 65
Gore Grn. Rd. ME3: High'm 7H 65 (7F 9)
Gore La. CT13: E'try 3J 183 (2F 33)
TN17: Goud 3G 37
Gore M. CT1: Cant 9A 168
Gore Rd. CT13: E'try 2K 183 (2F 33)
DA2: Dart 7C 60 (7J 7)
ME9: B'gar 5A 114 (6D 18)
Goresbrook Rd. RM9: Dag 2D 6
GORE STREET 4D 22
Gore St. CT12: Monk'n 5D 22
Gore Ter. CT13: E'try 2K 183
Gorham Cl. ME6: Snod 3D 108
Gorham Dr. ME15: Bear 8K 127
TN9: Tonb 7K 145
Gorley Ho. CT17: Dover 5J 181
Gorman Rd. SE18 4B 50
Gorrell Ct. CT5: Whits 5G 226
Gorrell Rd. CT5: Whits 4G 226
Gorringe Av. DA4: S Dar 5D 74
Gorse Av. ME5: Chat'm 7B 94
Gorse Cres. ME20: Dit 1H 125
Gorse Hill DA4: Farn'm, Fawk 1A 88 (3H 15)
Gorse La. CT6: H Bay 5K 195 (3K 21)
Gorse Mead TN23: Ashf 1D 160
Gorse Rd. BR5: St M Cry 3B 86 (4E 14)
CR0: Croy 5D 82
ME2: Strood 4K 79
ME10: Sit 6J 99
TN2: Tun W 9L 151

Gorse Way—Green La.

Gorse Way DA3: Hart'y .8M **75**
Gorsewood Rd. DA3: Hart'y .8M **75**
Gorse Wood Rd. DA3: Long .6N **75**
Gorst St. ME7: Gill .7F **80**
Goschen Rd. CT17: Dover .4G **180**
Gosfield Rd. CT6: H Bay .3H **195**
GOSMERE .1B **30**
GOSPEL OAK .1E **4**
Gospel Oak Station (Rail) .1E **4**
Gossage Rd. SE18 .5F **50**
Gosselin St. CT5: Whits .5F **226**
Gosset St. E2 .2G **5**
Goss Hall La. CT3: Ash .4F **216** (7E **22**)
Goss Hill BR8: Swanl .2K **73** (1G **15**)
Gosshill Rd. BR7: Chst .5C **70**
Gossington Cl. BR7: Chst .9D **56**
Goswell Rd. EC1 .2F **5**
Goteley Mere TN24: Kenn .3G **159**
Gothic Cl. CT14: Walm .9L **177**
DA1: Dart .8L **59**
Gothic Cotts. TN23: Gt Cha .9A **158**
GOUDHURST .3C **190** (4G **37**)
Goudhurst Cl. CT2: Cant .7N **167**
ME16: Maid .5B **126**
Goudhurst Rd. BR1: Brom .1H **69**
ME8: Gill .9L **81**
TN3: Lamb .4E **36**
TN12: Horsm .8C **196** (2F **37**)
TN12: Mard .4B **212** (2G **37**)
TN12: S'hrst .2J **37**
TN17: Cran, Goud, Siss .4H **37**
Gouge Av. DA11: Nflt .6D **62**
Gough Rd. CT20: S'gte .8E **188**
Gould Rd. ME5: Chat'm .8E **94**
Goulston ME15: W Far .2J **137**
Gourock Rd. SE9 .3C **56**
GOVER HILL .2D **134** (3B **26**)
Gover Hill ME18: W Peck .3C **134** (3B **26**)
TN11: S'brne .3C **134** (3B **26**)
Gover Vw. TN11: S'brne .1D **134**
Gower St. WC1 .2E **4**
Gowland Pl. BR3: Beck'm .5C **68**
Grace Av. DA7: Bexhth .9A **52**
ME16: Alltn .3A **126**
(not continuous)
Grace Cl. SE9 .8N **55**
Grace Ct. *CT20: F'stone .6K 189*
(off Grace Hill)
Grace Hill CT20: F'stone .6K **189** (4B **42**)
Grace Mdw. CT16: Whitf .6E **178**
Grace Rd. ME12: S'ness .3B **220**
Grace Wlk. CT14: Deal .5K **177**
Gracious La. TN13: S'oaks .3H **131** (3G **25**)
Gracious La. End TN14: S'oaks .3G **131**
Grafton Av. ME1: Roch .3B **94**
Grafton Ri. CT6: H Bay .4D **194**
Grafton Rd. CT10: B'stairs .5J **209**
KT4: Wor Pk .4A **12**
ME10: Sit .7G **99**
Grafton Way ME10: Sit .7H **99**
GRAFTY GREEN .9N **141** (5D **28**)
Graham Cl. CR0: Croy .3D **82**
ME4: Chat'm .6C **80**
Graham Rd. DA6: Bexhth .2A **58**
E8 .1H **5**
Graham Ter. *DA15: Sidc .4K 57*
(off Westerham Dr.)
GRAIN .7C **190** (5E **10**)
Grainey Fld. ME9: H'lip .7G **96**
Grainger Wlk. TN10: Tonb .1L **145**
Grain Rd. ME3: Isle G .9A **190** (6D **10**)
(Grain)
ME3: Isle G, Lwr Sto .9A **204**
(Middle Stoke)
ME3: Lwr Sto, Isle G .6B **10**
ME8: Gill .7L **95**
Grampian Cl. BR6: St M Cry .9H **71**
TN2: Tun W .9K **151**
Grampian Way ME15: Bear .8K **127**
Grampion Cl. TN24: Ashf .6G **158**
Gram's Rd. CT14: Walm .9L **177** (4J **33**)
Granada St. ME15: Maid .5D **126**
Granary TN12: Pad W .9N **147**
Granary Cl. ME8: Rain .2B **96**
ME14: Weav .4H **127**
Granary Ct. Rd. TN25: Sme .8M **165** (2E **40**)
Granary Mans. *SE28 .2E 50*
(off Erebus Dr.)
Granary Pl. CT5: Whits .6F **226**
Granby Rd. DA11: Nflt .4B **62**
(not continuous)
SE9 .9B **50**
Grand Acre CT4: Walt .6F **31**
Grand Ct. *CT20: F'stone .8H 189*
(off Earls Av.)
TN28: L'stne .4N **213**
Grand Dpt. Rd. SE18 .5C **50** (4B **6**)
Grand Dr. CT6: H Bay .2C **194** (3J **21**)
SS9: Lgh S .1C **10**
SW20 .2B **12**
Grand Pde. SS9: Lgh S .1C **10**
TN28: L'stne .5N **213** (3K **47**)
Grand Shaft .6J **181**
Grandshore La. TN17: Frit .2K **37**
Grandsire Gdns. ME3: Hoo .7H **67**
Grandstand Rd. KT18: Eps .7B **12**
Grand Vw. Av. TN16: Big H .5C **164**
GRANGE .6L **81** (2K **17**)
Grange Cl. DA15: Sidc .8J **57**
ME19: Leyb .8A **108**
TN8: Eden .6C **184**
TN16: Westrm .8E **116**
Grange Cotts. ME15: Otham .2M **139**
Grange Ct. CT11: Ram .6G **211**
CT20: F'stone .7J 189
(off Ingles Rd.)
Grange Cres. DA2: Dart .4B **60**
TN30: St Mic .4B **224**
Grange Dr. BR6: Prat B .9L **85**
BR7: Chst .2A **70**
Grange Gdns. TN4: R'hall .1D **156**
Grange Hill ME5: Chat'm .9E **80**
TN15: Plax .9L **121** (3A **26**)
Grangehill Pl. SE9 .1B **56**
Grangehill Rd. SE9 .2B **56**
Grange Ho. DA8: Erith .9H **53**
DA11: Grav'nd .5F **62**
ME16: Maid .7L **125**
Grange La. DA3: Hart'y .1N **89** (3A **16**)
ME14: S'lng .8C **110**
(not continuous)
ME14: S'lng, Boxf .7J **17**
(not continuous)
Grangemill Rd. SE6 .8D **54**
Grangemill Way SE6 .7D **54**
Grange Rd. BR6: Orp .3F **84**
CR7: Thor H .2G **13**
CT6: H Bay .3J **195**
(not continuous)
CT10: B'stairs .6K **209** (2K **23**)
CT11: Ram .5G **211** (4J **23**)
CT14: Deal .5L **177**
CT19: F'stone .5E **188**
CT21: Salt .4J **199** (5H **41**)
DA11: Grav'nd .5F **62**
E13 .2K **5**
ME2: Strood .5M **79**
ME7: Gill .6H **81**
ME7: Gill .2K **17**
(Gillingham, not continuous)
ME7: Gill .2K **17**
(Grange)
SE1 .4G **5**
SE25 .2G **13**
TN4: R'hall .1D **156**
TN11: S'brne .3K **133**
TN13: S'oaks .9H **119**
TN15: Bor G .2B **122** (1B **26**)
TN30: St Mic .4A **224**
TN30: St Mic .5D **38**
Grange Roundabout ME7: Gill .6L **81**
Grange, The CR0: Croy .3C **82**
CT5: Seas .7C **226**
CT15: Mart .3N **179**
CT15: S'wll .7K **219**
DA4: S Dar .4D **74**
ME19: E Mal .2E **124**
TN15: W King .9F **88**
Grange Way CT10: B'stairs .2K **211**
DA3: Hart'y .9M **75**
DA8: Erith .7J **53**
ME1: Roch .9N **79**
Grangeways Cl. DA11: Nflt .9E **62**
Grangewood DA5: Bex'y .6A **58**
Grangewood La. BR3: Beck'm .2C **68**
Granite St. SE18 .5H **51**
Grannies La. CT15: Chil'm .3D **32**
Granny's La. CT4: S Min .5G **31**
Grant Cl. CT10: B'stairs .7J **209**
ME8: Gill .2L **95**
Grant Dr. ME15: Maid .2G **138**
Grantham Av. CT14: Deal .5K **177**
Grantley Cl. TN23: Ashf .2E **160**
Granton Rd. DA14: Sidc .2L **71**
Grant Rd. ME3: Wain .1N **79**
Grants Cotts. ME17: Len .7K **201**
Grants La. RH8: Oxt .4A **24**
TN8: Eden .4A **24**
Granville Av. CT10: B'stairs .1M **211**
CT12: Ram .3F **210**
Granville Cl. ME13: Fav .5G **186**
Granville Ct. ME14: Maid .3D **126**
Granville Dr. CT6: H Bay .5C **194**
Granville Farm CT11: Ram .5K **211**
Granville Gro. SE13 .1F **54**
Granville Ho. *CT11: Ram .5K 211*
(off Victoria Pde.)
Granville Marina CT11: Ram .5K **211**
Granville Marina Ct. *CT11: Ram .5K 211*
(off Granville Marina)
Granville M. DA14: Sidc .9J **57**
Granville Pde. CT20: S'gte .8E **188**
Granville Pk. SE13 .1F **54**
Granville Pl. ME12: S'ness .2D **220**
Granville Rd. CT10: B'stairs .1M **211**
CT14: Kgdn .6F **200**
CT14: Walm .8M **177** (4J **33**)
CT15: St Marg .7J **33**
CT15: St Marg .8C **214**
DA11: Grav'nd .5E **62**
DA14: Sidc .9J **57**
DA16: Well .1L **57**
ME7: Gill .7H **81**
ME12: S'ness .2C **220** (6F **11**)
ME14: Maid .3D **126**
TN1: Tun W .9J **151**
TN13: S'oaks .6H **119**
TN16: Westrm .8E **116**
Granville Rd. E. CT20: S'gte .8F **188**
Granville Rd. W. CT20: S'gte .8E **188**
Granville St. CT14: Deal .5N **177**
CT16: Dover .3H **181**
Granville Theatre & Cinema .5K **211**
Grapple Rd. ME14: Maid .2C **126**
Grasdene Rd. SE18 .7J **51**
Grasmere Av. BR6: Farnb .4D **84**
CT11: Ram .5E **210**
Grasmere Gdns. BR6: Farnb .4D **84**
CT19: F'stone .4H **189**
Grasmere Gro. ME2: Strood .2N **79**
Grasmere Pk. CT5: Whits .5K **227**
Grasmere Rd. BR1: Brom .4J **69**
BR6: Farnb .4D **84**
CR8: Purl .6F **13**
CT5: Whits .4J **227**
DA7: Bexhth .9D **52**
TN24: Kenn .4G **159**
Grasmere Way CT3: Aysm .1D **162**
Grasshaven Way SE28 .1H **51**
(not continuous)
Grassington Rd. DA14: Sidc .9J **57**
Grasslands ME17: L'ly .4A **140**
TN23: Ashf .2B **160**
Grassmere ME19: Leyb .8D **108**
TN29: St M Bay .3L **215**
Grass Rd. DA3: Long .8B **76**
Grassy Glade ME7: Hpstd .5L **95**
Grassy La. TN13: S'oaks .8J **119**
Grave La. TN12: Mard, S'hrst .6J **27**
GRAVEL CASTLE .8E **162** (5A **32**)
Gravel Castle Rd. CT4: B'hm .9D **162** (5A **32**)
Gravel Hill CR0: Croy .7A **82** (5H **13**)
CT4: Cha H .3C **170** (1F **31**)
DA6: Bexhth .2C **58** (6E **6**)
Gravel Hill Cl. DA6: Bexhth .3C **58**
Gravel Hill Station (CT) .7B **82** (5J **13**)
Gravel La. CT15: Chu H, W Hou .3D **42**
Gravelly Bottom Rd.
ME17: Kgswd .5B **140** (4A **28**)
Gravelly Ways ME18: Pad W, Ladd .6E **26**
Gravel Pit La. SE9 .3D **56**
Gravel Pits La. TN8: Chid .5A **142**
Gravel Pit Way BR6: Orp .3J **85**
Gravel Rd. BR2: Shortl .4A **84** (4B **14**)
DA4: S at H .3B **74**
Gravel Wlk. ME1: Roch .7A **80**
TN23: Ashf .8F **158**
Gravelwood Cl. BR7: Chst .8E **56**
GRAVENEY .5C **20**
Graveney Cl. ME3: Cli W .6N **65**
Graveney Rd. ME13: Fav .5K **187** (6B **20**)
ME15: Maid .1J **139**
GRAVESEND .4G **63** (6C **8**)
Gravesend & Northfleet F.C.
(Stonebridge Road) .3N **61** (6A **8**)
Gravesend Rd. DA12: Shorne .8B **64** (1E **16**)
ME2: High'm .8B **64**
ME2: Strood .1G **17**
ME3: High'm .8B **64** (1E **16**)
TN15: Stans .3D **106**
TN15: Wro .6A **106**
Gravesend Sailing Club *.4J 63*
(off Gordon Prom. E.)
Gravesend Station (Rail) .4G **62** (7C **8**)
Gravesham Ct. DA12: Grav'nd .5G **63**
Gravesham Mus. .4G **63**
Gray Cl. CT18: H'nge .7L **193**
Grayland Cl. BR1: Brom .4N **69**
Graylen Cl. CT14: Deal .3M **177**
Grayling Ct. ME10: Sit .9D **98**
Graylings, The ME1: Roch .9M **79**
Grayne Av. ME3: Isle G .8C **190**
GRAYS .5A **8**
Grays Farm Production Village
BR5: St P .4K **71**
Grays Farm Rd. BR5: St P .4K **71**
Grayshott Cl. ME10: Sit .8G **99**
Gray's Inn Rd. WC1 .2F **5**
Grays Rd. TN14: Westrm .3D **116**
TN16: Westrm .3D **116**
TN16: Westrm, S'oaks .1B **24**
Grays Station (Rail) .5A **8**
Graystone Rd. CT5: Whits .2J **227**
Grays Way CT1: Cant .4H **171**
Grazeley Cl. DA6: Bexhth .3D **58**
Gt. Basin Rd. ME12: S'ness .2A **220**
Gt. Bounds Dr. TN4: S'bgh .3E **150**
Gt. Brooms Rd. TN4: Tun W .6H **151**
GREAT BUCKLAND .7M **91** (5D **16**)
GREAT BURGH .7B **12**
Gt. Burton Ho's *TN24: Kenn .5J 159*
(off Nettlefield)
Gt. Central Way HA9: Wemb .1A **4**
NW10 .1A **4**
GREAT CHART .9A **158** (1K **39**)
Gt. Chart By-Pass
TN23: Ashf, Gt Cha .1A **160** (2J **39**)
Gt. Chertsey Rd. W4 .5A **4**
Great Comp Garden .3D **122** (1B **26**)
Gt. Conduit St. CT21: Hythe .6K **199**
Gt. Courtlands TN3: Lang G .1A **156**
Great Dixter .3F **45**
Gt. Dover St. SE1 .4G **5**
Gt. Eastern Rd. E15 .1K **5**
Gt. Eastern St. EC2 .2G **5**
Great Elms TN11: Hdlw .7D **134**
Gt. Elms Rd. BR2: Shortl .7M **69**
Greatfield Cl. SE4 .2D **54**
Gt. Footway TN3: Lang G .2N **155**
Gt. Gatton Cl. CR0: Croy .1B **82**
Gt. Hall Arc. TN1: Tun W .2H **157**
Gt. Harry Dr. SE9 .8C **56**
Greathed Manor .1A **34**
Gt. Higham Farm Cotts. ME9: Dod .9K **115**
Gt. Hollanden Bus. Cen. TN15: Under .6C **132**
Great Holt TN25: Elms .7F **31**
Gt. Ivy Mill Cotts. ME15: Maid .1C **138**
GREAT JOB'S CROSS .1G **45**
GREAT LINES .8E **80**
Great Lines ME7: Gill .7D **80**
Gt. Lodge Retail Pk. TN2: Tun W .5L **151**
Gt. Marlborough St. W1 .3E **4**
Great Maytham Hall .4C **214** (7C **38**)
Great Mead TN8: Eden .4C **184**
GREAT MONGEHAM .4H **33**
GREATNESS .3K **119** (1G **25**)
Greatness La. TN14: S'oaks .3K **119**
Greatness Rd. TN14: S'oaks .3K **119**
Gt. Norman St. TN14: Ide H .2A **130** (3E **24**)
Gt. Oak Row TN23: Kgnt .5F **160**
Gt. Portland St. W1 .3E **4**
Great Portland Street Station (Tube) .2E **4**
Gt. Queen St. DA1: Dart .5N **59**
WC2 .3F **5**
Gt. South Av. ME4: Chat'm .2D **94**
GREAT STONAR .2M **217** (7G **23**)
GREATSTONE-ON-SEA .7H **213** (5K **47**)
Gt. Stour Pl. CT2: Cant .1M **171**
Gt. Tattenhams KT18: Eps .7B **12**
Great Thrift BR5: Pet W .7E **70**
Gt. Till Cl. TN14: Otf .7F **102**
Gt. Western Rd. W9 .2C **4**
W11 .3C **4**
Gt. West Rd. W4 .4A **4**
(Chiswick)
W4 .4A **4**
(Gunnersbury)
W6 .4B **4**
Greatwood BR7: Chst .3C **70**
Grebe Apartments *ME15: Maid .3H 139*
(off Wallis Av.)
Grebe Cl. CT18: H'nge .8K **193**
Grebe Cl. ME3: Lwr Sto .8C **204**
Grebe Ct. ME20: Lark .9D **108**
Grebe Cres. CT21: Hythe .8D **198**
Grecian Rd. TN1: Tun W .3H **157**
Grecian St. ME14: Maid .3D **126**
Greenacre CT4: Kgstn .4K **31**
DA1: Dart .7L **59**
Greenacre Cl. BR8: Swanl .7F **72**
Green Acre Cl. ME5: Chat'm .6D **94**
Greenacre Dr. CT14: Walm .9M **177**
Green Acres CT15: Eyt .9L **185**
Greenacres DA14: Sidc .9J **57**
SE9 .4C **56**
Greenacres Cl. BR6: Farnb .5E **84**
Green Acres Cl. CT6: H Bay .4J **195**
Greenbank ME5: Chat'm .3E **94**
TN24: Kenn .4H **159**
Grn. Bank Cl. ME7: Hpstd .6K **95**
Greenbank Lodge *BR7: Chst .5C 70*
(off Forest Cl.)
Greenbanks CT18: Lym'ge .8L **205**
DA1: Dart .7M **59**
Greenborough Cl. ME15: Maid .2H **139**
Green Cl. BR2: Shortl .6H **69**
CT18: H'nge .8L **193**
ME1: Roch .1A **94**
Green Cloth M. *CT1: Cant .9A 168*
(off Brymore Cl.)
Green Ct. CT4: Brid .8H **173**
CT19: F'stone .4L **189**
TN12: S'hrst .3K **223**
Greencourt Rd. BR5: Pet W .8F **70**
Green Ct. Rd. BR8: Crock'm .8E **72** (3F **15**)
Greencroft TN23: Ashf .3B **160**
Greendale Wlk. DA11: Nflt .8D **62**
Green Dell CT2: Cant .7M **167**
Grn. Farm Cl. BR6: Chels .7H **85**
Green Farm La. DA12: Shorne .7C **64** (7E **8**)
Greenfield TN8: Eden .6D **184**
Greenfield Cl. ME20: Burh .4L **109**
TN4: R'hall .9C **150**
Greenfield Cotts. CT1: Cant .3L **171**
ME14: Boxl .7F **110**
TN25: S'ndge .7D **218**
Greenfield Dr. BR1: Brom .5M **69**
Greenfield Gdns. BR5: Pet W .1F **84**
Greenfield Rd. CT12: Ram .2G **211**
CT19: F'stone .4L **189**
DA2: Dart .1E **72**
ME7: Gill .6H **81**
Greenfields ME15: Maid .9H **127**
TN25: S'ndge .7D **218**
Greenfields Cl. ME3: Wain .1A **80**
Greenfinches DA3: Long .6A **76**
ME7: Hpstd .5J **95**
Greenfrith Dr. TN10: Tonb .9H **133**
Green Gdns. BR6: Farnb .6E **84**
Greengates CT16: Whitf .5F **178**
Greengate St. E13 .2A **6**
GREEN HILL .9L **127** (3K **27**)
GREENHILL .5E **194** (3J **21**)
Green Hill BR6: Downe .3B **100**
ME15: Otham, Bear .9L **127**
SE18 .5B **50**
Greenhill TN12: S'hrst .1J **223**
Greenhill Bri. Rd. CT6: H Bay .4D **194**
Greenhill Cl. CT12: Minst .6E **212**
Greenhill Cotts. ME15: Otham .9L **127**
Greenhill Ct. SE18 .5B **50**
Greenhill Gdns. CT6: H Bay .4E **194**
CT12: Minst .6E **212**
Grn. Hill La. ME17: Graf G .8M **141**
TN27: Eger .7F **29**
Greenhill Pk. NW10 .2A **4**
Greenhill Rd. CT6: H Bay .5C **194** (3H **21**)
DA11: Nflt .7E **62**
TN14: Otf .6K **103**
Green Hills CT4: B'hm .9A **162** (5K **31**)
Greenhill Ter. SE18 .5B **50**
GREENHITHE .2H **61** (6K **7**)
Greenhithe ME15: Maid .6C **126**
Greenhithe Cl. DA15: Sidc .5G **56**
Greenhithe for Bluewater
Station (Rail) .3H **61** (6K **7**)
Greenholm Rd. SE9 .3D **56**
Greenhouse La. CT2: Cant .9L **167**
Greenhurst La. RH8: Oxt .4A **24**
Greening St. SE2 .4L **51**
Greenlands DA12: Sole S .8J **77**
TN15: Bor G .2A **122**
Greenlands Rd. TN15: Kems'g .1B **120**
Green La. BR7: Chst .1B **14**
BR7: Chst .7D **56**
CT3: Chill .2D **32**
CT3: Wickh .7B **22**
CT4: Old L .6K **175**
CT4: R Min .8H **183** (1G **41**)
CT5: Whits .5F **226**
CT9: Mgte .5H **209** (2J **23**)
CT10: B'stairs .8J **209** (2K **23**)
CT14: Walm .9L **177**
CT15: Eyt .9K **185** (5E **32**)
CT15: St Marg .9A **200**
CT16: Dover .2G **180** (1F **43**)
CT16: Temp E, Whitf .8C **178**
(not continuous)
CT18: Cap F .1B **174**
CT18: R Min .1G **41**
CT19: F'stone .5L **189**
CT21: Hythe .6H **199**
DA12: Shorne .2B **78**
DA13: Meop .1G **90** (3C **16**)
IG1: Ilf .1C **6**
IG3: Ilf .1C **6**
ME3: Cliffe .2C **176**
ME3: Isle G .7C **190** (5E **10**)
ME9: Rod .3J **115** (6F **19**)
ME9: S'bry .1G **113**
ME13: Stal .3H **29**
ME17: Bou Mo .5E **138** (4J **27**)
ME17: Cha S .5K **27**
ME17: L'ly .5A **140** (4A **28**)
ME17: S'wy .4D **28**
ME19: Tros .5E **106**

Green La.—Hacton La.

Green La. RM8: Dag 1E 6
SE9 7B 6
SE9 6D 56
SE20 3A 68 (1H 13)
SM4: Mord 3C 12
SW16: Thor H 1F 13
TN6: Crowb 7G 35
TN8: Four E 5D 24
TN12: Brenc 3D 36
TN12: Coll S 6F 27
TN12: Pad W 1M 153
TN14: Four E 8A 130 (5D 24)
TN17: Bendn 6B 38
(Beacon Hill)
TN17: Bendn 5B 38
(East End)
TN17: Frit 1B 38
TN23: Ashf 4C 160
TN25: C'lck 8B 174 (4K 29)
TN25: W Bra 1D 40
TN27: Smar 8C 222
Green La. Av. CT21: Hythe 6G 199
Green La. Bus. Pk. SE9 7C 56
Green La. Cotts. ME17: L'ly 5A 140
Green Lanes N16 1G 5
Green La., The TN11: Leigh 6N 143
Greenlaw St. SE18 3C 50
Green Leas CT5: Whits 4M 227
Greenleas TN2: Pem 8B 152
Greenlees Cl. ME10: Sit 6C 98
Greenleigh Av. BR5: St P 7K 71
Greenly Way TN28: New R 3L 213
Grn. Manor Way DA11: Nflt 2M 61
Greenmead DA18: Erith 3N 51
Green Mdws. TN29: Dym 5C 182
Greenoak Ri. TN16: Big H 6C 164
Green Park Station (Tube) 3E 4
Green Pl. DA1: Cray 3F 58
Grn. Porch Cl. ME10: Sit 4G 99
Green Rd. CT7: Birch 3E 206
DA2: Dart 1K 15
TN12: Horsm 7C 196
Green Rd., The CT4: Chart'm 7D 170
Greensands ME5: Chat'm 2F 110
Greensands Rd. ME15: Bear 7K 127
Greensand Way ME18: W Peck 3D 134
TN11: S'brne 3D 134
Green's Cotts. ME15: E Far 4L 137
Green's End SE18 4D 50
Greenshanks ME9: Iwade 9K 197
Greenside BR8: Swanl 5E 72
DA5: Bex'y 6N 57
ME15: Maid 6E 126
TN26: H Hald 2C 196
Greenside Cl. SE6 7G 54
Greenside Wlk. TN16: Big H 6B 164
Greensleeves Way ME19: W Mal 6A 124
Greensole La. CT12: Mans 4C 210
Green St. DA1: Dart 7H 7
DA2: Dart 1J 15
E7 1A 6
E13 2A 6
ME7: Gill 7F 80
GREEN STREET GREEN
Dartford 2G 74 (1K 15)
Orpington 7H 85 (5C 14)
Green Street Green Rd. DA1: Dart 6B 60
DA2: Dart 8C 60
Green, The BR1: Brom 8K 55
(not continuous)
BR2: Shortl 1K 83
BR5: St P 3K 71
BR6: Farnb 5D 84 (4B 14)
CR0: Croy 9C 82
CR6: Warl 7H 13
CT2: Blean 5G 167
CT2: Up Harb 1E 170
CT3: L'brne 3L 173 (1A 32)
CT4: Chart'm 2F 31
CT12: Mans 3B 210
CT15: Cold 6D 32
CT15: Eyt 9L 185
CT21: Salt 4J 199 (5H 41)
DA2: Dart 7D 60
DA7: Bexhth 8B 52
DA14: Sidc 9J 57 (1D 14)
DA16: Well 2G 56
ME9: Lwr Hal 3L 225
ME12: Minst 3J 221
ME14: Bear 5M 127 (2A 28)
ME15: E Far 1M 137
ME17: Bou Mo 5E 138 (4J 27)
ME18: W Peck 2F 134
ME19: Addtn 7J 107
ME19: W Mal 1A 124
RM18: W Til 5C 8
TN3: Groom 5K 155 (4G 35)
TN3: Lang G 2M 155 (3H 35)
TN11: Leigh 6N 143
TN12: Mat 6J 153 (2C 36)
TN13: S'oaks 4L 119
TN14: Otf 7J 103
TN15: Seal 3N 119
(off Church Rd.)
TN16: Westrm 8F 116
TN17: Bendn 6A 38
TN23: Bou L 6B 30
TN25: Wye 2M 159
TN26: Wdchu 7B 228 (5H 39)
TN29: Burm 3B 182
TN29: Lydd 3J 205
Greentrees Av. TN10: Tonb 2M 145
Green Va. DA6: Bexhth 3M 57
Greenvale Gdns. ME8: Gill 1L 95
Greenvale Rd. SE9 2B 56
Greenview Av. BR3: Beck'm 9B 68
CR0: Croy 9B 68
Green Vw. Av. TN11: Leigh 6A 144
Greenview Cres. TN11: Hild 3E 144
Greenview Wlk. ME7: Gill 8K 81
Green Wlk. DA1: Cray 3G 58
Green Way BR2: Shortl 9A 70
Greenway BR7: Chst 1C 70
Green Way DA3: Hart'y 8L 75
Greenway ME5: Chat'm 5A 94
ME13: Fav 4F 186
Green Way ME16: Maid 6M 125
SE9 3N 55
TN2: Tun W 6L 151
Greenway TN16: Tats 8C 164
TN17: Cran 8B 176
Green Way TN29: Lydd 4J 205
Greenway Ct. ME17: Holl 1H 141
Greenway Ct. Rd. ME17: Holl 7G 128 (2C 28)
Greenway Gdns. CR0: Croy 4C 82
Greenway La. ME17: Holl, H'shm 1H 141 (3C 28)
Greenways BR3: Beck'm 6D 68
DA3: Long 6C 76
ME10: Sit 8J 99
ME14: Weav 4J 127
Greenways, The TN12: Pad W 1L 153
Greenway, The BR5: St M Cry 9K 71
GREENWICH 5K 5
Greenwich Borough Mus. 5H 51 (4C 6)
Greenwich Cl. ME5: Chat'm 7E 94
ME16: Maid 5A 126
Greenwich High Rd. SE8 5J 5
Greenwich La. CT15: Ewe M 1C 42
Greenwich Pk. 5K 5
Greenwich Sth. St. SE10 5K 5
Greenwich Station (Rail & DLR) 5K 5
Greenwood Cl. BR5: Pet W 9G 70
DA15: Sidc 7J 57
Greenwood Ho. SE4 2A 54
Greenwood Ind. Est. ME13: Fav 2F 186
Greenwood Pl. TN15: Wro 8N 105
Greenwood Rd. DA5: Bex'y 9E 58
Greenwood Way TN13: S'oaks 7G 119
Green Wrythe La. SM5: Cars 3D 12
Greggs Wood Rd. TN2: Tun W 7K 151
Gregory Cl. BR2: Shortl 7H 69
ME8: Gill 7A 96
ME10: Kems'y 3H 99
TN14: S'ham 2G 103
Gregory Ct. TN25: Wye 2M 159
Gregory Cres. SE9 5N 55
Grenadier Cl. ME8: Rain 1D 96
ME15: Bear 7J 127
Grenadier St. E16 1C 50
Grenham Bay Av. CT7: Birch 3D 206
Grenham Rd. CT7: Birch 3D 206
Grenville Cl. DA13: Meop 3F 90
Grenville Gdns. CT7: Birch 3D 206
Grenville Rd. CR0: Croy 9F 82
Grenville Way CT10: B'stairs 9J 209
Gresham Av. CT9: Mgte 2M 207
DA3: Hart'y 7M 75
Gresham Cl. DA5: Bex'y 4N 57
ME8: Rain 2B 96
TN10: Tonb 9L 133
Gresham Rd. BR3: Beck'm 5B 68
ME17: Cox 5A 138
Greshams Way TN8: Eden 5A 184
Gresswell Cl. DA14: Sidc 8J 57
Greville Pl. NW6 2C 4
Greybury La. TN8: Marsh G 1B 34
Greycot Rd. BR3: Beck'm 1D 68
Greyfriars CT1: Cant 2M 171
ME16: Maid 4A 126
Grey Friars Cotts. CT1: Cant 2M 171
Grey Friars Ct. CT10: B'stairs 4K 209
Greyhound Commercial Cen., The
DA1: Cray 3F 58
Greyhound La. SW16 1E 12
Greyhound Rd. ME12: Minst 9K 221
Greyhound Ter. SW16 2E 12
Greyhound Way DA1: Cray 3F 58
Greys Pk. Cl. BR2: Kes 6N 83
Greystone Pk. TN14: Sund 7N 117
Greystones Cl. TN15: Kems'g 8M 103
Greystones Rd. CT12: C'snd 7B 210
ME15: Bear 7K 127
Grey Wethers ME14: S'lng 6B 110
Grey Willow Gdns. TN23: Ashf 1B 160
Gribble Bri. La. TN27: Bidd 4C 38
TN30: St Mic 4C 38
Grice Av. TN16: Big H 3A 164
Grice Cl. CT18: H'nge 9J 193
Grierson Rd. SE23 5A 54
Grieves Rd. DA11: Nflt 8E 62
Griffin Mnr. Way SE28 3F 50
Griffin Rd. SE18 5F 50 (4C 6)
Griffin St. CT14: Deal 3N 177
Griffin Wlk. DA9: G'hithe 3F 60
GRIGG 7C 28
Grigg La. TN27: H'crn 8M 191 (7C 28)
Griggs App. IG1: Ilf 1C 6
Griggs Way TN15: Bor G 2N 121
Grigsby La. TN27: Smar 9A 222 (2D 38)
Grimsby Gro. E16 2D 50
Grimshill Ct. CT2: Cant 7J 167
Grimshill Rd. CT5: Whits 5F 226
Grimston Av. CT20: F'stone 6H 189 (5A 42)
Grimston Gdns. CT20: F'stone 7H 189
Grimthorpe Av. CT5: Whits 6E 226
Grinsell Hill CT12: Ram, Minst 4G 23
Grisbrook Farm Cl. TN29: Lydd 3L 205
Grisbrook Rd. TN29: Lydd 3K 205
Grizedale Cl. ME1: Roch 3A 94
Gromenfield TN3: Groom 6K 155
GROOMBRIDGE 6K 155 (4G 35)
Groombridge Cl. DA16: Well 3J 57
Groombridge Hill TN3: Groom 5K 155 (4G 35)
Groombridge La. TN3: Epp G 5H 35
Groombridge Place 5K 155 (4G 35)
Groombridge Rd. TN3: A'hst, Groom 3G 35
TN3: Ford, Groom 4H 155
Groombridge Sq. ME15: Maid 2J 139
Groombridge Station
Spa Valley Railway 6K 155
Groom Cl. BR2: Shortl 7L 69
Grosmont Rd. SE18 5H 51
Grosvenor Av. ME4: Chat'm 9B 80
N5 1G 5
SM5: Cars 5D 12
Grosvenor Bri. TN1: Tun W 9H 151 (2K 35)
Grosvenor Cres. DA1: Dart 3L 59
Grosvenor Gdns. CT9: Mgte 4C 208 (1H 23)
Grosvenor Gdns. SW1 4E 4
Grosvenor Hill CT9: Mgte 3C 208
Grosvenor Ho. ME15: Maid 3J 139
Grosvenor Pk. TN1: Tun W 1G 157
Grosvenor Pl. CT9: Mgte 3C 208
SW1 4E 4
TN1: Tun W 8H 151
Grosvenor Rd. BR4: W W'ck 2E 82
BR5: St M Cry 9G 71
CT5: Whits 6F 226
CT10: B'stairs 9L 209
CT11: Ram 5G 210
DA6: Bexhth 3M 57
DA17: Belv 6B 52
ME8: Gill 2J 95 (3K 17)
SM5: Wall 4E 12
SW1 5E 4
TN1: Tun W 1G 157 (3K 35)
TN24: Kenn 3G 159
Grosvenor Sq. *DA3: Long 6L 75*
(off Park Dr.)
Grosvenor St. W1 3E 4
Grosvenor Ter. *CT20: F'stone 5L 189*
(off Tram Rd., The)
Grosvenor Wlk. TN1: Tun W 1G 157
Grotto Gdns. CT9: Mgte 3D 208
Grotto Hill CT9: Mgte 3D 208
Grotto Rd. CT9: Mgte 3D 208
GROVE 5B 22
Grove Av. ME12: Ley S 6M 203
TN1: Tun W 3G 157
Grovebury Cl. DA8: Erith 6E 52
Grovebury Ct. DA6: Bexhth 3C 58
Grovebury Rd. SE2 2K 51
Grove Cl. BR2: Shortl 3K 83
ME13: Fav 6E 186
SE23 6B 54
TN11: Hdlw 5H 135
Grove Cott. TN9: Tonb 5K 145
Grove Ct. ME13: Bou B 3K 165
GROVE END 6E 18
Grove End Rd. NW8 2D 4
GROVE FERRY 5B 22
Gro. Ferry Hill CT3: Ups 5B 22
Grove Ferry Picnic Site 5B 22
Grove Gdns. CT9: Mgte 4A 208
GROVE GREEN 4H 127 (1K 27)
Grove Grn. La. ME14: Weav 4H 127
Grove Grn. Rd. E10 1K 5
E11 1K 5
ME14: Weav 4J 127
Groveherst Rd. DA1: Dart 1N 59
GROVE HILL 6B 22
Grovehill Ct. BR1: Brom 2J 69
Grove Hill Gdns. TN1: Tun W 3H 157
Grove Hill Rd. TN1: Tun W 2H 157 (3K 35)
GROVEHURST
Sittingbourne 2F 98
Tonbridge 2F 37
Grovehurst Av. ME10: Kems'y 3G 98 (3F 19)
Grovehurst La. TN12: Horsm 8E 196 (2F 37)
Grovehurst Rd. ME9: Iwade 9K 197 (3F 19)
ME10: Kems'y, Sit 9K 197 (3F 19)
Groveland Rd. BR3: Beck'm 6C 68
Grovelands ME17: Len 7N 201
Grovelands Rd. BR5: St P 3J 71
Grove La. ME15: Hunt 8G 137
SE5 5G 5
TN29: Snar 2E 46
TN31: Iden 4B 46
Grove Mkt. Pl. SE9 4B 56
GROVE PARK
CHISWICK 5A 4
SE12 8L 55 (7A 6)
Grove Pk. Av. ME10: Sit 6C 98
Gro. Park Rd. SE9 8M 55 (7A 6)
W4 5A 4
Grove Park Station (Rail) 8L 55 (7A 6)
Grove Rd. CR4: Mitc 2E 12
CT3: S'le 1D 32
CT3: Sturry, Pres 5C 22
CT3: Wickh 7B 22
CT11: Ram 6H 211
CT14: Walm 7N 177
CT20: F'stone 5L 189
DA7: Bexhth 2D 58
DA11: Nflt 3A 62
DA17: Belv 6A 52
E3 2H 5
ME2: Hall'g 6C 92
ME2: Strood 4M 79
ME4: Chat'm 1E 94
ME7: Gill 6K 81
ME13: Sell'g 4M 219 (2B 30)
ME15: Maid 2F 138
SM1: Sutt 5C 12
TN8: Chid H 5E 148 (1F 35)
TN11: Pens 5E 148 (1F 35)
TN14: S'oaks 3K 119
TN15: Seal 3A 120 (1H 25)
TN16: Tats 8C 164
Grover St. SS1: Sth S 1E 10
TN1: Tun W 1H 157
Groves, The ME6: Snod 3D 108
Grove St. SE8 4J 5
Grove Ter. CT1: Cant 3L 171
GROVE, THE 1G 39
GROVE, THE 7H 5
Grove, The BR4: W W'ck 4E 82
BR8: Swanl 6G 72
CT4: B'hm 8D 162
CT6: H Bay 5D 194
CT8: Wgte S 3L 207
CT14: Deal 4M 177
CT16: Dover 3H 181
CT21: Hythe 6K 199
DA6: Bexhth 2M 57
DA10: Swans 3M 61
DA12: Grav'nd 5G 63
DA14: Sidc 1N 71
E15 1K 5
ME14: Bear 6K 127
TN2: Pem 6C 152
TN15: W King 1F 104
Grove, The TN16: Big H 6D 164
TN24: Kenn 4J 159
TN31: Rye 5B 46
Grove Va. BR7: Chst 2C 70
SE22 6G 5
Groveway ME12: Ley S 6L 203
Grovewood Ct. ME14: Weav 5H 127
Grovewood Dr. ME14: Weav 4H 127
GRUBB STREET 4H 75 (2K 15)
Grummock Av. CT11: Ram 5F 210
Grundy's Hill CT11: Ram 6J 211
Guardian Ct. ME8: Rain 2M 95
SE12 3H 55
Guardian Ind. Est. TN12: Mard 2C 212
Guernsey Way TN24: Kenn 3G 158
GUESTLING THORN 7H 45
Guestwick TN10: Tonb 2M 145
Guibal Rd. SE12 5L 55
Guildables La. TN8: Eden 8B 24
Guildcount La. CT13: S'wch 5L 217
Guildford Av. CT8: Wgte S 3J 207
Guildford Gdns. ME2: Strood 6G 79
Guildford Ho. ME15: Maid 1G 138
Guildford Lawn CT11: Ram 6H 211
Guildford Rd. CT1: Cant 4M 171
TN1: Tun W 2H 157
Guildhall Mus. 6N 79
(off High St., Rochester)
Guildhall Mus., The 7A 220
Guildhall St. CT1: Cant 2M 171
CT20: F'stone 6K 189
Guildhall St. Nth. CT20: F'stone 6K 189
Guild Rd. DA8: Erith 7G 52
SE7 6A 50
Guilford Av. CT16: Whitf 5E 178
Guilford Ct. CT14: Walm 8N 177
Guilford Rd. CT13: S'wch 1H 33
Guilford St. WC1 2F 5
GUILTON 5B 216 (7E 22)
Guilton CT3: Ash 5A 216 (7D 22)
Guinness Dr. ME3: Wain 2M 79
Gulbenkian Theatre 7K 167
Guldeford La. TN29: B'lnd 4D 46
TN31: B'lnd 4D 46
GULDEFORD LANE CORNER 4D 46
Guldeford Rd. TN31: E Guld 5B 46
Gullands ME17: L'ly 4A 140
Gulliver Rd. DA15: Sidc 7F 56
Gumping Rd. BR5: Farnb 3E 84
Gun Back La. TN12: Horsm 8C 196
Gundulph Ho. ME1: Roch 6N 79
Gundulph Rd. BR2: Shortl 6M 69
ME1: Chat'm 8B 80
ME4: Roch 8B 80
Gundulph Sq. ME1: Roch 6N 79
Gunfleet Cl. DA12: Grav'nd 5K 63
GUN GREEN 4F 192 (7J 37)
Gun Hill RM18: W Til 5C 8
Gunlands TN12: Horsm 7C 196
Gun La. ME2: Strood 5L 79 (2G 17)
Gunner La. SE18 5C 50
GUNNERSBURY 4A 4
Gunnersbury Av. W3 4A 4
W5 4A 4
Gunnersbury Dr. W5 4A 4
Gunnersbury La. W3 4A 4
GUNNERSBURY PARK 4A 4
Gunnersbury Station (Rail & Tube) 4A 4
Gunnery Ter. SE18 3E 50
Gunning St. SE18 4G 50
Gunnis Cl. ME8: Gill 7N 95
Gunn Rd. DA10: Swans 4L 61
Gunter Gro. SW10 5D 4
Gun Tower M. ME1: Roch 8M 79
Gurling Rd. CT15: St Marg 8B 200
GUSHMERE 1C 30
GUSTON 7K 179 (7G 33)
Guston La. CT15: E Lan 4L 179 (6G 33)
Guston Rd. CT15: E Lan 5M 179 (7G 33)
CT15: Gus 3K 181
CT16: Dover 1G 43
CT16: Gus 3K 181
ME14: Maid 4F 126
Guthrie Gdns. CT17: Dover 1D 180
Guy Barnett Gro. SE3 1K 55
Guy Cl. CT10: B'stairs 6L 209
Guyscliff Rd. SE13 3F 54
Gwillim Cl. DA15: Sidc 3J 57
Gwydor Rd. BR3: Beck'm 6A 68
Gwydyr Rd. BR2: Shortl 6J 69
Gwynne Av. CR0: Croy 1A 82
Gwynn Rd. DA11: Nflt 7B 62
Gwyn Rd. CT12: Ram 2G 210
Gybbon Ri. TN12: S'hrst 3J 223
Gybbons Rd. TN17: Rolv 3C 214
GYPSY CORNER 3A 4
Gypsy Way ME3: H Hals 2H 67

H

Haberdashers Ct. SE14 1A 54
HACKBRIDGE 4E 12
Hackbridge Rd. SM6: Wall 4E 12
Hackbridge Station (Rail) 3E 12
Hackfield TN23: Ashf 9D 158
Hackington Cl. CT2: Cant 7L 167
Hackington Cres. BR3: Beck'm 2D 68
Hackington Pl. CT2: Cant 9M 167
Hackington Rd.
CT2: Whits, T Hill 1K 167 (5G 21)
Hackington Ter. CT2: Cant 9M 167
HACKLINGE 2H 33
Hacklinge Rd. CT14: Worth, Hackl 2G 33
HACKNEY 2H 5
Hackney Central Station (Rail) 1H 5
Hackney Downs Station (Rail) 1H 5
Hackney Rd. E2 2G 5
ME16: Maid 7N 125 (2H 27)
HACKNEY WICK 1J 5
HACKNEY WICK 1J 5
Hackney Wick Station (Rail) 1J 5
HACTON 1H 7
Hacton La. RM12: H'church, Upm 1H 7

Hacton La.—Harrison Dr.

Hacton La. RM14: Upm 1H 7
Hadden Rd. SE28 3G 50
Haddington Rd. BR1: Brom 8G 55
Haddon Gro. DA15: Sidc 5H 57
Haddon Rd. BR5: St M Cry 8L 71
Hadleigh Castle 1A 10
Hadleigh Castle Country Pk. 1K 9
Hadleigh Ct. ME7: Hpstd 8K 95
Hadleigh Gdns. CT6: H Bay 2J 195
Hadleigh Rd. SS9: Lgh S 1B 10
Hadley Cl. DA13: Meop 3G 90
Hadley Ct. TN4: Tun W 8F 150
Hadley Gdns. ME17: Holl 7G 128
Hadley Rd. DA17: Belv 4A 52
HADLOW 8D 134 (5B 26)
Hadlow Dr. CT9: Clift 3J 209
Hadlow Pk. TN11: Hdlw 7D 134
Hadlow Rd. DA14: Sidc 9J 57
DA16: Well 7L 51
ME14: Maid 4F 126
TN9: Tonb 5J 145 (6K 25)
TN10: Hdlw, Tonb 2N 145 (6K 25)
TN11: Hdlw, Tonb 2N 145
Hadlow Rd. E. TN10: Tonb 2N 145
TN11: Tonb 2N 145 (5A 26)
HADLOW STAIR 3M 145 (6A 26)
Hadlow Stair Rd. TN10: Tonb 3M 145
Hadlow Way DA13: Ist R 3D 76
Hadrian Gdns. TN23: Ashf 4D 160
Haffenden Cl. TN12: Mard 2D 212
Haffenden Mdw. TN27: Char'g 2K 175
HAFFENDEN QUARTER 2D 38
Haffenden Rd. TN30: Tent 6B 224
Hafod Pas. CT21: Hythe 6K 199
Hafton Rd. SE6 6H 55
Hagger Dr. CT18: H'nge 7M 193
HAGGERSTON 2G 5
Ha Ha Rd. SE18 6B 50 (5B 6)
Haig Av. ME1: Roch 2A 94
ME4: Chat'm 1D 94
ME7: Gill 8H 81
Haig Gdns. DA12: Grav'nd 5H 63
Haig Rd. TN16: Big H 5E 164
Haig Vs. ME3: C'den 8D 66
Haileybury Rd. BR6: Chels 5J 85
Hailey Rd. DA18: Erith 2B 52
Hailey Rd. Bus. Pk. DA18: Erith 2B 52
Hailstone Cl. TN11: Hdlw 8D 134
Haimo Rd. SE9 3N 55
Hainault St. SE9 6D 56
HAINE 2D 210 (3J 23)
Haine Ind. Est. CT12: Ram 3D 210
Haine Rd. CT12: Ram 5D 210 (4H 23)
Hainford Cl. SE4 2A 54
Halcot Av. DA6: Bexhth 3C 58
Haldane Gdns. DA11: Nflt 6B 62
Halden Cl. ME15: Maid 2J 139
Halden La. TN17: Bendn, Rolv 5B 38
TN17: Rolv 2C 214
HALE
Birchington 7A 206 (3D 22)
Gillingham 3H 95 (4J 17)
Hale Cl. BR6: Farnb 5E 84
Hale Ct. TN12: E Peck 9M 135
Hale La. TN14: Otf 8G 102
Hale Oak Rd. TN8: Chid 5E 142
TN8: Chid, Weald 6F 25
TN14: Weald 7H 131 (6F 25)
Hale Rd. ME3: Cli W 6N 65
Hales Cl. TN30: Tent 7C 224
Hales Ct. TN30: Tent 7C 224
Hales Dr. CT2: Cant 8M 167
HALES PLACE 7N 167 (7H 21)
Hales Rd. ME10: Sit 1E 114
HALE STREET 9M 135 (5D 26)
Hale St. TN12: E Peck 8M 135 (5D 26)
Halesworth Rd. SE13 1E 54
Haleys Pl. ME1: Burh 2L 109
Halfmile Ride CT9: Mgte 6C 208
Half Moon La. SE24 6G 5
TN11: Hild 1D 144
TN11: Tude 2C 152
Half Moon Way ME3: H Hals 2H 67
Halford Cl. CT6: H Bay 5J 195
Halfpence La. DA12: Cobh 7M 77 (2D 16)
Halfpenny Cl. ME16: Barm 7L 125
HALFWAY HOUSES 6F 220 (7G 11)
Halfway Rd. ME12: Minst 3E 220 (7G 11)
HALFWAY STREET 9J 219 (6C 32)
Halfway St. DA15: Sidc 5F 56 (7C 6)
Half Yoke ME16: Maid 9M 125
Halifax Cl. ME5: Chat'm 5E 94
Halifield Dr. DA17: Belv 3N 51
Haling Pk. Rd. CR2: S Croy 4F 13
Hallam Cl. BR7: Chst 1B 70
Halland Ct. *TN8: Eden* 6C 184
(off Stangrove Rd.)
Hall Av. TN24: Ashf 3K 161
Hall By The Sea Rd. CT9: Mgte 3C 208
Hall Cl. ME10: Sit 5F 98
Hall Cres. CT14: Shol 5J 177
Hallcroft Ct. CT11: Ram 5G 210
Hallett Wlk. CT1: Cant 9A 168
Halley Gdns. SE13 2G 55
Hall Farm Cotts. TN26: Hoth 2K 197
Hallford Way DA1: Dart 4K 59
Hall Hill TN15: Seal 5B 120 (2H 25)
Halliday Ct. CT21: Hythe 6H 199
Halliday Dr. CT14: Walm 7M 177
Halliford St. N1 1G 5
HALLING 6E 92 (4F 17)
Halling By-Pass ME2: Hall'g 5E 92 (4F 17)
Halling Station (Rail) 6E 92 (4F 17)
Hall Place & Visitors Cen. 4D 58 (6F 7)
Hall Pl. Cres. DA5: Bex'y 3D 58
Hall Place Gardens 4D 58
Hall Rd. DA1: Dart 2N 59
DA11: Nflt, Sflt 7B 62 (7B 8)
E15 1K 5
ME1: Woul 9G 92 (5F 17)
ME3: St M Hoo 5A 10
ME5: Chat'm 8F 94
ME20: Aylfd 9J 109 (7G 17)
NW8 2D 4
Hall Rd. RM19: Avel 4J 7
Halls Cotts. ME14: Det 9K 111
Hallsfield Rd. ME5: Chat'm 8A 94
HALL'S GREEN 9H 131 (5G 25)
Hall's Hole Rd. TN2: Tun W 3K 157 (3K 35)
Hall, The SE3 1K 55
Hall Vw. SE9 7N 55
Hallwards TN12: S'hrst 4J 223
Hallwood Cl. ME8: Gill 6N 95
Hallwood Ho. ME5: Chat'm 9F 94
Halons Rd. SE9 5C 56
Halsbrook Rd. SE3 1M 55
Halstatt Rd. CT14: Deal 7K 177
HALSTEAD 4A 102 (6E 14)
Halstead Cl. CT2: Cant 7N 167
Halstead Gdns. CT9: Clift 2K 209
Halstead La. TN14: Hals 6N 101
TN14: Knock, Hals 7E 14
Halstead Rd. DA8: Erith 8F 52
Halstead Wlk. ME16: Alltn 2N 125
Halstow Cl. ME15: Maid 2E 138
Halstow La. ME9: Lwr Hal, Upc 3J 225 (3C 18)
Halstow Way TN23: Ashf 1D 160
Halt Robin La. DA17: Belv 4C 52
Halt Robin Rd. DA17: Belv 4B 52
(not continuous)
Halt, The CT4: Elham 7N 183
CT5: Whits 6H 227
HAM 2G 33
Hambledon Ct. ME16: Maid 6M 125
Hambledown Rd. DA15: Sidc 5F 56
Hamblehyrst BR3: Beck'm 5E 68
Hamble Rd. TN10: Tonb 2H 145
Hambro Av. BR2: Shortl 2K 83
Hambrook Cl. CT4: Chil'm 8J 175
Hambrook La. CT4: Chil'm 9J 175 (3D 30)
Hambrook Wlk. ME10: Sit 3G 98
Hamelin Rd. ME7: Gill 3J 95
Hamerton Rd. DA11: Nflt 3A 62
HAM GREEN
Sittingbourne 2C 18
Tenterden 2K 45
HAM HILL 4E 108 (6E 16)
Hamilton Cl. CT12: Ram 3E 210
TN28: L'stne 4N 213
Hamilton Ct. *DA8: Erith* 7G 53
(off Frobisher Rd.)
ME1: Roch 8M 79
(off Fennel Cl.)
ME5: Chat'm 2F 94
SE6 6J 55
TN4: Tun W 9G 151
Hamilton Cres. ME10: Sit 8D 98
Hamilton Ho. ME15: Maid 3J 139
TN4: Tun W 9G 151
Hamilton Rd. CT5: Whits 4F 226
CT14: Deal 6L 177 (4J 33)
CT17: Dover 4F 180
DA7: Bexhth 9N 51
DA15: Sidc 9J 57
ME7: Gill 5G 80
TN24: Ashf 3H 161
TN29: Lydd 3K 205
Hamilton Wlk. DA8: Erith 7G 53
Ham La. ME7: Gill 8G 95 (5J 17)
ME17: Len 7K 201 (3E 28)
Hamlea Cl. SE12 3K 55
Hamlet Cl. SE13 2H 55
Hamlet Ct. Rd. SS0: Wclf S 1D 10
Hamlet Ho. DA8: Erith 7F 52
Hamlet International Trad. Est.
DA8: Erith 5E 52
Hamlet Rd. SE19 1G 13
Hamlin Rd. TN13: Riv 4F 118
Hamlyn Ct. TN13: Dun G 3F 118
Hammelton Ct. *BR1: Brom* 4J 69
(off London Rd.)
Hammelton Rd. BR1: Brom 4J 69
HAMMERSMITH 4B 4
Hammersmith Bri. SW13 5B 4
W6 5B 4
HAMMERSMITH BROADWAY 4B 4
HAMMERSMITH FLYOVER 4B 4
Hammersmith Flyover W6 4B 4
Hammersmith Rd. W6 4B 4
W14 4B 4
Hammersmith Station (Tube) 4B 4
HAMMERWOOD 3B 34
Hammerwood Park 3C 34
Hammerwood Rd. RH19: A'hstw 4A 34
HAMMILL 2E 32
Ham Mill La. TN29: Snar 1E 46
Hammill Rd. CT13: Wdboro 9E 216 (1E 32)
Hammond Cl. CT15: Non 3D 32
Hammond Hill ME4: Chat'm 8B 80
Hammonds TN18: Hawkh 5D 192
Hammonds Rd. CT20: F'stone 6E 188
Hammond's Sq. ME6: Snod 2E 108
Hampden Av. BR3: Beck'm 5B 68
Hampden La. TN23: Ashf 2E 160
Hampden M. TN23: Ashf 3E 160
Hampden Rd. BR3: Beck'm 5B 68
TN23: Ashf 3E 160
Hampden Way ME19: W Mal 6L 123
Hampkins Hill Rd. TN8: Chid 5E 142 (7F 25)
Hampshire Cl. ME5: Chat'm 4F 94
Hampshire Dr. ME15: Maid 9F 126
Hampshire Rd. CT1: Cant 3C 172
Hampson Way ME14: Bear 5K 127
HAMPSTEAD 1D 4
Hampstead Cl. SE28 1K 51
Hampstead Cott. Cvn. Pk. ME18: Yald 7B 136
Hampstead Heath 1D 4
Hampstead Heath Station (Rail) 1D 4
Hampstead High St. NW3 1D 4
Hampstead La. ME18: W'bury, Yald 7N 135
ME18: Yald, W'bury 4E 26
Hampstead Rd. NW1 2E 4
Hampstead Station (Tube) 1D 4
HAMPTON 3C 194 (2H 21)
Hampton Cl. CT6: H Bay 4B 194
ME5: Chat'm 6D 94
Hampton Cres. DA12: Grav'nd 7K 63
Hampton Gdns. CT6: H Bay 4B 194
Hampton Ho. *DA7: Bexhth* 9C 52
(off Erith Rd.)
Hampton La. TN25: Brook, W Bra 1D 40
Hampton Pier Av. CT6: H Bay 2C 194 (3H 21)
Hampton Pier Yacht Club 2C 194
Hampton Rd. ME14: Maid 3F 126
HAMPTONS 3B 26
Hamptons Rd. TN11: Hdlw, S'brne 3M 133
TN11: S'brne, Hdlw 3A 26
Hampton Va. CT21: Hythe 7B 188
Ham River Hill ME3: Cli W 7L 65 (7G 9)
Ham Rd. ME13: Fav 3G 186 (5A 20)
HAMSEY GREEN 7H 13
Hamshades Cl. DA15: Sidc 8H 57
Ham Shades La. CT5: Whits 4J 227 (3G 21)
Hamstel Rd. SS2: Sth S 1E 10
HAMSTREET 3L 191 (6A 40)
Hamstreet By-Pass TN26: Hams 3K 191 (6A 39)
Hamstreet Rd. TN26: Ruck 3M 191 (6A 40)
TN26: Shad 4K 39
Ham Street Station (Rail) 2L 191 (6A 40)
Ham Vw. CR0: Croy 9B 68
Ham Wall ME3: Cliffe 1B 176
Hamwick Grn. ME5: Chat'm 1F 110
Hanbury Cl. ME18: W'bury 1C 136
Hanbury Dr. TN16: Big H 3A 164
Hanbury Wlk. DA5: Bex'y 8F 58
Hancock Cl. ME3: Wain 3M 79
Hancocks Fld. CT14: Deal 5K 177
Handcroft Rd. CR0: Croy 3F 13
Handel Wlk. TN10: Tonb 1L 145
Handen Rd. SE12 3H 55
Hanes Dene ME2: Hall'g 6D 92
HANGER HILL 2A 4
HANGER LANE 2A 4
HANGING BANK 5A 130 (4E 24)
Hanging Bank Nature Reserve 4C 130
Hangman's La. CT14: Mart, Ripp 4A 200
CT14: R'wld 4B 200
Hangmans La. CT15: Gus 7L 179
Hangrove Hill BR6: Downe 4D 100 (6B 14)
Hanley Pl. BR3: Beck'm 3D 68
Hanmer Way TN12: S'hrst 4J 223
Hannah Cl. BR3: Beck'm 6F 68
ME4: Chat'm 9D 80
Hanover Cl. CT9: Clift 3J 209
CT14: Walm 8N 177
ME10: Sit 9F 98
TN23: Ashf 8D 158
Hanover Ct. CT10: B'stairs 9K 209
CT20: F'stone 7J 189
(off Court App.)
CT21: Hythe 6K 199
ME14: Maid 4E 126
Hanover Dr. BR7: Chst 9E 56
ME8: Gill 7M 95
Hanover Grn. ME20: Lark 7C 108
Hanover Ho. TN9: Tonb 4J 145
Hanover Pk. SE15 5H 5
Hanover Pl. CT2: Cant 9M 167
DA3: New A 3M 89
Hanover Rd. ME17: Cox 5N 137
TN1: Tun W 1G 157
Hanover Sq. CT6: H Bay 2G 195
Hanover St. CT6: H Bay 2G 194
Hanover Way DA6: Bexhth 1M 57
Hanscomb Ho. CT2: Cant 9L 167
Hanslett's La. ME13: Osp 9A 186 (7K 19)
Hansol Rd. DA6: Bexhth 3N 57
Hansom Ter. *BR1: Brom* 4L 69
(off Freelands Gro.)
Hanson Cl. BR3: Beck'm 2E 68
Hanway ME8: Gill 1K 95
Harbex Cl. DA5: Bex'y 5C 58
HARBLEDOWN 1J 171 (7G 21)
Harbledown CT2: Harb 1J 171
Harbledown By-Pass CT2: Harb 1G 170
CT2: Harb, Cant, R Comn 7G 21
Harbledown Gdns. CT9: Clift 2J 209
Harbledown Ho. ME16: Maid 7M 125
Harbledown Mnr. *ME8: Gill* 9L 81
(off Goudhurst Rd.)
Harbledown Pk. CT2: Harb 1J 171
Harbledown Pl. BR5: St M Cry 7L 71
Harbledown Ter. CT2: Harb 1J 171
Harborne La. TN26: H Hald 3C 196
Harborough Av. DA15: Sidc 5G 57
Harbour App. Rd. CT20: F'stone 7L 189 (5B 42)
HARBOURLAND 1F 126 (7J 17)
Harbourland Cl. ME14: Boxl 1E 126
Harbourland Cotts. ME14: Boxl 1F 126
Harbourne La. TN26: H Hald 5E 38
TN30: H Hald 5E 38
TN30: St Mic 4B 196
Harbour Pde. CT11: Ram 6J 211
Harbour Point CT19: F'stone 6L 189
Harbour St. CT5: Whits 3F 226 (3F 21)
CT10: B'stairs 9M 209
CT11: Ram 6J 211
CT20: F'stone 6L 189
HARBOUR, THE 5A 28
Harbour, The ME17: Sut V 5A 28
Harbour Towers *CT11: Ram* 6J 211
(off Albert St.)
Harbour Vw. Rd. CT17: Dover 4G 180
Harbour Way CT20: F'stone 6L 189
Harcourt Av. DA15: Sidc 4L 57
Harcourt Dr. CT2: Cant 9K 167
CT6: H Bay 2C 194
Harcourt Gdns. ME8: Rain 7A 96
Harcourt Rd. CT19: F'stone 4F 188
DA6: Bexhth 2N 57
SE4 1C 54
Hardcourts Cl. BR4: W W'ck 8E 82
Harden Ct. SE7 4A 50
Harden Rd. DA11: Nflt 8E 62
TN29: Lydd 2L 205 (5H 47)
Hardens Vw. TN26: W'hrne 4H 191
Hardie Cl. ME19: E Mal 9D 108
Hardinge Av. TN4: S'bgh 3E 150
Hardinge Cl. ME8: Gill 7N 95
Hardinge Cres. SE18 3E 50
Hardinge Rd. TN24: Ashf 7G 158
Harding Rd. DA7: Bexhth 9A 52
Hardings La. SE20 2A 68
Hardres Ct. Rd. CT4: Lwr Har, Up Hard 3H 31
Hardres Rd. CT11: Ram 5J 211 (4K 23)
Hardres St. CT11: Ram 5J 211
Hardres Ter. BR5: Orp 2M 85
Hards Town ME4: Chat'm 8D 80
Hardwick Ct. DA8: Erith 6E 52
Hardwick Cres. DA2: Dart 4B 60
Hardwicke Rd. CT17: Dover 6G 180
Hardwick Ho. ME15: Maid 9H 127
Hardwick Rd. CT20: F'stone 7G 188
TN11: Hild 9E 132
Hardy Av. DA11: Nflt 7D 62
Hardy Cl. CT2: Cant 1K 171
ME5: Chat'm 5E 94
TN24: W'boro 2L 161
Hardy Ct. DA8: Erith 7G 53
Hardy Gro. DA1: Dart 2A 60
Hardy Lodge *ME1: Roch* 9L 79
(off Fennel Cl.)
Hardy Rd. CT15: St Marg 9A 200
(not continuous)
TN28: G'stne 6M 213
Hardy St. ME14: Maid 3D 126
Hardy's Yd. TN13: Dun G 3F 118
Hare & Billet Rd. SE3 5K 5
Harebell Cl. ME5: Chat'm 7B 94
ME12: Minst 8H 221
ME14: Weav 4H 127
Harebrook CT11: Ram 3K 211
Haredale Cl. ME1: Roch 4A 94
Haredon Cl. SE23 5A 54
Harefield M. SE4 1C 54
Harefield Rd. DA14: Sidc 7M 57
SE4 1C 54
Haremere Hill TN19: Etch'm, Hur G 2A 44
HAREPLAIN 3B 38
Hareplain Rd. TN27: Bidd 3B 38
Harescroft TN2: Tun W 5F 156
Hare St. ME4: Chat'm 9E 80
ME12: S'ness 2D 220
SE18 3C 50
Harfst Way BR8: Swanl 4D 72
Hargate Cl. TN2: Tun W 6F 156
Harkness Ct. ME10: Sit 7J 99
Harkness Dr. CT2: Cant 9K 167
Harland Av. DA15: Sidc 8F 56
Harland Rd. SE12 6K 55
Harlands Gro. BR6: Farnb 5D 84
Harland Way TN4: S'bgh 2E 150
Harlech Cl. ME2: Strood 3K 79
Harleighbury Rd. CT15: St Marg 7B 214
Harlequin Ho. *DA18: Erith* 3N 51
(off Kale Rd.)
Harlequin La. TN6: Crowb 7F 35
Harlescott Rd. SE15 2A 54
HARLESDEN 2A 4
Harlesden Rd. NW10 2B 4
Harlesden Station (Rail & Tube) 2A 4
Harleyford BR1: Brom 4L 69
Harleyford Rd. SE11 5F 5
Harley Gdns. BR6: Orp 5G 84
Harling Cl. ME15: Maid 3G 138
Harlinger St. SE18 3A 50
Harlington Rd. DA7: Bexhth 1N 57
Harlow Cl. TN8: Eden 4D 184
Harman Av. CT21: Lymp 5A 198
DA11: Grav'nd 1G 76
Harman Ct. ME5: Chat'm 8D 94
Harman Dr. DA15: Sidc 4H 57
HARMAN'S CORNER 9C 98 (5E 18)
Harmans Dr. RH19: E Grin 3A 34
Harmer Ct. TN4: S'bgh 4G 150
Harmer Rd. DA10: Swans 4M 61
Harmer St. DA12: Grav'nd 4H 63 (6C 8)
Harmers Way TN27: Eger 6F 29
Harmony St. TN4: R'hall 1D 156
Harmony Way BR2: Shortl 5K 69
Harmsworth Gdns. CT10: B'stairs 8L 209
Harness Rd. SE28 2J 51
Harnet St. CT13: S'wch 5L 217
Harnetts Cl. BR8: Crock'm 1E 86
Harold Av. CT8: Wgte S 3K 207
DA17: Belv 5A 52
ME7: Gill 8H 81
Harold Ct. ME13: Fav 6G 186
Harold Pas. CT16: Dover 4K 181
Harold Rd. CT7: Birch 3C 206
CT9: Clift 3F 208
CT14: Deal 2M 177
DA2: Dart 9N 59
ME2: Cux 9G 78
ME10: Sit 7J 99
SE19 1G 13
Harold's Rd. CT16: Dover 4K 181
Harold St. CT16: Dover 4J 181
(not continuous)
ME11: Queen 8B 220
Harold Wilson Ho. SE28 1K 51
Harper Rd. SE1 4G 5
TN23: Ashf 1D 160
Harp Farm Rd. ME14: Boxl 3F 110 (6J 17)
Harple La. ME14: Det 9J 111 (7K 17)
Harps Av. ME12: Minst 6J 221
Harps Wlk. ME12: Minst 6K 221
Harpswood La. CT21: Hythe 5H 199
Harptree Dr. ME5: Chat'm 6B 94
Harrier Dr. ME10: Sit 9H 99
Harrier M. SE28 2F 50
Harries Rd. TN2: Tun W 7K 151
Harriet Dr. ME1: Roch 9L 79
Harriets Cnr. CT5: Seas 9C 226
HARRIETSHAM 2M 141 (3D 28)
Harrietsham Station (Rail) 2M 141 (3D 28)
Harringe La. TN25: Lymp, S'ndge 5E 40
Harrington Road Station (CT) 2H 13
Harrington Way SE18 3A 50
Harriot Cl. CT19: F'stone 4H 189
Harris' All. CT3: Wing 8J 225
Harris Cl. DA11: Nflt 8E 62
Harris Gdns. ME10: Sit 6K 99
Harris Lodge SE6 6F 54
Harrison Dr. ME3: H Hals 1H 67
ME17: H'shm 2N 141

Hazlemere Rd.—Highfield Cl.

Hazlemere Rd. CT5: Seas .6C 226
Hazling Dane CT15: S'wll .7M 219
Hazlitt Dr. ME16: Maid .4A 126
Hazlitt Theatre .5D 126
HEADCORN .8K 191 (7B 28)
Headcorn Dr. CT2: Cant .7N 167
Headcorn Gdns. CT9: Clift .3J 209
Headcorn Rd. BR1: Brom .1J 69
ME8: Gill .8L 81
ME17: Graf G, Bou Ma .6D 28
ME17: Graf G, S'wy .9N 141
ME17: S'wy, Len .9J 201
ME17: Sut V .9A 140 (5A 28)
ME17: Ulc .6C 28
TN12: S'hrst .2K 223 (1K 37)
TN17: Frit, H'crn .2A 38
TN27: Bidd .6L 163 (2C 38)
TN27: Smar .1D 38
Headcorn Station (Rail) .9L 191 (1B 38)
Head Hill Rd. ME13: Fav, G'ney .6C 20
Headingley Rd. ME16: Alltn .3M 125
Headley Ct. TN8: Eden .5D 184
Headley Dr. CR0: Croy .8E 82 (5J 13)
Headley Rd. KT18: Eps .7A 12
Head Race, The ME15: Maid .7A 126
Heaf Gdns. ME20: Aylfd .9K 109
Healy Dr. BR6: Orp .5H 85
Heard Way ME10: Sit .6J 99
HEARNDEN GREEN .6B 28
Hearne Cl. ME10: Sit .6K 99
Hearn's Rd. BR5: St P .7L 71
Heartenoak Rd. TN18: Hawkh .3C 192 (7H 37)
Heart In Hand Rd. CT6: H Bay .5N 195 (3A 22)
HEARTS DELIGHT .1C 114 (5E 18)
Hearts Delight ME9: B'den .1C 114 (5E 18)
Hearts Delight La. CT3: Pres .7C 22
CT3: Wing .7C 22
Hearts Delight Rd.
ME9: B'den, T'stall .1C 114 (6E 18)
Heartwood Dr. TN23: Ashf .7C 158
Heath Av. DA7: Bexhth .6M 51
Heath Cl. BR5: Orp .1L 85
BR8: Swanl .5F 72
CT2: Sturry .4E 168
Heathclose Av. DA1: Dart .5J 59
Heathclose Rd. DA1: Dart .6H 59 (7G 7)
Heathcote Cl. ME20: Aylfd .8K 109
Heath Ct. CT15: St Marg .7B 214
Heathdene Dr. DA17: Belv .4C 52
Heath End Rd. DA5: Bex'y .6F 58
Heatherbank BR7: Chst .5C 70
SE9 .9B 50
Heather Bank TN12: Pad W .9M 147
Heatherbank Cl. DA1: Cray .4F 58
Heather Cl. CT9: Mgte .5A 208
ME5: Chat'm .7C 94
ME10: Sit .8H 99
SE13 .5G 54
Heather Ct. DA14: Sidc .2M 71
Heather Dr. DA1: Dart .5H 59
ME15: Maid .7E 126
TN30: St Mic .4C 224
Heather End BR8: Swanl .7E 72
Heather Rd. SE12 .7K 55
Heatherside Rd. DA14: Sidc .8L 57
Heathers, The TN17: Cran .9A 176
Heather Wlk. TN10: Tonb .9H 133
(not continuous)
Heather Way CR2: S Croy .9A 82
Heatherwood Cl. ME17: Kgswd .6G 140
Heathfield BR7: Chst .2E 70
ME17: L'ly .4A 140
Heathfield Av. CT16: Dover .2G 181
ME14: Pen H .2F 126
Heathfield Cl. BR2: Kes .6M 83
ME5: Chat'm .4E 94
ME14: Pen H .2E 126
Heathfield Gdns. TN32: Rob .4B 44
Heathfield La. BR7: Chst .2D 70 (1C 14)
Heathfield Pde. BR8: Swanl .5D 72
Heathfield Rd. BR1: Brom .3J 69
BR2: Kes .6M 83 (4A 14)
DA6: Bexhth .2A 58
ME14: Pen H .2E 126
TN13: S'oaks .4G 118
TN24: Ashf .7G 159
Heathfields TN2: Tun W .1K 157
Heathfield Ter. BR8: Swanl .5E 72
SE18 .6G 51
W4 .4A 4
Heathfield Va. CR2: S Croy .9A 82
Heathfield Way CT4: B'hm .8D 162
Heath Gdns. DA1: Dart .6K 59
Heath Gro. ME16: Barm .7L 125
Heath Ho. DA15: Sidc .9H 57
Heathlands Ri. DA1: Dart .4J 59
Heath La. (Lwr.) DA1: Dart .6K 59 (7G 7)
Heath La. (Up.) DA1: Dart .7H 59 (7G 7)
Heathlee Rd. DA1: Cray .4F 58
SE3 .2J 55
Heathley End BR7: Chst .2E 70
Heathorn St. ME14: Maid .4E 126
Heath Pk. Dr. BR1: Brom .6A 70
Heath Ri. BR2: Shortl .9J 69
Heath Rd. DA1: Cray .4G 59
DA5: Bex'y .6D 58
ME15: W Far, Hunt, E Far .3J 137 (4G 27)
ME16: Barm .6K 125 (2G 27)
ME17: Cox, Lint .5M 137 (4G 27)
ME17: L'ly .4A 140 (4A 28)
ME17: Lint, Bou Mo .4H 27
RM16: Ors, Grays .3B 8
TN26: App .7H 39
HEATH SIDE .8G 58
Heathside BR5: Pet W .2E 84
TN26: App .7H 39
Heathside Av. DA7: Bexhth .8N 51
ME17: Cox .4N 137
Heath St. DA1: Dart .5L 59
NW3 .1D 4
Heath Ter. TN12: Horsm .7B 196
Heath, The CT5: Whits .4K 227
ME19: E Mal .4C 124 (1E 26)
TN12: Horsm .7C 196
Heathview Av. DA1: Cray .4F 58
Heathview Cres. DA1: Dart .6H 59
Heathview Dr. SE2 .6M 51
Heath Vs. SE18 .5H 51
HEATHWAY .2E 6
Heathway CR0: Croy .4C 82
Heath Way DA8: Erith .8D 52
Heathway RM9: Dag .1E 6
RM10: Dag .1E 6
Heathwood Dr. CT11: Ram .3J 211
Heathwood Gdns. BR8: Swanl .5D 72
SE7 .4A 50
Heathwood Point SE23 .8A 54
Heathwood Wlk. DA5: Bex'y .6F 58
Heaton Rd. CT1: Cant .4L 171
HEAVERHAM .8E 104 (7J 15)
Heaverham Rd. TN15: Kems'g .8B 104 (7H 15)
Heavitree Cl. SE18 .5F 50
Heavitree Rd. SE18 .5F 50
(not continuous)
Hectorage Rd. TN9: Tonb .7J 145 (7K 25)
Hector St. SE18 .4G 50
Hedge Barton Countryside Home Pk.
TN3: Ford .9G 149
Hedgemans Rd. RM9: Dag .1D 6
Hedgend Ind. Est. CT7: St N .7M 215
Hedge Pl. Rd. DA9: G'hithe .4F 60 (6J 7)
Hedgerows TN23: Ashf .2B 160
Hedgerows, The DA11: Nflt .7D 62
Hedgerow, The ME14: Weav .4H 127
Hedges, The ME14: Pen H .2D 126
Hedge Wlk. SE6 .1E 68
Hedgley M. SE12 .3J 55
Hedgley St. SE12 .3J 55
Hedley St. ME14: Maid .4D 126
Heel La. CT2: B Oak .3B 168
Heel Rd. ME13: Throw .3J 29
Heights Ter. CT17: Dover .6H 181
Heights, The BR3: Beck'm .3F 68
(not continuous)
CT5: Whits .6E 226
Helder Gro. SE12 .5J 55
Helding Cl. CT6: H Bay .5J 195
Helegan Cl. BR6: Chels .5H 85
Helena Av. CT9: Mgte .5C 208 (1H 23)
Helena Corniche CT20: S'gte .8C 188
Helena Rd. CT18: Cap F .2C 174
Helena Vs. CT20: Hythe .8B 188
Helen Cl. DA1: Dart .5J 59
Helen Keller Cl. TN10: Tonb .2K 145
Helen St. SE18 .4D 50
Helen Thompson Cl. ME9: Iwade .8K 197
Hellfire Corner & Underground Hospital .4L 181
Hellyar Ct. ME1: Roch .8N 79
Helmdon Cl. CT12: Ram .2G 210
Helvellyn Av. CT11: Ram .5F 210
Helvetia St. SE6 .7C 54
Hemmings Cl. DA14: Sidc .7K 57
HEMPSTEAD .5K 95 (4K 17)
Hempstead La. ME9: Bap, Tonge .8M 99 (5G 19)
Hempstead Rd. ME7: Hpstd .8J 95
(not continuous)
ME7: Hpstd .5K 17
Hempstead Valley Dr. ME7: Hpstd .5K 95 (4K 17)
Hempstead Valley Shop. Cen. ME7: Hpstd .8K 95
Hempton Hill TN25: M Hor .3G 41
HEMSTED .2H 41
Hemsted Rd. DA8: Erith .7F 52
Henbane Cl. ME14: Weav .4H 127
Henbury La. CT4: Elham, Acr .7K 31
Hendal Hill TN3: Groom .7H 155 (4G 35)
Henderson Dr. DA1: Dart .2N 59 (6H 7)
Henderson Rd. TN16: Big H .2B 164
Hendley Dr. TN17: Cran .7C 176
Hendry Ho. ME3: C'den .7B 66
Hendy Rd. ME6: Snod .2F 108
Henfield Cl. DA5: Bex'y .4B 58
Hengist Av. CT9: Mgte .4F 208
Hengist Ct. ME14: Maid .5D 126
Hengist Fld. ME9: B'den .2A 114
Hengist Rd. CT7: Birch .4B 206
CT8: Birch, Wgte S .3J 207
CT14: Deal .3N 177
DA8: Erith .7C 52
SE12 .5L 55
Hengist Way BR2: Shortl .7H 69
Hengrave Rd. SE23 .5A 54
Hengrove Ct. DA5: Bex'y .6N 57
Henham Gdns. TN12: E Peck .1M 147
HENHURST .4K 77 (2D 16)
Henhurst Rd. DA12: Cobh .5J 77 (2D 16)
DA13: Cobh .5J 77
Heniker La. ME17: Sut V, E Sut .5A 28
Henley Bus. Pk. ME2: Med E .5A 80
Henley Cl. ME5: Chat'm .5D 94
ME8: Gill .3N 95
TN2: Tun W .9J 151
Henley Deane DA11: Nflt .9D 62
Henley Flds. ME14: Weav .3H 127
TN30: St Mic .5C 224
Henley Mdws. TN30: Tent .5B 224
Henley Rd. E16 .2B 50
TN12: Pad W .8M 147
HENLEY STREET .9L 77 (3D 16)
Henley St. DA13: Lud'n .9L 77 (3D 16)
Henley Vw. TN30: St Mic .5C 224
Hennel Cl. SE23 .8A 54
Henniker Cl. CT16: Dover .8E 178
Henniker Gdns. E6 .2A 6
Henrietta Chase ME4: Chat'm .2E 80
Henry Cooper Way SE9 .8N 55
Henry Ct. CT1: Cant .3M 171
Henryson Rd. SE4 .3D 54
Henry St. BR1: Brom .4L 69
ME4: Chat'm .9E 80
ME8: Rain .2C 96
Henry Tudor Ct. SE9 .5E 56
Henshill La. TN18: Hawkh .7B 192
Henson Cl. BR6: Farnb .3D 84
Henville Rd. BR1: Brom .4L 69
Henwick Rd. SE9 .1N 55
Henwood TN24: Ashf .7H 159
HENWOOD GREEN .8D 152 (2B 36)
Henwood Grn. Rd. TN2: Pem .7C 152 (2B 36)
Henwood Ind. Est. TN24: Ashf .7J 159
Henwoods Cres. TN2: Pem .8C 152
Henwoods Mt. TN2: Pem .8D 152
Hepburn Gdns. BR2: Shortl .2H 83
Hepplewhite M. ME5: Chat'm .1C 110
Herald Wlk. DA1: Dart .3N 59
Herbert Pl. SE18 .6D 50
Herbert Rd. BR2: Shortl .8N 69
BR8: Swanl .2J 73
CT11: Ram .6G 210
DA7: Bexhth .9N 51
DA10: Swans .4M 61
ME4: Chat'm .9D 80
ME8: Gill .3A 96
SE18 .5B 6
SE18 .7C 50
(not continuous)
TN24: Ashf .3H 161
Herberts Ct. ME3: Lwr Sto .8C 204
Herbert St. CT17: Dover .3G 181
Herdsdown ME3: Hoo .8G 66
Herdson Rd. CT20: F'stone .6G 188
Hereford Cl. ME8: Rain .1N 95
TN24: Kenn .3G 158
Hereford Gdns. CT7: Birch .5E 206
SE13 .3H 55
Hereford Rd. ME15: Maid .1F 138
HERESON .5J 211
Hereson Rd. CT11: Ram .4K 211 (4K 23)
Hereward Av. CT7: Birch .3D 206
Hereward Lincoln Ho. *DA11: Nflt* .*4C 62*
(off London Rd.)
Heritage Cl. CT5: Seas .7C 226
Heritage Dr. ME7: Gill .2J 95
Heritage Gdns. CT16: Dover .4K 181
Heritage Hill BR2: Kes .6M 83
Heritage Quay DA12: Grav'nd .4H 63
Heritage Rd. CT20: F'stone .5D 188
ME5: Chat'm .5D 94
Herman Ter. ME4: Chat'm .9D 80
Hermitage Cl. CT21: Hythe .6J 199
Hermitage Ct. TN9: Tonb .5J 145
Hermitage Ct. Bus. Cen. ME16: Maid .4K 125
Hermitage La. ME14: Det .8J 111 (7K 17)
ME16: Maid .1K 125 (1G 27)
ME17: Bou Mo .5K 27
ME20: Aylfd .1K 125
ME20: Aylfd, Barm .1G 27
NW2 .1C 4
SW16 .1F 13
Hermitage Rd. ME3: 'm .1G 79 (1F 17)
SE19 .1G 13
Hermit Rd. E16 .2K 5
HERNE .6H 195 (3K 21)
Herne Av. CT6: H Bay .4H 195
HERNE BAY .2F 194 (2J 21)
Herne Bay Angling .2D 194
Herne Bay Clock Tower .2G 194
Herne Bay Mus. & Art Gallery .2G 195
Herne Bay Pier .1F 194
Herne Bay Rd. CT2: Sturry .4D 168
CT2: Sturry .5J 21
CT3: B Oak, Sturry .5J 21
CT3: Sturry .4D 168
CT5: Whits .2K 227 (3G 21)
Herne Bay Rowing Club .2C 194
Herne Bay Sailing Club .2H 195
Herne Bay Station (Rail) .4F 194 (3J 21)
Herne Bay W. Ind. Est. CT6: H Bay .4D 194
HERNE COMMON .8G 195 (4J 21)
Herne Dr. CT6: H Bay .5D 194
HERNE HILL .6G 5
Herne Hill SE24 .6G 5
Herne Hill Rd. SE24 .6G 5
Herne Hill Station (Rail) .6F 5
HERNE POUND .7K 123 (2C 26)
Herne Rd. CT6: H Bay .9F 194 (4J 21)
ME8: Gill .1M 95
Herne St. CT6: H Bay .6H 195 (3K 21)
Herneville Gdns. CT6: H Bay .3J 195
Herne Windmill .5H 195 (3K 21)
HERNHILL .6D 20
Hern, The TN15: Bor G .4B 122
Heron Apartments ME15: Maid .3H 139
Heron Cl. ME9: Lwr Hal .3L 225
TN8: Eden .4C 184
Heron Ct. BR2: Shortl .7M 69
Heron Cres. DA14: Sidc .8G 56
Herondale CR2: S Croy .9A 82
HERONDEN .2E 32
Heronden Rd. CT13: E'try .4H 183 (2E 32)
ME15: Maid .4J 139
Heron Dr. ME12: Minst .7J 221
Heron Forstal Av. CT18: H'nge .8L 193
Herongate Rd. BR8: Swanl .2F 72
Heron Hill DA17: Belv .5A 52 (4E 6)
Heron Hill La. DA13: Meop .7E 90
Heron Ho. DA14: Sidc .8K 57
TN23: Ashf .9D 158
Heron Lodge CT16: Dover .2G 180
Heron Quays Station (DLR) .3J 5
Heron Rd. ME20: Lark .9D 108
Herons Cl. CT4: Chil'm .8K 175
Herons Swimming Pool .2G 195
Heron's Way CT21: Hythe .8D 198
Herons Way TN2: Pem .6D 152
Herontye Dr. RH19: E Grin .4A 34
Heron Wlk. TN23: Ashf .1C 160
Heron Way ME3: Lwr Sto .8C 204
ME5: Chat'm .6D 94
RM20: W Thur .4K 7
Hero Wlk. ME1: Roch .4N 93
Herron Ct. BR2: Shortl .7J 69
Herschell Rd. CT7: Birch .3E 206
SE23 .5B 54
Herschell Rd. E. CT14: Walm .7M 177
Herschell Rd. W. CT14: Walm .7M 177
Herschell Sq. CT14: Walm .7M 177
HERSDEN .2L 169 (5A 22)
Hertford Ct. CT1: Cant .2B 172
Hertford Ho. *CT11: Ram* .*6J 211*
(off Hertford Pl.)
Hertford Pl. CT11: Ram .6J 211
Hertford Rd. CT9: Mgte .5G 208
Hertford St. CT11: Ram .6H 211
Hertford Wlk. DA17: Belv .5B 52
Herts Cres. ME15: Loose .5C 138
Hertsfield Av. ME2: Strood .2L 79
Hertsfield Ho. *TN9: Tonb* .*7H 145*
(off Quarry Hill Rd.)
Herying Cl. ME2: Hall'g .7F 92
Hesiers Hill CR6: Warl .7K 13
Hesiers Rd. CR6: Warl .7K 13
Hesketh Av. DA2: Dart .6B 60
Heskett Pk. TN2: Pem .7D 152
Hestia Way *TN23: Kgnt* .*4C 160*
(off Forum Way)
Hetherhale Farm Rd. CT7: St N .3D 22
HEVER .7D 24
Hever Av. TN15: W King .6E 88
Hever Castle & Gardens .7D 24
Hever Cl. ME15: Maid .2J 139
Hever Cotts. DA12: Sole S .8K 77
Hever Ct. Rd. DA11: Grav'nd .1G 77
DA12: Grav'nd .2H 77 (1C 16)
Hever Cft. ME2: Strood .7K 79
SE9 .9C 56
Hever Gdns. BR1: Brom .5C 70
Heverham Rd. SE18 .4G 50
Hever Ho. ME2: Strood .3N 79
Hever La. TN8: Cowd, Hever .1D 34
Hever Pl. CT2: Cant .8N 167
ME10: Sit .8D 98
ME16: Maid .6B 126
Hever Rd. TN8: Eden, Hever .7D 184 (7C 24)
TN8: Hever .5A 142
TN8: Hever, Chid .7D 24
TN15: W King .7E 88
Heversham Rd. DA7: Bexhth .9B 52
Hever Station (Rail) .7D 24
Hever Wood Rd. TN15: W King .8E 88
Hewett Pl. BR8: Swanl .7E 72
Hewitt Cl. CR0: Croy .4D 82
ME7: Gill .6J 81
ME16: Alltn .2A 126
Hewitt Rd. CT16: Dover .4J 181
Hewitts Pl. TN24: W'boro .9K 159
Hewitts Rd. BR6: Chels .8A 86 (5E 14)
HEWITTS ROUNDABOUT .8A 86 (5E 14)
Hexal Rd. SE6 .8H 55
HEXTABLE .3G 73 (1F 15)
Hextable Cl. ME16: Alltn .2N 125
TN23: Ashf .3D 160
Hextable Heritage Cen. .3F 72
Heyford Cl. CT18: H'nge .8L 193
Heygate Av. SS1: Sth S .1E 10
Heywood M. CT1: Cant .1A 172
Hibbs Cl. BR8: Swanl .5E 72
Hibernia Dr. DA12: Grav'nd .8L 63
Hibernia Point *SE2* .*2M 51*
(off Wolvercote Rd.)
Hibernia St. CT11: Ram .6J 211
Hichisson Rd. SE15 .3A 54
HICKMANS GREEN .4K 165 (7D 20)
Hickory Dell ME7: Hpstd .5K 95
HICKS FORSTAL .5K 21
Hicks Forstal Rd. CT3: Hoath .5J 21
Hidden Mdw. ME13: Fav .5F 186
Higgins La. ME4: Chat'm .7C 80
HIGHAM
Higham Upshire .1G 78 (1F 17)
Lower Higham .4H 65
Chilton Hills .9G 65
Higham Cl. ME15: Maid .7A 126
Higham Gdns. TN10: Tonb .1M 145
Higham La. CT4: Bis .9J 173
TN10: Tonb .3L 145 (5A 26)
TN11: Tonb .7L 133 (4A 26)
TN32: Rob .3C 44
Higham Pk. House & Gardens .9K 173
Higham Rd. ME3: Cliffe .4B 176 (6G 9)
ME3: Wain .1A 80 (1H 17)
Higham School Rd. TN10: Tonb .1L 145
Higham Station (Rail) .7H 65 (7F 9)
HIGHAM UPSHIRE .1G 78
Higham Vw. ME14: S'lng .6B 110
HIGHAM WOOD .2L 145 (5A 26)
High Bank ME1: Roch .1A 94
High Banks ME15: Loose .3C 138 (3H 27)
Highbanks Cl. DA16: Well .7K 51
High Beeches BR6: Chels .7J 85
DA14: Sidc .1N 71
TN2: Tun W .8K 151
Highberry ME19: Leyb .8C 108
Highbourne Pk. ME17: Len .3G 29
Highbrook Rd. SE3 .1N 55
High Broom Cres. BR4: W W'ck .1E 82
High Broom Rd. TN6: Crowb .7F 35
HIGH BROOMS .7J 151 (2K 35)
High Brooms Rd. TN4: Tun W .6H 151 (2K 35)
High Brooms Station (Rail) .7J 151 (2K 35)
HIGHBURY .1F 5
Highbury & Islington Station (Rail & Tube) .1F 5
Highbury Cl. BR4: W W'ck .3E 82
HIGHBURY CORNER .1F 5
Highbury Gdns. CT12: Ram .1F 210
Highbury Gro. N5 .1F 5
Highbury La. TN30: Tent .8B 224
Highbury Pk. N5 .1F 5
Highbury Wlk. CT12: Ram .2F 210
Highclere St. SE26 .9B 54
Highcombe Cl. SE9 .6N 55
High Cft. Cotts. BR8: Swanl .7H 73
Highcroft Grn. ME15: Maid .4J 139
Highcross Rd. DA13: Sflt .1K 75 (1K 15)
High Cross Rd. TN15: Ivy H .8H 121 (2K 25)
High Dewar Rd. ME8: Rain .3C 96
High Elms ME8: Rain .1A 96
High Elms Country Pk. .8F 84
High Elms Nature Cen. .8F 84
High Elms Rd. BR6: Downe .2C 100 (6B 14)
Higher Dr. CR8: Purl .6F 13
Highfield Av. BR6: Chels .7H 85
DA8: Erith .6C 52
Highfield Cl. CT2: Blean .8H 167
CT12: Ram .1F 210
CT21: Salt .4H 199
ME8: Gill .4N 95

Hill St. Bottom—Hook Green

Hill St. Bottom CT4: Elms 6G 31
TN25: Elms, Bods 7F 31
Hill, The CT3: L'brne 2K 173 (1A 32)
DA11: Nflt 4B 62 (6B 8)
TN17: Cran 8D 176
TN27: Char'g 2K 175 (5H 29)
HILL TOP 5N 153
Hilltop CT5: Whits 6F 226
Hill Top ME15: Hunt 5H 137 (4F 27)
Hilltop TN9: Tonb 8H 145
Hill Top TN17: Goud 2H 37
Hill Top Cotts. ME17: Lint 6B 138
Hilltop Gdns. BR6: Orp 3G 84
DA1: Dart 3N 59
Hill Top Rd. CT6: H Bay 2J 195
Hilltop Rd. ME2: Strood 3N 79
ME12: Minst 7H 221
Hillview CT9: Mgte 6B 208
Hill Vw. TN15: Bor G 2N 121
Hillview TN15: Bor G 5M 121
Hill Vw. TN24: Ashf 6G 159
Hill Vw. Cl. TN15: Bor G 2N 121
Hill Vw. Cres. BR6: Orp 2G 85
Hill Vw. Dr. DA16: Well 9G 50
SE28 1G 50
Hillview Ho. DA12: Grav'nd 6H 63
Hill Vw. Rd. BR6: Orp 2H 85
Hillview Rd. BR7: Chst 1C 70
CT2: Cant 9J 167
CT5: Whits 5F 226
Hill Vw. Rd. DA3: Long 6A 76
TN4: R'hall 1C 156
TN11: Hild 2F 144
Hill Vw. Way ME5: Chat'm 6B 94
Hillworth BR3: Beck'm 5E 68
Hillydeal Rd. TN14: Otf 6K 103
Hillyfield Cl. ME2: Strood 3K 79
Hillyfield Rd. TN23: Ashf 1E 160
Hilly Flds. Cres. SE4 1D 54
Hillyfields Ri. TN23: Ashf 9E 158
Hilton Cl. ME13: Fav 6H 187
Hilton Dr. ME10: Sit 5C 98
Hilton Ho. SE4 2A 54
Hilton Rd. ME3: Cli W 6M 65
TN23: Ashf 8D 158
Hinchliffe Way CT9: Mgte 5H 209
Hind Cl. TN29: Dym 7B 182
Hind Cres. DA8: Erith 6E 52
Hinde Cl. ME10: Sit 4G 98
Hindmans Way RM9: Dag 2E 6
Hindsley's Pl. SE23 7A 54
Hines Ter. ME5: Chat'm 2F 94
Hinksden Rd. TN17: Bendn 7K 37
TN18: Hawkh 7K 37
Hinksey Path SE2 2M 51
Hinstock Rd. SE18 6E 50
Hinton Cl. SE9 6A 56
Hinton Cres. ME7: Hpstd 5K 95
Hinton Rd. SE24 6F 5
HINXHILL 1C 40
Hinxhill Rd. TN24: W'boro 1N 161
TN24: W'boro, Hin 1C 40
TN25: Hin 1C 40
Hirst Cl. CT16: Dover 9G 178
Historic Dockyard, The 5C 80 (2H 17)
Historic Dockyard Vis. Cen., The 5D 80
Hitchen Hatch La. TN13: S'oaks 6H 119
Hither Chantlers TN3: Lang G 3A 156
Hither Farm Rd. SE3 1M 55
Hitherfield TN27: Char'g 3J 175
HITHER GREEN 4H 55 (6K 5)
Hither Grn. La. SE13 3F 54 (6K 5)
Hither Green Station (Rail) 4H 55 (6K 5)
Hive La. DA11: Nflt 4A 62
(not continuous)
Hive, The DA11: Nflt 4A 62
HMP Aldington TN25: Aldtn 5D 40
HMP Cookham Wood ME1: Roch 3M 93
HMP Elmley ME12: E'chu 9B 202
HMP Maidstone 4D 126
HMP Standford Hill ME12: E'chu 7B 202
HMP Swaleside ME12: E'chu 8B 202
HM Young Offenders & Prison
East Sutton Pk. ME1: E Sut 9D 140
HM Young Offenders Institution
CT17: Dover 6G 180
ME1: Roch 2M 93
HOAD COMMON 4J 133
HOADEN 6D 22
Hoades Wood Rd. CT2: Sturry 4F 168
Hoadleys La. TN6: Crowb 6F 35
Hoads Wood Gdns. TN25: Ashf 4C 158
HOATH 4A 22
Hoath Cl. ME8: Gill 4K 95
HOATH CORNER 3C 148 (1E 34)
Hoath Hill TN32: Mount 5C 44
Hoath La. ME8: Gill 4L 95 (4K 17)
Hoath Mdw. TN12: Horsm 7C 196
Hoath Rd. CT2: Sturry 3G 168
CT3: Hoath, Sturry 3G 168 (6K 21)
Hoath Way ME8: Gill, Hpstd 4L 95 (4K 17)
Hobart Cres. CT16: Dover 1G 181
Hobart Gdns. ME10: Sit 7D 98
Hobart Rd. CT12: Ram 3E 210
Hobbs La. TN31: Beckl 3J 45
Hoblands End BR7: Chst 2G 71
HOCKENDEN 6B 72 (2E 14)
Hockenden La. BR8: Swanl 6B 72 (2E 14)
Hockeredge Gdns. CT8: Wgte S 3L 207
Hockers Cl. ME14: Det 1K 127
Hockers La. ME14: Weav 3J 127
ME14: Weav 1K 27
HOCKLEY 2K 29
Hockley Sole CT18: Cap F 2B 42
Hoddesdon Rd. DA17: Belv 5B 52
Hode La. CT4: Brid 6D 172 (2J 31)
Hodges Gap CT9: Clift 2G 208
Hodgson Cres. ME6: Snod 1E 108
Hodgson Rd. CT5: Seas 6A 226
Hodsoll Ct. BR5: St M Cry 8M 71
HODSOLL STREET 9C 90 (5B 16)
Hodsoll St. TN15: Ash 9C 90 (5B 16)
Hodson Cres. BR5: St M Cry 8M 71
Hoever Ho. SE6 9F 54
Hogarth Cl. CT6: H Bay 2M 195
Hogarth La. W4 4A 4
HOGARTH ROUNDABOUT 5A 4
Hogbarn Cvn. Site ME17: H'shm 6H 201
Hogbarn La. ME17: H'shm, Frin 2D 28
Hogben Cl. CT18: Lym'ge 7K 205
HOGBEN'S HILL 2M 219 (1B 30)
Hogbrook Hill La. CT15: Alk 2C 42
Hogg La. CT4: Up Hard 4H 31
RM17: Grays 4A 8
Hog Green CT4: Elham 7N 183
Hog Hill ME14: Bear 5L 127
TN36: Winch 7K 45
Hog Hole La. TN3: Lamb 5C 36
Hognore La. TN15: Wro 5C 106
Hogs La. DA11: Nflt 8C 62
Hogs Orchard BR8: Swanl 4J 73
Hogtrough Hill TN16: Bras 2H 117
TN16: Bras, S'oaks 1C 24
Holbeach Gdns. DA15: Sidc 4G 57
Holbeach Rd. SE6 5D 54
Holbeam Rd. ME13: E'lng 2J 29
HOLBORN 3F 5
Holborn EC1 3F 5
Holborn La. ME4: Chat'm 7C 80
Holborn Station (Tube) 3F 5
Holborn Viaduct EC1 3F 5
EC4 3F 5
HOLBOROUGH 9E 92 (5F 17)
Holborough M. ME6: Snod 1E 108
Holborough Rd. ME6: Snod 2E 108 (6F 17)
Holbourn Cl. CT6: H Bay 7J 195
Holbrook Dr. CT12: Ram 3F 210
Holbrook Ho. BR7: Chst 4F 70
Holbrook La. BR7: Chst 3F 70
Holbrook Way BR2: Shortl 9B 70 (3B 14)
Holburne Rd. SE3 8A 50
Holcombe Cl. TN16: Westrm 8F 116
Holcombe Pl. *SE4* *1B 54*
(off St Asaph Rd.)
Holcombe Rd. ME1: Roch 9N 79
ME4: Chat'm 1C 94
Holcote Cl. DA17: Belv 3N 51
Holdenby Rd. SE4 3B 54
Holden Cnr. TN4: S'bgh 5E 150
Holdenhurst TN23: Ashf 3C 160
Holden Pk. Rd. TN4: S'bgh 6F 150
Holden Rd. TN4: S'bgh 5E 150 (1J 35)
Holder Cl. ME5: Chat'm 5F 94
Holding St. ME8: Rain 2B 96
Hole La. TN8: Eden 1A 184 (5B 24)
Hole Pk. 6B 38
Holford St. TN9: Tonb 6H 145
Holiday Sq. CT9: Mgte 2C 208
HOLLAND 4A 24
Holland Av. SM2: Sutt 5C 12
Holland Cl. BR2: Shortl 3J 83
CT10: B'stairs 3L 209
ME12: S'ness 3C 220
Holland Dr. SE23 8B 54
Holland Ho. *ME1: Roch* *8A 80*
(off St Margarets Bank)
Holland La. RH8: Oxt 4A 24
Holland Pk. Av. W11 3C 4
HOLLAND PARK ROUNDABOUT 4C 4
Holland Park Station (Tube) 3C 4
Holland Rd. ME5: Chat'm 7B 94
ME14: Maid 4D 126 (1J 27)
RH8: Oxt 4A 24
W14 4C 4
Hollands Av. CT19: F'stone 4M 189
Hollands Cl. DA12: Shorne 1C 78
Hollands Hill CT15: Mart M 4N 179 (6G 33)
Holland Way BR2: Shortl 3J 83
HOLLICONDANE 3H 211
Hollicondane Rd. CT11: Ram 4H 211
Hollies Av. DA15: Sidc 7H 57
Hollies, The DA3: Long 6B 76
DA12: Grav'nd 2J 77
Holligrave Rd. BR1: Brom 4K 69
Hollin Cl. TN4: Tun W 1F 156
HOLLINGBOURNE 6G 129 (2C 28)
Hollingbourne Av. DA7: Bexhth 8A 52
Hollingbourne Hill
ME17: Holl 6H 129 (2C 28)
Hollingbourne Rd. ME8: Gill 9M 81
Hollingbourne Station (Rail) 6E 128 (2B 28)
HOLLINGROVE 5A 44
Hollington Ct. BR7: Chst 2D 70
Hollington Pl. TN24: Ashf 7F 158
Hollingworth Ct. *ME14: Maid* *5F 126*
(off Ashford Rd.)
Hollingworth Rd. BR5: Pet W 9D 70
ME15: Maid 3J 139
Hollingworth Way TN16: Westrm 8F 116
HOLLOWAY 1E 4
Holloway Rd. N7 1F 5
N19 1E 4
Holloway Road Station (Tube) 1F 5
Hollow La. CT1: Cant 4L 171 (1H 31)
ME6: Snod 3D 108 (6E 16)
ME9: H'lip 6G 96 (4C 18)
RH7: Dor'land 1A 34
RH19: E Grin 1A 34
Hollowmede CT1: Cant 4L 171
Hollow Rd. CT3: Hoath, C'let 4A 22
Hollow Shore ME13: Fav 5A 20
Hollows Trees Dr. TN11: Leigh 5A 144
HOLLOW STREET 4B 22
Hollow Wood Rd. CT17: Dover 4D 180
Holly Bank TN12: Brenc 6N 153
Hollybank Hill ME10: Sit 7F 98
Hollybrake Cl. BR7: Chst 3F 70
Holly Bush Cl. TN13: S'oaks 6K 119
Holly Bush Ct. TN13: S'oaks 6K 119
HOLLYBUSHES 1F 29
Holly Bush La. BR6: Chels 7B 86
Hollybush La. CT3: Sturry 8K 169 (7A 22)
Holly Bush La. TN13: S'oaks 6K 119
Hollybush Rd. DA12: Grav'nd 7H 63
Holly Bush Sports Complex 6K 119
Holly Cl. BR3: Beck'm 7F 68
CT10: B'stairs 9G 208
CT13: E'try 3L 183
Holly Cl. CT19: F'stone 4L 189
CT21: Hythe 5L 199
ME5: Chat'm 2F 94
ME7: Gill 6H 81
Holly Ct. *DA14: Sidc* *9K 57*
(off Sidcup Hill)
Holly Cres. BR3: Beck'm 8C 68
Hollycroft ME2: Cux 1G 92
Hollydale Dr. BR2: Shortl 4B 84
Hollydene *BR2: Shortl* *4J 69*
(off Beckenham Rd.)
Hollydown Way E11 1K 5
Holly Farm Rd. ME15: Otham 2M 139 (3A 28)
Hollyfield Rd. KT5: Surb 3A 12
Holly Gdns. CT9: Mgte 3G 209
DA7: Bexhth 2D 58
Holly Hedge Ter. SE13 3G 54
HOLLY HILL 5D 16
Holly Hill CT4: Elham 7K 31
Holly Hill Public Open Space 9L 91
Holly Hill Rd. CT2: Denst 1N 165
DA8: Erith 5C 52
DA13: Meop 8L 91 (5D 16)
DA17: Belv, Erith 5C 52
ME13: Denst 1N 165
Holly Ho. ME12: S'ness 2C 220
Holly La. CT9: Mgte 3G 209
SM7: Bans 7C 12
Holly Mdws. TN23: Ashf 7B 158
Hollymeoak Rd. CR5: Coul 7E 12
Holly Rd. BR6: Chels 8J 85
CT11: Ram 4J 211
DA1: Dart 6L 59
ME2: Strood 6J 79
ME2: Wain 2A 80
TN29: St M Bay 2M 215
Hollyshaw Cl. TN2: Tun W 3J 157
Hollytree Av. BR8: Swanl 5F 72
Hollytree Cl. ME17: Kgswd 6G 140
Hollytree Dr. ME3: High'm 1F 78
Holly Tree Ho. *SE4* *1C 54*
(off Brockley Rd.)
Hollytree Pde. *DA14: Sidc* *2L 71*
(off Sidcup Hill)
Holly Vs. ME15: W Far 2H 137
Hollywood La. ME3: Wain 2N 79 (1H 17)
TN15: W King 2F 104
Hollywoods CR0: Croy 9C 82
Hollywood Way DA8: Erith 7J 53
Holman M. CT1: Cant 3N 171
Holmbury Gro. CR0: Croy 8C 82
Holmbury Mnr. DA14: Sidc 9J 57
Holmbury Pk. BR1: Brom 3A 70
Holm Ct. SE12 8L 55
Holmcroft Way BR2: Shortl 8B 70
Holmdale Rd. BR7: Chst 1E 70
Holmdene Cl. BR3: Beck'm 5F 68
Holmdene Ct. BR1: Brom 6A 70
Holme Lacey Rd. SE12 4J 55
Holme Oak Cl. CT1: Cant 4M 171
Holmes Cl. ME3: H Hals 2H 67
Holmesdale Cl. ME15: Loose 5C 138
Holmesdale Hill DA4: S Dar 4C 74 (2J 15)
Holmesdale M. ME6: Snod 4D 108
Holmesdale Rd. DA4: S Dar 4C 74 (2J 15)
DA7: Bexhth 9M 51
TN13: S'oaks 5K 119
Holmesdale Ter. *CT20: F'stone* *7K 189*
(off Sandgate Rd.)
Holmesley Rd. SE23 4B 54
Holmes Place Bromley (Sports Club) 3D 180
Holmewood Ridge TN3: Lang G 2M 155
Holmewood Rd. TN4: Tun W 7J 151
Holmhurst Cl. TN4: Tun W 1F 156
Holmhurst Rd. DA17: Belv 5C 52
Holmlea Cl. TN24: W'boro 9K 159
Holmleigh Av. DA1: Dart 3K 59
Holm Mill La. ME17: H'shm 2K 141 (3C 28)
Holm Oak Gdns. CT10: B'stairs 9K 209
Holmoaks ME8: Rain 1A 96
ME14: Maid 4F 126
Holmoaks Ho. BR3: Beck'm 5F 68
Holmscroft Rd. CT6: H Bay 2L 195
Holmsdale Gro. DA7: Bexhth 9F 52
Holmshaw Cl. SE26 9B 54
Holmside ME7: Gill 1H 95
Holmside Av. ME12: Minst 6E 220
Holmwood Rd. TN23: Ashf 2C 160
Holness Rd. CT3: Ash 4C 216
Holstein Way DA18: Erith 3M 51
Holters La. CT2: Cant 9M 167
Holters Mill CT2: Cant 9M 167
HOLT HILL 1H 125
Holton Cl. CT7: Birch 5F 206
Holt Rd. E16 1A 50
Holt St. CT15: Aysm, Non 4F 162
CT15: Non, Aysm 4C 32
Holt Wood Av. ME20: Aylfd 1H 125
Holtwood Cl. ME8: Gill 6N 95
HOLTYE 3C 34
Holtye Cres. ME15: Maid 7E 126
Holtye Rd. RH19: E Grin 3A 34
RH19: Hamm 3C 34
TN8: Cowd 3C 34
Holwood Pk. Av. BR6: Farnb 5B 84
Holy Ghost All. *CT13: S'wch* *5M 217*
(off St Peter's St.)
Holyoake Mt. DA12: Grav'nd 6J 63
Holyoake Ter. TN13: S'oaks 6H 119
Holyrood Dr. ME12: Minst 7H 221
Holywell Av. CT19: F'stone 3J 189
Holywell Cl. BR6: Chels 5J 85
Holywell Ho. CT19: F'stone 3J 189
Holywell La. ME9: Upc 3J 225 (3C 18)
Home Cotts. CT4: Chart'm 7D 170
Homedean Rd. TN13: Riv 4D 118 (1F 25)
Home Farm BR6: Chels 6B 86
Home Farm Cl. TN11: Leigh 4A 144
Home Farm Ct. TN3: Frant 9J 157
Home Farm La. TN2: Tun W 6L 151
Homefern Ho. *CT9: Mgte* *2D 208*
(off Cobbs Pl.)
Homefield Av. CT14: Deal 4L 177
Homefield Cl. BR5: St P 7K 71
Homefield Cl. BR8: Swanl 6G 72
Homefield Dr. ME8: Rain 1D 96
Homefield Ho. SE23 8A 54
Homefield M. BR3: Beck'm 4D 68
Homefield Ri. BR6: Orp 2J 85
Homefield Rd. BR1: Brom 4M 69 (2A 14)
DA4: S at H 4A 74
TN13: Riv 4F 118
Homefield Row CT14: Deal 4L 177
Homefleet Ho. *CT11: Ram* *5K 211*
(off Wellington Cres.)
Home Gdns. DA1: Dart 4M 59 (6H 7)
Home Hill BR8: Swanl 3G 73
Homelands Cl. TN25: S'ndge 8C 218
Homelands Stadium, The 9D 160
Home Lea BR6: Chels 6H 85
Homeleigh Rd. CT12: Ram 1F 210
SE15 3A 54
Homemead DA9: G'hithe 4H 61
DA12: Grav'nd 5G 63
Home Mead Cl. DA12: Grav'nd 5G 63
Homemead Rd. BR2: Shortl 8B 70
Home Orchard DA1: Dart 4M 59
(not continuous)
Home Pk. Rd. SW19 1C 12
Homepeak Ho. *CT21: Hythe* *6J 199*
(off Bartholomew St.)
Homer Cl. DA7: Bexhth 8D 52
Homer Rd. CR0: Croy 9A 68
Homersham CT1: Cant 4K 171
HOMERTON 1H 5
Homerton High St. E9 1H 5
Homerton Rd. E9 1J 5
Homerton Station (Rail) 1H 5
Homesdale Rd. BR1: Brom 7M 69 (2A 14)
BR2: Shortl 7M 69 (2A 14)
BR5: Pet W 1G 84
Homeside Farm CT4: Up Hard 5H 31
Homespire Ho. *CT1: Cant* *1N 171*
(off Knott's La.)
Homestall Ct. CT2: Cant 7J 167
Homestall Honey Farm 6B 20
Homestall La. ME9: Lyn 7H 19
ME13: Fav 6M 187
Homestall Rd. ME13: Fav 6B 20
RH19: A'hstw 4B 34
SE22 6H 5
Homestead TN23: Ashf 1B 160
Homestead Cl. CT9: Mgte 4D 208
Homestead Ct. CT14: Deal 6K 177
Homestead La. CT15: Ashy 5F 33
Homestead Rd. BR6: Chels 8K 85
SW6 5C 4
TN8: Eden 2B 184
Homestead, The *DA1: Cray* *3F 58*
(off Crayford High St.)
DA1: Dart 4K 59
Homestead Vw. ME9: B'den 9C 98
Homestead Village CT11: Ram 6G 210
Homevale Ho's. CT20: S'gte 8E 188
Home Vw. ME10: Sit 7J 99
Homewards Rd. ME3: Allh 4B 204 (5B 10)
Homewood Av. ME10: Sit 8E 98 (5E 18)
Homewood Cres. BR7: Chst 2G 70
Homewood Rd. CT2: Sturry 5F 168
TN3: Lang G 2N 155
TN30: Tent 6C 224
Homing Leisure Pk. CT5: Seas 8C 226
Hompine Ho. CT20: F'stone 7J 189
Honduras Ter. ME14: Maid 2D 126
Hone St. ME2: Strood 4M 79
Honeyball Wlk. ME9: Tey 7K 223
Honey Bee Glade ME8: Rain 6A 96
Honeybourne Way BR5: Pet W 2F 84
Honey Cl. ME7: Hpstd 6K 95
Honeycrest Ind. Pk. TN12: S'hrst 1J 223
Honeycrock Hill ME9: S'bry 2H 113 (6C 18)
Honeyden Rd. DA14: Sidc 2N 71
Honeyfield BR8: Swanl 2G 72
TN23: Ashf 9C 158
HONEY HILL 4F 166 (6F 21)
Honey Hill CT2: Blean 5F 21
CT2: Blean 2E 166
CT5: Whits, Blean 2E 166 (5F 21)
Honey La. ME15: Otham 2L 139 (3K 27)
Honeypot Cl. ME2: Strood 4M 79
Honeypot La. TN8: Eden 6A 24
TN15: Ash 9B 90
TN15: Kems'g 1B 120 (1J 25)
Honeysuckle Cl. CT9: Mgte 5A 208
ME5: Chat'm 7B 94
ME7: Hpstd 7J 95
Honeysuckle Ct. ME10: Sit 6J 99
Honeysuckle Gdns. CR0: Croy 1A 82
Honeysuckle Rd. CT11: Ram 4K 211
Honeysuckle Way CT6: H Bay 5L 195
Honeywood CT21: S'lng 1E 198
Honeywood Cl. CT1: Cant 9A 168
CT16: Dover 7F 178
CT21: Lymp 5B 198
Honeywood Parkway CT16: Dover 8F 178 (7F 33)
Honeywood Rd. CT16: Dover 7F 178 (7F 33)
Honfleur Rd. CT13: S'wch 6L 217
Honiton Rd. DA16: Well 9H 51
Honley Rd. SE6 5E 54
Honner Cl. CT18: H'nge 9J 193
HONOR OAK 6H 5
Honor Oak Crematorium SE23 3B 54
HONOR OAK PARK 5B 54 (6J 5)
Honor Oak Pk. SE23 4A 54 (6H 5)
Honor Oak Park Station (Rail) 4A 54 (6H 5)
Honor Oak Rd. SE23 7H 5
HONR CORNER 1C 44
Honywood Rd. ME17: Len 8L 201
HOO 7B 212 (4E 22)
Hoo Comn. ME3: C'den 9D 66
Hood Av. BR5: St M Cry 8K 71
Hook Cl. CT20: F'stone 6F 188
ME5: Chat'm 6B 94
Hook Farm Rd. BR2: Shortl 8N 69
Hookfields DA11: Nflt 8D 62
HOOK GREEN
Gravesend 9G 76 (3C 16)
Southfleet 3N 75 (1A 16)

Hook Green—Ifield Rd.

HOOK GREEN
Tunbridge Wells . . . 4C 36
Wilmington . . . 9H 59
Hook Grn. La. DA2: Dart . . . 8G 59 (7F 7)
Hook Grn. Rd. DA13: Sflt . . . 3L 75 (1A 16)
Hook Hill TN5: Wadh . . . 6D 36
Hook La. DA16: Well . . . 2H 57 (6D 6)
ME17: H'shm . . . 2L 141
TN27: Char'g . . . 3H 175 (5H 29)
TN29: B'Ind . . . 3E 46
Hook Rd. KT19: Eps . . . 5A 12
ME6: Snod . . . 2D 108
Hookstead TN26: H Hald . . . 2A 196
Hook Wall TN29: Ivyc . . . 3E 46
Hookwood Cotts. BR6: Prat B . . . 2L 101
Hookwood Rd. BR6: Prat B . . . 2L 101 (6D 14)
Hoo Marina Pk. ME3: Hoo . . . 1H 81
Hoopers La. CT6: H Bay . . . 5L 195
ME3: Allh, St M Hoo . . . 6A 204
ME3: St M Hoo . . . 5A 10
Hooper's Pl. ME1: Roch . . . 8N 79
Hooper's Rd. ME1: Roch . . . 8N 79
Hoopers Yd. TN13: S'oaks . . . 8K 119
Hoo Rd. ME3: Wain . . . 1A 80 (1H 17)
HOO ST WERBURGH . . . 8H 67 (7K 9)
Hoo Swimming Pool . . . 8F 66
Hop Bine Cl. TN12: E Peck . . . 9M 135
Hope Av. TN11: Hdlw . . . 7C 134
Hope Cl. SE12 . . . 8L 55
Hope Cotts. ME15: Maid . . . 3D 138
TN25: Bra L . . . 7K 165
Hope La. TN28: New R . . . 1J 213 (2H 47)
TN29: New R . . . 2H 47
Hope Pk. BR1: Brom . . . 3J 69
Hope Rd. CT14: Deal . . . 5N 177
DA10: Swans . . . 4M 61
HOPE'S GREEN . . . 1J 9
Hopes Gro. TN26: H Hald . . . 2B 196
Hopes Hill ME9: Dod . . . 1G 29
Hopes La. CT12: Ram . . . 1G 210
Hope St. ME4: Chat'm . . . 9D 80
ME12: S'ness . . . 2C 220
(not continuous)
ME14: Maid . . . 3C 126
Hope Ter. ME3: High'm . . . 6H 65
Hope Vs. TN28: New R . . . 2J 213
Hopeville Av. CT10: B'stairs . . . 7H 209
Hopewell Bus. Cen. ME5: Chat'm . . . 3F 94
Hopewell Dr. DA12: Grav'nd . . . 1L 77
ME5: Chat'm . . . 3F 94
Hop Farm Country Pk. . . . 4M 147 (6D 26)
Hop Gdn. TN26: App . . . 7H 39
Hopgarden Cl. TN8: Eden . . . 4D 184
Hop Gdn. Cotts. CT1: Cant . . . 4L 171
Hopgarden La. TN13: S'oaks . . . 1H 131
Hopgarden Rd. TN10: Tonb . . . 2K 145
Hoppers TN12: Five G . . . 8G 147
Hoppers Way TN23: Ashf . . . 1B 160
Hop Pocket Cl. TN17: Siss . . . 3C 222
Hop Pocket La. TN12: Pad W . . . 8L 147
Hopsons Pl. ME12: Minst . . . 7K 221
Hopton Ct. BR2: Shortl . . . 2L 83
Hopton Rd. SE18 . . . 3D 50
Hopwood Gdns. TN4: Tun W . . . 8G 151
Horatio Pl. ME1: Roch . . . 8M 79
(off Fennel Cl.)
HORDEN . . . 2H 37
Horizon Cl. TN4: S'bgh . . . 6H 151
Horizon Ho. BR8: Swanl . . . 7F 72
Horley Cl. DA6: Bexhth . . . 3B 58
Horley Rd. SE9 . . . 9A 56
Horlingham Cl. TN10: Tonb . . . 9K 133
Hornash La. TN26: Shad . . . 9A 160 (3J 39)
Hornbeam Av. ME5: Chat'm . . . 9E 94
TN4: S'bgh . . . 5K 151
Hornbeam Cl. ME20: Lark . . . 9F 108
TN12: Pad W . . . 1L 153
TN23: Ashf . . . 7D 158
Hornbeam La. DA7: Bexhth . . . 9D 52
Hornbeams DA13: Meop . . . 2G 107
Hornbeam Way BR2: Shortl . . . 9C 70
Horncastle Cl. SE12 . . . 5K 55
Horncastle Rd. SE12 . . . 5K 55
Hornchurch Country Pk. . . . 1G 7
Hornchurch Station (Tube) . . . 1G 7
HORNDON ON THE HILL . . . 2D 8
Horndon Rd. SS17: Horn H . . . 2D 8
Hornes Place Chapel . . . 7H 39
Hornet Cl. CT10: B'stairs . . . 1H 211
Hornfair Rd. SE7 . . . 5A 6
Hornfield Cotts. DA13: Meop . . . 8G 91
Horniman Mus. . . . 7H 5
Horning Cl. SE9 . . . 9A 56
Horn La. W3 . . . 3A 4
HORN PARK . . . 3L 55
Horn Pk. Cl. SE12 . . . 3L 55
Hornpark La. SE12 . . . 3L 55
HORNS CROSS
Greenhithe . . . 4E 60 (6J 7)
Northiam . . . 4G 45
Hornsey Rd. N7 . . . 1F 5
N19 . . . 1F 5
HORNS GREEN . . . 8G 100 (7C 14)
HORNS HILL . . . 3C 24
Horns La. ME18: Mere . . . 7J 123 (2C 26)
Horns Lodge TN11: Tonb . . . 8J 133
Horns Lodge Rd. TN15: Stans . . . 1N 105 (5A 16)
Horn's Oak Rd. DA13: Meop . . . 5G 91 (4C 16)
Horns Rd. TN18: Hawkh . . . 7A 192 (1B 44)
HORN STREET
Hythe . . . 7B 188 (5K 41)
West Malling . . . 4C 108 (6E 16)
Horn St. CT19: F'stone . . . 6B 188
CT20: F'stone . . . 6B 188 (5K 41)
CT21: Hythe . . . 8B 188 (5K 41)
Horn Yd. DA12: Grav'nd . . . 4G 63
(off Bank St.)
Horsa Rd. CT7: Birch . . . 4C 206
CT14: Deal . . . 2N 177
DA8: Erith . . . 7C 52
SE12 . . . 5M 55
Horsebridge Rd. CT5: Whits . . . 3F 226
Horsecroft Cl. BR6: Orp . . . 2K 85
Horseferry Rd. SW1 . . . 4E 4
HORSELEES . . . 3K 165 (7D 20)
Horselees Rd. ME13: Bou B, Dunk . . . 4K 165 (7D 20)
Horsell Rd. BR5: St P . . . 4K 71
Horseshoe Cl. ME14: Weav . . . 4H 127
HORSESHOE GREEN . . . 1E 34
Horseshoe La. TN31: Beckl . . . 4H 45
Horseshoes La. ME17: L'ly . . . 4N 139 (4A 28)
Horseshore Cl. ME7: Hpstd . . . 6J 95
Horse Wash La. ME1: Roch . . . 6N 79
Horsfeld Gdns. SE9 . . . 3A 56
Horsfeld Rd. SE9 . . . 3N 55
Horsfield Cl. DA2: Dart . . . 5C 60
Horsford Wlk. ME13: Fav . . . 4E 186
Horsham La. ME8: Rain . . . 2H 225 (3B 18)
ME9: Upc . . . 2H 225 (3B 18)
Horsham Rd. DA6: Bexhth . . . 3B 58
Horshams, The CT6: H Bay . . . 2L 195
Horsley Cl. CT18: H'nge . . . 9L 193
Horsley Dr. CR0: Croy . . . 8F 82
Horsley Rd. BR1: Brom . . . 4L 69
ME1: Roch . . . 8M 79
HORSMONDEN . . . 7C 196 (2F 37)
Horsmonden Cl. BR6: Orp . . . 1H 85
Horsmonden Rd. SE4 . . . 3C 54
TN3: Lamb . . . 1L 201 (4D 36)
TN12: Brenc . . . 6N 153 (2D 36)
Horsmonden St. Works TN12: Horsm . . . 7F 196
Horsted Av. ME4: Chat'm . . . 2B 94
Horsted Keynes Rd. RH17: Hors K, Chel G . . . 7A 34
Horsted Retail Pk. ME5: Chat'm . . . 6A 94
Horsted Way ME1: Roch . . . 4A 94 (4H 17)
HORTON
Canterbury . . . 7F 170 (2F 31)
Ewell . . . 6A 12
Horton Country Pk. . . . 5A 12
Horton Downs ME15: Bear . . . 8J 127
HORTON KIRBY . . . 7C 74 (2J 15)
Horton Kirby Trad. Est. DA4: S Dar . . . 4C 74
Horton La. KT19: Eps . . . 6A 12
Horton Pk. Children's Farm . . . 5A 12
Horton Pl. TN16: Westrm . . . 8F 116
Horton Rd. CT4: Chart'm . . . 7E 170
DA4: Hort K, S Dar . . . 7C 74 (2J 15)
Hortons Cl. TN17: Bendn . . . 6A 38
Horton St. SE13 . . . 1E 54
Hortons Way TN16: Westrm . . . 8F 116
Horton Twr. BR5: St M Cry . . . 7L 71
(off Harbledown Pl.)
Horton Way CR0: Croy . . . 8A 68
DA4: Farn'm . . . 1N 87
Horwood Cl. ME1: Roch . . . 3M 93
Hoselands Vw. DA3: Hart'y . . . 7L 75
Hoser Av. SE12 . . . 7K 55
Hoser Gdns. CT7: Birch . . . 4F 206
Hosey Comn. La. TN16: Westrm . . . 3C 24
Hosey Comn. Rd. TN8: Crock H, Westrm . . . 4C 24
TN16: Westrm . . . 4C 24
HOSEY HILL . . . 3C 24
Hosey Hill TN16: Westrm . . . 9G 116 (3C 24)
Hospital Hill CT20: F'stone, Hythe . . . 8B 188
CT21: Hythe . . . 5K 41
Hospital La. CT1: Cant . . . 2M 171
ME1: Roch . . . 8B 80
Hospital Rd. ME17: Holl . . . 9G 128 (3C 28)
TN13: S'oaks . . . 3K 119
Hospital Way SE13 . . . 4G 54
Hostier Cl. ME2: Hall'g . . . 7F 92
Hotel Rd. CT15: St Marg . . . 7J 33
CT15: St Marg . . . 7D 214
ME8: Gill . . . 1K 95
Hotham Cl. BR8: Swanl . . . 4J 73
DA4: S at H . . . 3B 74
HOTHFIELD . . . 2M 197 (7J 29)
Hothfield Common Nature Reserve . . . 1L 197
Hothfield Rd. ME8: Rain . . . 2B 96
Hottsfield DA3: Hart'y . . . 6L 75
Hougham Ct. La. CT15: Chu H . . . 9A 180 (3D 42)
Hougham Top Rd. CT15: Chu H . . . 8A 180 (3D 42)
Houghton Av. ME7: Hpstd . . . 8L 95
HOUGHTON GREEN . . . 4B 46
Houghton Grn. La. TN31: Play . . . 4B 46
Houghton Ho. CT19: F'stone . . . 6J 189
Houghton La. TN31: Iden, Play . . . 4B 46
House Fld. TN24: W'boro . . . 8K 159
Housefield Rd. ME13: Stal, Throw . . . 3J 29
Houselands Rd. TN9: Tonb . . . 5H 145
Houston Rd. SE23 . . . 7B 54
Hovenden Cl. CT2: Cant . . . 7N 167
Hovendens TN17: Siss . . . 3C 222
Hoverspeed Stadium, The . . . 2E 180
Howard Av. DA5: Bex'y . . . 6L 57
ME1: Roch . . . 8A 80
ME10: Sit . . . 5E 98
Howard Cl. ME12: Minst . . . 5K 221
Howard Dr. ME16: Alltn . . . 3M 125
Howard Gdns. TN2: Tun W . . . 4G 156
Howard Rd. BR1: Brom . . . 3K 69
CT10: B'stairs . . . 1L 211
DA1: Dart . . . 4A 60
ME19: E Mal . . . 1D 124
Howards Crest Cl. BR3: Beck'm . . . 5F 68
Howarth Rd. SE2 . . . 5J 51
Howbury La. DA1: Erith . . . 5G 7
DA8: Erith . . . 9H 53
Howbury Wlk. ME8: Gill . . . 7N 95
Howells Cl. TN15: W King . . . 7E 88
Howerd Way SE18 . . . 8A 50
(not continuous)
Howe Rd. CT15: St Marg . . . 9B 200
Howfield La. CT4: Cha H . . . 4C 170
CT4: Cha H, Chart'm . . . 1F 31
HOW GREEN . . . 6D 24
How Grn. La. TN8: Four E, Hever . . . 6D 24
Howick Cl. ME20: Aylfd . . . 1K 125
Howland Cotts. TN12: Mard . . . 2E 212
Howland Rd. TN12: Mard . . . 3D 212 (7H 27)
Howlands TN15: Wro . . . 6M 105
How La. CR5: Chip . . . 7D 12
Howletts Wild Animal Pk. . . . 3J 173 (1K 31)
Howlsmere Cl. ME2: Hall'g . . . 8F 92
Howson Rd. SE4 . . . 2B 54
HOWT GREEN . . . 2E 98 (3E 18)
HOXTON . . . 2G 5
Hoxton Cl. TN23: Ashf . . . 1B 160
Hoystings Cl., The CT1: Cant . . . 3N 171
Hubart Pl. CT2: Sturry . . . 6E 168
Hubbards Hill ME17: Len . . . 3F 29
Hubbard's Hill TN13: Weald . . . 3J 131 (4G 25)
TN14: Weald . . . 4J 131 (4G 25)
Hubbard's La. ME17: Bou Mo . . . 6D 138 (4J 27)
Hubble Dr. ME15: Maid . . . 1H 139
Hubert Pas. CT16: Dover . . . 4K 181
Hubert Way CT10: B'stairs . . . 7J 209
HUCKING . . . 9G 113 (7B 18)
Huckleberry Cl. ME5: Chat'm . . . 8E 94
Hudson Cl. CT2: Sturry . . . 5E 168
CT16: Dover . . . 1G 181
ME8: Gill . . . 2M 95
Hudson Gdns. BR6: Chels . . . 7H 85
Hudson Pl. SE18 . . . 5E 50
Hudson Rd. CT1: Cant . . . 9A 168
DA7: Bexhth . . . 9A 52
Hughes Cotts. TN25: Sme . . . 8J 165
Hughes Dr. ME2: Wain . . . 2A 80
Hugh Pl. ME13: Fav . . . 5H 187
Hugh Price Cl. ME10: Sit . . . 6K 99
Hugin Av. CT10: B'stairs . . . 6J 209
Huguenot Pl. SW18 . . . 6D 4
HULBERRY . . . 3H 87
Hulkes La. ME1: Roch . . . 8B 80
Hull Pl. CT14: Shol . . . 4J 177
E16 . . . 1E 50
Hull Rd. TN29: G'stne . . . 8H 213
Hulsewood Cl. DA2: Dart . . . 8J 59
Humber Av. CT6: H Bay . . . 3A 194
Humber Cres. ME2: Strood . . . 5K 79
Humber Rd. DA1: Dart . . . 3L 59
Humboldt Ct. TN2: Tun W . . . 9K 151
Hume Av. RM18: Tilb . . . 1F 62 (6C 8)
Hume Cl. RM18: Tilb . . . 1F 62
Hume Ct. CT21: Hythe . . . 7L 199
Hump Bk. TN25: Wye, Elms . . . 6E 30
Hundredhouse La. TN31: B Oak, Bkld, Peas . . . 6H 45
Hundreds Cl. CT8: Wgte S . . . 4J 207
Hunger Hatch La. TN27: Char'g . . . 5G 29
HUNGERSHALL PARK . . . 3E 156 (3J 35)
Hungershall Pk. TN4: Tun W . . . 3D 156 (3J 35)
Hungershall Pk. Cl. TN4: Tun W . . . 3D 156
Hunsdon Dr. TN13: S'oaks . . . 5J 119
Hunstanton Cl. ME8: Rain . . . 8A 96
Hunt Cl. CT18: H'nge . . . 8K 193
Hunter Av. TN24: W'boro . . . 1J 161 (2B 40)
Hunter Cl. TN24: W'boro . . . 1J 161
Hunter Rd. TN24: W'boro . . . 9J 159 (1B 40)
Hunters Bank CT4: Elham . . . 7N 183
Hunters Chase CT5: Whits . . . 6G 226
CT6: H Bay . . . 5K 195
Hunters Cl. DA5: Bex'y . . . 8F 58
Hunters Ct. ME7: Gill . . . 5F 80
(off Milburn Rd.)
Hunter Seal TN11: Leigh . . . 5E 144
Huntersfield Cl. ME5: Chat'm . . . 1F 110
HUNTERS FORSTAL . . . 5J 195 (3K 21)
Hunters Forstal Rd. CT6: H Bay . . . 5J 195 (3K 21)
Hunters Gro. BR6: Farnb . . . 5E 84
Hunters Health and Fitness Club . . . 6H 145
(off Avebury Av.)
Hunters Wlk. CT14: Deal . . . 4K 177
TN14: Knock . . . 5N 101
Hunters Way ME7: Gill . . . 2H 95
ME13: Shel . . . 3H 219
TN2: Tun W . . . 4F 156
Hunters Way W. ME5: Chat'm . . . 1G 95
Huntingdon Wlk. ME15: Maid . . . 1H 139
Huntingfield CR0: Croy . . . 8C 82
Huntingfield Rd. DA13: Meop . . . 1F 90
Hunting Ga. CT7: Birch . . . 4E 206
Huntington Cl. TN17: Cran . . . 8D 176
Huntington Rd. ME17: Cox . . . 5M 137
Huntley Av. DA11: Nflt . . . 4A 62
Huntleys Gdns. TN4: Tun W . . . 8E 150
Huntley Mill Rd. TN5: Tice . . . 7E 36
Huntleys Pk. TN4: Tun W . . . 9F 150
HUNTON . . . 9H 137 (5F 27)
Hunton Gdns. CT2: Cant . . . 7N 167
Hunton Hill ME15: Hunt . . . 7K 137 (4G 27)
Hunton Rd. TN12: Mard . . . 5G 27
Hunt Rd. DA11: Nflt . . . 8D 62
TN10: Tonb . . . 1L 145
Hunts Farm Cl. TN15: Bor G . . . 2N 121
Huntsford Cl. ME8: Gill . . . 6N 95
Hunts La. TN17: Goud . . . 3C 190
Huntsman La. ME14: Maid . . . 5E 126
TN15: Wro . . . 9D 106
Huntsmans Cl. ME1: Roch . . . 2B 94
Huntsmans Cl. Ct. ME1: Roch . . . 2A 94
Huntsmead Cl. BR7: Chst . . . 3B 70
Hunts Slip Rd. SE21 . . . 7G 5
Hunt St. ME15: Yald . . . 3E 26
ME18: Yald, W Far . . . 4C 136
Huntswood TN23: Ashf . . . 1C 160
Hurlfield DA2: Dart . . . 8K 59
HURLINGHAM . . . 6C 4
Hurlingham Rd. DA7: Bexhth . . . 7A 52
Huron Cl. BR6: Chels . . . 7G 85
Huron Ter. CT16: Dover . . . 1G 181
(off Toronto Cl.)
Hurren Cl. SE3 . . . 1H 55
Hurricane Rd. ME19: W Mal . . . 6L 123
Hurstbourne Rd. SE23 . . . 6B 54
Hurst Cl. BR2: Shortl . . . 2J 83
ME5: Chat'm . . . 5B 94
TN12: S'hrst . . . 2K 223
TN30: Tent . . . 8A 224
Hurst Ct. DA15: Sidc . . . 7J 57
Hurstdene Av. BR2: Shortl . . . 2J 83
Hurst Farm Rd. RH19: E Grin . . . 4A 34
TN14: Weald . . . 5J 131
Hurstfield BR2: Shortl . . . 8K 69
Hurstford La. TN27: L Char . . . 6H 29
HURST GREEN
Etchingham . . . 2B 44
Limpsfield . . . 4A 24
Tonbridge . . . 6J 27
Hurst Grn. Rd. RH8: Oxt . . . 4A 24
Hurst Green Station (Rail) . . . 4A 24
Hurst Gro. CT12: Ram . . . 3G 210
Hurst Hill ME5: Chat'm . . . 9B 94
Hurstings, The ME15: Maid . . . 7A 126
Hurstlands RH8: Oxt . . . 4A 24
Hurst La. CT18: Cap F . . . 1B 174 (3C 42)
ME10: Kems'y . . . 2G 98
ME13: O'den . . . 3G 29
SE2 . . . 5M 51
TN14: Weald . . . 6J 131
(not continuous)
TN27: Char'g . . . 5G 29
TN33: Sed . . . 6E 44
Hurst La. Est. SE2 . . . 5M 51
Hurst Pl. DA1: Dart . . . 4K 59
ME8: Gill . . . 3B 96
Hurst Rd. DA5: Bex'y . . . 6M 57 (7D 6)
DA8: Erith . . . 8D 52
DA15: Bex'y, Sidc . . . 7J 57 (7D 6)
TN24: Kenn . . . 3F 158
Hurst Springs DA5: Bex'y . . . 6N 57
Hurst, The ME18: Bor G . . . 9C 122
ME18: S'brne . . . 2B 26
TN2: Tun W . . . 7L 151
TN11: S'brne . . . 9C 122
TN15: Bor G . . . 7B 122
TN15: Bor G, Tonb . . . 2B 26
Hurst Way ME16: Barm . . . 7K 125
TN13: S'oaks . . . 9K 119
Hurstwood ME5: Chat'm . . . 7B 94
Hurstwood Av. DA5: Bex'y . . . 6N 57
DA8: Erith . . . 8F 52
Hurstwood Dr. BR1: Brom . . . 6B 70
Hurstwood La. RH17: Sharp . . . 7A 34
TN4: Tun W . . . 1E 156
Hurstwood Pk. TN4: Tun W . . . 2F 156
Hurstwood Rd. ME7: B'hst . . . 1L 111 (5K 17)
ME14: B'hst, Det . . . 1L 111
Hurtis Hill TN6: Crowb . . . 7F 35
Husheath Hill TN12: S'hrst . . . 2H 37
TN17: Goud . . . 2H 37
Husseywell Cres. BR2: Shortl . . . 2K 83
Hustlings Dr. ME12: E'chu . . . 3A 202
Hutchings Cl. ME10: Sit . . . 6K 99
Hutchins Rd. SE28 . . . 1J 51
Hutsons Ct. TN18: Hawkh . . . 5D 192
Huxbear St. SE4 . . . 3C 54
Huxley Ct. ME1: Roch . . . 7A 80
(off King St.)
Huxley Rd. DA16: Well . . . 1H 57
Hyacinth Rd. ME2: Strood . . . 6H 79
Hybrid Cl. ME1: Roch . . . 2A 94
Hyde Cl. CT17: Dover . . . 5H 181
Hyde Dr. BR5: St P . . . 6K 71
Hyde Pk. . . . 3D 4
HYDE PARK CORNER . . . 3E 4
Hyde Park Corner Station (Tube) . . . 4E 4
Hyde Pk. St. W2 . . . 3D 4
Hyde Pl. CT3: Aysm . . . 2D 162
Hyde Rd. DA7: Bexhth . . . 9A 52
ME16: Alltn . . . 3A 126
N1 . . . 2G 5
Hyders Forge TN15: Plax . . . 9N 121
(not continuous)
Hyde's Orchard TN27: H'crn . . . 8M 191
Hyde, The CT4: Chart'm . . . 8B 170
Hyde Va. SE10 . . . 5K 5
Hylands Row TN26: Wdchu . . . 7B 228
Hylton St. SE18 . . . 4H 51
Hyndewood SE23 . . . 8A 54
Hyndford Cres. DA9: G'hithe . . . 3J 61
(off Calcroft Av.)
Hyperion Dr. ME2: Strood . . . 3K 79
HYTHE . . . 6K 199 (5J 41)
Hythe Av. DA7: Bexhth . . . 7N 51
Hythe Cl. BR5: St M Cry . . . 7L 71
CT20: F'stone . . . 6F 188
TN4: S'bgh . . . 5G 150
Hythe Cricket Club . . . 6K 199
Hythe Local History Room (Mus.) . . . 6K 199
Hythe Pl. CT13: S'wch . . . 6L 217
Hythe Rd. CT21: Lymp . . . 3C 198 (5G 41)
ME10: Sit . . . 6E 98
TN24: Ashf, W'boro . . . 8H 159 (1A 40)
TN25: Hin, Sme, E Bra . . . 2C 40
TN29: Dym . . . 7B 182 (7F 41)
Hythe Station
Romney, Hythe & Dymchurch Railway . . . 6H 199 (5H 41)
Hythe St. DA1: Dart . . . 4M 59
(not continuous)
Hythe St. (Lwr.) DA1: Dart . . . 3M 59
Hythe Swimming Pool . . . 7L 199
Hyton Cl. CT14: Deal . . . 4L 177
Hyton Dr. CT14: Deal . . . 4L 177

I

Ian's Wlk. CT21: Hythe . . . 8A 188
Ibis Cl. CT5: Whits . . . 7D 226
Ice Bowl . . . 2K 95
ICKHAM . . . 7A 22
ICKLESHAM . . . 7J 45
Ickleton Rd. SE9 . . . 9A 56
IDE HILL . . . 4A 130 (3E 24)
Ide Hill Rd. TN8: Chid . . . 2A 142 (5E 24)
TN8: Four E . . . 5D 24
TN14: Ide H . . . 4A 130 (3E 24)
IDEN . . . 4A 46
Iden Cl. BR2: Shortl . . . 6H 69
Iden Cres. TN12: S'hrst . . . 4J 223
Iden Croft Herb Gdns. . . . 1K 37
IDEN GREEN
Benenden . . . 7A 38
Cranbrook . . . 4H 37
Iden Grn. Rd. TN17: Bendn . . . 7A 38
Iden La. TN27: Eger . . . 5F 29
Iden Rd. ME2: Strood . . . 3N 79
TN31: Iden, Play . . . 4A 46
Idenwood Cl. ME8: Gill . . . 5N 95
Idleigh Ct. Rd. DA13: Hart'y, Meop . . . 3A 90 (4A 16)
Iffin La. CT4: Cant . . . 9L 171
CT4: P'hm . . . 3G 31
IFIELD . . . 3H 77
Ifield Cl. ME15: Maid . . . 1J 139
Ifield Rd. DA13: Meop . . . 6D 90

Ifield Way—Junction Rd.

Ifield Way DA12: Grav'nd .2J **77**
IGHTHAM .3K 121 (1K 25)
Ightham By-Pass TN15: Igh .3J **121** (1K **25**)
IGHTHAM COMMON .5H 121 (2K 25)
Ightham Ho. *BR3: Beck'm* .*3C* ***68***
(off Bethersden Cl.)
Ightham Mote .9G 121 (3K 25)
Ightham Rd. DA7: Erith .7B **52**
TN11: S'brne .2J **133** (3K **25**)
TN15: S'brne .2J **133** (3K **25**)
Ilderton Rd. SE15 .5H **5**
SE16 .4H **5**
Ilex Rd. CT19: F'stone .5F **188**
ILFORD .1B 6
Ilford Hill IG1: Ilf .1B **6**
Ilford La. IG1: Ilf .1B **6**
Ilford Station (Rail) .1B 6
Ilfracombe Rd. BR1: Brom .8J **55**
Illustrious Cl. ME5: Chat'm .6D **94**
Imbert Cl. TN28: New R .3L **213**
Impala Gdns. TN4: Tun W .8H **151**
Imperial Av. ME12: Minst .5L **221**
Imperial Bus. Est. DA11: Nflt .4E **62**
Imperial College at Wye
(University of London) .1M 159
Imperial Dr. DA12: Grav'nd .1L **77**
ME12: Ward .4K **203**
Imperial Ho. Mdw. TN23: Ashf .1A **160**
Imperial Pl. BR7: Chst .4C **70**
Imperial Retail Pk. DA11: Grav'nd .4F **62**
Imperial Rd. ME7: Gill .9F **80**
SW6 .5C **4**
Imperial Way BR7: Chst .8E **56**
TN23: Ashf .1A **160**
Inca Dr. SE9 .5D **56**
Ince Rd. CT2: Sturry .4E **168**
Inchmery Rd. SE6 .7E **54**
Inchwood CR0: Croy .5E **82**
Independents Rd. SE3 .1J **55**
Indoor Bowls Cen.
Maidstone .7F 126
Ingess Pk. Av. DA9: G'hithe .2H **61**
Ingham Cl. CR2: S Croy .9A **82**
Ingham Rd. CR2: S Croy .9A **82**
Ingleby Way BR7: Chst .1C **70**
Ingle Cl. CT7: Birch .4G **206**
INGLEDEN .6E 224
Ingleden Cl. ME10: Kems'y .3G **99**
Ingleden Cotts. TN30: Tent .5D **224**
Ingleden Pk. Rd. TN30: Tent .6C **224**
(not continuous)
Ingledew Rd. SE18 .5F **50**
Inglemere Rd. SE23 .8A **54**
Inglenorth Ct. BR8: Crock'm .9D **72**
Ingle Rd. ME4: Chat'm .1C **94**
Ingleside Cl. BR3: Beck'm .3D **68**
Ingles La. CT20: F'stone .6K **189**
Ingles M. CT20: F'stone .7J **189**
Ingles Pas. *CT20: F'stone* .*7J* ***189***
(off Ingles Pl.)
Ingles Pl. CT20: F'stone .7J **189**
Ingles Rd. CT20: F'stone .7J **189**
Ingles Way CT20: F'stone .6J **189**
Ingleton Av. DA16: Well .3J **57**
Ingleton Wood Rd. CT15: Hou, Alk, Dover .2D **42**
Inglewood BR8: Swanl .5E **72**
CR0: Croy .9B **82**
Inglewood Copse BR1: Brom .5A **70**
Inglewood Rd. DA7: Bexhth .2E **58**
Inglis Rd. W5 .3A **4**
Ingoldsby Rd. CT1: Cant .4K **171**
CT7: Birch .4C **206**
CT19: F'stone .4L **189**
DA12: Grav'nd .6K **63**
Ingram Cl. CT18: H'nge .9J **193**
Ingram Rd. CR7: Thor H .2G **13**
DA1: Dart .6M **59**
ME7: Gill .7H **81** (2K **17**)
Ingrebourne Ho. *BR1: Brom* .*1G* ***68***
(off Brangbourne Rd.)
Ingrebourne Rd. RM13: Rain .2G **7**
Ingress Gdns. DA9: G'hithe .3K **61**
INGRESS PARK .2J 61
Ingress Ter. DA13: Sflt .9L **61**
Inigo Jones Rd. SE7 .7A **50**
Inner Lines ME7: Gill .6D **80**
Inner London Rd. TN1: Tun W .2G **156**
Inner Pk. Rd. SW19 .7B **4**
Inspirations Way BR6: Orp .1J **85**
Institute Rd. ME4: Chat'm .8D **80**
ME13: Fav .5H **187**
Instone Rd. DA1: Dart .5L **59** (7G **7**)
Inverary Ct. CT11: Ram .3J **211**
Inverary Pl. SE18 .6F **50**
Invermore Pl. SE18 .4E **50**
Inverness Ct. SE6 .6J **55**
Inverness Ho. ME15: Maid .1H **139**
Inverness M. E16 .1E **50**
Inverness Ter. CT10: B'stairs .1L **211**
W2 .3C **4**
Inverton Rd. SE15 .2A **54**
Invicta Bus. Pk. TN15: Wro .8B **106**
Invicta Cl. BR7: Chst .1C **70**
Invicta Ct. ME10: Sit .4G **98**
Invicta Ho. CT1: Cant .3M **171**
CT9: Mgte .4F **208**
Invicta Pde. DA14: Sidc .9K **57**
Invicta Rd. CT5: Whits .5H **227**
CT9: Mgte .5F **208**
CT19: F'stone .4K **189**
DA2: Dart .4B **60**
ME12: S'ness .2D **220** (6G **11**)
Invicta Vs. ME14: Bear .5M **127**
Inward Car Lanes CT16: Dover .4M **181**
Inward Freight Lanes CT16: Dover .4M **181**
Inwood Cl. CR0: Croy .3B **82**
Iona Cl. ME5: Chat'm .1G **110**
SE6 .5D **54**
Iona Rd. ME15: Maid .1D **138**
Ionia Wlk. DA12: Grav'nd .8L **63**
Ipswich Ho. SE4 .3A **54**
Irchester St. *CT11: Ram* .*5K* ***211***
(off Balmoral Pl.)
Ireland Ter. TN23: Ashf .3E **160**
Irene Astor Ct. *CT20: F'stone* .*6K* ***189***
(off St John's St.)
Irene Rd. BR6: Orp .1H **85**
Iris Av. DA5: Bex'y .3N **57**
Iris Cl. CR0: Croy .2A **82**
ME5: Chat'm .2D **110**
Iris Cres. DA7: Bexhth .6A **52**
Iron Bar La. CT1: Cant .2N **171**
Iron Mill La. DA1: Cray .2F **58** (6F **7**)
Iron Mill Pl. DA1: Cray .2G **58**
Ironside Cl. ME5: Chat'm .3D **94**
Ironstones TN3: Lang G .2B **156**
Iron Wharf ME13: Fav .3J **187**
Irvine Dr. CT9: Mgte .5G **209**
Irvine Rd. ME3: High'm .1F **78**
Irvine Way BR6: Orp .1H **85**
Irving Ho. TN1: Tun W .9H **151**
Irving Wlk. DA10: Swans .5L **61**
Irving Way BR8: Swanl .5E **72**
Irwin Av. SE18 .7G **51**
Isabella Dr. BR6: Farnb .5E **84**
Isard Ho. BR2: Shortl .2L **83**
Isis Cl. CT21: Lymp .5B **198**
Island Gardens Station (DLR) .4K 5
Island Rd. CR3: Hersd .4H **169**
CT2: Sturry .6E **168** (6K **21**)
CT3: Ups .6K **21**
Island Wall CT5: Whits .4E **226**
Island Way E. ME4: Chat'm .2E **80**
Island Way W. ME4: Chat'm .2E **80**
Isla Rd. SE18 .6E **50**
Isledon Rd. N7 .1F **5**
Islehurst Cl. BR7: Chst .4C **70**
Islingham Farm Rd. ME3: Wain .1A **80** (1H **17**)
ISLINGTON .1F 5
Islington Pk. St. N1 .1F **5**
Ismays Rd. TN15: Igh, Ivy H .7H **121**
TN15: Ivy H, Igh .2K **25**
ISTEAD RISE .4E 76 (2B 16)
Istead Ri. DA13: Ist R .3E **76**
ITCHINGWOOD COMMON .4A 24
Itchingwood Comn. Rd. RH8: Oxt .4A **24**
Ito Way ME7: Gill .3K **17**
ME8: Gill .1J **95**
Ivanhoe Rd. CT6: H Bay .2E **190** (3G **37**)
CT8: Wgte S .2K **207**
Iveagh Ct. BR3: Beck'm .6F **68**
Ivedon Rd. DA16: Well .9L **51**
Ivens Way ME17: H'shm .2M **141**
Iverhurst Cl. DA6: Bexhth .3M **57**
Iversgate Cl. ME8: Rain .1B **96**
Iverson Rd. NW6 .1C **4**
Ivers Way CR0: Croy .8E **82**
Ives Ga. CT13: S'wch .5M **217**
Ives Rd. TN9: Tonb .6F **144**
Ivor Gro. SE9 .6D **56**
Ivory Cl. ME13: Fav .3E **186**
Ivorydown BR1: Brom .9K **55**
Ivy Bower Cl. DA9: G'hithe .3H **61**
Ivybridge Ct. *BR7: Chst* .*4C* ***70***
(off Old Hill)
IVYCHURCH .2G 47
Ivychurch Gdns. CT9: Clift .3J **209**
Ivychurch Rd. TN29: Bztt .2F **47**
Ivy Cl. CT18: Etch'l .2M **185** (3J **41**)
DA1: Dart .4A **60**
DA12: Grav'nd .9H **63**
ME17: Kgswd .6F **140**
Ivy Cott. Hill CT12: Minst .4G **23**
Ivy Cotts. TN23: Ashf .8E **158**
TN23: Gt Cha .1A **160**
Ivy Ct. CT2: T Hill .5L **167**
TN30: Tent .8C **224**
Ivydale Rd. SE15 .1A **54** (6H **5**)
IVY HATCH .8H 121 (2K 25)
Ivy Ho. La. TN13: Dun G, Otf .9E **102** (7F **15**)
Ivy Ho. Rd. CT5: Whits .4H **227**
Ivy La. CT1: Cant .2N **171**
CT11: Ram .6H **211**
TN3: Bell G .4A **36**
TN3: Bell G .8N **157**
TN14: Knock .7N **101**
Ivy M. ME17: Kgswd .6G **140**
Ivy Pl. CT1: Cant .3L **171**
CT14: Deal .3N **177**
ME1: Roch .1L **93**
Ivy Rd. SE4 .2C **54**
Ivy St. ME8: Rain .3B **96**
Ivy Vs. DA9: G'hithe .3G **61**
Ivy Way CT19: F'stone .4L **189**
IWADE .8K 197 (3E 18)
Iwade Rd. ME9: Bob, N'tn .4L **97** (4D **18**)
Izane Rd. DA6: Bexhth .2A **58**

J

Jacinth Dr. ME10: Sit .5D **98**
Jackass La. BR2: Kes .6L **83** (4A **14**)
Jacklin Cl. ME5: Chat'm .9C **94**
Jacks Hill TN7: Hartf .5D **34**
Jackson Av. ME1: Roch .3B **94**
Jackson Cl. DA9: G'hithe .3F **60**
ME8: Gill .2M **95**
Jackson Rd. BR2: Shortl .3B **84**
CT1: Cant .3L **171**
Jacksons La. TN30: Tent .8B **224**
Jackson St. SE18 .6C **50**
Jackson's Way CR0: Croy .4D **82**
Jackson Way TN17: Bendn .5B **38**
Jacob Cl. CT9: Mgte .6C **208**
Jacob Ho. *DA18: Erith* .*2M* ***51***
(off Kale Rd.)
Jacob's Ho. ME12: S'ness .2D **220**
Jacobs La. DA4: Hort K .6C **74**
Jacob's La. ME3: Hoo .6L **67** (7K **9**)
Jacob Yd. *ME13: Fav* .*5H* ***187***
(off Preston St.)
Jade Cl. ME10: Sit .4D **98**
Jade Hill ME2: Hall'g .5E **92**
Jaffa Ct. CT5: Whits .5F **226**
Jaffray Rd. BR2: Shortl .7N **69**
Jaggard Way TN12: S'hrst .3J **223**
Jagger Cl. DA2: Dart .5C **60**
Jago Cl. SE18 .6E **50**
Jail La. TN16: Big H .3D **164** (7B **14**)
Jamaica Rd. SE1 .4G **5**
SE16 .4H **5**
Jamaica Ter. ME14: Maid .2D **126**
James Allchin Gdns. TN24: Kenn .6K **159**
James Av. *TN15: W King* .*8E* ***88***
(off London Rd.)
James Cl. CT3: Ash .4C **216**
CT18: Lym'ge .7K **205**
TN11: Hdlw .7E **134**
James Ct. CT9: Clift .3F **208**
CT20: F'stone .7G **189**
ME4: Chat'm .1D **94**
James Hall Gdns. CT14: Walm .7M **177**
James Haney Dr. TN24: Kenn .5K **159**
James Newman Ct. SE9 .8C **56**
James Rd. DA1: Dart .5H **59**
ME2: Cux .1F **92**
James St. CT11: Ram .6H **211**
CT19: F'stone .4L **189**
ME1: Roch .8N **79**
ME4: Chat'm .8C **80**
(not continuous)
ME7: Gill .7F **80** (2J **17**)
ME12: S'ness .2E **220**
ME14: Maid .4D **126**
TN23: Ashf .8E **158**
W1 .3E **4**
James Watt Way DA8: Erith .6G **52**
James Whatman Ct. *ME14: Maid* .*6F* ***126***
(off Ashford Rd.)
James Whatman Way ME14: Maid .4C **126**
Jane Grn. M. CT1: Cant .9A **168**
Jane Seymour Ct. SE9 .5F **56**
Japonica Cl. ME5: Chat'm .9F **94**
Jarlen Rd. TN29: Lydd .3J **205**
Jarman's Fld. TN25: Wye .2N **159**
Jarrett Av. ME2: Wain .2N **79**
Jarrett Ho. CT20: F'stone .7J **189**
Jarretts Ct. *ME10: Sit* .*7J* ***99***
(off Wykeham Rd.)
JARVIS BROOK .7G 35
Jarvis Dr. TN24: W'boro .2L **161**
Jarvis La. TN17: Goud .2E **190** (3G **37**)
Jarvis Pl. TN30: St Mic .4C **224**
Jarvist Pl. CT14: Kgdn .3F **200**
Jashoda Ho. *SE18* .*5C* ***50***
(off Connaught M.)
Jasmin Ct. SE12 .4J **55**
Jasmine Cl. BR6: Farnb .3D **84**
CT4: Chart'm .9D **170**
ME5: Chat'm .7C **94**
ME19: E Mal .1D **124**
Jasmine Ct. TN15: W King .8E **88**
Jasmine Gdns. CR0: Croy .4E **82**
Jasmine Pl. CT3: Wing .7J **225**
Jasmine Rd. ME19: E Mal .1D **124**
Jason Wlk. SE9 .9C **56**
Jasper Av. ME1: Roch .1N **93**
Javelin Rd. ME19: W Mal .6L **123**
Jay Gdns. BR7: Chst .9B **56**
Jaynes Ind. Est., The CT17: Dover .4D **180**
Jayne Wlk. CT5: Whits .7D **226**
Jefferson Cl. TN23: Ashf .9D **158**
Jefferson Dr. ME8: Gill .2M **95**
Jefferson Rd. ME12: S'ness .3E **220**
Jefferson Wlk. SE18 .6C **50**
Jefferstone Gdns. TN29: St M Bay .2L **215**
Jefferstone La. TN29: St M Bay .3J **215**
TN29: St M Bay .2J **47**
Jefferstone Lane Station
Romney, Hythe
& Dymchurch Railway .2M 215 (2K 47)
Jeffery Cl. TN12: S'hrst .2J **223**
Jeffery St. ME7: Gill .6F **80** (2J **17**)
Jeffrey Row SE12 .3L **55**
Jeffrey St. ME14: Maid .4D **126**
Jeffries Cotts. ME15: Hunt .5H **137**
Jeken Rd. SE9 .2M **55**
Jellicoe Av. DA12: Grav'nd .8H **63**
Jellicoe Av. W. DA12: Grav'nd .8H **63**
Jellicoe Cl. TN24: W'boro .2L **161**
Jemmett La. TN25: Mers .3C **40**
Jemmett Rd. TN23: Ashf .2E **160**
Jenkins Dale ME4: Chat'm .9C **80** (3H **17**)
Jenkins Dr. ME15: Maid .3H **139**
Jenner Rd. ME1: Roch .8N **79**
Jenner's Way TN29: St M Bay .3L **215**
Jenner Way ME20: Burh .4K **109**
Jennifer Ct. ME3: Hoo .8H **67**
Jennifer Gdns. CT9: Mgte .5G **209**
Jennifer Rd. BR1: Brom .8J **55**
Jenningtree Rd. DA8: Erith .7J **53**
Jenningtree Way DA17: Belv .2D **52**
Jenton Av. DA7: Bexhth .8N **51**
Jermyn St. SW1 .3E **4**
Jerome Rd. ME20: Lark .6D **108**
Jerrard St. SE13 .1E **54**
Jersey Cl. TN24: Kenn .2G **159**
Jersey Dr. BR5: Pet W .9F **70**
Jersey La. CT4: P'hm .3G **31**
Jersey Rd. ME2: Strood .5L **79**
Jeskyns Rd. DA12: Cobh .2C **16**
DA12: Grav'nd .6H **77**
DA13: Sole S, Cobh .6H **77** (2C **16**)
Jesmond St. CT19: F'stone .5K **189**
Jessamine Pl. DA2: Dart .5C **60**
Jesse's Hill CT4: Kgstn .4K **31**
Jessett Cl. DA8: Erith .4E **52**
Jessica M. CT1: Cant .1A **172**
ME10: Sit .4F **98**
Jesson Ct. Cvn. Pk. TN29: St M Bay .2M **215**
Jessup Cl. SE18 .4E **50**
Jesuit Cl. CT2: Cant .7N **167**
Jetty Rd. ME3: Hoo .6N **67**
ME12: S'ness .1A **220**
ME12: Ward .4K **203** (1B **20**)
Jevington Way SE12 .6L **55**
Jewell Gro. TN12: Mard .3D **212**
Jewels Hill TN16: Big H .1A **164** (6A **14**)
Jewry La. CT1: Cant .2M **171**
Jeyes Rd. ME7: Gill .8F **80**
Jezreels Rd. ME7: Gill .9G **80**
Jillian Way TN23: Ashf .2C **160**
Jim Bradley Cl. SE18 .4C **50**
Jiniwin Rd. ME1: Roch .4A **94**
JJ's Gun Club .8F 60
Joan Cres. SE9 .5N **55**
Joanne Harmer Gallery .3N 177
Jockey La. TN17: Cran .7D **176**
Jodrell Rd. E3 .1J **5**
Johanesburg Rd. CT16: Dover .9H **179**
Johannesburg Ho. ME15: Maid .3H **139**
John Anderson Ct. *ME13: Fav* .*5H* ***187***
(off East St.)
John Badger Cl. TN24: Kenn .5J **159**
John Dutton Way TN24: Kenn .6J **159**
John Graham Ct. CT1: Cant .4N **171**
John Hall Ct. ME13: Fav .2F **186**
John Islip St. SW1 .4E **4**
John Nash Cl. ME9: Lyn .9J **223**
John Newington Cl. TN24: Kenn .5K **159**
John Newton Ct. DA16: Well .1K **57**
JOHN'S CROSS .5C 44
John's Grn. CT13: S'wch .8K **217**
JOHN'S HOLE .5C 60
Johnson Av. ME7: Gill .5E **80**
Johnson Cl. DA11: Nflt .8C **62**
TN24: W'boro .2L **161**
Johnson Ct. ME13: Fav .3F **186**
Johnson Rd. BR2: Shortl .8N **69**
ME10: Sit .7E **98**
Johnson's Av. TN14: Hals .1C **102**
Johnsons Ct. TN15: Seal .3N **119**
Johnson's Way DA9: G'hithe .4J **61**
Johnson Way ME12: Minst .5H **221**
John Spare Ct. *TN4: Tun W* .*8G* ***150***
(off Whitefield Rd.)
John's Rd. DA13: Meop .8E **76**
TN16: Tats .8D **164**
Johnstone Ho. *SE13* .*1G* ***54***
(off Belmont Hill)
John St. CT10: B'stairs .9M **209**
ME1: Roch .8N **79**
ME14: Maid .3D **126**
TN4: Tun W .9G **150**
John Tapping Cl. CT14: Walm .9L **177**
John Wilson Bus. Pk. CT5: Whits .4K **227**
John Wilson St. SE18 .3C **50** (4B **6**)
John Woolley Cl. SE13 .2N **55**
Joiners Ct. ME4: Chat'm .1E **94**
Jointon Rd. CT20: F'stone .7H **189**
Jonas La. TN5: Wadh .6B **36**
Jordan Cl. ME15: Maid .3H **139**
Jordan Ho. *SE4* .*2A* ***54***
(off St Norbert Rd.)
Joseph Conrad Ho. CT2: Cant .1K **171**
Joseph Wilson Ind. Est. & Retail Pk.
CT5: Whits .6H **227**
Joss Gap Rd. CT10: B'stairs .4M **209** (1K **23**)
Joyce Cl. TN17: Cran .8C **176**
JOYCE GREEN .2N 59 (6H 7)
Joyce Grn. La. DA1: Dart .1M **59**
(Dunlop Cl.)
DA1: Dart .8L **53**
(University Way)
Joyce Grn. Wlk. DA1: Dart .2N **59**
JOYDENS WOOD .9E 58 (1F 15)
Joydens Wood (Nature Reserve) .9C 58
Joydens Wood Rd. DA5: Bex'y .9E **58**
Joyes Cl. CT16: Whitf .6G **178**
CT19: F'stone .4L **189**
Joyes Rd. CT16: Whitf .6F **178**
CT19: F'stone .4K **189** (4B **42**)
Joy La. CT5: Whits .6C **226** (4E **20**)
Joy Rd. DA12: Grav'nd .6H **63**
Joywood ME15: Maid .3G **139**
Jubilee Cl. CT21: Hythe .8E **198**
DA9: G'hithe .4J **61**
Jubilee Cotts. CT2: Cant .7E **168**
CT3: S'le .8A **216**
TN14: S'oaks .2J **119**
Jubilee Country Pk. .7D 70
Jubilee Ct. *CT10: B'stairs* .*9M* ***209***
(off Oscar Rd.)
DA1: Dart .*5L* ***59***
(off Spring Va. Sth.)
Jubilee Cres. DA12: Grav'nd .7K **63**
ME11: Queen .7A **220**
TN15: Igh .3J **121**
Jubilee Dr. CT14: Walm .7N **177**
Jubilee Flds. TN30: Witter .2D **228**
Jubilee Ri. TN15: Seal .3N **119**
Jubilee Rd. BR6: Chels .7B **86** (5E **14**)
CT3: L'brne .2L **173** (1A **32**)
CT13: S'wch .6L **217**
CT14: Worth .9N **217** (2G **33**)
Jubilee St. E1 .3H **5**
ME10: Sit .6F **98**
Jubilee Ter. ME7: Gill .6F **80**
Jubilee Way CT15: Dover .4M **181**
CT15: Gus .7F **33**
CT16: Dover, Gus, Whitf .7F **178** (7F **33**)
DA14: Sidc .7J **57**
KT9: Chess .4A **12**
SW19 .2C **12**
Judd Rd. ME13: Fav .5E **186**
TN9: Tonb .8H **145**
Judd St. WC1 .2F **5**
Judeth Gdns. DA12: Grav'nd .1K **77**
Judkins Cl. ME5: Chat'm .5F **94**
Jug Hill TN16: Big H .4D **164**
Juglans Rd. BR6: Orp .2J **85**
Julian Rd. BR6: Chels .7J **85**
CT19: F'stone .6H **189**
Julians Cl. TN13: S'oaks .9H **119**
Julians Way TN13: S'oaks .9H **119**
Julie Cl. CT10: B'stairs .7L **209**
Julien Pl. TN24: W'boro .1L **161**
Julie Rose Stadium, The .6K 159
Juliette Way RM15: Avel .2N **53**
Jumpers Rebound Cen. (Trampoline Cen.) .6E 80
JUMPER'S TOWN .6D 34
Junction App. SE13 .1F **54**
Junction Rd. CT6: H Bay .5D **194**
DA1: Dart .4L **59**
ME7: Gill .8G **81**

Junction Rd.—Kingfisher Cl.

Junction Rd. NW5 .1E 4
TN32: Bdm, Ewh G .2D 44
Juniper Cl. CT1: Cant .4N 171
CT5: Whits .4H 227
ME5: Chat'm .7D 94
ME16: Alltn .3M 125
TN4: S'bgh .5K 151
TN16: Big H .5E 164
TN23: Ashf .8C 158
Juniper Wlk. BR8: Swanl .5E 72
Jupiter La. TN23: Kgnt .4C 160
JURY'S GAP .6E 46
Jury's Gap TN31: Camb .6E 46
Jury's Gap Rd. TN29: Lydd .4H 205 (6F 47)
Jury St. DA11: Grav'nd .4G 63
Jutland Cl. ME3: Allh .5D 204
Jutland Rd. SE6 .5F 54

K

Kake St. CT4: Walt .5F 31
Kale Rd. DA18: Erith .2M 51
Kane Hythe Rd. TN33: Neth, Batt .6A 44
Kangley Bri. Rd. SE26 .2C 68
Kangley Bus. Cen. SE26 .1C 68
Karen Ct. BR1: Brom .4J 69
Karlof Way ME3: Wain .2M 79
Kashgar Rd. SE18 .4H 51
Katherine Ct. ME5: Chat'm .9E 94
Katherine Gdns. SE9 .2N 55
Katherine Rd. E6 .1A 6
E7 .1A 6
TN8: Eden .7C 184
Kavanagh Cinema .2G 195
Kaysland Cvn Pk. TN15: W King .8E 88
Kays La. ME13: Hernh .6D 20
Kay St. DA16: Well .8K 51
KEARSNEY .9D 178 (7E 32)
Kearsney Av. CT16: Dover .9D 178
Kearsney Ct. CT16: Temp E .9B 178
Kearsney Station (Rail) .9C 178 (7E 32)
Keary Rd. DA10: Swans .5L 61
Keat Farm Cl. CT6: H Bay .2N 195
Keating Cl. ME1: Roch .9L 79
Keats Ho. DA1: Cray .3F 58
Keats Rd. DA16: Well .8G 51
DA17: Belv .3D 52
ME20: Lark .7D 108
Kechill Gdns. BR2: Shortl .1K 83
Keddow's Cl. CT21: Hythe .8E 198
Kedleston Dr. BR5: St M Cry .9H 71
Kedleston Rd. CT16: Dover .8F 178
Keeble Cl. SE18 .6D 50
Keedonwood Rd. BR1: Brom .1H 69
Keefe Cl. ME5: Chat'm .1A 110
Keel Ct. ME2: Med E .4B 80
Keel Gdns. TN4: S'bgh .6E 150
Keeling Rd. SE9 .3N 55
Keemor Cl. SE18 .7C 50
Keepers Cotts. ME14: Bear .3M 127
Keeper's Hill CT4: Brid .7H 173 (2K 31)
Keepers La. CT18: Acr .2K 41
Keightley Dr. SE9 .6E 56
Keith Av. CT12: Ram .4E 210
DA4: S at H .2B 74
Keith Pk. Cres. TN16: Big H .2A 164
Kelbrook Rd. SE3 .9A 50
Kelby Path SE9 .8D 56
Kelchers La. TN11: Gold G .2E 146
Kellaway Rd. ME5: Chat'm .9D 94
Kellerton Rd. SE13 .3H 55
Kelley Dr. ME7: Gill .5F 80
Kellner Rd. SE28 .3H 51
Kelly Ho. ME1: Roch .4N 93
Kelsey Ga. BR3: Beck'm .5E 68
Kelsey La. BR3: Beck'm .5D 68
Kelsey Pk. Av. BR3: Beck'm .5E 68
(not continuous)
Kelsey Pk. Rd. BR3: Beck'm .5D 68
Kelsey Rd. BR5: St P .5K 71
Kelsey Sq. BR3: Beck'm .5D 68
Kelsey Way BR3: Beck'm .6D 68
Kelso Dr. DA12: Grav'nd .9L 63
Kelvedon Rd. CT14: Walm .8M 177
SW6 .5C 4
Kelvin Cl. TN10: Tonb .9K 133
Kelvington Cl. CR0: Croy .1B 82
Kelvington Rd. SE15 .3A 54
Kelvin Pde. BR6: Orp .2G 84
Kelvin Rd. DA16: Well .1J 57
Kemble Cl. TN2: Tun W .7L 151
Kemble Dr. BR2: Shortl .4A 84
Kemble Rd. SE23 .6A 54
Kembleside Rd. TN16: Big H .6C 164
Kemerton Rd. BR3: Beck'm .5E 68
Kemnal Rd. BR7: Chst .9F 56
(not continuous)
Kemp All. *CT5: Whits* .*4F 226*
(off Middle Wall)
Kemp Cl. ME5: Chat'm .7B 94
KEMPE'S CORNER .6B 30
Kempes Pl. *TN25: Wye* .*2M 159*
(off Up. Bridge St.)
Kemp Rd. CT5: Whits .3L 227
Kemps Gdns. SE13 .3F 54
Kemps Wharf Rd. ME8: Rain .3A 18
Kempthorne St. DA11: Grav'nd .4G 62
Kempton Cl. DA8: Erith .6D 52
ME5: Chat'm .8F 94
(not continuous)
Kempton Wlk. CR0: Croy .9B 68
Kempt St. SE18 .6C 50
Kemsdale Rd. ME13: Hernh .1J 165 (6C 20)
KEMSING .8B 104 (7H 15)
Kemsing Cl. BR2: Shortl .3J 83
DA5: Bex'y .5N 57
Kemsing Down Nature Reserve .7N 103
Kemsing Gdns. CT2: Cant .7A 168
Kemsing Heritage Cen. .8B 104
Kemsing Rd. TN15: Kems'g .7F 104
TN15: Kems'g, Wro .7K 15
Kemsing Station (Rail) .1D 120 (1J 25)
KEMSLEY .2G 98 (3F 19)
Kemsley SE13 .3E 54
Kemsley Cl. DA9: G'hithe .4H 61
DA11: Nflt .9E 62
KEMSLEY DOWN .2J 99
Kemsley Down Station
Sittingbourne & Kemsley Light Railway .3F 19
Kemsley Rd. TN16: Tats .7D 164
Kemsley Station (Rail) .2F 98 (3F 19)
KEMSLEY STREET .1N 111 (5A 18)
Kemsley St. Rd. ME7: B'hst .1L 111 (5K 17)
KENARDINGTON .6J 39
Kenardington Rd. TN26: App .7H 39
Kenbrook TN24: Kenn .3G 159
Kencot Way DA18: Erith .2A 52
Kendal Cl. CT11: Ram .6E 210
TN9: Tonb .4J 145
Kendal Dr. TN9: Tonb .5J 145
Kendale Rd. BR1: Brom .1H 69
Kendall Av. BR3: Beck'm .5B 68
Kendall Ct. DA15: Sidc .8J 57
Kendall Lodge *BR1: Brom* .*4L 69*
(off Willow Tree Wlk.)
Kendall Rd. BR3: Beck'm .5B 68
SE18 .8A 50
Kendal Mdw. CT5: Whits .4N 227
Kendal Pk. TN4: Tun W .9E 150
Kendal Pl. ME15: Maid .9F 126
Kendal Ri. CT10: B'stairs .8L 209
Kendal Rd. NW10 .1B 4
Kendal Way ME8: Gill .3N 95
ME19: W Mal .6A 124
Kender St. SE14 .5H 5
Kendon Bus. Pk. ME2: Med E .4A 80
Kenfield Rd. CT4: P'hm .3F 31
Kengate Ind. Est. CT21: Hythe .7G 199
Kenia Wlk. DA12: Grav'nd .8L 63
Kenilworth Cl. CT15: St Marg .7C 214
Kenilworth Ct. *DA2: Dart* .*4B 60*
(off Bow Arrow La.)
ME10: Sit .6D 98
Kenilworth Dr. ME8: Gill .4N 95 (4A 18)
Kenilworth Gdns. ME8: Gill .4N 95
SE18 .9D 50
Kenilworth Ho. ME16: Maid .7M 125
Kenilworth Rd. BR5: Pet W .9E 70
SE20 .4A 68
KENLEY .6G 13
Kenley Airfield .7G 13
Kenley Cl. BR7: Chst .6G 71
DA5: Bex'y .5B 58
Kenley La. CR8: Kenl .6G 13
Kenley Rd. KT1: King T .2A 12
Kenley Station (Rail) .6G 13
Kenmere Rd. DA16: Well .9L 51
Kennard Cl. ME1: Roch .1K 93
Kennard St. E16 .1B 50
Kennedy Cl. BR5: Pet W .2F 84
ME13: Fav .3H 187
Kennedy Dr. CT14: Walm .8L 177
Kennedy Gdns. TN13: S'oaks .5K 119
Kennedy Ho. *CT11: Ram* .*5J 211*
(off Newcastle Hill)
DA11: Nflt .8D 62
Kennel Barn Rd. ME9: Bic, B'gar .6K 113 (7C 18)
Kennel Hill CT15: Eyt, W'share .9L 185 (5E 32)
Kennelling Rd. ME13: Stal .4H 29
TN27: Char'g .4H 29
Kennet La. TN25: Stanf .8F 218 (3G 41)
Kennet Rd. DA1: Cray .1H 59
TN10: Tonb .2J 145
Kennett Ct. *BR8: Swanl* .*6F 72*
(off Oakleigh Cl.)
Kennett Dr. CT14: Deal .8K 177
Kenninghall Rd. E5 .1H 5
KENNINGTON
Ashford .3H 159 (7A 30)
London .5F 5
Kennington Cl. ME8: Gill .8M 81
ME15: Maid .9J 127
Kennington La. SE11 .4F 5
KENNINGTON OVAL .5F 5
Kennington Oval SE11 .5F 5
Kennington Pk. Rd. SE11 .5F 5
Kennington Pl. TN24: Kenn .3H 159
Kennington Rd. SE1 .4F 5
SE11 .4F 5
TN24: W'boro .8L 159 (1B 40)
Kennington Station (Tube) .4F 5
KENSAL GREEN .2B 4
Kensal Green Station (Rail & Tube) .2B 4
KENSAL RISE .2B 4
Kensal Rise Station (Rail) .2B 4
Kensal Rd. W10 .2B 4
KENSAL TOWN .2C 4
KENSINGTON .4C 4
Kensington Av. CR7: Thor H .2F 13
Kensington Chu. St. W8 .3C 4
Kensington Gardens .3D 4
Kensington Gore SW7 .4D 4
Kensington High St. W8 .4C 4
W14 .4C 4
Kensington Ho. ME16: Maid .7L 125
Kensington Olympia Station (Rail & Tube) .4C 4
Kensington Palace .3C 4
Kensington Pk. Rd. W11 .3C 4
Kensington Rd. CT1: Cant .7B 168
W8 .4D 4
Kent & Sussex Crematorium
TN2: Tun W .5H 157 (4K 35)
Kent & Sussex Railway .7D 38
Kent Av. CT1: Cant .2B 172
DA16: Well .3H 57
ME10: Sit .8E 98
ME12: Minst .5J 221
ME15: Maid .8F 126
TN24: Ashf .7F 158
Kent Battle of Britain Mus. .8J 193 (3A 42)
Kent Boat & Ski Club .2G 92
Kent CC Club
(St Lawrence Ground) .4A 172 (1H 31)
Kent Cl. BR6: Chels .7G 85
ME1: Roch .3N 93
TN12: Pad W .9M 147
Kent Cl. TN15: W King .8E 88
Kent County Crematorium
TN27: Char'g .4L 175 (5H 29)
Kent County Show Ground .7M 111 (7A 18)
Kent Gdns. CT7: Birch .4E 206
Kent Ga. Way CR0: Croy .7C 82 (5J 13)
KENT HATCH .4B 24
Kent Hatch Rd. RH8: Oxt, Eden .3A 24
TN8: Crock H .3A 24
Kent Ho. CT20: F'stone .7H 189
ME15: Maid .6D 126
Kent Ho. La. BR3: Beck'm .2B 68 (1J 13)
Kent Ho. Rd. BR3: Beck'm .1H 13
SE26 .1B 68 (1J 13)
Kent House Station (Rail) .4B 68 (2J 13)
Kent Intl. Bus. Pk. CT12: Mans .9J 207
Kentish Ct. ME16: Maid .5B 126
Kentish Gdns. TN2: Tun W .5E 156
Kentish Rd. DA17: Belv .4B 52
KENTISH TOWN .1E 4
Kentish Town Rd. NW1 .1E 4
NW5 .1E 4
Kentish Town Station (Rail & Tube) .1E 4
Kentish Town West Station (Rail) .1E 4
Kentish Way BR1: Brom .5K 69 (2A 14)
BR2: Shortl .5L 69
Kent Kraft Ind. Est. DA11: Nflt .3M 61
Kent La. TN32: Brig .5A 44
Kentlea Rd. SE28 .2G 51
Kentmere Av. CT11: Ram .5D 210
Kentmere Rd. SE18 .4G 51
Kenton Ct. *SE26* .*9B 54*
(off Adamsrill Rd.)
Kenton Gdns. CT12: Minst .7E 212
Kenton Rd. E9 .1H 5
Kent Pl. CT11: Ram .6K 211
Kent Police Mus. .5C 80
Kent Rd. BR4: W W'ck .2E 82
BR5: St M Cry .9K 71 (3D 14)
CT9: Mgte .5F 208
CT19: F'stone .4E 188
DA1: Dart .4L 59
DA3: Long .5K 75
DA11: Grav'nd .6F 62
ME2: Hall'g .5E 92 (4F 17)
ME6: Snod .4E 108
ME12: S'ness .3C 220
TN4: Tun W .8G 150
KENT STREET
Battle .7E 44
Maidstone .7K 123 (2D 26)
Kent St. CT5: Whits .5F 226
ME18: Mere .7K 123 (2D 26)
TN33: Sed .7E 44
Kent Ter. CT11: Ram .6K 211
DA13: Meop .4F 90
ME3: High'm .6H 65
Kent Vw. Dr. ME12: E'chu .7C 202
Kentwell Cl. SE4 .2B 54
KENWARD .4E 26
Kenward Ct. TN11: Hdlw .8D 134
Kenward Rd. ME16: Alltn .4N 125
ME18: Yald .4C 136 (4E 26)
SE9 .3M 55
Kenwood Av. DA3: Long .6B 76
ME5: Chat'm .7D 94
Kenwood Dr. BR3: Beck'm .6F 68
Kenworthy Rd. E9 .1J 5
Kenwyn Rd. DA1: Dart .3L 59
Kenya Ter. ME14: Maid .2D 126
Kenyon Wlk. ME8: Gill .8L 95
Kerry Hill Way ME14: Maid .3B 126
Kersey Gdns. SE9 .9A 56
Kerton Rd. TN29: Lydd .6K 47
Kesteven Cl. ME2: Hall'g .6F 92
Kestlake Rd. DA5: Bex'y .4L 57
KESTON .6M 83 (4A 14)
Keston Av. BR2: Kes .6M 83
Keston Cl. DA16: Well .7L 51
Keston Ct. DA5: Bex'y .5A 58
ME8: Gill .1K 95
Keston Gdns. BR2: Kes .5M 83
KESTON MARK .5A 84 (4B 14)
KESTON MARK .4A 84 (4A 14)
Keston Pk. Cl. BR2: Kes .4B 84
Kestrel Cl. ME10: Sit .9H 99
TN8: Eden .4D 184
TN23: Kgnt .6G 160
Kestrel Ct. CT16: Dover .1G 181
Kestrel Ho. *ME7: Gill* .*7E 80*
(off Marlborough Rd.)
Kestrel Rd. ME5: Chat'm .9F 94
Kestrel Way CR0: Croy .9G 83
Keswick Av. ME10: Sit .8K 99
Keswick Cl. TN9: Tonb .5J 145
Keswick Ct. BR2: Shortl .7J 69
SE6 .6J 55
SE13 .3E 54
Keswick Dr. ME16: Alltn .4M 125
Keswick Rd. BR4: W W'ck .3H 83
BR6: Orp .2H 85
DA7: Bexhth .8B 52
Ketridge La. ME18: E Mal .7B 124
Kettle Cnr. ME15: E Far .1J 137
Kettle Dr. CT18: H'nge .7L 193
Kettle Hill ME13: E'lng .2J 29
Kettle Hill Rd. ME13: E'lng .1J 29
(not continuous)
Kettle La. ME15: E Far .3J 137 (3G 27)
Kettlewell Ct. BR8: Swanl .5G 72
Kevin Dr. CT11: Ram .6F 210
KEVINGTON .9N 71 (3E 14)
Kevington Cl. BR5: St P .7H 71
Kevington Dr. BR5: St P .7H 71
BR7: Chst .7G 71
KEW .5A 4
KEW BRIDGE .5A 4
Kew Bri. TW8: Bford .5A 4
TW9: Rich .5A 4
Kew Bri. Rd. TW8: Bford .5A 4
Kew Bridge Station (Rail) .4A 4
Kew Gdns. Rd. TW9: Rich .5A 4
Kew Gardens Station (Rail & Tube) .5A 4
KEW GREEN .5A 4
Kewlands ME14: Maid .3F 126
KEYCOL .6N 97 (4D 18)
Keycol Hill ME9: Bob, N'tn .6N 97 (4D 18)
Keyes Av. ME4: Chat'm .1C 94
Keyes Gdns. TN9: Tonb .8F 144
Keyes Pl. CT19: F'stone .3L 189
Keyes Rd. DA1: Dart .2N 59
Keymer Cl. TN16: Big H .4C 164
Keynes College
University of Kent at Canterbury .8K 167
Keynsham Gdns. SE9 .3A 56
Keynsham Rd. SE9 .3N 55
KEY'S GREEN .3C 36
Keys, The CT18: H'nge .7M 193
KEY STREET .6B 98 (4E 18)
Key St. ME9: Sit .6B 98
ME10: Sit .6B 98 (4E 18)
Keyworth Cl. TN12: Pad W .9L 147
Keyworth M. CT1: Cant .9A 168
Khalsa Dr. DA12: Grav'nd .5H 63
Khartoum Pl. DA12: Grav'nd .4H 63
Khartoum Rd. ME4: Chat'm .7C 80
ME7: Gill .7C 80
Khartoum Sq. CT16: Dover .8F 178
Khyber Rd. ME4: Chat'm .5D 80
ME7: Gill .6E 80
Kibbles La. TN4: S'bgh .5E 150 (1J 35)
KIDBROOKE .5A 6
Kidbrooke Est. SE3 .1M 55
Kidbrooke Green Nature Reserve .1M 55
Kidbrooke La. SE9 .2A 56
KIDBROOKE PARK .5A 34
Kidbrooke Pk. & Repton Grounds .5A 34
Kidbrooke Pk. Rd. SE3 .5A 6
Kidbrooke Station Station (Rail) .1L 55 (6A 6)
Kidd Pl. SE7 .5A 50
Kidd's Hill TN7: Cole H .6C 34
Kilbride Ct. CT11: Ram .3K 211
KILBURN .2C 4
Kilburn High Rd. NW6 .1C 4
Kilburn High Road Station (Rail) .2C 4
Kilburn Ho. ME14: Maid .4D 126
Kilburn La. W9 .2C 4
W10 .2B 4
Kilburn Pk. Rd. NW6 .2C 4
Kilburn Park Station (Tube) .2C 4
Kilburn Priory NW6 .2C 4
Kilburn Station (Tube) .1C 4
Kilgour Rd. SE23 .4B 54
Killearn Rd. SE6 .6G 54
Killewarren Way BR5: Orp .9L 71
Killick Cl. TN13: Dun G .2F 118
Killick Rd. ME3: Hoo .8G 67
Killigarth Ct. DA14: Sidc .9J 57
Kilmorie Rd. SE23 .6B 54
Kiln Barn Rd. ME19: E Mal .3G 125 (1F 27)
ME20: Dit, E Mal .1G 124 (1F 27)
Kilnbridge Cl. ME15: E Far .1M 137
Kiln Cl. ME10: Sit .8H 99
TN25: C'lck .8D 174
Kiln Ct. ME13: Fav .4E 186
KILNDOWN .5F 37
Kilndown DA12: Grav'nd .2J 77
Kilndown Cl. ME16: Alltn .2N 125
TN23: Ashf .3C 160
Kilndown Gdns. CT2: Cant .7N 167
CT9: Clift .3J 209
Kilndown Rd. TN17: Goud .4F 37
Kiln Fld. TN30: Tent .9D 224
Kilnfields BR6: Chels .7B 86
Kiln La. TN11: Leigh .6N 143
TN26: Beth .3L 163 (3G 39)
Kiln Rd. TN25: Aldtn .5C 40
Kiln Way TN12: Pad W .1M 153
Kilnwood TN14: Hals .4A 102
Kimbell Pl. SE3 .2M 55
Kimberley Av. SE15 .6H 5
Kimberley Cl. CT16: Dover .1H 181
Kimberley Ct. *CT8: Wgte S* .*2K 207*
(off Sea Rd.)
Kimberley Dr. DA14: Sidc .7M 57
Kimberley Ga. BR1: Brom .3H 69
Kimberley Gro. CT5: Seas .7B 226
Kimberley Rd. BR3: Beck'm .5A 68
CT12: Ram .3E 210
ME7: Gill .9G 80
Kimberley Ter. CT18: Lym'ge .7L 205
Kimberley Wlk. CT6: Dover .9H 179
Kimberley Way TN24: Ashf .2G 161 (2A 40)
Kimbolton Cl. SE12 .4J 55
Kimmeridge Gdns. SE9 .9A 56
Kimmeridge Rd. SE9 .9A 56
Kincraig Dr. TN13: S'oaks .5H 119
King Alfred Av. SE6 .9D 54
(not continuous)
King & Queen Cl. SE9 .9A 56
King Arthur Rd. CT12: C'snd .5B 210
King Arthurs Dr. ME2: Strood .3K 79
(not continuous)
King Charles Ct. CT14: Walm .8N 177
King Charles Rd. KT5: Surb .3A 12
Kingcup Cl. CR0: Croy .1A 82
King Edward Av. CT6: H Bay .3J 195
CT10: B'stairs .9L 209
DA1: Dart .4L 59
King Edward Ct. CT6: H Bay .3J 195
King Edward Rd. CT7: Birch .5E 206
CT11: Ram .6G 210
CT14: Deal .2N 177 (3J 33)
DA9: G'hithe .3G 60
(not continuous)
ME1: Roch .7N 79
ME4: Chat'm .1C 94
ME7: Gill .6J 81
ME15: Maid .7C 126
RM16: Grays .4B 8
King Edwards Rd. IG11: Bark .2C 6
King Edward St. CT5: Whits .4F 226
Kingfisher Apartments *ME15: Maid* .*3H 139*
(off Wallis Av.)
Kingfisher Av. CT21: Hythe .8D 198
Kingfisher Cl. BR5: St P .7M 71
CT5: Whits .6E 226
CT9: Mgte .3N 207

A-Z Kent Atlas 271

Lackenden Cotts. CT3: L'brne 4J 173
Lacton Oast TN24: W'boro 1M 161
Lacton Way TN24: W'boro 1L 161
Lacy Cl. ME16: Alltn 2A 126
Ladbroke Gdns. W11 3C 4
Ladbroke Gro. W10 2B 4
W11 2B 4
Ladbroke Grove Station (Tube) 3C 4
Ladbrooke Cres. DA14: Sidc 8M 57
Ladbrooke Ho. ME14: Maid 4D 126
LADDINGFORD 5E 26
Ladds La. ME2: Hall'g 5E 16
ME6: Hall'g 8B 92
Ladds Way BR8: Swanl 7E 72
LADE 8H 213 (5K 47)
Lade Fort Cotts. TN29: G'stne 8H 213
Lade Fort Cres. TN29: G'stne 8H 213
Ladesfield CT5: Whits 6E 226
Ladham House 1E 190 (3G 37)
Ladham Rd. TN17: Goud 2D 190 (3G 37)
Ladies Mile TN6: Lye G 5F 35
TN7: Withy 9D 154 (5F 35)
Ladies Wlk. CT21: Hythe 6K 199
Lady Amherst's Dr. TN14: Ide H 4C 130
Ladyclose Av. ME3: Cli W 6L 65
Ladycroft Gdns. BR6: Farnb 6E 84
Ladycroft Rd. SE13 1E 54
Ladycroft Way BR6: Farnb 6E 84
Ladyfields CT6: H Bay 5L 195
DA11: Nflt 9E 62
ME5: Chat'm 9G 95
Ladyfields Cl. ME9: Bob 6A 98
Lady Garne Rd. CT15: W Hou 2D 42
Ladygrove CR0: Croy 9B 82
Lady Margaret Mnr. Rd. ME9: Dod 2G 29
Lady Oak La. TN5: Flim 6F 37
TN17: Goud 6F 37
Lady's Gift Rd. TN4: S'bgh 6F 150
Ladysmith Gro. CT5: Seas 7B 226
Ladysmith Rd. CT5: Whits 8D 226
SE9 4C 56
Lady's Wlk. TN15: Igh, Ivy H 6G 120
Lady Vane Cl. TN11: S'brne 3J 133
LADYWELL 3E 54 (6J 5)
Ladywell Cl. SE4 3D 54
Ladywell Hgts. SE4 4C 54
Ladywell Ho. *CT16: Dover* *4J 181*
(off Park St.)
Ladywell Leisure Cen. 3F 54
Ladywell Pk. Pl. CT16: Dover 4J 181
Ladywell Rd. SE13 3D 54 (6J 5)
Ladywell Station (Rail) 3E 54 (6J 5)
Ladywood Av. BR5: Pet W 8G 71
Ladywood Rd. CT2: Sturry 4E 168
DA2: Dart 1E 74
ME2: Cux 1F 92
Lady Wootton's Grn. CT1: Cant 2N 171
L.A. Fitness 1H 157
Lagonda Way DA1: Dart 2K 59
Lagoon Rd. BR5: St M Cry 8L 71
Lagos Av. CT12: Ram 3E 210
Lake Av. BR1: Brom 2K 69
Lakedale Rd. SE18 6G 50 (5C 6)
Lake Dr. ME3: High'm 7G 65
Lake Footpath SE2 2M 51
Lake Ho. Rd. E11 1A 6
Lakelands ME15: Maid 1D 138
ME17: H'shm 2N 141
Lakeman Way TN4: Tun W 7H 151
Lakemead TN23: Ashf 1C 160
Laker Ind. Est. *SE26* *1B 68*
(off Kent Ho. La.)
Lake Rd. CR0: Croy 3C 82
ME20: Aylfd 2J 125
TN4: Tun W 1E 156
Laker Rd. ME1: Roch 6N 93
Lakeside BR3: Beck'm 6E 68
ME6: Snod 4D 108
TN2: Tun W 8L 151
Lakeside Av. SE28 1J 51
Lakeside Cl. DA15: Sidc 3L 57
TN8: Chid 3A 142
Lakeside Dr. BR2: Shortl 4A 84
Lakeside Pk. ME2: Med E 5B 80
Lakes Rd. BR2: Kes 6M 83
Lakes, The ME20: Lark 6E 108
Lake St. TN6: Mayf 7K 35
TN20: Mayf 7K 35
Lakesview International Bus. Pk.
CT3: Hersd 2M 169
Lakeswood Rd. BR5: Pet W 9D 70
Lakeview Cl. ME6: Snod 4E 108
Lakeview Rd. DA16: Well 2K 57
Lake Vw. Rd. TN13: S'oaks 5H 119
Lakewood Dr. ME8: Gill 5M 95
Laking Av. CT10: B'stairs 6L 209
Laleham Gdns. CT9: Mgte 3F 208
Laleham Rd. CT9: Mgte 4F 208 (1J 23)
SE6 5F 54
Laleham Wlk. CT9: Mgte 4F 208
Lambarde Av. SE9 9C 56
Lambarde Cl. ME2: Hall'g 7E 92
Lambarde Dr. TN13: S'oaks 5H 119
Lambarde Rd. TN13: S'oaks 4H 119
Lambardes DA3: New A 4M 89
Lambardes Cl. BR6: Prat B 2L 101
Lambard Ho. ME14: Maid 4D 126
Lambden Rd. TN27: P'ley 7G 29
LAMBERDEN 1G 45
LAMBERHURST 2L 201 (4D 36)
Lamberhurst Cl. BR5: Orp 2M 85
Lamberhurst Grn. ME8: Gill 9L 81
LAMBERHURST QUARTER 3C 36
Lamberhurst Rd. ME16: Alltn 2M 125
TN3: Lamb 4E 36
TN12: Horsm 9A 196 (4E 36)
Lamberhurst Vineyard Pk. 3K 201 (5D 36)
Lamberhurst Way CT9: Clift 2K 209
Lambersart Cl. TN4: S'bgh 5K 151
Lambert Cl. TN16: Big H 4D 164
Lambert Ct. *DA8: Erith* *6D 52*
(off Park Cres.)
Lambert Ho. CT14: Deal 7L 177
Lambert M. ME6: Snod 2E 108
Lamberts Pl. TN12: Horsm 8D 196
Lamberts Rd. TN2: Tun W 6K 151 (2K 35)
Lambert's Yd. TN9: Tonb 6H 145
Lambes Ct. ME8: Gill 6N 95
LAMBETH 4F 5
Lambeth Bri. SE1 4F 5
SW1 4F 5
Lambeth Cl. ME5: Chat'm 7E 94
Lambeth North Station (Tube) 4F 5
Lambeth Pal. Rd. SE1 4F 5
Lambeth Rd. CT1: Cant 7B 168
SE1 4F 5
Lambourne Dr. ME19: W Mal 7L 123
Lambourne Pl. ME8: Rain 1C 96
Lambourne Rd. ME15: Bear 7J 127
Lambourne Wlk. *CT1: Cant* *2B 172*
(off Sturmer Cl.)
Lambourn Way ME5: Chat'm 8F 94
TN2: Tun W 4K 157
Lambs Bank TN9: Tonb 8H 145
Lambscroft Av. SE9 8M 55
LAMB'S CROSS 5K 27
Lambsfrith Gro. ME7: Hpstd 8L 95
Lambs Mobile Home Pk. TN12: Pad W 7M 147
Lambs Wlk. CT5: Whits 7E 226
Lambton Rd. CT17: Dover 3F 180
Lamerock Rd. BR1: Brom 9J 55
Laming Rd. CT7: Birch 5G 206
Lamkin Wall CT3: Sturry 5N 169 (6A 22)
Lammas Dr. ME10: Sit 5F 98
Lammas Ga. ME13: Fav 4H 187
LAMORBEY 6H 57
Lamorbey Cl. DA15: Sidc 6H 57
Lamorbey Swimming Cen. 7J 57
Lamorna Av. DA12: Grav'nd 7J 63
Lamorna Cl. BR6: Orp 1J 85
Lampington Row TN3: Lang G 2M 155
Lampits Hill SS17: Corr 1F 9
Lamplighters Cl. DA1: Dart 4N 59
ME7: Hpstd 6J 95
Lampmead Rd. SE12 3J 55
Lamport Cl. SE18 4B 50
Lanain Ct. SE12 5J 55
Lanargate St. CT3: L'brne 3L 173 (1A 32)
Lanbury Rd. SE15 2A 54
Lanbury Wlk. TN25: Ashf 6D 158
Lancashire Rd. ME15: Maid 1H 139
Lancaster Av. CT18: Cap F 2B 174
SE27 7F 5
Lancaster Cl. BR2: Shortl 7J 69
TN26: Hams 2L 191
Lancaster Ct. DA12: Grav'nd 8H 63
ME8: Gill 4M 95
Lancaster Gdns. BR2: Shortl 8A 70
CT6: H Bay 2L 195
CT7: Birch 5E 206
Lancaster Gate Station (Tube) 3D 4
Lancaster Ho. CT14: Deal 5K 177
CT17: Dover *5J 181*
(off Lancaster Rd.)
Lancaster Pl. WC2 3F 5
Lancaster Rd. CT1: Cant 4M 171
CT17: Dover 5J 181
NW10 1B 4
SE25 2G 13
Lancaster Way ME19: W Mal 6L 123
Lance Cl. ME10: Kems'y 3G 98
Lance Cft. DA3: New A 3M 89
Lancelot Av. ME2: Strood 6J 79
Lancelot Cl. CT14: Deal 7K 177
ME2: Strood 6J 79
Lancelot Ct. BR6: Orp 3K 85
Lancelot Rd. DA16: Well 2J 57
Lances Cl. DA13: Meop 1F 90
Lancester Cl. CT12: Ram 3F 210
Lancet La. ME15: Maid 2C 138
Lancey Cl. SE7 4A 50
Lanchester Cl. CT6: H Bay 4B 194
Lancing Rd. BR6: Orp 3J 85
Landale Gdns. DA1: Dart 5K 59
Landau Way DA8: Erith 5L 53
Landgate TN31: Rye 5B 46
Landon Rd. CT6: H Bay 2K 195
Landor Ct. ME7: Hpstd 8K 95
Landrail Rd. ME9: Lwr Hal 3L 225
Landseer Av. DA11: Nflt 8C 62
Landseer Cl. TN10: Tonb 1L 145
Landstead Rd. SE18 7F 50
Land Way ME3: High'm 9H 65
Landway TN15: Seal 2N 119
Landway, The BR5: St P 6L 71
ME14: Bear 6J 127 (2K 27)
TN15: Bor G 2M 121
TN15: Kems'g 8A 104 (7H 15)
Lane Av. DA9: G'hithe 4J 61
LANE END 9D 60 (1J 15)
Lane End CT6: H Bay 2E 194
DA7: Bexhth 1C 58
Lanes Av. DA11: Nflt 8E 62
Laneside BR7: Chst 1D 70
Lanes, The CT12: Minst 4F 23
Lane's Wlk. CT5: Whits 3F 226
Lane, The CT15: Gus 7K 179 (7G 33)
SE3 1K 55
TN3: Ford 9K 149
Lanfranc Gdns. CT2: Harb 1J 171
Lanfranc Rd. CT14: Deal 2M 177
Langafel Cl. DA3: Long 5L 75
Langbrook Rd. SE3 9A 50
Lang Ct. CT5: Whits 2L 227
Langdale TN23: Ashf 9C 158
Langdale Av. CT11: Ram 5E 210
Langdale Cl. BR6: Farnb 4D 84
ME8: Rain 2M 95
Langdale Cres. DA7: Bexhth, Erith 7B 52
Langdale Ri. ME16: Maid 4N 125
Langdale Wlk. *DA11: Nflt* *8D 62*
(off Landseer Av.)
Langdon Av. CT3: Ash 5D 216
Langdon Cl. CT15: St Marg 8B 214
Langdon Rd. BR2: Shortl 6L 69
CT19: F'stone 4D 188
ME1: Roch 8N 79
Langdon Shaw DA14: Sidc 1H 71
Langford Pl. DA14: Sidc 8J 57
Langham Cl. CT9: Mgte 2N 207
Langham Gro. ME16: Maid 5N 125
Langham Pk. Pl. BR2: Shortl 7J 69
Langholm Rd. TN3: Lang G 1N 155
TN23: Ashf 2E 160
(not continuous)
Langhorne Gdns. *CT20: F'stone* *7J 189*
(off Leas, The)
LANGHURST 5B 24
Langland Gdns. CR0: Croy 3C 82
Langlands Dr. DA2: Dart 1E 74
LANGLEY 4M 139 (4A 28)
LANGLEY BOTTOM 7A 12
Langley Gdns. BR2: Shortl 7M 69
BR5: Pet W 9D 70
CT9: Clift 2J 209
Langley Gro. KT3: N Mald 2A 12
LANGLEY HEATH 4A 140 (4A 28)
Langley Pk. Farm Cotts. ME17: L'ly 4L 139
Langley Pk. Girls School Sports Cen. 9F 68
Langley Rd. BR3: Beck'm 7B 68
CR2: S Croy 9A 82
DA16: Well 6L 51
ME10: Sit 5G 98
Langley Va. Rd. KT18: Eps 7A 12
Langley Way BR4: W W'ck 2G 83
Langmore Ct. DA6: Bexhth 1M 57
Langney Dr. TN23: Ashf 3B 160
Langport Rd. TN28: New R 3L 213
Langthorne Ct. SE6: Brom 9F 54
Langthorne Rd. E11 1K 5
Langton Cliffs Viewpoint 3M 181 (1G 43)
Langton Cl. CT14: Deal 2M 177
ME14: Maid 4F 126
LANGTON GREEN 2N 155 (3H 35)
Langton La. CT1: Cant 6N 171
Langton Ridge TN3: Lang G 2B 156
Langton Rd. TN3: Lang G 3L 155
TN3: Lang G, Tun W 3H 35
TN3: Speld 9N 149 (2H 35)
TN4: R'hall, Tun W 3H 35
TN4: R'hall, Tun W 3L 155
Langworth Cl. DA2: Dart 8L 59
Lanier Rd. SE13 4G 54
Lankester Parker Rd. ME1: Roch 5N 93
Lankton Cl. BR3: Beck'm 4F 68
Lannoy Rd. SE9 6E 56
Lanridge Rd. SE2 3M 51
Lansbury Cres. DA1: Dart 3A 60
Lansdell Rd. CR4: Mitc 2E 12
Lansdown Cotts. CT1: Cant 3N 171
Lansdowne Av. BR6: Farnb 2D 84
DA7: Bexhth 7M 51
ME15: Maid 2F 138
(not continuous)
Lansdowne Ct. ME4: Chat'm 8C 80
Lansdowne Dr. E8 1H 5
Lansdowne Rd. BR1: Brom 3K 69
CR0: Croy 3G 13
ME4: Chat'm 1B 94
TN1: Tun W 1H 157 (3K 35)
TN9: Tonb 4H 145
TN13: S'oaks 4L 119
Lansdowne Sq. DA11: Nflt 4E 62
TN1: Tun W 1H 157
Lansdown Pl. DA11: Nflt 6E 62
Lansdown Rd. CT1: Cant 3N 171
DA11: Nflt 6E 62
DA14: Sidc 8K 57 (7D 6)
ME10: Sit 7K 99
Lanterns Shop. Cen., The CT20: F'stone 7K 189
Lanthorne M. TN1: Tun W 9H 151
Lanthorne Rd. CT10: B'stairs 6L 209 (2K 23)
Lapins La. ME19: W Mal 7L 123
Lapis Cl. DA12: Grav'nd 6N 63
La Providence ME1: Roch 7N 79
Lapwing Cl. CT18: H'nge 9K 193
DA8: Erith 7J 53
ME12: Minst 7J 221
Lapwing Dr. ME9: Lwr Hal 3L 225
TN23: Kgnt 7H 161
Lapwing Rd. ME3: Isle G 8C 190
Lapwings DA3: Long 6A 76
Lapwings, The DA12: Grav'nd 7J 63
Lapworth Cl. BR6: Chels 3L 85
Lara Cl. SE13 4F 54
Larch Cl. CT10: B'stairs 9H 209
ME20: Lark 8F 108
Larch Cres. TN10: Tonb 1J 145
Larchcroft ME5: Chat'm 7D 94
Larch Dene BR6: Farnb 3C 84
Larches, The CT5: Whits 5E 226
ME3: High'm 1G 79
ME13: Fav 4E 186
Larch Gro. DA15: Sidc 6H 57
TN12: Pad W 9L 147
Larch Ho. BR2: Shortl 4H 69
Larch Rd. CT15: Evtn 7J 185
DA1: Dart 5L 59
Larch Ter. ME12: S'ness 4B 220
Larch Tree Way CR0: Croy 4D 82
Larch Wlk. BR8: Swanl 5D 72
TN24: Kenn 4G 159
Larch Way BR2: Shortl 1C 84
Larch Wood Cl. ME5: Chat'm 1G 110
Larchwood Rd. SE9 7D 56
Largo Wlk. DA8: Erith 8F 52
Larkbere Rd. SE26 9B 54
Larkey Valley Wood Nature Reserve 7G 171
Larkey Vw. CT4: Chart'm 9E 170
LARKFIELD 8E 108 (7F 17)
Larkfield TN12: Five G 8F 146
Larkfield Av. ME7: Gill 8H 81
ME10: Sit 5F 98
Larkfield Cl. BR2: Shortl 3J 83
ME20: Lark 9E 108
Larkfield Leisure Cen. 7E 108
Larkfield Rd. DA14: Sidc 8H 57
ME20: Lark 9E 108
TN13: Riv 5D 118
Larkfields DA11: Nflt 8D 62
Larkfield Trad. Est. ME20: Lark 5F 108
Larkhill Ter. SE18 7C 50
Larkin Cl. ME2: Strood 2M 79
Larks Fld. DA3: Hart'y 7L 75
Larksfield Rd. ME13: Fav 3G 187
Larkspur Cl. BR6: Chels 3L 85
ME19: E Mal 9E 108
Larkspur Lodge DA14: Sidc 8K 57
Larkspur Rd. ME5: Chat'm 7B 94
ME19: E Mal 9D 108
Larkstore Pk. TN12: S'hrst 1J 223
Larkswood Cl. DA8: Erith 8H 53
Larkwell La. DA3: Hart'y 7M 75
Larkwing Cl. ME16: Alltn 2A 126
Larner Rd. DA8: Erith 7F 52
Lascelles Rd. CT17: Dover 6F 180
Laser Quay ME2: Med E 5A 80
LASHENDEN 2C 38
Lassa Rd. SE9 3A 56
Last La. *CT17: Dover* *5J 181*
(off Queen La.)
Latchgate CT20: S'gte 8C 188
Latchmere Rd. SW11 5D 4
La-Tene CT14: Deal 8L 177
Latham Cl. DA2: Dart 7E 60
TN16: Big H 4C 164
Latham Rd. DA6: Bexhth 3B 58
Lathe Barn Children's Farm 2C 182 (6F 41)
Lathkill Ct. BR3: Beck'm 4C 68
Latimer Cl. CT6: H Bay 5C 194
Latimer Ct. *BR2: Shortl* *7J 69*
(off Durham Rd.)
Latimer Pl. ME7: Gill 5F 80
Latimer Road Station (Tube) 3B 4
Latona Dr. DA12: Grav'nd 1L 77
La Tourne Gdns. BR6: Farnb 4E 84
Latters Flats TN11: Hdlw 8D 134
Latymers TN11: Pens 2J 149
Lauderdale Rd. W9 2C 4
Launcelot Rd. BR1: Brom 9K 55
Launder's La. RM13: Rain 2H 7
Launder Way ME15: Maid 7B 126
Laundry M. SE23 5B 54
Laundry Rd. CT12: Minst 4F 23
Launton Dr. DA6: Bexhth 2M 57
Laura Dr. BR8: Swanl 3H 73
Laura Pl. ME1: Roch 1K 93
Laureate Cl. CT9: Mgte 3F 208
Laurel Av. DA12: Grav'nd 7H 63
TN29: St M Bay 3L 215
Laurel Bank TN4: S'bgh 7H 151
Laurelbrook SE6 8H 55
Laurel Cl. CT20: F'stone 5E 188
DA1: Dart 6K 59
DA14: Sidc 8J 57
Laurel Cres. CR0: Croy 4D 82
Laurel Gdns. BR1: Brom 7A 70
Laurel Gro. ME17: Kgswd 6F 140
SE26 9A 54
Laurel Ho. BR2: Shortl 4H 69
Laurel La. TN36: Ickl 7J 45
Laurel Rd. ME7: Gill 5F 80
TN2: Tun W 7K 151
Laurels, The BR1: Brom 4L 69
BR2: Shortl 7K 69
DA2: Dart 8K 59
DA3: Long 6B 76
ME9: Mils 6G 115
ME16: Maid 7N 125
TN26: H Hald 2A 196
Laurel Wlk. ME8: Rain 5A 96
Laurel Way CT4: Chart'm 9E 170
TN2: Tun W 7K 151
Laurensfield CT12: Minst 6F 212
Laureston Pl. CT16: Dover 4K 181
Laurie Gray Av. ME5: Chat'm 1A 110
Lauriston Cl. CT11: Ram 7E 210
Lauriston Mt. CT10: B'stairs 8L 209
Lauriston Rd. E9 1H 5
Lausanne Rd. CT9: Mgte 3D 208
SE15 5H 5
Lavenda Cl. ME7: Hpstd 7K 95
Lavender Av. CR4: Mitc 2D 12
Lavender Cl. BR2: Shortl 9A 70
CT5: Whits 3L 227
CT9: Mgte 5A 208
ME5: Chat'm 7B 94
ME19: E Mal 1D 124
Lavender Ct. ME10: Sit 8H 99
TN2: Tun W 4E 156
Lavender Hill BR8: Swanl 6E 72
SW11 6D 4
TN9: Tonb 7J 145
Lavender La. CT12: C'snd 7A 210
Lavender M. CT1: Cant 2M 171
Lavender Rd. ME19: E Mal 1D 124
Lavenders Rd. ME19: W Mal 2A 124 (1E 26)
Lavender Wlk. ME19: E Mal 1D 124
Lavender Way CR0: Croy 9A 68
Lavernock Rd. DA7: Bexhth 9B 52
Lavidge Rd. SE9 7A 56
Lavinia Rd. DA1: Dart 4N 59
Lavisham Ho. BR1: Brom 1K 69
Lawford Gdns. DA1: Dart 3K 59
Lawley Cl. CT12: Ram 3G 211
Lawn Cl. BR1: Brom 3L 69
BR8: Swanl 5D 72
ME4: Chat'm 1E 94
TN30: Tent 8A 224
Lawn Pk. TN13: S'oaks 9J 119
Lawn Rd. BR3: Beck'm 3C 68
CT10: B'stairs 8L 209
CT14: Walm 9M 177
DA11: Nflt 4B 62
(not continuous)
TN9: Tonb 7H 145
Lawnside SE3 2J 55
Lawns, The CT11: Ram 5K 211
DA14: Sidc 9K 57
SE3 1J 55
TN12: Brenc 6N 153
Lawn Ter. SE3 1H 55
Lawn Vs. *CT11: Ram* *6J 211*
(off Guildford Lawn)
Lawrance Sq. DA11: Nflt 8E 62
Lawrence Av. CT11: Ram 7F 210

Lonesome—Luton High St.

LONESOME 2E 12
Lonewood Way TN11: Hdlw 6E 134
Long Acre BR6: Orp 3M 85
Longacre CT5: Whits 4M 227
Long Acre WC2 3F 5
Long Acre Cl. CT2: Cant 9L 167
Longacre Rd. TN23: Ashf 2B 160
Longage Hill CT4: R Min 9H 183 (1H 41)
CT18: Lym'ge 6K 205 (1H 41)
Long Barn Rd. TN14: Weald 6J 131 (4G 25)
Long Barrow, The TN24: Ashf 3J 161
Long Beech TN23: Ashf 9C 158
Longbridge TN24: W'boro 9M 159
Longbridge Rd. IG11: Bark 1C 6
RM8: Dag 1D 6
Longbridge Ter. CT21: Hythe 7G 199
Longbridge Way SE13 3F 54
Longbury Cl. BR5: St P 6K 71
Longbury Dr. BR5: St P 6K 71
Long Catlis Rd. ME8: Gill 8N 95
Longcroft SE9 8B 56
Longdon Wood BR2: Kes 4A 84
Longdown La. Nth. KT17: Eps 6B 12
Longdown La. Sth. KT17: Eps 6B 12
Longdown Rd. SE6 9D 54
Long Dr. CT13: E'try 3L 183
Longend La. TN12: Coll S 7F 27
Longfellow Rd. ME7: Gill 9F 80
LONGFIELD 5L 75 (2A 16)
Longfield BR1: Brom 4J 69
TN30: Tent 9B 224
Longfield Av. DA3: Long 5B 76
ME3: H Hals 1H 67
Longfield Cl. CT5: Whits 3M 227
Longfield Ct. CT5: Whits 3M 227
LONGFIELD HILL 7C 76 (2B 16)
Longfield Pl. ME15: Maid 9E 126
Longfield Rd. CT17: Dover 6G 180
DA3: Long, Meop 8C 76 (3B 16)
DA13: Meop 8C 76 (3B 16)
TN2: Tun W 6K 151 (2K 35)
Longfields Dr. ME14: Weav 4K 127
Longfield Station (Rail) 6L 75 (2A 16)
LONGFORD 2F 118
Longford Cl. ME8: Rain 3B 96
Longford Ct. ME8: Rain 3C 96
TN13: Dun G 2F 118
Longford Ho. BR1: Brom 1G 68
(off Brangbourne Rd.)
Longford Ter. CT20: F'stone 7K 189
ME1: Woul 7G 93
Longford Way CT20: F'stone 7K 189
Long Gro. Rd. KT19: Eps 5A 12
Longham Copse ME15: Bear 8J 127
Longheath Gdns. CR0: Croy 1A 82
Long Hill CT4: Chil'm, Old L 8J 175 (2D 30)
Longhill Av. ME5: Gill 8E 80
Longhill Rd. SE6 7G 55
Longhurst Dr. ME5: Chat'm 9C 94
Longhurst Rd. SE13 3G 55
LONGLANDS 8E 56 (7C 6)
Longlands Ct. DA15: Sidc 7H 57
Longlands Pk. Cres. DA15: Sidc 8G 56
Longlands Rd. DA14: Sidc 7C 6
DA15: Sidc 8G 56
Long La. CR0: Croy 8A 68 (3H 13)
CT15: Eyt, S'wll 6K 219 (5C 32)
DA7: Bexhth 7M 51 (5E 6)
ME17: Bou Mo 5J 27
RM16: Grays 3A 8
SE1 4G 5
Longleat M. BR5: St M Cry 7L 71
Longleigh La. DA7: Bexhth 5D 6
SE2 6L 51 (5D 6)
Long Length TN23: Kgnt 6B 160 (3K 39)
TN26: Kgnt 6B 160 (3K 39)
Longley Rd. ME1: Roch 8N 79
ME8: Rain 2B 96
SW17 1D 12
Longmarket CT1: Cant 2N 171
Longmarsh La. SE28 1G 51
Longmarsh Vw. DA4: S at H 4B 74
Longmead BR7: Chst 5C 70
Longmead Cl. CT6: H Bay 4D 194
Longmead Dr. DA14: Sidc 7M 57
Longmeade DA12: Grav'nd 6L 63
Long Mdw. TN13: Riv 3E 118
Long Mdw. Cl. BR4: W W'ck 1F 82
Longmeadow Rd. DA15: Sidc 6G 56
Long Mdw. Way CT2: Cant 7M 167
Longmead Rd. KT19: Eps 6A 12
Longmeads TN3: Lang G 1B 156
Longmead Stadium 2G 145
Long Mead Way TN10: Tonb 2H 145
Longmete Rd. CT3: Pres 6C 22
Long Mill La. TN11: S'brne 2N 133 (3A 26)
TN15: Bor G 2A 122 (1B 26)
TN15: Plax 9N 121 (3A 26)
Long Mill La. Crouch TN15: Bor G 4B 122
Longmore Dr. ME12: E'chu 7B 202
Longparish Cl. ME15: Maid 1J 139
Longport CT1: Cant 2N 171 (1H 31)
TN25: Crun 5D 30
Longport Rd. CT18: Peene 4B 188
Long Reach Cl. CT5: Whits 7E 226
Longreach Rd. DA8: Erith 7J 53
Long Rede La. ME16: Barm 6K 125
Longridge ME10: Sit 9J 99
Long Rd. SS8: Can I 2K 9
SW4 6E 4
Long Rock CT5: Whits 2M 227
Long's Acre TN25: Wye 3M 159
Longsfield TN25: Aldtn 4D 40
Longshaw Rd. ME15: Maid 3J 139
Long Slip TN3: Lang G 2A 156
Longsole Cotts. ME16: Barm 6K 125
Longspring Wood TN13: S'oaks 2H 131
Longstone Av. NW10 1A 4
Longtail Ri. CT6: H Bay 5F 194
Longtown Ct. DA2: Dart 4B 60
(off Osbourne Rd.)
Longtye Dr. CT5: Whits 5L 227
Longview Way TN2: Tun W 6K 151
Longwalk DA13: Ist R 4D 76
Long Wlk. SE18 6D 50
TN23: Ashf 6C 158
Longwood ME5: Chat'm 1E 110
(not continuous)
Lonsdale Av. CT9: Clift 2F 208
E6 2A 6
Lonsdale Cl. SE9 8N 55
Lonsdale Cres. DA2: Dart 6C 60
Lonsdale Dr. CT6: H Bay 2C 194
ME8: Gill 5N 95 (4A 18)
ME10: Sit 6D 98
Lonsdale Gdns. TN1: Tun W 2G 157
Lonsdale Rd. DA7: Bexhth 9A 52
SW13 5A 4
Lookers La. CT21: Hythe 5J 199
Loop Ct. M. CT13: S'wch 5L 217
Loop Rd. BR7: Chst 2E 70
Loop St. CT13: S'wch 5L 217
Loop, The CT12: Mans 9J 207 (3F 23)
LOOSE 3C 138 (3H 27)
Loose Bowls Club 1D 138
Loose Ct. ME15: Maid 1D 138
Loose Down Rd. ME13: Throw 3K 29
Loose Rd. ME15: Maid 7D 126 (3J 27)
Loraine Ct. BR7: Chst 1D 70
Lord Cornwalls Ct. CT19: F'stone 3J 189
Lordine La. TN32: Ewh G 3E 44
Lord Robert's Ter. SE18 5C 50
Lord Romney's Hill ME14: Bear 6J 127
Lords Cl. ME9: Bap 9M 99
Lord's Cricket Ground
Marylebone & Middlesex County Cricket Club 2D 4
Lordship La. SE22 6G 5
Lordship Pk. N16 1G 5
Lords of the Level 7B 182
Lord St. DA12: Grav'nd 5G 63
E16 1A 50
Lord's Wlk. ME19: Mere, W Mal 5J 123
ME19: W Mal 7L 123
LORDS WOOD 9F 94 (5J 17)
Lordswood Cl. DA2: Dart 9E 60
ME5: Chat'm 9E 94
Lordswood Ind. Est. ME5: Chat'm 2F 110
(not continuous)
Lordswood La. ME5: Chat'm 9E 94 (5J 17)
Lords Wood La. ME5: Chat'm 6E 94
Lordswood Leisure Cen. 8F 94
Lord Warden Av. CT14: Walm 8N 177
Lord Warden Sq. CT17: Dover 7J 181
Lord Warwick St. SE18 3B 50
Lorenden Pk. TN18: Hawkh 6C 192
Lorimar Ct. ME10: Sit 4D 98
Lorina Rd. CT12: Ram 4G 210
Lorne Av. CR0: Croy 1A 82
Lorne Gdns. CR0: Croy 1A 82
Lorne Rd. CT11: Ram 6G 211
CT16: Dover 2G 181
Lorraine Ct. CT19: F'stone 5L 189
(off Green La.)
Lorton Cl. DA12: Grav'nd 7K 63
LOSSENHAM 2H 45
Lossenham La. TN18: N'den 2G 45
Lothian Rd. SW9 5F 5
Lotus Rd. TN16: Big H 6F 164
Loudon Ct. TN23: Ashf 7C 158
Loudon Path TN23: Ashf 7C 158
Loudon Way TN23: Ashf 7C 158
Loudoun Rd. NW8 2D 4
Loughborough Ct. CT11: Ram 5J 211
Loughborough Junction Station (Rail) 5F 5
Loughborough La. CT18: Lym'ge 9H 205 (2H 41)
Loughborough Rd. SW9 5F 5
Louis Gdns. BR7: Chst 9B 56
Louisville Av. ME7: Gill 8G 81
Lourdes Mnr. Cl. TN25: S'ndge 8C 218
Louvain Rd. DA9: G'hithe 5E 60
Loveace Cl. ME8: Gill 7N 95
Lovelace Av. BR2: Shortl 9C 70
Lovelace Cl. TN15: W King 7E 88
Lovelace Ct. TN26: Beth 2H 163
Lovelace Grn. SE9 1B 56
Lovelace Rd. SE21 7G 5
Love La. BR1: Brom 6L 69
CT1: Cant 2N 171
CT3: Adm 2B 32
CT9: Mgte 2C 208
CT13: S'wch 5M 217
(off Strand St.)
DA5: Bex'y 4A 58
(not continuous)
DA12: Grav'nd 5H 63
ME1: Roch 7N 79
ME12: Minst 5L 221
ME13: Fav 7K 187 (6B 20)
ME18: W'bury 1B 136
RM18: E Til 5E 8
RM19: Avel 4J 7
SE18 4C 50
SM4: Mord 3C 12
TN27: H'crn 9N 191 (7C 28)
Lovel Av. DA16: Well 9J 51
Lovell Rd. CT2: R Comn 8H 167
ME12: Minst 7H 221
Lovers La. DA9: G'hithe 2J 61
TN17: Goud 2C 190 (3G 37)
Lover's Wlk. TN9: Tonb 4J 145
Loves Holiday Camp ME12: Ley S 6L 203
Love St. Cl. CT6: H Bay 5D 194
Lovibonds Av. BR6: Farnb 5D 84
Low Cl. DA9: G'hithe 3G 60
Lwr. Addiscombe Rd. CR0: Croy 3G 13
Lwr. Bell La. ME20: Dit 8F 108
LOWER BITCHET 8C 120
Lwr. Blackhouse Hill CT21: Hythe 5L 199
Lwr. Boxley Rd. ME14: Maid 4C 126 (1H 27)
Lwr. Bridge St. CT1: Cant 2N 171 (1H 31)
LOWER BUSH 9D 78 (3E 16)
Lower Camden BR7: Chst 3B 70
Lwr. Chantry La. CT1: Cant 2N 171 (1H 31)
Lwr. Church Hill DA9: G'hithe 3E 60
LOWER CLAPTON 1H 5
Lwr. Clapton Rd. E5 1H 5
Lwr. Court Rd. KT19: Eps 6A 12
LOWER COUSLEY WOOD 6D 36
LOWER COX STREET 6A 18
Lower Cft. BR8: Swanl 7G 73
Lwr. Denmark Rd. TN23: Ashf 1F 160
Lwr. Downs Rd. SW20 2B 12
Lwr. Dunton Rd. SS17: Horn H 1D 8
Lwr. Ensden Rd. CT4: Old L 2D 30
LOWER EYTHORNE 8J 185 (5D 32)
Lwr. Fant Rd. ME16: Maid 6A 126
Lwr. Farm Rd. ME17: Bou Mo 5J 27
LOWER GOLDSTONE 6E 22
Lwr. Gravel Rd. BR2: Shortl 2A 84
LOWER GREEN
Pembury 6C 152 (2B 36)
Rusthall 9C 150 (2J 35)
Lower Grn. TN11: Leigh 6N 143 (6H 25)
Lwr. Green Rd. TN2: Pem 8C 152 (2B 36)
TN3: Speld, Tun W 7B 150 (2J 35)
TN4: R'hall 9C 150 (2J 35)
Lwr. Guild Hall DA9: Bluew 5F 60
LOWER HALSTOW 3L 225 (3C 18)
LOWER HARDRES 3H 31
LOWER HARTLIP 7G 96 (4C 18)
Lwr. Hartlip Rd. ME9: H'lip 7F 96 (5B 18)
Lwr. Hayesbank TN24: Ashf 7G 158
LOWER HAYSDEN 7D 144 (7J 25)
Lwr. Haysden La. TN11: Tonb 8C 144 (7J 25)
Lwr. Hazelhurst TN5: Tice 7D 36
LOWER HEPPINGTON 3H 31
Lwr. Herne Rd. CT6: H Bay 7F 194 (4J 21)
LOWER HIGHAM 7G 65 (7F 9)
Lwr. Higham Rd.
DA12: Grav'nd, Shorne 6L 63 (7D 8)
Lower High St. TN5: Wadh 7C 36
LOWER HOLLOWAY 1F 5
LOWER ISLAND 4F 226 (3F 21)
Lwr. Lake TN33: Batt 7C 44
Lwr. Lea Crossing E14 3K 5
Lwr. Lees Rd. CT4: Old L 6K 175 (2D 30)
LOWER LUDDESDOWN 1M 91 (3D 16)
Lwr. Mill La. CT14: Deal 5M 177
Lwr. Morden La. SM4: Mord 3B 12
Lwr. Northdown Av. CT9: Mgte 3F 208
Lwr. Norton Rd. ME9: Tey 5J 19
Lwr. Park Rd. CR5: Chip 7D 12
DA17: Belv 4B 52
LOWER PLACE 2A 4
Lwr. Platts TN5: Tice 7E 36
Lwr. Queens Rd. TN24: Ashf 7G 158
LOWER RAINHAM 3A 18
Lwr. Rainham Rd. ME7: Gill, Rain 6K 81 (2K 17)
ME8: Rain 1D 96 (2K 17)
Lwr. Range Rd. DA12: Grav'nd 5K 63
Lwr. Richmond Rd. SW13 5B 4
SW14 6A 4
SW15 6B 4
TW9: Rich 6A 4
Lower Rd. BR5: St M Cry 9K 71 (3D 14)
BR8: Swanl 3G 73 (1G 15)
CT3: S'le 8A 216 (1D 32)
CT16: Temp E 8C 178 (1E 42)
CT17: Dover 9C 178 (1E 42)
DA8: Erith 3C 52 (4F 7)
DA11: Nflt 2L 61
(not continuous)
DA12: Shorne 7C 64 (7E 8)
DA17: Belv 3C 52 (4E 6)
ME9: Tonge, Tey 6J 223 (5G 19)
ME12: E'chu 5A 202
ME12: Minst 8K 221 (1G 19)
(Forty Acres Hill)
ME12: Minst 8F 220
(Queenborough Rd.)
ME13: Fav 5E 186 (6A 20)
ME13: Lud'm 4A 186 (5J 19)
ME15: Maid 7E 126
ME15: W Far, E Far 2G 137 (3F 27)
ME17: Sut V 9A 140 (5A 28)
SE16 4H 5
(not continuous)
SM1: Sutt 4D 12
TN26: Wdchu 8C 228 (5H 39)
TN30: Ston C E 1B 46
Lower Rd. E. CT16: Dover 4N 181
Lower Rd. Est. ME13: Fav 5D 186
Lower Rd. W. CT16: Dover 4M 181
Lwr. Rochester Rd. ME3: High'm 7H 65 (7F 9)
Lwr. Rose Gallery DA9: Bluew 5F 60
Lwr. Sandgate CT20: F'stone 7K 189
Lwr. Sandgate Rd. CT20: F'stone 8H 189
Lower Sands TN29: Dym 5D 182
Lwr. Santon La. CT3: Pres 6C 22
LOWER SHORNE 9C 64 (7E 8)
Lwr. Sloane St. SW1 4E 4
Lwr. Station Rd. DA1: Cray 4F 58
LOWER STOKE 8C 204 (5B 10)
Lwr. Stone St. ME15: Maid 5D 126
Lower St. CT13: E'try 3K 183 (2F 33)
CT14: Tilm 4F 33
ME17: Leeds 3F 140 (3B 28)
(Broomfield)
ME17: Leeds 1C 140 (3B 28)
(Leeds)
TN11: Hild 2M 143 (5H 25)
LOWER SYDENHAM 9A 54 (1H 13)
Lwr. Sydenham Ind. Est. SE26 1C 68
Lower Sydenham Station (Rail) 1C 68 (1J 13)
Lower Ter. NW3 1D 4
Lwr. Thames St. EC3 3G 5
Lwr. Thames Wlk. DA9: Bluew 6F 60
Lower Tovil ME15: Maid 7B 126 (2H 27)
LOWER TWYDALL 7M 81 (2A 18)
Lwr. Twydall La. ME7: Gill 8L 81 (2A 18)
ME8: Gill 8M 81
LOWER UPNOR 1D 80 (1J 17)
Lwr. Vicarage Rd. TN24: Kenn 3G 159
Lwr. Wall Rd. CT21: W Hyt 9A 198 (6D 40)
TN25: Aldtn 6D 40
LOWER WALMER 7M 177
Lwr. Warren Rd. ME5: Aylfd, Boxl 4A 110 (6H 17)
Lwr. Woodlands Rd.
ME7: Gill 6J 81
Lowestoft M. E16 2D 50
Lowfield Rd. ME12: Minst 6F 220
Lowfield St. DA1: Dart 5M 59 (7H 7)
Low Mdw. ME2: Hall'g 6E 92
Lownds Ct. BR1: Brom 5K 69
Lowry Cl. DA8: Erith 4E 52
Lowry, The TN9: Tonb 7H 145
Lowslip Hill CT15: W Hou 6A 180 (2D 42)
Low St. La. RM16: W Til 4D 8
Lowther Hill SE23 5B 54
Lowther Rd. CT17: Dover 4G 181
LOXFORD 1C 6
Loxford La. IG1: Ilf 1C 6
Loxley Cl. SE26 1A 68
Loxton Rd. SE23 6A 54
Loxwood Cl. BR5: Orp 3M 85
CT16: Whitf 6G 178
Lubbock Cl. ME15: Maid 3H 139
Lubbock Rd. BR7: Chst 3B 70 (1B 14)
Lubbock Wlk. ME8: Gill 6N 95
Lucas Ct. SE26 1B 68
Lucas Cres. DA9: G'hithe 2J 61
(off Ingress Pk. Av.)
Lucas Rd. ME6: Snod 3C 108
Lucerne Ct. CT5: Seas 7B 226
DA18: Erith 3N 51
Lucerne Dr. CT5: Seas 7B 226
Lucerne La. CT15: Mart M, Mart 6H 33
Lucerne Rd. BR6: Orp 2H 85
Lucerne St. ME14: Maid 4D 126
Lucilina Dr. TN8: Eden 7C 184
Lucilla Av. TN23: Ashf 5D 160
Luckhurst Gdns. CT9: Clift 2J 209
Luckhurst Rd. CT17: Dover 1D 180
TN24: W'boro 2L 161
Lucknow Cl. CT15: Gus 1L 181
Lucknow Rd. TN12: Pad W 7M 147
Lucknow St. SE18 7G 50
Luck's Hill ME19: W Mal 1A 124 (1E 26)
Lucks La. ME17: Bou Mo 5K 27
TN12: Pad W 6M 147 (7D 26)
Luck's Way TN12: Mard 2B 212
Lucorn Cl. SE12 4J 55
Lucy Av. CT19: F'stone 4G 189 (4A 42)
Lucy's Av. CT21: Hythe 6L 199
Lucys Hill CT21: Hythe 6J 199
LUDDENHAM 1C 186 (5K 19)
Luddenham Cl. ME14: Maid 3F 126
TN23: Ashf 3D 160
Luddesdon Rd. DA8: Erith 7B 52
LUDDESDOWN 2L 91 (3D 16)
Luddesdown Rd. DA13: Lud'n 2M 91 (3D 16)
Ludgate Hill EC4 3F 5
Ludgate La. ME9: Lyn 6M 115 (7G 19)
Ludley Hill TN31: Peas 5H 45
Ludlow Cl. BR2: Shortl 6K 69
Ludpit La. TN19: Etch'm 3A 44
TN32: Rob, Brig 3A 44
Luffield Rd. SE2 3K 51
Luffman Rd. SE12 8L 55
Lughorse La. ME15: Hunt, Yald 7E 136 (4F 27)
ME18: Yald 7E 136 (4F 27)
Lukes Cl. CT17: Dover 3G 180
Lukin Ho. CT21: Hythe 7G 198
Lullarook Cl. TN16: Big H 4C 164
LULLENDEN 2B 34
LULLINGSTONE 6K 87 (4G 15)
Lullingstone Av. BR8: Swanl 6G 72
Lullingstone Castle 6K 87 (4G 15)
Lullingstone Cl. BR5: St P 3K 71
ME7: Hpstd 8L 95
Lullingstone Ct. CT1: Cant 2M 171
(off St John's La.)
Lullingstone Cres. BR5: St P 3J 71
Lullingstone La. DA4: Eyns 4K 87 (4G 15)
SE13 4G 54
Lullingstone Pk. Vis. Cen. 7H 87 (5G 15)
Lullingstone Rd. DA17: Belv 6A 52
ME16: Alltn 2N 125
Lullingstone Roman Villa 4J 87 (4G 15)
Lullington Gth. BR1: Brom 3H 69
Lulworth Rd. DA16: Well 9H 51
SE9 7A 56
Lumley Cl. DA17: Belv 5B 52
Lumsden Ter. ME4: Chat'm 8B 80
Lunar Cl. TN16: Big H 4D 164
Lunedale Rd. DA2: Dart 6C 60
Lunghurst Rd. CR3: Wold 7J 13
LUNSFORD 6D 108 (7E 16)
Lunsford District Cen.
ME20: Lark 6E 108
Lunsford La. ME20: Lark 5D 108 (7E 16)
LUNSFORD PARK 6D 108 (7F 17)
Lupin Cl. CR0: Croy 2A 82
Lupton Cl. SE12 8L 55
Lupus St. SW1 4E 4
Lurkins Ri. TN17: Goud 4B 190
Luscombe Ct. BR2: Shortl 5H 69
Lushington Rd. ME14: Maid 2B 126
SE6 9E 54
Lusted Hall La. TN16: Tats, Big H 8C 164 (1A 24)
Lusted Rd. TN13: Dun G 2F 118
LUTON 2F 94 (3J 17)
Luton Av. CT10: B'stairs 1K 211
Luton Ct. CT10: B'stairs 1K 211
Luton High St. ME5: Chat'm 1F 94 (3J 17)

Manford Ind. Est.—Marlowe Theatre, The

Manford Ind. Est. DA8: Erith 6J 53
Manger's La. CT16: Dover 2F 180
Mangers Pl. CT16: Dover 1F 180
Mangold Way DA18: Erith 3M 51
MANGRAVET 1F 138
Mangravet Av. ME15: Maid 1F 138
Manister Rd. SE2 3J 51
Manitoba Gdns. BR6: Chels 7H 85
Manitoba Ho. *CT16: Dover* 1H 181
(off Winnipeg Cl.)
Manley Cl. CT16: Whitf 6F 178
Manley Ho. CT16: Whitf 6F 178
Mannering Cl. CT17: Dover 1E 180
Manning Ct. *SE28* 1K 51
(off Titmuss Av.)
Manningham Ho. ME19: E Mal 3E 124
Manning Rd. BR5: St M Cry 8M 71
Mannock Ho. CT1: Cant 1A 172
Mannock Rd. DA1: Dart 1N 59
Manns Hill CT4: Up Hard 5H 31
Mann Sq. TN9: Tonb 8K 145
Manor Av. CT14: Deal 6L 177
Manor Brook SE3 2K 55
MANOR CIRCUS 6A 4
Manor Cl. CT1: Cant 5J 171
CT6: H Bay 1N 195
CT14: Deal 6K 177
DA1: Cray 2E 58
DA2: Dart 8H 59
DA12: Grav'nd 7N 63
ME11: Queen 9A 220
ME14: Bear 6L 127
TN4: Tun W 1E 156
Manor Cotts. ME17: E Sut 8E 140
ME17: L'ly 3M 139
Manor Ct. BR4: W W'ck 2E 82
DA7: Bexhth 2C 58
DA13: Sole S 8J 77
ME7: Gill 8M 81
ME14: Bear 6L 127
Manor Ct. Flats CT1: Cant 3M 171
Manor Dr. CT7: Birch 5E 206
DA3: Hart'y 9M 75
Mnr. Farm Cl. CT21: Lymp 4B 198
Mnr. Farm Cotts. TN15: Igh 3G 121
Manor Fld. DA12: Shorne 1C 78
Manorfield TN23: Ashf 1C 160
Manorfields Cl. BR7: Chst 6H 71
Manor Forstal DA3: New A 4M 89
Manor Gdns. CT16: Whitf 5F 178
ME5: Chat'm 8C 94
Manor Gro. BR3: Beck'm 5E 68
ME10: Sit 8E 98
TN10: Tonb 4J 145
Manor Ho. DA3: New A 4M 89
ME7: Gill 6D 80
Manor Ho. Dr. ME16: Maid 6A 126
TN23: Kgnt 5G 161
Manor Ho. Gdns. TN8: Eden 6C 184
Manor Ho. La. CT18: Cap F 2C 42
Manor La. DA3: Fawk 1J 89 (3K 15)
DA3: Hart'y 9N 75
ME1: Roch 9K 79
ME17: Holl 6G 129
SE12 3H 55 (6K 5)
SE13 3H 55
TN15: Ash 3K 15
TN15: Fawk 1J 89
Manor La. Ter. SE13 2H 55
Manor Lea Rd. CT7: St N 9M 215
Manor Leaze TN25: Sme 8L 165
Manor M. CT14: R'wld 4B 200
MANOR PARK 1B 6
Manor Pk. BR7: Chst 5F 70
DA8: Erith 6H 53
SE13 2G 55
TN4: Tun W 2E 156
Manor Pk. Cl. BR4: W W'ck 2E 82
Manor Pk. Country Pk. 2N 123 (1E 26)
Mnr. Park Pde. *SE13* 2G 55
(off Lee High Rd.)
Manor Pk. Rd. BR4: W W'ck 2E 82 (3J 13)
BR7: Chst 4E 70 (2C 14)
NW10 2A 4
Manor Park Station (Rail) 1A 6
Manor Pl. BR7: Chst 5F 70
DA1: Dart 6M 59
Mnr. Pound La. TN25: E Bra 6K 165 (2E 40)
Manor Ri. CT17: Dover 6F 180
ME14: Bear 5L 127
Manor Rd. BR3: Beck'm 5E 68 (2J 13)
BR4: W W'ck 3E 82
CR4: Mitc 2E 12
CT5: Whits 2J 227
CT6: H Bay 1N 195
CT7: St N 8M 215 (3D 22)
CT10: B'stairs 9K 209
CT14: Deal 6K 177 (4J 33)
CT17: Dover 6F 180
CT20: F'stone 7J 189
DA1: Cray 2F 58 (6F 7)
DA3: Long, Long H 8B 76 (3B 16)
DA5: Bex'y 6C 58
DA8: Erith 6G 52 (5F 7)
DA10: Swans 4K 61 (7K 7)
DA12: Grav'nd 4G 63
DA13: Sole S 8H 77
DA15: Sidc 8H 57
E15 2K 5
E16 2K 5
ME4: Chat'm 8C 80
ME9: Mils 8F 114 (7F 19)
ME11: Queen 9A 220
ME12: E'chu 2H 203
SE25 2H 13
SM6: Wall 4E 12
TN4: R'hall 1C 156
TN4: S'bgh 5E 150
TN8: Eden 6B 184
Manor Rd. TN14: Sund 6M 117
TN15: W King 2F 104
TN16: Tats 8E 164
TN29: Lydd 4K 205
TW9: Rich 6A 4
Manor Row TN30: Tent 8B 224
Manorside Cl. SE2 4L 51
Manor St. ME7: Gill 6D 80
Manor Vw. DA3: Hart'y 9N 75
Manor Way BR2: Shortl 9A 70
BR3: Beck'm 5D 68
BR5: Pet W 7E 70
CT20: F'stone 7J 189
DA5: Bex'y 6B 58
DA7: Bexhth 1E 58
DA10: Swans 2K 61
DA11: Nflt 2N 61
ME12: E'chu 2H 203 (1A 20)
ME12: Ley S 6M 203
RM13: Rain 2F 7
SE3 2J 55
TN23: Ashf 6D 158
Manorway, The SS17: Stan H, Corr 2E 8
Manover Ct. ME13: Fav 4F 186
Manse Fld. TN25: Bra L 8K 165
Mansel Dr. ME1: Roch 1L 93
Mansell La. CT15: S'fld 1A 42
Mansell St. E1 3G 5
Manse Pde. BR8: Swanl 7H 73
Mansergh Cl. SE18 7A 50
Manse Way BR8: Swanl 7H 73
Mansfield Cl. BR5: St M Cry 1M 85
Mansfield Cl. CT4: Brid 8H 173
Mansfield Dr. ME9: Iwade 9J 197
Mansfield Rd. BR8: Swanl 2F 72
NW3 1D 4
Mansfield Wlk. ME16: Maid 7B 126
Mansion Cotts. ME15: Maid 6H 127
Mansion Gdns. CT16: Dover 9F 178
Mansion Ho. Cl. TN27: Bidd 7K 163
Mansion House Station (Tube) 3G 5
Mansion Row ME7: Gill 6D 80
Mansions, The CT10: B'stairs 9J 209
Mansion St. CT9: Mgte 2C 208
MANSTON 3B 210 (3H 23)
MANSTON AIRPORT 4A 210 (3G 23)
Manston Camping & Cvn. Pk. CT12: Mans 2B 210
Manston Ct. Rd. CT9: Mgte 3A 210 (3H 23)
CT12: Mans, Mgte 3A 210 (3H 23)
Manston Pk. Bungs. CT12: Mans 9L 207
Manston Rd. CT7: Birch 7G 206 (3F 23)
CT9: Mgte 8A 208 (3H 23)
CT11: Ram 3G 23
CT12: Mans, Mgte 3A 210 (3G 23)
CT12: Ram 4D 210
Mantelow Ct. CT10: Ram 2K 211
Manthorp Rd. SE18 5E 50
Mantle Rd. SE4 1B 54 (6J 5)
Mantles Hill CT14: Ripp 4H 33
Manton Rd. SE2 4J 51
Manwarings, The TN12: Horsm 7C 196
Manwood Av. CT2: Cant 8M 167
Manwood Cl. ME10: Sit 9G 98
Manwood Rd. CT13: S'wch 6M 217
SE4 3C 54 (6J 5)
Manwood St. E16 1B 50
Mapesbury Rd. NW2 1C 4
Maple Av. ME7: Gill 7H 81
ME16: Alltn 3N 125
Maple Cl. BR5: Pet W 8F 70
BR8: Swanl 5F 72
CT2: R Comn 8H 167
CT10: B'stairs 4J 209
ME20: Lark 8E 108
TN2: Tun W 4G 156
TN23: Ashf 8C 158
Maple Cotts. TN26: Beth 3K 163
Maple Ct. CT3: Hersd 2K 169
DA9: G'hithe 5E 60
SE6 6E 54
Maple Cres. DA15: Sidc 4J 57
Mapledene BR7: Chst 1E 70
Maple Dr. CT18: H'nge 7M 193
TN29: St M Bay 3M 215
Maple Gdns. CT3: Hersd 3K 169
Maple Ho. CT2: R Comn 8H 167
Maplehurst BR2: Shortl 5H 69
Maplehurst Cl. DA5: Bex'y 7F 58
Maple Leaf Cl. TN16: Big H 4D 164
Maple Leaf Dr. DA15: Sidc 6H 57
Maple Rd. DA1: Dart 6K 59
DA12: Grav'nd 9H 63
ME2: Strood 6K 79
SE20 2H 13
MAPLESCOMBE 6C 88 (4H 15)
Maplescombe La. DA4: Farn'm 4A 88 (4H 15)
TN15: Farn'm 4A 88 (4H 15)
Maplesden Cl. ME16: Barm 6K 125
Maples, The CT10: B'stairs 9H 209
DA3: Long 5A 76
ME12: Minst 6J 221
Maple St. ME12: S'ness 3D 220
Mapleton Cl. BR2: Shortl 9K 69
Mapleton Rd. TN8: Four E, Westrm 3C 24
TN16: Westrm 3C 24
Maple Way SS8: Can I 2K 9
Maplin Ho. *SE2* 2M 51
(off Wolvercote Rd.)
Maplins Cl. ME8: Rain 2B 96
Maplin Way SS1: Sth S 1G 11
Maplin Way Nth. SS1: Sth S 1G 11
Mara Ct. ME4: Chat'm 2C 94
Maran Way DA18: Erith 2M 51
Marathon Paddock ME7: Gill 8G 81
Marathon Way SE28 2H 51
MARBLE ARCH 3D 4
Marble Arch Station (Tube) 3D 4
Marble Ho. SE18 5H 51
Marbrook Ct. SE12 8M 55
Marcellina Way BR6: Orp 4G 85
Marcet Rd. DA1: Dart 3K 59
Marcilly Rd. SW18 6D 4
Marconi Rd. DA11: Nflt 8C 62
Marconi Way ME1: Roch 4A 94
Marcus Rd. DA1: Dart 5H 59
Mardale Cl. ME8: Rain 2C 96
Mardell Rd. CR0: Croy 8A 68
MARDEN 2D 212 (7H 27)
Marden Av. BR2: Shortl 9J 69
CT12: Ram 4F 210
MARDEN BEECH 1G 37
Marden Cres. DA5: Bex'y 3D 58
Marden Rd. ME2: Strood 3N 79
TN12: S'hrst 2H 223 (7J 27)
TN17: Siss 3H 37
MARDEN'S HILL 6E 34
Marden's Hill TN6: Crowb 6E 34
Marden Station (Rail) 2C 212 (7H 27)
MARDEN THORN 1J 37
Mardol Rd. TN24: Kenn 5G 158
Marechal Niel Av. DA15: Sidc 8F 56
Marechal Niel Pde. *DA14: Sidc* 8F 56
(off Main Rd.)
Maresfield Cl. CT16: Dover 2G 181
Mare St. E8 2H 5
Margaret Barr Row DA10: Swans 5L 61
Margaret Ct. CT6: H Bay 3G 195
Margaret Gardner Dr. SE9 7B 56
Margaret Rd. DA5: Bex'y 4M 57
Margaret St. CT20: F'stone 6L 189
MARGATE 3C 208 (1H 23)
Margate Caves 2D 208
Margate Cl. ME7: Gill 6H 81
Margate Crematorium CT9: Mgte 2H 23
Margate F.C. (Hartsdown Pk.) 4B 208 (1H 23)
Margate Hill CT7: Acol 8G 207 (3F 23)
Margate Lifeboat Station 2C 208
Margate Old Town Hall Mus. 2C 208
(off Market St.)
Margate Rd. CT6: H Bay 4J 195 (3K 21)
(Reculver Rd.)
CT6: H Bay 5K 195 (3K 21)
(Hunters Forstal Rd.)
CT10: B'stairs, Ram 9E 208 (3J 23)
CT11: Ram 9E 208 (3J 23)
CT12: Ram 3J 23
Margate Station (Rail) 3B 208 (1H 23)
Margery St. WC1 2F 5
Margetts La. ME1: Burh 1H 109 (5F 17)
Margetts Pl. ME2: Upnor 1D 80
Marian Av. ME12: Minst 5H 221
Marian Sq. TN12: S'hrst 2K 223
Marigold Way CR0: Croy 2A 82
Marilyn Cres. CT7: Birch 4G 207
Marina Cl. BR2: Shortl 6K 69
Marina Ct. CT14: Deal 2N 177
Marina Dr. DA1: Dart 6A 60
DA11: Nflt 5E 62
DA16: Well 9G 50
ME12: Minst 5H 221
Marina Esplanade CT11: Ram 6K 211
Marina Rd. CT11: Ram 5K 211
Marina, The CT14: Deal 1N 177 (3J 33)
Marine Av. SS0: Wclf S 1D 10
TN29: Dym 4E 182
Marine Ct. CT16: Dover 5K 181
DA8: Erith 7G 53
RM19: Purf 4N 53
Marine Cres. CT5: Whits 2K 227
CT20: F'stone 7K 189
Marine Dr. CT9: Mgte 3C 208 (1H 23)
CT10: B'stairs 2L 209
SE18 4B 50
Marine Gap CT5: Whits 4E 226
Marine Gdns. CT9: Mgte 3C 208
CT20: F'stone 7L 189
Marine Pde. CT5: Whits 2H 227 (3F 21)
CT16: Dover 5K 181 (2G 43)
(not continuous)
CT20: F'stone 7K 189 (5B 42)
CT21: Hythe 7K 199
ME12: S'ness 2E 220 (6G 11)
SS1: Sth S 1E 10
SS9: Lgh S 1B 10
TN28: L'stne 4N 213 (3K 47)
Marine Pde. M. CT20: F'stone 7L 189
Marine Point CT20: F'stone 8H 189
Marine Prom. CT20: F'stone 7K 189
Marine Rd. CT14: Walm 6N 177
Mariners Ct. CT5: Whits 4F 226
DA9: G'hithe 2H 61
(off High St.)
Mariners Lea CT10: B'stairs 9H 209
Mariners, The ME1: Roch 8M 79
Mariners Vw. ME7: Gill 5J 81
Mariners Wlk. DA8: Erith 6G 53
ME13: Oare 2F 186
Mariners Way DA11: Nflt 5D 62
Marine Ter. CT5: Whits 4E 226
CT9: Mgte 3B 208 (1H 23)
CT20: F'stone 7L 189 (5B 42)
MARINE TOWN 3E 220 (6G 11)
Marine Vw. ME4: Chat'm 3E 80
Marine Wlk. CT20: F'stone 8H 189
Marine Wlk. Sth. CT21: Hythe 6K 199
Marion Cl. ME5: Chat'm 9D 94
Marion Cres. BR5: St M Cry 8J 71
ME15: Maid 8E 126
Marischal Rd. SE13 1G 54
Maritime Av. CT6: H Bay 3K 195
Maritime Bus. Cen. ME2: Med E 4A 80
Maritime Cl. DA9: G'hithe 3H 61
ME2: Med E 4A 80
Maritime Ga. DA11: Nflt 5D 62
Maritime Way ME4: Chat'm 4D 80
Marjan Cl. CT17: Dover 3F 180
Mark Av. CT11: Ram 7F 210
MARKBEECH 1D 34
Mark Brunel Way ME4: Chat'm 5D 80
Mark Cl. DA7: Bexhth 8N 51
MARK CROSS 7K 35
Marke Cl. BR2: Kes 5A 84
Market All. DA12: Grav'nd 4G 63
Market Bldgs. ME14: Maid 5C 126
Market Hill CT21: Hythe 6K 199
SE18 3C 50
Market La. *TN23: Ashf* 8F 158
(off Queen St.)
Market Mdw. & William Pl. BR5: St M Cry 7L 71
Market Pde. *BR1: Brom* 4K 69
(off East St.)
DA14: Sidc 9K 57
Market Pl. CT3: Aysm 2D 162 (3B 32)
CT9: Mgte 2C 208
(off Market St.)
CT20: F'stone 6K 189
DA1: Dart 5M 59
DA6: Bexhth 2B 58
ME4: Chat'm 8D 80
ME13: Fav 5H 187
TN2: Tun W 3G 156
TN12: S'hrst 1K 223
TN27: Char'g 3K 175
Market Pl. (Sth.) *CT9: Mgte* 2C 208
(off Market St.)
Market Rd. N7 1F 5
Market Sq. BR1: Brom 5K 69 (2A 14)
(not continuous)
CT16: Dover 5J 181
TN1: Tun W 1H 157
TN16: Westrm 8F 116 (2C 24)
Market St. CT6: H Bay 2G 194
CT9: Mgte 2C 208
CT13: S'wch 5L 217
(not continuous)
CT14: Deal 4N 177
CT17: Dover 5J 181
DA1: Dart 5M 59 (7H 7)
ME13: Fav 5H 187
SE18 4C 50
TN2: Tun W 3G 156
TN12: S'hrst 1K 223
Market Vw. CT3: Aysm 2D 162
Market Way CT2: Cant 9N 167
TN16: Westrm 8F 116
Markham Cotts. ME15: W Far 2J 137
Markland Rd. CT17: Dover 5E 180
Mark La. DA12: Grav'nd 5K 63
(not continuous)
Marks Sq. DA11: Nflt 9E 62
Mark St. ME4: Chat'm 1D 94
Mark Way BR8: Swanl 8H 73
Marlborough Cl. BR6: Orp 9H 71
CT10: B'stairs 1J 211
TN4: Tun W 1E 156
TN28: L'stne 2M 213
Marlborough Ct. *CT20: F'stone* 7H 189
(off Earls Av.)
CT21: Hythe 7L 199
TN16: Westrm 8E 116
(off Croydon Rd.)
Marlborough Cres. TN13: S'oaks 6F 118
Marlborough Pde. ME16: Barm 7K 125
Marlborough Pk. Av. DA15: Sidc 5J 57
Marlborough Rd. BR2: Shortl 7M 69
CT5: Whits 8F 226
CT9: Mgte 4C 208
CT11: Ram 6H 211
CT14: Deal 8K 177
CT17: Dover 5E 180
DA1: Dart 4K 59
DA7: Bexhth 1M 57
ME7: Gill 8E 80
N19 1E 4
SE18 3D 50
Marlborough Way TN24: Kenn 3K 159
Marle Place Gardens & Gallery 3D 36
Marle Pl. Rd.
TN12: Brenc, Horsm 9N 153 (2D 36)
Marler Ho. DA8: Erith 9G 52
Marler Rd. CT19: F'stone 5E 188
SE23 6B 54
MARLEY
Canterbury 4K 31
Deal 3G 33
Marley Av. DA7: Bexhth 6M 51
Marley Ct. CT2: Cant 7J 167
Marley La. CT3: Hoath, C'let 4A 22
CT4: Kgstn 6A 162 (5J 31)
CT14: Fin 3G 33
TN33: Batt 7C 44
Marley Rd. ME3: Hoo 7G 67
ME17: H'shm 2N 141 (3D 28)
Marley Vw. ME1: Roch 3H 17
Marley Way ME1: Roch 1N 93
Marlfield TN12: S'hrst 2J 223
Marlhurst TN8: Eden 3B 184
Marlie Farm Holiday Village
TN28: New R 1L 213
Marlings Cl. BR7: Chst 7G 71
Marlings Pk. Av. BR7: Chst 7G 71
Marling Way DA12: Grav'nd 2K 77
Marlow Cl. CT5: Whits 4K 227
Marlow Copse ME5: Chat'm 1C 110
Marlowe Arc. CT1: Cant 2M 171
Marlowe Av. CT1: Cant 2M 171
Marlowe Cl. BR7: Chst 2F 70
Marlowe Ct. *CT1: Cant* 1M 171
(off King St.)
Marlowe Gdns. SE9 4C 56
Marlowe Mdws. CT2: Cant 7E 168
Marlowe Rd. CT9: Mgte 5G 208
CT16: Dover 1G 180
ME20: Lark 7D 108
TN23: Ashf 8F 158
Marlowes, The DA1: Cray 2E 58
Marlowe Theatre, The 1M 171

Marlow Ho.—Mead Way

Marlow Ho. *CT7: Birch* 4G 206
(off Sutherland Dr.)
MARLPIT 6H 139
Marlpit Cl. TN8: Eden 3C 184
MARLPIT HILL 3B 184 (5C 24)
Marlpit La. CR5: Coul 7F 13
Marlwood Cl. DA15: Sidc 7G 56
Marmadon Rd. SE18 4H 51
Marne Av. DA16: Well 1J 57
Marnock Rd. SE4 3C 54
Maroons Way SE6 1D 68
Marquis Dr. ME7: Hpstd 8L 95
Marrabon Cl. DA15: Sidc 6J 57
Marr Cl. ME12: Minst 5G 221
Marriett Ho. SE6 9F 54
Marriott Rd. DA1: Dart 5N 59
Marriotts Wharf DA11: Grav'nd 3G 62
Marrose Av. CT12: Ram 1F 210
Marsala Rd. SE13 2E 54
Marsden Way BR6: Orp 5H 85
Marshall Cres. CT10: B'stairs 9J 209
ME11: Queen 9A 220
Marshall Gdns. TN11: Hdlw 7D 134
Marshall Rd. ME8: Gill 4M 95
Marshalls Gro. SE18 4A 50
Marshalls Land TN30: St Mic 4B 224
Marshall St. CT19: F'stone 4K 189
Marsham Cl. BR7: Chst 1D 70
ME17: H'shm 2N 141
Marsham Cres. ME17: Cha S 7L 139
Marsham M. *CT1: Cant* 1A 172
(off Clement Cl.)
Marsham St. ME14: Maid 5D 126
SW1 4E 4
Marsham Way ME2: Hall'g 6E 92
MARSHBOROUGH 6F 216 (1F 33)
Marshborough Rd.
CT13: Ash, S'wch, Wdboro 6E 216 (1F 33)
Marshbrook Cl. SE3 1N 55
Marsh Cres. ME3: H Hals 1H 67
TN28: New R 3K 213
Marsh Farm Rd. CT12: Minst 9E 212 (5F 23)
Marshfoot Rd. RM16: Grays 4B 8
RM17: Grays 4B 8
Marshgate La. E15 1J 5
Marshgate Path SE28 3E 50
MARSH GREEN
Edenbridge 7B 24
Hartfield 6D 34
Marsh Grn. Rd. TN8: Marsh G 9C 184 (1B 34)
Marsh Hill E9 1J 5
Marshlands TN29: Dym 8A 182
Marshlands Cl. TN29: Dym 8A 182
Marshland Vw. ME3: Lwr Sto 7C 204
Marsh La. CT14: Deal, Shol 4J 177
ME3: Cliffe 2C 176
Marsh Quarter La. TN18: Sandh 4D 218 (2F 45)
Marsh Ri. ME10: Kems'y 2H 99
Marsh Rd. ME2: Hall'g 6E 92
TN26: Hams 3L 191 (6A 40)
TN26: Ruck 6B 40
MARSHSIDE 3B 22
Marsh St. DA1: Dart 1A 60
(Chaucer Way)
DA1: Dart 3N 59
(Hilltop Gdns.)
ME2: Strood 5M 79
Marsh Vw. CT21: Hythe 8D 198
DA12: Grav'nd 6L 63
Marsh Wall E14 4J 5
Marsh Way ME20: Lark 6E 108
RM13: Rain 2F 7
Marshwood Cl. CT1: Cant 8B 168
Marstan Cl. ME9: Upc 4H 225
Marston Cl. ME5: Chat'm 8B 94
Marston Dr. ME14: Maid 4E 126
Marston Wlk. ME5: Chat'm 8B 94
Martello Cotts. CT21: Hythe 7F 198
Martello Dr. CT21: Hythe 7G 198
Martello Ind. Cen. CT19: F'stone 5M 189
Martello Rd. CT20: F'stone 5L 189
(Dover Rd.)
CT20: F'stone 8D 188
(West Rd.)
Martello Ter. CT20: S'gte 8F 188
Martello Tower no. 1 4N 189
Martello Tower no. 2 4M 189
Martello Tower no. 3 5N 189
Martello Tower no. 4 8G 188
Martello Tower no. 5 7F 188
Martello Tower no. 6 8E 188
Martello Tower no. 7 8D 188
Martello Tower no. 8 8C 188
Martello Tower no. 9 8B 188
Martello Tower no. 13 8J 199
Martello Tower no. 23 6D 182
Martello Tower no. 24 8B 182 (7F 41)
Martello Tower no. 25 9B 182
Marten Rd. CT20: F'stone 6H 189
Martens Av. DA7: Bexhth 2C 58
Martens Cl. DA7: Bexhth 2D 58
Martens La. TN26: H Hald 2F 196 (4F 39)
Martha Cl. CT19: F'stone 4H 189
Martime Way ME4: Chat'm 2J 17
MARTIN 2N 179 (6G 33)
Martin Bowes Rd. SE9 1B 56
Martin Ct. ME7: Hpstd 8L 95
Martindale Av. BR6: Chels 6J 85
Martindale Cl. CT1: Cant 3N 171
Martin Dene DA6: Bexhth 3A 58
Martindown Rd. CT5: Whits 7E 226
Martin Dr. DA2: Dart 5C 60
Martin Hardie Way TN10: Tonb 2L 145
Martin Ho. DA11: Nflt 8F 62
TN25: Wye 3M 159
MARTIN MILL 6H 33
Martin Mill Station (Rail) 6H 33
Martin Pl. *SE28* 1G 50
(off Martin St.)
Martin Ri. DA6: Bexhth 3A 58
Martin Rd. DA2: Dart 8K 59
ME2: Strood 4M 79
Martins Cl. BR4: W W'ck 2G 83
BR5: St P 6M 71
Martin's Cl. CT12: Ram 2G 211
Martins Cl. ME3: High'm 7H 65
TN30: Tent 8D 224
Martin's Dr. TN11: Leigh 8L 143
Martins La. TN12: E Peck 7K 135 (4D 26)
Martin Sq. ME20: Lark 8E 108
(not continuous)
Martin's Rd. BR2: Shortl 5H 69
Martins Shaw TN13: Riv 4D 118
Martins, The TN26: H Hald 1E 196
Martin St. SE28 1G 50
Martin's Way CT21: Hythe 8E 198
Martin Wlk. *SE28* 1G 50
(off Martin St.)
Martin Way SM4: Mord 2C 12
SW20 2C 12
Marton Cl. SE6 8D 54
MARTYRS FIELD 3L 171
Martyr's Fld. Rd. CT1: Cant 3L 171
Marvels Cl. SE12 7L 55
Marvels La. SE12 7L 55 (7A 6)
(not continuous)
Marvillion Ct. TN12: E Peck 1L 147
Marwell TN16: Westrm 8D 116
Marwell Cl. BR4: W W'ck 3J 83
Marwood Cl. DA16: Well 1K 57
Mary Ann Cotts. *CT19: F'stone* 4E 188
(off Ashley Av.)
Mary Bank SE18 4B 50
Mary Burrows Gdns. TN15: Kems'g 8B 104
Mary Day's TN17: Goud 4C 190
Mary Dukes Pl. ME15: Maid 6E 126
Maryfield Cl. DA5: Bex'y 2F 58
Mary Grn. Wlk. CT1: Cant 9A 168
Maryland Ct. CT21: Hythe 5L 199
ME8: Rain 6A 96
Maryland Dr. ME16: Barm 7K 125
Maryland Gro. CT1: Cant 4A 172
Maryland Rd. TN2: Tun W 4K 157
Maryland Station (Rail) 1K 5
Mary Last Cl. ME6: Snod 3C 108
MARYLEBONE 3E 4
MARYLEBONE FLYOVER 2D 4
Marylebone High St. W1 3E 4
Marylebone Rd. W2 3D 4
Marylebone Station (Rail & Tube) 2D 4
Mary Magdalene Ho. TN9: Tonb 7H 145
Maryon Gro. SE7 4A 50
Maryon Rd. SE7 4A 50
SE18 4A 50
Mary Rd. CT14: Deal 7K 177
Maryville DA16: Well 9H 51
MASCALLS 1D 36
Mascall's Ct. La. TN12: Pad W 2N 153 (1D 36)
Mascall's Ct. Rd. TN12: Pad W 1M 153 (7D 26)
Mascalls Pk. TN12: Pad W 1L 153
Masefield Cl. DA8: Erith 8G 53
Masefield Dr. ME3: Cli W 5M 65
Masefield Rd. DA1: Dart 3B 60
DA11: Nflt 8C 62
ME20: Lark 6D 108
Masefield Vw. BR6: Farnb 4E 84
Masefield Way TN9: Tonb 7F 144
Masham Ho. *DA18: Erith* 2M 51
(off Kale Rd.)
Mason Cl. DA7: Bexhth 1C 58
Masons Hill BR2: Shortl 6K 69 (2A 14)
SE18 4D 50
Masons Ri. CT10: B'stairs 8L 209
Masons Rd. CT17: Dover 3G 180
Mason Way ME3: Wain 2M 79
Master Gunners Pl. SE18 7A 50
Masters La. ME19: Birl 5N 107
Masthead Cl. DA2: Dart 2C 60
Matchless Dr. SE18 7C 50
MATFIELD 6J 153 (2C 36)
Matfield Cl. BR2: Shortl 8K 69
Matfield Cres. ME14: Maid 4F 126
Matfield Rd. DA17: Belv 6B 52
Mathon Ct. TN24: Kenn 5G 159
Matilda Cl. ME8: Gill 2L 95
Matterdale Gdns. ME16: Barm 7J 125
Matthews Cl. CT14: Deal 4M 177
Matthews Ct. ME7: Gill 7G 80
Matthews La. ME18: W Peck 3E 134 (4B 26)
TN11: Hdlw 3E 134 (4B 26)
Matthew's Pl. CT16: Dover 3H 181
Matthews Rd. CT6: H Bay 5D 194
Matthias Rd. N16 1G 5
Mattinson Pl. ME9: Worm 1D 28
Matts Hill Rd. ME9: H'lip 9N 95 (5A 18)
Maud Cashmore Way SE18 3B 50
Maude Rd. BR8: Swanl 2H 73
Maudslay Rd. SE9 1B 56
Maugham Ct. CT5: Whits 5F 226
Maunders Cl. ME5: Chat'm 3F 94
Maunsell Pl. TN24: Ashf 2H 161
Maureen Ct. BR3: Beck'm 5A 68
Maury Rd. N16 1H 5
Mavelstone Cl. BR1: Brom 4A 70
Mavelstone Rd. BR1: Brom 4N 69
Maxey Rd. SE18 4E 50
Maximfeldt Rd. DA8: Erith 5F 52
Maximilian Dr. ME2: Hall'g 7F 92
Maxim Rd. DA1: Cray 3F 58
DA8: Erith 4F 52
Maxine Gdns. CT10: B'stairs 8K 209
Maxted Ct. CT6: H Bay 3K 195
MAXTED STREET 7G 31
Maxted St. CT4: Elms 7G 31
MAXTON 6F 180 (2F 43)
Maxton Cl. ME14: Weav 4J 127
Maxton Ct. CT17: Dover 6F 180
Maxton Rd. CT17: Dover 6F 180
Maxwell Dr. ME16: Alltn 3M 125
Maxwell Gdns. BR6: Orp 4H 85
Maxwell Pl. CT14: Deal 6M 177
Maxwell Rd. DA16: Well 1H 57
ME7: Gill 7D 80
May Av. BR5: St M Cry 8K 71
DA11: Nflt 6E 62
May Av. Ind. Est. *DA11: Nflt* 6E 62
(off May Av.)
Mayberry Ct. *BR3: Beck'm* 3C 68
(off Copers Cope Rd.)
Maybrook Ind. Est. CT1: Cant 8B 168
Maybury Av. DA2: Dart 6C 60
Maybury Cl. BR5: Pet W 8D 70
Maycotts La. TN12: Mat 5J 153 (1C 36)
Mayday Gdns. SE3 9A 50
Maydowns Rd. CT5: Whits 3M 227
Mayerne Rd. SE9 3N 55
Mayers Rd. CT14: Walm 9K 177
Mayes Cl. BR8: Swanl 7H 73
Mayeswood Rd. SE12 9M 55
MAYFAIR 3E 4
Mayfair ME2: Strood 3N 79
Mayfair Av. DA7: Bexhth 8M 51
ME15: Maid 9D 126
Mayfair Cl. BR3: Beck'm 4E 68
Mayfair Rd. DA1: Dart 3L 59
Mayfield DA7: Bexhth 1A 58
Mayfield Av. BR6: Orp 2H 85
CT16: Dover 2G 181
Mayfield Cl. ME5: Chat'm 1D 110
ME8: Rain 1A 96
Mayfield Cotts. ME14: Bear 5M 127
Mayfield Ct. CT16: Dover 2G 181
Mayfield Gdns. CT16: Dover 2H 181
Mayfield La. TN5: Wadh 7B 36
Mayfield Rd. BR1: Brom 8A 70
CR2: S Croy 5G 13
CT6: H Bay 4H 195
CT16: Whitf 7F 178
CT18: Lym'ge 8L 205 (2J 41)
DA11: Grav'nd 5E 62
DA17: Belv 4D 52
TN3: Frant, Mark C 6K 35
TN4: Tun W 1F 156
TN6: Mark C 6K 35
TN6: Roth 7H 35
W3 3A 4
Mayfields DA10: Swans 4L 61
Mayfield Vs. DA14: Sidc 2L 71
Mayfly Cl. BR5: St P 7M 71
Mayfly Dr. CT18: H'nge 8K 193
Mayford Cl. BR3: Beck'm 6A 68
Mayford Rd. ME5: Chat'm 9G 95
Mayforth Gdns. CT11: Ram 6F 210
Maygrove Rd. NW6 1C 4
Mayhew Cl. TN23: Ashf 1E 160
Maylam Ct. TN10: Tonb 3J 145
Maylam Gdns. ME10: Sit 7C 98
Maylands Dr. DA14: Sidc 8M 57
Maymills Cotts. CT13: E'try 3J 183
Maynard TN26: H Hald 2B 196
Maynard Av. CT9: Mgte 3N 207
Maynard Cl. DA8: Erith 7G 52
Maynard Pl. ME5: Chat'm 1G 95
Maynard Rd. CT1: Cant 3K 171
Maynards TN12: Mard 3C 212
Mayor Cotts. TN3: Blkm 9C 148
Mayor's La. DA2: Dart 9K 59
Mayor's Pl. *TN30: Tent* 8B 224
(off Woodbury Gdns.)
Mayow Rd. SE23 9A 54 (7H 5)
SE26 9A 54 (1H 13)
Maypits TN23: Ashf 1D 160
May Pl. DA12: Sole S 8J 77
Mayplace Av. DA1: Cray 2H 59
Mayplace Cl. DA7: Bexhth 1C 58
Mayplace La. SE18 6D 50
(not continuous)
Mayplace Rd. E. DA1: Cray 2F 58 (6F 7)
DA7: Bexhth 1C 58 (6E 6)
Mayplace Rd. W. DA6: Bexhth 6E 6
DA7: Bexhth 2B 58
MAYPOLE
Bexley 7E 58
Canterbury 9M 195 (4A 22)
Orpington 7B 86 (5E 14)
Maypole Cres. DA8: Erith 6L 53
Maypole Dr. ME19: W Mal 6A 124
Maypole La. CT3: Hoath 8M 195 (4A 22)
TN17: Goud 3C 190 (4G 37)
Maypole Rd. BR6: Chels 6A 86 (4E 14)
CT3: Hoath 9M 195 (4K 21)
DA12: Grav'nd 6L 63
RH19: A'hstw 4B 34
May Rd. DA2: Dart 9N 59
ME1: Roch 9N 79
ME7: Gill 8E 80
Mays Cotts. ME15: E Far 9J 125
May's Cotts. ME15: E Far 4L 137
Mays Hill Rd. BR2: Shortl 5H 69
May's Rd. CT11: Ram 6G 211
Maystreet CT6: H Bay 3N 195
(not continuous)
May St. ME2: Cux 1F 92
ME6: Snod 2F 108
May Ter. ME7: Gill 5D 80
Maytham Rd. TN17: Rolv, Rolv L 3C 214 (7C 38)
Mayton La. CT2: B Oak 2A 168 (5H 21)
Maytree Cotts. TN24: Svgtn 4M 161
May Tree Ho. *SE4* 1C 54
(off Wickham Rd.)
Maytum's Cotts. ME17: Lint 8A 138
Mayville Rd. CT10: B'stairs 7J 209
Mayweed Av. ME5: Chat'm 7B 94
Maywood Cl. BR3: Beck'm 3E 68
Maze Hill SE3 5K 5
SE10 5K 5
Maze Hill Station (Rail) 5K 5
Mead Cl. BR8: Swanl 8H 73
Mead Cres. DA1: Dart 6L 59
Meades Cl. TN12: Mard 2B 212
Meade, The CT18: H'nge 8J 193
Meadfield Rd. DA13: Meop 3F 90
Mead Grn. ME5: Chat'm 8F 94
Meadow Av. CR0: Croy 9A 68
Meadow Bank ME19: W Mal 1A 124
SE3 1J 55
TN11: Leigh 6N 143
Meadow Bank Cl. TN15: W King 9F 88
Mdw. Bank M. ME19: W Mal 1A 124
Meadowbank Rd. ME4: Chat'm 8E 80
Meadowbrook CT20: S'gte 7E 188
Meadowbrook Cl. TN24: Kenn 4H 159
Meadowbrook Ct. CT20: S'gte 7E 188
Meadowbrook Rd. TN24: Kenn 4H 159
Meadow Cl. BR7: Chst 1D 70
CT4: Brid 8H 173
CT4: Chil'm 8M 175
CT6: H Bay 3K 195
CT18: H'nge 8L 193
DA6: Bexhth 3A 58
ME2: Hall'g 7C 92
ME5: Chat'm 6C 94
ME9: Iwade 8J 197
SE6 1D 68
TN13: S'oaks 5H 119
Meadow Ct. CT21: Wnhgr 2C 198
Meadowcourt Rd. SE3 2J 55
Meadow Cres. ME2: Hall'g 7C 92
Meadowcroft BR1: Brom 6B 70
Meadowdown ME14: Weav 5H 127
Meadowdown Cl. ME7: Hpstd 7K 95
Meadow Dr. CT5: Whits 5M 227
Meadow Gro. TN25: S'ndge 9C 218
Meadow Hill Rd. TN1: Tun W 2H 157
Meadowlands TN15: Seal 2N 119
Meadow La. DA3: New A 3M 89
DA13: Meop 1E 106
SE12 8L 55
TN8: Eden 3B 184
MEADOW LAWN 7G 145
Meadow Pk. ME3: Allh 3E 204
Meadow Ri. ME9: Iwade 8J 197
Meadow Rd. BR2: Shortl 5H 69
CT2: Cant 9J 167
CT2: Sturry 5E 168
CT9: Mgte 2N 207
DA11: Grav'nd 7F 62
DA11: Nflt 6B 62
TN1: Tun W 1G 157
TN3: Groom 6K 155
TN4: R'hall 1C 156 (3J 35)
TN4: S'bgh 5F 150
TN9: Tonb 7G 145
TN23: Ashf 6E 158
Meadows Ct. DA14: Sidc 2K 71
Meadowside DA1: Dart 6L 59
SE9 2M 55
Meadowside Leisure Cen. 2M 55
Meadows, The BR6: Chels 7L 85
CT6: H Bay 5K 195
ME10: Sit 9G 98
ME15: Maid 7B 126
TN11: Hild 3D 144
TN14: Hals 4A 102
TN27: Bidd 7K 163
TN28: New R 3L 213
TN30: Witter 2C 228
Meadowsweet Ho. TN23: Ashf 9E 158
Meadowsweet Vw. ME4: Chat'm 2E 80
Meadow, The BR7: Chst 2E 70
TN2: Pem 6C 152
Meadow Vw. BR5: St P 6L 71
DA15: Sidc 5K 57
TN13: Dun G 9E 102
TN26: Hoth 3L 197
Meadow Vw. Rd. CT15: S'wll 6L 219
Meadowview Rd. DA5: Bex'y 4N 57
Meadow Vw. Rd. ME17: Bou Mo 5E 138
Meadowview Rd. SE6 1C 68
Meadow Wlk. CT5: Whits 6E 226
DA2: Dart 9K 59
(not continuous)
ME6: Snod 3D 108
ME15: Maid 6E 126
Meadow Way BR6: Farnb 4C 84
CT15: Eyt 8K 185
CT21: Hythe 8E 198
DA2: Dart 5C 60
ME1: Woul 6G 93
TN12: Mard 2D 212
Mead Rd. BR7: Chst 2E 70
CT19: F'stone 5K 189
DA1: Dart 6L 59
DA11: Grav'nd 7G 62
TN8: Eden 8D 184
TN24: Ashf 2J 161 (2B 40)
Meads Av., The ME10: Sit 4E 98
Meadside Cl. BR3: Beck'm 4B 68
Meadside Wlk. ME5: Chat'm 5C 94
Meads, The TN2: Tun W 3J 157
TN17: Cran 5H 37
Meads Way TN29: St M Bay 3L 215
Mead, The BR3: Beck'm 4F 68
BR4: W W'ck 2G 82
DA3: New A 3L 89
ME19: Leyb 8C 108
Mead Wlk. TN23: Ashf 1C 160
(Oxen Lease)
TN23: Ashf 1C 160
(Tithe Barn La.)
Mead Wall ME3: Cliffe 1A 176
Mead Way BR2: Shortl 9J 69 (3K 13)
Meadway BR3: Beck'm 4F 68
Mead Way CR0: Croy 3B 82
CR5: Coul 7F 13
CT2: Cant 1L 171

Meadway—Mill Farm Cotts.

Meadway CT17: Dover . . . 1C 180
TN11: Hild . . . 2E 144
TN14: Hals . . . 4A 102
Meadway, The BR6: Chels . . . 7K 85
TN13: S'oaks . . . 4G 119
Meath Cl. BR5: St M Cry . . . 8K 71
Medbury Rd. DA12: Grav'nd . . . 6L 63
Medebourne Cl. SE3 . . . 1K 55
Mede Ho. *BR1: Brom* . . . *1L 69*
(off Pike Cl.)
Medfield St. SW15 . . . 7B 4
Medhurst Cres. DA12: Grav'nd . . . 8K 63
Medhurst Gdns. DA12: Grav'nd . . . 8L 63
MEDHURST ROW . . . 6D 24
Median Rd. E5 . . . 1H 5
Medina Av. CT5: Whits . . . 6D 226
Medina Ho. DA8: Erith . . . 7F 52
Medina Rd. ME20: Dit . . . 9G 109
TN10: Tonb . . . 1J 145
Medlar Cl. ME9: B'gar . . . 4B 114
Medlar Gro. ME7: Hpstd . . . 7K 95
Medlar Ho. DA15: Sidc . . . 8J 57
Medlars, The DA13: Meop . . . 9F 76
ME14: Maid . . . 3G 126
Medlar St. SE5 . . . 5G 5
Medusa Rd. SE6 . . . 4E 54
Medway Av. ME3: H Hals . . . 1H 67
ME18: Yald . . . 7D 136
MEDWAY CITY ESTATE . . . 5B 80
Medway Cl. ME10: Sit . . . 7E 98
Medway Crematorium
ME5: Chat'm . . . 1B 110 (5H 17)
Medway Ent. Cen. ME2: Med E . . . 4A 80
Medway Gdns. ME4: Chat'm . . . 5C 80
Medway Heritage Cen. . . . 7C 80
Medway Little Theatre . . . 8A 80
Medway Mdws. TN12: E Peck . . . 1M 147
Medway Outdoor Cen. . . . 5H 81
Medway Pl. ME1: Woul . . . 7G 93
ME6: Snod . . . 1F 108
Medway Rd. DA1: Cray . . . 1H 59
ME7: Gill . . . 5F 80 (2J 17)
(not continuous)
ME12: S'ness . . . 3C 220
TN1: Tun W . . . 9H 151
Medway St. ME4: Chat'm . . . 7C 80 (2H 17)
ME14: Maid . . . 5C 126
Medway Ter. *ME18: W'bury* . . . *2B 136*
(off Maidstone Rd.)
Medway Trad. Est. ME16: Maid . . . 6C 126
Medway Tunnel ME2: Med E . . . 4C 80
ME4: Chat'm . . . 4C 80
Medway Valley Leisure Pk. ME2: Strood . . . 8J 79
Medway Vw. ME3: Lwr Sto . . . 9C 204
TN11: Gold G . . . 2F 146
Medway Vs. ME15: E Far . . . 1M 137
Medway Wharf Rd. TN9: Tonb . . . 6J 145
Medway Yacht Club . . . 1D 80
Meehan Rd. TN28: G'stne, L'stne . . . 5N 213
Meehan Rd. Sth. TN28: G'stne . . . 6M 213
Meerbrook Rd. SE3 . . . 1M 55
Meeres Ct. La. ME10: Sit . . . 6K 99
Meesons Cl. ME13: E'lng . . . 1J 29
Meeting Ct. *CT9: Mgte* . . . *2C 208*
(off Love La.)
Meeting Ho. La. ME4: Chat'm . . . 8C 80
Meeting St. CT11: Ram . . . 5J 211
Megabowl
Bexleyheath . . . 2A 58
Megan Cl. TN29: Lydd . . . 2L 205
Megby Cl. ME8: Gill . . . 5N 95
Meggett La. CT15: Alk . . . 2C 42
Megone Cl. CT18: H'nge . . . 8K 193
Megrims Hill TN18: Sandh . . . 2B 218 (1E 44)
Melanda Cl. BR7: Chst . . . 1B 70
Melanie Cl. DA7: Bexhth . . . 8N 51
Melbourne Av. CT12: Ram . . . 4E 210
CT16: Dover . . . 8G 178 (7F 33)
Melbourne Cl. BR6: Orp . . . 1G 85
Melbourne M. SE6 . . . 5F 54
Melbourne Quay DA11: Grav'nd . . . 4G 62
Melbourne Rd. ME4: Chat'm . . . 9D 80
Melbury Cl. BR7: Chst . . . 2A 70
Melbury M. TN28: New R . . . 1L 213
Meldrum Cl. BR5: Orp . . . 9L 71
Melfield Gdns. SE6 . . . 9F 54
Melford Dr. ME16: Maid . . . 5M 125
Melfort Rd. CR7: Thor H . . . 2F 13
Meliot Rd. SE6 . . . 7G 55
Mellanby Cl. CT7: Birch . . . 5F 206
Melliker La. DA3: Meop . . . 9E 76
DA13: Meop . . . 9E 76 (3B 16)
Melling St. SE18 . . . 6G 51
Mellor Row ME10: Kems'y . . . 2G 98
Mells Cres. SE9 . . . 9B 56
Melody Cl. ME8: Gill . . . 7M 95
ME12: Ward . . . 4K 203
Melody Rd. TN16: Big H . . . 6C 164
Melon La. TN26: Newchu . . . 2G 47
TN29: Ivyc, Newchu . . . 2G 47
Melrose Av. DA1: Cray . . . 5F 58
ME19: W Mal . . . 6A 124
Melrose Cl. ME15: Maid . . . 1D 138
SE12 . . . 6K 55
Melrose Cres. BR6: Orp . . . 5F 84
Melrose Rd. TN16: Big H . . . 4C 164
Melsetter Cl. CT7: Birch . . . 4G 206
Melthorpe Gdns. SE3 . . . 8A 50
Melton St. NW1 . . . 2E 4
Melville Ct. ME4: Chat'm . . . 6C 80
Melville Lea CT13: Wdboro . . . 7H 217
Melville Rd. DA14: Sidc . . . 7L 57
ME15: Maid . . . 6D 126
Memel Pl. CT11: Ram . . . 6H 211
Memess Path SE18 . . . 6C 50
Mendfield St. ME13: Fav . . . 5G 186
Mendip TN24: Ashf . . . 6F 158
Mendip Rd. DA7: Erith . . . 8F 52
Mendip Wlk. TN2: Tun W . . . 9K 151
Menin Rd. ME10: Kems'y . . . 2G 98
Mentmore Ho. CT12: Ram . . . 1G 210
Mentmore Rd. CT12: Ram . . . 1G 210
Menzies Av. CT14: Walm . . . 9L 177
Menzies Ct. ME12: Minst . . . 7H 221
Menzies Rd. CT16: Dover . . . 9E 178 (7F 33)
MEOPHAM . . . 3F 90 (3C 16)
Meopham Cotts. TN14: Weald . . . 5J 131
Meopham Ct. DA13: Meop . . . 2G 90
MEOPHAM GREEN . . . 4F 90 (4C 16)
Meopham Leisure Cen. . . . 3F 90
MEOPHAM STATION . . . 8F 76 (3B 16)
Meopham Station (Rail) . . . 8F 76 (3C 16)
Meopham Windmill . . . 4E 90 (4B 16)
Mera Dr. DA7: Bexhth . . . 2B 58
Merantun Way SW19 . . . 2D 12
Merbury Cl. SE13 . . . 3F 54
Merbury Rd. SE28 . . . 2G 50 (3C 6)
Mercator Rd. SE13 . . . 2G 54
Mercer Dr. ME17: H'shm . . . 6H 201
Mercer La. ME20: Lark . . . 6F 108
Mercers TN3: Lang G . . . 2A 156
TN18: Hawkh . . . 6D 192
Mercers Cl. TN12: Pad W . . . 9K 147
Mercers Pl. ME19: W Mal . . . 7M 123
Mercer St. TN1: Tun W . . . 9H 151
Mercer Way ME17: Cha S . . . 7L 139
Mercery La. CT1: Cant . . . 2M 171
Merchant Pl. TN12: Mard . . . 3C 212
Merchants Way CT2: Cant . . . 3J 171
Merchiston Rd. SE6 . . . 7G 54
Merchland Rd. SE9 . . . 6E 56
Mercia Gro. SE13 . . . 2F 54
Mercury Cl. ME1: Roch . . . 1L 93
Mercy Ter. SE13 . . . 3E 54
Mere Cl. BR6: Farnb . . . 3C 84
Meredith M. SE4 . . . 2C 54
Mere End CR0: Croy . . . 1A 82
Mere Ga. CT9: Mgte . . . 4C 208
MERESBOROUGH . . . 6B 96 (4B 18)
Meresborough La. ME8: Rain . . . 6C 96 (4B 18)
Meresborough Rd. ME8: Rain . . . 8B 96 (5A 18)
Mere Side BR6: Farnb . . . 3C 84
Meretone Cl. SE4 . . . 2B 54
Merewood Cl. BR1: Brom . . . 5C 70
Merewood Rd. DA7: Bexhth . . . 9D 52
MEREWORTH . . . 9J 123 (3C 26)
Mereworth Cl. BR2: Shortl . . . 8J 69
ME8: Gill . . . 9K 81
Mereworth Dr. SE18 . . . 7D 50
Mereworth Ho. *ME2: Strood* . . . *3N 79*
(off Cypress Ct.)
Mereworth Rd.
ME18: Mere, W Peck . . . 2G 134 (3C 26)
TN4: Tun W . . . 8G 151
Merganser Gdns. SE28 . . . 3F 50
Meriden Cl. BR1: Brom . . . 3N 69
Meriden Wlk. *CT18: Etch'l* . . . *2M 185*
(off St Mary's Dr.)
Meridian Ct. ME16: Maid . . . 5B 126
TN23: Ashf . . . 1C 160
Meridian Pk. ME2: Med E . . . 6B 80
Meriel Wlk. DA9: G'hithe . . . 2H 61
Merifield Rd. SE9 . . . 2M 55
Merino Pl. DA15: Sidc . . . 4J 57
Merino Way TN23: Kgnt . . . 4C 160
Merivale Gro. ME5: Chat'm . . . 7D 94
Merland Ri. KT18: Eps . . . 7B 12
KT20: Tad . . . 7B 12
Merleburgh Dr. ME10: Kems'y . . . 3G 99
MERLE COMMON . . . 5A 24
Merlewood TN13: S'oaks . . . 5J 119
Merlewood Dr. BR7: Chst . . . 4B 70
Merleys Cl. DA3: Long . . . 6B 76
Merlin Av. ME20: Lark . . . 8D 108
Merlin Cl. ME10: Sit . . . 8H 99
TN10: Tonb . . . 2L 145
Merlin Ct. BR2: Shortl . . . 6J 69
Merlin Gdns. BR1: Brom . . . 8K 55
Merlin Gro. BR3: Beck'm . . . 7C 68
Merlin Rd. DA16: Well . . . 2J 57
Merlin Rd. Nth. DA16: Well . . . 2J 57
Mermaid Cl. DA11: Nflt . . . 5C 62
ME5: Chat'm . . . 5D 94
Mermerus Gdns. DA12: Grav'nd . . . 9L 63
Merrals Wood Ct. *ME2: Strood* . . . *7H 79*
(off Merrals Wood Rd.)
Merrals Wood Rd. ME2: Strood . . . 7H 79
Merriams Farm Cotts. ME17: Leeds . . . 9N 127
Merrick Way ME2: Med E . . . 4B 80
Merrielands Cres. RM9: Dag . . . 2E 6
Merrilees Rd. DA15: Sidc . . . 5G 56
Merrimans Vw. ME5: Chat'm . . . 9F 80
Merriments Gardens . . . 2B 44
Merriments La. TN19: Hur G . . . 2B 44
Merrion Cl. TN4: Tun W . . . 7H 151
Merrion Way TN4: Tun W . . . 7H 151
Merritt Rd. SE4 . . . 3C 54
TN28: G'stne . . . 7M 213
Merrivale Hgts. CT10: B'stairs . . . 2L 211
Merrow Way CR0: Croy . . . 7F 82 (5K 13)
Merry Boys Cotts. ME3: Cliffe . . . 5N 65
Merryboys Rd. ME3: Cli W . . . 5M 65 (7G 9)
Merrydown Way BR7: Chst . . . 4A 70
Merryfield Ct. TN9: Tonb . . . 7G 145
Merryfield Ho. *SE9* . . . *8M 55*
(off Grove Pk. Rd.)
Merryfields ME2: Strood . . . 3L 79
Merryfields Cl. DA3: Hart'y . . . 7M 75
Merryfields Way SE6 . . . 5E 54
MERRY HILL . . . 5H 91
Merryhills Cl. TN16: Big H . . . 4D 164
Merryweather Cl. DA1: Dart . . . 4N 59
Merrywood Gro. CT6: H Bay . . . 5L 195
Mersey Rd. TN10: Tonb . . . 2H 145
MERSHAM . . . 8M 161 (3C 40)
Merston Ct. ME3: High'm . . . 1G 78
MERTON . . . 1D 12
Merton Av. DA3: Hart'y . . . 7L 75
Merton Cl. ME5: Chat'm . . . 6F 94
Merton Cotts. CT1: Cant . . . 5N 171
Merton Ct. DA16: Well . . . 9K 51
Merton Gdns. BR5: Pet W . . . 8D 70
Merton High St. SW19 . . . 1D 12
Merton La. CT4: Cant . . . 6L 171 (2H 31)
Merton La. Nth. CT4: Cant . . . 7N 171
MERTON PARK . . . 2C 12
Merton Park Stop (CT) . . . 2C 12
Merton Rd. ME15: Bear . . . 7J 127
SW18 . . . 6C 4
SW19 . . . 1C 12
Merttins Rd. SE4 . . . 3A 54
SE15 . . . 3A 54 (6H 5)
Mervyn Av. SE9 . . . 8E 56
Meryl Gdns. CT14: Walm . . . 9L 177
Mesne Way TN14: S'ham . . . 3G 102
Messent Rd. SE9 . . . 3M 55
Messeter Pl. SE9 . . . 4C 56
Metcalfe-Hofmann Studio Gallery . . . *4N 177*
(off St George's Pas.)
Metcalfe M. CT1: Cant . . . 9A 168
Meteor Av. CT5: Whits . . . 6D 226
Meteor Cl. ME10: Sit . . . 3F 98
Meteor Rd. ME19: W Mal . . . 6L 123
Methuen Rd. DA6: Bexhth . . . 2A 58
DA17: Belv . . . 4C 52
Metro Bus. Cen., The SE26 . . . 2C 68
Metro Cen. BR5: St M Cry . . . 9K 71
Metropole Ct. CT20: F'stone . . . 8H 189
Metropole Galleries, The . . . 8H 189
Metropole Rd. E. CT20: F'stone . . . 8H 189
Metropole Rd. W. CT20: F'stone . . . 8H 189
Meverall Av. CT12: C'snd . . . 7B 210 (4H 23)
Mews End TN16: Big H . . . 6D 164
Mews, The *DA3: Long* . . . *6L 75*
(off Bramblefield Cl.)
DA14: Sidc . . . 9J 57
ME2: Strood . . . 5K 79
ME10: Sit . . . 9G 98
ME16: Maid . . . 4B 126
ME18: Yald . . . 7D 136
TN1: Tun W . . . 2H 157
TN2: Pem . . . 8B 152
TN13: S'oaks . . . 5H 119
(Hartslands Rd.)
TN13: S'oaks . . . 5H 119
(Hitchen Hatch La.)
Meyer Rd. DA8: Erith . . . 6E 52
Meyrick Rd. ME12: S'ness . . . 2D 220
Miall Wlk. SE26 . . . 9B 54
Micawber Cl. ME5: Chat'm . . . 1D 110
Michael Av. CT11: Ram . . . 4L 211
Michael Gdns. DA12: Grav'nd . . . 1K 77
Michaels Cl. SE13 . . . 2H 55
Michaels La. DA3: Fawk . . . 3H 89 (4K 15)
TN15: Fawk . . . 3H 89 (4K 15)
Micheldever Rd. SE12 . . . 4H 55
Michele Cotts. ME3: High'm . . . 7G 64
Michelle Ct. *BR1: Brom* . . . *4J 69*
(off Blyth Rd.)
Michelle Gdns. CT9: Mgte . . . 3M 207
Micketts Gdns. ME10: Sit . . . 7C 98
Mick Jagger Cen., The . . . *4K 59*
(off Shepherd's La.)
Mickleburgh Av. CT6: H Bay . . . 4J 195
Mickleburgh Hill CT6: H Bay . . . 3H 195 (3K 21)
Mickleham Cl. BR5: St P . . . 5H 71
Mickleham Rd. BR5: St P . . . 4H 71
Mickleham Way CR0: Croy . . . 8G 82
Mid Comp Cotts. TN15: Bor G . . . 3E 122
Middelburg Ho. CT19: F'stone . . . 5D 188
Middelburg Sq. CT20: F'stone . . . 5B 42
Middleburg Sq. CT20: F'stone . . . 7K 189
Middle Cl. TN23: Gt Cha . . . 9A 158
MIDDLE DEAL . . . 4M 177
Middle Deal Rd. CT14: Deal . . . 5K 177 (3J 33)
Middlefield TN2: Pem . . . 6D 152
Middle Fld. TN4: R'hall . . . 1C 156
Middlefields CR0: Croy . . . 9B 82
ME8: Rain . . . 3C 96
Middleham Ct. *DA2: Dart* . . . *4B 60*
(off Osbourne Rd.)
Middle La. TN15: Seal . . . 3N 119
Middle Mead CT19: F'stone . . . 4H 189
Middle Mill Rd. ME19: E Mal . . . 2D 124
Middle Pk. Av. SE9 . . . 4N 55 (6A 6)
MIDDLE QUARTER . . . 3E 38
Middle Rd. TN3: Bell G . . . 8N 157
Middle Roe *TN24: Ashf* . . . *8G 158*
(off High St.)
Middle Row ME13: Fav . . . 5H 187
Middlesex Rd. ME15: Maid . . . 1G 139
MIDDLE STOKE . . . 9C 204 (6B 10)
Middle St. CT14: Deal . . . 4N 177
(Broad St.)
CT14: Deal . . . 3N 177
(Exchange St.)
ME7: Gill . . . 6D 80
Middleton Av. DA14: Sidc . . . 2K 71
Middleton Cl. ME8: Gill . . . 7A 96
Middleton Ct. ME10: Sit . . . 7F 98
Middleton Rd. SM4: Mord, Cars . . . 3C 12
Middleton Way SE13 . . . 2G 55
Middletune Av. ME10: Sit . . . 4F 98
Middle Wlk. TN2: Tun W . . . 6L 151
Middle Wall CT5: Whits . . . 3F 226
Middle Way DA18: Erith . . . 3N 51
Middleway ME10: Sit . . . 8J 99
Middlings Ri. TN13: S'oaks . . . 7G 119
Middlings, The TN13: S'oaks . . . 8G 119
Middlings Wood TN13: S'oaks . . . 7H 119
Midfield Av. BR8: Swanl . . . 2H 73
DA7: Bexhth . . . 1D 58
Midfield Pde. DA7: Bexhth . . . 1D 58
Midfield Way BR5: St P . . . 4K 71 (2D 14)
Midholm Rd. CR0: Croy . . . 3B 82
Midhurst Ct. ME15: Maid . . . 6D 126
Midhurst Hill DA6: Bexhth . . . 4B 58
Mid Kent Bus. Pk. ME6: Snod . . . 3F 108
ME16: Alltn . . . 3M 125
Mid Kent Shop. Cen., The ME16: Alltn . . . 2N 125
Midland Rd. NW1 . . . 2E 4
Midley Cl. ME16: Alltn . . . 2N 125
Midsummer Hill TN24: Kenn . . . 4H 159
Midsummer Rd. ME6: Snod . . . 2C 108
Midway, The TN4: Tun W . . . 2D 156
Midwinter Cl. DA16: Well . . . 1J 57
Mierscourt Cl. ME8: Rain . . . 3C 96
Mierscourt Rd. ME8: Gill . . . 7A 96 (5A 18)
Miers Ct. Rd. ME8: Rain . . . 5A 96
Mike Spring Ct. DA12: Grav'nd . . . 9J 63
Milborough Cres. SE12 . . . 4H 55
Milbourne Gro. ME10: Sit . . . 4F 98
Milburn Rd. ME7: Gill . . . 5F 80
Mildmay Gro. N1 . . . 1G 5
Mildmay Pk. N1 . . . 1G 5
Mildmay Pl. TN14: S'ham . . . 2G 102
Mildred Cl. DA1: Dart . . . 4A 60
Mildred Cotts. CT19: F'stone . . . 4F 188
Mildred Rd. DA8: Erith . . . 5F 52
Milebush La. TN12: Mard . . . 6H 27
MILE END . . . 2J 5
MILE END GREEN . . . 4K 75 (2K 15)
Mile End Rd. E1 . . . 2H 5
E3 . . . 2J 5
Mile End Station (Tube) . . . 2J 5
Mile La. TN17: Goud . . . 2F 190 (3G 37)
MILE OAK . . . 1E 36
Miles Ct. CT3: Wing . . . 7J 225
Miles Dr. SE28 . . . 1G 50
Miles Pl. ME1: Roch . . . 9A 80
Milestone Cl. CT19: F'stone . . . 4G 189
MILESTONE GREEN . . . 6A 4
Milestone Rd. DA2: Dart . . . 4B 60
Miles Way CT7: Birch . . . 4E 206
MILE TOWN . . . 2C 220 (6F 11)
Mile Town Ind. Pk. ME12: S'ness . . . 3B 220
Milford Cl. ME16: Maid . . . 4N 125
SE2 . . . 6N 51
Milford Gdns. CR0: Croy . . . 8A 68
Milford Towers SE6 . . . 5E 54
Military Rd. CT1: Cant . . . 1N 171 (7H 21)
CT11: Ram . . . 6J 211
CT17: Dover . . . 5J 181
CT20: F'stone, S'gte . . . 6D 188 (4K 41)
CT21: Hythe . . . 6H 199 (5H 41)
ME4: Chat'm . . . 8C 80
TN30: Iden, Ston C E . . . 5B 46
TN31: Rye, Play, Iden . . . 5B 46
Milk Ho. Cotts. TN17: Siss . . . 3C 222
Milking La. BR2: Kes . . . 6A 14
BR6: Downe . . . 3A 100
Milk St. BR1: Brom . . . 2L 69
E16 . . . 1D 50
Milkwood Rd. SE24 . . . 6F 5
Millais Rd. CT16: Dover . . . 3H 181
MILLBANK . . . 8M 195 (4A 22)
Millbank SW1 . . . 4F 5
Mill Bank TN9: Tonb . . . 5J 145
TN27: H'crn . . . 7K 191 (7B 28)
TN29: Lydd . . . 3J 205
Millbank La. TN29: Old R . . . 3F 47
Millbank Rd. TN23: Ashf . . . 2K 39
TN23: Kgnt . . . 4D 160
(not continuous)
Millbank Way SE12 . . . 3K 55
Mill Bay CT20: F'stone . . . 6K 189
Millbro BR8: Swanl . . . 4H 73
Millbrook CT21: Hythe . . . 5L 199
ME19: Leyb . . . 9B 108
Millbrook Av. DA16: Well . . . 2F 56
Millbrook Cl. ME15: Maid . . . 8C 126
Millbrook Hill TN22: Chel G, Nut . . . 7B 34
Millbrook Mdw. TN23: Ashf . . . 9C 158
Mill Brook Rd. BR5: St M Cry . . . 7L 71 (2D 14)
Mill Bus. Pk., The TN26: Hoth . . . 3B 158
Mill Cl. CT3: Ickh . . . 7B 22
CT13: S'wch . . . 4K 217
CT17: Dover . . . 2E 180
ME2: Strood . . . 3M 79
ME17: Len . . . 8L 201
MILL CORNER . . . 4G 45
Mill Cotts. CT11: Ram . . . 6G 211
CT16: Temp E . . . 8C 178
Mill Ct. DA4: S Dar . . . 5C 74
ME10: Sit . . . 8H 99
Mill Ct. Cl. CT6: H Bay . . . 5J 195
Mill Cres. TN9: Tonb . . . 5J 145
Millcroft Ho. *SE6* . . . *9F 54*
(off Melfield Gdns.)
Millcroft Rd. ME3: Cliffe . . . 4C 176
Milldale Cl. CT14: Deal . . . 6L 177
Millen Ct. DA4: Hort K . . . 7C 74
Millennium Dome . . . 3K 5
Millennium Green Open Space . . . *3A 126*
(off Cloudberry Cl.)
Millennium Way CT10: B'stairs . . . 9G 208
ME12: S'ness . . . 2C 220 (6F 11)
SE10 . . . 4K 5
Millen Rd. ME10: Sit . . . 6F 98
Miller Av. CT2: Cant . . . 2K 171
Miller Cl. CT14: Deal . . . 2M 177
ME10: Kems'y . . . 3H 99
TN24: Ashf . . . 8H 159
Miller Cotts. TN24: Ashf . . . 8H 159
Miller Ct. DA7: Bexhth . . . 1D 58
ME12: Minst . . . 7H 221
TN24: Ashf . . . 8H 159
Miller Rd. DA12: Grav'nd . . . 7M 63
Millers Ct. CT5: Whits . . . 6F 226
Miller's Hill TN35: W'fld . . . 7F 45
Millers La. CT12: Monk'n . . . 4E 22
Millers Mdw. Cl. SE3 . . . 3J 55
Millers Wlk. DA13: Meop . . . 3F 90
Millers Wharf ME15: Maid . . . 7A 126
Miller Way ME2: Wain . . . 2N 79
Mill Farm Cotts. ME3: Hoo . . . 7F 66

Montgomery Av. ME5: Chat'm .4D 94
Montgomery Cl. DA15: Sidc .4H 57
Montgomery Rd. DA4: S Dar .4D 74
ME7: Gill .8F 80
TN4: Tun W .7H 151
Montgomery Way CT19: F'stone .3K 189
Montpelier Av. CT5: Whits .8F 226
DA5: Bex'y .5M 57
Montpelier Bus. Pk. TN23: Ashf .9D 158
Montpelier Ct. *BR2: Shortl .7J 69*
(off Westmoreland Rd.)
Montpelier Ga. ME16: Alltn .4M 125
Montpelier Row SE3 .5K 5
Montreal Cl. CT16: Dover .1G 181
Montreal Rd. RM18: Tilb .1F 62
TN13: Riv .5F 118
Montrose Av. DA15: Sidc .5J 57
DA16: Well .1F 56
ME5: Chat'm .1H 95
Montrose Cl. DA16: Well .1H 57
Montrose Ct. SE6 .6J 55
Montrose Way SE23 .6A 54
Mont St Aignan Way TN8: Eden .7C 184
Monument Gdns. SE13 .3F 54
Monument Station (Tube) .3G 5
Monument Way TN24: Ashf .3J 161
Monypenny TN17: Rolv .3C 214
Monypenny Cl. TN11: Hdlw .8C 134
Moon Ct. SE12 .2K 55
Moonfleet Cl. ME10: Kems'y .2H 99
Moon Hill CT15: S'wll .8L 219
MOON'S GREEN .2K 45
Moonstone Dr. ME5: Chat'm .9E 94
Moorcroft Gdns. BR2: Shortl .8A 70
Moorden La. TN11: Chid .6H 143 (6G 25)
Moordown SE18 .7D 50
Moore Cl. DA2: Dart .7D 60
TN29: Bztt .2F 47
Moorehead Way SE3 .1K 55
Mooreland Rd. BR1: Brom .3J 69
Moore Rd. DA10: Swans .4L 61
Moore's La. TN31: Beckl .5H 45
Moore St. ME2: Strood .4L 79
Moorfield CT2: Cant .7M 167
Moorfield Rd. BR6: Orp .1J 85
Moorgate EC2 .3G 5
Moorgate Station (Rail & Tube) .3G 5
Moorhen Cl. DA8: Erith .7J 53
Moor Hill TN18: Hawkh .7C 192 (1C 44)
MOORHOUSE .9B 116 (3B 24)
MOORHOUSE BANK .3B 24
Moorhouse Rd. RH8: Oxt, Westrm .4B 24
TN16: Westrm .4B 24
Mooring Rd. ME1: Roch .2A 94
Moorings, The ME9: Tey .4J 19
TN18: Sandh .4A 218
Moorland Rd. CT15: S'wll .8K 219
Moorlands .6E 34
Moor La. RH7: Dor'land .1A 34
TN8: Dor'land, Marsh G .1A 34
TN26: Wdchu .9A 228 (6G 39)
TN29: Bztt, Ivyc .2F 47
TN35: W'fld .7F 45
Moor Pk. Cl. ME8: Rain .3C 96
Moor Rd. TN14: S'oaks .2J 119
Moorside Rd. BR1: Brom .8H 55
MOORSTOCK .7B 218 (3F 41)
Moorstock La. TN25: S'ndge .8B 218 (3F 41)
MOOR STREET .3D 96 (4B 18)
Moor St. ME8: Rain .3D 96 (4B 18)
MOOR, THE
Cranbrook .7C 192 (1C 44)
Hastings .7F 45
Moor, The TN18: Hawkh .7C 192 (1C 44)
Moorwell Dr. CT15: S'wll .7K 219
Morants Ct. Rd. TN13: Dun G .9D 102 (7F 15)
TN14: Dun G .9D 102
Moray Av. CT7: Birch .3E 206
Mordaunt Av. CT8: Wgte S .3K 207
MORDEN .2C 12
Morden Ct. ME1: Roch .8N 79
Morden Hall Rd. SM4: Mord .2D 12
MORDEN PARK .3C 12
Morden Rd. CR4: Mitc .2D 12
SW19 .2C 12
Morden Station (Tube) .2C 12
Morden Road Station (CT) .2C 12
Morden South Station (Rail) .3C 12
Morden St. ME1: Roch .8N 79
Mordred Rd. SE6 .7H 55
MOREHALL .4F 188 (4A 42)
Morehall Av. CT19: F'stone .5F 188
Moreland St. EC1 .2F 5
Morel Ct. TN13: S'oaks .4J 119
Morella Wlk. ME17: Len .7L 201
Morello Cl. BR8: Swanl .7E 72
ME9: Tey .7K 223
Moremead Rd. SE6 .9C 54
Morement Rd. ME3: Hoo .7G 66
Morena St. SE6 .5E 54
Moreton Almshouses TN16: Westrm .8F 116
Moreton Cl. BR8: Swanl .5F 72
Moreton Ct. DA1: Cray .1G 58
Moreton Ind. Est. BR8: Swanl .7J 73
Morewood Cl. TN13: S'oaks .5G 119
Morewood Cl. Ind. Est. TN13: S'oaks .5G 119
Morgan Dr. DA9: G'hithe .5E 60
Morgan Kirby Gdns. ME13: Shel .3J 219
Morgan Rd. BR1: Brom .3K 69
ME2: Strood .4L 79
Morgan Wlk. BR3: Beck'm .7E 68
Morhen Cl. ME6: Snod .3C 108
Morland Av. DA1: Dart .3J 59
Morland Dr. ME2: Strood .3L 79
TN3: Lamb .2L 201
Morland Rd. CR0: Croy .3G 13
SE20 .2A 68
Morley Cl. BR6: Farnb .3D 84
Morley Ct. BR2: Shortl .7J 69
Morley Dr. TN12: Horsm .7B 196
Morley Hill SS17: Stan H .1E 8
Morley Rd. BR7: Chst .4E 70
SE13 .2F 54
TN9: Tonb .6K 145
Morley's Rd. TN14: Weald .6K 131 (4G 25)
Morning Cross Cotts. ME3: Cliffe .4C 176
Morning La. E9 .1H 5
Mornington Av. BR1: Brom .6M 69
Mornington Cl. TN16: Big H .5D 164
Mornington Ct. DA5: Bex'y .6E 58
Mornington Crescent Station (Tube) .2E 4
Morris Av. CT6: H Bay .3A 194
Morris Cl. BR6: Orp .4G 84
CR0: Croy .8B 68
ME15: Maid .3G 139
ME19: E Mal .9D 108
Morris Ct. Cl. ME9: Bap .9L 99
Morris Gdns. DA1: Dart .3A 60
Morrison Rd. CT20: F'stone .5L 189
Morris Rd. E14 .3J 5
Morry La. ME17: E Sut .7F 140 (5B 28)
Morston Gdns. SE9 .9B 56
Mortgramit Sq. SE18 .3C 50
Mortimer Cl. TN23: Ashf .2F 160
Mortimer Rd. BR6: Orp .2J 85
CT16: Dover .4L 181
DA8: Erith .6E 52
NW10 .2B 4
TN16: Big H .2B 164
Mortimers Av. ME3: Cli W .5L 65
Mortimer St. CT6: H Bay .2G 194
W1 .3E 4
MORTLAKE .6A 4
Mortlake High St. SW14 .6A 4
Mortlake Rd. TW9: Rich .5A 4
Mortlake Station (Rail) .6A 4
Mortley Cl. TN9: Tonb .5J 145
Morton Cl. ME15: Maid .2G 138
Morvale Cl. DA17: Belv .4A 52
Morval Rd. SW2 .6F 5
Moselle Rd. TN16: Big H .6E 164
Mosquito Rd. ME19: W Mal .6L 123
Mossbank ME5: Chat'm .8D 94
Mossdown Cl. DA17: Belv .4B 52
Moss End M. CT11: Ram .2J 211
Moss Gdns. CR2: S Croy .8A 82
Mosslea Rd. BR2: Shortl .8N 69
BR6: Farnb .4E 84
Moss Way DA2: Dart .9D 60
Mossy Glade ME8: Rain .5A 96
Mostyn Rd. ME14: Maid .5F 126
Mosul Way BR2: Shortl .9A 70
Mosyer Dr. BR5: Orp .3M 85
Mote Av. ME15: Maid .6E 126
Mote Hall Vs. ME14: Bear .5M 127
Mote Pk. .7G 126
Mote Rd. ME15: Maid .6D 126 (2J 27)
TN11: S'brne .3F 132 (3J 25)
TN15: Ivy H .1G 133 (3J 25)
TN15: S'brne .3F 132
Mote, The DA3: New A .3M 89
Motherwell Way RM20: W Thur .5K 7
MOTNEY HILL .2B 18
Motney Hill Rd. ME8: Rain .3B 18
MOTSPUR PARK .3B 12
Motspur Pk. KT3: N Mald .3A 12
Motspur Park Station (Rail) .3B 12
MOTTINGHAM .7A 56 (7B 6)
Mottingham Gdns. SE9 .6N 55
Mottingham La. SE9 .6M 55 (7A 6)
SE12 .6M 55 (7A 6)
Mottingham Rd. SE9 .7A 56 (7B 6)
Mottingham Station (Rail) .6B 56 (7B 6)
Mottins Hill TN6: Jar B .7G 35
Mottisfont Rd. SE2 .3J 51
MOTT'S DOWN .5F 35
MOTT'S MILL .5G 35
Mouat Ct. ME5: Chat'm .8D 94
Mouchotte Cl. TN16: Big H .2A 164
Moultain Hill BR8: Swanl .7H 73
Mound, The SE9 .8C 56
Mountain Bungs. TN26: Hams .4M 191
Mountain Cl. *TN15: Wro .7M 105*
(off West St.)
Mountain St. CT4: Chil'm .9J 175 (3D 30)
Mt. Arlington *BR2: Shortl .5H 69*
(off Pk. Hill Rd.)
Mount Av. ME18: Yald .7E 136
Mountbatten Av. ME3: High'm .9G 64
ME5: Chat'm .4D 94
Mountbatten Cl. SE18 .6G 50
Mountbatten Gdns. BR3: Beck'm .7B 68
Mountbatten Pav. ME20: Aylfd .1K 125
Mountbatten Way TN25: Bra L .7K 165
Mt. Castle La. ME17: Len .4F 29
Mt. Charles Wlk. CT4: Brid .9E 172
Mount Cl. BR1: Brom .4A 70
TN13: S'oaks .5G 119
Mount Cotts. ME14: Bear .5L 127
Mount Ct. BR4: W W'ck .3H 83
Mt. Culver Av. DA14: Sidc .2M 71
Mount Dr. DA6: Bexhth .3N 57
ME14: Bear .5L 127
Mt. Edgecombe Rd. TN4: Tun W .2G 156
Mt. Ephraim TN1: Tun W .2F 156
TN4: Tun W .3J 35
Mount Ephraim Gardens .2L 165 (6D 20)
Mt. Ephraim Rd. TN1: Tun W .1G 157
Mount Farm .6A 36
MOUNTFIELD .5B 44
Mount Fld. ME11: Queen .7B 220
ME13: Fav .6F 186
Mountfield TN15: Bor G .2N 121
Mountfield Cl. DA13: Meop .9E 90
SE6 .5G 54
Mountfield Ct. *TN1: Tun W .2H 157*
(off Mountfield Gdns.)
Mountfield Gdns. TN1: Tun W .2H 157
Mountfield Ind. Est. TN28: New R .3L 213
Mountfield La. TN32: Mount .5A 44
Mountfield Pk. TN9: Tonb .7J 145
Mountfield Pl. TN12: Mard .3D 212
Mountfield Rd. TN1: Tun W .2H 157
TN28: New R .4L 213
Mountfield Row TN28: New R .3L 213
Mountfield Way BR5: St M Cry .7L 71
CT8: Wgte S .5J 207
Mt. Green Av. CT12: C'snd .7B 210
Mountgrove Rd. N5 .1G 5
Mt. Harry Rd. TN13: S'oaks .5H 119 (2G 25)
Mount Hill TN14: Knock .8J 101
Mounthurst Rd. BR2: Shortl .1J 83
Mountjoy Cl. SE2 .2K 51
Mount La. ME9: H'lip .8F 96 (5B 18)
ME14: Bear .5L 127
Mount Lodge *ME1: Roch .1M 93*
(off Valley Vw. Rd.)
MOUNT PLEASANT .4F 23
Mt. Pleasant CT2: Blean .5G 166
ME5: Chat'm .8E 80
ME13: Oare .2F 186
ME20: Aylfd .7L 109
TN6: Crowb .7G 35
TN11: Hild .1D 144
TN12: Pad W .8L 147
TN14: Ide H .4A 130
TN16: Big H .5D 164
TN25: Aldtn .4D 40
TN30: Tent .8D 224
Mt. Pleasant Av. TN1: Tun W .2H 157
Mt. Pleasant Cl. CT18: Lym'ge .7L 205
Mt. Pleasant Ct. TN11: Hild .1D 144
Mt. Pleasant Dr. ME14: Bear .4M 127
Mt. Pleasant La. TN3: Lamb .1H 201 (4C 36)
Mt. Pleasant Pl. SE18 .4F 50
Mt. Pleasant Rd. CT20: F'stone .6K 189
DA1: Dart .4N 59
SE13 .4E 54
TN1: Tun W .2G 157 (3K 35)
TN14: Weald .6J 131
Mt. Pleasant Wlk.
DA5: Bex'y .3D 58
Mount Rd. CT1: Cant .4B 172
CT17: Dover .7F 180
DA1: Cray .4G 59
ME1: Roch .1L 93
ME4: Chat'm .9C 80
Mounts Cl. CT14: Deal .5K 177
Mountsfield Cl. ME16: Maid .4A 126
Mountsfield Ct. SE13 .4G 54
Mounts Hill TN17: Bendn .6K 37
Mount Sion TN1: Tun W .3G 157
Mounts La. TN17: Rolv L, Rolv .1E 214 (7C 38)
Mounts Rd. DA6: Bexhth .3M 57
DA9: G'hithe .3H 61 (6K 7)
Mount St. CT21: Hythe .6K 199
TN33: Batt .7C 44
Mount, The DA6: Bexhth .3C 58
ME4: Chat'm .8C 80
ME13: Fav .6F 186
TN5: Flim .7F 37
Mount Top CT4: Elham .7J 183 (1H 41)
Mountview ME9: B'den .9C 98
Mountview Rd. BR6: St M Cry .1J 85
(not continuous)
Mount Vw. Rd. CT6: H Bay .5H 195
Mount Vs. ME18: Yald .7E 136
MOVERS LANE .2C 6
Movers La. IG11: Bark .2C 6
MOWSHURST .3E 184 (6C 24)
Moyes Cl. CT12: C'snd .7B 210
Moyle Cl. ME8: Gill .7N 95
Moyle Ct. CT21: Hythe .7K 199
Moyle Twr. Rd. CT21: Hythe .7K 199
Mozart Ct. ME4: Chat'm .9B 80
MUCKING .3E 8
MUCKINGFORD .4D 8
Muckingford Rd. RM18: W Til .4C 8
SS17: Linf .4D 8
Mucking Wharf Rd. SS17: Stan H .3E 8
Mudchute Station (DLR) .4J 5
Muddy La. ME10: Sit .9J 99
Muggins La. DA12: Grav'nd, Shorne .9A 64
Muirkirk Rd. SE6 .6F 54
Muir Rd. CT11: Ram .3K 211
ME15: Maid .6D 126
Muir St. E16 .1A 50
(not continuous)
Mulberry Cl. CT11: Ram .4K 211
DA13: Meop .9G 76
ME7: Hpstd .7K 95
TN4: S'bgh .5K 151
Mulberry Cotts. CT4: Chil'm .7L 175
Mulberry Ct. CT1: Cant .2M 171
CT21: Hythe .5K 199
ME14: Maid .4E 126
TN28: L'stne .4N 213
Mulberry Dr. RM19: Purf .4N 53
Mulberry Fld. CT13: S'wch .5L 217
Mulberry Hill CT4: Chil'm .8L 175 (2D 30)
Mulberry Ho. BR2: Shortl .4H 69
Mulberry Rd. DA11: Nflt .8D 62
TN23: Ashf .7B 158
Mulberry Way DA17: Belv .2D 52
Mulgrave Rd. SE18 .4B 50
SM2: Sutt .5C 12
Mullender Ct. DA12: Grav'nd .6M 63
Muller Ho. SE18 .5C 50
Multon Rd. TN15: W King .7E 88
Muncies M. SE6 .7F 54
Munday Works Est. TN9: Tonb .6J 145
MUNDY BOIS .7F 29
Mundy Bois La. TN27: P'ley .7F 29
Mundy Bois Rd. TN27: Eger .6E 28
Munford Dr. DA10: Swans .5L 61
Mungean Ho. *ME1: Roch .8N 79*
(off Hooper's Rd.)
Mungo Pk. Rd. DA12: Grav'nd .1J 77
RM13: Rain .1G 7
Mungo Pk. Way BR5: Orp .1L 85
Munnery Way BR6: Farnb .4C 84
Munn's La. ME9: H'lip .5G 96 (4C 18)
Munsgore La. ME9: B'den .1N 113 (5D 18)
Munster Rd. SW6 .5C 4
Murchison Av. DA5: Bex'y .6M 57 (7D 6)
Murillo Rd. SE13 .2G 55
Murrain Dr. ME15: Bear .8K 127
Murray Av. BR1: Brom .6L 69
Murray Bus. Cen. BR5: St P .6K 71
Murray Ho. *SE18 .4B 50*
(off Rideout St.)
Murray Rd. BR5: St P .6K 71
ME2: Strood .3N 79
MURSTON .7J 99 (4F 19)
Murston Rd. ME10: Sit .8J 99 (5F 19)
Murthwaite Ct. ME12: Minst .7H 221
Murton Neale Cl. TN18: Hawkh .5D 192
Murton Pl. ME13: G'ney .5C 20
Muscovy Ho. *DA18: Erith .2N 51*
(off Kale Rd.)
Muscovy Rd. TN25: Kenn .3G 158
Muscovy Way CT6: H Bay .4F 194
Museum Av. ME14: Maid .4C 126
Mus. of Artillery in the Rotunda .5B 50
Mus. of Canterbury, The .2M 171
Mus. of Kent Life .9A 110 (7H 17)
Musgrave Cl. CT12: Mans .9L 207
Musgrave Rd. ME10: Sit .5G 98
Musgrove TN23: Ashf .1E 160
Muskerry Ct. TN4: R'hall .1B 156
Musket La. ME17: Holl .7C 128 (2B 28)
(not continuous)
Mussenden La. DA4: Hort K .8C 74 (3J 15)
Mustang Rd. ME19: W Mal .6L 123
Mustards Rd. ME12: Ley S .6J 203
Mutrix Gdns. CT9: Mgte .2M 207
Mutrix Rd. CT9: Mgte .3N 207
Mutton Hill RH7: Dor'land .2A 34
Mutton La. ME13: Osp .7E 186 (6A 20)
Mymms Cl. CT5: Whits .5L 227
Mynn Cres. ME14: Bear .5K 127
Myra St. SE2 .4J 51
Myron Pl. SE13 .1F 54
Myrtle Cl. DA8: Erith .7F 52
Myrtle Cotts. TN30: St Mic .4C 224
Myrtle Cres. ME5: Chat'm .6C 94
Myrtledene Rd. SE2 .5J 51
Myrtle Grn. TN23: Ashf .6B 158
Myrtle Pl. DA2: Dart .5D 60
Myrtle Rd. CR0: Croy .4D 82
CT19: F'stone .5L 189
DA1: Dart .6L 59
TN6: Crowb .7F 35
Mystole La. CT4: Chart'm .9C 170 (3E 30)

N

NACCOLT .7C 30
Naccolt Rd. TN25: Brook, Hin .7C 30
Nacholt Cl. CT5: Whits .3J 227
NACKINGTON .8N 171 (2H 31)
Nackington Ct. CT1: Cant .4A 172
Nackington Rd. CT1: Cant .9N 171 (2H 31)
CT4: Lwr Har, Cant .9N 171 (2H 31)
Nagpur Ho. ME15: Maid .3H 139
NAG'S HEAD .1F 5
Nags Head La. DA16: Well .1K 57
ME1: Roch .8A 80
Nailbourne Cl. CT4: Kgstn .4K 31
Nailbourne Ct. CT18: Lym'ge .7L 205
Naildown Cl. CT21: Hythe .8A 188
Naildown Rd. CT21: Hythe .8A 188
Nairne Cl. TN26: Shad .4J 39
Namur Pl. CT15: Gus .1L 181
Nansen Rd. DA12: Grav'nd .9J 63
NAPCHESTER .2H 179 (6F 33)
Napchester Rd. CT15: Whitf .5F 178 (7F 33)
CT16: Whitf .5F 178 (7F 33)
Napier Cl. ME10: Sit .7D 98
Napier Ct. ME14: Maid .2C 126
SE12 .8L 55
Napier Gdns. CT21: Hythe .7K 199
Napier Rd. BR2: Shortl .7L 69
CT10: B'stairs .7J 209
CT16: Dover .1G 181
DA11: Nflt .6E 62
DA17: Belv .4A 52
ME7: Gill .8G 80 (3J 17)
TN2: Tun W .3K 157
Napier Ter. *ME12: S'ness .2E 220*
(off Marine Pde.)
Napleton Ct. CT11: Ram .6G 211
Napleton Rd. CT11: Ram .6G 210
ME13: Fav .5G 186
Napoleon Dr. TN12: Mard .3D 212
Napoleon Wlk. ME17: Len .7K 201
Napwood Cl. ME8: Gill .5N 95
Narboths Nursery ME13: Fav .7J 187
Nares Rd. ME8: Gill .7N 95
Nargate Cl. CT3: L'brne .2M 173
Narrabeen Rd. CT19: F'stone .5E 188
Narrow Boat Cl. SE28 .2F 50
Narrowbush La. TN29: Ivyc .3F 47
Narrow St. E14 .3J 5
Narrow Way BR2: Shortl .9A 70
Naseby Av. CT20: F'stone .6D 188
Naseby Ct. DA14: Sidc .9H 57
NASH .7K 83 (4A 14)
Nash CT3: Ash .7D 22
Nash Bank DA13: Meop, Ist R .5E 76 (2B 16)
Nash Cl. ME5: Chat'm .9F 94
Nash Ct. Cotts. TN25: Westw .1C 158
Nash Ct. Gdns. CT9: Mgte .5C 208
Nash Ct. Rd. CT9: Mgte .5D 208
Nash Cft. DA11: Nflt .9D 62

Norwood Av. CR7: Thor H . . . 2F 13
Norwood Cl. ME3: Cliffe . . . 4C 176
Norwood Ct. DA1: Dart . . . 3A 60
(off Farnol Rd.)
Norwood Gdns. TN23: Ashf . . . 8F 158
Norwood High St. SE27 . . . 7F 5
Norwood Junction Station (Rail) . . . 2H 13
Norwood La. DA13: Meop . . . 8F 76 (3C 16)
TN29: Newchu . . . 7C 40
NORWOOD NEW TOWN . . . 1G 13
Norwood Ri. ME12: Minst . . . 5K 221
Norwood Rd. SE24 . . . 7F 5
SE27 . . . 7F 5
Norwood St. TN23: Ashf . . . 8F 158
Norwood Wlk. ME10: Sit . . . 6C 98
Norwood Wlk. E. ME10: Sit . . . 6D 98
Norwood Wlk. W. ME10: Sit . . . 5C 98
Notley St. CT1: Cant . . . 1N 171
Notley Ter. CT1: Cant . . . 1N 171
(off Notley St.)
Nottidge Rd. TN4: Tun W . . . 4D 156
Nottingham Av. ME15: Maid . . . 1G 139
Nottingham Rd. CT7: Birch . . . 6E 206
Nottingham Wlk. ME2: Strood . . . 6H 79
NOTTING HILL . . . 3C 4
Notting Hill Ga. W11 . . . 3C 4
Notting Hill Gate Station (Tube) . . . 3C 4
Nouds La. ME9: Lyn . . . 6H 19
Nouds Rd. ME9: Lyn . . . 9L 223
Novar Cl. BR6: Orp . . . 1H 85
Novar Rd. SE9 . . . 6E 56
Nower, The TN14: Knock . . . 1H 117 (1C 24)
Nubia Way BR1: Brom . . . 8H 55
Nuding Cl. SE13 . . . 1D 54
Nuffield Rd. BR8: Swanl . . . 2H 73
Nugent Ind. Pk. BR5: St M Cry . . . 7L 71
NUNHEAD . . . 6H 5
Nunhead La. SE15 . . . 6H 5
Nunhead Station (Rail) . . . 5H 5
Nunnery Flds. CT1: Cant . . . 4N 171 (1H 31)
Nunnery La. TN11: Pens . . . 6G 149 (2F 35)
Nunnery Rd. CT1: Cant . . . 3M 171
Nunnington Cl. SE9 . . . 8A 56
Nuralite Ind. Cen. ME3: High'm . . . 5E 64
Nursery Av. CR0: Croy . . . 3A 82
DA7: Bexhth . . . 1A 58
ME14: Bear . . . 6L 127
ME16: Alltn . . . 3M 125
Nursery Cl. BR6: Orp . . . 1H 85
BR8: Swanl . . . 5D 72
CR0: Croy . . . 3A 82
CT5: Whits . . . 4J 227
CT11: Ram . . . 5G 210
CT18: D'sole . . . 5K 193
DA2: Dart . . . 5C 60
ME12: S'ness . . . 3E 220
TN10: Tonb . . . 3K 145
TN13: S'oaks . . . 4K 119
Nursery Flds. CT7: Acol . . . 8G 206
CT21: Hythe . . . 6G 199
Nursery Gdns. BR7: Chst . . . 2D 70
CT10: B'stairs . . . 4J 209
ME3: Hoo . . . 8H 67
Nursery Ind. Est. CT6: H Bay . . . 4D 194
Nurserylands CT6: H Bay . . . 4G 194
Nursery La. CT16: Whitf . . . 6E 178 (7E 32)
CT18: D'sole . . . 5K 193
ME13: Shel . . . 3H 219
Nursery Pl. TN13: Riv . . . 4E 118
Nursery Rd. DA13: Meop . . . 8F 76
ME8: Gill . . . 3N 95
ME20: Dit . . . 9G 109
TN4: Tun W . . . 6H 151
TN12: Pad W . . . 7L 147
Nursery, The DA8: Erith . . . 7G 52
Nursery Wlk. CT2: Cant . . . 9L 167
NURSTEAD . . . 6E 76 (2B 16)
Nurstead Av. DA3: Long . . . 7C 76
Nurstead Chu. La.
DA13: Meop, Sole S . . . 7E 76 (2C 16)
Nurstead Court . . . 7F 76
Nurstead La. DA3: Long H, Meop . . . 7C 76 (2B 16)
Nurstead Rd. DA8: Erith . . . 7B 52
Nutberry Cl. ME9: Tey . . . 7L 223
Nutfield Cl. ME5: Chat'm . . . 3E 94
Nutfield Ct. BR1: Brom . . . 6K 69
Nutfields ME10: Sit . . . 8J 99
TN15: Igh . . . 5H 121
Nutfield Way BR6: Farnb . . . 3D 84
Nuthatch DA3: Long . . . 6A 76
Nuthatch Gdns. SE28 . . . 2F 50
(not continuous)
Nutley Cl. BR8: Swanl . . . 4G 73
TN24: Ashf . . . 7G 159
Nutmead Cl. DA5: Bex'y . . . 6D 58
Nut Tree Cl. BR6: Chels . . . 4M 85
Nutts Av. ME12: Ley S . . . 6M 203
Nutts Cvn. Site ME12: Ley S . . . 7N 203
Nutwood Cl. ME14: Weav . . . 5H 127
Nuxley Rd. DA17: Belv . . . 6A 52 (5E 6)
Nyanza St. SE18 . . . 6F 50
Nyon Gro. SE6 . . . 7C 54

O

OAD STREET . . . 1M 113 (5D 18)
Oad Street Craft Cen. . . . 1N 113
Oak Apple Ct. SE12 . . . 6K 55
Oakapple Ho. ME16: Barm . . . 6L 125
Oakapple La. ME16: Barm . . . 5K 125
Oak Av. CR0: Croy . . . 2D 82
ME7: Gill . . . 6H 81
ME12: Minst . . . 6N 221
TN13: S'oaks . . . 1J 131
Oak Bank CR0: Croy . . . 7F 82
Oakbrook Cl. BR1: Brom . . . 9L 55
Oak Bungs. TN29: Lydd . . . 3K 205
Oak Caer TN25: Aldtn . . . 5C 40
Oak Cl. DA1: Cray . . . 2G 58
Oak Cott. Cl. SE6 . . . 6J 55
Oak Cotts. ME17: Bou Mo . . . 5E 138
TN11: Leigh . . . 6M 143
Oakdale La. TN8: Crock H . . . 4B 24
Oakdale Rd. CT6: H Bay . . . 3H 195
TN4: Tun W . . . 1F 156
Oakdene Av. BR7: Chst . . . 1C 70
DA8: Erith . . . 6D 52
Oakdene Rd. BR5: St M Cry . . . 8H 71
CT12: Ram . . . 3G 210
TN13: S'oaks . . . 4H 119
Oak Dr. CT18: H'nge . . . 7L 193
ME3: High'm . . . 1F 78
ME13: Bou B . . . 3K 165
ME20: Lark . . . 8E 108
TN29: St M Bay . . . 3M 215
Oak End Cl. TN4: S'bgh . . . 4G 151
Oakenden La. TN8: Chid H . . . 5C 148
Oakenden Rd. DA13: Meop, Lud'n . . . 2J 91 (3C 16)
Oakenholt Ho. SE2 . . . 1M 51
Oakenpole TN23: Ashf . . . 9C 158
Oak Farm Gdns. TN27: H'crn . . . 7L 191
Oak Farm La. TN15: Stans . . . 1D 106 (5B 16)
Oakfield TN18: Hawkh . . . 5C 192
Oakfield Cotts. TN17: Bendn . . . 7A 38
Oakfield Ct. CT12: Ram . . . 4F 210
TN2: Tun W . . . 2J 157
Oakfield Ct. Rd. TN2: Tun W . . . 2H 157
Oakfield Gdns. BR3: Beck'm . . . 8E 68
Oakfield La. BR2: Kes . . . 5M 83
DA1: Dart . . . 7F 59 (7F 7)
DA2: Dart . . . 7J 59 (7F 7)
Oakfield Pk. Rd. DA1: Dart . . . 7L 59
Oakfield Pl. DA1: Dart . . . 7L 59
Oakfield Rd. BR6: Orp . . . 1J 85
CR0: Croy . . . 3G 13
SE20 . . . 1H 13
TN8: Eden . . . 2B 184
TN12: Mat . . . 6J 153
TN24: Kenn . . . 5H 159
Oakfields ME10: Sit . . . 8D 98
TN13: S'oaks . . . 8J 119
Oak Gdns. CR0: Croy . . . 3D 82
Oak Gro. BR4: W W'ck . . . 2F 82
CT15: Evtn . . . 6J 185
Oak Hall Pas. CT21: Hythe . . . 6K 199
Oakham Cl. SE6 . . . 7C 54
Oakham Dr. BR2: Shortl . . . 7J 69
TN29: Lydd . . . 2L 205
Oak Hill CT13: Wdboro . . . 8G 217 (1F 33)
TN13: S'oaks . . . 6H 119
Oakhill Rd. BR3: Beck'm . . . 5F 68
BR6: Orp . . . 2H 85
TN13: S'oaks . . . 6H 119
Oak Ho. ME5: Chat'm . . . 7C 94
(off Gorse Av.)
Oakhouse Rd. DA6: Bexhth . . . 3B 58
OAKHURST . . . 4H 25
Oakhurst Av. DA7: Bexhth . . . 7N 51
Oakhurst Cl. BR7: Chst . . . 4B 70
ME5: Chat'm . . . 8C 94
Oakhurst Gdns. DA7: Bexhth . . . 7N 51
Oakington Av. HA9: Wemb . . . 1A 4
Oakland Cl. ME5: Chat'm . . . 8C 94
Oakland Ct. CT6: H Bay . . . 2F 194
CT12: C'snd . . . 7A 210
Oaklands BR3: Beck'm . . . 4E 68
TN17: Cran . . . 8D 176
TN23: Ashf . . . 9D 158
TN25: Mers . . . 8M 161
Oaklands Av. BR4: W W'ck . . . 4E 82
CT10: B'stairs . . . 8J 209
DA15: Sidc . . . 5H 57
Oaklands Cl. BR5: Pet W . . . 9G 70
DA6: Bexhth . . . 3A 58
TN15: W King . . . 7E 88
Oaklands Cotts. CT21: Hythe . . . 8F 198
Oaklands La. TN16: Big H . . . 3A 164 (6A 14)
Oaklands Rd. BR1: Brom . . . 3H 69
DA2: Dart . . . 6B 60
DA6: Bexhth . . . 2A 58
DA11: Nflt . . . 9E 62
TN3: Groom . . . 7J 155
TN18: Hawkh . . . 6D 192
Oaklands Way CT2: Sturry . . . 4G 168
TN11: Hild . . . 2F 144
Oak La. ME9: Upc . . . 4H 225 (4B 18)
ME12: Minst . . . 6M 221 (7J 11)
TN13: S'oaks . . . 1G 131 (3G 25)
TN27: H'crn . . . 8L 191 (7B 28)
TN29: Lydd . . . 3J 205
Oaklea Rd. TN12: Pad W . . . 9L 147
Oakleigh Cl. BR8: Swanl . . . 6F 72
ME5: Chat'm . . . 9B 94
Oakleigh Gdns. BR6: Orp . . . 5G 85
Oakleigh Ho. TN23: Ashf . . . 1C 160
Oakleigh La. CT4: Bek . . . 5G 173
Oakleigh Pk. Av. BR7: Chst . . . 4C 70
Oakley Dr. BR2: Shortl . . . 4A 84
SE9 . . . 6F 56
SE13 . . . 4G 54
Oakley Pk. DA5: Bex'y . . . 5L 57
Oakley Rd. BR2: Shortl . . . 4A 84 (4B 14)
Oakley Sq. NW1 . . . 2E 4
Oakleys, The CT15: S'wll . . . 7K 219
Oakley St. SW3 . . . 5D 4
Oak Lodge TN13: S'oaks . . . 6H 119
Oak Lodge Dr. BR4: W W'ck . . . 1E 82
Oak Lodge La. TN16: Westrm . . . 7F 116
Oak Lodge Rd. TN28: New R . . . 2K 213
Oakmead DA13: Meop . . . 3F 90
TN10: Tonb . . . 1J 145
Oakmead Av. BR2: Shortl . . . 9K 69
Oakmere Rd. SE2 . . . 6J 51
Oakmont Pl. BR6: Orp . . . 2F 84
Oakridge CT10: B'stairs . . . 4L 209
Oak Ridge TN26: Ruck . . . 6B 40
Oakridge La. BR1: Brom . . . 1G 69
Oakridge Rd. BR1: Brom . . . 9G 55
Oak Rd. BR6: Chels . . . 8J 85
DA8: Erith . . . 7D 52
(Mill Rd.)
DA8: Erith . . . 8H 53
(Moat La.)
DA9: G'hithe . . . 4E 60
DA12: Grav'nd . . . 8H 63
ME2: Strood . . . 6J 79
ME10: Sit . . . 6K 99
TN2: Tun W . . . 7J 151
TN12: Five G . . . 8G 146
TN16: Westrm . . . 7F 116
Oaks Av. CT6: H Bay . . . 5E 194
Oaks Bus. Village, The ME5: Chat'm . . . 1F 110
Oaks Dene ME5: Chat'm . . . 1C 110
Oaks Forstal TN18: Sandh . . . 3D 218
Oakshade Rd. BR1: Brom . . . 9G 55
Oakside Rd. CT3: Aysm . . . 2C 162
Oaks Pk. CT2: R Comn . . . 8H 167
Oak Sq. TN13: S'oaks . . . 8K 119
Oaks Rd. CR0: Croy . . . 5A 82 (4H 13)
CT20: F'stone . . . 5D 188
TN30: Tent . . . 7C 224 (6E 38)
Oaks, The BR2: Shortl . . . 9C 70
BR8: Swanl . . . 5F 72
CT3: Hersd . . . 2L 169
CT7: St N . . . 8M 215
CT10: B'stairs . . . 6K 209
CT18: H'nge . . . 9L 193
DA2: Dart . . . 4B 60
ME20: Aylfd . . . 9J 109
SE18 . . . 5E 50
TN27: Smar . . . 8B 222
Oak St. CT14: Deal . . . 4N 177
Oaks Vw. CT21: Hythe . . . 8D 198
Oak Ter. ME5: Chat'm . . . 9D 94
TN18: Hawkh . . . 5C 192
Oak Tree Av. DA9: Bluew . . . 5F 60
ME15: Maid . . . 1F 138
Oak Tree Cl. TN2: Tun W . . . 4G 157
TN12: Mard . . . 3D 212
Oak Tree Gdns. BR1: Brom . . . 1L 69
Oak Tree Gro. CT9: Mgte . . . 3M 207
Oaktree Ho. ME10: Sit . . . 8J 99
(off Woodberry Dr.)
Oak Tree Rd. TN23: Ashf . . . 1D 160
Oakum Ct. ME4: Chat'm . . . 1E 94
Oakvale Cl. CT17: Dover . . . 5G 180
Oak Vw. TN8: Eden . . . 5B 184
Oakview Gro. CR0: Croy . . . 2B 82
Oakview Rd. SE6 . . . 1E 68
Oak Wlk. CT21: Hythe . . . 6K 199
Oak Warren TN13: S'oaks . . . 2H 131
Oakway BR2: Shortl . . . 5G 68
Oak Way CR0: Croy . . . 9A 68
Oakway Cl. DA5: Bex'y . . . 4N 57
Oakways SE9 . . . 4D 56
Oakwood Av. BR2: Shortl . . . 6L 69
BR3: Beck'm . . . 5F 68 (2K 13)
Oakwood Cl. BR7: Chst . . . 2B 70
DA1: Dart . . . 6B 60
Oakwood Ct. BR8: Swanl . . . 5D 72
(off Lawn Cl.)
ME16: Maid . . . 6A 126
Oakwood Dr. CT5: Whits . . . 4J 227
DA7: Bexhth . . . 2D 58
TN13: S'oaks . . . 5J 119
Oakwood Gdns. BR6: Farnb . . . 3E 84
Oakwood Ri. DA3: Long . . . 6L 75
TN2: Tun W . . . 6L 151
Oakwood Rd. BR6: Farnb . . . 3E 84
CT2: Sturry . . . 4F 168
ME16: Maid . . . 6N 125 (2H 27)
OARE . . . 2F 186 (5A 20)
Oare Meadow . . . 2F 186
Oare Rd. ME13: Fav . . . 2F 186 (5A 20)
Oasis, The BR1: Brom . . . 5M 69
Oast Cl. TN2: Tun W . . . 7K 151
Oast Cotts. CT1: Cant . . . 3L 171
CT3: Wing . . . 8J 225
TN13: S'oaks . . . 4H 119
Oast Ct. CT9: Mgte . . . 5D 208
ME10: Sit . . . 9F 98
ME18: Yald . . . 7D 136
Oasthouse Fld. TN29: Ivyc . . . 2G 47
Oasthouse Way BR5: St M Cry . . . 7K 71
Oast La. ME13: Throw . . . 3K 29
TN10: Tonb . . . 3G 144
Oast Mdw. TN24: W'boro . . . 9K 159
Oast, The CT1: Cant . . . 4A 172
Oast Theatre . . . 3G 144
Oastview ME8: Rain . . . 3C 96
Oast Vw. TN12: Horsm . . . 7C 196
Oast Way DA3: Hart'y . . . 9L 75
Oaten Hill CT1: Cant . . . 3N 171
Oaten Hill Pl. CT1: Cant . . . 3N 171
Oates Cl. BR2: Shortl . . . 6G 68
Oatfield Cl. TN17: Cran . . . 7C 176
Oatfield Dr. TN17: Cran . . . 7C 176
Oatfield Rd. BR6: Orp . . . 2H 85
Oaze, The CT5: Whits . . . 7E 226
Occupation La. SE18 . . . 8D 50
Occupation Rd. TN25: Wye . . . 2N 159
Ocean Cl. CT7: Birch . . . 3G 206
Ocean Ter. ME12: Minst . . . 5L 221
Ocean Vw. CT6: H Bay . . . 1M 195
CT10: B'stairs . . . 3L 211
Ocelot Ct. ME4: Chat'm . . . 9E 80
Ockendon Rd. RM14: Upm, N Ock . . . 1J 7
Ockendon Station (Rail) . . . 2K 7
OCKHAM . . . 3E 44
Ockham Dr. BR5: St P . . . 3J 71
OCKLEY . . . 4D 192
Ockley Ct. DA14: Sidc . . . 8G 57
Ockley La. TN18: Hawkh . . . 3D 192
Ockley Rd. TN18: Hawkh . . . 5D 192 (7J 37)
Octavia Ct. ME5: Chat'm . . . 8E 94
Octavian Dr. CT21: Lymp . . . 5B 198
Octavian Way TN23: Kgnt . . . 4C 160
(off Forum Way)
Odeon Cinema
Beckenham . . . 5C 68
Bromley . . . 5K 69
(off High St.)
London . . . 2A 56
(off Well Hall Rd.)
Maidstone . . . 6C 126
Tunbridge Wells . . . 6M 151
Odeon Pde. SE9 . . . 2A 56
(off Well Hall Rd.)
Odessa Rd. E7 . . . 1K 5
Odiham Dr. ME16: Alltn . . . 2N 125
Odo Rd. CT17: Dover . . . 4G 181
Offenham Rd. SE9 . . . 9B 56
Offen's Dr. TN12: S'hrst . . . 3J 223
OFFHAM . . . 1J 123 (1C 26)
Offham Rd. ME19: W Mal . . . 2L 123 (1D 26)
Officers' Rd. ME4: Chat'm . . . 4E 80
Officers Ter. ME4: Chat'm . . . 5C 80
Offley Cl. CT9: Mgte . . . 4G 209
Offord Rd. N1 . . . 1F 5
Ogilby St. SE18 . . . 4B 50
Ogilvy Ct. CT10: B'stairs . . . 6J 209
Okehampton Cl. TN24: Kenn . . . 3K 159
Okehampton Cres. DA16: Well . . . 8K 51 (5D 6)
Okemore Gdns. BR5: St M Cry . . . 7L 71
Olantigh Ct. CT7: Birch . . . 4F 206
Olantigh Rd. TN25: Wye . . . 2N 159 (6C 30)
Olave Rd. CT9: Mgte . . . 4E 208
Old Ash Cl. TN24: Kenn . . . 5G 158
Old Ashford Rd. ME17: Len . . . 7M 201 (3F 29)
TN27: Char'g . . . 3K 175
Old Badgins Rd. ME13: Shel, Throw . . . 1A 30
Old Bailey, The ME17: H'shm . . . 2N 141
Old Bakery Cl. TN29: St M Bay . . . 2M 215
Old Bakery M. ME13: Bou B . . . 3J 165
Old Barn Cl. ME7: Hpstd . . . 5J 95
TN9: Tonb . . . 7F 144
TN15: Kems'g . . . 8A 104
Old Barn Rd. ME19: Leyb . . . 8B 108
Old Barn Way DA7: Bexhth . . . 1E 58
Old Bethnal Grn. Rd. E2 . . . 2H 5
OLD BEXLEY . . . 5C 58 (7F 7)
Old Bexley Bus. Pk. DA5: Bex'y . . . 5C 58
Old Bexley La. DA1: Bex'y . . . 6G 58
DA2: Bex'y . . . 7F 7
DA5: Bex'y, Dart . . . 7E 58 (7F 7)
Old Billet La. ME12: E'chu . . . 2B 202
Old Boundary Rd. CT8: Wgte S . . . 2L 207
Old Bri. Rd. CT5: Whits . . . 4G 226 (3F 21)
Old Bromley Rd. BR1: Brom . . . 1G 69
Old Brompton Rd. SW5 . . . 4C 4
SW7 . . . 4D 4
Old Brook Pumping Station . . . 8C 80
OLDBURY . . . 4H 121 (1K 25)
Oldbury Cl. BR5: St M Cry . . . 7L 71
TN15: Igh . . . 4H 121
Oldbury Cotts. TN15: Igh . . . 3H 121
Oldbury Hill . . . 4G 120
Oldbury La. TN15: Igh . . . 3H 121 (1K 25)
Oldbury Vs. TN15: Igh . . . 4H 121
Oldbury Wood . . . 5G 120
Old Carriage Way, The
ME7: Hpstd . . . 7J 95
Old Carriageway, The TN13: Riv . . . 4D 118
Old Castle Wlk. ME8: Gill . . . 7N 95
Old Chapel Rd. BR8: Crock'm . . . 1D 86 (3F 15)
Old Charlton Rd. CT16: Dover . . . 2J 181 (1F 43)
Old Chatham Rd. ME14: S'lng . . . 6B 110 (6H 17)
(Boarley)
ME14: S'lng . . . 5B 110 (7H 17)
(Sandling)
ME20: Aylfd . . . 4A 110
Oldchurch Ct. ME16: Maid . . . 6B 126
Old Church Hill SS16: Lang H . . . 1D 8
Old Church La. NW9 . . . 1A 4
TN12: E Peck . . . 3K 135 (3D 26)
Old Church Rd. ME1: Burh . . . 1G 109 (5F 17)
ME1: Woul . . . 9G 92
ME18: W Peck . . . 3J 135
TN2: Pem . . . 4C 152 (1B 36)
TN12: E Peck . . . 3J 135
Old Church Way CT4: Chart'm . . . 9E 170
Old Clem Sq. SE18 . . . 6C 50
Old Coach Rd. TN15: Wro . . . 5L 105
Old Coal Yd. SE28 . . . 4F 50
Old Cotts. ME15: Maid . . . 7B 126
TN15: Igh . . . 4H 121
OLD COULSDON . . . 7F 13
Old Ct. Hill CT3: Aysm . . . 1F 162 (3C 32)
CT15: Aysm . . . 1F 162
CT15: Non . . . 3C 32
Old Courtyard, The BR1: Brom . . . 4L 69
Old Crossing Rd. CT9: Mgte . . . 2N 207
OLD CRYALS . . . 2D 36
Old Dairy Cl. CT11: Ram . . . 5K 211
Old Dartford Rd. DA4: Farn'm . . . 9N 73
Old Dover Rd. CT1: Cant . . . 3N 171 (1H 31)
CT18: Cap F . . . 3B 174 (3C 42)
SE3 . . . 5A 6
Old Downs DA3: Hart'y . . . 8L 75
Old Dr. ME15: Maid . . . 2C 138
Old Farleigh Rd. CR2: S Croy . . . 5H 13
CR6: Warl . . . 5H 13
Old Farm Av. DA15: Sidc . . . 6F 56
Old Farm Cl. CT5: Whits . . . 7E 226
Old Farm Gdns. BR8: Swanl . . . 6G 72
Old Farm Rd. CT7: Birch . . . 4C 206
Old Farm Rd. E. DA15: Sidc . . . 7J 57
Old Farm Rd. W. DA15: Sidc . . . 7H 57
Old Ferry Rd. ME9: Iwade . . . 7K 197 (2F 19)
Oldfield Cl. BR1: Brom . . . 7B 70
ME8: Gill . . . 3N 95
ME15: Maid . . . 8H 127
Oldfield Dr. ME1: Woul . . . 6G 93

Pennine Way—Pitfold Rd.

Pennine Way ME15: Bear . . . 8K **127**
TN24: Ashf . . . 6F **158**
Pennington Cl. CT2: Sturry . . . 4H **169**
Pennington Mnr. TN4: S'bgh . . . 4G **150**
Pennington Pl. TN4: S'bgh . . . 4H **151**
Pennington Rd. TN4: S'bgh . . . 4F **150**
Pennington Way SE12 . . . 7L **55**
Pennis La. DA3: Fawk . . . 9K **75**
Penn La. DA5: Bex'y . . . 3M **57**
(not continuous)
TN14: Ide H, Sund . . . 9N **117**
Penn St. N1 . . . 2G **5**
Penn's Yd. TN2: Pem . . . 8B **152**
Penny Cress Gdns. ME16: Maid . . . 6N **125**
Penny Cress Rd. ME12: Minst . . . 8H **221**
Pennycroft CR0: Croy . . . 9B **82**
Pennyfields TN17: Cran . . . 8D **176**
PENNYPOT . . . 7G 199
Pennypot Ind. Est. CT21: Hythe . . . 7G **199**
Penny Pot La.
CT4: P'hm, Chart'm, Walt . . . 4E **30**
Penpool La. DA16: Well . . . 1K **57**
Penrith Cl. BR3: Beck'm . . . 4E **68**
Penrose Ct. CT21: Hythe . . . 7K **199**
Penruddocke Ho. TN10: Tonb . . . 3J **145**
Penryn Mnr. *ME7: Gill . . . 6F 80*
(off Skinner St.)
Pensand Ho. CT21: Hythe . . . 7L **199**
PENSHURST . . . 2J 149 (1G 35)
Penshurst Av. DA15: Sidc . . . 4J **57**
Penshurst Cl. CT2: Cant . . . 8N **167**
DA3: Long . . . 5C **76**
ME8: Rain . . . 1A **96**
TN15: W King . . . 7E **88**
Penshurst Ent. Cen. TN11: Pens . . . 2K **149**
Penshurst Gdns. CT9: Clift . . . 3K **209**
Penshurst Grn. BR2: Shortl . . . 8J **69**
Penshurst Off Road Cycling . . . 4G 148
Penshurst Place & Gardens . . . 1J 149 (7G 25)
Penshurst Ri. ME13: Fav . . . 4F **186**
Penshurst Rd. CT11: Ram . . . 5K **211**
DA7: Bexhth . . . 8A **52**
TN3: Bidb . . . 3L **149** (1G **35**)
TN3: Pens, Speld . . . 6M **149** (2H **35**)
TN11: Pens . . . 6M **149** (2H **35**)
(Poundsbridge)
TN11: Pens, Bidb . . . 3L **149** (1G **35**)
(Printstile)
TN11: Pens, Leigh . . . 9H **143** (7G **25**)
(Penshurst)
Penshurst Station (Rail) . . . 6G 143 (6F 25)
Penshurst Vineyards . . . 4G 148 (1F 35)
Penshurst Wlk. BR2: Shortl . . . 8J **69**
Penshurst Way BR5: St M Cry . . . 7L **71**
Penstocks, The ME15: Maid . . . 7A **126**
Pentagon Shop. Cen. ME4: Chat'm . . . 7C **80**
Penton Ho. SE2 . . . 1M **51**
Penton St. N1 . . . 2F **5**
Pentonville Rd. N1 . . . 2F **5**
Pent Rd. CT19: F'stone . . . 4F **188**
Pentstemon Dr. DA10: Swans . . . 3L **61**
Pentvale Cl. CT19: F'stone . . . 5G **189**
Pen Way TN10: Tonb . . . 2L **145**
Penwith Rd. SW18 . . . 7C **4**
Pepingstraw Cl. ME19: Off . . . 2J **123**
Pepper All. ME14: Maid . . . 1B **126**
PEPPER HILL . . . 8C 62
Pepperhill DA11: Nflt . . . 8B **62**
Pepperhill La. DA11: Nflt . . . 8B **62**
Peppermead Sq. SE4 . . . 3D **54**
Pepys Av. ME12: S'ness . . . 2C **220** (6F **11**)
Pepys Cl. DA1: Dart . . . 2A **60**
DA11: Nflt . . . 8C **62**
Pepys Ri. BR6: Orp . . . 2H **85**
Pepys Rd. SE14 . . . 1A **54** (5H **5**)
Pepy's Way ME2: Strood . . . 4K **79**
Perch La. TN3: Lamb . . . 3C **36**
Percival Rd. BR6: Farnb . . . 3D **84**
Percival St. EC1 . . . 2F **5**
Percival Ter. CT17: Dover . . . 5G **181**
Percy Av. CT10: B'stairs . . . 4K **209**
Percy Rd. CT9: Clift . . . 2E **208**
CT10: B'stairs . . . 8K **209**
CT11: Ram . . . 4H **211**
DA7: Bexhth . . . 9N **51**
SE20 . . . 4A **68**
Peregrine Cl. CT21: Hythe . . . 8E **198**
Peregrine Ct. DA16: Well . . . 8H **51**
Peregrine Dr. ME10: Sit . . . 8H **99**
Peregrine Gdns. CR0: Croy . . . 3B **82**
Peregrine Rd. ME19: W Mal . . . 7M **123**
Peri Ct. CT1: Cant . . . 4L **171**
Perie Row *ME7: Gill . . . 6D 80*
(off W. Court St.)
Perimeter Rd. CT16: Dover . . . 4M **181**
ME20: Lark . . . 7G **108**
Periton Rd. SE9 . . . 2N **55**
Periwinkle Cl. ME10: Sit . . . 6F **98**
Perkins Av. CT9: Mgte . . . 5D **208**
Perkins Cl. DA9: G'hithe . . . 3F **60**
Perks Cl. SE3 . . . 1H **55**
Perpins Rd. SE9 . . . 4G **56**
Perran Cl. DA3: Hart'y . . . 7M **75**
Perries Mead CT19: F'stone . . . 4H **189**
Perrott St. SE18 . . . 4E **50**
PERRY . . . 7C 22
Perryfield St. ME14: Maid . . . 3C **126**
Perry Gro. DA1: Dart . . . 2A **60**
Perry Hall Cl. BR6: St M Cry . . . 1J **85**
Perry Hall Rd. BR6: St M Cry . . . 9H **71** (3C **14**)
Perry Hill ME3: Cliffe . . . 4N **65** (6H **9**)
SE6 . . . 8C **54** (7J **5**)
Perry La. CT3: Pres . . . 7C **22**
Perry Ri. SE23 . . . 8B **54** (7J **5**)
Perrys La. BR6: Prat B . . . 4K **101** (6D **14**)
PERRY STREET . . . 6D 62 (7B 8)
Perry St. BR7: Chst . . . 2F **70** (1C **14**)
DA1: Cray . . . 2F **58** (6F **7**)
DA11: Nflt . . . 6D **62** (7B **8**)
Perry St. ME4: Chat'm . . . 9B **80**
ME14: Maid . . . 3C **126**
Perry St. Gdns. BR7: Chst . . . 2G **71**
Perry St. Shaw BR7: Chst . . . 3G **71**
Perry Va. SE23 . . . 7A **54** (7H **5**)
PERRYWOOD . . . 2C 30
Persant Rd. SE6 . . . 7H **55**
Perth Gdns. ME10: Sit . . . 7D **98**
Perth Rd. BR3: Beck'm . . . 5F **68**
Perth Way CT16: Dover . . . 1H **181**
Pescot Av. DA3: Long . . . 6N **75**
PESTED . . . 4A 30
Pested Bars Rd. ME17: Bou Mo . . . 3F **138** (3J **27**)
Pested La. TN25: C'lck . . . 6E **174** (4A **30**)
Petchell M. *CT1: Cant . . . 9A 168*
(off Teddington Cl.)
Peterborough Gdns. ME2: Strood . . . 6G **79**
Peter Candler Way TN24: Kenn . . . 6J **159**
Peter Kennedy Ct. CR0: Croy . . . 9C **68**
Peters Cl. DA16: Well . . . 9G **51**
Petersfield TN2: Pem . . . 6D **152**
Petersfield Dr. DA13: Meop . . . 1E **106**
PETER'S GREEN . . . 2E 44
Petersham Dr. BR5: St P . . . 5H **71**
Petersham Gdns. BR5: St P . . . 5H **71**
Peterstone Rd. SE2 . . . 2K **51**
Peter St. CT14: Deal . . . 3N **177**
CT16: Dover . . . 4H **181**
CT20: F'stone . . . 6L **189**
DA12: Grav'nd . . . 5G **63**
Peters Works ME1: Woul . . . 8G **92**
Petfield Cl. ME12: Minst . . . 6K **221**
PETHAM . . . 4G 31
Petham Grn. ME8: Gill . . . 9M **81**
Petherton Rd. N5 . . . 1G **5**
Petlands ME15: Maid . . . 3G **139**
Petley Ct. Almshouses *TN9: Tonb . . . 7H 145*
(off Pembury Rd.)
Petrel Cl. CT6: H Bay . . . 3N **195**
Petrel Way CT18: H'nge . . . 9K **193**
Petrie Ho. *SE18 . . . 6C 50*
(off Woolwich Comn.)
PETT BOTTOM . . . 3J 31
Pett Bottom Rd. CT4: Bis, Brid . . . 9D **172** (4J **31**)
CT4: Up Hard . . . 5J **31**
Petten Cl. BR5: Orp . . . 2M **85**
Petten Gro. BR5: Orp . . . 2L **85**
PETTERIDGE . . . 8L 153 (2D 36)
Petteridge La. TN12: Brenc, Mat . . . 8K **153** (2D **36**)
Pettfield Hill Rd. ME13: Throw . . . 2J **29**
Pett Hill CT4: Brid . . . 9E **172** (2J **31**)
PETTINGS . . . 8A 90 (5A 16)
Pettits Row ME13: Fav . . . 5F **186**
Pett La. ME9: S'bry . . . 2J **113** (6C **18**)
TN27: Char'g . . . 3L **175** (5H **29**)
Pett Level Rd. TN36: Pett, Winch . . . 7A **46**
Pettman Cl. CT6: H Bay . . . 4G **195**
Pettman Ct. CT10: B'stairs . . . 8J **209**
Pettman Cres. SE28 . . . 3F **50** (4C **6**)
Pettmans M. CT5: Whits . . . 3E **226**
Petts Cres. CT12: Minst . . . 8E **212**
Petts La. CT3: Wing . . . 6H **225**
Pett St. SE18 . . . 4J **49**
PETTS WOOD . . . 8E 70 (3C 14)
Petts Wood Rd. BR5: Pet W . . . 8E **70** (3C **14**)
Petts Wood Station (Rail) . . . 8E 70 (3C 14)
Petworth Rd. DA6: Bexhth . . . 3B **58**
Peverel Dr. ME14: Weav . . . 4J **127**
Peverel Grn. ME8: Gill . . . 7N **95**
Peverell Rd. CT16: Dover . . . 9G **178**
Peveril Ct. *DA2: Dart . . . 4B 60*
(off Clifton Wlk.)
Pewter Rd. CT1: Cant . . . 3M **171**
Phalarop Way ME4: Chat'm . . . 2F **80**
Pharos Dr. CT16: Dover . . . 3K **181**
Pharos, The . . . 4L 181 (2G 43)
Pheasant La. ME15: Maid . . . 1E **138** (3J **27**)
Pheasant Rd. ME4: Chat'm . . . 1F **94**
Pheasants' Hall Rd. CT4: Kgstn, Bis . . . 4J **31**
Phelps Cl. TN15: W King . . . 7E **88**
Philimore Cl. SE18 . . . 5G **51**
Philip Av. BR8: Swanl . . . 7E **72**
Philip Corby Cl. CT9: Clift . . . 3F **208**
Philip Gdns. CR0: Croy . . . 3C **82**
Philipot Path SE9 . . . 4B **56**
Philippa Gdns. SE9 . . . 3N **55**
Philippa Ho. CT19: F'stone . . . 5M **189**
Philippine Village Craft Cen. . . . 3D 46
Philip Rd. CT19: F'stone . . . 5E **188**
Phillippa Ct. ME10: Sit . . . 3F **98**
Phillips Cl. DA1: Dart . . . 4J **59**
Phillips Ct. ME8: Gill . . . 1L **95**
Phillips Rd. CT7: Birch . . . 5F **206**
Philpots La. TN11: Leigh, Hild . . . 2L **143** (5G **25**)
Phineas Pett Rd. SE9 . . . 1A **56**
Phipps Bridge Station (CT) . . . 2D 12
Phoebeth Rd. SE13 . . . 3D **54**
Phoenix Cl. BR4: W W'ck . . . 3G **83**
Phoenix Cotts. *ME18: W'bury . . . 2B 136*
(off Maidstone Rd.)
Phoenix Dr. BR2: Kes . . . 5N **83**
ME18: W'bury . . . 1C **136**
Phoenix Ind. Est. ME2: Med E . . . 5A **80**
Phoenix Pk. Bus. Cen. ME15: Maid . . . 4J **139**
Phoenix Pl. DA1: Dart . . . 5L **59**
Phoenix Rd. ME5: Chat'm . . . 9E **94**
Phoenix Wharf ME2: Med E . . . 5A **80**
Picardy Manorway DA17: Belv . . . 3C **52** (4E **6**)
Picardy Rd. DA17: Belv . . . 5B **52** (4E **6**)
Picardy St. DA17: Belv . . . 3B **52** (4E **6**)
Piccadilly W1 . . . 3E **4**
Piccadilly Circus Station (Tube) . . . 3E 4
Pickelden La.
CT4: Chilw, Chart'm . . . 8M **175** (3E **30**)
Pickering Ct. *DA2: Dart . . . 4B 60*
(off Osbourne Rd.)
Pickering St. ME15: Maid . . . 2D **138**
Pickford Cl. DA7: Bexhth . . . 9N **51**
Pickford La. DA7: Bexhth . . . 9N **51** (5E **6**)
Pickford Rd. DA7: Bexhth . . . 1N **57**
Pickhurst Grn. BR2: Shortl . . . 1J **83**
Pickhurst La. BR2: Kes . . . 2K **83**
BR2: Shortl . . . 9H **69** (3K **13**)
BR4: W W'ck . . . 8H **69** (3K **13**)
Pickhurst Mead BR2: Shortl . . . 1J **83**
Pickhurst Pk. BR2: Shortl . . . 8H **69**
Pickhurst Ri. BR4: W W'ck . . . 1F **82**
Pickle's Way ME3: Cliffe . . . 2B **176**
Pickmoss La. TN14: Otf . . . 7H **103**
Pickwick Ct. SE9 . . . 6A **56**
Pickwick Cres. ME1: Roch . . . 1N **93**
Pickwick Gdns. DA11: Nflt . . . 8C **62**
Pickwick Ho. DA11: Nflt . . . 8C **62**
Pickwick Way BR7: Chst . . . 2E **70**
Picney Bush La. TN29: St M Mar, Newchu . . . 1H **47**
Picton Rd. CT11: Ram . . . 6G **211**
Piedmont Rd. SE18 . . . 5F **50**
(not continuous)
Pie Factory Rd. CT15: Non . . . 4D **32**
Pier App. CT10: B'stairs . . . 9M **209**
Pier App. Rd. ME7: Gill . . . 5G **80**
Pier Av. CT5: Whits . . . 2J **227**
CT6: H Bay . . . 2F **194**
Pierce Mill La. TN11: Hdlw . . . 2G **146**
Pierce Mill Rd. TN11: Hdlw . . . 5C **26**
Pier Chine CT6: H Bay . . . 3F **194**
Piermont Pl. BR1: Brom . . . 5A **70**
Pier Pde. *E16 . . . 1C 50*
(off Pier Rd.)
Pier Pavilion Leisure Cen. . . . 2F 194
Pier Pl. ME2: Upnor . . . 1D **80**
Pierpoint Rd. CT5: Whits . . . 6F **226**
Pierremont Av. CT10: B'stairs . . . 9L **209**
Pier Rd. DA8: Erith . . . 6F **52**
(not continuous)
DA9: G'hithe . . . 2H **61**
DA11: Nflt . . . 4E **62**
E16 . . . 2B **50** (4B **6**)
ME4: Chat'm . . . 4E **80** (2J **17**)
ME7: Gill . . . 5G **80** (2J **17**)
ME11: Queen . . . 6A **220**
Pier Rd. Ind. Est. ME7: Gill . . . 5G **81**
Pier, The CT16: Whitf . . . 5E **178**
Pier Way SE28 . . . 2E **50**
Pigdown La. TN8: Hever . . . 1D **34**
Pigeon Hoo La. TN30: Tent . . . 6F **39**
Pigeon La. CT6: H Bay . . . 5H **195**
Pigsdean Rd. DA13: Lud'n . . . 1N **91**
Pigs Pas. TN18: Hawkh . . . 5D **192**
PIGTAIL CORNER . . . 7J 11
Pike Cl. BR1: Brom . . . 1L **69**
CT19: F'stone . . . 4G **189**
ME20: Lark . . . 6E **108**
Pikefields ME8: Gill . . . 1M **95**
Pikefish La. ME18: Ladd . . . 6E **26**
TN12: Pad W . . . 6E **26**
Pike La. RM14: Upm . . . 1J **7**
Pike Rd. CT14: Tilm . . . 4E **32**
CT15: Eyt . . . 7L **185** (4E **32**)
Pikes La. RH7: Ling . . . 6A **24**
Pikethorne SE23 . . . 7A **54**
Pikey La. ME19: E Mal . . . 4B **124** (1E **26**)
Pilckem Cl. CT1: Cant . . . 1C **172**
Pile La. TN12: S'hrst . . . 2L **223** (1K **37**)
Pilgrim's Ct. DA1: Dart . . . 3A **60**
Pilgrims Ct. TN27: Char'g . . . 3K **175**
Pilgrims Lakes ME17: H'shm . . . 2N **141**
Pilgrims La. CT4: Chil'm . . . 7M **175**
CT5: Seas . . . 8D **226**
RH8: Tats . . . 2A **24**
RM16: N Stif . . . 3K **7**
TN16: Tats, Westrm . . . 5A **116** (2A **24**)
Pilgrim Spring CT19: F'stone . . . 3J **189**
Pilgrims Rd. DA10: Nflt, Swans . . . 2L **61**
ME2: Hall'g . . . 5C **92** (4E **16**)
Pilgrims Vw. DA9: G'hithe . . . 4J **61**
ME6: Snod . . . 2D **108**
ME14: S'lng . . . 7B **110**
Pilgrims Way CT1: Harb . . . 3A **172** (1F **31**)
CT2: Harb . . . 2F **170** (1F **31**)
CT4: Cha H . . . 5B **170**
CT16: Dover . . . 1E **180**
DA1: Dart . . . 6A **60**
ME1: Burh . . . 3L **109**
ME1: Woul . . . 7H **93**
ME2: Cux . . . 9G **79**
ME2: Hall'g . . . 8B **92** (5E **16**)
ME14: Boxl, Det . . . 6E **110** (7J **17**)
ME14: Det, T'hm . . . 9K **111** (7K **17**)
ME17: H'shm, Len . . . 3D **28**
ME17: Holl . . . 6E **110** (7K **17**)
ME19: Tros . . . 4E **106** (6B **16**)
ME20: Aylfd . . . 3L **109** (6J **17**)
Pilgrim's Way TN13: Dun G . . . 8E **102**
TN14: Dun G . . . 8D **102**
(not continuous)
Pilgrims Way TN14: Otf . . . 7L **103** (7H **15**)
TN14: Sund . . . 5B **116** (1D **24**)
TN15: Kems'g . . . 7C **104** (7H **15**)
TN15: Wro . . . 7M **105**
(Battlefields Rd.)
TN15: Wro . . . 7A **106** (7A **16**)
(London Rd.)
TN16: Bras, Westrm . . . 5B **116** (2B **24**)
TN25: Bou L . . . 6B **30**
TN25: W Bra, E Bra . . . 1E **40**
TN27: Char'g . . . 2L **175** (5H **29**)
Pilgrims Way Cotts. TN15: Kems'g . . . 8A **104**
Pilgrims Way E. TN14: Otf . . . 6K **103** (7G **15**)
Pilgrims Way W. TN13: Otf . . . 8E **102**
TN14: Otf . . . 7F **102** (7F **15**)
Pilkington Rd. BR6: Farnb . . . 4E **84**
Pillar Box La. TN11: Hdlw . . . 3C **134**
Pillar Box Rd. TN15: Seal . . . 4E **120** (1J **25**)
Pilot Rd. ME1: Roch . . . 3N **93**
Pilots Av. CT14: Deal . . . 6K **177**
Pilot's Farm Rd. CT4: Lwr Har, Up Hard . . . 4H **31**
Pilots Pl. DA12: Grav'nd . . . 4H **63**
PIMLICO . . . 4E 4
Pimlico Rd. SW1 . . . 4E **4**
Pimlico Station (Tube) . . . 4E 4
Pimpernel Cl. ME14: Bear . . . 5L **127**
Pimpernel Way ME5: Chat'm . . . 7B **94**
Pimps Ct. Cotts. ME15: Loose . . . 2B **138**
Pinchbeck Rd. BR6: Chels . . . 7H **85**
Pincott Pl. SE4 . . . 1A **54**
Pincott Rd. DA6: Bexhth . . . 3B **58**
Pincroft Wood DA3: Long . . . 6B **76**
PINDEN . . . 5J 75 (2K 15)
Pine Av. BR4: W W'ck . . . 2E **82**
DA12: Grav'nd . . . 6J **63**
Pine Cl. BR8: Swanl . . . 7G **73**
ME20: Lark . . . 8E **108**
Pine Coombe CR0: Croy . . . 5A **82**
Pine Cotts. CT4: Elham . . . 6N **183**
ME16: Alltn . . . 1B **126**
Pinecrest Gdns. BR6: Farnb . . . 5D **84**
Pinecroft Ct. DA16: Well . . . 7J **51**
Pine Glade BR6: Farnb . . . 5B **84**
Pine Gro. ME7: Hpstd . . . 5K **95**
ME14: Pen H . . . 3E **126**
TN8: Eden . . . 5B **184**
PINEHAM . . . 6J 179 (7F 33)
Pineham Rd. CT15: Whitf, Gus . . . 5H **179** (7F **33**)
Pine Ho. ME5: Chat'm . . . 6C **94**
Pinehurst TN14: S'oaks . . . 3M **119**
Pinehurst Wlk. BR6: Orp . . . 2F **84**
Pine Lodge ME16: Maid . . . 6N **125**
Pine Lodge Cvn. Pk. ME17: Holl . . . 7B **128**
Pine Lodge Ct. CT14: Deal . . . 5L **177**
Pine Needle La. TN13: S'oaks . . . 5J **119**
Pine Pl. ME15: Maid . . . 8B **126**
Pine Ridge TN10: Tonb . . . 1H **145**
Pine Ri. DA13: Meop . . . 9F **76**
Pine Rd. ME2: Strood . . . 6K **79**
Pinesfield La. ME19: Tros . . . 3G **107** (6C **16**)
Pines Gardens, The . . . 8D 214 (1J 43)
Pineside Rd. CT3: L'brne . . . 2K **173**
Pines Rd. BR1: Brom . . . 5A **70** (2B **14**)
Pines, The *CT1: Cant . . . 4N 171*
(off Puckle St.)
CT2: Up Harb . . . 1E **170**
Pine, The CT10: B'stairs . . . 9H **209**
Pine Tree Av. CT2: Cant . . . 9L **167**
Pinetree Cl. CT5: Whits . . . 2H **227**
Pine Tree Cl. *CT7: Birch . . . 4G 206*
(off Parkway, The)
Pine Tree La. TN15: Ivy H . . . 7G **121** (2K **25**)
Pine Tree Lodge BR2: Shortl . . . 7J **69**
Pine Vw. TN15: Bor G . . . 2B **122**
Pine Wlk. CT6: H Bay . . . 2M **195**
Pine Way CT19: F'stone . . . 4D **188**
Pinewood Av. DA15: Sidc . . . 6G **57**
TN14: S'oaks . . . 3L **119**
Pinewood Cl. BR6: Orp . . . 2F **84**
CR0: Croy . . . 4B **82**
CT12: Ram . . . 3G **210**
TN12: Pad W . . . 9L **147**
Pinewood Ct. TN4: S'bgh . . . 5G **150**
Pinewood Dr. BR6: Orp . . . 6G **84**
ME5: Chat'm . . . 2G **110**
Pinewood Gdns. TN4: S'bgh . . . 5G **150**
Pinewood Pl. DA5: Bex'y . . . 7F **58**
Pinewood Rd. BR2: Shortl . . . 7K **69**
SE2 . . . 6M **51**
TN2: Tun W . . . 9K **151**
Pin Hill CT1: Cant . . . 3M **171** (1H **31**)
Pink All. *TN2: Tun W . . . 3G 156*
(off Nevill St.)
Pinkham TN12: E Peck . . . 2M **147**
Pinkham Gdns. TN12: E Peck . . . 1M **147**
Pink's Hill BR8: Swanl . . . 8F **72**
Pinnacle Hill DA7: Bexhth . . . 2C **58**
Pinnacle Hill Nth. DA7: Bexhth . . . 2C **58**
Pinnacles Cl. TN10: Tonb . . . 2J **145**
Pinnacles, The ME4: Chat'm . . . 3F **80**
Pinnell Rd. SE9 . . . 2N **55**
Pinners Hill CT3: Aysm . . . 3C **32**
CT15: Non . . . 3C **32**
Pinners La. CT15: Non . . . 3C **32**
Pinnock La. TN12: S'hrst . . . 1K **37**
Pinnocks Av. DA11: Grav'nd . . . 6G **62**
Pinnock, The TN27: P'ley . . . 7F **29**
Pintail Cl. ME3: Isle G . . . 7C **190**
Pintail Dr. ME9: Iwade . . . 9K **197**
Pintails, The ME4: Chat'm . . . 3E **80**
Pintail Way CT6: H Bay . . . 5K **195**
Pinto Way SE3 . . . 2L **55**
Pioneer Bus. Pk. CT11: Ram . . . 4H **211**
Pioneer Pl. CR0: Croy . . . 9D **82**
Pioneer Rd. CT17: Dover . . . 1F **180**
Pioneer Way BR8: Swanl . . . 6F **72**
Pipers Cl. CT18: Lym'ge . . . 7L **205**
Piper's Cotts. ME15: Loose . . . 4B **138**
Piper's Gdns. CR0: Croy . . . 1B **82**
Piper's Grn. Rd. TN16: Bras . . . 3D **24**
Pipers La. TN16: Bras . . . 9J **117**
(not continuous)
Pippenhall SE9 . . . 4D **56**
Pippin Av. CT4: Bis . . . 9J **173**
Pippin Cl. CR0: Croy . . . 2C **82**
ME10: Sit . . . 5E **98**
ME17: Cox . . . 6M **137**
Pippin Rd. TN12: E Peck . . . 1L **147**
Pippins, The DA13: Meop . . . 9F **76**
Pippin Way ME19: W Mal . . . 7M **123**
Pippon Cft. ME7: Hpstd . . . 5K **95**
PIPSDEN . . . 7J 37
Pirbright Cl. ME5: Chat'm . . . 9G **95**
Pirbright Cres. CR0: Croy . . . 7F **82**
Pirrip Cl. DA12: Grav'nd . . . 6L **63**
Pitfield DA3: Hart'y . . . 7M **75**
Pitfield Cres. SE28 . . . 1J **51**
Pitfield Dr. DA13: Meop . . . 4E **90**
Pitfield St. N1 . . . 2G **5**
Pitfold Cl. SE12 . . . 4K **55**
Pitfold Rd. SE12 . . . 4K **55**

Pit La.—Pratling St.

Pit La. TN8: Eden 3C 184
Pitstock Rd. ME9: Rod 7J 115 (7F 19)
Pittlesden TN30: Tent 8B 224
Pittlesden Pl. TN30: Tent 8B 224
Pittock Ho. CT14: Deal 7L 177
Pitt Rd. BR6: Farnb 5E 84
KT17: Eps 6A 12
ME16: Maid 8M 125
ME17: Kgswd 5B 140 (4A 28)
Pittsmead Av. BR2: Shortl 1K 83
PITTSWOOD 8N 133 (5A 26)
Pittswood TN11: Hdlw 8A 134
Pittswood Cotts. TN11: Hdlw 8N 133
Pivington La. TN27: P'ley 6F 29
Pixfield Ct. *BR2: Shortl* *5J 69*
(off Beckenham La.)
Pixot Hill TN12: Brenc 5N 153 (1D 36)
Pix's Cotts. TN17: Rolv 3D 214
Pix's La. TN17: Rolv 3C 214 (7C 38)
Pixton Way CR0: Croy 9B 82
PIZIEN WELL 1N 135 (3D 26)
Pizien Well Rd. ME18: W'bury 2M 135 (3D 26)
PJ's Fitness & Squash Club 5C 202
Place Farm Av. BR6: Orp 2F 84
Placehouse La. CR5: Coul 7F 13
Place La. ME9: H'lip 6F 96 (4B 18)
TN26: Wdchu 7C 228 (5H 39)
Plain Cotts. CT20: F'stone 7G 189
Plain Rd. CT20: F'stone 7G 189
TN12: Mard 4C 212 (1H 37)
TN25: Sme 8K 165 (2E 40)
Plains Av. ME15: Maid 8E 126
Plains of Waterloo CT11: Ram 5J 211
Plain, The TN17: Goud 3C 190
PLAISTOW
Bromley 3K 69 (1A 14)
London 2A 6
Plaistow Gro. BR1: Brom 3L 69
Plaistow La. BR1: Brom 3K 69 (1A 14)
(not continuous)
Plaistow Rd. E13 2A 6
E15 2K 5
Plaistow Sq. ME14: Maid 3F 126
Plaistow Station (Tube) 2K 5
Plane Av. DA11: Nflt 5C 62
Plane Ho. BR2: Shortl 5H 69
Plane Wlk. TN10: Tonb 9J 133
Plantagenet Ho. *SE18* *3B 50*
(off Leda Rd.)
Plantation Cl. DA9: G'hithe 4F 60
TN26: Hoth 2M 197
Plantation Dr. BR5: Orp 2M 85
Plantation La. ME14: Bear 5K 127
Plantation Rd. BR8: Swanl 3H 73
CT5: Whits 3M 227
DA8: Erith 8H 53
ME7: Gill 6K 81
ME13: Fav 5G 186
Plantin Ho. TN24: Ashf 7G 159
PLASHET 1B 6
Plashet Gro. E6 1A 6
Plashet Rd. E13 2A 6
Plassy Rd. SE6 5E 54
Platt Comn. TN15: Bor G 2B 122
Platters Farm Lodge ME8: Gill 4M 95
Platters, The ME8: Gill 3M 95
Plat, The TN8: Eden 6D 184
Platt Ho. La. TN15: Stans, Wro 4B 106 (6B 16)
Platt Ind. Est. TN15: Bor G 1A 122
Platt Mill Cl. TN15: Bor G 2A 122
Platt Mill Ter. TN15: Bor G 2A 122
PLATT'S HEATH 4D 28
Platt's La. NW3 1C 4
PLATT, THE 5K 35
Platt, The ME17: Sut V 9A 140
Plaw Hatch La. RH19: F Row 6A 34
Plawsfield Rd. BR3: Beck'm 4A 68
Plaxdale Grn. Rd. TN15: Stans 4K 105 (6K 15)
PLAXTOL 9L 121 (3A 26)
Plaxtol Cl. BR1: Brom 4M 69
Plaxtol La. TN11: S'brne 3K 25
TN15: Plax 9J 121
Plaxtol Rd. DA8: Erith 7B 52
PLAXTOL SPOUTE 9M 121
PLAYDEN 4B 46
Playden La. TN31: Iden 4A 46
Playgreen Way SE6 8D 54
Playground Cl. BR3: Beck'm 5A 68
Playhouse, The 4F 226
Playstool Cl. ME9: N'tn 5K 97
Playstool Rd. ME9: N'tn 5J 97
Pleasance Rd. BR5: St P 5K 71
Pleasance Rd. Cen. TN29: Lydd 6K 47
Pleasance Rd. Nth. TN29: G'stne 9H 213
Pleasance Rd. Sth. TN29: Lydd 6K 47
Pleasant Courts ME14: Det 9K 111
Pleasant Gro. CR0: Croy 4C 82
Pleasant Pl. ME12: Minst 6F 220
Pleasant Row ME1: Roch 7N 79
ME7: Chat'm 6D 80
Pleasant Valley La. ME15: E Far 4M 137
Pleasant Vw. DA8: Erith 5F 52
Pleasant Vw. Pl. BR6: Farnb 6D 84
Pleasure Ho. Rd. ME17: Sut V 9C 140 (5B 28)
Pleasure Pit Rd. KT21: Asht 7A 12
Plenty Brook Rd. CT6: H Bay 4G 194
Pleydell Ct. *CT20: F'stone* *7K 189*
(off Pleydell Gdns.)
Pleydell Cres. CT2: Sturry 4E 168
Pleydell Gdns. CT20: F'stone 7K 189
Plimsoll Av. CT19: F'stone 3K 189
Plomley Cl. ME8: Gill 7N 95
Plough Cotts. ME17: Sut V 6N 139
Plough Ct. CT6: H Bay 5K 195
Plough Hill CT15: Chu H 8B 180 (3D 42)
TN15: Bor G 5M 121 (2A 26)
Plough La. CR8: Purl 5F 13
CT2: Up Harb 1E 170
CT5: Whits 2M 227
Plough La. SM6: Wall 4F 13
SW17 1D 12
SW19 1D 12
Ploughmans Way ME5: Chat'm 1D 110
ME8: Rain 5A 96
Plough Rd. ME12: Minst, E'chu 3A 202 (7J 11)
RH7: Dor'land 1A 34
SW11 6D 4
Plough Wlk. *TN8: Eden* *4C 184*
(off Fircroft Way)
Plough Way SE16 4J 5
Plough Wents Rd. ME17: Cha S 6J 139 (4K 27)
Plover Cl. CT6: H Bay 2N 195
ME5: Chat'm 1G 110
TN8: Eden 4D 184
Plover Rd. CT18: H'nge 9J 193
ME12: Minst 7H 221
ME20: Lark 8D 108
Plowenders Cl. ME19: Addtn 7J 107
PLUCKLEY 7G 29
Pluckley Cl. ME8: Gill 9M 81
Pluckley Gdns. CT9: Clift 3J 209
Pluckley Rd. TN26: Beth 1J 163 (2G 39)
TN27: Char'g 4J 175 (6H 29)
TN27: P'ley 7H 29
TN27: Smar 7D 222 (1E 38)
Pluckley Station (Rail) 1G 39
PLUCKLEY THORNE 7F 29
PLUCK'S GUTTER 5D 22
Plug La. DA13: Meop 6J 91 (4C 16)
PLUMFORD 7A 20
Plumford Rd. ME13: Osp 9E 186 (7A 20)
ME13: Shel 1H 219
Plum La. SE18 7D 50
Plummer La. TN30: Tent 9A 224
Plummers Cft. TN13: Dun G 3F 118
Plumpton Wlk. CT1: Cant 1A 172
ME15: Maid 2J 139
Plumpudding La. ME13: Darg 6D 20
PLUMSTEAD 4G 50 (4C 6)
PLUMSTEAD COMMON 6E 50 (5C 6)
Plumstead Comn. Rd. SE18 6D 50 (5B 6)
Plumstead High St. SE18 4F 50 (4C 6)
Plumstead Leisure Cen. 5H 51
Plumstead Rd. SE18 4D 50 (4C 6)
Plumstead Station (Rail) 4F 50 (4C 6)
Plumstone Rd.
CT12: Acol, Monk'n 9E 206 (3E 22)
Plum Tree Cotts. TN18: Hawkh 7B 192
Plumtree Gdns. CT7: Birch 4E 206
Plum Tree Gdns. TN26: Wdchu 8C 228
PLUMTREE GREEN 7A 28
Plumtree Gro. ME7: Hpstd 7K 95
Plum Tree Rd. ME9: S'bry 2D 112 (6B 18)
Plumtree Rd. TN27: H'crn 6H 191 (7A 28)
Plumtrees ME16: Barm 7L 125
Plurenden Rd.
TN26: H Hald 2F 196 (4G 39)
Plymouth Dr. TN13: S'oaks 6K 119
Plymouth Pk. TN13: S'oaks 6K 119
Plymouth Rd. BR1: Brom 4L 69
Plympton Cl. DA17: Belv 3N 51
Plymstock Rd. DA16: Well 7L 51
Poachers Cl. ME5: Chat'm 6F 94
Pochard Cl. ME4: Chat'm 3E 80
Pochard Cres. CT6: H Bay 4F 194
Pocket Hill TN13: S'oaks 1H 131
Podkin Wood ME5: Chat'm 2C 110
Podlinge La. TN25: Elms 6F 31
Poets' Cnr. CT9: Mgte 4D 208
Poets Wlk. CT14: Walm 9L 177
Point Cnr. TN11: S'brne 3M 133
Point Rd. SS8: Can I 2A 10
Poldark Ct. *CT11: Ram* *5K 211*
(off Victoria Pde.)
Polebrook Rd. SE3 1M 55
Pole Cat All. BR2: Shortl 3J 83
Polecroft La. SE6 7C 54
Polesden Rd. TN2: Tun W 3K 157
Polesteeple Hill TN16: Big H 5D 164 (7A 14)
Poles, The ME9: Upc 2H 225
Polhill TN14: Hals 6D 102 (7F 15)
Polhill Dr. ME5: Chat'm 9C 94
Police Sta. Rd. ME19: W Mal 1A 124
Pollard Cl. TN23: Ashf 1D 160
Pollard Ct. ME7: Gill 7F 80
Pollard Pl. CT5: Whits 7E 226
Pollards Wood Hill RH8: Oxt 3A 24
Pollards Wood Rd. RH8: Oxt 4A 24
Pollard Wlk. DA14: Sidc 2L 71
Polley Cl. TN2: Pem 7C 152
Pollyhaugh DA4: Eyns 4L 87
Polo Way CT5: Whits 4M 227
Polperro Cl. BR6: St M Cry 9H 71
Polsted Rd. SE6 5C 54
Polthorne Gro. SE18 4E 50
Polytechnic St. SE18 4C 50
Pomeroy St. SE14 5H 5
Pomfret Ho. CT4: Chart'm 9D 170
Pomfret Rd. CT4: Chart'm 9D 170
Pommeus La. CT14: Ripp 5H 33
Poncia Rd. TN23: Ashf 2E 160
Pond Cott. La. BR3: Beck'm 2D 82
Pond Cotts. CT6: H Bay 5L 195
Pond Dr. ME10: Sit 9H 99
Pond Farm Rd. ME9: B'den 1A 114 (5D 18)
ME17: Holl 9F 112 (7B 18)
Pondfield La. DA12: Shorne 3C 78
Pondfield Rd. BR2: Shortl 2H 83
BR6: Farnb 4D 84
Pond Hill CT3: Adm 2B 32
ME3: Cliffe 2C 176
Pond Hill Rd. CT20: F'stone 6C 188 (4K 41)
Pondicherry All. *CT13: S'wch* *5M 217*
(off Up. Strand St.)
Pond La. CT3: Aysm 4B 162 (4B 32)
CT4: Wom 4B 32
CT15: St Marg 7H 33
TN15: Ivy H 7E 120 (2J 25)
Pondmore Way TN25: Ashf 6D 158
Pond Path BR7: Chst 2D 70
Pond Rd. SE3 1J 55
Pond St. NW3 1D 4
PONDTAIL 2C 34
Pondwood Ri. BR6: Orp 1G 84
Pontefract Rd. BR1: Brom 1J 69
Pontoise Cl. TN13: S'oaks 4G 119
Pont St. SW1 4D 4
Pony Cart La. CT4: S Min 6H 31
Pook La. TN27: Bidd, Smar 2C 38
Pool Cl. BR3: Beck'm 1D 68
Pool Ct. SE6 7D 54
Poona Rd. TN1: Tun W 3H 157
Poorhole La. CT10: B'stairs 8F 208 (2J 23)
POOTINGS 5C 24
Pootings Rd. TN8: Four E, Crock H 5C 24
Poot La. ME9: Upc 1H 225 (2C 18)
Pope Dr. TN12: S'hrst 2J 223
Pope Ho. La. TN30: St Mic 3C 224
Pope Rd. BR2: Shortl 8N 69
Popes Gro. CR0: Croy 4C 82
Popes La. CT2: Sturry 4D 168 (6J 21)
RH8: Oxt 4A 24
Pope St. CT4: Godm 4D 30
ME16: Maid 7N 125
Popes Wood ME14: Weav 3K 127
POPLAR 3J 5
Poplar Av. BR6: Farnb 3D 84
DA12: Grav'nd 9H 63
Poplar Cl. ME2: Strood 7K 79
TN23: Ashf 7D 158
Poplar Dr. CT6: H Bay 5D 194
CT15: Evtn 6J 185
Poplar Gro. ME16: Alltn 4M 125
Poplar High St. E14 3J 5
Poplar Ho. *SE4* *2C 54*
(off Wickham Rd.)
Poplar La. TN29: Lydd 2K 205
Poplar Mt. DA17: Belv 4C 52
Poplar Pl. SE28 1L 51
Poplar Rd. CT10: B'stairs 7J 209
CT11: Ram 5H 211
ME2: Strood 7J 79
TN30: Witter 2C 228 (2K 45)
Poplars Cl. DA3: Long 6B 76
Poplar Station (DLR) 3J 5
Poplars, The CT3: Hersd 2L 169
DA12: Grav'nd 5K 63
TN26: Beth 2K 163
Poplar Vw. ME13: Bou B 3H 165
Poplar Wlk. DA13: Meop 9G 76
Poplicans Rd. ME2: Cux 9F 78
Poppinghole La. TN32: Rob 4C 44
Poppy Cl. DA17: Belv 3C 52
ME7: Gill 7H 81
ME16: Maid 6A 126
Poppy Mdw. TN12: Pad W 1M 153
Popsal La. CT3: Wing 1C 32
CT3: Wing 8K 225 (1C 32)
(not continuous)
Porchester Cl. DA3: Hart'y 7M 75
ME15: Maid 2D 138
Porchester Mead BR3: Beck'm 2D 68
Porchester Rd. W2 3C 4
Porchfield Cl. DA12: Grav'nd 7H 63
Porcupine Cl. SE9 7A 56
Porrington Cl. BR7: Chst 4B 70
Porson Ct. SE13 1E 54
Port Av. DA9: G'hithe 4H 61
Port Cl. ME5: Chat'm 8E 94
ME14: Weav 4K 127
Porter Cl. ME12: Minst 6H 221
Porters Av. RM8: Dag 1D 6
RM9: Dag 1D 6
Porters Cl. TN12: Mat 1K 153
Porter's La. ME13: Osp 9E 186 (7A 20)
Porters Wlk. ME17: L'ly 4A 140
Porters Wood TN12: Mat 8K 153
Porthallow Cl. BR6: Chels 5H 85
Porthcawe Rd. SE26 9B 54
Port Hill BR6: Prat B 3K 101 (6D 14)
Porthkerry Av. DA16: Well 2J 57
Portland Av. DA12: Grav'nd 7G 63
DA15: Sidc 4J 57
ME10: Sit 7K 99
Portland Cl. CT21: Hythe 6J 199
TN10: Tonb 9K 133
TN24: Kenn 3F 158
Portland Ct. CT11: Ram 5J 211
CT21: Hythe *6J 199*
(off Portland Cl.)
Portland Cres. SE9 7A 56
Portland Pl. *DA3: Long* *6L 75*
(off Park Dr.)
ME6: Snod 2E 108
W1 3E 4
Portland Rd. BR1: Brom 9M 55
CT9: Mgte 8B 208
CT21: Hythe (5H 41) 6J 199
DA11: Nflt 4C 62
DA12: Grav'nd 6G 62
ME1: Woul 7G 92
ME7: Gill 6H 81
SE9 7A 56
SE25 2H 13
Portland St. ME4: Chat'm 1E 94
Portland Ter. *ME12: S'ness* *2D 220*
(off Millennium Way)
Port Lympne Wild Animal Pk. 5F 41
Portman Cl. DA5: Bex'y 6F 58
DA7: Bexhth 1N 57
Portman Pk. TN9: Tonb 4J 145
Portman Sq. W1 3D 4
Portmeadow Wlk. SE2 2M 51
Portnalls Rd. CR5: Coul 7E 12
Portobello Ct. CT14: Deal 3N 177
Portobello Pde. TN15: W King 9G 88
Port Ri. ME4: Chat'm 9C 80
Portsdown Cl. ME16: Maid 7M 125
Portsmouth Cl. ME2: Strood 6H 79
Port Victoria Rd. ME3: Isle G 8C 190
Portway CT5: Whits 5E 226
E15 2K 5
Port Way ME3: Cliffe, Cli W 5A 66
Portway Rd. ME3: Cli W 6M 65
Post Barn Rd. ME4: Chat'm 1C 94
Postern Ind. Est. TN9: Tonb 5K 145
Postern La. TN11: Tonb 5K 145
Postley Commercial Cen. ME15: Maid 7D 126
Postley Ind. Cen. ME15: Maid 8D 126
Postley Rd. ME15: Maid 7D 126
POSTLING 3H 185 (3H 41)
Postling TN23: Ashf 9C 158
Postling Ct. CT21: Post 3H 185 (3H 41)
POSTLING GREEN 5D 40
Postling Rd. CT19: F'stone 4E 188
Postmill Cl. CR0: Croy 4A 82
Postmill Dr. ME15: Maid 8C 126
Post Office Rd. TN18: Hawkh 5C 192
Post Office Sq. TN1: Tun W 2G 157
Post Ter. CT5: Whits 3G 226
Potash La. TN15: Bor G 3B 122 (1B 26)
Pot Kiln La. TN26: H Hald, Beth 3E 38
TN27: H Hald 3E 38
POTMAN'S HEATH 2J 45
POTTEN STREET 6K 215 (3C 22)
Potten St. CT7: St N 6K 215 (3C 22)
Potten St. Rd. CT7: St N 6K 215 (3C 22)
Potters Cl. CR0: Croy 2B 82
TN25: Ashf 4C 158
POTTERS CORNER 4C 158 (7K 29)
POTTER'S FORSTAL 6E 28
Potters La. TN18: Hawkh 1C 192 (6H 37)
Potter St. CT13: S'wch 5M 217
Pottery La. TN31: Brede 6F 45
Pottery Rd. DA5: Bex'y 7D 58
ME3: Hoo 8G 66
Potyn Ho. ME1: Roch 8N 79
Poulders Gdns. CT13: S'wch 7K 217
(not continuous)
Poulders Rd. CT13: S'wch 6K 217
Poulsen Ct. ME10: Sit 7J 99
Poulters Wood BR2: Kes 6N 83
Poulton Ct. CT17: Dover 3D 180 (2E 42)
Poulton Cl. Bus. Pk. CT17: Dover 3D 180
Poulton La. CT3: Ash 5B 216
Pound Bank Cl. TN15: W King 9F 88
Pound Cl. BR6: Orp 3F 84
Pound Ct. TN23: Kgnt 6E 160
Pound Ct. Dr. BR6: Orp 3F 84
Poundfield Rd. TN18: Sandh 3C 218
Poundfield Wlk. TN23: Ashf 1B 160
(not continuous)
Pound Grn. DA5: Bex'y 5B 58
Pound Ho. *TN11: Hdlw* *8D 134*
(off Maidstone Rd.)
TN23: Ashf 1F 160
Poundhurst Rd. TN26: Ruck 5A 40
Pound La. CT1: Cant 1M 171
CT4: Elham 7N 183
CT4: Mol 4B 30
KT19: Eps 6A 12
NW10 1B 4
TN13: S'oaks 6K 119
TN14: Knock 6M 101 (7D 14)
TN23: Kgnt 4D 160 (3K 39)
TN25: Bra L, Sme 7L 165 (2E 40)
Pound Pl. SE9 4C 56
Pound Rd. TN12: E Peck 9K 135 (5D 26)
POUNDSBRIDGE 6L 149 (2G 35)
Poundsbridge Hill
TN3: Ford, Pens 8L 149 (2G 35)
TN11: Pens 8L 149 (2G 35)
Poundsbridge La. TN11: Pens 4L 149 (1G 35)
Pound St. SM5: Cars 4D 12
Pound, The TN12: E Peck 1L 147
Pound Way BR7: Chst 3E 70
CT20: F'stone 7K 189
Pounsley Rd. TN13: Dun G 3F 118
Pout Rd. ME6: Snod 3D 108
POVEREST 7J 71 (3D 14)
Poverest Rd. BR5: St M Cry 8H 71 (3C 14)
Povey Av. ME2: Wain 2N 79
Powder Mill Cl. TN4: S'bgh 6J 151
Powder Mill La. DA1: Dart 7M 59
TN4: S'bgh, Tun W 7G 151 (2K 35)
TN11: Leigh 5A 144 (6H 25)
(Hildenborough Rd.)
TN11: Leigh 5D 144
(Leigh Rd.)
Powdermill La. TN31: B Oak 5F 45
TN33: Batt 7C 44
POWDER MILLS 5E 144 (6J 25)
Powell Av. DA2: Dart 7E 60
Powell Cl. ME20: Aylfd 7L 109
Powell Cotton Dr. CT7: Birch 5G 206
Powell-Cotton Mus. 6G 207
Powerscroft Rd. DA14: Sidc 2L 71
(not continuous)
E5 1H 5
Power Station Rd. ME3: Isle G 8B 190 (5E 10)
ME12: Minst 5F 220
Power Works DA8: Erith 8H 53
Powis St. SE18 3C 50
Powlett Rd. ME2: Strood 3N 79
Powster Rd. BR1: Brom 1K 69
Powys Cl. DA7: Bexhth 6M 51
Poynders Rd. SW4 6E 4
Poynings Cl. BR6: Chels 3L 85
Poyntell Cres. BR7: Chst 4F 70
Poyntell Rd. TN12: S'hrst 2K 223
Poynters La. SS3: Shoe 1G 11
Praed St. W2 3D 4
Pragnell Rd. SE12 7L 55
Prall's La. TN12: Mat 4K 153
PRATLING STREET 7N 109 (7H 17)
Pratling St. ME20: Aylfd 7M 109 (7G 17)

Pratt's Bottom—Queen Anne Rd.

PRATT'S BOTTOM 1L 101 (5D 14)
PRATT'S BOTTOM 9L 85 (5D 14)
Pratt St. NW1 2E 4
Prebend St. N1 2G 5
Precincts, The CT1: Cant 1N 171
Precinct, The ME1: Roch 6N 79
Precinct Toy Collection 5M 217
(off Butchery, The)
Premier Bus. Pk. ME4: Chat'm 2E 94
Premier Pde. ME20: Aylfd 9J 109
Prendergast Rd. SE3 1H 55
Prentis Cl. ME10: Sit 6D 98
Prentis Quay ME10: Sit 6F 98
Prescott Av. BR5: Pet W 9D 70
Prescott Cl. CT15: Gus 7K 179
Prescott Ho. TN28: New R 2J 213
Prestbury Sq. SE9 9B 56
Prestedge Av. CT11: Ram 2J 211
PRESTON
Canterbury 6C 22
Faversham 6H 187 (6A 20)
Preston Av. ME7: Gill 2H 95
ME13: Fav 7J 187
Preston Ct. DA14: Sidc 9H 57
(off Crescent, The)
Preston Dr. DA7: Bexhth 8M 51
Preston Gro. ME13: Fav 6H 187
Preston Hall Gdns. ME12: Ward 4J 203
Preston Hill CT3: Wing 6J 225 (7C 22)
Preston La. CT3: Pres 7C 22
ME13: Fav 6H 187
(Preston Pk.)
ME13: Fav 6G 187
(Preston St.)
TN30: Tent 9F 224 (6F 39)
Preston Malthouse ME13: Fav 6H 187
Preston Pde. CT5: Seas 6A 226
Preston Pk. ME13: Fav 6H 187
Preston Pl. ME13: Fav 6H 187
(off Chapel St.)
Preston Rd. CT3: Pres 7C 22 (6K 225)
(Preston La.)
CT3: Pres 5C 22
(Church La.)
CT3: Wing 6K 225
CT12: Mans 1B 210 (3H 23)
DA11: Nflt 6D 62
TN9: Tonb 6G 145
Prestons Rd. BR2: Shortl 4K 83 (4A 14)
Preston's Rd. E14 3K 5
Preston St. ME13: Fav 6G 187 (6A 20)
Preston Way ME8: Gill 1M 95
Prestwood Cl. SE18 6J 51
Pretoria Ho. DA8: Erith 7F 52
ME15: Maid 3H 139
Pretoria Rd. CT1: Cant 2A 172
ME4: Chat'm 1C 94
ME7: Gill 9G 80
Prettymans La. TN8: Eden 3F 184 (6C 24)
Price's Av. CT9: Mgte 3E 208
CT11: Ram 6G 210
Prices Cotts. ME3: Cliffe 5N 65
Prices Ct. ME10: Sit 7J 99
Prickley Wood BR2: Shortl 2J 83
Pridmore Rd. ME6: Snod 2D 108
Priest Av. CT2: Cant 2J 171
Priestfield ME1: Roch 3G 17
Priestfield Rd. ME7: Gill 7H 81
SE23 8B 54
Priest Flds. CT6: H Bay 2N 195
Priestfields ME1: Roch 9M 79
Priestfield Stadium 7H 81 (2K 17)
Priestlands Pk. Rd. DA15: Sidc 8H 57
Priestley Dr. ME20: Lark 6D 108
TN10: Tonb 9K 133
Priestly Hill CT4: Elham 7K 31
Priests Bri. SW14 6A 4
SW15 6A 4
Priest's Wlk. DA12: Grav'nd 7M 63
Priest Wlk. CT5: Whits 2K 227
PRIESTWOOD
Gravesend 6G 91
Meopham Green 4C 16
PRIESTWOOD GREEN 6H 91 (4C 16)
Priestwood Rd. DA13: Meop 7G 91 (5C 16)
Primmett Cl. TN15: W King 7E 88
Primrose Av. ME8: Gill 6L 95
Primrose Cl. ME4: Chat'm 4B 94
SE6 1F 68
Primrose Cotts. ME15: Otham 9L 127
Primrose Cotts. Cvn. Pk. CT5: Whits 6H 227
Primrose Dr. ME20: Dit 9H 109
TN23: Kgnt 5F 160
PRIMROSE HILL 2D 4
Primrose Hill CT4: Cha H 3A 170 (1E 30)
Primrose Hill Rd. NW3 1D 4
Primrose La. CR0: Croy 2A 82
ME9: B'gar 4B 114 (6E 18)
Primrose Pl. CT17: Dover 3G 180
Primrose Rd. CT17: Dover 3F 180
ME2: Hall'g 6C 92
Primrose Ter. DA12: Grav'nd 6H 63
Primrose Wlk. TN12: Pad W 1M 153
Primrose Way CT5: Whits 4L 227
CT12: C'snd 7A 210
Prince Albert Rd. NW1 2E 4
NW8 2D 4
Prince Andrew Rd. CT10: B'stairs 6J 209
Prince Arthur Indoor Bowls Cen. 6E 80
Prince Arthur Rd. ME7: Gill 6E 80 (2J 17)
Prince Charles Av. DA4: S Dar 5D 74
ME5: Chat'm 7E 94 (5J 17)
ME10: Sit 8J 99
ME12: Minst 6K 221
RM16: Ors 2C 8
Prince Charles Rd. CT10: B'stairs 6J 209
SE3 5K 5
Prince Consort Dr. BR7: Chst 4F 70
Prince Edward's Prom. CT11: Ram 7F 210
Prince Henry Rd. SE7 7A 50
Prince Imperial Rd. BR7: Chst 4D 70 (1B 14)
SE18 8B 50
Prince John Rd. SE9 3A 56
Prince of Wales Dr. SW11 5D 4
Prince of Wales Res. Mobile Home Pk.
CT21: Hythe 8F 198
Prince of Wales Rd. NW3 1E 4
SE3 5K 5
Prince of Wales Rdbt. CT17: Dover 6J 181
Prince of Wales Ter. CT14: Deal 5N 177 (3J 33)
Prince of Wales Youth Club & Sports Cen. 9A 168
Prince Regent La. E13 2A 6
E16 3A 6
Prince Regent Station (DLR) 3A 6
Prince Rupert Rd. SE9 2B 56
Princes Av. BR5: Pet W 8G 70
Prince's Av. CT12: Ram 3F 210
Princes Av. DA2: Dart 6B 60
ME5: Chat'm 8D 94 (5J 17)
ME12: Minst 5L 221
Princes Cl. CT7: Birch 4C 206
DA14: Sidc 8M 57
Princes Cres. CT9: Mgte 3D 208
Prince's Gdns. CT9: Clift 3G 208
Princes Golf & Leisure Club 6A 60
Princes Pde. CT20: Hythe 9A 188
CT21: Hythe 7L 199 (5J 41)
PRINCES PARK 5E 94 (4J 17)
Prince's Plain BR2: Shortl 1A 84
Princes Rd. BR8: Swanl 2H 73
Prince's Rd. CT11: Ram 4H 211 (4J 23)
Princes Rd. CT13: S'wch 7H 23
DA1: Dart 4H 59 (6G 7)
DA2: Dart 6B 60 (7H 7)
DA12: Grav'nd 9H 63
SE20 2A 68
PRINCES ROAD INTERCHANGE 6B 60 (7H 7)
Princess Alice Way SE28 2F 50
Princess Anne Rd. CT10: B'stairs 6J 209
Princess Cl. CT5: Whits 2L 227
Princesses Pde. DA1: Cray 3F 58
(off Waterside)
Princess Margaret Av. CT9: Clift 3H 209 (1J 23)
CT12: Ram 3E 210
Princess Margaret Rd. RM18: E Til 4D 8
SS17: Linf, E Til 4D 8
Princess Mary Av. ME4: Chat'm 5E 80
Princess of Wales Royal Regiment Mus. 4K 181
Princess Pde. BR6: Farnb 4C 84
Princess Pocahontas Memorial 4G 62
(off Church St.)
Princess Rd. CT5: Whits 2L 227
Princess St. CT19: F'stone 5L 189
Princes St. CT9: Mgte 3D 208
Prince's St. CT11: Ram 6J 211
Princes St. CT14: Deal 3N 177
CT17: Dover 5J 181
DA7: Bexhth 1A 58
DA11: Grav'nd 4G 62
(not continuous)
Prince's St. ME1: Roch 8N 79
Princes St. ME14: Maid 4D 126
TN2: Tun W 2J 157
Princes Ter. CT21: Hythe 7G 198
Princes Vw. DA1: Dart 6A 60
Princes Vs. TN12: Mard 2D 212
Prince's Wlk. CT9: Clift 2J 209
Princes Wlk. ME2: Strood 2M 79
Princes Way BR4: W W'ck 5J 83
CT2: Cant 1K 171
ME14: Det 9K 111
Princethorpe Rd. SE26 9A 54
Prince William Ct. CT14: Deal 3N 177
Print Room, The 4N 177
(off Beach St.)
PRINTSTILE 1H 35
Prinys Dr. ME8: Gill 7M 95
Prioress Cres. DA9: G'hithe 2J 61
Prioress Rd. CT2: Cant 2K 171
Prioress Wlk. CT16: Dover 1F 180
Prior Rd. TN28: G'stne 7H 213
Priors Dean Cl. ME16: Barm 8J 125
Priorsford Av. BR5: St M Cry 7J 71
Priors Ga. ME1: Roch 7N 79
(off Precinct, The)
PRIORS HEATH 5F 37
Priors Leas CT20: F'stone 7K 189
Prior's Way TN8: Cowd 2D 34
Priory Apartments, The SE6 6E 54
Priory Av. BR5: Pet W 9F 70
Priory Cl. BR3: Beck'm 6B 68
BR7: Chst 4B 70
CT10: B'stairs 1K 211
DA1: Dart 3K 59
ME15: E Far 9M 125
TN28: New R 3H 213
Priory Ct. DA1: Dart 4L 59
ME8: Gill 1K 95
Priory Dr. SE2 5M 51
Priory Flds. DA4: Eyns 3N 87
Priory Gardens 1K 85
Priory Gdns. CT1: Cant 4N 171
CT20: F'stone 7K 189
DA1: Dart 3L 59
Priory Ga. ME14: Maid 4D 126
Priory Ga. Rd. CT17: Dover 4H 181
Priory Gro. CT17: Dover 4H 181
ME20: Dit 9H 109
TN9: Tonb 7H 145
Priory Hill CT17: Dover 4H 181
DA1: Dart 4L 59
Priory Hill Holiday Camp ME12: Ley S 7N 203
Priory La. CT6: H Bay 4H 195
DA4: Eyns 2N 87
SW15 6A 4
TN25: M Hor 6C 218 (3F 41)
Priory Leas SE9 6A 56
Priory Leisure Cen., The 2L 85
Priory of St Jacob CT1: Cant 4L 171
Priory Pk. SE3 1J 55
Priory Parks ME20: Aylfd 2H 125
Priory Pl. CT17: Dover 4J 181
(off Biggin St.)
DA1: Dart 4L 59
ME13: Fav 3G 186
Priory Rd. CT11: Ram 6H 211
CT17: Dover 4J 181 (2F 43)
ME2: Strood 6L 79 (2G 17)
ME8: Gill 1K 95
ME13: Fav 4F 186 (6A 20)
ME15: Maid 6D 126
NW6 2C 4
RH18: F Row 6A 34
SM3: Sutt 4B 12
TN9: Tonb 7H 145 (7K 25)
TN25: Bils 5C 40
Priory Rd. Nth. DA1: Dart 2L 59
Priory Rd. Sth. DA1: Dart 4L 59 (6G 7)
Priory Row ME13: Fav 4G 186 (5A 20)
Priory Shop. Cen. DA1: Dart 4M 59
Priory Sta. App. Rd. CT17: Dover 4H 181
Priory St. CT17: Dover 4J 181 (2F 43)
TN9: Tonb 7H 145
Priory, The ME15: E Far 9N 125
SE3 2J 55
Priory Wlk. TN9: Tonb 7H 145
Priory Way TN30: Tent 9D 224
Pristling La. TN12: S'hrst 2J 37
Pritchard Dr. CT18: H'nge 8K 193
Pritchard's Rd. E2 2H 5
Procter Rd. TN29: Lydd 2K 205
Proctor Wlk. CT18: H'nge 8J 193
Progress Est., The ME15: Maid 3K 139
Promenade CT5: Whits 2H 227
(not continuous)
CT7: Birch 3E 206
CT9: Mgte 2C 208
CT14: Deal 1N 177
CT14: Walm 7N 177
CT16: Dover 5K 181
Promenade, The CT9: Clift 2E 208
CT10: B'stairs 1M 211
ME12: Ley S 6M 203 (1B 20)
Prospect Av. ME2: Strood 4M 79
Prospect Cl. CT8: Wgte S 4K 207
DA17: Belv 4B 52
Prospect Cotts. CT15: S'wll 8K 219
TN26: Beth 2K 163
Prospect Gdns. CT12: Minst 6E 212
Prospect Gro. DA12: Grav'nd 5J 63
Prospect Hill CT6: H Bay 2H 195
Prospect M. CT21: Hythe 6K 199
Prospect Pk. TN4: S'bgh 5F 150
Prospect Pl. BR2: Shortl 6L 69
CT1: Cant 3N 171
CT7: St N 9L 215
CT10: B'stairs 9M 209
CT17: Dover 3G 181
DA12: Grav'nd 5J 63
(not continuous)
ME1: Roch 1L 93
ME16: Maid 6B 126
TN26: Hams 3K 191
Prospect Pl. Retail Pk. DA1: Dart 4M 59
Prospect Rd. CT7: Birch 4E 206 (2E 22)
CT10: B'stairs 9M 209
CT12: Minst 7E 212
CT20: S'gte 8D 188
CT21: Hythe 6K 199 (5J 41)
TN2: Tun W 2H 157 (3K 35)
TN4: S'bgh 5F 150
TN13: S'oaks 5K 119
Prospect Row ME4: Chat'm 9D 80
ME7: Gill 6D 80
Prospect Ter. CT4: Elham 6N 183
CT11: Ram 6J 211
Prospect Va. SE18 4A 50
Prospect Way TN25: Bra L 7K 165
Provender Rd. ME13: Lyn 6J 19
Provender Way ME14: Weav 4H 127
Providence Cotts. ME3: High'm 2F 78
ME7: B'hst 2K 111
TN3: Groom 6K 155
(off Corseley Rd.)
Providence Pl. ME1: Woul 7G 93
Providence Row CT1: Cant 3L 171
Providence St. DA9: G'hithe 3G 60
TN23: Ashf 1G 160
Prudence Cotts. TN14: Weald 6J 131
Prudhoe Ct. DA2: Dart 4B 60
(off Osbourne Rd.)
Puckle La. CT1: Cant 4N 171
Pucknells Cl. BR8: Swanl 4D 72
Puddingcake La. TN17: Rolv 1F 214 (6D 38)
Pudding La. CT3: Ash 5C 216
ME14: Maid 5C 126
TN15: Seal 3N 119
Pudding Mill Lane Station (DLR) 2J 5
Pudding Rd. ME8: Rain 3B 96
PUDDLEDOCK
Bexley 2F 72
Hextable 2G 73
Toys Hill 4D 24
Puddledock La. DA2: Dart 1F 72 (1F 15)
TN16: Westrm 4C 24
Puffin Cl. BR3: Beck'm 8A 68
Puffin Ct. CT18: H'nge 9K 193
Puffin Rd. CT6: H Bay 3M 195
ME3: Isle G 8C 190
Pullington Cotts. TN17: Bendn 6A 38
Pullman Cl. CT12: Ram 3G 211
Pullman M. SE12 8L 55
Pullman Pl. SE9 3A 56
Pulton Ho. SE4 2B 54
(off Turnham Rd.)
Pump Cl. ME19: Leyb 9B 108
Pump Ho. Cl. BR2: Shortl 5H 69
Pump La. BR6: Orp 6C 86
CT9: Mgte 3D 208
ME8: Rain 2M 95 (3A 18)
(not continuous)
Pump St. SS17: Horn H 2D 8
Punch Cft. DA3: New A 4L 89
Purbeck Rd. ME4: Chat'm 1B 94
Purcell Av. TN10: Tonb 1M 145
Purchas Ct. CT2: Cant 7J 167
Purelake M. SE13 1G 54
(off Marischal Rd.)
PURFLEET 4H 7
Purfleet By-Pass RM19: Purf 4J 7
Purfleet Ind. Pk. RM15: Avel 1N 53
(Centre Pl.)
RM15: Avel 2N 53
(Kirby Av.)
Purfleet Rd. RM15: Avel 4H 7
Purfleet Station (Rail) 4H 7
Purland Rd. SE28 2H 51
PURLEY 6F 13
PURLEY CROSS 6F 13
Purley Downs Rd. CR2: S Croy 5G 13
CR8: Purl 5G 13
Purley Oaks Station (Rail) 5G 13
Purley Rd. CR8: Purl 6F 13
Purley Station (Rail) 6F 13
Purley Way CR0: Croy 3F 13
CR8: Purl 5F 13
Purneys Rd. SE9 2N 55
Purrett Rd. SE18 5H 51
Purser Way ME7: Gill 5F 80
Putlands Sports & Leisure Cen. 1L 153
PUTNEY 6C 4
Putney Bri. SW6 6C 4
SW15 6C 4
Putney Bri. Rd. SW15 6C 4
SW18 6C 4
Putney Bridge Station (Tube) 6C 4
PUTNEY HEATH 6B 4
Putney Heath SW15 6B 4
Putney High St. SW15 6B 4
Putney Hill SW15 6B 4
Putney Station (Rail) 6C 4
PUTNEY VALE 7B 4
Puttenden Rd. TN11: S'brne 4M 133 (4A 26)
Puttney Dr. ME10: Kems'y 3G 99
Pychers Pl. TN2: Pem 8C 152
Pye All. La. CT5: Whits 9F 226
Pye All. Rd. CT5: Whits 5E 20
PYE CORNER 5C 28
Pym Ho. TN27: Char'g 3L 175
Pym Orchard TN16: Bras 6L 117
Pynham Cl. SE2 3K 51
Pyott M. CT1: Cant 1A 172
Pyrus Cl. ME5: Chat'm 2E 110
Pyson's Rd. CT10: B'stairs, Ram 2G 210 (3J 23)
CT12: Ram 2G 210 (3J 23)
Pyson's Rd. Ind. Est. CT10: B'stairs 1H 211

Q

QUADBROOK 5C 34
Quadrant, The DA7: Bexhth 7M 51
Quaggy Wlk. SE3 2K 55
Quain Ct. CT20: F'stone 7J 189
Quaker Cl. TN13: S'oaks 5L 119
Quaker Dr. TN17: Cran 6D 176
Quaker La. TN17: Cran 6D 176 (4J 37)
Quakers Cl. DA3: Hart'y 6L 75
Quakers Hall La. TN13: S'oaks 4K 119 (1G 25)
Quantock Cl. TN2: Tun W 9K 151
Quantock Dr. TN24: Ashf 7F 158
Quantock Gdns. CT12: Ram 1F 210
Quantock Rd. DA7: Bexhth 9F 52
QUARRIES, THE 4F 138
Quarries, The ME17: Bou Mo 4F 138 (4J 27)
Quarrington La. TN25: W Bra 2C 40
Quarry Av. CT21: Hythe 5J 199
Quarry Bank TN9: Tonb 8G 144
Quarry Cotts. ME17: Bou Mo 4E 138
TN13: S'oaks 5G 119
Quarry Farm 3D 44
Quarry Gdns. TN9: Tonb 7G 145
Quarry Hill TN15: S'oaks 5L 119
Quarry Hill Pde. TN9: Tonb 7H 145
Quarry Hill Rd. TN9: Tonb 8G 145 (7K 25)
(not continuous)
TN15: Bor G 3M 121 (1A 26)
Quarry La. CT21: Hythe 5J 199
Quarry Ri. TN9: Tonb 8G 145
Quarry Rd. ME15: Maid 7D 126
TN1: Tun W 9H 151 (2K 35)
Quarry Sq. ME14: Maid 4D 126
Quarry Vw. ME19: Off 2H 123
TN23: Ashf 2B 160
Quarry Wlk. CT21: Hythe 8A 188
QUARRY WOOD 1J 125
Quarry Wood TN25: Aldtn 4D 40
Quarry Wood Ind. Est. ME20: Aylfd 1J 125
QUARTER, THE 7E 28
Quay La. CT13: S'wch 5M 217
DA9: G'hithe 2H 61
ME13: Fav 4H 187 (6A 20)
Quayside ME4: Chat'm 3E 80
(not continuous)
Quay, The CT13: S'wch 5M 217 (7G 23)
ME9: Tey 4J 19
TN31: Rye 5A 46
Quebec Av. TN16: Westrm 8F 116
Quebec Cotts. TN16: Westrm 9F 116
Quebec House 8F 116 (2C 24)
Quebec Sq. TN16: Westrm 8F 116
Quebec Ter. CT16: Dover 1G 181
(off Winnipeg Cl.)
Queen Anne Av. BR2: Shortl 6J 69 (2K 13)
Queen Anne Rd. ME14: Maid 5D 126

Queen Anne's Ga.—Reading Cl.

Queen Anne's Ga. DA7: Bexhth 1M 57
Queen Bertha Rd. CT11: Ram 6G 210
Queen Bertha's Av. CT7: Birch 3H 207
QUEENBOROUGH 7B 220 (7F 11)
Queenborough Dr. ME12: Minst 5J 221
Queenborough Gdns. BR7: Chst 2F 70
Queenborough Rd. ME12: Minst 7C 220 (7G 11)
Queenborough Station (Rail) 7B 220 (7F 11)
Queen Ct. ME1: Roch 8N 79
Queendown Av. ME8: Gill 6N 95
Queendown Warren Nature Reserve 8D 96
Queen Elizabeth Av. CT9: Mgte 4H 209 (1J 23)
Queen Elizabeth II Bri. DA1: Dart 1D 60
Queen Elizabeth Rd. CT16: Dover 4L 181
Queen Elizabeth's Dr. CR0: Croy 9G 82
Queen Elizabeth Sq. ME15: Maid 2G 138
Queen Mother Ct., The ME1: Roch 8M 79
Queens Arms Yd. *CT9: Mgte* *2C 208*
(off Market St.)
Queens Av. CT2: Cant 1K 171
CT6: H Bay 2L 195
Queen's Av. CT7: Birch 4C 206
CT9: Mgte 4C 208 (1H 23)
CT10: B'stairs 7M 209
CT12: Ram 3F 210
Queens Av. CT17: Dover 5E 180
CT20: F'stone 5B 188
Queen's Av. ME6: Snod 2E 108
ME16: Maid 4A 126
Queensbridge Dr. CT6: H Bay 2D 194
Queensbridge Rd. E2 1G 5
E8 1G 5
Queen's Club (Tennis) 4C 4
Queen's Ct. CT6: H Bay 3H 195
Queens Ct. CT9: Clift 2E 208
CT21: Hythe *7J 199*
(off Albert Ct.)
Queen's Ct. TN8: Eden 6D 184
Queens Ct. TN18: Hawkh 5D 192
Queen's Ct. TN24: Ashf 7G 158
Queenscroft Rd. SE9 3N 55
QUEENSDOWN 8L 207
Queensdown Rd. CT7: Wdchu 7L 207
CT14: Kgdn 5E 200
Queens Dr. TN14: S'oaks 2K 119
W3 3A 4
W5 3A 4
Queen's Farm Rd.
DA12: Shorne, Grav'nd 7C 64 (7E 8)
Queens Gdns. CT6: H Bay 2G 195
Queen's Gdns. CT9: Clift 2E 208
CT10: B'stairs 1M 211
Queens Gdns. CT17: Dover 4J 181
DA2: Dart 6B 60
Queen's Gdns. TN4: Tun W 8H 151
Queens Ga. SW7 4D 4
Queensgate Gdns. BR7: Chst 4F 70
Queen's Ga. Rd. CT11: Ram 4G 211 (4J 23)
Queens Ho. ME16: Maid 6M 125
Queensland Ho. *E16* *1C 50*
(off Rymill St.)
Queen's Lea CT18: Cap F 3D 42
Queen's Mead Rd. BR2: Shortl 5J 69 (2K 13)
Queens M. CT14: Deal 4N 177
TN18: Hawkh 5D 192
Queen's Pde. CT9: Clift 2E 208 (1J 23)
Queen's Pde. ME12: S'ness 4B 220
ME13: Fav *5H 187*
(off East St.)
Queen's Pk. Rangers F.C. (Loftus Road) 3B 4
Queens Park Station (Rail & Tube) 2C 4
Queens Pas. BR7: Chst 2D 70
Queens Ride SW13 6B 4
SW15 6B 4
Queen's Ri. CT14: R'wld 4B 200
Queens Rd. BR1: Brom 5K 69
BR3: Beck'm 5B 68
BR7: Chst 2D 70
CR0: Croy 3F 13
Queen's Rd. CT3: Ash 4C 216 (7E 22)
Queens Rd. CT3: Aysm 2D 162
CT5: Whits 3H 227 (3F 21)
CT8: Wgte S 3L 207
Queen's Rd. CT10: B'stairs 9L 209 (3K 23)
CT11: Ram 5K 211
DA8: Erith 6F 52 (5F 7)
Queens Rd. DA12: Grav'nd 8H 63
Queen's Rd. DA16: Well 9K 51
Queens Rd. KT2: King T 1A 12
ME5: Chat'm 1G 94
Queen's Rd. ME6: Snod 2E 108
Queens Rd. ME7: Gill 8F 80
ME12: Minst 5L 221 (7H 11)
ME13: Fav 5F 186
Queen's Rd. ME16: Maid 6M 125 (2G 27)
SE14 5H 5
SE15 5H 5
Queens Rd. SW19 1C 12
Queen's Rd. TN4: Tun W 9G 151 (2K 35)
Queens Rd. TN6: Crowb 7F 35
Queen's Rd. TN18: Hawkh 5D 192 (7J 37)
Queens Rd. TN24: Ashf 7G 159
TN24: W'boro 9L 159
Queen's Rd. TN28: L'stne 3L 213
Queens Rd. TN29: Lydd 3K 205 (5H 47)
Queens Road (Peckham) Station (Rail) 5H 5
Queens St. ME3: Hoo 4E 66
TN18: Sandh 1E 44
Queensthorpe Rd. SE26 9A 54
Queenstown Rd. SW8 5E 4
Queenstown Road Station (Rail) 5E 4
QUEEN STREET 7E 26
Queen St. CT6: H Bay 2G 194
CT9: Mgte 3C 208 (1H 23)
CT11: Ram 6H 211 (4K 23)
CT14: Deal 4M 177 (3J 33)
CT17: Dover 5J 181
CT20: F'stone 6L 189
DA7: Bexhth 1A 58
Queen St. DA8: Erith 6F 52
DA12: Grav'nd 4G 63
ME1: Roch 8N 79
(not continuous)
ME4: Chat'm 8D 80
ME19: W Mal 6M 123
TN12: Pad W 7E 26
TN18: Sandh 2B 218
TN23: Ashf 8F 158
Queensway BR4: W W'ck 4H 83
BR5: Pet W 8E 70 (3C 14)
ME3: Allh 3D 204
Queen's Way ME12: S'ness 4B 220 (7F 11)
Queensway ME14: Det 9K 111
SS1: Sth S 1E 10
SS2: Sth S 1D 10
TN29: Dym 5C 182
TN29: Lydd 3K 205
W2 3C 4
Queensway Station (Tube) 3C 4
Queenswood Rd. DA15: Sidc 3H 57
ME20: Aylfd 3A 110
SE23 8A 54
QUEEN VICTORIA 4B 12
Queen Victoria St. EC4 3F 5
Quentin Pl. SE13 1H 55
Quentin Rd. SE13 1H 55
Quentins Dr. TN16: Big H 7D 100
Quentins Wlk. *TN16: Big H* *7D 100*
(off St Anns Way)
Quernmore Cl. BR1: Brom 2K 69
Quernmore Rd. BR1: Brom 2K 69
Quern Rd. CT14: Deal 7K 177
Querns Pl. CT1: Cant 2A 172
Querns Rd. CT1: Cant 2B 172
Quern, The ME15: Maid 8B 126
Quested Rd. CT19: F'stone 5E 188
Quested Way ME17: H'shm 2L 141
Questor DA1: Dart 7M 59
Quetta Rd. CT12: Ram 3D 210
Quex Cvn. Pk. CT7: Birch 6J 207
Quex Ct. *CT7: Birch* *5G 206*
(off Powell Cotton Dr.)
Quex House Gardens 6G 207 (2F 23)
Quex Rd. CT8: Wgte S 3L 207
NW6 2C 4
Quex Vw. Rd. CT7: Birch 5E 206
Quickbourne La. TN31: N'thiam 3G 45
Quickrells Av. ME3: Cliffe 3C 176
Quickstep Cl. ME10: Sit 3G 98
Quicks, The CT3: Ash 4C 216
Quickthorn Cres. ME5: Chat'm 6B 94
Quiet Nook BR2: Kes 4N 83
Quilter Gdns. BR5: Orp 2L 85
Quilter Rd. BR5: Orp 2L 85
Quilter St. SE18 5H 51
Quince Orchard TN26: Hams 2L 191
Quincewood Gdns. TN10: Tonb 9H 133
Quinion Cl. ME5: Chat'm 2C 110
Quinnell St. ME8: Rain 2A 96
Quinton Cl. BR3: Beck'm 6F 68
Quinton Rd. ME9: Sit 4D 98
ME10: Sit 4D 98 (4E 18)
Quixote Cres. ME2: Strood 3M 79

R

Rabbit Hole CT4: B'hm 9D 162 (5A 32)
RABBIT'S CROSS 6K 27
Rabbits Rd. DA4: S Dar 5D 74 (2J 15)
Racecourse Rd. RH7: Ling, Dor'land 1A 34
Racefield Cl. DA12: Shorne 3C 78
Rackham Cl. DA16: Well 9K 51
Radcliffe Ct. CT21: Hythe 6J 199
Radcot Point SE23 8A 54
RADFALL 8M 227 (4G 21)
Radfall CT5: Whits 7L 227
Radfall Hill CT5: Whits 7L 227
Radfall Ride CT5: Whits 8L 227
Radfall Rd. CT5: Whits 7L 227 (4G 21)
(not continuous)
RADFIELD 5G 19
Radfield Way DA15: Sidc 5E 56
(not continuous)
Radford Rd. SE13 4F 54
Radleigh Gdns. ME1: Roch 2B 94
Radley Cl. CT10: B'stairs 7L 209
Radley Ho. *SE2* *2M 51*
(off Wolvercote Rd.)
Radnor Av. DA16: Well 3K 57
Radnor Bri. Rd. CT19: F'stone 6L 189
CT20: F'stone 6L 189 (4B 42)
Radnor Cliff CT20: F'stone 8G 188
Radnor Cliff Cres. CT20: F'stone 8G 188
Radnor Cl. BR7: Chst 2G 71
CT6: H Bay 6J 195
Radnor Cres. SE18 7J 51
Radnor M. CT1: Cant 9A 168
Radnor Pk. Av. CT19: F'stone 5H 189
Radnor Pk. Cres. CT19: F'stone 6J 189
Radnor Pk. Gdns. CT19: F'stone 5J 189
Radnor Pk. Rd. CT19: F'stone 6J 189 (4B 42)
Radnor Pk. W. CT19: F'stone 6H 189
Radnor St. CT19: F'stone 6L 189
Radnor Wlk. CR0: Croy 9B 68
Radzan Cl. DA5: Bex'y 7F 58
Raeburn Av. DA1: Dart 3J 59
KT5: Surb 3A 12
Raeburn Cl. TN10: Tonb 1L 145
Raeburn Pl. DA10: Swans 3L 61
Raeburn Rd. DA15: Sidc 4G 57
Rafford Way BR1: Brom 5L 69
R.A.F. Manston History Mus. 9M 207
Raggatt Pl. ME15: Maid 7E 126
Ragge Way TN15: Seal 2N 119
Raggleswood BR7: Chst 4C 70
Rag Hill Cl. TN16: Tats 9E 164
Rag Hill Rd. TN16: Tats 9D 164 (1A 24)
Raglan Ct. SE12 3K 55
Raglan Pl. CT10: B'stairs 9M 209
Raglan Rd. BR2: Shortl 7M 69
DA17: Belv 4A 52
SE18 5E 50
Ragstone Ct. ME20: Dit 1G 125
Ragstone Hollow TN25: Aldtn 4D 40
Ragstone Rd. ME15: Bear 7K 127
Railmania Mus. *CT5: Whits* *4F 226*
(off High St.)
Railton Rd. SE24 6F 5
Railway App. RH19: E Grin 3A 34
TN9: Tonb 6H 145
Railway Av. CT5: Whits 4G 226 (3F 21)
Railway Children Wlk. BR1: Brom 7K 55
SE12 7K 55
Railway Cotts. TN12: Mard 2D 212
Railway Hill CT4: B'hm 9B 162 (5K 31)
Railway Pl. DA12: Grav'nd 4G 63
DA17: Belv 3B 52
Railway Rd. ME12: S'ness 2C 220 (6F 11)
Railway Sidings DA13: Meop 8F 76
Railway Sidings Ind. Est. DA13: Sole S 8F 76
Railway St. DA11: Nflt 3N 61
ME4: Chat'm 8C 80 (3H 17)
ME7: Gill 7G 80 (2J 17)
Railway St. Ind. Est. ME7: Gill 6G 81
Railway Ter. CT9: Mgte 4B 208
ME11: Queen 7B 220
SE13 3E 54
TN16: Westrm 7F 116
Rainbow La. SS17: Stan H 2E 8
Rainbow Rd. RM16: Chaf H 4K 7
RAINHAM
Dagenham 2G 7
Gillingham 3B 96 (4A 18)
Rainham Cl. ME15: Maid 8C 126
SE9 4G 56
Rainham Hall 2G 7
Rainham Rd. ME5: Chat'm 9F 80 (3J 17)
ME7: Gill 9F 80 (3J 17)
RM12: H'church, Rain 1F 7
RM13: Rain 1F 7
Rainham Rd. Nth. RM10: Dag 1E 6
Rainham Rd. Sth. RM10: Dag 1F 7
Rainham Shop. Cen. ME8: Rain 2B 96
Rainham Station (Rail)
Essex 2G 7
Kent 2B 96 (3A 18)
Raleigh Cl. DA8: Erith 6G 53
ME5: Chat'm 5D 94
TN24: W'boro 1L 161
Raleigh Ct. BR3: Beck'm 4E 68
DA8: Erith 7G 53
Raleigh M. BR6: Chels 6H 85
Raleigh Rd. SE20 3A 68
Raleigh Way ME12: Minst 6F 220
Ralph Grimshaw Ct. CT8: Wgte S 3K 207
Ralph Perring Ct. BR3: Beck'm 7D 68
Ramillies Cl. ME5: Chat'm 6D 94
Ramillies Rd. DA15: Sidc 4K 57
RAM LANE 6J 29
Ram La. TN25: Hoth 7H 29
TN27: L Char 1H 197 (7H 29)
Rammell M. TN17: Cran 8D 176
Ramp A CT16: Dover 4N 181
Rampart Rd. CT21: Hythe 6J 199
Ramp B CT16: Dover 4M 181
Ramp C CT16: Dover 4M 181
Rampion Cl. ME14: Weav 4H 127
RAMSDEN 2L 85 (3D 14)
Ramsden Cl. BR5: Orp 2L 85
Ramsden La. TN17: Bendn 7A 38
Ramsden Rd. BR5: Orp 2K 85
BR6: Orp 1K 85
DA8: Erith 7E 52
Ramsey Cl. CT2: Cant 1L 171
Ramsey Ho. *CT1: Cant* *3M 171*
(off Station Rd. E.)
RAMSGATE 5J 211 (4K 23)
Ramsgate Maritime Mus. 6K 211 (4K 23)
Ramsgate Model Village 7H 211
Ramsgate Motor Mus. CT11: Ram 7H 211
Ramsgate Mus. 6J 211 (4J 23)
Ramsgate Rd.
CT9: B'stairs, Mgte 4D 208 (2H 23)
CT10: B'stairs, Ram 1K 211 (3K 23)
CT11: Ram 3K 23
CT12: Ram 7G 23
CT13: S'wch, C'snd 5M 217 (7G 23)
Ramsgate Sports Cen. 5H 211
Ramsgate Station (Rail) 4G 211 (4J 23)
Ramsgate Swimming Pool 4G 210
RAMS HILL 1F 37
RAMSLYE 4E 156 (3J 35)
Ramslye Rd. TN4: Tun W 4D 156
Ramstone Cl. TN25: Sme 8K 165
Ram St. SW18 6C 4
Ramuswood Av. BR6: Chels 6G 84
Rancliffe Gdns. SE9 2A 56
Rancliffe Rd. E6 2B 6
Rancorn Rd. CT9: Mgte 4A 208
Randall Cl. DA8: Erith 6D 52
Randall Hill Rd. TN15: Wro 7M 105
Randall Rd. ME4: Chat'm 2B 94
Randalls Row ME15: Loose 3C 138
Randall St. ME14: Maid 3C 126
Randal Way ME9: Bap 9M 99
Randisbourne Gdns. SE6 8E 54
Randlesdown Rd. SE6 9D 54
(not continuous)
Randles La. TN14: Knock 6M 101 (6D 14)
Randolph Cl. CT1: Cant 4N 171
DA7: Bexhth 1D 58
Randolph Cotts. ME2: Strood 3M 79
Randolph Gdns. TN24: Kenn 5J 159
Randolph Ho. *CT20: F'stone* *6L 189*
(off Tram Rd., The)
ME7: Gill 7F 80
Randolph Rd. BR2: Shortl 2B 84
CT17: Dover 3F 180
ME7: Gill 7F 80
Randolphs TN27: Bidd 9L 163
Randolph's La. TN16: Westrm 8D 116
Randolph Sq. CT9: Mgte 2D 208
Ranelagh Gdns. CT10: B'stairs 8J 209
DA11: Nflt 5E 62
Ranelagh Gro. CT10: B'stairs 8J 209
Ranelagh Rd. CT14: Deal 5N 177
ME12: S'ness 2D 220
Rangefield Rd. BR1: Brom 1H 69
Range Rd. CT21: Hythe 7J 199
DA12: Grav'nd 5K 63
ME12: E'chu 7C 202
Range Rd. Ind. Est. CT21: Hythe 7H 199
Rangeworth Pl. DA15: Sidc 8H 57
Rankine Rd. TN2: Tun W 7K 151
Ranleigh Gdns. DA7: Bexhth 7A 52
Ranmore Path BR5: St M Cry 7J 71
Ranscombe Cl. ME2: Strood 7H 79
Ransley TN26: H Hald 1C 196
Ransley Grn. TN26: Ruck 6B 40
Ransome Way CT7: Birch 5F 206
Ranters La. TN17: Goud, Kiln 4A 190 (5F 37)
Ranworth Cl. DA8: Erith 9F 52
Raphael Ct. TN11: Hild 9D 132
Raphael Rd. DA12: Grav'nd 5J 63
Rapier Cl. RM19: Purf 4N 53
Rashleigh Way DA4: Hort K 7C 74
Raspberry Hill La. ME9: Iwade 6H 197 (2E 18)
Ratcliffe Cl. SE12 5K 55
Ratcliffe Highway ME3: Allh, St M Hoo 5A 204
ME3: C'den, St M Hoo 8D 66 (7J 9)
Rathfern Rd. SE6 6C 54
Rathmore Rd. DA11: Grav'nd 5G 62
RATLING 3C 32
Ratling Rd. CT3: Aysm 1D 162 (3B 32)
Rattington St. CT4: Chart'm 8D 170 (2F 31)
Rattray Ct. SE6 7J 55
Raven Cl. ME20: Lark 9D 108
Raven Knowle ME1: Woul 7H 93
Ravenlea Rd. CT20: F'stone 6G 189
Ravensbourne Av. BR2: Shortl 3G 68
CT6: H Bay 4J 195
Ravensbourne Ct. SE6 5D 54
Ravensbourne Ho. BR1: Brom 1G 68
Ravensbourne Pk. SE6 5D 54 (7J 5)
Ravensbourne Pk. Cres. SE6 5C 54
Ravensbourne Rd. BR1: Brom 6K 69
DA1: Cray 1H 59
SE6 5C 54
Ravensbourne Station (Rail) 3G 68 (1K 13)
Ravensbury Rd. BR5: St P 6H 71
Ravenscar Rd. BR1: Brom 9H 55
Ravens Cl. BR2: Shortl 5J 69
Ravenscourt Gro. RM12: H'church 1H 7
Ravenscourt Park Station (Tube) 4B 4
Ravenscourt Rd. BR5: St P 6J 71
CT2: R Comn 8H 167
CT14: Deal 5M 177
Ravenscroft Cres. SE9 8B 56
Ravenscroft Rd. BR3: Beck'm 5A 68
Ravens Dane Cl. ME15: Bear 8K 127
Ravenshill BR7: Chst 4D 70
Ravensleigh Gdns. BR1: Brom 1L 69
Ravensmead Rd. BR2: Shortl 3G 69
Ravens M. SE12 3K 55
Ravensquay Bus. Cen. BR5: St M Cry 8K 71
Ravens Way SE12 3K 55
Ravenswood DA5: Bex'y 6N 57
Ravenswood Av. BR4: W W'ck 2F 82
ME2: Strood 4M 79
TN2: Tun W 8J 151
Ravenswood Cres. BR4: W W'ck 2F 82
Ravensworth Rd. BR4: W W'ck 3K 13
SE9 8B 56
Ravine Gro. SE18 6G 50
Rawdon Rd. CT11: Ram 6F 210
ME15: Maid 6D 126
Rawlings Cl. BR3: Beck'm 8F 68
BR6: Chels 6H 85
Rawling St. ME9: Mils 8F 114 (7F 19)
Rawlins Cl. CR2: S Croy 8B 82
Rawlinson Ho. *SE13* *2G 55*
(off Mercator Rd.)
Rawsthorne Cl. E16 1B 50
Rayfield Cl. BR2: Shortl 9A 70
Rayfield Ct. ME6: Snod 1E 108
Rayford Av. SE12 5J 55
Rayford Cl. DA1: Dart 3K 59
Rayham Rd. CT5: Whits 5J 227
Ray Lamb Way DA8: Erith 6J 53
Rayleas Cl. SE18 8D 50
Rayleigh Cl. ME16: Alltn 2A 126
Rayleigh Ho. *BR1: Brom* *4K 69*
(off Hammelton Rd.)
Raymere Gdns. SE18 7F 50
Rayner Rd. ME14: Pen H 1E 126
Raymond Av. CT1: Cant 4N 171
Raymond Fuller Way TN24: Kenn 6J 159
Raymond Rd. BR3: Beck'm 7B 68
Raymoor Av. TN29: St M Bay 2N 215
Raymouth Rd. SE16 4H 5
Rayner's Ct. DA11: Nflt 3A 62
Rayners Hill ME17: Len 4F 29
RAYNES PARK 2B 12
Raynes Park Station (Rail) 2B 12
Rays Hill DA4: Hort K 7C 74 (2J 15)
Rays Rd. BR4: W W'ck 1F 82
Reach Cl. CT15: St Marg 7B 214
Reachfields CT21: Hythe 7H 199
Reach Mdw. CT15: St Marg 7C 214
Reach Rd. CT15: St Marg 8B 214 (7H 33)
Readers Bri. Rd. TN30: St Mic 3A 224 (5D 38)
Readers Ct. ME18: Tstn 9E 124
Readers La. TN31: Iden 4A 46
Reading Cl. CT14: Walm 9L 177

Reading Ho.—Rigden's Ct.

Reading Ho. ME15: Maid 3J 139
Reading Rd. CT17: Dover 5E 180
READING STREET
Broadstairs 6K 209 (2K 23)
Tenterden 7G 39
Reading Street CT10: B'stairs 6K 209
Reading St. CT10: B'stairs 5K 209 (2K 23)
TN26: App 7G 39
TN30: Tent 7G 39
Reading St. Rd. CT10: B'stairs 4J 209 (1K 23)
Readscroft Rd. ME8: Gill 6N 95
Read Way DA12: Grav'nd 1J 77
Rear, The *TN2: Tun W* 3G 156
(off Pantiles, The)
Rebecca Ct. CT9: Mgte 3F 208
DA14: Sidc 9K 57
Recreation Av. ME6: Snod 2E 108
Recreation Cl. ME14: Maid 3E 126
Recreation Ground Rd.
TN30: Tent 8C 224
Recreation Rd. BR2: Shortl 5J 69
DA15: Sidc 8G 57
SE26 9A 54
Recreation Way ME10: Kems'y 2G 99
Rectory Bus. Cen. DA14: Sidc 9K 57
Rectory Cl. DA1: Cray 2F 58
DA14: Sidc 9K 57
ME1: Woul 6G 93
ME6: Snod 2E 108
TN26: Wdchu 7B 228
TN29: Newchu 7C 40
Rectory Cotts. CT15: Eyt 8K 185
Rectory Ct. CT5: Whits 3M 227
Rectory Dr. TN3: Bidb 3C 150
Rectory Fields TN17: Cran 7D 176
Rectory Gdns. *BR3: Beck'm* 4D 68
(off Rectory Rd.)
CT5: Whits 3M 227
Rectory Grange ME1: Roch 1M 93
Rectory Grn. BR3: Beck'm 4C 68
Rectory Gro. SS9: Lgh S 1B 10
Rectory La. CT4: B'hm 7D 162 (4A 32)
CT18: Lym'ge 8L 205
CT21: Salt 4J 199
DA14: Sidc 9K 57 (1D 14)
ME16: Maid 8K 125 (2G 27)
ME17: Cha S 9M 139
ME17: H'shm 3N 141
ME17: Sut V 9A 140 (5A 28)
SM7: Bans 7D 12
SW17 1E 12
TN8: Hever 7D 24
TN13: S'oaks 8J 119
TN15: Igh 4J 121 (1K 25)
TN16: Bras 6L 117 (2D 24)
TN16: Tats 5A 116 (2B 24)
TN17: Cran 7D 176
TN31: Beckl 3H 45
TN36: Winch 7A 46
Rectory La. Nth. ME19: Leyb 8C 108
Rectory La. Sth. ME19: Leyb 8C 108
Rectory Mdw. DA13: Sflt 2N 75
Rectory Pk. CR2: S Croy 6G 13
Rectory Pk. Rd. TN12: Horsm 3F 37
Rectory Pl. SE18 4C 50
Rectory Rd. BR2: Kes 8N 83
BR3: Beck'm 5D 68 (2J 13)
CT10: B'stairs 8M 209
CT14: Deal 6J 177 (4H 33)
DA10: Swans 5L 61
ME3: Cliffe 2L 65 (6G 9)
ME10: Sit 8J 99
N16 1G 5
RM16: Ors 3C 8
RM17: Grays 4B 8
RM18: W Til 4C 8
TN15: Ash 6A 90 (4A 16)
TN29: St M Mar 1H 215
Rectory Road Station (Rail) 1G 5
Rectory Wlk. TN26: Hams 3L 191
Rectory Way TN24: Kenn 5G 158
RECULVER 2B 22
Reculver Av. CT7: Birch 3D 206
Reculver Cl. CT6: H Bay 1N 195
Reculver Dr. CT6: H Bay 2M 195
Reculver La. CT6: Rec 2A 22
Reculver Rd. CT6: H Bay 4K 195 (3K 21)
Reculver Roman Fort (Regulbium) 2B 22
Reculvers Rd. CT8: Wgte S 4L 207
Reculver Wlk. ME15: Maid 1J 139
Redan Pl. ME12: S'ness 2E 220
Redbank ME19: Leyb 8C 108
Red Barracks Rd. SE18 4B 50
Redberry Rd. TN23: Kgnt 4F 160
Redbridge Cl. ME5: Chat'm 7E 94
Redbrook St.
TN26: H Hald, Wdchu 2F 196 (4G 39)
Redbrooks Way CT21: Hythe 5G 199
Red Cedars Rd. BR6: Orp 1G 84
Redcliffe Gdns. SW5 4C 4
SW10 4C 4
Redcliffe La. ME14: Pen H 2E 126
Redcot La. CT2: Sturry 4G 168
Red Cotts. ME16: Alltn 1B 126
Redding Cl. DA2: Dart 7E 60
Redding Ho. SE18 3A 50
Reddons Rd. BR3: Beck'm 3B 68
Reddy Rd. DA8: Erith 6G 52
Rede Ct. Rd. ME2: Strood 4H 79 (2G 17)
Rede Wood Rd. ME16: Barm 6J 125
Redfern Av. ME7: Gill 7H 81
Redfern Rd. SE6 5F 54
Redgate Dr. BR2: Shortl 3L 83
Redgates CT6: H Bay 2H 195
RED HILL 8D 124 (2E 26)
Red Hill BR7: Chst 1D 70 (1B 14)
ME18: W'bury 7D 124 (3E 26)
Redhill Rd. CT8: Wgte S 3K 207
DA3: New A 4L 89 (4A 16)
Redhill Wood DA3: New A 4N 89
(not continuous)
Red House 2N 57
Redhouse Bungs. CT14: Deal 1L 177
Red Ho. Cotts. TN13: S'oaks 7K 119
Red Ho. Gdns. ME18: W'bury 1A 136
Redhouse La. CT4: P'hm 3G 31
CT14: Deal 1L 177
Red Ho. La. DA6: Bexhth 2M 57
Redhouse Rd. TN16: Tats 8C 164
Redhouse Wall CT14: Deal 1L 177
Redington TN24: Ashf 7G 159
Redlands Ct. BR1: Brom 3J 69
CT17: Dover 9D 178
Redland Shaw ME1: Roch 2B 94
Redlands La. TN32: Rob 4C 44
Redlands Rd. TN13: S'oaks 6G 119
Redlands, The BR3: Beck'm 5E 68
Red La. RH8: Oxt 4A 24
Redleaf Cl. DA17: Belv 6B 52
TN2: Tun W 8K 151
Red Lion Cl. BR5: St M Cry 9L 71
Red Lion La. CT5: Whits 3F 226
SE18 7C 50 (5B 6)
Red Lion Pl. SE18 8C 50
Red Lion Rd. KT6: Surb 4A 12
Red Lion Sq. CT21: Hythe 6J 199 (5H 41)
Red Lion St. WC1 3F 5
Red Lodge BR4: W W'ck 2F 82
Red Lodge Cres. DA5: Bex'y 8E 58
Red Lodge Rd. BR4: W W'ck 2F 82 (3K 13)
DA5: Bex'y 8E 58
Redmans La. TN14: S'ham 7D 86 (5F 15)
Redmill Cl. CT20: F'stone 6E 188
Red Oak TN18: Hawkh 7B 192
Red Oak Cl. BR6: Farnb 4D 84
Redoubt Sailing Club 8D 198
Redoubt Way TN29: Dym 8E 182
Redpoll Wlk. TN12: Pad W 1M 153
Redpoll Way DA18: Erith 3M 51
Red Post Hill SE24 6G 5
Redriff Rd. SE16 4H 5
Red Rd. CT2: Denst 1N 165
Redroofs Cl. BR3: Beck'm 4E 68
RED ROVER 6A 4
Redruth Mnr. *ME7: Gill* 6F 80
(off Cross St.)
Redsells Cl. ME15: Bear 8K 127
Redshank Rd. ME4: Chat'm 3D 80
REDSTREET 2A 76
Red St. DA13: Sflt 1N 75 (1A 16)
Redsull Av. CT14: Deal 7K 177
Red Tree Orchard TN23: Ashf 2C 160
Redvers Cotts. CT16: Dover 8D 178
Redvers Rd. ME4: Chat'm 1D 94
Redwall La. ME15: Hunt 9L 137 (5G 27)
ME17: Hunt, Lint 9B 138 (5G 27)
Redwell Cotts. TN15: Igh 5J 121
Redwell Gro. ME19: W Mal 7A 124
Redwell La. TN15: Igh 5H 121 (2K 25)
Redwing Cl. ME20: Lark 7D 108
Redwing Path SE28 2F 50
Redwing Rd. ME5: Chat'm 5E 94
Redwings La. TN2: Pem 5C 152 (1B 36)
Redwood Cl. CT2: Cant 9L 167
CT4: Chart'm 9E 170
DA15: Sidc 6J 57
ME5: Chat'm 9E 94
Redwood Ct. DA1: Dart 4A 60
Redwood Glade ME7: B'hst 1K 111
Redwood Pk. TN12: Five G 1F 152
Redyear Ct. TN24: W'boro 9L 159
Reece Adams Ho. CT18: Cap F 3A 174
Reece La. CT18: Acr 7A 32
Reed Av. BR6: Orp 4G 84
CT1: Cant 9B 168
Reed Cl. ME20: Lark 6E 108
SE12 3K 55
Reed Cres. TN23: Kgnt 6G 160
Reede Rd. RM10: Dag 1E 6
Reedham Cres. ME3: Cli W 6N 65
Reedham Station (Rail) 6F 13
Reedland Cres. ME13: Fav 4G 186
Reedmace Cl. TN23: Ashf 1B 160
Reed Mill La. CT4: Kgstn 5J 31
Reeds Cl. CT6: H Bay 3J 195
Reeds La. TN11: S'brne 3L 133 (3A 26)
Reeds Mill La. CT4: Kgstn 5J 31
Reeds Mill Rd. CT4: Kgstn 6A 162 (4K 31)
Reed St. ME3: Cliffe 2C 176 (5G 9)
Reeves All. *CT5: Whits* 4F 226
(off Middle Wall)
Reeves Cl. TN12: S'hrst 2J 223
Reeves Corner Stop (CT) 4G 13
Reeves Ct. ME19: E Mal 9E 108
Reeves Cres. BR8: Swanl 6E 72
Reeves Rd. SE18 6D 50
Reeves Way CT5: Whits 4L 227
Reflection, The *E16* 2D 50
(off Woolwich Mnr. Way)
Reform Rd. ME4: Chat'm 9E 80
Regency Cl. CT5: Whits 6G 227
ME8: Gill 8M 95
ME12: S'ness 1B 220
TN15: W King 7E 88
Regency Ct. ME10: Sit 7E 98
Regency Hall TN2: Tun W 3G 156
Regency M. BR3: Beck'm 3F 68
Regency Pl. CT1: Cant 9A 168
Regency Wlk. CR0: Croy 9C 68
Regency Way DA6: Bexhth 1M 57
Regent Dr. ME15: Maid 9D 126
Regent Pl. TN2: Tun W 2K 157
Regent Rd. ME7: Gill 8F 80
Regents Ct. BR1: Brom 3J 69
DA11: Grav'nd 3G 62
TN23: Ashf 8F 158
(off Regents Pl.)
Regents Dr. BR2: Kes 6N 83
REGENT'S PARK 2E 4
Regent's Pk. 2D 4
Regent's Pk. Rd. NW1 2D 4
Regent's Park Station (Tube) 2E 4
Regents Pl. *ME12: S'ness* 2C 220
(off Cross St.)
TN23: Ashf 8F 158
Regent Sq. DA17: Belv 4C 52
Regent St. CT5: Whits 3F 226
SW1 3E 4
TN17: Rolv 2B 214 (7C 38)
W1 3E 4
Regents Wlk. CT6: H Bay 2L 195
Regent Way ME19: W Mal 6A 124
Regina Ct. TN4: Tun W 1F 156
Regina Ho. SE20 4A 68
Reginald Av. ME2: Cux 9G 78
Reginald Rd. ME16: Maid 6B 126
Regis Bus. Pk. ME12: S'ness 3B 220
Regis Cres. ME10: Sit 5F 98
Regis Ind. Est. ME12: S'ness 4B 220
Reidhaven Rd. SE18 4G 50
Reigate Av. SM1: Sutt 3C 12
Reigate Rd. BR1: Brom 8J 55
KT17: Eps 5A 12
KT20: Tad 7B 12
Reinden Gro. ME15: Bear 8J 127
Reinickendorf Av. SE9 4E 56
Rembrandt Cl. TN10: Tonb 1L 145
Rembrandt Dr. DA11: Nflt 8C 62
Rembrandt Rd. SE13 2H 55
Remston M. CT1: Cant 9A 168
Remus Cl. TN23: Ashf 5D 160
Renault Cl. CT6: H Bay 3B 194
Rendezvous St. CT20: F'stone 6K 189
Rendezvous, The CT9: Mgte 2C 208
Rennell St. SE13 1F 54
Rennets Cl. SE9 3G 56
Rennets Wood Rd. SE9 3F 56
Renovation, The *E16* 2D 50
(off Woolwich Mnr. Way)
Renown Rd. ME5: Chat'm 9F 94
Renshaw Cl. DA17: Belv 6A 52
Rentain Rd. CT4: Chart'm 8D 170
Renton Dr. BR5: Orp, St M Cry 1M 85
Renwick Rd. IG11: Bark 2D 6
Replingham Rd. SW18 7C 4
Repository Rd. SE18 6B 50 (5B 6)
Repton Cl. CT10: B'stairs 7K 209
Repton Ct. BR3: Beck'm 4E 68
Repton Mnr. Rd. TN23: Ashf 7E 158
Repton Rd. BR6: Chels 4J 85
Repton Way ME5: Chat'm 7C 94
Reservoir Cl. DA9: G'hithe 4J 61
Reservoir Cotts. ME2: Hall'g 7C 92
Reservoir La. TN31: Sed, B Oak 6E 44
TN33: Sed 6E 44
Reservoir Rd. CT5: Whits 3G 226
Resolution Cl. ME5: Chat'm 6D 94
Resolution Wlk. SE18 3B 50
Restavon Cvn. Site TN16: Big H 7D 100
Rest Harrow ME13: Shel 3H 219
Restharrow Rd. ME14: Weav 5H 127
Restharrow Way ME4: Chat'm 3F 80
Restons Cres. SE9 4F 56
Restoration House 7N 79
(off Crow La.)
Retreat Cvn. Pk., The ME18: W'bury 2B 136
Retreat Club & Cvn. Pk., The
ME12: E'chu 2E 202
Retreat, The BR6: Chels 7K 85
CT7: Birch 3G 206
CT12: Ram 4F 210
TN13: S'oaks 7J 119
Rettendon Dr. ME10: Sit 3G 98
Revell Ri. SE18 6H 51
Revelon Rd. SE4 2B 54
Revenge Rd. ME5: Chat'm 2F 110
ME5: Chat'm 1F 110
Reventlow Rd. SE9 6E 56
Reynard Cl. BR1: Brom 6C 70
SE4 1B 54
Reynolds Cl. CT6: H Bay 3J 195
TN10: Tonb 1L 145
Reynolds Flds. ME3: High'm 7G 65
Reynolds Health & Fitness 7F 58
Reynolds La. CT3: M'sde 3B 22
TN4: Tun W 7F 150 (2J 35)
Rhee Wall TN29: Bztt, Old R, Ivyc 5F 47
Rheims Ct. CT2: Cant 1K 171
Rheims Way CT2: Cant 1K 171 (7H 21)
Rhodaus Cl. CT1: Cant 3M 171
Rhodaus Town CT1: Cant 3M 171 (1H 31)
RHODE COMMON 1D 30
Rhode Ct. ME10: Sit 6D 98
Rhodes Gdns. CT10: B'stairs 7L 209
Rhodes Ho. *ME5: Chat'm* 1F 94
(off Beacon Hill)
RHODES MINNIS 9H 183 (1H 41)
Rhode St. ME4: Chat'm 8D 80
Rhodeswell Rd. E14 3J 5
Rhodewood Cl. ME15: Bear 8K 127
Rhododendron Av. DA13: Meop 8F 90
Ribblesdale Rd. DA2: Dart 6C 60
Ribston Cl. BR2: Shortl 2B 84
Ribston Gdns. TN12: Pad W 8K 147
Ricard M. TN3: Lamb 2L 201
Ricardo Path SE28 1L 51
Riccards La. TN33: What 6D 44
Rice Pde. BR5: Pet W 8F 70
Richard Cl. SE18 4A 50
Richard Ct. CT9: Mgte 3F 208
Richard Meech Dr. TN24: Kenn 6J 159
Richard Neve Ho. *SE18* 4G 50
(off Plumstead High St.)
Richards Cl. TN11: Chid 5G 143
Richardson Cl. DA9: G'hithe 3F 60
Richardson Rd. TN4: Tun W 8G 151
Richardson Way CT12: C'snd 6A 210
Richard St. ME1: Roch 9N 79
ME4: Chat'm 8C 80
Richard Watts Ct. *ME4: Chat'm* 7C 80
(off Medway St.)
Richborough Bus. Pk. CT13: S'wch 3L 217
Richborough Castle 6G 23
Richborough Cl. BR5: St M Cry 7M 71
Richborough Dr. ME2: Strood 3L 79
RICHBOROUGH PORT 6G 23
Richborough Rd. CT3: Ash 1C 216
CT3: S'wch 1J 217
CT8: Wgte S 4L 207
CT13: S'wch 1J 217 (6F 23)
Richborough Roman Fort 2J 217 (7F 23)
Richborough Way TN23: Kgnt 4C 160
Richdore Rd. CT4: Walt 5F 31
Richmer Rd. DA8: Erith 7H 53
Richmond Av. CT9: Mgte 4F 208
Richmond Cl. ME2: Upnor 3C 80
ME5: Chat'm 7E 94
TN16: Big H 7B 164
Richmond Ct. CT16: Dover 3J 181
Richmond Dr. CT6: H Bay 3M 195
DA12: Grav'nd 7K 63
ME10: Sit 4F 98
TN28: New R 1K 213
Richmond Gdns. CT2: Cant 9J 167
Richmond Ho. *CT20: F'stone* 6L 189
(off Parade, The)
Richmond Pk. 7A 4
Richmond Pl. SE18 4E 50
TN2: Tun W 4H 157
Richmond Rd. CT5: Whits 4K 227
CT11: Ram 6H 211
E8 1G 5
ME7: Gill 6F 80 (2J 17)
Richmond St. CT6: H Bay 2G 194
CT19: F'stone 5D 188
ME12: S'ness 2E 220 (6G 11)
Richmond Way ME15: Maid 9D 126
Richmount Gdns. SE3 1K 55
Ricketts Hill Rd. TN16: Tats 6D 164 (7A 14)
Rickyard Path SE9 2A 56
Riddlesdale Av. TN4: Tun W 8G 151
RIDDLESDOWN 6G 13
Riddlesdown Rd. CR8: Purl 6G 13
Riddlesdown Station (Rail) 6G 13
Riddles Rd. ME10: Sit 8D 98 (5E 18)
Riddons Rd. SE12 8M 55
Rideout St. SE18 4B 50
Rider Cl. DA15: Sidc 4G 56
Ridge Av. DA1: Cray 4G 58
Ridgebrook Rd. SE3 1N 55
Ridge Cl. SE28 2F 50
Ridgecroft Cl. DA5: Bex'y 6D 58
Ridgelands TN3: Bidb 2C 150
Ridge La. DA13: Meop 8F 90
Ridgemount Av. CR0: Croy 2A 82
Ridge Rd. SM3: Sutt 3C 12
RIDGE ROW 3J 193 (1A 42)
Ridge, The BR6: Orp 3F 84
DA5: Bex'y 5A 58
TN3: Groom 7H 155
TN24: Kenn 4J 159
Ridgeway BR2: Shortl 3K 83
CT5: Whits 4K 227
Ridge Way DA1: Cray 4G 58
Ridgeway DA2: Dart 1E 74
TN2: Pem 7C 152
Ridge Way TN8: Eden 3C 184
Ridgeway TN18: Hawkh 7A 192
Ridgeway Av. DA12: Grav'nd 8G 63
Ridgeway Bungs. DA12: Shorne 3D 78
Ridgeway Cliff CT6: H Bay 2D 194
Ridgeway Cres. BR6: Orp 4G 85
TN10: Tonb 3K 145
Ridgeway Cres. Gdns. BR6: Orp 3G 85
Ridgeway Dr. BR1: Brom 9L 55
Ridgeway E. DA15: Sidc 3H 57
Ridgewaye, The TN4: S'bgh 5G 151
Ridgeway Rd. CT6: H Bay 8H 195 (4K 21)
Ridgeway Ter. TN25: Sme 8H 165
Ridgeway, The CT9: Mgte 4F 208
CT10: B'stairs 1K 211
CT17: Dover 2D 180
CT21: Lymp 5B 198
DA12: Shorne 3C 78 (1E 16)
ME4: Chat'm 4B 94 (4H 17)
ME7: Gill 5F 80
ME13: Bou B 3K 165
SS0: Wclf S 1C 10
TN10: Tonb 2J 145 (6K 25)
TN25: Sme 2D 40
Ridgeway Wlk. CT6: H Bay 8H 195
Ridgeway W. DA15: Sidc 3G 56
Ridgewell Cl. SE26 9C 54
Ridgewood DA3: Long 5B 76
Ridgway ME16: Maid 7M 125
SW19 1B 12
Ridgy Fld. Cl. TN15: Wro 8N 105
Ridham Av. ME10: Kems'y 2G 99 (3F 19)
Riding Hill TN24: Kenn 4G 159
Riding La. TN11: Hild 1D 144 (5J 25)
Riding Pk. TN11: Hild 9D 132
Ridings, The CT1: Cant 1A 172
CT5: Whits 4M 227
CT9: Clift 2J 209
TN2: Tun W 8M 151
TN12: Pad W 8M 147
TN16: Big H 5E 164
Ridlands La. RH8: Oxt 3A 24
RIDLEY 6A 90 (4A 16)
Ridley Cl. CT6: H Bay 7H 195
Ridley Rd. BR2: Shortl 6J 69
DA16: Well 8K 51
ME1: Roch 8M 79
Riefield Rd. SE9 2E 56 (6C 6)
Rigden Rd. TN23: Ashf 2F 160
Rigden's Ct. ME10: Sit 6F 98

Riggs Way—Ropemakers Ct.

Riggs Way TN15: Wro 7M 105
Rigshill Rd. ME13: O'den, Char'g 3H 29
Riley Av. CT6: H Bay 3A 194
Ring Cl. BR1: Brom 3L 69
Ringden Av. TN12: Pad W 1K 153
Ringers Ct. BR1: Brom 6K 69
(off Ringers Rd.)
Ringers Rd. BR1: Brom 6K 69
Ringle Grn. TN18: Sandh 3D 218
Ringlemere Farm Rd. CT13: Wdboro 8E 216
RINGLESTONE
Harrietsham 2D 28
Maidstone 2C 126 (1H 27)
Ringlestone Cres. ME14: Maid 1C 126
Ringlestone Rd. ME17: Holl 4K 129 (1C 28)
Ringlet Rd. ME4: Chat'm 2E 80
Ringmer Way BR1: Brom 8A 70
Ringold Av. CT12: Ram 4E 210
Ringshall Rd. BR5: St P 6J 71
Rings Hill TN11: Hild 1B 144 (5H 25)
Ringsloe Ct. CT7: Birch 3C 206
(off Parade, The)
Ringstead Rd. SE6 5E 54
Ringwold Cl. BR3: Beck'm 3B 68
Ringwood Av. BR6: Prat B 1L 101
Ringwood Cl. CT2: Cant 8L 167
ME8: Gill 3N 95
Ringwood Rd. ME15: Maid 9F 126
RINGWOULD 4B 200 (5H 33)
Ringwould Rd. CT14: Kgdn, R'wld 4C 200 (5J 33)
CT14: Ripp 5A 200 (6H 33)
CT15: Mart, R'wld 5A 200 (6H 33)
Ringwould Windmill 5H 33
Ripley Cl. BR1: Brom 8B 70
CR0: Croy 7F 82
Ripley Rd. DA17: Belv 4B 52
TN24: W'boro 1L 161
Ripleys Mkt. DA1: Dart 5M 59
Ripleys Mus. 3B 44
Ripon Cl. ME8: Rain 9N 81
Ripon Rd. SE18 6D 50
RIPPER'S CROSS 1H 39
Rippersley Rd. DA16: Well 8J 51
RIPPLE 4H 33
Ripple La. CT4: Crun 5D 30
Ripple Rd. CT14: Ripp, Walm 3A 200 (5H 33)
IG11: Bark 2C 6
RM9: Dag 2D 6
RIPPLE ROAD JUNCTION 2D 6
Rippolson Rd. SE18 5H 51
Ripton Cotts. ME18: Tstn 1E 136
Risborough La. CT19: F'stone 6D 188
CT20: F'stone 6D 188
(Military Rd.)
CT20: F'stone 7D 188 (4K 41)
(North Rd.)
Risborough Way CT20: F'stone 5E 188 (4A 42)
Risden La. TN18: Hawkh 8F 192 (1D 44)
Risdon Cl. CT2: Sturry 5E 168
Risedale Rd. DA7: Bexhth 1D 58
RISEDEN
Cranbrook 4F 37
Wadhurst 7B 36
Riseden Rd. TN5: Tide, Wadh 7B 36
Riseldine Rd. SE23 4B 54
Rise, The CT14: Kgdn 4E 200 (5J 33)
CT15: St Marg 7D 214
DA1: Cray 2G 59
DA5: Bex'y 5L 57
DA12: Grav'nd 9K 63
ME1: Roch 9A 80
ME4: Chat'm 5D 80
ME7: Hpstd 8K 95
ME9: B'den 9C 98
ME12: Minst 7D 220
TN13: S'oaks 2K 131
TN23: Ashf 2C 160
Rising Rd. TN23: Ashf 9E 158
Ritch Rd. ME6: Snod 2C 108
Ritter St. SE18 6C 50
Rivendell Cl. ME3: Isle G 8C 190
RIVER 1D 180 (1E 42)
River Bank Cl. ME15: Maid 5E 126
Riverbank Pk. ME12: Minst 3H 221
Riverbank Rd. BR1: Brom 8K 55
River Cen., The TN9: Tonb 6J 145
(off Medway Wharf Rd.)
River Cl. ME15: E Far 1L 137
River Ct. CT4: Chart'm 7D 170
CT17: Dover 2E 180
RM19: Purf 4N 53
TN13: Riv 4F 118
Riverdale CT17: Dover 1E 180
SE13 2F 54
Riverdale Est. TN9: Tonb 7K 145
Riverdale Rd. CT1: Cant 9A 168
DA5: Bex'y 5A 58
DA8: Erith 5C 52
SE18 5H 51
Riverdale Shop. Cen. SE13 1F 54
River Dr. CT17: Dover 2E 180
ME2: Strood 5J 79
River Gro. Pk. BR3: Beck'm 4C 68
Riverhall Hill TN5: Wadh 6A 36
River Hall Rd. TN27: Bidd 6N 163 (3D 38)
RIVERHEAD 4F 118 (1F 25)
Riverhead Cl. CT9: Mgte 4F 208
ME10: Sit 8D 98
ME16: Alltn 3N 125
Riverhead M. TN13: Riv 5F 118
River Hill TN15: S'oaks 3L 131 (3H 25)
Riverhill House & Gardens 4M 131 (4H 25)
Riverhope Mans. SE18 3A 50
River Lawn Rd. TN9: Tonb 6H 145
Rivermead ME4: Chat'm 2F 80
River Mdw. CT17: Dover 1E 180
River Pde. TN13: Riv 4F 118
River Pk. Gdns. BR2: Shortl 3G 69
River Pk. Vw. BR6: Orp 1K 85
River Rd. IG11: Bark 2C 6
Rivers Cl. ME18: W'bury 1C 136
Rivers Ct. CT12: Minst 8F 212
Riversdale DA11: Nflt 7D 62
Riversdale Rd. CT12: Ram 3E 210
TN23: Ashf 1G 160
Riverside CT4: Chart'm 7C 170
CT16: Temp E 8B 178
CT17: Dover 1E 180
DA4: Eyns 3L 87 (4G 15)
TN8: Eden 6C 184
Riverside Bus. Pk. TN24: Ashf 8H 159
Riverside Cvn. Pk. ME16: E Far 9L 125
Riverside Cl. BR5: St P 5L 71
CT4: Brid 8H 173
TN23: Kgnt 5E 160
Riverside Cotts. CT4: Chart'm 7C 170
Riverside Country Pk. 6M 81 (2A 18)
Riverside Country Pk. Vis. Cen. 7N 81
Riverside Ct. CT2: Cant 1M 171
SE3 2J 55
TN8: Eden 6D 184
TN9: Tonb 6J 145
Riverside E. Rd. ME4: Chat'm 2F 80
Riverside Est. ME2: Med E 6B 80
Riverside Ind. Est. CT2: Cant 8A 168
CT21: W Hyt 7C 198
DA1: Dart 3M 59
Riverside M. CT4: Brid 8H 173
Riverside Rail Freight Terminal
RM18: Tilb 2F 62
Riverside Retail Pk. CT1: Cant 4K 171
TN14: S'oaks 1K 119
Riverside Rd. DA14: Sidc 8N 57
Riverside Swimming Cen. 5F 52
Riverside Vw. ME20: Aylfd 8M 109
Riverside Wlk. BR4: W W'ck 2E 82
Riverside Way DA1: Dart 3M 59
Rivers Rd. ME9: Tey 7L 223
River St. CT17: Dover 1D 180
ME7: Gill 6D 80
Rivers Wlk. ME17: Len 7L 201
River Vw. CT2: Sturry 4E 168
Riverview DA1: Dart 2A 60
(off Henderson Dr.)
River Vw. ME8: Gill 9N 81
ME11: Queen 9A 220
ME15: Maid 7C 126
RM16: Grays 4C 8
Riverview TN23: Ashf 9C 158
River Vw. Cl. ME4: Chat'm 9C 80
RIVERVIEW PARK 9L 63 (1D 16)
Riverview Pk. SE6 7D 54
Riverview Rd. DA9: G'hithe 3G 61
River Wlk. TN9: Tonb 6H 145
River Way ME20: Lark 6E 108
River Wharf Bus. Pk. DA17: Belv 1E 52
Riverwood La. BR7: Chst 4F 70
Riviera Ct. CT20: S'gte 8E 188
Riviera, The CT20: S'gte 8F 188
Rixon Ho. SE18 6D 50
Roach St. ME2: Strood 5L 79
Road of Remembrance CT20: F'stone 5B 42
Road of Remembrance Rd.
CT20: F'stone 7K 189
Roan Ct. ME2: Strood 4K 79
Robert Bean Lodge ME1: Roch 2B 94
Robert Brundett Cl. TN24: Kenn 5J 159
Roberton Dr. BR1: Brom 4M 69
ROBERTSBRIDGE 4B 44
Robertsbridge Station (Rail) 4B 44
Roberts Cl. BR5: St M Cry 8L 71
ME10: Sit 4E 98
SE9 6F 56
Roberts M. BR6: Orp 2J 85
Roberts Orchard Rd. ME16: Barm 6K 125
Roberts Rd. CT5: Seas 7B 226
DA17: Belv 5B 52
ME6: Snod 2D 108
ME8: Gill 3A 96
TN28: G'stne 7M 213
Robert St. CT14: Deal 3N 177
E16 1D 50
NW1 2E 4
SE18 5F 50
(not continuous)
Robeshaw ME9: Mils 8F 114
ROBHURST 5G 39
Robina Av. DA11: Nflt 5C 62
Robina Cl. DA6: Bexhth 2M 57
Robina Ct. BR8: Swanl 7H 73
Robin Hill Dr. BR7: Chst 2A 70
ROBIN HOOD 7A 4
Robin Hood Grn. BR5: St M Cry 8J 71
Robin Hood La. DA6: Bexhth 3N 57
ME5: Chat'm 9C 94 (5H 17)
TN29: Lydd 4K 205 (5H 47)
Robin Hood La. Lwr. ME5: Chat'm 1B 110
Robin Hood La. Up. ME5: Chat'm 1A 110
Robin Hood Way SW15 1A 12
SW20 1A 12
Robin Ho. ME16: Maid 5B 126
Robin La. TN29: Lydd 3K 205
Robins Av. ME17: Len 8L 201
Robin's Cl. CT21: Hythe 8D 198
Robins Cl. ME17: Len 8L 201
Robin's Ct. BR3: Beck'm 5G 68
Robins Ct. ME14: Pen H 2E 126
SE12 8M 55
Robins Cft. DA11: Nflt 8D 62
Robins Gro. BR4: W W'ck 4K 83
Robin Way BR5: St P 6K 71
Robinwood Dr. TN15: Seal 1N 119
Robson Av. NW10 1B 4
Robson Dr. ME3: Hoo 8G 66
ME20: Aylfd 8H 109
Robson Rd. SE27 7G 5
Robus Cl. CT18: Lym'ge 7L 205
Robus Ter. CT18: Lym'ge 7L 205
Robyn Cotts. TN26: H Hald 1C 196
Robyns Way TN8: Eden 7D 184
TN13: S'oaks 4G 119
Rocfort Rd. ME6: Snod 2E 108 (6F 17)
Rochdale Rd. SE2 5K 51
TN1: Tun W 9J 151
ROCHESTER 7N 79 (2H 17)
ROCHESTER AIRPORT 4H 17
Rochester Airport Ind. Est. ME1: Roch 5N 93
Rochester Av. BR1: Brom 5L 69 (2A 14)
CT1: Cant 4A 172
ME1: Roch 8N 79
Rochester Castle 6N 79 (2G 17)
Rochester Cathedral 6N 79
Rochester Cl. DA15: Sidc 4K 57
Rochester Ct. CT1: Cant 4A 172
ME2: Med E 4A 80
Rochester Cres. ME3: Hoo 7G 67
Rochester Dr. DA5: Bex'y 4A 58
Rochester Ga. ME1: Roch 7A 80
(off High St.)
Rochester Ho. ME15: Maid 1G 138
Rochester Rd. DA1: Dart 5A 60
DA12: Grav'nd 5K 63 (7D 8)
ME1: Burh, Woul 9J 93 (5F 17)
ME1: Roch, Chat'm 5N 93 (4H 17)
ME1: Woul 7H 93 (4F 17)
ME2: Cux 2F 92 (3F 17)
ME5: Chat'm, Roch 6N 93 (4H 17)
ME20: Aylfd 7L 109 (7G 17)
TN10: Tonb 3K 145
Rochester Row SW1 4E 4
Rochester Station (Rail) 7A 80 (2H 17)
Rochester St. ME4: Chat'm 1B 94
Rochester Way DA1: Dart 5E 58 (7F 7)
SE3 6A 6
SE9 1M 55 (6B 6)
Rochester Way Relief Rd. SE3 5A 6
SE9 2M 55 (5A 6)
Rock Av. ME7: Gill 8F 80 (3J 17)
Rockbourne M. SE23 6A 54
Rockbourne Rd. SE23 6A 54
Rockdale TN13: S'oaks 7J 119
Rockdale Gdns. TN13: S'oaks 7J 119
Rockdale Pleasance
TN13: S'oaks 8J 119
Rockdale Rd. TN13: S'oaks 7K 119
Rockfield Rd. RH8: Oxt 3A 24
Rock Hill BR6: Orp 7C 86 (5E 14)
TN32: S'cross 4E 44
Rock Hill Rd. TN27: Eger 6E 28
Rockingham Pl. CT6: H Bay 5J 195
Rock La. TN17: Winch 7K 45
Rockmount Rd. SE18 5H 51
Rock Rd. ME10: Sit 7F 98
ME14: Pen H 2D 126
TN15: Bor G 2M 121 (1A 26)
Rocks Cl. ME19: E Mal 3E 124
Rocks Hill TN17: Frit 3K 37
TN31: N'thiam 5G 45
TN32: Rob 3C 44
Rock's Hill TN35: W'fld 7F 45
Rocks La. SW13 6B 4
Rocks Rd., The ME19: E Mal 3E 124 (1F 27)
Rockstone Way CT12: Ram 3E 210
Rock Villa Rd. TN1: Tun W 1G 157
Rocky Bourne Rd. TN25: Aldtn 4C 40
Rocky Hill ME16: Maid 5B 126
Rocky Hill Ter. ME16: Maid 5B 126
Rocque La. SE3 1J 55
Rodeo Cl. DA8: Erith 8J 53
Rodmell Rd. TN2: Tun W 3G 157
Rodmer Cl. ME12: Minst 4K 221
RODMERSHAM 2L 115 (5G 19)
RODMERSHAM GREEN 3J 115 (6F 19)
Rodmersham Grn. ME9: Rod 3J 115 (6F 19)
Rodmersham Squash & Fitness Club 4H 115
Rodney Av. TN10: Tonb 3L 145
Rodney Gdns. BR4: W W'ck 5K 83
Rodney Rd. SE17 4G 5
Rodney St. CT11: Ram 6H 211
Rodway Rd. BR1: Brom 4L 69
Roebourne Way E16 1C 50
Roebuck Rd. ME1: Roch 7N 79
ME13: Fav 5E 186
Roedean Cl. BR6: Chels 5K 85
Roedean Rd. TN2: Tun W 4G 157
ROEHAMPTON 7B 4
Roehampton Cl. DA12: Grav'nd 5K 63
Roehampton Dr. BR7: Chst 2E 70
Roehampton High St. SW15 7B 4
ROEHAMPTON LANE 7B 4
Roehampton La. SW15 6B 4
Roehampton Va. SW15 7A 4
Roethorne Gdns. TN30: Tent 7C 224
Roffen Rd. ME1: Roch 1N 93
Rogers Ct. BR8: Swanl 7H 73
Rogersmead TN30: Tent 8A 224
Rogers Rough Rd. TN17: Kiln, Goud 5F 37
Rogers Wood La. DA3: Fawk 5G 88 (4K 15)
Rogues Hill TN11: Pens 2J 149 (1G 35)
Rojack Rd. SE23 6A 54
Rokell Ho. BR3: Beck'm 1E 68
(off Beckenham Hill Rd.)
Rokesby Cl. DA16: Well 9F 50
Rokesley Rd. CT16: Dover 8G 178
Rolfe La. TN28: New R 2J 213 (3J 47)
Rolinsden Way BR2: Kes 6N 83
Rolleston Av. BR5: Pet W 9D 70
Rolleston Cl. BR5: Pet W 1D 84
Rollo Rd. BR8: Swanl 3G 72
Roll's Av. ME12: E'chu 7A 202
Rolls Rd. SE1 4G 5
ROLVENDEN 3B 214 (7C 38)
Rolvenden Av. ME8: Gill 9M 81
Rolvenden Dr. ME10: Sit 6C 98
Rolvenden Gdns. BR1: Brom 3N 69
Rolvenden Hill TN17: Rolv 1E 214 (6C 38)
ROLVENDEN LAYNE 7C 38
Rolvenden Rd. ME2: Wain 2N 79
TN17: Bendn 6A 38
TN30: Tent 8A 224 (6D 38)
Rolvenden Station (Rail) 6D 38
Roly Eckhoff Ho. CT16: Dover 1G 181
Roman Cl. CT14: Deal 4L 177
ME5: Chat'm 1A 110
Roman Ct. TN15: Bor G 2M 121
Roman Hgts. ME14: Maid 3F 126
Romanhurst Av. BR2: Shortl 7H 69
Romanhurst Gdns. BR2: Shortl 7H 69
Roman Mus. 2N 171
(off Butchery La.)
Roman Painted House, The 5J 181
(off New St.)
Roman Rd. CT12: Ram 2F 210
CT15: E Stu, Ashy 1H 179 (4F 33)
CT15: Whitf 4J 179
CT16: Dover 2J 181 (1F 43)
DA11: Nflt 8B 62
E2 2H 5
E3 2H 5
ME6: Snod 2D 108
ME13: Fav 5G 187 (6A 20)
TN8: Marsh G 9D 184 (7C 24)
TN25: Aldtn 4D 40
Roman Sq. ME10: Sit 8G 98
SE28 1J 51
Roman Villa Rd. DA2: Dart 1C 74 (1J 15)
DA4: S Dar, S at H 1B 74 (1J 15)
Roman Way CR0: Croy 4F 13
CT15: Evtn 6J 185
CT15: St Marg 8B 214
CT19: F'stone 5C 188
DA1: Cray 3F 58
ME2: Strood 8K 79
TN23: Kgnt 5F 160 (3A 40)
Romany Ct. ME5: Chat'm 1G 94
Romany Ri. BR5: Farnb 2E 84
Romany Rd. ME8: Gill 1L 95
Romborough Gdns. SE13 3F 54
Romborough Way SE13 3F 54
ROMDEN 8F 222 (1E 38)
Romden Rd. TN27: Smar 9D 222 (2E 38)
Rome Rd. TN28: New R 3J 213
Romero Sq. SE3 2M 55
Rome Ter. ME4: Chat'm 8C 80
ROMFORD 7E 152 (2B 36)
Romford Rd. E7 1K 5
E15 1K 5
RM15: Avel 3J 7
TN2: Pem 7C 152 (2B 36)
Romily Gdns. CT12: Ram 2G 211
Romney Av. CT20: F'stone 6F 188 (4A 42)
Romney Cl. CT7: Birch 4F 206
ME14: Bear 6K 127
Romney Ct. ME10: Sit 6E 98
Romney Dr. BR1: Brom 3N 69
Romney Gdns. DA7: Bexhth 8A 52
Romney, Hythe & Dymchurch Railway 7F 41
Romney Marsh Ho. TN29: Dym 8B 182
Romney Marsh Rd. TN23: Ashf 9G 158
TN23: Kgnt 5E 160 (2A 40)
Romney Pl. ME15: Maid 5D 126
Romney Rd. DA11: Nflt 8D 62
ME5: Chat'm 6E 94
SE10 5K 5
TN24: W'boro 9J 159
TN26: Hams 3L 191
TN29: Lydd 1L 205 (5H 47)
Romney Sands Holiday Village
TN28: G'stne 8M 213
Romney Sands Station
Romney, Hythe & Dymchurch Railway
6H 213 (5K 47)
ROMNEY STREET 2A 104 (6H 15)
Romney St. TN15: Knat 2A 104 (6H 15)
Romney St. Cvn. Pk. TN15: Knat 3A 104
Romney Toy & Model Mus., The 3J 47
Romney Way CT21: Hythe 7G 198
TN10: Tonb 2L 145
Romsey Cl. BR6: Farnb 5D 84
ME2: Strood 4J 79
TN24: W'boro 8L 159
Romulus Gdns. TN23: Ashf 5D 160
Ronald Cl. BR3: Beck'm 7C 68
Ronald Ho. SE3 2M 55
Ronalds Ct. ME10: Sit 7H 99
Ronalds Rd. BR1: Brom 4K 69
Ronaldstone Rd. DA15: Sidc 4G 57
Rondel Ct. DA5: Bex'y 4N 57
Ronfearn Av. BR5: St M Cry 8M 71
Ron Grn. Ct. DA8: Erith 6E 52
Ron Leighton Way E6 2B 6
Ronley Ct. TN13: S'oaks 3K 119
(off Hillingdon Av.)
Ronver Rd. SE12 6J 55
Roodlands La. TN8: Four E 6D 24
Rookdean TN13: Riv 4D 118
Rookery Cl. ME9: B'gar 4B 114
TN24: Kenn 3H 159
Rookery Cres. ME3: Cliffe 2C 176
Rookery Dr. BR7: Chst 4C 70
Rookery Gdns. BR5: St M Cry 8L 71
Rookery Hill SS17: Corr 2F 9
Rookery La. BR2: Shortl 9N 69
Rookery Lodge ME3: Cliffe 3C 176
Rookery Rd. BR6: Downe 1B 100 (5B 14)
Rookesley Rd. BR5: St M Cry 1M 85
Rook La. ME9: Bob 6N 97 (4D 18)
Rookley Cl. TN2: Tun W 3K 157
Rooks Hill TN15: Under 2C 132
(not continuous)
Roonagh Ct. ME10: Sit 9F 98
Roopers TN3: Speld 7A 150
Roosevelt Av. ME5: Chat'm 4C 94
Roosevelt Rd. CT16: Dover 1G 180
ROOTING STREET 2H 197 (7H 29)
Ropemakers Ct. ME4: Chat'm 2D 94

Roper Cl.—Rutland Gdns.

Roper Cl. CT2: Cant 1L 171
ME8: Gill 8M 95
Roper Rd. CT2: Cant 1L 171
ME9: Tey 6L 223
Roper's Ga. TN4: Tun W 4E 156
Roper's Grn. La. ME3: H Hals 5K 67
Roper's La. ME3: Hoo 5J 67 (7K 9)
Roper St. SE9 3B 56
Rope Wlk. ME4: Chat'm 7C 80
Ropewalk TN17: Cran 7C 176
Rope Wlk. M. CT13: S'wch 5L 217
Rope Wlk., The TN18: Sandh 3C 218
Rope Yd. Rails SE18 3D 50
ROSEACRE 5K 127 (2K 27)
Roseacre Cl. CT2: Cant 1L 171
Roseacre Ct. CT9: Clift 3J 209
Roseacre Gdns. ME14: Bear 5K 127
Roseacre La. ME14: Bear 6K 127 (2K 27)
Rose Acre Rd. CT3: L'brne 3L 173
Roseacre Rd. DA16: Well 1K 57
Rose Av. DA12: Grav'nd 6K 63
Rosebank Gdns. DA11: Nflt 6D 62
Rosebank Wlk. SE18 4A 50
Roseberry Gdns. BR6: Orp 4G 85
DA1: Dart 5K 59
Rosebery Av. CT6: H Bay 2M 195
CT11: Ram 3K 211
DA15: Sidc 5G 56
EC1 2F 5
Rosebery Cl. ME10: Sit 7L 99
Rosebery Ct. DA11: Grav'nd 6E 62
Rosebery Rd. ME4: Chat'm 1B 94
ME7: Gill 5G 80
Rose Cott. CT6: H Bay 4L 195
Rose Cotts. ME2: Roch 4F 78
Rosecroft Cl. BR5: St M Cry 9L 71
TN16: Big H 6F 164
Rosecroft Pk. TN3: Lang G 1A 156
Rose Dale BR6: Farnb 3D 84
Rosedale Cl. DA2: Dart 5B 60
SE2 3K 51
Rosedale Pl. CR0: Croy 1A 82
Rosedale Rd. CT9: Mgte 4E 208
Rosedene Ct. DA1: Dart 5K 59
Rose Farm Rd. TN27: P'ley 7F 29
Rosefield TN13: S'oaks 6H 119
Rose Gdns. CT6: H Bay 3K 195
CT7: Birch 5E 206
CT12: Minst 7E 212
CT15: Eyt 9L 185
Rosegarth DA13: Ist R 4D 76
ROSEHILL 3D 12
Rose Hill CT11: Ram 6J 211
CT15: Chill 3D 32
CT15: W Lan 2K 179 (6G 33)
SM1: Sutt 4C 12
TN30: Ston C E, Witter 3F 228 (2A 46)
Rosehill Rd. TN16: Big H 5C 164
ROSE HILL ROUNDABOUT 3D 12
Rosehill Wlk. TN1: Tun W 2G 156
Roseholme ME16: Maid 7A 126
Roselands CT14: Walm 9M 177
Roselands Gdns. CT2: Cant 9K 167
Rose La. CT1: Cant 2M 171
CT4: Bis 3K 31
ME17: Len 5F 29
Roselawn Gdns. CT9: Mgte 3N 207
Roselea Av. CT6: H Bay 4G 195
Roseleigh Av. ME16: Alltn 5N 125
Roseleigh Rd. ME10: Sit 1E 114
Rosemary Av. CT10: B'stairs 2K 211
ME12: Minst 6E 220
Rosemary Cl. ME5: Chat'm 7C 94
Rosemary Gdns. CT5: Whits 5J 227
CT10: B'stairs 2K 211
Rosemary La. CT1: Cant 2M 171
TN5: Flim 6F 37
TN15: Ash 9C 90 (5B 16)
TN27: Smar 7D 28
Rosemary Rd. DA16: Well 8H 51
ME15: Bear 6K 127
ME19: E Mal 9D 108
Rosemary Vs. CT20: F'stone 6L 189
(off Saffron's Pl.)
Rosemead Gdns. TN27: H'crn 7J 191
Rosemount Cl. ME15: Loose 4C 138
Rosemount Ct. ME2: Strood 3L 79
Rosemount Dr. BR1: Brom 7B 70
Rosemount Point SE23 8A 54
Rosendale Rd. SE21 7G 5
SE24 7G 5
Roseneath Cl. BR6: Chels 8L 85
Rosenthal Rd. SE6 4E 54
Rosenthorpe Rd. SE15 3A 54
Rosery, The CR0: Croy 9A 68
Rose St. DA11: Nflt 4A 62
ME1: Roch 9A 80
ME12: S'ness 2C 220
TN9: Tonb 7J 145
Rose Ter. ME3: Isle G 8C 190
ME13: Fav 7H 187
(off Canterbury Rd.)
Rosetower Ct. CT10: B'stairs 5K 209
Roseveare Rd. SE12 9M 55
Rose Vs. DA1: Dart 5B 60
TN28: New R 3K 213
Rose Wlk. BR4: W W'ck 3F 82
CT18: H'nge 8K 193
Rose Way SE12 3K 55
Rosewood DA2: Dart 9F 58
Rosewood Cl. DA14: Sidc 8L 57
Rosewood Ct. BR1: Brom 4M 69
Rosewood Dr. TN25: Ashf 6C 158
Rosewood Way CT7: Birch 4G 207
Rose Yd. ME14: Maid 5D 126
Rosher Ho. DA11: Nflt 4E 62
ROSHERVILLE 4E 62 (6B 8)
Rosherville Way DA11: Nflt 5D 62 (7B 8)
Rosiers Ct. CT2: Cant 1L 171
Roslin Way BR1: Brom 1K 69
Ross Ct. TN23: Ashf 3E 160
Rossdale TN2: Tun W 9J 151
Rossendale Ct. CT20: F'stone 5L 189
(off Dover Rd.)
Rossendale Gdns. CT20: F'stone 5L 189
Rossendale Rd. CT20: F'stone 5L 189
Rossetti Gdns. TN2: Tun W 4H 157
Rossetti Rd. CT7: Birch 3E 206
Ross Gdns. CT2: R Comn 8G 167
Rossland Cl. DA6: Bexhth 3C 58
Rossland Rd. CT12: Ram 4E 210
Rosslare Cl. TN16: Westrm 7F 116
Rosslyn Cl. BR4: W W'ck 4J 83
Rosslyn Grn. ME16: Alltn 4M 125
Rosslyn Hill NW3 1D 4
Rossmore Rd. NW1 2D 4
Ross Rd. DA1: Dart 4H 59
Ross St. ME1: Roch 8A 80
Ross Way CT20: F'stone 6E 188
SE9 1A 56
Rothbrook Dr. TN24: Kenn 3G 158
Rothbury Rd. E9 1J 5
ROTHERFIELD 7H 35
Rotherfield Rd. TN6: Jar B, Roth 7G 35
ROTHERHITHE 4H 5
Rotherhithe New Rd. SE16 4H 5
Rotherhithe Station (Tube) 4H 5
Rothermere Cl. TN17: Bendn 6A 38
Rother Rd. TN10: Tonb 2H 145
Rother Va. ME5: Chat'm 8F 94
Rothesay Ct. SE6 7J 55
(off Cumberland Pl.)
SE12 8L 55
Rothley Cl. TN30: Tent 7C 224
Rothsay Ct. CT11: Ram 3K 211
Rouge La. DA12: Grav'nd 6G 63
Rougemont ME19: W Mal 7A 124
ROUGH COMMON 8H 167 (7G 21)
Rough Comn. Rd. CT2: R Comn 9G 167 (7G 21)
Roughetts Rd. ME19: Rya 6K 107 (7D 16)
ROUGHWAY 2A 134 (3A 26)
Roughway La.
TN11: S'brne, Rough 2N 133 (3A 26)
Round Ash Way DA3: Hart'y 9L 75
Roundel Cl. ME9: Tey 7L 223
SE4 2C 54
Roundell Way TN12: Mard 3C 212
Roundels, The ME9: Lyn 9H 223
Roundel, The ME10: Sit 9G 98
ROUND GREEN 3H 37
Round Grn. La. TN17: Goud, Siss 3H 37
Round Gro. CR0: Croy 1A 82
Roundhay ME19: Leyb 9B 108
Roundhay Cl. SE23 7A 54
Roundhill Rd. TN2: Tun W 4K 157
Roundlyn Gdns. BR5: St M Cry 7K 71
ROUNDSHAW 5F 13
ROUND STREET 7J 77 (2C 16)
Round St. DA13: Sole S 6H 77 (2C 16)
Roundtable Rd. BR1: Brom 8J 55
Roundway TN16: Big H 4C 164
Roundwell ME14: Bear 5N 127 (2A 28)
Roundwood BR7: Chst 5D 70
Round Wood Cl. ME5: Chat'm 1D 110
Roundwood Rd. NW10 1A 4
Rover Rd. ME5: Chat'm 9E 94
Rowan Cl. CT2: Sturry 5E 168
CT3: S'le 1D 32
DA13: Meop 9G 76
ME20: Aylfd 9J 109
TN12: Pad W 1L 153
TN23: Ashf 8C 158
Rowan Cres. DA1: Dart 6K 59
Rowan Ho. BR2: Shortl 5H 69
DA14: Sidc 8H 57
ME5: Chat'm 6C 94
(off Gorse Av.)
ME16: Barm 6K 125
Rowan Lea ME5: Chat'm 3E 94
Rowan Rd. BR8: Swanl 6E 72
DA7: Bexhth 1N 57
SW16 2E 12
Rowans Cl. DA3: Long 5K 75
Rowan Shaw TN10: Tonb 1K 145
Rowans, The ME12: Minst 5J 221
Rowan Tree Pk. CT5: Seas 7C 226
Rowan Tree Rd. TN2: Tun W 4E 156
Rowan Wlk. BR2: Shortl 4B 84
ME4: Chat'm 9B 80
Rowanwood Av. DA15: Sidc 6J 57
Rowbrocke Cl. ME8: Gill 8N 95
Rowden Rd. BR3: Beck'm 4B 68
Rowdow TN14: Otf 7L 103 (7H 15)
Row Dow La. TN14: Knat 4L 103 (6G 15)
TN15: Knat 4L 103 (6G 15)
Rowdown Cres. CR0: Croy 9G 83
Rowe Cl. CT9: Mgte 6D 208
Rowena Rd. CT8: Wgte S 2K 207
Rowe Pl. ME20: Burh 4K 109
Rowetts Way ME12: E'chu 5B 202 (1K 19)
Rowfield TN8: Eden 4D 184
Rowhill Rd. BR8: Swanl 2G 73
DA2: Dart 2G 73
Rowland Av. ME7: Gill 1H 95
Rowland Cl. ME7: Gill 2H 95
ME16: Maid 6B 126
Rowland Cotts. CT21: Lymp 5A 198
Rowland Cres. CT6: H Bay 2M 195
Rowland Dr. CT6: H Bay 5D 194
Rowlatt Cl. DA2: Dart 9K 59
Rowlatt Rd. DA2: Dart 9K 59
Rowley Av. DA15: Sidc 5K 57
Rowley Hill TN2: Pem 5C 152
Rowley Rd. RM16: Ors 3C 8
ROWLING 2D 32
ROWLING STREET 4A 40
Rowman Ct. CT10: B'stairs 8L 209
Rownmarsh Cl. DA11: Nflt 8C 62
Rowntree Path SE28 1K 51
Row, The CT4: Elham 7N 183 (7J 31)
DA3: New A 3M 89
TN8: Eden 3B 184
Rowton Rd. SE18 7E 50
Rowzill Rd. BR8: Swanl 2G 72
Roxborough Rd. CT8: Wgte S 2L 207
Roxley Rd. SE13 4E 54
Roxton Gdns. CR0: Croy 6D 82
Royal Albert Station (DLR) 3A 6
Royal Albert Way E16 3A 6
Royal Av. CT5: Whits 8E 226
TN9: Tonb 7J 145
Royal Brass Foundry 3D 50
ROYAL BRITISH LEGION VILLAGE
1L 125 (1G 27)
Royal Chase TN4: Tun W 1F 156
Royal Cinema, The 5H 187
(off Middle Row)
Royal Cinque Ports Golf Course 2J 33
Royal Cl. BR6: Farnb 5D 84
CT10: B'stairs 9K 209
Royal Ct. ME12: S'ness 2D 220
SE9 6B 56
Royal Cres. CT9: Mgte 3B 208
CT11: Ram 7H 211
Royal Docks Rd. E6 3B 6
IG11: Bark 3B 6
Royal Eagle Cl. ME2: Med E 5B 80
Royal Engineers Mus. 5E 80 (2J 17)
Royal Engineers Rd.
ME14: S'lng, Maid 9B 110 (1H 27)
Royal Esplanade CT9: Mgte 2L 207 (1G 23)
CT11: Ram 7F 210
Royal Harbour App. CT11: Ram 6E 210 (4J 23)
CT12: Ram 4J 23
Royal Herbert Pavilions SE18 8B 50
Royal Hill SE10 5K 5
Royal Hospital Rd. SW3 5D 4
Royal Military Av. CT20: F'stone 6D 188 (4K 41)
Royal Military Rd. CT21: Hythe 6L 199
(Twiss Rd.)
CT21: Hythe, W Hyt 7A 198
(Aldergate La.)
TN36: Winch 7A 46
Royal Mint St. E1 3G 5
Royal Mus. & Art Gallery, The 2M 171
Royal Oak Camping and Cvn.
CT2: B Oak 3C 168
Royal Oak Hill TN14: Knock 9H 101
Royal Oak Rd. DA6: Bexhth 3A 58
(not continuous)
Royal Oak Station (Tube) 3C 4
Royal Oak Ter. DA12: Grav'nd 6H 63
(off Constitution Hill)
Royal Pde. BR7: Chst 3E 70 (1C 14)
CT11: Ram 6J 211 (4K 23)
SE3 5K 5
Royal Pde. M. BR7: Chst 3E 70
(off Royal Pde.)
Royal Pier M. DA12: Grav'nd 4H 63
Royal Pier Rd. DA12: Grav'nd 4G 63
Royal Ri. TN9: Tonb 7J 145
Royal Rd. CT11: Ram 6H 211 (4J 23)
DA2: Dart 1A 74
DA14: Sidc 8M 57
ME12: S'ness 2D 220
Royal St George's Golf Course 1H 33
Royal Sovereign Av. ME4: Chat'm 5E 80
Royal Star Arc. ME14: Maid 5C 126
ROYAL TUNBRIDGE WELLS 3G 157 (3K 35)
Royal Tunbridge Wells Bus. Pk.
TN2: Tun W 5L 151
Royal Tunbridge Wells District
Indoor Bowls Club, The 3L 157
Royal Victoria Hall 5G 150
Royal Victoria Pl. CT16: Dover 4J 181
(off Maison Dieu Pl.)
TN1: Tun W 1H 157
Royal Victoria Station (DLR) 3A 6
Royal W. Kent Av. TN10: Tonb 3K 145
Royal West Kent Regiment Mus.
ME14: Maid 4C 126
Roydene Rd. SE18 6G 50
Roydon Hall Rd. TN12: E Peck 3K 135 (4D 26)
Royds Rd. TN24: Ashf 3H 161
Royston Gdns. CT15: St Marg 7B 214
Royston Rd. DA1: Cray 4G 58
ME15: Bear 6K 127
SE20 4A 68
Roystons Cl. ME8: Rain 1B 96
Roystons, The KT5: Surb 3A 12
Royton Av. ME17: Len 7M 201
Rubens St. SE6 7C 54
Rubery Drove CT13: Ash 6F 23
Rubin Pl. ME19: W Mal 6N 123
Ruckholt Rd. E10 1J 5
RUCKINGE 6J 40
Ruckinge Rd. TN25: Bils 5B 40
TN26: Hams 3L 191 (6A 40)
Ruckinge Way ME8: Gill 9M 81
Ruck La. TN12: Horsm 3E 36
Ruddstreet Cl. SE18 4E 50
Rudge Cl. ME5: Chat'm 9G 94
Rudgwick Ct. SE18 4A 50
(off Woodville St., not continuous)
Rudland Rd. DA7: Bexhth 1C 58
Ruegg Ho. SE18 6C 50
(off Woolwich Comn.)
Ruffets Wood DA12: Grav'nd 2H 77
Ruffetts Wood TN23: Kgnt 6G 160
Rugby Cl. CT10: B'stairs 8K 209
ME5: Chat'm 7C 94
Rugby Gdns. TN23: Ashf 1G 160
Rugby Rd. CT17: Dover 6F 180
Ruggles Cl. ME3: H Hals 2H 67
Ruins Barn Rd. ME9: B'gar, T'stall 6D 114 (7E 18)
ME10: T'stall 6D 114 (7E 18)
Rule Ct. ME12: S'ness 4C 220
Rumania Wlk. DA12: Grav'nd 8L 63
Rumfields Rd. CT10: B'stairs 9G 209 (3J 23)
Rumstead La. ME9: S'bry 8E 112 (7B 18)
Rumstead Rd. ME9: S'bry 6F 112 (7B 18)
Rumwood Ct. ME17: L'ly 3M 139
Runcie Ho. CT1: Cant 3M 171
(off Station Rd. E.)
Runcie Pl. CT2: Cant 1K 171
Runciman Cl. BR6: Prat B 1L 101
Runham La. ME17: H'shm 6N 141 (4D 28)
Running Horse Rdbt.
ME14: S'lng 9B 110
Runnymede Ct. DA2: Dart 6C 60
Runnymede Gdns. ME15: Maid 9D 126
Runnymede M. ME13: Fav 5G 186
Rural Ter. TN25: Wye 2M 159
Rural Va. DA11: Nflt 5D 62
Ruscombe Cl. TN4: S'bgh 4F 150
Rusham Rd. CT3: Shtng 6L 225 (7C 22)
Rushbrook TN27: P'ley 7G 29
Rushbrook Rd. SE9 7E 56
Rush Cl. ME5: Chat'm 8D 94
TN29: Dym 9A 182
Rushdean Rd. ME2: Strood 7H 79
Rushdene SE2 3M 51
(not continuous)
Rushdene Wlk. TN16: Big H 5D 164
RUSHENDEN 9A 220 (1F 19)
Rushenden Ct. ME11: Queen 9A 220
Rushenden Rd. ME11: Queen 9A 220 (1F 19)
Rushes, The ME20: Lark 6F 108
Rushet Rd. BR5: St P 5J 71
RUSHETT 5B 24
Rushett La. ME13: Osp 6J 19
Rushetts TN3: Lang G 1N 155
Rushetts Rd. TN15: W King 8E 88
Rushey Grn. SE6 5E 54 (7J 5)
Rushey Mead SE4 3D 54
Rushford Cl. TN27: H'crn 8K 191
Rushford Rd. SE4 4C 54
Rushgrove St. SE18 4B 50
Rushley Cl. BR2: Kes 5N 83
Rushlye Cl. TN3: Bell G 8M 157
Rushmead Cl. CT2: Cant 9K 167
Rushmead Dr. ME15: Maid 1D 138
Rushmere Ct. TN15: Igh 2K 121
Rushmore Cl. BR1: Brom 6A 70
Rushmore Hill BR6: Prat B 9L 85 (5D 14)
TN14: Knock, Prat B 3M 101 (5D 14)
Rushymead TN15: Kems'g 9A 104
Ruskin Av. DA16: Well 9J 51
Ruskin Cl. ME19: E Mal 1D 124
Ruskin Dr. BR6: Orp 4G 84
DA16: Well 1J 57
Ruskin Gro. DA1: Dart 3A 60
DA16: Well 9J 51
Ruskin Rd. DA17: Belv 4B 52
SM5: Cars 4E 12
Ruskins Vw. CT6: H Bay 6H 195
Ruskin Ter. CT16: Dover 1G 181
Ruskin Wlk. BR2: Shortl 9B 70
Rusland Av. BR6: Orp 4F 84
Russell Cl. BR3: Beck'm 6E 68
DA1: Cray 2H 59
DA7: Bexhth 2B 58
ME10: Sit 8D 98
Russell Ct. ME4: Chat'm 9E 80
Russell Dr. CT5: Whits 2M 227
Russell Pl. DA4: S at H 4A 74
ME13: Oare 1F 186
Russell Rd. CT19: F'stone 5K 189
DA12: Grav'nd 4J 63
ME20: Aylfd 3A 110
Russell's Av. ME8: Rain 3C 96
Russell Sq. DA3: Long 6K 75
Russell Square Station (Tube) 2F 5
Russell St. CT16: Dover 4K 181
ME12: S'ness 2C 220
(not continuous)
WC1 3F 5
Russells Yd. TN17: Cran 8D 176
Russell Ter. DA4: Hort K 7C 74
Russet Av. ME13: Fav 7J 187
Russet Cl. ME2: Strood 4J 79
Russet Ct. ME17: Cox 5N 137
Russet Dr. CR0: Croy 2B 82
Russets, The CT5: Whits 4M 227
DA13: Meop 9F 76
ME16: Alltn 4M 125
Russett Cl. BR6: Chels 6K 85
ME20: Aylfd 1J 125
Russett Rd. CT1: Cant 3B 172
TN12: E Peck 1L 147
Russett Way BR8: Swanl 5E 72
Russet Way ME19: W Mal 7L 123
RUSTHALL 1C 156 (3J 35)
Rusthall Grange TN4: R'hall 1D 156
Rusthall Pk. TN4: R'hall, Tun W 1D 156
(not continuous)
Rusthall Pl. TN4: R'hall 2D 156
Rusthall Rd. TN4: R'hall 1C 156 (3J 35)
Ruston Rd. SE18 3A 50
Rustwick TN4: R'hall 1D 156
Rutherford College
University of Kent at Canterbury 7L 167
Rutherford Rd. TN25: Ashf 5F 158
Rutherford Way TN10: Tonb 9K 133
Rutherglen Rd. SE2 6J 51
Ruth Ho. ME16: Maid 4B 126
Ruth St. ME4: Chat'm 1D 94
Rutland Av. CT9: Clift 3F 208
DA15: Sidc 5J 57
Rutland Cl. DA1: Dart 5L 59
DA5: Bex'y 7M 57
Rutland Cotts. ME17: Leeds 3A 140
Rutland Ct. BR7: Chst 4C 70
SE9 7E 56
Rutland Gdns. CT7: Birch 4E 206
CT9: Clift 3G 208

A-Z Kent Atlas 295

Rutland Ga.—St John's Rd.

Rutland Ga. BR2: Shortl 7J 69
DA17: Belv 5C 52
Rutland Ho. CT1: Cant 3N 171
Rutland Pk. SE6 7C 54
Rutland Pl. ME8: Gill 8M 95
Rutland Rd. CT1: Cant 3C 172
CT16: Dover 1G 180
Rutland Wlk. SE6 7C 54
Rutland Way BR5: St M Cry 9L 71
ME15: Maid 9H 127
RUXLEY 3N 71 (1E 14)
Ruxley Cl. DA14: Sidc 2M 71
Ruxley Cnr. Ind. Est. DA14: Sidc 2M 71
Ruxley La. KT19: Eps 5A 12
Ruxton Cl. BR8: Swanl 6F 72
Ruxton Ct. BR8: Swanl 6F 72
Ryan Cl. SE3 2L 55
Ryan Dr. ME15: Bear 7K 127
RYARSH 6M 107 (7D 16)
Ryarsh Cres. BR6: Orp 5G 85
Ryarsh La. ME19: W Mal 9N 107
Ryarsh Pk. Ind. Est. ME19: Rya 6L 107
Ryarsh Rd. ME19: Birl 5N 107 (6D 16)
Rycault Cl. ME16: Maid 6B 126
Rycaut Cl. ME8: Gill 8N 95
Rycroft La. TN14: S'oaks 3F 130 (3F 25)
Rydal Av. CT11: Ram 5E 210
Rydal Cl. TN4: Tun W 9E 150
Rydal Dr. BR4: W W'ck 3H 83
DA7: Bexhth 8B 52
TN4: Tun W 9E 150
Rydal Ho. ME15: Maid 1G 139
Rydal Mt. BR2: Shortl 7J 69
Ryde Cl. ME5: Chat'm 3E 94
Rydens Ho. SE9 8M 55
(off Gro. Park Rd.)
Ryder Cl. BR1: Brom 1L 69
Ryders TN3: Lang G 2A 156
Ryder's Av. CT8: Wgte S 3J 207
Ryde St. CT2: Cant 1L 171
Rydons Cl. SE9 1A 56
RYE 5B 46
Rye Cl. DA5: Bex'y 4C 58
Rye Ct. TN23: Ashf 2B 160
Rye Cres. BR5: Orp 2L 85
Ryecroft DA3: Long H 7C 76
DA12: Grav'nd 1K 77
Ryecroft Rd. BR5: Pet W 9F 70
SE13 3F 54
TN14: Otf 8H 103
Rye Fld. BR5: Orp 2M 85
RYE FOREIGN 4K 45
Rye Golf Course 6C 46
Ryegrass Cl. ME5: Chat'm 5F 94
RYE HARBOUR 6B 46
Rye Harbour Rd. TN31: Rye 6B 46
Rye Hill TN31: Play, Rye 5A 46
Ryelands Cres. SE12 4M 55
Rye La. SE15 5H 5
TN14: Dun G, Otf 2G 118 (1F 25)
Rye Lane Pottery 2G 119
Rye Rd. SE15 2A 54
TN18: Hawkh, Sandh 1A 218 (7J 37)
TN18: Sandh 3D 218 (1F 45)
TN29: B'lnd 3E 46
(not continuous)
TN30: Witter 4F 228 (3A 46)
TN31: N'thiam 3G 45
TN31: Rye F 4K 45
Rye Station (Rail) 5A 46
Rye St. ME3: Cliffe 3E 176
Rye Wlk. CT6: H Bay 5K 195
Ryewood Cotts. TN14: Dun G 2G 118
Ryland Ct. CT20: F'stone 6L 189
(off Ryland Pl.)
Ryland Pl. CT20: F'stone 6L 189
Rylands Rd. TN24: Kenn 4H 159
Rymers Cl. TN2: Tun W 7K 151
Rymill St. E16 1C 50
Rype Cl. TN29: Lydd 4K 205
(not continuous)
Rysted La. TN16: Westrm 8E 116
Ryswick M. TN28: New R 1L 213

S

Sabre Ct. ME8: Gill 2K 95
Sackett's Gap CT9: Clift 2G 209
Sacketts Hill CT10: B'stairs 7F 208
Sackville Av. BR2: Shortl 2K 83
Sackville Cl. TN13: S'oaks 4J 119
TN26: Hoth 2M 197
Sackville Cres. TN23: Ashf 8E 158
Sackville Rd. DA2: Dart 7L 59
Saddington St. DA12: Grav'nd 5G 63
Saddlers Cl. ME14: Weav 4H 127
Saddlers Hill CT3: Good 2C 32
Saddlers M. CT5: Whits 4M 227
Saddler's Pk. DA4: Eyns 4L 87
Saddlers, The TN25: S'ndge 8A 218
Saddlers Wall La. TN29: Snar, B'lnd 3D 46
Saddlers Way TN23: Kgnt 4F 160
Saddleton Gro. CT5: Whits 5F 226
Saddleton Rd. CT5: Whits 5F 226
Sadlers Cl. ME5: Chat'm 9A 94
Saffron's Pl. CT20: F'stone 6L 189
Saffron Way ME5: Chat'm 6C 94
ME10: Sit 4G 99 (4F 19)
Sage Rd. ME1: Roch 9L 79
Sail Fld. Ct. ME4: Chat'm 5D 80
Sail Lofts, The CT5: Whits 3F 226
Sailmakers Ct. ME4: Chat'm 1E 94
St Agnes Gdns. ME12: S'ness 3D 220
St Aidan's Way DA12: Grav'nd 8K 63
St Alban's Cl. DA12: Grav'nd 8J 63
St Albans Cl. ME7: Gill 5H 81
St Albans Downs Rd. CT15: Non, Chill 4D 32
St Alban's Gdns. DA12: Grav'nd 8J 63
St Albans Rd. CT3: Hersd 2K 169
St Alban's Rd. DA1: Dart 5N 59
ME2: Strood 6H 79
St Albans Wlk. ME4: Chat'm 9B 80
St Alphege Cl. CT5: Whits 6D 226
St Alphege La. CT1: Cant 1M 171
St Alphege Rd. CT16: Dover 3H 181
St Ambrose Grn. TN25: Wye 2M 159
St Ames Levett Sports Cen. 4A 172
St Amunds Cl. SE6 9D 54
St Andrews CT19: F'stone 6L 189
St Andrews Cl. CT1: Cant 3L 171
St Andrew's Cl. CT5: Whits 6G 226
CT6: H Bay 3H 195
CT9: Mgte 6D 208
CT19: F'stone 4H 189
ME16: Maid 7L 125
TN12: Pad W 9M 147
St Andrews Ct. BR8: Swanl 6F 72
St Andrew's Ct. DA12: Grav'nd 4G 63
(off Queen St.)
St Andrews Ct. TN4: S'bgh 5G 150
St Andrew's Dr. BR5: St M Cry 9K 71
St Andrew's Gardens 4G 63
St Andrew's Gdns. CT15: S'wll 7L 219
St Andrews Gdns. CT17: Dover 2F 180
St Andrews Ho. ME16: Maid 6L 125
St Andrews Lees CT13: S'wch 6M 217
St Andrew's Pk. Rd. TN4: S'bgh 5G 150
St Andrew's Rd. CT11: Ram 4K 211
CT14: Deal 4M 177
DA12: Grav'nd 5G 63
DA14: Sidc 8M 57
St Andrews Rd. ME7: Gill 5G 80
St Andrew's Rd. ME16: Maid 7L 125
RM18: Tilb 1E 62 (5B 8)
TN12: Pad W 9M 147
TN28: L'stne 3M 213 (3J 47)
St Andrew's Wlk. ME3: Allh 4D 204
St Andrews Way CT14: Tilm 4F 33
St Andrew Ter. CT17: Dover 2F 180
St Anne Ct. ME16: Maid 5B 126
St Anne's Ct. BR4: W W'ck 5H 83
CT6: H Bay 2F 194
St Anne's Dr. CT6: H Bay 3E 194
St Anne's Gdns. CT9: Mgte 5D 208
St Anne's Rd. CT5: Whits 2H 227 (3F 21)
TN23: Ashf 2D 160
ST ANN'S GREEN 7H 27
St Ann's Grn. La. TN12: Mard 7H 27
St Ann's Hill SW18 6C 4
St Ann's Rd. ME13: Fav 5F 186
TN29: Dym 8A 182
St Anns Way TN16: Big H 7D 100
St Anthony's Ct. BR6: Farnb 3D 84
St Anthony's Way CT9: Mgte 4G 208
St Asaph Ho. ME15: Maid 1G 139
St Asaph Rd. SE4 1A 54 (6H 5)
St Aubyn's Cl. BR6: Orp 4H 85
St Aubyn's Gdns. BR6: Orp 3H 85
St Audrey Av. DA7: Bexhth 9B 52
St Augustine Ho. TN9: Tonb 7H 145
(off Priory Rd.)
St Augustine's Abbey (Ruins) 2N 171 (1H 31)
St Augustine's Av. BR2: Shortl 8A 70
CT9: Mgte 5D 208
St Augustines Bus. Pk. CT5: Whits 3N 227
St Augustine's Ct. CT1: Cant 1A 172
St Augustines Ct. CT6: H Bay 4G 195
St Augustine's Cres. CT5: Whits 2M 227
St Augustine's Cross 7A 210
St Augustine's Pk. CT11: Ram 6G 210
St Augustine's Rd. CT1: Cant 3A 172
CT11: Ram 7H 211 (4J 23)
CT14: Deal 6J 177
DA17: Belv 4A 52 (4E 6)
St Barnabas Cl. BR3: Beck'm 5F 68
ME7: Gill 9G 81
ME16: Alltn 1N 125
TN1: Tun W 9J 151
TN23: Ashf 2D 160
St Barnabas Rd. SM1: Sutt 4D 12
St Bartholomews CT13: S'wch 6M 217
St Bartholomew's Cl. CT17: Dover 4H 181
St Bartholomews La. ME1: Roch 8B 80
St Bartholomews Ter. ME1: Roch 8B 80
St Bart's Rd. CT13: S'wch 6K 217 (1G 33)
St Benedict Rd. ME6: Snod 3C 108
St Benedict's Av. DA12: Grav'nd 7J 63
St Benedict's Lawn CT11: Ram 7H 211
St Benets Ct. TN30: Tent 7C 224
St Benet's Rd. CT8: Wgte S 4K 207
St Benets Way TN30: Tent 7C 224
St Benjamins Dr. BR6: Prat B 9L 85
St Bernards Rd. TN10: Tonb 1J 145
St Blaise Av. BR1: Brom 5L 69 (2A 14)
St Botolph Rd. DA11: Nflt 8C 62
St Botolph's Av. TN13: S'oaks 6H 119
St Botolph's Rd. TN13: S'oaks 6J 119 (2G 25)
St Brelade's Mobile Home Pk. TN8: Eden 4A 184
St Brides Cl. DA18: Erith 2M 51
St Catherine's TN29: Old R 3G 47
(off Swamp Rd.)
St Catherines Ct. CT11: Ram 3J 211
St Catherine's Dr. ME13: Fav 6H 187
St Catherine's Gro. CT12: Mans 3B 210
St Catherines Hospital ME1: Roch 8A 80
St Chad's Dr. DA12: Grav'nd 8K 63
St Chads Rd. RM16: Grays 5C 8
RM18: Grays, Tilb 5C 8
St Christopher Cl. CT9: Mgte 5H 209
St Christopher's Grn. CT10: B'stairs 8K 209
St Clare Rd. CT14: Walm 9M 177 (4J 33)
St Clements CT13: S'wch 6M 217
St Clement's Ct. DA11: Nflt 8E 62
St Clements Cl. ME12: Ley S 6J 203
St Clements Ct. CT6: H Bay 4H 195
CT10: B'stairs 8J 209
CT19: F'stone 6M 189
St Clements Ho. ME1: Roch 7A 80
St Clements Rd. CT8: Wgte S 2K 207
ME12: Ward 5K 203
St Clements Way DA2: Bean, Bluew 7G 61
DA9: Bluew 3G 61 (7K 7)
St Clere Hill Rd. TN15: W King 3F 104 (6J 15)
St Columba's Cl. DA12: Grav'nd 8J 63
(not continuous)
St Cosmus Cl. TN25: C'lck 8D 174
St Crispin's Rd. CT8: Wgte S 4K 207
St Daniel Ct. BR3: Beck'm 3D 68
(off Brackley Rd.)
St David's Av. CT17: Dover 8F 180
St David's Bri. TN17: Cran 8D 176 (5J 37)
St David's Cl. BR4: W W'ck 1E 82
CT5: Whits 5G 227
CT7: Birch 3G 207
St David's Cres. DA12: Grav'nd 9J 63
St David's Ho. ME15: Maid 1G 139
St Davids Rd. BR8: Swanl 2G 72 (1F 15)
St David's Rd. CT11: Ram 3K 211
CT14: Deal 4M 177
ME3: Allh 4D 204
TN4: Tun W 7H 151
St Denys Rd. CT18: H'nge 7L 193
St Domingo Ho. SE18 3B 50
(off Leda Rd.)
ST DUNSTAN'S 1K 171 (7G 21)
ST DUNSTAN'S 5C 12
St Dunstans Av. W3 3A 4
St Dunstans Cl. CT2: Cant 1L 171
St Dunstans Ct. CT2: Cant 1L 171
St Dunstan's Dr. DA12: Grav'nd 9K 63
St Dunstan's Hill SM1: Sutt 5C 12
St Dunstan's La. BR3: Beck'm 9F 68
St Dunstan's Rd. CT9: Mgte 3E 208
St Dunstan's St. CT2: Cant 1L 171 (7H 21)
St Dunstan's Ter. CT2: Cant 1L 171
St Dunstan's Wlk. TN17: Cran 8D 176
St Eanswythe's Way CT20: F'stone 6K 189
St Edith Cotts. TN15: Kems'g 7H 105
St Edith's Farm Cotts. TN15: Kems'g 9B 104
St Edith's Rd. TN15: Kems'g 9A 104 (7H 15)
St Edmunds Cl. DA18: Erith 2M 51
St Edmund's Ct. TN15: W King 9F 88
St Edmunds Rd. CT1: Cant 2M 171
St Edmund's Rd. CT14: Deal 6H 177
DA1: Dart 2A 60
St Edmunds Wlk. CT17: Dover 4J 181
(off Priory Rd.)
St Edmunds Way ME8: Rain 2C 96
St Faith's La. ME14: Bear 5L 127
St Faith's St. ME14: Maid 5C 126
St Fidelis Rd. DA8: Erith 4E 52
St Fillans Rd. SE6 6F 54
St Francis Av. DA12: Grav'nd 9K 63
St Francis Cl. BR5: Pet W 9G 70
CT9: Mgte 5H 209
CT14: Deal 6H 177
ME2: Strood 6J 79
ME14: Pen H 2E 126
St Francis Rd. CT19: F'stone 5F 188
DA8: Erith 4E 52
DA13: Meop 8G 91
St Gabriel's Ct. CT20: F'stone 6L 189
(off Dover Rd.)
St George's Av. CT6: H Bay 3D 194
St Georges Av. ME12: E'chu 6C 202
St George's Av. ME12: S'ness 4C 220 (7F 11)
St Georges Bus. Cen. TN23: Ashf 8D 158
St Georges Bus. Pk. ME10: Sit 7J 99
St Georges Cen. 4D 80
St George's Cen. CT1: Cant 2N 171
St Georges Cl. CT5: Whits 6G 227
St Georges Ct. CT17: Dover 2F 180
ME12: S'ness 4C 220
TN15: Wro 7M 105
St George's Cres. CT17: Dover 7G 180
DA12: Grav'nd 9J 63
St George's Dr. SW1 4E 4
St George's La. CT1: Cant 2M 171 (1H 31)
St George's Lees CT13: S'wch 6M 217
(not continuous)
St George's M. TN9: Tonb 7H 145
St Georges Pde. SE6 7C 54
St George's Pk. TN2: Tun W 5F 156
St George's Pas. CT14: Deal 4N 177
St George's Path SE4 2D 54
(off Adelaide Av.)
St George's Pl. CT1: Cant 2N 171 (1H 31)
St Georges Pl. CT13: S'wch 6N 217
CT15: St Marg 7B 214
St George's Pl. CT21: Hythe 8E 198
St George's Rd. BR1: Brom 5B 70
BR3: Beck'm 4E 68
BR5: Pet W 9F 70
St Georges Rd. BR8: Swanl 7G 72
St George's Rd. CT10: B'stairs 9L 209
CT11: Ram 4K 211
CT13: S'wch 6M 217 (1G 33)
CT14: Deal 4M 177
St Georges Rd. CT19: F'stone 5F 188
St George's Rd. DA14: Sidc 2M 71
E7 1A 6
ME7: Gill 6F 80
SE1 4F 5
TN13: S'oaks 4J 119
St George's Rd. W. BR1: Brom 4A 70
St George's Shop. Cen. DA11: Grav'nd 4G 62
St Georges Sq. DA3: Long 6L 75
DA11: Grav'nd 4G 62
St George's Sq. ME16: Maid 6A 126
St Georges Sq. TN24: Ashf 8F 158
(off Castle St.)
St George's St. CT1: Cant 2N 171
St George's Ter. CT6: H Bay 2E 194
St Georges Ter. CT19: F'stone 5F 188
St George's Wlk. ME3: Allh 4D 204
St German's Rd. SE23 6B 54
St Giles Cl. BR6: Farnb 6F 84
CT17: Dover 7G 180
St Giles Rd. CT17: Dover 7G 180
St Giles Wlk. CT17: Dover 7G 180
St Gregory's Cl. CT14: Deal 6J 177
St Gregory's Ct. CT1: Cant 1A 172
DA12: Grav'nd 7K 63
St Gregory's Cres. DA12: Grav'nd 7K 63
St Gregory's Rd. CT1: Cant 1A 172
St Helen's Cotts. ME15: E Far 9J 125
St Helens La. ME15: E Far 9J 125 (3G 27)
St Helen's Rd. DA18: Erith 2M 51
St Helens Rd. ME3: Cliffe 3C 176
St Helen's Rd. ME12: S'ness 3D 220 (6G 11)
ST HELIER 3D 12
St Helier Av. SM4: Mord 3D 12
St Helier's Cl. ME16: Maid 7M 125
St Helier Station (Rail) 3C 12
St Hilda Rd. CT19: F'stone 5E 188
St Hildas TN15: Plax 9M 121
St Hildas Rd. CT21: Hythe 7J 199
St Hilda's Way DA12: Grav'nd 9J 63
St Hugh Ter. CT18: H'nge 8J 193
(off St Michael's Wlk.)
St Jacob's Pl. CT1: Cant 4K 171
St James Av. CT10: B'stairs 8J 209
St Jame's Av. CT12: Ram 2F 210
St James Cl. ME3: Isle G 7C 190
ME12: Ward 4K 203
ME19: E Mal 1D 124
SE18 5E 50
TN10: Tonb 9K 133
St James Ct. DA9: G'hithe 4F 60
TN1: Tun W 1H 157
St James Gdns. CT5: Whits 5F 226
St James La. CT16: Dover 5K 181
DA9: Dart, G'hithe 6E 60 (7J 7)
St James Oak DA11: Grav'nd 5F 62
St James' Pk. TN1: Tun W 9J 151
St James Pk. Rd. CT9: Mgte 3M 207
St James Pl. DA1: Dart 4L 59
St James Rd. CT14: Kgdn 4F 200
ME3: Isle G 8C 190
St James' Rd. TN1: Tun W 9H 151
St James Rd. TN13: S'oaks 4J 119
ST JAMES'S 3E 4
St James's Av. BR3: Beck'm 6B 68
DA11: Grav'nd 5F 62
St James's Church 4K 181
St James's Dr. SW17 7D 4
St James's Pk. 4E 4
St James's Park Station (Tube) 4E 4
St James Sq. DA3: Long 6L 75
(off Park Dr.)
TN5: Wadh 7C 36
St James's Rd. CR0: Croy 3F 13
DA11: Grav'nd 4F 62
SE1 4H 5
St James's St. DA11: Grav'nd 4F 62
W1 3E 4
St James's Ter. CT7: Birch 3G 207
(Sea Rd.)
St James St. CT16: Dover 5K 181
(not continuous)
St James Ter. BR6: Prat B 9L 85
(off St Benjamins Dr.)
CT7: Birch 3G 207
(Canterbury Rd.)
St James Way DA14: Sidc 1N 71
St Jean's Rd. CT8: Wgte S 4K 207
St John Fisher Rd. DA18: Erith 3M 51
ST JOHN'S
Crowborough 7F 35
Sevenoaks 4K 119 (1G 25)
Tunbridge Wells 9G 150 (2K 35)
ST JOHNS 5J 5
St John's Almshouses CT1: Cant 1N 171
St John's Av. CT12: Ram 3D 210
ME10: Sit 8J 99
St John's Chu. Rd. CT19: F'stone 5J 189
St John's Cl. CT18: D'sole 5K 193
DA3: Hart'y 8M 75
ME3: High'm 9G 65
St Johns Cl. TN16: Big H 7D 100
St John's Cotts. TN26: Beth 2J 163
St John's Ct. CT1: Cant 2M 171
DA8: Erith 4E 52
TN13: S'oaks 4K 119
TN24: Svgtn 2L 161
St Johns Cres. CT2: T Hill 4K 167
St John's Gro. N19 1E 4
St John's Hill SW11 6D 4
TN13: S'oaks 3K 119 (1G 25)
St John's Jerusalem Garden 3B 74 (1H 15)
St John's La. CT1: Cant 2M 171
DA3: Hart'y 9M 75
St Johns La. TN23: Ashf 8G 158
St Johns Pde. DA14: Sidc 9J 57
(off Sidcup High St.)
St John's Pk. TN4: Tun W 6G 150
St John's Pl. CT1: Cant 1N 171
St Johns Ri. TN16: Big H 7D 100
St John's Rd. BR5: Pet W 9F 70
CT5: Whits 3M 227 (3G 21)
CT9: Mgte 3D 208
St Johns Rd. CT15: Evtn 6J 185
St John's Rd. CT17: Dover 5H 181
CT21: Hythe 5H 199
DA2: Dart 5C 60
DA8: Erith 5E 52
DA12: Grav'nd 5J 63
DA14: Sidc 9K 57
DA16: Well 1K 57
ME3: High'm 9G 65
St Johns Rd. ME3: Hoo 7G 67
St John's Rd. ME7: Gill 9F 80
ME13: Fav 6H 187
TN4: S'bgh 6G 150
TN4: Tun W 8G 150 (2K 35)

St John's Rd.—Salter Rd.

St John's Rd. TN6: Crowb .7F 35
TN13: S'oaks .3J 119
TN28: New R .3J 213
St Johns Station (Rail) .5J 5
St John's St. CT9: Mgte .3D 208
CT20: F'stone .6K 189
St John's Ter. CT19: F'stone .5K 189
(off St John's Chu. Rd.)
SE18 .6E 50
St John St. EC1 .2F 5
St John's Way CT18: D'sole .5J 193
St Johns Way ME1: Roch .1L 93
(not continuous)
ST JOHN'S WOOD .2D 4
St John's Wood Rd. NW8 .2D 4
St John's Wood Station (Tube) .2D 4
St Joseph's Cl. BR6: Orp .5H 85
St Joseph's Va. SE3 .1G 55
St Julians Rd.
TN15: S'oaks, Under .3M 131 (3H 25)
St Julien Av. CT1: Cant .1C 172
St Justin Cl. BR5: St P .6M 71
St Katherine Rd. ME12: Minst .5F 220
St Katherine's La. ME6: Snod .3D 108 (6E 16)
St Katherine's Rd. DA18: Erith .2M 51
St Keverne Rd. SE9 .9A 56
St Kilda Rd. BR6: Orp .2H 85
St Laurence Av. ME16: Alltn .1M 125
St Laurence Cl. BR5: St P .6M 71
ST LAWRENCE .5G 210 (4J 23)
St Lawrence Av. CT11: Ram .6F 210
TN4: Bidb .3D 150
St Lawrence Cl. CT1: Cant .4A 172
ME9: Bap .9L 99
St Lawrence Ct. CT1: Cant .4A 172
CT11: Ram .5F 210
St Lawrence Forstal CT1: Cant .4A 172
St Lawrence Ground .4A 172
St Lawrence Ind. Est. CT12: Ram .4F 210
St Lawrence Pk. Rd. CT11: Ram .5G 210 (4J 23)
St Lawrence Rd. CT1: Cant .4A 172 (1H 31)
St Lawrence Ter. CT16: Dover .1G 181
(off Montreal Cl.)
St Leonards Av. ME4: Chat'm .1C 94 (3H 17)
St Leonard's Church Crypt .6K 199
St Leonard's Cl. DA16: Well .1J 57
St Leonard's Ct. CT21: Hythe .7J 199
(off St Leonard's Rd.)
St Leonard's M. CT21: Hythe .7J 199
St Leonard's Ri. BR6: Orp .5G 84
St Leonard's Rd. CT14: Deal .6L 177 (4J 33)
CT21: Hythe .8J 199 (5H 41)
St Leonards Rd. ME16: Alltn .1N 125
ST LEONARD'S STREET .3N 123
St Leonard's St. ME19: W Mal .3M 123 (1D 26)
St Leonard's Tower .2M 123
St Louis Gro. CT6: H Bay .3D 194
ST LUKE'S .2G 5
St Luke's Av. CT11: Ram .4H 211 (4J 23)
St Lukes Av. ME14: Maid .4E 126
St Luke's Cl. BR8: Swanl .5E 72
St Lukes Cl. CT5: Whits .6G 226
St Luke's Cl. CT8: Wgte S .3K 207
DA2: Dart .1E 74
St Luke's Rd. CT11: Ram .4J 211
St Lukes Rd. ME14: Maid .4E 126
St Luke's Rd. TN4: Tun W .8H 151
St Lukes Wlk. CT18: H'nge .8J 193
St Luke's Way ME3: Allh .4D 204
St Magnus Cl. CT7: Birch .3E 206
St Magnus Ct. CT7: Birch .3F 206
ST MARGARETS .3E 74
ST MARGARET'S AT CLIFFE .7B 214 (7H 33)
St Margaret's At Cliffe CT15: St Marg .7B 214
St Margaret's Av. DA15: Sidc .8F 56
St Margarets Av. TN16: Big H .7D 100
St Margarets Banks ME1: Roch .7A 80
St Margaret's Cl. BR6: Chels .5K 85
St Margarets Cl. CT5: Seas .7C 226
St Margaret's Cl. DA2: Dart .7D 60
ME16: Maid .7M 125
St Margaret's Ct. CT20: F'stone .6H 189
St Margaret's Ct. ME3: H Hals .2H 67
St Margaret's Cres. DA12: Grav'nd .8K 63
St Margarets Dr. CT14: Walm .9L 177
ME8: Gill .6M 95
St Margaret's Gro. SE18 .6E 50
St Margaret's M. ME1: Roch .7N 79
St Margaret's Mus., The .8D 214
St Margaret's Pas. SE13 .1H 55
(not continuous)
St Margarets Path SE18 .5E 50
St Margarets Rd. CT7: Wdchu .8L 207
St Margaret's Rd. CT8: Wgte S .4K 207
CT15: St Marg .8C 214
St Margarets Rd. CT15: St Marg .7C 200
DA2: Dart, S Dar .3E 74 (1J 15)
DA4: S Dar .3E 74 (1J 15)
DA11: Nflt .6D 62
SE4 .2C 54
(not continuous)
St Margaret's St. CT1: Cant .2M 171
ME1: Roch .8M 79 (3G 17)
St Margaret's Ter. SE18 .5E 50
St Margaret St. SW1 .4F 5
St Mark's Av. DA11: Nflt .5D 62
St Mark's Cl. CT5: Whits .5G 227
St Marks Cl. CT20: F'stone .6D 188
St Mark's Cl. ME9: N'tn .4L 97
St Marks Ct. ME20: Burh .4K 109
St Mark's Ho's. ME7: Gill .7F 80
St Mark's Rd. BR2: Shortl .6K 69
St Marks Rd. CR4: Mitc .2D 12
St Mark's Rd. TN2: Tun W .5F 156 (4J 35)
W10 .3B 4
ST MARTIN'S .2A 172
St Martin's Av. CT1: Cant .2A 172
St Martin's Cl. CT1: Cant .2A 172
CT17: Dover .7G 180
St Martin's Cl. DA18: Erith .2M 51
ME9: N'tn .4L 97
ME14: Det .9K 111
St Martin's Ct. CT1: Cant .2A 172
St Martin's Dr. DA4: Eyns .5L 87
St Martins Gdns. CT17: Dover .5H 181
(off Clarendon Rd.)
St Martin's Hill CT1: Cant .2A 172 (1J 31)
St Martin's La. BR3: Beck'm .8E 68
WC2 .3F 5
St Martins Mdw. TN16: Bras .5L 117
St Martin's Path CT17: Dover .6H 181
St Martin's Pl. CT1: Cant .2A 172
ST MARTIN'S PLAIN .5B 188
St Martin's Priory .2A 172
St Martin's Rd. CT1: Cant .2A 172
CT14: Deal .6J 177
CT15: Gus .9K 179
St Martins Rd. CT20: F'stone .5D 188
St Martin's Rd. DA1: Dart .4N 59
TN28: New R .3K 213
St Martin's Smockmill .2B 172
St Martin's Steps CT17: Dover .6H 181
St Martin's Ter. CT1: Cant .2A 172
St Martin's Vw. CT6: H Bay .7H 195
ST MARY CRAY .7L 71 (2D 14)
St Mary Cray Station (Rail) .7K 71 (2D 14)
ST MARY HOO .5A 10
ST MARY IN THE MARSH .2H 215 (2J 47)
St Mary's Abbey .1A 124
St Mary's Av. BR2: Shortl .6H 69
CT9: Mgte .4H 209
(not continuous)
ST MARY'S BAY .2M 215 (2K 47)
St Mary's Cl. BR5: St P .5K 71
CT13: E'try .3L 183
CT13: Wdboro .8G 216
CT15: Non .3C 32
CT18: Etch'l .2M 185
DA12: Grav'nd .7H 63
St Marys Cl. ME18: Ladd .6E 26
St Mary's Cl. TN15: Bor G .2B 122
TN26: Hams .2L 191
St Mary's Cotts. ME3: St M Hoo .5A 10
St Mary's Ct. CT1: Cant .2L 171
CT6: H Bay .3F 194
ME19: W Mal .1N 123
TN16: Westrm .8F 116
St Mary's Dr. CT18: Etch'l .2M 185
TN13: Riv .5F 118
St Mary's Gdns. CT3: Ups .5B 22
ME4: Chat'm .5E 80
TN29: Dym .1N 215
St Mary's Ga. CT13: S'wch .5M 217
St Mary's Grn. TN16: Big H .6C 164
TN24: Kenn .3J 159
St Mary's Gro. CT5: Seas .7A 226
CT14: Tilm .4F 33
TN16: Big H .6C 164
St Mary's-in-Castro Church .4L 181
ST MARY'S ISLAND .3F 80 (1J 17)
St Mary's La. RM14: Upm, Bwood .1H 7
TN3: Speld .6A 150
St Marys Mdw. CT3: Wing .7J 225
St Mary's M. TN24: W'boro .1K 161
St Mary's Pas. CT16: Dover .4J 181
St Mary's Pl. CT3: Wing .7J 225
.4B 56
ST MARYS PLATT .2B 122 (1B 26)
St Mary's Rd. BR8: Swanl .7E 72
CT4: Brid .7G 173
CT4: Elham .7N 183
CT10: B'stairs .9M 209
CT12: Minst .7E 212
CT14: Walm .9M 177
CT21: W Hyt .7C 198
DA5: Bex'y .6D 58
DA9: G'hithe .3E 60
ME2: Strood .5M 79
ME7: Gill .6F 80
ME13: Fav .6H 187
SW19 .1C 12
TN9: Tonb .8H 145
TN15: Wro .8N 105
TN28: New R .4J 215 (3J 47)
TN29: Dym .8A 182 (1J 47)
TN29: St M Mar .1J 215 (3J 47)
St Mary's Row ME12: Minst .6H 221
St Mary's St. CT1: Cant .2M 171
St Mary St. SE18 .4B 50
St Mary's Vw. ME9: N'tn .4L 97
St Mary's Wlk. ME1: Burh .1K 109
St Mary's Way DA3: Long .6L 75
St Matthew's Cl. ME9: N'tn .4L 97
St Matthew's Dr. BR1: Brom .6B 70
St Matthews Dr. ME1: Roch .1L 93
St Matthews Rd. SW2 .6F 5
St Matthew's Way ME3: Allh .4D 204
St Merryn Cl. SE18 .7F 50
St Merryn Ct. BR3: Beck'm .3D 68
ST MICHAELS .4C 224 (5E 38)
St Michaels All. CT11: Ram .6J 211
St Michael's Av. CT9: Mgte .5H 209
St Michael's Cl. BR1: Brom .6A 70
St Michaels Cl. CT2: R Comn .1G 171
St Michael's Cl. DA18: Erith .2M 51
St Michaels Cl. ME4: Chat'm .9C 80
St Michael's Cl. ME10: Sit .7G 99
ME20: Aylfd .7N 109
St Michael's Ct. CT20: F'stone .6L 189
(off Harbour Way)
St Michaels Ct. ME2: Strood .4M 79
TN11: Hild .9D 132
St Michael's Dr. TN14: Otf .7L 103
St Michael's Pl. CT2: Cant .9L 167
St Michael's Ri. DA16: Well .8K 51
St Michael's Rd. CT2: Cant .8L 167
(not continuous)
DA16: Well .1K 57
St Michael's Rd. ME10: Sit .7F 98 (5F 19)
(not continuous)
ME16: Maid .6A 126
TN4: Tun W .8H 151
St Michaels St. CT20: F'stone .6L 189
St Michael's Ter. TN30: St Mic .4B 224
St Michael's Wlk. CT18: H'nge .8J 193
(not continuous)
St Mildred's Av. CT7: Birch .4D 206
CT10: B'stairs .9L 209
St Mildreds Cl. TN30: Tent .8B 224
St Mildreds Ct. CT1: Cant .2L 171
St Mildred's Ct. CT8: Wgte S .2L 207
(off Beach Rd.)
St Mildreds Ct. CT14: Walm .9M 177
St Mildred's Gdns. CT8: Wgte S .2L 207
St Mildred's Pl. CT1: Cant .3L 171
St Mildred's Rd. CT8: Wgte S .2K 207 (1G 23)
CT9: Mgte .3E 208
CT11: Ram .6G 210
CT12: Minst .8E 212
St Mildreds Rd. SE6 .5H 55
SE12 .5J 55 (7K 5)
St Monicas CT17: Dover .5H 181
St Monica's Rd. CT14: Kgdn .3F 200
ST NICHOLAS AT WADE .8M 215 (3D 22)
St Nicholas Cvn. & Camping Site
CT7: St N .8L 215
St Nicholas Cl. CT2: Sturry .4E 168
CT14: Deal .6J 177
St Nicholas Ct. TN13: S'oaks .7J 119
(off Lime Tree Wlk.)
St Nicholas Dr. TN13: S'oaks .8J 119
St Nicholas Gdns. ME2: Strood .5K 79
St Nicholas Ho. SE18 .7A 50
(off Shrapnel Cl.)
St Nicholas Rd. CT1: Cant .4J 171 (1G 31)
CT21: Hythe .6H 199
ME13: Fav .5E 186
SE18 .5H 51
TN28: L'stne .3M 213
St Nicholas Ter. CT21: Hythe .6J 199
St Nicholas Way SM1: Sutt .4C 12
St Nicolas La. BR7: Chst .4A 70
St Norbert Grn. SE4 .2B 54
St Norbert Rd. SE4 .3A 54 (6H 5)
ST PANCRAS .2F 5
St Pancras Station (Rail) .2F 5
St Pancras Way NW1 .1E 4
St Patricks Cl. CT5: Whits .6G 227
St Patrick's Cl. CT14: Deal .4M 177
St Patrick's Gdns. DA12: Grav'nd .8J 63
St Patrick's Rd. CT11: Ram .4K 211
CT14: Deal .4M 177
CT17: Dover .8F 180
St Patricks Row ME9: Rod .3J 115
(off Rodmersham Grn.)
St Paul's Av. ME13: Fav .5E 186
NW2 .1B 4
St Paul's Cl. DA10: Swans .5L 61
ME2: Strood .7H 79
TN10: Tonb .2K 145
St Paul's Ct. CT20: S'gte .7E 188
St Pauls Ct. TN4: R'hall .1C 156
ST PAUL'S CRAY .5K 71 (2D 14)
St Paul's Cray Rd. BR7: Chst .4F 70 (2C 14)
St Pauls Cres. ME13: Bou B .3K 165
St Paul's M. CT9: Clift .2E 208
(off St Paul's Rd.)
St Paul's Rd. CT9: Clift .2E 208
DA8: Erith .7D 52
St Pauls Rd. IG11: Bark .2C 6
ME13: Bou B .3K 165
St Paul's Rd. N1 .1F 5
St Paul's Sq. BR2: Shortl .5J 69
St Paul's Station (Tube) .3G 5
St Paul's St. ME10: Sit .6F 98 (4F 19)
(not continuous)
TN4: R'hall .1C 156
St Paul's Ter. CT1: Cant .2N 171
St Paul's Way CT20: F'stone .7E 188
E3 .3J 5
St Paul's Wood Hill BR5: St P .5G 71 (2C 14)
ST PETER'S .8J 209 (2K 23)
St Peters Av. TN16: Big H .7D 100
St Peter's Bri. ME14: Maid .5C 126
St Peter's Cl. BR7: Chst .3F 70
DA10: Swans .5M 61
ME12: Minst .6E 220
ME20: Dit .9F 108
St Peter's Ct. CT10: B'stairs .7K 209
ME13: Fav .5E 186
ME20: Dit .9F 108
St Peters Ct. SE12 .3J 55
St Peter's Footpath CT9: Mgte .4D 208
(not continuous)
St Peter's Gro. CT1: Cant .2M 171
St Peter's La. BR5: St P .5J 71
CT1: Cant .1M 171
St Peter's Pk. Rd. CT10: B'stairs .8K 209 (2K 23)
St Peter's Path ME1: Roch .7N 79
St Peter's Pl. CT1: Cant .2L 171 (1H 31)
ME20: Burh .4K 109
St Peter's Rd. CR0: Croy .4G 13
CT5: Whits .3F 226
CT9: Mgte .4D 208 (1H 23)
CT10: B'stairs .8J 209 (2K 23)
St Peters Rd. ME13: Bou B .3K 165
St Peter's Rd. ME20: Dit .9F 108
St Peter's Row TN3: Ford .9J 149
TN26: Beth .2J 163
St Peter's St. CT1: Cant .1M 171
CT13: S'wch .5M 217
St Peters St. TN2: Tun W .2J 157
St Peter St. ME1: Roch .8A 80
ME16: Maid .4C 126 (1H 27)
St Philip's Av. ME15: Maid .6E 126 (2J 27)
St Philips Ct. TN2: Tun W .8K 151
St Pier's La. RH7: Ling .1A 34
St Piers La. TN8: Ling .1A 34
St Quentin Rd. DA16: Well .1H 57
St Quintin Av. W10 .3B 4
ST RADIGUND'S .3F 180
St Radigund's Abbey Farm Cotts.
CT15: Dover .3A 180
(Abbey Rd.)
St Radigund's Ct. CT17: Dover .3F 180
St Radigund's Pl. CT1: Cant .1N 171
St Radigund's Rd. CT17: Dover .3E 180
St Radigund's St. CT1: Cant .1M 171 (7H 21)
St Radigunds Wlk. CT17: Dover .3G 180
(off Bunkers Hill Av.)
St Richard's Rd. CT14: Deal .6H 177 (4H 33)
St Richard's Wlk. CT17: Dover .8F 180
St Saviours Cl. CT19: F'stone .4K 189
St Saviour's Cl. ME13: Fav .5J 187
St Saviours Rd. ME15: Maid .2G 139
St Saviours Wlk. DA1: Dart .4M 59
(off Bullace La.)
SAINT'S HILL .6H 149
Saint's Hill TN11: Pens .5H 149 (2G 35)
ST STEPHEN'S .9M 167
St Stephen's Cl. CT2: Cant .9M 167
ME9: N'tn .4L 97
St Stephen's Cotts. ME15: W Far .2J 137
St Stephen's Ct. CT2: Cant .9M 167
St Stephens Ct. TN1: Tun W .9H 151
St Stephen's Flds. CT2: Cant .1M 171
St Stephen's Grn. CT2: Cant .8M 167
St Stephens Gro. SE13 .1F 54
St Stephen's Hill CT2: Cant .6L 167 (6H 21)
St Stephens M. ME1: Roch .3B 94
St Stephen's Pathway CT2: Cant .9M 167
(not continuous)
St Stephen's Rd. CT2: Cant .8M 167 (7H 21)
St Stephen's Sq. ME15: Maid .7B 126
St Stephen's St. TN9: Tonb .7H 145
St Stephen's Trad. Est. CT2: Cant .9M 167
St Stephen's Wlk. TN23: Ashf .2D 160
St Stephen's Way CT20: F'stone .7F 188
St Swithin's Rd. CT5: Whits .3K 227
St Swithun's Rd. SE13 .4G 54
St Theresa's Cl. TN24: Ashf .7F 158
St Thomas' Almshouses DA11: Grav'nd .6F 62
St Thomas Ct. DA5: Bex'y .5B 58
St Thomas Dr. BR5: Farnb .2E 84
St Thomas' Hill CT2: Cant .8J 167 (7G 21)
St Thomas Rd. DA11: Nflt .7D 62
DA17: Belv .2D 52
St Thomas's Av. DA11: Grav'nd .6G 62
St Thomas St. SE1 .3G 5
St Timothys M. BR1: Brom .4L 69
St Vincent Rd. CT15: St Marg .6A 214
St Vincents Av. DA1: Dart .3A 60 (6H 7)
St Vincent's Cl. CT3: L'brne .1L 173
St Vincents Cl. CT5: Whits .6G 227
St Vincent's La. ME19: Addtn .9F 106 (7C 16)
St Vincents Rd. DA1: Dart .4A 60 (6H 7)
St Vincents Vs. DA1: Dart .4N 59
St Welcume's Way ME17: H'shm .2N 141
St Werburgh Cl. ME3: Hoo .8G 66
St Werburgh Cres. ME3: Hoo .8G 66
St Werburgh Ter. ME3: Hoo .8H 67
St William's Way ME1: Roch .9A 80 (3H 17)
St Winifred Rd. CT19: F'stone .5F 188
St Winifred's Rd. TN16: Big H .6F 164
Sala Ho. SE3 .2L 55
Salamons Rd. TN4: R'hall .1C 156
Salbris Cl. TN29: Dym .7C 182
Salcote Rd. DA12: Grav'nd .1K 77
SALEHURST .3C 44
Salehurst Rd. SE4 .4C 54
Salem Pl. DA11: Nflt .5C 62
Salem St. ME15: Maid .6D 126
Salisbury Av. BR8: Swanl .7H 73
CT10: B'stairs .1K 211
CT11: Ram .4K 211
ME8: Gill .3N 95
Salisbury Cl. ME10: Sit .7K 99
TN10: Tonb .2K 145
Salisbury Ho. ME15: Maid .1G 139
Salisbury Rd. BR2: Shortl .8A 70
CT2: Cant .9L 167
CT5: Whits .5F 226
CT6: H Bay .2J 195
CT14: Walm .8L 177 (4J 33)
CT15: St Marg .7D 214
CT16: Dover .3H 181
CT19: F'stone .4E 188
DA2: Dart .6C 60
DA5: Bex'y .6B 58
DA11: Grav'nd .6E 62
KT4: Wor Pk .4A 12
ME4: Chat'm .9D 80
ME14: Maid .3D 126
ME20: Aylfd .2A 110
TN3: Lang G .2N 155
TN4: Tun W .6J 151
TN10: Tonb .3K 145
Sallow Cl. ME4: Chat'm .3F 80
Sallows Shaw DA13: Sole S .8H 77
Sally Port ME7: Gill .6D 80
Sally Port Gdns. ME7: Gill .6D 80
Salmans La. TN11: Pens .2H 149
Salmestone Ri. CT9: Mgte .5C 208
Salmestone Rd. CT9: Mgte .5C 208
Salmon Cres. ME12: Minst .6G 221
Salmon La. E14 .3J 5
Salmon Rd. DA1: Dart .1N 59
DA17: Belv .5B 52
Salmons La. CR3: Whyt .7G 13
Salmons La. W. CR3: Cat'm .7G 13
Salmon St. NW9 .1A 4
Saltash Rd. DA16: Well .8L 51
Saltbox Hill CR6: Big H .6A 14
TN16: Big H .3A 164
Saltcote Cl. DA1: Cray .4F 58
Salter Rd. SE16 .3H 5

Sea App.—Shepherds Ga. Dr.

Sea App. CT10: B'stairs 9M 209
ME12: Ward 4J 203
Seabourne Cl. TN29: Dym 9A 182
Seabourne Way TN29: Dym 9A 182
SEABROOK 9B 188
Seabrook Ct. CT21: Hythe 8B 188
Seabrook Dr. BR4: W W'ck 3H 83
Seabrook Gdns. CT21: Hythe 9A 188
Seabrook Gro. CT21: Hythe 9A 188
Seabrook Rd. CT20: Hythe 9A 188
CT21: Hythe 6L 199 (5J 41)
TN10: Tonb 3G 144
Seabrook Va. CT21: Hythe 7B 188
Seacliff Cvn. Pk. ME12: Minst 5M 221
Seacourt Rd. SE2 2M 51
Seacroft Rd. CT10: B'stairs 3L 211
Seadown Cl. CT21: Hythe 7A 188
Seafield Ho. TN28: New R 3J 213
Seafield Rd. CT5: Whits 2K 227
CT10: B'stairs 9K 209
CT11: Ram 5G 210
Seaford Ct. ME1: Roch 8M 79
Seafront ME3: Allh 2C 204
(not continuous)
Seager Rd. ME12: S'ness 2F 220
ME13: Fav 3F 186
Seagull Rd. ME2: Strood 6G 79
SEAL 3N 119 (1H 25)
Sealand Ct. ME1: Roch 8M 79
SEAL CHART 5C 120 (2J 25)
Sealcroft Cotts. TN15: Seal 1N 119
Seal Dr. TN15: Seal 3N 119
Seal Hollow Rd. TN13: S'oaks 6K 119 (2G 25)
Seal Rd. TN14: S'oaks 3K 119 (1G 25)
Seamark Cl. CT12: Monk'n 4E 22
Seamark Rd. CT7: Birch, Monk'n 9D 206
CT12: Monk'n, Birch 4E 22
Seamew Ct. ME2: Strood 5G 79
Seaplane Ho. ME2: Med E 6B 80
Seapoint Rd. CT10: B'stairs 1M 211
Sea Rd. CT8: Wgte S 3G 207 (2F 23)
CT14: Kgdn 3E 200
(not continuous)
CT21: Hythe 6M 199
(Cannongate Cl.)
CT21: Hythe 6N 199
(Ferguson Cl.)
CT21: Hythe 9A 188
(Seabrook Gro.)
TN36: Winch 7A 46
SEASALTER 6C 226 (4E 20)
Seasalter Beach CT5: Whits 6C 226
Seasalter Cl. ME12: Ward 4K 203
Seasalter La. CT5: Seas 9B 226 (5E 20)
Seasalter Rd. ME13: G'ney 5C 20
Seaside Av. ME12: Minst 4K 221
Seaside Cvn. Pk. CT6: H Bay 3B 194
Sea St. CT5: Whits 3F 226 (3F 21)
CT6: H Bay 4C 194 (3H 21)
CT15: St Marg 7C 214 (7J 33)
Seathorpe Av. ME12: Minst 5K 221
Seaths Cnr. CT3: Wing 8J 225
SEATON 7B 22
Seaton Av. CT21: Hythe 5J 199
Seaton Rd. CT3: Wickh, Ickh 7B 22
DA1: Dart 5H 59
DA16: Well 7L 51
ME7: Gill 9H 81
Seaview ME3: Isle G 8C 190
Sea Vw. Av. CT7: Birch 3D 206
Seaview Av. ME12: Ley S 7N 203
Seaview Cvn. & Chalet Pk. CT5: Whits 1N 227
Sea Vw. Cl. CT18: Cap F 3B 174
Seaview Ct. *CT10: B'stairs* *1M 211*
(off W. Cliff Rd.)
Sea Vw. Gdns. ME12: Ward 5K 203
Sea Vw. Hgts. *CT7: Birch* *3C 206*
(off Ethelbert Rd.)
Seaview Hgts. TN29: Dym 7B 182
Seaview Holiday Camp ME12: Ley S 5K 203
Sea Vw. Rd. CT6: H Bay 2K 195 (2K 21)
CT7: Birch 3D 206
CT10: B'stairs 7L 209
CT12: C'snd 6B 210
CT15: St Marg 9B 214
(not continuous)
Seaview Rd. ME7: Gill 8F 80
SS8: Can I 2A 10
TN28: G'stne 8M 213
Sea Vw. Sq. CT6: H Bay 2G 194
Sea Vw. Ter. CT9: Mgte 3A 208
CT17: Dover 2F 180
CT20: S'gte *8D 188*
(off Wellington Pl.)
Seaview Ter. *ME11: Queen* *7B 220*
(off North Rd.)
Seaville Dr. CT6: H Bay 2M 195
Sea Wlk. CT20: S'gte 8E 188
Sea Wall CT5: Whits 3F 226
TN29: Dym 8B 182
(not continuous)
Seaway Cotts. CT5: Whits 4E 226
Seaway Cres. TN29: St M Bay 2M 215
Seaway Gdns. TN29: St M Bay 2M 215
(not continuous)
Seaway Rd. TN29: St M Bay 2M 215
Second Av. CT9: Clift 2F 208
CT10: B'stairs 3L 209
ME4: Chat'm 2E 94
ME7: Gill 9H 81
ME11: Queen 9A 220
ME12: E'chu 3E 202
ME12: S'ness 3C 220
Secretan Rd. ME1: Roch 2M 93
Sedcombe Cl. DA14: Sidc 9K 57
Sedgebrook Rd. SE3 1N 55
Sedge Cres. ME5: Chat'm 7B 94
Sedgehill Rd. SE6 9D 54
Sedgemere Rd. SE2 3L 51
Sedgemoor Ho. ME1: Roch 7B 80
Sedgeway SE6 6J 55
Sedgewood Cl. BR2: Shortl 1J 83
SEDLESCOMBE 6E 44
Sedlescombe Vineyard 5D 44
Sedley DA13: Sflt 2N 75
Sedley Cl. ME3: Cli W 6N 65
ME8: Gill 8M 95
ME20: Aylfd 8K 109
SEED 1H 29
Seed Rd. ME9: Dod, Newn 1H 29
Seeshill Cl. CT5: Whits 5G 227
Sefton Cl. BR5: St M Cry 7H 71
Sefton Rd. BR5: St M Cry 7H 71
Segal Cl. SE23 5B 54
Segrave Cres. CT19: F'stone 5M 189
Segrave Rd. CT19: F'stone 6M 189
Selah Dr. BR8: Swanl 4D 72
Selborne Av. DA5: Bex'y 6N 57
Selborne Rd. CT9: Mgte 4F 208
DA14: Sidc 9K 57
Selbourne Cl. DA3: Long 6C 76
Selbourne Rd. ME7: Gill 5G 80
Selbourne Ter. CT17: Dover 5H 181
Selbourne Wlk. ME15: Maid 2J 139
Selby Cl. BR7: Chst 2C 70
CT6: H Bay 3K 195
Selby Rd. ME15: Maid 4J 139
Selby's Cotts. TN11: Hild 3D 144
SELGROVE 7A 20
SELHURST 3G 13
Selhurst Rd. SE25 3G 13
Selhurst Station (Rail) 3G 13
Selkirk Dr. DA8: Erith 8F 52
Selkirk Rd. CT16: Dover 1G 181
Sellbourne Pk. TN3: Frant 9J 157
SELLINDGE 8C 218 (3F 41)
Sellindge Cl. BR3: Beck'm 3C 68
SELLING 2N 219 (1C 30)
Selling Ct. ME13: Sell'g 1C 30
Sellinge Grn. ME8: Gill 9M 81
Selling Rd. CT4: Old L 6K 175 (2D 30)
ME13: Fav 7J 187 (7B 20)
ME13: Sell'g 2N 219 (1B 30)
Selling Station (Rail) 1C 30
Selling St. ME13: Sell'g 2M 219
SELSDON 5H 13
Selsdon Pk. Rd. CR0: Croy 9A 82 (5J 13)
CR2: S Croy 9A 82 (5H 13)
Selsdon Rd. CR2: S Croy 4G 13
Selsea Av. CT6: H Bay 2E 194
Selsey Cres. DA16: Well 8M 51
SELSON 2J 183 (2F 33)
Selson Rd. CT13: E'try, Wdboro 1H 183 (2E 32)
Selstead Cl. ME8: Gill 2L 95
SELSTED 7A 32
Selway Ct. CT14: Deal 7L 177
Selwood Cl. ME12: Minst 6F 220
Selworthy Rd. SE6 8C 54
Selwyn Ct. CT10: B'stairs 8K 209
SE3 1J 55
Selwyn Cres. DA16: Well 1K 57
Selwyn Dr. CT10: B'stairs 8K 209
Selwyn Pl. BR5: St P 6K 71
Semaphore Rd. CT7: Birch 3E 206
Semple Cl. CT12: Minst 6F 212
Semple Gdns. ME4: Chat'm 9B 80
Sempstead La. TN31: Ewh G, N'thiam 4F 45
TN32: Ewh G 4F 45
Senacre La. ME15: Maid 2H 139
Senacres Cotts. ME15: Maid 2J 139
Senacre Sq. ME15: Maid 1J 139
SENACRE WOOD 2H 139
Senator Wlk. SE28 3F 50
Sene Pk. CT21: Hythe 5L 199
Senlac Cl. CT11: Ram 6F 210
Senlac Pl. *TN3: Groom* *6K 155*
(off Meadow Rd.)
Senlac Rd. SE12 6L 55
Sennen Wlk. SE9 8A 56
Sennocke Ct. TN13: S'oaks 7J 119
Sequoia Gdns. BR6: Orp 1H 85
Serene Ct. CT10: B'stairs 9M 209
Serene Pl. *CT10: B'stairs* *9M 209*
(off Raglan Pl.)
Sermon Dr. BR8: Swanl 6D 72
Serpentine Ct. TN13: S'oaks 4L 119
Serpentine Rd. TN13: S'oaks 5K 119
Serviden Dr. BR1: Brom 4N 69
Servite Ho. BR3: Beck'm 4C 68
Sessions Ho. Sq. ME14: Maid 4C 126
Setford Rd. ME5: Chat'm 5F 94
Setterfield Ho. CT21: Hythe 6L 199
Setterfield Rd. CT9: Mgte 4D 208
Settington Av. ME5: Chat'm 2F 94
Sevastapol Pl. CT1: Cant 1C 172
Sevenacre Rd. ME13: Fav 4G 187
Seven Acres BR8: Crock'm 9E 72
DA3: New A 4L 89
Seven Kings Rd. IG3: Ilf 1C 6
Seven Mile La. ME18: E Peck 2J 135
ME18: Mere 1E 122 (1B 26)
TN12: E Peck 2J 135 (3C 26)
(not continuous)
TN15: Wro 1E 122 (1B 26)
SEVENOAKS 7K 119 (2G 25)
Sevenoaks Bus. Cen. TN14: S'oaks 3K 119
Sevenoaks By-Pass
TN14: Riv, S'oaks 5D 118 (2F 25)
Sevenoaks Cl. DA7: Bexhth 2C 58
SEVENOAKS COMMON 2J 131 (3G 25)
Sevenoaks Leisure Cen. 7K 119
Sevenoaks Mus. & Art Gallery 2G 25
Sevenoaks Rd. BR6: Chels, Orp 6H 85 (4C 14)
BR6: Prat B 8H 85 (5C 14)
SE4 4B 54
TN14: Hals 9N 85
TN14: Hals 9N 85 (5E 14)
TN14: Otf, S'oaks 7J 103 (7G 15)
Sevenoaks Rd. TN15: Bor G 2M 121
TN15: Igh, Seal 5F 120 (2J 25)
(not continuous)
Sevenoaks Station (Rail) 6H 119 (2G 25)
Sevenoaks Way BR5: St P 3L 71 (2D 14)
DA14: Sidc 3L 71
SEVENOAKS WEALD 6J 131 (4G 25)
Sevenoaks Wildfowl Reserve 3G 119
Sevenoaks Wildfowl Reserve Vis. Cen. 3G 119
Seven Post All. *CT13: S'wch* *5M 217*
(off St Peter's St.)
Seven Sisters Rd. N4 1F 5
N7 1F 5
Seven Stones Dr. CT10: B'stairs 3L 211
Severn Cl. TN10: Tonb 2J 145
Severn Rd. ME5: Chat'm 6F 94
SEVINGTON 3M 161 (2B 40)
Sevington La. TN24: Mers, Svgtn 6L 161
TN24: W'boro 1K 161
TN25: Mers, Svgtn 3B 40
Sevington Pk. ME15: Maid 2C 138
Seward Rd. BR3: Beck'm 5A 68
Sewardstone Rd. E2 2H 5
Sewell Cl. CT7: Birch 5F 206
Sewell Rd. SE2 3J 51
Sexburga Dr. ME12: Minst 4J 221
Sextant Pk. ME2: Med E 6B 80
Seymour Av. CT5: Whits 4G 227
CT9: Mgte 2L 207
Seymour Cl. CT6: H Bay 6J 195
Seymour Dr. BR2: Shortl 2B 84
Seymour Gdns. SE4 1B 54
Seymour Pl. CT1: Cant 3L 171
NW1 3D 4
Seymour Rd. CT15: St Marg 9B 200
DA11: Nflt 6E 62
ME5: Chat'm 9E 80
ME8: Rain 3E 96 (4B 18)
Seymour's Cotts. ME17: Leeds 1A 140
Seymour St. SE18 3E 50
W1 3D 4
Seymour Wlk. DA10: Swans 5L 61
Shab Hall Cotts. TN13: Dun G 9D 102
Shacklands Rd.
TN14: Hals, S'ham 2C 102 (6F 15)
Shackleton Cl. ME5: Chat'm 5E 94
SHACKLEWELL 1G 5
Shacklewell La. E8 1G 5
Shades, The ME2: Strood 5F 78
Shadler Ho. ME7: Gill 5G 80
SHADOXHURST 3J 39
Shadoxhurst Rd. TN26: Wdchu 5H 39
SHADWELL 3H 5
Shadwell Station (DLR & Tube) 3H 5
Shaftesbury Av. CT19: F'stone 4D 188
W1 3E 4
WC2 3E 4
Shaftesbury Cl. ME19: E Mal 9D 108
Shaftesbury Ct. CT14: Walm 8N 177
Shaftesbury Dr. ME16: Maid 5N 125
Shaftesbury La. DA1: Dart 2B 60
Shaftesbury Rd. BR3: Beck'm 5C 68
CT2: Cant 8L 167
CT3: Hersd 2K 169
CT5: Whits 4F 226
TN4: Tun W 8G 151
Shaftsbury Ct. *DA8: Erith* *8G 52*
(off Selkirk Dr.)
Shaftsbury St. CT11: Ram 5K 211
Shah Pl. CT11: Ram 4H 211
Shakespeare Farm Rd.
ME3: St M Hoo 5A 10
Shakespeare Pas. CT9: Mgte 3B 208
Shakespeare Rd. CT7: Birch 3E 206
CT9: Mgte 4D 208
CT17: Dover 6G 180
DA1: Dart 2A 60
DA7: Bexhth 8N 51
ME7: Gill 8F 80
ME10: Sit 7H 99
TN9: Tonb 7F 144
Shakespeare Ter. CT20: F'stone 7J 189
Shalford Cl. BR6: Farnb 5E 84
Shalloak Rd. CT2: B Oak 6C 168 (6J 21)
Shallons Rd. SE9 9D 56
Shallows Rd. CT10: B'stairs 7G 209
Shalmsford Ct. CT4: Chart'm 8B 170
Shalmsford Rd. CT4: Chil'm 6M 175 (2E 30)
SHALMSFORD STREET 8B 170 (2E 30)
Shalmsford St. CT4: Chart'm 8A 170 (2E 30)
Shambles, The TN13: S'oaks 7K 119
Shamel Bus. Cen. ME2: Strood 5N 79
Shamley Rd. ME5: Chat'm 9G 94
Shamrock Av. CT5: Whits 6D 226
Shamrock Rd. DA12: Grav'nd 5K 63
Shandon Cl. TN2: Tun W 1J 157
Shanklin Cl. ME5: Chat'm 3F 94
SHANNON CORNER 2B 12
Shannon Way BR3: Beck'm 2E 68
Shapland Cl. CT6: H Bay 4K 195
Shardeloes Rd. SE4 5J 5
SE14 1C 54 (5J 5)
Share & Coulter Rd. CT5: Whits 4M 227
Sharfleet Dr. ME2: Strood 5F 78
Sharland Rd. DA12: Grav'nd 7H 63
Sharman Ct. *DA14: Sidc* *9J 57*
(off Carlton Rd.)
Sharnal La. ME6: Snod 3E 108
SHARNAL STREET 4K 67 (6K 9)
Sharnal St. ME3: H Hals 4K 67
Sharnbrooke Cl. DA16: Well 1L 57
Sharon Cres. ME5: Chat'm 7C 94
Sharp's Fld. TN27: H'crn 8M 191
Sharp Way DA1: Dart 1N 59
Sharsted Hill ME9: Newn 1H 29
Sharsted Way ME7: Hpstd 8K 95 (5K 17)
ME14: Bear 4L 127
SHATTERLING 6N 225 (7D 22)
Shawbrooke Rd. SE9 3M 55
Shaw Cl. ME3: Cli W 5M 65
ME14: Maid 2F 126
SE28 1K 51
Shaw Cross TN24: Kenn 5H 159
Shawdon Av. CT13: S'wch 1J 33
Shawfield Pk. BR1: Brom 5N 69
Shaw Ho. DA17: Belv 5A 52
E16 *1C 50*
(off Claremont St.)
Shaw Path BR1: Brom 8J 55
Shaw Rd. BR1: Brom 8J 55
TN16: Tats 8C 164
Shaws Cotts. SE23 8B 54
Shawstead Rd. ME5: Chat'm 4J 17
ME7: Gill 4F 94
Shaws Way ME1: Roch 9N 79
Shaws Wood ME2: Strood 3M 79
Shaw, The TN2: Tun W 3J 157
Shaxton Cres. CR0: Croy 9F 82
Sheafe Dr. TN17: Cran 7C 176
Sheal's Ct. ME15: Maid 7D 126
Sheal's Cres. ME15: Maid 7D 126 (2J 27)
Shearers Cl. ME14: Weav 5H 127
Shearman Rd. SE3 2J 55
Shears Cl. DA1: Dart 7K 59
Shears Grn. Ct. DA11: Nflt 7F 62
Shearwater DA3: Long 6A 76
ME16: Alltn 4M 125
Shearwater Av. CT5: Whits 6E 226
Shearwater Cl. ME2: Strood 5G 78
Shearwater Ct. ME12: S'ness 4B 220
Shearwater Ho. TN29: St M Bay 3N 215
Shear Way TN29: Burm 2B 182 (6F 41)
Shearway Bus. Pk. CT19: F'stone 3G 188
Shearway Rd. CT19: F'stone 3F 188
Shearwood Cres. DA1: Cray 1G 59
Sheen Ct. CT9: Mgte 3C 208
Sheen La. SW14 6A 4
Sheen Rd. BR5: St M Cry 7H 71
TW10: Rich 6A 4
Sheepbarn La. CR6: Big H 6K 13
Sheepcote La. BR5: St M Cry 8A 72 (3E 14)
BR8: Swanl 7B 72
Sheepfold La. TN23: Kgnt 6G 160 (3A 40)
Sheephurst La. TN12: Mard, Coll S 7F 27
Sheep Plain TN6: Crowb 7F 35
Sheepstreet La. TN5: Etch'm 1A 44
TN19: Etch'm 1A 44
SHEERNESS 2D 220 (6G 11)
Sheerness Harbour Est. ME12: S'ness 1A 220
Sheerness Heritage Cen. *2D 220*
(off Rose St.)
Sheerness M. E16 2D 50
Sheerness-on-Sea Station (Rail)
2C 220 (6F 11)
Sheerness Rd. ME9: Lwr Hal 3M 225 (3D 18)
Sheerstone ME9: Iwade 8J 197
SHEERWATER 6D 22
Sheerwater Rd. CT3: Pres 6D 22
Sheerways ME13: Fav 5E 186
Sheet Glass Rd. ME11: Queen 9B 220
SHEET HILL 7M 121 (2A 26)
Sheet Hill TN15: Plax 7K 121 (2A 26)
Sheffield Gdns. CT14: Walm 6M 177
Sheffield Rd. TN4: S'bgh 4F 150
Sheilings, The TN15: Seal 2N 119
Shelbourne Pl. BR3: Beck'm 3C 68
Shelbury Cl. DA14: Sidc 8J 57
Sheldon Bus. Cen. ME2: Med E 4A 80
Sheldon Cl. CT3: Aysm 1D 162
SE12 3L 55
Sheldon Dr. ME8: Rain 3B 96
(not continuous)
Sheldon Rd. DA7: Bexhth 8A 52
Sheldon Way ME20: Lark 7E 108
Sheldrake Cl. E16 1B 50
SHELDWICH 2H 219 (1A 30)
Sheldwich Cl. TN23: Ashf 3D 160
SHELDWICH LEES 3H 219 (1A 30)
Sheldwich Ter. BR2: Shortl 9A 70
Shellbank La. DA2: Bean, Dart 2G 75 (1K 15)
Shell Cl. BR2: Shortl 9A 70
Shelldrake Cl. ME3: Isle G 8C 190
Shelley Av. CT1: Cant 9B 168
Shelley Cl. BR6: Orp 4G 85
Shelley Dr. DA16: Well 8G 51
Shelley Ri. ME1: Roch 9L 79
Shelley Rd. ME16: Maid 7N 125
Shelleys La. TN14: Knock 7H 101 (7D 14)
Shell Grotto 3D 208
Shellness Rd. ME12: Ley S 7N 203 (1B 20)
Shellons St. CT20: F'stone 6K 189 (5B 42)
Shell Rd. SE13 1E 54
Shelton Cl. TN10: Tonb 2J 145
Shelvingford Farm Rd. CT3: Hoath 4A 22
Shelvin La. CT4: Woot 6B 32
Shenden Cl. TN13: S'oaks 9K 119
Shenden Way TN13: S'oaks 1K 131
Shenley Gro. ME14: S'lng 8C 110
Shenley Rd. DA1: Dart 4A 60
TN27: H'crn, Smar 1C 38
Shenstone Cl. DA1: Cray 2E 58
Shepherd Cl. TN23: Kgnt 4C 160
Shepherd Cotts. TN17: Cran 7C 176
Shepherd Dr. TN24: W'boro 1L 161
Shepherdess Wlk. N1 2G 5
Shepherd Neame Brewery 4H 187
SHEPHERD'S BUSH 4B 4
Shepherd's Bush Grn. W12 4B 4
Shepherd's Bush Rd. W6 4B 4
Shepherd's Bush Station (Tube)
Central Line 3B 4
Hammersmith & City Line 3B 4
Shepherd's Cl. BR6: Orp 4H 85
Shepherd's Cl. Rd. CT4: Brid 2K 31
Shepherds Ga. CT2: Cant 1M 171
ME7: Gill 6J 95
Shepherdsgate Dr. CT6: H Bay 7H 195
Shepherds Ga. Dr. ME14: Weav 4H 127

Shepherds Grn.—Sissinghurst Dr.

Shepherds Grn. BR7: Chst . . . 3F 70
Shepherdsgrove La. RH19: E Grin, Hamm . . . 2B 34
SHEPHERDS HILL . . . 4M 219 (2B 30)
Shepherd's Hill TN7: Cole H . . . 5C 34
Shepherd's La. DA1: Dart . . . 6H 59 (7G 7)
Shepherds Leas SE9 . . . 2E 56
Shepherds Ley SE28 . . . 1G 50
Shepherd St. DA11: Nflt . . . 5C 62
Shepherds Wlk. CT5: Whits . . . 5L 227
CT21: Hythe . . . 8F 198
TN2: Tun W . . . 1K 157
Shepherds Way CR2: S Croy . . . 8A 82
CT5: Whits . . . 5L 227
ME3: Lwr Sto . . . 8C 204
ME17: L'ly . . . 4A 140
SHEPHERDSWELL . . . 7K 219 (6D 32)
Shepherds Well Rd. CT4: Wom . . . 5B 32
Shepherdswell Rd. CT15: Eyt . . . 6M 219 (5D 32)
Shepherds Well Station
East Kent Railway . . . 7K 219 (5C 32)
Shepherds Well Station (Rail) . . . 7K 219 (5C 32)
Sheppards Coll. BR1: Brom . . . 4K 69
(off London Rd.)
Shepperton Cl. ME5: Chat'm . . . 7F 94
Shepperton Rd. BR5: Pet W . . . 9E 70
N1 . . . 2G 5
Sheppey Beach Vs. ME12: Ley S . . . 6N 203
Sheppey Cl. CT7: Birch . . . 4F 206
DA8: Erith . . . 7J 53
Sheppey Holiday Camp ME12: Ley S . . . 6L 203
Sheppey Leisure Complex . . . 2D 220
Sheppey Little Theatre . . . 2D 220
Sheppey Rd. ME15: Maid . . . 1C 138
Sheppey St. ME12: S'ness . . . 2B 220
Sheppey Vw. CT5: Whits . . . 7E 226
Sheppey Way ME9: Bob . . . 6B 98 (4E 18)
(not continuous)
ME9: Iwade, Minst . . . 7K 197 (2F 19)
ME11: Minst . . . 2F 19
ME12: Minst . . . 9E 220 (2F 19)
Sheppy Ct. ME12: Minst . . . 5E 220
Sheppy Pl. DA12: Grav'nd . . . 5G 62
SHEPWAY . . . 9G 126 (3J 27)
Shepway TN24: Kenn . . . 5J 159
Shepway Cl. CT19: F'stone . . . 5K 189
Shepway Ct. ME15: Maid . . . 9F 126
Sherard Rd. SE9 . . . 3A 56 (6B 6)
Sheraton Ct. ME5: Chat'm . . . 1C 110
Sherborne Cl. TN2: Tun W . . . 3K 157
Sherborne Rd. BR5: St M Cry . . . 7H 71
Sherbourne Cl. TN15: W King . . . 7E 88
Sherbourne Dr. ME2: Strood . . . 3L 79
ME16: Maid . . . 7M 125
Sherbourne Gro. TN15: Kems'g . . . 8A 104
Sherbrooke Cl. DA6: Bexhth . . . 2B 58
Sherenden La. TN12: Mard, S'hrst . . . 1G 37
Sherenden Pk. TN11: Gold G . . . 2F 146
(not continuous)
Sherenden Rd. TN11: Tude . . . 6B 146 (6B 26)
Sherfield Rd. RM17: Grays . . . 5A 8
Sheridale Bus. Cen. ME2: Strood . . . 6L 79
Sheridan Cl. BR8: Swanl . . . 7G 73
ME5: Chat'm . . . 4F 94
ME14: Maid . . . 1B 126
Sheridan Ct. DA1: Dart . . . 2A 60
ME1: Roch . . . 1L 93
TN11: Hild . . . 3F 144
Sheridan Cres. BR7: Chst . . . 5D 70
Sheridan Lodge BR2: Shortl . . . 7M 69
(off Homesdale Rd.)
Sheridan Rd. CT16: Dover . . . 1G 180
DA7: Bexhth . . . 1N 57
DA17: Belv . . . 4B 52
Sheridan Way BR3: Beck'm . . . 4C 68
Sheriff Dr. ME5: Chat'm . . . 9D 94
Sheriffs Ct. La. CT12: Minst . . . 8B 212 (4E 22)
Sheriff's La. TN6: Roth . . . 7J 35
Sheringham Cl. ME16: Alltn . . . 2A 126
Sherlies Av. BR6: Orp . . . 3G 85
Shermanbury Pl. DA8: Erith . . . 7G 52
Sherman Cl. ME8: Gill . . . 2L 95
Sherman Rd. BR1: Brom . . . 4K 69
Shernden La. TN8: Marsh G . . . 9C 184 (7C 24)
(not continuous)
Shernolds ME15: Maid . . . 1E 138
Sheron Cl. CT14: Deal . . . 5K 177
Sherway Cl. TN27: H'crn . . . 8M 191
Sherway Rd. TN27: H'crn, Smar . . . 7D 28
Sherwood Av. ME5: Chat'm . . . 9D 94
Sherwood Cl. CT5: Whits . . . 7E 226
CT6: H Bay . . . 5K 195
DA5: Bex'y . . . 4L 57
ME13: Fav . . . 3F 186
TN24: Kenn . . . 3H 159
Sherwood Cotts. TN2: Tun W . . . 8L 151
Sherwood Ct. CT8: Wgte S . . . 2K 207
Sherwood Dr. CT5: Whits . . . 7E 226
Sherwood Gdns. CT11: Ram . . . 3J 211
Sherwood Ho. ME5: Chat'm . . . 8C 94
SHERWOOD PARK . . . 8K 151 (2A 36)
Sherwood Pk. TN2: Tun W . . . 9L 151
Sherwood Pk. Av. DA15: Sidc . . . 5J 57
Sherwood Pk. Rd. CR4: Mitc . . . 2E 12
Sherwood Pl. TN3: Lang G . . . 2M 155
Sherwood Rd. CT7: Birch . . . 6E 206
DA16: Well . . . 9G 50
TN2: Tun W . . . 8K 151
Sherwoods ME5: Chat'm . . . 1A 110
Sherwood Trust Homes CT20: F'stone . . . 6L 189
(off St Michaels St.)
Sherwood Way BR4: W W'ck . . . 3F 82
TN2: Tun W . . . 8K 151
Shieldhall St. SE2 . . . 4L 51
Shifford Path SE23 . . . 8A 54
Shillingheld Cl. ME14: Weav . . . 4J 127
Shinecroft TN14: Otf . . . 7H 103
Shingle Barn La. ME15: W Far . . . 5G 136 (4F 27)
Shinglewell Rd. DA8: Erith . . . 7B 52
SHIPBOURNE . . . 3J 133 (3K 25)
Shipbourne Rd. TN10: Tonb . . . 4J 145 (6K 25)
TN11: Tonb . . . 5K 133 (6K 25)
Ship Cl. TN29: Dym . . . 7B 182
Shipfield Cl. TN16: Tats . . . 9C 164
Ship Hill TN16: Tats . . . 9C 164 (1A 24)
Ship La. DA4: Swanl, S at H . . . 4L 73 (2H 15)
RM15: Avel, Purf . . . 4J 7
RM19: Purf . . . 4J 7
Shipley Ct. ME14: Maid . . . 5D 126
Shipley Hills Rd. DA3: Meop . . . 3B 16
DA13: Meop . . . 3C 90
Shipley Mill Cl. TN23: Kgnt . . . 5G 160
Shipman Av. CT2: Cant . . . 2J 171
Shipman Rd. SE23 . . . 7A 54
Shipman's Way CT16: Dover . . . 1F 180
Shipp La. ME1: Roch . . . 8B 80
Ship St. CT19: F'stone . . . 6K 189
RH19: E Grin . . . 4A 34
Shipwrights Av. ME4: Chat'm . . . 2D 94
Ship Yd. CT3: Ash . . . 5C 216
Shipyard, The ME13: Fav . . . 3H 187
Shirebrook Rd. SE3 . . . 1N 55
Shire Ct. DA18: Erith . . . 3M 51
Shirehall Rd. DA2: Dart . . . 1K 73 (1G 15)
Shire La. BR2: Kes . . . 9A 84 (5B 14)
BR6: Downe . . . 9A 84 (5B 14)
(not continuous)
ME13: Stal . . . 3H 29
Shires, The TN12: Pad W . . . 8M 147
Shireway Cl. CT19: F'stone . . . 4G 189
SHIRKOAK . . . 4G 39
Shirland Rd. W9 . . . 2C 4
SHIRLEY . . . 4H 13
Shirley Av. CR0: Croy . . . 2A 82
DA5: Bex'y . . . 5M 57
ME5: Chat'm . . . 6A 94
Shirley Chu. Rd. CR0: Croy . . . 4A 82 (4H 13)
Shirley Cl. DA1: Dart . . . 2K 59
DA12: Grav'nd . . . 7N 63
Shirley Cotts. TN4: Tun W . . . 9G 151
Shirley Ct. ME15: Maid . . . 3H 139
Shirley Cres. BR3: Beck'm . . . 7B 68
Shirley Gdns. TN4: R'hall . . . 1C 156
Shirley Gro. TN4: R'hall . . . 9C 150
Shirley Hills Rd. CR0: Croy . . . 6A 82 (4H 13)
SHIRLEY OAKS . . . 3H 13
Shirley Oaks Rd. CR0: Croy . . . 2A 82
Shirley Rd. CR0: Croy . . . 3H 13
DA15: Sidc . . . 8G 56
Shirley Way CR0: Croy . . . 4B 82 (4J 13)
ME15: Bear . . . 6K 127
Shoebury Comn. Rd. SS3: Shoe . . . 1G 11
SHOEBURYNESS . . . 1G 11
Shoeburyness Station (Rail) . . . 1G 11
SHOLDEN . . . 4J 177 (3H 33)
Sholden Bk. CT14: Gt Mon . . . 6H 177
Sholden Gdns. BR5: St M Cry . . . 8L 71
Sholden New Rd. CT14: Shol . . . 4J 177 (3H 33)
Sholden Rd. ME2: Strood . . . 3N 79
SHOOTERS HILL . . . 8C 50 (5B 6)
Shooters Hill CT15: Eyt . . . 8K 185 (5E 32)
Shooter's Hill CT17: Dover . . . 3H 181
Shooters Hill DA16: Well . . . 8B 50 (5C 6)
SE18 . . . 8B 50 (5B 6)
Shooters Hill Rd. SE3 . . . 5K 5
SE7 . . . 5K 5
SE10 . . . 5K 5
SE18 . . . 8A 50 (5A 6)
Shoot Up Hill NW2 . . . 1C 4
Shore Cl. CT6: H Bay . . . 4C 194
SHOREDITCH . . . 2G 5
Shoreditch High St. E1 . . . 2G 5
Shoreditch Station (Tube) . . . 2G 5
Shorefield Rd. SS0: Wclf S . . . 1D 10
Shorefields ME8: Rain . . . 1C 96
Shoregate La. ME9: Upc . . . 2C 18
SHOREHAM . . . 2G 103 (6F 15)
Shoreham Aircraft Mus., The . . . 2G 103
Shoreham Cl. DA5: Bex'y . . . 6M 57
Shoreham Countryside Cen. . . . 2H 103
Shoreham La. BR6: Chels . . . 7B 86 (5E 14)
TN13: Riv, S'oaks . . . 4G 118
TN14: Hals . . . 3A 102 (6E 14)
TN30: St Mic . . . 4B 224 (5E 38)
TN32: Ewh G . . . 4E 44
Shoreham Pl. TN14: S'ham . . . 3H 103
Shoreham Rd. BR5: St P . . . 4K 71
DA4: Eyns . . . 7K 87 (5G 15)
TN14: Eyns . . . 7K 87
TN14: Otf, S'ham . . . 2J 103 (5G 15)
Shoreham Station (Rail) . . . 2J 103 (6G 15)
Shoreham Wlk. ME15: Maid . . . 1J 139
Shoreham Way BR2: Shortl . . . 9K 69
Shorehill Ct. TN15: Kems'g . . . 8N 103
Shorehill La. TN15: Kems'g, Knat . . . 6N 103
(not continuous)
Shore, The DA11: Nflt . . . 3B 62 (6B 8)
(not continuous)
Shoreway, The ME4: Chat'm . . . 2E 80
Shorland Ct. ME1: Roch . . . 8M 79
Shorncliffe Cres. CT20: F'stone . . . 6E 188
Shorncliffe Ind. Est. CT20: F'stone . . . 6E 188
Shorncliffe Rd. CT20: F'stone . . . 6E 188 (4A 42)
Shorndean St. SE6 . . . 6F 54
SHORNE . . . 1C 78 (1E 16)
Shorne Cl. BR5: St M Cry . . . 7M 71
DA15: Sidc . . . 4K 57
Shornefield Cl. BR1: Brom . . . 6C 70
Shorne Ifield Rd. DA12: Shorne . . . 2M 77 (1D 16)
Shornells Way SE2 . . . 4L 51
SHORNE RIDGEWAY . . . 2C 78 (1E 16)
Shorne Wood Country Pk. . . . 3N 77 (1D 16)
Shorne Wood Country Pk. Vis. Cen.
. . . 4A 78
SHORTLANDS . . . 5H 69 (2K 13)
Shortlands Cl. DA17: Belv . . . 3A 52
Shortlands Gdns. BR2: Shortl . . . 5H 69
Shortlands Grn. ME15: Maid . . . 3J 139
Shortlands Gro. BR2: Shortl . . . 6G 69
Shortlands Rd. BR2: Shortl . . . 6G 68 (2K 13)
ME10: Sit . . . 7H 99
Shortlands Station (Rail) . . . 5H 69 (2K 13)
Short La. CT15: Alk . . . 1C 42
ME7: Gill . . . 6K 81
RH8: Oxt . . . 4A 24
TN12: Brenc . . . 2E 36
TN15: Igh . . . 5H 121
TN29: Snar . . . 1E 46
Short Path SE18 . . . 6D 50
Short's Prospect ME12: E'chu . . . 8A 202
Shorts Reach ME1: Roch . . . 7M 79
(off Esplanade)
Short St. CT3: Chill . . . 3D 32
CT13: S'wch . . . 5M 217
ME4: Chat'm . . . 9E 80
ME12: S'ness . . . 2C 220
Shorts Way ME1: Roch . . . 9L 79 (3G 17)
Short Way SE9 . . . 1A 56
Shotfield Cl. CT3: Pres . . . 6C 22
Shottendane Rd. CT7: Birch . . . 6J 207 (2F 23)
CT9: Mgte . . . 5M 207 (2F 23)
SHOTTENDEN . . . 2C 30
Shottenden La. CT4: Mol, Chilw . . . 3B 30
Shottenden Rd. ME7: Gill . . . 5G 80
ME13: Bad . . . 3A 30
Shottery Cl. SE9 . . . 8A 56
SHOVER'S GREEN . . . 7C 36
Showcase Cinema
Bluewater . . . 6F 60
Showfields Rd. TN2: Tun W . . . 4F 156
Shrapnel Cl. SE18 . . . 7A 50
Shrapnel Rd. SE9 . . . 1B 56
Shrewsbury La. SE18 . . . 8D 50
Shrewsbury Rd. BR3: Beck'm . . . 6B 68
Shrimp Brand Cotts. DA13: Grav'nd . . . 1F 76
Shrimpton Cl. CT4: Old L . . . 2D 30
Shroffold Rd. BR1: Brom . . . 9H 55
Shropshire Ter. ME15: Maid . . . 1H 139
Shrubbery Rd. DA4: S Dar . . . 4D 74 (2J 15)
DA12: Grav'nd . . . 6G 63
Shrubbery, The CT14: B'hm . . . 7C 162
CT14: Walm . . . 9M 177
Shrubcote TN30: Tent . . . 9D 224
(not continuous)
Shrub Hill Rd. CT5: Whits . . . 6M 227
Shrublands Av. CR0: Croy . . . 4D 82
Shrublands Ct. TN2: Tun W . . . 1J 157
TN9: Tonb . . . 5K 145
Shrubsall Cl. SE9 . . . 6A 56
Shrubsole Av. ME12: S'ness . . . 3D 220
Shrubsole Dr. ME14: S'lng . . . 7B 110
Shuart La. CT7: St N . . . 8M 215 (3D 22)
(not continuous)
Shurland Av. ME10: Sit . . . 1G 114
ME12: Ley S . . . 7N 203
ME12: Minst . . . 6J 221
Shurland Cvn. Pk. ME12: E'chu . . . 3D 202
Shurlock Av. BR8: Swanl . . . 5E 72
Shurlock Dr. BR6: Farnb . . . 5E 84
Shuttle Cl. DA15: Sidc . . . 5H 57
TN27: Bidd . . . 7L 163
Shuttlemead DA5: Bex'y . . . 5A 58
Shuttle Rd. CT10: B'stairs . . . 8M 209
DA1: Cray . . . 1H 59
SHUTTLESFIELD . . . 2K 41
Shuttlesfield La. CT4: O'nge . . . 1J 41
Sibert's Cl. CT15: S'wll . . . 8M 219
SIBERTSWOLD . . . 7K 219 (6D 32)
Sibley Cl. DA6: Bexhth . . . 3N 57
Sibthorpe Rd. SE12 . . . 4L 55
SIDCUP . . . 9J 57 (7D 6)
Sidcup By-Pass BR5: St P . . . 8F 56
BR7: Chst . . . 8F 56
DA14: Sidc . . . 2J 71 (1C 14)
Sidcup High St. DA14: Sidc . . . 9J 57
Sidcup Hill DA14: Sidc . . . 9K 57 (1D 14)
Sidcup Hill Gdns. DA14: Sidc . . . 1L 71
Sidcup Pl. DA14: Sidc . . . 1J 71
Sidcup Rd. SE9 . . . 6B 56 (7A 6)
SE12 . . . 4M 55 (6A 6)
Sidcup Station (Rail) . . . 7J 57 (7D 6)
Sidcup Technical Cen. DA14: Sidc . . . 1M 71
Siddons Rd. SE23 . . . 7B 54
Side Hills CT4: Woot . . . 5B 32
Sidewood Rd. SE9 . . . 6F 56
Sidings, The CT18: Lym'ge . . . 7L 205
Sidmouth Ct. DA1: Dart . . . 6B 60
(off Churchill Cl.)
Sidmouth Rd. BR5: St M Cry . . . 8K 71
(not continuous)
DA16: Well . . . 7L 51
NW2 . . . 1B 4
Sidmouth St. WC1 . . . 2F 5
Sidney Cl. TN2: Tun W . . . 5E 156
Sidney Gdns. TN14: Otf . . . 7K 103
Sidney Rd. BR3: Beck'm . . . 5B 68
ME1: Roch . . . 1L 93
ME7: Gill . . . 5F 80
Sidney St. CT19: F'stone . . . 5L 189
E1 . . . 3H 5
ME16: Maid . . . 7N 125
Signal Ct. ME8: Rain . . . 2B 96
Sign Post Fld. TN11: Gold G . . . 2F 146
Silchester Ct. ME14: Pen H . . . 2F 126
Silecroft Ct. TN23: Ashf . . . 9C 158
Silecroft Rd. DA7: Bexhth . . . 8B 52
Silk Cl. SE12 . . . 3K 55
Silk Mills Cl. TN14: S'oaks . . . 3K 119
Silvanus Ho. CT11: Ram . . . 5H 211
(off High St.)
Silver Av. CT7: Birch . . . 5G 206
Silverbank ME5: Chat'm . . . 5D 94
Silver Birch Av. DA13: Meop . . . 1E 106
Silver Birch Cl. DA2: Dart . . . 9F 58
SE6 . . . 8C 54
SE28 . . . 1J 51
Silver Birches ME5: Chat'm . . . 8D 94
ME12: Minst . . . 3H 221
Silver Birch Gro. TN23: Kgnt . . . 5F 160
Silver Birch Wlk. ME18: W'bury . . . 2B 136
Silver Cl. TN9: Tonb . . . 9H 145
Silverdale DA3: Hart'y . . . 7M 75
ME16: Barm . . . 7K 125
SE26 . . . 9A 54
Silverdale Av. ME12: Minst . . . 6H 221
Silverdale Dr. CT6: H Bay . . . 5L 195
ME8: Gill . . . 4B 96
SE9 . . . 7A 56
Silverdale Gro. ME10: Sit . . . 8D 98
Silverdale La. TN4: Tun W . . . 7H 151
Silverdale Rd. BR5: Pet W . . . 7E 70
BR5: St P . . . 6J 71
CT11: Ram . . . 7E 210
DA7: Bexhth . . . 9C 52
TN4: Tun W . . . 8H 151 (2K 35)
Silverden La. TN18: Sandh . . . 4A 218 (2E 44)
SILVER HILL
Etchingham . . . 2C 44
Maidstone . . . 7A 128
Silver Hill ME1: Roch . . . 1K 93
ME4: Chat'm . . . 9C 80
TN30: Tent . . . 6C 224
Silver Hill Gdns. ME4: Chat'm . . . 9C 80
TN24: W'boro . . . 9L 159
Silver Hill Rd. TN24: W'boro . . . 9L 159 (1B 40)
Silverhurst Dr. TN10: Tonb . . . 1J 145
Silverlands Rd. CT18: Lym'ge . . . 7K 205
Silverland St. E16 . . . 1B 50
Silver La. BR4: W W'ck . . . 3G 82
Silvermere Rd. SE6 . . . 5E 54
Silver Rd. DA12: Grav'nd . . . 7K 63
SE13 . . . 1E 54
(not continuous)
Silver Screen Cinema
Dover . . . 5J 181
(off Market Sq.)
Folkestone . . . 6K 189
Silverspot Cl. ME8: Rain . . . 4B 96
Silver Spring Cl. DA8: Erith . . . 6C 52
Silverstead La. TN16: Westrm . . . 3F 116 (1C 24)
Silvers, The CT10: B'stairs . . . 9G 208
SILVER STREET . . . 5A 114 (6D 18)
Silver St. CT14: Deal . . . 3N 177
ME3: Wain . . . 8M 65 (7G 9)
ME9: B'gar . . . 5A 114 (6D 18)
Silverthorne Rd. SW8 . . . 5E 4
SILVERTOWN . . . 3A 6
Silvertown Station (Rail) . . . 3A 6
Silvertown Way E16 . . . 3K 5
Silver Tree Cl. ME5: Chat'm . . . 1D 110
Silverweed ME5: Chat'm . . . 6C 94
Silverweed Rd. ME5: Chat'm . . . 7B 94
Silverwood Cl. BR3: Beck'm . . . 3D 68
CR0: Croy . . . 9C 82
Silwood Cl. TN2: Tun W . . . 7L 151
Simmonds Ct. TN4: R'hall . . . 1B 156
Simmonds Dr. DA3: Hart'y . . . 8N 75
Simmonds La. ME14: Otham . . . 3K 27
ME15: Otham . . . 2L 139
Simmonds Rd. CT1: Cant . . . 3K 171
Simmons Rd. SE18 . . . 5D 50
Simnel Rd. SE12 . . . 5L 55
Simon Av. CT9: Clift . . . 3H 209
Simone Cl. BR1: Brom . . . 4N 69
Simone Weil Av. TN24: Ashf . . . 6E 158 (1A 40)
Simon's Av. TN23: Ashf . . . 2D 160
Simpson Rd. ME6: Snod . . . 4E 108
ME10: Sit . . . 6D 98
Simpsons Rd. BR2: Shortl . . . 6K 69
Sims Wlk. SE3 . . . 2J 55
Sinclair Cl. ME8: Gill . . . 6A 96
Sinclair Pl. SE4 . . . 4D 54
Sinclair Way DA2: Dart . . . 9D 60
Sincoe Ter. CT16: Dover . . . 1G 181
(off Toronto Cl.)
Sindal Shaw Ho. ME5: Chat'm . . . 7B 94
Sindals La. ME5: Chat'm . . . 1H 111
Singapore Dr. ME7: Gill . . . 7D 80
(not continuous)
Singer Av. CT6: H Bay . . . 3C 194
Singledge Av. CT16: Whitf . . . 7E 178
Singledge La. CT15: Cold, Whitf . . . 1A 178 (6D 32)
CT16: Whitf . . . 1A 178 (6D 32)
Singles Cross La. TN14: Knock . . . 5L 101 (6D 14)
SINGLE STREET . . . 6D 100 (7B 14)
Single St. TN16: Big H . . . 6D 100 (7B 14)
SINGLETON . . . 1B 160 (2K 39)
Singleton Cen., The TN23: Ashf . . . 1B 160
Singleton Cl. CT12: Minst . . . 7E 212
Singleton Hill TN23: Ashf . . . 2A 160 (2K 39)
Singleton Rd. TN23: Gt Cha . . . 9A 158
SINGLEWELL . . . 1J 77 (1C 16)
Singlewell Rd. DA11: Grav'nd . . . 6G 63 (7C 8)
SINKHURST GREEN . . . 1A 38
Sion Hill CT11: Ram . . . 6J 211
Sion Pas. CT11: Ram . . . 6J 211
(off Albert St.)
Sion Wlk. TN1: Tun W . . . 3G 157
(off Mount Sion)
Sirdar Strand DA12: Grav'nd . . . 1L 77
Sir David's Pk. TN4: S'bgh . . . 5E 150
Sir Evelyn Rd. ME1: Roch . . . 2M 93
Sir John Hawkins Way ME4: Chat'm . . . 8C 80
Sir John Moore Av. CT21: Hythe . . . 6H 199
Sir John Moore Ct. CT20: S'gte . . . 8E 188
Sir John's Boy's House . . . 1M 171
(off King St.)
Sir Thomas Longley Rd.
ME2: Med E . . . 5B 80
Siskin Cl. CT18: H'nge . . . 8J 193
TN25: Kenn . . . 3F 158
Siskin Gdns. TN12: Pad W . . . 1M 153
Siskin Wlk. ME20: Lark . . . 8D 108
SISSINGHURST . . . 3C 222 (4K 37)
Sissinghurst Castle Garden . . . 2F 222 (3A 38)
Sissinghurst Cl. BR1: Brom . . . 1H 69
Sissinghurst Dr. ME16: Maid . . . 5M 125

Sissinghurst Rd.—South Stifford

Sissinghurst Rd. TN17: Siss 4A 222 (4K 37)
TN27: Siss, Bidd 8H 163 (4A 38)
SITTINGBOURNE 7G 98 (5F 19)
Sittingbourne & Kemsley Light Railway 4F 19
Sittingbourne F.C. & Maidstone United F.C. (Central Pk.) 5K 99
Sittingbourne Heritage Mus. 7H 99
Sittingbourne Ind. Pk. ME10: Sit 6G 99
Sittingbourne Retail Pk. ME10: Sit 6G 98
Sittingbourne Rd. ME14: Det 1H 127 (1K 27) (Detling)
ME14: Det, S'bry 8N 111 (7A 18) (Friningham)
ME14: Maid 4E 126 (1J 27) (not continuous)
Sittingbourne Station
Sittingbourne & Kemsley Light Railway 6F 98 (4F 19)
Sittingbourne Station (Rail) 7G 98 (5F 19)
Siviter Way RM10: Dag 1E 6
Siward Rd. BR2: Shortl 6L 69
Six Bells La. TN13: S'oaks 8K 119
Six Bells Pk. TN26: Wdchu 6B 228
Six Flds. Path TN30: Tent 8B 224
SIXMILE 7G 31
Six Penny Cl. TN8: Eden 7C 184
Six Poor Travellers House 6N 79
Sixth Av. ME12: E'chu 3G 202
SKEETE 2H 41
Skeete Rd. CT18: Lym'ge 8H 205 (2H 41)
Skeet Hill La. BR5: Orp 2N 85 (4E 14)
BR6: Orp 2N 85 (4E 14)
Skeffington St. SE18 3E 50
Skeleton Hill ME1: Woul 7H 93
Skene Cl. ME8: Rain 2C 96
Skeynes Rd. TN8: Eden 6B 184
Skibbs La. BR5: Chels 3A 86 (4E 14)
BR6: Chels 6N 85 (4E 14)
Skid Hill La. CR6: Warl 6K 13
Skinner Gdns. TN17: Siss 3C 222
Skinner Rd. TN29: Lydd 3K 205 (5H 47)
Skinners All. CT5: Whits 4F 226 (off King Edward St.)
Skinners Cl. ME20: Burh 4L 109
Skinner's La. TN8: Eden 4D 184
Skinner's Ter. TN9: Tonb 7H 145
Skinner St. EC1 2F 5
ME4: Chat'm 9C 80
ME7: Gill 7F 80 (not continuous)
Skinners Way ME17: L'ly 4A 140
Skinney La. DA4: Hort K, S Dar 6D 74 (2J 15)
Skippers Cl. DA9: G'hithe 3H 61
Skipton Ho. SE4 2B 54
Skua Ct. ME2: Strood 5G 79
Skye Cl. ME15: Maid 1D 138
Skylark Way TN23: Kgnt 6H 161
SLADE 2G 29
Sladebrook Rd. SE3 1N 55
Slade Cl. ME5: Chat'm 9E 94
Sladedale Rd. SE18 5G 50
Slade Gdns. DA8: Erith 8G 53
SLADE GREEN 9H 53 (5G 7)
Slade Grn. Rd. DA8: Erith 7J 53 (5G 7)
Slade Green Station (Rail) 8H 53 (5G 7)
Slade Rd. ME9: O'den 3G 29
ME17: O'den 3G 29
Slades Cl. CT5: Whits 5L 227
Slades Dr. BR7: Chst 9E 56
Slade, The SE18 6G 50 (5C 6)
TN3: Lamb 4K 201 (5D 36)
TN9: Tonb 5H 145
Slagrove Pl. SE4 3D 54
Slaithwaite Rd. SE13 2F 54
Slaney Rd. TN12: S'hrst 2K 223
Slater Cl. SE18 5C 50
Slatin Rd. ME2: Strood 4L 79
Sleepers Stile Rd. TN5: Cous W 5C 36
Sleigh Rd. CT2: Sturry 5E 168
Slicketts Hill ME4: Chat'm 8D 80
Slines New Rd. CR3: Wold 7H 13
Slines Oak Rd. CR6: Warl 7J 13
Slip La. CT15: Alk 1C 42
Slip Mill Rd. TN18: Hawkh 5B 192 (7H 37)
Slip Pas. CT17: Dover 5J 181
Slip, The TN16: Westrm 8E 116
Slipway Rd. ME12: S'ness 1A 220
Sloane Gdns. BR6: Farnb 4E 84
Sloane Sq. DA3: Long 6L 75
Sloane Square Station (Tube) 4E 4
Sloane St. SW1 4D 4
Sloane Wlk. CR0: Croy 9C 68
Sloe La. CT10: Mgte 8F 208
Slough Rd. ME9: Mils 6H 115 (7F 19)
Smacks All. ME13: Fav 4H 187
Smallbridge Rd. TN12: Horsm 1A 190 (3F 37)
Small Grains DA3: Fawk 4H 89
SMALL HYTHE 7E 38
Small Hythe Cl. ME15: Bear 7L 127
Smallhythe Place 7E 38
Smallhythe Rd. TN30: Tent 9B 224 (6E 38)
Small Profits ME18: Yald 3D 136 (4E 26)
SMARDEN 8C 222 (1E 38)
SMARDEN BELL 6A 222 (1D 38)
Smarden Bell Rd. TN27: Smar 1D 38
Smarden Cl. DA17: Belv 5B 52
Smarden Gro. SE9 9B 56
Smarden Rd. TN27: Bidd, Smar 3C 38
TN27: H'crn 9M 191 (7C 28)
TN27: Smar, P'ley 7F 29
Smarden Wlk. ME8: Rain 2D 96
Smarts Cotts. ME14: Bear 5M 127 (off Green, The)
SMART'S HILL 5H 149 (1G 35)
Smarts Hill TN11: Pens 5H 149 (1G 35)
Smarts Rd. DA12: Grav'nd 8G 63
Smeed Cl. ME10: Sit 7J 99
Smeed Dean Cen. ME10: Sit 7H 99
SMEETH 9H 165 (3D 40)
Smetham Gdns. ME2: Strood 3M 79
Smitham Bottom La. CR8: Purl 6E 12
Smitham Downs Rd. CR8: Purl 6E 12
Smitham Station (Rail) 7F 13
Smithers Cl. TN11: Hdlw 7D 134
Smithers Ct. TN12: E Peck 9M 135
Smithers La. TN12: E Peck 9M 135
Smithfield Ct. ME4: Chat'm 5D 80
Smithfield Rd. ME3: Isle G 8D 190
Smithies Rd. SE2 4K 51
Smith Rd. ME5: Chat'm 8E 94
Smiths Est. ME14: S'lng 7B 110
Smith's Hill ME15: W Far 4F 136 (4F 27)
Smith's Hospital Almshouses CT1: Cant 2A 172
Smiths La. TN8: Crock H 4C 24
Smiths Orchard ME9: B'gar 5A 114
Smith St. ME2: Strood 6L 79
SS3: Shoe 1G 11
Smithy Dr. TN23: Kgnt 5G 160
Smithyfield TN8: Eden 4D 184
Smugglers TN18: Hawkh 6D 192
Smugglers Wlk. DA9: G'hithe 3H 61
Smugglers Way CT7: Birch 3F 206
Smythe Cl. TN4: S'bgh 3E 150
Smythe Rd. DA4: S at H 4A 74
Snag La. BR6: Cud, Prat B 3F 100
TN14: Cud 3F 100 (6C 14) (not continuous)
SNAGSHALL 3E 44
Snake Hill TN3: Epp G 5H 35
Snakes Hill CT3: Wing 1C 32
CT15: E Stu 4F 33
Snape La. TN5: Wadh 7B 36
SNARGATE 1E 46
Snargate La. TN29: Snar 2E 46
Snargate St. CT17: Dover 6J 181 (2F 43)
SNAVE 1F 47
Snelgrove Ho. CT16: Dover 4J 181
Snell Gdns. CT6: H Bay 5C 194
Snelling Av. DA11: Nflt 7D 62
Snipe Cl. DA8: Erith 7J 53
TN2: Pem 6D 152
TN25: Kenn 3G 158
Snipe Ct. ME2: Strood 5G 79
SNIPESHILL 8K 99 (5G 19)
SNOAD HILL 1H 39
Snoad La. TN12: S'hrst 2J 37
Snode Hill CT4: Woot 6A 32
Snodhurst Av. ME5: Chat'm 6B 94
Snodhurst Ho. ME5: Chat'm 4C 94
SNODLAND 3E 108 (6F 17)
Snodland By-Pass
ME6: Hall'g, Snod 5D 108 (6F 17)
Snodland Cl. BR6: Downe 1C 100
Snodland Rd. ME6: Snod 4A 108 (6E 16)
ME19: Birl 4A 108 (6E 16)
Snodland Station (Rail) 2F 108 (5F 17)
SNOLL HATCH 2K 147
Snoll Hatch Rd. TN12: E Peck 2K 147 (5D 26)
Snowbell Rd. TN23: Kgnt 5F 160
Snowdon Av. ME14: Maid 4E 126
Snowdon Cl. ME5: Chat'm 4E 94
Snowdon Pde. ME14: Maid 4F 126
SNOWDOWN 4E 162 (4C 32)
Snowdown Cvn. Site CT15: Aysm 3E 162
Snowdown Cl. SE20 4A 68
Snowdown Ct. CT3: Aysm 2D 162
Snowdown Station (Rail) 4F 162 (4C 32)
Snowdrop Cl. CT19: F'stone 3J 189
Snughorne La. TN27: Smar 2D 38
Sobraon Way CT1: Cant 1C 172
Socket La. BR2: Shortl 9L 69
SOHO 3E 4
Solefields Rd. TN13: S'oaks 1J 131 (3G 25)
Solent Gdns. ME5: Chat'm 4E 94
Soleoak Dr. TN13: S'oaks 9J 119
Soleshill Farm Cotts. CT4: Chil'm 8H 175
Soleshill Rd. CT4: Chil'm 8H 175 (2C 30)
SOLE STREET
Canterbury 5E 30
Gravesend 8J 77
Meopham 8J 77 (3C 16)
Sole St. CT4: Crun 5D 30
DA12: Sole S, Cobh 8J 77 (3C 16)
DA13: Sole S, Grav'nd 9H 77 (3C 16)
Sole Street Station (Rail) 8J 77 (3C 16)
Soloman Ho. CT14: Deal 7L 177
Solomon Rd. ME8: Rain 2B 96
Solomons La. ME13: Fav 5H 187
Solomon's La. TN32: Mount 6C 44
Solomon's Rd. ME4: Chat'm 8C 80
Solton La. CT15: E Lan 5M 179 (7G 33)
Somerden Rd. BR5: St M Cry 1M 85
Somerfield Barn Ct. TN25: S'ndge 9B 218
Somerfield Cl. ME16: Maid 5A 126
Somerfield La. ME16: Maid 4A 126
Somerfield Rd. ME16: Maid 5A 126
SOMERHILL 9M 145
Somerhill Av. DA15: Sidc 5K 57
Somerhill Rd. DA16: Well 9K 51
TN9: Tonb 7K 145
Somerset Av. DA16: Well 3H 57
Somerset Cl. CT5: Whits 6D 226
ME5: Chat'm 3F 94
ME10: Sit 7D 98
Somerset Ct. CT10: B'stairs 9K 209
CT14: Walm 7L 177
Somerset Rd. BR6: Orp 1J 85
CT1: Cant 2C 172
CT14: Walm 7M 177
CT19: F'stone 5E 188
DA1: Dart 4J 59
ME15: Maid 9F 126
TN4: Tun W 8G 150
TN24: Ashf 8G 158 (1A 40)
Somerset Vs. TN3: Groom 6K 155 (off Corseley Rd.)
Somersham Rd. DA7: Bexhth 9N 51
SOMERS TOWN 2E 4
Somertrees Av. SE12 7L 55
Somerville Gdns. TN4: Tun W 1F 156
Somerville Rd. DA1: Dart 4N 59
SE20 3A 68
Somme Ct. CT1: Cant 1C 172
Sommerville Cl. ME13: Fav 5J 187
Somner Cl. CT2: Cant 1K 171
Somner Wlk. ME15: Maid 4J 139
Somnes Av. SS8: Can I 1K 9
Sondes Cl. CT6: H Bay 5H 195
Sondes Rd. CT14: Deal 5N 177 (3J 33)
Sonnet Wlk. TN16: Big H 6B 164
Sonora Way ME10: Sit 5D 98
Soper Cl. SE23 6A 54
Soper's La. TN18: Hawkh 3A 192 (not continuous)
Sophurst La. TN12: Mat 8H 153 (2C 36)
Sopwith Cl. TN16: Big H 4D 164
Sorceress 6J 181 (off Waterloo Cres.)
Sorrel Cl. SE28 1J 51
Sorrell Cl. TN8: Eden 4D 184
Sorrel Rd. ME5: Chat'm 7B 94
Sorrells, The SS17: Stan H 2E 8
Sorrel Way DA11: Nflt 9D 62
Sortmill Rd. ME6: Snod 3F 108
Sotherton TN24: W'boro 2J 161
Souberg Cl. CT14: Deal 2M 177
Sounds Lodge BR8: Crock'm 9D 72
SOUTH ACTON 4A 4
South Acton Station (Rail) 4A 4
SOUTH ALKHAM 1C 42
Southall Cl. CT12: Minst 6F 212
Southampton Rd. NW5 1D 4
Southampton Row WC1 3F 5
Southampton Way SE5 5G 5
SOUTH ASHFORD 1F 160 (2A 40)
Sth. Ash Rd. TN15: Ash 1K 105 (5K 15)
Sth. Audley St. W1 3E 4
South Av. CT15: Aysm 4E 162
ME8: Gill 1K 95
ME10: Sit 8H 99 (5F 19)
Sth. Aylesford Retail Pk. ME20: Aylfd 1J 125
South Bank ME3: Cliffe 3M 65
ME17: Sut V 9A 140
TN12: S'hrst 4J 223
TN16: Westrm 8F 116
Sth. Barham Rd.
CT4: Elham, B'hm 9C 162 (6K 31)
SOUTH BEDDINGTON 5E 12
SOUTH BENFLEET 1J 9
South Bermondsey Station (Rail) 4H 5
SOUTHBOROUGH
Bromley Common 8B 70 (3B 14)
Tunbridge Wells 5G 150 (1K 35)
Southborough Ct. TN4: S'bgh 5F 150
Southborough La. BR2: Shortl 8A 70 (3B 14)
Southborough Rd. BR1: Brom 6A 70 (3B 14)
Southbourne BR2: Shortl 1K 83
TN23: Ashf 4C 160
Southbourne Gdns. SE12 3L 55
Southbourne Gro. ME5: Chat'm 7D 94
SS0: Wclf S 1C 10
Sth. Bourne Rd. CT19: F'stone 5L 189
Southbridge Rd. CR0: Croy 4G 13
SOUTH BROMLEY 3K 5
Southbrook M. SE12 4J 55
Southbrook Rd. SE12 4J 55 (6K 5)
Sth. Bush La. ME8: Rain 5D 96 (4B 18)
Sth. Camber Way CT16: Dover 4N 181
Sth. Canterbury Rd. CT1: Cant 4N 171 (1H 31)
SOUTHCHURCH 1F 11
Southchurch Av. SS1: Sth S 1E 10
Southchurch Blvd. SS2: Sth S 1F 11
Southchurch Hall & Mus. 1E 10
Southchurch Rd. SS1: Sth S 1E 10
Sth. Cliff Pde. CT10: B'stairs 3L 211
South Cl. CT1: Cant 2N 171
DA6: Bexhth 2M 57
South Ct. CT14: Deal 4N 177
Sth. Court Dr. CT3: Wing 8J 225
South Cres. ME17: Cox 5N 137
Southcroft Av. BR4: W W'ck 3F 82
DA16: Well 1G 57
Southcroft Rd. BR6: Orp 4G 85
SW16 1E 12
SW17 1E 12
Sth. Croxted Rd. SE21 7G 5
SOUTH CROYDON 4G 13
South Croydon Station (Rail) 4G 13
SOUTH DARENTH 4C 74 (2J 15)
Southdene TN14: Hals 4A 102 (not continuous)
Southdown Rd. ME12: Minst 6F 220
Southdowns DA4: S Dar 5D 74
South Dr. BR6: Orp 6G 84
Sth. Eastern Rd. CT11: Ram 6G 211 (4J 23)
ME2: Strood 5N 79
Sth. Eden Pk. Rd. BR3: Beck'm 9E 68 (3J 13)
Southenay La. TN25: S'ndge 6A 218 (3E 40)
SOUTHEND 9G 54 (1K 13)
South End CR0: Croy 4G 13
Southend Central Station (Rail) 1E 10
Southend Cl. SE9 4D 56
Southend Cres. SE9 4D 56 (6B 6)
Southend East Station (Rail) 1E 10
Southend La. SE6 9C 54 (1J 13)
SE26 9C 54 (1J 13)
SOUTHEND-ON-SEA 1E 10
Southend Pier 1E 10
Southend Rd. BR3: Beck'm 4D 68 (1J 13)
Sth. End Rd. NW3 1D 4
RM12: H'church 2G 7
RM13: H'church, Rain 2G 7
Southend Rd. RM17: Grays 4B 8
SS17: Corr, Fob 2E 8
Southend Sea Life Cen. 1E 10
Southend United F.C. 1D 10
Southend Victoria Station (Rail) 1E 10
SOUTHERNDEN 7D 28
Southernden Rd. TN27: H'crn, Bou Ma 6D 28
Southern Pl. BR8: Swanl 7E 72
Southern Way CT20: F'stone 5L 189
Southernwood Ri. CT20: F'stone 7F 188
South Essex Crematorium RM14: Upm 1J 7
Sth. Exit Rd. CT16: Dover 4M 181
Southey St. SE20 3A 68
Southey Way ME20: Lark 6D 108
South Farm La. TN3: Tun W 6N 155 (4H 35)
Southfield La. TN27: Char'g 5G 29
Southfield Rd. BR7: Chst 6J 71
TN4: Tun W 8G 150
W4 4A 4
SOUTHFIELDS 7C 4
Southfields ME1: Roch 9M 79
TN3: Speld 7A 150
Southfield Shaw DA13: Meop 1G 106
Southfield Shaw Pk. Homes DA13: Meop 1F 106
Southfields Rd. TN15: W King 8F 88
Southfields Station (Tube) 7C 4
Southfields Way TN4: S'bgh 6H 151
SOUTHFLEET 1N 75 (1A 16)
Southfleet Av. DA3: Long 5A 76
Southfleet Rd. BR6: Orp 4G 85
DA2: Bean 9J 61 (1K 15)
DA10: Swans 5M 61 (7A 8)
DA11: Nflt 6E 62
South Foreland Lighthouse 1J 43
Southgate Rd. N1 2G 5
TN30: Tent 9D 224
Sth. Gipsy Rd. DA16: Well 1M 57
Sth. Glade, The DA5: Bex'y 6A 58
Sth. Goodwin Ct. CT14: Deal 2N 177
SOUTH GREEN 5J 113 (6C 18)
South Grn. La. ME9: S'bry 3H 113 (6C 18)
South Gro. TN1: Tun W 3G 157
SOUTH HACKNEY 1H 5
Sth. Hall Cl. DA4: Farn'm 1N 87
SOUTH HAMPSTEAD 1D 4
South Hampstead Station (Rail) 1D 4
South Hill BR7: Chst 2B 70
SS16: Horn H, Lang H 1D 8
SS17: Horn H 2D 8 (Square, The)
SS17: Horn H 1D 8 (High Rd.)
TN25: H'lgh 7E 30
Sth. Hill Rd. BR2: Shortl 6H 69
DA12: Grav'nd 6H 63
SOUTH HORNCHURCH 2F 7
Southill Ct. BR2: Shortl 8J 69
Southill Rd. BR7: Chst 3A 70
ME4: Chat'm 9C 80
SOUTH KENSINGTON 4D 4
South Kensington Station (Tube) 4D 4
Sth. Kent Av. DA11: Nflt 4B 62
SOUTH LAMBETH 5F 5
Sth. Lambeth Rd. SW8 5F 5
Southland Rd. SE18 7H 51 (not continuous)
Southlands Av. BR6: Orp 5F 84
Southlands Gro. BR1: Brom 6A 70
Southlands Rd. BR1: Brom 7A 70 (2A 14)
BR2: Shortl 8M 69 (2A 14)
South La. KT3: N Mald 2A 12
ME17: Sut V 9A 140 (5A 28)
South La. W. KT3: N Mald 2A 12
South Lea TN23: Kgnt 6E 160
Southlees La. ME9: S'bry 7H 113 (7C 18)
South Lodge CT5: Whits 2G 227
Sth. Lodge Av. CR4: Mitc 2F 13
Sth. Lodge Cl. CT5: Whits 2G 227
Sth. Lodge Hill CT4: S Min 6J 31
Sth. Lodge Rd. CT4: S Min, Elham 6H 31
Southmead Cl. CT19: F'stone 5G 189
South Merton Station (Rail) 2C 12
Sth. Military Rd. CT17: Dover 7H 181 (2F 43)
South Motto TN23: Kgnt 5F 160
SOUTH NORWOOD 2H 13
South Norwood Country Pk. 7A 68 (2H 13)
Sth. Norwood Hill SE25 2G 13
SOUTH OCKENDON 3K 7
South of England Rare Breeds Cen. 8E 228 (5H 39)
Southold Ri. SE9 8B 56
Southover BR1: Brom 1K 69
South Pde. W4 4A 4
South Pk. TN13: S'oaks 7J 119
South Pk. Bus. Village ME15: Maid 8D 126
Sth. Park Ct. BR3: Beck'm 3D 68
Sth. Park Cres. SE6 6H 55
Sth. Park Dr. IG3: Ilf 1C 6
IG11: Bark 1C 6
Sth. Park Hill Rd. CR2: S Croy 4G 13
South Pk. Rd. ME15: Maid 8E 126
Sth. Pondside Rd. ME4: Chat'm 4D 80
Southport Rd. SE18 4F 50
Sth. Promenade CT14: Deal 4N 177
South Quay Station (DLR) 4J 5
South Ri. Way SE18 5F 50
South Rd. CT6: H Bay 3H 195
CT14: Kgdn 4F 200
CT17: Dover 4G 181
CT20: F'stone 8C 188
CT21: Hythe 7K 199 (5J 41)
DA8: Erith 7G 52
ME4: Chat'm 4E 80
ME4: Gill 5D 80
ME13: Fav 5G 186 (6A 20)
RM15: S Ock 3K 7
SE23 7A 54
TN12: Mard 2E 212
Southsea Av. ME12: Minst 3J 221
Southsea Dr. CT6: H Bay 3E 194
Southside Comn. SW19 1B 12
Sth. Side Three Rd. ME4: Chat'm 4E 80
Southspring DA15: Sidc 5F 56
SOUTH STIFFORD 4A 8

Southstone Ct.—Standen Street

Southstone Ct. CT21: Hythe 7K **199**
SOUTH STOUR 3B 40
Sth. Stour Av. TN23: Ashf 1G **160**
SOUTH STREET
Faversham 1C 30
Gravesend 7E 90 (5B 16)
Sittingbourne 4E 112 (6B 18)
Westerham 1C 116 (1B 24)
Whitstable 5J 227 (4G 21)
South St. BR1: Brom 5K **69**
CT1: Cant 8B **168**
CT5: Whits 5J **227** (4G **21**)
CT14: Deal 4N **177**
CT20: F'stone 6L **189**
DA12: Grav'nd 5G **63**
DA13: Meop 7E **90** (5B **16**)
KT18: Eps 6A **12**
ME11: Queen 7A **220**
ME13: Bou B 9N **187** (7C **20**)
ME16: Barm 8J **125** (2G **27**)
TN6: Roth 7H **35**
TN29: Lydd 3K **205**
South St. Rd. ME9: S'bry 3C **112** (6B **18**)
SOUTH TANKERTON 4J 227
South Ter. DA4: Farn'm 1N **87**
South Trench TN10: Tonb 2J **145**
South Undercliff TN31: Rye 5B **46**
South Vw. BR1: Brom 5M **69**
CT3: Hersd 3K **169**
ME14: Bear 5M **127**
Southview Camping CT3: Hoath 9M **195**
Southview Cl. BR8: Swanl 7H **73**
Sth. View Cl. DA5: Bex'y 4A **58**
Southview Gdns. ME12: S'ness 4D **220**
Southview Rd. BR1: Brom 9G **55**
Sth. View Rd. CT5: Whits 7F **226**
DA2: Dart 8L **59**
TN4: Tun W 6H **151**
TN5: Wadh 6B **36**
Southview Rd. TN6: Crowb 7F **35**
Southviews CR2: S Croy 9A **82**
South Vw. Ter. TN17: Goud 3C **190**
South Wlk. BR4: W W'ck 4H **83**
South Wall CT14: Deal 2K **177** (3J **33**)
(not continuous)
Southwall Ind. Est. CT14: Deal 3L **177**
South Wall Rd. CT14: Deal 4L **177** (3J **33**)
SOUTHWARK 3G 5
Southwark Bri. EC4 3G **5**
SE1 3G **5**
Southwark Bri. Rd. SE1 4F **5**
Southwark Pk. Rd. SE16 4H **5**
Southwark Pl. BR1: Brom 6B **70**
Southwark Rd. ME2: Strood 6H **79**
Southwark Station (Tube) 3F 5
Southwark St. SE1 3F **5**
Southwater Cl. BR3: Beck'm 3E **68**
South Way BR2: Shortl 1K **83**
CR0: Croy 4B **82**
HA9: Wemb 1A **4**
South Ways ME17: Sut V 9A **140**
Southwell Rd. ME2: Strood 6G **79**
SOUTH WILLESBOROUGH 2J 161 (2B 40)
SOUTH WIMBLEDON 1C 12
South Wimbledon Station (Tube) 2C 12
Southwold Pl. CT8: Wgte S 4K **207**
Southwold Rd. DA5: Bex'y 4C **58**
Southwood ME16: Barm 7K **125**
Southwood Av. TN4: Tun W 8G **151**
Southwood Cl. BR1: Brom 7B **70**
Sth. Woodford to Barking Relief Rd. E6 1B **6**
E12 1B **6**
IG11: Bark 1B **6**
Southwood Gdns. CT11: Ram 5F **210**
Southwood Hgts. CT11: Ram 6G **210**
Southwood Rd. CT5: Whits 3K **227**
CT11: Ram 5G **210**
SE9 7D **56** (7B **6**)
SE28 1K **51**
TN4: R'hall 9B **150**
SOVAL 6B 180
Sovereign Blvd. ME7: Gill 1H **95** (3K **17**)
Sovereign Ct. *DA4: S at H* *4B 74*
(off Ship La.)
ME2: Strood 5G **78**
Sovereign Ho. *SE18* *3B 50*
(off Leda Rd.)
Sovereigns, The ME16: Maid 5A **126**
Sovereigns Way TN12: Mard 2B **212**
Sovereign Way TN9: Tonb 6J **145**
Sowell St. CT10: B'stairs 8K **209** (2K **23**)
Sowerby Cl. SE9 3A **56**
Spa at Beckenham, The 4C 68
Spa Cl. TN11: Hdlw 7E **134**
Spade Ho. *CT20: S'gte* *8F 188*
(off Radnor Cliff Cres.)
Spade La. ME9: H'lip 6E **96** (4B **18**)
Spa Esplanade CT6: H Bay 2D **194**
Spa Hill SE19 2G **13**
Spa Ind. Pk. TN2: Tun W 6L **151**
Spalding Ho. SE4 2B **54**
Spaniards Rd. NW3 1D **4**
Spanton Cres. CT21: Hythe 5H **199**
Sparepenny La.
DA4: Eyns, Farn'm 3L **87** (4G **15**)
SPARKESWOOD 3C 214
Sparkeswood Av. TN17: Rolv 2C **214**
Sparkeswood Cl. TN17: Rolv 3C **214**
Sparrow Castle CT9: Mgte 4D **208**
Sparrow Dr. BR5: Farnb 2E **84**
Sparrow's Farm Leisure Cen. 5E 56
SPARROW'S GREEN 6C 36
Sparrows Grn. Rd. TN5: Wadh 6B **36**
Sparrows La. SE9 5E **56**
Spa Valley Railway 6L 155 (4G 35)
Speakman Ct. *CT11: Ram* *6G 211*
(off St Mildred's Rd.)
Speakman Ho. *SE4* *1B 54*
(off Arica Rd.)
Spearhead Rd. ME14: Maid 2C **126**
Spearman St. SE18 6C **50**
Spectrum Bus. Cen. ME2: Med E 4B **80**
Spectrum Bus. Est. ME15: Maid 4J **139**
Spectrum W. ME16: Alltn 1A **126**
Speedgate Hill DA3: Fawk 3G **88** (4K **15**)
Speedwell Av. ME5: Chat'm 7B **94**
Speedwell Cl. ME7: Gill 7H **81**
ME14: Weav 5H **127**
TN8: Eden *4D 184*
(off Woodpecker Cl.)
Speedwell Rd. CT5: Whits 7D **226**
Speke Hill SE9 8B **56**
Speke Rd. CT10: B'stairs 7J **209**
Spekes Rd. ME7: Hpstd 5L **95**
Spelders Hill TN25: Brook 1C **40**
SPELDHURST 6A 150 (2H 35)
Speldhurst Cl. BR2: Shortl 8J **69**
TN23: Ashf 4C **160**
Speldhurst Ct. ME16: Maid 5A **126**
Speldhurst Gdns. CT9: Clift 2K **209**
Speldhurst Hill TN3: Speld 7A **150** (2H **35**)
Speldhurst Rd. TN3: Lang G 2M **155** (3H **35**)
TN4: S'bgh, Tun W 6D **150** (2J **35**)
Spelmonden Rd. TN12: Horsm 9B **196** (3E **36**)
Spence Cl. CT18: H'nge 8K **193**
Spencer Cl. BR6: Orp 3G **85**
ME5: Chat'm 6D **94**
Spencer Ct. BR6: Farnb 6E **84**
CT20: S'gte 8C **188**
Spencer Flats ME5: Chat'm 3E **94**
Spencer Gdns. SE9 3B **56**
Spencer Ho. *CT20: F'stone* *6F 188*
(off Coolinge La.)
Spencer M. *TN1: Tun W* *3G 157*
(off Berkeley Rd.)
Spencer Pk. SW18 6D **4**
Spencer Rd. BR1: Brom 3J **69**
CT7: Birch 3E **206**
Spencers Cotts. TN15: Bor G 2M **121**
Spencer Sq. CT11: Ram 6H **211**
Spencer St. CT11: Ram 6H **211**
DA11: Grav'nd 5F **62**
EC1 2F **5**
Spencer Way ME15: Maid 1H **139**
SPENDIFF 4B 66 (6H 9)
Spenlow Dr. ME5: Chat'm 1D **110**
Spenny La. TN12: Coll S 7F **27**
Spenser Rd. CT6: H Bay 3F **194** (3J **21**)
Speranza Rd. SE18 5H **51**
Speyside TN10: Tonb 2H **145**
Spicers Ct. CT21: Hythe 7K **199**
Spicer's Pl. CT3: Wickh 7B **22**
Spielman Rd. DA1: Dart 2N **59**
Spiers, The ME7: Gill 7M **81**
Spillet Cl. ME13: Fav 5F **186**
Spillway, The ME15: Maid 7A **126**
Spindle Cl. SE18 3A **50**
Spindle Glade ME14: Maid 4F **126**
Spindlewood Cl. ME5: Chat'm 8E **94**
Spindlewood End TN23: Ashf 6B **158**
Spinel Cl. SE18 5H **51**
Spinnaker Ct. ME1: Roch 2N **93**
Spinners Cl. TN27: Bidd 7L **163**
Spinney Cl. BR3: Beck'm 7E **68**
Spinney La. CT3: Aysm 4B **162** (4B **32**)
(not continuous)
Spinney Oak BR1: Brom 5A **70**
Spinneys, The BR1: Brom 5B **70**
Spinney, The BR8: Swanl 5F **72**
CT9: Clift 4J **209**
CT17: Dover 2D **180**
DA14: Sidc 1N **71**
ME5: Chat'm 1D **110**
ME15: Maid 7E **126**
TN9: Tonb 8G **144**
TN23: Ashf 7C **158**
Spinney Way TN14: Cud 2F **100**
Spire Av. CT5: Whits 5H **227**
Spire Cl. DA12: Grav'nd 6G **63**
Spires, The CT2: Cant 9M **167**
DA1: Dart 7L **59**
ME2: Strood 7H **79**
ME16: Barm 4A **126**
Spitalfield La. TN28: New R 3H **213**
SPITALS CROSS 4C 184 (6C 24)
SPITALS CROSS ESTATE 4D 184
Spital St. DA1: Dart 4L **59**
Spitfire & Hurricane Memorial 9M 207 (3G 23)
Spitfire Cl. ME5: Chat'm 5E **94**
Spitfire Rd. ME19: W Mal 6L **123**
Spitfire Way CT18: H'nge 9K **193** (3A **42**)
SPITTALFIELDS 3H 5
Splashes Leisure Pool 2N 95
Splashworld 2M 57
Split Ho. CT17: Dover 3F **180**
Split La. CT4: S Min 5H **31**
Spode La. TN8: Cowd 1C **34**
Sponden La. TN18: Sandh 1B **218** (1E **44**)
Spongs La. TN17: Siss 2C **222** (3K **37**)
Sportsbank St. SE6 5F **54**
Sportsfield ME14: Maid 4E **126**
Sportsmans Cotts. ME19: W Mal 4N **123**
Spot Farm Cotts. ME15: Otham 1N **139**
Spothouse La. TN26: Wdchu 6F **228** (5J **39**)
Spot La. ME15: Bear 7J **127** (2K **27**)
Spout Hill CR0: Croy 6D **82** (4J **13**)
TN6: Town R 7J **35**
Spout La. TN8: Crock H 4C **24**
TN12: Brenc 9N **153** (2D **36**)
Spratling La. CT12: Mans 3D **210** (3H **23**)
Spratling St. CT12: Mans, Ram 3B **210** (3H **23**)
Spray Hill TN3: Lamb 2L **201** (5D **36**)
Spray's La. TN33: Sed 7E **44**
Spray St. SE18 4D **50**
Sprig, The ME14: Bear 5K **127**
Springbank Rd. SE13 4G **55**
Springbourne Ct. BR3: Beck'm 4F **68**
(not continuous)
Spring Cotts. TN26: Hams 3K **191**
Springcroft DA3: Hart'y 9N **75**
Spring Cross DA3: New A 4N **89**
(not continuous)
Springett Almshouses TN18: Hawkh 7B **192**
Springett Cl. ME20: Burh 4K **109**
SPRINGETTS HILL 2B 124
Springett Way ME17: Cox 4A **138**
Springfarm Rd. TN29: Bztt 1F **47**
Springfield Av. BR8: Swanl 7G **73**
ME14: Maid 3B **126**
TN30: St Mic 6D **224**
Springfield Cl. CT11: Ram 2J **211**
Springfield Cotts. CT4: Bek 4F **172**
Springfield Gdns. BR1: Brom 7B **70**
BR4: W W'ck 3E **82**
Springfield Ind. Est. TN18: Hawkh 4C **192**
Springfield Pas. CT21: Hythe 6J **199**
Springfield Pl. *TN3: Groom* *6K 155*
(off Corseley Rd.)
Springfield Rd. BR1: Brom 7B **70**
CT9: Clift 2J **209** (1K **23**)
CT16: Dover 2G **181**
DA7: Bexhth 2C **58**
DA16: Well 1K **57**
ME7: Gill 6H **81**
ME10: Sit 6E **98**
ME20: Lark 6D **108**
TN3: Groom 6K **155**
TN4: S'bgh 5F **150**
TN8: Eden 6B **184**
Springfield Ter. ME4: Chat'm 8C **80**
TN25: S'ndge 9C **218**
Springfield Wlk. *BR6: Orp* *2F 84*
(off Place Farm Av.)
Springfield Way CT21: Hythe 8B **188**
Spring Gdns. BR6: Chels 7K **85**
CT1: Cant 3L **171**
TN4: R'hall 1B **156**
TN16: Big H 6C **164**
Spring Gro. DA12: Grav'nd 6G **63**
Springhead TN2: Tun W 9K **151**
Springhead Ent. Pk. DA11: Nflt 6A **62**
Springhead Rd. DA8: Erith 6G **53**
DA11: Nflt 7B **62** (7B **8**)
ME13: Fav 3G **187**
Spring Head Rd. TN15: Kems'g 8N **103**
Spring Hill TN3: Ford 8H **149** (2G **35**)
TN11: Pens 8H **149** (2G **35**)
Spring Hollow TN29: St M Bay 2N **215**
Springholm Cl. TN16: Big H 6C **164**
Spring Ho. Flats *CT21: Hythe* *6K 199*
(off Dental St.)
Springhouse La. SS17: Corr 2F **9**
Springhouse Rd. SS17: Corr 2E **8**
Springhurst Cl. CR0: Croy 5C **82**
Spring La. CT1: Cant 2A **172**
CT2: Cant 7F **168**
CT21: Hythe 7A **188**
RH8: Oxt 4A **24**
SE25 3H **13**
TN3: Bidb 3C **150**
TN15: Igh 4H **121** (1K **25**)
SPRING PARK 4D 82 (4J 13)
Spring Pk. Av. CR0: Croy 3A **82**
Springpark Dr. BR3: Beck'm 6F **68**
Spring Pk. Rd. CR0: Croy 3A **82**
Springrice Rd. SE13 4G **54**
Springshaw Cl. TN13: Riv 5E **118**
Springshaw Ct. TN2: Tun W 8K **151**
Spring Shaw Rd. BR5: St P 4J **71**
Springside La. CT18: Lym'ge 8L **205**
Spring St. KT17: Eps 5A **12**
W2 3D **4**
Spring Ter. *CT20: F'stone* *6K 189*
(off Foord Rd. Sth.)
Spring Va. DA7: Bexhth 2C **58**
DA9: G'hithe 4J **61**
Springvale ME8: Gill 5M **95** (4A **18**)
ME9: Iwade 8J **197**
Spring Va. ME16: Maid 5B **126**
Spring Va. Cl. BR8: Swanl 4G **73**
Springvale Ct. DA11: Nflt 7B **62**
Spring Va. Nth. DA1: Dart 5L **59**
Springvale Retail Pk. BR5: St P 6L **71**
(not continuous)
Spring Va. Sth. DA1: Dart 5L **59**
Springvale Way BR5: St P 6L **71**
Spring Wlk. CT5: Whits 6E **226**
Springwater Cl. SE18 8C **50**
Springwell Rd. TN9: Tonb 7H **145**
Springwood Cl. ME16: Barm 6L **125**
TN23: Ashf 7C **158**
Springwood Ct. TN28: New R 3K **213**
Springwood Dr. TN23: Ashf 7B **158**
Springwood Pk. TN11: Tonb 7K **133**
Springwood Rd. ME16: Barm 6L **125**
Sprivers 9A 196 (3E 36)
Sprotlands Av. TN24: W'boro 9K **159**
Sprotshill Cl. ME10: Sit 5F **98**
Spruce Cl. ME20: Lark 8E **108**
Sprucedale Cl. BR8: Swanl 5F **72**
Sprucedale Gdns. CR0: Croy 5A **82**
Spruce Pk. BR2: Shortl 7J **69**
Spruce Rd. TN16: Big H 4D **164**
Sprules Rd. SE4 1B **54**
Spurgeon's Cotts. ME17: Lint 6B **138**
Spurrell Av. DA5: Bex'y 9E **58**
Spur Rd. BR6: Orp 3J **85** (4D **14**)
Spurway ME14: Bear 5K **127**
Spurway, The TN4: Tun W 3D **156**
Square Hill ME15: Maid 5E **126**
Square Hill Rd. ME15: Maid 6E **126** (2J **27**)
Square, The BR8: Swanl 6E **72**
CT3: Wing 8J **225**
CT4: Chil'm 8J **175**
CT4: Elham 7N **183**
CT7: Birch 4F **206**
ME10: Kems'y 2G **99**
Square, The ME15: Hunt 9H **137**
ME17: Len 7M **201** (3E **28**)
TN8: Cowd 2D **34**
TN11: Hdlw 8D **134**
TN11: Leigh 6N **143**
TN13: Riv 4F **118**
TN16: Tats 8C **164**
Squeeze Gut All. *CT5: Whits* *3F 226*
(off Island Wall)
Squerryes Court Manor House & Garden
3C 24
Squerryes Mede TN16: Westrm 9E **116**
Squerryes Pk. Cotts. TN16: Westrm 9E **116**
Squids Ga. TN25: C'lck, Westw 5J **29**
Squire Av. CT2: Cant 2J **171**
Squires Cl. ME2: Strood 5F **78**
Squires Ct. ME12: E'chu 5D **202**
Squires Fld. BR8: Swanl 4H **73**
Squires Way CT16: Dover 1F **180**
DA2: Dart 9E **58**
Squires Wood Dr. BR7: Chst 3A **70**
Squirrel Cl. BR6: Orp 2G **84**
Squirrel La. TN25: Ashf 5D **158**
Squirrels Drey *BR2: Shortl* *5H 69*
(off Pk. Hill Rd.)
Squirrels, The SE13 1G **54**
Squirrel Way TN2: Tun W 9L **151**
Stable Cl. ME5: Chat'm 6F **94**
Stable Cotts. ME15: E Far 1N **137**
Stable Ct. CT4: Chil'm 9J **175**
ME13: Fav *6H 187*
(off St Mary's Rd.)
TN13: S'oaks 8K **119**
Stabledene Way TN2: Pem 8C **152**
Stable Mead CT19: F'stone 4G **189**
Stable M. CT18: Etch'l 1M **185**
Stables End BR6: Farnb 4E **84**
Stable Yd. TN15: Kems'g 8A **104**
Stace Cl. TN30: Tent 8D **224**
Stacey Cl. DA12: Grav'nd 1K **77**
Stacey Rd. TN10: Tonb 3F **144**
Staceys St. ME14: Maid 4C **126**
Stackfield TN8: Eden 4D **184**
Stacklands Cl. TN15: W King 7E **88**
Stack La. DA3: Hart'y 8L **75**
DA4: Hort K 2J **15**
Stack Rd. DA4: Hort K 7D **74**
Stade St. CT21: Hythe 7K **199** (5J **41**)
Stade, The CT19: F'stone 6L **189**
Stadium Rd. SE18 7B **50**
Stadium Way DA1: Cray 3F **58**
ME10: Sit 5K **99**
Stadler Cl. ME16: Alltn 2A **126**
Staffa Rd. ME15: Maid 1D **138**
Staffhurst Wood La. TN8: Oxt 5A **24**
Stafford Cl. DA9: G'hithe 3F **60**
TN23: Ashf 8D **158**
Stafford Rd. CR0: Croy 4F **13**
DA14: Sidc 9G **57**
SM6: Wall 5E **12**
TN2: Tun W 1L **157**
TN9: Tonb 5H **145**
Staffordshire St. CT11: Ram 5J **211**
Stafford St. ME7: Gill 7E **80**
Stafford Way TN13: S'oaks 9K **119**
STAG LANE 7A **4**
Stag Rd. ME5: Chat'm 6E **94**
TN2: Tun W 6K **151**
Stagshaw Cl. ME15: Maid 7D **126**
Stag Theatre & Cinema 7J 119
Stainer Ho. SE3 2M **55**
Stainer Rd. TN10: Tonb 1L **145**
Staines Hill CT2: Sturry 4G **168**
Staines Pl. CT1: Cant 2M **171**
CT10: B'stairs 8M **209**
Staines Wlk. DA14: Sidc 2L **71**
Stainmore Cl. BR7: Chst 4F **70**
Stainton Rd. SE6 4G **54**
Stairfoot La. TN13: Riv 4D **118**
Stair Rd. TN10: Tonb 3M **145**
Stake La. ME2: Hall'g 5E **92**
Staleys Acre TN15: Bor G 2M **121**
Staleys Rd. TN15: Bor G 2L **121**
Stalham Bus. Cen.
ME11: Queen 9B **220**
Stalham Ct. ME7: Hpstd 7L **95**
Stalin Av. ME5: Chat'm 3E **94**
STALISFIELD GREEN 3H 29
Stalisfield Pl. BR6: Downe 1C **100**
Stalisfield Rd. ME13: E'lng, Osp 2K **29**
(Throwley)
ME13: Stal 4H **29**
TN27: Char'g 4H **29**
STALLIONS GREEN 6B 134 (4B 26)
Stambourne Way BR4: W W'ck 3F **82**
Stamford Bridge (Chelsea F.C.) 5C 4
Stamford Brook Rd. W6 4A **4**
Stamford Brook Station (Tube) 4A 4
Stamford Dr. BR2: Shortl 7J **69**
Stamford Rd. N1 1G **5**
Stamford St. SE1 3F **5**
Stampers, The ME15: Maid 7A **126**
Stanbridge Rd. TN8: Eden 5B **184**
Stanbrook Rd. DA11: Grav'nd 6E **62**
SE2 2K **51**
Stanbury Cres. CT19: F'stone 4M **189**
Stancomb Av. CT11: Ram 7G **211**
Standard Av. CT6: H Bay 3B **194**
Standard Ind. Est. E16 2B **50**
Standard La. TN26: Beth 3G **39**
Standard Quay ME13: Fav 4H **187**
Standard Rd. BR6: Downe 1C **100**
DA6: Bexhth 2N **57**
DA17: Belv 5B **52**
Standard Sq. ME13: Fav 4H **187**
STANDEN 2C 38
Standen Cl. ME8: Rain 7A **96**
Standen La. CT18: H'nge 7N **193** (2B **42**)
STANDEN STREET 7A 38

Standen St.—Stoddards La.

Standen St. TN4: Tun W 9G **150**
TN17: Bendn, Sandh 7A **38**
Standish Ho. *SE3* *2L 55*
(off Elford Cl.)
Standlake Point SE23 . . . . .8A **54**
Staner Ct. CT12: Ram 4E **210**
Stane Way SE18 . . . . .7A **50**
STANFORD 4G 41
Stanford Dr. ME16: Maid 6N **125**
Stanford La. TN11: Hdlw 4C **26**
STANFORD-LE-HOPE 2E 8
Stanford-le-Hope By-Pass
SS17: Horn H, Lang H, Stan H, Van 1E **8**
Stanford-le-Hope Station (Rail) 2E 8
Stanford Rd. RM16: Grays, Horn H, Ors 4B **8**
SS17: Stan H 4B **8**
TN11: Hdlw 6G **134**
Stanford Way ME2: Cux 1G **92**
Stangate Dr. ME9: Iwade 8J **197**
Stangate Rd. ME2: Strood 5G **78**
ME19: Birl 2N **107** (6D **16**)
Stangrove Lodge TN8: Eden 6C **184**
Stangrove Pde. *TN8: Eden* *6C 184*
(off Stangrove Rd.)
Stangrove Rd. TN8: Eden 6C **184** (6C **24**)
Stanham Pl. DA1: Cray 2H **59**
Stanham Rd. DA1: Dart 3K **59**
TN2: Pem 8D **152**
Stanhill Cotts. DA2: Dart 3E **72**
STANHOPE 3D 160 (2K 39)
Stanhope Av. BR2: Shortl 2J **83**
ME10: Sit 8G **99** (5F **19**)
Stanhope Cl. ME14: Maid 2B **126**
Stanhope Gdns. SW7 . . . . .4D **4**
Stanhope Gro. BR3: Beck'm 8C **68**
Stanhope Rd. CT14: Deal 4N **177**
CT16: Dover 2H **181**
DA7: Bexhth 9N **51**
DA10: Swans 4M **61** (6A **8**)
DA15: Sidc 9J **57**
ME2: Strood 5L **79**
TN1: Tun W 9J **151**
TN23: Ashf 3C **160** (2K **39**)
Stanhope Sq. TN23: Ashf 3D **160**
Stanhope Vs. TN23: Kgnt 4E **160**
Stanhope Way TN13: Riv 4E **118**
Stan La. ME18: W Peck 1F **134** (3C **26**)
Stanley Av. BR3: Beck'm 5F **68**
ME11: Queen 8B **220**
ME12: Minst 5L **221**
Stanley Cl. DA9: G'hithe 3E **60**
TN12: S'hrst 2H **223**
TN29: Dym 9E **182**
Stanley Cotts. DA2: Dart 1E **74**
Stanley Cres. DA12: Grav'nd 1J **77**
Stanley Gdns. CT6: H Bay 3G **195**
Stanley Pk. Rd. SM5: Cars 5D **12**
SM6: Wall 5D **12**
Stanley Pl. CT10: B'stairs 9L **209**
CT11: Ram 4J **211**
Stanley Rd. BR2: Shortl 7L **69**
BR6: Orp 2J **85**
CT5: Whits 6F **226**
CT6: H Bay 3G **195**
CT9: Clift 2E **208**
CT10: B'stairs 7L **209**
CT11: Ram 4H **211**
CT14: Deal 5N **177**
CT19: F'stone 5E **188**
DA10: Swans 4M **61**
DA11: Nflt 7D **62**
DA14: Sidc 8J **57**
ME5: Chat'm 5F **94**
ME7: Gill 6F **80**
RM17: Grays 4A **8**
TN1: Tun W 9H **151**
TN12: Mard 3D **212**
Stanley Sykes Cl. CT9: Mgte 5F **208**
Stanley Ter. DA6: Bexhth 2B **58**
Stanley Way BR5: St M Cry 8K **71**
Stanmore Ct. CT1: Cant 3A **172**
Stanmore Rd. DA17: Belv 4D **52**
Stanmore Ter. BR3: Beck'm 5D **68**
Stansfeld Av. CT18: H'nge 8K **193**
Stansfeld Rd. E6 . . . . .3A **6**
Stanstead Cl. BR2: Shortl 8J **69**
Stanstead Gro. SE6 .6C **54**
Stanstead Rd. SE6 . . . . .6C **54** (7J **5**)
SE23 . . . . .6A **54** (7H **5**)
STANSTED 1M 105 (5A 16)
Stansted Cl. ME16: Alltn 2N **125**
Stansted Cres. DA5: Bex'y 6M **57**
Stansted Hill TN15: Stans 1M **105** (5A **16**)
Stansted La. TN15: Ash 1H **105** (5K **15**)
Stanton Cl. BR5: Orp 1L **85**
Stanton Rd. SE26 . . . . .9C **54**
Stanton Sq. SE26 . . . . .9C **54**
Stanton Way SE26 . . . . .9C **54**
Stanyhurst SE23 . . . . .6B **54**
STAPLE 1D 32
Staple Cl. DA5: Bex'y 8E **58**
ME10: Sit 6F **98**
STAPLECROSS 4D 44
Staple Dr. TN12: S'hrst 2K **223**
Stapleford Ct. TN13: S'oaks 6G **119**
STAPLEHURST 1K 223 (1K 37)
Staplehurst Av. CT10: B'stairs 2L **211**
Staplehurst Gdns. CT9: Clift 2J **209**
Staplehurst Lodge Ind. Est. ME10: Sit 6D **98**
Staplehurst Rd. ME8: Gill 9L **81**
ME10: Sit 5C **98** (4E **18**)
(Bobbing)
ME10: Sit 6D **98**
(Chalkwell)
SE13 . . . . .3G **55**
SM5: Cars 5D **12**
TN12: Mard 6H **27**
TN17: Frit 1A **38**
Staplehurst Station (Rail) 1J 223 (7K 27)
Staple La. CT21: Post 2H **185** (3H **41**)
Staple Rd. CT3: Wing 8K **225** (1C **32**)
Staplers Ct. ME14: Pen H 1E **126**
Staples, The BR8: Swanl 4J **73**
STAPLESTREET 1J 165 (6C 20)
Staplestreet Rd. ME13: Hernh 1J **165** (6C **20**)
Stapleton Rd. BR6: Orp 5H **85**
DA7: Bexhth 7A **52**
Staple Vineyard 1D 32
Stapley Rd. DA17: Belv 5B **52**
Starboard Av. DA9: G'hithe 4H **61**
Starborough Rd. TN8: Eden, Marsh G 7A **24**
Star Hill DA1: Cray 3F **58**
ME1: Roch 7A **80** (2H **17**)
Star Hill Rd. TN14: Dun G 7A **102** (7E **14**)
Star La. BR5: St M Cry 7L **71** (2D **14**)
CT9: Mgte 8E **208** (2J **23**)
CT19: F'stone 4D **188**
E16 . . . . .2K **5**
ME7: Gill 3J **95** (4K **17**)
Starle Cl. CT1: Cant 1A **172**
Starling Cl. DA3: Long 6A **76**
Star Mill Ct. ME5: Chat'm 1G **95**
Star Mill La. ME5: Chat'm 1G **95**
Starnes Ct. ME14: Maid 4D **126**
Star Rd. TN24: Ashf 8H **159**
STARR'S GREEN 7C 44
Starts Cl. BR6: Farnb 4C **84**
Starts Hill Av. BR6: Farnb 5D **84**
Starts Hill Rd. BR6: Farnb 4C **84** (4B **14**)
Starveacre La. ME9: B'den 1C **114**
Starvecrow La. TN31: Peas 5H **45**
Starve Goose La. TN17: Cran 5H **37**
Starvenden La. TN17: Siss 1A **222**
State Farm Av. BR6: Farnb 5D **84**
Stately Pk. ME18: W'bury 7A **136**
STATENBOROUGH 1L 183 (2F 33)
Statenborough La. CT13: E'try 1K **183** (2F **33**)
Station App. *BR1: Brom* *6K 69*
(off High St.)
BR2: Shortl 2K **83** (3A **14**)
BR3: Beck'm 4D **68**
BR4: W W'ck 1F **82**
BR5: St M Cry 7K **71**
BR6: Chels 6K **85**
BR6: Orp 3H **85**
BR7: Chst 2A **70**
(Elmstead La.)
BR7: Chst 4C **70**
(Vale Rd.)
BR8: Swanl 7F **72**
CT4: Bek 5G **173**
CT4: Chil'm 8L **175**
CT7: Birch .4E **206** (2E **22**)
CT12: Minst 8F **212** (4F **23**)
CT15: Mart M 6H **33**
DA1: Cray 4G **58**
DA1: Dart 4M **59**
DA5: Bex'y 6B **58**
DA7: Bexhth 9D **52**
(Barnehurst Rd.)
DA7: Bexhth 9N **51**
(Pickford La.)
DA13: Meop 8F **76**
DA16: Well 9J **51**
(not continuous)
KT19: Eps 6A **12**
ME2: Hall'g 6E **92**
ME14: Maid 4C **126**
ME16: Maid 6C **126**
ME19: W Mal 1B **124**
RH8: Oxt 3A **24**
SE3 . . . . .1L **55**
SE9 . . . . .6B **56**
(Mottingham Station)
SE9 . . . . .7E **56**
(New Eltham Station)
SE12 . . . .*4K 55*
(off Burnt Ash Hill)
SE26 . . . . .1C **68**
TN1: Tun W 2G **157**
TN8: Eden 5C **184**
TN12: Pad W 8M **147**
TN12: S'hrst 1J **223**
TN15: Bor G 2M **121**
TN27: H'crn 8L **191**
TN28: L'stne 3L **213**
Station App. Nth. DA15: Sidc 7J **57**
Station App. Rd. CT11: Ram 4G **211** (4J **23**)
CT12: Ram 4J **23**
Station Chine CT6: H Bay 3F **194**
Station Cotts. BR6: Orp 3H **85**
Station Ct. *TN15: Bor G* *1M 121*
(off Station App.)
Station Dr. CT14: Walm 9K **177**
Station Est. BR3: Beck'm 6A **68**
Station Hill BR2: Shortl 3K **83** (4A **14**)
ME15: E Far 1L **137** (3G **27**)
TN5: Wadh 6B **36**
TN11: Chid 6G **143** (6G **25**)
Station Hill Cotts. ME15: E Far 1L **137**
Station La. RM12: H'church 1H **7**
Station Pde. CT7: Birch 4E **206**
DA7: Bexhth *9N 51*
(off Pickford La.)
DA8: Erith 5F **52**
DA14: Sidc 7J **57**
TN13: S'oaks 6H **119**
Station Rd. BR1: Brom 4K **69**
BR2: Shortl 5H **69** (2K **13**)
BR4: W W'ck 2F **82** (3K **13**)
BR5: St P .7L **71** (2D **14**)
BR6: Orp .3H **85** (4C **14**)
BR8: Swanl 7F **72**
CT3: Adm 2B **32**
CT4: Brid .9D **172** (2J **31**)
(Pett Hill)
CT4: Brid, Bek 7G **173** (2K **31**)
(Street, The)
Station Rd. CT4: Chart'm 7D **170** (2F **31**)
CT5: Whits 3G **226**
CT6: H Bay 3F **194** (3J **21**)
CT7: Birch .4F **206** (2F **23**)
CT8: Wgte S 2K **207**
CT9: Mgte 3B **208**
CT12: Minst 8F **212** (4F **23**)
CT14: Walm 9K **177** (4J **33**)
CT15: S'wll 7K **219**
CT15: St Marg, Mart M 6A **214** (6H **33**)
CT18: Lym'ge 8L **205** (2J **41**)
CT19: F'stone 5F **188**
CT21: Hythe 6L **199** (5J **41**)
DA1: Cray 5G **58** (6F **7**)
DA3: Long .6L **75** (2A **16**)
DA4: Eyns .4L **87** (4G **15**)
DA4: S Dar 5B **74** (2H **15**)
DA7: Bexhth 1N **57**
DA9: G'hithe 3G **61** (6K **7**)
(not continuous)
DA11: Nflt 4A **62**
DA13: Meop 8F **76**
DA13: Sflt 9M **61** (1A **16**)
DA15: Sidc 7J **57** (7D **6**)
DA17: Belv 3B **52**
E12 . . . . .1B **6**
ME2: Cux 1G **92** (3F **17**)
ME2: Strood 4M **79** (2G **17**)
ME3: Cliffe .4C **176** (6G **9**)
ME8: Rain 2B **96** (3A **18**)
ME9: N'tn 5K **97**
ME9: Tey .7K **223** (5H **19**)
ME13: Fav .6H **187** (6A **20**)
ME14: Maid 4C **126**
ME17: H'shm 2M **141**
ME17: Len 8L **201**
ME18: W'bury 6A **136** (4E **26**)
ME20: Dit, Aylfd 9G **109** (7F **17**)
NW10 . . . . .2A **4**
RH7: C'hrst, Ling 7A **24**
RH7: Dor'land 2A **34**
RH19: E Grin 3A **34**
RM14: Upm 1J **7**
RM18: E Til, W Til .5D **8**
SE13 . . . . .1F **54**
SM2: Sutt 5C **12**
SS0: Wclf S 1D **10**
SS1: Sth S 1F **11**
SS9: Lgh S 1C **10**
(not continuous)
SW13 . . . . .5A **4**
TN3: Groom 6K **155** (4G **35**)
TN5: Wadh 6A **36**
(not continuous)
TN6: Roth 7H **35**
TN7: Withy .9C **154** (4E **34**)
TN8: Cowd 2D **34**
TN8: Eden .4C **184** (6C **24**)
TN12: Pad W 8L **147** (7D **26**)
TN12: S'hrst 1K **223** (7K **27**)
TN13: Dun G 2F **118** (1F **25**)
TN14: Hals 1A **102** (6E **14**)
TN14: Otf .7J **103** (7G **15**)
TN14: S'ham 2H **103** (6G **15**)
TN15: Bor G 2M **121** (1A **26**)
TN16: Bras 5K **117** (2D **24**)
TN17: Goud 4A **190** (4F **37**)
TN19: Hur G 2B **44**
TN23: Ashf 9G **158** (1A **40**)
TN25: Sme 4D **40**
TN26: App, Kena 1C **46**
TN26: Hoth 2M **197** (7J **29**)
TN27: Char'g 3K **175** (5H **29**)
TN27: H'crn 8L **191** (7B **28**)
TN27: P'ley 1G **39**
TN28: New R 3K **213** (3J **47**)
TN29: Dym 8A **182**
TN29: Lydd 2K **205** (5H **47**)
TN30: Tent 8B **224**
TN31: N'thiam 3G **45**
TN32: Rob 4B **44**
TN36: Winch 6A **46**
Station Rd. Cl. CT14: Walm 9L **177**
Station Rd. E. CT1: Cant 3M **171**
RH8: Oxt 3A **24**
Station Rd. Nth. DA17: Belv 3C **52**
Station Rd. W. CT2: Cant 1L **171** (7H **21**)
RH8: Oxt 3A **24**
Station Row ME9: Tey 6L **223**
Station Sq. BR5: Pet W 8E **70**
Station St. E16 . . . . .1D **50**
ME10: Sit 7F **98**
Station Way SM3: Sutt 5C **12**
Staveley Rd. W4 . . . . .5A **4**
Staverton Rd. NW2 .1B **4**
Steadman Cl. ME3: High'm 7G **65**
Steam Packet Cotts. *CT2: Cant* *1M 171*
(off North La.)
Stede Hill ME17: H'shm 5N **129** (2D **28**)
(not continuous)
STEDE QUARTER 3D 38
Stedman Cl. DA5: Bex'y 8F **58**
Steed Cl. CT6: H Bay 7J **195**
Steeds Cl. TN26: Kgnt 7E **160**
Steeds La. TN26: Kgnt 8E **160** (3A **40**)
STEEL CROSS 7G 35
Steele Av. DA9: G'hithe 3F **60**
Steele's La. DA13: Meop 5E **90**
Steele St. ME2: Strood 4L **79**
Steele Wlk. DA8: Erith 7C **52**
Steep Cl. BR6: Chels 7H **85**
Steeple Hgts. Dr. TN16: Big H 5D **164**
Steerforth Cl. ME1: Roch 1N **93**
Steers Pl. TN11: Hdlw 6D **134**
Stella Cl. TN12: Mard 3D **212**
STELLING MINNIS 6H 31
Stelling Minnis Windmill 6H 31
Stelling Rd. DA8: Erith 7E **52**
Stembrook CT16: Dover 4J **181**
Stembrook Ct. CT16: Dover 4K **181**
Stempe Cl. CT18: H'nge 9L **193**
Stenning Ct. *TN10: Tonb* *3J 145*
(off Uridge Cres.)
Stephen Cl. BR6: Orp 4H **85**
CT10: B'stairs 9L **209**
Stephen Ct. *CT20: F'stone* *6K 189*
(off Foord Rd.)
Stephen Rd. DA7: Bexhth 1D **58**
Stephen's Cl. CT9: Mgte 4N **207**
CT11: Ram 4G **211**
Stephens Cl. ME13: Fav 4F **186**
Stephens Ct. SE4 . . . . .1B **54**
Stephenson Rd. CT2: Cant 8M **167**
Stephenson St. E16 .2K **5**
Stephen's Rd. TN4: Tun W 8G **151**
STEPNEY 3H 5
Stepneyford La. TN17: Bendn 6B **38**
Stepney Grn. E1 . . . . .3H **5**
Stepney Green Station (Tube) 2H 5
Stepney Way E1 . . . . .3H **5**
Steps Hill Rd. ME9: S'bry 4E **112** (6B **18**)
Step Style ME10: Sit 9J **99**
Sterling Av. ME16: Alltn 4N **125**
Sterling Cl. CT10: B'stairs 8J **209**
Sterling Ho. SE3 . . . . .2L **55**
Sterling Rd. ME10: Sit 1E **114**
ME11: Queen 7B **220**
Sterndale Rd. DA1: Dart 5N **59**
Sternhold Av. SW2 .7F **5**
Sterry Gdns. ME15: Maid 1H **139**
Steucers La. SE23 .6B **54**
Stevannie Ct. DA17: Belv 5A **52**
Steve Biko La. SE6 .9D **54**
Stevedale Rd. DA16: Well 9L **51**
Steven Cl. ME4: Chat'm 9D **80**
Steven Ct. CT11: Ram 7F **210**
Stevens Cl. BR3: Beck'm 2D **68**
DA2: Dart 1E **74**
DA5: Bex'y 9E **58**
ME6: Snod 2E **108**
TN27: Eger 6F **29**
STEVEN'S CROUCH 7A 44
Stevenson Cl. DA8: Erith 7J **53**
ME15: Maid 6C **126**
Stevenson Way ME20: Lark 6D **108**
Stevens Rd. ME20: Burh 4K **109**
Stewart Cl. BR7: Chst 1D **70**
Stewart Ho. ME3: C'den 7B **66**
Stewart Rd. TN4: Tun W 7J **151**
Steyne Rd. W3 . . . . .3A **4**
Steyning Gro. SE9 .9B **56**
Steynton Av. DA5: Bex'y 7M **57**
Stickens La. ME19: E Mal 3C **124** (1E **26**)
Stickfast La. ME9: Bob 1A **98** (3D **18**)
ME17: E Sut, Ulc 6B **28**
STICK HILL 1D 34
Stickland Rd. DA17: Belv 4B **52**
Stifford Clays Rd. RM16: Grays 3A **8**
RM16: Ors 3B **8**
Stifford Hill RM15: N Stif, S Ock 3K **7**
RM16: N Stif 3K **7**
Stifford Rd. RM15: Avel, S Ock 3J **7**
STIFF STREET 3N 113 (6D 18)
STILEBRIDGE 6J 27
Stilebridge La. TN12: Bou Mo 5J **27**
TN12: Mard 6H **27**
(not continuous)
Stiles Cl. BR2: Shortl 9B **70**
CT19: F'stone 4G **189**
DA8: Erith 5C **52**
ME12: Minst 6H **221**
Still La. TN4: S'bgh 4F **150**
Stillness Rd. SE23 .4B **54**
Stillwater M. *ME4: Chat'm* *2E 80*
(off Causeway, The)
Stirling Cl. ME1: Roch 9L **79**
ME8: Gill 7A **96**
Stirling Dr. BR6: Chels 6K **85**
Stirling Ho. SE18 . . . . .5D **50**
Stirling Rd. ME19: W Mal 6L **123**
TN24: Ashf 2H **161**
Stirling Sports Cen. .4N 93
Stirling Way CT12: Ram 3D **210**
Stisted Way TN27: Eger 6F **29**
Stites Hill Rd. CR5: Coul 7F **13**
Stoats Nest Rd. CR5: Coul 6F **13**
STOCKBURY 2F 112 (6C 18)
Stockbury Dr. ME16: Alltn 2A **126**
Stockbury Gdns. CT9: Clift 3J **209**
Stockbury Valley ME9: S'bry 5E **112** (6B **18**)
Stockdale Gdns. CT14: Deal 6M **177**
Stockenbury TN12: E Peck 1L **147**
Stockers Brow ME9: Rod 3H **115**
STOCKER'S HEAD 1N 175 (4J 29)
Stockers Hill ME9: Rod 3H **115** (6F **19**)
Stocker's Hill ME13: Bou B 2H **165** (7C **20**)
Stockett La. ME15: E Far, Maid 5N **137** (2H **27**)
ME17: Cox .5N **137** (4H **27**)
Stockham CT15: S'fld 7B **32**
Stockham Ct. CT19: F'stone 4E **188**
Stock Hill TN16: Big H 4D **164** (7A **14**)
STOCKLAND GREEN 5C 150 (1J 35)
Stockland Grn. Rd. TN3: S'bgh 6B **150** (2H **35**)
Stock La. DA2: Dart .8K **59**
TN25: Sme 3D **40**
STOCKS GREEN 2B 144 (5H 25)
Stocks Grn. Rd. TN11: Hild 2B **144** (5H **25**)
Stocks Mill .3F 228 (2A 46)
Stocks Rd. TN30: Witter 3D **228** (2A **46**)
STOCKS, THE 3F 228 (2A 46)
Stockton Cl. ME14: Pen H 1E **126**
STOCKWELL 5F 5
Stockwell Cl. BR1: Brom 5L **69**
Stockwell Rd. SW9 . . . . .5F **5**
Stockwell Station (Tube) 5F 5
Stockwood Chase CT2: R Comn 9G **167**
Stockwood Hill CT2: R Comn 9G **167**
Stoddards La. TN31: Beckl 3H **45**

Summerville Av.—Tannsfeld Rd.

Summerville Av. ME12: Minst 7G 221
Sumner Cl. BR6: Farnb 5E 84
TN17: Rolv 3C 214
Sumner Rd. CR0: Croy 3F 13
Sump Cotts. TN23: Kgnt 8F 160
Sumpter Way ME13: Fav 5D 186
Sunbeam Av. CT6: H Bay 3A 194
Sunburst Cl. TN12: Mard 3D 212
Sunbury St. SE18 3B 50
Sun Ct. DA8: Erith 9G 53
Sundale Av. CR2: S Croy 9A 82
Sunderland Cl. ME1: Roch 9L 79
Sunderland Dr. ME8: Rain 3C 96
Sunderland Ho. *ME7: Gill* *5F 80*
(off Strover St.)
Sunderland Mt. SE23 7A 54
Sunderland Quay ME2: Med E 6A 80
Sunderland Rd. SE23 6A 54 (7H 5)
Sundew Gro. CT11: Ram 4J 211
SUNDRIDGE
Bromley 2L 69 (1A 14)
Sevenoaks 6N 117 (2E 24)
Sundridge Av. BR1: Brom, Chst 4N 69 (2A 14)
BR7: Chst 4N 69
DA16: Well 9F 50
Sundridge Cl. CT2: Cant 7N 167
DA1: Dart 4A 60
Sundridge Dr. ME5: Chat'm 7D 94
Sundridge Hill ME2: Cux, Strood 1G 92 (3F 17)
TN14: Knock, Sund 9L 101 (7D 14)
Sundridge La. TN14: Knock 8K 101 (7D 14)
Sundridge Pde. BR1: Brom 3L 69
SUNDRIDGE PARK 3L 69
Sundridge Park Station (Rail) 3L 69 (1A 14)
Sundridge Rd. TN14: Dun G 2B 118 (1E 24)
Sun Hill DA3: Fawk 4G 88 (4K 15)
Sunhill Ct. TN2: Pem 8B 152
SUN-IN-THE-SANDS 5A 6
Sunland Av. DA6: Bexhth 2N 57
Sun La. CT7: St N 8M 215
CT21: Hythe 6K 199
DA12: Grav'nd 7H 63
Sunningdale Av. CT19: F'stone 4G 189
Sunningdale Cl. ME8: Gill 5N 95
Sunningdale Ct. ME15: Maid 5E 126
Sunningdale Dr. ME8: Gill 5N 95
Sunningdale Rd. BR1: Brom 7A 70
Sunningdale Wlk. CT6: H Bay 6E 194
Sunninghill DA11: Nflt 7D 62
Sunnings La. RM14: Upm 1J 7
Sunningvale Av. TN16: Big H 3C 164 (7A 14)
Sunningvale Cl. TN16: Big H 3D 164
Sunnybank CR6: Warl 7J 13
Sunny Bank CT15: Eyt 8J 185
CT21: Hythe 6G 199
ME10: Sit 6J 99
Sunny Cnr. CT17: Dover 7G 180
Sunnydale BR6: Farnb 3C 84
Sunnydale Rd. SE12 3L 55
Sunnydene St. SE26 9B 54
Sunnyfield Rd. BR7: Chst 6J 71
Sunnyfields Cl. ME8: Gill 3A 96
Sunnyfields Dr. ME12: Minst 6D 220
Sunnyhill Rd. CT6: H Bay 4C 194
Sunnymead CT2: T Hill 4K 167
Sunnymead Av. ME7: Gill 7H 81
Sunnymead Cvn. Pk. ME12: E'chu 3E 202
Sunny Side DA13: Meop 4F 90
Sunnyside ME9: Dod 1G 29
TN8: Eden 4B 184
Sunnyside Av. ME12: Minst 6H 221
Sunnyside Cl. CT14: Ripp 4H 33
Sunnyside Cotts. CT2: Sturry 6E 168
CT14: Deal 4M 177
Sunnyside Gdns. CT13: S'wch 6K 217
Sunnyside Holiday Pk.
ME12: E'chu 3D 202
Sunnyside Pl. *CT20: F'stone* *6L 189*
(off Tram Rd., The)
Sunnyside Rd. CT20: S'gte 8D 188
TN4: R'hall 1C 156
Sunnyside Vs. *CT20: F'stone* *6L 189*
(off Tram Rd., The)
TN23: Gt Cha 9A 158
Sunray Av. BR2: Shortl 9A 70
CT5: Whits 6D 226
SE24 6G 5
Sun Ri. TN25: Ashf 5D 158
Sunrise Cotts. TN13: S'oaks 4G 118
Sun Rd. DA10: Swans 4M 61
Sunset Cl. CT5: Whits 7E 226
DA8: Erith 7J 53
ME12: E'chu 2E 202
Sunset Rd. SE28 1J 51
Sunstone Dr. ME10: Sit 4D 98
Sun St. CT1: Cant 2M 171
EC2 3G 5
Sun Ter. ME5: Chat'm 7E 94
Sun Valley Way CT15: Eyt 8K 185
Superabbey Est. ME20: Aylfd 8M 109
Superior Dr. BR6: Chels 7H 85
Surbiton Hill Pk. KT5: Surb 3A 12
Surf Cres. ME12: E'chu 2E 202
Surrenden Pk. TN27: P'ley 7G 29
Surrenden Rd. CT19: F'stone 5F 188
TN12: S'hrst 3J 223
Surrey Canal Rd. SE14 5H 5
SE15 4H 5
Surrey Cl. CT12: Ram 3F 210
TN2: Tun W 5F 156
TN15: W King 8E 88
Surrey County Cricket Club
(Oval Cricket Ground, The) 5F 5
Surrey Gdns. CT7: Birch 4E 206
Surrey Quays Rd. SE16 4H 5
Surrey Quays Station (Tube) 4H 5
Surrey Rd. BR4: W W'ck 2E 82
CT1: Cant 3C 172
CT9: Clift 2F 208
Surrey Rd. ME15: Maid 9G 126
SE15 3A 54
Surtees Cl. TN24: Ashf 3J 161
Susan's Hill TN26: Wdchu 6A 228 (5G 39)
Susans La. ME9: Upc 1K 225 (2C 18)
Susan Wood BR7: Chst 4C 70
Sussex Av. CT1: Cant 3B 172
CT9: Mgte 4D 208
TN24: Ashf 7F 158
Sussex Cl. CT6: H Bay 3C 194
TN2: Tun W 4J 157
TN15: W King 8E 88
Sussex Dr. ME5: Chat'm 7D 94
Sussex Gdns. CT6: H Bay 3C 194
CT7: Birch 4E 206
CT8: Wgte S 2L 207
W2 3D 4
Sussex M. SE6 5D 54
TN2: Tun W 3G 156
Sussex Pl. W2 3D 4
Sussex Rd. BR4: W W'ck 2E 82
BR5: Orp 9L 71
CT19: F'stone 5K 189
DA1: Dart 5A 60
DA8: Erith 7C 52
DA14: Sidc 1K 71
ME15: Maid 8G 126
TN9: Tonb 7G 144
TN28: New R 3J 213 (3H 47)
(not continuous)
Sussex St. CT11: Ram 5J 211
Sussex Wlk. CT1: Cant 3C 172
Sutcliffe Pk. Athletics Track 3M 55
Sutcliffe Rd. DA16: Well 9L 51
SE18 6G 51
Sutherland Av. BR5: St M Cry 9H 71
DA16: Well 2G 56
TN16: Big H 5D 164
W9 2C 4
Sutherland Cl. CT21: Hythe 6H 199
DA9: G'hithe 3F 60
DA12: Grav'nd 7N 63
Sutherland Dr. CT7: Birch 4G 206
Sutherland Gdns. ME8: Gill 5A 96
Sutherland Rd. CT14: Deal 4M 177
DA17: Belv 3B 52
TN1: Tun W 2H 157
SUTTON
Cheam 4C 12
Dover 5G 33
SUTTON AT HONE 3B 74 (1H 15)
Sutton Baron Rd. ME9: B'den 2A 114 (6D 18)
Sutton Cl. BR3: Beck'm 4E 68
CT19: F'stone 4G 188
ME8: Rain 3C 96
Sutton Comn. Rd. SM1: Sutt 4C 12
SM3: Sutt 3C 12
Sutton Common Station (Rail) 4C 12
Sutton Ct. TN12: Mard 3C 212
Sutton Ct. Rd. W4 5A 4
Sutton Forge TN12: Mard 3D 212
Sutton La. CT14: R'wld, Ripp 3B 200 (5H 33)
SM2: Sutt 6C 12
SM7: Bans 6C 12
Sutton Pk. Rd. SM1: Sutt 4C 12
Sutton Rd. CT3: Hersd 2K 169
CT14: Ripp 5H 33
ME15: Maid 9E 126 (3J 27)
ME17: L'ly, Sut V 9E 126 (3J 27)
Suttons Av. RM12: H'church 1G 7
Suttons La. RM12: H'church 1G 7
Sutton Station (Rail) 5D 12
Sutton St. ME14: Bear 6N 127
SUTTON VALENCE 9A 140 (5A 28)
Sutton Valence Hill ME17: Sut V 9A 140
Swadelands Cl. ME17: Len 7L 201
Swaffield Rd. TN13: S'oaks 4K 119
SWAILE'S GREEN 5D 44
Swain Cl. ME2: Strood 4K 79
Swain Rd. ME8: Gill 5L 95
TN26: St Mic, Wdchu 5E 38
TN30: St Mic 4C 224 (5E 38)
Swaisland Dr. DA1: Cray 3G 58
Swaisland Rd. DA1: Dart 3J 59
Swakeley Wlk. CT5: Whits 2L 227
Swale Av. ME11: Queen 9A 220
ME12: S'ness 3C 220
SWALECLIFFE 3M 227 (3G 21)
Swalecliffe Av. CT6: H Bay 3C 194
Swalecliffe Ct. Dr. CT5: Whits 3M 227
Swalecliffe Rd. CT5: Whits 3J 227
DA17: Belv 5C 52
Swale Cl. CT6: H Bay 4H 195
Swaledale Rd. DA2: Dart 6C 60
Swale Ho. ME10: Sit 7H 99
Swale Rd. DA1: Cray 2H 59
ME2: Strood 5G 78
Swale Station (Rail) 2F 19
Swale Vw. ME13: Hernh 6D 20
Swallands Rd. SE6 8D 54
(not continuous)
Swallow Av. CT5: Whits 7D 226
Swallow Cl. CT9: Mgte 5A 208
DA8: Erith 8F 52
DA9: G'hithe 3F 60
Swallow Ct. *CT6: H Bay* *8F 194*
(off Nightingale Rd.)
SE12 5K 55
TN27: Bidd 9L 163
Swallowdale CR2: S Croy 9A 82
Swallow Dr. TN2: Tun W 8M 151
Swallowfield TN24: Ashf 2J 161
Swallowfields DA11: Nflt 8D 62
Swallow Ri. ME5: Chat'm 6D 94
Swallow Rd. ME20: Lark 8D 108
Swallows Leisure Cen., The 8G 98
Swallowtail Cl. BR5: St P 7M 71
Swamp Rd. TN29: Old R, Lydd 3G 47
SWAMSCOMBE 3M 61 (6A 8)
Swan Apartments *ME15: Maid* *3H 139*
(off Wallis Av.)
Swanbridge Rd. DA7: Bexhth 8B 52
Swan Bus. Pk. DA1: Dart 2L 59
Swan Cl. BR5: St P 6J 71
ME10: Sit 7J 99
Swan Cotts. TN30: Witter 3C 228
Swandon Way SW18 6C 4
Swanfield Rd. CT5: Whits 5F 226
Swan Grn. TN25: S'ndge 8C 218
Swanland Dr. TN9: Tonb 8F 144
Swan La. DA1: Dart 5G 58 (7F 7)
TN8: Eden 3C 184 (6C 24)
TN17: Goud 3G 37
TN25: S'ndge 8C 218 (3F 41)
TN27: P'ley, L Char 7G 29
SWANLEY 6F 72 (2F 15)
Swanley By-Pass BR8: Swanl 4C 72 (2E 14)
DA14: Swanl 4C 72 (2E 14)
Swanley Cen. BR8: Swanl 6F 72
SWANLEY INTERCHANGE 8J 73 (3G 15)
Swanley La. BR8: Swanl 6G 72 (2F 15)
Swanley Rd. DA16: Well 8L 51
Swanley Station (Rail) 7E 72 (2F 15)
SWANLEY VILLAGE 4J 73 (2G 15)
Swanley Village Rd. BR8: Swanl 4J 73 (2G 15)
Swanmead Way TN9: Tonb 5K 145
Swann Way CT18: H'nge 8K 193
Swan Ridge TN8: Eden 3D 184
Swanscombe Bus. Cen. DA10: Swans 3L 61
Swanscombe Leisure Cen. 4K 61
Swanscombe Skull Site Nature Reserve 4K 61
Swanscombe Station (Rail) 3M 61 (6A 8)
Swanscombe St. DA10: Swans 5L 61 (6A 8)
Swansea Ct. E16 1D 50
Swanstree Av. ME10: Sit 9J 99
Swan St. ME19: W Mal 1A 124 (1E 26)
TN30: Witter 3A 228 (2K 45)
SWAN, THE 3F 82 (4K 13)
SWANTON 3C 26
Swanton La. CT3: Sturry 1H 173 (7K 21)
CT15: Ewe M, Lyd'n 7C 32
ME18: S'brne, W Peck 1C 134
Swanton Mill 3B 40
Swanton Rd. DA8: Erith 7B 52
ME18: W Peck 1E 134 (3C 26)
SWANTON STREET 7N 113 (7D 18)
SWANTON VALLEY 9F 122
Swanton Valley La. ME18: S'brne 3B 26
Swanzy Rd. TN14: S'oaks 2K 119
Sward Rd. BR5: St M Cry 9J 71
Swarling Hill Rd. CT4: P'hm 3G 31
Swattenden La. TN17: Cran 5J 37
Swaylands Rd. DA17: Belv 6B 52
Swaynesland Rd. TN8: Eden 4B 24
Swaynes Way CT13: E'try 3K 183
Sweechbridge Rd. CT6: H Bay 4N 195 (3A 22)
Sweechgate CT2: B Oak 4C 168 (6J 21)
Sweeps Hill Cl. TN2: Pem 7C 152
Sweeps La. BR5: St M Cry 8M 71 (3D 14)
Sweet Bay Cres. TN23: Ashf 7B 158
Sweetbriar La. CT15: Evtn 6J 185
Sweethaws La. TN6: Crowb 7F 35
Sweetings La. TN5: Cous W 5C 36
Sweetlands La. TN12: S'hrst 1L 223 (7K 27)
Sweetlove Pl. CT3: Wing 7J 225
Sweets La. ME19: E Mal 5E 124 (2F 27)
Swetenham Wlk. SE18 5E 50
Sweyne Rd. DA10: Swans 4L 61
Sweyn Rd. CT9: Clift 2E 208 (1J 23)
Swievelands Rd. TN16: Big H 7B 164
Swift Cl. ME20: Lark 8E 108
Swift Ct. TN15: Seal 3A 120
Swift Cres. ME5: Chat'm 5E 94 (4J 17)
Swift Pl. ME2: Med E 4B 80
SWIFTSDEN 1B 44
Swiftsden Way BR1: Brom 2H 69
SWIFT'S GREEN 7D 28
Swifts Vw. TN17: Cran 6D 176
Swiller's La. DA12: Shorne 1C 78
Swinburne Av. CT10: B'stairs 1L 211
Swinford Gdns. CT9: Mgte 5G 209
Swingate Av. ME3: Cliffe 2C 176
Swingate Cl. ME5: Chat'm 9E 94
Swingate La. SE18 6G 51 (5C 6)
Swinge Hill CT18: Cap F 3C 42
SWINGFIELD MINNIS 1L 193 (1A 42)
SWINGFIELD STREET 1B 42
Swinton Av. ME3: C'den 7C 66
Swires Shaw BR2: Kes 5N 83
SWISS COTTAGE 1D 4
Swiss Cottage Station (Tube) 1D 4
Swiss Way CT19: F'stone 4N 189
Swithland Gdns. SE9 9C 56
Sycamore Av. CT3: Aysm 2C 162
DA15: Sidc 4H 57
Sycamore Cl. CT4: Chart'm 9F 170
CT6: H Bay 2K 195
CT9: Mgte 6C 208
CT10: B'stairs 9G 209
CT21: Hythe 7F 198
DA12: Grav'nd 5J 63
SE9 7A 56
TN29: Dym 7B 182
TN29: Lydd 2K 205
Sycamore Cotts. TN2: Pem 8B 152
Sycamore Ct. *DA8: Erith* *5E 52*
(off Sandcliff Rd.)
DA9: G'hithe 5E 60
Sycamore Cres. ME16: Alltn 4N 125
Sycamore Dr. BR8: Swanl 6F 72
CT14: Deal 6L 177
ME20: Aylfd 9J 109
Sycamore Gdns. TN12: Pad W 1L 153
TN29: Dym 7B 182
Sycamore Grange CT11: Ram 3K 211
Sycamore Gro. SE6 4F 54
Sycamore Ho. BR2: Shortl 5H 69
Sycamore La. TN23: Ashf 6C 158
Sycamore Lodge BR6: Orp 3H 85
Sycamore M. *DA8: Erith* *5E 52*
(off St John's Rd.)
Sycamore Rd. DA1: Dart 6L 59
ME2: Strood 7J 79
Sycamores, The CT3: Hersd 3K 169
Sychem La. TN12: Five G 8F 146 (7C 26)
Sychem Pl. TN12: Five G 8F 146
Sydcot Dr. CT14: Deal 2N 177
SYDENHAM 1H 13
Sydenham Cotts. SE12 7M 55
Sydenham Hill SE23 7H 5
SE26 1H 13
Sydenham Hill Station (Rail) 7G 5
Sydenham Rd. CR0: Croy 3G 13
CT14: Deal 3N 177
SE26 1A 68 (1H 13)
Sydenham Station (Rail) 1H 13
Sydenham St. CT5: Whits 3F 226
Sydney Av. ME10: Sit 7D 98
Sydney Cooper Cl. CT2: R Comn 9H 167
Sydney Rd. CT5: Whits 5G 226
CT11: Ram 4K 211
CT14: Walm 9K 177
DA6: Bexhth 2M 57
DA14: Sidc 9G 57
ME4: Chat'm 9D 80
SE2 3L 51
Sydney St. SW3 4D 4
TN23: Ashf 1F 160
Sylewood Cl. ME1: Roch 3M 93
Sylvan Glade ME5: Chat'm 2D 110
Sylvan Hill SE19 2G 13
Sylvan M. *DA9: G'hithe* *2H 61*
(off Watermans Way)
Sylvan Rd. ME8: Gill 3M 95
Sylvan Wlk. BR1: Brom 6B 70
Sylvan Way BR4: W W'ck 5H 83
Sylvester Av. BR7: Chst 2B 70
Sylvestre Cl. ME2: Hall'g 7E 92
Sylvestres TN13: Riv 3E 118
Symmonds Dr. ME10: Sit 6H 99
Symonds Cl. TN15: W King 6E 88
Symonds La. ME18: Ladd 9C 136 (5E 26)
Symonds Rd. ME3: Cliffe 4B 176
Symons Av. ME4: Chat'm 1C 94
Syndale Pl. CT11: Ram 5K 211
Syon Lodge SE12 5K 55
Syringa Ho. SE4 1C 54

T

Tabret Cl. TN24: Kenn 4H 159
Tack M. SE4 1D 54
Tadburn Grn. ME5: Chat'm 7E 94
Taddington ME5: Chat'm 5H 17
Taddington Wood La. ME5: Chat'm 9B 94
Taddy Gdns. CT9: Mgte 5G 209
Tadworth Rd. TN24: Kenn 5H 159
Taillour Cl. ME10: Kems'y 4G 99
Tail Race, The ME15: Maid 7B 126
Tainter Rd. TN11: Hdlw 7D 134
Talavera Rd. CT1: Cant 2B 172
Talbot Av. CT6: H Bay 4C 194
Talbot Pk. TN2: Tun W 9K 151
Talbot Rd. CT9: Mgte 3F 208
ME16: Alltn 3N 125
TN18: Hawkh 7C 192 (1C 44)
Talgarth Rd. W. W6 4B 4
Tall Elms Cl. BR2: Shortl 8J 69
Tallents Cl. DA4: S at H 3B 74
Tall Trees Cl. ME17: Kgswd 6F 140
Tally Ho Rd. TN26: Shad, Stu X 7A 160 (3J 39)
Tally Rd. RH8: Oxt 4B 24
Tamar Dr. ME2: Strood 6K 79
Tamarind Cl. ME7: Hpstd 7K 95
Tamar Rd. TN10: Tonb 2H 145
Tamar St. SE7 3A 50
Tame La. TN29: Burm 6E 40
Tamesis Strand DA12: Grav'nd 1K 77
Tamley La. TN25: H'lgh 7E 30
Tams Gdns. ME12: Minst 6L 221
Tamworth La. CR4: Mitc 2E 12
Tandridge Dr. BR6: Orp 2F 84
Tandridge Pl. BR6: Orp 2F 84
Tanfield Av. NW2 1A 4
Tangier Cl. CT15: Gus 1K 181
Tangier La. TN3: Tun W 7G 157
Tangleberry Cl. BR1: Brom 7B 70
Tanglewood Cl. ME8: Gill 5M 95
Tanglewood Ct. BR5: St P 6L 71
Tangmere Cl. ME7: Gill 7J 81
Tanhouse La. TN31: Peas 4J 45
Tanhouse Rd. RH8: Oxt 4A 24
Tanhurst Wlk. *SE2* *3M 51*
(off Alsike Rd.)
Tanker Hill ME8: Gill 5N 95
TANKERTON 3J 227 (3G 21)
Tankerton Bay Sailing Club 2K 227
Tankerton Cir. CT5: Whits 2H 227
Tankerton Ct. CT5: Whits 2J 227
Tankerton Hgts. CT5: Whits 2G 227
Tankerton Rd. CT5: Whits 2G 227 (3F 21)
Tankerton Slopes CT5: Whits 2J 227
Tank Hill Rd. RM19: Avel, Purf 4H 7
Tanner's Hill CT21: Hythe 4K 199 (5J 41)
Tanner's Hill Gdns. CT21: Hythe 4K 199
Tanners M. TN8: Eden 6C 184
Tanners St. ME13: Fav 5G 186 (6A 20)
Tanner St. SE1 4G 5
Tannery Cl. BR3: Beck'm 8A 68
Tannery Ct. *ME10: Sit* *6F 98*
(off Kings Mill Cl.)
Tannery La. CT13: S'wch 5L 217
TN23: Ashf 8G 159
Tannery Rd. TN9: Tonb 6J 145
Tannery Rd. Ind. Est. TN9: Tonb 6J 145
Tannsfeld Rd. SE26 1A 68

Tanyard—Three Gates Rd.

Tanyard TN18: Sandh 3C 218
Tanyard Cotts. DA12: Shorne 2C 78
Tanyard Hill DA12: Shorne 2C 78 (1E 16)
Tanyard La. DA5: Bex'y 5B 58
TN4: S'bgh 5F 150
(not continuous)
TN36: Winch 7A 46
Tanyard, The TN17: Cran 8D 176
Tapleys Hill CT4: Lwr Har 3H 31
Tappan Dr. ME4: Chat'm 2E 80
Tapsells La. TN5: Wadh 6B 36
Tara Ct. BR3: Beck'm 5E 68
Target Bus. Cen. ME15: Maid 4K 139
Target Firs CT16: Temp E 8C 178
Tarland Ho. TN2: Tun W 2K 157
Tarling Cl. DA14: Sidc 8K 57
Tarnwood Pk. SE9 5B 56
Tar Path CT14: Deal 4M 177
Tarpot La. TN25: Bils 6B 40
TN26: Ruck, Bils 6B 40
Tarragon Gro. SE26 2A 68
Tarragon Rd. ME16: Maid 6L 125
Tartane La. TN29: Dym 7B 182
Tasker Cl. ME15: Bear 6L 127
Tassell Cl. ME19: E Mal 9E 108
Tassell's Wlk. CT5: Whits 2M 227
Taswell Cl. CT16: Dover 4K 181
Taswell Rd. ME8: Rain 2C 96
Taswell St. CT16: Dover 4K 181
Tate Rd. E16 1B 50
(not continuous)
SM1: Sutt 4C 12
Tates TN18: Hawkh 6D 192
Tates Orchard DA3: Hart'y 9M 75
Tatler Cl. ME5: Chat'm 9G 94
Tatnell Rd. SE23 4B 54
TATSFIELD 9C 164 (1A 24)
Tatsfield Cl. ME8: Gill 1K 95
TATSFIELD GREEN 9D 164 (1B 24)
Tatsfield La. TN16: Tats 9F 164 (1B 24)
TATTENHAM CORNER 7B 12
Tattenham Cnr. Rd. KT18: Eps 7A 12
Tattenham Corner Station (Rail) 7B 12
Tattenham Cres. KT18: Eps 7B 12
Tattenham Way KT20: Tad 7C 12
Tattersall Cl. SE9 3A 56
Tattersall Gdns. SS9: Lgh S 1B 10
Tattershall Rd. ME15: Maid 8D 126
Tattlebury La. TN17: Goud 2D 190 (3G 37)
Tattlebury Rd. TN27: H'crn 7B 28
Taunton Cl. DA7: Bexhth 9E 52
ME15: Maid 2J 139
Taunton Rd. DA11: Nflt 3N 61
SE12 3H 55
Taunton Va. DA12: Grav'nd 8J 63
Tavern Cl. TN15: Bor G 2M 121
Taverners Rd. ME8: Gill 4N 95
Tavernors La. CT17: Dover 5J 181
Tavistock Cl. ME5: Chat'm 1C 110
ME8: Gill 4A 96
ME10: Sit 7E 98
Tavistock Pl. WC1 2F 5
Tavistock Rd. BR2: Shortl 7J 69
CT11: Ram 3J 211
DA16: Well 8L 51
Tavistock Sq. WC1 2E 4
Tavy Bri. SE2 2L 51
Tay Cl. ME5: Chat'm 6E 94
Taylor Cl. BR6: Orp 5H 85
ME17: H'shm 2M 141
Taylor Rd. CT12: Minst 7E 212
CT19: F'stone 5E 188
TN29: G'stne 8H 213
Taylor Row DA2: Dart 8J 59
Taylors Bldgs. SE18 4D 50
Taylors Cl. DA14: Sidc 8H 57
TN29: St M Bay 3M 215
Taylors Hill CT4: Chil'm 8J 175 (3D 30)
Taylor's La. ME2: Strood 5M 79
ME3: High'm 8G 64 (1F 17)
ME19: Tros 4E 106 (6B 16)
Taylors La. TN29: St M Bay 3L 215
Taylors Pl. ME19: Tros 5F 106
Taylor St. TN4: S'bgh 6F 150
Taylors Yd. TN25: Wye 2M 159
Taywood Cl. TN24: W'boro 9K 159
Tea Gdn. La. TN3: R'hall 4B 156 (3J 35)
Teal Av. BR5: St P 7M 71
Teal Cl. CT18: H'nge 9J 193
ME3: Isle G 8C 190
Teal Dr. CT6: H Bay 5F 194
Teal Way ME9: Iwade 9K 197
Teapot La. ME20: Aylfd 8J 109
Teardrop Ind. Est. BR8: Swanl 8J 73
Teasaucer ME15: Maid 3H 27
Teasaucer Hill ME15: Maid 9C 126
Teasel Cl. CR0: Croy 2A 82
ME14: Weav 5J 127
Teasel Cres. SE28 1G 51
Teasel Rd. ME5: Chat'm 7C 94
TEASLEY MEAD 3F 35
Teasley Mead TN3: Blkm 1D 154
Tebbs Way TN15: Igh 6J 121
Teddars Leas Rd. CT18: Etch'l 2M 185 (3J 41)
Tedder Av. ME5: Chat'm 4D 94
Tedder Rd. CR2: S Croy 8A 82
TN4: Tun W 7H 151
Teddington Cl. CT1: Cant 9A 168
Teelin Cl. TN29: St M Bay 2M 215
Teesdale Rd. DA2: Dart 6C 60
Teeswater Ct. DA18: Erith 3M 51
Teignmouth Rd. DA16: Well 9L 51
Teise Cl. TN2: Tun W 3J 157
TELEGRAPH HILL 5N 99 (4G 19)
Telegraph Hill ME3: High'm 2G 78 (1F 17)
Telegraph Hill Ind. Est. CT12: Minst 4F 23
Telegraph Path BR7: Chst 1D 70
Telegraph Rd. CT14: Deal 8L 177
Telemann Sq. SE3 2L 55
Telescope All. ME12: S'ness 2E 220
Telford Ct. CT6: H Bay 5D 194
CT19: F'stone 5L 189
Telford Ho. ME14: Maid 4D 126
Telford M. *CT6: H Bay* *2F 194*
(off Telford St.)
Telford Rd. SE9 7F 56
Telford St. CT6: H Bay 2F 194
Telham Av. CT12: Ram 4F 210
Tellson Av. SE18 8A 50
Telscombe Cl. BR6: Orp 3G 85
Telston La. TN14: Otf 8F 102
(not continuous)
Temeraire Hgts. CT20: F'stone 8C 188
Temeraire Mnr. *ME7: Gill* *6D 80*
(off Middle St.)
Temperance Row ME1: Woul 7G 92
Tempest Rd. ME19: W Mal 6L 123
Templar Ct. *TN8: Eden* *4C 184*
(off Farmstead Dr.)
Templar Dr. DA11: Grav'nd 1F 76
Templar Rd. CT16: Temp E 8C 178
Templars Ct. DA1: Dart 3A 60
Templar St. CT17: Dover 4H 181
Temple Av. CR0: Croy 3C 82
Temple Boat Yd. ME2: Strood 7L 79
Temple Cl. CT16: Temp E 7C 178
SE28 3E 50
TN23: Ashf 4D 160
Temple Ct. CT2: Cant 1K 171
ME2: Strood 6L 79
TEMPLE EWELL 8C 178 (7E 32)
Temple Gdns. ME2: Strood 6K 79
ME10: Sit 8J 99
TEMPLE HILL 3N 59 (6H 7)
Temple Hill DA1: Dart 4N 59 (6H 7)
Temple Hill Sq. DA1: Dart 3N 59 (6H 7)
Temple Ind. Est. ME2: Strood 6M 79
Temple Manor 6L 79
Temple M. *CT1: Cant* *2M 171*
(off Stour St.)
Temple Mill La. E10 1K 5
E15 1K 5
TEMPLE MILLS 1J 5
Temple Rd. CT2: Cant 1K 171
KT19: Eps 6A 12
TN16: Big H 5D 164
Templer Way TN23: Ashf 7E 158 (1K 39)
Temple Side CT16: Temp E 8C 178
Temple Station (Tube) 3F 5
Temple St. ME2: Strood 5L 79
Temple Way CT14: Worth 2G 33
ME19: E Mal 1D 124
Ten Acre Ct. ME17: H'shm 2M 141
Ten Acre Way ME8: Rain 1D 96
Tenby Rd. DA16: Well 8M 51
Tennison Rd. SE25 2G 13
Tennyson Av. CT1: Cant 8C 168
ME3: Cli W 6M 65
Tennyson Cl. DA16: Well 8G 51
Tennyson Gdns. CT3: Aysm 1D 162
Tennyson Ho. DA17: Belv 5A 52
Tennyson Pl. CT19: F'stone 4L 189
Tennyson Rd. DA1: Dart 3A 60
ME7: Gill 9F 80
SE20 3A 68
TN23: Ashf 3E 160
Tennyson Wlk. DA11: Nflt 8C 62
Ten Perch Rd. CT1: Cant 4K 171
Tensing Av. DA11: Nflt 8D 62
TENTERDEN 8B 224 (6E 38)
Tenterden Cl. SE9 9B 56
Tenterden Dr. CT2: Cant 7M 167
Tenterden Leisure Cen. 8C 224
Tenterden Mus. 7B 224 (6E 38)
Tenterden Rd. ME5: Chat'm 6L 79
TN17: Rolv 2B 214 (7C 38)
TN26: App 7G 39
TN27: Bidd 5C 38
(Benenden Rd.)
TN27: Bidd 8L 163 (3C 38)
(North St.)
Tenterden Town Station
Kent & East Sussex Railway 7B 224 (6E 38)
Tenterden Vineyard Pk. 7E 38
Tenterden Way CT9: Mgte 4G 208
Tent Peg La. BR5: Pet W 8E 70
Terance Butler Av. ME2: Med E 4B 80
Terence Cl. DA12: Grav'nd 6L 63
ME4: Chat'm 1D 94
Terence Ct. *DA17: Belv* *6A 52*
(off Stream Way)
Terminus Dr. CT6: H Bay 2L 195
Terminus Rd. ME16: Maid 7L 125
Terminus Wlk. *CT20: F'stone* *5L 189*
(off Tram Rd., The)
Tern Cres. ME2: Strood 6G 79
Terrace Rd. CT15: Evtn 7J 185
ME10: Sit 8J 99
ME16: Maid 5B 126
Terraces, The DA2: Dart 5C 60
Terrace St. DA12: Grav'nd 4G 63
Terrace, The CT2: Cant 8M 167
CT15: S'wll 7K 219
DA11: Grav'nd 4G 63 (6C 8)
(not continuous)
DA12: Grav'nd 4G 63
(not continuous)
ME1: Roch 7N 79
ME13: Fav 5E 186
SE23 5B 54
SW13 5A 4
TN11: Hdlw 8D 134
TN13: Riv 4E 118
TN29: Lydd 2K 205
Terry's La. CT5: Whits 3F 226
Terry's Lodge Rd. TN15: Wro 5H 105 (6K 15)
Terry's Yd. ME14: Maid 4D 126
Terry Wlk. ME19: Leyb 8C 108
TESTON 9E 124 (3F 27)
Teston Bridge Country Pk. 1F 136
TESTON CORNER 7F 124
Teston Ho. ME18: Tstn 1E 136
Teston La. ME15: W Far 1F 136 (3F 27)
ME18: Tstn 1F 136 (3F 27)
Teston Rd. ME18: E Mal 6B 124 (2E 26)
ME19: Wro, W Mal 1E 122 (1C 26)
Tetty Way BR2: Shortl 5K 69
Teviot Cl. DA16: Well 8K 51
Tewson Rd. SE18 5G 51
TEYNHAM 7K 223 (5H 19)
Teynham Cl. CT9: Clift 3K 209
Teynham Ct. BR3: Beck'm 6E 68
Teynham Dr. CT5: Whits 3H 227
Teynham Grn. BR2: Shortl 8K 69
ME8: Gill 8K 81
Teynham Rd. CT5: Whits 3H 227 (3F 21)
Teynham Station (Rail) 6L 223 (5H 19)
TEYNHAM STREET 4J 19
Thackeray Rd. ME20: Lark 7D 108
Thames Av. ME3: H Hals 1H 67
ME8: Gill 3A 96
ME12: S'ness 3C 220
Thames Barrier Visitors Cen. 4A 6
Thames Ct. ME12: Ley S 6M 203
Thames Dr. SS9: Lgh S 1B 10
Thames Ga. DA1: Dart 3A 60
Thames Gateway RM9: Dag 2E 6
RM15: Avel, Purf 1N 53
Thames Gateway Bri. E6 3C 6
SE28 3C 6
THAMES HAVEN 3G 9
Thameside Ind. Est. DA8: Erith 6L 53
THAMESMEAD 1J 51 (3D 6)
THAMESMEAD CENTRAL 1H 51 (3D 6)
THAMESMEAD EAST 2B 52
THAMESMEAD SOUTH 2M 51
THAMESMEAD SOUTH WEST 2H 51
THAMESMEAD WEST 3E 50
THAMESPORT 6D 10
Thames Rd. DA1: Cray 9G 53 (5F 7)
IG11: Bark 2C 6
TN10: Tonb 2H 145
Thames Ter. ME3: Cliffe 2C 176
Thames Vw. ME3: Cli W 6N 65
Thames Way DA11: Nflt, Grav'nd 4N 61 (6A 8)
Thanet Cl. CT10: B'stairs 8M 209
Thanet Crematorium CT9: Mgte 6C 208
Thanet Dr. BR2: Kes 4N 83
Thanet Gdns. CT19: F'stone 5M 189
Thanet Ho. DA11: Nflt 6E 62
ME15: Maid 3J 139
Thanet Indoor Bowls Cen. 2F 208
Thanet Pl. CT10: B'stairs 7M 209
Thanet Pl. Gdns. CT10: B'stairs 7M 209
Thanet Reach Bus. Pk. CT10: B'stairs 9F 208
Thanet Rd. CT8: Wgte S 2J 207
CT9: Mgte 3D 208
CT10: B'stairs 9M 209
CT11: Ram 5K 211 (4K 23)
DA5: Bex'y 5B 58
DA8: Erith 7F 52
ME8: Gill 7M 95
Thanet Ter. TN26: Hoth 3L 197
Thanet Vw. CT15: Eyt 8J 185
Thanet Way CT5: Seas 7N 187 (6C 20)
CT5: Whits 8D 226 (4E 20)
CT6: H Bay 5A 194 (3K 21)
CT7: St N 7H 215
ME13: Bou B 7N 187 (6C 20)
ME13: Hernh 9C 226
Thanet Way Cvn. Company CT7: St N 8M 215
Thanet Way Retail Pk. CT5: Whits 4L 227
Thanington Ct. CT1: Cant 4J 171
DA15: Sidc 4G 56
Thanington Rd. CT1: Cant 4J 171 (1G 31)
THANINGTON WITHOUT 4J 171 (1G 31)
Thatch Barn Rd. TN27: H'crn 7L 191
Thatcher Ct. DA1: Dart 5L 59
Thatcher Rd. TN12: S'hrst 2J 223
Thatcher's La. ME3: Cliffe 3C 176
(not continuous)
Thatchers, The ME16: Alltn 4M 125
Thaxted Rd. SE9 8E 56
Thayers Farm Rd. BR3: Beck'm 4B 68
Theatre Royal *3D 208*
(off Addington St.)
Theatre Sq. TN30: Tent 8B 224
Theatre St. CT21: Hythe 6K 199
Theberton St. N1 2F 5
Thelma Cl. DA12: Grav'nd 1L 77
Theobalds TN18: Hawkh 5C 192
Theobalds Cl. TN15: Kems'g 9A 104
Theobalds Rd. WC1 3F 5
Theodore Cl. TN2: Tun W 7L 151
Theodore Ct. SE13 4G 54
Theodore Pl. ME7: Gill 7F 80
Theodore Rd. SE13 4G 54
Therapia Lane Stop (CT) 3F 13
Theresa Rd. CT21: Hythe 7J 199
Thesiger Rd. SE20 3A 68 (1H 13)
Thicket Rd. SE20 1H 13
Thicketts TN13: S'oaks 5K 119
Third Av. CT9: Clift 2F 208
DA11: Nflt 6D 62
ME5: Chat'm 2F 94
ME7: Gill 9H 81
ME12: E'chu 2E 202
Third St. TN3: Lang G 2N 155
Thirlemere Rd. TN4: Tun W 9D 150
Thirlmere TN24: Kenn 4H 159
Thirlmere Av. CT11: Ram 5E 210
Thirlmere Cl. ME2: Strood 3N 79
ME7: Gill 7K 81
ME16: Alltn 1A 126
Thirlmere Gdns. CT3: Aysm 2D 162
Thirlmere Ri. BR1: Brom 2J 69
Thirlmere Rd. DA7: Bexhth 9D 52
Thirsk Ho. *ME15: Maid* *2J 139*
(off Fontwell Cl.)
Thirza Rd. DA1: Dart 4N 59
Thistlebank ME5: Chat'm 8D 94
Thistlebrook SE2 3L 51
Thistlebrook Ind. Est. SE2 3L 51
Thistle Ct. *DA1: Dart* *6B 60*
(off Churchill Cl.)
Thistledown DA12: Grav'nd 2J 77
ME14: Weav 5J 127
Thistledown Cl. ME7: Hpstd 7K 95
Thistlefield Cl. DA5: Bex'y 6M 57
Thistle Hill Way ME12: Minst 8H 221
(Bellflower Av.)
ME12: Minst 7J 221
(Heron Dr.)
Thistlemead BR7: Chst 5D 70
Thistle Rd. DA12: Grav'nd 5K 63
Thistle Wlk. ME10: Sit 6J 99
Thomas Dean Rd. SE26 9C 54
Thomas Dinwiddy Rd. SE12 7L 55
Thomas Dr. DA12: Grav'nd 7J 63
Thomas Dunk Almshouses *TN18: Hawkh* *5D 192*
(off Rye Rd.)
Thomas La. SE6 5D 54
Thomas More St. E1 3H 5
Thomas Rd. ME10: Sit 7J 99
ME13: Fav 5G 187
Thomas Seth Bus. Pk. ME11: Queen 9B 220
Thomas Spencer Hall of Residence *4C 50*
(off Grand Depot Rd.)
Thomas St. ME1: Roch 9N 79
SE18 4D 50
TN4: Tun W 9G 150
Thomas Wyatt Way TN15: Wro 7M 105
Thompson Cl. CT14: Walm 1D 200
CT19: F'stone 4H 189
ME8: Rain 3C 96
Thompson Rd. TN24: Ashf 5F 158
Thomson Cl. ME6: Snod 1E 108
THONG 2M 77 (1D 16)
Thong La. DA12: Grav'nd, Shorne 9L 63 (1D 16)
TN15: Bor G 3L 121 (1A 26)
Thorden Wood Rd. CT6: H Bay 5H 21
Thorn Cl. BR2: Shortl 9C 70
ME5: Chat'm 1A 110
Thorndale Cl. ME5: Chat'm 6A 94
Thornden Cl. CT6: H Bay 5B 194
Thornden Ct. CT2: Cant 7J 167
TN17: Rolv L 1H 45
Thornden La. TN17: Rolv L 1H 45
Thornden Wood Rd. CT2: Whits 1K 167
CT6: H Bay 9B 194
Thorndike Cl. ME4: Chat'm 3C 94
Thorndike Ho. ME4: Chat'm 3C 94
Thorndike Rd. TN29: Burm 3B 182 (7F 41)
Thorndon Cl. BR5: St P 5H 71
Thorndon Rd. BR5: St P 5H 71
Thorndyke Way TN15: Wro 7M 105
Thornebridge Rd. CT14: Deal 7K 177
Thorne Cl. DA8: Erith 6C 52
Thorne Est. TN27: P'ley 7G 29
Thorne Rd. CT12: Minst 7E 212
Thornes Cl. BR3: Beck'm 6F 68
Thornet Wood Rd. BR1: Brom 6C 70
Thorney Bay Rd. SS8: Can I 2K 9
Thorney Cft. Cl. ME17: Kgswd 6F 140
Thorneycroft Rd. ME13: Stal 3H 29
Thornfield Gdns. TN2: Tun W 9M 151
Thornford Rd. SE13 3F 54
Thorn Gdns. CT11: Ram 3J 211
Thornham Rd. ME8: Gill 9M 81
Thorn Hill CT12: Ram 4G 23
Thornhill Av. SE18 7G 51 (5C 6)
Thornhill Pl. ME14: Maid 3D 126
Thorn Hill Rd. ME12: Ward 3J 203 (1A 20)
Thornhill Rd. N1 1F 5
Thornhurst CT6: H Bay 3L 195
Thorn La. CT4: Elms 6G 31
Thornlea TN23: Ashf 8C 158
Thorn Rd. TN12: Mard 3D 212 (1H 37)
Thornsbeach Rd. SE6 6F 54
Thorns Mdw. TN16: Bras 5L 117
Thornton Av. SW2 7E 4
Thornton Cl. TN24: W'boro 9L 159
Thornton Dene BR3: Beck'm 5D 68
THORNTON HEATH 2G 13
THORNTON HEATH POND 3F 13
Thornton Heath Station (Rail) 2G 13
Thornton La. CT13: E'try 4H 183 (3E 32)
CT14: E'try 3E 32
Thornton Rd. BR1: Brom 1K 69
CR0: Croy 3F 13
CR7: Thor H 3F 13
DA17: Belv 4C 52
SW12 7E 4
Thorn Wlk. ME10: Sit 6K 99
Thornwood Rd. SE13 3H 55
Thorold Rd. ME5: Chat'm 9E 80
Thorpe Av. TN10: Tonb 2J 145
THORPE BAY 1F 11
Thorpe Bay Station (Rail) 1F 11
Thorpe Cl. BR6: Orp 3G 84
SE26 9A 54
Thorpe Esplanade SS1: Sth S 1F 11
Thorpe Hall Av. SS1: Sth S 1F 11
Thorpe Wlk. ME8: Gill 8M 95
(not continuous)
Thrale Rd. SW16 1E 12
Thrale Way ME8: Gill 7A 96
Thread La. ME13: Dunk, Hernh 2L 165 (7D 20)
Three Acres Site CT19: F'stone 4J 189
THREE CHIMNEYS 3B 38
Three Colts La. E2 2H 5
Three Corners DA7: Bexhth 9C 52
Three Elm La. TN11: Gold G 2E 146
TN11: Tonb, Gold G 1A 146 (5A 26)
Three Flds. Path TN30: Tent 9B 224
Three Gates Rd. DA3: Fawk 4F 88 (4J 15)

Three Kings Yd.—Trenchard Cl.

Three Kings Yd. CT13: S'wch 5M 217
THREE LEG CROSS 7E 36
Three Oaks La. TN5: Wadh 6B 36
Three Post La. CT21: Hythe 6K 199
THREE TREES 2L 139
Three Ways TN9: Tonb 7J 145
Threshers Dr. ME14: Weav 4G 127
Thriffwood SE26 . . . . . 8A 54
Thrift La. TN14: Cud 8G 100
Thrift, The DA2: Bean 8J 61
Thriftwood Cvn. Pk. TN15: Stans 4K 105
THROWLEY 2K 29
Throwley Cl. SE2 . . . . . 3L 51
(not continuous)
Throwley Cotts. CT9: Mgte 4N 207
Throwley Dr. CT6: H Bay 3D 194
THROWLEY FORSTAL 2K 29
Throwley Rd. ME13: Throw 2K 29
Throwley Way SM1: Sutt 4C 12
Thrupp Paddock CT10: B'stairs 4L 209
Thrush Cl. ME5: Chat'm 4E 94
Thruxted La. CT4: Chart'm 8A 170 (2E 30)
Thundersland Rd. CT6: H Bay 3J 195
(not continuous)
Thurbarn Rd. SE6 . . . . . 1E 68
Thurlestone Ct. ME14: Maid 3C 126
Thurlow Av. CT6: H Bay 2K 195
Thurlow Pk. Rd. SE21 . . . . . 7F 5
Thurlow St. SE17 . . . . . 4G 5
THURNHAM 1N 127 (1A 28)
Thurnham Castle 9N 111
Thurnham La.
ME14: Bear, T'hm 4M 127 (1A 28)
Thurrock Commercial Cen. RM15: Avel 2N 53
THURROCK LAKESIDE 4K 7
Thurrock Mus. 4A 8
Thursland Rd. DA14: Sidc 1N 71
Thursley Cres. CR0: Croy 8F 82
Thursley Rd. SE9 . . . . . 8B 56
Thurston Dr. ME2: Strood 5H 79
Thurston Ind. Est. SE13 . . . . . 1E 54
THURSTON PARK 4G 227
Thurston Pk. CT5: Whits 4G 227
Thurston Rd. SE13 . . . . . 1E 54 (5J 5)
Thwaite Cl. DA8: Erith 6D 52
Thyer Cl. BR6: Farnb 5E 84
Tibbenham Pl. SE6 . . . . . 7D 54
TIBBET'S CORNER 7B 4
Tibbet's Ride SW15 . . . . . 7B 4
Tibb's Ct. La. TN12: Brenc, Mat 7L 153 (2D 36)
Tiber Cl. CT19: F'stone 5C 188
TICEHURST 7E 36
Ticehurst Cl. BR5: St P 3J 71
Ticehurst Rd. SE23 . . . . . 7B 54
TN19: Hur G 1A 44
Tichborne Cl. ME16: Alltn 3N 125
TICKENHURST 2E 32
Tickford Cl. SE2 . . . . . 2L 51
TICKHAM 6H 19
Tickham La. ME9: Lyn 7H 19
Tickner's La. TN29: B'lnd 2F 47
Tiddymotts La. TN17: Goud 3C 190
TIDEBROOK 7A 36
Tidebrook TN5: Tide 7A 36
Tidebrook Rd. TN5: Tide, Wadh 7A 36
Tidelea Twr. SE28 . . . . . 2E 50
(off Erebus Dr.)
Tideside Ct. SE18 . . . . . 3A 50
Tides Leisure Pool 5M 177
Tideswell Rd. CR0: Croy 4D 82
Tideway, The ME1: Roch 4N 93 (4H 17)
Tidford Rd. DA16: Well 9H 51
Tidlock Ho. SE28 . . . . . 2F 50
(off Erebus Dr.)
Tiepigs La. BR2: Brom 3H 83
BR4: W W'ck 3H 83 (4K 13)
Tiger La. BR2: Shortl 7L 69
Tilbrook Rd. SE3 . . . . . 1M 55
TILBURY 5C 8
Tilbury Cl. BR5: St P 5K 71
Tilbury Fort 2H 63 (6C 8)
Tilbury Rd. ME8: Rain 1C 96
Tilbury Town Station (Rail) 5B 8
Tilden Chapel La. TN27: Smar 2D 38
Tilden Cl. TN26: H Hald 2B 196
Tilden Cotts. TN27: H'crn 6L 191
Tilden Ct. TN26: H Hald 2C 196
Tilden Gill Rd. TN30: Tent 9D 224
Tilden La. ME17: Ulc 7B 28
TN12: Mard 6H 27
TN27: H'crn, Ulc 7B 28
Tilebarn Cnr. TN10: Tonb 3L 145
Tile Farm Rd. BR6: Orp 4F 84
Tile Flds. ME17: Holl 7F 128
Tile Ho., The CT21: Hythe 6K 199
(off Mount St.)
Tilehurst Point SE2 . . . . . 2M 51
(Blewbury Ho.)
SE2 . . . . . 2L 51
(Tavy Bri.)
Tile Kiln Hill CT2: Blean 6H 167 (6G 21)
Tile Kiln La. CT19: F'stone 4F 188 (4A 42)
DA5: Bex'y 7D 58 (7F 7)
(not continuous)
Tile Kiln Rd. TN24: Kenn 3G 159
Tile Lodge Rd. TN27: Char'g 5G 29
Tilford Av. CR0: Croy 9F 82
Tilghman Way ME6: Snod 1F 108
Tillard Cl. CT4: P'hm 4G 31
Till Av. DA4: Farn'm 1N 87
Tillery La. TN29: Ivyc 3E 46
Tilley Cl. ME3: Hoo 8G 67
Tillingbourne Grn. BR5: St M Cry 7H 71
Tillmans TN15: Bor G 2N 121
Tilmans Mead DA4: Farn'm 2N 87
TILMANSTONE 4F 33
Tilsden La. TN17: Cran 9E 176 (5J 37)
Tilton Rd. TN15: Bor G 2M 121
Tilt Yd. App. SE9 . . . . . 4B 56
Timber Bank DA13: Meop 3E 106
Timberbank ME5: Chat'm 5D 94
Timber Cl. BR7: Chst 5C 70
Timbercroft La. SE18 . . . . . 6G 50 (5C 6)
TIMBERDEN BOTTOM 1F 102 (5F 15)
Timbertop Rd. TN16: Big H 6C 164
Timber Tops ME5: Chat'm 2G 111
Timber Yd. Ind. Est. CT12: Ram 5D 210
Time Ball Tower Mus. 5N 177
(off Victoria Pde.)
Times Sq. TN1: Tun W 1G 157
Timothy Cl. DA6: Bexhth 3N 57
Timothy Ho. DA18: Erith 2N 51
(off Kale Rd.)
Timperley Cl. CT14: Deal 4K 177
Tina Gdns. CT10: B'stairs 7L 209
Tinbridge Oast ME13: Fav 7L 187
Tinker Pot La.
TN15: Knat, W King 5B 104 (6J 15)
Tinkerpot Ri. TN15: W King 4C 104
Tinker's All. ME4: Chat'm 5C 80
Tinkers La. TN5: Tice 7E 36
Tin Shop Hill ME13: Fav 3D 186 (5K 19)
Tintagel Gdns. ME2: Strood 5K 79
Tintagel Mnr. ME7: Gill 6F 80
Tintagel Rd. BR5: Orp 3L 85
Tintern Rd. ME16: Alltn 3N 125
Tippens Cl. TN17: Cran 8D 176
Tippledore La. CT10: B'stairs 8J 209
Titchfield Cl. ME15: Maid 2J 139
Titchfield Rd. ME15: Maid 2J 139
Tithe Barn La. TN23: Ashf 1B 160 (2K 39)
Tithepit Shaw La. CR6: Warl 7H 13
Titmuss Av. SE28 . . . . . 1K 51
TITSEY 2A 24
Titsey Hill RH8: Tats 2A 24
Titsey Place 2A 24
Titsey Rd. RH8: Oxt, Tats 3A 24
Tiverton Dr. SE9 . . . . . 6E 56
Tiverton Rd. NW10 . . . . . 2B 4
Tivoli Brooks CT9: Mgte 4C 208
Tivoli Gdns. DA12: Grav'nd 6G 63
SE18 . . . . . 4A 50
(not continuous)
Tivoli Pk. Av. CT9: Mgte 4B 208 (1H 23)
Tivoli Rd. CT9: Mgte 5C 208 (2H 23)
Tobruk Way ME5: Chat'm 5C 94
Toby Gdns. TN11: Hdlw 8D 134
Toby Rd. TN29: G'stne 8H 213
Tockwith Ct. TN13: S'oaks 5K 119
Todd Cres. ME10: Kems'y 3H 99
Toddington Cres. ME5: Chat'm 1A 110
Toke Cl. TN23: Gt Cha 9A 158
Tolcairn Ct. DA17: Belv 5B 52
Toledo Paddock ME7: Gill 7G 81
Tolgate La. ME2: Strood 5M 79
Tolgate Rd. TN33: Sed 7E 44
Tolhurst Rd. TN12: Five G 8F 146
Tollemache Cl. CT12: Mans 9L 207
Tollgate CT14: Deal 6K 177
Tollgate Cl. CT5: Whits 5E 226
Tollgate M. TN15: Bor G 2N 121
Tollgate Pl. TN27: H'crn 8M 191
Tollgate Rd. DA2: Dart 5D 60
E6 . . . . . 3A 6
E16 . . . . . 3A 6
TN33: Sed 7E 44
Tollgate Way ME14: S'lng 7B 110
TOLLHURST 7D 36
Tollington Pk. N4 . . . . . 1F 5
Tollington Rd. N7 . . . . . 1F 5
Tollington Way N7 . . . . . 1F 5
Toll La. TN27: Char'g 3M 175 (5J 29)
Tollwood Rd. TN6: Crowb 7G 35
Tolputt Ct. CT19: F'stone 5L 189
Tolsey Mead TN15: Bor G 1N 121
Tolsford Cl. CT18: Etch'l 2M 185 (3J 41)
CT19: F'stone 5D 188
TOLWORTH 4A 12
TOLWORTH JUNCTION (TOBY JUG) 4A 12
Tolworth Ri. Nth. KT5: Surb 3A 12
Tolworth Ri. Sth. KT5: Surb 3A 12
Tolworth Station (Rail) 4A 12
Tombridge Chambers TN9: Tonb 7H 145
Tom Coombs Cl. SE9 . . . . . 2A 56
Tom Cribb Rd. SE28 . . . . . 3E 50
Tom Joyce Cl. ME6: Snod 3D 108
Tomlin Cl. ME6: Snod 2E 108
TN12: S'hrst 2J 223
Tomlin Gdns. CT9: Mgte 5G 209
TOMPSET'S BANK 6B 34
Tomson's Pas. CT11: Ram 5H 211
Tom Thumb Theatre 2F 208
TONBRIDGE 5H 145 (6K 25)
Tonbridge Angels F.C. (Longmead Stadium)
. . . . . 2G 145
Tonbridge By-Pass TN11: Hild, Leigh 1A 144
(Tonbridge)
TN11: Hild, S'oaks 6N 131
(Sevenoaks)
TN11: Tonb 7C 144
TN14: S'oaks, Tonb 4H 25
Tonbridge Castle 5H 145 (6K 25)
Tonbridge Ct. ME16: Maid 6N 125
Tonbridge Ho. ME2: Strood 3N 79
(off Cypress Ct.)
Tonbridge Ind. Est. TN9: Tonb 6K 145
Tonbridge Rd. ME16: Barm, Tstn, Maid 6B 126
ME16: Maid 6B 126
ME18: Mere, W'bury 1J 135 (3D 26)
TN2: Pem 5N 151 (1A 36)
TN8: Chid 5C 142 (6E 24)
TN11: Chid 5C 142 (6E 24)
TN11: Gold G 3H 147 (5C 26)
TN11: Hdlw 9A 134 (5A 26)
TN11: Hild 1C 144 (5J 25)
TN11: Pem, Tun W 5N 151 (1A 36)
TN11: S'brne, Tonb 4J 133 (4K 25)
TN12: E Peck 3H 147
Tonbridge Rd. TN13: S'oaks 9K 119 (3G 25)
TN15: Igh, Plax 8J 121 (2K 25)
Tonbridge Station (Rail) 6H 145 (6K 25)
Tonbridge Swimming Pool 5H 145
Tonford La. CT1: Harb 4H 171 (1G 31)
CT2: Harb 2F 170 (1G 31)
(not continuous)
TONG 6B 28
TONGE 8N 99 (5G 19)
Tonge Castle 7M 99
Tonge Cl. BR3: Beck'm 8D 68
TONGE CORNER 4N 99 (4G 19)
Tonge Rd. ME10: Sit 7J 99 (5F 19)
TONG GREEN 2J 29
Tong La. ME13: E'lng 1H 29
TN3: Lamb 3E 36
Tong Rd. TN12: Brenc 9N 153 (2D 36)
Tongswood Dr. TN18: Hawkh 6F 192 (7J 37)
Tonics Fitness Cen. 4F 114
Tontine St. CT20: F'stone 6K 189 (4B 42)
Tookey Rd. TN28: New R 3K 213
Tooley St. DA11: Nflt 5C 62
SE1 . . . . . 3G 5
TOOTING 1D 12
TOOTING BEC 7E 4
Tooting Bec Gdns. SW16 . . . . . 1E 12
Tooting Bec Rd. SW16 . . . . . 1E 12
SW17 . . . . . 7E 4
Tooting Bec Station (Tube) 7E 4
Tooting Broadway Station (Tube) 1D 12
TOOTING GRAVENEY 1D 12
Tooting High St. SW17 . . . . . 1D 12
Tooting Station (Rail) 1E 12
Tootswood Rd. BR2: Shortl 8H 69
Topaz Dr. ME10: Sit 5D 98
Topcliffe Dr. BR6: Farnb 5F 84
Top Dartford Rd. BR8: Swanl 3G 73 (1F 15)
DA2: Dart 3G 73 (1F 15)
Topley Dr. ME3: H Hals 2H 67
Topley St. SE9 . . . . . 2M 55
Top Pk. BR3: Beck'm 8H 69
Top Rd. TN30: Ston C E 2B 46
Torbay TN12: Pad W 2N 147 (5D 26)
Torbrook Cl. DA5: Bex'y 4N 57
Tor Gro. SE28 . . . . . 1G 50
Tormore M. CT14: Deal 6K 177
Tormore Pk. CT14: Deal 6K 177
Tormount Rd. SE18 . . . . . 6G 50
Toronto Cl. CT16: Dover 1G 181
Toronto Rd. ME7: Gill 8H 81
Torrens Wlk. DA12: Grav'nd 1K 77
Torriano Av. NW5 . . . . . 1E 4
Torridon Rd. SE6 . . . . . 5G 55 (7K 5)
SE13 . . . . . 7K 5
Torrington Cl. ME18: Mere 9J 123
Torrington Pl. WC1 . . . . . 2E 4
Torrington Rd. TN23: Ashf 1F 160
Tor Rd. DA16: Well 8L 51
Torr Rd. SE20 . . . . . 3A 68
Torver Way BR6: Orp 4F 84
Tothill Rd. CT12: Minst 7E 212
Tothill St. CT12: Minst 4F 23
Totnes Rd. DA16: Well 7K 51
Tottenham Ct. Rd. W1 . . . . . 2E 4
Tottenham Court Road Station (Tube) 3E 4
Tourist Info. Cen.
Ashford 8F 158 (1A 40)
Battle 7C 44
Bexley 4D 58 (6F 7)
Bexleyheath 2B 58 (6E 6)
Broadstairs 9M 209 (3K 23)
Canterbury 2M 171 (1H 31)
Cranbrook 7D 176 (4J 37)
Croydon 4G 13
Deal 3J 33
Deal 4N 177
Dover 5K 181 (2F 43)
Edenbridge 5C 184
Faversham 5H 187 (6A 20)
Folkestone 6L 189 (4B 42)
Gillingham 6F 80
Gravesend 5G 63 (6C 8)
Gravesend 4G 63
Greenwich 5K 5
Herne Bay 2G 194 (2J 21)
Hythe 6J 199 (5H 41)
Lewisham 2F 54 (6K 5)
Maidstone 5C 126 (2H 27)
Margate 3C 208 (1H 23)
New Romney 3J 213 (3J 47)
Ramsgate 6J 211 (4K 23)
Redbridge 1B 6
Rochester 6N 79 (2H 17)
Rye 5B 46
Sandwich 5L 217 (1G 33)
Sevenoaks 7K 119 (2G 25)
Southend-on-Sea 1E 10
Swanley 6F 72
Tenterden 8B 224 (6E 38)
Thurrock Services 4K 7
Tonbridge 5H 145 (6K 25)
Tunbridge Wells 3G 156 (3K 35)
Tourist Info. Cen. CT6: H Bay 2G 194
CT16: Dover 5K 181
Tourmaline Dr. ME10: Sit 5D 98
Tournay Cl. TN23: Ashf 1D 160
Tourney Cl. CT21: Lymp 5A 198
Tourney Rd. TN29: Lydd 4J 205 (5G 47)
Tourtel Rd. CT1: Cant 1N 171 (7H 21)
TOVIL 7B 126 (2H 27)
Tovil Grn. ME15: Maid 7B 126
Tovil Green Bus. Pk.
ME15: Maid 8B 126
Tovil Hill ME15: Maid 8B 126 (2H 27)
Tovil Rd. ME15: Maid 7C 126 (2H 27)
Tower Bri. E1 . . . . . 3G 5
SE1 . . . . . 3G 5
Tower Bri. Rd. SE1 . . . . . 4G 5
Tower Bungs. CT7: Birch 3F 206
Tower Cl. BR6: Orp 3H 85
DA12: Grav'nd 1K 77
Tower Ct. CT20: S'gte 8E 188
Tower Cft. DA4: Eyns 3M 87
Tower Est. TN29: Dym 5D 182
Tower Gdns. CT21: Hythe 7K 199
ME14: Bear 5L 127
Tower Gateway Station (DLR) 3G 5
TOWER HAMLETS 4H 181 (2F 43)
Tower Hamlets Rd. CT17: Dover 4H 181 (2F 43)
Tower Hamlets St. CT17: Dover 4H 181
TOWER HILL 3G 5
Tower Hill CT5: Whits 2G 227 (3F 21)
CT17: Dover 4H 181
ME19: Off 3J 123 (1C 26)
Tower Hill Station (Tube) 3G 5
Tower Ind. Est. TN15: Wro 5K 105
Tower La. ME14: Bear 5K 127
Tower Pde. CT5: Whits 2G 226 (3F 21)
Tower Pk. Rd. DA1: Cray 3G 59
Tower Retail Pk. DA1: Cray 3G 58
Tower Rd. BR6: Orp 3H 85 (4C 14)
CT5: Whits 3G 227
DA1: Dart 5K 59
DA7: Bexhth 2B 58
DA17: Belv 4D 52
Tower St. CT17: Dover 4H 181 (2F 43)
TN31: Rye 5B 46
Towers Vw. TN24: Kenn 3G 159
Towers Wood DA4: S Dar 4D 74
Tower Vw. CR0: Croy 1B 82
ME19: W Mal 5N 123 (1D 26)
Tower Way CT1: Cant 2M 171
Town Acres TN10: Tonb 3J 145
Towncourt Cres. BR5: Pet W 8E 70
Towncourt La. BR5: Pet W 9F 70 (3C 14)
Townfield Cnr. DA12: Grav'nd 6H 63
Towngate Wood Pk. TN10: Tonb 9L 133
Town Hill CT4: Brid 8E 172 (2J 31)
ME19: W Mal 9A 108 (7E 16)
RH7: Ling 1A 34
TN3: Lamb 3K 201 (5D 36)
Town Hill Cl. ME19: W Mal 9A 108
Townland Cl. TN27: Bidd 7L 163
TOWNLAND GREEN 7A 228 (5H 39)
Town La. CT4: Cha H 4C 170 (1F 31)
Townley Rd. DA6: Bexhth 3A 58 (6E 6)
Townley St. CT11: Ram 6H 211
Town Lock Ho. TN9: Tonb 5J 145
Town Lock M. TN9: Tonb 5J 145
Townmead Rd. SW6 . . . . . 6C 4
Town Rd. CT4: P'hm 4G 31
ME3: Cli W 9L 65 (7G 9)
TOWN ROW 7J 35
Townsend Farm Rd. CT15: St Marg 7B 214
Townsend Rd. ME6: Snod 1C 108
Townsend Sq. ME19: W Mal 7M 123
Townsend Ter. CT17: Dover 7G 180
Townshend Cl. DA14: Sidc 2K 71
Townshend Rd. BR7: Chst 1D 70
Town Sq. DA8: Erith 6F 52
Town Wlk. CT20: F'stone 7K 189
Townwall St. CT16: Dover 5K 181 (2G 43)
Toy & Model Mus. 4E 36
Toynbec Cl. BR7: Chst 9D 56
TOY'S HILL 4D 24
Toy's Hill TN8: Four E, Westrm 4D 24
TN16: Westrm 4D 24
Tracies, The ME9: N'tn 5L 97
Tradescant Dr. DA13: Meop 9G 76
Trafalgar Av. SE15 . . . . . 4G 5
Trafalgar Cl. ME1: Woul 6G 92
Trafalgar Ct. DA8: Erith 7G 53
(off Frobisher Rd.)
Trafalgar Pde. ME12: Minst 6J 221
Trafalgar Rd. CT7: Wdchu 8L 207
CT15: St Marg 8B 200
DA1: Dart 7M 59
DA11: Grav'nd 5F 62
SE10 . . . . . 5K 5
Trafalgar Sq. SW1 . . . . . 3E 4
Trafalgar St. ME7: Gill 7F 80
Tram Rd., The CT20: F'stone 6L 189 (4B 42)
Tramways ME5: Chat'm 1F 94
Tranquil Ri. DA8: Erith 5F 52
Tranquil Va. SE3 . . . . . 5K 5
Transfesa Rd. TN12: Pad W 7M 147
Transmere Cl. BR5: Pet W 9E 70
Transmere Rd. BR5: Pet W 9E 70
Transom Ho. ME1: Roch 2N 93
Trapfield Cl. ME14: Bear 5M 127
Trapfield La. ME14: Bear 5M 127
(not continuous)
Trapham Rd. ME16: Maid 4A 126
Traps La. KT3: N Mald 2A 12
Travers Gdns. ME9: B'gar 5A 114
Travers Rd. CT14: Deal 5K 177
Travertine Rd. ME5: Chat'm 1E 110
Treasury Vw. CT3: Ickh 1A 32
Trebble Rd. DA10: Swans 4L 61
Trebilco Cl. TN2: Tun W 7K 151
Treblers Rd. TN6: Jar B 7G 35
Tredegar Rd. DA2: Dart 7H 59
E3 . . . . . 2J 5
Tredwell Cl. BR2: Shortl 7A 70
Treebourne Rd. TN16: Big H 5C 164
Tree La. TN15: Plax 9L 121 (3A 26)
Treetops DA12: Grav'nd 1G 77
Tree Tops TN9: Tonb 8H 145
Treetops TN15: Kems'g 8A 104
Treetops Cl. SE2 . . . . . 5N 51
Treewall Gdns. BR1: Brom 9L 55
Trefoil Ho. DA18: Erith 2N 51
(off Kale Rd.)
Trefor Jones Ct. CT16: Dover 2G 180
Tregony Rd. BR6: Chels 5H 85
Trelawn Cres. ME5: Chat'm 9E 94
Trellyn Cl. ME16: Barm 7K 125
Trenchard Cl. TN24: W'boro 1K 161

V

Victoria Ter.—Warren La.

Victoria Ter. CT21: Hythe 9B 188
ME1: Roch 1L 93
Victor Rd. SE20 3A 68
Victory Cotts. TN14: Weald 6K 131
Victory Ct. DA8: Erith 7G 53
(off Frobisher Rd.)
Victory Mnr. ME7: Gill 5D 80
(off Middle St.)
Victory Pk. ME2: Med E 5B 80
Victory Rd. CT15: St Marg 9A 200
Victory St. ME12: S'ness 2C 220
Victory Way DA2: Dart 2C 60
Vidal Mnr. ME7: Gill 7F 80
(off Britton St.)
Vidgeon Av. ME3: Hoo 7F 66
View Cl. TN16: Big H 4C 164
View Ct. SE12 8M 55
Viewfield Rd. DA5: Bex'y 6L 57
Viewland Rd. SE18 5H 51
Viewlands ME5: Chat'm 9F 80
Viewlands Av. TN16: Westrm 2G 117
View Rd. ME3: Cli W 6L 65 (7G 9)
View, The SE2 5N 51
Vigilant Way DA12: Grav'nd 1L 77 (1D 16)
Vigo Hill ME19: Tros 4D 106 (6B 16)
Vigo La. ME9: B'gar, B'den 5M 113 (6D 18)
Vigo Rd. TN15: Stans 2A 106 (6A 16)
Vigo Ter. ME9: Tey 8J 223
VIGO VILLAGE 2F 106 (6C 16)
Viking Cl. CT7: Birch 3C 206
ME2: Strood 8K 79
Viking Ct. CT2: Cant 9M 167
(off St Stephen's Cl.)
CT9: Mgte 3E 208
CT10: B'stairs 1M 211
Viking Rd. DA11: Nflt 8B 62
Viking Way DA8: Erith 3D 52
TN15: W King 6E 88
Villa Cl. DA12: Grav'nd 7N 63
Villa Ct. DA1: Dart 7M 59
Villacourt Rd. SE18 7J 51
Village Ct. SE3 1H 55
(off Hurren Cl.)
Village Cres., The DA9: Bluew 5F 60
Village Grn. Av. TN16: Big H 5E 164
Village Grn. Rd. DA1: Cray 2H 59
Village Grn. Way TN16: Big H 5E 164
Village, The DA9: Bluew 5F 60
SE7 5A 6
Village Vw. ME5: Chat'm 1F 94
Village Way BR3: Beck'm 5D 68 (2J 13)
SE21 6G 5
TN26: Hams 3L 191
Villa Rd. ME3: High'm 1F 78 (1F 17)
Villas Rd. SE18 5E 50
(not continuous)
Villas, The CT3: Hersd 2M 169
Villiers Ct. CT17: Dover 5H 181
Villiers Ho. CT10: B'stairs 6M 209
Villiers Rd. BR3: Beck'm 5A 68
CT1: Cant 1C 172
Vincent Cl. BR2: Shortl 7L 69
CT10: B'stairs 1G 210
CT20: F'stone 7E 188
DA15: Sidc 6G 56
Vincent Ct. ME12: S'ness 3D 220
Vincent Gdns. ME12: S'ness 3D 220
Vincent Pl. TN24: Kenn 6K 159
Vincent Rd. CT9: Mgte 9A 208 (3H 23)
ME10: Sit 8K 99
ME20: Aylfd 3N 109
SE18 4D 50
Vincent Sq. TN16: Big H 3B 164
Vincers Cotts. TN25: Sme 8K 165
Vine Av. TN13: S'oaks 6J 119
Vine Cl. CT11: Ram 2J 211
Vine Ct. ME18: W'bury 9C 124
Vine Ct. Rd. TN13: S'oaks 6K 119
Vinehall Rd. TN32: Mount 5C 44
VINEHALL STREET 5C 44
Vinelands TN29: Lydd 3J 205
Vine Lodge TN13: S'oaks 6K 119
Vine Lodge Ct. TN13: S'oaks 6K 119
Vineries, The ME7: Gill 7H 81
SE6 6D 54
Vine Rd. BR6: Chels 7H 85 (5C 14)
Viners Cl. ME10: Sit 1F 114
Vines La. ME1: Roch 7N 79 (2H 17)
TN11: Hild 7C 132 (4J 25)
Vine, The TN13: S'oaks 6J 119
Vine Way TN12: S'hrst 3J 223
Vineyard Cl. SE6 6D 54
Vineyard Cres. ME8: Rain 2D 96
Vineyard La. TN5: Tice 7D 36
Viney Bank CR0: Croy 9C 82
Viney Cotts. ME17: Leeds 2B 140
Viney Rd. SE13 1E 54
Vineys Gdns. TN30: Tent 7D 224
Vinson Cl. BR6: Orp 2J 85
ME13: G'ney 5C 20
Vinten Cl. CT6: H Bay 7J 195
VINTERS PARK 1J 27
Vinters Pk. Crematorium
ME14: Weav 3G 127 (1J 27)
Vinters Rd. ME14: Maid 4E 126
Vinters Valley Nature Reserve 4G 126
Vintners Ct. ME14: Weav 5H 127
Vintners Way ME14: Weav 5H 127
Viola Av. SE2 4K 51
Violet Av. CT12: Ram 2G 210
Violet Cl. ME5: Chat'm 2D 110
Violet Rd. E3 2J 5
Violets, The TN12: Pad W 1M 153
Virginia Rd. CR7: Thor H 2F 13
CT5: Whits 5J 227
ME7: Gill 5F 80
Virginia Wlk. DA12: Grav'nd 2J 77
Virgins La. TN33: Batt 7C 44
Visitors' Cen. (Summer Only) 5N 189
Vista, The DA14: Sidc 1H 71
SE9 4N 55
Vixen Cl. ME5: Chat'm 4F 94
Vlissingen Dr. CT14: Deal 2M 177
Voce Rd. SE18 7F 50
Vogue Ct. BR1: Brom 4L 69
Volante Dr. ME10: Sit 4F 98
Vulcan Bus. Cen. CR0: Croy 9H 83
Vulcan Cl. CT5: Whits 6E 226
ME5: Chat'm 4E 94
Vyne, The DA7: Bexhth 1C 58
Vyvyan Cotts. TN17: Bendn 7A 38

W

Wacher Cl. CT2: Cant 9M 167
Wadard Ter. BR8: Swanl 8K 73
Wadden Hall CT4: Walt 6G 31
Waddington Dr. CT18: H'nge 8K 193
WADDON 4F 13
Waddon Marsh Stop (CT) 3F 13
Waddon New Rd. CR0: Croy 4F 13
Waddon Rd. CR0: Croy 4F 13
Waddon Station (Rail) 4F 13
Waddon Way CR0: Croy 5F 13
Wade Av. BR5: Orp 1M 85
Wade Ct. TN29: St M Mar 2H 215
Wades Cl. TN12: Mard 2D 212
Wadeville Cl. DA17: Belv 5B 52
Wadham Pl. ME10: Sit 9J 99
WADHURST 6B 36
Wadhurst Rd. TN3: Frant 5K 35
TN5: Wadh 7K 35
TN6: Mark C 7K 35
Wadhurst Station (Rail) 6B 36
Wadlands Rd. ME3: Cliffe 3C 176
Waghorn Rd. ME6: Snod 2E 108
Waghorn St. ME4: Chat'm 9E 80
Wagoners Cl. ME14: Weav 5H 127
Wagon La. TN12: Pad W 6N 147 (6D 26)
Wagstaff La. TN27: Bidd 3D 38
Wagtail Wlk. BR3: Beck'm 8F 68
Wagtail Way BR5: St P 7M 71
Waid Cl. DA1: Dart 4N 59
Wain Ct. ME12: Minst 7H 221
Wainhouse Cl. TN8: Eden 4D 184
WAINSCOTT 2A 80 (1H 17)
Wainscott Eastern By-Pass
ME2: Wain 2A 80 (1H 17)
Wainscott Northern By-Pass
ME2: Strood 4E 78 (1F 17)
Wainscott Rd. ME2: Wain 2A 80 (1H 17)
Wainscott Wlk. ME2: Wain 1A 80
Wainwright Pl. TN24: Ashf 1H 161
Waite Davies Rd. SE12 5J 55
Wakefield Cl. ME2: Strood 6H 79
Wakefield Rd. DA9: G'hithe 3J 61
Wakefield St. DA11: Grav'nd 4G 62
Wakefield Wlk. CT21: Hythe 7K 199
Wakefield Way CT21: Hythe 7J 199
Wakehurst Cl. ME17: Cox 5M 137
Wakeley Rd. ME8: Rain 2C 96
Wakelin Ho. SE23 5B 54
(off Brockley Pk.)
Wakely Cl. TN16: Big H 6C 164
Wakering Rd. SS1: Gt W 1F 11
SS3: Shoe 1H 11
Wake Rd. ME1: Roch 3N 93
Walcheren Cl. CT14: Deal 1M 177
Walcott Pl. CT6: H Bay 4J 195
Waldair Ct. E16 2D 50
Waldeck Rd. DA1: Dart 5N 59
Waldegrave Rd. BR1: Brom 7A 70
Walden Av. BR7: Chst 9B 56
Walden Cl. DA17: Belv 5A 52
Waldenhurst Rd. BR5: St M Cry 1M 85
Walden Pde. BR7: Chst 2B 70
(not continuous)
Walden Rd. BR7: Chst 2B 70
Waldens Cl. BR5: St M Cry 1M 85
Waldens Rd. BR5: St M Cry 1N 85 (3E 14)
Waldens, The ME17: Kgswd 6G 140
Walder Chain CT4: B'hm, Woot 5A 32
Waldershare Av. CT13: S'wch 1J 33
Waldershare La.
CT15: W Lan, E Lan 3K 179 (6G 33)
Waldershare Rd. CT15: Ashy 5F 33
WALDERSLADE 8D 94 (5J 17)
WALDERSLADE BOTTOM 8D 94
Walderslade Cen. ME5: Chat'm 8D 94
Walderslade Rd. ME4: Chat'm 3C 94 (4H 17)
ME5: Chat'm 3C 94 (4H 17)
Walderslade Village By-Pass
ME5: Chat'm 8C 94
Walderslade Woods ME5: Chat'm 8A 94 (5H 17)
Waldo Ind. Est. BR1: Brom 6N 69
Waldo Rd. BR1: Brom 6N 69
Waldram Pk. Rd. SE23 6A 54 (7H 5)
Waldrist Way DA18: Erith 2A 52
Waldron Dr. ME15: Maid 2C 138
Waldron Gdns. BR2: Shortl 6G 68
Waldron Rd. CT10: B'stairs 2M 211
Walerand Rd. SE13 1F 54
Wales Farm Rd. W3 3A 4
WALHAM GREEN 5C 4
Walkden Rd. BR7: Chst 1C 70
Walker Cl. DA1: Cray 1G 58
SE18 4E 50
Walker La. CT7: Birch 3C 206
Walker Pl. TN15: Igh 3K 121
Walkhurst Rd. TN17: Bendn 6A 38
Walkley Rd. DA1: Dart 3J 59
Walks, The TN3: Groom 5K 155
Walk, The ME17: Kgswd 6G 140
Wallace Cl. TN2: Tun W 5G 157
Wallace Gdns. DA10: Swans 4L 61
Wallace M. CT19: F'stone 4K 189
Wallace Rd. ME1: Roch 3B 94
Wallace Way CT10: B'stairs 9J 209
Wallbridge La. ME8: Rain 1F 96 (3B 18)
Wallbutton Rd. SE4 1B 54
Wall Cl. ME3: Hoo 6G 66
WALLCROUCH 7D 36
Walled Gdn. Cl. BR3: Beck'm 7E 68
WALL END 5B 22
WALLEND 1B 6
Waller Rd. TN28: G'stne 7H 213
Wallers TN3: Speld 7A 150
Wallers Cotts. ME15: E Far 4K 137
Wallers Rd. ME13: Fav 5E 186
Walleys Cl. ME8: Rain 2D 96
WALL HILL 4B 34
Wall Hill Rd. RH18: F Row 4B 34
RH19: A'hstw 4B 34
Wallhouse Rd. DA8: Erith 7J 53
WALLINGTON 5E 12
WALLINGTON GREEN 4E 12
Wallington Station (Rail) 5E 12
Wallis Av. ME15: Maid 3H 139 (3K 27)
Wallis Cl. DA2: Dart 8G 59
Wallis Fld. TN3: Groom 7J 155
Wallis Pk. DA11: Nflt 3A 62
Wallis Rd. TN24: Ashf 8H 159
Wall Rd. TN24: Ashf 7F 158
Wall, The ME10: Sit 6F 98
Wallwood Rd. CT11: Ram 4K 211
WALMER 9L 177 (4J 33)
Walmer Castle & Gardens 9N 177 (4J 33)
Walmer Castle Rd. CT14: Walm 9M 177
Walmer Cl. BR6: Farnb 5F 84
Walmer Ct. CT14: Walm 9L 177
ME14: Maid 4D 126
Walmer Gdns. CT12: C'snd 7A 210
CT14: Walm 8K 177
ME10: Sit 6E 98
Walmer Ho. ME2: Strood 3N 79
(off Cypress Ct.)
Walmer Rd. CT5: Whits 5G 226
Walmers Av. ME3: High'm 9E 64
Walmer Station (Rail) 9K 177 (4J 33)
Walmer Ter. SE18 4E 50
Walmer Way CT14: Walm 8K 177
CT20: F'stone 6F 188
Walmestone Rd. CT3: Pres, Ash 7C 22
Walm La. NW2 1B 4
Walmsley Ho. CT19: F'stone 5L 189
(off Princess St.)
Walmsley Rd. CT10: B'stairs 8K 209
Walner Gdns. TN28: New R 2K 213
Walner La. TN28: New R 2K 213
Walnut Cl. CT10: B'stairs 2K 211
DA4: Eyns 4L 87
ME5: Chat'm 3E 94
ME18: Yald 7D 136
TN12: Pad W 9M 147
TN24: Kenn 4H 159
Walnut Hill Rd.
DA13: Meop, Ist R 6D 76 (2B 16)
Walnut Ridge TN25: Aldtn 4D 40
Walnut Row ME20: Dit 1F 124
Walnuts Leisure Cen. 2J 85
Walnuts Rd. BR6: Orp 2K 85
Walnuts, The 2J 85
(off High St.)
Walnut Tree Av. DA1: Dart 7M 59
ME15: Maid 3D 138
Walnut Tree Cl. BR7: Chst 4F 70
CT7: Birch 4F 206
Walnut Tree Cott. ME18: Yald 7D 136
Walnut Tree Cotts. ME15: Maid 3D 138
Walnut Tree Ct. ME20: Lark 9F 108
Walnut Tree Dr. ME10: Sit 7E 98
Walnut Tree La. CT2: Sturry 4J 169
ME15: Maid 3D 138
Walnut Tree Rd. DA8: Erith 5F 52
RM8: Dag 1E 6
Walnut Tree Way DA13: Meop 9F 76
Walnut Way BR8: Swanl 5E 72
TN4: S'bgh 6K 151
Walpole Bay Living Mus. 2F 208
Walpole Cl. ME19: E Mal 9D 108
Walpole Pl. SE18 4D 50
Walpole Rd. BR2: Shortl 8N 69
CT9: Mgte 2D 208
Walsby Dr. ME10: Kems'y 3H 99
Walsham Rd. ME5: Chat'm 1C 110
Walshaw Ho. ME14: Maid 3D 126
Walshes Rd. TN6: Crowb 7G 35
Walsingham Cl. ME8: Gill 8N 95
Walsingham Ho. ME14: Maid 3D 126
Walsingham Pk. BR7: Chst 5F 70
Walsingham Rd. BR5: St P 4K 71
Walsingham Wlk. DA17: Belv 6B 52
Walter Burke Av. ME1: Woul 6G 93
Walter's Farm Rd. TN9: Tonb 6J 145
WALTER'S GREEN 8F 148 (2F 35)
Walters Grn. Rd. TN11: Pens 8F 148 (2F 35)
Walters Rd. ME3: Hoo 7H 67
Walters Way SE23 4A 54
Walters Yd. BR1: Brom 5K 69
Walterton Rd. W9 2C 4
WALTHAM 5F 31
Waltham Cl. BR5: Orp 2M 85
CT9: Clift 3J 209
DA1: Dart 4H 59
TN24: W'boro 8L 159
Waltham Rd. CT4: P'hm 4F 31
ME8: Gill 9L 81
Walton Cotts. CT13: E'try 2L 183
Walton Gdns. CT19: F'stone 4K 189
Walton Grn. CR0: Croy 9E 82
Walton Hall Farm Mus. 3D 8
Walton Mnr. Cl. CT19: F'stone 3K 189
Walton Rd. CT19: F'stone 5K 189
DA14: Sidc 7L 57
TN10: Tonb 1M 145
Walton's Hall Rd. SS17: Stan H 4D 8
Waltons, The CT19: F'stone 3J 189
WALWORTH 4G 5
Walworth Rd. SE1 4G 5
Walwyn Av. BR1: Brom 6N 69
WANDEN 7E 28
Wanden La. TN27: Eger 7E 28
Wandle Ho. BR1: Brom 1G 68
Wandle Park Station (CT) 4F 13
Wandle Rd. SM4: Mord 2D 12
WANDSWORTH 6C 4
Wandsworth Bri. SW6 6C 4
SW18 6D 4
Wandsworth Bri. Rd. SW6 5C 4
WANDSWORTH COMMON 7D 4
Wandsworth Common Station (Rail) 7D 4
WANDSWORTH GYRATORY 6C 4
Wandsworth High St. SW18 6C 4
Wandsworth Rd. SW8 6E 4
Wandsworth Road Station (Rail) 5E 4
Wandsworth Town Station (Rail) 6C 4
Wansbury Way BR8: Swanl 8H 73
WANSHURST GREEN 7J 27
Wanstead Cl. BR1: Brom 5M 69
Wanstead Park Station (Rail) 1A 6
Wanstead Rd. BR1: Brom 5M 69
Wansum Ct. CT7: St N 8M 215
Wansunt Rd. DA5: Bex'y 6D 58
Wantage Rd. SE12 3J 55
Wantsum Cl. CT6: H Bay 2N 195
Wantsume Lees CT13: S'wch 4K 217
Wantsum M. CT13: S'wch 5L 217
Wantsum Way CT7: St N 8L 215 (3D 22)
WAPPING 3H 5
Wapping High St. E1 3H 5
Wapping La. E1 3H 5
Wapping Station (Tube) 3H 5
Wapping Wall E1 3H 5
WAPSES ROUNDABOUT 7H 13
Warberry Pk. Gdns. TN4: Tun W 1E 156
Warbler's Cl. ME2: Strood 5L 79
Ward Cl. DA8: Erith 6E 52
WARDEN 4K 203 (1B 20)
Warden Bay Cvn. Pk. ME12: Ley S 6K 203
Warden Bay Holiday Camp
ME12: Ley S 6K 203
Warden Bay Rd. ME12: Ward 5K 203 (1B 20)
Warden Cl. ME16: Maid 5N 125
Warden Ct. CT17: Dover 3H 181
Warden Ho. M. CT14: Deal 6K 177
Warden Mill Cl. ME18: W'bury 1B 136
Warden Point Way CT5: Whits 7E 226
Warden Rd. ME1: Roch 9N 79
ME12: E'chu 5C 202 (1K 19)
Wardens Fld. Cl. BR6: Chels 7G 85
Warden Spring Cvn. Pk. ME12: Ward 3J 203
Warden Ter. ME18: W'bury 2B 136
(off Maidstone Rd.)
Warden Vw. Gdns. ME12: Ley S 7J 203
Warde's ME18: Yald 6D 136
Warde's Cotts. ME15: Otham 9L 127
Wardona Ho. DA10: Swans 4M 61
Wardour Cl. CT10: B'stairs 9M 209
Wardour Ct. DA2: Dart 4B 60
(off Bow Arrow La.)
Wardour St. W1 3E 4
Wards Hill Rd. ME12: Minst 4J 221 (7H 11)
Ward's La. TN5: Wadh 7C 36
Wardwell La. ME9: N'tn 4M 225 (4D 18)
WARE 6D 22
Wareham Wlk. TN17: Bendn 5B 38
WAREHORNE 4H 191 (6K 39)
Warehorne Rd. TN26: Hams 3K 191 (6K 39)
Warehorn Rd. CT3: Ash 2C 22
Warepoint Dr. SE28 2F 50 (4C 6)
WARE STREET 4K 127 (1K 27)
Ware St. ME14: Weav, Bear 4J 127 (1K 27)
Warham Rd. CR2: S Croy 4F 13
TN14: Otf 7J 103
Waring Cl. BR6: Chels 7H 85
Waring Dr. BR6: Chels 7H 85
Waring Rd. DA14: Sidc 2L 71
Warland Rd. SE18 7F 50
TN15: W King 9F 88
WARLINGHAM 7H 13
Warlingham Cl. ME8: Rain 2C 96
Warm Ho. La. ME13: G'ney 2M 187
WARMLAKE 7A 140 (4A 28)
Warmlake ME17: Sut V 7B 140
Warmlake Bus. Est. ME17: Sut V 7A 140
Warmlake Rd.
ME17: Cha S, Sut V 7L 139 (4K 27)
Warne Pl. DA15: Sidc 4K 57
Warner Pl. E2 2H 5
Warner Rd. BR1: Brom 3J 69
Warner St. ME4: Chat'm 9C 80
Warnett Ct. ME6: Snod 1E 108
Warnford Gdns. ME15: Maid 9D 126
Warnford Rd. BR6: Chels 6H 85
Warre Av. CT11: Ram 7G 210
Warren Av. BR1: Brom 3H 69 (1K 13)
BR6: Chels 6H 85
CR2: S Croy 8A 82
Warren Cl. CT19: F'stone 5M 189
DA6: Bexhth 3B 58
ME10: Sit 9J 99
Warren Ct. BR3: Beck'm 3D 68
TN13: S'oaks 6K 119
Warren Ct. Farm TN14: Hals 4N 101
Warren Dr. BR6: Chels 6K 85
CT10: B'stairs 8J 209
Warren Dr., The CT8: Wgte S 4J 207
Warren Farm La. TN3: Eri G 9A 156
Warren Gdns. BR6: Chels 6J 85
Warren Hastings Ct. DA11: Nflt 4E 62
(off Pier Rd.)
Warren La. CT15: Ewe M, Lyd'n 7C 32
ME9: H'lip 8E 96 (5B 18)
RH8: Oxt 4A 24
RM16: Chad H 4K 7

Warren La.—Well Rd.

Warren La. SE18 . . . . . 3D 50
TN24: Ashf 6E 158
Warren La. Ga. SE18 . . . . . 3D 50
Warren Retail Pk., The TN24: Ashf 6F 158
Warren Ridge TN3: Frant 5K 35
Warren Rd. BR2: Shortl 3K 83 (4A 14)
BR6: Chels 6H 85 (4C 14)
CR8: Purl 6F 13
CT19: F'stone 5M 189
DA1: Dart 8M 59
DA6: Bexhth 3B 58
DA13: Lud'n 9A 78 (3E 16)
DA13: Sflt 1A 76 (1A 16)
DA14: Sidc 8L 57
E10 . . . . . 1K 5
ME2: Lud'n 9A 78 (3E 16)
ME5: Aylfd 2A 110 (6H 17)
TN24: Ashf 7A 30
TN28: L'stne 3M 213
Warrens, The DA3: Hart'y 9M 75
WARREN STREET 3G 29
Warren St. ME17: Len 3G 29
Warren St. Rd. TN27: Len, Char'g 4G 29
Warren Street Station (Tube) 2E 4
WARREN, THE 5E 158
Warren, The CT5: Whits 7E 226
CT18: F'stone 4N 189
CT19: F'stone 4N 189
DA12: Grav'nd 9J 63
TN11: Pens 2H 149
TN25: Bra L 8K 165
Warren Vw. DA12: Shorne 1C 78
TN25: Ashf 6D 158
Warren Way CT19: F'stone 5M 189
Warren Wood Cl. BR2: Shortl 3J 83
Warren Wood Rd. ME1: Roch 4N 93
Warrington Rd. TN12: Pad W 9L 147
Warrior Av. DA12: Grav'nd 9H 63
Warsop Trad. Est. TN8: Eden 7D 184
Warspite Rd. SE18 . . . . . 3A 50
Warten Rd. CT11: Ram 3K 211
Warwick Av. W9 . . . . . 2C 4
Warwick Avenue Station (Tube) 2D 4
Warwick Cl. BR6: Chels 4J 85
DA5: Bex'y 5A 58
Warwick Ct. BR2: Shortl 5H 69
DA8: Erith 7G 52
TN13: S'oaks 7J 119
Warwick Cres. ME1: Roch 1K 93
ME10: Sit 6D 98
Warwick Dr. CT11: Ram 7F 210
Warwick Gdns. DA13: Meop 3F 90
W14 . . . . . 4C 4
Warwick Ho. BR8: Swanl 7F 72
Warwick La. RM13: Rain 2H 7
RM14: Avel, Upm 2H 7
Warwick Pk. TN2: Tun W 3G 156 (3K 35)
Warwick Pl. DA11: Nflt 3A 62
ME16: Maid 5B 126
Warwick Rd. CT1: Cant 2B 172
CT5: Whits 3F 226
CT9: Clift 3F 208
CT14: Walm 8N 177
DA14: Sidc 1K 71
DA16: Well 1L 57
SW5 . . . . . 4C 4
TN1: Tun W 3G 157
TN24: Kenn 4J 159
W14 . . . . . 4C 4
Warwick Ter. SE18 . . . . . 6F 50 (5C 6)
Warwick Way DA1: Dart 7M 59
SW1 . . . . . 4E 4
Washford Farm Rd. TN23: Ashf 4C 160
Washingstool Hill TN3: Eri G 8C 156 (4J 35)
Washington Cl. CT16: Dover 1G 180
Washington Ho. ME15: Maid 3H 139
Washington La. TN29: Old R 3F 47
Washneys Rd. BR6: Prat B 5J 101 (6D 14)
Washpond La. CR6: Warl 7K 13
Wasps R.U.F.C. (Queen's Pk. Rangers F.C.) 3B 4
Wassall La. TN17: Rolv L 1G 45
Wass Drove CT3: Ash 6D 22
Wastdale Rd. SE23 . . . . . 6A 54
Watchester Av. CT11: Ram 7G 211
Watchester La. CT12: Minst 8E 212 (4F 23)
Watchgate DA2: Dart 1D 74
(not continuous)
Watchmans Ter. ME5: Chat'm 1G 94
Waterbank Rd. SE6 . . . . . 8E 54
WATERBROOK 4L 161 (2B 40)
Waterbrook Av. TN24: Ashf 4K 161 (2B 40)
Water Cir. DA9: Bluew 6F 60
Watercress Cl. TN14: S'oaks 2K 119
Watercress Dr. TN14: S'oaks 2K 119
Watercress La. CT3: Wing 9H 225
TN23: Ashf 1C 160
Watercroft Rd. TN14: Hals 1A 102 (5E 14)
Waterdale Rd. SE2 . . . . . 6J 51
Waterdales DA11: Nflt 7B 62
Waterden Rd. E15 . . . . . 1J 5
Waterditch La. ME17: Len 3G 29
Waterdown Rd. TN4: Tun W 4D 156
Waterer Ho. SE6 . . . . . 9F 54
Waterfall La. TN26: Hoth 3M 197 (7J 29)
Water Farm CT4: Elham 7N 183
Waterfield TN2: Tun W 6G 156
Waterfield Cl. DA17: Belv 3B 52
SE28 . . . . . 1K 51
Waterfront Leisure Cen.
Gillingham 4H 81
Woolwich 3C 50
WATERHAM 5D 20
Waterham Rd. ME13: Hernh 5D 20
Waterhead Cl. DA8: Erith 7F 52
WATERINGBURY 1C 136 (3E 26)
Wateringbury Cl. BR5: St P 6K 71
Wateringbury Rd. ME19: E Mal 7D 124 (2E 26)
Wateringbury Station (Rail) 2C 136 (3E 26)
Waterlakes TN8: Eden 7C 184
Water La. CT1: Cant 2M 171
CT2: Sturry 6E 168 (6J 21)
DA14: Sidc 7A 58
E15 . . . . . 1K 5
IG3: Ilf 1C 6
ME13: Fav 5G 187
(off West St.)
ME13: Osp 8D 186 (7K 19)
ME14: Bear, T'hm 5N 127 (2A 28)
ME15: Hunt 9H 137
ME15: Maid 5D 126
ME17: H'shm 2J 141
ME19: W Mal 1A 124 (1E 26)
TN8: Eden 7A 24
TN14: S'ham 3G 102
TN16: Westrm 9F 116
TN18: Hawkh 1E 192 (6J 37)
TN27: H'crn 9H 191 (1B 38)
TN27: Smar 7A 222 (1D 38)
Waterlock Cotts. CT3: Wing 8J 225
Waterloo Bri. SE1 . . . . . 3F 5
Waterloo Cotts. CT4: Brid 8H 173
Waterloo Cres. CT16: Dover 6J 181
CT17: Dover 6J 181
Waterloo East Station (Rail) 3F 5
Waterloo Hill ME12: Minst 6K 221
Waterloo International Station (Rail) 4F 5
Waterloo Mans. CT17: Dover 5J 181
Waterloo Pl. CT11: Ram 5K 211
ME3: Hoo 4E 66
TN9: Tonb 7H 145
Waterloo Rd. CT5: Whits 3F 226
CT20: F'stone 6D 188
KT19: Eps 6A 12
ME7: Gill 8F 80
ME10: Sit 6E 98
SE1 . . . . . 4F 5
TN9: Tonb 7H 145
TN17: Cran 7D 176 (4J 37)
Waterloo Station (Rail & Tube) 4F 5
Waterloo St. DA12: Grav'nd 5H 63
ME15: Maid 6D 126
Waterloo Ter. TN25: S'ndge 8B 218
Waterlow Rd. DA13: Meop 3D 106 (6B 16)
ME14: Maid 3D 126
Waterman Ho. TN23: Ashf 1F 160
WATERMAN QUARTER 1B 38
Waterman's La.
TN12: Pad W, Brenc 2M 153 (1D 36)
Watermans Way DA9: G'hithe 2H 61
Watermead Cl. TN23: Ashf 2D 160
Watermeadow Cl. DA8: Erith 7J 53
ME7: Hpstd 5J 95
Water Mdws. CT2: Cant 7E 168
Watermead Rd. SE6 . . . . . 9F 54
Water Mill Cl. ME2: Strood 4N 79
Watermill Cl. ME16: Alltn 4M 125
Watermill La. TN35: Pett, Ickl 7J 45
TN36: Ickl 7J 45
Water Mill Way DA4: S Dar 5B 74
Watermint Cl. BR5: St P 7M 71
Waters Edge ME15: Maid 7C 126
Waters Edge Ct. DA8: Erith 5G 52
Watersend CT16: Temp E 8B 178
WATERSIDE 7A 24
Waterside BR3: Beck'm 4C 68
DA1: Cray 3F 58
DA11: Nflt 4D 62
ME14: Maid 4C 126
TN24: W'boro 9K 159
Waterside Av. BR3: Beck'm 8F 68
(off Adamson Way)
Waterside Ct. CT21: Hythe 6J 199
ME2: Med E 6C 80
ME4: Chat'm 4D 80
ME19: Leyb 7C 108
Waterside Dr. CT8: Wgte S 2L 207
Waterside La. ME7: Gill 5J 81
Waterside M. ME18: W'bury 2B 136
Waterside Vw. ME12: Ward 4K 203
Water Slippe TN11: Hdlw 7C 134
Watersmeet Cl. ME15: Maid 8D 126
Waters Pl. ME7: Hpstd 5K 95
Waters Rd. SE6 . . . . . 8H 55
Waterstone Pl. ME13: Fav 6E 186
(off Grove Cl.)
Water St. CT14: Deal 3N 177
Waterton BR8: Swanl 7E 72
Waterton Av. DA12: Grav'nd 5K 63
Water Works Cotts. ME1: Roch 3L 93
Waterworks Cotts. ME14: Boxl 7F 110
ME14: Weav 2J 127
Waterworks Hill CT15: Mart 2L 179 (6G 33)
Waterworks La. CT15: Mart 2N 179 (6G 33)
Waterworks Vs. TN13: S'oaks 8J 119
Watery La. CT4: P'hm 3G 31
DA14: Sidc 2K 71 (1D 14)
TN15: Kems'g, Seal 4B 120 (1J 25)
TN25: Westw 2A 158 (7J 29)
Watkin Rd. CT19: F'stone 5J 189
Watkins Cl. TN12: S'hrst 1J 223
Watling Av. ME5: Chat'm 1G 95
Watling Pl. ME10: Sit 8H 99
Watlings Cl. CR0: Croy 9B 68
Watling St. CT1: Cant 2M 171 (1H 31)
DA1: Dart 5A 60 (7H 7)
(Brent, The)
DA1: Dart 4J 59
(Dartford Rd.)
DA1: Dart 5N 59
(East Hill)
DA2: Bean, Bluew, Dart, G'hithe . . . 6D 60 (7A 8)
(Darenth Wood Rd.)
DA2: Bean, Sflt 7L 61
(Sandy La.)
DA6: Bexhth 2C 58
DA7: Bexhth 6E 6
DA9: G'hithe, Bluew 7H 7
Watling St. DA11: Grav'nd 1G 76
(Orchard Av.)
DA11: Grav'nd, Nflt, Nflt G 8B 62
(Springhead Rd.)
DA11: Nflt G 8B 62
DA11: Sflt, Cobh 7N 61 (7A 8)
ME2: Strood 2E 16
ME5: Chat'm, Gill 1G 95 (3J 17)
ME7: Chat'm 3J 17
ME8: Gill 1K 95 (3K 17)
Watlington Gro. SE26 . . . . . 1B 68
Watney's Rd. CR4: Mitc 3E 12
Watson Av. ME5: Chat'm 6A 94
Watsons Cl. TN25: Ashf 2G 159
Watsons Hill ME10: Sit 6F 98
Watsons Yd. BR6: Orp 1K 85
Watts Almshouses ME1: Roch 8N 79
Watts Av. ME1: Roch 8N 79 (3H 17)
Watts Bri. Rd. DA8: Erith 6G 52
Watts Cl. ME6: Snod 2F 108
Watts Cotts. TN24: Kenn 3H 159
WATT'S CROSS 9B 132 (5H 25)
Watt's Cross Rd. TN11: Hild 1B 144 (5H 25)
Watts La. BR7: Chst 4D 70 (2C 14)
Watts' Pal. La. TN31: B Oak, N'thiam 5F 45
Watts' St. ME4: Chat'm 9B 80
Wat Tyler Rd. SE10 . . . . . 5K 5
Wat Tyler Way ME15: Maid 5D 126 (2J 27)
Wauchope Rd. CT5: Seas 7B 226
Wave Crest CT5: Whits 4E 226
Wavell Dr. DA15: Sidc 4G 57
Waveney Rd. TN10: Tonb 2H 145
Waverley Av. ME12: Minst 5J 221
Waverley Cl. BR2: Shortl 8N 69
ME5: Chat'm 9G 95
ME17: Cox 6N 137
Waverley Cres. SE18 . . . . . 5F 50 (5C 6)
Waverley Dr. TN2: Tun W 8M 151
Waverley Rd. CT9: Mgte 2N 207
SE18 . . . . . 5E 50
WAY 4G 23
Wayborough Hill CT12: Minst 4F 23
Wayfares CT13: S'wch 7L 217
WAYFIELD 4H 17
Wayfield Link SE9 . . . . . 4F 56
Wayfield Rd. ME5: Chat'm 5C 94 (4H 17)
Way Hill CT12: Minst 4G 23
Waylands BR8: Swanl 7G 72
ME14: Bear 5L 127
Waylands Cl. TN14: Knock 6N 101
Waylands Mead BR3: Beck'm 4E 68
Wayne Cl. BR6: Orp 4H 85
CT10: B'stairs 8J 209
Wayne Ct. ME2: Wain 2A 80
Wayside CR0: Croy 7E 82
TN30: St Mic 5C 224
Wayside Av. TN30: St Mic 4C 224
Wayside Dr. TN8: Eden 4D 184
Wayside Flats TN30: St Mic 5C 224
Wayside Gro. SE9 . . . . . 9B 56
Wayville Rd. DA1: Dart 5B 60
Way Volante DA12: Grav'nd 9K 63
Weald Cl. BR2: Shortl 3A 84
DA13: Ist R 3D 76
ME15: Maid 2F 138
TN14: Weald 6K 131
Weald Ct. ME10: Sit 9E 98
TN11: Hild 1D 144
Wealden Av. TN30: Tent 5C 224
Wealden Cl. TN11: Hild 2E 144
Wealden Ct. ME5: Chat'm 9E 80
Wealden Forest Pk. CT6: H Bay 5J 21
Wealden Pl. TN13: S'oaks 3K 119
Wealden Vw. TN17: Goud 3C 190
TN27: H'crn 7J 191
Wealden Way ME20: Aylfd 2J 125
Wealdhurst Pk. CT10: B'stairs 8H 209
Weald Rd. TN13: S'oaks 2J 131 (3G 25)
Weald Sports Cen. 6C 176
Weald, The BR7: Chst 2B 70
TN24: Ashf 7G 158
Weald Vw. TN12: Brenc 1E 36
Weald Vw. Rd. TN9: Tonb 8H 145
Wear Bay Cres. CT19: F'stone 5M 189
Wear Bay Rd. CT19: F'stone 4M 189 (4B 42)
Weardale Av. DA2: Dart 7C 60
Weardale Rd. SE13 . . . . . 2G 55
Weare Rd. TN4: Tun W 6J 151
Wearside Rd. SE13 . . . . . 2E 54
Weatherall Cl. ME13: Dunk 4L 165
Weatherly Cl. ME1: Roch 8N 79
Weatherly Dr. CT10: B'stairs 2K 211
WEAVERING 1K 27
Weavering Cl. ME2: Strood 2M 79
Weavering Cotts. ME14: Weav 6H 127
WEAVERING STREET 4J 127
Weavering St. ME14: Weav 5H 127
Weavers Cl. DA11: Grav'nd 6F 62
TN12: S'hrst 2K 223
Weavers La. TN14: S'oaks 3K 119
Weavers Orchard DA13: Sflt 2N 75
Weavers, The CT1: Cant 2M 171
(off All Saints La.)
ME16: Alltn 4M 125
TN27: Bidd 8L 163
Weavers Way CT16: Dover 1F 180
TN23: Ashf 2C 160
Webb Cl. CT19: F'stone 4G 188
ME3: Hoo 7G 66
Webber Cl. DA8: Erith 7J 53
Webb's All. TN13: S'oaks 7K 119
(not continuous)
Webbs Mdw. TN13: S'oaks 7K 119
Webster Rd. ME8: Rain 2B 96
Webster Way CT18: H'nge 7L 193
WEDDINGTON 3D 216 (7E 22)
Weddington La. CT3: Ash 2D 216 (7E 22)
(not continuous)
Wedgewood Cl. ME16: Alltn 4M 125
Wedgewood Ct. BR2: Shortl 6J 69
(off Cumberland Rd.)
DA5: Bex'y 5A 58
Wedgewood Dr. ME5: Chat'm 4D 94
Wedgwoods TN16: Tats 9C 164
WEEDS WOOD 6C 94 (5H 17)
Weeds Wood Rd. ME5: Chat'm 7C 94
Weekes Ct. ME11: Queen 7B 220
(off Mount Fld.)
Weekes La. TN25: W Bra 1E 40
Weeks La. TN27: Bidd 2C 38
Week St. ME14: Maid 4D 126
Weigall Pl. CT11: Ram 5G 210
Weigall Rd. SE12 . . . . . 3K 55 (6A 6)
Weighbridge Cotts.
CT2: Cant 1M 171
Weighbridge Way CT16: Dover 3N 181
Weird Wood DA3: Long 6B 76
Weir Rd. DA5: Bex'y 5C 58
Welbeck Av. BR1: Brom 9K 55
DA15: Sidc 6J 57
TN4: Tun W 6J 151
Welcombe Ct. ME8: Gill 3N 95
(off Derwent Way)
Weld Cl. TN12: S'hrst 2K 223
Weldon Way DA9: G'hithe 3H 61
Wellan Cl. DA15: Sidc 3K 57
Welland Ct. SE6 . . . . . 7C 54
(off Oakham Cl.)
Welland Rd. TN10: Tonb 3H 145
Wellands Cl. BR1: Brom 5B 70
Wellbrook Rd. BR6: Farnb 5C 84 (4B 14)
Well Cl. CT2: Sturry 5F 168
TN11: Leigh 6N 143
Wellcome Av. DA1: Dart 2M 59
Well Cotts. ME14: Det 9K 111
Weller Av. ME1: Roch 1A 94 (3H 17)
Weller Pl. BR6: Downe 2C 100
Weller Rd. TN4: R'hall 1C 156
Wellers Cl. TN16: Westrm 9E 116
WELLER'S TOWN 1E 148 (7F 25)
Wellers Town Rd.
TN8: Chid, Chid H 3C 148 (1E 34)
Wellesley Av. CT14: Walm 7M 177
Wellesley Cl. CT8: Wgte S 4K 207
CT10: B'stairs 1K 211
Wellesley Ct. CT11: Ram 5J 211
(off King St.)
Wellesley Rd. CR0: Croy 3G 13
CT8: Wgte S 4L 207
CT9: Mgte 4F 208
CT16: Dover 5K 181
ME12: S'ness 2E 220
TN24: Ashf 8G 158 (1A 40)
(not continuous)
TW8: Bford 4A 4
Wellesley Road Station (CT) 4G 13
Wellesley Ter. CT13: S'wch 6M 217
Wellesley Vs. TN24: Ashf 7G 158
(off Wellesley Rd.)
Well Fld. DA3: Hart'y 7M 75
Wellfield Rd. CT20: F'stone 6G 188
Well Hall Pde. SE9 . . . . . 2B 56
Well Hall Rd. SE9 . . . . . 1A 56 (6B 6)
WELL HALL ROUNDABOUT 2A 56 (6B 6)
WELL HILL 7C 86 (5E 14)
Well Hill BR6: Orp 7C 86 (4E 14)
Well Hill La. BR6: Orp 7C 86
Wellhouse La. CT4: Mol 3B 30
ME13: Mol 3B 30
Wellhouse Rd. BR3: Beck'm 7D 68
WELLING 1K 57 (6D 6)
Welling High St. DA16: Well 1K 57 (6D 6)
Welling Station (Rail) 9J 51 (5D 6)
Wellington Av. DA15: Sidc 4J 57
Wellington Cl. CT8: Wgte S 2K 207
Wellington Cotts. DA13: Meop 4F 90
TN18: Hawkh 3B 192
Wellington Cres. CT11: Ram 6K 211 (4K 23)
Wellington Gdns. CT9: Mgte 2D 208
CT16: Dover 1G 180
Wellington Ho. ME15: Maid 3H 139
Wellingtonia Way TN8: Eden 5C 184
Wellington Pde. CT14: Kgdn, Walm 1F 200
DA15: Sidc 3J 57
Wellington Pl. CT20: S'gte 8D 188
ME14: Maid 3C 126
Wellington Rd. BR2: Shortl 7M 69
BR5: St M Cry 9K 71
CT8: Wgte S 4K 207
CT14: Deal 5N 177
CT16: Temp E 8C 178
CT20: F'stone 6D 188
DA1: Dart 4K 59
DA5: Bex'y 3M 57
DA17: Belv 5A 52
ME7: Gill 8F 80
ME10: Sit 6C 98
NW8 . . . . . 2D 4
Wellington St. CT5: Whits 8F 226
DA12: Grav'nd 5H 63 (7C 8)
SE18 . . . . . 4C 50 (4B 6)
WC2 . . . . . 3F 5
Wellington Way ME19: W Mal 6L 123
Welling United F.C. (Pk. View Road) 1L 57 (6D 6)
Welling Way DA16: Well 1G 56 (6C 6)
SE9 . . . . . 1E 56 (6C 6)
Wellis Gdns. CT9: Mgte 4A 208
Well La. CT2: Cant 8F 168 (7K 21)
CT15: St Marg 7B 214
ME13: Osp 9A 186 (7J 19)
Wellmeade Dr. TN13: S'oaks 9J 119
Wellmeadow Rd. SE13 . . . . . 4H 55
(not continuous)
Well Penn Rd. ME3: Cliffe 4C 176
Well Rd. CT18: Lym'ge 8L 205 (2J 41)
ME11: Queen 7B 220
(Castle St.)

Well Rd.—West St.

Well Rd. ME11: Queen 9A 220 (Swale Av.)
ME14: Maid 4D 126 (1J 27)
TN14: Otf 7K 103
Wells Av. CT1: Cant 3A 172
Wells Cl. TN1: Tun W 2G 156
TN10: Tonb 3K 145
TN28: New R 3L 213
TN30: Tent 7B 224
Wells Cotts. ME18: W'bury 6A 136
TN11: Hild 3D 144
Wells Ct. ME2: Strood 7H 79
Wells Farm Cotts. CT13: E'try 2K 183
Wells Ho. *BR1: Brom* *1L 69* (off Pike Cl.)
ME10: Sit 7J 99
ME15: Maid 1G 139
Wellsmoor Gdns. BR1: Brom 6C 70
Wells Pk. Rd. SE26 7H 5
Wells Pl. TN16: Westrm 9E 116
Wells Rd. BR1: Brom 5B 70
CT19: F'stone 5F 188
ME2: Strood 7H 79
WELL STREET 3C 124 (1E 26)
Well St. E9 1H 5
ME15: Loose 4B 138 (4H 27)
ME19: E Mal 3B 124 (1E 26)
Wells Way ME13: Fav 3F 186
SE5 5G 5
Wellwinch Rd. ME10: Sit 6E 98
Welsdene Rd. CT9: Mgte 3N 207
Welson Rd. CT20: F'stone 6F 188
Welton Gdns. TN9: Tonb 8F 144
Welton Rd. SE18 7G 50
WEMBLEY PARK 1A 4
Wembley Pk. Dr. HA9: Wemb 1A 4
Wembley Park Station (Tube) 1A 4
Wembley Stadium 1A 4
Wembley Stadium Station (Rail) 1A 4
Wemmick Cl. ME1: Roch 4A 94
Wemyss Way CT1: Cant 1B 172
Wenbans La. TN5: Wadh 7B 36
Wenderton La. CT3: Wing 6K 225 (7C 22)
Wendover Cl. ME2: Hall'g 6F 92
Wendover Ct. *BR2: Shortl* *6L 69* (off Wendover Rd.)
Wendover Rd. BR2: Shortl 7L 69
SE9 1N 55
Wendover Way BR6: St M Cry 9J 71
DA16: Well 3J 57 (6D 6)
Wenham La. TN29: Old R, Ivyc 2F 47
WENNINGTON 3H 7
Wennington Rd. RM13: Rain, Wenn 2G 7
Wensley Cl. SE9 4B 56
Wentland Cl. SE6 7G 55
Wentland Rd. SE6 7G 55
Wents, The ME15: E Far 5L 137
Went Woods ME14: Weav 4J 127
Wentworth Av. CT9: Mgte 2M 207
Wentworth Cl. BR2: Shortl 3K 83
BR6: Farnb 6G 84
CT18: Lym'ge 8L 205
DA11: Grav'nd 1F 76
Wentworth Ct. ME10: Sit 6H 99
Wentworth Dr. CT12: Ram 3E 210
DA1: Dart 4H 59
ME3: Cli W 5M 65
ME8: Gill 4A 96
ME10: Sit 6D 98
Wentworth Gdns. CT6: H Bay 5E 194
Wenvoe Av. DA7: Bexhth 9C 52
Wernbrook St. SE18 6E 50
Wesley Cl. BR5: St P 6L 71
ME16: Barm 6K 125
Wesley Ter. CT18: Lym'ge 7L 205
Wessex Ct. BR3: Beck'm 4B 68
Wessex Dr. DA8: Erith 9F 52
Wessex Wlk. DA5: Bex'y 7F 58
WEST ACTON 3A 4
West Acton Station (Tube) 3A 4
West App. BR5: Pet W 8E 70
WEST BARNES 2B 12
W. Barnes La. KT3: N Mald 2B 12
West Beach CT5: Whits 4E 226
W. Beach Cvn. Pk. CT5: Whits 5D 226
WESTBERE 4H 169 (6K 21)
Westbere La. CT2: Sturry 5G 168 (6K 21)
Westbere Rd. NW2 1C 4
Westboro' Sports Cen. 6N 125
Westbourne TN23: Ashf 3B 160
Westbourne Dr. SE23 7A 54
Westbourne Gdns. CT20: F'stone 7H 189
WESTBOURNE GREEN 3C 4
Westbourne Gro. SS0: Wclf S 1C 10
W2 3C 4
W11 3C 4
Westbourne Pk. Rd. W11 3C 4
Westbourne Park Station (Tube) 3C 4
Westbourne Rd. DA7: Bexhth 7M 51
N7 1F 5
SE26 2A 68
Westbourne St. ME10: Sit 7F 98
Westbourne Ter. *SE23* *7A 54* (off Westbourne Dr.)
W2 3D 4
Westbridge Rd. SW11 5D 4
WEST BROMPTON 5C 4
West Brompton Station (Rail & Tube) 5C 4
WESTBROOK 4A 208 (1G 23)
Westbrook Av. CT9: Mgte 2L 207 (1G 23)
Westbrook Cotts. CT9: Mgte 4A 208
Westbrook Dr. BR5: Orp 2M 85
Westbrooke Cl. ME4: Chat'm 1D 94
Westbrooke Cres. DA16: Well 1L 57
Westbrooke Rd. DA15: Sidc 7F 56
DA16: Well 1K 57
Westbrook Gdns. CT9: Mgte 4A 208 (1H 23)
Westbrook Ind. Est. CT6: H Bay 4C 194
Westbrook La. CT6: H Bay 4C 194
Westbrook Prom. CT9: Mgte 1M 207
Westbrook Rd. CT9: Mgte 3A 208
Westbrook Ter. TN2: Tun W 4K 157
Westbury Cres. CT17: Dover 6G 180
Westbury Hgts. CT17: Dover 6G 180
Westbury Rd. BR1: Brom 4N 69
BR3: Beck'm 6B 68
CT8: Wgte S 3K 207
CT17: Dover 6G 180
SE20 4A 68
Westbury Ter. TN16: Westrm 9E 116
Westchurch Ho. TN23: Ashf 9F 158
West Cliff CT5: Whits 5E 226
W. Cliff Arc. CT11: Ram 6J 211
W. Cliff Av. CT10: B'stairs 1M 211
Westcliff Av. SS0: Wclf S 1D 10
W. Cliff Ct. *CT10: B'stairs* *1M 211* (off W. Cliff Rd.)
W. Cliff Dr. CT6: H Bay 3C 194
W. Cliff Dr. ME12: Minst 4L 221
WEST CLIFFE 7H 33
W. Cliff Gdns. CT6: H Bay 3C 194
Westcliff Gdns. CT9: Mgte 2N 207
W. Cliff Gdns. CT20: F'stone 7K 189
Westcliff Ho. *CT20: F'stone* *7K 189* (off W. Cliff Gdns.)
W. Cliff Mans. *CT11: Ram* *6J 211* (off Cliff St.)
W. Cliff M. *CT10: B'stairs* *1M 211* (off W. Cliff Rd.)
WESTCLIFF-ON-SEA 1D 10
Westcliff Pde. SS0: Wclf S 1D 10
W. Cliff Prom. CT10: B'stairs 2M 211
CT11: Ram 7H 211
Westcliff Rd. CT9: Mgte 4A 208
W. Cliff Rd. CT10: B'stairs 1L 211 (3K 23)
CT11: Ram 6H 211 (4J 23)
Westcliff Station (Rail) 1D 10
W. Cliff Ter. CT11: Ram 7F 210
Westcliff Ter. Mans. CT11: Ram 7F 210
Westcombe Hill SE3 5A 6
Westcombe Park Station (Rail) 5K 5
West Comn. Rd. BR2: Shortl 2K 83 (4A 14)
Westcote Rd. SW16 1E 12
Westcott Av. DA11: Nflt 8E 62
Westcott Cl. BR1: Brom 8B 70
CR0: Croy 9E 82
WESTCOURT 7J 63 (7D 8)
West Ct. ME15: Maid 8D 126
West Ct. Downs CT15: S'wll 7H 219 (5C 32)
W. Court La. CT4: S'wll 6B 32
CT15: S'wll 6B 32
Westcourt La. CT15: S'wll 7H 219 (5C 32)
DA12: Grav'nd 6L 63
Westcourt Pde. DA12: Grav'nd 8K 63
Westcourt St. ME7: Gill 6D 80
West Cres. Rd. DA12: Grav'nd 4G 63
WEST CROSS 2A 214 (7B 38)
West Cross TN30: Tent 8B 224 (6D 38)
W. Cross Gdns. TN30: Tent 8A 224
W. Cross M. TN30: Tent 8A 224
West Croydon Station (Rail & CT) 3G 13
Westdale Pas. SE18 6D 50
Westdale Rd. SE18 6D 50
Westdean Av. SE12 6L 55
Westdean Cl. CT17: Dover 2D 180
West Down TN25: H'gh 7E 30
Westdown Rd. SE6 5D 54
West Dr. ME5: Chat'm 6A 94
ME17: E Sut 9D 140
SW16 1E 12
WEST DULWICH 7G 5
West Dulwich Station (Rail) 7G 5
WEST DUMPTON 3J 211
West Dumpton CT11: Ram 2J 211
W. Dumpton La. CT11: Ram 2J 211 (3K 23)
Wested La. BR8: Crock'm 1H 87 (3G 15) (not continuous)
WEST END 4H 21
West End TN12: Mard 2C 212 (7H 27)
TN15: Kems'g 8N 103 (7H 15)
TN16: Bras 7K 117
W. End La. NW6 1C 4
WESTENHANGER 2C 198 (4G 41)
Westenhanger Station (Rail) 1C 198 (4G 41)
Westergate Rd. ME2: Strood 3K 79
SE2 6N 51
WESTERHAM 8F 116 (2C 24)
Westerham Cl. CT2: Cant 7N 167
CT9: Clift 4K 209
ME8: Gill 8L 81
Westerham Dr. DA15: Sidc 4K 57
WESTERHAM HILL 2C 116 (1B 24)
Westerham Hill TN16: Westrm 3C 116 (1B 24)
Westerham Lodge *BR3: Beck'm* *3D 68* (off Park Rd.)
Westerham Rd. BR2: Kes 8N 83 (4B 14)
ME10: Sit 8D 98
RH8: Oxt, Westrm 3A 24
TN13: Riv 5D 118 (2E 24)
TN14: Sund 5C 118 (2E 24)
TN16: Oxt 9C 116 (3A 24)
TN16: Westrm, Bras 7H 117 2D 24
Westerham Trade Cen.
TN16: Westrm 7F 116
Westerhill Rd. ME17: Lint, Cox 7N 137 (4H 27)
Westerhout Cl. CT14: Deal 2M 177
Westerley Cres. SE26 1C 68
Westerly M. CT2: Cant 1L 171
Western Av. CT4: Brid 8H 173
CT6: H Bay 3E 194 (3J 21)
ME4: Chat'm 4D 80 (2J 17)
ME12: Minst 6E 220
TN18: Hawkh 5C 192
TN23: Ashf 8E 158
WESTERN CIRCUS 3A 4
Western Cl. CT17: Dover 6H 181
Western Cross Cl. DA9: G'hithe 4J 61
Western Docks CT17: Dover 6K 181
Western Esplanade CT6: H Bay 2C 194 (2J 21)
CT10: B'stairs 2M 211
SS0: Wclf S 1D 10
SS1: Sth S 1D 10
SS8: Can I 2K 9
Western Gdns. TN24: W'boro 1J 161
WESTERN HEIGHTS 6H 181 (2F 43)
Western Hgts. Rdbt. CT17: Dover 7H 181
Western Ho. CT14: Deal 3M 177
Western Link ME13: Fav 5D 186
Western Link Rd. ME13: Fav 6K 19
Western Rd. CR4: Mitc 2D 12
CT9: Mgte 5G 208
CT14: Deal 4M 177 (3J 33)
ME16: Maid 7N 125
SW19 2D 12
TN1: Tun W 9J 151
TN4: S'bgh 5F 150
TN6: Jar B 7G 35
TN15: Bor G 2M 121 (1A 26)
TN18: Hawkh 5C 192
Western Service Rd. CT16: Dover 4M 181
Western Vs. TN24: Kenn 4H 159
Western Way SE28 3F 50 (4C 6)
WEST EWELL 5A 12
WEST FARLEIGH 2G 136 (3F 27)
Westferry Rd. E14 3J 5
Westferry Station (DLR) 3J 5
WESTFIELD 7F 45
Westfield CT2: Blean 5G 166
DA3: New A 5M 89
TN13: S'oaks 4K 119
Westfield Bus. Cen. ME2: Strood 5N 79
Westfield Cl. DA12: Grav'nd 2H 77
Westfield Cotts. CT2: Cant 7E 168
ME9: Lwr Hal 4K 225
Westfield Gdns. ME9: B'den 8L 97
Westfield La. CT18: Etch'l 3L 185
Westfield Rd. BR3: Beck'm 5C 68
CT7: Birch 4E 206
CT9: Mgte 3N 207
DA7: Bexhth 1D 58
Westfields TN27: P'ley 7G 29
WESTFIELD SOLE 3F 110 (6J 17)
Westfield Sole Rd. ME14: Chat'm 2F 110 (6J 17)
Westfield St. SE18 3A 50
Westfield Ter. TN17: Cran 5H 37
Westfield Wood Nature Reserve 4C 110
Westgate ME4: Chat'm 2E 80
Westgate Av. CT7: Wdchu 7M 207
Westgate Bay Av. CT8: Wgte S 2J 207 (1G 23)
Westgate Cl. CT2: Cant 1J 171
Westgate Ct. *SE12* *6K 55* (off Burnt Ash Hill)
Westgate Ct. Av. CT2: Cant 1J 171
Westgate Gdn. Flats CT1: Cant 2L 171
Westgate Gro. CT2: Cant 1M 171
Westgatehall Rd. CT1: Cant 1M 171
West Gate Mus. 1M 171
WESTGATE ON SEA 2K 207 (1G 23)
Westgate on Sea Station (Rail) 2K 207 (1G 23)
Westgate Pavilion & Theatre 1K 207
Westgate Rd. BR3: Beck'm 4F 68
DA1: Dart 4L 59 (6G 7)
ME13: Fav 5J 187
Westgate Ter. CT5: Whits 3F 226
West Gate Towers 1M 171
West Grn. ME10: Kems'y 2G 99
West Hallowes SE9 6N 55
Westhall Rd. CR6: Warl 7H 13
WEST HAM 2A 6
W. Ham La. E15 1K 5
WEST HAMPSTEAD 1C 4
West Hampstead Station (Rail) 1C 4
West Hampstead Station (Tube) 1C 4
West Hampstead Thameslink Station (Rail) 1C 4
West Ham Station (Rail & Tube)
District and Hammersmith & City Lines 2K 5
Jubilee Line 2K 5
West Ham United F.C. (Upton Park) 2A 6
Westharold BR8: Swanl 6E 72
WEST HEATH 6M 51 (5D 6)
W. Heath Cl. DA1: Cray 4G 59
W. Heath Cotts. TN13: S'oaks 1J 131
W. Heath La. TN13: S'oaks 1J 131
W. Heath Rd. DA1: Cray 4G 59
NW3 1C 4
SE2 6L 51 (5D 6)
WEST HILL 6C 4
West Hill BR6: Downe 3B 100
DA1: Dart 4L 59 (6G 7)
KT19: Eps 6A 12
RH8: Oxt 3A 24
RH19: E Grin 4A 34
SW15 6C 4
SW18 6C 4
Westhill Cl. DA12: Grav'nd 6G 63
W. Hill Dr. DA1: Dart 4K 59
W. Hill Ri. DA1: Dart 4L 59
W. Hill Rd. CT6: H Bay 2D 194
W. Hoathly Rd. RH19: E Grin 4A 34
Westholme BR6: Orp 1G 85
West Holme DA8: Erith 8D 52
Westhorne Av. SE9 5K 55 (6A 6)
SE12 5K 55 (6A 6)
WEST HOUGHAM 2D 42
Westhurst Dr. BR7: Chst 1D 70
WEST HYTHE 7C 198 (5G 41)
W. Hythe Rd. CT21: W Hyt 8B 198 (6G 41)
W. India Dock Rd. E14 3J 5
West India Quay Station (DLR) 3J 5
WEST KENSINGTON 4C 4
West Kensington Station (Tube) 4C 4
W. Kent Av. DA11: Nflt 4B 62
W. Kent Cold Storage Dpt. TN14: Dun G 2G 118
WEST KILBURN 2C 4
WEST KINGSDOWN 7E 88 (5J 15)
W. Kingsdown Ind. Est. TN15: W King 9E 88
Westland Dr. BR2: Shortl 3J 83
Westland Ho. *E16* *1C 50* (off Rymill St.)
Westlands Av. ME10: Sit 7C 98
Westlands Cvn. Pk. CT6: H Bay 9F 194
Westlands Rd. CT6: H Bay 4D 194
Westland Way CT18: H'nge 9L 193
West La. ME3: Isle G 7B 190 (5E 10)
ME10: Sit 7H 99 (Castle Rd.)
ME10: Sit 7H 99 (East St.)
ME12: S'ness 2B 220
West La. Trad. Est. ME10: Sit 6H 99
WEST LANGDON 2K 179 (6G 33)
W. Lawn Gdns. CT20: S'gte 8D 188
West Lea CT14: Deal 3M 177
Westlea Ct. CT20: F'stone 8G 189
Westleigh Dr. BR1: Brom 4A 70
Westleigh Rd. CT8: Wgte S 3J 207
Westley Heights Country Pk. 1E 8
WEST MALLING 1A 124 (1E 26)
W. Malling By-Pass ME19: W Mal 3A 124
W. Malling Ind. Pk. ME19: W Mal 8K 107
West Malling Station (Rail) 1B 124 (1E 26)
WESTMARSH 6D 22
Westmarsh Cl. ME15: Maid 1J 139
Westmarsh Dr. CT9: Clift 3J 209
Westmead ME20: Lark 6G 108
Westmead Rd. SM1: Sutt 4D 12
Westmeads Rd. CT5: Whits 3G 226
West Mill DA11: Grav'nd 4E 62
W. Mill Rd. ME20: Lark 7G 108
WEST MINSTER 4B 220 (7F 11)
WESTMINSTER 4F 5
Westminster Bri. SE1 4F 5
SW1 4F 5
Westminster Bri. Rd. SE1 4F 5
Westminster Rd. CT1: Cant 7B 168
Westminster Sq. ME16: Maid 5M 125
Westminster Station (Tube) 4F 5
Westminster Wlk. CT12: Ram 3G 210
Westmoat Cl. BR3: Beck'm 3F 68
West Moors TN23: Ashf 3C 160
Westmore Grn. TN16: Tats 8C 164
Westmoreland Av. DA16: Well 1G 57
Westmoreland Dr. ME9: Lwr Hal 3L 225
Westmoreland Pl. BR1: Brom 6K 69
Westmoreland Rd. BR2: Shortl 8H 69 (3K 13)
Westmore Rd. TN16: Tats 9C 164
Westmorland Cl. ME15: Maid 1H 139
Westmorland Grn. ME15: Maid 1H 139
Westmorland Rd. ME15: Maid 1H 139
W. Motney Way ME8: Rain 3B 18
Westmount Av. ME4: Chat'm 8C 80
Westmount Rd. SE9 9B 50 (5B 6)
W. Norman Rd. CT16: Dover 4K 181
WEST NORWOOD 1G 13
West Norwood Station (Rail) 1F 13
West Oak BR3: Beck'm 4G 68
Weston Av. RM20: W Thur 4J 7
Weston Gro. BR1: Brom 4J 69
Weston Rd. BR1: Brom 3J 69
ME2: Strood 5L 79
Westonville Av. CT9: Mgte 2N 207
Westover Gdns. CT10: B'stairs 6J 209
Westover Rd. CT10: B'stairs 6J 209 (2K 23)
Westow Hill SE19 1G 13
Westow St. SE19 1G 13
West Pde. CT21: Hythe 8J 199 (5H 41)
West Pk. SE9 7A 56 (7B 6)
W. Park Av. CT9: Mgte 4H 209
TN4: S'bgh 5F 150
West Pk. Rd. ME15: Maid 7E 126
West Pas. *ME12: S'ness* *2B 220* (off West La.)
ME12: S'ness *1B 220* (off Charles St.)
WEST PECKHAM 2F 134 (3C 26)
West Pl. CT2: Cant 1L 171
TN29: B'lnd 3E 46
West Ramp CT16: Dover 4M 181
Westree Ct. ME16: Maid 6B 126
Westree Pl. ME16: Maid 7B 126
Westree Rd. ME16: Maid 6B 126
West Ridge ME10: Sit 8E 98
West Ri. CT12: Ram 3F 210
Westrise TN9: Tonb 8G 144
West Rd. CT20: F'stone 7C 188 (5K 41)
ME4: Gill 5D 80
RM15: S Ock 2K 7
SS0: Wclf S 1D 10
TN17: Goud 3C 190 (4G 37)
TN17: Kiln 5E 36
W. Roman Ditch CT16: Dover 4L 181
West Shaw DA3: Long 5K 75
West Side CT15: E Lan 4M 179 (not continuous)
W. Side Comn. SW19 1B 12
West Smithfield EC1 3F 5
WEST STOURMOUTH 5C 22
WEST STREET
Deal 2G 33
Rochester 3B 176 (5G 9)
West St. BR1: Brom 4K 69 (2A 14)
CT14: Deal 3N 177 (3J 33)
CT17: Dover 4H 181
DA7: Bexhth 1A 58
DA8: Erith 4E 52 (4F 7)
DA11: Grav'nd 4F 62 (6C 8)
ME2: Strood 3M 79
ME7: Gill 6G 80
ME10: Sit 7F 98 (5F 19)
ME11: Queen 7A 220
ME12: S'ness 2B 220
ME13: Fav 5G 186 (6A 20) (not continuous)
ME15: Hunt 8F 136 (5F 27)

West St.—Wilderwick Rd.

West St. ME17: H'shm . . . 2L 141 (3D 28)
ME17: Len . . . 3F 29
ME18: Yald . . . 8F 136 (5F 27)
ME19: W Mal . . . 1N 123 (1D 26)
RH19: E Grin . . . 4A 34
SM1: Sutt . . . 4C 12
SM5: Cars . . . 4D 12
SS2: Sth S . . . 1D 10
TN15: Wro . . . 7M 105
TN23: Ashf . . . 8F 158 (1A 40)
TN26: Hoth . . . 2J 197 (7H 29)
TN28: New R . . . 3J 213
West Street Gallery . . . 5G 187
(off West St.)
West Sutton Station (Rail) . . . 4C 12
West Ter. CT20: F'stone . . . 7K 189
DA15: Sidc . . . 6G 57
WEST THURROCK . . . 5K 7
W. Thurrock Way
RM20: Chaf H, Grays, W Thur . . . 4K 7
WEST TILBURY . . . 4D 8
West Vw. CT19: F'stone . . . 3K 189
Westview ME4: Chat'm . . . 2E 80
West Vw. Cl. CT6: H Bay . . . 5D 194
West Vw. Cotts. ME17: Cha S . . . 6M 139
West Vw. Rd. BR8: Crock'm . . . 9E 72
BR8: Swanl . . . 7H 73
DA1: Dart . . . 4N 59
West Wlk. ME16: Maid . . . 6M 125
West Way BR4: W W'ck . . . 9G 69
Westway BR5: Pet W . . . 8F 70
West Way CR0: Croy . . . 3B 82
Westway ME17: Cox . . . 5N 137
SW20 . . . 2B 12
TN2: Pem . . . 7C 152
W12 . . . 3B 4
W. Way Gdns. CR0: Croy . . . 3A 82
Westways TN8: Eden . . . 5C 184
TN16: Westrm . . . 8E 116
WESTWELL . . . 6K 29
Westwell Cl. BR5: Orp . . . 2M 85
Westwell Ct. TN30: Tent . . . 8A 224
Westwell La. TN25: C'lck . . . 9A 174
TN25: Char'g, Westw . . . 4M 175 (5J 29)
TN25: Hoth . . . 4C 158
TN25: Westw . . . 1B 158 (6K 29)
(not continuous)
TN26: Hoth . . . 6J 29
WESTWELL LEACON . . . 6H 29
WEST WICKHAM . . . 2F 82 (3K 13)
West Wickham Pools . . . 2F 82
West Wickham Station (Rail) . . . 1F 82 (3K 13)
WESTWOOD
Broadstairs . . . 8E 208 (2J 23)
Canterbury . . . 4J 31
Dartford . . . 3K 75
Westwood Cl. BR1: Brom . . . 5N 69
WESTWOOD COURT . . . 9J 187
Westwood Hill SE26 . . . 1H 13
Westwood Ind. Est. CT9: Mgte . . . 7E 208
Westwood La. DA15: Sidc . . . 3J 57
DA16: Well . . . 1H 57 (6C 6)
Westwood Pl. ME13: Fav . . . 7H 187
Westwood Retail Pk. CT10: B'stairs . . . 8F 208
Westwood Rd. CT10: B'stairs . . . 9F 208 (3J 23)
DA13: Sflt . . . 3L 75 (1A 16)
W. Wood Rd. ME9: S'bry . . . 3C 112 (6B 18)
Westwood Rd. ME15: Maid . . . 1D 138
TN4: R'hall . . . 9B 150
TN12: E Peck . . . 1K 147
West Woodside DA5: Bex'y . . . 5N 57
Westwood Wlk. ME9: N'tn . . . 4K 97
Westwood Way TN13: S'oaks . . . 4G 119
WEST YOKE . . . 4L 89 (4K 15)
West Yoke TN15: Ash . . . 3K 89 (4K 15)
W. Yoke Rd. DA3: New A . . . 4L 89 (4A 16)
Wet End Rd. ME20: Lark . . . 7G 108
WETHAM GREEN . . . 1J 225 (2C 18)
Wetheral Dr. ME5: Chat'm . . . 7E 94
Wetland Cen., The . . . 5B 4
Weybridge Cl. ME5: Chat'm . . . 7F 94
Weyburn Dr. CT12: Ram . . . 3E 210
Wey Cl. ME5: Chat'm . . . 6F 94
Weyhill Cl. ME14: Maid . . . 3F 126
Weymouth Cl. CT19: F'stone . . . 4D 188
Weymouth Ho. BR2: Shortl . . . 5J 69
(off Beckenham La.)
Weymouth Rd. CT19: F'stone . . . 5D 188
Weymouth St. W1 . . . 3E 4
Weymouth Ter. CT19: F'stone . . . 4D 188
(off Biggins Wood Rd.)
WEY STREET . . . 6C 20
Wey St. TN26: Bztt, Ruck . . . 7A 40
Wharfdale Rd. N1 . . . 2F 5
Wharfedale Rd. CT9: Mgte . . . 4E 208
DA2: Dart . . . 6C 60
Wharf La. ME3: Cliffe . . . 2C 176
Wharf Rd. DA12: Grav'nd . . . 4K 63
ME7: Gill . . . 5F 80 (2J 17)
(not continuous)
ME15: Maid . . . 7B 126
SS17: Fob . . . 2F 9
Wharfside Cl. DA8: Erith . . . 5G 52
Wharf, The DA9: G'hithe . . . 2G 61
Wharf Way ME10: Sit . . . 6G 99
Wharncliffe Rd. SE25 . . . 2G 13
Wharnecliffe DA9: G'hithe . . . 4H 61
Wharton Gdns. TN24: W'boro . . . 1J 161
Wharton Rd. BR1: Brom . . . 4L 69
Whatcote Cotts. TN15: Bor G . . . 2B 122
Whateley Rd. SE20 . . . 3A 68
WHATLINGTON . . . 7D 44
Whatlington Rd. TN33: Batt, What . . . 7C 44
Whatman Cl. ME14: Maid . . . 3F 126
Whatman Rd. SE23 . . . 5A 54
Whatmer Cl. CT2: Sturry . . . 5F 168
WHATSOLE STREET . . . 7F 31
Whatsole St. TN25: Elms . . . 7F 31
Wheatcroft Cl. ME10: Sit . . . 7J 99
Wheatcroft Gro. ME8: Gill . . . 4B 96
Wheatear Way ME5: Chat'm . . . 4E 94
Wheatfield ME19: Leyb . . . 9C 108
Wheatfield Cl. TN17: Cran . . . 7C 176
Wheatfield Dr. TN17: Cran . . . 7C 176
Wheatfield Lea TN17: Cran . . . 7C 176
Wheatfields ME5: Chat'm . . . 9G 95
ME14: Weav . . . 5G 127
Wheatfield Way TN17: Cran . . . 7C 176
Wheatley Cl. DA9: G'hithe . . . 3G 60
Wheatley Rd. CT5: Whits . . . 3G 226
CT12: Ram . . . 3G 210
Wheatley Ter. DA8: Erith . . . 6G 53
Wheatsheaf Cl. ME13: Bou B . . . 3K 165
ME15: Maid . . . 9E 126
Wheatsheaf Farm Rd.
ME9: S'bry . . . 9H 113 (7C 18)
ME17: Holl . . . 9H 113 (1C 28)
Wheatsheaf Gdns. ME12: S'ness . . . 3C 220
Wheatsheaf Hill BR6: Orp . . . 9A 86
Wheatsheaf La. CT15: Mart . . . 3N 179
Wheatsheaf Way TN10: Tonb . . . 1K 145
Wheatstone Rd. DA8: Erith . . . 5E 52
Wheelbarrow Pk. Est. TN12: Mard . . . 2B 212
WHEELBARROW TOWN . . . 6H 31
Wheeler Pl. ME19: W Mal . . . 7M 123
Wheeler's La. ME17: Lint . . . 8A 138 (5H 27)
Wheelers, The ME8: Gill . . . 5L 95
Wheeler St. ME14: Maid . . . 4D 126
TN27: H'crn . . . 8L 191 (7B 28)
Wheeler St. Hedges ME14: Maid . . . 3E 126
(not continuous)
Wheel La. TN35: W'fld . . . 7F 45
Wheelock Cl. DA8: Erith . . . 7C 52
Wheelwrights TN15: Plax . . . 1L 133
Wheelwrights, The ME17: H'shm . . . 2M 141
Wheelwrights Way CT13: E'try . . . 3K 183
Wheler Ct. ME13: Fav . . . 5E 186
Wheler Rd. TN27: Char'g . . . 2K 175
Whenman Av. DA5: Bex'y . . . 7D 58
WHETSTED . . . 7J 147 (6C 26)
Whetsted Rd. TN12: Five G . . . 8G 147 (7C 26)
Whiffen's Av. ME4: Chat'm . . . 7C 80
Whiffen's Av. W. ME4: Chat'm . . . 7C 80
Whiffen Wlk. ME19: E Mal . . . 9F 108
Whigham Cl. TN23: Ashf . . . 1B 160
Whimbrel Cl. ME10: Sit . . . 3G 98
Whimbrel Grn. ME20: Lark . . . 8D 108
Whimbrels, The ME4: Chat'm . . . 3E 80
Whimbrel Wlk. ME5: Chat'm . . . 1F 110
Whinchat Rd. SE28 . . . 3F 50 (4C 6)
Whinfell Av. CT11: Ram . . . 5D 210
Whinfell Way DA12: Grav'nd . . . 9L 63
Whinless Rd. CT17: Dover . . . 4F 180
Whinyates Rd. SE9 . . . 1A 56
Whippendell Cl. BR5: St P . . . 4K 71
Whippendell Way BR5: St P . . . 4K 71
Whistler Rd. TN10: Tonb . . . 9K 133
Whiston Av. TN26: Beth . . . 3H 163
Whiston Rd. E2 . . . 2G 5
Whitbourne Ct. CT5: Whits . . . 5F 226
Whitbread Rd. SE4 . . . 2B 54
Whitburn Rd. SE13 . . . 2E 54
Whitby Cl. DA9: G'hithe . . . 3G 60
TN16: Big H . . . 7B 164
Whitby Rd. CT20: F'stone . . . 5D 188
SE18 . . . 4B 50
Whitby Ter. CT16: Dover . . . 1G 181
(off Toronto Cl.)
Whitchurch Cl. ME16: Maid . . . 5B 126
Whitcombe Cl. ME5: Chat'm . . . 9F 94
Whiteacre Dr. CT14: Walm . . . 1D 200
Whiteacre La. CT4: Walt . . . 5F 31
White Av. DA11: Nflt . . . 8E 62
Whitebeam Av. BR2: Shortl . . . 1C 84
Whitebeam Cl. TN15: Kems'g . . . 8A 104
TN23: Ashf . . . 6B 158
Whitebeam Dr. ME17: Cox . . . 5M 137
White Bear Pas. TN1: Tun W . . . 3G 156
Whitebine Gdns. TN12: E Peck . . . 1M 147
Whitebread La. TN31: N'thiam, Bkld . . . 3G 45
WHITECHAPEL . . . 3H 5
Whitechapel Rd. E1 . . . 3H 5
Whitechapel Station (Tube) . . . 3H 5
WHITE CITY . . . 3B 4
White City . . . 3B 4
White City Station (Tube) . . . 3B 4
White Cliffs CT20: F'stone . . . 7K 189
White Cliffs Bus. Pk. CT16: Dover . . . 8F 178
White Cliffs Pk. CT18: Cap F . . . 2D 174
(not continuous)
Whitecliff Way CT19: F'stone . . . 5M 189
White Cott. Rd. TN10: Tonb . . . 1J 145
White Cotts. ME15: S'lng . . . 9B 110
White Ct. CT20: S'gte . . . 8E 188
Whitecroft BR8: Swanl . . . 5F 72
Whitecroft Cl. BR3: Beck'm . . . 7G 68
Whitecroft Way BR3: Beck'm . . . 8F 68
Whitedyke Rd. ME6: Hall'g, Snod . . . 9B 92
Whitefield Cl. BR5: St P . . . 6L 71
Whitefield Rd. TN4: Tun W . . . 8G 150
Whitefoot La. BR1: Brom . . . 9F 54 (1K 13)
Whitefoot Ter. BR1: Brom . . . 8H 55
White Friars TN13: S'oaks . . . 9H 119
Whitefriars Mdw. CT13: S'wch . . . 6L 217
Whitefriars Shop. Cen. CT1: Cant . . . 2N 171
Whitefriars Way CT13: S'wch . . . 5L 217
Whitefriars Wharf TN9: Tonb . . . 6J 145
White Ga. ME2: Strood . . . 3K 79
Whitegate Ct. CT21: Hythe . . . 7K 199
TN4: Tun W . . . 6G 150
Whitegate Cl. ME8: Gill . . . 6N 95
Whitegates Av. TN15: W King . . . 7E 88
Whitegates La. TN5: Wadh . . . 5B 36
WHITEHALL . . . 3F 210
Whitehall SW1 . . . 3F 5
TN29: B'lnd . . . 3E 46
Whitehall Bri. Rd. CT2: Cant . . . 1L 171
Whitehall Cl. CT2: Cant . . . 2L 171
Whitehall Dr. ME17: Kgswd . . . 6F 140
Whitehall Gdns. CT2: Cant . . . 1L 171
Whitehall La. DA8: Erith . . . 9G 53 (5F 7)
ME14: T'hm . . . 2C 128
Whitehall Pde. DA12: Grav'nd . . . 8H 63
Whitehall Rd. BR2: Shortl . . . 8N 69
CT2: Cant . . . 3J 171
CT12: Ram . . . 4F 210
ME10: Sit . . . 9F 98
ME14: T'hm . . . 2C 128
Whitehall Way TN25: S'ndge . . . 8C 218
White Hart Cl. TN13: S'oaks . . . 1K 131
White Hart La. SW13 . . . 6A 4
White Hart Mans. CT9: Mgte . . . 2C 208
(off Parade, The)
White Hart Pde. TN13: Riv . . . 4F 118
White Hart Rd. BR6: Orp . . . 1J 85
SE18 . . . 4G 51
White Hart Slip BR1: Brom . . . 5K 69
White Hart Wood TN13: S'oaks . . . 2K 131
Whitehaven Cl. BR2: Shortl . . . 7K 69
Whitehead Cl. DA2: Dart . . . 8K 59
Whiteheads La. ME14: Bear . . . 5L 127
WHITEHILL
Crowborough . . . 7F 35
Faversham . . . 9E 186 (7A 20)
Whitehill TN15: Wro . . . 7A 106
White Hill Cl. CT4: Lwr Har . . . 3H 31
Whitehill La. DA12: Grav'nd . . . 8H 63 (7C 8)
Whitehill Rd. DA1: Cray . . . 3H 59
DA12: Grav'nd . . . 7H 63 (7C 8)
DA13: Long . . . 5K 75 (2K 15)
White Hill Rd. DA13: Meop . . . 3G 90
Whitehill Rd. DA13: Meop . . . 3F 90 (4C 16)
DA13: Sflt . . . 5K 75
White Hill Rd. ME14: Det . . . 1N 111 (5A 18)
Whitehill Rd. TN6: Crowb . . . 7F 35
White Horse Hill BR7: Chst . . . 9C 56 (1B 14)
CT18: H'nge . . . 9M 193 (3B 42)
Whitehorse Hill ME5: Chat'm . . . 9E 80
White Horse Hill TN25: C'lck, Bou L . . . 4B 30
White Horse La. CT1: Cant . . . 2M 171
CT4: R Min . . . 8H 183 (1H 41)
DA13: Meop . . . 9H 91
E1 . . . 2H 5
ME15: Otham . . . 2K 139 (3K 27)
Whitehorse La. SE25 . . . 2G 13
Whitehorse Rd. CR0: Croy . . . 3G 13
CR7: Thor H . . . 2G 13
White Horse Rd. DA13: Meop . . . 1H 107 (5C 16)
White Horse Stone . . . 5B 110
White Ho. CT15: Non . . . 3D 32
Whitehouse Cl. ME3: Hoo . . . 9H 67
Whitehouse Cres. ME1: Burh . . . 2L 109
Whitehouse Drove CT13: S'wch . . . 6F 23
White Ho. La. TN14: S'oaks . . . 3G 131
White Ho. Rd. TN14: S'oaks . . . 3G 130 (3F 25)
Whitelake Rd. TN10: Tonb . . . 2J 145
White La. RH8: Tats . . . 2A 24
TN16: Tats . . . 2A 24
White Leaves Ri. ME2: Cux . . . 9F 78
Whitelocks Cl. CT4: Kgstn . . . 4K 31
White Lodge TN1: Tun W . . . 1J 157
TN13: S'oaks . . . 1H 131
White Lodge Cl. TN13: S'oaks . . . 5J 119
Whitemarsh Ct. CT5: Whits . . . 3G 226
White Mill Folk Mus. . . . 4K 217
Whitenbrook CT21: Hythe . . . 8A 188
Whitenbrook Dell CT21: Hythe . . . 8A 188
Whiteness Grn. CT10: B'stairs . . . 4K 209
Whiteness Rd. CT10: B'stairs . . . 4L 209 (1K 23)
White Oak Cl. TN9: Tonb . . . 7H 145
Whiteoak Ct. BR7: Chst . . . 2C 70
White Oak Ct. BR8: Swanl . . . 6F 72
White Oak Dr. BR3: Beck'm . . . 5F 68
White Oak Gdns. DA15: Sidc . . . 5H 57
White Oak Leisure Cen. . . . 5E 72
White Oak Sq. BR8: Swanl . . . 6F 72
(off London Rd.)
WHITE POST . . . 7E 148 (2F 35)
Whitepost Gdns. CT3: Ash . . . 5D 216
White Post Hill DA4: Farn'm . . . 1A 88
Whitepost La. DA13: Meop . . . 9E 90 (5B 16)
White Post La. DA13: Sole S . . . 7G 76 (2C 16)
White Rd. ME4: Chat'm . . . 2D 94
White Rock Ct. ME16: Maid . . . 6B 126
White Rock Pl. ME16: Maid . . . 6B 126
Whites Cl. DA9: G'hithe . . . 4J 61
Whites Hill CT14: Tilm . . . 4F 33
White's La. TN18: Hawkh . . . 5D 192 (7J 37)
White's Mdw. BR1: Brom . . . 7C 70
Whitewall Cen. ME2: Med E . . . 4A 80
Whitewall Rd. ME2: Med E . . . 4A 80
Whitewall Way ME2: Med E . . . 5A 80
(not continuous)
Whiteway Rd. ME11: Queen . . . 6A 220 (7F 11)
Whitewebbs Way BR5: St P . . . 4H 71
Whitewell La. TN17: Cran . . . 6D 176 (4J 37)
Whitewood Cotts. TN16: Tats . . . 8C 164
White Wood Rd. CT13: E'try . . . 4K 183
Whitfeld Rd. TN23: Ashf . . . 1F 160
WHITFIELD . . . 6F 178 (7F 33)
Whitfield Av. CT10: B'stairs . . . 6J 209
CT16: Dover . . . 2G 180 (1F 43)
Whitfield Cotts. TN23: Ashf . . . 1G 160
Whitfield Ct. CT16: Dover . . . 7F 178
Whitfield Hill CT16: Dover . . . 9D 178 (1E 42)
(not continuous)
Whitfield Rd. DA7: Bexhth . . . 7A 52
Whitfield Rdbt. CT16: Dover . . . 7F 178
Whitgift Ct. CT2: Cant . . . 1K 171
Whiting Cres. ME13: Fav . . . 4E 186
Whiting Ho. TN29: Lydd . . . 4K 205
WHITLEY ROW . . . 5F 34
Whitley Wlk. CT16: Whitf . . . 6G 178
Whitmore Rd. BR3: Beck'm . . . 6C 68
Whitmore St. ME16: Maid . . . 7N 125
Whitney Wlk. DA14: Sidc . . . 2N 71
WHITSTABLE . . . 3F 226 (3F 21)
Whitstable Ct. CT5: Whits . . . 3F 226
Whitstable Cl. BR3: Beck'm . . . 4C 68
Whitstable Mus. & Art Gallery . . . 4F 226 (3F 21)
Whitstable Rd. CT2: Blean, Cant . . . 7H 167 (7G 21)
CT2: Cant . . . 9K 167 (7G 21)
CT6: H Bay . . . 4A 194 (3H 21)
ME13: Fav . . . 5J 187 (6B 20)
(Love La.)
ME13: Fav . . . 6M 187 (6C 20)
(Homestall La.)
Whitstable Sports Cen. . . . 5H 227
Whitstable Station (Rail) . . . 4G 226 (3F 21)
Whitstable Swimming Pool . . . 2F 226
Whitstable Vis. Info. Cen. . . . 4F 226 (3F 21)
Whitstable Yacht Club . . . 3E 226
Whitstable Youth & Sailing Cen. . . . 2G 226
Whitstone La. BR3: Beck'm . . . 8E 68
Whittaker St. ME4: Chat'm . . . 8D 80
Whittington Ter. CT15: S'wll . . . 8K 219
Whitworth Rd. SE18 . . . 7C 50
SE25 . . . 2G 13
Whybornes Chase ME12: Minst . . . 5K 221
Whybourne Crest TN2: Tun W . . . 4J 157
Whydown Hill TN33: Sed . . . 7E 44
Whyman Av. ME4: Chat'm . . . 2D 94
Whytecliffs CT10: B'stairs . . . 2L 211
WHYTELEAFE . . . 7G 13
Whyteleafe Hill CR3: Whyt . . . 7G 13
Whyteleafe South Station (Rail) . . . 7H 13
Whyteleafe Station (Rail) . . . 7G 13
WICHLING . . . 1F 29
Wichling Cl. BR5: Orp . . . 2M 85
CT2: Cant . . . 8N 167
Wickenden Cres. TN24: W'boro . . . 1L 161
Wickenden Rd. TN13: S'oaks . . . 4K 119
Wicken Ho. ME16: Maid . . . 5B 126
Wicken La. TN27: Char'g . . . 4M 175 (5J 29)
(not continuous)
Wickens Cvn. Site TN14: Dun G . . . 1H 119
Wickens Mdw. TN14: Dun G . . . 1G 119
Wickens Pl. ME19: W Mal . . . 1A 124
Wickets, The TN14: Weald . . . 5K 131
TN24: W'boro . . . 2K 161
Wicket, The CR0: Croy . . . 6D 82
Wickham Av. CR0: Croy . . . 3B 82
CT11: Ram . . . 4L 211
WICKHAMBREAUX . . . 9N 169 (7A 22)
Wickham Chase BR4: W W'ck . . . 2G 82
Wickham Cl. ME9: N'tn . . . 5K 97
Wickham Ct. La. CT3: Wickh . . . 7M 169 (7A 22)
Wickham Ct. Rd. BR4: W W'ck . . . 3F 82 (4K 13)
Wickham Cres. BR4: W W'ck . . . 3F 82
Wickham Fld. TN14: Otf . . . 7G 102
Wickham Gdns. SE4 . . . 1C 54
TN4: R'hall . . . 9D 150
Wickham La. CT3: Ickh . . . 9N 169 (7A 22)
SE2 . . . 5J 51 (4D 6)
Wickham Pl. ME17: Len . . . 7M 201
Wickham Rd. BR3: Beck'm . . . 5E 68 (2J 13)
CR0: Croy . . . 3A 82 (4H 13)
CT3: Wickh . . . 1N 173 (7A 22)
SE4 . . . 2C 54 (6J 5)
Wickham Rock La. TN36: Winch, Ickl . . . 7J 45
Wickham St. DA16: Well . . . 9G 51 (5D 6)
ME1: Roch . . . 9A 80
Wickhams Way DA3: Hart'y . . . 8M 75
Wickham Ter. ME11: Queen . . . 7A 220
(off North Rd.)
Wickham Way BR3: Beck'm . . . 7F 68 (2K 13)
WICKHURST . . . 5G 25
Wickhurst Rd. TN14: Weald . . . 4G 130
Wick La. CT4: Wom . . . 5B 32
E3 . . . 2J 5
(not continuous)
Wick Rd. E9 . . . 1H 5
Wicks Cl. SE9 . . . 9N 55
Wicksteed Cl. DA5: Bex'y . . . 8E 58
Widbury TN3: Lang G . . . 2N 155
Widecombe Rd. SE9 . . . 8A 56
Wide Way CR4: Mitc . . . 2E 12
Widgeon Rd. DA8: Erith . . . 7J 53
ME2: Strood . . . 6H 79
Widgeon Wlk. CT18: H'nge . . . 9L 193
WIDMORE . . . 6M 69 (2A 14)
WIDMORE GREEN . . . 5N 69
Widmore Lodge Rd. BR1: Brom . . . 5N 69
Widmore Rd. BR1: Brom . . . 5K 69 (2A 14)
Widred Rd. CT17: Dover . . . 4H 181
WIERTON . . . 5K 27
Wierton Hill ME17: Bou Mo . . . 9G 139 (5J 27)
Wierton Rd. ME17: Bou Mo . . . 6H 139 (4K 27)
Wife of Bath Hill CT2: Cant . . . 2J 171
Wigeon Path SE28 . . . 3F 50
WIGMORE . . . 7L 95 (5K 17)
Wigmore Cotts. CT15: Eyt . . . 8K 185
Wigmore La. CT15: Eyt . . . 8K 185 (5E 32)
Wigmore Rd. ME8: Gill . . . 7L 95 (4K 17)
(not continuous)
Wigmore St. W1 . . . 3E 4
Wigmore Wood CT15: Eyt . . . 8K 185
Wigwam Paddocks CT7: Birch . . . 3F 206
Wihtred Rd. ME9: Bap . . . 9L 99
Wilberforce Rd. CT20: S'gte . . . 8E 188
ME17: Cox . . . 5A 138
Wilberforce Way DA12: Grav'nd . . . 1J 77
Wilbrough Rd. CT7: Birch . . . 4F 206
Wilcox Cl. CT3: Aysm . . . 2B 162
Wildage Ct. CT4: Elham . . . 6J 31
Wilden Pk. Rd. TN12: S'hrst, Mard . . . 1H 37
WILDERNESSE . . . 4M 119 (1H 25)
Wildernesse Av. TN15: Seal, S'oaks . . . 4M 119
Wildernesse Mt. TN13: S'oaks . . . 4L 119
Wildernesse Sports Cen. . . . 3M 119
Wilderness Hill CT9: Mgte . . . 3E 208
Wilderness La. TN8: Hever, Mark . . . 1E 34
Wilderness Rd. BR7: Chst . . . 3D 70
Wilde Rd. DA8: Erith . . . 7C 52
Wilderwick Rd. RH7: E Grin . . . 2A 34

Wildfell Cl.—Wises La.

Wildfell Cl. ME5: Chat'm 2E 110
Wildfell Rd. SE6 5E 54
Wildish Rd. ME13: Fav 4E 186
Wildman Cl. ME8: Gill 8N 95
Wildwood Cl. ME17: Kgswd 6G 140
SE12 5J 55
Wildwood Glade ME7: Hpstd 7L 95
Wildwood Rd. CT2: Sturry 5E 168
Wiles Av. TN28: New R 3K 213
Wiles Ho. TN28: New R 3K 213
Wilfred Rd. CT11: Ram 5G 211
Wilfred St. DA12: Grav'nd 4G 63
WILGATE GREEN 1K 29
Wilgate Grn. Rd. ME13: Throw 1K 29
Wilkes Rd. CT10: B'stairs 1J 211
Wilkie Rd. CT7: Birch 3F 206
Wilkinson Cl. DA1: Dart 2N 59
(not continuous)
Wilkinson Dr. CT14: Walm 7N 177
Wilkins Way TN16: Bras 6K 117
Wilks Av. DA1: Dart 7N 59
Wilks Cl. ME8: Rain 1D 96
Wilks Gdns. CR0: Croy 2B 82
Will Adams Ct. ME7: Gill 6F 80
Will Adams Memorial 1H 95
Will Adams Roundabout ME8: Gill 1J 95
Will Adams Way ME8: Gill 2J 95 (3K 17)
WILLARD'S HILL 3A 44
Will Crooks Gdns. SE9 2M 55
Willement Rd. ME13: Fav 5F 186
Willenhall Rd. SE18 5D 50
Willersley Av. BR6: Orp 4F 84
DA15: Sidc 6H 57
Willersley Cl. DA15: Sidc 6H 57
WILLESBOROUGH 1K 161 (2B 40)
Willesborough Ct. TN24: W'boro 8L 159
Willesborough Ind. Pk. TN24: W'boro 9L 159
WILLESBOROUGH LEES 9L 159 (1B 40)
Willesborough Rd.
TN24: Kenn, W'boro 5K 159 (7B 30)
Willesborough Smockmill 9L 159
WILLESDEN 1B 4
WILLESDEN GREEN 1B 4
Willesden Green Station (Tube) 1B 4
Willesden Junction Station (Rail & Tube) 2A 4
Willesden La. NW2 1B 4
NW6 1B 4
Willesley Gdns. TN17: Cran 6D 176
Willett Cl. BR5: Pet W 9G 70
Willetts Hill CT12: Monk'n 6A 212 (4E 22)
Willetts La. TN3: Blkm 1D 154
Willett Way BR5: Pet W 8F 70
William Av. CT9: Mgte 5G 209
CT19: F'stone 4H 189 (4A 42)
William Baker Ho. ME20: Aylfd 1K 125
William Barefoot Dr. SE9 9C 56 (1B 14)
William Cl. SE13 1F 54
William Cory Prom. DA8: Erith 5F 52
William Gibbs Ct. ME13: Fav 5H 187
William Ho. DA12: Grav'nd 5G 63
William Judge Cl. TN30: Tent 9E 224
William Luck Cl. TN12: E Peck 1K 147
William Nash Ct. BR5: St P 6L 71
William Pitt Av. CT14: Deal 4L 177
William Pitt Cl. CT21: Hythe 6L 199
William Rigby Dr. ME12: Minst 5F 220
William Rd. ME2: Cux 1G 92
TN23: Ashf 1F 160
William Smith Ho. DA17: Belv 3B 52
(off Ambrooke Rd.)
Williamson Rd. TN29: G'stne 8H 213
William St. CT5: Whits 3F 226
CT6: H Bay 3G 195
DA12: Grav'nd 5G 63
ME8: Rain 1C 96
ME10: Sit 8F 98
ME13: Fav 5H 187
TN4: Tun W 9G 150
Williams Way DA5: Bex'y 7E 58
Willicombe Pk. TN2: Tun W 1K 157
Willingdon TN23: Ashf 4C 160
Willingdon Pl. CT14: Walm 9M 177
Willingdon Rd. CT16: Dover 8F 178
WILLINGTON 9H 127 (3K 27)
Willington Grn. ME15: Maid 1H 139
Willington St. ME15: Maid 6J 127 (3K 27)
Willis Cotts. ME7: B'hst 2K 111
Willis Ct. BR4: W W'ck 3G 83
ME12: Minst 7G 221
Willis Ho. ME1: Roch 8N 79
(off Hooper's Rd.)
Willis Rd. DA8: Erith 4D 52
Willop Cl. TN29: Dym 4E 182
Willop Way TN29: Dym 4E 182
Willoughby Ct. CT1: Cant 2M 171
Willow Av. BR8: Swanl 6G 73
CT10: B'stairs 9H 209
DA15: Sidc 4J 57
ME13: Fav 5E 186
Willowbank Ct. TN29: St M Bay 2N 215
Willowbank Dr. ME3: H Hals 1H 67
Willow Bank Ind. Est. ME9: Iwade 6J 197
Willow Brook Rd. SE15 5G 5
Willowby Gdns. ME8: Rain 7A 96
Willow Cl. BR2: Shortl 8B 70
BR5: St M Cry 1K 85
CT2: Cant 9N 167
CT9: Mgte 3G 209
CT21: Hythe 7F 198
DA5: Bex'y 4A 58
ME3: Allh 3E 204
SE6 6J 55
Willow Cott. ME2: Hall'g 5K 92
Willow Ct. CT10: B'stairs 8K 209
CT20: S'gte 7E 188
ME15: Maid 2D 138
Willow Cres. TN12: Five G 8F 146
TN12: S'hrst 1K 223
Willow Dr. TN26: Hams 3L 191
TN29: St M Bay 3M 215
Willow Farm Way CT6: H Bay 5K 195
Willowfields Cl. SE18 5G 50
Willow Grange DA14: Sidc 8K 57
ME3: Hoo 8G 67
Willow Gro. BR7: Chst 2C 70
Willowherb Cl. ME4: Chat'm 3F 80
Willow Ho. BR2: Shortl 5H 69
ME5: Chat'm 7C 94
ME10: Sit 8J 99
ME12: S'ness 2C 220
(off Hope St.)
ME16: Barm 6L 125
TN23: Ashf 9D 158
Willow Industries ME14: S'lng 7C 110
Willow La. SE18 4B 50
TN12: Pad W 7E 26
Willow Lea TN10: Tonb 9J 133
Willowmead ME19: Leyb 8C 108
Willow Pk. TN14: Otf 8G 102
Willow Ri. ME15: Bear 8J 127
Willow Rd. CT5: Whits 8E 226
CT14: Gt Mon 4H 33
DA1: Dart 6K 59
DA8: Erith 8H 53
ME2: Strood 6J 79
ME20: Lark 7D 108
Willows Ct. CT2: Cant 7J 167
Willowside ME6: Snod 1E 108
Willows, The BR3: Beck'm 4D 68
ME3: Isle G 7C 190
ME8: Rain 1A 96
ME9: N'tn 5K 97
ME10: Kems'y 2G 98
ME12: Minst 3J 221
TN15: Igh 3K 121
TN24: Kenn 4H 159
TN27: Bidd 7L 163
Willow Ter. DA4: Eyns 3M 87
Willow Tree Cl. CT6: H Bay 2L 195
TN24: W'boro 9K 159
Willow Tree Ct. DA14: Sidc 1J 71
Willow Tree Farm Cvn. Pk. CT21: Hythe 8E 198
Willow Tree Rd. TN2: Tun W 4E 156
Willow Tree Wlk. BR1: Brom 4L 69
Willow Va. BR7: Chst 2D 70
Willow Wlk. BR6: Farnb 4D 84
DA1: Cray 2K 59
DA1: Dart 3K 59
DA13: Meop 8E 90
TN2: Tun W 6L 151
Willow Way CT5: Whits 5L 227
CT9: Mgte 5A 208
ME15: Maid 6E 126
Willow Waye CT15: Eyt 9L 185
Willow Wents ME18: Mere 8H 123 (2C 26)
Willow Wood Rd. DA13: Meop 9E 90
Willow Woods Rd. CT14: E Stu, L Mon 5F 33
CT15: W'share, E Stu 5F 33
Willrose Cres. SE2 5K 51
Wills La. TN25: Bils 6C 40
TN29: Bils, Newchu 6C 40
Willson's Rd. CT11: Ram 6G 211
Wilman Rd. TN4: Tun W 7G 151
Wilmar Gdns. BR4: W W'ck 2E 82
Wilmar Way TN15: Seal 2N 119
Wilmay Copse Nature Reserve 3G 88
Wilmecote Ct. ME8: Gill 3N 95
Wilmerhatch La. KT18: Eps 7A 12
WILMINGTON 8K 59 (1G 15)
Wilmington Av. BR6: Orp 3L 85
Wilmington Ct. Rd. DA2: Dart 8H 59
Wilmington Way ME8: Gill 1L 95
Wilmot Rd. DA1: Dart 3H 59
Wilmott Pl. CT13: E'try 3K 183
Wilmount St. SE18 4D 50
WILSLEY GREEN 6D 176 (4J 37)
WILSLEY POUND 3A 222 (4K 37)
Wilson Av. CT14: Deal 7J 177
ME1: Roch 2A 94
Wilson Cl. ME15: Maid 1H 139
TN11: Hild 2E 144
TN24: W'boro 9L 159
Wilson La. DA4: S Dar 5F 74 (2J 15)
Wilson Rd. TN10: Tonb 1L 145
Wilsons La. ME15: E Far 4L 137 (3G 27)
Wilson St. EC2 3G 5
Wilson's Way DA13: Meop 8E 90
Wiltie Gdns. CT19: F'stone 6J 189
Wilton Cl. CT14: Deal 5L 177
Wilton Dr. ME20: Dit 1F 124
Wilton Rd. CT12: Ram 3D 210
CT19: F'stone 5H 189
SE2 4L 51
Wilton Ter. ME10: Sit 6C 98
Wiltshire Cl. DA2: Dart 5D 60
ME5: Chat'm 3F 94
Wiltshire Rd. BR6: Orp 1J 85
Wiltshire Way ME15: Maid 9H 127
TN2: Tun W 7K 151
WIMBLEDON 1C 12
Wimbledon (All England Lawn Tennis & Croquet Club) 1C 12
Wimbledon Chase Station (Rail) 2C 12
Wimbledon Common 1B 12
Wimbledon Hill Rd. SW19 1C 12
Wimbledon Lawn Tennis Mus.
Centre Court, All England Lawn Tennis & Croquet Club 1C 12
WIMBLEDON PARK 7C 4
Wimbledon Pk. Rd. SW18 7C 4
SW19 7C 4
Wimbledon Pk. Side SW19 7B 4
Wimbledon Park Station (Tube) 7C 4
Wimbledon Rd. SW17 1D 12
Wimbledon Station (Rail, CT & Tube) 1C 12
Wimborne Av. BR5: St P 7H 71
BR7: Chst 6H 71
Wimborne Cl. SE12 3J 55
Wimborne Pl. CT12: Ram 4F 210
Wimborne Way BR3: Beck'm 6A 68
Wimbourne Dr. ME8: Gill 5N 95
Wimpole Cl. BR2: Shortl 7M 69
Winant Way CT16: Dover 1G 180
Winch Cl. TN17: Cran 9D 176
Winchcomb Gdns. SE9 1N 55
Wincheap CT1: Cant 4K 171 (1G 31)
Wincheap Grn. CT1: Cant 3M 171
Wincheap Ind. Est. CT1: Cant 3K 171
WINCHELSEA 7A 46
Winchelsea Av. DA7: Bexhth 7A 52
WINCHELSEA BEACH 7A 46
Winchelsea Ct. CT17: Dover 5H 181
Winchelsea La. TN31: Udim 6J 45
Winchelsea Mus. 7A 46
Winchelsea Rd. CT17: Dover 5G 181
ME5: Chat'm 5E 94
NW10 2A 4
TN35: Gues T 7H 45
Winchelsea Station (Rail) 6K 45
Winchelsea St. CT17: Dover 5G 181
Winchelsea Ter. CT17: Dover 5G 181
Winchester Av. ME5: Chat'm 7C 94
Winchester Cl. BR2: Shortl 6J 69
Winchester Cres. DA12: Grav'nd 8J 63
Winchester Gdns. CT1: Cant 4N 171
Winchester Gro. TN13: S'oaks 5J 119
Winchester Ho. ME15: Maid 1G 139
Winchester Pk. BR2: Shortl 6J 69
Winchester Pl. ME14: Maid 4D 126
Winchester Rd. BR2: Shortl 6J 69
BR6: Chels 5L 85
DA7: Bexhth 9M 51
TN10: Tonb 2K 145
TN18: Hawkh 5D 192
Winchester St. W3 4A 4
Winchester Way ME8: Rain 2C 96
WINCHET HILL 2G 37
Winchfield Rd. SE26 1B 68
Winch's Gth. TN12: S'hrst 1K 223
Wincliff Rd. TN9: Tonb 7H 145
Wincrofts Dr. SE9 2F 56
Windermere ME13: Fav 6J 187
Windermere Av. CT11: Ram 5D 210
Windermere Cl. BR6: Farnb 4D 84
DA1: Dart 6J 59
Windermere Ct. TN24: Ashf 6G 158
Windermere Dr. ME8: Gill 4N 95
Windermere Gdns. CT3: Aysm 2D 162
Windermere Gro. ME10: Sit 8E 98
Windermere Ho. ME15: Maid 1G 139
Windermere Rd. BR4: W W'ck 3H 83
DA7: Bexhth 9D 52
Windfield Cl. SE26 9A 54
Windham Av. CR0: Croy 9G 83
Windhill TN27: Char'g 5G 29
Wind Hill La. TN27: Char'g 5G 29
Windhover Way DA12: Grav'nd 9K 63
Winding Hill ME13: Sell'g, Shel 1K 219 (1B 30)
Windmill Av. CT12: Ram 1F 210
Windmill Bus. Cen. DA13: Meop 4E 90
Windmill Cl. CT1: Cant 2B 172
CT4: Brid 8H 173
CT6: H Bay 5H 195
ME2: Strood 3M 79
TN24: W'boro 9L 159
Windmill Cotts. ME3: Lwr Sto 7C 204
TN14: Weald 6J 131
(off Windmill Rd.)
TN17: Cran 6D 176
Windmill Ct. CT5: Whits 6E 226
ME17: Bou Mo 5E 138
TN2: Tun W 2J 157
(off North St.)
Windmill Dr. BR2: Kes 5M 83
Windmill Gdns. TN27: H'crn 8L 191
Windmill Grange TN15: W King 8E 88
Windmill Hgts. ME14: Bear 5L 127
Windmill Hill ME17: Ulc, H'shm 9J 141 (5C 28)
TN12: Brenc 5N 153 (1D 36)
TN15: Bor G, Wro 3C 122 (1B 26)
Windmill La. E15 1K 5
KT17: Eps 6A 12
TN5: Cous W 6C 36
Windmill La. Cvn. Site
ME19: W Mal 4M 123
Windmill La. E. ME19: W Mal 3N 123
Windmill La. W. ME19: W Mal 4N 123
Windmill Pk. TN15: Bor G 2D 122
Windmill Quay Rd. ME12: Minst 9N 221
Windmill Ri. ME12: Minst 6M 221
Windmill Rd. CR0: Croy 3G 13
CR4: Mitc 2E 12
CT1: Cant 2B 172
CT5: Whits 6F 226
CT6: H Bay 5H 195
ME7: Gill 9E 80
ME10: Sit 5E 98
SW18 6D 4
TN13: S'oaks 3J 131 (3G 25)
TN14: Weald 6J 131 (4G 25)
Windmill St. CT21: Hythe 7J 199
DA11: Grav'nd 5G 62
(not continuous)
DA12: Grav'nd 4G 63 (7C 8)
(not continuous)
ME2: Strood 3M 79
TN2: Tun W 2J 157
Windmill Vw. CT9: Mgte 5E 208
Windmill Wlk. CT12: Ram 3F 210
Windrush SE28 1K 51
Windrush La. SE23 8A 54
Windsor Av. CT9: Mgte 4F 208
ME4: Chat'm 1C 94
SW19 2D 12
Windsor Cinema 9M 209
(off Harbour St.)
Windsor Cl. BR7: Chst 1D 70
CT10: B'stairs 8J 209
ME14: Maid 3E 126
Windsor Ct. CT9: Mgte 4F 208
CT14: Walm 8M 177
Windsor Dr. BR6: Chels 7J 85 (5D 14)
DA1: Dart 4H 59
ME10: Sit 9E 98
Windsor Gdns. CT6: H Bay 4C 194
ME12: Ward 4J 203
Windsor Ho. CT5: Whits 4F 226
CT14: Deal 5K 177
CT17: Dover 5J 181
(off Durham Cl.)
Windsor M. SE6 6F 54
SE23 6B 54
TN28: New R 1L 213
Windsor Rd. CT1: Cant 4J 171
CT12: C'snd 5B 210
DA6: Bexhth 2N 57
DA12: Grav'nd 8G 63
ME7: Gill 7G 81
Windward Rd. ME1: Roch 2N 93
Windy Ridge BR1: Brom 4A 70
Windyridge ME7: Gill 2H 95
Winehouse La. CT18: Cap F 1C 174 (3C 42)
Wine Pine Ho. CT21: Hythe 7H 199
Wineycock ME9: Newn 1H 29
Winfield La. TN15: Bor G 7L 121 (2A 26)
Winford M. ME1: Roch 1L 93
Winfreds Cl. TN17: Rolv 3B 214
Wingate Ct. ME10: Sit 7F 98
(off Anselm Cl.)
Wingate Hill CT2: Harb 1G 170
Wingate Rd. CT19: F'stone 4K 189
DA14: Sidc 2L 71
Wingfield Bank DA11: Nflt 7B 62
Wingfield Ct. DA15: Sidc 7H 57
Wingfield Rd. DA12: Grav'nd 5G 62
WINGHAM 7J 225 (1C 32)
Wingham Cl. ME8: Gill 9M 81
ME15: Maid 1J 139
Wingham Ct. CT3: Wing 8J 225
WINGHAM GREEN 1B 32
Wingham Rd. CT3: Ickh 1B 32
WINGHAM WELL 1B 32
Wingham Well La.
CT3: Wing, Bram 1B 32
Wingham Wildlife Pk. 6L 225 (7C 22)
Wingleton La. CT14: Ripp 3A 200 (5H 33)
CT15: Sutt 5H 33
WINGMORE 6K 31
Wing Rd. ME12: Ley S 7N 203
Wingrove Dr. ME2: Strood 4N 79
ME14: Weav 4H 127
Wingrove Hill CT17: Dover 2D 180
Wingrove Rd. SE6 7H 55
Wings Cl. CT10: B'stairs 8M 209
Wings Ct. CT10: B'stairs 8M 209
Winifred Av. CT12: Ram 2G 210
Winifred Rd. DA1: Dart 3J 59
DA8: Erith 5F 52
ME15: Bear 6J 127
Winifred St. E16 1B 50
WINKHURST GREEN 9C 130 (5E 24)
Winkhurst Grn. Rd.
TN8: Ide H, Chid 9C 130 (5E 24)
Winkland Oaks Rd. CT14: Sutt 6G 33
CT15: Sutt 1N 179 (6G 33)
Winkle Cl. CT6: H Bay 4C 194
Winkworth Rd. SM7: Bans 6C 12
Winlaton Rd. BR1: Brom 9G 54
Winnipeg Cl. CT16: Dover 1H 181
Winnipeg Dr. BR6: Chels 7H 85
Winn Rd. SE12 6K 55 (7A 6)
Winns Comn. Rd. SE18 6G 51
Winser Rd. TN17: Rolv L 7C 38
Winsford Rd. SE6 8C 54
Winslade Way SE6 5E 54
Winstanley Cres. CT11: Ram 4H 211
Winstanley Rd. ME12: S'ness 2D 220
Winston Av. ME19: W Mal 6N 123
Winston Cl. CT1: Cant 3B 172
CT7: Birch 3F 206
DA9: G'hithe 4F 60
Winston Ct. BR1: Brom 4L 69
(off Widmore Rd.)
Winston Dr. ME2: Wain 2A 80
Winston Gdns. CT6: H Bay 3L 195
Winston Ho. CT20: F'stone 6F 188
Winston Rd. ME2: Strood 7H 79
Winston Scott Av. TN3: Lang G 1M 155
Winston Way IG1: Ilf 1B 6
Winterage La. CT18: Acr 5H 193 (2K 41)
Winterborne Av. BR6: Orp 4F 84
WINTERBOURNE 1D 30
Winterbourne Rd. SE6 6C 54
Winter Dr. CT18: H'nge 7L 193
Winterfield La. ME19: W Mal 1C 124 (1E 26)
Wintergarden Cres. DA9: Bluew 5G 60
WINTER GARDENS 1K 9
Winter Gardens 2D 208
Wintergreen Cl. ME4: Chat'm 3F 80
Winters Cft. DA12: Grav'nd 2J 77
Winterstoke Cres. CT11: Ram 4L 211
Winterstoke Rd. SE6 6C 54
Winterstoke Undercliff CT11: Ram 5L 211
Winterstoke Way CT11: Ram 4K 211
Winterton Ct. TN16: Westrm 9F 116
(off Market Sq.)
Winton Ct. BR8: Swanl 7F 72
Winton Rd. BR6: Farnb 5D 84
Winton Way TN29: Dym 1N 215
Wireless Rd. TN16: Big H 3D 164
Wirrals, The ME5: Chat'm 7D 94
Wirral Wood Cl. BR7: Chst 2C 70
Wiseacre TN3: Lamb 4K 201
Wises La. ME9: B'den 8B 98 (5E 18)
ME10: Sit 6B 98 (5E 18)

Wise's La.—Wordsworth Way

Wise's La. TN15: Ash 9K 89
TN15: Stans 9L 89
Wish St. TN31: Rye 5A 46
Wish, The TN26: Kena 6J 39
Wisley Rd. BR5: St P 3J 71
WISSENDEN 2F 39
Wissenden La. TN26: Beth 2H 163 (2F 39)
Wistaria Cl. BR6: Farnb 3D 84
Wisteria Gdns. BR8: Swanl 5E 72
Wisteria Rd. SE13 2G 54
Witches La. TN13: Riv 4E 118 (2F 25)
Witham Way ME2: Strood 5K 79
Withens Cl. BR5: St M Cry 7L 71
WITHERSDANE 7C 30
Witherston Way SE9 7C 56
WITHYHAM 9B 154 (5E 34)
Withyham Rd.
TN3: Groom, Withy 6G 155 (4F 35)
Witley Cres. CR0: Croy 7F 82
Witney Path SE23 8A 54
WITTERSHAM 3D 228 (2A 46)
Wittersham Cl. ME5: Chat'm 6E 94
Wittersham La. TN31: Iden 3A 46
Wittersham Rd. BR1: Brom 1J 69
TN30: Iden 3A 46
TN30: Witter 1A 228 (1J 45)
(Potman's Heath)
TN30: Witter, Ston C E 3F 228 (2A 46)
(Stocks, The)
TN31: Iden 3A 46
TN31: Peas 3J 45
Wittersham Road Station
Kent & East Sussex Railway 1J 45
Wivenhoe TN23: Ashf 4C 160
Wivenhoe Cl. ME8: Rain 1C 96
Wixom Ho. SE3 2M 55
Woburn Pl. WC1 2F 5
Wodehouse Cl. ME20: Lark 6D 108
Wodehouse Rd. DA1: Dart 2A 60
Wold Chalet & Cvn. Pk., The
ME12: E'chu 2E 202
Woldham Pl. BR2: Shortl 7M 69
Woldham Rd. BR2: Shortl 7M 69
Woldingham Rd. CR3: Wold 7H 13
Wolds Dr. BR6: Farnb 5C 84
Wolfe Cl. BR2: Shortl 9K 69
Wolfe Cotts. TN16: Westrm 9F 116
Wolfe Rd. ME16: Maid 7M 125
Wolfe Ter. *CT16: Dover 1G 181*
(off Montreal Cl.)
Wolfram Cl. SE13 3H 55
Wolf's Hill RH8: Oxt 4A 24
Wolf's Rd. RH8: Oxt 3A 24
Wolf's Row RH8: Oxt 3A 24
Wollaston Cl. ME8: Gill 8N 95
Wollaston Rd. CT14: Walm 6N 177
Wolseley Av. CT6: H Bay 3B 194
Wolseley Pl. TN24: Ashf 7F 158
Wolseley Rd. TN4: Tun W 7J 151
Wolseley Ter. TN29: Lydd 4K 205
Wolsey Cres. CR0: Croy 9F 82
Wolsey M. BR6: Chels 6H 85
Wolsley Cl. DA1: Cray 3F 58
Wolvercote Rd. SE2 2M 51
WOLVERTON 1D 42
Wolverton Hill CT15: Alk 1D 42
Wombwell Gdns. DA11: Nflt 7D 62
WOMBWELL PARK 7C 62
Women's Land Army Mus., The 7D 180 (2E 42)
WOMENSWOLD 4B 32
Wood Av. CT19: F'stone 4K 189
Woodbank Rd. BR1: Brom 8J 55
Woodbastwick Rd. SE26 1A 68
Woodberry Dr. ME10: Sit 8J 99
Woodberry Gro. DA5: Bex'y 8E 58
Woodbine Rd. DA15: Sidc 6G 56
Woodbridge Dr. ME15: Maid 8B 126
Woodbrook TN27: Char'g 3L 175
Woodbrook Rd. SE2 6J 51
Woodbury Av. RH19: E Grin 4A 34
Woodbury Cl. TN4: Tun W 9G 151
TN16: Big H 6F 164
Woodbury Gdns. TN30: Tent 8B 224
Woodbury La. TN30: Tent 8B 224
Woodbury Pk. Gdns. TN4: Tun W 9H 151
Woodbury Pk. Rd. TN4: Tun W 9G 151
Woodbury Rd. ME5: Chat'm 1B 110
TN16: Big H 6F 164
TN18: Hawkh 5D 192
WOODCHURCH
Ashford 7B 228 (5H 39)
Birchington 6L 207 (3G 23)
Woodchurch Cl. DA14: Sidc 8F 56
ME5: Chat'm 6E 94
Woodchurch Cres. ME8: Gill 1M 95
Woodchurch Dr. BR1: Brom 3N 69
Woodchurch Ho. ME8: Gill 1M 95
Woodchurch Rd. CT7: Wdchu 8L 207 (3G 23)
(not continuous)
CT9: Wdchu 2G 23
TN26: App 7H 39
TN26: Shad 4J 39
TN30: Tent 8D 224 (6E 38)
Woodchurch Village Life Mus. 6A 228 (5G 39)
Woodchurch Windmill 6B 228 (5H 39)
Wood Cl. DA5: Bex'y 8F 58
ME20: Aylfd 1J 125
Woodclyffe Dr. BR7: Chst 5C 70
Woodcock Gdns. CT18: H'nge 8J 193
Woodcock La. ME17: Graf G 5D 28
TN17: Bendn 7A 38
Woodcocks TN27: H'crn 8L 191
WOODCOTE
Epsom 7A 12
Purley 6E 12
Woodcote CT5: Whits 4M 227
Woodcote Dr. BR6: Orp 2F 84
WOODCOTE GREEN 5E 12
Woodcote Grn. SM6: Wall 5E 12
Woodcote Grn. Rd. KT18: Eps 7A 12
Woodcote Gro. Rd. CR5: Coul 7E 12
Woodcote Rd. CR8: Purl 5E 12
KT18: Eps 6A 12
SM6: Wall 5E 12
Woodcote Side KT18: Eps 7A 12
Woodcote Valley Rd. CR8: Purl 6E 12
Wood Cottage La. CT19: F'stone 4D 188
Woodcourt Cl. ME10: Sit 9F 98
Woodcroft SE9 8B 56
Woodcut ME14: Pen H 1D 126
Woodcut Cotts. ME17: Holl 7B 128
Wood Dr. BR7: Chst 2A 70
TN13: S'oaks 8G 119
Wood End BR8: Swanl 7D 72
Wooden Spoon Preserving Company, The
6D 30
Woodfall Dr. DA1: Cray 2F 58
Woodfalls Ind. Est. ME18: Ladd 5E 26
Woodfield Av. CT19: F'stone 4E 188
DA11: Grav'nd 6G 62
SW16 7E 4
TN11: Hild 2E 144
Woodfield Cl. CT19: F'stone 4D 188
Woodfield Ho. *SE23 8A 54*
(off Dacres Rd.)
Woodfield Rd. TN9: Tonb 7H 145
Woodfields TN13: Riv 4E 118
Woodfield Way ME3: C'den, Wain 9A 66
Woodford Av. CT12: Ram 3H 211
Woodford Ct. CT7: Birch 4F 206
Woodford Gro. ME19: W Mal 6N 123
Woodford Rd. E7 1A 6
ME16: Maid 7M 125
Woodgate CT4: Bis 4J 31
Woodgate Cl. ME13: Fav 4G 187
Woodgate La. ME9: B'den 9L 97
Woodgate Rd. ME19: Rya 6H 107 (7C 16)
Woodgates Cl. TN26: H Hald 2B 196
Woodgate Way TN9: Tonb 7L 145
TN11: Tonb 8K 145 (7K 25)
Woodgers Gro. BR8: Swanl 5G 73
Woodgrange Dr. SS1: Sth S 1E 10
Woodgrange Park Station (Rail) 1A 6
Woodgrange Rd. E7 1A 6
Woodhall Ter. ME11: Queen 7B 220
Woodham Rd. SE6 8F 54
Woodhayes Rd. SW19 1B 12
Woodhead Dr. BR6: Orp 4G 85
Wood Hill CT2: T Hill 5L 167 (6H 21)
DA13: Meop 4C 16
Woodhill DA13: Meop 5H 91
SE18 4A 50
Woodhill Pk. TN2: Pem 8B 152
Woodhurst ME5: Chat'm 7A 94
Woodhurst Av. BR5: Pet W 9E 70
Woodhurst Cl. ME2: Cux 1F 92
Woodhurst La. RH8: Oxt 4A 24
Woodhurst Rd. SE2 5J 51
Woodington Cl. SE9 4C 56
Woodknoll Dr. BR7: Chst 4B 70
WOODLAND 2H 41
Woodland Av. CT3: Aysm 2C 162
CT7: Birch 5G 206
DA3: Hart'y 8M 75
Woodland Cl. CT17: Dover 2D 180
DA3: Long 6B 76
ME19: W Mal 1M 123
TN4: Tun W 7H 151
Woodland Cotts. CT18: Lym'ge 7K 205
Woodland Dr. ME12: Minst 5J 221
TN8: Eden 4D 184
Woodland Ri. CT21: W Hyt 7B 198
TN15: Seal, S'oaks 5M 119
Woodland Rd. CT6: H Bay 5C 194
CT18: Lym'ge 6H 205 (2G 41)
TN4: Tun W 7J 151
WOODLANDS 4C 104 (6J 15)
Woodlands BR2: Shortl 7J 69
DA6: Bexhth 3C 58
ME5: Chat'm 9D 94
ME13: Darg 6D 20
ME17: Cox 5M 137
TN2: Pem 7E 152
TN12: Pad W 8L 147
TN17: Cran 6D 176
Woodlands Av. DA15: Sidc 6G 57
ME6: Snod 2D 108
Woodlands Cl. BR1: Brom 5B 70
BR8: Swanl 6G 72
ME14: Pen H 2D 126
ME18: Tstn 9F 124
TN2: Tun W 1K 157
Woodlands Cotts. ME17: H'shm 1N 141
Woodlands Ct. BR1: Brom 4J 69
ME5: Chat'm 9C 94
(off Walderslade Rd.)
TN4: S'bgh 4G 150
Woodlands Dr. CT21: Hythe 7A 188
Woodlands Est. Res. Pk.
CT2: Blean 4F 166
Woodlands La. DA12: Shorne 3B 78 (1E 16)
Woodlands Pde. ME20: Dit 1H 125
Woodlands Pk. DA5: Bex'y 9E 58
TN27: Bidd 4D 38
Woodlands Ri. BR8: Swanl 5G 72
Woodlands Rd. BR1: Brom 5A 70
BR6: Chels 7J 85
CT3: Adm 3A 32
CT4: Adm 3A 32
DA7: Bexhth 1N 57
ME7: Gill 1J 95 (3K 17)
ME10: Sit 8J 99
ME20: Aylfd, Dit 9G 108
TN9: Tonb 8G 145
TN24: W'boro 8K 159
Woodlands St. SE13 5G 55
Woodlands Ter. BR8: Crock'm 9C 72
ME7: Gill 9J 81
Woodlands, The BR6: Chels 7K 85
SE13 5G 54
TN2: Tun W 1J 157
Woodlands Vw. TN14: Hals 1C 102
TN30: Witter 2D 228
Woodlands Wlk. ME17: H'shm 2N 141
Woodland Ter. SE7 4A 50
Woodland Wlk. BR1: Brom 9G 55
(not continuous)
Woodland Way BR4: W W'ck 5E 82
BR5: Pet W 7E 70
CR0: Croy 2B 82
CT2: Cant 7K 167
CT10: B'stairs 4L 209
CT13: Wdboro 8H 217
DA9: G'hithe 3G 61
ME14: Pen H 2E 126
SE2 4M 51
TN4: Bidb 2D 150
TN29: Dym 8D 182
Wood La. DA2: Dart 9D 60
(not continuous)
ME5: Chat'm 5H 17
RM8: Dag 1D 6
RM12: H'church 1G 7
TN17: Bendn 5B 38
TN23: Kgnt 6G 161
W12 3B 4
Woodlark Rd. ME4: Chat'm 3E 80
Woodlawn St. CT5: Whits 3F 226
Woodlea DA3: Long 6B 76
ME19: Leyb 8D 108
TN24: Ashf 7G 159
Woodlea Dr. BR2: Shortl 8H 69
Woodleas ME16: Barm 7K 125
Woodley Rd. BR6: Chels 3L 85
Wood Lodge Gdns. BR1: Brom 3A 70
Wood Lodge Grange TN13: S'oaks 4K 119
Wood Lodge La. BR4: W W'ck 4F 82
Woodman Av. CT5: Whits 2M 227
Woodman Pde. *E16 1C 50*
(off Woodman St.)
WOODMANS GREEN 6D 44
WOODMANSTERNE 7D 12
Woodmansterne La. SM5: Cars 6D 12
(Croydon La.)
SM6: Wall 6E 12
SM7: Bans 6D 12
(Park Rd.)
Woodmansterne Rd. SM5: Cars 5D 12
Woodmansterne Station (Rail) 7E 12
Woodmansterne St. SM7: Bans 7D 12
Woodman St. E16 1C 50
(not continuous)
Woodman Vs. DA3: Fawk 4H 89
Woodmere SE9 6B 56
Woodmere Av. CR0: Croy 1A 82
Woodmere Cl. CR0: Croy 1A 82
Woodmere Gdns. CR0: Croy 1A 82
Woodmere Way BR3: Beck'm 8G 68
Woodmount BR8: Crock'm 1E 86
WOODNESBOROUGH 8G 217 (1F 33)
Woodnesborough La. CT13: E'try 2K 183 (2F 33)
Woodnesborough Rd.
CT13: S'wch 7K 217 (1G 33)
Woodpecker Cl. TN8: Eden 4D 184
Woodpecker Dr. ME9: Iwade 8K 197
Woodpecker Glade ME8: Gill 5N 95
Woodpecker Mt. CR0: Croy 9B 82
Woodpecker Rd. ME20: Lark 9D 108
Woodplace La. CR5: Coul 7E 12
Wood Retreat SE18 7F 50
Wood Ride BR5: Pet W 7F 70
Wood Rd. CT21: Hythe 7J 199
TN16: Big H 6C 164
Woodrow SE18 4B 50
Woodrow Chase CT6: H Bay 1N 195
Woodruff Cl. ME8: Rain 3B 18
Woodrush Pl. ME4: Chat'm 3E 80
WOODSDEN 7J 37
Woodsgate Way TN2: Pem 8A 152
WOOD'S GREEN 6B 36
Woods Hill CT4: Walt 5F 31
Woods Hill La. RH19: A'hstw 4A 34
Woodshole Cotts. ME9: Bob 2E 98
WOODSIDE 3H 13
Woodside BR6: Chels 6J 85
DA13: Meop 2E 106
ME8: Gill 5L 95 (4A 18)
ME13: Dunk 4L 165
SW19 1C 12
TN23: Ashf 3C 160
Woodside Av. BR7: Chst 1E 70
CT4: Chart'm 8D 170
Woodside Cl. CT16: Dover 9D 178
DA7: Bexhth 2E 58
TN2: Pem 8D 152
Woodside Cres. DA15: Sidc 8G 57
Woodside Dr. DA2: Dart 9F 58
Woodside Gdns. ME10: Sit 9E 98
WOODSIDE GREEN 3F 29
Woodside Grn. ME3: Cli W 6M 65
(not continuous)
SE25 3H 13
Woodside La. DA5: Bex'y 4M 57
Woodside Pde. DA15: Sidc 8G 57
Woodside Rd. BR1: Brom 8A 70
CT2: Sturry 4E 168
DA7: Bexhth 2E 58
DA15: Sidc 8G 57
ME15: Maid 1F 138
TN2: Pem 8D 152
TN4: R'hall 1D 156
TN9: Tonb 8H 145
TN13: S'oaks 5H 119
TN14: Sund 6N 117
Woodside Stop (CT) 3H 13
Woodside Vw. CT16: Dover 8D 178
Woods Ley CT3: Ash 4C 216
Wood's Pl. CT17: Dover 2G 180
WOODSTOCK 6E 18
Woodstock Cl. DA5: Bex'y 5A 58
Woodstock Cotts. ME9: Mils 5F 114
Woodstock Ct. SE12 4K 55
Woodstock Gdns. BR3: Beck'm 4E 68
Woodstock Rd. CT14: Deal 6M 177
ME2: Strood 5L 79
ME10: Sit 1F 114 (5F 19)
WOODSTOCK, THE 3C 12
Woodstock Way TN24: Kenn 4G 159
Wood St. BR8: Swanl 5K 73 (2G 15)
CT16: Dover 4H 181
ME2: Cux 1F 92
ME7: Gill 6D 80 (2J 17)
ME9: Tonge 2N 115 (6G 19)
ME12: S'ness 2D 220
TN1: Tun W 1H 157
Wood Va. SE23 7H 5
Woodvale Av. CT5: Whits 5L 227
Woodvale Ct. *BR1: Brom 4L 69*
(off Widmore Rd.)
Woodview DA2: Dart 2G 74
Wood Vw. RM16: Grays 4B 8
Woodview Cl. BR6: Farnb 3E 84
TN15: W King 7E 88
Woodview Cres. TN11: Hild 2E 144
Woodview Ri. ME2: Strood 3K 79
Woodview Rd. BR8: Swanl 5D 72
Woodville Cl. CT1: Cant 4K 171
SE12 3K 55
Woodville Gro. DA16: Well 1J 57
Woodville Halls Theatre *5G 62*
(off Woodville Pl.)
Woodville Pl. DA11: Grav'nd 5G 62
DA12: Grav'nd 5G 62
Woodville Rd. CT12: Ram 3G 210
ME15: Maid 7D 126
Woodville St. SE18 4A 50
Woodward Rd. RM9: Dag 1D 6
Woodward Ter. DA9: G'hithe 4E 60
Wood Way BR6: Farnb 3C 84
Wood Yd. CT14: Deal 4N 177
Woodyates Rd. SE12 4K 55
WOOLAGE GREEN 5B 32
Woolage Grn. Rd. CT4: Wom 5B 32
CT15: S'wll 6H 219 (5C 32)
WOOLAGE VILLAGE 4B 32
Woolaston Cl. ME15: Maid 8C 126
Woolbrook Cl. ME8: Rain 1D 96
Woolbrook Rd. DA1: Cray 4F 58
Woolcomber St. CT16: Dover 4K 181 (2G 43)
Wooldeys Rd. ME8: Rain 1B 96
Woolett Rd. ME10: Sit 6D 98
Woolf Cl. SE28 1K 51
Woolies, The CT18: Lym'ge 7L 205
Woollets Cl. CT6: H Bay 4D 194
Woollett Cl. DA1: Cray 2H 59
Woollett St. ME14: Maid 4D 126
Woolley Cl. TN4: S'bgh 5F 150
Woolley Rd. ME15: Maid 9H 127
TN4: S'bgh 5F 150
Woolmans Wood Caravan Pk.
ME5: Chat'm 7A 94
Woolmer Dr. TN24: W'boro 2L 161
WOOLPACK CORNER 4C 38
Woolpack Hill TN25: Sme 8J 165 (2D 40)
Woolpack Hill Cotts. TN25: Sme 8J 165
Woolreeds Rd. TN23: Ashf 2E 160
Woolstone Rd. SE23 7B 54 (7J 5)
WOOLWICH 3C 50 (4B 6)
Woolwich Arsenal Station (Rail) 4D 50 (4B 6)
Woolwich Chu. St. SE18 3A 50 (4B 6)
Woolwich Cl. ME5: Chat'm 4D 94
Woolwich Comn. SE18 6C 50 (5B 6)
Woolwich Dockyard Ind. Est. SE18 3A 50
Woolwich Dockyard Station (Rail) 4B 50 (4B 6)
Woolwich High St. SE18 3C 50
Woolwich Ind. Est. SE28 3G 50
(not continuous)
Woolwich Mnr. Way E6 3B 6
E16 2D 50 (3B 6)
Woolwich New Rd. SE18 5C 50 (4B 6)
Woolwich Rd. DA7: Bexhth 1B 58 (6E 6)
DA17: Belv 5A 52 (4E 6)
SE2 6M 51 (5D 6)
SE7 4A 6
SE10 4K 5
Wooton Cl. CT4: P'hm 4G 31
Wooton Dr. CT4: P'hm 3G 31
WOOTTON 6B 32
Wootton Grn. ME8: Gill 9N 81
Wootton Hill CT4: Woot 6A 32
Wootton La. CT4: Woot 7B 32
CT15: S'fld 7B 32
Wopsle Cl. ME1: Roch 4A 94
Worcester Av. ME19: W Mal 7M 123
Worcester Cl. CR0: Croy 3D 82
DA9: G'hithe 2H 61
DA13: Ist R 3E 76
ME2: Strood 4J 79
ME12: Minst 6K 221
ME13: Fav 6J 187
Worcester Dr. ME10: Sit 5E 98
Worcester La. CT3: Cant 3D 172
WORCESTER PARK 4B 12
Worcester Pk. Rd. KT4: Wor Pk 4A 12
Worcester Park Station (Rail) 3B 12
Worcester Rd. ME15: Maid 1G 139
Wordsworth Cl. ME5: Chat'm 4F 94
Wordsworth Gdns. CT3: Aysm 1D 162
Wordsworth Ho. *SE18 6C 50*
(off Woolwich Comn.)
Wordsworth Rd. DA16: Well 8G 51
ME14: Pen H 2E 126
SE20 3A 68
Wordsworth Way DA1: Dart 2A 60
(not continuous)
ME20: Lark 6E 108

HOSPITALS and HOSPICES
covered by this atlas.

N.B. Where Hospitals and Hospices are not named on the map, the reference
given is for the road in which they are situated.

ALEXANDRA BUPA HOSPITAL, THE 2D **110**
Impton Lane
CHATHAM
ME5 9PG
Tel: 01634 687166

ARCHERY HOUSE 4B **60**
Bow Arrow Lane
DARTFORD
DA2 6PB
Tel: 01322 622222

BECKENHAM HOSPITAL 5C **68**
379 Croydon Road
BECKENHAM
BR3 3QL
Tel: 01689 863000

BELVEDERE PRIVATE CLINIC 5L **51**
Knee Hill
LONDON
SE2 0AT
Tel: 020 83114464

BENENDEN HOSPITAL 5B **38**
Goddards Green Road
Benenden
CRANBROOK
TN17 4AX
Tel: 01580 240333

BETHLEM ROYAL HOSPITAL, THE 1D **82**
Monks Orchard Road
BECKENHAM
BR3 3BX
Tel: 020 87776611

BLACKHEATH BMI HOSPITAL, THE 1H **55**
40-42 Lee Terrace
LONDON
SE3 9UD
Tel: 020 83187722

BRACTON CENTRE, THE 7G **58**
Bracton Lane
Leyton Cross Road
BEXLEY
DA2 7AF
Tel: 01322 294300

BUCKLAND HOSPITAL 4F **180**
Coombe Valley Road
Buckland
DOVER
CT17 0HD
Tel: 01304 201624

BURRSWOOD 5H **155**
Groombridge
TUNBRIDGE WELLS
TN3 9PU
Tel: 01892 863637

CHAUCER BMI HOSPITAL, THE 6N **171**
Nackington Road
CANTERBURY
CT4 7AR
Tel: 01227 825100

CHELSFIELD PARK HOSPITAL 6N **85**
Bucks Cross Road
ORPINGTON
BR6 7RG
Tel: 01689 877855

CHILDREN'S HOSPITAL, THE (LEWISHAM) 3E **54**
Lewisham University Hospital
Lewisham High Street
LONDON
SE13 6LH
Tel: 020 83333000

DARENT VALLEY HOSPITAL 6E **60**
Darenth Wood Road
DARTFORD
DA2 8DA
Tel: 01322 428100

DEMELZA HOUSE CHILDREN'S HOSPICE 5A **98**
Rook Lane
Bobbing
SITTINGBOURNE
ME9 8DZ
Tel: 01795 845200

EDENBRIDGE & DISTRICT WAR MEMORIAL HOSPITAL 8C **184**
Mill Hill
EDENBRIDGE
TN8 5DA
Tel: 01732 862137

ELLENOR FOUNDATION (HOSPICE) 5N **59**
Livingstone Hospital
East Hill
DARTFORD
DA1 1SA
Tel: 01322 221315

ERITH & DISTRICT HOSPITAL 6E **52**
Park Crescent
ERITH
DA8 3EE
Tel: 020 83083131

FAVERSHAM COTTAGE HOSPITAL 5G **187**
Stone Street
FAVERSHAM
ME13 8PS
Tel: 01795 562000

FAWKHAM MANOR BMI HOSPITAL 2J **89**
Manor Lane
Fawkham
LONGFIELD
DA3 8ND
Tel: 01474 879900

GRAVESEND & NORTH KENT HOSPITAL 4F **62**
Bath Street
GRAVESEND
DA11 0DG
Tel: 01474 564333

GREENWICH & BEXLEY COTTAGE HOSPICE 5L **51**
185 Bostall Hill
LONDON
SE2 0QX
Tel: 020 83122244

HAWKHURST COTTAGE HOSPITAL 5A **192**
High Street, Hawkhurst
CRANBROOK
TN18 4PU
Tel: 01580 753345

HAYES GROVE PRIORY HOSPITAL 3K **83**
Prestons Road
BROMLEY
BR2 7AS
Tel: 020 84627722

HEART OF KENT HOSPICE 1K **125**
Preston Hall
Royal British Legion Village
AYLESFORD
ME20 7NJ
Tel: 01622 792200

HEATHVIEW DAY CENTRE 6L **51**
Lodge Hill
LONDON
SE2 0AY
Tel: 020 83197100

HOMOEOPATHIC HOSPITAL 2G **156**
Church Road
TUNBRIDGE WELLS
TN1 1JU
Tel: 01892 542977

HOSPICE IN THE WEALD 5D **152**
Maidstone Road, Pembury
TUNBRIDGE WELLS
TN2 4TA
Tel: 01892 820500

KENT & CANTERBURY HOSPITAL 5N **171**
Ethelbert Road
CANTERBURY
CT1 3NG
Tel: 01227 766877

KENT & SUSSEX HOSPITAL 1G **156**
Mount Ephraim
TUNBRIDGE WELLS
TN4 8AT
Tel: 01892 526111

LEWISHAM UNIVERSITY HOSPITAL 3E **54**
Lewisham High Street
LONDON
SE13 6LH
Tel: 020 83333000

LIONS HOSPICE, THE 9E **62**
Coldharbour Road
Northfleet
GRAVESEND
DA11 7HQ
Tel: 01474 320007

LITTLE BROOK HOSPITAL 4C **60**
Bow Arrow Lane
DARTFORD
DA2 6PH
Tel: 01322 622222

LIVINGSTONE HOSPITAL 5N **59**
East Hill
DARTFORD
DA1 1SA
Tel: 01322 622222

MAIDSTONE HOSPITAL 5L **125**
Hermitage Lane
MAIDSTONE
ME16 9QQ
Tel: 01622 729000

MEDWAY MARITIME HOSPITAL 8E **80**
Windmill Road
GILLINGHAM
ME7 5NY
Tel: 01634 830000

MEMORIAL HOSPITAL 9C **50**
Shooters Hill
LONDON
SE18 3RZ
Tel: 020 88366000

ORPINGTON HOSPITAL 5H **85**
Sevenoaks Road
ORPINGTON
BR6 9JU
Tel: 01689 815000

PEMBURY HOSPITAL 7N **151**
Tonbridge Road
Pembury
TUNBRIDGE WELLS
TN2 4QJ
Tel: 01892 823535

PILGRIMS HOSPICE IN ASHFORD 2N **161**
Hythe Road
Willesborough
ASHFORD
TN24 0NE
Tel: 01233 504100

PILGRIMS HOSPICE IN CANTERBURY 1K **171**
56 London Road
CANTERBURY
CT2 8JA
Tel: 01227 459700

PILGRIMS HOSPICE IN THANET 6D **208**
Ramsgate Road
MARGATE
CT9 4AD
Tel: 01843 233920

PRESTON HALL HOSPITAL 9K **109**
London Road
British Legion Village
AYLESFORD
ME20 7NJ
Tel: 01622 710161

PRINCESS ROYAL UNIVERSITY HOSPITAL 4C **84**
Farnborough Common
ORPINGTON
BR6 8ND
Tel: 01689 814100

PRIORITY HOUSE 5M **125**
Hermitage Lane
MAIDSTONE
ME16 9PH
Tel: 01622 725000

QUEEN ELIZABETH HOSPITAL 7A **50**
Stadium Road
LONDON
SE18 4QH
Tel: 020 88366000

QUEEN ELIZABETH THE QUEEN MOTHER HOSPITAL 5D **208**
St Peter's Rd.
MARGATE
CT9 4AN
Tel: 01843 225544

QUEEN MARY'S HOSPITAL 1J **71**
Frognal Avenue
SIDCUP
DA14 6LT
Tel: 020 83022678

QUEEN VICTORIA MEMORIAL HOSPITAL 3J **195**
King Edward Avenue
HERNE BAY
CT6 6EB
Tel: 01227 594700

ROYAL VICTORIA HOSPITAL 5J **189**
Radnor Park Avenue
FOLKESTONE
CT19 5BN
Tel: 01303 850202

ST BARTHOLOMEW'S HOSPITAL 8B **80**
New Road
ROCHESTER
ME1 1DS
Tel: 01634 810900

ST MARTIN'S HOSPITAL 2C **172**
Littlebourne Road
CANTERBURY
CT1 1TD
Tel: 01227 459371

ST SAVIOUR'S BUPA HOSPITAL 6N **199**
73 Seabrook Road
HYTHE
CT21 5QW
Tel: 01303 265581

SEVENOAKS HOSPITAL 3K **119**
Hospital Road
SEVENOAKS
TN13 3PG
Tel: 01732 455155

SHEPPEY COMMUNITY HOSPITAL 7H **221**
Plover Road, Minster On Sea
SHEERNESS
ME12 3LT
Tel: 01795 879100

SITTINGBOURNE MEMORIAL HOSPITAL 8G **98**
Bell Rd., SITTINGBOURNE
ME10 4DT
Tel: 01795 418300

SLOANE BMI HOSPITAL, THE 4G **69**
125-133 Albemarle Road
BECKENHAM
BR3 5HS
Tel: 020 84666911

SOMERFIELD BMI HOSPITAL 4A **126**
71 London Road
MAIDSTONE
ME16 0DU
Tel: 01622 208000

SOUTH BROMLEY HOSPICE CARE 5H **85**
Orpington Hospital
109 Sevenoaks Road
ORPINGTON
BR6 9JX
Tel: 01689 605300

STONE HOUSE HOSPITAL 4C **60**
Cotton Lane, DARTFORD
DA2 6AU
Tel: 01322 622222

TONBRIDGE COTTAGE HOSPITAL 9J **145**
Vauxhall Lane, TONBRIDGE
TN11 0NE
Tel: 01732 353653

TUNBRIDGE WELLS BUPA HOSPITAL 2J **155**
Fordcombe Road
Fordcombe
TUNBRIDGE WELLS
TN3 0RD
Tel: 01892 740047

TUNBRIDGE WELLS NUFFIELD HOSPITAL, THE 2J **157**
Kingswood Road
TUNBRIDGE WELLS
TN2 4UL
Tel: 01892 531111

UPTON CENTRE 2N **57**
14 Upton Road
BEXLEYHEATH
DA6 8LQ
Tel: 020 83017900

VICTORIA HOSPITAL 5L **177**
London Road
DEAL
CT14 9UA
Tel: 01304 865400

WEST VIEW HOSPITAL 9A **224**
Plummer Lane
TENTERDEN
TN30 6TX
Tel: 01580 763677

WHITSTABLE & TANKERTON HOSPITAL 3J **227**
Northwood Road
WHITSTABLE
CT5 2HN
Tel: 01227 594400

WILLIAM HARVEY HOSPITAL 9N **159**
Kennington Road
Willesborough
ASHFORD
TN24 0LZ
Tel: 01233 633331

WISDOM HOSPICE 1A **94**
High Bank
ROCHESTER
ME1 2NU
Tel: 01634 830456

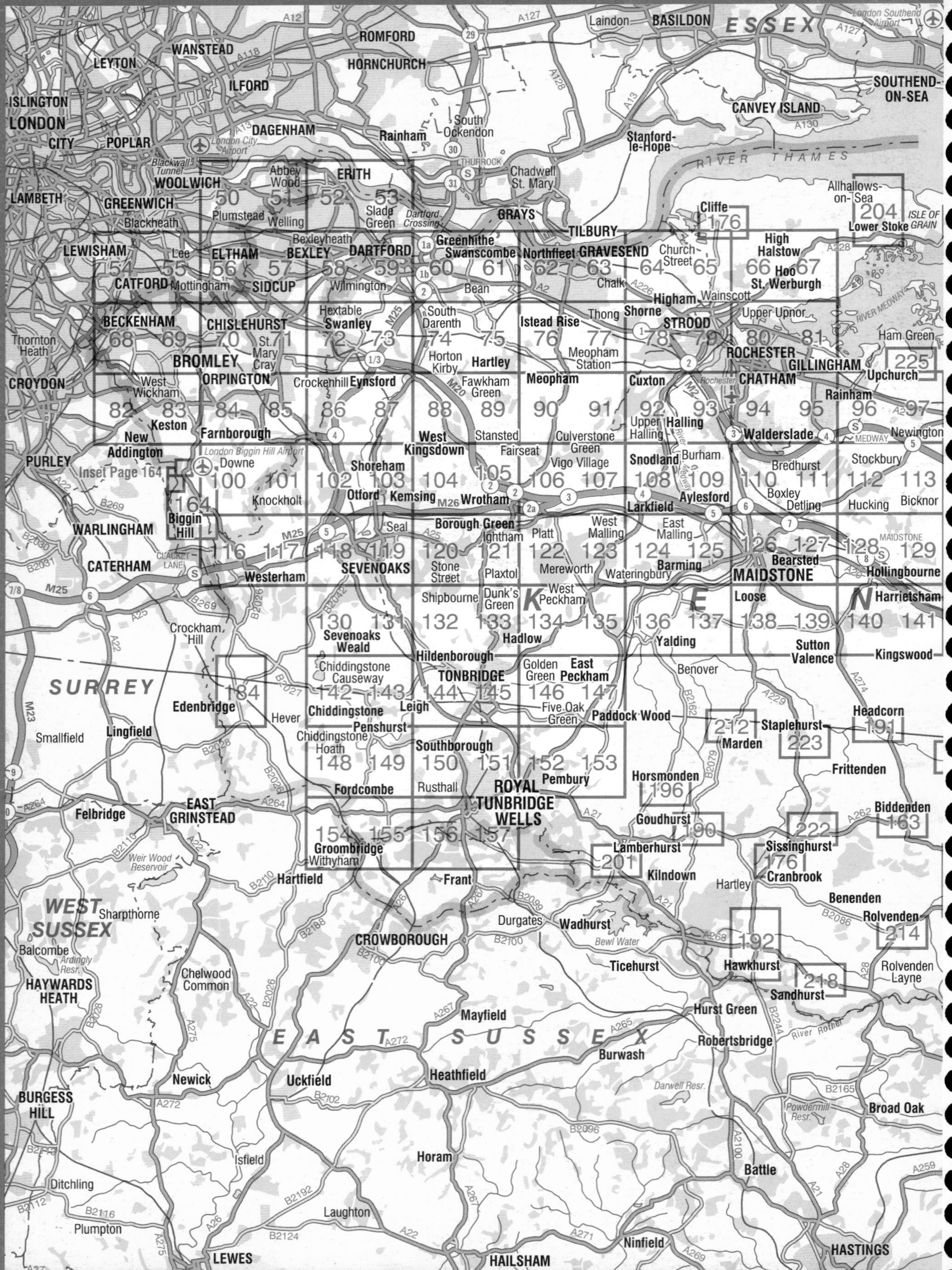
ESSEX
Laindon
BASILDON
London Southend Airport
ROMFORD
HORNCHURCH
WANSTEAD
LEYTON
ILFORD
ISLINGTON
LONDON
CITY
POPLAR
DAGENHAM
London City Airport
Blackwall Tunnel
Rainham
South Ockendon
THURROCK
SOUTHEND-ON-SEA
CANVEY ISLAND
Stanford-le-Hope
RIVER THAMES
Chadwell St. Mary
LAMBETH
WOOLWICH
GREENWICH
Blackheath
Abbey Wood
Plumstead
Welling
ERITH
Slade Green
Dartford Crossing
GRAYS
TILBURY
Cliffe
Allhallows-on-Sea
Lower Stoke
ISLE OF GRAIN
LEWISHAM
Lee
ELTHAM
BEXLEY
Bexleyheath
DARTFORD
Greenhithe
Swanscombe
Northfleet
GRAVESEND
Church Street
High Halstow
Hoo St. Werburgh
CATFORD
Mottingham
SIDCUP
Wilmington
Bean
Chalk
Higham
Wainscott
BECKENHAM
CHISLEHURST
Hextable
Swanley
South Darenth
Istead Rise
Thong
Shorne
STROOD
Upper Upnor
RIVER MEDWAY
Ham Green
Thornton Heath
BROMLEY
St. Mary Cray
Horton Kirby
Hartley
Meopham Station
ROCHESTER
GILLINGHAM
Upchurch
CROYDON
West Wickham
ORPINGTON
Crockenhill
Eynsford
Fawkham Green
Meopham
Cuxton
CHATHAM
Rainham
Keston
New Addington
Farnborough
West Kingsdown
Stansted
Culverstone Green
Upper Halling
Halling
Walderslade
Newington
PURLEY
London Biggin Hill Airport
Downe
Inset Page 164
Shoreham
Fairseat
Vigo Village
Snodland
Burham
Bredhurst
Stockbury
Knockholt
Otford
Kemsing
Wrotham
Larkfield
Aylesford
Boxley
Detling
Hucking
Bicknor
WARLINGHAM
Biggin Hill
Seal
Borough Green
Ightham
Platt
West Malling
East Malling
MAIDSTONE
CATERHAM
CLACKET LANE
Westerham
SEVENOAKS
Stone Street
Plaxtol
Mereworth
Wateringbury
Barming
Bearsted
Hollingbourne
M25
Shipbourne
Dunk's Green
West Peckham
Loose
Harrietsham
K E N
Crockham Hill
Sevenoaks Weald
Hadlow
Yalding
Sutton Valence
Kingswood
SURREY
Hildenborough
Chiddingstone Causeway
TONBRIDGE
Golden Green
East Peckham
Benover
Edenbridge
Hever
Chiddingstone
Leigh
Five Oak Green
Paddock Wood
Headcorn
Staplehurst
Marden
Smallfield
Lingfield
Penshurst
Chiddingstone Hoath
Southborough
Pembury
Frittenden
Horsmonden
Fordcombe
Rusthall
ROYAL TUNBRIDGE WELLS
Felbridge
EAST GRINSTEAD
Goudhurst
Biddenden
Groombridge
Withyham
Lamberhurst
Sissinghurst
Cranbrook
Weir Wood Reservoir
Hartfield
Frant
Kilndown
Hartley
Benenden
WEST SUSSEX
Sharpthorne
Durgates
Wadhurst
Bewl Water
Rolvenden
Balcombe
Ardingly Resr.
CROWBOROUGH
Ticehurst
Hawkhurst
Rolvenden Layne
HAYWARDS HEATH
Chelwood Common
Sandhurst
Mayfield
Hurst Green
EAST SUSSEX
Robertsbridge
River Rother
Burwash
Newick
Uckfield
Heathfield
Darwell Resr.
BURGESS HILL
Powdermill Resr.
Broad Oak
Isfield
Horam
Battle
Ditchling
Laughton
Plumpton
Ninfield
LEWES
HAILSHAM
HASTINGS
50 51 52 53
54 55 56 57 58 59 60 61 62 63 64 65 66 67
68 69 70 71 72 73 74 75 76 77 78 79 80 81
82 83 84 85 86 87 88 89 90 91 92 93 94 95 96 97
100 101 102 103 104 105 106 107 108 109 110 111 112 113
116 117 118 119 120 121 122 123 124 125 126 127 128 129
130 131 132 133 134 135 136 137 138 139 140 141
142 143 144 145 146 147
148 149 150 151 152 153
154 155 156 157
164 176 184 190 191 192 196 201 204 212 214 218 222 223 225